Medical Physiology

6th
EDITION

Review of
Medical
Physiology

WILLIAM F. GANONG, MD

Professor of Physiology
Chairman, Department of Physiology
University of California School of Medicine
San Francisco, California

LANGE Medical Publications   Los Altos, California

A Concise Medical Library for Practitioner and Student

Review of Medical Physiology, 6th ed. $9.00

Current Diagnosis & Treatment 1973 (12th annual revision). Edited by M.A. Krupp and M.J. Chatton. 996 pp. — 1973

Current Pediatric Diagnosis & Treatment, 2nd ed. Edited by C.H. Kempe, H.K. Silver, and D. O'Brien. 1008 pp, *illus.* — 1972

Review of Physiological Chemistry, 14th ed. H.A. Harper. About 540 pp, *illus.* — 1973

Review of Medical Microbiology, 10th ed. E. Jawetz, J.L. Melnick, and E.A. Adelberg. 518 pp, *illus.* — 1972

Review of Medical Pharmacology, 3rd ed. F.H. Meyers, E. Jawetz, and A. Goldfien. 688 pp, *illus.* — 1972

General Urology, 7th ed. D.R. Smith. 436 pp, *illus.* — 1972

General Ophthalmology, 6th ed. D. Vaughan, T. Asbury, and R. Cook. 316 pp, *illus.* — 1971

Principles of Clinical Electrocardiography, 8th ed. M.J. Goldman. 400 pp, *illus.* — 1973

Correlative Neuroanatomy & Functional Neurology, 15th ed. J.G. Chusid. 429 pp, *illus.* — 1973

Handbook of Psychiatry, 2nd ed. Edited by P. Solomon and V.D. Patch. 648 pp. — 1971

Handbook of Surgery, 5th ed. Edited by J.L. Wilson. About 780 pp, *illus.* — 1973

Handbook of Obstetrics & Gynecology, 4th ed. R.C. Benson. 774 pp, *illus.* — 1971

Physician's Handbook, 17th ed. M.A. Krupp, N.J. Sweet, E. Jawetz, E.G. Biglieri, and R.L. Roe. About 660 pp, *illus.* — 1973

Handbook of Medical Treatment, 13th ed. Edited by M.J. Chatton. 648 pp. — 1972

Handbook of Pediatrics, 10th ed. H.K. Silver, C.H. Kempe, and H.B. Bruyn. 693 pp, *illus.* — 1973

Handbook of Poisoning: Diagnosis & Treatment, 7th ed. R.H. Dreisbach. 515 pp. — 1971

Preface

This book is designed to provide a concise summary of mammalian and, particularly, of human physiology which medical students and others can supplement with readings in current texts, monographs, and reviews. Pertinent aspects of general and comparative physiology are also included. Summaries of relevant anatomic considerations will be found in each section, but this book is written primarily for those who have some knowledge of anatomy, chemistry, and biochemistry.

Examples from clinical medicine are given where pertinent to illustrate physiologic points. Physicians desiring to use this book as a review will find short discussions of important symptoms produced by disordered function in several sections.

It has not been possible to be complete and concise without also being dogmatic. I believe, however, that the conclusions presented without a detailed discussion of the experimental data on which they are based are those supported by the bulk of the currently available evidence. Much of this evidence can be found in the papers cited in the credit lines of the illustrations. Further discussions of particular subjects and information on subjects not considered in detail in this book can be found in the references listed at the end of each section. Information about serial review publications which provide up-to-date discussions of various physiologic subjects is included in the note on general references in the appendix.

In the interest of brevity and clarity, I have in most instances omitted the names of the many investigators whose work made possible the view of physiology presented here. This is in no way intended to slight their contributions, but including their names and specific references to original papers would greatly increase the length of this book.

I am greatly indebted to many individuals who helped in the preparation of this book. Those whom I wish especially to thank for their help with the Sixth Edition include Drs. James Meyer and Ralph Kellogg. I am also indebted to my wife, who labored long hours reading proof, and Annette Lowe, who drew many of the illustrations. I also wish to thank all the students and others who took the time to write to me offering helpful criticisms and suggestions. Such comments are always welcome. Many associates and friends provided unpublished illustrative materials, and numerous authors and publishers generously granted permission to reproduce illustrations from other books and journals.

With the appearance of the Sixth Edition I am pleased to be able to announce that the following translations have been published: Portuguese, German (second edition), Italian (second edition), Spanish (third edition), and Japanese (second edition). Polish, Serbo-Croatian, Greek, and Turkish translations are under way.

William F. Ganong

San Francisco, California
June, 1973

Table of Contents

V. GASTROINTESTINAL FUNCTION

VI. CIRCULATION

I. Introduction

1...

Physiologic Principles

In unicellular organisms, all vital processes occur in a single cell. As the evolution of multicellular organisms has progressed, various cell groups have taken over particular functions. In higher animals and man, the specialized cell groups include a gastrointestinal system to digest and absorb food, a respiratory system to take up O_2 and eliminate CO_2, a urinary system to remove wastes, a cardiovascular system to distribute food, O_2, and the products of metabolism, a reproductive system for perpetuating the species, and nervous and endocrine systems to coordinate and integrate the functions of the other systems. This book is concerned with the way these systems function and the way each contributes to the functions of the body as a whole.

CELLULAR STRUCTURE & FUNCTION

Revolutionary advances in the understanding of cell structure and function have been made through the use of electron microscopy, x-ray diffraction, and the other technics of modern cellular and molecular biology. The specialization of the cells in the various organs of higher animals is very great, and no cell can be called "typical" of all cells in the body. However, a number of structures, or **organelles**, are common to most cells. These structures are shown in Fig 1–1.

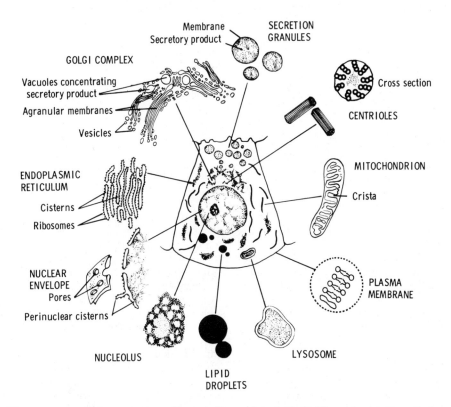

FIG 1–1. Ultrastructure of the common cell organelles and inclusions. The endoplasmic reticulum illustrated here is the granular type, with ribosomes attached to it. Some cells also contain tubes of membrane without ribosomes (agranular endoplasmic reticulum). The pores in the nuclear envelope are closed by a thin, homogeneous membrane. (Modified and reproduced, with permission, from Bloom & Fawcett: *A Textbook of Histology,* 9th ed. Saunders, 1968.)

Cell Membrane

The membrane which surrounds the cell is a remarkable structure. It is not only semipermeable, allowing some substances to pass through it and excluding others, but its permeability can be varied. It is generally referred to as the **plasma membrane**. The nucleus is also surrounded by a membrane, and the organelles are surrounded by or made up of membrane.

Although the chemical structure of membranes and their properties vary considerably from one location to another, they have certain common features. They are generally about 7.5 nm (75 Angstrom units) thick. They are made up primarily of protein and lipids, and the major lipids are phospholipids such as phosphatidyl choline and phosphatidyl ethanolamine. The chemistry of proteins and lipids is discussed in Chapter 17. The shape of the phospholipid molecule is roughly that of a clothespin (Fig 1–2). The head end of the molecule contains the phosphate portion, is positively charged, and is quite soluble in water (polar,

or **hydrophilic**). The tails are quite insoluble (nonpolar, or **hydrophobic**). In the membrane, the hydrophilic ends are exposed to the aqueous environment that bathes the exterior of the cells and the aqueous cytoplasm; the hydrophobic ends meet in the water-poor interior of the membrane.

There are many different proteins embedded in the membrane. They exist as separate globular units and stud the inside and outside of the membrane in a random array (Fig 1–2). Some are located in the inner surface of the membrane; some are located on the outer surface; and some extend through the membrane (**through and through proteins**). In general, the uncharged, hydrophobic portions of the protein molecules are located in the interior of the membrane and the charged, hydrophilic portions are located on the surfaces. Many of the proteins are enzymes concerned with various biochemical reactions. Some can be removed by relatively mild chemical treatments (**peripheral proteins**), whereas others are difficult to remove (**integral proteins**). Some contain lipids (lipoproteins) and some carbohydrates (glycoproteins).

The protein structure—and particularly the enzyme content—of biologic membranes varies not only from cell to cell but also within the same cell. For example, plasma membranes contain relatively large quantities of magnesium adenosine triphosphatase, whereas monoamine oxidase is found in high concentration in the outer membranes of mitochondria. The membranes are dynamic structures, and their constituents are being constantly renewed at different rates. In addition, the composition of some membranes changes during development. Finally, evidence has now accumulated that some proteins can move laterally within the membrane along the cell surface. Thus, the picture of membrane structure that emerges is not one of a static structure but rather one of a dynamic fluid mosaic in which components change and even move.

On the external surface of most cells is a **basement membrane**, a thin layer which under the electron microscope has a homogeneously fuzzy appearance.

Intercellular Connections

An interesting recent development has been the demonstration that, in tissues, connections form between cells. Two types of connections are associated with cell-to-cell adhesion and maintenance of tissue strength and organization. One of these is the **tight junction**, in which the membranes of 2 cells become apposed and the outer layers of the membranes fuse. The other is the **adherens** type of junction in which there are various forms of membrane specialization but the 2 membranes are separated by a 15–35 nm space. A third junction, the **gap junction** or **nexus**, permits the direct transfer of ions and other small molecules between cells without traversing the extracellular space. The gap junction is characterized by a 2 nm space between the opposing membranes. This gap is bridged by hexagonally arranged fibrils. The nexus permits rapid propagation of electrical potential changes from one cell to another.

FIG 1–2. Biologic membrane. *Top:* Model of membrane structure. The phospholipid molecules each have 2 fatty acid chains (wavy lines) attached to a phosphate head (open oval). The proteins, indicated by the heavy lines, are partly in the *α*-helical configuration and partly folded, with the charged ends (+ and − signs) on the exterior or interior sides of the membrane. *Bottom:* Three-dimensional view of membrane. Proteins are shown as irregular shaded globules. (Reproduced, with permission, from Singer & Nicolson: The fluid mosaic model of the structure of cell membranes. Science 175:720, 1972. Copyright 1972 by the American Association for the Advancement of Science.)

When 2 separate cells are brought together in tissue culture, they develop areas of increased permeability in the regions where their membranes are apposed. There is evidence that this change occurs when the calcium concentration, normally low on the inside of the membrane, is also reduced on the outside. It is of interest that intercellular connections are apparently absent in tumor cells.

Nucleus & Related Structures

A nucleus is present in all cells that divide. If a cell is cut in half, the anucleate portion eventually dies without dividing. The nucleus is made up in large part of the **chromosomes,** the structures in the nucleus which carry a complete blueprint for all the heritable species and individual characteristics of the animal. During cell division, the pairs of chromosomes become visible, but between cell divisions the irregular clumps of the dark material called **chromatin** are the only evidence of their presence. Each chromosome is made up of supporting protein and a giant molecule of **deoxyribonucleic acid (DNA).** The ultimate units of heredity are the **genes** on the chromosomes, and each gene is a portion of the DNA molecule.

During normal cell division by **mitosis,** the chromosomes duplicate themselves and then divide in such a way that each daughter cell receives a full complement **(diploid number)** of chromosomes. During their final maturation, germ cells undergo a division in which half the chromosomes go to each daughter cell (see Chapter 23). This reduction division, or **meiosis,** is actually a 2-stage process; but the important consideration is that, as a result of it, mature sperms and ova contain half the normal number (the **haploid number)** of chromosomes. When a sperm and ovum unite, the resultant cell **(zygote)** has a full (diploid) complement of chromosomes, one-half from the female parent and one-half from the male. The chemistry of DNA and the way the base chains of DNA split during mitosis and meiosis are discussed in Chapter 17.

The nucleus of most cells contains a **nucleolus** (Fig 1–1), a patchwork of granules rich in **ribonucleic acid (RNA).** In some cells, the nucleus contains several of these structures. Nucleoli are most prominent and numerous in growing cells. The DNA in the nucleus serves as a template for the synthesis of RNA, which then moves to the cytoplasm, where it regulates the synthesis of proteins by the cell. The nucleolus is probably the site where the RNA found in the ribosomes (see below) is synthesized. Since the enzymes that control the metabolism of the cell are proteins, the synthesis of protein is the key to the control of the development of the cell. The chemistry of RNA and the subject of protein synthesis are discussed further in Chapter 17.

The nucleus is surrounded by a **nuclear membrane,** or **envelope** (Fig 1–1). This membrane is double, and the spaces between the 2 folds are called **perinuclear cisterns.** The nuclear membrane is apparently quite permeable, since it permits passage of mole-

FIG 1–3. Cutaway drawing of a mitochondrion, showing the inner and outer membranes. The inner membrane is folded, forming shelves (cristae). The coiled structures represent possible arrangements of the mitochondrial DNA. Mitochondrial branching of the type shown here is not present in all cells. (Reproduced, with permission, from Nass: Mitochondrial DNA: Advances, problems and goals. Science 165:25, 1969. Copyright 1969 by the American Association for the Advancement of Science.)

cules as large as RNA from the nucleus to the cytoplasm. There are areas of discontinuity in the nuclear membrane, but these "pores" are closed by a thin, homogeneous membrane.

Endoplasmic Reticulum

The endoplasmic reticulum is a complex series of tubules in the cytoplasm of the cell (Fig 1–1). The tubule walls appear to be made up of membrane. In **granular** endoplasmic reticulum, granules called **ribosomes** are attached to the membrane, whereas in **agranular** endoplasmic reticulum the granules are absent. The ribosomes are about 15 nm in diameter. Each is made up of a large and a small subunit called, on the basis of their rates of sedimentation in the centrifuge, the 50 S and the 30 S subunits, respectively. Sometimes, 3–5 ribosomes are clumped together, forming **polyribosomes (polysomes).** The ribosomes contain about 65% RNA and 35% protein. They are the sites of protein synthesis. The agranular endoplasmic reticulum is the site of steroid synthesis in steroid-secreting cells and the site of detoxification processes in other cells. As the sarcoplasmic reticulum (see Chapter 3), it plays an important role in skeletal and cardiac muscle.

Golgi Complex

The Golgi complex is a collection of membranous tubules and vesicles. It is usually located near the nucleus, and is particularly prominent in actively secreting gland cells. The function of the Golgi complex is believed to be the "packaging" of proteins secreted by the cell. Hormones and enzymes are stored in protein-secreting cells as membrane-enclosed **secretion granules,** and these granules are probably produced in the Golgi complex. The complex is also the site of formation of lysosomes (see below), and it adds certain carbohydrates to proteins to form glycoproteins (see Chapter 17). These carbohydrate-containing proteins on the cell surface are believed to play important roles in the association of cells to form tissues.

Mitochondria

Although their morphology varies somewhat from cell to cell, each mitochondrion (Figs 1–1, 1–3) is in essence a sausage-shaped structure. It is made up of an outer membrane and an inner membrane that is folded to form shelves (**cristae**). The mitochondria are the power-generating units of the cell and are most plentiful and best developed in parts of cells where energy-requiring processes take place. The chemical reactions occurring in them are discussed in detail in Chapter 17. The outer membrane of each mitochondrion is studded with the enzymes concerned with biologic oxidations, providing raw materials for the reactions occurring inside the mitochondrion. The interior of the mitochondrion contains the enzymes concerned with the citric acid cycle and the respiratory chain enzymes by which the 2-carbon fragments produced by metabolism are burned to CO_2 and water (see Chapter 17). In this process electrons are transferred along the respiratory enzyme chain. Coupled with the electron transfer is **oxidative phosphorylation**, the synthesis of the high-energy phosphate compound, **adenosine triphosphate (ATP)**. This ubiquitous molecule is the principal energy source for energy-requiring actions in animals and plants. The inner membrane of the mitochondrion appears to be made up of repeating units, each of which contains a basepiece, a stalk, and a spherical headpiece. The basepieces contain the enzymes of the electron transfer chain, and the stalks and headpieces contain an enzyme complex concerned with the synthesis of ATP from adenosine diphosphate (ADP) and inorganic phosphate.

The mitochondria contain DNA and can synthesize protein. It now appears that the mitochondrial DNA represents a second genetic system in the cell. However, the mitochondrial DNA alone does not contain enough genetic information to code for all mitochondrial components, and the nuclear and mitochondrial genetic systems apparently interact in the formation of the protein systems in the mitochondria.

Lysosomes

In the cytoplasm of the cell, there are large, somewhat irregular structures surrounded by membrane which may contain fragments of other cell structures. These organelles are the **lysosomes**. Some of the granules of the granulocytic white blood cells are lysosomes. Each lysosome contains a variety of enzymes (Table 1–1) which would cause the destruction of most cellular components if the enzymes were not separated from the rest of the cell by the membrane of the lysosome.

The lysosomes are believed to function as a form of digestive system for the cell. Exogenous substances such as bacteria which become engulfed by the cell end up in membrane-lined vacuoles. A vacuole of this type (**phagocytic vacuole**) may merge with a lysosome, per-

TABLE 1–1. Some of the enzymes found in lysosomes and the cell components which are their substrates.

Enzyme	Substrate
Ribonuclease	RNA
Deoxyribonuclease	DNA
Phosphatase	Phosphate esters
Glycosidases	Complex carbohydrates: glycosides and polysaccharides
Aryl sulfatases	Sulfate esters
Collagenase	Proteins
Cathepsins	Proteins

mitting the contents of the vacuole and the lysosome to mix within a common membrane. Some of the products of the "digestion" of the engulfed material are absorbed through the walls of the vacuole, and the remnants are dumped from the cell by rupture of the vacuole to the exterior of the cell. The lysosomes also appear to engulf worn out components of the cell in which they are located, forming **autophagic vacuoles**. When a cell dies, lysosomal enzymes cause autolysis of the remnants. In vitamin A intoxication and certain other conditions, lysosomal enzymes are released to the exterior of the cell with resultant breakdown of intercellular material. There is evidence that in gout, phagocytes ingest uric acid crystals, and that such ingestion triggers the release of lysosomal enzymes which contribute to the inflammatory response in the joints. Lysosomal enzymes also play a role in rheumatoid arthritis. One form of **glycogen storage disease**, a condition in which glycogen accumulates in excess in cells, is thought to be due to the congenital absence of a lysosomal enzyme that breaks down glycogen.

Centrioles

In the cytoplasm of most cells there are 2 short cylinders called **centrioles**. The centrioles are located near the nucleus, and they are arranged so that they are at right angles to each other. Tubules in groups of 3 run longitudinally in the walls of the centriole (Fig 1–1). There are 9 of these triplets spaced at regular intervals around the circumference. **Cilia**, the hair-like motile processes which in higher animals extend from various types of epithelial cells, also have an array of 9 tubular structures in their walls, but they have in addition a pair of tubules in the center and there are 2 rather than 3 tubules in each of the 9 circumferential structures. The **basal granule**, on the other hand, which is the structure to which a cilium is anchored, has 9 circumferential triplets, like a centriole.

The centrioles seem to be concerned with the movement of the chromosomes during cell division. They duplicate themselves at the start of mitosis, and the pairs move apart to form the poles of the mitotic spindle. In multinucleate cells, there is a pair of centrioles near each nucleus.

Microtubules & Microfilaments

Many cells contain **microtubules**, long hollow structures about 25 nm in diameter, and **microfilaments**, solid fibers 4–6 nm in diameter. The microtubules are found in the mitotic spindles of dividing cells and in structures such as the axons of growing nerve cells. They are thought to provide structural stability. Their function is disrupted by the drug colchicine. Microfilaments appear to be responsible for cell movement. They seem to contain a protein that resembles the contractile protein actin in muscle (see Chapter 2), and they have been called the muscle of the cell. Their function is disrupted by cytochalasin, a compound secreted by certain fungi.

Secretion Granules

Secretion granules in cells which secrete proteins have been mentioned in the section on the Golgi complex. Typical examples include the granules of tropic hormones in the anterior lobe of the pituitary gland (see Chapter 22), the granules of renin in the juxtaglomerular cells of the kidney (see Chapter 24), and the granules of proteolytic enzyme precursors in the exocrine cells of the pancreas (see Chapter 26).

The proteins in these granules are synthesized in the endoplasmic reticulum, packaged into membrane-enclosed granules in the Golgi apparatus, and stored in the cytoplasm until they are extruded from the cell by exocytosis (see below).

Other Structures in Cells

If cells are homogenized and the resulting suspension is centrifuged, various cellular components can be isolated. The nuclei sediment first, followed by the mitochondria. High-speed centrifugation that generates forces of 100,000 times gravity or more causes a fraction made up of granules called the **microsomes** to sediment. This fraction includes the ribosomes, but it is not homogeneous and includes other granular material as well. The ribosomes and other components can be isolated from the microsomal fraction by further ultracentrifugation or other technics.

BODY FLUID COMPARTMENTS

Organization of the Body

The cells which make up the bodies of all but the simplest multicellular animals, both aquatic and terrestrial, exist in an "internal sea" of **extracellular fluid (ECF)** enclosed within the integument of the animal. From this fluid the cells take up O_2 and nutrients; into it, they discharge metabolic waste products. The ECF is more dilute than present-day sea water, but its composition closely resembles that of the primordial oceans in which, presumably, all life originated.

In animals with a closed vascular system, the ECF is divided into 2 components: the **interstitial fluid** and the circulating **blood plasma**. The plasma and the cellu-

lar elements of the blood, principally red blood cells, fill the vascular system, and together they constitute the **total blood volume**. The interstitial fluid is that part of the ECF which is outside the vascular system, bathing the cells. The special fluids lumped together as transcellular fluids are discussed below. About a third of the **total body water (TBW)** is extracellular; the remaining two-thirds are intracellular (**intracellular fluid**).

Size of the Fluid Compartments

In the average young adult male, 18% of the body weight is protein and related substances, 7% is mineral, and 15% is fat. The remaining 60% is water. The distribution of this water is shown in Fig 1–4.

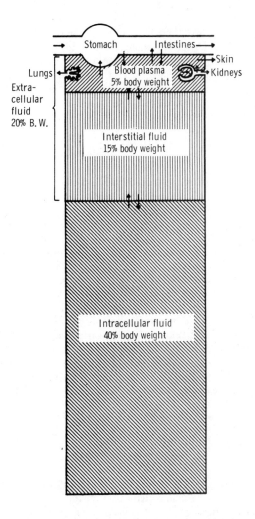

FIG 1–4. Body fluid compartments. Arrows represent fluid movement, B.W., body weight. Transcellular fluids, which constitute a very small percentage of total body fluids, are not shown. (Modified and reproduced, with permission, from Gamble: *Chemical Anatomy, Physiology, and Pathology of Extracellular Fluid,* 6th ed. Harvard Univ Press, 1954.)

The intracellular component of the body water accounts for about 40% of body weight and the extracellular component about 20%. Approximately 25% of the extracellular component is in the vascular system (plasma = 5% of body weight), and 75% outside the blood vessels (interstitial fluid = 15% of body weight). The total blood volume is about 8% of body weight.

Measurement of Body Fluid Volumes

It is theoretically possible to measure the size of each of the body fluid compartments by injecting substances which will stay in only one compartment and then calculating the volume of fluid in which the test substance is distributed (the **volume of distribution** of the injected material). The volume of distribution is equal to the amount injected (minus any which has been removed from the body by metabolism or excretion during the time allowed for mixing) divided by the concentration of the substance in the sample. *Example:* 150 mg of sucrose are injected into a 70 kg man. The plasma sucrose level after mixing is 0.01 mg/ml, and 10 mg have been excreted or metabolized during the mixing period. The volume of distribution of the sucrose is

$$\frac{150 \text{ mg} - 10 \text{ mg}}{0.01 \text{ mg/ml}} = 14{,}000 \text{ ml}$$

Since 14,000 ml is the space in which the sucrose was distributed, it is also called the **sucrose space.**

Volumes of distribution can be calculated for any substance that can be injected into the body provided the concentration in the body fluids and the amount removed by excretion and metabolism can be accurately measured.

Although the principle involved in such measurements is simple, there are a number of complicating factors which must be considered. The material injected must be nontoxic, must mix evenly throughout the compartment being measured, must have no effect of its own on the distribution of water or other substances in the body, and must be unchanged by the body during the mixing period. It also should be relatively easy to measure.

Plasma Volume, Total Blood Volume, & Red Cell Volume

Plasma volume has been measured by using dyes which become bound to plasma protein—particularly Evans blue (T-1824). Plasma volume can also be measured by injecting serum albumin labeled with radioactive iodine. Suitable aliquots of the injected solution and plasma samples obtained after injection are counted in a scintillation counter. An average value is 3500 ml (5% of the body weight of a 70 kg man, assuming unit density).

If the plasma volume and the hematocrit are known, **total blood volume** can be calculated by multiplying the plasma volume by

$$\frac{100}{100 - \text{hematocrit}}$$

Example: The hematocrit is 38 and the plasma volume 3500 ml. The total blood volume is

$$3500 \times \frac{100}{100 - 38} = 5645 \text{ ml}$$

The **red cell volume** (volume occupied by all the circulating red cells in the body) can be determined by subtracting the plasma volume from the total blood volume. It may also be measured independently, by injecting tagged red blood cells and, after mixing has occurred, measuring the fraction of the red cells that is tagged. A commonly used tag is ^{51}Cr, a radioactive isotope of chromium which is attached to the cells by incubating them in a suitable chromium solution. Isotopes of iron and phosphorus (^{59}Fe and ^{32}P) and antigenic tagging have also been employed.

Extracellular Fluid Volume

The ECF volume is difficult to measure because the limits of this space are ill-defined and because few substances mix rapidly in all parts of the space while remaining exclusively extracellular. The lymph cannot be separated from the ECF, and is measured with it. Many substances enter the cerebrospinal fluid (CSF) slowly because of the blood-brain barrier (see Chapter 32). Equilibration is slow with joint fluid and aqueous humor and with the ECF in relatively avascular tissues such as dense connective tissue, cartilage, and some parts of bone. Substances which distribute in ECF appear in glandular secretions and in the contents of the gastrointestinal tract. Because they are not strictly part of the ECF, these fluids, as well as CSF, the fluids in the eye, and a few other special fluids, are called **transcellular fluids.** Their volume is relatively small.

Perhaps the most accurate measurement of ECF volume is that obtained by using inulin. Radioactive inulin has been prepared by substituting ^{14}C for one of the carbon atoms of the molecule; and when this material is used, inulin levels are easily determined by counting the samples with suitable radiation detectors. Mannitol and sucrose have also been used to measure ECF volume. Because chloride ions, for example, are largely extracellular in location, radioactive isotopes of chloride (^{36}Cl and ^{38}Cl) have been used for determination of ECF volume. However, some chloride is known to be intracellular. The same objection applies to ^{82}Br, which interchanges with chloride in the body. Other anions which have been used include sulfate, thiosulfate, thiocyanate, and ferrocyanide.

Careful measurement with each of these substances gives a range of values, which indicates that each has a slightly different volume of distribution. A generally accepted value for ECF volume is 20% of the body weight, or about 14 liters in a 70 kg man (3.5 liters = plasma; 10.5 liters = interstitial fluid).

Interstitial Fluid Volume

The interstitial fluid space cannot be measured directly since it is difficult to sample interstitial fluid and since substances which equilibrate in interstitial fluid also equilibrate in plasma. The volume of the interstitial fluid can be calculated by subtracting the plasma volume from the ECF volume. The ECF volume/intracellular fluid volume ratio is larger in infants and children than it is in adults, but the absolute volume of ECF in children is, of course, smaller than it is in adults. Therefore, dehydration develops more rapidly and is frequently more severe in children than in adults.

Intracellular Fluid Volume

The intracellular fluid volume cannot be measured directly, but it can be calculated by subtracting the ECF volume from the total body water (TBW). TBW can be measured by the same dilution principle used to measure the other body spaces. Deuterium oxide (D_2O, heavy water) is most frequently used. D_2O has properties which are slightly different from H_2O, but in equilibration experiments for measuring body water it gives accurate results. Tritium oxide and aminopyrine have also been used for this purpose.

The water content of lean body tissue is constant at $71-72$ ml/100 g of tissue, but since fat is relatively free of water the ratio of TBW to body weight varies with the amount of fat present. In young adult males water constitutes about 60% of body weight. The values for females are somewhat lower. In both sexes the values tend to decrease with age (see Table $1-2$).

TABLE 1−2. TBW (as percentage of body weight) in relation to age and sex.*

Age	Male	Female
10−18	59%	57%
18−40	61%	51%
40−60	55%	47%
Over 60	52%	46%

*Modified and reproduced, with permission, from Edelman & Liebman: Anatomy of body water and electrolytes. Am J Med 27:256, 1959.

UNITS FOR MEASURING CONCENTRATION OF SOLUTES

In considering the effects of various physiologically important substances and the interactions between them, the number of molecules, electrical charges, or particles of a substance per unit volume of a particular body fluid are often more meaningful than simply the weight of the substance per unit volume. For this reason, concentrations are frequently expressed in mols, equivalents, or osmols.

Mols

The mol is defined as the gram-molecular weight of a substance, ie, the molecular weight of the substance in grams. The millimol (mM) is 1/1000 of a mol and the micromol (μM) is 1/1,000,000 of a mol. Thus, 1 mol of NaCl = 23 + 35.5 g = 58.5 g, and 1 mM = 58.5 mg.

Equivalents

The concept of electrical equivalence is important in physiology because many of the important solutes in the body are in the form of charged particles. One equivalent (Eq) is 1 mol of an ionized substance divided by its valence. The milliequivalent (mEq) is 1/1000 of an equivalent. Thus, 1 Eq of Na^+ = 23 g/1 = 23 g; but 1 Eq of Ca^{++} = 40 g/2 = 20 g.

Electrical equivalence is not necessarily the same as chemical equivalence. A gram equivalent is that weight of a substance which is chemically equivalent to 8.000 g of oxygen. The normality (N) of a solution is the number of gram equivalents in 1 liter. A 1 N solution of hydrochloric acid contains 1 + 35.5 g/liter = 36.5 g/liter.

Osmols

When dealing with concentrations of osmotically active particles, the amounts of these particles are usually expressed in osmols. One osmol (Osm) equals the molecular weight of the substance in grams divided by the number of freely moving particles each molecule liberates in solution. The milliosmol (mOsm) is 1/1000 of 1 osmol. Osmosis is discussed in detail in a later section of this chapter.

The **osmolal concentration** of a substance in a fluid is measured by the degree to which it depresses the freezing point, 1 mol/liter of ideal solute depressing the freezing point 1.86° C. The number of mOsm/liter in a solution equals the freezing point depression divided by 0.00186. The **osmolarity** is the number of osmols per liter of solution—eg, plasma—while the **osmolality** is the number of osmols per kg of solvent. Therefore, osmolarity is affected by the volume of the various solutes in the solution and the temperature, while the osmolality is not. Osmotically active substances in the body are dissolved in water, and the density of water is 1, so osmolal concentrations can be expressed as Osm/liter of water. In this book, osmolal (rather than osmolar) concentrations are considered, and osmolality is expressed in mOsm/liter (of water).

COMPOSITION OF BODY FLUIDS

The distribution of electrolytes in the various compartments of the body fluid is shown in Fig 1−5. The figures for the intracellular phase ("cell fluid") are approximations. The composition of intracellular fluid varies somewhat depending upon the nature and function of the cell.

It is apparent from Fig 1−5 that electrolyte concentrations differ markedly in the various compartments. The most striking differences are the relatively

FIG 1–5. Electrolyte composition of human body fluids. Note that the values are in mEq/liter of water, not of body fluid. (Reproduced, with permission, from Leaf & Newburgh: *Significance of Body Fluids in Clinical Medicine,* 2nd ed. Thomas, 1955.)

low content of protein anions in interstitial fluid compared to intracellular fluid and plasma, and the fact that Na^+ and Cl^- are largely extracellular, whereas most of the K^+ is intracellular.

FORCES PRODUCING MOVEMENT OF SUBSTANCES BETWEEN COMPARTMENTS

The differences in composition of the various body fluid compartments are due in large part to the nature of the barriers separating them. The membranes of the cells separate the interstitial fluid and intracellular fluid, and the capillary wall separates the interstitial fluid from the plasma. The forces producing movement of water and other molecules across these barriers are diffusion, solvent drag, filtration, osmosis, active transport, and the processes of pinocytosis, phagocytosis, and emeiocytosis.

Diffusion

Diffusion is the process by which a gas or a substance in solution expands, because of the motion of its particles, to fill all of the available volume. The particles (molecules or ions) of a substance dissolved in a solvent are in continuous random movement. In regions where they are abundant, they frequently collide. They therefore tend to spread from areas of high concentration to areas of low concentration until the concentration is uniform throughout the solution.

Solute particles are, of course, moving both into and out of the area of high concentration; however, since more molecules move out than in, there is a **net flux** of the molecular species to the area of low concentration. The magnitude of the diffusing tendency from one area to another is proportionate to the difference in concentration of the substance in the 2 areas (the **concentration, or chemical gradient**). Diffusion of ions is also affected by their electrical charge. Whenever there is a difference in potential between 2 areas, positively charged ions move along this **electrical gradient** to the more negatively charged area; negatively charged ions move in the opposite direction.

In the body, diffusion occurs not only within fluid compartments but also from one compartment to another provided the barrier between the compartments is permeable to the diffusing substances. The diffusion rate of most solutes across the barriers is much slower than the diffusion rate in water, but diffusion is still a major force affecting the distribution of water and solutes.

Donnan Effect

When there is an ion on one side of a membrane that cannot diffuse through the membrane, the distribution of other ions to which the membrane is permeable is affected in a predictable way. For example, the negative charge of a nondiffusible anion hinders diffusion of the diffusible cations and favors diffusion of the diffusible anions. This situation may be represented diagrammatically as follows:

X		Y
	m	
K^+		K^+
Cl^-		Cl^-
$Prot^-$		

in which the membrane (m) between compartments X and Y is impermeable to $Prot^-$ but freely permeable to K^+ and Cl^-. Cl^- tends to diffuse down its concentration gradient from Y to X and some K^+ moves with the negatively charged Cl^-. Therefore,

$$[K^+_X] > [K^+_Y] \text{ and } [Cl^-_X] < [Cl^-_Y]$$

Furthermore,

$$[K^+_X] + [Cl^-_X] + [Prot^-_X] > [K^+_Y] + [Cl^-_Y]$$

ie, there are more osmotically active particles on side X than on side Y.

Donnan and Gibbs showed that in the presence of a nondiffusible ion, the diffusible ions distribute themselves so that, at equilibrium, their concentration ratios are equal:

$$\frac{[K^+_X]}{[K^+_Y]} = \frac{[Cl^-_Y]}{[Cl^-_X]}$$

In the case of single cations and anions of the same valence, the product of the concentration of the diffusible ions on one side equals that on the other side. Thus,

$$[K^+_X] \ [Cl^-_X] = [K^+_Y] \ [Cl^-_Y]$$

Electrochemical neutrality would require that the sum of the anions on each side of the membrane equal the sum of the cations on that side:

$$[K^+_X] = [Cl^-_X] + Prot^-_X], \text{ and}$$
$$[K^+_Y] = [Cl^-_Y]$$

This condition hinders the movement of ions. It is not met when the diffusible ions are distributed so that the product of their concentrations on the 2 sides of the membrane are equal. There is a slight excess of cations on side Y and a slight excess of anions on side X at equilibrium, and therefore a difference in electrical potential exists between X and Y. However, it should be emphasized that the difference between the number of anions and the number of cations on either side of the membrane is extremely small relative to the total numbers of anions and cations present.

The **Donnan effect** on the distribution of diffusible ions is important in the body because of the presence in cells and in plasma, but not in interstitial fluid, of large quantities of nondiffusible protein anions (see Chapters 35 and 38).

Solvent Drag

When solvent is moving in one direction (**bulk flow**), the solvent tends to drag along some molecules of solute. This force is called **solvent drag**. In most situations in the body, its effects are very small.

Filtration

Filtration is the process by which fluid is forced through a membrane or other barrier due to a difference in hydrostatic pressure on the 2 sides. The amount of fluid filtered in a given interval is proportionate to the difference in pressure and the surface area of the membrane. Molecules which are smaller in diameter than the pores of the membrane pass through with the fluid, and larger molecules are retained. Filtration of small molecules across the capillary walls occurs when the hydrostatic pressure in the vessels is greater than that in the extravascular tissues.

Osmosis

Osmosis is the movement of **solvent** molecules across a membrane into an area in which there is a higher concentration of a **solute** to which the membrane is impermeable. It is an immensely important factor in physiologic processes. The tendency for movement of solvent molecules to a region of greater solute concentration can be prevented by applying pressure to the more concentrated solution. The pressure necessary to prevent solvent migration is the **effective osmotic pressure** of the solution.

Osmotic pressure, like vapor pressure lowering, freezing point depression, and boiling point elevation, depends upon the number rather than the type of particles in a solution, ie, it is a fundamental colligative property of solutions. In effect, it is due to a reduction in the **activity** of the solvent molecules in a solution. The activity of a substance is its effective concentration as evaluated by its behavior in solution. When a solute is dissolved in a solvent, the activity of the solvent molecules is decreased. A homogeneous solution of a single substance has an osmotic pressure, but this pressure can be expressed—ie, the solution has an effective osmotic pressure—only when the solution is in contact with a more dilute solution across a membrane permeable to the solvent but not to the solute. In this situation, solvent molecules will diffuse from the area in which their activity is greater (the **dilute** solution) to the area in which their activity is less (the **concentrated** solution). Thus, if a 10% aqueous solution of glucose is placed in contact with distilled water across a membrane permeable to water but not to glucose, the volume of the glucose solution increases and its glucose concentration decreases as water molecules move into it from the water compartment (see Fig 1–6).

Osmotic pressure (P) is related to temperature and volume in the same way as the pressure of a gas:

$$P = \frac{nRT}{V}$$

where n is the number of particles, R the gas constant, T the absolute temperature, and V the volume. If T is held constant, it is clear that the osmotic pressure is proportionate to the number of particles in solution

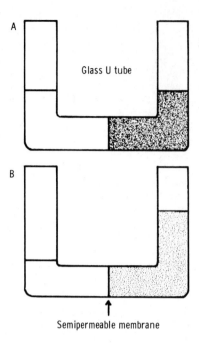

A

Glass U tube

B

↑
Semipermeable membrane

FIG 1–6. Demonstration of osmotic pressure. *A:* Immediately after adding a solution of glucose (shaded area) to the right arm of the **U** tube and an equal volume of water (clear space) to the other. *B:* After equilibration has taken place. The water has entered the glucose solution which has increased in volume and decreased in concentration.

per unit volume of solution. If the solute is a nonionizing compound such as glucose, the osmotic pressure is a function of the number of glucose molecules present. If the solute ionizes and forms an **ideal** solution, each ion is an osmotically active particle. For example, NaCl would dissociate into Na^+ and Cl^- ions, so that each mol in solution would supply 2 Osm. Na_2SO_4 would dissociate into Na^+, Na^+, and $SO_4^=$, supplying 3 Osm/mol. However, the body fluids are not ideal solutions, and although the dissociation of strong electrolytes is complete, the number of particles free to exert an osmotic effect is reduced due to interactions between the ions. Thus, it is actually the effective concentration, or activity in the body fluids, rather than the number of equivalents of an electrolyte in solution that determines its osmotic effect. This is why, for example, 1 mM/liter of NaCl in the body fluids contributes somewhat less than 2 mOsm/liter of osmotically active particles.

Osmolal Concentration of Plasma: Tonicity

The freezing point of normal human plasma averages $-0.54°$ C, which corresponds to an osmolal concentration in plasma of 290 mOsm/liter. This is equivalent to an osmotic pressure of 7.3 atmospheres. The osmolality might be expected to be higher than this, because the sum of all the cation and anion equivalents

in plasma is over 300. It is not this high because plasma is not an ideal solution, and ionic interactions reduce the number of particles free to exert an osmotic effect. Except when there has been insufficient time after a sudden change in composition for equilibration to occur, all fluid compartments of the body are apparently in or nearly in osmotic equilibrium. The term **tonicity** is used to describe the effective osmotic pressure of a solution relative to plasma. Solutions which have the same effective osmotic pressure as plasma are said to be **isotonic**; those with greater pressures are **hypertonic**; and those with lesser pressure are **hypotonic**. All solutions which are isosmotic with plasma—ie, have the same actual osmotic pressure or freezing point depression as plasma—would also be isotonic if it were not for the fact that some solutes diffuse into cells and others are metabolized. Thus a 0.9% saline solution is isotonic because there is no net movement of the osmotically active particles in the solution into cells and the particles are not metabolized. However, urea diffuses rapidly into cells, so that the effective osmotic pressure drops when cells are suspended in an aqueous solution that initially contains 290 mOsm/liter of urea. Similarly, a 5% glucose solution is isotonic when initially infused intravenously, but glucose is metabolized, so the net effect is that of infusing a hypotonic solution.

It is important to note the relative contributions of the various plasma components to the total osmolal concentration of plasma. Glucose, for example, is normally present to the extent of about 80 mg/100 ml of plasma, but glucose does not dissociate and it has a molecular weight of 180. Therefore, the osmolal concentration of glucose in normal plasma is only

$$\frac{80 \text{ mg} \times 10}{180} = 4.4 \text{ mOsm/liter}$$

The plasma proteins have a high molecular weight but are present in large quantities, so they do make a small contribution to the plasma osmolality. The osmolal concentration of protein derivatives (other than electrolytes) is about 0.36 times the plasma nonprotein nitrogen level in mg/100 ml, or, in normal plasma, 0.36×30 mg/100 ml = 10.8 mOsm/liter. On the other hand, the contribution due to Na^+ and Cl^- is about 250 mOsm/liter.

Nonionic Diffusion

Some weak acids and bases are quite soluble in cell membranes in the undissociated form, whereas in the ionic form they cross membranes with difficulty. Consequently, molecules of the undissociated substance diffuse from one side of the membrane to the other and then dissociate, effectively moving ions from one side of the membrane to another. This phenomenon, which occurs in the gastrointestinal tract (see Chapter 25) and kidneys (see Chapter 38), is called **nonionic diffusion**.

Carrier-Mediated Transport

In addition to moving across cell membranes by diffusion, osmosis, and the processes described above, ions and larger nonionized molecules are transported by carrier molecules in the membranes. When such **carrier-mediated transport** is from an area of greater concentration of the transported molecule to an area of lesser concentration, energy is not required and the process is called **facilitated diffusion.** In many instances, facilitated diffusion is regulated by hormones; eg, insulin increases the facilitated diffusion of glucose into muscle cells (see Chapter 19). When, on the other hand, the transport is from an area of lesser to an area of greater concentration, the process requires energy and is referred to as **active transport.** The energy is supplied by the metabolism of the cells, generally through adenosine triphosphate (ATP; see Chapter 17). Active transport is of major importance throughout the body.

Transport of Proteins & Other Large Molecules

There is little doubt that in certain situations proteins enter cells, and a number of hormones secreted by endocrine cells are proteins or large polypeptides. Current evidence supports the hypothesis that large molecules enter cells by the processes of phagocytosis and pinocytosis or endocytosis, and that proteins and polypeptides are secreted by reverse pinocytosis, or exocytosis.

Phagocytosis ("cell eating") is the process by which bacteria, dead tissue, or other bits of material visible under the microscope are engulfed by cells such as the polymorphonuclear leukocytes of the blood. The material makes contact with the cell membrane, which then invaginates. The invagination is pinched off, leaving the engulfed material in a membrane-enclosed vacuole. **Pinocytosis** ("cell drinking") is essentially the same process, the only difference being that the substances ingested are in solution and hence not visible under the microscope. The process is summarized diagrammatically in Fig 1–7. In the cell, the membrane around a **pinocytic** or **phagocytic vacuole** may fuse with that of a lysosome, mixing the "digestive" enzymes in the lysosome with the contents of the vacuole. It has also been assumed that the membrane around vacuoles can be digested away, but the ultimate fate of the vacuoles is uncertain. In **exocytosis**, which has also been called **reverse pinocytosis, or emeiocytosis** ("cell vomiting"), the membrane around a vacuole or secretion granule fuses with the cell membrane and the region of fusion then breaks down, leaving the contents of the vacuole or secretion granule outside the cell and the cell membrane intact.

The rate of pinocytosis is greatly increased by substances called **inducers.** In mammalian cells, proteins such as albumins and globulins are potent inducers. Insulin apparently acts as an inducer in fat cells. There is evidence that pinocytosis and, presumably, phagocytosis are active processes in the sense that they do not occur when the energy-producing processes in the cell are blocked.

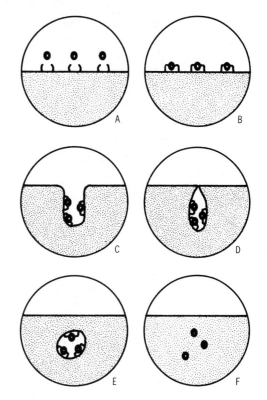

FIG 1–7. **One concept of pinocytosis ("membrane vesiculation").** Particles in solution attach to "receptors" on the cell surface (A, B), and the membrane invaginates and is pinched off (C, D, E). The membrane around the particles may then be removed by cellular processes (F), although the occurrence of such removal has not been proved. (Redrawn and reproduced, with permission, from Bennett: The concepts of membrane flow and membrane vesiculation as mechanisms for active transport and ion pumping. J Biophys Biochem. Cytology 2 [Suppl]:99, 1956.)

Pinocytosis and phagocytosis provide an explanation of how large molecules can enter cells without disrupting their cell membranes. In infants, protein may be absorbed from the gastrointestinal tract by this process (see Chapter 25). Other examples may be the ingestion of colloid by thyroid cells (see Chapter 18) and of osteoid by osteoclasts (see Chapter 21). Exocytosis has been observed in the case of the secretion of the pancreatic enzymes that enter the pancreatic juice, and most of the protein hormones in the body.

CELL MEMBRANE & RESTING MEMBRANE POTENTIALS

Ion Distribution Across Cell Membranes

The unique properties of the cell membranes are responsible for the differences in the composition of

TABLE 1–3. Concentration of some ions inside and outside frog skeletal muscle cells.*

Ion	Concentration (mM/kg H$_2$O)		Equilibrium Potential (mv)
	Inside Cell	Outside Cell	
Na$^+$	20	120	+45
K$^+$	139	2.5	−101
Cl$^-$	3.8	120	−87
Resting membrane potential = −88 mv			

*Data from various authors, compiled by Davies: Membrane theory and resting potential. Chap 52 in: *Medical Physiology,* 12th ed. Vol 2. Mountcastle VB (editor). Mosby, 1968.

intracellular and interstitial fluid. Average values for the composition of intracellular fluid in humans are shown in Fig 1–5, and specific values for frog skeletal muscle are shown in Table 1–3.

Membrane Potentials

There is a potential difference across the membranes of most if not all cells, with the inside of the cells negative to the exterior. By convention, this **resting membrane potential** or **steady potential** is written with a minus sign, signifying that the inside is negative to the exterior. Its magnitude varies considerably from tissue to tissue, ranging from −10 to −100 mv.

Membrane Permeability

Cell membranes are practically impermeable to intracellular protein and other organic anions, which make up most of the intracellular anions and are usually represented by the symbol A$^-$. However, they are moderately permeable to Na$^+$, and rather freely permeable to K$^+$ and Cl$^-$. K$^+$ permeability is 50–100 times greater than Na$^+$ permeability. The permeability values listed in Table 1–4 for the cell membrane of frog skeletal muscle are representative. It should be noted that permeability of these ions in the membrane,

TABLE 1–4. Permeability coefficients (P) for cell membrane of frog skeletal muscle. Values are equivalents diffusing through 1 sq cm of membrane under specified conditions and have the dimensions of cm/sec. For purposes of comparison, P$_{K^+}$ in water is 10.*

P$_{A^-}$	~ 0
P$_{Na^+}$	2 × 10^{-8}
P$_{K^+}$	2 × 10^{-6}
P$_{Cl^-}$	4 × 10^{-6}

*Data from Hodgkins & Horowicz: The influence of potassium and chloride ions on the membrane potential of single muscle fibers. J Physiol 148:127, 1959.

although appreciable, is a fraction of their permeability in water.

The reason for the differences in the permeability of cell membranes to various small ions is unknown. It is tempting to speculate that the membranes contain pores and that the differences in permeability can be explained on the basis of ion size. As noted above, most nonjunctional cell membranes behave as if they contained pores approximately 0.7 nm in diameter. The sizes of some of the principal inorganic ions are listed in Table 1–5.

TABLE 1–5. Sizes of hydrated ions relative to K$^+$ = 1.00. The diameter of the hydrated K$^+$ is about 0.4 nm.*

Cl$^-$	0.96	CH$_3$COO$^-$	1.80
K$^+$	1.00	SO$_4^=$	1.84
Na$^+$	1.47	H$_2$PO$_4^-$	2.04
HCO$_3^-$	1.65	HPO$_4^=$	2.58

*Data from Eccles: *The Physiology of Nerve Cells.* Johns Hopkins Univ Press, 1957.

The ions in the body are hydrated, and although the atomic weight of potassium (39) is greater than that of sodium (23), the hydrated sodium ion, ie, Na$^+$ with its full complement of water, is larger than the hydrated potassium ion. Therefore, one might expect sodium ions to move through membranes with greater difficulty than potassium ions. However, the postulated membrane pores have not been visualized, and ions may traverse the membrane attached to carriers, or by some other method. Fortunately, an exact explanation of the way ions move passively across membranes is not necessary for an analysis of ion fluxes; for this purpose, the empiric data on ion permeability are sufficient.

Forces Acting on Ions

The forces acting across the cell membrane on each ion can be analyzed. Chloride ions are present in higher concentration in the ECF than in the cell interior, and they tend to diffuse along this **concentration gradient** into the cell. The interior of the cell is negative relative to the exterior, and chloride ions are pushed out of the cell along this **electrical gradient**. An equilibrium is reached at which Cl$^-$ influx and Cl$^-$ efflux are equal. The membrane potential at which this equilibrium exists is the **equilibrium potential.** Its magnitude can be calculated from the **Nernst equation,** as follows:

$$E_{Cl} = \frac{RT}{FZ_{Cl}} \ln \frac{[Cl_o^-]}{[Cl_i^-]}$$

Where E$_{Cl}$ = equilibrium potential for Cl$^-$
R = gas constant
T = absolute temperature

F = the faraday (number of coulombs per mol of charge)

Z_{Cl} = valence of Cl⁻ (−1)

$[Cl_i^-]$ = Cl⁻ concentration inside the cell

$[Cl_o^-]$ = Cl⁻ concentration outside the cell

Converting from the natural log to the base 10 log and replacing some of the constants with numerical values, the equation becomes:

$$E_{Cl} = 61.5 \log \frac{[Cl_i^-]}{[Cl_o^-]} \text{ at } 37° \text{ C}$$

Note that in converting to the simplified expression, the concentration ratio is reversed because the minus 1 valence of Cl⁻ has been removed from the expression.

The equilibrium potential for Cl⁻ (E_{Cl}) can be calculated in this fashion for frog skeletal muscle fibers; using the data in Table 1–3, the calculated value is −87 mv. This figure is almost identical with the experimentally measured resting membrane potential for these cells. It can therefore be concluded that no forces other than those represented by the chemical and electrical gradients affect the movement of Cl⁻ across the membrane.

A similar equilibrium potential can be calculated for K⁺.

$$E_K = \frac{RT}{FZ_K} \ln \frac{[K_o^+]}{[K_i^+]} = 61.5 \log \frac{[K_o^+]}{[K_i^+]} \text{ at } 37°C$$

Where E_K = equilibrium potential for K⁺

Z_K = valence of K⁺ (+1)

$[K_i^+]$ = K⁺ concentration inside the cell

$[K_o^+]$ = K⁺ concentration outside the cell

R, T, and F as above

In this case, the concentration gradient is outward and the electrical gradient inward. In the frog muscle cells, the calculated equilibrium potential for potassium (E_K) is −101 mv. Since the resting membrane potential is only −88 mv, $[K_i^+]$ is greater in these cells than it would be if only the concentration and electrical gradients were affecting K⁺ movement through the membrane. Therefore, some other force must be keeping $[K_i^+]$ elevated. This force is an active transport of K⁺ into the nerve cell.

The situation for Na⁺ is quite different from that for K⁺ and Cl⁻. The direction of the chemical gradient for Na⁺ is inward, to the area where it is in lesser concentration, and the electrical gradient is in the same direction. Experiments with radioactive sodium have established the fact that the membrane has a relatively low but definite permeability to Na⁺ (Table 1–4). However, the intracellular Na⁺ remains low. Therefore, Na⁺ must be actively transported out of the cell against its electrical and chemical gradients. The fluxes across nerve cell membranes are summarized in Fig 1–8.

The Sodium-Potassium Pump

The mechanism responsible for the active trans-

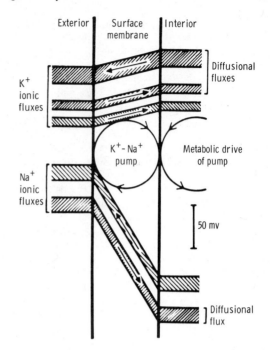

FIG 1–8. Na⁺ and K⁺ fluxes through the resting nerve cell membrane. The Na⁺ and K⁺ fluxes that are not labeled "diffusional fluxes" are due to active transport of these ions. The diffusional efflux of Na⁺, less than 1% of the influx, has been omitted. (Reproduced, with permission, from Eccles: *The Physiology of Nerve Cells*. Johns Hopkins Univ Press, 1957.)

port of sodium out of the cell and potassium into the cell is a **sodium-potassium pump** that is sometimes referred to simply as the **sodium pump**. The pump is located in the membrane. The energy for pumping is provided by ATP, and an adequate supply of ATP depends on the metabolic processes in the cell. Application of ATP by micropipet to the inside of the membrane increases transport, while application to the outside has no effect. The transport of Na⁺ is generally but not invariably coupled to that of K⁺ on a one for one basis; the rate of pumping is reduced, although not abolished, by removal of K⁺ from the fluid bathing the exterior of the cell. The activity of the pump is also directly proportional to the intracellular concentration of Na⁺. The rate of Na⁺ extrusion from the cell is thus proportionate to the amount of Na⁺ in it, a feedback arrangement which tends to keep the internal ionic composition of the cell constant. The transport mechanism is inhibited by ouabain and related cardiac glycosides, and by metabolic poisons which prevent the formation of ATP. It is also markedly temperature dependent, as would be expected in view of its dependence on metabolic processes. When the temperature is reduced, Na⁺ efflux and K⁺ influx are reduced several times as much as the passive processes of Na⁺ influx and K⁺ efflux.

The details of the operation of the Na^+ and K^+ pump are currently the subject of intensive research. The actual process by which the ions are actively transported is still unknown, but an enzyme that is intimately related to the pumping mechanism has been identified in red blood cells, brain cells, and the membranes of a great many other types of cells in a wide variety of species. This enzyme hydrolyzes ATP to adenosine diphosphate (ADP; see Chapter 17), and it is activated by Na^+ and K^+. It is therefore known as the **sodium-potassium-activated adenosine triphosphatase,** or **Na^+-K^+ ATPase.** It has 2 sites with affinities for cations: one where the affinity for Na^+ exceeds the affinity for K^+, and one where the affinity for K^+ exceeds the affinity for Na^+. For maximum activity, one site must be occupied by Na^+ and one by K^+. The enzyme is a large lipoprotein with a molecular weight of 670,000 which requires Mg^{++} for activity and is inhibited by ouabain. Its concentration in cell membranes is proportionate to the rate of Na^+ and K^+ transport in the cells. Its properties closely resemble those of the sodium-potassium pump, and it must in some way be intimately associated with it.

Genesis of the Action Potential

The distribution of ions across the cell membrane and the nature of this membrane provide the explanation for the membrane potential. K^+ diffuses out of the cell along its concentration gradient, while the nondiffusible anion component stays in the cell, creating a potential difference across the membrane. There is thus a slight excess of cations outside of the membrane and a slight excess of anions inside it. It should be emphasized, however, that the number of ions responsible for the membrane potential is a minute fraction of the total number present. Na^+ influx does not compensate for the K^+ efflux because the membrane at rest is much less permeable to Na^+ than K^+. Cl^- diffuses inward down its concentration gradient, but its movement is balanced by the electrical gradient. Generally, the action of the sodium pump is electrically neutral since it normally transports a K^+ into the cell for each Na^+ it pumps out. However, the pump maintains the concentration gradients on which the existence of the membrane potential depends. If the pump is shut off by the administration of metabolic inhibitors, Na^+ enters the cell, K^+ leaves it, and the membrane potential declines. The rate of this decline varies with the size of the cell. In large cells, it takes hours, but in nerve fibers with diameters of less than 1 μm, complete depolarization can occur in less than 4 minutes.

The magnitude of the membrane potential at any given time depends, of course, upon the distribution of Na^+, K^+, and Cl^-, and the permeability of the membrane to each of these ions. An equation that describes this relationship with considerable accuracy is the **Goldman constant-field equation:**

$$V = \frac{RT}{F} \ln\left(\frac{P_{K^+}[K_o^+] + P_{Na^+}[Na_o^+] + P_{Cl^-}[Cl_i^-]}{P_{K^+}[K_i^+] + P_{Na^+}[Na_i^+] + P_{Cl^-}[Cl_o^-]}\right)$$

where V is the membrane potential, R the gas content, T the absolute temperature, F the faraday, and P_{K^+}, P_{Na^+}, and P_{Cl^-} the permeability of the membrane to K^+, Na^+, and Cl^-, respectively. The brackets signify concentration, and i and o refer to the inside and outside of the cell. Since P_{Na^+} is low relative to P_{K^+} and P_{Cl^-} in the resting cells, Na^+ contributes little to the value of V. As would be predicted from the Goldman equation, changes in external Na^+ produce little change in the resting membrane potential whereas increases in external K^+ decrease it.

Variations in Membrane Potential

If the resting membrane potential is decreased by the passage of a current through the membrane, the electrical gradient which keeps K^+ inside the cell is decreased and there is an increase in K^+ diffusion out of the cell. This K^+ efflux and the simultaneous movement of Cl^- into the cell result in a net movement of positive charge out of the cell, with consequent restoration of the resting membrane potential. When the membrane potential increases, these ions move in the opposite direction. These processes occur in all polarized cells, and tend to keep the resting membrane potential of the cells constant within narrow limits. However, in nerve and muscle cells, reduction of the membrane potential triggers a sudden increase in Na^+ permeability. This unique feature permits these cells to generate self-propagating impulses which are transmitted along their membranes for great distances. These impulses are considered in detail in Chapter 2.

Effects of the Sodium-Potassium Pump on Metabolic Rate

Active transport of Na^+ and K^+ is one of the major energy-using processes in the body, and probably accounts for a large part of the basal metabolism. Furthermore, there is a direct link between Na^+ and K^+ transport and metabolism; the greater the rate of pumping, the more ADP is formed, and the available supply of ADP determines the rate at which ATP is formed by oxidative phosphorylation (see Chapter 17).

Effects of the Sodium-Potassium Pump on Cell Volume

In animals, the maintenance of normal cell volume and pressure depend on Na^+ and K^+ pumping. In the absence of such pumping, Cl^- and Na^+ would enter the cells down their concentration gradients, and water would follow along the osmotic gradient thus created, causing the cells to swell until the pressure inside them balanced the influx. This does not occur, and the osmolality and pressure of the cells remain the same as those of the interstitial fluid because Na^+ and K^+ are actively transported, the membrane potential is maintained, and $[Cl_i^-]$ remains low.

THE CAPILLARY WALL

The capillary wall, the barrier between the plasma and the interstitial fluid, permits free movement of water and small molecules. It has been postulated that pores are present in it, and their presumed size has been calculated. The structure of the capillary wall varies in different capillary beds, but in most sites the pores are too small to permit plasma proteins and other colloids to pass through in significant quantities. The colloids have a high molecular weight but are present in large amounts. The capillary wall therefore behaves like a membrane impermeable to colloids, which exert an osmotic pressure of about 25 mm Hg. The osmotic pressure due to the plasma colloids is called the **colloid osmotic pressure** or the **oncotic pressure**. Filtration across the capillary membrane due to the hydrostatic pressure head in the vascular system is opposed by the oncotic pressure. The way the balance between the hydrostatic and oncotic pressures controls exchanges across the capillary wall is considered in detail in Chapter 30.

Moderate amounts of protein do cross the capillary walls and enter the lymph. The size and frequency of the pores necessary to explain this movement have been calculated. Studies with the electron microscope have failed to demonstrate pores of the necessary size, but there are numerous vesicles in the capillary endothelium. Tagged protein molecules have been found in these vesicles, suggesting that proteins are transported out of capillaries across endothelial cells by pinocytosis followed by exocytosis on the interstitial side of the cells.

SODIUM & POTASSIUM DISTRIBUTION & TOTAL BODY OSMOLALITY

The foregoing discussion of the various compartments of the body fluids and the barriers between them facilitates consideration of the total body stores of the principal cations, Na^+ and K^+.

Total Body Sodium

The total amount of exchangeable Na^+ in the body (Na_E)—as opposed to its concentration in any particular body fluid—can be determined by the same dilution principle used to measure the body fluid compartments. A radioactive isotope of sodium (usually ^{24}Na) is injected, and after equilibration the fraction of the sodium in the body which is radioactive is determined. The fraction of a substance that is radioactive—ie, the concentration of radioactive molecules divided by the concentration of radioactive plus nonradioactive molecules—is the **specific activity** (SA) of the substance. The SA of sodium in plasma after the injection of ^{24}Na, for example, is

$$\frac{^{24}Na \text{ (counts per minute/liter)}}{^{24}Na + \text{nonradioactive Na (mEq/liter)}}$$

The total exchangeable body sodium (Na_E) =

$$\frac{^{24}Na \text{ injected} - {}^{24}Na \text{ excreted}}{SA \text{ of plasma}}$$

The average normal value for Na_E in healthy adults is 41 mEq/kg, whereas the total amount of Na^+ in the body is about 58 mEq/kg. Therefore, approximately 17 mEq/kg are not available for exchange. The vast majority of this nonexchangeable Na^+ is in the hydroxyapatite crystal lattice of bone. The amount of Na^+ in the various body compartments is summarized in Table 1−6.

TABLE 1−6. Distribution of sodium in the body in mEq/kg body weight and percentage of total body sodium.*

	mEq/kg	% of Total
Total	58	100
Exchangeable body sodium (Na_E)	41	70.7
Total intracellular	5.2	9.0
Total extracellular	52.8	91.0
Plasma	6.5	11.2
Interstitial fluid	16.8	29.0
Dense connective tissue and cartilage	6.8	11.7
Bone sodium		
Exchangeable	6.4	11.0
Nonexchangeable	14.8	25.5
Transcellular	1.5	2.6

*Data courtesy of IS Edelman.

Total Body Potassium

The total exchangeable body K^+ can be determined by measuring the dilution of radioactive potassium (^{42}K). The average value in young adult men is about 45 mEq/kg body weight. It is somewhat less in women, and declines slightly with advancing age. About 10% of the total body K^+ is bound, mostly in red blood cells, brain, and bone, and the remaining 90% is exchangeable (Fig 1−9).

Interrelationships of Sodium & Potassium

Since the salts of sodium and potassium dissociate in the body to such a great extent, and since they are so plentiful, they determine in large part the osmolality of the body fluids. A change in the amount of electrolyte in one compartment is followed by predictable changes in the electrolyte concentration of the others. Fig 1−10 shows, for example, the changes in osmolal concentration and volume of the intracellular and extracellular fluid spaces that follow removal of

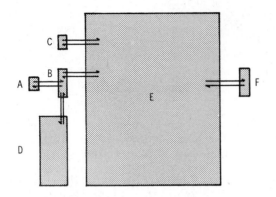

A: Plasma potassium, 0.4% of total body
   potassium
B: Interstitial lymph potassium, 1%
C: Dense connective tissue and cartilage
   potassium, 0.4%
D: Bone potassium, 7.6%
E: Intracellular potassium, 89.6%
F: Transcellular potassium, 1%

FIG 1—9. Body potassium distribution. Figures are percentages of total body potassium. (Data from Edelman & Liebman: Am J Med 27:256, 1959.)

500 mOsm of extracellular electrolyte. Loss of electrolyte in excess of water from the ECF leads to hypotonicity of the ECF relative to the intracellular fluid. Consequently, water moves into the cells by osmosis until osmotic equilibrium between the ECF and the intracellular fluid is again attained.

Total Body Osmolality

Since Na^+ is the principal cation of the plasma, the plasma osmotic pressure correlates well with the plasma Na^+ level. However, plasma Na^+ does not necessarily correlate well with Na_E. Total body osmolality reflects the electrolyte concentration in the body, ie, the total exchangeable body sodium plus the total exchangeable body potassium divided by the total body water:

$$\frac{Na_E + K_E}{TBW}$$

Because this latter figure has been found to correlate well with plasma Na^+, plasma Na^+ is a relatively accurate measure of total body osmolality. It is worth noting that plasma Na^+ can be affected by changes in any of 3 body components: Na_E itself, K_E, or TBW. A detailed discussion of the effects of disease on electrolyte and water balance is beyond the scope of this book, but the facts discussed above are basic to any consideration of pathologic water and electrolyte changes.

Plasma K^+ levels are not a good indicator of the total body K^+ since most of the K^+ is in the cells. There

is a correlation between the K^+ and H^+ content of plasma, the 2 rising and falling together.

pH & BUFFERS

The maintenance of a stable pH in the body fluids is essential to life. The pH of a solution is the logarithm to the base 10 of the reciprocal of the H^+ concentration ($[H^+]$), ie, the negative logarithm of the $[H^+]$. The pH of water, in which H^+ and OH^- ions are present in equal numbers, is 7.0. For each pH unit less than 7.0, the $[H^+]$ is increased tenfold; and for each pH unit above 7.0, it is decreased tenfold.

Buffers

The pH of the ECF is maintained at 7.40. In health, this value usually varies less than ±0.05 pH unit. Body pH is stabilized by the buffering capacity of the body fluids. A buffer is a substance which has the ability to bind or release H^+ in solution, thus maintaining the pH of the solution relatively constant despite the addition of considerable quantities of acid or base. One buffer in the body is carbonic acid, which is normally only slightly dissociated into H^+ and bicarbonate: $H_2CO_3 \rightleftarrows H^+ + HCO_3^-$. If H^+ is added to a solution of carbonic acid, the equilibrium shifts and most of the added H^+ is removed from solution. If OH^- is added, H^+ and OH^- combine and more H_2CO_3 dissociates. Other buffers include the blood proteins and the proteins in cells. The quantitative aspects of buffering and the respiratory and renal adjustments that operate with the buffers to maintain a stable ECF pH of 7.40 are discussed in Chapters 35 and 40.

HOMEOSTASIS

The actual environment of the cells of the body is the interstitial component of the ECF. Since normal cell function depends upon the constancy of this fluid, it is not surprising that in higher animals an immense number of regulatory mechanisms have evolved to maintain it. To describe "the various physiologic arrangements which serve to restore the normal state, once it has been disturbed," W.B. Cannon coined the term homeostasis. The buffering properties of the body fluids and the renal and respiratory adjustments to the presence of excess acid or alkali are examples of homeostatic mechanisms. There are countless other examples, and a large part of physiology is concerned with regulatory mechanisms which act to maintain the constancy of the internal environment. Many of these regulatory mechanisms operate on the principle of negative feedback; deviations from a given normal setpoint are detected by a sensor, and signals from the sensor trigger compensatory changes which continue until the setpoint is again reached.

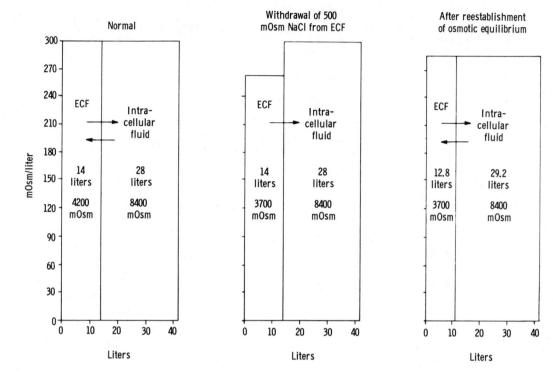

FIG 1–10. Response of body fluid to removal of 500 mOsm from ECF without change in total body water in a 70 kg man. The hypotonicity of the ECF causes water to enter cells until osmotic equilibrium is reestablished. Total mOsm in body after removal of 500 mOsm = (14 × 300) + (28 × 300)−500 = 12,100 mOsm. New osmotic equilibrium = 12,000/(28 + 14) = 288 mOsm/liter. This means that the new volume of the ECF will be (4200−500)/288 = 12.8 liters, and the new volume of the intracellular fluid will be 8400/288 = 29.2 liters. (After Darrow & Yannet. Modified and reproduced, with permission, from Gamble: *Chemical Anatomy, Physiology, and Pathology of Extracellular Fluid.* Harvard Univ Press, 1942.)

• • •

References: Section I.
Introduction

Bloom W, Fawcett DW: *A Textbook of Histology,* 9th ed. Saunders, 1968.

Cannon WB: *The Wisdom of the Body.* Norton, 1932.

Cohen SS: Are/were mitochondria and chloroplasts microorganisms? Am Scientist 58:281, 1970.

Davson H: *A Textbook of General Physiology,* 4th ed. Williams & Wilkins, 1970.

De Robertis EDP, Nowinski WW, Saez FA: *Cell Biology,* 5th ed. Saunders, 1970.

Haggis GH & others: *Introduction to Molecular Biology.* Wiley, 1964.

Katz AI, Epstein FH: Physiologic role of sodium-potassium-activated adenosine triphosphatase in the transport of cations across biologic membranes. New England J Med 278:253, 1968.

Moore FD & others: *The Body Cell Mass and Its Supporting Environment.* Saunders, 1963.

Siekevitz P: The organization of biological membranes. New England J Med 283:1035, 1970.

Watson JD: *Molecular Biology of the Gene,* 2nd ed. Benjamin, 1970.

Welt L: *Clinical Disorders of Hydration and Acid-Base Equilibrium,* 2nd ed. Little, Brown, 1959.

Wessells NK: How living cells change shape. Scientific American 225:76, Oct 1971.

Whaley WG, Dauwalder M, Kephart JE: Golgi apparatus: Influence on cell surfaces. Science 175:596, 1972.

Symposium: Comparative aspects of transport of hypertonic, isotonic and hypotonic solutions by epithelial membranes. Fed Proc 30:3, 1971.

Symposium: Membrane structure and its biological applications. Ann New York Acad Sci 195:5, 1972.

Symposium: The nature and function of peroxisomes (microbodies, glyoxysomes). Ann New York Acad Sci 168:209, 1969.

II. Physiology of Nerve & Muscle Cells

2...

Excitable Tissue: Nerve

The human nervous system contains about 10 billion neurons. These basic building blocks of the nervous system have evolved from primitive neuroeffector cells which respond to various stimuli by contracting. In higher animals, contraction has become the specialized function of muscle cells, while transmission of nerve impulses has become the specialized function of neurons.

NERVE CELLS

Morphology

A typical spinal motor neuron such as that shown in Fig 2–1 has many processes called **dendrites** which extend out from the cell body and arborize extensively. It also has a long fibrous **axon** which originates from a somewhat thickened area of the cell body, the **axon hillock**. A short distance from its origin, the axon acquires a sheath of **myelin**, a protein-lipid complex made up of many layers of unit membrane (Fig 2–2). The myelin sheath envelops the axon except at its ending and at periodic constrictions about 1 mm apart called the **nodes of Ranvier**. The axon ends in a number of **synaptic knobs**, which are also called **terminal buttons** or **axon telodendria**. These knobs contain granules or vesicles in which the synaptic

transmitter secreted by the nerve is stored (see Chapter 4). Some mammalian neurons and most neurons in invertebrates are unmyelinated; the axons are invested in Schwann cells, but there has been no rotation of the axon to produce multiple layers of membrane (Fig 2–2).

The conventional terminology used above for the parts of a neuron works well enough for spinal motor neurons and interneurons, but it has obvious shortcomings in terms of "dendrites" and "axons" when it is applied to other types of neurons found in the nervous system (Fig 2–3). A terminology for the parts of neurons which harmonizes morphologic and functional considerations is shown in Fig 2–4. According to this terminology, the **dendritic zone** of the neuron is the receptor membrane of the neuron (see below and Chapters 4 and 5). The axon is the single, elongated cytoplasmic neuronal extension with the specialized function of conducting impulses away from the dendritic zone. The cell body is often located at the dendritic zone end of the axon, but it can be within the axon (eg, auditory neurons) or attached to the side of the axon (eg, cutaneous neurons). Its location makes no difference as far as the receptor function of the dentritic zone and the transmission function of the axon are concerned.

The size of the neurons and the length of their processes vary considerably in different parts of the nervous system. In some cases, the dimensions of the

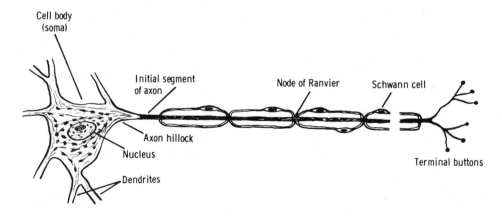

FIG 2–1. Motor neuron with myelinated axon.

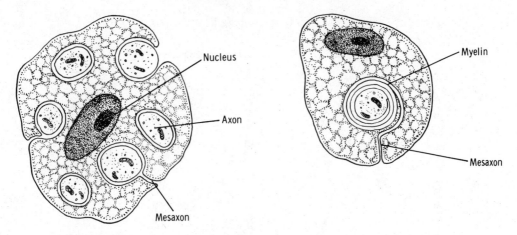

FIG 2–2. Relation of axons to Schwann cell in unmyelinated *(left)* and myelinated nerve *(right)*. In the former, the axons are simply buried in the cell. In the latter, the Schwann cell membrane is coiled many times around the axon, forming the multiple layers of unit membrane that make up myelin. (Redrawn and reproduced, with permission, from Wyburn: *The Nervous System.* Academic Press, 1960.)

neurons are truly remarkable. In the case of spinal motor neurons supplying the muscles of the foot, for example, it has been calculated that if the cell body were the size of a tennis ball the dendrites of the cell would fill an average-sized living room and the axon would be up to 1.6 km (almost a mile) long though only 13 mm (½ inch) in diameter.

Protein Synthesis & Axoplasmic Transport

Despite the extremely long axons of some

neurons, it is the cell body that maintains the functional and anatomic integrity of the axon; if the axon is cut, the part distal to the cut degenerates (**Wallerian degeneration**). The materials responsible for maintaining the axon, probably mostly proteins, are formed in the cell body and transported down the axon (**axoplasmic transport**). Proteins associated with synaptic transmitters are also synthesized in the endoplasmic reticulum of the cell body and transported to the axon terminals.. There is both fast (400 mm/day)

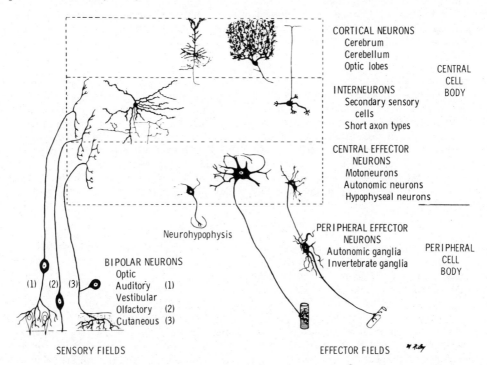

FIG 2–3. Types of neurons in the mammalian nervous system. (Reproduced, with permission, from Bodian: Introductory survey of neurons. *In:* Cold Spring Harbor Symposium on Quantitative Biology 17:1, 1952.)

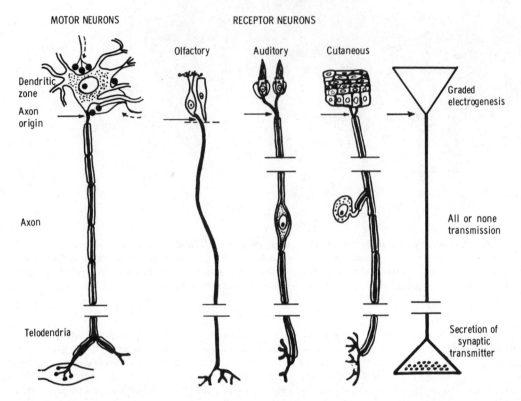

FIG 2—4. A variety of mammalian receptor and effector neurons. The neurons are arranged to illustrate the concept that impulse origin (indicated in each case by the arrow) rather than location of the cell body is the logical point of departure for analyzing neuronal structure in functional terms. Thus the dendritic zone, the area where the activity that generates the impulses occurs, may be dendrites or cell body. The axon conducts the impulses to the axon telodendria. The location of the cell body varies, and has no direct effect on impulse generation or transmission. (Modified after Grundfest and reproduced, with permission, from Bodian: The generalized vertebrate neuron. Science 137:323, 1962. Copyright 1962 by the American Association for the Advancement of Science.)

and slow (approximately 200 mm/day) transport. The fast transport mechanism depends on the oxidative metabolism of the neuron and probably on ATP (see Chapter 17). It appears to depend on the microtubules, and, since it has some similarities to the contraction of muscle, the hypothesis has been advanced that the transported material is attached to filaments formed in the cell body and slides along the microtubules in a manner analogous to the way actin slides along myosin in skeletal muscle.

Excitation

The nerve cell has a low threshold for excitation. The stimulus may be electrical, chemical, or mechanical. The physicochemical disturbance created by the stimulus, the **impulse**, is normally transmitted (or **conducted**) along the axon to its termination. Nerves are not "telephone wires" which transmit impulses passively; and conduction of nerve impulses, although rapid, is much slower than that of electricity. Nerve tissue is in fact a relatively poor passive conductor, and it would take a potential of many volts to produce a signal of a fraction of 1 volt at the other end of a 1

meter axon in the absence of active processes in the nerve. Conduction is an active, self-propagating process which requires expenditure of energy by the nerve, and the impulse moves along the nerve at a constant amplitude and velocity. The process is often compared to what happens when a match is applied to one end of a train of gunpowder; by igniting the powder particles immediately in front of it, the flame moves steadily down the train to its end.

ELECTRICAL PHENOMENA IN NERVE CELLS

For over 100 years it has been known that there are electrical potential changes in a nerve when it conducts impulses, but it was not until suitable equipment was developed that these electrical events could be measured and studied in detail. Special instruments are necessary because the events are rapid, being measured in **milliseconds (msec)**; and the potential changes are

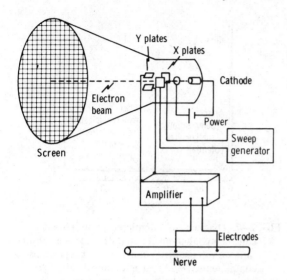

FIG 2–5. Cathode ray oscilloscope. Simplified diagram of principal connections when arranged to record potential changes in nerve. (Modified and reproduced, with permission, from Erlanger & Gasser: *Electrical Signs of Nervous Activity.* University of Pennsylvania Press, 1937.)

small, being measured in **millivolts (mv)**. The principal advances which made detailed study of the electrical activity in nerves possible were the development of electronic amplifiers and the cathode ray oscilloscope. Modern amplifiers magnify potential changes 1000 times or more, and the cathode ray oscilloscope provides an almost inertialess and almost instantaneously responding "lever" for recording electrical events.

The Cathode Ray Oscilloscope

The cathode ray oscilloscope (CRO) is used to measure the electrical events in living tissue. A cathode emits electrons when a high voltage is applied across it and a suitable anode in a vacuum. In the CRO the electrons are directed into a focused beam which strikes the face of the glass tube in which the cathode is located. The face is coated with one of a number of substances (phosphors) which emit light when struck by electrons. A vertical metal plate is placed on either side of the electron beam. When a voltage is applied across these plates, the negatively charged electrons are drawn toward the positively charged plate and repelled by the negatively charged plate. If the voltage applied to the vertical plates (X plates) is increased slowly and then reduced suddenly and increased again, the beam moves steadily toward the positive plate, snaps back to its former position, and moves toward the positive plate again. Application of a "saw-tooth voltage" of this type thus causes the beam to sweep across the face of the tube, and the speed of the sweep is proportionate to the rate of rise of the applied voltage.

In the CRO (Fig 2–5), another set of plates (Y plates) is arranged horizontally, with one plate above

and one below the beam. Voltages applied to these plates move the beam up and down as it sweeps across the face of the tube, the magnitude of the vertical deflection being proportionate to the potential difference between the horizontal plates at any given instant. In practice, electrodes placed on or in the nerve are connected through a suitable amplifier to the horizontal plates of the oscilloscope. Any changes in potential occurring in the nerve are thus recorded as vertical deflections of the beam as it moves across the tube. The tracing of the beam on the face of the oscilloscope may be photographed to make a permanent record.

Recording From Single Axons

With the CRO the electrical events occurring in a piece of peripheral nerve dissected from a laboratory animal can be demonstrated. However, such preparations contain many axons, and it is important to be able to study the properties of a single axon. Mammalian axons are relatively small (20 µm or less in diameter) and are difficult to separate from other axons, but giant unmyelinated nerve cells exist in a number of invertebrate species. Such giant cells are found, for example, in crabs (Carcinus) and cuttlefish (Sepia), but the largest known axons are found in the squid (Loligo). The neck region of the muscular mantle of the squid contains single axons up to 1 mm in diameter. It appears that their fundamental properties are similar to those of mammalian axons.

Another important technical advance in neurophysiology has been the development of microelectrodes which can be inserted into nerve cells. These electrodes are made by drawing out glass capillary pipets so that the diameter of the tip is very small. They are filled with a solution of electrolyte, usually potassium chloride. Electrodes with tip diameters of a few micrometers can be inserted into invertebrate giant axons, and ultramicroelectrodes with tip diameters of less than 1 µm can be inserted into mammalian nerve cells.

Resting Membrane Potential

When 2 electrodes are connected through a suitable amplifier to a CRO and placed on the surface of a single axon, no potential difference is observed. However, if one electrode is inserted into the interior of the cell, a constant potential difference is observed between the inside and the outside of the cell at rest. The magnitude of this **resting membrane potential** in most neurons is approximately 70 mv. It is expressed as a negative potential, −70 mv, because the inside of the cell is negatively charged relative to the exterior.

Latent Period

If the axon is stimulated and a conducted impulse occurs, a characteristic series of potential changes is observed as the impulse passes the exterior electrode. When the stimulus is applied there is a brief irregular deflection of the baseline, the **stimulus artifact.** This artifact is due to current leakage from the stimulating electrodes to the recording electrodes. It usually occurs despite careful shielding, but it is of value because it marks on the cathode ray screen the point at which the stimulus was applied.

The stimulus artifact is followed by an isopotential interval or **latent period** which ends with the next potential change and corresponds to the time it takes the impulse to travel along the axon from the site of stimulation to the recording electrodes. Its duration is proportionate to the distance between the stimulating and recording electrodes and the speed of conduction of the axon. If the duration of the latent period and the distance between the electrodes are known, the speed of conduction in the axon can be calculated. For example, assume that the distance between the cathodal stimulating electrode and the exterior electrode in Fig 2–6 is 4 cm. The cathode is normally the stimulating electrode, as described below. If the latent period is 2 msec long, the speed of conduction is 4 cm/2 msec, or 20 meters/sec.

Action Potential

The first manifestation of the approaching impulse is a beginning depolarization of the membrane. After an initial 15 mv of depolarization, the rate of depolarization increases. The point at which this change in rate occurs is called the **firing level**. Thereafter, the tracing on the oscilloscope rapidly reaches and **overshoots** the isopotential (zero potential) line to approximately +35 mv. It then reverses and falls rapidly toward the resting level. When repolarization is about 70% completed, the rate of repolarization decreases and the tracing approaches the resting level

FIG 2–6. Action potential ("spike potential") recorded with one electrode inside cell.

FIG 2–7. Diagram of complete action potential of large mammalian myelinated fiber, drawn without time or voltage distortion to show proportions of components. (Modified and redrawn from Gasser: The control of excitation in the nervous system. Harvey Lectures 32:169, 1957.)

more slowly. The sharp rise and rapid fall are the **spike potential** of the axon, and the slower fall at the end of the process is the **after-depolarization,** or **negative after-potential.** After reaching the previous resting level, the tracing overshoots slightly in the hyperpolarizing direction to form the small but prolonged **after-hyperpolarization,** or **positive after-potential.** The whole sequence of potential changes is called the **action potential.**

The proportions of the tracing in Fig 2–6 are intentionally distorted to illustrate these various components of the action potential. A tracing with the components plotted on exact temporal and magnitude scales for a mammalian neuron is shown in Fig 2–7. Note that the rise of the action potential is so rapid that it fails to show clearly the change in depolarization rate at the firing level, and also that the after-hyperpolarization is only about 1–2 mv in amplitude although it lasts about 35–40 msec. The duration of the after-depolarization is about 4 msec. Changes may occur in the after-polarizations without changes in the rest of the action potential. For example, if the nerve has been conducting repetitively for a long time, the after-hyperpolarization is usually quite large. These potentials are therefore thought to represent recovery processes in the neuron rather than the events responsible for the spike portion of the action potential.

"All or None" Law

If an axon is arranged for recording as shown in Fig 2–6 with the recording electrodes at an appreciable distance from the stimulating electrodes, it is possible to determine the minimal intensity of stimulating current (**threshold intensity**) which will just produce an impulse. This threshold varies with the experimental conditions and the type of axon, but once it is reached, a full-fledged action potential is produced. Further increases in the intensity of a stimulus produce no increment or other change in the action potential as long as the other experimental conditions remain constant. The action potential fails to occur if the stimulus is subthreshold in magnitude, and it occurs with a constant amplitude and form regardless of the strength of the stimulus if the stimulus is at or above threshold intensity. The action potential is therefore "all or none" in character, and is said to obey the **"all or none law."**

Strength-Duration Curve

In a preparation such as that in Fig 2−6, it is possible to determine experimentally the relationship between the strength of the stimulating current and the length of time it must be applied to the nerve to produce a response. Stimuli of extremely short duration will not excite the axon no matter how intense they may be. With stimuli of longer duration, threshold intensity is related to the duration of stimulus as shown in Fig 2−8. With weak stimuli, a point is reached where no response occurs no matter how long the stimulus is applied. The relationship shown in Fig 2−8 applies only to currents that rise to peak intensity rapidly. Slowly rising currents sometimes fail to fire the nerve because the nerve in some way adapts to the applied stimulus. This process is called **accommodation.**

Classically, the magnitude of the current just sufficient to excite a given nerve or muscle is called the **rheobase** and the time for which it must be applied the **utilization time.** Another common measurement is the **chronaxie,** ie, the length of time a current of twice rheobasic intensity must be applied to produce a response. Within limits, the chronaxie of any given excitable tissue is constant for that tissue, and chronaxie values have been used to compare excitability of various tissues.

Duration (time)

A: Rheobase
B: Utilization time
C: Chronaxie

FIG 2−8. Strength-duration curve. The curve relates the strength of a stimulus to the time for which it must be applied to an excitable tissue to produce a response.

Electrotonic Potentials, Local Response, & Firing Level

Although subthreshold stimuli do not produce an action potential, they do have an effect on the membrane potential. This can be demonstrated by placing recording electrodes within a few millimeters of a stimulating electrode and applying subthreshold stimuli of fixed duration. Application of such currents with a cathode leads to a localized depolarizing potential change which rises sharply and decays exponentially with time. The magnitude of this response drops off rapidly as the distance between the stimulating and recording electrodes is increased. Conversely, an anodal current produces a hyperpolarizing potential change of similar duration. These potential changes are called **electrotonic potentials,** those produced at a cathode being **catelectrotonic** and those at an anode **anelectrotonic.** They are passive changes in membrane polarization caused by addition or subtraction of charge by the particular electrode. At low current intensities producing up to about 7 mv of depolarization or hyperpolarization, their size is proportionate to the magnitude of the stimulus. With stronger stimuli, this relationship remains constant for anelectrotonic responses but not for responses at the cathode. The cathodal responses are greater than would be expected from the magnitude of the applied current. Finally, when the cathodal stimulation is great enough to produce about 15 mv of depolarization, ie, at a membrane potential of −55 mv, the membrane potential suddenly begins to fall rapidly and a propagated action potential occurs. The disproportionately greater response at the cathode to stimuli of sufficient strength to produce 7−15 mv of depolarization indicates active participation by the membrane in the process and is called the **local response** (Fig 2−9). The point at which a runaway spike potential is initiated is the **firing level.** Thus, cathodal currents which produce up to 7 mv of depolarization have a purely passive effect on the membrane caused by addition of negative charges. Those producing 7−15 mv of depolarization produce in addition a slight active change in the membrane, and this change contributes to the depolarizing process. However, the repolarizing forces are still stronger than the depolarizing forces, and the potential decays. At 15 mv of depolarization, the depolarizing forces are strong enough to overwhelm the repolarizing processes and an action potential results. These facts indicate that at 15 mv of depolarization some fundamental change which leads to runaway depolarization occurs in the membrane.

Stimulation normally occurs at the cathode because cathodal stimuli are depolarizing. Anodal currents, by taking the membrane potential farther away from the firing level, actually inhibit impulse formation. However, cessation of an anodal current may lead to an overshoot of the membrane potential in the depolarizing direction. This rebound is sometimes large enough to cause the nerve to fire at the end of an anodal stimulus.

FIG 2–9. Electrotonic potentials and local response. The changes in the membrane potential of a neuron following application of stimuli of 0.2, 0.4, 0.6, 0.8, and 1.0 times threshold intensity are shown superimposed on the same time scale. The responses below the horizontal line are those recorded near the anode, and the responses above the line are those recorded near the cathode. The stimulus of threshold intensity was repeated twice. Once it caused a propagated action potential (top line), and once it did not. (Based on a diagram from Hodgkin: The subthreshold potentials in a crustacean nerve fiber. Proc Roy Soc London s.B 126:87, 1938.)

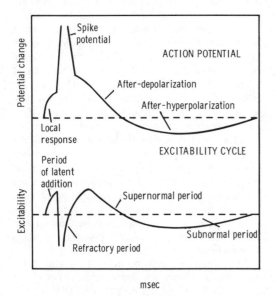

FIG 2–10. Relative changes in excitability of a nerve cell membrane during the passage of an impulse. Note that excitability is the reciprocal of threshold. (Redrawn and reproduced, with permission, from Morgan: *Physiological Psychology.* McGraw-Hill, 1943.)

Changes in Excitability During Electrotonic Potentials & the Action Potential

During the action potential as well as during catelectrotonic and anelectrotonic potentials and the local response, there are changes in the threshold of the neuron to stimulation. Hyperpolarizing anelectrotonic responses elevate the threshold and catelectrotonic potentials lower it as they move the membrane potential closer to the firing level. During the local response the threshold is also lowered, but during the rising and the early portion of the falling phases of the spike potential the neuron is refractory to stimulation. This **refractory period** is divided into an **absolute refractory period**, corresponding to the period from the time the firing level is reached until repolarization is about one-third complete; and a **relative refractory period**, lasting from this point to the start of after-depolarization. During the absolute refractory period no stimulus, no matter how strong, will excite the nerve, but during the relative refractory period stronger than normal stimuli can cause excitation. During after-depolarization the threshold is again decreased, and during after-hyperpolarization it is increased. These changes in threshold are correlated with the phases of the action potential in Fig 2–10.

Electrogenesis of the Action Potential

The descriptive data discussed above may be formulated into a picture of the electrical events underlying the action potential. The nerve cell membrane is polarized at rest, with positive charges lined up along the outside of the membrane and negative charges along the inside. During the action potential, this polarity is abolished and for a brief period is actually reversed (Fig 2–11). Positive charges from the membrane ahead of and behind the action potential flow into the area of negativity represented by the action potential ("current sink"). By drawing off positive charges, this flow decreases the polarity of the membrane ahead of the action potential. Such electrotonic depolarization initiates a local response, and when the firing level is reached a propagated response occurs which in turn electrotonically depolarizes the membrane in front of it. This sequence of events moves regularly along an unmyelinated axon to its end. Thus, the self-propagating nature of the nerve impulse is due to circular current flow and successive electrotonic depolarizations to the firing level of the membrane ahead of the action potential.

The action potentials produced at synaptic junctions also depend upon electrotonic depolarization of the nerve cell membrane to the firing level. The details of the process by which the nerve cell body and dendrites serve as a large current sink to draw off positive charges from the axon are described in Chapter 4.

Saltatory Conduction

Conduction in myelinated axons depends upon a similar pattern of circular current flow. However, myelin is a relatively effective insulator, and current flow through it is negligible. Instead, depolarization in

FIG 2–11. Local current flow around an impulse in an axon. Note that current flow is represented as movement of positive charges. *A* represents the situation in nonmyelinated nerves, *B* that in myelinated nerves (saltatory conduction). IM = impulse.

myelinated axons jumps from one node of Ranvier to the next, with the current sink at the active node serving to electrotonically depolarize to the firing level the node ahead of the action potential (Fig 2–11). This jumping of depolarization from node to node is called **saltatory conduction.** It is a rapid process, and myelinated axons conduct up to 50 times faster than the fastest unmyelinated fibers.

Orthodromic & Antidromic Conduction

An axon can conduct in either direction. When an action potential is initiated in the middle of it, 2 impulses traveling in opposite directions are set up by electrotonic depolarization on either side of the initial current sink. Once initiated, a moving impulse does not

depolarize the area behind it to the firing level (as it does the area ahead of it) because the area behind is refractory.

In a living animal impulses normally pass in one direction only, ie, from synaptic junctions or receptors along axons to their termination. Such conduction is called **orthodromic.** Conduction in the opposite direction is called **antidromic.** Since synapses, unlike axons, permit conduction in one direction only, any antidromic impulses that are set up fail to pass the first synapse they encounter (see Chapter 4) and die out at that point.

Biphasic & Monophasic Action Potentials

The descriptions of the resting membrane potential and action potential outlined above are based on recording with 2 electrodes, one on the surface of the axon and the other inside the axon. If both recording electrodes are placed on the surface of the axon, there is no potential difference between them at rest. When the nerve is stimulated and an impulse is conducted past the 2 electrodes, a characteristic sequence of potential changes results. As the wave of depolarization reaches the electrode nearest the stimulator, this electrode becomes negative to the other electrode (Fig 2–12). When the impulse passes to the portion of the nerve between the 2 electrodes, the potential returns to zero and then, as it passes the second electrode, the first electrode becomes positive to the second. It is conventional to connect the leads in such a way that when the first electrode becomes negative to the second an upward deflection is recorded. Therefore, the record shows an upward deflection followed by an iso-electric interval and then a downward deflection. This sequence is called a **biphasic action potential** (Fig 2–12). The duration of the iso-electric interval is proportionate to the speed of conduction of the nerve and the distance between the 2 recording electrodes.

If the axon under one of the external electrodes is damaged (eg, by crushing), the damaged area becomes negative relative to the healthy portion at rest. The potential difference between the 2 electrodes is called the **demarcation potential.** Its magnitude is variable, depending upon the extent of the disruption of the membrane. The negativity of the damaged area is due to breakdown of the membrane. If such a preparation is stimulated, an upward deflection is recorded as the

Cathode ray oscilloscope

FIG 2–13. Monophasic action potential.

impulse passes under the electrode on healthy tissue. No downward deflection is observed because the impulse stops at the damaged area. The single deflection produced in this way is called a **monophasic action potential** (Fig 2–13).

Conduction in a Volume Conductor

Because the body fluids contain large quantities of electrolytes, the nerves in the body function in a conducting medium which is often called a **volume conductor.** The monophasic and biphasic action potentials described above are those seen when an axon is stimulated in a nonconducting medium outside the body. The potential changes observed during extracellular recording in a volume conductor are basically similar to these action potentials, but they are complicated by the effects of current flow in the volume conductor. These effects are complex, depending upon such factors as the orientation of the electrodes relative to the direction the action potential is moving and the distance between the recording electrode over active tissue and the indifferent electrode. In general, when an action potential is recorded in a volume conductor, there are positive deflections before and after the negative spike. A simplified diagram of the genesis of these deflections is shown in Fig 2–14.

IONIC BASIS OF EXCITATION & CONDUCTION

Ionic Basis of Resting Membrane Potential

The ionic basis of the resting membrane potential has been discussed in Chapter 1, using frog skeletal muscle cells as an example. In nerve, as in other tissues, Na^+ is actively transported out of the cell and K^+ is actively transported in. K^+ diffuses back out of the cell down its concentration gradient, and Na^+ diffuses back in, but since the permeability of the membrane to K^+ is much greater than it is to Na^+ at rest, the passive K^+ efflux is much greater than the passive Na^+ influx. Since the membrane is impermeable to most of the anions in the cell, the K^+ efflux is not accompanied by

FIG 2–12. **Biphasic action potential.** Both recording electrodes are on the outside of the nerve membrane.

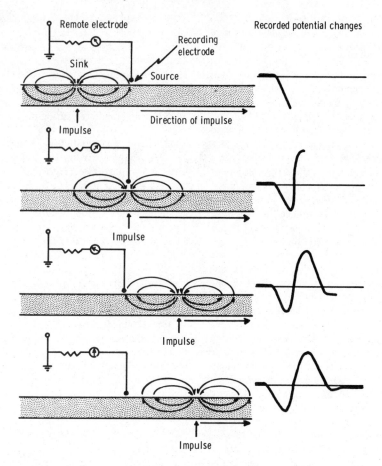

FIG 2–14. Potential changes recorded during passage of an impulse along an axon in a volume conductor. One electrode (recording electrode) is on the surface of the axon; the other (remote or indifferent electrode) is on inactive tissue at a distance in the conducting medium. (Reproduced, with permission, from Brazier: *The Electrical Activity of the Nervous System,* 3rd ed. Pitman, 1968.)

an equal flux of anions and the membrane is maintained in a polarized state with the outside positive to the inside. The ion fluxes across the nerve cell membrane at rest are summarized in Fig 1–8.

Ionic Fluxes During the Action Potential

In nerve, as in other tissues, a slight decrease in resting membrane potential leads to increased movement of K^+ out of and Cl^- into the cell, restoring the resting membrane potential. In the case of nerve and muscle, however, there is a unique change in the cell membrane when depolarization exceeds 7 mv. This change is a voltage-dependent increase in membrane permeability to Na^+, so that the closer the membrane potential is to the firing level the greater the Na^+ permeability. The electrical and concentration gradients for Na^+ are both directed inward. During the local response, Na^+ permeability is slightly increased, but K^+ efflux is able to restore the potential to the resting value. When the firing level is reached, permeability is great enough so that Na^+ influx further lowers the membrane potential and Na^+ permeability is

further increased. The consequent Na^+ influx swamps the repolarizing processes, and runaway depolarization results, producing the spike potential.

The equilibrium potential for Na^+ in mammalian neurons calculated by using the Nernst equation is about +60 mv. With the great increase in Na^+ permeability at the start of the action potential, the membrane potential approaches this value. It does not reach it, however, primarily because the change in Na^+ permeability is short-lived. Na^+ permeability starts to return to the resting value during the rising phase of the spike potential. In addition, the direction of the electrical gradient for Na^+ is reversed during the overshoot because the membrane potential is reversed. Both factors limit Na^+ influx and help initiate repolarization.

Another important factor producing repolarization of the nerve membrane is the increase in K^+ permeability that accompanies the increase in Na^+ permeability. The change in K^+ permeability starts more slowly and reaches a peak during the falling phase of the action potential. The increase in permeability decreases the barrier to K^+ diffusion, and K^+ consequently leaves the cell. The resulting net transfer of positive charge out of the cell serves to complete repolarization.

The changes in membrane permeability during the action potential have been documented in a number of ways, perhaps most clearly by the voltage clamp technic. This research technic, the details of which are beyond the scope of this book, has made it possible to measure the **conductance** of the membrane for various ions. The conductance of an ion is the reciprocal of its electrical resistance in a membrane, and is a measure of membrane permeability to that ion. The changes in Na^+ and K^+ conductance during the action potential are shown in Fig 2–15. Additional evidence that this ionic hypothesis of the basis of the action potential is correct is provided by the observation that decreasing the external Na^+ concentration decreases the size of the action potential but has little effect on the resting membrane potential. The lack of much effect on the resting membrane potential would be predicted from the Goldman equation (see Chapter 1) since the permeability of the membrane to Na^+ at rest is relatively low. Conversely, increasing the external K^+ concentration decreases the resting membrane potential. The way in which partial depolarization causes the change in membrane permeability to Na^+ has not been determined.

Although Na^+ enters the nerve cell and K^+ leaves it during the action potential, the number of ions involved is not large relative to the total numbers present. The fact that the nerve gains Na^+ and loses K^+ during activity has been demonstrated experimentally, but significant differences in ion concentrations can be measured only after prolonged, repeated stimulation.

FIG 2–15. **Changes in sodium and potassium conductance during the action potential in giant squid axon.** The dotted line represents the action potential superimposed on the same time coordinate. The unit of conductance, the mmho, is the reciprocal of the unit of resistance, the mohm (milliohm). (Redrawn and reproduced, with permission, from Hodgkin: Ionic movements and electrical activity in giant nerve fibers. Proc Roy Soc London s.B 148:1, 1958.)

As noted above, the after-depolarization (negative after-potential) and the after-hyperpolarization (positive after-potential) represent restorative processes in the cell. Relatively little is known about their origin. The after-depolarization is reduced by agents that inhibit metabolism and seems to be associated with a transient accumulation along the membrane of some of the K^+ leaving the nerve during the repolarization.

Energy Sources & Metabolism of Nerve

The major part of the energy requirement of nerve is the portion used to maintain polarization of the membrane. The energy for the sodium-potassium pump is derived from the hydrolysis of ATP. During maximal activity, the metabolic rate of the nerve doubles; by comparison, that of skeletal muscle increases as much as 100-fold. Inhibition of lactic acid production does not influence nerve function.

Like muscle, nerve has a resting heat while inactive, an initial heat during the action potential, and a recovery heat that follows activity. However, in nerve, the recovery heat after a single impulse is about 30 times the initial heat. There is some evidence that the initial heat is produced during the after-depolarization rather than the spike. The metabolism of muscle is discussed in detail in Chapter 3.

PROPERTIES OF MIXED NERVES

Peripheral nerves in mammals are made up of many axons bound together in a fibrous envelope called the **epineurium.** Potential changes recorded from such nerves therefore represent an algebraic summation of the all or none action potentials of many axons. The thresholds of the individual axons in the nerve and their distance from the stimulating electrodes vary. With subthreshold stimuli, none of the axons are stimulated and no response occurs. When the stimuli are of threshold intensity, axons with low thresholds fire and a small potential change is observed. As the intensity of the stimulating current is increased, the axons with higher thresholds are also discharged. The electrical response increases proportionately until the stimulus is strong enough to excite all of the axons in the nerve. The stimulus which produces excitation of all the axons is the **maximal stimulus,** and further application of greater, **supramaximal** stimuli produces no further increase in the size of the observed potential.

Compound Action Potentials

Another property of mixed nerves, as opposed to single axons, is the appearance of multiple peaks in the action potential. The multi-peaked action potential is called a **compound action potential.** Its shape is due to the fact that a mixed nerve is made up of families of fibers with varying speeds of conduction. Therefore, when all the fibers are stimulated, the activity in fast-

Action potential

Stimulator   Mixed nerve   Direction of impulse ⟶

FIG 2–16. Compound action potential. *Above:* Record obtained with recording electrodes at various distances from the stimulating electrodes along a mixed nerve. *Left:* Reconstruction of a compound action potential to show relative sizes and time relationships of the components. (Redrawn and reproduced, with permission, from Erlanger & Gasser: *Electrical Signs of Nervous Activity.* University of Pennsylvania Press, 1937.)

conducting fibers arrives at the recording electrodes sooner than the activity in slower fibers; and the farther away from the stimulating electrodes the action potential is recorded, the greater is the separation between the fast and slow fiber peaks. The number and size of the peaks vary with the types of fibers in the particular nerve being studied. If less than maximal stimuli are used, the shape of the compound action potential also depends upon the number and type of fibers stimulated.

Erlanger and Gasser have divided mammalian nerve fibers into A, B, and C groups, further subdividing the A group into *a*, *β*, *γ*, and *δ* fibers. The relative latencies of the electrical activity due to each of these components are shown in Fig 2–16. It should be emphasized that the drawing is not the compound action potential of any particular peripheral nerve; none of the peripheral nerves show all the components

illustrated in this composite diagram because none contain all of the fiber types.

NERVE FIBER TYPES & FUNCTION

By comparing the neurologic deficits produced by careful dorsal root section and other nerve cutting experiments with the histologic changes in the nerves, the functions and histologic characteristics of each of the families of axons responsible for the various peaks of the compound action potential have been established. In general, the greater the diameter of a given nerve fiber, the greater its speed of conduction. The larger axons are concerned with proprioceptive sensation and somatic motor function, while the smaller

TABLE 2–1. Nerve fiber types in mammalian nerve.

Fiber Type	Function	Fiber Diameter (μm)	Conduction Velocity (m/sec)	Spike Duration (msec)	Absolute Refractory Period (msec)
A *a*	Proprioception; somatic motor	12–20	70–120		
β	Touch, pressure	5–12	30–70	0.4–0.5	0.4–1
γ	Motor to muscle spindles	3–6	15–30		
δ	Pain, temperature	2–5	12–30		
B	Preganglionic autonomic	<3	3–15	1.2	1.2
C dorsal root	Pain, reflex responses	0.4–1.2	0.5–2	2	2
sympathetic	Postganglionic sympathetics	0.3–1.3	0.7–2.3	2	2

TABLE 2–2. Numerical classification sometimes used for sensory neurons.

Number		Origin	Fiber Type
I	a	Muscle spindle, annulo-spiral ending	A α
	b	Golgi tendon organ	A α
II		Muscle spindle, flower-spray ending; touch, pressure	A β
III		Pain and temperature receptors	A δ
IV		Pain and other receptors	Dorsal root C

TABLE 2–3. Relative susceptibility of mammalian A, B, and C nerve fibers to conduction block produced by various agents.

	Most Susceptible	Intermediate	Least Susceptible
Sensitivity to hypoxia	B	A	C
Sensitivity to pressure	A	B	C
Sensitivity to cocaine and local anesthetics	C	B	A

TABLE 2–4. Types of fibers in peripheral and cranial nerves.

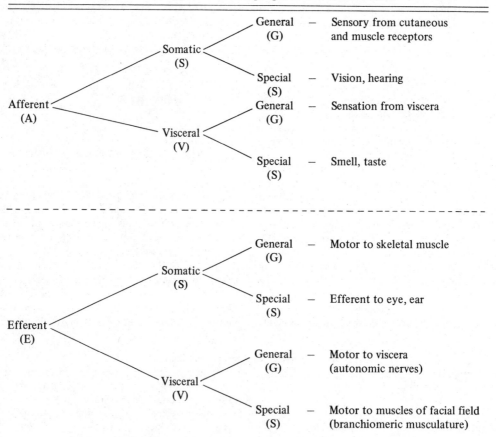

Thus, GVA = general visceral afferent; SVE = special visceral efferent; etc.

axons subserve pain sensation and autonomic function. In Table 2–1, the various fiber types are listed with their diameters, electrical characteristics, and functions. There is evidence that the dorsal root C fibers conduct impulses generated by touch and other cutaneous receptors in addition to pain receptors, but only the latter are relayed to consciousness. The other fibers presumably are concerned with reflex responses integrated in the spinal cord and brain stem.

Further research has shown that not all the classically described lettered components are homogeneous, and a numerical system (Ia, Ib, II, III, IV) has been used by some physiologists to classify sensory fibers. Unfortunately, this has led to some confusion. A comparison of the number system and the letter system is shown in Table 2–2.

In addition to variations in speed of conduction and fiber diameter, the various classes of fibers in peripheral nerves differ in their sensitivity to hypoxia and anesthetics (Table 2–3). This fact has clinical as well as physiologic significance. Local anesthetics depress transmission in the group C fibers before they affect the touch fibers in the A group. Conversely, pressure on a nerve can cause loss of conduction in motor, touch, and pressure fibers while pain sensation remains relatively intact. Patterns of this type are sometimes seen in individuals who sleep with their arms under their heads for long periods of time, causing compression of the nerves in the arms. Because of the association of deep sleep with alcoholic intoxication, the syndrome is common on weekends, and has acquired the interesting name Saturday night or Sunday morning paralysis.

Peripheral nerve fibers in man are also classified on a physio-anatomic basis. This classification (Table 2–4) divides nerves into afferent and efferent categories, and further subdivides them according to whether they have somatic or visceral and general or special functions. The term special is applied to nerves which supply the organs of the special senses and the musculature which is branchiomeric in origin, ie, musculature arising from the branchial arches during embryonic development.

GLIA

In addition to neurons, the nervous system contains glial cells, or neuroglia. Glial cells are very numerous; indeed, there are approximately 10 times as many glial cells as neurons. The Schwann cells which invest axons in peripheral nerves are classified as glia. In the CNS, there are 3 types of glia. **Microglia** are scavenger cells that enter the nervous system from the blood vessels. The **oligodendroglia** are involved in myelin formation. The **astrocytes** are found throughout the brain and many send end feet to blood vessels (see Chapter 32). They have a membrane potential which varies with the external K^+ concentration, but do not generate propagated potentials. Despite many theories, their function remains uncertain.

3 . . .
Excitable Tissue: Muscle

Muscle cells, like neurons, can be excited chemically, electrically, and mechanically to produce an action potential which is transmitted along their cell membrane. Unlike neurons, they have a contractile mechanism which is activated by the action potential.

Muscle is generally divided into 3 types, **skeletal**, **cardiac**, and **smooth**, although smooth muscle is not a homogeneous single category. Skeletal muscle comprises the great mass of the somatic musculature. It has well developed cross-striations, does not normally contract in the absence of nervous stimulation, lacks anatomic and functional connections between individual muscle fibers, and is generally under voluntary control. Cardiac muscle also has cross-striations, but it is functionally syncytial in character and contracts rhythmically even when denervated. Smooth muscle lacks cross-striations. The type found in most hollow viscera is functionally syncytial in character and has inherent semirhythmic contractile activity. The type found in the eye and in some other locations is not spontaneously active and resembles skeletal muscle.

FIG 3–1. Structure of skeletal muscle fiber. The fiber is made up of a number of fibrils and surrounded by a membrane, the sarcolemma. Each fibril is surrounded by sarcoplasmic reticulum and by the T system of tubules, which opens to the exterior of the fiber. (Reproduced, with permission, from: How is muscle turned on and off? by Hoyle. Scientific American 222:84 [April], 1970. Copyright © 1970 by Scientific American, Inc. All rights reserved.)

SKELETAL MUSCLE

MORPHOLOGY

Organization

Skeletal muscle is made up of individual muscle fibers which are the "building blocks" of the muscular system in the same sense that the neurons are the building blocks of the nervous system. Most skeletal muscles begin and end in tendons, and the muscle fibers are arranged in parallel between the tendinous ends so that the force of contraction of the units is additive. Each muscle fiber is a single cell, multinucleated, long, and cylindrical in shape. There are no syncytial bridges between cells.

The muscle fibers are made up of fibrils, as shown in Fig 3–1, and the fibrils are divisible into individual filaments about 15 nm in diameter. The filaments are made up of the contractile proteins.

Muscle contains the proteins **myosin** (molecular weight probably about 500,000), **actin** (molecular weight about 60,000), **tropomyosin**, and **troponin**. Tropomyosin binds troponin to actin. When actin and myosin are mixed, they form a unique complex with contractile properties called **actomyosin**.

Striations

The cross-striations characteristic of skeletal muscle are due to differences in the refractive indexes of the various parts of the muscle fiber. The parts of the cross-striations are identified by letters (Fig 3–2). The light I band is divided by the dark Z line, and the dark A band has the lighter H band in its center. A transverse M line is seen in the middle of the H band, and this line plus the narrow light areas on either side of it are sometimes called the pseudo-H zone. The area between 2 adjacent Z lines is called a **sarcomere**. The arrangement of thick and thin filaments that is responsible for the striations is diagrammed in Fig 3–3. The

FIG 3–2. Electron micrograph of skeletal muscle of rabbit (X 24,000), showing various lines, bands, and zones. (Photograph reproduced, with permission, from: The contraction of muscle, by Huxley. Scientific American 199:66 [Nov], 1958. Copyright © 1958 by Scientific American, Inc. All rights reserved.)

FIG 3–3. *Top left:* Arrangement of actin and myosin filaments in skeletal muscles. ***Right:*** Cross-sections through I band and through A band lateral to H band. ***Bottom left:*** Probable fine structure of actin and myosin, showing cross-linkages. Myosin appears to be made up of units arranged on either side of the sarcomere in such a way that their heads form the cross-linkages. Actin appears to be made up of 2 helical chains of globular units.

thick filaments are made up of myosin; the thin filaments are made up of actin and tropomyosin. The
thick myosin filaments are lined up to form the A
bands, whereas the array of thin actin filaments forms
the less dense I bands. The lighter H bands in the
center of the A bands are the regions where, when the
muscle is relaxed, the actin filaments do not overlap
the myosin filaments. The Z lines transect the fibrils
and connect to the actin filaments. If a transverse section through the A band is examined under the electron microscope, each myosin filament is found to be
surrounded by 6 actin filaments in a regular hexagonal
pattern.

Observations with x-ray diffraction technics and
the electron microscope indicate that the individual
myosin molecules have enlarged "heads" and that they
are arranged as shown in the lower right hand portion
of Fig 3–3. Cross-linkages between the myosin and
actin filaments have been demonstrated, and it seems
likely that these links are formed by the heads of the
myosin molecules. The molecules are arranged sym-
metrically on either side of the center of the sarcomere, and it is this arrangement which creates the light
areas in the pseudo-H zone. The M line is due to a
central bulge in each of the thick filaments. At these
points, there are slender cross-connections which hold
the myosin filaments in proper array. The actin filaments are apparently made up of 2 chains of globular
units which form a long double helix.

Sarcotubular System

The muscle fibrils are surrounded by structures
made up of membrane which appear in electron photo-
micrographs as vesicles and tubules. These structures
form the **sarcotubular system**, which is made up of a **T
system** and a **sarcoplasmic reticulum**. The T system,
which is continuous with the membrane of the muscle
fiber, forms a grid perforated by the individual muscle
fibrils (Fig 3–1). The space between the 2 layers of the
T system is an extension of the extracellular space. The
sarcoplasmic reticulum forms an irregular curtain
around each of the fibrils between its contacts with the
T system, which in mammalian skeletal muscle is at the
junction of the A and I bands. At these junctions, the
arrangement of the central T system with sarcoplasmic
reticulum on either side has led to the use of the term
triads to describe the system. The function of the T
system is the rapid transmission of the action potential
from the cell membrane to all the fibrils in the muscle.
The sarcoplasmic reticulum is concerned with calcium
movement and muscle metabolism (see below).

timing and magnitude. The resting membrane potential
of skeletal muscle is about -90 mv. The action potential lasts 2–4 msec, and is conducted along the muscle
fiber at about 5 meters/sec. The absolute refractory
period is 1–3 msec long and the after-polarizations,
with their related changes in threshold to electrical
stimulation, are relatively prolonged. The chronaxie of
skeletal muscle is generally somewhat longer than that
of nerve. The initiation of impulses at the myoneural
junction is discussed in Chapter 4.

Although the electrical properties of the individual fibers in a muscle do not differ sufficiently to produce anything resembling a compound action potential, there are slight differences in the thresholds of the
various fibers. Furthermore, in any stimulation experiment some fibers are farther from the stimulating
electrodes than others. Therefore, the size of the
action potential recorded from a whole muscle preparation is proportionate to the intensity of the stimulating current between threshold and maximal current
intensities.

Ion Distribution & Fluxes

The distribution of ions across the muscle fiber
membrane is similar to that across the nerve cell membrane. The values for the various ions and their equilibrium potentials are shown in Tables 1–3 and 3–1.
Depolarization is a manifestation of Na^+ influx and
repolarization of K^+ efflux (as described in Chapter 2
for nerve).

**TABLE 3–1. Steady-state distribution of ions in the
intracellular and extracellular compartments of
mammalian skeletal muscle, and the equilibrium
potentials for these ions.* A^- represents organic
anions. The value for intracellular Cl^- is calculated from the membrane potential, using the
Nernst equation.**

| Ion | Concentration, mM/liter | | Equilibrium Potential (mv) |
	Intracellular Fluid	Extracellular Fluid	
Na^+	12	145	$+65$
K^+	155	4	-95
H^+	13×10^{-5}	3.8×10^{-5}	-32
Cl^-	3.8	120	-90
HCO_3^-	8	27	-32
A^-	155	0	. . .

Membrane Potential = -90 mv

*Data from Ruch TC, Patton HD (editors): *Physiology and
Biophysics,* 19th ed. Saunders, 1965.

ELECTRICAL PHENOMENA
& IONIC FLUXES

Electrical Characteristics of Skeletal Muscle

The electrical events in skeletal muscle and the
ionic fluxes underlying them are similar to those in
nerve although there are quantitative differences in

CONTRACTILE RESPONSES

It is important to distinguish between the electrical and mechanical events in muscle. Although one
response does not normally occur without the other,
their physiologic basis and characteristics are different.

Muscle fiber membrane depolarization normally starts at the motor end-plate, the specialized structure under the motor nerve ending (see Chapter 4); the action potential is transmitted along the muscle fiber and initiates the contractile response.

The Muscle Twitch

A single action potential causes a brief contraction followed by relaxation. This response is called a **muscle twitch**. In Fig 3–4, the action potential and the twitch are plotted on the same time scale. The twitch starts about 2 msec after the start of depolarization of the membrane, before repolarization is complete. The duration of the twitch varies with the type of muscle being tested. "Fast" muscle fibers, primarily those concerned with fine, rapid, precise movement, have twitch durations as short as 7.5 msec. "Slow" muscle fibers, principally those involved in strong, gross, sustained movements, have twitch durations up to 100 msec in duration.

FIG 3–4. The electrical and mechanical responses of a mammalian skeletal muscle fiber to a single maximal stimulus. The mechanical response (tension) and the electrical response (mv potential change) are plotted on the same abscissa (time). T = tension in arbitrary units.

Molecular Basis of Contraction

The process by which the shortening of the contractile elements in muscle is brought about is a sliding of the myosin filaments over the actin filaments. The width of the A bands is constant, whereas the Z lines move closer together when the muscle contracts and farther apart when it is stretched (Fig 3–5). As the muscle shortens, the actin filaments from the opposite ends of the sarcomere approach each other; when the shortening is marked, these filaments apparently overlap. The sliding during muscle contraction is produced by breaking and reforming of the cross-linkages between actin and myosin.

The process by which depolarization of the

FIG 3–5. Muscle contraction. Calcium ions (represented by black dots) are normally stored in the cisterns of the sarcoplasmic reticulum. The action potential spreads via the transverse tubules and releases Ca^{++}. The actin filaments (thin lines) slide on the myosin filaments, and the Z lines move closer together. Ca^{++} is then pumped into the sarcoplasmic reticulum and the muscle relaxes. (Modified from Layzer & Rowland: Cramps. New England J Med 285:31, 1971.)

muscle fiber initiates contraction is called **excitation-contraction coupling**. The action potential is transmitted to all the fibrils in the fiber via the T system. It triggers the release of calcium ions from the **terminal cisterns**, the portions of the sarcoplasmic reticulum next to the T system (Fig 3–5). The Ca^{++} activates the contractile mechanism. It now appears that muscle is maintained in the relaxed state by a "relaxing protein" which inhibits the interaction between actin

FIG 3–6. *A:* Muscle preparation arranged for recording isotonic contractions. *B:* Preparation arranged for recording isometric contractions. In A, the muscle is fastened to a writing lever which swings on a pivot. In B, it is attached to a steel spring to which is fastened a writing lever. Contraction deforms the spring and the slight motion is indicated by deflection of the writing lever.

FIG 3–7. *Above:* Isotonic (free) contraction. Biceps shortens freely, weight is lifted. *Below:* Isometric contraction. Biceps generates force but cannot shorten and raise weight.

and myosin. The relaxing protein is made up of troponin and tropomyosin, which attaches the troponin to actin. Ca^{++} binds to troponin and, in so doing, inhibits its inhibitory effect on contraction, permitting the actin to slide on the myosin.

Shortly after releasing Ca^{++}, the sarcoplasmic reticulum begins to reaccumulate Ca^{++}. The Ca^{++} is actively pumped into longitudinal portions of the reticulum and diffuses from there to the cisterns, where it is stored (Fig 3–5). Once the Ca^{++} concentration outside of the reticulum has been lowered sufficiently, chemical interaction between myosin and actin ceases and the muscle relaxes. If the active transport of Ca^{++} is inhibited, relaxation does not occur even though there are no more action potentials; the resulting sustained contraction is called a **contracture.**

The immediate source of energy for muscle contraction is ATP (Fig 17–3). Hydrolysis of the bonds between the phosphate residues of this compound is associated with the release of a large amount of energy, and the bonds are therefore referred to as high-energy phosphate bonds. In muscle, the hydrolysis of ATP to adenosine diphosphate (ADP) is catalyzed by the contractile protein, myosin; and this **adenosine triphosphatase** activity is found in the heads of the myosin molecules, where they are in contact with actin. ATP also provides the energy for the active transport of Ca^{++} into the sarcoplasmic reticulum. Thus, both contraction and relaxation of muscle require ATP.

Types of Contraction

Muscular contraction involves shortening of the contractile elements, but because muscles have elastic and viscous elements in series with the contractile mechanism it is possible for contraction to occur without an appreciable decrease in the length of the whole muscle. Such a contraction is called **isometric** ("same measure" or length). Contraction against a constant load, with approximation of the ends of the muscle, is **isotonic** ("same tension").

A whole muscle preparation arranged for recording isotonic contractions is shown in Fig 3–6A. The muscle lifts the lever, and the distance the lever moves indicates the degree of shortening. In this situation, the muscle does external work, since the lever is being moved a certain distance. The muscle preparation in Fig 3–6B is arranged for recording isometric contractions. It is attached to a strong metal spring, and contraction deforms the spring. The slight motion produced is proportionate to the tension developed. Since the product of force times distance in this situation is very small, little external work is done by the muscle. In other situations, it is possible for muscles to do no external work (Fig 3–7) or even negative work while contracting. This happens, for example, when a heavy weight is lowered onto a table. In this case the biceps muscles actively resist the descent of the object, but the net effect of the effort is to lengthen the biceps muscle while it is contracting.

FIG 3–8. Tetanus. Isometric tension of a single muscle fiber during continuously increasing and decreasing stimulation frequency. Dots at top are at 0.2 sec intervals. (Reproduced, with permission, from Buchtal: Dan Biol Medd 17:1, 1942.)

Summation of Contractions

The electrical response of a muscle fiber to repeated stimulation is like that of nerve. The fiber is electrically refractory only during the rising and part of the falling phase of the spike potential. At this time, the contraction initiated by the first stimulus is just beginning. However, because the contractile mechanism does not have a refractory period, repeated stimulation before relaxation has occurred produces additional activation of the contractile elements and a response which is added to the contraction already present. This phenomenon is known as **summation of contractions**. The tension developed during summation is considerably greater than that during the single muscle twitch. With rapidly repeated stimulation, activation of the contractile mechanism occurs repeatedly before any relaxation has occurred and the individual responses fuse into one continuous contraction. Such a response is called a **tetanus**, or **tetanic contraction**. It is a **complete tetanus** when there is no relaxation between stimuli, and an **incomplete tetanus** when there are periods of incomplete relaxation between the summated stimuli. During a complete tetanus, the tension developed is about 4 times that developed by the individual twitch contractions. The development of an incomplete and a complete tetanus in response to stimuli of increasing frequency is shown in Fig 3–8.

The stimulation frequency at which summation of contractions will occur is determined by the twitch duration of the particular muscle being studied. For example, if the twitch duration is 10 msec, frequencies less than 1 per 10 msec (100/sec) will cause discrete responses interrupted by complete relaxation, and frequencies greater than 100/sec will cause summation.

Treppe

When a series of maximal stimuli are delivered to skeletal muscle at a frequency just below the tetanizing frequency, there is an increase in the tension developed during each twitch until, after several contractions, a uniform tension per contraction is reached. This phenomenon is known as **treppe**, or the "staircase" phenomenon (German *Treppe* = "staircase"). It also occurs in cardiac muscle. Treppe is caused by a poorly understood "warming up" process in the actomyosin whereby its ability to develop tension increases with use. It should not be confused with summation of contractions and tetanus.

Relation Between Muscle Length, Tension, & Velocity of Contraction

Both the tension that a muscle develops when stimulated to contract isometrically (the **total tension**), and the **passive tension** exerted by the unstimulated muscle vary with the length of the muscle fiber. This relationship can be studied in a whole skeletal muscle preparation such as that shown in Fig 3–6B. The length of the muscle can be varied by changing the distance between the 2 rods to which it is attached. At each length, the passive tension is measured and the muscle is then stimulated electrically and the total tension measured. The difference between the 2 values at any length is the amount of tension actually generated by the contractile process, the **active tension**. The records obtained by plotting passive tension and total tension against muscle length are shown in Fig 3–9. Similar curves are obtained when single muscle

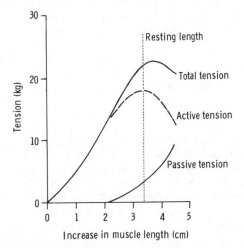

FIG 3–9. Length-tension diagram for skeletal muscle. The passive tension curve measures the tension exerted by the muscle at each length when it is not stimulated. The total tension curve represents the tension developed when the muscle contracts isometrically in response to a maximal stimulus. The active tension is the difference between the 2. (Drawn from data on human triceps muscle, with permission, from *Report to the NRC, Committee on Artificial Limbs, on Fundamental Studies of Human Locomotion and Other Information Relating to Design of Artificial Limbs.* University of California [Berkeley], 1947, vol 2.)

fibers are studied. Passive tension rises slowly at first, and then rapidly as the muscle is stretched. Rupture of the muscle occurs when it is stretched to about 3 times its **equilibrium length,** ie, the length of the relaxed muscle cut free from its bony attachments.

The total tension curve rises to a maximum and then declines until it reaches the passive tension curve, ie, until no additional tension is developed upon further stimulation. The length of the muscle at which the active tension is maximal is usually called its **resting length.** The term comes originally from experiments demonstrating that the length of many of the muscles in the body at rest is the length at which they develop maximal tension. Other definitions of resting length are sometimes used, but that given here is the most widely accepted and has the greatest physiologic validity.

The observed length-tension relation in skeletal muscle is explained by the sliding filament mechanism of muscle contraction. When the muscle fiber contracts isometrically, the tension developed is proportionate to the number of cross-linkages between the actin and the myosin molecules. When muscle is stretched, the overlap between actin and myosin is reduced and the number of cross-linkages is reduced. Conversely, when the muscle is shorter than resting length, the actin filaments overlap, and this also reduces the number of cross-linkages.

The velocity of muscle contraction varies inversely with the load on the muscle. At a given load, the velocity is maximal at the resting length and declines if the muscle is shorter or longer than this length.

ENERGY SOURCES & METABOLISM

Muscle contraction requires energy, and muscle has been called "a machine for converting chemical into mechanical energy." The immediate source of this energy is the energy-rich organic phosphate derivatives in muscle; the ultimate source is the intermediary metabolism of carbohydrate and lipids. The hydrolysis of ATP to provide the energy for contraction has been discussed above.

Phosphocreatine

ATP is resynthesized from ADP by the addition of a phosphate group. Under normal conditions the energy for this endothermic reaction is supplied by the breakdown of glucose to CO_2 and H_2O, but there also exists in muscle another energy-rich phosphate compound which can supply this energy. This compound is **phosphocreatine** (Fig 17–25), which is hydrolyzed to creatine and phosphate groups with the release of considerable energy. At rest, some ATP transfers its phosphate to creatine, so that a phosphocreatine store is built up. During exercise the phosphocreatine is hydrolyzed, forming ATP from ADP and thus permitting contraction to continue.

$$ATP + H_2O \rightarrow ADP + H_3PO_4 + 12{,}000 \text{ calories}$$

$$Phosphocreatine + ADP \rightleftarrows Creatine + ATP$$

$$Glucose + 2\,ATP \text{ (or glycogen } + 1\,ATP)$$
$$\xrightarrow[\text{Anaerobic}]{} 2\,Lactic\ acid + 4\,ATP$$

$$Glucose + 2\,ATP \text{ (or glycogen } + 1\,ATP)$$
$$\xrightarrow[\text{Oxygen}]{} 6\,CO_2 + 6\,H_2O + 40\,ATP$$

$$FFA \xrightarrow[\text{Oxygen}]{} CO_2 + H_2O + ATP$$

FIG 3–10. Energy sources for muscle contractions. The amount of ATP formed per mol of free fatty acid (FFA) oxidized varies with the size of the FFA (see Chapter 17).

Carbohydrate Breakdown

Much of the energy for phosphocreatine and ATP resynthesis comes from the breakdown of glucose to CO_2 and H_2O. An outline of the major metabolic pathways involved is presented in Chapter 17. For the purposes of the present discussion, it is sufficient to point out that glucose in the blood stream enters cells, where it is degraded through a series of chemical reactions to pyruvic acid. Another source of intracellular glucose, and consequently of pyruvic acid, is glycogen, the carbohydrate polymer which is especially abundant in liver and skeletal muscle. When adequate O_2 is present, pyruvic acid enters the citric acid cycle and is metabolized—through this cycle and the so-called respiratory enzyme pathway—to CO_2 and H_2O. This process is called **aerobic glycolysis.** The metabolism of glucose or glycogen to CO_2 and H_2O liberates sufficient energy to form large quantities of ATP from ADP. If O_2 supplies are insufficient, the pyruvic acid formed from glucose does not enter the tricarboxylic acid cycle but is reduced to lactic acid. This process of **anaerobic glycolysis** is associated with the net production of much smaller quantities of energy-rich phosphate bonds, but it does not require the presence of O_2. Skeletal muscle also takes up free fatty acids (FFA) from the blood and oxidizes them to CO_2 and H_2O. Indeed, FFA are probably the major substrates for muscle at rest and during recovery after contraction. The various reactions involved in supplying energy to skeletal muscle are summarized in Fig 3–10.

The Oxygen Debt Mechanism

During muscular exercise, the muscle blood vessels dilate and blood flow is increased so that the available O_2 supply is increased. Up to a point, the increase in O_2 consumption is proportionate to the energy expended, and all the energy needs are met by aerobic processes. However, when muscular exertion is very great, aerobic resynthesis of energy stores cannot keep pace with their utilization. Under these conditions, phosphocreatine is used to resynthesize ATP. Phosphocreatine resynthesis is accomplished by using the energy released by the anaerobic breakdown of glucose to lactic acid. This use of the anaerobic pathway is self-limiting, because in spite of rapid diffusion of lactic acid into the blood stream, enough accumulates in the muscles to eventually exceed the capacity of the tissue buffers and produce an enzyme-inhibiting decline in pH. However, for short periods, the presence of an anaerobic pathway for glucose breakdown permits muscular exertion of a far greater magnitude than would be possible without it. Without this pathway, for example, walking or running at a slow jog would be possible but sprinting and all other forms of short-term, violent exertion would not.

After a period of exertion is over, extra O_2 is consumed to remove the excess lactic acid and replenish the ATP and phosphocreatine stores. The amount of extra O_2 consumed is proportionate to the extent to which the energy demands during exertion exceeded the capacity for the aerobic synthesis of energy stores, ie, the extent to which an **oxygen debt** was incurred. The O_2 debt is measured experimentally by determining O_2 consumption after exercise until a constant, basal consumption is reached, and subtracting the basal consumption from the total. The amount of this debt may be 6 times the basal O_2 consumption, which indicates that the subject is capable of 6 times the exertion that would have been possible without it. Obviously, the maximal debt can be incurred rapidly or slowly; violent exertion is possible for only short periods of time, whereas less strenuous exercise can be carried on for longer periods of time.

Trained athletes are able to increase the O_2 consumption of their muscles to a greater degree than untrained individuals. Consequently, they are capable of greater exertion without increasing their lactic acid production, and they contract smaller oxygen debts for a given amount of exertion.

Heat Production in Muscle

Thermodynamically, the energy supplied to a muscle must equal its energy output. The energy output appears in work done by the muscle, in energy-rich phosphate bonds formed for later use, and in heat. The overall mechanical efficiency of skeletal muscle (work done/total energy expenditure) ranges up to 50% while lifting a weight during isotonic contraction and is essentially 0% during isometric contraction. Energy storage in phosphate bonds is a small factor. Consequently, heat production is considerable. The heat produced in muscle can be measured accurately with suitable thermocouples.

Resting heat, the heat given off at rest, is the external manifestation of basal metabolic processes. The heat produced in excess of resting heat during contraction is called the **initial heat.** This is made up of **activation heat,** the heat that muscle produces whenever it is contracting; and **shortening heat,** which is proportionate in amount to the distance the muscle shortens. Shortening heat is apparently due to some change in the structure of the muscle during shortening.

Following contraction, heat production in excess of resting heat continues for as long as 30 minutes. This **recovery heat** is the heat liberated by the metabolic processes which restore the muscle to its precontraction state. The recovery heat of muscle is approximately equal to the initial heat, ie, the heat produced during recovery is equal to the heat produced during contraction.

If a muscle which has contracted isotonically is restored to its previous length, extra heat in addition to recovery heat is produced (**relaxation heat**). External work must be done on the muscle to return it to its previous length, and relaxation heat is mainly a manifestation of this work.

PROPERTIES OF MUSCLES IN THE INTACT ORGANISM

Effects of Denervation

In the intact animal or human, healthy skeletal muscle does not contract except in response to stimulation of its motor nerve supply. Destruction of this nerve supply causes muscle atrophy. It also leads to abnormal excitability of the muscle and increases its sensitivity to circulating acetylcholine (denervation hypersensitivity; see Chapter 4). Fine, irregular contractions of individual fibers (**fibrillations**) appear. If the motor nerve regenerates, these disappear. Such contractions usually are not visible grossly and should not be confused with **fasciculations**, which are jerky, visible contractions of groups of muscle fibers due to pathologic discharge of spinal motor neurons.

The Motor Unit

Since the axons of the spinal motor neurons supplying skeletal muscle each branch to innervate several muscle fibers, the smallest possible amount of muscle which can contract in response to the excitation of a single motor neuron is not one muscle fiber but all the fibers supplied by the neuron. Each single motor neuron and the muscle fibers it innervates constitute a **motor unit.** The number of muscle fibers in a motor unit varies. In muscles such as those of the hand and those concerned with motion of the eye—ie, muscles concerned with fine, graded, precise movement—there are 3–6 muscle fibers per motor unit. On the other hand, values of 120–165 fibers per unit have been reported in cat leg muscles, and some of the large muscles of the back in man probably contain even more.

Electromyography

Activation of motor units in experimental animals and man can be studied by **electromyography,** the process of recording the electrical activity of muscle on a cathode ray oscilloscope. This may be done in unanes-

BICEPS

TRICEPS

500 μv

0.5 sec

FIG 3–11. Electromyographic tracings from human biceps and triceps muscles during alternate flexion and extension of the elbow. (Courtesy of BC Garoutte.)

thetized humans by using small metal disks on the skin overlying the muscle as the pick-up electrodes, or by using hypodermic needle electrodes. The record obtained with such electrodes is the **electromyogram (EMG)**. With needle electrodes, it is usually possible to pick up the activity of single muscle fibers. A typical EMG is shown in Fig 3–11.

Factors Responsible for Grading of Muscular Activity

It has been shown by electromyography that there is little if any spontaneous activity in the skeletal muscles of normal individuals at rest. With minimal voluntary activity, a few motor units discharge, and with increasing voluntary effort more and more are brought into play. This process is sometimes called **recruitment of motor units**. Gradation of muscle response is therefore in part a function of the number of motor units activated. In addition, the frequency of discharge in the individual nerve fibers plays a role, the tension developed during a tetanic contraction being greater than that during individual twitches. The length of the muscle is also a factor. Finally, the motor units fire asynchronously, ie, out of phase with each other. This asynchronous firing causes the individual muscle fiber responses to merge into a smooth contraction of the whole muscle.

Muscle Types in Man

The properties of the various muscles in the human vary with the character of the muscle. There are 3 general types of skeletal muscle: red, white, and intermediate. The **red** ("slow") fibers contain more myoglobin, have less evident striations, respond more slowly, and have a longer latency than white. They are adapted for long, slow, posture-maintaining contractions. The long muscles of the back contain many red fibers. The **intermediate** fibers resemble the white fibers in some ways, but they also have a high myoglo-

bin content and respond slowly; the soleus muscle has a high content of these fibers. **White** ("fast") fibers have short twitch durations. They are specialized for fine, skilled movements. The extraocular muscles and some of the hand muscles contain large numbers of white fibers. Each spinal motor neuron innervates only one kind of muscle fiber, so that all the muscle fibers in a motor unit are of the same type.

It has generally been supposed that the differences between these types of muscles are inherent, but it now appears that the character of the muscle is determined in part by its innervation. A "trophic" effect of motor nerves has long been recognized. Denervation of skeletal muscle leads to atrophy and flaccid paralysis, with the appearance of fibrillations. These effects are the classical consequences of a **lower motor neuron lesion**. The muscle also becomes hypersensitive to acetylcholine (denervation hypersensitivity: see Chapter 4).

The nerves to fast and slow muscles have been crossed and allowed to regenerate. When regrowth was complete and the nerve which previously supplied the slow muscle innervated the fast one, the fast muscle became slow. The reverse change occurred in the previously slow muscle. It appears, therefore, that even the biochemical characteristics of muscle depend in part upon the type of innervation it receives. There is evidence that substances can flow down neurons and enter muscle.

The Strength of Skeletal Muscles

Skeletal muscle in man can exert 3–4 kg of tension per sq cm of cross-sectional area. This figure is about the same as that obtained in a variety of experimental animals, and seems to be constant for all mammalian species. Since many of the muscles in man have a relatively large cross-sectional area, the tension they can develop is quite large. The gastrocnemius, for example, not only supports the weight of the whole body during climbing but resists a force several times this great when the foot hits the ground during running or jumping. An even more striking example is the gluteus maximus, which can exert a tension of 1200 kg. The total tension that could be developed by all muscles in the body of an adult man is approximately 22,000 kg (nearly 25 tons).

Body Mechanics

Body movements are generally organized in such a way that they take maximal advantage of the physiologic principles outlined above. For example, the attachments of the muscles in the body are such that many of them are normally at or near their resting length when they start to contract. In the case of muscles that extend over more than one joint, movement at one joint may compensate for movement at another in such a way that relatively little shortening of the muscle occurs during contraction. Nearly isometric contractions of this type permit development of maximal tension per contraction. The hamstring muscles extend from the pelvis over the hip joint and the knee

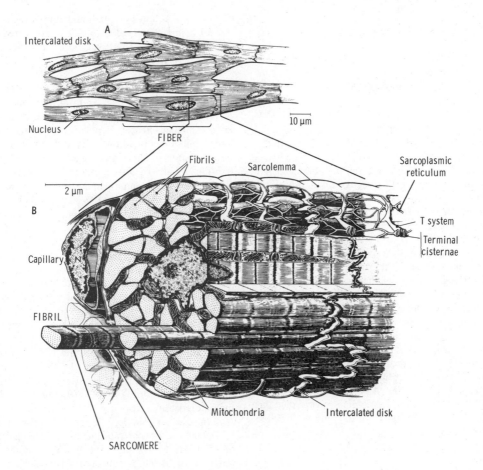

FIG 3–12. *Top:* Electron photomicrograph of cardiac muscle. The fuzzy thick lines are intercalated disks (×
12,000). (Reproduced, with permission, from Bloom & Fawcett: *A Textbook of Histology,* 9th ed. Saunders, 1968.) *Bottom:* Diagram of cardiac muscle as seen under the light microscope (**A**) and the electron
microscope (**B**). N: nucleus. (Reproduced, with permission, from Braunwald & others: Mechanisms of
contraction of the normal and failing heart. New England J Med 277:794, 853, 910, 1012, 1967. Courtesy
of Little, Brown, Inc.)

joint to the tibia and fibula. Hamstring contraction produces flexion of the leg on the thigh. If the thigh is flexed on the pelvis at the same time, the lengthening of the hamstrings across the hip joint tends to compensate for the shortening across the knee joint. In the course of walking and other activities, the body moves in a way which takes advantage of this.

Such factors as momentum and balance are integrated into body movement in ways which make possible maximal motion with minimal muscular exertion. In walking, for example, there is a brief burst of activity in the leg flexors at the start of each step, and then the leg is swung forward with little more active muscular contraction. Therefore, the muscles are active for only a fraction of each step, and walking for long periods of time causes relatively little fatigue.

FIG 3–13. Action potentials and contractile response of mammalian cardiac muscle fiber plotted on the same time axis. ARP, absolute refractory period; RRP, relative refractory period.

CARDIAC MUSCLE

MORPHOLOGY

The striations in cardiac muscle are similar to those in skeletal muscle, and Z lines are present. The muscle fibers branch and interdigitate, but each is a complete unit surrounded by a cell membrane. Where the end of one muscle fiber abuts on another, the membranes of both fibers parallel each other through an extensive series of folds. These areas, which always occur at Z lines, are called **intercalated disks** (Fig 3–12). They provide a strong union between fibers, maintaining cell to cell cohesion, so that the pull of one contractile unit can be transmitted along its axis to the next. Along the sides of the muscle fibers next to the disks, the cell membranes of adjacent fibers fuse for considerable distances. These junctions provide low resistance bridges for the spread of excitation from one fiber to another (see Chapter 1). They permit cardiac muscle to function as if it were a syncytium, even though there are no protoplasmic bridges between cells. The T system in cardiac muscle is located at the Z lines rather than at the A–I junction (as it is in mammalian skeletal muscle). Cardiac muscle contains large numbers of elongated mitochondria in close contact with the fibrils.

ELECTRICAL PROPERTIES

Resting Membrane & Action Potentials
The resting membrane potential of individual mammalian cardiac muscle cells is about −80 mv (interior negative to exterior). Stimulation produces a propagated action potential which is responsible for

initiating contraction. Depolarization proceeds rapidly and overshoot is present, as in skeletal muscle and nerve, but repolarization is a slow process (Fig 3–13). In mammalian hearts, depolarization lasts about 2 msec, but repolarization lasts 200 msec or more. Repolarization is therefore not complete until the contraction is half over. With extracellular recording, the electrical events include a spike and a later wave that bear a resemblance to the QRS complex and T wave of the electrocardiogram. Intracellular records indicate that repolarization is a 3-phase process. After the spike, repolarization starts rapidly but then becomes prolonged, with a final more rapid return to the resting membrane potential. It has been suggested, but not proved, that depolarization and the first rapid phase of repolarization are due to a rapid change in Na^+ permeability similar to that occurring in nerve and skeletal muscle, whereas the second phase or prolonged repolarization is due to a slower starting, less intense, and more prolonged increase in Na^+ permeability. According to this hypothesis, the third phase is the manifestation of a delayed increase in K^+ permeability. This increase produces the K^+ efflux which completes the repolarization process.

In cardiac muscle, the repolarization time decreases as the cardiac rate increases. At a cardiac rate of 75 beats per minute, the duration of the action potential (0.25 sec) is almost 70% longer than it is at a cardiac rate of 200 (0.15 sec).

MECHANICAL PROPERTIES

Refractory Period
The contractile response of cardiac muscle begins

FIG 3–14. "Length-tension" relationship for cardiac muscle. The values are for dog heart. (Modified from Patterson & others: The regulation of the heart beat. J Physiol 48:465, 1914.)

just after the start of depolarization and lasts about 1½ times as long as the action potential (Fig 3–13). The role of Ca^{++} in excitation-contraction coupling is similar to its role in skeletal muscle (see above); however, it appears that the Ca^{++} is largely extracellular in diastole and must cross the cell membrane to initiate contraction. Responses of the muscle are all or none in character, ie, the muscle fibers contract fully if they respond at all. Since cardiac muscle is absolutely refractory during most of the action potential, the contractile response is more than half over by the time a second response can be initiated. Therefore, tetanus of the type seen in skeletal muscle cannot occur. Of course, tetanization of cardiac muscle for any length of time would have lethal consequences, and in this sense the fact that cardiac muscle cannot be tetanized is a safety feature. Ventricular muscle is said to be in the "vulnerable period" just at the end of the action potential, because stimulation at this time will sometimes initiate ventricular fibrillation.

Correlation Between Muscle Fiber Length & Tension

The relation between initial fiber length and total tension in cardiac muscle is similar to that in skeletal muscle; there is a resting length at which the tension developed upon stimulation is maximal. In the body, the initial length of the fibers is determined by the degree of diastolic filling of the heart and the pressure developed in the ventricle is proportionate to the total tension developed. As the diastolic filling increases, the force of contraction of the ventricles is increased (Fig 3–14). The homeostatic value of this response is discussed in Chapter 29.

METABOLISM

Although the general pattern of cardiac muscle metabolism resembles that of skeletal muscle, there are differences. Mammalian hearts have an abundant blood supply, numerous mitochondria, and a high content of myoglobin, a muscle pigment that may function as an O_2 storage mechanism (see Chapter 35). Normally, less than 1% of the total energy liberated is provided by anaerobic metabolism. During hypoxia, this figure may increase to nearly 10%; but under totally anaerobic conditions the energy liberated is inadequate to sustain ventricular contractions. Under basal conditions, 35% of the caloric needs of the human heart are provided by carbohydrate, 5% by ketones and amino acids, and 60% by fat. However, the proportions of substrates utilized vary greatly with the nutritional state. After feeding large amounts of glucose, more lactic acid and pyruvic acid are used; during prolonged starvation, more fat is used. Circulating free fatty acids normally account for almost 50% of the lipid utilized. In untreated diabetics, the carbohydrate utilization of cardiac muscle is reduced and that of fat increased. The factors affecting the O_2 consumption of the human heart are discussed in Chapter 29.

PACEMAKER TISSUE

The heart can be cut into small pieces and the pieces will continue to beat. Therefore, inherent rhythmicity is a characteristic of all parts of cardiac muscle. In the intact heart, however, 2 areas of tissue are specialized for originating impulses: the atrioventricular (AV) node and the sinoatrial (SA) node. The inherent rate of the AV node is faster than that of cardiac muscle, and the rate of the SA node is faster than that of the AV node. Consequently, impulses arising in the SA node normally spread to the rest of

FIG 3–15. Diagram of the membrane potential of pacemaker tissue.

the heart, depolarizing it before it discharges spontaneously. There are also multiple but anatomically poorly defined and shifting pacemakers in visceral smooth muscle (see below).

Pacemaker tissue is characterized by an unstable membrane potential. Instead of a steady value between impulses, the membrane potential declines steadily after each action potential until the firing level is reached and another action potential is triggered. This slow depolarization between action potentials is called a **pacemaker potential** or **prepotential** (Figs 3–15, 28–2). The steeper its slope, the faster the rate at which the pacemaker fires. The prepotential has been shown to be due to a slow decrease in K⁺ permeability. This causes a progressive decline in K⁺ efflux and a resultant reduction in membrane potential. Prepotentials are not seen in atrial and ventricular muscle cells; and in these cells, K⁺ permeability is constant during diastole.

SMOOTH MUSCLE

MORPHOLOGY

Smooth muscle is distinguished anatomically from skeletal and cardiac muscle because it lacks visible cross-striations. Studies with the electron microscope show many thin parallel filaments but no organization of these filaments into patterns. There is a sarcoplasmic reticulum, but it is poorly developed.

FIG 3–16. Spontaneous electrical activity in individual smooth muscle cells of tenia coli of guinea pig colon. *a:* Pacemaker type; *b:* sinusoidal waves with action potentials on the rising phases; *c:* sinusoidal waves with action potentials on the falling phases; *d:* mixture of pacemaker, oscillatory, and conducted action potentials. (Reproduced, with permission, from Bulbring: Physiology and pharmacology of intestinal smooth muscle. Lectures on the Scientific Basis of Medicine 7:374, 1957.)

Types

There are various types of smooth muscle in the body. In general, smooth muscle can be divided into **visceral smooth muscle** and **multi-unit smooth muscle.** Visceral smooth muscle occurs in large sheets, has low resistance bridges between individual muscle cells, and functions in a syncytial fashion. The bridges, like those in cardiac muscle, are junctions where the membranes of the 2 adjacent cells fuse to form a single membrane. Visceral smooth muscle is found primarily in the walls of hollow viscera. The musculature of the intestine, the uterus, and the ureters are examples. Multi-unit smooth muscle is made up of individual units without interconnecting bridges. It is found in structures such as the iris of the eye in which fine, graded contractions occur. It is usually not under voluntary control, but it has many functional similarities to skeletal muscle.

VISCERAL SMOOTH MUSCLE

Electrical & Mechanical Activity

Visceral smooth muscle is characterized by the instability of its membrane potential and by the fact that it shows continuous, irregular contractions that are independent of its nerve supply. This maintained state of partial contraction is called **tonus,** or **tone.** The membrane potential has no true "resting" value, being relatively low when the tissue is active and higher when it is inhibited; but in periods of relative quiescence it averages about −50 mv. Superimposed on the membrane potential are waves of various types (Fig 3–16). There are slow sine wave-like fluctuations a few millivolts in magnitude and spikes that sometimes overshoot the zero potential line and sometimes do not. In many tissues the spikes have a duration of about 50 msec. However, in some tissues the action potentials have a prolonged plateau during repolarization, like the action potentials in cardiac muscle. The spikes may occur on the rising or falling phases of the sine wave oscillations. There are, in addition, pacemaker potentials similar to those found in the cardiac pacemakers. However, in visceral smooth muscle, these potentials are generated in multiple foci which shift from place to place. Spikes generated in the pacemaker foci are conducted for some distance in the muscle. Because of the continuous activity, it is difficult to study the relation between the electrical and mechanical events in visceral smooth muscle; but in some relatively inactive preparations, a single spike can be generated. The muscle starts to contract about 200 msec after the start of the spike and 150 msec after the spike is over. The peak contraction is reached as long as 500 msec after the spike. Thus, the excitation-contraction coupling in visceral smooth muscle is a very slow process compared to skeletal and cardiac muscle, in which the time from initial depolarization to initiation of contraction is less than 10 msec.

Visceral smooth muscle is unique in that, unlike

INTESTINAL SMOOTH MUSCLE

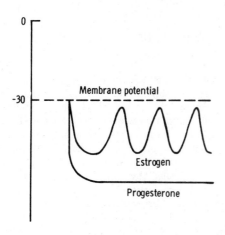

UTERINE SMOOTH MUSCLE

FIG 3–17. *Above:* Effects of various agents on the membrane potential of intestinal smooth muscle. *Below:* Effects of estrogens and of progesterone on the membrane potential of the uterus of the ovariectomized rabbit or rat. (Modified and reproduced, with permission, from Burnstock & others: Electrophysiology of smooth muscle. Physiol Rev 43:482, 1963.)

other types of muscle, it contracts when stretched in the absence of any extrinsic innervation. Stretch is followed by a decline in membrane potential, an increase in the frequency of spikes, and a general increase in tone.

If epinephrine is added to a preparation of intestinal smooth muscle arranged for recording of intracellular potentials in vitro, the membrane potential becomes larger, the spikes decrease in frequency, and the muscle relaxes (Fig 3–17). Norepinephrine is the chemical mediator released at adrenergic nerve endings (see Chapter 13), and stimulation of the adrenergic nerves to the preparation has a similar effect. Stimula-

tion of the adrenergic nerves to the intestine inhibits contractions in vivo.

Acetylcholine has an effect opposite to that of norepinephrine on the membrane potential and contractile activity of intestinal smooth muscle. If acetylcholine is added to the fluid bathing a smooth muscle preparation in vitro, the membrane potential decreases and the spikes become more frequent (Fig 3–17). The muscle becomes more active, with an increase in tonic tension and the number of rhythmic contractions. In the intact animal, stimulation of cholinergic nerves causes release of acetylcholine and increased intestinal contractions. In vitro, similar effects are produced by cold and stretch.

Relatively little is known about the ionic events underlying the electrical activity of smooth muscle. The spikes depend on the external concentration of Na^+, although this must be reduced considerably before they are affected. A K^+ efflux has been demonstrated during contraction, and the greater the tension developed by the muscle, the greater the magnitude of this efflux.

Function of the Nerve Supply to Smooth Muscle

The effects of acetylcholine and norepinephrine on visceral smooth muscle serve to emphasize 2 of its important properties: (1) its spontaneous activity in the absence of nervous stimulation, and (2) its sensitivity to chemical agents released from nerves locally or brought to it in the circulation. In mammals, visceral muscle usually has a dual nerve supply from the 2 divisions of the autonomic nervous system..The function of this nerve supply is not to initiate activity in the muscle but rather to modify it. Stimulation of one division of the autonomic nervous system usually increases smooth muscle activity, whereas stimulation of the other decreases it. However, in some organs adrenergic stimulation increases and cholinergic stimulation decreases smooth muscle activity; in others the reverse is true. The details of transmission from the autonomic endings to smooth muscle are considered in Chapter 4.

Other chemical agents also affect smooth muscle. An interesting example is the uterus. Uterine smooth muscle is relatively inexcitable during diestrus and in the ovariectomized animal. During estrus or in the estrogen-treated ovariectomized animal, excitability is enhanced and tonus and spontaneous contractions occur. However, estrogen increases rather than decreases the membrane potential (Fig 3–17). Progesterone increases the membrane potential even further and inhibits the electrical and contractile activity of uterine muscle (see Chapter 23).

Relation of Length to Tension; Plasticity

Another special characteristic of smooth muscle is the variability of the tension it exerts at any given length. If a piece of visceral smooth muscle is stretched, it first exerts increased tension (see above). However, if the muscle is held at the greater length after stretching, the tension gradually decreases. Some-

FIG 3–18. **Change in pressure in the bladder in man during filling and emptying.** Water was instilled into the bladder by catheter 50 ml at a time, the inflow being stopped and the pressure measured after each increment (upper left curve). After 700 ml had been instilled, the bladder was allowed to empty 50 ml at a time (lower right curve). (Reproduced, with permission, from Denny-Brown & Robertson: Physiology of micturition. Brain 56:149, 1933.)

times the tension falls to or below the level exerted before the muscle was stretched. It is consequently impossible to correlate length and developed tension accurately, and no resting length can be assigned. In some ways, therefore, smooth muscle behaves more like a viscous mass than a rigidly structured tissue, and it is this property which is referred to as the **plasticity** of smooth muscle.

The consequences of plasticity can be demon-strated in the intact animal. For example, the tension exerted by the smooth muscle walls of the bladder can be measured at varying degrees of distention. To obtain the data shown in Fig 3–18, a catheter was inserted into the empty bladder of an intact human and fluid introduced in 50 ml increments. After each addition of fluid, the tension was measured for a period of time. Immediately after each increment of fluid, the tension was higher but after a short period of time it decreased. Therefore, the filling curve in Fig 3–18 is not a smooth curve but a jagged line. After 700 ml had been infused into the bladder, the subject voided in 50 ml increments and the tension was recorded after each increment. Plotting these tensions produced an emptying curve which was different from the filling curve, again due to the absence of any con-stant relationship between fiber length and tension.

MULTI-UNIT SMOOTH MUSCLE

Unlike visceral smooth muscle, multi-unit smooth muscle is nonsyncytial and contractions do not spread widely through it. Because of this, the contractions of multi-unit smooth muscle are more discrete, fine, and localized than those of visceral smooth muscle. Like visceral smooth muscle, multi-unit smooth muscle is very sensitive to circulating chemical substances and is normally activated by chemical mediators (acetyl-choline and norepinephrine) released at the endings of its motor nerves. Especially in the case of norepineph-rine, the mediator tends to persist and to cause repeated firing of the muscle after a single stimulus rather than a single action potential. Therefore, the contractile response produced is usually an irregular tetanus rather than a single twitch. When a single twitch response is obtained, it resembles the twitch contraction of skeletal muscle except that its duration is 10 times as long.

4 . . .

Synaptic & Junctional Transmission

The all or none type of conduction seen in axons and skeletal muscle has been discussed in Chapters 2 and 3. Impulses are transmitted from one nerve cell to another at **synapses**, the junctions where the axon of one cell (the **presynaptic cell**) terminates on the soma or dendrites (or both) of another cell (the **postsynaptic cell**). Transmission at most of these junctions is chemical—the impulse in the terminals of the presynaptic axon liberates a **chemical** mediator which alters the permeability of the membrane of the postsynaptic neuron. At some of the junctions, however, transmission is **electrical**, and at a few **conjoint synapses** it is both electrical and chemical. In any case, impulses in the presynaptic fibers contribute to the initiation of conducted responses in the postsynaptic cell, but transmission is not a simple jumping of one action potential from the presynaptic to the postsynaptic neuron. It is a complex process which permits the grading and modulation of neural activity necessary for normal function.

In the case of electrical synapses, the membranes of the presynaptic and postsynaptic neurons fuse. Like the intercellular junctions in other tissues (see Chapter 1), these junctions form low-resistance bridges through which ions pass with relative ease. In the case of conjoint synapses, the membranes are partly fused and partly separate. Since electrical and conjoint synapses are apparently rare in mammals and most synaptic transmission is chemical, consideration in this chapter is limited, unless otherwise specified, to chemical transmission.

Transmission from nerve to muscle resembles chemical synaptic transmission. The **myoneural junction**, the specialized area where a motor nerve terminates on a skeletal muscle fiber, is the site of a stereotyped transmission process. The contacts between autonomic neurons and smooth and cardiac muscle are less specialized, and transmission is a more diffuse process.

SYNAPTIC TRANSMISSION

SYNAPTIC ANATOMY

There is considerable variation in the anatomic structure of synapses in various parts of the mammalian nervous system. The ends of the presynaptic fibers are enlarged to form **terminal buttons**, or **synaptic knobs** (Fig 4–1). In some instances the terminal branches of the axon of the presynaptic neuron form a basket or net around the soma of the postsynaptic cell ("basket cells" of the cerebellum and autonomic ganglia). In other locations they intertwine with the dendrites of the postsynaptic cell (climbing fibers of the cerebellum) or end on the dendrites directly (apical dendrites of cortical pyramids). In the spinal cord, the presynaptic endings are closely applied to the soma and the proximal portions of the dendrites of the postsynaptic neuron. The number of synaptic knobs varies from one per postsynaptic cell (in the midbrain) to a very large number. The number of synaptic knobs applied to a single spinal motor neuron has been calculated to be about 5500; there are so many knobs that the neuron appears to be encrusted with them. The portion of the soma membrane covered by any single synaptic knob is small, but the synaptic knobs are so numerous that, in aggregate, the area covered by them all is often 40% of the total membrane area (Fig 4–2).

Synaptic Knobs

Under the electron microscope, the synaptic knobs at synapses where transmission is chemical are found to be separated from the soma of the postsynaptic cell by a definite **synaptic cleft** about 20 nm wide. The synaptic knob and the soma each have an intact membrane. Inside the knob, there are many mitochondria and small vesicles or granules, the latter being especially numerous in the part of the knob closest to the synaptic cleft (Fig 4–1). The vesicles or granules contain small "packets" of the chemical transmitter responsible for synaptic transmission (see below). They vary in morphology depending on the particular transmitter they contain.

The transmitter is released from the synaptic knobs when action potentials pass along the axon to the endings. There is debate about the actual release process, but most of the evidence indicates that the membranes of the vesicles or granules fuse to the nerve cell membrane and the area of fusion breaks down, releasing the contents by the process of exocytosis (see Chapter 1).

Convergence & Divergence

Only a few of the synaptic knobs on a postsynaptic neuron are endings of any single presynaptic neuron. The inputs to the cell are multiple. In the case of

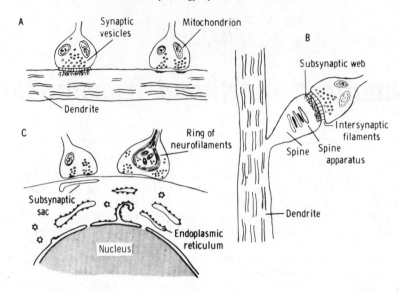

FIG 4–1. Various forms of contact at chemical synapses. *A:* Two types of contact with a dendrite (axodendritic synapses). *B:* Synapse on dentritic spine. *C:* Axosomatic contacts. The functions of the subsynaptic sac and the spine apparatus are unknown, although both contain ribosomes and would therefore seem to be associated with protein synthesis. (Redrawn and reproduced, with permission, from Whittaker & Gray: The synapse: biology and morphology. Brit Med Bull 18:223, 1962.)

spinal motor neurons, for example, some inputs come directly from the dorsal root, some from the long descending spinal tracts, and many from **interneurons**, the short interconnecting neurons of the spinal cord. Thus, many presynaptic neurons **converge** on any single postsynaptic neuron. Conversely, the axons of most presynaptic neurons divide into many branches which **diverge** to end on many postsynaptic neurons.

Convergence and divergence are the anatomic substrates for facilitation, occlusion, and reverberation (see below). It has been calculated that there are approximately 10^{14} synapses in the human brain and that, on the average, each of the 10 billion neurons in the nervous system has 100 inputs converging on it while it in turn diverges to 100 other neurons. The number of possible paths an impulse can take through a neuron net of this complexity is astronomically large.

ELECTRICAL EVENTS AT SYNAPSES

Synaptic activity in the spinal cord has been studied in detail by inserting a microelectrode into the soma of a motor neuron in the cat and recording the electrical events that follow stimulation of the excitatory and inhibitory inputs to these cells. Activity at other synapses has not been so well studied in mammals, but the events occurring at these synapses are apparently similar to those occurring at spinal synapses.

Penetration of an anterior horn cell is achieved by advancing a microelectrode through the ventral portion of the spinal cord. Puncture of a cell membrane is signalled by the appearance of a steady 70 mv potential difference between the microelectrode and an electrode outside the cell. The cell can be identified as a spinal motor neuron by stimulating the appropriate ventral root and observing the electrical activity of the cell. Such stimulation initiates an antidromic impulse (see Chapter 2) which is conducted to the soma and

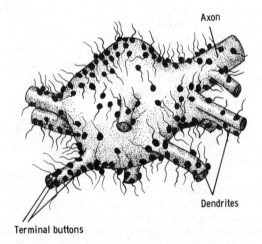

FIG 4–2. Drawing of a model of an anterior horn cell from the lumbar spinal cord of a cat. The dark objects are terminal buttons of presynaptic neurons. (Drawn from a photograph in Haggar & Barr: Quantitative data on the size of synaptic endbulbs in the cat's spinal cord. J Comp Neurol 93:17, 1950.)

FIG 4–3. Arrangement of recording electrodes and stimulators for studying synaptic activity in spinal motor neurons in mammals. One stimulator (S_2) is used to produce antidromic impulses for identifying the cell; the other (S_1) is used to produce orthodromic stimulation via reflex pathways.

stops at this point. Therefore, the presence of an action potential in the cell after antidromic stimulation indicates that the cell that has been penetrated is a motor neuron rather than an interneuron. Activity in some of the presynaptic terminals impinging on the impaled spinal motor neuron (Fig 4–3) can be initiated by stimulating the dorsal roots.

Excitatory Postsynaptic Potentials

Single stimuli applied to the sensory nerves in the experimental situation described above characteristically do not lead to the formation of a propagated action potential in the postsynaptic neuron. Instead, the stimulation produces either a transient, partial depolarization or a transient hyperpolarization.

The depolarizing response produced by a single stimulus to the proper input begins about 0.5 msec after the afferent impulse enters the spinal cord. It reaches its peak 1–1.5 msec later, and then declines exponentially, with a **time constant** (time required for the response to decay to 1/e, or 1/2.718 of its maximum) of about 4 msec. During this potential, the excitability of the neuron to other stimuli is increased, and consequently the potential is called an **excitatory postsynaptic potential (EPSP)**.

The EPSP is due to depolarization of the postsynaptic cell membrane immediately under the active synaptic knob. The current sink thus created is so small that it will not drain off enough positive charges to depolarize the whole membrane. Instead, an EPSP is

inscribed. The EPSP due to activity in one synaptic knob is small, but the depolarizations produced by each of the active knobs summate.

Summation may be **spatial** or **temporal**. When activity is present in more than one synaptic knob at the same time, spatial summation occurs and activity in one synaptic knob is said to **facilitate** activity in another to approach the firing level. Temporal summation occurs if repeated afferent stimuli cause new EPSPs before previous EPSPs have decayed. Spatial and temporal facilitation are illustrated in Fig 4–4. The EPSP is therefore not an all or none response but is proportionate in size to the strength·of the afferent stimulus. If the EPSP is large enough to reach the firing level of the cell, a full-fledged action potential is produced.

Synaptic Delay

When an impulse reaches the presynaptic terminals, there is an interval of at least 0.5 msec, the **synaptic delay**, before a response is obtained in the postsynaptic neuron. The delay following maximal stimulation of the presynaptic neuron corresponds to the latency of the EPSP, and is due to the time it takes for the synaptic mediator to be released and to act on the membrane of the postsynaptic cell. Because of it, conduction along a chain of neurons is slower if there are many synapses in the chain than if there are only a few. This fact is important in comparing, for example, transmission in the lemniscal sensory pathways to the cerebral cortex and transmission in the reticular activating system (see Chapter 11). Since the minimum time for transmission across one synapse is 0.5 msec, it is also possible to determine whether a given reflex

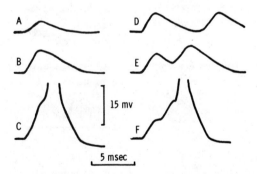

FIG 4–4. Spatial summation (A–C) and temporal summation (D–F) of EPSPs. Records are potential changes recorded with one electrode inside the postsynaptic cell. In A–C, afferent volleys of increasing strength were delivered. In C, the firing level was reached and an action potential generated. In D–F, 2 different volleys of the same strength were delivered but the time interval between them was shortened. In F, the firing level was reached and an action potential generated. (Based on Eccles: *The Physiology of Nerve Cells.* Johns Hopkins Univ Press, 1957.)

pathway is monosynaptic or polysynaptic (contains more than one synapse) by measuring the delay in transmission from the dorsal to the ventral root across the spinal cord.

Ionic Basis of EPSPs

The ionic events underlying excitatory synaptic activity have been worked out in considerable detail. Depolarization of the synaptic knob of an excitatory input is followed by an increase in the permeability of the soma membrane underlying it to K^+, Cl^-, and Na^+. Consequently, Na^+ moves along its concentration and electrical gradients into the cell (see Chapter 2) and a depolarizing potential is produced. However, the area in which this influx occurs is so small that the repolarizing forces are able to overcome its influence, and runaway depolarization of the whole membrane does not result. If more excitatory synaptic knobs are active, more Na^+ enters and the depolarizing potential is greater. If Na^+ influx is great enough, the firing level is reached and a propagated action potential results.

Inhibitory Postsynaptic Potentials

An EPSP is usually produced by afferent stimulation, but stimulation of certain presynaptic fibers regularly initiates a hyperpolarizing response in spinal motor neurons. This response begins 1—1.25 msec after the afferent stimulus enters the cord, reaches its peak in 1.5—2 msec, and declines exponentially with a time constant of 3 msec. During this potential, the excitability of the neuron to other stimuli is decreased; consequently, it is called an **inhibitory postsynaptic potential (IPSP)**. Spatial summation of IPSPs occurs, as shown by the increasing size of the response as the

strength of an inhibitory afferent volley is increased (Fig 4—5). Temporal summation also occurs. This type of inhibition is called **postsynaptic** or **direct inhibition**.

Ionic Basis of IPSPs

At least in spinal motor neurons, the IPSP is apparently due to a localized increase in membrane permeability to K^+ and Cl^-, but not to Na^+. When an inhibitory synaptic knob becomes active, the area of the postsynaptic cell membrane under the knob permits increased K^+ efflux and Cl^- influx as the ions flow down their concentration gradients. The net effect is the transfer of negative charge into the cell, so that membrane potential increases. The equilibrium potential for K^+ is −90 mv in spinal motor neurons, and that for Cl^- is −70 mv (see Chapter 2). The potential apparently moves toward a balance between the 2 of −80 mv. However, the permeability change is short-lived, and the Na^+-K^+ pump restores resting conditions rapidly. This explanation is supported by the experimental observation that if the membrane potential of the cell is artificially held at −80 mv by passage of a current while inhibitory input is stimulated, the IPSP is flat. If the membrane potential is held at −90 mv, the IPSP becomes a depolarizing potential. In some invertebrates, certain IPSPs are due to an increase in Cl^- permeability; and in mammalian hearts the hyperpolarizing effect of vagal stimulation on nodal tissue is due to an increase in K^+ permeability.

The decreased excitability of the nerve cell during the IPSP is due in part to moving the membrane potential away from the firing level. Consequently, more

FIG 4—5. Inhibitory postsynaptic potentials. The lower tracing in each case is the intracellular response of a biceps semitendinosus motor neuron to stimulation of the nerve from the quadriceps. The upper tracing is the externally recorded response from the dorsal root. Note that the IPSPs increase in size as the stimulus strength is increased from A to D. All records were obtained by superimposing about 40 traces. (Reproduced, with permission, from Eccles, in: *Handbook of Physiology.* Field J, Magoun HW [editors]. Washington: American Physiological Society, 1959. Section 1, pp 59—74.)

Excitatory transmitter ⟶ increased permeability of postsynaptic cell membrane to all small ions (Na^+, K^+, Cl^-)

Inhibitory transmitter ⟶ increased permeability of postsynaptic cell membrane to K^+ and Cl^-, not to Na^+

FIG 4—6. Summary of events occurring at synapses in mammals.

excitatory (depolarizing) activity is necessary to reach the firing level. However, additional factors are involved; when the membrane potential is held at −80 mv, inhibitory stimulation still decreases excitability even though the membrane potential does not change. The actions of excitatory and inhibitory synaptic activity on the membrane of the postsynaptic cell are summarized in Fig 4−6.

Neurons Responsible for Postsynaptic Inhibition

Stimulation of certain sensory nerve fibers known to pass directly to motor neurons in the spinal cord produces EPSPs in these neurons and IPSPs in other neurons. If these afferent fibers also pass directly to the neurons in which IPSPs are produced, it is necessary to postulate that a single presynaptic neuron has 2 kinds of endings, some excitatory and some inhibitory, or, alternatively, that the soma membrane of the postsynaptic cell is a patchwork of 2 kinds of membrane. However, evidence has accumulated that a single interneuron is inserted between afferent dorsal root fibers and inhibitory endings. This special interneuron, called a Golgi bottle neuron, is short and plump and has a thick axon. Discharge of the chemical mediator from the synaptic knobs of this neuron causes formation of an IPSP due to increase in the permeability of the postsynaptic cell membrane to K^+ and Cl^- but not to Na^+. In this way, excitatory input is "converted" into inhibitory input by interposing a single Golgi bottle neuron between the excitatory ending and the spinal motor neuron.

Electrogenesis of the Action Potential in the Postsynaptic Neuron

The constant interplay of excitatory and inhibitory activity on the postsynaptic neuron produces a fluctuating membrane potential that is the algebraic sum of the hyperpolarizing and depolarizing activity. The soma of the neuron thus acts as a sort of integrator. When the 10−15 mv of depolarization sufficient to reach the firing level is attained, a propagated spike results. However, the discharge of the neuron is slightly more complicated than this. The portion of the neuron with the lowest threshold for the production of a full-fledged action potential is the **initial segment,** the portion of the axon at and just beyond the axon hillock. This unmyelinated segment is depolarized or hyperpolarized electronically by the current sinks and sources under the excitatory and inhibitory synaptic knobs. It is the first part of the neuron to fire, and its discharge is propagated in 2 directions: down the axon and back into the soma. Retrograde firing of the soma in this fashion probably has value in "wiping the slate clean" for subsequent renewal of the interplay of excitatory and inhibitory activity on the cell.

Function of the Dendrites

Evidence is accumulating that in the CNS the dendrites do not conduct like the axons. Instead, they are usually part of the "receptor membrane" of the neuron (see Chapter 2), the site of current sources or sinks which electrotonically change the membrane potential of the axon hillock region or other locus from which the action potentials are generated. When the dendritic tree is extensive and has multiple presynaptic knobs ending on it, there is room for a great interplay of inhibitory and excitatory activity. Current flow to and from the dendrites in these situations waxes and wanes. The role of the dendrites in the genesis of the electroencephalogram is discussed in Chapter 11.

Electrical Transmission

At synaptic junctions where transmission is electrical, the impulse reaching the presynaptic terminal generates an EPSP in the postsynaptic cell which, because of the low-resistance bridge between the 2, has a much shorter latency than the EPSP at a synapse where transmission is chemical. In conjoint synapses, there is both a short latency response and a longer latency, chemically mediated, postsynaptic response.

CHEMICAL TRANSMISSION OF SYNAPTIC ACTIVITY

The nature of the chemical mediators at many of the synapses is not known. However, acetylcholine is the mediator at all synapses between preganglionic and postganglionic fibers of the autonomic nervous system, at the myoneural junction, at all postganglionic parasympathetic and at some postganglionic sympathetic endings. It is also a mediator in the CNS. The chemical and biophysical events occurring at synapses where it is a mediator are relatively well understood, and the mediator function of acetylcholine provides a good example of chemical mediation of synaptic activity. It should be emphasized, however, that acetylcholine is only one of the mediators in the nervous system.

Acetylcholine

The relatively simple structure of acetylcholine, which is the acetyl ester of choline, is shown in Fig 4−7. It exists, largely enclosed in clear synaptic vesicles, in high concentration in the terminal buttons of cholinergic neurons. Neurons which release acetylcholine are known as **cholinergic** neurons. The arrival of impulses at a synaptic knob apparently causes liberation of acetylcholine into the synaptic cleft by the process of exocytosis. The transmitter crosses the cleft, and, at those synaptic junctions where acetylcholine is an excitatory mediator, it acts on receptors on the membrane of the postsynaptic cell to increase the permeability of the membrane to Na^+ and all other small ions.

Cholinesterases

Acetylcholine must be rapidly removed from the synapse if repolarization is to occur. Some is taken up again by the presynaptic terminals, but most is hydrolyzed by a process catalyzed by the enzyme **acetylcholinesterase.** This enzyme is also called **true** or

$$CH_3\overset{+}{\underset{\underset{\textstyle CH_3}{\diagdown}\overset{}{\diagup}}{N}}\!-\!CH_2CH_2\!-\!O\!-\!\overset{\overset{\textstyle O}{\|}}{C}\!-\!CH_3$$

Acetylcholine

$$HS\text{-}Co\ A\ +\ ATP\ +\ Acetate\ \xrightarrow[\textstyle Acetyl\text{-}Co\ A\ +\ H_2O\ +\ ADP]{\textstyle Acetylthiokinase}$$

$$Acetyl\text{-}Co\ A\ +\ Choline\ \xrightarrow[\textstyle }]{\substack{\textstyle Choline\\ \textstyle acetylase}}\ Acetylcholine\ +\ HS\text{-}Co\ A$$

$$Acetylcholine\ +\ H_2O\ \xrightarrow[\textstyle]{\substack{\textstyle Acetylcholin\text{-}\\ \textstyle esterase}}\ Choline\ +\ Acetate$$

FIG 4—7. Summary of reactions involved in the breakdown and synthesis of acetylcholine. Acetyl-Co A, acetyl-coenzyme A; HS-Co A, reduced coenzyme A.

specific cholinesterase. It is present in high concentrations in the cell membranes at nerve terminals which are cholinergic, but it is also found in some other membranes, in red blood cells, and in the placenta. Its greatest affinity is for acetylcholine, but it also hydrolyzes other choline esters. There are a variety of esterases in the body. One found in plasma is capable of hydrolyzing acetylcholine but has different properties from acetylcholinesterase. It is therefore called **pseudocholinesterase** or **nonspecific cholinesterase**. The plasma moiety is partly under endocrine control and is affected by variations in liver function. On the other hand, the specific cholinesterase at nerve endings is highly localized. Hydrolysis of acetylcholine by this enzyme is rapid enough to explain the observed changes in Na^+ permeability and electrical activity during synaptic transmission.

Acetylcholine Synthesis

Synthesis of acetylcholine involves the reaction of choline with acetate. There is an active uptake of choline into cholinergic neurons (Fig 13—4). The acetate is activated by the combination of acetate groups with reduced coenzyme A. The reaction between active acetate (acetyl-coenzyme A) and choline is catalyzed by the enzyme **choline acetylase**. This enzyme is found in high concentration in the cytoplasm of cholinergic nerve endings; indeed, its localization is so specific that the presence of a high concentration in any given neural area has been taken as evidence that the synapses in that area are cholinergic.

Inhibitory Mediator

The chemical mediator released at the endings of the inhibitory interneurons in the spinal cord produces IPSPs in the postsynaptic neurons. The chemical nature of this **inhibitory mediator** has not been conclusively determined, although it appears to be the amino acid **glycine**. The action of the mediator is inhibited, possibly competitively, by strychnine and tetanus toxin. Thus, the action of these 2 poisons is to inhibit inhibition, with consequent unopposed play of excitatory impulses. The clinical picture of convulsions and muscular hyperactivity produced by tetanus toxin and strychnine emphasize the importance of postsynaptic inhibition in normal neural function.

Other Chemical Mediators

Norepinephrine is the mediator of activity at most postganglionic sympathetic endings in the autonomic nervous system. Its synthesis and metabolism are discussed in Chapter 13. Neurons which liberate norepinephrine are called **adrenergic neurons**. Dopamine-secreting neurons which modulate the activity of the adrenergic neurons are found in sympathetic ganglia. Norepinephrine, dopamine, and 5-hydroxytryptamine (serotonin) are mediators in the CNS. Unlike acetylcholine, these amines are found in vesicles containing a dense core (granulated vesicles). Histamine, the polypeptide "substance P," and other agents may also be mediators in the brain (see Chapter 15).

One-Way Conduction

Synapses permit conduction of impulses in one direction only, from the presynaptic to the postsynaptic neurons. An impulse conducted antidromically up the axons of the ventral root dies out after depolarizing the cell bodies of the spinal motor neurons. Since axons will conduct in either direction with equal facility, the one-way gate at the synapses is necessary for orderly neural function. Chemical mediation at synaptic junctions explains one-way conduction. The mediator is located in the synaptic knobs of the presynaptic fibers, and very little if any is present in the postsynaptic membrane. Therefore, an impulse arriving at the postsynaptic membrane cannot liberate synaptic mediator. Progression of impulse traffic occurs only when the action potential arrives in the presynaptic terminals and causes liberation of stored chemical transmitter.

Pharmacologic Implications

The fact that transmission at most if not all synapses is chemical is of great pharmacologic importance. Transmission is also chemical at the endings of motor neurons on skeletal muscles, and at the points of contact between autonomic nerve fibers and smooth muscle (see below and Chapter 13). The biochemical events occurring at the synapse are much more sensitive than the events in the nerve fibers themselves to hypoxia and to drugs. For instance, polysynaptic pathways are more affected by anesthesia than those with few synapses, a factor which probably helps to explain the mechanism by which general anesthesia is produced (see Chapter 11). During deep anesthesia, synaptic transmission is blocked but long fibers still conduct impulses.

Nerve endings have been called biologic transducers that convert electrical energy into chemical energy. In broad terms, this conversion process involves the synthesis of the transmitter agents, their storage in the synaptic knobs, their release by the nerve impulses into the synaptic cleft, their action on the membrane of the postsynaptic cell, and their removal or their destruction, which is catalyzed by enzymes concentrated in the area around the endings. In theory, at least, all these processes can be inhibited or facilitated by drugs, with resultant changes in synaptic transmission. The synapses are thus a logical point for pharmacologic manipulation of neural function. Since transmission is chemical not only in the autonomic nervous system and at the myoneural junction but in the CNS as well, the pharmacologist can look forward to eventually regulating not only somatic and visceral motor activity but also emotions, behavior, and the other complex functions of the brain.

INHIBITION & FACILITATION AT SYNAPSES

Direct & Indirect Inhibition

Postsynaptic inhibition during the course of an IPSP is also called **direct inhibition** because it is not a consequence of previous discharges of the postsynaptic neuron. Various forms of **indirect inhibition**, inhibition due to the effects of previous postsynaptic neuron dis-

charge, also occur. For example, the postsynaptic cell can be refractory to excitation because it has just fired and is in its refractory period. During after-hyperpolarization it is also less excitable; and in spinal neurons, especially after repeated firing, this after-hyperpolarization may be large and prolonged. In addition, there is evidence that with repeated stimulation of a given pathway the amount of transmitter released or the sensitivity of postsynaptic membrane to the transmitter decreases.

Postsynaptic Inhibition in the Spinal Cord

The various pathways in the nervous system which are known to mediate postsynaptic inhibition are discussed in Chapter 6, but one illustrative example will be presented here. Afferent fibers from the muscle spindles (stretch receptors) in skeletal muscle are known to pass directly to the spinal motor neurons of the motor units supplying the same muscle. Impulses in this afferent supply cause EPSPs and, with summation, propagated responses in the postsynaptic motor neurons. At the same time, IPSPs are produced in motor neurons supplying the antagonistic muscles. This latter response is probably mediated by collaterals of the afferent fibers which end on Golgi bottle neurons. These interneurons, in turn, end on the motor neurons which supply the antagonist (Fig 4–8). Therefore, activity in the afferent fibers from the muscle spindles excites the motor neurons supplying the muscle from which the impulses come and inhibits those supplying its antagonists.

Presynaptic Inhibition

Another type of inhibition occurring in the CNS is **presynaptic inhibition**, a process which reduces the amount of synaptic mediator liberated by action

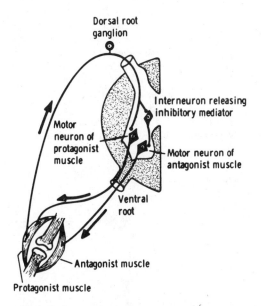

FIG 4–8. Diagram illustrating the probable anatomic connections responsible for inhibiting the antagonists to a muscle contracting in response to stretch. Activity is initiated in the spindle in the protagonist muscle. Impulses pass directly to the motor neurons supplying the same muscle and, via collaterals, to Golgi bottle neurons which end on the motor neurons of the antagonist muscle.

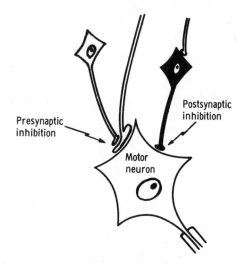

FIG 4–9. Arrangement of neurons producing presynaptic and postsynaptic inhibition. The neuron producing presynaptic inhibition is shown ending on an excitatory synaptic knob. Many of these neurons actually end higher up along the axon of the excitatory cell.

potentials arriving at excitatory synaptic knobs. It has been demonstrated that the amount of mediator liberated at a nerve ending is markedly reduced if the magnitude of the action potential reaching the ending is reduced. The neurons producing presynaptic inhibition end on the excitatory endings (Fig 4–9). When they discharge, they produce a partial depolarization of the excitatory endings. Reducing the membrane potential of the excitatory endings to a level closer to the firing level makes the endings more excitable, but it also reduces the size of the action potentials reaching the ending by an amount equal to the amount of depolarization. Consequently, less mediator is released and there is less excitation of the postsynaptic cell. The neurons producing presynaptic inhibition often fire repetitively, and the partial depolarization may last 100 msec or more.

The chemical mediator released by the neurons responsible for presynaptic inhibition is antagonized by the convulsant drug picrotoxin, and there is reason to believe that it is γ-aminobutyric acid (GABA).

Organization of Inhibitory Systems

Presynaptic and postsynaptic inhibition are usually produced by stimulation of certain systems converging on a given postsynaptic neuron ("afferent inhibition"). Neurons may also inhibit themselves in a negative feedback fashion ("negative feedback inhibition"). For instance, spinal motor neurons regularly give off a recurrent collateral which synapses with an inhibitory interneuron that terminates on the cell body of the spinal neuron and other spinal motor neurons (Fig 4–10). This particular inhibitory neuron is sometimes called the Renshaw cell after its discoverer. Impulses generated in the motor neuron activate the inhibitory interneuron to liberate inhibitory mediator, and this slows or stops the discharge of the motor neuron. Similar inhibition via recurrent collaterals is seen in the cerebral cortex and limbic system. Presynaptic inhibition appears to be in most cases a negative feedback inhibition in which cutaneous and other sensory neurons make connections which bring about presynaptic inhibition of their own terminals and surrounding terminals. In addition, fibers descending from the medulla in the pyramidal tract end on the excitatory endings of the afferent fibers from the muscle spindles. The muscle spindles are the receptors for the stretch reflex (see Chapter 6), and so impulses in the descending fibers presumably decrease stretch reflex activity.

Another type of inhibition is seen in the cerebellum. In this part of the brain, stimulation of basket cells produces IPSPs in the Purkinje cells. However, the basket cells and the Purkinje cells are excited by the same excitatory input. This arrangement, which has been called "feed-forward inhibition," presumably limits the duration of the excitation produced by any given afferent volley.

Summation & Occlusion

The interplay between excitatory and inhibitory influences at synaptic junctions in a nerve net illustrates the integrating and modulating activity of the nervous system.

In the hypothetical nerve net shown in Fig 4–11, neurons A and B converge on X, and neuron B diverges on X and Y. A stimulus applied to A or to B will set up an EPSP in X. If A and B are stimulated at the same time, 2 areas of depolarization will be produced in X and their actions will sum. The resultant EPSP in X will be twice as large as that produced by stimulation of A or B alone, and the membrane potential may well reach the firing level of X. The effect of the depolarization caused by the impulse in A is facilitated by that due to activity in B, and vice versa; spatial facilitation has taken place. In this case, Y has not fired, but its excitability has been increased, and it is easier for activity in neuron C to fire it during the duration of

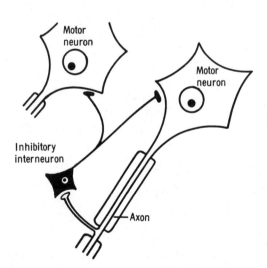

FIG 4–10. Negative feedback inhibition of a spinal motor neuron via an inhibitory interneuron (Renshaw cell).

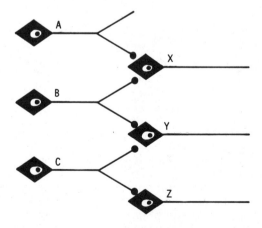

FIG 4–11. Simple nerve net. Neurons A, B, and C have excitatory endings on neurons X, Y, and Z.

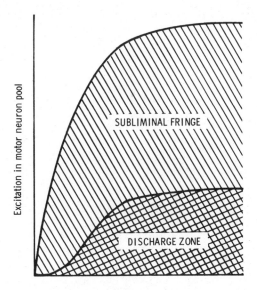

FIG 4–12. **Relation of the size of the discharge zone and subliminal fringe to the strength of the presynaptic volley.** (Redrawn and reproduced, with permission, from Lloyd: Reflex action in relation to pattern and peripheral source of afferent stimulation. J Neurophysiol 6:111, 1943.)

the EPSP. Y is therefore said to be in the **subliminal fringe** of X. More generally stated, neurons are in the subliminal fringe if they are not discharged by an afferent volley (not in the **discharge zone**) but do have their excitability increased. The neurons that have few active knobs ending on them are in the subliminal fringe and those with many are in the discharge zone. However, this does not mean that with increasing strength of afferent stimulus the discharge zone becomes the same size as the subliminal fringe. In the case of stimulation of a dorsal root, the number of neurons discharged increases to a maximum with increasing strength of stimulation of the root, but so does the size of the subliminal fringe (Fig 4–12). Inhibitory impulses show similar temporal and spatial facilitation and subliminal fringe effects.

If neuron B in Fig 4–11 is stimulated repetitively, X and Y will discharge as a result of temporal summation of the EPSPs produced. If C is stimulated repetitively, Y and Z will discharge. If B and C are fired repetitively at the same time, X, Y, and Z will discharge. Thus, the response to stimulation of B and C together is not as great as the sum of responses to stimulation of B and C separately, because B and C both end on neuron Y. This decrease in expected response, due to presynaptic fibers sharing postsynaptic neurons, is called **occlusion.**

Excitatory and inhibitory subliminal effects and occlusive phenomena can have pronounced effects on

transmission in any given pathway. Because of these effects, temporal patterns in peripheral nerves are usually altered as they pass through synapses on the way to the brain. In addition, these effects may explain such important phenomena as referred pain (see Chapter 7).

POST-TETANIC POTENTIATION

The shifting patterns of facilitation and inhibition described above produce effects on neuronal excitability that are of relatively short duration. Another form of synaptic activity which has much more prolonged effects on excitability is the process of **post-tetanic potentiation.** This term refers to the decreased threshold for afferent stimulation of neurons in the CNS after their input has been subjected to prolonged repeated stimulation. It also occurs at autonomic ganglia and myoneural junctions. The potentiation may last several hours, and is localized to the afferent input that is stimulated. It does not spread to other afferent inputs. Inhibitory inputs also show post-tetanic potentiation, and the potentiation extends not only to the neurons directly fired but also to the subliminal fringe zone. This facilitation of transmission with repeated use of a pathway is in a sense an elementary form of learning. There is considerable evidence that the potentiation is due to an increase in transmitter release.

NEUROMUSCULAR TRANSMISSION

THE MYONEURAL JUNCTION

Anatomy

As the axon supplying a skeletal muscle fiber approaches its termination, it loses its myelin sheath and divides into a number of terminal buttons or end feet (Fig 4–13). The end feet contain many small clear vesicles which appear to contain acetylcholine, the transmitter at these junctions. The endings fit into depressions in the **motor end-plate**, the thickened portion of the muscle membrane of the junction. Underneath the nerve ending, the muscle membrane of the end-plate is thrown into folds, the **palisades**. The space between the nerve and the thickened muscle membrane is comparable to the synaptic cleft at synapses. The whole structure is known as the **myoneural junction.** Only one nerve fiber ends on each end-plate, with no convergence of multiple inputs.

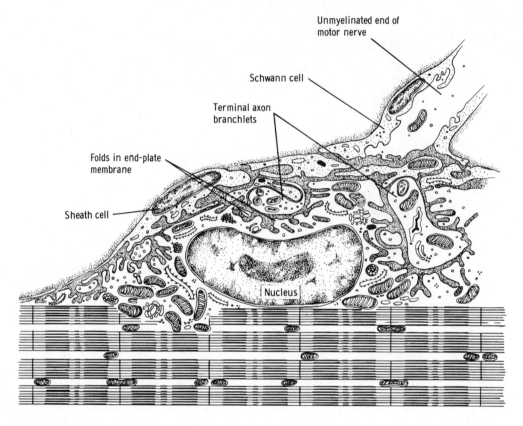

FIG 4–13. Myoneural junction. The drawing is based on electron micrographs of tissue from mice, and shows the terminal ends of a motor neuron axon buried in the end-plate cytoplasm, with the much folded end-plate membrane around them. (Modified and redrawn, with permission, from Anderson-Cedergren: Ultrastructure of motor end plate and sarcoplasmic components of skeletal muscle fiber. J Ultrastructure Res, Suppl 1, 1959.)

Sequence of Events During Transmission

The events occurring during transmission of impulses from the motor nerve to the muscle are somewhat similar to those occurring at synapses. The impulse arriving in the end of the motor neuron evokes liberation of acetylcholine from the vesicles in the nerve terminals. The acetylcholine increases the permeability of the underlying membrane, and Na$^+$ influx produces a depolarizing potential, the **end-plate potential**. The current sink created by this local potential depolarizes the adjacent muscle membrane to its firing level. Action potentials are generated on either side of the end-plate and are conducted away from the end-plate in both directions along the muscle fiber. The muscle action potential, in turn, initiates muscle contraction, as described in Chapter 3.

End-Plate Potential

The end-plate potential is normally obscured by the propagated response initiated from the muscle fiber, but it can be seen if its magnitude is reduced to a size that is insufficient to fire the adjacent muscle membrane. Curare competes with acetylcholine for receptors on the end-plate membrane and forms a strong complex with the receptors. With small doses of curare, not all of the receptors are blocked, and acetylcholine acting at the unblocked receptors produces a small end-plate potential. The response is recorded only at the end-plate region, and decrements exponentially away from it. Under these conditions, end-plate potentials can be shown to undergo temporal summation. Normally, however, the magnitude of the end-plate potential is sufficient to discharge the muscle membrane, and each impulse in the nerve ending produces a response in the muscle. Consequently, summation is not a usual phenomenon at the end-plate.

At the motor end-plate, it appears to be the complex formed by acetylcholine and the membrane receptor that induces the change in membrane permeability. There is a simultaneous increase in Na$^+$ and K$^+$ permeability, and the potential of the end-plate moves toward an equilibrium value of about −10 mv rather than the positive value reached during the action potential in nerve and muscle in which the peak increase in K$^+$ permeability follows the increase in Na$^+$ permeability. After triggering depolarization of the end-plate, the acetylcholine is probably bound to acetylcholinesterase, which hydrolyzes it. The end-plate membrane is depolarized if acetylcholine is dropped on it from a micropipet; but if the pipet is inserted through the muscle and the acetylcholine is applied to the underside of the end-plate membrane, no depolarization results.

Mediator Release at Rest

Small quanta, or "packets" of acetylcholine are released randomly from the nerve cell membrane at rest, each producing a minute depolarizing spike called a **miniature end-plate potential**, which is about 0.5 mv in amplitude. The number of quanta of acetylcholine released in this way varies directly with the Ca^{++} concentration and inversely with the Mg^{++} concentration at the end-plate. When a nerve impulse reaches the ending, the number of quanta released increases by several orders of magnitude, and the result is the large end-plate potential that exceeds the firing level of the muscle fiber. Current evidence indicates that the nerve impulse increases the permeability of the ending to Ca^{++} and that the Ca^{++} is responsible for the increased quantal release.

Quantal release of acetylcholine similar to that seen at the myoneural junction has been observed at other cholinergic synapses, and similar processes are presumably operating at these locations.

NERVE ENDINGS IN SMOOTH & CARDIAC MUSCLE

Anatomy

The postganglionic neurons in the various smooth muscles that have been studied in detail branch extensively and come in close contact with the muscle cells. Some of these nerve fibers contain vesicles and are cholinergic, while others contain the characteristic dense-core granules that are known to contain norepinephrine (see Chapter 13). There are no recognizable end-plates, and no discrete endings have been found; but the nerve fibers run along the membrane of the muscle cells and sometimes groove their surface. The adrenergic neurons have many branches and are beaded with enlargements or **varicosities** which contain adrenergic granules (Fig 4–14). The cholinergic neurons are probably similar. It has been suggested that transmitter is liberated at each varicosity, ie, at many locations along each axon. This arrangement permits one neuron to innervate many effector cells. The type of contact in which a neuron grooves the surface of a smooth muscle cell and then passes on to make similar contacts with other cells has been called a **synapse en passant**.

In the heart, cholinergic and adrenergic nerve fibers end on the sinoatrial node, the atrioventricular node, and the bundle of His. Adrenergic fibers also innervate the ventricular muscle. The exact nature of the endings on nodal tissue is not known. In the ventricle, the contacts between the adrenergic fibers and the cardiac muscle fibers resemble those found in smooth muscle.

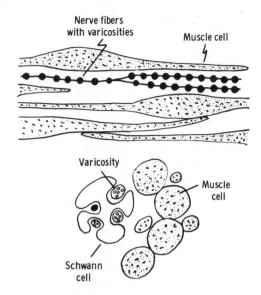

FIG 4–14. Relation of smooth muscle to autonomic nerve fibers. Longitudinal section (*top*) and transverse section (*bottom*). The Schwann cells which envelop the nerve fibers have been omitted from the top diagram. Note the areas of membrane fusion between muscle cells. (modified from Bennett & Burnstock in: *Handbook of Physiology.* Code CF [editor]. Washington: The American Physiological Society, 1968. Section 6, pp 1709–1732.)

Electrical Responses

In smooth muscles in which adrenergic discharge is excitatory, stimulation of the adrenergic nerves produces discrete partial depolarizations that look like small end-plate potentials and are called **excitatory junction potentials (EJPs)**. These potentials summate with repeated stimuli. Similar EJPs are seen in tissues excited by cholinergic discharges. In tissues inhibited by adrenergic stimuli, hyperpolarizing **inhibitory junction potentials (IJPs)** have been produced by stimulation of the adrenergic nerves.

These electrical responses are observed in many smooth muscle cells when a single nerve is stimulated, but their latency varies. This finding is consistent with the synapse en passant arrangement described above, but it could also be explained by transmission of the junction responses from cell to cell across low-resistance junctions or by diffusion of transmitter from its site of release to many smooth muscle cells. Miniature excitatory junction potentials similar to the miniature end-plate potentials in the skeletal muscle have been observed in some smooth muscle preparations, but they show considerable variation in size and duration. They may represent responses to single packets of transmitter, with the variation due to diffusion of the transmitter for variable distances.

DENERVATION HYPERSENSITIVITY

When the motor nerve to skeletal muscle is cut and allowed to degenerate, the muscle gradually becomes extremely sensitive to acetylcholine. This **denervation hypersensitivity** is also seen in smooth muscle. Smooth muscle, unlike skeletal muscle, does not atrophy when denervated, but it becomes hyperresponsive to the chemical mediator that normally activates it. Denervated glands, except for sweat glands, also become hypersensitive. A good example of denervation hypersensitivity is the response of the denervated iris. If the postganglionic sympathetic nerves to one pupil are cut in an experimental animal and, after several weeks, norepinephrine is injected intravenously, the denervated pupil dilates widely. A much smaller, less prolonged response is observed on the intact side. There is considerable evidence that other neural structures show a similar reaction to loss of their nerve supply. When higher centers in the nervous system are destroyed, the activity of the lower centers they control is generally increased ("release phenomenon"). The increased activity may be due in part to denervation hypersensitivity of the lower centers. Indeed, one theory holds that many of the signs and symptoms of neurologic disease are due to denervation hypersensitivity of various groups of neurons in the brain.

Hypersensitivity is limited to the structures immediately innervated by the destroyed neurons, and fails to develop in neurons and muscle farther "downstream." Suprasegmental spinal cord lesions do not lead to hypersensitivity of the paralyzed skeletal muscles to acetylcholine, and destruction of the preganglionic autonomic nerves to visceral structures does not cause hypersensitivity of the denervated viscera. This fact has practical implications in the treatment of diseases due to spasm of the blood vessels in the extremities. For example, if the upper extremity is sympathectomized by removing the upper part of the ganglion chain and the stellate ganglion, the hypersensitive smooth muscle in the vessel walls is stimulated by circulating norepinephrine and episodic vasospasm continues to occur. However, if preganglionic sympathectomy of the arm is performed by cutting the ganglion chain below the third ganglion (to interrupt ascending preganglionic fibers) and the white rami of the first 3 thoracic nerves, no hypersensitivity results.

The cause of denervation hypersensitivity is still obscure. In skeletal muscle it is associated with an increase in the area of the muscle membrane sensitive to acetylcholine. Normally, only the end-plate region is depolarized by this mediator; after denervation, the sensitivity of the end-plate is no greater, but large portions of the muscle membrane respond. The sensitivity returns to normal if the nerve regrows. A similar spread of acetylcholine sensitivity has been demonstrated in denervated postganglionic cholinergic neurons. The hypersensitivity in smooth muscle may be due in part to loss of monoamine oxidase activity. Another factor is lack of re-uptake of liberated catecholamines; the nerve endings in normal tissue take up large amounts of norepinephrine, and after they have degenerated more norepinephrine is available to act on the receptors in the tissue (see Chapter 13).

5...

Initiation of Impulses in Sense Organs

SENSE ORGANS & RECEPTORS

Information about the internal and external environment reaches the CNS via the various **sense organs.** Within the sense organs are **receptor cells** or elements which convert various forms of energy in the environment into action potentials in the sensory nerves. The terms sense organ and receptor have sometimes been used interchangeably, but in order to avoid confusion it seems wise to use them only as defined above. The forms of energy converted by the receptors include, for example, mechanical (pressure or touch), thermal (degrees of warmth), electromagnetic (light), and chemical energy (odor, taste, O_2 and CO_2 content of blood). The receptors in each of the sense organs are adapted to respond to one particular form of energy at a much lower threshold than other receptors respond to this form of energy. The particular form of energy to which a receptor is most sensitive is called its **adequate stimulus.** The adequate stimulus for the rods and cones in the eye, for example, is light. Receptors do respond to forms of energy other than their adequate stimulus, but the threshold for these nonspecific responses is much higher. Pressure on the eyeball will stimulate the rods and cones, for example, but the threshold of these receptors to pressure is much higher than the threshold of the pressure receptors in the skin.

THE SENSES

Sensory Modalities

Because the receptors in sense organs are specialized to respond to one particular form of energy and because many variables in the environment are perceived, it follows that there must be many different types of sense organs. We learn in elementary school that there are "5 senses," but the inadequacy of this dictum is apparent if we list the major sensory modalities and the sense organs for each in man. The list (Table 5–1) contains over 20 senses. The existence of other senses is suspected on both anatomic and physiologic grounds, and future research will undoubtedly add to the list. Furthermore, any listing is bound to be arbitrary. The rods and cones, for example, respond

maximally to light of different wavelengths, and there probably are different cones for each of the 3 primary colors. There are 4 different modalities of taste—sweet, salt, sour, and bitter—and each is subserved by a physiologically, if not histologically, distinct type of taste bud. Sounds of different pitches are heard primarily because different groups of hair cells in the organ of Corti are activated maximally by sound waves of different frequencies. Whether these various responses to light, taste, and sound should be considered separate senses is a semantic question that in the present context is largely academic.

Specificity of Cutaneous Sense Organs

The sense organs listed in Table 5–1 for the various cutaneous senses are not present in some parts of the integument, and there is controversy about the degree to which histologically distinct sense organs for the cutaneous senses exist. The cornea, for example, is sensitive to touch and pain, although only free nerve endings are present; no Meissner corpuscles or other organized sensory endings have been found. Parts of the lip and the lobe of the ear also lack the classically described endings for each of these modalities. It should be emphasized, however, that this controversy involves the histologic specificity of the sensory endings rather than their physiologic specificity. No concrete evidence has been presented which calls into question the principle that in the skin, as elsewhere, functionally specific receptors exist for each of the sensory modalities.

Classifications of Sense Organs

Numerous attempts have been made to classify the senses into groups, but none have been entirely successful. The most commonly used classifications are listed in Table 5–1. Traditionally, the special senses are smell, vision, hearing, equilibrium, and taste; the cutaneous senses are those with receptors in the skin; and the visceral senses are those concerned with perception of the internal environment. Pain from visceral structures is usually classified as a visceral sensation. Another classification of the various receptors divides them into (1) teleceptors ("distance receivers"), the receptors concerned with events at a distance; (2) exteroceptors, those concerned with the external environment near at hand; (3) interoceptors, those concerned with the internal environment; and (4) proprioceptors, those which provide information about

TABLE 5–1. Principal sensory modalities and sense organs.*

Sensory Modality	Sense Organ	Classification	
		Receptors	Senses
Vision	Eye	Teleceptor	Special senses
Audition	Ear		
Smell	Olfactory mucous membrane		
Taste	Taste buds	Interoceptor	
Rotational acceleration	Semicircular canals		
Linear acceleration	Utricle		
Pain	Naked nerve endings	Exteroceptors	Cutaneous senses
Touch	Meissner's corpuscles, etc		
Pressure	Pacinian corpuscles		
Warmth	Ruffini's end organs		
Cold	Krause's end bulbs		
Muscle stretch	Golgi tendon organs	Proprioceptors	
Muscle stretch	Muscle spindles		
Joint position	Nerve endings around joints		
Arterial blood pressure	Wall of carotid sinus and aortic arch	Interoceptors	Visceral senses
"Central" venous pressure	Wall of great veins, atria		
Inflation of lung	Vagal endings in lung parenchyma		
Temperature of blood in head	Cells in hypothalamus		
Partial pressure of O_2 (P_{O_2})	Carotid and aortic bodies		
pH of CSF	Receptors on ventral surface of medulla oblongata		
Osmotic pressure of plasma	Receptors in anterior hypothalamus		
Arteriovenous blood glucose difference	Cells in hypothalamus (glucostats)		

*The histologic specificity of the cutaneous endings is probably not as definite as the traditional listing given here (see text).

the position of the body in space at any given instant. However, the conscious component of proprioception, or "body image," is actually synthesized from information coming not only from receptors in and around joints but from cutaneous touch and pressure receptors as well.

In addition to the classifications listed in Table 5–1, certain other special terms are sometimes used. Deep pressure and pain, the pressure and pain sensations elicited from muscles, tendons, and deep fasciae, are sometimes listed as separate sensory modalities because they differ in quality from their cutaneous counterparts. Because pain fibers have connections which mediate strong and prepotent withdrawal reflexes (see Chapter 6), and because pain is initiated by potentially noxious or damaging stimuli, pain receptors are sometimes called **nociceptors**. Finally, the term **chemoreceptor** is used to refer to those receptors in sense organs which are stimulated by a change in the chemical composition of the environment in which they are located. These include receptors for taste and smell as well as visceral receptors such as those sensitive to changes in the plasma level of O_2, CO_2, and osmolality.

ELECTRICAL & IONIC EVENTS IN RECEPTORS

Anatomic Relationships

The problem of how receptors convert energy into action potentials in the sensory nerves has been the subject of intensive study. In the complex sense organs such as those concerned with vision, hearing, equilibrium, and taste, there are separate receptor cells and synaptic junctions between receptors and afferent nerves. However, in most of the cutaneous sense organs, the receptors are specialized, histologically modified ends of sensory nerve fibers.

Pacinian corpuscles have been studied in detail. Because of their relatively large size and accessibility in the mesentery of experimental animals, they can be isolated, studied with microelectrodes, and subjected to microdissection. These capsules consist of the straight, unmyelinated ending of the sensory nerve fiber, 2 μm in diameter, surrounded by concentric lamellas of connective tissue which give the organ the appearance of a minute cocktail onion. The myelin sheath of the sensory nerve begins inside the corpuscle. The first node of Ranvier is also located inside, whereas the second is usually near the point at which the nerve fiber leaves the corpuscle (Fig 5–1).

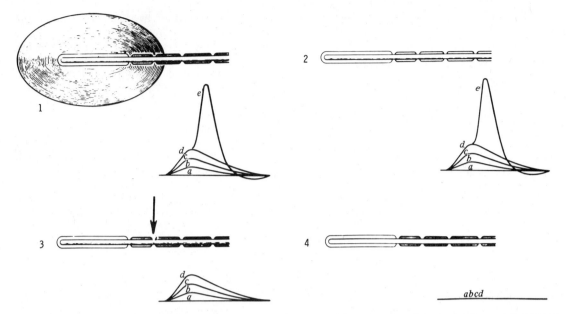

FIG 5–1. Demonstration that the generator potential in a pacinian corpuscle originates in the nonmyelinated nerve terminal. In 1, the electrical responses to a pressure of x (record a), 2 x (b), 3 x (c), and 4 x (d) were recorded. The strongest stimulus produced an action potential in the sensory nerve (e). In 2, the same responses persisted after removal of the connective tissue capsule. In 3, the generator responses persisted but the action potential was absent when the first node of Ranvier was blocked with pressure or narcotics (arrow). In 4, all responses disappeared when the sensory nerve was cut and allowed to degenerate before the experiment. (Reproduced, with permission, from Biological transducers, by Lowenstein. Scientific American 203:98, Aug 1960. Copyright © 1960 by Scientific American, Inc. All rights reserved.)

Generator Potentials

Recording electrodes can be placed on the sensory nerve as it leaves a pacinian corpuscle and graded pressure applied to the corpuscle. When a small amount of pressure is applied, a nonpropagated depolarizing potential resembling an EPSP is recorded. This is called the **generator potential**, or **receptor potential**. As the pressure is increased, the magnitude of the receptor potential increases. When the magnitude of the generator potential is about 10 mv, an action potential is generated in the sensory nerve. As the pressure is further increased, the generator potential becomes even larger and the sensory nerve fires repetitively. Eventually, in the case of the pacinian corpuscle, the size of the generator potential reaches a maximum, but its rate of rise continues to increase as the magnitude of the applied pressure is increased.

Source of the Generator Potential

By microdissection technics it has been shown that removal of the connective tissue lamellas from the unmyelinated nerve ending in a pacinian corpuscle does not abolish the generator potential. When the first node of Ranvier is blocked by pressure or narcotics, the generator potential is unaffected but conducted impulses are abolished (Fig 5–1). When the sensory nerve is sectioned and the nonmyelinated terminal is allowed to degenerate, no generator potential is formed. These and other experiments have established the fact that the generator potential is produced in the

unmyelinated nerve terminal. This potential electrotonically depolarizes the first node of Ranvier. The receptor therefore converts mechanical energy into an electrical response, the magnitude of which is proportionate to the intensity of the stimulus. The generator potential in turn depolarizes the sensory nerve at the first node of Ranvier one or more times. It thus converts the graded response of the receptor into action potentials, the frequency of which is proportionate to the magnitude of the applied stimuli.

Similar generator potentials have been studied in the muscle spindle. The relationship between the stimulus intensity and the size of the generator potential and between the stimulus intensity and the frequency of the action potentials in the afferent nerve fiber from a spindle is shown in Fig 5–2. The frequency of the action potentials is generally related to the intensity of the stimulus by a power function (see below). Generator potentials have also been observed in the organ of Corti, the olfactory and taste organs, and other sense organs. Presumably, they are in most cases the mechanism by which sensory nerve fibers are activated.

Ionic Basis of Excitation

The biophysical events underlying the generator potential have not been completely clarified, but it is known that sodium depletion diminishes and eventually abolishes the generator potential in pacinian cor-

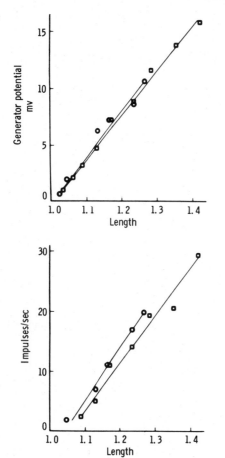

of cutaneous sense organs by an action that is independent of any effect on smooth muscle. However, the available evidence indicates that neither acetylcholine nor epinephrine is responsible for the formation of the generator potential in pacinian corpuscles, carotid sinus receptors, and a number of other sense organs.

Adaptation

When a maintained stimulus of constant strength is applied to a sense organ, the frequency of the action potentials in its sensory nerve declines over a period of time. This phenomenon is known as **adaptation**. The degree to which adaptation occurs varies with the type of sense organ (Fig 5–3). Touch and pressure adapt rapidly. It is interesting in this regard that application of a maintained pressure to a pacinian corpuscle produces a generator potential that decays rapidly. On the other hand, the carotid sinus, the muscle spindles, and the organs for cold, pain, and lung inflation adapt very slowly and incompletely. This correlates with the fact that the generator potential of the muscle spindle is prolonged and decays very slowly when a steady stimulus is applied to it. Maintained pressure applied to the outside of a pacinian corpuscle causes steady displacement in the outer lamellas, but the lamellas near the nerve fiber slip back to their original position, presumably ending the distortion of the nerve ending and causing the generator potential to decline. However, this is not the only factor producing adaptation; there is still a decline in the number of action poten-

FIG 5–2. Relation between muscle length and size of generator potential (*above*) and impulse frequency (*below*) in crayfish stretch receptor. Squares and circles indicate values in 2 different preparations. (Reproduced, with permission, from Terzuolo & Washizu: Relation between stimulus strength, generator potential, and impulse frequency in stretch receptor of crustacea. J Neurophysiol 25:56, 1962.)

puscles. Presumably, the stimulus initiates an increase in the permeability of the membrane of the unmyelinated terminal to Na^+, the resultant influx of Na^+ produces the generator potential, and the magnitude of the permeability change is proportionate to the intensity of the stimulus.

Relation of Chemical Mediators to Receptor Function

How the mechanical stimulus is converted into a change in membrane permeability is not known. It is possible that the change is due to stretching or distortion of the membrane, or it could be due to the release of some chemical mediator. It has been argued that acetylcholine is liberated during stimulation of the cutaneous sense organs. Perfusion of a pacinian corpuscle with acetylcholine does lower its threshold to stimulation. Epinephrine also decreases the threshold

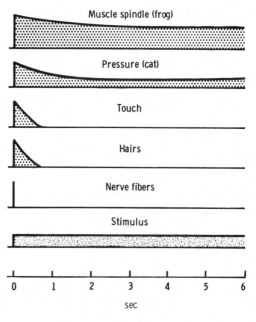

FIG 5–3. Adaptation. The height of the curve in each case indicates the frequency of the discharge in afferent nerve fibers at various times after beginning sustained stimulation. (Reproduced, with permission, from Adrian: *Basis of Sensation*. Christophers, 1928.)

tials generated over a period of time by a steady stimulus after removal of the outer lamellas from the pacinian corpuscle. This decline is due to accommodation of the sensory nerve fiber to the generator potential, and does not occur in the case of the slowly accommodating muscle spindle.

The slow, incomplete adaptation of the carotid sinus and the organs for muscle stretch, pain, and cold is of some value to the animal. Muscle stretch plays a role in prolonged postural adjustments. The sensations of pain and cold are initiated by potentially noxious stimuli, and they would lose some of their warning value if their receptors showed marked adaptation. Carotid and aortic receptors operate continuously in the regulation of blood pressure, and adaptation of these receptors would limit the precision with which the regulatory system operates.

"CODING" OF SENSORY INFORMATION

There are minor variations in the speed of conduction and other characteristics of sensory nerve fibers (see Chapter 2), but in general action potentials are similar in all nerves. The action potentials in the nerve from a pressure receptor, for example, are essentially identical to those in the nerve from a warmth receptor. This raises the question of why stimulation of a pressure receptor causes a sensation of pressure and not of warmth and how it is possible to tell whether the pressure is light or heavy.

Doctrine of Specific Nerve Energies

The sensation evoked by impulses generated in a receptor depends upon the specific part of the brain they ultimately activate. The specific sensory pathways are discrete from sense organ to cortex. Therefore, when the nerve pathways from a particular sense organ are stimulated, the sensation evoked is that for which the receptor is specialized no matter how or where along the pathway the activity is initiated. This principle, first enunciated by Müller, has been given the rather cumbersome name of the **doctrine of specific nerve energies**. For example, if the sensory nerve from a pacinian corpuscle in the hand is stimulated by pressure at the elbow or by irritation from a tumor in the brachial plexus, the sensation evoked is one of pressure. Similarly, if a fine enough electrode could be inserted into the appropriate fibers of the dorsal columns of the spinal cord, the thalamus, or the postcentral gyrus of the cerebral cortex, the sensation produced by stimulation would be pressure. This doctrine has been questioned from time to time, especially by those who claim that pain is produced by overstimulation of a variety of sense organs. However, the overstimulation hypothesis has been largely discredited and the principle of specific nerve energies remains one of the cornerstones of sensory physiology.

Projection

No matter where a particular sensory pathway is stimulated along its course to the cortex, the conscious sensation produced is referred to the location of the receptor. This principle is called the **law of projection**. Cortical stimulation experiments during neurosurgical procedures on conscious patients illustrate this phenomenon. For example, when the cortical receiving area for impulses from the left hand is stimulated, the patient reports sensation in his left hand, not in his head. Another dramatic example is seen in amputees. These patients may complain, often bitterly, of pain and proprioceptive sensations in the absent limb ("phantom limb"). These sensations are due in part to pressure on the stump of the amputated limb. This pressure initiates impulses in nerve fibers which previously came from sense organs in the amputated limb, and the sensations evoked are projected to where the receptors used to be.

Intensity Discrimination

There are 2 ways in which information about intensity of stimuli is transmitted to the brain: by variation in the frequency of the action potentials generated by the activity in a given receptor, and by variation in the number of receptors activated. It has long been taught that the magnitude of the sensation felt is proportionate to the log of the intensity of the stimulus (**Weber-Fechner law**). It now appears, however, that a power function more accurately describes this relation. In other words, $R = KS^A$, where R is the sensation felt, S is the intensity of the stimulus, and for any specific sensory modality, K and A are constants. The frequency of the action potentials a stimulus generates in a sensory nerve fiber is also related to the intensity of the initiating stimulus by a power function. An example of this relation is shown in Fig 5–2, in which the exponent is approximately 1.0. Another example is shown in Fig 5–4, in which the calculated exponent is 0.52. Current evidence indicates that in the CNS the relation between stimulus and sensation is linear; consequently, it appears that for any given sensory modality the relation between sensation and stimulus intensity is determined primarily by the properties of the peripheral receptors themselves.

Sensory Units

The term sensory unit is applied to a single sensory axon and all its peripheral branches. The number of these branches varies, but they may be numerous, especially in the case of the cutaneous senses. In the cornea, and adjacent sclera of the eye, the surface area supplied by a single sensory unit is 50–200 sq mm. Generally, the areas supplied by one unit overlap and interdigitate with the areas supplied by others.

Recruitment of Sensory Units

As the strength of a stimulus is increased, it tends to spread over a large area and generally activates not only the sense organs immediately in contact with it

FIG 5—4. Relation between magnitude of touch stimulus (S) and frequency of action potentials in sensory nerve fibers (R). Dots are individual values from cats plotted on linear coordinates (*left*) and log-log coordinates (*right*). The equation shows the calculated power function relationship between R and S. (Reproduced, with permission, from Werner & Mountcastle: Neural activity in mechanoreceptive cutaneous afferents, stimulus-response relations, Weber functions, and information transmission. J Neurophysiol 28:359, 1965.)

but "recruits" those in the surrounding area as well. Furthermore, weak stimuli activate the receptors with the lowest thresholds, whereas stronger stimuli also activate those with higher thresholds. Some of the receptors activated are part of the same sensory unit, and impulse frequency in the unit therefore increases.

Because of overlap and interdigitation of one unit with another, however, receptors of other units are also stimulated and consequently more units fire. In this way more afferent pathways are activated, and this is interpreted in the brain as an increase in intensity of the sensation.

●   ●   ●

References: Section II
Physiology of Nerve & Muscle Cells

Brazier MAB: *The Electrical Activity of the Nervous System,* 3rd ed. Pitman, 1968.

Bulbring E (editor): *Smooth Muscle.* Williams & Wilkins, 1970.

Caldwell PC: Factors governing movement and distribution of inorganic ions in nerve and muscle. Physiol Rev 48:1, 1968.

Close RI: Dynamic properties of mammalian skeletal muscles. Physiol Rev 52:129, 1972.

Davson H: *A Textbook of General Physiology,* 4th ed. Williams & Wilkins, 1970.

Eccles JC: The synapse. Scientific American 212:56, Jan 1965.

Geffen LB, Livett BG: Synaptic vesicles in sympathetic neurons. Physiol Rev 51:98, 1971.

Hodgkin AL: The ionic basis of nervous conduction. Science 145:1148, 1964.

Hoffman BF, Cranefield PF: *Electrophysiology of the Heart.* McGraw-Hill, 1960.

Hubbard JI: Mechanism of transmitter release from nerve terminals. Ann New York Acad Sci 183:131, 1971.

Huxley AF: Excitation and conduction in nerve: Quantitative analysis. Science 145:1154, 1964.

Kandel ER, Kupferman I: The functional organization of invertebrate ganglia. Ann Rev Physiol 32:193, 1970.

Katz B: Quantal mechanism of neural transmitter release. Science 173:123, 1971.

Langer GA: The intrinsic control of myocardial contraction—ionic factors. New England J Med 285:1065, 1971.

Ochs S: Fast transport of materials in mammalian nerve fibers. Science 176:252, 1972.

Pappas GD, Purpura DP (editors): *Structure and Function of Synapses.* Raven, 1972.

Sonnenblick EH, Stam AC Jr: Cardiac muscle: Activation and contraction. Ann Rev Physiol 31:647, 1969.

III. Functions of the Nervous System

6 . . .

Reflexes

THE REFLEX ARC

The basic unit of integrated neural activity is the reflex arc. This arc consists of a sense organ, an afferent neuron, one or more synapses in a central integrating station, an efferent neuron, and an effector. In mammals and man, the connection between afferent and efferent somatic neurons is in the brain or spinal cord. The afferent neurons enter via the dorsal roots or cranial nerves, and have their cell bodies in the dorsal root ganglia or in the homologous ganglia on the cranial nerves. The efferent fibers leave via the ventral roots or corresponding motor cranial nerves. The principle that in the spinal cord the dorsal roots are sensory and the ventral roots are motor is known as the **Bell-Magendie law.**

In previous chapters the function of each of the components of the reflex arc has been considered in detail. As noted in Chapters 2 and 3, impulses generated in the axons of the afferent and efferent neurons and in muscle are "all or none" in character. On the other hand, there are 3 junctions or junction-like areas in the reflex arc where responses are graded (Fig 6–1). These are the receptor-afferent neuron region, the synapse between the afferent and efferent neurons, and the myoneural junction. At each of these points, a nonpropagated potential proportionate in size to the magnitude of the incoming stimulus is generated. The graded potentials serve to electrotonically depolarize the adjacent nerve or muscle membrane and set up all or none responses. The number of action potentials in the afferent nerve is proportionate to the magnitude of the applied stimulus at the sense organ. There is also a rough correlation between the magnitude of the stimulus and the frequency of action potentials in the efferent nerve; however, since the connection between the afferent and efferent neurons is in the CNS, activity in the reflex arc is modified by the multiple inputs converging on the efferent neurons.

The simplest reflex arc is one with a single synapse between the afferent and efferent neurons. Such arcs are **monosynaptic,** and reflexes occurring in them are **monosynaptic reflexes.** Reflex arcs in which one or more interneurons are interposed between the afferent and efferent neurons are **polysynaptic,** the number of synapses in the arcs varying from 2 to many hundreds. In both types, but especially in polysynaptic reflex arcs, activity is modified by spatial and temporal facilitation, occlusion, and subliminal fringe effects.

MONOSYNAPTIC REFLEXES: THE STRETCH REFLEX

When a skeletal muscle with an intact nerve supply is stretched, it contracts. This response is called the

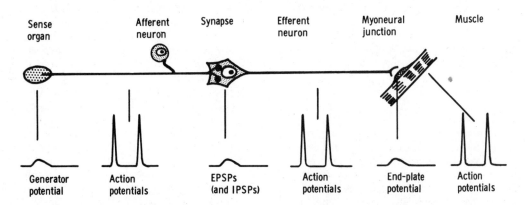

FIG 6–1. The reflex arc. Note that at the receptor and at each of the junctions in the arc there is a nonpropagated graded response which is proportionate to the magnitude of the stimulus, whereas in the portions of the arc specialized for transmission (axons, muscle membrane) the responses are all or none action potentials.

stretch reflex. The stimulus that initiates the reflex is stretch of the muscle, and the response is contraction of the muscle being stretched. The sense organ is the muscle spindle. The impulses originating in the spindle are conducted to the CNS by fast sensory fibers which pass directly to the motor neurons which supply the same muscle. Stretch reflexes are the only monosynaptic reflexes in the body.

Clinical Examples

Tapping the patellar tendon elicits the **knee jerk,** a stretch reflex of the quadriceps femoris muscle, because the tap on the tendon stretches the muscle. A similar contraction is observed if the quadriceps is stretched manually. Stretch reflexes can also be elicited from most of the large muscles of the body. Tapping on the tendon of the triceps brachii, for example, causes an extensor response at the elbow due to reflex contraction of the triceps; tapping on the Achilles tendon causes an ankle jerk due to reflex contraction of the gastrocnemius; and tapping on the side of the face causes a stretch reflex in the masseter. Other examples of stretch reflexes are listed in neurology textbooks.

Muscle Spindles

Each muscle spindle consists of 2–10 muscle fibers enclosed in a connective tissue capsule. These fibers are more embryonal in character and have less distinct striations than the rest of the fibers in the muscle. They are called **intrafusal fibers** to distinguish them from the **extrafusal fibers,** the regular contractile units of the muscle. The intrafusal fibers are in parallel with the rest of the muscle fibers because the ends of the capsule of the spindle are attached to the tendons at either end of the muscle or to the sides of the extrafusal fibers.

The 2 ends of each intrafusal fiber are contractile, but the middle portion is filled with nuclei (**nuclear bag region**) and is probably noncontractile (Fig 6–2). In this middle portion are located the **primary** or **annulospiral endings.** These are the endings of afferent neurons with large, rapidly conducting processes. The processes, which are 8–12 μm in diameter, form the Ia component in the classification scheme for sensory fibers described in Chapter 2. The endings, which are wrapped around the intrafusal fibers in a complex manner, are the receptors for the stretch reflex.

On either side of the annulospiral endings are the **secondary** or **flower-spray endings,** which are the receptor ends of smaller myelinated fibers (6–9 μm in diameter) belonging to the group II sensory fiber category. These receptors also respond to stretch. Activity in them leads to increased flexor and decreased extensor motor neuron activity. The possible functional significance of the polysynaptic connections of these endings in walking is discussed below.

The muscle spindles also have a motor nerve supply of their own. These nerves are 3–6 μm in diameter, constitute about 30% of the fibers in the ventral roots, and belong in Erlanger and Gasser's A γ group. They are distributed to the motor end-plates on

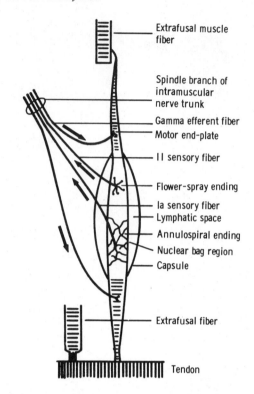

Extrafusal muscle fiber

Spindle branch of intramuscular nerve trunk

Gamma efferent fiber

Motor end-plate

II sensory fiber

Flower-spray ending

Ia sensory fiber

Lymphatic space

Annulospiral ending

Nuclear bag region

Capsule

Extrafusal fiber

Tendon

FIG 6–2. Muscle spindle (highly diagrammatic).

the contractile ends of the intrafusal fibers. Because of their characteristic size, they are called the **gamma efferents** of Leksell, or the **small motor nerve system.** There also appears to be a sparse innervation of spindles by motor fibers of intermediate size. The function of this **beta innervation** is unknown.

Stimulation of the Spindle

When the nuclear bag region of the spindle is stretched, the annulospiral endings are distorted and receptor potentials are generated. These in turn set up action potentials in the Ia sensory fibers at a frequency which is proportionate to the degree of stretching. The spindle is in parallel with the extrafusal fibers, and, as long as the rate of gamma efferent discharge remains constant, active contraction of the muscle causes tension on the spindle to decrease. When a muscle is stretched under these conditions, there is a burst of activity in the fibers from the spindle and then, as the muscle contracts reflexly, a silent period in which all discharge ceases. Similarly, direct stimulation of the extrafusal muscle fibers causes inhibition of spindle discharge as the muscle contracts.

Spindles respond both to static and dynamic phasic events in muscle; the receptors are stimulated by steady stretch and changes in the rate of stretching. There is evidence that the annulospiral endings respond to steady stretch and the velocity of stretching, whereas the flower-spray endings respond primarily to steady stretch.

It is evident that the spindle mechanism and its reflex connections constitute a feedback device which operates to maintain muscle length; if the muscle is stretched, spindle discharge increases and reflex shortening is produced, whereas if the muscle is shortened, spindle discharge decreases and the muscle relaxes. In such a feedback loop, the sensitivity to the velocity of stretch counteracts the consequences of time lag in the circuit. One of these consequences is oscillation. There is normally a small oscillation in this feedback loop during voluntary contractions: this is the **physiologic tremor,** which has a frequency of approximately 10 hz. However, the tremor would be worse if it were not for the sensitivity of the spindle to velocity of stretch.

Effects of Gamma Efferent Discharge

Stimulation of the gamma efferent system produces a very different picture from that produced by stimulation of the extrafusal fibers. Such stimulation does not lead directly to detectable contraction of the muscles because the intrafusal fibers are not strong enough or plentiful enough to cause shortening. However, stimulation does cause the contractile ends of the intrafusal fibers to shorten and therefore stretches the nuclear bag portion of the spindles, deforming the annulospiral endings and initiating impulses in the Ia fibers. If the whole muscle is then stretched during stimulation of the gamma efferents, additional action potentials are generated due to the additional stretch of the nuclear bag region, and the rate of discharge in the Ia fibers is further increased (Fig 6–3). Therefore, increased gamma efferent discharge increases spindle sensitivity and the sensitivity of the spindles to stretch varies directly with the rate of gamma efferent discharge.

Control of Gamma Efferent Discharge

The motor neurons of the gamma efferent system are regulated to a large degree by descending tracts from a number of areas in the brain. Via these pathways, the sensitivity of the muscle spindles and hence the threshold of the stretch reflexes in various parts of

the body can be adjusted and shifted to meet the needs of postural control (see Chapter 12).

Other factors also influence gamma efferent discharge. Anxiety causes an increased discharge, a fact which probably explains the hyperactive tendon reflexes sometimes seen in anxious patients. Stimulation of the skin, especially by noxious agents, increases gamma efferent discharge to ipsilateral flexor muscle spindles while decreasing that to extensors, and produces the opposite pattern in the opposite limb. It is well known that having a subject try to pull his hands apart when his flexed fingers are hooked together facilitates his knee jerk reflex (Jendrassik's maneuver), and this may also be due to increased gamma efferent discharge initiated by afferent impulses from the hands. Stimulation of certain gamma efferent fibers has been shown to increase the sensitivity of the spindles to dynamic changes and stimulation of other fibers to increase their sensitivity to static events.

There is considerable evidence that there is increased gamma efferent discharge along with the increased discharge in the alpha motor neurons that initiates movements. Because of this "alpha-gamma linkage," the spindle shortens with the muscle, and spindle discharge may continue throughout the contraction. The physiologic significance of this simultaneous contraction of the extrafusal and intrafusal fibers of the muscle is uncertain, but it appears to be related to the stabilization and coordination of movement.

Central Connections of Afferent Fibers

It can be proved experimentally that the fibers from the annulospiral endings end directly on motor neurons supplying the extrafusal fibers of the same muscle. The time between the application of the stimulus and the response in a reflex is the **reaction time.** In man, the reaction time for a stretch reflex such as the knee jerk is 19–24 msec. Weak stimulation of the sensory nerve from the muscle, known to stimulate only

FIG 6–3. Effect of various conditions on muscle spindle discharge. In *A* the spindle is stretched the same amount as the extrafusal fibers. In *B* it is relaxed and hence longer than the contracted extrafusal fibers. In *C* the contractile portions of the spindle are shortened, and the pull on the nuclear bag portion causes sensory nerve discharge. In *D* the nuclear bag region, already stretched due to the γ efferent discharge, is stretched further, causing the very high rate of discharge in the sensory nerve. (Drawn in part from Patton, in: *Physiology and Biophysics,* 19th ed. Ruch TC, Patton HD [editors]. Saunders, 1965.)

FIG 6—4. **Discharge frequency of a motor neuron supplying a leg muscle in a cat.** Discharge frequency is plotted against muscle length at various magnitudes of stimulation of the nerve from the antagonist to the muscle. (Reproduced, with permission, from Henneman & others: Excitability and inhibitability of motor neurons of different sizes. J Neurophysiol 28:599, 1965.)

Ia fibers, causes a contractile response with a similar latency. Since the conduction velocity of the afferent and efferent fiber types are known and the distance from the muscle to the spinal cord can be measured, it is possible to calculate how much of the reaction time was taken up by conduction to and from the spinal cord. When this value is subtracted from the reaction time, the remainder, called the **central delay,** is the time taken for the reflex activity to traverse the spinal cord. In man, the central delay for the knee jerk is 0.6–0.9 msec, and figures of similar magnitude have

been found in experimental animals. Since the minimal synaptic delay is 0.5 msec (see Chapter 4), only one synapse could have been traversed.

Reciprocal Innervation

When a stretch reflex occurs, the muscles that antagonize the action of the muscle involved (antagonists) relax. This phenomenon is said to be due to **reciprocal innervation.** Impulses in the Ia fibers from the muscle spindles of the protagonist muscle cause postsynaptic inhibition of the motor neurons to the antagonists. Although there is still some argument on the point, it appears that the pathway mediating this effect is a simple bisynaptic one. A collateral from each Ia fiber passes in the spinal cord to an inhibitory interneuron (Golgi bottle neuron) which synapses directly on one of the motor neurons supplying the antagonist muscles. This example of postsynaptic inhibition is discussed in Chapter 4, and the pathway is illustrated in Fig 4—8. The interaction of spindle discharge, tendon organ discharge, and reciprocal innervation in determining the rate of discharge of a motor neuron is shown in Fig 6—4.

Inverse Stretch Reflex

Up to a point, the harder a muscle is stretched, the stronger is the reflex contraction. However, when the tension becomes great enough, contraction suddenly ceases and the muscle relaxes. This relaxation in response to strong stretch is called the **inverse stretch reflex,** or **autogenic inhibition.** It may protect the muscle from disruption or rupture of its attachments.

The receptor for the inverse stretch reflex is in the **Golgi tendon organ** (Fig 6—5). This organ consists of a net-like collection of knobby nerve endings among the fascicles of a tendon. There are 3—25 muscle fibers per tendon organ. The fibers from the Golgi tendon organs make up the Ib group of myelinated, rapidly conducting sensory nerve fibers. Stimulation of these Ib fibers leads to the production of IPSPs on the motor neurons that supply the muscle from which the fibers arose. The Ib fibers apparently end in the spinal cord on inhibitory interneurons which, in turn, terminate directly on the motor neurons (Fig 6—6). They also

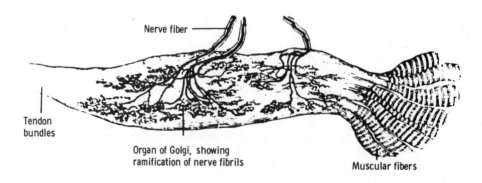

FIG 6—5. **Golgi tendon organ.** (After Ciaccio. Reproduced, with permission, from: *Gray's Anatomy of the Human Body,* 29th ed. Goss CM [editor]. Lea & Febiger, 1973.)

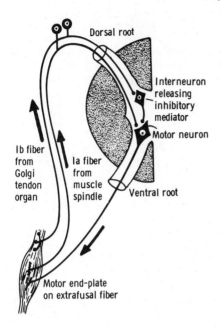

FIG 6–6. Diagram illustrating the pathways responsible for the stretch reflex and the inverse stretch reflex. Stretch stimulates the spindle, and impulses pass up the Ia fiber to excite the motor neuron. It also stimulates the Golgi tendon organ, and impulses passing up the Ib fiber activate the interneuron to release inhibitory mediator. With strong stretch, the resulting hyperpolarization of the motor neuron is so great that it stops discharging.

make excitatory connections with motor neurons supplying antagonists to the muscle.

Since the Golgi tendon organs, unlike the spindles, are in series with the muscle fibers, they are stimulated by both passive stretch and active contraction of the muscle. The threshold of the Golgi tendon organs is low. The degree of stimulation by passive stretch is not great because the more elastic muscle fibers take up much of the stretch, and this is why it takes a strong stretch to produce relaxation. However, discharge is regularly produced by contraction of the muscle, and it now appears that the Golgi tendon organ functions as a transducer in a feedback circuit which regulates muscle tension in a fashion analogous to the spindle feedback circuit which regulates muscle length.

Muscle Tone

The resistance of a muscle to stretch is often referred to as its **tone** or **tonus**. If the motor nerve to a muscle is cut, the muscle offers very little resistance and is said to be **flaccid**. A **hypertonic** or **spastic** muscle is one in which the resistance to stretch is high. Somewhere between the states of flaccidity and spasticity is the ill-defined area of normal tone. The muscles are generally **hypotonic** when the rate of gamma

efferent discharge is low and hypertonic when it is high.

Lengthening Reaction

When the muscles are hypertonic the sequence of moderate stretch → muscle contraction, strong stretch → muscle relaxation is clearly seen. Passive flexion of the elbow, for example, meets immediate resistance due to the stretch reflex in the triceps muscle. Further stretch activates the inverse stretch reflex. The resistance to flexion suddenly collapses, and the arm flexes. Continued passive flexion stretches the muscle again, and the sequence may be repeated. This sequence of resistance followed by give when a limb is moved passively is known clinically as the **clasp-knife effect** because of its resemblance to the closing of a pocket knife. The physiologic name for it is the **lengthening reaction** because it is the response of a spastic muscle (in the example cited, the triceps) to lengthening.

Clonus

Another finding characteristic of states in which increased gamma efferent discharge is present is **clonus**. This neurologic sign is the occurrence of regular, rhythmic contractions of a muscle subjected to sudden, maintained stretch. Ankle clonus is a typical example. This is initiated by brisk dorsiflexion of the foot, and the response is rhythmic plantar flexion at the ankle. The stretch reflex-inverse stretch reflex sequence described above may contribute to this response. However, it can occur on the basis of synchronized motor neuron discharge without Golgi tendon organ discharge. The spindles of the tested muscle are hyperactive, and the burst of impulses from them discharges all the motor neurons supplying the muscle at once. The consequent muscle contraction stops spindle discharge. However, the stretch has been

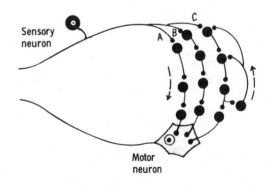

FIG 6–7. Diagram of polysynaptic connections between afferent and efferent neurons in the spinal cord. The dorsal root fiber activates pathway A with 3 interneurons, pathway B with 4 interneurons, and pathway C with 4 interneurons. Note that one of the interneurons in pathway C connects to a neuron which doubles back to other interneurons, forming reverberating circuits.

maintained, and as soon as the muscle relaxes it is again stretched and the spindles stimulated.

POLYSYNAPTIC REFLEXES: THE WITHDRAWAL REFLEX

Polysynaptic reflex paths branch in a complex fashion (Fig 6–7). The number of synapses in each of their branches is variable. Because of the synaptic delay incurred at each synapse, activity in the branches with fewer synapses reaches the motor neurons first, followed by activity in the longer pathways. This causes prolonged bombardment of the motor neurons from a single stimulus and consequently prolonged responses. Furthermore, as shown in Fig 6–7, at least some of the branch pathways turn back on themselves, permitting activity to reverberate until it becomes unable to cause a propagated transsynaptic response and dies out. Such **reverberating circuits** are common in the brain and spinal cord.

Withdrawal Reflex

The withdrawal reflex is a typical polysynaptic reflex which occurs in response to a noxious and usually painful stimulation of the skin or subcutaneous tissues and muscle. The response is flexor muscle contraction and inhibition of extensor muscles, so that the part stimulated is flexed and withdrawn from the stimulus. When a strong stimulus is applied to a limb, the response includes not only flexion and withdrawal of that limb but also extension of the opposite limb. This **crossed extensor response** is properly part of the withdrawal reflex. It can also be shown in experimental animals that strong stimuli generate activity in the interneuron pool which spreads to all 4 extremities. This is difficult to demonstrate in normal animals, but is easily demonstrated in an animal in which the modulating effects of impulses from the brain have been abolished by prior section of the spinal cord (**spinal animal**). For example, when the hind limb of a spinal cat is pinched, the stimulated limb is withdrawn, the opposite hind limb extended, the ipsilateral forelimb extended, and the contralateral forelimb flexed. This spread of excitatory impulses up and down the spinal cord to more and more motor neurons is called **irradiation of the stimulus,** and the increase in the number of active motor units is called **recruitment of motor units.**

Importance of the Withdrawal Reflex

Flexor responses can be produced by innocuous stimulation of the skin or by stretch of the muscle via the flower-spray endings, but strong flexor responses with withdrawal are initiated only by stimuli that are noxious or at least potentially harmful to the animal. These stimuli are therefore called **nociceptive stimuli.** Sherrington pointed out the survival value of the withdrawal response. Flexion of the stimulated limb gets it away from the source of irritation, and extension of the other limb supports the body. The pattern assumed by all 4 extremities puts the animal in position to run away from the offending stimulus. Withdrawal reflexes are **prepotent,** ie, they preempt the spinal pathways from any other reflex activity taking place at the moment.

Many of the characteristics of polysynaptic reflexes can be demonstrated by studying the withdrawal reflex in the laboratory. A weak noxious stimulus to one foot evokes a minimal flexion response; stronger stimuli produce greater and greater flexion as the stimulus irradiates to more and more of the motor neuron pool supplying the muscles of the limb. Stronger stimuli also cause a more prolonged response. A weak stimulus causes one quick flexion movement; a strong stimulus causes prolonged flexion and sometimes a series of flexion movements. This prolonged response is due to prolonged, repeated firing of the motor neurons. The repeated firing is called **afterdischarge,** and is due to continued bombardment of motor neurons by impulses arriving by complicated and circuitous polysynaptic paths.

As the strength of a noxious stimulus is increased, the reaction time is shortened. Spatial and temporal facilitation occur at the various synapses in the polysynaptic pathway. Stronger stimuli produce more action potentials per second in the active branches and cause more branches to become active; summation of the EPSPs to the firing level therefore occurs more rapidly.

Local Sign

The exact flexor pattern of the withdrawal reflex in a limb varies with the part of the limb which is stimulated. If the medial surface of the limb is stimulated, for example, the response will include some abduction, whereas stimulation of the lateral surface will produce some adduction with flexion. The reflex response in each case generally serves to effectively remove the limb from the irritating stimulus. This dependence of the exact response on the location of the stimulus is called **local sign.** The degree to which local sign determines the particular response pattern is illustrated in Fig 6–8.

Fractionation & Occlusion

Another characteristic of the withdrawal response is the fact that supramaximal stimulation of any of the sensory nerves from a limb never produces as strong a contraction of the flexor muscles as that elicited by direct electrical stimulation of the muscles themselves. This indicates that the afferent inputs **fractionate** the motor neuron pool, ie, each input goes to only part of the motor neuron pool for the flexors of that particular extremity. On the other hand, if all the sensory inputs are dissected out and stimulated one after the other, the sum of the tension developed by stimulation of each is greater than that produced by direct electrical stimulation of the muscle or stimulation of all inputs at once. This fact indicates that the various

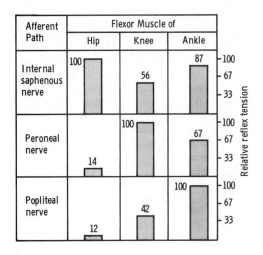

Afferent Path	Flexor Muscle of		
	Hip	Knee	Ankle
Internal saphenous nerve	100	56	87
Peroneal nerve	14	100	67
Popliteal nerve	12	42	100

Relative reflex tension

FIG 6−8. The importance of local sign in determining the character of the withdrawal response in a leg. When afferent fibers in each of the 3 nerves on the left were stimulated, hip, knee, and ankle flexors contracted but the relative tension developed in each case (shaded bars) varied. (Data from Creed & Sherrington: Observations on concurrent contraction of flexor muscles in the flexion reflex. Proc Roy Soc London s.B 100:258, 1926.)

afferent inputs share some of the motor neurons, and that occlusion (see Chapter 4) occurs when all inputs are stimulated at once.

Flower-Spray Endings & Stepping

Impulses in the group II afferent fibers from the flower-spray endings in the muscle spindles cause ipsilateral flexor stimulation and extensor inhibition, and the reverse pattern on the contralateral side. The pattern is thus similar to the withdrawal response. The step-like pattern of flexion of one leg and extension of the other has led to speculation that the flower-spray endings play a role in walking. However, walking is a complex phenomenon. Stepping movements occur in animals after spinal cord transection, but they also occur during spinal cord stimulation in animals in which the limbs have been deafferented. This indicates that the flower-spray endings, although they may contribute, are not essential for stepping responses.

Other Polysynaptic Reflexes

There are many polysynaptic reflexes in addition to the withdrawal reflex, all with similar properties. Such reflexes as the abdominal and cremasteric reflexes are forms of the withdrawal reflex. Others include visceral components. Numerous polysynaptic reflexes that relate to specific regulatory functions are described in other sections of this book, and comprehensive lists can be found in neurology textbooks.

GENERAL PROPERTIES OF REFLEXES

It is apparent from the preceding description of the properties of monosynaptic and polysynaptic reflexes that reflex activity is stereotyped and specific in terms of both the stimulus and the response; a particular stimulus elicits a particular response.

Adequate Stimulus

The stimulus that triggers a reflex is generally very precise. This stimulus is called the **adequate stimulus** for the particular reflex. A dramatic example is the scratch reflex in the dog. This spinal reflex is adequately stimulated by multiple linear touch stimuli such as those produced by an insect crawling across the skin. The response is vigorous scratching of the area stimulated. (Incidentally, the precision with which the scratching foot goes to the site of the irritant is a good example of local sign.) If the multiple touch stimuli are widely separated or are not in a line, the adequate stimulus is not produced and no scratching occurs. Fleas crawl, but they also jump from place to place. This jumping separates the touch stimuli so that an adequate stimulus for the scratch reflex is not produced. It is doubtful if the flea population would long survive without the ability to jump.

Final Common Path

The motor neurons that supply the extrafusal fibers in skeletal muscles are the efferent side of the reflex arc. All neural influences affecting muscular contraction ultimately funnel through them to the muscles, and they are therefore called the **final common paths**. Numerous inputs converge on them. Indeed, it has been reported that the surface of the average motor neuron accommodates 5500 synaptic knobs. The inputs from the same spinal segment to a typical spinal motor neuron are listed in Fig 6−9. In addition to these, there are excitatory and inhibitory inputs, generally relayed via interneurons, from other levels of the spinal cord and multiple long descending tracts from the brain. All of these pathways converge on and determine the activity in the final common paths.

Central Excitatory & Inhibitory States

The spread up and down the spinal cord of subliminal fringe effects from excitatory stimulation has already been mentioned. Direct and presynaptic inhibitory effects can also be widespread. These effects are generally transient. However, the spinal cord also shows prolonged changes in excitability, possibly because of activity in reverberating circuits or prolonged effects of synaptic mediators. The terms **central excitatory state** and **central inhibitory state** have been used to describe prolonged states in which excitatory influences overbalance inhibitory influences and vice versa. When the central excitatory state is marked, excitatory impulses irradiate not only to many somatic areas of the spinal cord but also to autonomic areas and vice versa. In chronically paraplegic humans, for example, a mild noxious stimulus may cause, in addi-

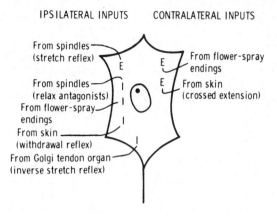

IPSILATERAL INPUTS   CONTRALATERAL INPUTS

From spindles
(stretch reflex)
From spindles
(relax antagonists)
From flower-spray
endings
From skin
(withdrawal reflex)
From Golgi tendon organ
(inverse stretch reflex)

From flower-spray
endings
From skin
(crossed extension)

FIG 6–9. Diagram of major segmental afferent inputs to a motor neuron supplying an extensor muscle. E, excitatory; I, inhibitory. All inputs except that mediating the stretch reflex traverse a Golgi bottle neuron or one or more other interneurons. The pathways from Renshaw cells, those mediating Phillipson's reflex, and some crossed pathways not discussed in the text are omitted. In addition, there are multiple inputs from other spinal segments and from the brain. (Redrawn and reproduced, with permission, from Patton, in: *Physiology and Biophysics,* 19th ed. Ruch TC, Patton HD [editors]. Saunders, 1965.)

tion to prolonged withdrawal-extension patterns in all 4 limbs, urination, defecation, sweating, and blood pressure fluctuations (**mass reflex**).

In view of the multiple, shifting, and often antagonistic influences which constantly bombard the final common paths, it is surprising that chaos does not result. Yet, as Mountcastle has expressed it, "Order reigns. The end result of reflex action is always one of some functional meaning to the organism, and reflex actions occurring one after the other in time are coordinated in sequences of some purposeful character. Such coordination of neural activity into spatial and sequential patterns which serve a useful end is the essence of the integrative activity of the nervous system."*

*In Bard P (editor): *Medical Physiology,* 11th ed, p 1104. Mosby, 1961.

7...

Cutaneous, Deep, & Visceral Sensation

PATHWAYS

The sense organs for touch, pressure, warmth, cold, and pain have been discussed in Chapter 5, and the types of fibers which carry impulses generated in them to the CNS are listed in Chapter 2. These afferent fibers end on interneurons which make polysynaptic reflex connections to motor neurons at many levels in the spinal cord as well as on the neurons of ascending pathways which relay impulses to the cerebral cortex.

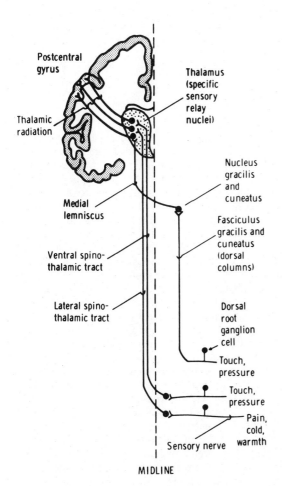

FIG 7–1. Touch, pressure, pain, and temperature pathways.

The principal pathways to the cerebral cortex for these senses are shown in Fig 7–1. Upon entering the spinal cord, the dorsal root fibers become segregated according to function. Fibers mediating fine touch, pressure, and proprioception ascend in the dorsal columns to the medulla, where they synapse in the gracile and cuneate nuclei. Other touch and pressure fibers synapse on neurons in the dorsal horn. The axons of these neurons cross the midline and ascend principally in the ventral spinothalamic tracts. Fibers carrying pain, warmth, and cold impulses are more laterally located in the dorsal roots. They synapse in the dorsal gray matter of the spinal cord, and the axons of the second order neurons cross the midline and ascend in the lateral spinothalamic tracts. Collaterals from the fibers that enter the dorsal columns pass to the **substantia gelatinosa,** a lightly staining area that caps each dorsal gray column. Evidence is accumulating that these collaterals can modify the input into other cutaneous sensory systems, including the pain system. The dorsal horn represents a "gate" in which impulses in the sensory nerve fibers are translated into impulses in ascending tracts, and it now appears that passage through this gate is dependent on the nature and pattern of impulses reaching the substantia gelatinosa. This gate is also affected by impulses in descending tracts from the brain.

Axons of the spinothalamic tracts from sacral and lumbar segments of the body are pushed laterally by axons crossing the midline at successively higher levels. On the other hand, sacral and lumbar dorsal column fibers are pushed medially by fibers from higher segments (Fig 7–2). Consequently, both of these ascending systems are laminated, with cervical to sacral segments represented from medial to lateral in the anterolateral pathways, and sacral to cervical segments from medial to lateral in the dorsal columns. Because of this lamination, tumors arising outside the spinal cord first compress the spinothalamic fibers from sacral and lumbar areas, causing the early symptom of loss of pain and temperature sensation in the sacral region. Intraspinal tumors cause anesthesia first in higher segments.

The second order neurons from the gracile and cuneate nuclei cross the midline and ascend in the medial lemniscus to end in the thalamus. They are joined in the brain stem by spinothalamic fibers and the sensory fibers from the head, principally those of the trigeminal nerve. Pain and temperature impulses

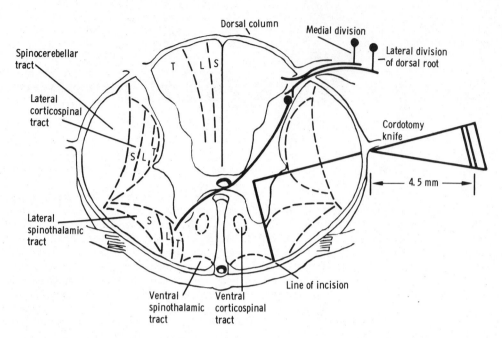

FIG 7–2. Major spinal pathways. The solid line on the right represents the line of incision in performing an anterolateral cordotomy. Note the lamination of the tracts. S, sacral; L, lumbar; T, thoracic.

are relayed via the spinal nucleus of this nerve, and touch, pressure, and proprioception mostly via its main sensory and mesencephalic nuclei.

Thalamic Connections

The thalamic nuclei are discussed in detail in Chapter 11. The spinothalamic tracts, the medial lemnisci, and associated specific ascending sensory systems terminate in the specific sensory relay nuclei. There they synapse on the neurons whose axons form the thalamic radiation to the postcentral gyrus. In the

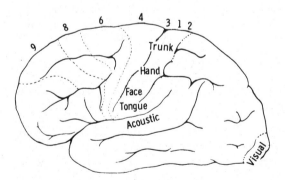

FIG 7–3. Cortical receiving areas for various sensory modalities in the human brain. The numbers are those of Brodmann's cortical areas. The auditory (acoustic) area is actually located in the fissure, on the top of the superior temporal gyrus, and is not normally visible in man. (Reproduced, with permission, from Brazier: *The Electrical Activity of the Nervous System,* 3rd ed. Pitman, 1968.)

thalamus, as elsewhere in the specific sensory systems, there is discrete representation of the various parts of the body.

Cortical Representation

The arrangement of the thalamic radiation fibers is such that the parts of the body are represented in order along the postcentral gyrus, with the legs on top and the head at the foot of the gyrus (Fig 7–3). Not only is there detailed localization of the fibers from the various parts of the body in the postcentral gyrus, but the size of the cortical receiving area for impulses from a particular part of the body is proportionate to the number of receptors in the part. The relative sizes of the cortical receiving areas are shown dramatically in Fig 7–4, in which the proportions of the homunculus have been distorted to correspond to the size of the cortical receiving areas for each. Note that the cortical areas for sensation from the trunk and back are small, whereas very large areas are concerned with impulses from the hand and the parts of the mouth concerned with speech.

Studies of the sensory receiving area emphasize the very discrete nature of the point-for-point localization of peripheral areas in the cortex and provide further evidence for the validity of the doctrine of specific nerve energies (see Chapter 5). Stimulation of the various parts of the postcentral gyrus gives rise to sensations projected to appropriate parts of the body. The sensations produced are usually those of numbness, tingling, or a sense of movement, but with fine enough electrodes it has been possible to produce relatively pure sensations of touch, warmth, cold, and pain. The cells in the postcentral gyrus appear to be

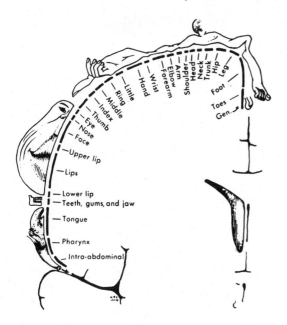

FIG 7—4. Sensory homunculus, drawn overlying a coronal section through the postcentral gyrus. Gen., genitalia. (Reproduced, with permission, from Penfield & Rasmussen: *The Cerebral Cortex of Man.* Macmillan, 1950.)

organized in vertical columns, like cells in the visual cortex (see Chapter 8), with a given sensory stimulus activating all the cells in a particular column.

There is a secondary sensory receiving area in the superior wall of the sylvian fissure. The head is represented at the inferior end of the postcentral gyrus, and the feet at the bottom of the sylvian fissure. The representation of the body parts is not as complete or detailed as it is in the postcentral gyrus. The function of the secondary receiving area is not known, although it may play a role in the perception of pain. Its ablation in animals does not cause any detectable deficit in other sensory modalities.

Many impulses from cutaneous receptors also reach the motor area in the precentral gyrus. There is some evidence that there are rapidly conducting ascending pathways for pain in addition to the classical, specific systems described above and the slowly conducting ascending reticular system (see Chapter 11).

Effects of Cortical Lesions

In animals and man, lesions of the postcentral gyrus decrease but do not entirely abolish sensation. Proprioception and fine touch are most affected by cortical lesions. Temperature sensibility is less affected, and pain sensibility is only slightly affected. This suggests that a certain degree of perception is possible in the absence of the cortex. Upon recovery, pain sensibility returns first, followed by temperature sense and, finally, proprioception and fine touch.

Principles of Sensory Physiology

The important general principles that relate to the physiology of sensory systems have been discussed in detail in Chapter 5. Each sense organ is specialized to convert one particular form of energy into action potentials in the sensory nerves. Each modality has a discrete pathway to the brain, and the sensation perceived as well as the part of the body to which it is localized is determined by the particular part of the brain activated. Differences in intensity of a given sensation are signaled in 2 ways: by changes in the frequency of action potentials in the sensory nerves, and by changes in the number of receptors activated. An increase in the intensity of stimulation of a sense organ has very little (if any) effect on the quality of the sensation produced.

Another principle that applies to cutaneous sensation is that of punctate representation. If the skin is carefully mapped, millimeter by millimeter, with a fine hair, a sensation of touch is evoked from spots overlying touch receptors. None is evoked from the intervening areas. Similarly, pain, pressure, and temperature sensations are produced by stimulation of the skin only over the spots where the sense organs for these modalities are located.

TOUCH & PRESSURE

Touch receptor organs adapt rapidly. They are most numerous in the fingers and lips and relatively scarce on the trunk. There are many receptors around hair follicles in addition to those in the subcutaneous tissues of hairless areas. When a hair is moved, it acts as a lever with its fulcrum at the edge of the follicle so that slight movements of the hairs are magnified into relatively potent stimuli to the nerve endings around the follicles. The stiff vibrissae on the snouts of some animals are highly developed examples of hairs that act as levers to magnify tactile stimuli. The pacinian corpuscles, the pressure receptors, are found in the subcutaneous tissues, muscles, and joints. They also abound in the mesentery, where their function is not known.

The group II sensory fibers that transmit touch and pressure impulses to the nervous system are 5—12 μm in diameter and have conduction velocities of 30—70 meters/sec. There is evidence that some touch impulses are conducted via C fibers. Some of the touch fibers ascend 1—3 segments from their points of entrance into the spinal cord, ending on the dorsal horn neurons whose axons form the ventral spinothalamic tract. Other touch fibers ascend in the dorsal columns as far as the medulla before synapsing. Therefore, disruption of both the dorsal columns and the ventral spinothalamic tracts must occur before tactile sensation is abolished, and only very large spinal lesions do this.

There are differences in the type of touch information transmitted in the dorsal columns and the ventral spinothalamic tracts. When the dorsal columns are destroyed, vibratory sensation and proprioception are lost, the touch threshold is elevated, and the number of touch-sensitive areas in the skin is decreased. In addition, localization of touch sensation is impaired. An increase in touch threshold and a decrease in the number of touch spots in the skin are also observed after interrupting the ventral spinothalamic tracts, but the touch deficit is slight and touch localization remains normal. The information carried in the dorsal columns is concerned with the detailed localization, spatial form, and temporal pattern of tactile stimuli. The information carried in the ventral spinothalamic tract, on the other hand, is concerned with poorly localized, gross tactile sensations. Along with the lateral spinothalamic tract, it projects in part to the reticular formation and mediates the alerting, arousal effects of tactile stimuli (see Chapter 11).

While lesions limited to the postcentral gyrus produce loss of fine touch discrimination on the opposite side of the body, lesions of the parietal lobe on the nondominant side produce contralateral disorders of spatial orientation, and lesions of the dominant parietal lobe produce agnosias. These abnormalities are discussed in Chapter 16.

PROPRIOCEPTION

Proprioceptive information is transmitted up the spinal cord in the dorsal columns. A good deal of the proprioceptive input goes to the cerebellum, but some passes via the medial lemnisci and thalamic radiations to the cortex. There is some evidence that proprioceptive information passes to consciousness in the anterolateral columns of the spinal cord as well. Since stimulation of group I fibers produces no electrical response in the cerebral cortex, impulses initiated in the muscle spindles and Golgi tendon organs apparently do not reach consciousness. Conscious awareness of the position of the various parts of the body in space depends instead upon impulses from sense organs in and around the joints. The organs involved are slowly adapting "spray" endings, Golgi tendon organ-like structures, and probably pacinian corpuscles in the synovia and ligaments. Impulses from these organs and those from touch and pressure receptors are synthesized in the cortex into a conscious picture of the position of the body in space. Diseases of the dorsal columns produce ataxia because of the interruption of proprioceptive input to the cerebellum.

TEMPERATURE

There are 2 types of temperature sense organs: those responding maximally to temperatures slightly above body temperature, and those responding maximally to temperatures slightly below body temperature. The former are the sense organs for what we call warmth, and the latter for what we call cold. However, the adequate stimuli are actually 2 different degrees of warmth, since cold is not a form of energy.

Although the exact structure of the warm and cold sense organs remains in some doubt, mapping experiments show that there are discrete cold-sensitive and warmth-sensitive spots in the skin. Cold spots outnumber the warm. The small myelinated fibers transmitting temperature sensibility are 2–5 μm in diameter and are in Erlanger and Gasser's A δ group (group III fibers; see Chapter 2). Impulses in them pass to the postcentral gyrus via the lateral spinothalamic tract and the thalamic radiation.

Because the sense organs are located subepithelially, it is the temperature of the subcutaneous tissues that determines the responses. Cool metal objects feel colder than wooden objects of the same temperature because the metal conducts heat away from the skin more rapidly, cooling the subcutaneous tissues to a greater degree.

Isolation of single fibers from warmth and cold receptors in the cat has permitted analysis of their responses. Both warmth and cold receptors respond to steady temperatures. Warmth receptors discharge at temperatures between 20° and 45° C, but their maximal discharge rate is at a temperature of 37.5–40° C. Cold receptors discharge between 10° and 41° C, with their maximum in the 15–20° C range. Adaptation is moderately rapid. Both receptor types also show increased activity with changes in temperature. Above 45° C, the warmth receptors stop discharging; paradoxically, however, the cold receptors start to discharge and pain receptors are stimulated. The sensation of heat is believed to be due to the combined discharge of the cold and pain receptors.

PAIN

The sense organs for pain are the naked nerve endings found in almost every tissue of the body. Pain impulses are transmitted to the CNS by 2 fiber systems. One system is made up of small myelinated A δ fibers, 2–5 μm in diameter, which conduct at rates of 12–30 meters/sec. The other consists of unmyelinated C fibers, 0.4–1.2 μm in diameter. These latter fibers are found in the lateral division of the dorsal roots, and are often called dorsal root C fibers. They conduct at the slow rate of 0.5–2 meters/sec. Both fiber groups end on the lateral spinothalamic tract neurons, and pain impulses ascend via this tract to the ventral posteromedial and posterolateral nuclei of the thalamus. From there, they relay to the postcentral gyri of the cerebral cortex.

Fast & Slow Pain

The presence of 2 pain pathways, one slow and one fast, explains the physiologic observation that there are 2 kinds of pain. A painful stimulus causes a "bright," sharp, localized sensation followed by a dull, aching, diffuse, and unpleasant feeling. These 2 sensations are variously called fast and slow pain or first and second pain. The farther from the brain the stimulus is applied, the greater the temporal separation of the 2 components. This and other evidence make it clear that fast pain is due to activity in the A δ pain fibers, while slow pain is due to activity in the C pain fibers.

Subcortical Perception & Affect

There is considerable evidence that sensory stimuli are perceived in the absence of the cerebral cortex, and this is especially true of pain. The cortical receiving areas are apparently concerned with the discriminative, exact, and meaningful interpretation of pain, but perception alone does not require the cortex.

Pain was called by Sherrington the "psychical adjunct of an imperative protective reflex." Stimuli which are painful generally initiate potent withdrawal and avoidance responses. Furthermore, pain is peculiar among the senses in that it is associated with a strong emotional component. Information transmitted via the special senses may secondarily evoke pleasant or unpleasant emotions, depending largely upon past experience, but pain alone has a "built-in" unpleasant affect. Present evidence indicates that this affective response depends upon connections of the pain pathways in the thalamus. Damage to the thalamus may be associated with a peculiar over-reaction to painful stimuli known as the **thalamic syndrome**. In this condition, usually due to blockage of the thalamogeniculate branch of the posterior cerebral artery with consequent damage to the posterior thalamic nuclei, minor stimuli lead to prolonged, severe, and very unpleasant pain. Such bouts of pain may occur spontaneously, or at least without evident external stimuli. Another interesting fact is that at least in some cases pain can be dissociated from its unpleasant subjective affect by cutting the deep connections between the frontal lobes and the rest of the brain (**prefrontal lobotomy**). After this operation patients report that they feel pain but that it "doesn't bother" them. The operation is sometimes useful in the treatment of intractable pain caused by terminal cancer.

Lobotomy is, of course, only one of the many neurosurgical procedures employed to relieve intractable pain in terminal cancer patients, and it produces extensive personality changes (see Chapter 16). Other operations are summarized in Fig 7–5. One of the most extensively used is **anterolateral cordotomy**. In this procedure, a knife is inserted into the lateral aspect of the spinal cord and swept anteriorly and laterally as shown in Fig 7–2. When properly per-

FIG 7–5. Diagram of various surgical procedures designed to alleviate pain. 1, nerve section; 2, sympathectomy (for visceral pain); 3, myelotomy to section spinothalamic fibers in anterior white commissure; 4, posterior rhizotomy; 5, anterolateral cordotomy; 6, medullary tractotomy; 7, mesencephalic tractotomy; 8, thalamotomy; 9, gyrectomy; 10, prefrontal lobotomy. (Modified from MacCarty & Drake: Neurosurgical procedures for the control of pain. Proc Staff Meet Mayo Clin 31:208, 1956.)

formed, this procedure cuts the lateral spinothalamic pain fibers while leaving the ventral spinothalamic touch fibers intact. Even if there is damage to the ventral system, touch is very little impaired because the dorsal column touch system is intact.

Deep Pain

The main difference between superficial and deep sensibility is the different nature of the pain evoked by noxious stimuli. Unlike superficial pain, deep pain is poorly localized, nauseating, and frequently associated with sweating and changes in blood pressure. Pain can be elicited experimentally from the periosteum and ligaments by injecting hypertonic saline into them. The pain produced in this fashion initiates reflex contraction of nearby skeletal muscles. This reflex contraction is similar to the muscle spasm associated with injuries to bones, tendons, and joints. The steadily contracting muscles become ischemic, and ischemia stimulates the pain receptors in the muscles (see below). The pain in turn initiates more spasm, and a vicious cycle is set up.

Adequate Stimulus

Pain receptors are specific, and pain is not produced by overstimulation of other receptors. On the other hand, the adequate stimulus for pain receptors is not as specific as that for others because they can be stimulated by a variety of strong stimuli. For example, pain receptors respond to warmth, but it has been calculated that their threshold for thermal energy is over 100 times that of the warmth receptors. Pain receptors also respond to electrical, mechanical, and, especially, chemical energy.

It has been suggested that pain is chemically mediated, and that stimuli which provoke it have in common the ability to liberate a chemical agent which stimulates the nerve endings. The chemical agent might be a kinin. The kinins are polypeptides that are liberated from proteins by proteolytic enzymes. Their formation and metabolism are discussed in detail in Chapter 31. They are known to be liberated in tissues by noxious stimuli, and they are capable of producing severe pain. However, the pain produced by injected kinins is usually transient. Histamine has also been suspected of being a chemical mediator of pain, but there is some evidence that it causes local liberation of kinins when it is injected into the tissues.

Muscle Pain

Kinins have been postulated to be responsible for muscle pain. If a muscle contracts rhythmically in the presence of an adequate blood supply, pain does not usually result. However, if the blood supply to a muscle is occluded, contraction soon causes pain. The pain persists after the contraction until blood flow is reestablished. If a muscle with a normal blood supply is made to contract continuously without periods of relaxation, it also begins to ache because the maintained contraction compresses the blood vessels supplying the muscle.

These observations are difficult to interpret except in terms of the release during contraction of a chemical agent (Lewis' "P factor") that causes pain when its local concentration is high enough. When the blood supply is restored, the material is washed out or metabolized. The identity of the P factor is not settled, but it could be a kinin or possibly potassium.

Clinically, the substernal pain that develops when the myocardium becomes ischemic during exertion (angina pectoris) is a classic example of the accumulation of P factor in a muscle. Angina is relieved by rest because this decreases the myocardial O_2 requirement and permits the blood supply to remove the factor. Intermittent claudication, the pain produced in the leg muscles of persons with occlusive vascular disease, is another example. It characteristically comes on while the patient is walking and disappears when he rests.

Hyperalgesia

In pathologic conditions the sensitivity of the pain receptors is altered. There are 2 important types of alteration, primary and secondary hyperalgesia. In the area surrounding an inflamed or injured area, the threshold for pain is lowered so that trivial stimuli cause pain. This phenomenon, **primary hyperalgesia,** is seen in the area of the **flare,** the region of vasodilatation around the injury. In the area of actual tissue damage, the vasodilatation and, presumably, the pain are due to substances liberated from injured cells, but the flare in surrounding undamaged tissue is due to a chemical agent liberated by antidromic impulses in sensory nerve fibers. This agent is postulated to be a proteolytic enzyme which causes the liberation of vasodilator kinins in the tissues. The kinins also lower the threshold of the pain fibers in the area and may themselves produce pain. Evidence for this hypothesis is the observation that stimulation of the peripheral end of a cut dorsal root produces vasodilatation in the area served by the root, and if the subcutaneous tissues are perfused during such stimulation, the perfusate contains a peptide that causes pain upon injection into innervated skin.

Another aberration of sensation following injury is **secondary hyperalgesia.** In the area affected, the threshold for pain is actually elevated but the pain produced is unpleasant, prolonged, and severe. The area from which this response is obtained extends well beyond the site of injury, and the condition does not last as long as primary hyperalgesia. It is probably due to some sort of central facilitation by impulses from the injured area of the pathways responsible for the unpleasant affect component of pain. Such facilitation or alteration of pathways may be a spinal subliminal fringe effect, or it may occur at the thalamic or even the cortical level.

DIFFERENCES BETWEEN SOMATIC & VISCERAL SENSORY MECHANISMS

The autonomic nervous system, like the somatic, has afferent components, central integrating stations, and effector pathways. The visceral afferent mechanisms play a major role in homeostatic adjustments. In the viscera there are a number of special receptors—osmoreceptors, baroreceptors, chemoreceptors, etc—which respond to changes in the internal environment. The afferent nerves from these receptors make reflex connections that are intimately concerned with regulating the function of the various systems with which they are associated, and their physiology is discussed in the chapters on these systems.

The receptors for pain and the other sensory modalities present in the viscera are similar to those in skin, but there are marked differences in their distribution. There are no proprioceptors in the viscera, and few temperature and pressure sense organs. If the abdominal wall is infiltrated with a local anesthetic, the abdomen can be opened and the intestines can be handled, cut, and even burned without eliciting any discomfort. Pain receptors are present in the viscera, however, and although they are more sparsely distributed than in somatic structures, certain types of stimuli cause severe pain. There are many pacinian corpuscles in the mesentery, but their function in this location is not known.

Afferent fibers from visceral structures reach the CNS via sympathetic and parasympathetic pathways. Their cell bodies are located in the dorsal roots and the homologous cranial nerve ganglia. Specifically, there are visceral afferents in the facial, glossopharyngeal, and vagus nerves, in the thoracic and upper lumbar dorsal roots, and in the sacral roots (Fig 7–6). There may also be visceral afferent fibers from the eye in the trigeminal nerve. There are A β and A δ afferent fibers in the splanchnic nerves, but only A δ fibers in the pelvic and vagus nerves. Visceral sensation travels along the same pathways as somatic sensation in the spinothalamic tracts and thalamic radiations, and the cortical receiving areas for visceral sensation are intermixed with the somatic receiving areas in the postcentral gyri.

VISCERAL PAIN

Pain from visceral structures is poorly localized, unpleasant, associated with nausea and autonomic symptoms, and often radiates or is referred to other areas.

Stimulation of Pain Fibers

Because there are relatively few pain receptors in the viscera, visceral pain is poorly localized. However, as almost everyone knows from personal experience, visceral pain can be very severe. The receptors in the walls of the hollow viscera are especially sensitive to distention of these organs. Such distention can be produced experimentally in the gastrointestinal tract by inflation of a swallowed balloon attached to a tube. This produces pain which waxes and wanes (intestinal colic) as the intestine contracts and relaxes on the balloon. Similar colic is produced in intestinal obstruction by the contractions of the dilated intestine above the obstruction. When a viscus is inflamed or hyperemic, relatively minor stimuli cause severe pain. This is

FIG 7–6. Pain innervation of the viscera. Pain afferents from structures above the thoracic pain line and below the pelvic pain line traverse parasympathetic pathways. (After White. Reproduced, with permission, from Patton, in: *Physiology and Biophysics,* 19th ed. Ruch TC, Patton HD [editors]. Saunders, 1965.)

probably a form of primary hyperalgesia similar to that which occurs in somatic structures. Traction on the mesentery is also claimed to be painful, but the significance of this observation in the production of visceral pain is not clear. Visceral pain is particularly unpleasant not only because of the affective component it has in common with all pain but also because so many visceral afferents excited by the same process that causes the pain have reflex connections that initiate nausea, vomiting, and other autonomic effects.

Pathways

Pain impulses from the thoracic and abdominal viscera are almost exclusively conducted through the sympathetic nervous system and the dorsal roots of the first thoracic to the second lumbar spinal nerves. This is why sympathectomy effectively abolishes pain from the heart, stomach, and intestines. However, pain impulses from the esophagus, trachea, and pharynx are mediated via vagal afferents, and pain from the structures deep in the pelvis is transmitted in the sacral parasympathetic nerves (Fig 7–6).

Muscle Spasm & Rigidity

Visceral pain, like deep somatic pain, initiates reflex contraction of nearby skeletal muscle. This reflex spasm is usually in the abdominal wall, and is most marked when visceral inflammatory processes involve the peritoneum. However, it can occur without such involvement. The anatomic details of the reflex pathways by which impulses from diseased viscera initiate skeletal muscle spasm are still obscure. The spasm protects the underlying inflamed structures from inadvertent trauma. Indeed, this reflex spasm is sometimes called "guarding."

The classical signs of inflammation in an abdominal viscus are pain, tenderness, autonomic changes such as hypotension and sweating, and spasm of the abdominal wall. From the preceding discussion, the genesis of each of these signs is apparent. The tenderness is due to the heightened sensitivity of the pain receptors in the viscus, the autonomic changes due to activation of visceral reflexes, and the spasm due to reflex contraction of skeletal muscle in the abdominal wall.

REFERRAL & INHIBITION OF PAIN

Referred Pain

Irritation of a viscus frequently produces pain which is felt not in the viscus but in some somatic structure that may be a considerable distance away. Such pain is said to be **referred** to the somatic structure. Deep somatic pain may also be referred, but superficial pain is not. When visceral pain is both local and referred, it sometimes seems to spread or **radiate** from the local to the distant site.

Obviously, a knowledge of referred pain and the common sites of pain referral from each of the viscera is of great importance to the physician. Perhaps the best known example is referral of cardiac pain to the inner aspect of the left arm. Other dramatic examples include pain in the tip of the shoulder due to irritation of the central portion of the diaphragm and pain in the testicle due to distention of the ureter. Other examples abound in the practice of medicine, surgery, and dentistry. However, sites of reference are not stereotyped, and unusual reference sites occur with considerable frequency. Heart pain, for instance, may be purely abdominal, may be referred to the right arm, and may even be referred to the neck. Referred pain can be produced experimentally by stimulation of the cut end of a splanchnic nerve.

Dermatomal Rule

When pain is referred it is usually to a structure that developed from the same embryonic segment or dermatome as the structure in which the pain originates. This principle is called the **dermatomal rule**. For example, the diaphragm migrates from the neck region during embryonic development to its adult location in the abdomen and takes its nerve supply, the phrenic nerve, with it. One-third of the fibers in the phrenic nerve are afferent, and they enter the spinal cord at the level of the second to fourth cervical segments, the same location at which afferents from the tip of the shoulder enter. Similarly, the heart and the arm have the same segmental origin, and the testicle has migrated with its nerve supply from the primitive urogenital ridge from which the kidney and ureter also developed.

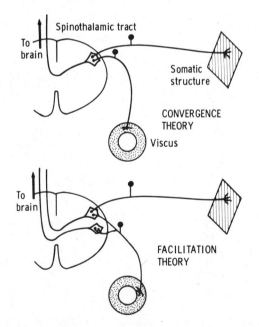

FIG 7–7. Diagram of convergence and facilitation theories of referred pain.

Role of Convergence in Referred Pain

Not only do the nerves from the visceral structures and the somatic structures to which pain is referred enter the nervous system at the same level, but there are many more sensory fibers in the peripheral nerves than there are axons in the lateral spinothalamic tracts. Therefore, a considerable degree of convergence of peripheral sensory fibers on the spinothalamic neurons must occur. One theory of the mechanism underlying referred pain is based on this fact. It holds that somatic and visceral afferents converge on the same spinothalamic neurons (Fig 7–7). Since somatic pain is much more common than visceral pain, the brain has "learned" that activity arriving in a given pathway is due to a pain stimulus in a particular somatic area. When the same pathway is stimulated by activity in visceral afferents, the signal reaching the brain is no different and the pain is projected to the somatic area.

Past experience does play an important role in referred pain. Although pain originating in an inflamed abdominal viscus is usually referred to the midline, in patients who have had previous abdominal surgery the pain of abdominal disease is frequently referred to their surgical scars. Pain originating in the maxillary sinus is usually referred to nearby teeth, but in patients with a history of traumatic dental work such pain is regularly referred to the previously traumatized teeth. This is true even when the teeth are a considerable distance away from the sinus.

Facilitation Effects

Another theory of the origin of referred pain holds that, owing to subliminal fringe effects, incoming impulses from visceral structures lower the threshold of spinothalamic neurons receiving afferents from somatic areas, so that minor activity in the pain pathways from the somatic areas—activity which would normally die out in the spinal cord—passes on to the brain.

If convergence alone were the explanation for referred pain, anesthetizing the somatic area of reference with procaine should have no effect on the pain, whereas if subliminal fringe effects were responsible the pain should disappear. The effects of local anesthesia in the area of reference vary. When the pain is severe, it is usually unaffected, but when the pain is mild it may be completely abolished. Therefore, it appears that both convergence and facilitation play a role in the pathogenesis of referred pain.

Central Inhibition & Counterirritants

There is experimental evidence that transmission in the pain pathways can be blocked by inhibition or occlusion. It is of course well known that soldiers wounded in the heat of battle may feel no pain until the battle is over. Stimulation of the splanchnic nerves, for example, produces evoked potentials (see Chapter 11) in the postcentral gyrus; but such stimulation produces no cortical response if it is preceded or accompanied by stimulation of somatic afferents.

Another fact that suggests that central inhibition occurs in afferent systems is the experimental observation that if an area of secondary hyperalgesia is repeatedly stimulated it shrinks in size.

One site of inhibition of pain transmission is probably the substantia gelatinosa. Touching an area from which pain is being initiated reduces the pain. Collateral fibers from the dorsal column touch fibers enter the substantia gelatinosa, and it has been postulated that impulses in these collaterals or interneurons on which they end inhibit transmission from the dorsal root pain fibers to the spinothalamic neurons. The mechanism involved appears to be presynaptic inhibition (see Chapter 2). Chronic stimulation of the dorsal columns has been used clinically as a method of relieving intractable pain. The pain relief could be due to antidromic conduction to the "gate" in the substantia gelatinosa or to the orthodromic conduction to a similar gate somewhere in the brain stem.

Inhibition in central sensory pathways may explain the efficacy of counterirritants. Stimulation of the skin over an area of visceral inflammation produces some relief of the pain due to the visceral disease. The old-fashioned mustard plaster works on this principle. Some similar mechanism may explain the "anesthesia" produced in dental patients by loud sound, although much of this effect is admittedly due to suggestion.

Itch & Tickle

Itching is probably produced by repetitive low-frequency stimulation of C fibers. Very mild stimulation of this system, especially if produced by something that moves across the skin, produces tickle. Itch spots can be identified on the skin by careful mapping; like the pain spots, they are in regions in which there are many naked endings of unmyelinated fibers. Itch persists along with burning pain in nerve block experiments when only C fibers are conducting, and itch, like pain, is abolished by section of the spinothalamic tracts. However, the distribution of itch and pain are different; itching occurs only in the skin, the eyes, and certain mucous membranes, and not in the deep tissues or viscera. Furthermore, low-frequency stimulation of pain fibers generally produces pain, not itch, and high-frequency stimulation of itch spots on the skin may merely increase the intensity of the itching without producing pain. These observations suggest that the C fiber system responsible for itching is not the same as that responsible for pain. It is interesting that a tickling sensation is usually regarded as pleasurable, whereas itching is at least annoying, and pain is unpleasant.

Itching can be produced not only by repeated local mechanical stimulation of the skin but by a variety of chemical agents. Histamine produces intense itching, and various injuries cause its liberation in the skin. However, in most instances of itching, histamine does not appear to be the responsible agent; doses of histamine that are too small to produce itching still produce redness and swelling on injection into the skin, and severe itching frequently occurs without any visible change in the skin. The kinins cause severe itching, and it may be that they are the chemical mediators responsible for the sensation. It is interesting in this regard that itch powder, which is made up of the spicules from the pods of the tropical plant cowhage, contains a proteolytic enzyme, and the powder presumably acts by liberating itch-producing peptides.

OTHER SENSATIONS

"Synthetic Senses"

The cutaneous senses for which separate receptors exist are touch, pressure, warmth, cold, pain, and possibly itching. Combinations of these sensations plus, in some cases, cortical components, are synthesized into the sensations of vibratory sensation, 2-point discrimination, and stereognosis.

Vibratory Sensibility

When a vibrating tuning fork is applied to the skin, a buzzing or thrill is felt. The sensation is most marked over bones, but it can be felt when the tuning fork is placed in other locations. The receptors involved are the pressure receptors, but a time factor is also necessary. A pattern of rhythmic pressure stimuli is interpreted as vibration. The impulses responsible for the vibrating sensation are carried in the dorsal columns. Degeneration of this part of the spinal cord occurs in poorly controlled diabetes, pernicious anemia, some vitamin deficiencies, and occasionally in other conditions, and depression of the threshold for vibratory stimuli is an early symptom of this degenera-

tion. Vibratory sensation and proprioception are closely related; when one is depressed, so is the other.

Two-Point Discrimination

The minimal distance by which 2 touch stimuli must be separated to be perceived as separate is called the **2-point threshold**. It depends upon touch plus the cortical component of identifying 1 rather than 2 stimuli. Its magnitude varies from place to place on the body, and is smallest where the touch receptors are most abundant. Points on the back, for instance, must be separated by 65 mm or more before they can be distinguished as separate points, whereas on the fingers 2 stimuli can be resolved if they are separated by as little as 3 mm. On the hands, the magnitude of the 2-point threshold is approximately the diameter of the area of skin supplied by a single sensory unit. However, the peripheral neural basis of discriminating 2 points is not completely understood, and in view of the extensive interdigitation and overlapping of the sensory units, it is probably complex.

Stereognosis

The ability to identify objects by handling them without looking at them is called **stereognosis**. Normal persons can readily identify objects such as keys and coins of various denominations. This ability obviously depends upon relatively intact touch and pressure sensation, but it also has a large cortical component. Impaired stereognosis is an early sign of damage to the cerebral cortex, and sometimes occurs in the absence of any defect in touch and pressure sensation when there is a lesion in the parietal lobe posterior to the postcentral gyrus.

8 ...

Vision

ANATOMIC CONSIDERATIONS

The eyes are complex sense organs that have evolved from primitive light-sensitive spots on the surface of invertebrates. Within its protective casing, each eye has a layer of receptors, a lens system for focusing light on these receptors, and a system of nerves for conducting impulses from the receptors to the brain. The principal structures are shown in Fig 8–1. The outer protective layer of the eyeball, the **sclera**, is modified anteriorly to form the transparent **cornea**,

through which light rays enter the eye. Inside the sclera is the **choroid**, a pigmented layer that contains many of the blood vessels which nourish the structures in the eyeball. Lining the posterior two-thirds of the choroid is the **retina**, the neural tissue containing the receptor cells.

The **crystalline lens** is a transparent structure held in place by a circular **lens ligament,** or **zonule.** The zonule is attached to the thickened anterior part of the choroid, the **ciliary body.** The ciliary body contains circular muscle fibers and longitudinal fibers which attach near the corneoscleral junction. In front of the

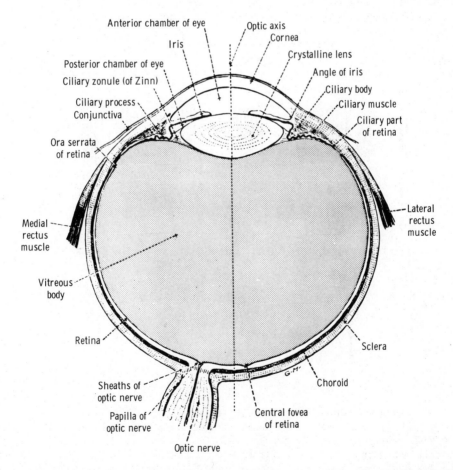

FIG 8–1. Section through right eye in horizontal plane magnified about 4 times. (After Eycleshymer & Jones. Reproduced, with permission, from Jones & Shepard: *A Manual of Surgical Anatomy.* Saunders, 1945.)

lens is the pigmented and opaque **iris,** the colored portion of the eye. The iris contains circular muscle fibers which constrict and radial fibers which dilate the **pupil.** Variations in the diameter of the pupil can produce up to 5-fold changes in the amount of light reaching the retina.

The anterior chamber of the eye between the cornea and the lens is filled with the **aqueous humor,** a fluid with a low protein content which is formed partly by diffusion and partly by active transport of components from the plasma. The space between the lens and the retina is filled with a clear gelatinous material called the **vitreous (vitreous humor).**

Retina

The retina is a complex 10-layered structure which extends anteriorly almost to the ciliary body. Its major neural components are the **rods,** the **cones,** the **bipolar cells,** and the **ganglion cells.**

The rods and cones are the visual receptors. Their elongated inner processes synapse with the processes of the bipolar cells (Fig 8–2). The bipolar cells in turn synapse with the ganglion cells. The axons of the ganglion cells converge, and leave the eye as the optic nerve. The receptor layer of the retina is apposed to the choroid, and light rays must pass through the ganglion cell and bipolar cell layers to reach the rods and cones. The pigmented layer of the choroid next to the retina absorbs light rays, preventing the reflection of rays back through the retina. Such reflection would produce blurring of the visual images.

The optic nerve leaves the eye and the retinal blood vessels enter it at a point 3 mm medial to and slightly above the posterior pole of the globe. This region is visible through the ophthalmoscope as the **optic disk** (Fig 8–3). There are no visual receptors overlying the disk, and consequently this spot is blind (the **blind spot).** At the posterior pole of the eye there is a yellowish pigmented spot, the **macula lutea.** This marks the location of the **fovea centralis,** a thinned-out, rod-free portion of the retina where the cones are densely packed and there are very few cells and no blood vessels overlying the receptors. The fovea is highly developed in man. It is the point where visual acuity is greatest. When attention is attracted to or fixed on an object, the eyes are normally moved so that light rays coming from the object fall on the fovea.

The arteries, arterioles, and veins in the superficial layers of the retina near its vitreous surface can be seen through the ophthalmoscope. Since this is the one place in the body where arterioles are readily visible, ophthalmoscopic examination is of great value in the diagnosis and evaluation of diabetes mellitus, hypertension, and other diseases that affect the blood vessels. The retinal vessels supply the bipolar and ganglion cells, but the receptors are nourished for the most part by the capillary plexus in the choroid.

Neural Pathways

The axons of the ganglion cells pass caudally in the **optic nerve** and **optic tract** to end in the **lateral**

FIG 8–2. Chief synaptic connections in the retina. *A:* Pure cone path from the fovea. *B:* Mainly cone paths. *C:* Mainly rod path. 1, midget bipolar cell. 2, midget ganglion cell. 3, 5, 6, 9, 12, various other types of bipolar cells. 4, 7, 8, various other types of ganglion cells. 10, horizontal cell. 11, amacrine cell. (After Polyak. Reproduced, with permission, from Best & Taylor: *The Physiological Basis of Medical Practice,* 8th ed. Williams & Wilkins, 1966.)

FIG 8–3. Retina seen through the ophthalmoscope in a normal human. Diagram at left identifies the landmarks in the photograph on the right. (Reproduced, with permission, from Vaughan, Cook, & Asbury: *General Ophthalmology,* 6th ed. Lange, 1971.)

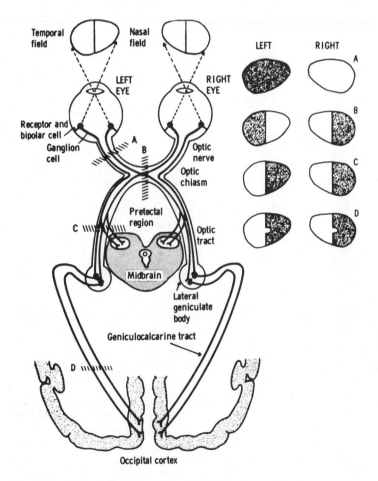

FIG 8–4. Visual pathways. Lesions at the points marked by the letters cause the visual field defects shown in the diagrams on the right (see text). Occipital lesions may spare the fibers from the macula (as in D) because of the separation in the brain of these fibers from the others subserving vision.

geniculate body, a part of the thalamus. The fibers from each nasal hemiretina decussate in the optic chiasm. In the geniculate body, the fibers from the nasal half of one retina and the temporal half of the other synapse in a highly specific fashion on the cells whose axons form the geniculocalcarine tract. This tract passes to the occipital lobe of the cerebral cortex. The primary visual receiving area, or visual cortex (Brodmann's area 17), is located principally on the sides of the calcarine fissure. Some of the optic nerve fibers, or possibly their collaterals, pass from the optic tract to the pretectal region of the midbrain and the superior colliculus, where they form connections which mediate visual reflexes (Fig 8–4).

Outer segments

Inner segments

Nuclear region

Synaptic zone

FIG 8–5. Rods from guinea pig retina. Note the comb-like structure and the complexity of the junctions with bipolar cells in the synaptic zone. The inner segments contain many filamentous mitochondria. (Reproduced, with permission, from Sjöstrand: The ultrastructure of cells as seen with the electron microscope. Internat Rev Cytol 5:455, 1956.)

Receptors

Each rod and cone is divided into an inner and an outer segment, a nuclear region, and a synaptic zone (Fig 8–5). The outer segments are modified cilia, and are made up of regular arrays of flat plates, or sacs, containing photosensitive pigment. The inner segments are rich in mitochondria. The rods are named for the thin, rod-like appearance of their outer segments. Cones generally have thick inner segments and conical outer segments, although their morphology varies from place to place in the retina.

The fovea contains no rods, and each foveal cone has a single bipolar cell connecting it to a single ganglion cell, so that each foveal cone is connected to a single fiber in the optic nerve. In other portions of the retina, rods predominate (Fig 8–6), and there is a good deal of convergence. Since there are approximately 6 million cones and 120 million rods in each human eye, but only 400,000 nerve fibers in each optic nerve, the overall convergence of receptors through bipolar cells on ganglion cells is about 315:1. In the peripheral portions of the retina, rods and cones often converge on the same ganglion cell. The retina contains horizontal cells (Fig 8–2), which connect receptor cells to other receptor cells, and amacrine cells, which connect ganglion cells to one another. These cells provide the pathways for complex shunting of electrical activity within the retina and for divergence of electrical activity from single receptors to several ganglion cells.

The rods are extremely sensitive to light, and are the receptors for night vision (scotopic vision). The scotopic visual apparatus is not capable of resolving the details and boundaries of objects or determining their color. The cones have a much higher threshold, but the cone system has a much greater acuity and is the system responsible for vision in bright light (photopic vision) and for color vision.

Eye Muscles

The eye is moved within the orbit by 6 ocular muscles (Fig 8–7). These are innervated by the oculomotor, trochlear, and abducens nerves. The muscles and the directions in which they move the eyeball are discussed at the end of this chapter.

Protection

The eye is well protected from injury by the bony walls of the orbit. The cornea is moistened and kept clear by tears which course from the lacrimal gland in the upper portion of each orbit across the surface of the eye to empty via the lacrimal duct into the nose. Blinking helps keep the cornea moist.

THE IMAGE-FORMING MECHANISM

The eyes convert energy in the visible spectrum into action potentials in the optic nerve. The wavelengths of visible light are approximately 397–723 nm.

FIG 8—6. **Rod and cone density along the horizontal meridian through the human retina.** A plot of the relative acuity of vision in the various parts of the light-adapted eye would parallel the cone density curve; a similar plot of relative acuity of the dark-adapted eye would parallel the rod density curve. (Modified and reproduced, with permission, from Osterberg: Topography of the rods and cones in the human retina. Acta ophth, Suppl 16, 1935.)

FIG 8—7. **Muscles of the right orbit.** The 6 muscles that move the eyeball and the levator palpebrae superioris, which raises the upper lid, are shown. (Reproduced, with permission, from: *Gray's Anatomy of the Human Body,* 29th ed. Goss CM [editor]. Lea & Febiger, 1973.)

The images of objects in the environment are focused on the retina. The light rays striking the retina generate potentials in the rods and cones. Impulses initiated in the retina are conducted to the cerebral cortex, where they produce the sensation of vision.

Principles of Optics

Light rays are bent, or refracted, when they pass from one medium into a medium of a different density, except when they strike perpendicular to the interface. Parallel light rays striking a biconvex lens (Fig 8—8) are refracted to a point, or **principal focus**, behind the lens. The principal focus is on a line passing through the centers of curvature of the lens, the **principal axis**. The distance between the lens and the principal focus is the **principal focal distance.** For practical purposes, light rays from an object that strike a lens more than 20 ft away are considered to be parallel. The rays from an object closer than 20 ft are diverging, and are therefore brought to a focus farther back on the principal axis than the principal focus (Fig 8—8). Biconcave lenses cause light rays to diverge.

The greater the curvature of a lens, the greater its refractive power. The refractive power of a lens is conveniently measured in **diopters**, the number of diopters being the reciprocal of the principal focal distance in meters. For example, a lens with a principal focal distance of 0.25 meters has a refractive power of 1/0.25, or 4 diopters. The human eye has a refractive power of approximately 66.7 diopters at rest.

Accommodation

When the ciliary muscle is relaxed, parallel light rays striking the optically normal (**emmetropic**) eye are brought to a focus on the retina. As long as this relaxation is maintained, rays from objects closer to the observer are brought to a focus behind the retina, and consequently the objects appear blurred. The problem of bringing diverging rays from objects closer than 6 meters (20 ft) to a focus on the retina can be solved by increasing the distance between the lens and the retina or by increasing the curvature or refractive power of the lens. In bony fish, the problem is solved by increasing the length of the eyeball, a solution analogous to the manner in which the images of objects closer than

FIG 8–9. Accommodation. The solid lines represent the shape of the lens, iris, and ciliary body at rest and the dotted lines represent the shape during accommodation.

FIG 8–8. Refraction of light rays by lenses. A: Biconvex lens. B: Biconvex lens of greater strength than A. C: Same lens as A, showing effect on light rays from a near point. D: Biconcave lens. The center line in each case is the principal axis. X is the principal focus.

6 meters are focused on the film of a camera by moving the lens away from the film. In mammals, the problem is solved by increasing the curvature of the lens.

The process by which the curvature of the lens is increased is called **accommodation**. At rest, the lens is held under tension by the lens ligaments. Because the lens substance is malleable and the lens capsule has considerable elasticity, the lens is pulled into a flattened shape. When the gaze is directed at a near object, the ciliary muscle contracts. This decreases the distance between the edges of the ciliary body and relaxes the lens ligaments, so that the lens springs into a more convex shape. This change in shape may add as many as 12 diopters to the refractive power of the eye. The relaxation of the lens ligaments produced by contraction of the ciliary muscle is due partly to the sphincter-like action of the circular muscle fibers in the ciliary body and partly to the contraction of longitudinal muscle fibers that attach anteriorly, near the corneoscleral junction. When these fibers contract, they pull the whole ciliary body forward and inward. This motion brings the edges of the ciliary body closer together.

The change in lens curvature during accommodation affects principally the anterior surface of the lens (Fig 8–9). This can be demonstrated by a simple experiment first described many years ago. If an observer holds an object in front of the eyes of an individual who is looking into the distance, 3 reflections of the object are visible in the subject's eye. A clear, small upright image is reflected from the cornea; a larger, fainter upright image is reflected from the anterior surface of the lens; and a small inverted image is reflected from the posterior surface of the lens. If the subject then focuses his vision on something nearby, the large, faint upright image becomes smaller and moves toward the other upright image whereas the other 2 images change very little. The change in size of the image is due to the increase in curvature of the reflecting surface, the anterior surface of the lens (Fig 8–9). The fact that the small upright image does not change and the inverted image changes very little shows that the corneal curvature is unchanged and that the curvature of the posterior lens surface is changed very little by accommodation.

Near Point

Accommodation is an active process, requiring muscular effort, and can therefore be tiring. Indeed, the ciliary muscle is one of the most used muscles in the body. The degree to which the lens curvature can be increased is, of course, limited, and light rays from an object very near the individual cannot be brought to a focus on the retina even with the greatest effort. The nearest point to the eye at which an object can be brought into clear focus by accommodation is called the **near point of vision**. The near point recedes throughout life, slowly at first and then rapidly with advancing age. For example, at age 8 the average normal near point is 8.6 cm from the eye and at age 20 it is 10.4 cm from the eye; but at age 60 it is 83.3 cm from the eye. This recession of the near point is due principally to increasing hardness of the lens substance, with a resulting steady decrease in the degree to which the curvature of the lens can be increased. By the time the normal individual reaches the age of 40–45, the near point often recedes far enough so that reading and close work become difficult. This condition, which is known as **presbyopia**, can be corrected by wearing glasses with convex lenses (see below).

The Near Response

In addition to accommodation, the visual axes

FIG 8–10. Reduced eye. n: nodal point. AnB and anb are similar triangles. In this reduced eye, the nodal point is 15 mm from the retina. All refraction is assumed to take place at the surface of the cornea, 5 mm from the nodal point, between a medium of density 1.000 (air) and a medium of density 1.333 (water). The dotted lines represent rays of light diverging from A and refracted at the cornea so that they are focused on the retina at a.

converge and the pupil constricts when an individual looks at a near object. This 3-part response—accommodation, convergence, and pupillary constriction—is called the **near response.**

Other Pupillary Reflexes

When light is directed into one eye, the pupil constricts (**pupillary light reflex**). The pupil of the other eye also constricts (**consensual light reflex**). The optic nerve fibers that carry the impulses initiating pupillary responses end in the pretectal region and the superior colliculi. The pathway for the light reflex, which presumably passes from the pretectal region to the oculomotor nuclei (Edinger-Westphal nuclei) bilaterally, is different from that for accommodation. In some pathologic conditions, notably neurosyphilis, the pupillary response to light may be absent while the response to accommodation remains intact. This phenomenon, the so-called **Argyll Robertson pupil**, is said to be due to a destructive lesion in the tectal region.

Retinal Image

In the eye, light is actually refracted at the anterior surface of the cornea and at the anterior and posterior surfaces of the lens. The process of refraction can be represented diagrammatically, however, without introducing any appreciable error, by drawing the rays of light as if all refraction occurs at the anterior surface of the cornea. Fig 8–10 is a diagram of such a "reduced" or "schematic" eye. In this diagram, the **nodal point** or optical center of the eye coincides with the junction of the middle and posterior third of the lens, 15 mm from the retina. This is the point through which the light rays from an object pass without refraction. All other rays entering the pupil from each point on the object are refracted and brought to a focus on the retina. If the height of the object (**AB**), and its distance from the observer (**Bn**) are known, the size of its retinal image can be calculated because **AnB** and **anb** in Fig 8–10 are similar triangles. The angle AnB is the **visual angle** subtended by object AB. It should be noted that the retinal image is inverted. The connections of the retinal receptors are such that from birth any inverted image on the retina is viewed right side up and projected to the visual field on the side opposite to the retinal area stimulated. This perception is innate. It is present in infants and immediately after restoration of vision in previously blind individuals who have had congenital cataracts removed surgically. If retinal images are turned right side up by means of special lenses, the objects viewed look as if they were upside down.

Common Defects of the Image-Forming Mechanism

In some individuals, the eyeball is shorter than normal and parallel rays of light are brought to a focus behind the retina. This abnormality is called **hyperopia**, or farsightedness (Fig 8–11). Sustained accommodation, even when viewing distant objects, can partially compensate for the defect, but the prolonged

FIG 8–11. Common defects of the optical system of the eye. In hyperopia the eyeball is too short, and light rays come to a focus behind the retina. A biconvex lens corrects this by adding to the refractive power of the lens of the eye. In myopia the eyeball is too long, and light rays focus in front of the retina. Placing a biconcave lens in front of the eye causes the light rays to diverge slightly before striking the eye, so that they are brought to a focus on the retina.

muscular effort is tiring and may cause headaches and blurring of vision. The prolonged convergence of the visual axes associated with the accommodation may lead eventually to squint, or **strabismus** (see below). The use of glasses with convex lenses to aid the refractive power of the eye in shortening the focal distance corrects the defect.

In **myopia**, or nearsightedness, the anteroposterior diameter of the eyeball is too long. This defect can be corrected by the use of glasses with biconcave lenses so that parallel light rays are made to diverge slightly before they strike the eye.

Astigmatism is a common condition in which the curvature of the cornea is not uniform. When the curvature in one meridian is different from that in others, light rays in that meridian are refracted to a different focus so that part of the retinal image is blurred. A similar defect may be produced if the lens is pushed out of alignment or the curvature of the lens is not uniform, but these conditions are rare. Astigmatism can usually be corrected with cylindric lenses placed in such a way that they equalize the refraction in all meridians. **Presbyopia** has been mentioned above.

THE PHOTORECEPTOR MECHANISM: GENESIS OF NEURAL ACTIVITY

The potential changes that initiate action potentials in the retina are generated by the action of light on photosensitive compounds in the rods and cones.

When light is absorbed by these substances, their structure changes, and some aspect of this change is responsible for initiating neural activity.

The photosensitive compounds in the eyes of man and most mammals are made up of a protein, called an **opsin**, and **retinene$_1$**, the aldehyde of vitamin A$_1$. The term retinene$_1$ is used to distinguish this compound from retinene$_2$, which is found in the eyes of some animal species. Since the retinenes are aldehydes, they are also called **retinals**. The A vitamins themselves are alcohols and are therefore called **retinols**.

Rhodopsin

The photosensitive pigment in the rods is called **rhodopsin**, or **visual purple**. Its opsin is called **scotopsin**. Light bleaches rhodopsin by breaking the retinene-scotopsin bond, the reaction proceeding through a series of short-lived intermediates to retinene and scotopsin.

A current view of the mechanism of action of light on rhodopsin is shown diagrammatically in Fig 8–12. The retinene in rhodopsin is in the form of the 11-cis isomer. The only action of light is conversion of the retinene to the 11-trans isomer, forming **prelumirhodopsin**. This straightens out the retinene and permits the spontaneous occurrence of the next step, a change in the shape of the opsin. The opening up of the opsin presumably exposes reactive groups which catalyze the reactions producing electrical activity. The last step in the sequence of reactions is the bleaching proper, the separation of the retinene from the opsin by hydrolysis. Some of the rhodopsin is regenerated directly, while some of the retinene$_1$ is reduced by the

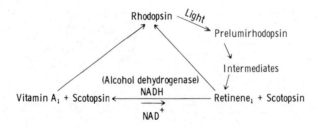

FIG 8–12. *Top:* Diagrammatic representation of events believed to occur in rods. Light converts retinene from the cis to the trans isomer, straightening out the molecule and permitting the opsin to open up. SH, HS, and X represent hypothetical active groups in the opsin that are exposed by the straightening of the retinene molecule. *Bottom:* Rhodopsin cycle in man. The iodopsin cycle is presumably similar. (Modified from Brown in: *Medical Physiology,* 13th ed. Mountcastle VB [editor]. Mosby, 1973.)

enzyme alcohol dehydrogenase in the presence of NADH to vitamin A_1, and this in turn reacts with scotopsin to form rhodopsin.

All of these reactions except the formation of prelumirhodopsin are independent of light, proceeding equally well in light or darkness. The amount of rhodopsin in the receptors therefore varies inversely with the incident light.

In vitro, solutions of rhodopsin absorb light maximally at a wavelength of 505 nm (Fig 8–13). The curve relating the sensitivity in dim light of the intact eye to light of different wavelengths also reaches a maximum at 505 nm. The fact that this **scotopic visibility curve** and the absorption curve of rhodopsin in vitro coincide is strong evidence that the rod pigment responsible for dim light vision is indeed rhodopsin.

Cone Pigments

There are 3 different types of cones in primates (see below), and there are in all probability 3 different cone pigments. One cone pigment, **iodopsin**, has been isolated from chicken retinas. It is also found in human cones, and appears to be the pigment most sensitive to red light. It is made up of $retinene_1$ and **photopsin**, a protein which is different from scotopsin. The other cone pigments also appear to contain $retinene_1$, and the differences between them are probably due to differences in the structures of the opsins. The **photopic visibility curve** (Fig 8–13) is the composite curve of the 3 cone systems.

Dark Adaptation

If an individual who has spent considerable time in a brightly lighted environment is placed in dim light, his retina slowly becomes more sensitive to light as, to use the layman's term, he "becomes accustomed to the dark." This decline in visual threshold is known as **dark adaptation**. It is nearly maximal in about 20 minutes, although there is some further decline over longer periods. On the other hand, when one passes suddenly from a dim to a brightly lighted environment, the light seems intensely and even uncomfortably bright until the eyes adapt to the increased illumination and the visual threshold rises. This adaptation occurs over a period of about 5 minutes, and is called **light adaptation** although, strictly speaking, it is merely the disappearance of dark adaptation.

There are actually 2 components to the dark adaptation response (Fig 8–14). The first drop in visual threshold, rapid but small in magnitude, is known to be due to dark adaptation of the cones because when only the foveal, rod-free portion of the retina is tested the decline proceeds no further. In the peripheral portions of the retina, a further drop occurs due to adaptation of the rods. The total change in threshold between the light-adapted and the fully dark-adapted eye is very great.

Radiologists, aircraft pilots, and others who need maximal visual sensitivity in dim light can avoid having to wait 20 minutes in the dark to become dark-adapted if they wear red goggles when in bright light. Light

FIG 8-13. *Top:* Scotopic and photopic visibility curves. Both curves are adjusted so that at peak sensitivity they have a relative sensitivity value of 1.0. In terms of absolute values, rod (scotopic) sensitivity is, of course, much greater than cone (photopic) sensitivity. *Bottom:* Correspondence between absorption of human rhodopsin and rod sensitivity. The rod sensitivity curves have been plotted with and without the lens. (Reproduced, with permission, from Wald & Brown: Human rhodopsin. Science 127:222, 1958.)

wavelengths in the red end of the spectrum stimulate the rods to only a slight degree while permitting the cones to function reasonably well (Fig 8–13). Therefore, a person wearing red glasses can see in bright light while his rods are becoming dark-adapted.

The time required for dark adaptation is determined in part by the time required to build up the rhodopsin stores. In bright light, much of the pigment is continuously being broken down and some time is

FIG 8–14. **Dark adaptation.** The curve shows the change in the intensity of a stimulus necessary to just excite the retina in dim light as a function of the time the observer has been in the dark.

FIG 8–15. **Electroretinogram recorded with an electrode in the vitreous humor of a cat.** Note that, by convention in electroretinography, positive deflections are upward. The onset and termination of the stimulus are indicated by the vertical lines in the lower record. (Reproduced, with permission, from Brown: The electroretinogram: Its components and their origins. Vision Research 8:633, 1968.)

required in dim light for accumulation of the amounts necessary for optimal rod function. However, dark adaptation also occurs in the cones, and additional factors are undoubtedly involved.

Effect of Vitamin Deficiencies on the Eye

In view of the importance of vitamin A in the synthesis of rhodopsin and iodopsin, it is not surprising that avitaminosis A produces visual abnormalities. Among these, one of the earliest is night blindness, or **nyctalopia**. This fact first called attention to the role of vitamin A in rod function, but it is now clear that concomitant cone degeneration occurs as vitamin A deficiency develops when dietary intake of this fat-soluble vitamin is reduced or its intestinal absorption is depressed. Prolonged deficiency is associated with anatomic changes in the rods and cones followed by degeneration of the neural layers of the retina. Treatment with vitamin A can restore retinal function if given before the receptors are destroyed.

Other vitamins, especially those of the B complex, are necessary for the normal functioning of the retina and other neural tissues. Nicotinamide is part of the nicotinamide adenine dinucleotide (NAD^+) molecule, and this coenzyme plays a role in the interconversion of retinene and vitamin A in the rhodopsin cycle.

TRANSMISSION IN THE OPTIC PATHWAYS & OTHER NEURAL PHENOMENA

Electroretinogram

The electrical activity of the eye has been studied by recording fluctuations in the potential difference between an electrode in the eye and another on the back of the eye. At rest there is a 6 mv potential difference between the front and the back of the eye, with the front positive. When light strikes the eye, a characteristic sequence of potential changes follows. The record of this sequence is known as the **electroretinogram (ERG)**. Turning on the light stimulus elicits the **a** and **b** waves, as shown in Fig 8–15, and also the **c** wave, which is so slow that with short stimuli its peak occurs after the stimulus. When the stimulus is turned off, a negative off-deflection occurs.

Through careful analysis of the effects of drugs and records obtained with microelectrodes inserted to varying depths in the retina, the ERG has been resolved into its components. The **c** wave is generated in the pigment epithelium. The neural components which summate to give the other deflections of the ERG are summarized in Fig 8–16. The negative **rod receptor potential** has a sudden onset, the leading edge of which is seen as the **a** wave, whereas the slow decay of this receptor potential produces the **remnant negativity** that appears in the ERG of a predominantly rod retina. A component that arises in the inner nuclear layer has been called the DC component because of its resemblance to a direct current pulse, and its decay creates the simple **off response** that is typical of the rod ERG. The **b** wave also comes from the inner nuclear layer. The ERG from retinas containing only cones is similar, except that the **cone receptor potential** has a faster decay. Since this decay precedes that of the oppositely directed DC component, a positive deflection called the **d** wave occurs after the stimulus.

The cone and rod receptor potentials are remarkable in that, during the potentials, the outer and inner segments of the receptors are positive relative to the axon terminals. Thus, extracellular current flows from the outer and inner segments toward the axon terminals. This is opposite from the current flow of receptor

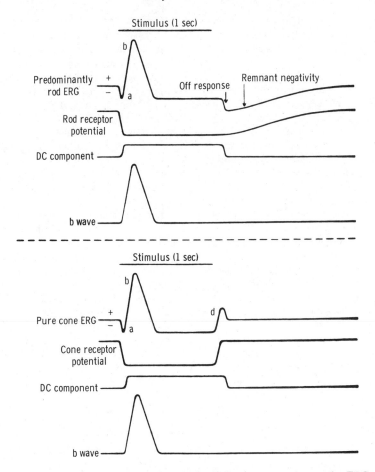

FIG 8—16. Components other than the c wave that algebraically sum to make up the ERG. The ERGs and the components are all plotted on the same time scale. The plus and minus signs indicate that positive deflections are plotted upward and negative deflections downward. (Reproduced, with permission, from Brown: The electroretinogram: Its components and their origins. Vision Research 8:633, 1968).

potentials that function, in structures such as the pacinian corpuscle (see Chapter 5), as generator potentials for nerve impulses. Furthermore, intracellular recordings have shown that the membranes of the outer and inner segments hyperpolarize during the receptor potential, and vertebrate photoreceptors do not fire impulses. In darkness, steady photoreceptor currents have been demonstrated that maintain the outer and inner segments in a partially depolarized state. It appears that light decreases the Na^+ permeability of the outer segments, thus decreasing the depolarizing current that flows in the dark and consequently hyperpolarizing the outer and inner segments. The hyperpolarization appears to be transmitted along the photoreceptors by electrotonic or similar means, and at their axon terminals it probably initiates the synaptic activation of bipolar cells.

The receptor potentials of both rods and cones have been shown to be preceded by an earlier biphasic electrical response. This response has no detectable latency by presently available methods and has been named the **early receptor potential**. It is closely associated with rapid molecular events that follow the absorption of light by the photopigment. It provides a convenient method for recording these rapid events, and its amplitude indicates accurately the concentration of photopigment. At the present time, however, it appears not to be in the direct sequence of excitatory events in retinal photoreceptors.

The exact cells that generate the **b** wave and DC component are not known. The **b** wave may result from activity in bipolar cells, and glial cells may also be involved.

Electroretinograms can be recorded in humans with one electrode on the cornea and the other on the skin of the head. Electroretinographic records are helpful in the diagnosis of certain ophthalmologic disorders, but most of these diseases are more readily diagnosed by simpler methods.

Synaptic Mediators in the Retina

Although the identities of the mediators at the synapses in the retina are not known for certain, there is evidence that acetylcholine is a transmitter at some junctions. The retina also contains relatively large amounts of dopamine, 5-hydroxytryptamine, gamma-aminobutyric acid (GABA), and the polypeptide, substance P. The evidence that these substances are synaptic mediators in the brain is discussed in Chapter 15. The presence of dopamine in some of the neurons in the retina has been established by histochemical technics. It has been reported that one of the drugs which inhibits monoamine oxidase impairs red-green color discrimination. Monoamine oxidase is the enzyme that catalyzes the oxidation of 5-hydroxytryptamine and dopamine (see Chapter 15).

Response Patterns of Ganglion Cells

The extensive convergence and divergence of neural pathways in the retina have been described above. This permits considerable organization and structuring of visual information before it leaves the retina. The characteristic patterns of ganglion cell responses are shown in Fig 8–17. The particular portion of the retina that produces a response in a ganglion cell is the **receptive field** of the cell. Ganglion cells generally discharge at a slow rate in the absence of stimulation. Some cells respond with increased discharge when a small, more or less circular beam of light is shined on their receptive fields ("on" center cells), and some cells respond with inhibition of discharge ("off" center cells). This inhibition is sometimes followed by a burst of impulses when the stimulus is turned off.

If the light is shined on the area surrounding the retinal spot where stimulation produced an "on" response, the ganglion cell discharge is inhibited; conversely, if a light is shined on the area surrounding the retinal spot where stimulation produced an "off" response, the ganglion cell discharge rate is increased. This inhibitory interaction is an example of **lateral or afferent inhibition**—that form of inhibition in which activation of a particular neural unit is associated with inhibition of the activity of surrounding units. It is a general phenomenon in mammalian sensory systems, and helps to sharpen the edges of a stimulus and improve discrimination.

Activity of Neurons in the Visual Cortex

In the visual cortex, single cells respond to lines and edges in their receptive fields rather than to circular spots. On the basis of the characteristics of their responses, the cells have been classified as simple or complex.

The **simple cells** respond maximally to slits of light, dark lines, or edges, but a particular cell responds only when the stimulus has a particular orientation. The farther the stimulating line is turned from the

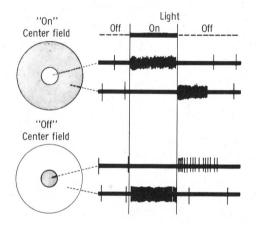

FIG 8–17. **Organization of "on" center and "off" center receptive fields of ganglion cells.** In the former case, stimulation of the center increases the number of action potentials generated (upper oscilloscope trace), while stimulation of the surrounding zone inhibits discharge but is followed by an "off" burst (lower oscilloscope trace). In the case of the "off" center field, the response patterns are reversed. (Reproduced, with permission, from: The visual cortex of the brain, by Hubel. Scientific American 209:54, Nov 1963. Copyright © 1963 by Scientific American, Inc. All rights reserved.)

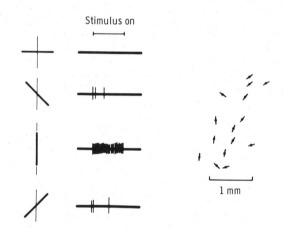

FIG 8–18. *Left:* Diagrammatic representation of the response of a single neuron in the occipital cortex to a linear visual stimulus with various orientations. The records show the number of action potentials generated when the eye was stimulated. Discharge was maximal when the orientation of the stimulus was vertical, as indicated on the left, and nil when it was horizontal. (Data from Hubel & Wiesel: Receptive fields of single neurons in the cat's striate cortex. J Physiol 148:574, 1959). *Right:* Receptive field orientation of superficial neurons in a small portion of the occipital cortex. The locations of the neurons are indicated by the dots on this map of the cortical surface, and the orientation of the stimulus to which each neuron responded maximally is indicated by the line through the dot. (Data from Hubel & Wiesel: Shape and arrangement of columns in cat's striate cortex. J Physiol 165:559, 1963.)

optimal orientation, the less the discharge it creates (Fig 8–18), and discharge is minimal when it is perpendicular to the optimal orientation. Like the ganglion cells, the simple cells show patterns of on-off interaction in their receptive fields. Typically, a long narrow "on" area is sandwiched between 2 "off" areas. Other patterns are also found, but the organization is always linear. Simple cells respond to movement of the stimulus, but with only a transient burst of activity.

The **complex cells** also respond to edges and lines in a particular orientation, but they discharge in a sustained fashion when the stimulus is moved. Other more complex cell types have also been described. Since these various types of cells in the visual cortex respond to one or another of the features of the stimulus, they have been called **feature detectors**. Feature detectors are also found in the cortical areas for other sensory modalities.

It now appears that the visual cortex is organized in vertically oriented columns of cells, with many simple cells projecting onto each complex cell. Presumably, among the many millions of neurons in the visual cortex there are simple cells with maximum rates of discharge for all the possible orientations in all the portions of the visual field. The complex cells integrate the discharges of the simple cells and the output of the complex cells is in turn elaborated by as yet unknown mechanisms into the sensation of vision.

Physiologic Nystagmus

Even when a subject stares fixedly at a stationary object, the eyeballs are not still; there are continuous jerky motions and other movements. This **physiologic nystagmus** appears to have an important function. Although individual visual receptors do not adapt rapidly to constant illumination, their neural connections do. Indeed, it has been shown that if, by means of an optical lever system, the image of an object is fixed so that it falls steadily on the same spot in the retina, the object disappears from view. Continuous visualization of objects apparently requires that the retinal images be continuously and rapidly shifted from one receptor to another.

Visual Acuity

Physiologic nystagmus is one of the many factors that determine **visual acuity**. This parameter of vision should not be confused with **visual threshold**. Visual threshold is the minimal amount of light that elicits a sensation of light; visual acuity is the degree to which the details and contours of objects are perceived. Although there is evidence that other measures are more accurate, visual acuity is usually defined in terms of the **minimum separable**—ie, the shortest distance by which 2 lines can be separated and still be perceived as 2 lines. Clinically, visual acuity is often determined by use of the familiar Snellen letter charts viewed at a distance of 20 ft (6 meters). The individual being tested reads aloud the smallest line he can distinguish. The results are expressed as a fraction. The numerator of the fraction is 20, the distance at which the subject

reads the chart. The denominator is the greatest distance from the chart at which a normal individual can read the smallest line the subject can read. Normal visual acuity is 20/20; a subject with 20/15 visual acuity has better than normal vision (not farsightedness); and one with 20/100 visual acuity has subnormal vision. The Snellen charts are designed so that the height of the letters in the smallest line a normal individual can read at 20 ft subtends a visual angle of 5 min. Each line in the letters subtends 1 min of arc, and the lines in the letters are separated by 1 min of arc. Thus the minimum separable in a normal individual corresponds to a visual angle of about 1 min.

Visual acuity is a complex phenomenon, and is influenced by a large variety of factors. These include optical factors such as the state of the image-forming mechanisms of the eye, retinal factors such as the state of the cones, and stimulus factors including the illumination, brightness of the stimulus, contrast between the stimulus and background, and the length of time the subject is exposed to the stimulus.

Visual Fields & Binocular Vision

The visual field of each eye is the portion of the external world visible out of that eye. Theoretically it should be circular, but actually it is cut off medially by the nose and superiorly by the roof of the orbit (Fig 8–19). Mapping the visual fields is important in neurologic diagnosis. The peripheral portions of the visual fields are mapped with an instrument called a **perimeter**, and the process is referred to as **perimetry**. One eye is covered while the other is fixed on a central point. A small target is moved toward this central point along selected meridians, and, along each, the location where it first becomes visible is plotted in

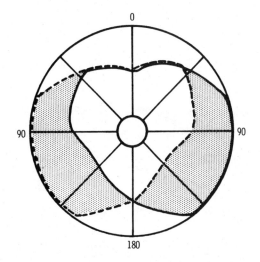

FIG 8–19. Monocular and binocular visual fields. The dotted line encloses the visual field of the left eye; the solid line that of the right eye. The common area (heart-shaped clear zone in the center) is viewed with binocular vision. The shaded areas are viewed with monocular vision.

degrees of arc away from the central point (Fig 8–19). The central visual fields are mapped with a **tangent screen,** a black felt screen across which a white target is moved. By noting the locations where the target disappears and reappears, the blind spot and any **scotomas** (blind spots due to disease) can be outlined.

The central parts of the visual fields of the 2 eyes coincide; therefore, anything in this portion of the field is viewed with **binocular vision.** The impulses set up in the 2 retinas by light rays from an object are fused at the cortical level into a single image (**fusion**). The points on the retina on which the image of an object must fall if it is to be seen binocularly as a single object are called **corresponding points.** If one eye is gently pushed out of line while staring fixedly at an object in the center of the visual field, double vision (**diplopia**) results; the image on the retina of the eye that is displaced no longer falls on the corresponding point. When visual images chronically fall on noncorresponding points in the 2 retinas in children under the age of 6, one is eventually suppressed and diplopia disappears. This suppression is a cortical phenomenon, and it usually does not develop in adults.

Binocular vision is often assigned an important role in the perception of depth. Actually, depth perception is to a large degree monocular, depending upon the relative sizes of objects, their shadows, and, in the case of moving objects, their movement relative to one another (movement parallax). However, binocular vision does add some appreciation of depth and proportion.

Effect of Lesions in the Optic Pathways

The anatomy of the pathways from the eyes to the brain is shown in Fig 8–4. Lesions along these pathways can be localized with a high degree of accuracy by the effects they produce in the visual fields.

The fibers from the nasal half of each retina decussate in the optic chiasm, so that the fibers in the optic tracts are those from the temporal half of one retina and the nasal half of the other. In other words,

each optic tract subserves half of the field of vision. Therefore, a lesion that interrupts one optic nerve causes blindness in that eye, but a lesion in one optic tract causes blindness in half of the visual field (Fig 8–4). This defect is classified as a **homonymous** (same side of both visual fields) **hemianopsia** (half-blindness). Lesions affecting the optic chiasm, such as pituitary tumors expanding out of the sella turcica, cause destruction of the fibers from both nasal hemiretinas, and produce a **heteronymous** (opposite sides of the visual fields) **hemianopsia.** Since the fibers from the maculas are located posteriorly in the optic chiasm, hemianopsic scotomas develop before there is complete loss of vision in the 2 hemiretinas. Selective visual field defects are further classified as bitemporal, binasal, and right or left.

The optic nerve fibers from the upper retinal quadrants subserving vision in the lower half of the visual field terminate in the medial half of the lateral geniculate body, while the fibers from the lower retinal quadrants terminate in the lateral half. The geniculocalcarine fibers from the medial half of the lateral geniculate terminate on the superior lip of the calcarine fissure, while those from the lateral half terminate on the inferior lip. Furthermore, the fibers from the lateral geniculate body which subserve macular vision separate from those which subserve peripheral vision and end more posteriorly on the lips of the calcarine fissure (Fig 8–20). Because of this anatomic arrangement, occipital lobe lesions may produce discrete quadrantic visual field defects (upper and lower quadrants of each half visual field). **Macular sparing,** ie, loss of peripheral vision with intact macular vision, is also common with occipital lesions (Fig 8–4) because the macular representation is separate from that of the peripheral fields and very large relative to that of the peripheral fields. Therefore, occipital lesions must extend considerable distances to destroy macular as well as peripheral vision.

Bilateral destruction of the occipital cortex in man causes essentially complete blindness, although in

Upper peripheral quadrant of retina

Upper quadrant of macula

Lower peripheral quadrant of retina

Lower quadrant of macula

FIG 8–20. Medial view of cerebral hemisphere showing projection of the retina on the calcarine fissure in man. (Redrawn and reproduced, with permission, from Brouwer: Projection of the retina on the cortex in man. Res Publ A Nerv Ment Dis 13:529, 1934.)

lower mammals considerable vision (especially rod vision) remains. The primary visual receiving area, Brodmann's area 17, also plays a role in visual discrimination. Areas 18 and 19, the so-called visual association areas, are apparently concerned with visual orientation, depth perception, and the relay of information from the visual cortex to other parts of the brain.

The fibers subserving the reflex pupillary constriction produced by shining a light into the eye leave the optic tracts in front of the geniculate bodies to enter the pretectal region. Therefore, blindness with preservation of the pupillary light reflex is almost invariably due to a lesion behind the optic tracts.

COLOR VISION

Although there is much that is still unknown about color vision, it seems clear that there are 3 types of cones in the retina, and that in some way the interactions of these 3 cone systems determine the color perceived.

Characteristics of Color

Any theory of color vision must be based on and explain a considerable number of physical, biophysical, and psychologic observations about color. Colors have 3 attributes: **hue**, **intensity**, and **saturation**, or degree of freedom from dilution with white. For any color there is a **complementary color** which, when properly mixed with it, produces a sensation of white. Black is the sensation produced by the absence of light, but it is probably a positive sensation because the blind eye does not "see black," it "sees nothing." Such phenomena as successive and simultaneous contrasts, optical tricks which produce a sensation of color in the absence of color, negative and positive after-images, and various psychologic aspects of color vision are also pertinent. Detailed discussion of these phenomena can be found in textbooks of physiologic optics.

Another observation of basic importance is the demonstration that the sensation of any spectral color, white, and even the extraspectral color, purple, can be produced by mixing various proportions of red light (wavelength 723–647 nm), green light (575–492 nm), and blue light (492–450 nm). Red, green, and blue are therefore called the **primary colors.**

Retinal Mechanisms

Before the turn of the century, color vision was believed to be subserved by 3 types of cones, each type containing a different photosensitive substance and being maximally sensitive to one of the 3 primary colors. This view, generally called the **Young-Helmholtz theory,** also held that the sensation of any given color was determined by the relative frequency of the impulses reaching the brain from each of the 3 cone systems.

The existence of 3 types of cones in the eyes of

FIG 8–21. Spectral sensitivity curves of the 3 types of cones found in primates, including man. They peak in the blue-violet (left curve), green (middle curve), and yellow (right curve) portions of the spectrum. (Modified and reproduced, with permission, from: Three-pigment color vision, by MacNichol. Scientific American 211:48, Dec 1964. Copyright © 1964 by Scientific American, Inc. All rights reserved.)

fish, monkeys, and humans has been proved by measuring the absorption spectra of individual cones. One type of human cone absorbs light maximally at wavelengths of 440–450 nm, another at 525–540 nm, and a third at 565–575 nm (Fig 8–21). The first peak is in the blue-violet portion of the spectrum; the second is in the green portion; and the third is in the yellow portion. Blue, green, and red are the primary colors, but the cones with their maximal sensitivity in the yellow portion of the spectrum are sensitive enough in the red portion to respond to red light at a lower threshold than green. This is all the Young-Helmholtz theory requires.

On the other hand, current evidence does not support the view that there are separate pathways from each of the cone systems to the brain. Apparently, there is some sort of coding process in the retina that converts color information into "on" and "off" responses in individual optic nerve fibers. Color vision is not fully developed in the fovea. There is a great degree of convergence of the extrafoveal visual receptors on the ganglion cells, and some of the connections seem to be excitatory while others are inhibitory.

Color Blindness

There are numerous tests for detecting color blindness. The most commonly used routine tests are the yarn matching test and the Ishihara charts. In the former test the subject is presented with a skein of yarn and asked to pick out the ones which match it from a pile of variously colored skeins. The Ishihara charts and similar polychromatic plates are plates on which are printed figures made up of colored spots on a background of similarly shaped colored spots. The figures are intentionally made up of colors that are liable to look the same as the background to an individual who is color blind.

The most common classification of the types of color blindness is based on the Young-Helmholtz 3-receptor theory. Some individuals are unable to distinguish certain colors, whereas others have only a color weakness. The suffix -anomaly denotes color weakness and the suffix -anopia color blindness. The prefixes prot-, deuter-, and trit- refer to defects of the red, green, and blue cone systems, respectively. Individuals with normal color vision and those with protanomaly, deuteranomaly, and tritanomaly are called **trichromats**; they have all 3 cone systems, but one may be weak. **Dichromats** are individuals with only 2 cone systems; they may have protanopia, deuteranopia, or tritanopia. **Monochromats** have only one cone system. Dichromats can match their color spectrum by mixing only 2 primary colors, and monochromats match theirs by varying the intensity of only one. Apparently monochromats see only black and white and shades of gray.

Inheritance of Color Blindness

Abnormal color vision is present in the human population in about 8% of males and 0.4% of females. Some cases arise as a complication of various eye diseases, but most are inherited. Deuteranomaly is the most common form followed by deuteranopia, protanopia, and protanomaly. These abnormalities are inherited as recessive and X-linked characteristics, ie, they are due to a mutant gene on the X chromosome. Since all of the male's cells except germ cells contain one X and one Y chromosome in addition to the 44

somatic chromosomes (see Chapter 23), color blindness will be present in males if the X chromosome has the abnormal gene. On the other hand, the normal female's cells have 2 X chromosomes, one from each parent, and since color blindness is recessive, females will show the defect only when both X chromosomes contain the abnormal gene. However, female children of a color blind male are carriers of color blindness, and will pass the defect on to half of their sons. Therefore, color blindness skips generations and appears in males of every second generation. Hemophilia, Duchenne muscular dystrophy, and a variety of other inherited disorders are caused by mutant genes on the X chromosome.

EYE MOVEMENTS

The direction in which each of the eye muscles moves the eye and the definitions of the terms used in describing eye movements are summarized in Table 8–1. Since the oblique muscles pull medially (Fig 8–7), their actions vary with the position of the eye. When the eye is turned nasally, the obliques elevate and depress it, while the superior and inferior recti rotate it; when the eye is turned temporally, the superior and inferior recti elevate and depress it and the obliques rotate it.

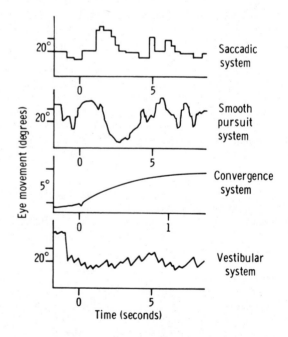

FIG 8–22. Types of eye movements. (Modified and reproduced, with permission, from Robinson: Eye movement control in primates. Science 161 [No. 3847]:1219–1224, 1968. Copyright 1968 by the American Association for the Advancement of Science.)

TABLE 8–1. Actions of the external ocular muscles. Abduction and adduction refer to rotation of the eyeball around the vertical axis with the pupil moving away from or toward the midline, respectively; elevation and depression refer to rotation around the transverse horizontal axis, with the pupil moving up or down; and torsion refers to rotation around the anteroposterior horizontal axis with the top of the pupil moving toward the nose (intorsion) or away from the nose (extorsion). (Reproduced, with permission, from Vaughan & others: *General Ophthalmology,* 6th ed. Lange, 1971.)

Muscle	Primary Action	Secondary Action
Lateral rectus	Abduction	None
Medial rectus	Adduction	None
Superior rectus	Elevation	Adduction, intorsion
Inferior rectus	Depression	Adduction, extorsion
Superior oblique	Depression	Intorsion, abduction
Inferior oblique	Elevation	Extorsion, abduction

Since much of the visual field is binocular, it is clear that a very high order of coordination of the movements of the 2 eyes is necessary if visual images are to fall at all times on corresponding points in the 2 retinas and diplopia is to be avoided.

There are 4 types of eye movements, each controlled by a different neural system but sharing the same final common path, the motor neurons that supply the external ocular muscles (Fig 8–22). **Saccades,** sudden jerky movements, occur as the gaze shifts from one object to another. **Smooth pursuit movements** are tracking movements of the eyes as they follow moving objects. **Vestibular movements,** adjustments which occur in response to stimuli initiated in the semicircular canals, maintain visual fixation as the head moves. **Convergence movements** bring the visual axes toward each other as attention is focused on objects near the observer. The similarity to a man-made tracking system on an unstable platform such as a ship is apparent; saccadic movements seek out visual targets, pursuit movements follow them as they move about, and vestibular movements stabilize the tracking device as the platform on which the device is mounted (ie, the head) moves about.

Strabismus

Abnormalities of the coordinating mechanisms can be due to a variety of causes. When the visual axes no longer are maintained in a position that keeps the visual images on corresponding retinal points, **strabismus** or squint is said to be present. Successful treatment of some types of strabismus is possible by careful surgical shortening of some of the eye muscles, by eye muscle training exercises, and by the use of glasses with prisms which bend the light rays sufficiently to compensate for the abnormal position of the eyeball.

9...

Functions of the Ear

ANATOMIC CONSIDERATIONS

Receptors for 2 sensory modalities, hearing and equilibrium, are housed in the ear. The external ear, the middle ear, and the cochlea of the inner ear are concerned with hearing. The semicircular canals, the utricle, and probably the saccule of the inner ear are concerned with equilibrium.

EXTERNAL & MIDDLE EAR

The external ear funnels sound waves into the **external auditory meatus.** In some animals the ears can be moved like radar antennas to seek out sound. From the meatus, the **external auditory canal** passes inward to the **tympanic membrane,** or ear drum (Fig 9–1).

The middle ear is an air-filled cavity in the temporal bone that opens via the eustachian tube into the nasopharynx and through the nasopharynx to the exterior. The tube is usually closed, but during swallowing, chewing, and yawning it opens, keeping the air pressure on the 2 sides of the ear drum equalized. The 3 **auditory ossicles,** the **malleus, incus,** and **stapes,** are located in the middle ear. The **manubrium,** or handle of the malleus, is attached to the back of the tympanic membrane. Its head is attached to the wall of the middle ear and its short process is attached to the incus, which in turn articulates with the head of the stapes. The stapes is named for its resemblance to a stirrup. Its **foot plate** is attached by an annular ligament to the walls of the **oval window** (Fig 9–2). Two small skeletal muscles, the **tensor tympani** and the **stapedius,** are also located in the middle ear. Contraction of the former pulls the manubrium of the malleus medially and decreases the vibrations of the tympanic membrane; contraction of the latter pulls the foot plate of the stapes out of the oval window.

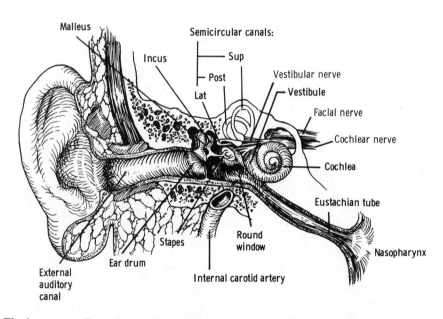

FIG 9–1. **The human ear.** To make the relationships clear, the cochlea has been turned slightly and the middle ear muscles have been omitted. Sup, superior; Post, posterior; Lat, lateral. (Modified and redrawn from Brödel: *Three Unpublished Drawings of The Anatomy of The Human Ear.* Saunders, 1946.)

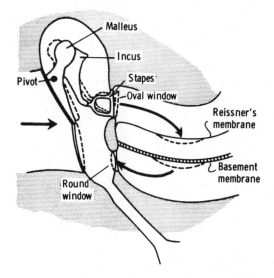

INNER EAR

The inner ear, or **labyrinth**, is made up of 2 parts, one within the other. The **bony labyrinth** is a series of channels in the petrous portion of the temporal bone. Inside these channels, surrounded by a fluid called **perilymph**, is the **membranous labyrinth**. The membranous labyrinth more or less duplicates the shape of the bony channels (Fig 9–3). It is filled with a fluid called **endolymph**, and there is no communication between the spaces filled with endolymph and those filled with perilymph.

Cochlea

The cochlear portion of the labyrinth is a coiled tube, 35 mm long, which in man makes 2¾ turns. Throughout its length the basement membrane and Reissner's membrane divide it into 3 chambers, or **scalae** (Fig 9–4). The upper **scala vestibuli** and the lower **scala tympani** contain perilymph and communicate with each other at the apex of the cochlea through a small opening called the **helicotrema**. At the base of the cochlea, the scala vestibuli ends at the oval window, which is closed by the foot plate of the stapes. The scala tympani ends at the **round window**, a foramen on the medial wall of the middle ear which is closed by the flexible **secondary tympanic membrane**. The **scala media**, the middle cochlear chamber, is continuous with the membranous labyrinth and does not communicate with the other 2 scalae. It contains endolymph (Figs 9–3, 9–4).

Organ of Corti

Located on the basement membrane is the organ of Corti, the structure that contains the auditory

FIG 9–2. Schematic representation of the auditory ossicles and the way their movement translates movements of the tympanic membrane into a wave in the fluid of the inner ear. The wave is dissipated at the round window. The movements of the ossicles, the membranous labyrinth, and the round window are indicated by dashed lines. (Redrawn from an original by Netter in Ciba Clinical Symposia, copyright © 1962, Ciba Pharmaceutical Co. Reproduced with permission.)

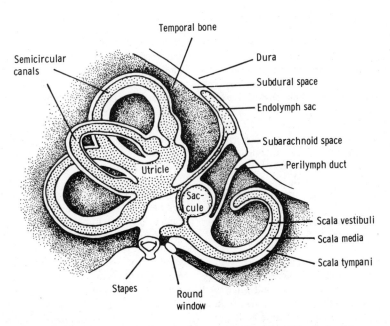

FIG 9–3. **Relationship between the membranous and osseous labyrinths (diagrammatic).**

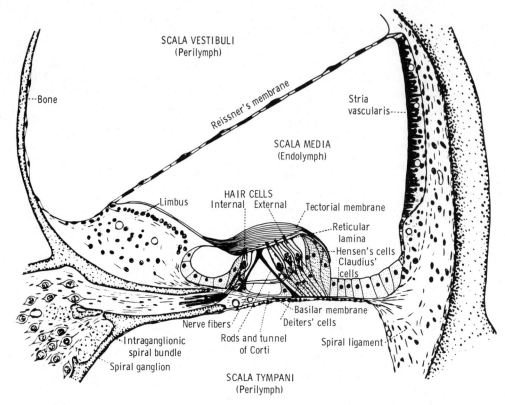

FIG 9–4. Cross-section of one turn of the cochlea of a guinea pig. (Reproduced, with permission, from Davis & others: Acoustic trauma in the guinea pig. J Acoust Soc Am 25:1180, 1953.)

receptor cells. This organ extends from the apex to the base of the cochlea, and consequently has a spiral shape. The auditory receptors are hair cells arranged in 2 rows (Fig 9–4), with their processes piercing the tough, membrane-like **reticular lamina**. There are 3500 inner and 20,000 outer hair cells in each human cochlea. The reticular lamina is supported by the **rods of Corti**. Covering the rows of hair cells is a thin, viscous but elastic **tectorial membrane** in which the tips of the hair cell processes are embedded. The cell bodies of the afferent neurons that arborize extensively around the hair cells are located in the **spiral ganglion** within the **modiolus**, the bony core around which the cochlea is wound. Their axons form the auditory division of the acoustic nerve and terminate in the **dorsal** and **ventral cochlear nuclei** of the medulla oblongata. There are approximately 28,000 fibers in each auditory nerve, and so there is no net convergence of receptors on first order neurons; most of the fibers, however, supply more than one cell and, conversely, most cells are supplied by more than one fiber.

Central Auditory Pathways

From the cochlear nuclei, axons carrying auditory impulses pass via a variety of crossed and uncrossed pathways to the **inferior colliculi**, the centers for auditory reflexes; and via the **medial geniculate body** in the thalamus to the **auditory cortex**. Others enter the reticular formation (Fig 9–5). In man, the primary auditory cortex, Brodmann's area 41, is located in the superior portion of the temporal lobe, buried in the floor of the lateral cerebral fissure (Fig 7–3). There is reason to believe that there are several additional auditory receiving areas, just as there is a secondary receiving area for cutaneous sensation (see Chapter 7). The auditory association areas adjacent to the primary auditory receiving area are widespread, extending onto the insula. The **olivocochlear bundle**, a prominent bundle of efferent fibers in each auditory nerve, arises in the olivary nucleus of the opposite side and ends around the hair cells of the organ of Corti.

Semicircular Canals

On each side of the head, the semicircular canals are perpendicular to each other so that they are oriented in the 3 planes of space. Inside the bony canals, the membranous canals are suspended in perilymph. A receptor structure, the **crista ampullaris**, is located in the expanded end or **ampulla** of each of the membranous canals. Each crista consists of hair cells and sustentacular cells surmounted by a gelatinous partition, or **cupula**, that closes off the ampulla like a swinging door (Fig 9–6). Endings of the afferent fibers of the vestibular division of the acoustic nerve are in close contact with the hair cells.

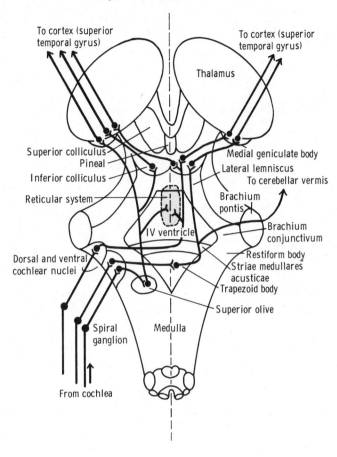

To cortex (superior temporal gyrus)

Thalamus

To cortex (superior temporal gyrus)

Superior colliculus
Pineal
Inferior colliculus
Reticular system
IV ventricle
Dorsal and ventral cochlear nuclei
Spiral ganglion
Medulla
From cochlea

Medial geniculate body
Lateral lemniscus
To cerebellar vermis
Brachium pontis
Brachium conjunctivum
Restiform body
Striae medullares acusticae
Trapezoid body
Superior olive

FIG 9–5. Simplified diagram of main auditory pathways superimposed on a dorsal view of the brain stem. Cerebellum and cerebral cortex removed.

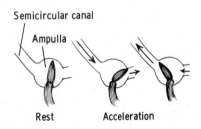

Semicircular canal

Ampulla

Rest   Acceleration

FIG 9–6. Ampullar crista. *Above:* Movements of cupula in ampullar crista during rotational acceleration. Arrows indicate direction of fluid movement. *Left:* Schematic 3-dimensional drawing of a cross-section of an ampullar crista. (Redrawn and reproduced, with permission, from Wersäll: Studies on the structure and innervation of the sensory epithelium of the cristae ampullares in the guinea pig. Acta oto-laryng, Suppl 126:1, 1956.)

Utricle & Saccule

Within each membranous labyrinth, on the floor of the utricle, there is an **otolithic organ** or **macula**. Another macula is located on the wall of the saccule, tilted 30° from the vertical plane. The maculas contain sustentacular cells and hair cells, surmounted by a membrane in which are embedded crystals of calcium carbonate, the **otoliths**. The nerve fibers from the hair cells join those from the cristae.

Neural Pathways

The cell bodies of the 19,000 neurons supplying the cristae and maculas on each side are located in the vestibular ganglion. Each vestibular nerve terminates in the ipsilateral 4-part vestibular nucleus and in the flocculonodular lobe of the cerebellum. Second order neurons pass down the spinal cord from the vestibular nuclei in the vestibulospinal tracts and ascend through the **medial longitudinal fasciculi** to the motor nuclei of the cranial nerves concerned with the control of eye movement. There are also anatomically poorly defined pathways by which impulses from the vestibular receptors are relayed via the thalamus to the cerebral cortex (Fig 9–7).

HEARING

AUDITORY RESPONSES

Sound Waves

Sound is the sensation produced when longitudinal vibrations of the molecules in the external environment, ie, alternate phases of condensation and rarefaction of the molecules, strike the tympanic membrane. A plot of these movements as changes in pressure on the tympanic membrane per unit of time is a series of waves (Fig 9–8), and such movements in the environment are generally called sound waves. The waves travel through air at a speed of approximately 344 meters/sec (775 miles/hour) at 20° C at sea level. The speed of sound increases with temperature and with altitude. Other media in which man occasionally finds himself also conduct sound waves, but at different speeds. For example, the speed of sound in water is 1428 meters/sec (3215 miles/hour).

Generally speaking, the **loudness** of a sound is correlated with the **amplitude** of a sound wave and its

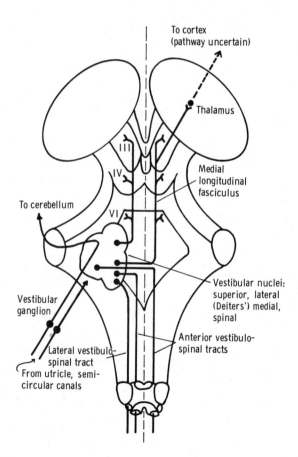

FIG 9–7. Principal vestibular pathways superimposed on a dorsal view of the brain stem. Cerebellum and cerebral cortex removed.

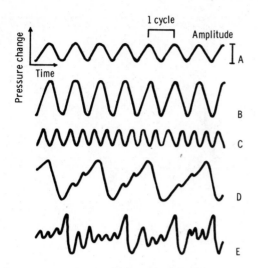

FIG 9–8. Characteristics of sound waves. *A* is the record of a pure tone. *B* has a greater amplitude and is louder than A. *C* has the same amplitude as A but a greater frequency, and its pitch is higher. *D* is a complex wave form which is regularly repeated. Such patterns are perceived as musical sounds, whereas waves like that shown in *E*, which have no regular pattern, are perceived as noise.

pitch with the **frequency**, or number of waves per unit of time. The greater the amplitude, the louder the sound; and the greater the frequency, the higher the pitch. Sound waves that have repeating patterns, even though the individual waves are complex, are perceived as musical sounds; aperiodic nonrepeating vibrations cause a sensation of noise. Most musical sounds are made up of a wave with a primary frequency which determines its pitch plus a number of harmonic vibrations, or **overtones**, which give the sound its characteristic **timbre** or quality. Variations in timbre permit us to identify the sounds of the various musical instruments even though they are playing notes of the same pitch.

The amplitude of a sound wave can be expressed in terms of the maximum pressure change or the root mean square pressure at the ear drum, but a relative scale is more convenient. The **decibel scale** is such a scale. The intensity of a sound in **bels** is the logarithm of the ratio of the intensities of that sound and a standard sound:

$$\text{bel} = \log \frac{\text{intensity of sound}}{\text{intensity of standard sound}}$$

The intensity is proportionate to the square of the sound pressure. Therefore,

$$\text{bel} = 2 \log \frac{\text{pressure of sound}}{\text{pressure of standard sound}}$$

A decibel is 0.1 bel. The standard sound reference level adopted by the Acoustical Society of America corresponds to 0 decibels at a pressure level of 0.000204 dyne/sq cm, a value that is just at the auditory threshold for the average human. In Fig 9–9, the decibel levels of various common sounds are compared. It is important to remember that the decibel scale is a log scale. Therefore, a value of 0 decibels does not mean the absence of sound but a sound level of an intensity equal to that of the standard. Furthermore, the 0–140 decibel range from threshold intensity to an intensity that is potentially damaging to the organ of Corti actually represents a 10^{14}, or 100 trillion-fold variation in sound intensity.

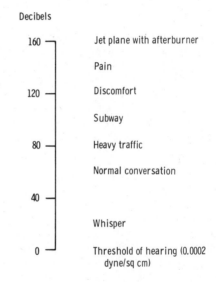

FIG 9–9. **Decibel scale for common sounds.** The reference standard is that adopted by the Acoustical Society of America, 10^{-16} watt/sq cm. (Modified from Stevens: Some similarities between hearing and seeing. Laryngoscope 68:512, 1958.)

The sound frequencies audible to the human range from about 20 to a maximum of 20,000 cycles per second (cps or hz). In other animals, notably the bat and the dog, much higher frequencies are audible. The threshold of the human ear varies with the pitch of the sound (Fig 9–10), the greatest sensitivity being in the 1000–3000 hz range. The pitch of the average male voice in conversation is about 120 hz and that of the average female voice about 250 hz. The number of pitches that can be distinguished by an average individual is about 2000, but trained musicians can improve on this figure considerably. Pitch discrimination is best in the 1000–3000 hz range and is poor at high and low pitches.

Masking

It is common knowledge that the presence of one sound decreases an individual's ability to hear other

FIG 9–10. **Audibility curve in man.** The middle curve
is that obtained by audiometry under the usual
conditions. The lower curve is that obtained
under ideal conditions. At about 140 decibels
(top curve), sounds are felt as well as heard.
(Redrawn and reproduced, with permission, from
Licklider, in: *Handbook of Experimental Psychology.* Stevens SS [editor]. Wiley, 1951.)

FIG 9–11. **Diagrammatic representation of the transmission of vibrations from the outer to the inner
ear.** (Reproduced, with permission, from Lippold
& Winton: *Human Physiology,* 6th ed. Churchill,
1970.)

sounds. This phenomenon is known as **masking.** It is
believed to be due to the relative or absolute refractori-
ness of previously stimulated auditory receptors and
nerve fibers to other stimuli. The degree to which a
given tone masks other tones is related to its pitch. The
masking effect of the background noise in all but the
most carefully soundproofed environments raises the
auditory threshold a definite and measurable amount.

SOUND TRANSMISSION

The ear converts sound waves in the external
environment into action potentials in the auditory
nerves. The waves are transformed by the ear drum and
auditory ossicles into movements of the foot plate of
the stapes. These movements set up waves in the fluid
of the inner ear. The action of the waves on the organ
of Corti generates action potentials in the nerve fibers.

Functions of the Tympanic Membrane & Ossicles

In response to the pressure changes produced by
sound waves on its external surface, the tympanic
membrane moves in and out. The membrane therefore
functions as a **resonator** which reproduces the vibrations of the sound source. It stops vibrating almost
immediately when the sound wave stops, ie, it is very
nearly **critically damped.** The motions of the tympanic
membrane are imparted to the manubrium of the
malleus. The malleus rocks on an axis through the
junction of its long and short processes, so that the

short process transmits the vibrations of the manubrium to the incus. The incus moves in such a way that
the vibrations are transmitted to the head of the
stapes. Movements of the head of the stapes swing its
foot plate to and fro like a door hinged at the posterior
edge of the oval window. The auditory ossicles thus
function as a lever system which converts the resonant
vibrations of the tympanic membrane into movements
of the stapes against the perilymph-filled scala vestibuli
of the cochlea (Figs 9–2, 9–11).

Tympanic Reflex

When the middle ear muscles—the tensor tympani
and the stapedius—contract, they pull the manubrium
of the malleus inward and the foot plate of the stapes
outward. This decreases sound transmission. Loud
sounds initiate a reflex contraction of these muscles
generally called the **tympanic reflex.** Its function is
protective, preventing strong sound waves from causing
excessive stimulation of the auditory receptors.

Bone & Air Conduction

Conduction of sound waves to the fluid of the
inner ear via the tympanic membrane and the auditory
ossicles is called **ossicular conduction.** Sound waves
also initiate vibrations of the secondary tympanic
membrane that closes the round window. This process,
unimportant in normal hearing, is called **air conduction.** A third type of conduction, **bone conduction,** is
the transmission of vibrations of the bones of the skull
to the fluid of the inner ear. When tuning forks or
other vibrating bodies are applied directly to the skull,
considerable conduction occurs in this fashion, and
this route also plays some role in the transmission of
extremely loud sounds.

Traveling Waves

The movements of the foot plate of the stapes set
up a series of traveling waves in the perilymph of the

FIG 9–12. Traveling waves. *Above:* The solid and the short-dashed lines represent the wave at 2 instants of time. The long-dashed line shows the "envelope" of the wave formed by connecting the wave peaks at successive instants. ***Below:*** Displacement of the basement membrane by the waves generated by stapes vibration of the frequencies shown at the top of each curve. (Data from Bekesy & Rosenblith, in: *Handbook of Experimental Psychology.* Stevens SS [editor]. Wiley, 1951.)

scala vestibuli. A diagram of such a wave is shown in Fig 9–12. As the wave moves up the cochlea, its height increases to a maximum and then drops off rapidly. The distance from the stapes to this point of maximum height varies with the frequency of the vibrations initiating the wave. High-pitched sounds generate waves that reach maximum height near the base of the cochlea; low-pitched sounds generate waves that peak near the apex. The bony walls of the scala vestibuli are rigid, but Reissner's membrane is flexible. The basement membrane is not under tension, and it also is readily depressed into the scala tympani by the peaks of waves in the scala vestibuli. Displacements of the

fluid in the scala tympani are dissipated into air at the round window. Therefore, sound produces distortion of the basement membrane, and the site at which this distortion is maximal is determined by the frequency of the sound wave. The tops of the hair cells in the organ of Corti are held rigid by the reticular lamina, and their hairs are embedded in the tectorial membrane (Figs 9–4, 9–13). When the basement membrane is depressed, the motion of the tectorial membrane relative to the reticular lamina bends the hairs. This bending in some way generates action potentials in the auditory nerves.

ELECTRICAL PHENOMENA

Endocochlear Potential

At rest, there is a steady 80 mv potential difference, the **endocochlear potential**, between the endolymph of the scala media and the perilymph. The endolymph is positive to the perilymph, whereas the interiors of the large cells of the organ of Corti, including the hair cells, are 65–75 mv negative to the perilymph. The total potential difference between the cells and the endolymph is therefore 150 mv. The boundaries of the space from which the endocochlear potential can be recorded are shown in Fig 9–14. The tunnel of Corti and the bases of the hair cells, which are bathed in perilymph, are outside this space. The ionic compositions of endolymph and perilymph are very different, endolymph being the only ECF in the body with a high K^+ content (Table 9–1). The significance of this fact in terms of potential differences is unsettled; the difference in ionic composition exists not only in the cochlea, where the potential difference between endolymph and perilymph is 80 mv, but in the utricle, where the potential difference between the 2 is only 5 mv. However, it seems clear that the endocochlear potential is generated by and depends upon an ion pump in the stria vascularis. A sodium-potassium activated adenosine triphosphatase system (see Chapter 1) has been demonstrated in this structure.

FIG 9–13. Effect of movement on the organ of Corti. The shearing action between 2 stiff structures, the tectorial membrane and the reticular lamina, bends the processes of the hair cells. (Reproduced, with permission, from Davis, in: *Physiological Triggers and Discontinuous Rate Processes.* Bullock TH [editor]. American Physiological Society, 1957.)

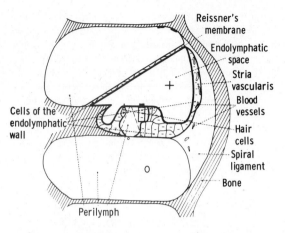

FIG 9–14. **Distribution of the positive endocochlear potential (the area within the heavy black line).** This potential is positive (+) relative to the peri-lymph (0). The minus signs inside the cells indi-cate that they are negative relative to the peri-lymph. (Reproduced, with permission, from Tasaki & others: Exploration of cochlear poten-tials in guinea pig with a microelectrode. J Acoust Soc Am 26:765, 1954.)

TABLE 9–1. **Composition of endolymph, perilymph, and spinal fluid.***

	Endolymph	Perilymph	Spinal Fluid
K^+	144.8	4.8	4.2
Na^+	15.8	150.3	152
Cl^-	107.1	121.5	122.4
Protein	15	50	21

*Data from Smith & others: Laryngoscope 64:141, 1954. K^+, Na^+, Cl^-, mEq/liter; protein, mg/100 ml.

Cochlear Microphonic & Summating Potentials

One of the electrical responses of the cochlea to sound is the **cochlear microphonic**, a potential fluctua-tion that can be recorded between an electrode on or near the cochlea and an indifferent electrode. It is generated by deformation of the processes of the hair cells, and is linearly proportionate to the magnitude of the basement membrane displacement. Consequently, it reproduces the wave form of the sound stimulus. Indeed, the reproduction of the frequency and amplitude of the sound is so faithful that if music is played into an experimental animal's ear a faithful rendition of the song can be produced by simply feed-ing the cochlear microphonic into an audio amplifier. The microphonic can be recorded from the auditory nerve close to the cochlea, but it is not a neural response. Indeed, it can be obtained from a recently killed animal in which neural activity has ceased. It is probably produced by mechanical distortion (**piezo-electric effect**) affecting the hair cells or some other structure in the cochlea. Two additional potentials, the

FIG 9–15. **Responses (vertical lines) of a guinea pig single auditory nerve fiber to tones of different frequencies and intensities.** The sound intensity is expressed in decibels below an arbitrary standard. The dotted line encloses the "response area" of this fiber. Note the sharp cut-off at higher fre-quencies and the relatively greater response spec-trum at higher sound intensities on the low-fre-quency side. (Reproduced, with permission, from Tasaki: Nerve impulses in individual auditory nerve fibers of guinea pig. J Neurophysiol 17:97, 1954.)

negative and **positive summating potentials**, are generated when sound strikes the ear. They are prin-cipally direct current baseline shifts on which the cochlear microphonic is superimposed.

Action Potentials in Auditory Nerve Fibers

The frequency of the action potentials in single auditory nerve fibers is proportionate to the loudness of the sound stimuli. At low sound intensities, each axon discharges to sounds of only one frequency, and this frequency varies from axon to axon depending upon the part of the cochlea from which the fiber comes. At higher sound intensities, the individual axons discharge to a wider spectrum of sound frequen-cies (Fig 9–15)–particularly to frequencies lower than that at which threshold stimulation occurs. The "response area" of each unit, the area above the line that defines its threshold at various frequencies, resem-bles the shape of the traveling wave in the cochlea.

Genesis of Action Potentials

The way the various cochlear potentials are inter-related in the genesis of action potentials in the afferent nerves is still unsettled. Apparently the cochlear microphonic, possibly in association with the negative summating potential, serves as the generator potential. The endocochlear potential probably keeps the receptors in a ready state by maintaining the potential difference between the hair cells and their processes.

The major determinant of the pitch perceived when a sound wave strikes the ear is the place in the organ of Corti that is maximally stimulated. The traveling wave set up by a tone produces peak depression of the basement membrane, and consequently maximal receptor stimulation, at one point. The distance between this point and the stapes is inversely related to the pitch of the sound, low tones producing maximal stimulation at the apex of the cochlea and high tones producing maximal stimulation at the base. The pathways from the various parts of the cochlea to the brain are distinct. An additional factor involved in pitch perception at sound frequencies of less than 2000 hz may be the pattern of the action potentials in the auditory nerve. When the frequency is low enough, the nerve fibers begin to respond with an impulse to each cycle of a sound wave. The importance of this **volley effect**, however, is limited; and the frequency of the action potentials in a given auditory nerve fiber determines principally the loudness, rather than the pitch, of a sound.

BRAIN MECHANISMS

Auditory Responses of Neurons in the Medulla Oblongata

The responses of individual second order neurons in the cochlear nuclei to sound stimuli are like those of the individual auditory nerve fibers. The frequency at which sounds of lowest intensity evoke a response varies from unit to unit; with increased sound intensities, the band of frequencies to which a response occurs becomes wider. The major difference between the responses of the first and second order neurons is the presence of a sharper "cut-off" on the low-frequency side in the medullary neurons (Fig 9−16). This greater specificity of the second order neurons is

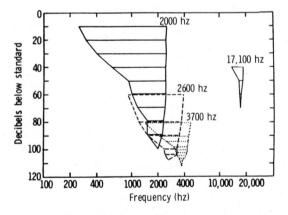

FIG 9−16. "Response areas" of 4 second order auditory neurons in the cochlear nuclei of the cat. The sound intensity is expressed in decibels below an arbitrary standard. Compare with Fig 9−15. (Reproduced, with permission, from Galambos & Davis: The response of single auditory nerve fibers to acoustic stimulation. J Neurophysiol 6:39, 1943.)

probably due to some sort of inhibitory process in the brain stem, but how it is achieved is not known.

Although the pitch of a sound depends primarily on the frequency of the sound wave, loudness also plays a part; low tones (below 500 hz) seem lower, and high tones (above 4000 hz) seem higher as their loudness increases. Duration also affects pitch to a minor degree. The pitch of a tone cannot be perceived unless it lasts for more than 0.01 sec, and with durations between 0.01 and 0.1 sec pitch rises as duration increases.

Auditory Cortex

The pathways from the cochlea to the auditory cortex are described in the first section of this chapter. Impulses ascend from the dorsal and ventral cochlear nuclei through complex paths that are both crossed and uncrossed. In deeply anesthetized animals, there is an organized pattern of tonal localization in the primary auditory cortex, as if the cochlea had been unrolled upon it. In man, low tones are represented anterolaterally and high tones posteromedially in the auditory cortex. However, individual neurons in the auditory cortex respond to such parameters as the onset, duration, and repetition rate of an auditory stimulus and particularly to the direction from which it came. In this way, they are analogous to some of the neurons in the visual cortex (see Chapter 8). Many animals species have better hearing than man in the absence of any auditory cortex. In the common laboratory mammals, destruction of the auditory cortex not only fails to cause deafness but also fails to obliterate established conditioned responses to sound of a given frequency. On the other hand, responses to a given sequence of 3 or more tones are absent. All of this suggests that the auditory cortex is concerned with recognition of tonal patterns, with analysis of properties of sounds, and with sound localization.

Sound Localization

Determination of the direction from which a sound emanates depends, at least in theory, upon detecting the difference in time between the arrival of the stimulus in the 2 ears and the difference in phase of the sound waves on the 2 sides, as well as upon the fact that the sound is louder on the side closest to the source. The time difference is said to be the most important factor at frequencies below 1000 hz, and the loudness difference the most important at frequencies above 1000 hz. Many neurons in the auditory cortex receive input from both ears, and they respond maximally or minimally when the time of arrival of a stimulus at one ear is delayed by a fixed time period relative to the time of arrival at the other ear. This fixed time period varies from neuron to neuron. Sounds coming from directly in front of the individual presumably differ in quality from those coming from behind, because the external ears are turned slightly forward. Sound localization is markedly disrupted by lesions of the auditory cortex in many experimental animals and in man.

Inhibitory Mechanisms

Stimulation of the efferent olivocochlear bundle in the auditory nerve decreases the neural response to auditory stimuli, possibly because of the liberation from the endings of the olivocochlear fibers of a hyperpolarizing inhibitory mediator. Other mechanisms inhibit transmission at the synaptic relays in the brain stem. These and similar mechanisms which operate as "volume controls" in all the specific sensory systems are discussed in detail in Chapter 11.

DEAFNESS

Clinical deafness may be due to impaired sound transmission in the external or middle ear (**conduction deafness**) or to damage to the neural pathways (**nerve deafness**). Among the causes of conduction deafness are plugging of the external auditory canals with wax or foreign bodies, destruction of the auditory ossicles, thickening of the ear drum following repeated middle ear infections, and abnormal rigidity of the attachments of the stapes to the oval window. Causes of nerve deafness include toxic degeneration of the acoustic nerve produced by streptomycin, tumors of the acoustic nerve and cerebellopontine angle, and vascular damage in the medulla.

Conduction and nerve deafness can be distinguished by a number of simple tests with a tuning fork. Three of these tests, named for the men who developed them, are outlined in Table 9–2. The Weber and Schwabach tests demonstrate the important masking effect of environmental noise on the auditory threshold.

Audiometry

Auditory acuity is commonly measured with an **audiometer**. This device presents the subject with pure tones of various frequencies through earphones. At each frequency, the threshold intensity is determined and plotted on a graph as a percentage of normal

hearing. This provides an objective measurement of the degree of deafness and a picture of the tonal range most affected.

Fenestration Procedures

A common form of conduction deafness is that due to **otosclerosis**, a disease in which the attachments of the foot plate of the stapes to the oval window become abnormally rigid. In patients with this disease, air conduction (see above) can be utilized to bring about some restoration of hearing. A membrane-covered outlet from the bony labyrinth is created so that waves set up by vibrations of the secondary tympanic membrane can be dissipated. In the "fenestration operation," an outlet is created by drilling a hole in the horizontal semicircular canal and covering it with skin.

VESTIBULAR FUNCTION

RESPONSES TO ROTATIONAL & LINEAR ACCELERATION

Semicircular Canals

Rotational acceleration in the plane of a given semicircular canal stimulates its crista. The endolymph, because of its inertia, is displaced in a direction opposite to the direction of rotation. The fluid pushes on the cupula and swings it like a door (Fig 9–6), bending the processes of the hair cells. When a constant speed of rotation is reached, the fluid spins at the same rate as the body and the cupula swings back into the upright position. When rotation is stopped, deceleration produces displacement of the endolymph in the direction of the rotation, and the cupula swings in a direction opposite to that during acceleration. It returns to midposition in 25–30 sec. Movement of the

TABLE 9–2. Common tests with a tuning fork to distinguish between nerve and conduction deafness.

	Weber	Rinne	Schwabach
Method	Base of vibrating tuning fork placed on vertex of skull.	Base of vibrating tuning fork placed on mastoid process until subject no longer hears it, then held in air next to ear.	Bone conduction of patient compared to that of normal subject.
Normal	Heard equally on both sides.	Hears vibration in air after bone conduction is over.	
Conduction deafness (one ear)	Sound louder in diseased ear because masking effect of environmental noise is absent on diseased side.	Does not hear vibrations in air after bone conduction is over.	Bone conduction better than normal (conduction defect excludes masking noise).
Nerve deafness (one ear)	Sound louder in normal ear.	Hears vibration in air after bone conduction is over.	Bone conduction less than normal.

FIG 9—17. Ampullary responses to rotation. Average time course of impulse discharge from ampulla of 2 semicircular canals during rotational acceleration, steady rotation, and deceleration. (Reproduced, with permission, from Adrian: Discharges from vestibular receptors in the cat. J Physiol 101:389, 1943.)

cupula in one direction commonly causes increased impulse traffic in single nerve fibers from its crista, whereas movement in the opposite direction commonly inhibits neural activity (Fig 9—17).

Rotation causes maximal stimulation of the semicircular canals most nearly in the plane of rotation. Since the canals on one side of the head are a mirror image of those on the other side, the endolymph is displaced toward the ampulla on one side and away from it on the other. The pattern of stimulation reaching the brain therefore varies with the direction as well as the plane of rotation. Linear acceleration probably fails to displace the cupula and therefore does not stimulate the cristae. However, there is considerable evidence that when one part of the labyrinth is destroyed other parts take over its functions. Experimental localization of labyrinthine functions is therefore difficult.

The tracts that descend from the vestibular nuclei into the spinal cord are concerned primarily with postural adjustments (see Chapter 12); the ascending connections to cranial nerve nuclei are largely concerned with eye movements.

Nystagmus

The characteristic jerky movement of the eye observed at the start and end of a period of rotation is called **nystagmus**. It is actually a reflex which maintains visual fixation on stationary points while the body rotates, although it is not initiated by visual impulses and is present in blind individuals. When rotation starts, the eyes move slowly in a direction opposite to the direction of rotation. When the limit of this movement is reached, the eyes quickly snap back to a new fixation point and then again move slowly in the other direction. The slow component is initiated by impulses from the labyrinths; the quick component is triggered by a center in the brain stem. Nystagmus is frequently horizontal, ie, the eyes move in the horizontal plane; but it can also be vertical, when the head is tipped sidewise during rotation, or rotatory, when the head is tipped forward. By convention, the direction of eye movement in nystagmus is identified by the direction of the quick component. The direction of the quick component during rotation is the same as that of the rotation, but the **postrotatory nystagmus** that occurs due to displacement of the cupula when rotation is stopped is in the opposite direction.

Macular Responses

In mammals, the utricular and saccular maculas respond to linear acceleration. The otoliths are more dense than the endolymph, and acceleration in any direction causes them to be displaced in the opposite direction, distorting the hair cells and generating activity in the nerve fibers. The maculas also discharge tonically in the absence of head movement, because of the pull of gravity on the otoliths. The impulses generated from these receptors are partly responsible for reflex righting of the head and other important postural adjustments discussed in Chapter 12.

Although most of the responses to stimulation of the maculas are reflex in nature, vestibular impulses also reach the cerebral cortex. These impulses are presumably responsible for conscious perception of motion and supply part of the information necessary for orientation in space. The nausea, blood pressure changes, sweating, pallor, and vomiting that are the well-known accompaniments of excessive vestibular stimulation are probably due to reflexes mediated via vestibular connections in the brain stem. **Vertigo** is the sensation of rotation in the absence of actual rotation.

Caloric Stimulation

The semicircular canals can be stimulated by instilling water that is hotter or colder than body temperature into the external auditory meatus. The temperature difference sets up convection currents in the endolymph, with consequent motion of the cupula. This technic of **caloric stimulation**, which is sometimes used diagnostically, causes some nystagmus, vertigo, and nausea. To avoid these symptoms, it is important when irrigating the ear canals in the treatment of ear infections to be sure that the fluid used is at body temperature.

ORIENTATION IN SPACE

Orientation in space depends in large part upon input from the vestibular receptors, but visual cues are also important. When the horizon is manipulated so that the vestibular and visual cues are conflicting, women are said to place more reliance on their visual sensations and men on their vestibular. Pertinent information is also supplied by impulses from proprioceptors in joint capsules, which supply data about the relative position of the various parts of the body, and impulses from cutaneous exteroceptors, especially touch and pressure receptors. These 4 inputs are synthesized at a cortical level into a continuous picture of the individual's orientation in space.

EFFECTS OF LABYRINTHECTOMY

The effects of unilateral labyrinthectomy are presumably due to unbalanced discharge from the remaining normal side. They vary from species to species and with the speed at which the labyrinth is destroyed. Rats develop abnormal body postures and roll over and over as they continuously attempt to right themselves. Postural changes are less marked in man, but the symptoms are distressing. Motion aggravates the symptoms, but efforts to minimize stimulation by lying absolutely still are constantly thwarted by waves of nausea, vomiting, and even diarrhea. Fortunately, compensation for the loss occurs, and after 1–2 months the symptoms disappear completely.

Symptoms of this type are absent after bilateral destruction of the labyrinths, but defects in orientation are present. For this reason, diving is hazardous for persons who lack vestibular function. The only means these individuals have of finding the surface is vision, because in the water the pressure sensed by the cutaneous exteroceptors is equal all over the body. If for any reason vision is obscured, a person whose vestibular apparatus is impaired has no mechanism for orienting himself. Therefore, he may swim away from rather than toward the surface and, consequently, he may drown.

10 . . .

Smell & Taste

Smell and taste are generally classified as visceral senses because of their close association with gastrointestinal function. Physiologically, they are related to each other. The flavors of various foods are in large part a combination of their taste and smell. Consequently, foods may taste "different" if one has a cold which depresses his sense of smell. Both taste and smell receptors are chemoreceptors which are stimulated by molecules in solution in the fluids of the nose and mouth. However, these 2 senses are anatomically quite different. The smell receptors are distance receptors (teleceptors); the smell pathways have no relay in the thalamus; and there is no neocortical projection area for olfaction. The taste pathways pass up the brain stem to the thalamus and project to the postcentral gyrus along with those for touch and pressure sensibility from the mouth.

SMELL

RECEPTORS & PATHWAYS

Olfactory Mucous Membrane

The olfactory receptors are located in a specialized portion of the nasal mucosa, the yellowish-pigmented **olfactory mucous membrane.** In the dog and other animals in which the sense of smell is highly developed (macrosmatic animals), the area covered by this membrane is large; in microsmatic animals such as man, it is small, covering an area of 5 sq cm in the roof of the nasal cavity near the septum (Fig 10–1). The supporting cells secrete the layer of mucus which constantly overlies the epithelium and send many microvilli into this mucus. Interspersed among the supporting cells of this mucous membrane are 10–20 million receptor cells. Each olfactory receptor is a neuron, and the olfactory mucous membrane is said to be the place in the body where the nervous system is closest to the external world. The neurons have short, thick dendrites with expanded ends called olfactory rods (Fig 10–2). From these rods cilia project to the surface of the mucus. The cilia are unmyelinated processes, about 2 μm long and 0.1 μm in diameter.

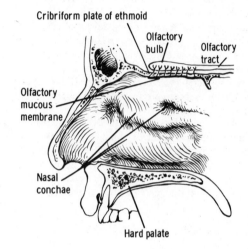

FIG 10–1. Olfactory mucous membrane. (Modified, redrawn, and reproduced, with permission, from Chusid: *Correlative Neuroanatomy & Functional Neurology,* 15th ed. Lange, 1973.)

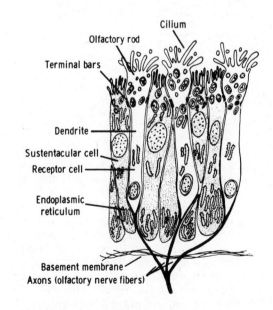

FIG 10–2. Structure of the olfactory mucous membrane. (Reproduced, with permission, from de Lorenzo, in: *Olfaction and Taste.* Zotterman Y [editor]. Macmillan, 1963.)

There are 10–20 cilia per receptor neuron. The axons of the olfactory receptor neurons pierce the cribriform plate of the ethmoid bone and enter the olfactory bulbs.

Olfactory Bulbs

In the olfactory bulbs the axons of the receptors terminate among the dendrites of the **mitral** and **tufted cells** (Fig 10–3) to form the complex globular synapses called **olfactory glomeruli**. An average of 26,000 receptor cell axons converge on each glomerulus. The axons of the tufted cells pass posteriorly through the **medial olfactory stria**, cross the midline in the **anterior commissure**, and enter the opposite olfactory bulb. The functional significance of this peculiar fiber arrangement is not known. In experimental animals, section of the anterior commissure apparently produces considerable olfactory deficit, but destruction of one olfactory bulb produces only unilateral loss of olfaction (**anosmia**).

Another group of fibers passes through the **intermediate olfactory stria** to end in the **anterior perforated substance** and the **area of the diagonal band**. Impulses concerned with olfactory reflexes pass from this region to the rest of the limbic system and hypothalamus. A third band of fibers, mostly axons of mitral cells, passes from the glomeruli through the **lateral olfactory stria** to the cortical and medial portions of the ipsilateral **amygdaloid nucleus** and to the prepyriform and periamygdaloid cortex. There are no direct connections to the hippocampal formation or the hippocampal gyrus, and the **cortical olfactory area** is in the prepyriform and periamygdaloid cortex (Fig 10–4). Evoked potentials have been recorded in the amygdaloid nuclei in response to olfactory stimuli in humans.

Limbic System

The inferior frontal and perihilar portions of the cerebral cortex and the associated deep nuclei in these regions have been called the **rhinencephalon** because this part of the brain was presumed to subserve only olfactory functions. In mammals and man, only a small part of the rhinencephalon is directly concerned with olfaction. The rest of the rhinencephalon is concerned with the emotional responses, instincts, and complex neuroendocrine regulatory functions discussed in Chapter 15. For this reason, the term rhinencephalon has generally been dropped and this part of the brain is now called the **limbic system** or **limbic lobe** (Fig 15–2).

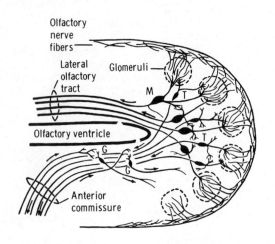

FIG 10–3. Neural pathways in the olfactory bulb. Olfactory nerve fibers enter the glomeruli from the surface. They synapse there with the dendrites of mitral cells (M) and tufted cells (T). The axons of the mitral cells form the lateral olfactory tract, while those of the tufted cells form primarily the medial olfactory tract to the opposite bulb via the anterior commissure. The granule cells (G) are the termini of fibers from the opposite bulb. The olfactory ventricle is a projection of the cerebral ventricles present in lower animals but not in man. (Reproduced, with permission, from Adey, in: *Handbook of Physiology.* Field J, Magoun HW [editors]. Washington: The American Physiological Society, 1959. Section 1, pp 535–548.)

FIG 10–4. Diagram of olfactory pathways.

Inhibitory Pathways

There are efferent fibers in the olfactory striae, and stimulation of these fibers decreases the electrical activity of the olfactory bulbs. Presumably, therefore, inhibitory mechanisms analogous to those in the eye, ear, and other sensory systems exist in the olfactory system.

PHYSIOLOGY OF OLFACTION

Stimulation of Receptors

Olfactory receptors respond only to substances that are in contact with the olfactory epithelium and are dissolved in the thin layer of mucus that covers it. The olfactory thresholds for the representative substances shown in Table 10–1 illustrate the remarkable sensitivity of the olfactory receptors to some substances. For example, methyl mercaptan, the substance that gives garlic its characteristic odor, can be smelled at a concentration of less than one-millionth of a milligram per liter of air. On the other hand, discrimination of differences in the intensity of any given odor is poor. The concentration of an odor-producing substance must be changed by about 30% before a difference can be detected. The comparable visual discrimination threshold is a 1% change in light intensity.

When odoriferous molecules react with a receptor, they generate a receptor potential; but the mechanism by which the molecules generate the potential is not known. Odor-producing molecules are generally those containing from 3–4 up to 18–20 carbon atoms, and molecules with the same number of carbon atoms but different structural configurations have different odors. Relatively high water and lipid solubility are characteristic of substances with strong odors. One theory holds that odoriferous molecules inactivate enzyme systems in the epithelium, altering its chemical reactions. Another theory holds that the molecules alter the surface of the receptor cells, thus changing their electrical state. A third theory holds that the molecules simply alter the Na^+ permeability of the receptor membrane.

TABLE 10–1. Some olfactory thresholds.*

Substance	mg/liter of Air
Ethyl ether	5.83
Chloroform	3.30
Pyridine	0.03
Oil of peppermint	0.02
Iodoform	0.02
Butyric acid	0.009
Propyl mercaptan	0.006
Artificial musk	0.00004
Methyl mercaptan	0.0000004

*Data from Allison & Katz: J Indust Chem 11:336, 1919.

Discrimination of Different Odors

Man can distinguish between 2000 and 4000 different odors. The physiologic basis of this olfactory discrimination is not known. A number of attempts have been made to divide olfactory receptors into different fundamental types. It is true that in the rabbit, receptors in the posterior portion of the olfactory epithelium respond more strongly to lipid-soluble substances whereas those in the anterior portion respond with some selectivity to water-soluble compounds, but attempts to further classify olfactory receptors have not been successful. There is evidence that the direction from which a smell comes can be detected by the slight difference in the time of arrival of odoriferous molecules in the 2 nostrils.

There is a close relationship between smell and sexual function in animals, and the perfume ads are ample evidence that a similar relationship exists in humans. The sense of smell is generally more acute in women than in men, and in women it is most acute at the time of ovulation. Olfaction and taste are both hypersensitive in patients with adrenal insufficiency (see Chapter 20).

Sniffing

The portion of the nasal cavity containing the olfactory receptors is poorly ventilated. Most of the air normally moves quietly through the lower part of the nose with each respiratory cycle, although eddy currents, probably set up by convection as cool air strikes the warm mucosal surfaces, pass some air over the olfactory mucous membrane. The amount of air reaching this region is greatly increased by sniffing, an action which includes contraction of the lower part of the nares on the septum to help deflect the air stream upward. Sniffing is a semireflex response that usually occurs when a new odor attracts attention.

Role of Pain Fibers in the Nose

Naked endings of many trigeminal pain fibers are found in the olfactory mucous membrane. They are stimulated by irritating substances, and an irritative, trigeminally mediated component is part of the characteristic "odor" of such substances as peppermint, menthol, and chlorine. These endings are also responsible for initiating sneezing, lacrimation, respiratory inhibition, and other reflex responses to nasal irritants.

Adaptation

It is common knowledge that when one is continuously exposed to even the most disagreeable odor, perception of the odor decreases and eventually ceases. This sometimes beneficent phenomenon is due to the fairly rapid adaptation which occurs in the olfactory system. It is specific for the particular odor being smelled, and the threshold for other odors is unchanged. Olfactory adaptation is in part a central phenomenon, but it is also due to a change in the receptors.

TASTE

RECEPTOR ORGANS & PATHWAYS

Taste Buds

The taste buds, the sense organs for taste, are ovoid bodies measuring 50–70 μm. Each taste bud is made up of supporting cells and 5–18 hair cells, the **gustatory receptors**. The receptor cells each have a number of hairs projecting into the **taste pore**, the opening at the epithelial surface of the taste bud (Fig 10–5). The unmyelinated ends of the sensory nerve fibers are wrapped around the receptor cells in intimate fashion. Each taste bud is innervated by about 50 nerve fibers, and, conversely, each nerve fiber receives input from an average of 5 taste buds. If the sensory nerve is cut, the taste buds it innervates degenerate and eventually disappear. However, if the nerve regenerates, the cells in the neighborhood become organized into new taste buds, presumably as a result of some sort of chemical inductive effect from the regenerating fiber.

The taste buds are located in the mucosa of the epiglottis and pharynx and in the lateral walls of the **fungiform** and **vallate papillae** of the tongue. The fungiform papillae are rounded structures on the tip and edges of the tongue; the vallate papillae are prominent structures arranged in a V on the back of the tongue. The small conical **filiform papillae** which cover the dorsum of the tongue do not usually contain taste buds. There are a total of about 9000 taste buds in man.

Taste Pathways

The sensory nerve fibers from the taste buds on the anterior two-thirds of the tongue travel in the chorda tympani branch of the facial nerve. The fibers from the posterior third of the tongue reach the brain stem via the glossopharyngeal nerve. The fibers from areas other than the tongue reach the brain stem via the vagus nerve. On each side, the myelinated but relatively slow-conducting taste fibers in these 3 nerves unite in the medulla oblongata to form the **tractus solitarius** (Fig 10–6). The second order neurons are located in the nucleus of this tract, and their axons cross the midline and join the medial lemniscus, ending with the fibers for touch, pain, and temperature sensibility in the specific sensory relay nuclei of the thalamus. Impulses are relayed from there to the taste projection area in the cerebral cortex at the foot of the postcentral gyrus. Taste does not have a separate cortical projection area, but is represented in the portion of the postcentral gyrus that subserves cutaneous sensation from the face.

PHYSIOLOGY OF TASTE

Receptor Stimulation

Taste receptors are chemoreceptors that respond to substances dissolved in the oral fluids bathing them. These substances appear to evoke generator potentials,

FIG 10–5. Taste bud.

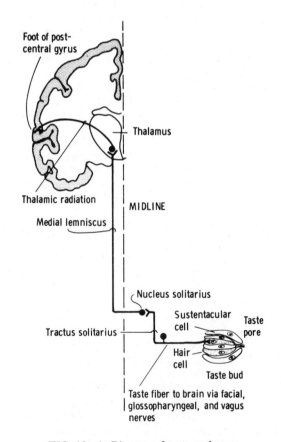

FIG 10–6. Diagram of taste pathways.

but how the molecules in solution interact with the receptor cells to produce these potentials is not known. One theory is based on the hypothesis that the receptor hairs have a polyelectrolyte surface film. According to this theory, binding of ions to this film causes a distortion in the spatial arrangement of the film with a consequent change in the distribution of charge density. There is also evidence that taste-provoking molecules bind to specific proteins in taste buds. The binding of substances to the receptors must be weak because it usually takes relatively little washing with water to abolish a taste.

Basic Taste Modalities

In man there are 4 basic tastes: sweet, sour, bitter, and salt. Bitter substances are tasted on the back of the tongue, sour along the edges, sweet at the tip, and salt on the dorsum anteriorly (Fig 10–7). Sour

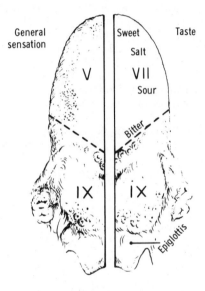

FIG 10–7. Sensory innervation of the tongue. The numbers refer to cranial nerves. (Modified and reproduced, with permission, from Chusid: *Correlative Neuroanatomy & Functional Neurology,* 15th ed. Lange, 1973.)

and bitter substances are also tasted on the palate. The taste buds are not histologically different in the different areas, but the existence of physiologic differences has been demonstrated by recording the electrical activity of nerve fibers from single taste buds in animals. These studies show that some taste buds respond only to bitter stimuli whereas others respond only to salt, sweet, or sour stimuli. Some respond to more than one modality, but none to all four. A curious finding of unknown physiologic significance is the demonstration that in the cat, dog, pig, and rhesus monkey there are taste buds that respond to the application of distilled water. Presumably, therefore, these animals can "taste water." Taste buds of this type are absent in the rat and man (Fig 10–8).

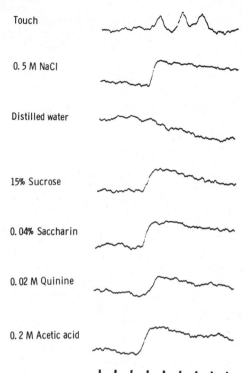

FIG 10–8. Integrated responses of the whole chorda tympani of man to various solutions poured over the tongue. The height of each curve is proportionate to the firing rate. The dots at the bottom are at 1-second intervals. (Reproduced, with permission, from Zotterman: The nervous mechanism of taste. Ann New York Acad Sci 81:358, 1959.)

Taste Thresholds & Intensity Discriminations

In man the ability to discriminate differences in the intensity of tastes, like intensity discrimination in olfaction, is relatively crude. A 30% change in the concentration of the substance being tasted is necessary before an intensity difference can be detected. The threshold concentrations of substances to which the taste buds respond vary with the particular substance (Table 10–2). These thresholds are lowered in patients with adrenal insufficiency (see Chapter 20).

Substances Evoking Primary Taste Sensations

Acids taste **sour**. The H^+, rather than the associated anion, stimulates the receptors. For any given acid, sourness is generally proportionate to the H^+ concentration, but organic acids are often more sour for a given H^+ concentration than are mineral acids. This is probably because they penetrate cells more rapidly than the mineral acids.

A **salty** taste is produced by the anion of inorganic salts. The halogens are particularly effective, but some organic compounds also taste salty.

The substance usually used to test the **bitter** taste is quinine sulfate. This compound can be detected in a

TABLE 10–2. Some taste thresholds.

Substance	Taste	Threshold Concentration (mols/liter)
Hydrochloric acid	Sour	0.0001
Sodium chloride	Salt	0.02
Strychnine hydrochloride	Bitter	0.0000016
Glucose	Sweet	0.08
Sucrose	Sweet	0.01
Saccharin	Sweet	0.000023

concentration of 0.000008 mols, although the threshold for strychnine hydrochloride is even lower (Table 10–2). Other organic compounds, especially morphine, nicotine, caffeine, and urea, taste bitter. Inorganic salts of magnesium, ammonium, and calcium also taste bitter. The taste is due to the cation. Thus, there is no readily apparent common feature of the molecular structure of substances that taste bitter.

Most **sweet** substances are organic. Sucrose, maltose, lactose, and glucose are the most familiar examples, but polysaccharides, glycerol, some of the alcohols and ketones, and a number of compounds with no apparent relation to any of these, such as chloroform and beryllium salts, also taste sweet. The sweetest compound known is the n-propyl derivative of 4-alkoxy-3-aminonitrobenzene. Saccharin is in demand as a sweetening agent in reducing diets because it produces satisfactory sweetening in an amount that is a minute fraction of the amount of calorie-rich sucrose required for the same purpose. Lead salts also taste sweet, which is why a cloying sweet taste is common when one is spray painting with lead-containing paints.

Flavor

The almost infinite variety of tastes so dear to the gourmet are mostly synthesized from the 4 basic taste components. In some cases a desirable taste includes an element of pain stimulation (eg, "hot" sauces). In addition, smell plays an important role in the overall sensation produced by food, and the consistency (or texture) and temperature of foods also contribute to their "flavor."

Taste Variation & After-Effects

There is considerable variation in the distribution of the 4 basic taste buds in various species and, within a given species, from individual to individual. In humans, there is an interesting variation in ability to taste **phenylthiocarbamide (PTC)**. In dilute solution, PTC tastes sour to about 70% of the Caucasian population but is tasteless to the other 30%. Inability to taste PTC is inherited as an autosomal recessive trait. Testing for this trait is of considerable value in studies of human genetics.

Taste exhibits after-reactions and contrast phenomena that are similar in some ways to visual after-images and contrasts. Some of these are chemical "tricks," but others may be true central phenomena.

11...

The Reticular Activating System & the Electrical Activity of the Brain

THE RETICULAR FORMATION & THE RETICULAR ACTIVATING SYSTEM

The various sensory pathways described in Chapters 7–10 relay impulses from sense organs via 3- and 4-neuron chains to particular loci in the cerebral cortex. The impulses are responsible for perception and localization of individual sensations. Impulses in these systems also relay via collaterals to the **reticular activating system (RAS)** in the brain stem reticular formation. Activity in this system produces the conscious, alert state that makes perception possible.

The **reticular formation**, the phylogenetically old reticular core of the brain, occupies the midventral portion of the medulla and midbrain. It is made up of myriads of small neurons arranged in complex, intertwining nets. Located within it are centers which regulate respiration, blood pressure, heart rate, and other vegetative functions. In addition, it contains ascending and descending components that play important roles in the adjustment of endocrine secretion, the formation of conditioned reflexes, and the regulation of sensory input, learning, and consciousness. The components concerned with consciousness and the modulation of sensory input are discussed in this chapter. The vegetative functions of the reticular core are considered in the chapters on the endocrine, gastrointestinal, cardiovascular, and respiratory systems. The functions related to learning are discussed in Chapter 16, "Higher Functions of the Nervous System."

The reticular activating system is a complex polysynaptic pathway. Collaterals funnel into it not only from the long ascending sensory tracts but also from the trigeminal, auditory, and visual systems and the olfactory system. The complexity of the neuron net and the degree of convergence in it abolish modality specificity, and most reticular neurons are activated with equal facility by different sensory stimuli. The system is therefore **nonspecific**, whereas the classical sensory pathways are **specific** in that the fibers in them are activated only by one type of sensory stimulation. Activity in the RAS percolates upward, and part of it bypasses the thalamus to project diffusely to the cortex. Another part of the RAS ends in the intralaminar and related thalamic nuclei, and from them is projected diffusely and nonspecifically to the whole neocortex (Fig 11–1). The RAS is intimately concerned with the electrical activity of the cortex.

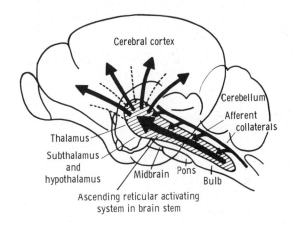

Cerebral cortex

Cerebellum

Afferent collaterals

Thalamus

Subthalamus and hypothalamus

Midbrain

Pons

Bulb

Ascending reticular activating system in brain stem

FIG 11–1. Diagram of ascending reticular system projected on a sagittal section of the cat brain. (Reproduced, with permission, from Starzl & others: Collateral afferent excitation of reticular formation of brain stem. J Neurophysiol 14:479, 1951.)

THE THALAMUS & THE CEREBRAL CORTEX

Thalamic Nuclei

On developmental and topographic grounds, the thalamus can be divided into 3 parts: the epithalamus, the dorsal thalamus, and the ventral thalamus. The **epithalamus** has connections to the olfactory system, and the projections and functions of the **ventral thalamus** are undetermined. The **dorsal thalamus** can be divided into nuclei which project diffusely to the whole neocortex and nuclei which project to specific discrete portions of the neocortex and limbic system. The nuclei which project to all parts of the neocortex are the midline and intralaminar nuclei. They are called collectively the **nonspecific projection nuclei**. They receive input from the reticular activating system. Impulses responsible for the diffuse secondary response and the alerting effect of reticular activation (see below) are relayed through them. The nuclei of the dorsal thalamus that project to specific areas can be divided into 3 groups: the specific sensory relay nuclei, the nuclei concerned with efferent control mechanisms, and the nuclei concerned with complex integrative functions. The **specific sensory relay nuclei** include the medial and lateral geniculate bodies that relay auditory and visual impulses to the auditory and visual cortices and the ventrobasal group of nuclei that relay somatesthetic information to the postcentral gyrus. The **nuclei concerned with efferent control mechanisms** include several nuclei that are concerned with motor function. They receive input from the basal ganglia and the cerebellum and project to the motor cortex. Also included in this group are the anterior nuclei, which receive afferents from the mammillary bodies and project to the limbic cortex as part of the limbic circuit which appears to be concerned with recent memory and emotion (see Chapters 15 and 16). The **nuclei concerned with complex integrative functions** are the dorsolateral nuclei that project to the cortical association areas and are concerned primarily with functions such as language.

Cortical Organization

The neocortex is generally arranged in 6 layers (Fig 11–2). The neurons are mostly pyramidal cells with extensive vertical dendritic trees (Figs 11–2, 11–3) that may reach to the cortical surface. The axons of these cells usually give off recurrent collaterals which turn back and synapse on the superficial portions of the dendritic trees. Afferents from the specific nuclei of the thalamus terminate primarily in cortical layer IV, whereas the nonspecific afferents are distributed to all cortical layers.

FIG 11–2. Neuronal connections in the neocortex. On the left are afferent fibers from the thalamus. The numbers identify the cortical layers. Note the extensive dendritic processes of the cells, especially those in the deep layers. (Based on drawing of Lonente de No, in Fulton: *Physiology of the Nervous System.* Oxford Univ Press, 1943.)

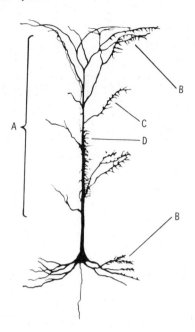

FIG 11–3. Cortical pyramidal cell, showing the distribution of presynaptic terminals. A, nonspecific afferents from the reticular formation and the thalamus; B, recurrent collaterals of pyramidal cell axons; C, commissural fibers from mirror image sites in contralateral hemisphere; D, specific afferents from thalamic sensory relay nuclei. (Reproduced, with permission, from Chew & Leiman: The structural and functional organization of the neocortex. Neurosciences Research Program Bulletin 8:157, 1970.)

EVOKED CORTICAL POTENTIALS

The electrical events that occur in the cortex after stimulation of a sense organ can be monitored with an exploring electrode connected to another electrode at an indifferent point some distance away. A characteristic response is seen in animals under barbiturate anesthesia. If the exploring electrode is over the primary receiving area for the particular sense, a surface-positive wave appears with a latency of 5–12 msec. This is followed by a small negative wave and then by a larger, more prolonged positive deflection with a latency of 20–80 msec. This sequence of potential changes is illustrated in Fig 11–4. The first positive-negative wave sequence is the **primary evoked potential**; the second is the **diffuse secondary response.**

Primary Evoked Potential

The primary evoked potential is highly specific in its location and can be observed only where the pathways from a particular sense organ end. Indeed, it is so discrete that it has been used to map the specific cortical sensory areas. It was thought at one time that the primary response was due to activity ascending to the

200 μv

0 10 20 30 40 50 60 70 80
msec

FIG 11–4. Response evoked in the contralateral sensory cortex by stimulation (at the arrow) of the sciatic nerve in a cat under barbiturate anesthesia. Upward deflection is surface-negative. (Modified from Forbes & Morrison: Cortical response to sensory stimulation under deep barbiturate narcosis. J Neurophysiol 2:112, 1939.)

cortex in the thalamic radiations. However, an electrode on the pial surface of the cortex samples activity to a depth of only 0.3–0.6 mm. The primary response is negative rather than positive when it is recorded with a microelectrode inserted in layers 2–6 of the underlying cortex, and the negative wave within the cortex is followed by a positive wave. This indicates depolarization on the dendrites and somas of the cells in the cortex, followed by hyperpolarization. The positive-negative wave sequence recorded from the surface of the cortex is due to the fact that the superficial cortical layers are positive relative to the initial negativity, then negative to the deep hyperpolarization. In unanesthetized animals the primary evoked potential is largely obscured by the spontaneous activity of the brain, but it can be demonstrated with special technics. It is somewhat more diffuse in unanesthetized animals, but still well localized compared to the diffuse secondary response.

Diffuse Secondary Response

The surface-positive diffuse secondary response is sometimes followed by a negative wave or series of waves. Unlike the primary response, the secondary response is not highly localized. It appears at the same time over most of the cortex and in many other parts of the brain. The uniform latency in different parts of the cortex and the fact that it is not affected by a circular cut through the cortical gray matter that isolates an area from all lateral connections indicates that the secondary response cannot be due to lateral spread of the primary evoked response. It therefore must be due to activity ascending from below the cortex. The pathway involved appears to be the nonspecific thalamic projection system from the midline and related thalamic nuclei.

The diffuse secondary response is present in unanesthetized animals, and in them is influenced by a variety of emotional and motivational factors. When the animal is presented with a stimulus to which it has become accustomed, the diffuse secondary response produced by it is small and inconspicuous. However, if the stimulus is followed a number of times by an electric shock, the diffuse secondary response to the same stimulus is large and is present not only in all parts of the cortex but in a variety of subcortical loci as well.

THE ELECTROENCEPHALOGRAM

The background electrical activity of the brain in unanesthetized animals was described in the 19th century, but it was first analyzed in a systematic fashion by the German psychiatrist Hans Berger, who introduced the term **electroencephalogram (EEG)** to denote the record of the variations in potential recorded from the brain. The EEG can be recorded with scalp electrodes through the unopened skull, or with electrodes on or in the brain. The term **electrocorticogram (ECoG)** is sometimes used to refer to the record obtained with electrodes on the pial surface of the cortex.

EEG records may be **bipolar** or **unipolar**. The former is the record of potential fluctuations between 2 cortical electrodes; the latter is the record of potential differences between a cortical electrode and a theoretically indifferent electrode on some part of the body distant from the cortex.

Alpha Rhythm

In an adult human who is at rest and letting his mind wander with his eyes closed, the most prominent component of the EEG is a fairly regular pattern of waves at a frequency of 8–12/sec and an amplitude of about 50 μv when recorded from the scalp. This pattern is the **alpha rhythm**. It is most marked in the parieto-occipital area, although it is sometimes observed in other locations. A similar rhythm has been observed in a wide variety of mammalian species (Fig 11–5). In the cat it is slightly more rapid than in the human, and there are other minor variations from species to species, but in all mammals the pattern is remarkably similar.

Other Rhythms

In addition to the dominant alpha rhythm, 18–30/sec patterns of lower voltage are sometimes seen over the frontal regions. This rhythm, the **beta rhythm,** may be a harmonic of the alpha. A pattern of large, regular 4–7/sec waves called the **theta rhythm** occurs in normal children and is generated in the hippocampus in experimental animals (see below). Large, slow waves with a frequency of less than 4/sec are sometimes called **delta waves.**

Variations in the EEG

In man, the frequency of the dominant EEG

Guinea pig:

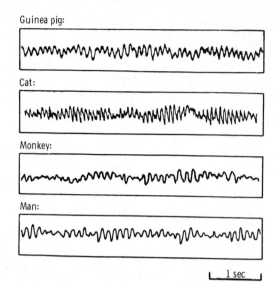

Cat:

Monkey:

Man:

1 sec

FIG 11–5. EEG records showing alpha rhythm from 4 different species. (Reproduced, with permission, from Brazier: *Electrical Activity of the Nervous System,* 2nd ed. Pitman, 1960.)

rhythm at rest varies with age. In infants there is fast, beta-like activity, but the occipital rhythm is a slow 0.5–2/sec pattern. During childhood this latter rhythm speeds up, and the adult alpha pattern gradually appears during adolescence. The frequency of the alpha rhythm is decreased by a low blood glucose level, a low body temperature, a low level of adrenal gluco-corticoid hormones, and a high arterial partial pressure of CO_2 (P_{CO_2}). It is increased by the reverse conditions. Forced overbreathing to lower the arterial P_{CO_2} is sometimes used clinically to bring out latent EEG abnormalities.

Alpha Block

When the eyes are opened, the alpha rhythm is replaced by fast, irregular low-voltage activity with no dominant frequency. This phenomenon is called **alpha block.** A breakup of the alpha pattern is also produced by any form of sensory stimulation (Fig 11–6) or mental concentration such as solving arithmetic problems. A common term for this replacement of the regular alpha rhythm with irregular low-voltage activity is **desynchronization,** because it represents a breaking up of the synchronized activity of neural elements responsible for the wave pattern. Because desynchronization is produced by sensory stimulation and is correlated with the aroused, alert state, it is also called the **arousal** or **alerting response.**

Sleep Patterns

When an individual in a relaxed, inattentive state becomes drowsy and falls asleep, the alpha rhythm is replaced by slower, larger waves (Fig 11–7). In deep sleep, very large, somewhat irregular delta waves at a frequency of less than 4/sec are observed. Interspersed with these waves during moderately deep sleep are bursts of alpha-like, 10–14/sec, 50 μv waves–the **sleep spindles.** The alpha rhythm and the patterns of the drowsy and sleeping individual are **synchronized,** in contrast to the desynchronized, irregular activity seen in the alert state.

Paradoxical (REM) Sleep

The high-amplitude slow waves seen in the EEG during sleep are sometimes replaced by rapid, low-voltage, irregular EEG activity that resembles that seen in alert animals and humans. However, sleep is not interrupted; indeed, the threshold for arousal by sensory stimuli and by stimulation of the reticular formation is elevated. The condition has therefore come to be called **paradoxical sleep** (Fig 11–8). There are rapid, roving movements of the eyes during paradoxical sleep, and for this reason it is also called rapid eye movement or **REM sleep.** Conversely, "spindle" or "synchronized" sleep is frequently called non-rapid eye movement or **NREM sleep.** It is also called **slow**

Excited

Relaxed

Drowsy

Asleep

Deep sleep

1 sec   50 μv

FIG 11–7. EEG records during excitement and sleep. Note sleep spindles, in this case at 14/sec, in fourth tracing from top. Vertical calibration mark at end of each record is 50 μv. (Reproduced, with permission, from Jasper, in: *Epilepsy and Cerebral Localization.* Penfield & Erickson [editors]. Thomas, 1941.)

Olf

FIG 11–6. Desynchronization of the cortical EEG of a rabbit by an olfactory stimulus (indicated by the line after Olf). (Reproduced, with permission, from Green & Arduini: Hippocampal electrical activity during arousal. J Neurophysiol 17:533, 1954.)

FIG 11–8. EEG and other changes in slow wave and paradoxical sleep. CORT, cortical EEG; HIPP, hippocampal EEG; PRF, electrical activity of pontine reticular formation; EMG, electromyogram of neck muscles; EYES, electromyogram of eye muscles; RESP, respiration. Vertical lines at right: 50 µv calibration marks. Note that during paradoxical sleep there is theta rhythm in the hippocampus, phasic activity in the pontine reticular formation, loss of tone in the neck muscles, eye movements at irregular intervals, and shallow respiration. (Reproduced, with permission, from Jouvet: Recherches sur les structures nerveuses et les mécanismes responsables des différentes phases du sommeil physiologique. Arch ital biol 100:125, 1962.)

wave sleep. REM sleep is found in all species of mammals that have been studied and in birds, but it probably does not occur in other animals. Humans aroused at a time when they show the low-voltage EEG activity generally report that they were dreaming, whereas individuals wakened from spindle sleep do not. This observation and other evidence indicate that REM sleep and dreaming are closely associated. During REM sleep, there is a marked reduction in skeletal muscle tone despite the rapid eye movements. There is a high incidence of penile erections in males during REM sleep, and the teeth-grinding (**bruxism**) that occurs in some individuals is also associated with dreaming.

REM periods occur about every 90 minutes during the night and occupy a total of about 20% of the usual night's sleep in young adults. The REM periods average about 20 minutes in length, but characteristically become longer toward morning. There is even more REM sleep in children and a great deal in newborn infants, who are probably too young to have the usual type of visual dreams (Table 11–1).

If humans are awakened every time they show REM sleep, they become somewhat anxious and irritable. If they are then permitted to sleep without interruption, they show a great deal more than the normal amount of paradoxical sleep for a few nights. The same "rebound" effect is seen in animals treated the same way. These observations have led some investigators to conclude that dreaming is necessary to maintain mental health. However, prolonged treatment with drugs that depress REM sleep (see below) does not produce adverse psychologic effects.

Sleep Walking & Bed-Wetting

Sleep walking (somnambulism) and bed-wetting (nocturnal enuresis) have been shown to occur during slow wave sleep or, more specifically, during arousal from slow wave sleep. They are not associated with REM sleep. Episodes of sleep walking may last several minutes. Somnambulists walk with their eyes open and avoid obstacles, but when awakened they cannot recall the episodes.

TABLE 11–1. Effect of age on total amount of daily sleep and REM sleep in humans.*

Age	Total Daily Sleep (Hours)	REM Sleep (% of Total Sleep)
1–15 days	16	50
3–5 months	14	40
2–3 years	13	25
5–9 years	11	19
10–14 years	9	20
19–30 years	8	22
33–45 years	7	19
50–70 years	6	15

*Data from Roffwarg & others: Ontogenetic development of the human sleep-dream cycle. Science 152:604, 1966. Copyright 1966 by the American Association for the Advancement of Science.

PHYSIOLOGIC BASIS OF THE EEG
& CONSCIOUSNESS

The presence of rhythmic waves in the alpha and slow wave sleep patterns indicates a priori that neural components of some sort are discharging rhythmically, since random discharges of individual units would cancel out and no waves would be produced. The main questions to be answered are which units are discharging synchronously, and what mechanisms are responsible for desynchronization and synchronization.

Source of the EEG

EEG waves were originally thought to be the summed action potentials of cortical cells discharging in a volume conductor. However, the activity recorded in the EEG is mostly that of the most superficial layers of the cortical gray substance, and there are relatively few cell bodies in these layers. Present evidence indicates that the potential changes in the cortical EEG are due to current flow in the fluctuating dipoles formed on the dendrites of the cortical cells and the cell bodies. The dendrites of the cortical cells are a forest of similarly oriented, densely packed units in the superficial layers of the cerebral cortex (Fig 11–2). As pointed out in Chapter 4, dendrites are generally not conducting processes that produce propagated all or none spikes; rather, they are the site of nonpropagated hypopolarizing and hyperpolarizing local potential changes. As excitatory and inhibitory endings on the dendrites of each cell become active, current flows into and out of these current sinks and sources from the rest of the dendritic processes and the cell body. The cell-dendrite relationship is therefore that of a constantly shifting dipole. Current flow in this dipole would be expected to produce wave-like potential fluctuations in a volume conductor (Fig 11–9). When the sum of the dendritic activity is negative relative to the cell, the cell is hypopolarized and hyperexcitable; when it is positive, the cell is hyperpolarized and less excitable. The cerebellar cortex and the hippocampus are 2 other parts of the CNS where many complex, parallel dendritic processes are located subpially over a layer of cells. In both of them there is a characteristic rhythmic fluctuation in surface potential similar to that observed in the cortical EEG.

Desynchronizing Mechanisms

Desynchronization, the replacement of a rhythmic EEG pattern with irregular low-voltage activity, is produced by stimulation of the specific sensory systems up to the level of the midbrain, but stimulation above this level, stimulation of the specific sensory relay nuclei of the thalamus, or stimulation of the cortical receiving areas themselves does not have this effect. On the other hand, high-frequency stimulation of the reticular formation in the midbrain tegmentum and of the nonspecific projection nuclei of the thalamus desynchronizes the EEG and arouses a sleeping animal. Large lesions of the lateral and superior portions of the midbrain which interrupt the medial

FIG 11–9. Diagrammatic comparison of the electrical responses of the axon and the dendrites of a nerve cell. Current flow to and from active synaptic knobs on the dendrites produces wave activity, while all or none action potentials are transmitted down the axon. (Modified and redrawn, with permission, from Bickford: Computational aspects of brain function. Institute of Radio Engineers, Medical Electronics Series [IRE, ME] 6:164, 1959.)

lemnisci and other ascending specific sensory systems fail to prevent the desynchronization produced by sensory stimulation, but lesions in the midbrain tegmentum which disrupt the RAS without damaging the specific systems are associated with a synchronized pattern which is unaffected by sensory stimulation (Fig 11–10). Animals with the former type of lesion are awake; those with the latter type are comatose for

FIG 11–10. Typical EEG records of cat with lesion of lemniscal pathways (above) and cat with lesion of midbrain tegmentum (below). (Reproduced, with permission, from Lindsley & others: Behavioral and EEG changes following chronic brain stem lesions in the cat. Electroenceph Clin Neurophysiol 2:483, 1950.)

long periods. It therefore appears that the ascending activity responsible for desynchronization following sensory stimulation passes up the specific sensory systems to the midbrain, enters the RAS via collaterals, and continues through the thalamus and the nonspecific thalamic projection system to the cortex.

Generalized & Localized Cortical Arousal

There is some evidence for localization of function within the RAS. The hypothesis has been advanced that the lower part of the reticular system is responsible for relatively crude sleep-wakefulness changes, whereas the thalamic portions of the system mediate shifting, localized alerting of the various parts of the cortex in response to the panorama of highly specific stimuli demanding attention in any active individual. The ways in which selected parts of the brain can be alerted under certain conditions, and the relationship of these responses to conditioned learning, are discussed in Chapter 16.

Effect of RAS Stimulation on Cortical Neurons

It is not known how impulses ascending in the RAS break up synchronized cortical activity. Stimulation of the RAS inhibits burst activity, the recruiting response, and the cortical waves produced by the application of strychnine to certain parts of the brain. RAS stimulation arouses and alerts the animal, and, a priori, one might expect it to produce a heightened rather than a depressed excitability of cortical neurons. However, some of the neurons in the cortical sensory projection areas fire randomly during sleep whereas they discharge only in response to specific stimuli when the animal is awake. It is possible that RAS activity abolishes this random firing by producing some degree of cortical inhibition, leaving these neurons free to respond only to specific sensory signals. The net effect of RAS activity, therefore, might be an increase in the "signal/noise ratio" at the expense of a slight decrease in absolute excitability.

Arousal Following Cortical Stimulation

Electrical stimulation of certain portions of the cerebral cortex causes increased reticular activity and EEG arousal. The most effective cortical loci in the monkey are the superior temporal gyrus and the orbital surface of the frontal lobe. Stimulation of these regions wakes a sleeping animal but causes no movements and has few visible effects in the conscious animal. Stimulation of other cortical areas, even with strong currents, does not produce electrical or behavioral arousal. These observations indicate that a system of **corticofugal fibers** feeds into the reticular formation, providing a pathway by which intracortical events can initiate arousal. The system may be responsible for the alerting responses to emotions and related psychic phenomena which occur in the absence of any apparent external stimulus.

Alerting Effects of Epinephrine & Related Compounds

An interesting pharmacologic effect on the RAS is the arousal response produced by agents that mimic the action of the sympathetic nervous system. Epinephrine, norepinephrine, and amphetamine produce EEG arousal and behavioral alerting by lowering the threshold of reticular neurons in the brain stem. Epinephrine and norepinephrine secreted from the adrenal medulla in the stressed individual have the same effect. Therefore, one of the effects of the mass adrenergic discharge in emergency situations (see Chapter 13) is reinforcement of the alert, attentive state necessary for effective action. The anxiety associated with excessive epinephrine secretion may be related to the hyperalerting of the cortex, but this possibility requires further study.

It was originally thought that the alerting effect was due to a direct action of pressor agents on the neurons in the midbrain, but it has been demonstrated that any increase in blood pressure increases the excitability of the reticular formation. Apparently there are blood pressure-sensitive neurons in the midbrain because pressor agents produce EEG arousal in animals in which the brain has been transected at the top of the pons, but not in animals in which transection has been carried out at higher levels.

Clinical Correlates

Patients with tumors or other lesions that interrupt the RAS are generally comatose. This system is especially vulnerable at the top of the midbrain and in the posterior hypothalamus, where it is pushed medially by other fiber systems. Relatively small lesions in this location may cause prolonged coma while producing very few other symptoms. In animals it has been demonstrated that concussion depresses activity in the RAS and produces a sleep pattern in the EEG which persists as long as the unconsciousness lasts.

The RAS & General Anesthesia

The ability of general anesthetics to produce unconsciousness appears to be due, at least in part, to their action in depressing conduction in the RAS. The effect of ether on the response of the reticular formation and the medial lemnisci to a sensory stimulus is shown in Fig 11–11. Similar blocking effects are produced by anesthetic doses of barbiturates. These effects may be simply a manifestation of general synaptic depression by these drugs. There are hundreds of synapses in the reticular pathways, whereas the specific systems have only 2–4. At each synapse, the EPSPs must build up until the firing level of the postsynaptic neurons is reached (see Chapter 4). Any agent which has a moderate depressant effect on this process will block conduction in multisynaptic paths before blocking it in those with only a few synapses.

Synchronizing Mechanisms

The wave pattern of the alpha rhythm indicates that the activity of many of the dendritic units is synchronized. Two factors contribute to this synchronization: the synchronizing effect on each unit of activity in neighboring parallel fibers, and the influence of impulses from the thalamus and related parts of the brain stem.

Stimulate

	ML	RAS
Before ether		
Ether for 2 min		
10 min after ether		

FIG 11–11. Effect of ether anesthesia on lemniscal (ML) and reticular (RAS) response to stimulation of the sciatic nerve. (Redrawn and reproduced, with permission, from French & King: Mechanisms involved in the anesthetic state. Surgery 38:228, 1955.)

If 2 nerve fibers are placed side by side in a volume conductor, depolarization of one of them rarely if ever causes a propagated discharge in the other but does influence its excitability. This is because external current flow into the area of depolarization in the active fiber hyperpolarizes the membrane of the neighboring fiber at 2 points and partially depolarizes it at another. Current flow in the opposite direction creates areas of positivity in fibers adjacent to sites where inhibitory endings are active (Fig 11–12). In a large population of similarly oriented neural processes this formation of current sinks and sources in neighboring

FIG 11–12. Effect of activity in one nerve fiber on the activity of a neighboring fiber in a volume conductor. Current flows into the area of depolarization (S) on fiber 2 from the surrounding membrane. At X and Z on the membrane of fiber 1, positive charges pile up, hyperpolarizing the membrane; at Y, positive charges are pulled off, partly depolarizing it.

fibers tends to synchronize current flow.

The dendritic potentials of the cerebral cortex are also influenced by projections from the thalamus. A circular cut around a piece of cortex does not alter its synchronized activity if the blood supply is intact, but the rhythmicity is markedly decreased if the deep connections of the cortical "button" are severed. Large lesions of nonspecific projection nuclei of the thalamus disrupt the EEG synchrony on the side of the lesion. Stimulation of these nuclei at a frequency of about 8/sec produces a characteristic 8/sec response throughout most of the ipsilateral cortex. Because the amplitude of this response waxes and wanes, it is called the **recruiting response** (Fig 11–13). Stimulation of the

FIG 11–13. Recruiting response in cortex produced by 8/sec stimulation of intralaminar thalamic region. (Based on recordings of Morrison & Dempsey: A study of thalamo-cortical relations. Am J Physiol 135:281, 1942.)

specific projection nuclei does not have this effect. The recruiting response has many similarities to the alpha rhythm and to **burst activity**, the occurrence of short trains of alpha-like waves superimposed on slower rhythms. The records of burst activity such as sleep spindles are essentially identical when recorded simultaneously from the cortex and the thalamic nonspecific projection nuclei, but these waves are absent from the other thalamic nuclei. Conscious, unrestrained animals, receiving 8/sec stimuli to the midline nuclei of the thalamus develop EEG synchrony and go to sleep. All of these observations point to activity projected from the thalamus via the nonspecific thalamic projection system, or possibly reverberating activity between the thalamus and the cortex, as being of importance in the genesis of the synchronized EEG rhythm. Stimulation of other parts of the brain stem at low frequencies also produces EEG synchronization and sleep in animals.

It should be noted that slow wave sleep is not solely a passive phenomenon that occurs when sensory stimuli are withdrawn; the synchronizing mechanisms must be active. It is also worth noting that high-frequency stimulation of the thalamic structures produces desynchrony, whereas low-frequency (8/sec) stimulation produces synchrony. These observations are not necessarily inconsistent; the important point is that low-frequency stimulation produces one response whereas high-frequency stimulation produces another.

The relation of these observations, if any, to the production of **electrosleep** or **electric anesthesia** is not known. These terms refer to the unconscious state produced in some humans by the application of small amounts of current to the head in the form of pulses at a frequency of 20–40 hz. However, sleep and insensibility to pain are not produced by the current in all individuals.

Role of the Raphe Nuclei & Serotonin

Lesions of the raphe nuclei in the brain stem cause prolonged wakefulness. These nuclei contain appreciable quantities of serotonin, and it has been demonstrated that treatment with *p*-chlorophenylalanine, a drug which selectively inhibits serotonin synthesis (see Chapter 15), causes wakefulness in cats. On the other hand, administration of compounds which increase brain serotonin causes increased slow wave sleep. This suggests that serotoninergic nerve fibers from the raphe nuclei are in some way capable of inhibiting the arousal system or stimulating the synchronizing system.

Genesis of REM Sleep

REM sleep appears to be initiated from nuclei in the pons. Phasic spike discharges from this region herald its onset, and destruction of the medial portion of the oral reticular nucleus of the pons abolishes REM sleep without usually affecting slow wave sleep or arousal. It is not known what initiates the discharge from the pons or how this discharge brings about the various phenomena associated with REM sleep. There is some evidence that an adrenergic mechanism in the brain is involved, since REM sleep is suppressed by brain stem lesions which deplete the forebrain of norepinephrine, presumably by interrupting ascending adrenergic fibers. However, drugs which inhibit monoamine oxidase increase brain norepinephrine and they also decrease REM sleep.

Clinical Uses of the EEG

The EEG is sometimes of value in localizing pathologic processes. When a collection of fluid overlies a portion of the cortex, activity over this area may be damped. This fact may aid in diagnosing and localizing conditions such as subdural hematomas. Lesions in the cortex cause local formation of irregular or slow waves which can be picked up in the EEG leads. Epileptogenic foci sometimes generate high-voltage waves which can be localized.

The waves recorded from corresponding anatomic loci on the 2 hemispheres are normally remarkably similar in timing and shape. This is presumably due to a central subcortical "pacemaker" that keeps the activity of both hemispheres in phase. A lesion in one hemisphere distorts the pattern; consequently, if records from homologous points on the 2 hemispheres are out of phase with each other, focal cortical damage is indicated.

In epileptics there are characteristic EEG patterns during seizures; between attacks, however, abnormalities are often difficult to demonstrate. **Grand mal** seizures, epileptic attacks in which an aura precedes a generalized convulsion with tonic muscular contraction and clonic jerks, have a characteristic EEG pattern. There is fast activity during the tonic phase. Slow waves, each preceded by a spike, occur at the time of each clonic jerk. For a while after the attack, slow waves are present. Similar changes are seen in experimental animals during convulsions produced by electric shocks. **Petit mal** epileptic attacks, seizures characterized by a momentary loss of responsiveness, are associated with 3/sec doublets, each consisting of a typical spike and rounded wave (Fig 11–14). **Psychomotor seizures**, attacks in which emotional lability and stereotyped behavior are seen due to discharge from a temporal lobe focus, are not associated with any typical EEG changes. During the various types of diencephalic seizures that originate in the brain stem, there are also no characteristic EEG abnormalities.

FIG 11–14. Petit mal epilepsy. Record of 4 cortical EEG leads from a 6-year-old boy who during the recording had one of his "blank spells" in which he was transiently unaware of his surroundings and blinked his eyelids. (Reproduced, with permission, from Chusid: *Correlative Neuroanatomy & Functional Neurology,* 15th ed. Lange, 1973.)

MODULATION OF SENSORY INPUT

The first evidence that the brain regulates the generation of sensory impulses or their transmission in the specific sensory systems was the observation that stimulation of the bulbar reticular formation inhibited transmission at the first synapse in the lemniscal and spinothalamic systems and the trigeminal nuclei. Inhibitory effects on transmission in the cochlear nucleus have also been observed. It has been claimed that some of the inhibitory effects in the auditory system are due to contraction of the stapedius and tensor tympani muscles (see Chapter 9). However, efferent fibers in the auditory nerve pass all the way to the cochlea, and stimulation of these efferent fibers inhibits the initiation of impulses in the organ of Corti. There are efferent fibers in the optic nerve which when stimulated either inhibit or augment retinal activity. These observations establish the existence of brain mechanisms that can turn up or down the volume of afferent input by effects on the specific sensory pathways or the sense organs themselves. Some of these mechanisms are reticular, but others are not. Stimulation of the sensory cortex produces presynaptic inhibition at synaptic junctions in the gracile and cuneate nuclei. There are other inhibitory mechanisms which affect transmission in the dorsal horns, the specific thalamic nuclei, and in the cortex itself.

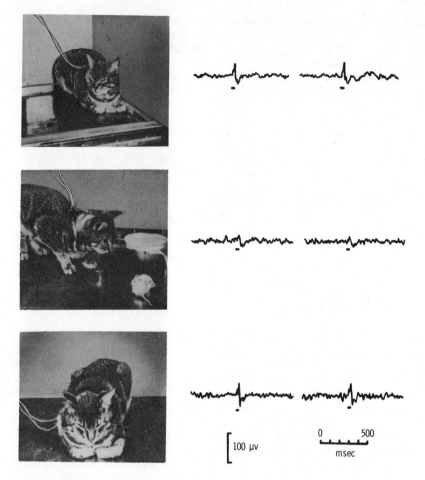

FIG 11–15. Changes in response of cochlear nucleus to repeated click stimuli (at dashes) before (top), during (middle), and after (bottom) attention is fixed on mice in a bell jar. (Reproduced, with permission, from Hernandéz-Péon, Scherrer, & Jouvet: Modification of electrical activity in cochlear nucleus during "attention." Science 123:331, 1956.)

Additional effects of brain stimulation on sensory input include the effect of epinephrine released by such stimulation in lowering the threshold of cutaneous receptors (see Chapter 5). This effect promotes maximal excitability of the receptors in the emergency states in which this hormone is released.

Some of these modulating mechanisms are brought into play when the individual's attention is focused on a particular object. In the experiment illustrated in Fig 11–15, electrodes were implanted in the cochlear nucleus of a cat. After the animal recovered, the electrical activity of the cochlear nucleus was recorded while a clicker was sounded at regular intervals. While the cat sat quietly in its cage, a spike was observed with each click. However, when the animal's attention was focused on a pair of mice placed in front of it, the click response in the cochlear nucleus practically disappeared. It returned when the mice were removed, but disappeared again when the cat's attention was attracted by the smell of fish. These observations indicate that—contrary to some theories—part of the narrowing of the field of awareness during focused attention is due to "turning off" some of the incoming stimuli before they reach the cerebral cortex.

Another example of central control of sensory input is the regulatory effect of brain centers on muscle spindle sensitivity. The effect of changes in the rate of gamma efferent discharge on the sensitivity of the spindles is described in Chapter 6. The gamma efferent neurons are subjected to both facilitatory and inhibitory influences via descending tracts in the lateral funiculus of the spinal cord. Stimulation of one part of the brain stem reticular formation facilitates gamma efferent discharge, whereas stimulation of another portion inhibits it. There are also inhibitory centers in the cerebellum, basal ganglia, and motor cortex. Their function in the regulation of body posture is discussed in the next chapter.

12...

Control of Posture & Movement

Somatic motor activity depends ultimately upon the pattern and rate of discharge of the spinal motor neurons and homologous neurons in the motor nuclei of the cranial nerves. These neurons, the final common paths to skeletal muscle, are bombarded by impulses from an immense array of pathways. There are at least 10 inputs to each spinal motor neuron from the same spinal segment (see Chapter 6). Numerous suprasegmental inputs also converge on these cells, in part via interneurons and in part via the neurons of the gamma efferent system to the muscle spindles and back through the Ia afferent fibers to the spinal cord. It is the integrated activity of these multiple inputs from spinal, medullary, midbrain, and cortical levels that regulates the posture of the body and makes coordinated movement possible.

The inputs converging on the motor neurons subserve 3 semidistinct functions: they initiate skilled, voluntary activity; they adjust body posture to provide a stable background for movement; and they coordinate the action of the various muscles to make movements smooth and precise. The first of these functions is in general that of the **pyramidal system** and the related parts of the brain that are concerned with the genesis and patterning of movement; the second is that of the multiple pathways grouped together as the **corticostrioreticular** or **extrapyramidal system**; and the third is that of the **cerebellum** with its afferent and efferent connections. Actually, this tripartite function-structure correlation is an oversimplification and may have to be modified as more information becomes available. For example, current research indicates that rapid ballistic movements (saccadic movements) may be generated in the cerebellum and that slow steady movements (ramp movements) are generated in the basal ganglia. However, from the heuristic, clinical, and pedagogic points of view, the correlation provides a useful basis for the analysis of motor function.

Encephalization

In species in which the cerebral cortex is highly developed, the process of **encephalization**, ie, the relatively greater role of the cerebral cortex in various functions, is an important phenomenon. For this reason the effects of cortical ablation in primates are generally more severe and sometimes quite different from those in cats, dogs, and other laboratory animals. Because this chapter is concerned primarily with motor function in man, pathologic and clinical observations

in humans and experiments in laboratory primates are emphasized.

Upper & Lower Motor Neurons

The motor system is commonly divided into **upper** and **lower motor neurons.** Lesions of the lower motor neurons—the spinal and cranial motor neurons that directly innervate the muscles—are associated with flaccid paralysis, muscular atrophy, and absence of reflex responses. The syndrome of spastic paralysis and hyperactive stretch reflexes in the absence of muscle atrophy is said to be due to destruction of the "upper motor neurons," the neurons in the brain and spinal cord which activate the motor neurons. However, there are 3 types of "upper motor neurons" to consider. Lesions in the extrapyramidal posture-regulating pathways do cause spastic paralysis, but lesions limited to the pyramidal tracts produce weakness (**paresis**) rather than paralysis, and the affected musculature is generally hypotonic, whereas cerebellar lesions produce incoordination. The unmodified term upper motor neuron is therefore confusing and should not be used.

PYRAMIDAL SYSTEM

ANATOMY

The nerve fibers of the pyramidal system descend in the internal capsule and pyramids from their origin in the precentral gyrus of the frontal lobe and related cortical areas. About 80% of them cross the midline in the pyramidal decussation to form the **lateral corticospinal tract**; the remainder descend as the **anterior corticospinal tract**, decussating just before their termination (Fig 12—1). Additional uncrossed corticospinal fibers may exist. There are valid anatomic objections to using the term pyramidal. However, it and the term extrapyramidal are retained in this text because of their convenience and the sanction of long clinical usage.

In most animals, the corticospinal axons do not end on the motor neurons but on interneurons. In man, however, at least 10% of them do make direct synaptic connections with the motor neurons.

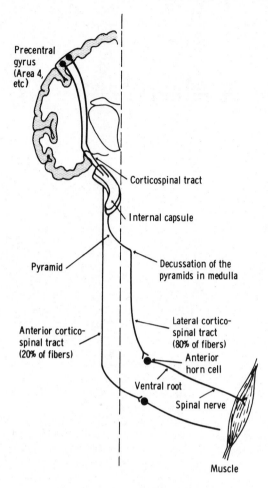

FIG 12–1. The corticospinal tracts.

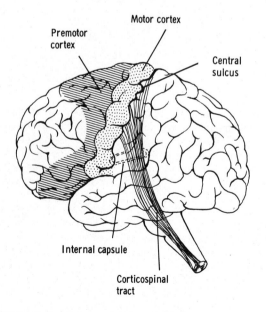

FIG 12–2. Diagram showing classical cortical motor areas.

Cortical Motor Areas

The cortical areas from which the pyramidal system originates are generally held to be those where stimulation produces prompt discrete movement. Although there is debate on the point, it is probable that individual muscles, rather than movements, are represented in the cortex. The Betz cells of layers 4 and 5 of the cortical mantle in the precentral gyrus (Brodmann's area 4) are said to be the neurons that give rise to the corticospinal fibers (Fig 12–2), but stimulation of the pyramids produces antidromic spikes not only in area 4 but also in areas 6 and 44 in front of it and even in the sensory area in the postcentral gyrus.

By means of stimulation experiments in patients undergoing craniotomy under local anesthesia, it has been possible to outline much of the cortical area from which the pyramidal system originates (Fig 12–3). The various parts of the body are represented in the precentral gyrus, with the feet at the top of the gyrus and the face at the bottom. There is evidence that the facial area is represented bilaterally, but the rest of the representation is unilateral, the cortical motor area controlling the musculature on the opposite side of the body. The cortical representation of each body part is proportionate in size to the skill with which the part is used in fine, voluntary movement. The muscles involved in speech and hand movements are especially

FIG 12–3. Motor homunculus. The figure represents, on a coronal section of the precentral gyrus, the location of the cortical representation of the various parts. The size of the various parts is proportionate to the amount of cortical area devoted to them. (Reproduced, with permission, from Penfield & Rasmussen: *The Cerebral Cortex of Man: A Clinical Study of Localization of Function.* Macmillan, 1950.)

FIG 12—4. Motor "simunculi," presenting, by the technic used in Fig 12—3, the cortical localization of motor function in the monkey. *B* is an enlarged view of *A,* the various lines representing the sulci and medial edge of the hemisphere as indicated in *A.* c = central sulcus; c′ = bottom of central sulcus; d = medial edge of hemisphere; e = sulcus cinguli; e′ = bottom of sulcus cinguli; i = inferior precentral sulcus; i′ = bottom of inferior precentral sulcus; s = superior precentral sulcus. (Reproduced, with permission, from Woolsey & others: Patterns of localization in pre-central and "supplementary" motor areas and their relation to the concept of a pre-motor area. Res Publ A Nerv Ment Dis 30:238, 1950.)

well represented in the cortex; use of the pharynx, lips, and tongue to form words, and the fingers and opposable thumbs to manipulate the environment are activities in which man is especially skilled.

The conditions under which these human studies were performed precluded stimulation of the banks of the sulci and other inaccessible areas. In monkeys, meticulous study has shown that the hand area is not interposed between the trunk and face areas (Fig 12—4). Instead, there is a regular representation of the body, with the axial musculature and the proximal portions of the limbs represented along the anterior edge of the precentral gyrus and the distal part of the limbs along the posterior edge. There is also a **supplementary motor area** of unknown significance on and above the superior bank of the cingulate sulcus on the medial side of the hemisphere (Fig 12—4). The organization of the motor cortex in man is probably similar.

Premotor Cortex

Brodmann's area 6, the region anterior to the precentral gyrus, has traditionally been called the **premotor cortex** or **premotor area** (Fig 12—2). Under certain conditions, stimulation in this region produces **adversive movements**, ie, gross rotation of the eyes, head, and trunk to the opposite side. These movements may be due to stimulation of extrapyramidal pathways, but they may also be due to intracortical spread of the stimuli to the pyramidal system. On this basis the existence of the premotor area as a separate entity has been questioned.

Other Areas

Stimulation of the frontal cortex anterior to and below area 6 causes eye movements in primates. The most common response is movement of both eyes in the same direction (**conjugate deviation**), but pupillary dilatation and nystagmus have also been observed. It is probable that this **frontal eye field** is a center concerned with integration of eye movements, but the details of the way it functions are not known. Stimulation of the occipital lobe near the visual cortex also causes conjugate deviation of the eyes to the opposite side. In primates, body movements can be evoked by stimulation of the sensory cortex in the postcentral gyrus and even by stimulation of the parietal lobe behind this region. However, these responses are probably due to impulses traveling in association fibers to the precentral motor area.

FUNCTION

Role in Movement

The pyramidal system appears to be concerned with the initiation of skilled, voluntary, fine movement. This emphatically does not mean that movement—even skilled movement—is impossible without it. Nonmammalian vertebrates have essentially no pyramidal system, but they move with great agility nonetheless. Cats and dogs stand, walk, run, and even eat if food is presented to them after complete destruction of the pyramidal system.

In primates it is difficult to produce selective disruption of pyramidal function, and this fact is responsible for much of the confusion about the role of the pyramidal system in man. Even the most circumscribed lesions in the cortical motor area destroy cells concerned with extrapyramidal and cerebellar functions. Careful surgical section of the pyramids in the medulla is probably the most selective experimental approach, but even this procedure damages other fibers.

After section of one pyramid in monkeys, the limbs on the opposite side of the body hang limply much of the time. However, they are not paralyzed. The hopping and placing postural reactions are defective (see below), but otherwise the monkey uses his limbs to maintain his posture and to right himself in the normal fashion. Furthermore, if use of the normal arm is prevented, he will occasionally reach for food and other objects with the affected arm, especially when motivation is strong. The motions lack precision; there is a loss of accuracy in the use of the digits, and a particular inability to maneuver objects into the palm of the hand, so that the grasp is clumsy. The main defects produced by destruction of the pyramidal system are therefore weakness, clumsiness, and difficulty in initiating voluntary movement.

What, then, is the role of the precentral motor cortex in skilled, voluntary movement? It appears reasonable, on the basis of present information, to hypothesize that movement patterns are generated in structures such as the basal ganglia and the cerebellum; that the patterns are modulated in the cortex in terms of the somatosensory input provided by afferents from the periphery; and that the pyramidal system is a final common path for these patterns to the spinal motor neurons. The fact that movements (such as those of the fingers) which require the most somatosensory input are most compromised by pyramidal lesions supports this hypothesis.

Effects on Stretch Reflexes

Section of the pyramids in monkeys produces prolonged hypotonia and flaccidity rather than spasticity. In man, the anatomic arrangements are such that disease processes rarely if ever damage the pyramidal system anywhere along its course without also destroying extrapyramidal posture-regulating pathways. When spasticity is present, it is probably due to damage to these latter pathways rather than to the pyramidal system itself.

Relation of Movement to Perception

If the apparent position of objects in the visual field is displaced by looking at them through prisms, an individual at first has trouble reaching for them. He gradually corrects the misreaching, but correction is not simply a result of recognizing the error and correcting it. The correction and that of other experimentally produced visual and auditory displacements have been shown to be independent of their recognition and dependent on the active movements made by the individual. Without movements no correction occurs, and passive movements fail to provide the necessary information input to the perceptual apparatus; only active movements by the subject will suffice. This indicates a close connection between the sensory areas and the motor areas concerned with active movement, but the nature of the connection is at present unknown.

EXTRAPYRAMIDAL MECHANISMS

The extrapyramidal mechanisms are integrated at various levels all the way from the spinal cord to the cerebral cortex. At the spinal cord level, afferent impulses produce simple reflex responses. At higher levels in the nervous system, neural connections of increasing complexity mediate increasingly complicated motor responses. This principle of levels of motor integration is illustrated in Table 12−1. In the intact animal, the individual motor responses are fitted into or "submerged" in the total pattern of motor activity. When the neural axis is transected, the activities integrated below the section are cut off or **released** from the "control of higher brain centers," and often appear to be accentuated. Release of this type, long a cardinal principle in neurology, may in some situations

TABLE 12−1. Summary of levels of integration of various neural functions.*

Functions	Normal	Preparation					Level of Integration
		Decorticate	Midbrain	Hindbrain (Decerebrate)	Spinal	Decerebellate	
Initiative, memory, etc	+	0	0	0	0	+	Cerebral cortex
Conditioned reflexes	+	+**	0	0	0	+	Cerebral cortex
Emotional responses	+	++	0	0	0	+	Hypothalamus, limbic system
Locomotor reflexes	+	++	+	0	0	Incoordinate	Midbrain, thalamus
Righting reflexes	+	+	++	0	0	Incoordinate	Midbrain
Antigravity reflexes	+	+	+	++	0	Incoordinate	Medulla
Respiration	+	+	+	+	0	+	Lower medulla
Spinal reflexes‡	+	+	+	+	++	+	Spinal cord

Legend: 0 = absent; + = present; ++ = accentuated.

*Modified from Cobb: *Foundations of Neuropsychiatry*, 6th ed. Williams & Wilkins, 1958.

**Conditioned reflexes can be established in decorticate animals but special technics are required.

‡Other than stretch reflexes.

be due to removal of an inhibitory control by higher neural centers. A more important cause of the apparent hyperactivity is loss of differentiation of the reaction, so that it no longer fits into the broader pattern of motor activity. An additional factor may be denervation sensitization of the centers below the transection, but the role of this component remains to be determined.

Postural Control

It is impossible to separate postural adjustments from voluntary movement in any rigid way, but it is possible to differentiate a series of postural reflexes (Table 12–2) that not only maintain the body in an upright, balanced position but also provide the constant adjustments necessary to maintain a stable postural background for voluntary activity. These adjustments include maintained **static** reflexes and dynamic, short-term **phasic** reflexes. The former involve sustained contraction of the musculature, whereas the latter involve transient movements. Both are integrated at various levels in the CNS from the spinal cord to the cerebral cortex, and are effected largely through extrapyramidal motor pathways. A major factor in postural control is variation in the threshold of the spinal stretch reflexes caused in turn by changes in the excitability of motor neurons and, indirectly, by changes in the rate of discharge in the small motor nerve system.

SPINAL INTEGRATION

The responses of animals and humans after spinal cord transection in the cervical region illustrate the integration of reflexes at the spinal level. The individual spinal reflexes are discussed in detail in Chapter 6.

Spinal Shock

In all vertebrates, transection of the spinal cord is followed by a period of **spinal shock** during which all spinal reflex responses are profoundly depressed. During it, the resting membrane potential of the spinal motor neurons is 2–6 mv greater than normal. Subsequently, reflex responses return and become relatively hyperactive. The duration of spinal shock is proportionate to the degree of encephalization of motor function in the various species. In frogs it lasts for minutes, in dogs and cats it lasts for 1–2 hours, in monkeys it lasts for days, and in man it usually lasts for a minimum of 2 weeks.

The cause of spinal shock is uncertain. Cessation of tonic bombardment of spinal neurons by excitatory impulses in descending pathways undoubtedly plays a role, but the subsequent return of reflexes and their eventual hyperactivity also need to be explained. The recovery of reflex excitability may possibly be due to the development of denervation hypersensitivity to the

TABLE 12–2. Principal postural reflexes.

Reflex	Stimulus and Receptor	Response	Center
Stretch reflexes	Stretch. Muscle spindles.	Contraction of muscle.	Spinal cord, medulla.
Positive supporting (magnet) reaction	Contact with sole or palm. Proprioceptors in distal flexors.	Foot extended to support body.	Spinal cord.
Negative supporting reaction	Stretch. Proprioceptors in extensors.	Release of positive supporting reaction.	Spinal cord.
Tonic labyrinthine reflexes	Gravity. Otolithic organs.	Extensor rigidity.	Medulla.
Tonic neck reflexes	Head turned (neck proprioceptors): (1) To side (2) Up (3) Down	Change in pattern of rigidity: (1) Extension of limbs on side to which head is turned (2) Hind legs flex (3) Forelegs flex	Medulla.
Labyrinthine righting reflexes	Gravity. Otolithic organs.	Head kept level.	Midbrain.
Neck righting reflexes	Stretch of neck muscles. Spindles.	Righting of thorax and shoulders, then pelvis.	Midbrain.
Body on head righting reflex	Pressure on side of body. Exteroceptors.	Righting of head.	Midbrain.
Body on body righting reflexes	Pressure on side of body. Exteroceptors.	Righting of body even when head held sideways.	Midbrain.
Optical righting reflexes	Visual cues.	Righting of head.	Cerebral cortex.
Placing reactions	Various visual, exteroceptive, and proprioceptive cues.	Foot placed on supporting surface in position to support body.	Cerebral cortex.
Hopping reactions	Lateral displacement while standing. Stretch receptors in muscles.	Hops, maintaining limbs in position to support body.	Cerebral cortex.

mediators released by the remaining spinal excitatory endings. Another possibility for which there is some evidence is the sprouting of collaterals from existing neurons with the formation of additional excitatory endings on interneurons and motor neurons.

In man the first reflex response to reappear as spinal shock wears off is frequently a slight contraction of the leg flexors and adductors in response to a noxious stimulus. In some patients, the knee jerks come back first. The interval between cord transection and the beginning return of reflex activity is about 2 weeks in the absence of any complications, but if complications are present it is much longer. It is not known why infection, malnutrition, and other complications of cord transection inhibit spinal reflex activity.

Complications of Cord Transection

The problems in the management of paraplegic and quadriplegic humans are complex. Like all immobilized patients, they develop a negative nitrogen balance and catabolize large amounts of body protein. The weight of the body compresses the circulation to the skin over bony prominences, so that unless the patient is moved frequently the skin breaks down at these points and **decubitus ulcers** form. The ulcers heal poorly and are prone to infection because of body protein depletion. The tissues broken down include the protein matrix of bone, and calcium is liberated in large amounts. The hypercalcemia leads to hypercalciuria, and calcium stones often form in the urinary tract. The stones and the paralysis of bladder function both cause urinary stasis, which predisposes to urinary infection. Therefore, the prognosis in patients with transected spinal cords used to be very poor, and death from septicemia, uremia, or inanition was the rule. Since World War II, however, the use of antibiotics and meticulous attention to nutrition, fluid balance, skin care, bladder function, and general nursing care have made it possible for many of these patients to survive.

Responses in Chronic Spinal Animals & Humans

Once the spinal reflexes begin to reappear after spinal shock, their threshold steadily drops. In chronically quadriplegic humans the threshold of the withdrawal reflex is especially low. Even minor noxious stimuli may cause not only prolonged withdrawal of one extremity but marked flexion-extension patterns in the other 3 limbs. Repeated flexion movements may occur for prolonged periods, and contractures of the flexor muscles develop. Stretch reflexes are also hyperactive, as are more complex reactions based on this reflex as well. For example, if a finger is placed on the sole of the foot of an animal after the spinal cord has been transected (**spinal animal**), the limb usually extends, following the examining finger. This **magnet reaction** or **positive supporting reaction** involves proprioceptive as well as tactile afferents and transforms the limb into a rigid pillar to resist gravity and support the animal. Its disappearance is also in part an active phenomenon (**negative supporting reaction**) initiated by stretch of the extensor muscles. On the basis of the positive supporting reaction, spinal cats and dogs can

be made to stand, albeit awkwardly, for as long as 2–3 minutes.

Autonomic Reflexes

Reflex contractions of the full bladder and rectum occur in spinal animals and humans, although the bladder is rarely emptied completely. Hyperactive bladder reflexes can keep the bladder in a shrunken state long enough for hypertrophy and fibrosis of its wall to occur. Blood pressure is generally normal at rest, but the precise feedback regulation normally supplied by the baroreceptor reflexes is absent and wide swings in pressure are common. Bouts of sweating and blanching of the skin also occur.

The intermediolateral gray columns of the spinal cord are relatively rich in norepinephrine and serotonin. Seven days after cord section in rabbits, when the autonomic reflexes are hyperactive, the norepinephrine and serotonin content of the spinal cord below the transection is markedly reduced. These observations suggest that norepinephrine and serotonin are mediators in descending pathways which normally inhibit autonomic function.

Sexual Reflexes

Other reflex responses are present in the spinal animal, but in general they are only fragments of patterns that are integrated in the normal animal into purposeful sequences. The sexual reflexes are an example. Coordinated sexual activity depends upon a series of reflexes integrated at many neural levels, and is absent after cord transection. However, genital manipulation in the male spinal animal and human will produce erection and even ejaculation. In the female spinal dog, vaginal stimulation causes tail deviation and movement of the pelvis into the copulatory position.

Mass Reflex

In chronic spinal animals, afferent stimuli irradiate from one reflex center to another. When even a relatively minor noxious stimulus is applied to the skin, it may irradiate to autonomic centers and produce evacuation of the bladder and rectum, sweating, pallor, and blood pressure swings in addition to the withdrawal response. This distressing **mass reflex** can sometimes be used to give paraplegic patients a degree of bladder and bowel control. They can be trained to initiate urination and defecation by stroking or pinching their thighs, thus producing an intentional mild mass reflex.

MEDULLARY COMPONENTS

In experimental animals in which the hindbrain and spinal cord are isolated from the rest of the brain by transection of the brain stem at the superior border of the pons, the most prominent finding is marked spasticity of the body musculature. The operative procedure is called **decerebration,** and the resulting pattern of spasticity is called **decerebrate rigidity.** Decerebration produces no phenomenon akin to spinal shock, and the rigidity develops as soon as the brain stem is transected. Flexor and extensor muscles are both involved, but in the dog and cat the spasticity is most prominent in the extensor muscles. This produces the characteristic posture of decerebration: neck and limbs extended, back arched, and tail elevated.

Mechanism of Decerebrate Rigidity

On analysis, decerebrate rigidity is found to be due to a diffuse facilitation of stretch reflexes. The facilitation is due to 2 factors: increased general excitability of the motor neuron pool and increase in the rate of discharge in the gamma efferent neurons.

Supraspinal Regulation of Stretch Reflexes

The brain areas which facilitate and inhibit stretch reflexes are shown in Fig 12–5. Except for the vestibular nuclei, these areas act by increasing or decreasing spindle sensitivity (Fig 12–6). The large facilitatory area in the brain stem reticular formation discharges spontaneously, possibly in response to afferent input like the reticular activating system. However, the smaller brain stem area which inhibits gamma efferent discharge does not discharge spontaneously but is driven instead by fibers from the cerebral cortex and the cerebellum. The inhibitory area in the basal ganglia may act through descending connections, as shown in Fig 12–5, or by stimulating the cortical inhibitory center. From the reticular inhibitory and facilitatory areas, impulses descend in the lateral funiculus of the spinal cord. When the brain stem is transected at the level of the top of the pons, 2 of the 3 inhibitory areas that drive the reticular inhibi-

Intact Excited Inhibited De-efferented

2 mm

3–5 mm

8 mm

13 mm

50 hz

FIG 12–6. Response of single afferent fiber from muscle spindle dorsal root to various degrees of muscle stretch. Figures at left indicate amount of stretch. The upward deflections are action potentials; the downward deflections are stimulus artifacts. Records were obtained before brain stimulation (first column), during stimulation of brain areas facilitating (second column) and inhibiting (third column) stretch reflexes, and after section of the motor nerve (fourth column). (Reproduced, with permission, from Eldred, Granit, & Merton: Supraspinal control of muscle spindles. J Physiol 122:498, 1953.)

tory center are removed. Discharge of the facilitatory area continues, but that of the inhibitory area is decreased. Consequently, the balance of facilitatory and inhibitory impulses converging on the gamma efferent neurons shifts toward facilitation. Gamma efferent discharge is increased, and stretch reflexes become hyperactive. The cerebellar inhibitory area is still present, and in decerebrate animals removal of the cerebellum increases the rigidity. The influence of the cerebellum is complex, however, and destruction of the cerebellum in man produces hypotonia rather than spasticity.

The vestibulospinal pathways are also facilitatory to stretch reflexes and promote rigidity. Unlike the reticular pathways, they pass primarily in the anterior funiculus of the spinal cord, and the rigidity due to increased discharge in them is not abolished by deafferentation of the muscles. This indicates that this rigidity is due to a direct action on the motor neurons rather than an effect mediated through the small motor nerve system which would, of course, be blocked by deafferentation.

Significance of Decerebrate Rigidity

Sherrington pointed out that the extensor muscles are those with which the cat and dog resist gravity; the decerebrate posture in these animals is, as he put it, "a caricature of the normal standing position." What has been uncovered by decerebration, then, are the tonic, static postural reflex mechanisms that support the animal against gravity. Additional evidence that this is the correct interpretation of the phenomenon comes from the observation that decerebration in the sloth, an arboreal animal which hangs upside down

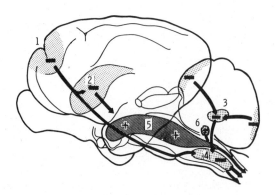

FIG 12–5. Areas in the cat brain where stimulation produces facilitation (plus signs) or inhibition (minus signs) of stretch reflexes. *1,* motor cortex; *2,* basal ganglia; *3,* cerebellum; *4,* reticular inhibitory area; *5,* reticular facilitatory area; *6,* vestibular nuclei. (Reproduced, with permission, from Lindsley, Schreiner, & Magoun: An electromyographic study of spasticity. J Neurophysiol 12:197, 1949.)

from branches most of the time, causes rigidity in flexion. In man, the pattern in true decerebrate rigidity is extensor in all 4 limbs, like that in the cat and dog. Apparently man is not far enough removed from his quadruped ancestors to have changed the pattern in his upper extremities even though the main antigravity muscles of the arms in the upright position are flexors. However, decerebrate rigidity in man is rare and the defects which produce it are usually incompatible with life. The more common pattern of extensor rigidity in the legs and moderate flexion in the arms is actually **decorticate rigidity** due to lesions of the cerebral cortex, with most of the brain stem intact (Fig 12–7).

FIG 12–7. Decorticate rigidity *(A–C)* **and true decerebrate rigidity** *(D)* **in man.** In *A* the patient is lying supine with head unturned. In *B* and *C,* the tonic neck reflex patterns produced by turning of the head to the right or left are shown. (Reproduced, with permission, from: *Textbook of Physiology,* 17th ed. Fulton JF [editor]. Saunders, 1955.)

Tonic Labyrinthine Reflexes

In the decerebrate animal the pattern of rigidity in the limbs varies with the position. No righting responses are present, and the animal stays in the position in which it is put. If the animal is placed on its back, the extension of all 4 limbs is maximal. As the animal is turned to either side, the rigidity decreases, and when it is prone the rigidity is minimal though still present. These changes in rigidity, the **tonic labyrinthine reflexes,** are initiated by the action of gravity on the otolithic organs and are effected via the vestibulospinal tracts. They are rather surprising in view of the role of rigidity in standing, and their exact physiologic significance remains obscure.

Tonic Neck Reflexes

If the head of a decerebrate animal is moved relative to the body, changes in the pattern of rigidity occur. If the head is turned to one side, the limbs on that side ("jaw limbs") become more rigidly extended while the contralateral limbs become less so. This is the position often assumed by a normal animal looking to one side. Flexion of the head causes flexion of the forelimbs and continued extension of the hindlimbs, the posture of an animal looking into a hole in the ground. Extension of the head causes flexion of the hindlimbs and extension of the forelimbs, the posture of an animal looking over an obstacle. These responses are the **tonic neck reflexes.** They are initiated by stretch of the proprioceptors in the upper part of the neck, and they can be sustained for long periods of time.

MIDBRAIN COMPONENTS

After section of the neural axis at the superior border of the midbrain **(midbrain animal),** extensor rigidity like that seen in the decerebrate animal is present only when the animal lies quietly on its back. In the decerebrate animal the rigidity, which is a static postural reflex, is prominent because there are no modifying phasic postural reflexes. Chronic midbrain preparations can rise to the standing position, walk, and right themselves. While the animals are engaged in these phasic activities, the static phenomenon of rigidity is not seen.

Righting Reflexes

All higher animals have righting reflexes that operate to maintain their normal standing position and keep their heads upright. These are a series of responses integrated for the most part in the nuclei of the midbrain.

When a midbrain animal is held by its body and tipped from side to side, the head stays level in response to the **labyrinthine righting reflexes.** The stimulus is tilting of the head, which stimulates the otolithic organs; the response is compensatory contraction of the neck muscles to keep the head level. If the animal is laid on its side, the pressure on that side of the body initiates reflex righting of the head even if the labyrinths have been destroyed. This is the **body on head righting reflex.** If the head is righted by either of these mechanisms and the body remains tilted, the neck muscles are stretched. Their contraction rights the thorax and initiates a wave of similar stretch reflexes which pass down the body, righting the abdomen and the hind quarters **(neck righting reflexes).** Pressure on the side of the body may cause body righting even if the head is prevented from righting **(body on body righting reflex).**

In cats, dogs, and primates, visual cues can initiate **optical righting reflexes** which right the animal in the absence of labyrinthine or body stimulation. Unlike the other righting reflexes, these responses depend upon an intact cerebral cortex.

Grasp Reflex

When a primate in which the brain tissue above the thalamus has been removed lies on its side, the limbs next to the supporting surface are extended. The upper limbs are flexed, and the hand on the upper side grasps firmly any object brought in contact with it (**grasp reflex**). This whole response is probably a supporting reaction that steadies the animal and aids in pulling him upright.

Other Midbrain Responses

Animals with intact midbrains show pupillary light reflexes if the optic nerves are also intact. Nystagmus, the reflex response to rotational acceleration described in Chapter 9, is also present. If a blindfolded animal is lowered rapidly, its forelegs extend and its toes spread. This response to linear acceleration is a **vestibular placing reaction** which prepares the animal to land on the floor.

CORTICAL COMPONENTS

Effects of Decortication

Removal of the cerebral cortex (**decortication**) produces little motor deficit in lower mammals. In primates the deficit is more severe, but a great deal of movement is still possible. Decorticate animals have all the reflex patterns of midbrain animals, and the responses generally are present in the immediate postoperative period whereas in midbrain preparations they take 2–3 weeks to appear. This suggests that centers between the top of the midbrain and the cerebral cortex facilitate brain stem reflexes. In addition, decorticate animals are easier to maintain than midbrain animals because temperature regulation and other visceral homeostatic mechanisms integrated in the hypothalamus (see Chapter 14) are present. The most striking defect is inability to react in terms of past experience. With certain special types of training, conditioned reflexes can be established in the absence of the cerebral cortex, but under normal laboratory conditions there is no evidence that learning or conditioning occurs.

Decorticate Rigidity

Moderate rigidity is present in the decorticate animal as a result of the loss of the cortical area that inhibits gamma efferent discharge via the reticular formation. Like the rigidity present after transection of the neural axis anywhere above the top of the midbrain, this **decorticate rigidity** is obscured by phasic postural reflexes and is only seen when the animal is at rest. Decorticate rigidity is seen on the hemiplegic side in man after hemorrhages or thromboses in the internal

capsule. Probably because of their anatomy, the small arteries in the internal capsule are especially prone to rupture or thrombotic obstruction, so this type of decorticate rigidity is common.

Suppressor Areas

The exact site of origin in the cerebral cortex of the fibers that inhibit stretch reflexes is a subject of debate. Under certain experimental conditions, stimulation of the anterior edge of the precentral gyrus is said to cause inhibition of stretch reflexes and cortically evoked movements. This region, which also projects to the basal ganglia, has been named area 4s, or the **suppressor strip**. Four other suppressor regions (Brodmann's areas 2, 8, 19, and 24) have also been described. However, the stimulation experiments on which the hypothesis of discrete suppressor areas is based have not been uniformly confirmed. Ablation of area 4s does cause spasticity in the trunk and proximal limb muscles of the contralateral side of the body, but destruction of the caudal part of area 4 produces spasticity in the distal limb muscles. Mapping experiments show that the musculature of the trunk and proximal portions of the limbs is represented in the anterior portion of the precentral gyrus, whereas that of the distal portions is represented posteriorly. It is therefore probable that the inhibitory fibers originate with the pyramidal fibers from all of the precentral motor area and that the distribution of the spasticity produced by lesions in this area depends upon the particular portion of the motor cortex destroyed.

Placing & Hopping Reactions

Two types of postural reactions are seriously disrupted by decortication, the **hopping** and **placing reactions**. The former are the hopping movements that keep the limbs in position to support the body when a standing animal is pushed laterally. The latter are the reactions that place the foot firmly on a supporting surface. They can be initiated in a blindfolded animal held suspended in the air by touching the supporting surface with any part of the foot. Similarly, when the snout or vibrissae of a suspended animal touch a table, the animal immediately places both forepaws on the table; and if one limb of a standing animal is pulled out from under it the limb is promptly replaced on the supporting surface. The vestibular placing reaction has already been mentioned. In cats, dogs, and primates, the limbs are extended to support the body when the animal is lowered toward a surface it can see. These various placing reactions are abolished on one side by unilateral decortication, but some of them reappear after subsequent removal of the other hemisphere. This casts doubt on the claim that they are entirely dependent upon an intact motor cortex, but this portion of the brain is certainly important in their regulation.

BASAL GANGLIA

Anatomic Considerations

The term **basal ganglia** is generally applied to the **caudate nucleus, putamen,** and **globus pallidus**—the 3 large nuclear masses underlying the cortical mantle (Fig 12–8)—and the functionally related **subthalamic nucleus** (body of Luys), **substantia nigra,** and **red nucleus** on each side. Parts of the thalamus are intimately related to this system, but the claustrum and the amygdala probably are not properly included although they have been in some classifications. The caudate nucleus and the putamen are sometimes called the **striatum;** the putamen and the globus pallidus are sometimes called the **lenticular nucleus** (Table 12–3).

The interconnections of these nuclei are complex (Fig 12–9). On each side, the caudate nucleus projects in part to the putamen, the putamen to the globus pallidus, and the globus pallidus via the **ansa lenticularis,** the major efferent pathway from the lenticular nucleus, to the thalamus, subthalamic nuclei, red nuclei, and other structures. There is considerable evidence for a feedback circuit that projects from the motor cortex to the caudate nucleus and from there back to the cortex via the lenticular nucleus, the ansa lenticularis, and the ventrolateral nuclei of the thalamus. There is a prominent system of dopaminergic neurons that project from the substantia nigra to the striatum (nigrostriatal pathway; see Chapter 15).

Metabolic Considerations

The metabolism of the basal ganglia is unique in a

TABLE 12–3. The basal ganglia.

Lenticular nucleus	Caudate nucleus	Striatum (neostriatum)
	Putamen	
	Globus pallidus (pallidum)	

Subthalamic nucleus (body of Luys)
Substantia nigra
Red nucleus

number of ways. These structures have an O_2 consumption per gram of tissue which in dogs exceeds that of the cerebral cortex (see Chapter 32). The copper content of the substantia nigra and the nearby locus ceruleus is particularly high. In Wilson's disease, a familial disorder of copper metabolism in which the plasma copper-binding protein, **ceruloplasmin,** is usually low, there is severe degeneration of the lenticular nucleus.

Function

The precise functions of the basal ganglia are a physiologic enigma. In birds, reptiles, and other animals in which the motor cortex is rudimentary or absent, these nuclear masses are prominent and take the place of a motor cortex. Removal of the striatum and pallidum in decorticate animals does not produce any additional gross impairment in motor function. Stimulation studies in animals have generally produced

FIG 12–8. The basal ganglia. AC: anterior commissure. OC: optic chiasm.

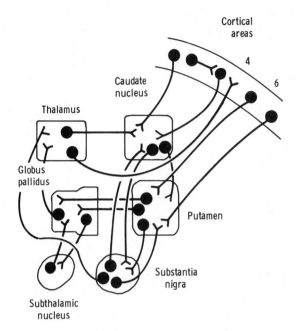

FIG 12—9. Some of the interconnections of the cerebral cortex and basal ganglia. (Modified from Carman: Anatomic basis of surgical treatment of Parkinson's disease. New England J Med 279:919, 1968. Courtesy of Little, Brown, Inc.)

negative results, although stimulation of the caudate nucleus inhibits stretch reflexes. This inhibition is probably mediated by activation of the cortical inhibitory areas through the thalamocortical feedback pathways. Stimulation of the globus pallidus and caudate nucleus also inhibits movements evoked by cortical stimulation. More recently, it has been shown that some neurons in the basal ganglia fire throughout slow, steady ramp movements and are silent during rapid saccadic movements. Thus, it appears that the basal ganglia are involved in the regulation of movement. The abnormalities in humans with basal ganglion disease also support this hypothesis.

Diseases of the Basal Ganglia in Man

Disorders of movement associated with diseases of the basal ganglia in man are of 2 general types: **hyperkinetic** and **hypokinetic**. The hyperkinetic conditions, those in which there is excessive and abnormal movement, include chorea, athetosis, and ballism. In Parkinson's disease, there are both hyperkinetic and hypokinetic features.

Hyperkinetic Disorders

Chorea is associated with degeneration of the caudate nucleus. It is characterized by rapid, involuntary "dancing" movements that may be a mixture of unrelated or conflicting cortical automatisms. **Athetosis** is due to lesions in the lenticular nucleus and is characterized by continuous slow, writhing movements

that may be tonic avoiding or grasping reactions. In **ballism**, the involuntary movements are flailing, intense, and violent. They appear when the subthalamic nuclei are damaged, and a sudden onset of the movements on one side of the body **(hemiballism)** due to hemorrhage in the contralateral subthalamic nucleus is one of the most dramatic syndromes in clinical medicine.

Parkinson's Disease (Paralysis Agitans)

In the syndrome originally described by James Parkinson and named for him, there are pathologic changes in the nigrostriatal system of dopaminergic neurons. Parkinsonism was a common late complication of the type of influenza that was epidemic during World War I, and it occurs also in patients with cerebral arteriosclerosis. It is now being seen as a complication of treatment with the phenothiazine group of tranquilizer drugs. The hallmarks of parkinsonism are **akinesia** or **poverty of movement** (a hypokinetic feature) and the hyperkinetic features **rigidity** and **tremor.** The absence of motor activity can be quite striking. There is difficulty in initiating voluntary movements, and there is also a decrease in **associated movements,** the normal, unconscious movements such as swinging of the arms during walking, the panorama of facial expressions related to the emotional content of thought and speech, and the multiple "fidgety" actions and gestures that occur in all of us. The rigidity is different from spasticity. In parkinsonism the stretch reflexes are normal. Passive motion of an extremity meets with a plastic, dead-feeling resistance that has been likened to bending a lead pipe and is therefore called **lead-pipe rigidity.** Sometimes there is a series of "catches" during passive motion (**cogwheel rigidity**), but the sudden loss of resistance seen in a spastic extremity is absent. The tremor, which is present at rest and disappears with activity, is due to regular, alternating, 8/sec contractions of antagonistic muscles.

It has been difficult to reproduce parkinsonism by means of lesions in laboratory animals. An interesting feature of the syndrome in man is the fact that even though it is due to lesions in parts of the basal ganglia, further destruction of these nuclei and other motor systems often brings about clinical improvement. Ablation of the motor cortex, section of the cerebral peduncles, posterolateral spinal cordotomy, destruction of the medial part of the globus pallidus, interruption of the ansa lenticularis, and lesions of the ventrolateral nucleus of the thalamus produced by electrocoagulation or the injection of alcohol (chemopallidectomy, etc) have all been reported to diminish the rigidity and the tremor. The low dopamine content of the basal ganglia in this disease and its treatment with levodopa and anticholinergic agents are discussed in Chapter 15.

Conclusion

The experimental and clinical data described above suggest that the basal ganglia function in some way to prevent oscillation and afterdischarge in motor systems. Recent evidence indicates that they play a role in the genesis of movement. They are also involved in the control of stretch reflexes and possibly in the generation of mannerisms and automatisms. Except for these necessarily vague speculations, however, the functions of the basal ganglia remain unclear.

CEREBELLUM

The cerebellum is concerned primarily with the coordination, adjustment, and smoothing out of movement. It receives afferent impulses from the motor cortex, proprioceptors, cutaneous tactile receptors, auditory and visual receptors, and even visceral receptors, but the way that it affects movement is uncertain.

ANATOMIC & FUNCTIONAL DIVISIONS

Orientation

The cerebellum sits astride the main sensory and motor systems in the brain stem (Fig 12–10). It is connected to the brain stem on each side by a **superior peduncle** (brachium conjunctivum), **middle peduncle** (brachium pontis), and **inferior peduncle** (restiform body). The medial **vermis** and lateral **cerebellar hemi-**

FIG 12–10. Diagrammatic representation of the principal parts of the brain. The parts are distorted to show the cerebellar peduncles and the way the cerebellum, pons, and middle peduncle form a napkin ring around the brain stem. (Reproduced, with permission, from: *Gray's Anatomy of the Human Body,* 27th ed. Goss CM [editor]. Lea & Febiger, 1959.)

spheres are more extensively folded and fissured than the cerebral cortex; the cerebellum weighs only 10% as much as the cerebral cortex, but its surface area is about 75% of that of the cerebral cortex.

The names given to the various lobes and lobules of the cerebellum by various authors are confusing. From a phylogenetic point of view, there are 10 primary lobules in the vermis. These are numbered I–X from superior to inferior in Fig 12–11.

Histology

The **cerebellar cortex** consists of an external, 3-layered gray mantle separated by white matter from the deep **cerebellar nuclei.** Many afferent nerve fibers enter the cortex and relay impulses through **granule cells** to the very extensive dendritic processes of the **Purkinje cells** (Fig 12–12). Others (the climbing fibers) connect directly to Purkinje cells. Granule cells also synapse on **basket cells** which diverge to many Purkinje cells. From the cerebellar cortex, impulses pass along the axons of the Purkinje cells to the deep nuclei, the **fastigial nuclei** receiving fibers from the vermis, the **globose** and **emboliform nuclei** receiving fibers from the medial part of the hemispheres, and the **dentate nuclei** receiving fibers from the lateral hemispheric areas. These nuclei project in turn to the brain stem.

Afferent & Efferent Cerebellar Connections

The major afferent pathways to the cerebellum are listed in Table 12–4. Impulses from proprioceptors in muscles, tendons, and joints and from cutaneous, visceral, visual, and auditory receptors reach the cerebellar cortex through the inferior and superior peduncles. Through the pons, impulses from the motor portion of the cerebral cortex are distributed to all parts of the cerebellar cortex except the flocculonodular lobes. The efferent pathways via the Purkinje cell axons and the deep cerebellar nuclei enter the brain stem. The fastigial nuclei project to the reticular formation via the fastigiobulbar tract. Pathways from the dentate, emboliform, and globose nuclei ascend in the superior peduncle to end in the red nuclei and other portions of the midbrain. They also ascend to the ventrolateral nucleus of the thalamus, which in turn projects to area 4 and related portions of the cerebral cortex (Fig 12–13). These latter fibers thus complete a feedback loop between the motor cortex and the cerebellum.

Functional Localization

On phylogenetic grounds the cerebellum can be divided into 3 parts: the flocculonodular lobe, or **archicerebellum;** the **paleocerebellum,** sometimes called the "physiologic anterior lobe"; and the **neocerebellum,** or "physiologic posterior lobe." It was thought for some time that the flocculonodular lobe had exclusively vestibular connections and functions; that the paleocerebellum had proprioceptive connections and was concerned with the regulation of stretch reflexes; and that the neocerebellum received the corticopontocerebellar fibers from the motor cortex and functioned in

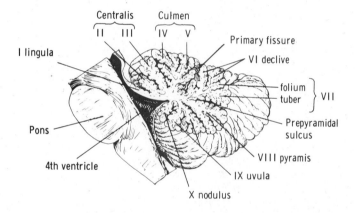

MIDSAGITTAL SECTION

FIG 12–11. Superior and inferior views and sagittal section of the human cerebellum. The 10 principal lobules are identified by name and by number (I–X), on the basis of the comparative studies of the mammalian cerebellum by Larsell: The cerebellum of the cat and monkey. J Comp Neurol 99:135, 1953. (Modified from Chusid JG: *Correlative Neuroanatomy and Functional Neurology,* 15th ed. Lange, 1973.)

the coordination of voluntary movement. However, this outline of the connections and functions of the paleocerebellum and neocerebellum must be revised. The corticopontocerebellar fibers project not only to the neocerebellum but also to the whole cerebellar cortex except for the flocculonodular lobe. Furthermore, cerebellar control of stretch reflexes cannot be clearly separated from control of voluntary movement; the 2 are intimately related and are controlled from the same cerebellar areas. It now appears that folia I–VI plus the pyramis and the paramedian lobules on the inferior surface of the cerebellum are a functional unit concerned generally with movement. The folium and tuber and the associated ansiform lobules in the hemispheres are also related in some way to movement. The function of the flocculonodular lobe is vestibular. The function of the uvula and paraflocculus has not been settled.

TABLE 12—4. Function and major terminations of the principal afferent systems to the cerebellum.

Afferent Tracts	Transmits	Distribution	Peduncle by Which Enters Cerebellum
Dorsal spinocerebellar	Proprioceptive and exteroceptive impulses	Folia I–VI, pyramis and paramedian lobule	Inferior
Ventral spinocerebellar	Proprioceptive and exteroceptive impulses	Folia I–VI, pyramis and paramedian lobule	Superior
External arcuate	Proprioceptive impulses, especially from head and neck	Folia I–VI, pyramis and paramedian lobule	Inferior
Tectocerebellar	Auditory and visual impulses via inferior and superior colliculi	Folium, tuber, ansiform lobule	Superior
Vestibulocerebellar	Vestibular impulses from labyrinths direct and via vestibular nuclei	Principally flocculonodular lobe	Inferior
Pontocerebellar	Impulses from motor and other parts of cerebral cortex via pontine nuclei	All cerebellar cortex except flocculonodular lobe	Middle
Olivocerebellar	?	All cerebellar cortex and deep nuclei	Superior

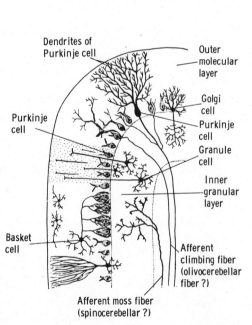

FIG 12–12. Cross-section of a folium of the cerebellum, showing cellular connections. (Reproduced, with permission, from Wyburn: *The Nervous System.* Academic Press, 1960.)

FIG 12–13. Corticopontocerebellar system.

PHYSIOLOGY

Flocculonodular Lobe

The phylogenetically oldest part of the cerebellum, the **flocculonodular lobe,** consists of the central **nodule** and lateral **flocculus** on either side. Its connections are essentially all vestibular. Animals in which it has been destroyed walk in a staggering fashion on a broad base. They tend to fall and are reluctant to move without support. Similar defects are seen in children as the earliest signs of a midline cerebellar tumor called a medulloblastoma. This malignant tumor arises from cell rests in the nodule and early in its course produces damage that is generally localized to the flocculonodular lobe.

Motion Sickness

Selective ablation of the flocculonodular lobe in dogs abolishes the syndrome of **motion sickness,** whereas extensive lesions in other parts of the cerebellum and the rest of the brain fail to affect it. This "disease," an ubiquitous if minor complication of modern travel, is a consequence of excessive and repetitive labyrinthine stimulation due to the motion of a vehicle. It can be controlled in man, of course, by a number of antiemetic tranquilizing drugs without recourse to surgery.

Uvula & Paraflocculus

According to some authors, the uvula and paraflocculus are part of the cerebellar area coordinating movement. Although the uvula is a constant anatomic feature throughout the phylogenetic scale, the paraflocculus is variable in size. It is rudimentary or absent in most terrestrial animals, including man, but it is large in aquatic diving mammals. It may play some role in the extensive reflex adjustments necessary for diving.

Folium, Tuber, & Ansiform Lobules

Auditory and visual stimuli evoke electrical responses in the folium, tuber, and ansiform lobules, and often in the adjoining portion of the lobulus simplex. This portion of the cerebellum is neocerebellar, and its size parallels the growth of the cerebral cortex. It is very large in primates, and the ansiform lobules make up a large part of the cerebellar hemispheres in man. The auditory and visual impulses apparently reach the cerebellum via the tectocerebellar tract from the inferior and superior colliculi. Each stimulus causes a response in 2 areas: one in the tuber (area II in Fig 12–14) and another in the folium and adjacent areas (area I in Fig 12–14). The significance of this elaborate projection is far from clear. Stimulation of the region produces turning of the head and eyes to the ipsilateral side. Localized lesions of the region gener-

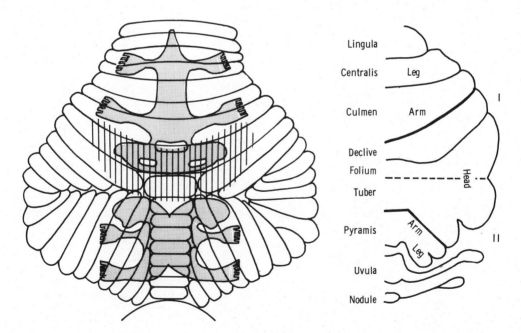

FIG 12–14. *Left:* Cerebellar homunculi. Proprioceptive and tactile stimuli are projected as shown in the figure above and the split figure below. The striped area represents the region from which evoked responses to auditory and visual stimuli are observed. (Redrawn and reproduced, with permission, from: The cerebellum, by Snider. Scientific American 199:84 [Aug], 1958. Copyright © 1958 by Scientific American, Inc. All rights reserved.) *Right:* Projection of the body on the cerebellum. Areas I and II (above and below the dotted line) are the 2 areas where auditory and visual stimuli are projected. (Redrawn and reproduced, with permission, from Hampson & others: Cerebro-cerebellar projections and the somatotopic localization of motor function in the cerebellum. Res Publ A Nerv Ment Dis 30:299, 1950.)

ally have little effect, although it has been reported that monkeys with such lesions crash into walls while running in spite of excellent vision and good coordination. These observations suggest that this part of the cerebellum is concerned in some way with integrating visual and auditory input with motor function.

Folia I–VI, Pyramis, & Paramedian Lobules

The portions of the cerebellum most concerned with the adjustment of posture and movement are folia I–VI of the vermis and their associated areas in the hemispheres plus the pyramis and the paramedian lobules. These areas receive impulses from the motor cortex via the pons. They also receive proprioceptive input from the entire body, as well as tactile and other sensory impulses. In both the superior (folia I–VI) and inferior (paramedian) areas, there is a point-for-point projection of peripheral sensory receptors, so that homunculi can be plotted on the cerebellar surface (Fig 12–14).

Effects on Stretch Reflexes

Stimulation of the cerebellar areas that receive proprioceptive input sometimes inhibits and sometimes facilitates movements evoked by stimulation of the cerebral cortex. In resting animals, cerebellar stimulation leads to changes in muscle tone through variations in the rate of gamma efferent discharge. Stretch reflexes are usually inhibited, especially if the site of stimulation is near the midline. However, more lateral stimuli may augment spasticity, and the response also varies with the parameters of stimulation. Lesions in folia I–VI and the paramedian areas in experimental animals cause spasticity localized to the part of the body that is represented in the part of the cerebellum destroyed. In man, however, hypotonia is characteristic of cerebellar destruction.

Effects on Movement

Except for the changes in stretch reflexes, animals with cerebellar lesions show no abnormalities as long as they are at rest. However, pronounced abnormalities are apparent when they move. There is no paralysis. and no sensory deficit, but all movements are characterized by a marked **ataxia,** a defect defined as incoordination due to errors in the rate, range, force, and direction of movement. With circumscribed lesions, the ataxia may be localized to one part of the body. If only the cortex of the cerebellum is involved, the movement abnormalities gradually disappear as **compensation** occurs. Lesions of the cerebellar nuclei produce more generalized defects, and the abnormalities are permanent.

Defects Produced by Cerebellar Lesions in Man

The signs of cerebellar deficit in man provide additional illustrations of the importance of the cerebellar mechanisms in the control of movement. The defects may be localized if the pathologic process is localized. Compensation for the effects of cortical lesions occurs in man and animals, but compensation

for the effects of lesions in the cerebellar nuclei does not occur. For this reason, care should be taken to avoid damaging the nuclei when surgical removal of parts of the cerebellum is necessary.

The hypotonia and the early symptoms of relatively selective destruction of the flocculonodular lobe have been mentioned above. The common denominator of most cerebellar signs in man and animals is inappropriate rate, range, force, and direction of movement. Ataxia is manifest not only in the wide-based, unsteady, "drunken" gait of patients but also in defects of the skilled movements involved in the production of speech, so that slurred or **scanning speech** results. Other voluntary movements are also highly abnormal. For example, if the patient attempts to touch an object with his finger his motion toward the object overshoots to one side or the other. This **dysmetria** or **past-pointing** promptly initiates a gross corrective action, but the correction overshoots to the other side. Consequently, the finger oscillates back and forth, and the farther it travels the greater the excursions become. This oscillation is the **intention tremor** of cerebellar disease. Unlike the resting tremor of parkinsonism, it is absent at rest; however, it appears whenever the patient attempts to perform some voluntary action. Another characteristic of cerebellar disease is inability to "put on the brakes," to stop movement promptly. For example, if a normal subject flexes his forearm against resistance and the resistance is suddenly released, movement of the limb is quickly checked. The patient with cerebellar disease cannot brake the movement, and the released forearm flies backward in a wide arc. This abnormal response is known as the **rebound phenomenon,** and similar impairment is detectable in other motor activities. This is one of the important reasons these patients show **adiadokokinesia,** the inability to perform rapidly alternating opposite movements such as repeated pronation and supination of the hands. Finally, patients with cerebellar disease have difficulty performing actions that involve simultaneous motion at more than one joint. They dissect such movements and carry them out one joint at a time, a phenomenon known as **decomposition of movement.**

Nature of Cerebellar Control

Movement depends not only on the coordinated activity of the muscles primarily responsible for the movement (**agonists** or **protagonists**) but also on that of **antagonistic** muscles, **synergistic** muscles, and muscles that anchor various parts of the body to form a base for movement (**fixation** muscles). Phasic reflex responses as well as skilled voluntary motion require a delicately adjusted interaction of all these muscles. Organizing this "cooperation in movement" has generally been regarded to be the function of the cerebellum.

In general terms, the motor cortex projects to the cerebellum and the cerebellum in turn projects to the cerebral cortex via the ventrolateral nucleus of the thalamus. The basal ganglia, the cerebral cortex, and the

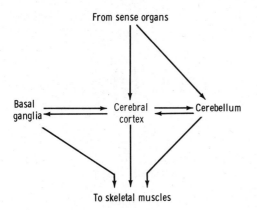

FIG 12—15. **Relationships between the cerebellum, cerebral cortex, and basal ganglia.**

cerebellum project to the skeletal muscles via the motor neurons of the spinal cord and the brain stem (Fig 12—15). The cerebral cortex and the cerebellum receive input from the sense organs. It has generally been held that whenever a "command" goes out over the pyramidal system, a signal also passes to the cerebellum. This hypothesis holds that, by continuous comparison of the command to the actual performance, motion is adjusted and perfected so that it is precise

and smooth. However, the concept of a feedback or stabilizing comparator circuit of this sort has been challenged. It now appears that the cerebellum is involved in the generation of rapid, ballistic movements (saccadic movements) and that these movements, unlike slow ramp movements, are not subject to feedback control. Instead, it has been hypothesized that it is the function of the cerebellar cortex to convert the energies needed for different movements into the requisite different durations of action potential trains to the motor neurons. This interesting concept—that the cerebellar cortex functions as a clock preprogramming the duration of fast movements—should stimulate additional research into the problem of how the cerebellum exerts its effects on movement.

The relation of the electrical events in the cerebellum to its function in motor control is another interesting problem. The cerebellar cortex has a basic, 150—300/sec, 200 μv electrical rhythm and, superimposed on this, a 1000—2000/sec component of smaller amplitude. The frequency of the basic rhythm is thus more than 10 times as great as that of the similarly recorded cerebral cortical EEG, and the amplitude is considerably less. Incoming stimuli generally alter the amplitude of the cerebellar rhythm, like a broadcast signal modulating a carrier frequency in radio transmission. However, the significance of these electrical phenomena in terms of cerebellar function is not known.

13...

Efferent Pathways to Visceral Effectors

The autonomic nervous system, like the somatic nervous system, is organized on the basis of the reflex arc. Impulses initiated in visceral receptors are relayed via afferent autonomic pathways to the CNS, integrated within it at various levels, and transmitted via efferent pathways to visceral effectors. This organization deserves emphasis because the functionally important afferent components have often been ignored. The visceral receptors and afferent pathways have been considered in Chapters 5 and 7, and the major autonomic effector, smooth muscle, in Chapter 3. The efferent pathways to the viscera are the subject of this chapter. Autonomic integration in the CNS is considered in Chapter 14.

ANATOMIC ORGANIZATION OF AUTONOMIC OUTFLOW

The peripheral motor portions of the autonomic nervous system are made up of **preganglionic** and **post-**ganglionic neurons (Figs 13–1 and 13–2). The cell bodies of the preganglionic neurons are located in the visceral efferent (lateral gray) column of the spinal cord or the homologous motor nuclei of the cranial nerves. Their axons are mostly myelinated, relatively slow-conducting B fibers. The axons synapse on the cell bodies of postganglionic neurons which are located in all cases outside the CNS. Each preganglionic axon diverges to an average of 8–9 postganglionic neurons. In this way, autonomic output is diffused. The axons of the postganglionic neurons, mostly unmyelinated C fibers, end on the visceral effectors.

Anatomically, the autonomic outflow is divided into 2 components: the **sympathetic** and **parasympathetic** divisions of the autonomic nervous system.

Sympathetic Division

The axons of the sympathetic preganglionic neurons leave the spinal cord with the ventral roots of the first thoracic to the third or fourth lumbar spinal nerves. They pass via the **white rami communicantes** to

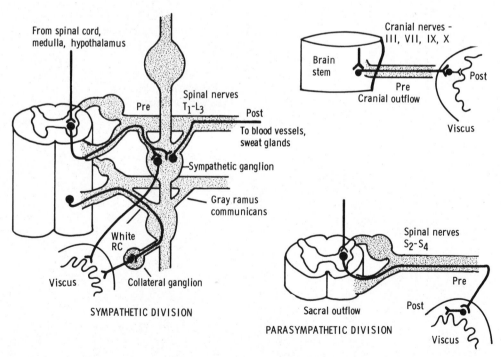

FIG 13–1. Autonomic nervous system. Pre, preganglionic neuron; Post, postganglionic neuron; RC, ramus communicans.

FIG 13–2. Diagram of the efferent autonomic pathways. Preganglionic neurons are shown as solid lines, post-ganglionic neurons as dotted lines. The heavy lines are parasympathetic fibers; the light lines are sympathetic. (Reproduced, with permission, from Youmans: *Fundamentals of Human Physiology,* 2nd ed. Year Book, 1962.)

the **paravertebral sympathetic ganglion chain,** where most of them end on the cell bodies of the postganglionic neurons. Some pass through the ganglion chain and end on postganglionic neurons located in the **collateral ganglia** close to the viscera. The axons of some of the postganglionic neurons pass to the viscera in the various sympathetic nerves. Others reenter the spinal nerves via the **gray rami communicantes** from the chain ganglia and are distributed to autonomic effectors in the areas supplied by these spinal nerves. The postganglionic sympathetic nerves to the head originate in the **superior, middle,** and **stellate** ganglia in the cranial extension of the sympathetic ganglion chain and travel to the effectors with the blood vessels.

Parasympathetic Division

The **cranial outflow** of the parasympathetic division supplies the visceral structures in the head via the oculomotor, facial, and glossopharyngeal nerves, and those in the thorax and upper abdomen via the vagus nerves. The **sacral outflow** supplies the pelvic viscera via the pelvic branches of the second to fourth sacral spinal nerves. The preganglionic fibers in both outflows end on short postganglionic neurons located on or near the visceral structures (Fig 13–2).

CHEMICAL TRANSMISSION AT AUTONOMIC JUNCTIONS

Transmission at the synaptic junctions between pre- and postganglionic neurons and between the postganglionic neurons and the autonomic effectors is chemically mediated. The principal transmitter agents involved are **acetylcholine** and **norepinephrine.**

Acetylcholine

The mediator liberated at all preganglionic endings and at anatomically parasympathetic postganglionic endings is acetylcholine. The biosynthesis and metabolism of this transmitter and its mechanism of action are described in detail in Chapter 4. It is stored in clear vesicles in the synaptic terminals of cholinergic neurons. It is released from the terminals by the nerve impulses. The secreted acetylcholine is in turn hydrolyzed. The enzyme responsible for the hydrolysis is acetylcholinesterase, and choline acetylase catalyzes the synthesis of acetylcholine from choline and active acetate. There are a number of esterases in the body, including a pseudocholinesterase in plasma that is capable of hydrolyzing acetylcholine, but only acetylcholinesterase is found in high concentration in cholinergic nerve endings.

Norepinephrine

The chemical transmitter at most sympathetic postganglionic endings is norepinephrine (levarterenol). It is stored in the synaptic knobs of adrenergic neurons in characteristic vesicles that have a dense core (granulated vesicles). Norepinephrine and its methyl derivative, epinephrine, are secreted by the adrenal medulla (see Chapter 20), but—contrary to previously accepted theories—epinephrine is not normally a mediator at sympathetic endings. There are in addition small, intensely flourescent cells (**SIF cells**) in the sympathetic ganglia that secrete dopamine. These cells modulate the discharge of the postganglionic neurons.

The endings of sympathetic postganglionic neurons in smooth muscle are discussed in Chapter 4; each neuron has multiple varicosities along its course, and each of these varicosities appears to be a site at which norepinephrine is liberated.

Biosynthesis of Catecholamines

The principal **catecholamines** found in the body—norepinephrine, epinephrine, and dopamine—are formed by hydroxylation and decarboxylation of the amino acids phenylalanine and tyrosine (Fig 13–3). Phenylalanine hydroxylase is found in the liver. Tyrosine is transported into adrenergic nerve endings by a concentrating mechanism. It is converted to dopa and then to dopamine by tyrosine hydroxylase and aromatic L-amino acid decarboxylase, which are located in the cytoplasm of the neurons. The dopamine then enters the granulated vesicles, within which it is converted to norepinephrine. L-Dopa is the isomer involved and it is the L isomer of norepinephrine that is produced. The rate-limiting step in synthesis is the conversion of tyrosine to dopa. The synthesis in adrenal medullary cells is presumably similar; however, unlike the adrenergic endings, some of these cells also contain the cytoplasmic enzyme phenylethanolamine-N-methyltransferase (PNMT). This enzyme, which catalyzes the conversion of norepinephrine to epinephrine, is found in high concentration only in the adrenal medulla, and consequently it is only in the adrenal medulla that appreciable quantities of epinephrine are produced. In the granulated vesicles, norepinephrine and epinephrine are bound to ATP and protein. The amines are held in the granulated vesicles by an active transport system, and this transport system is inhibited by the drug reserpine.

Some of the norepinephrine in nerve endings is manufactured there, but some of it is also norepinephrine that has been secreted and then taken up again into the adrenergic neurons. An active **reuptake mechanism** is characteristic of adrenergic neurons. Circulating norepinephrine and epinephrine are also picked up in small amounts by adrenergic neurons in the autonomic nervous system. In this regard, adrenergic neurons differ from cholinergic neurons. Acetylcholine is not taken up to any appreciable degree, but the choline formed by the action of acetylcholinesterase is actively taken up and recycled (Fig 13–4).

The pathways involved in the metabolism of phenylalanine are of considerable clinical importance because they are the site of several **inborn errors of metabolism,** diseases caused by congenital absence of various specific enzymes. Each of these diseases is believed to be due to inheritance from both parents of

FIG 13–3. Biosynthesis of catecholamines.

FIG 13–4. Comparison of the biochemical events at cholinergic endings with those at adrenergic endings. ACH, acetylcholine; ACE, acetylcholinesterase; NE, norepinephrine; X, receptor. Note that monoamine oxidase (MAO) is intracellular, so that some norepinephrine is being constantly deaminated in adrenergic endings. Catechol-O-methyltransferase (COMT) acts on norepinephrine after it is secreted.

FIG 13–5. *Top:* Catabolism of circulating epinephrine and norepinephrine. The main site of catabolism is the liver. The conjugates are mostly glucuronides and sulfates. *Bottom:* Catabolism of norepinephrine in adrenergic nerve endings. The acid and the glycol enter the circulation, and may be subsequently O-methylated to VMA and 3-methoxy-4-hydroxyphenylglycol. MAO, monoamine oxidase; COMT, catechol-O-methyltransferase.

a particular mutant gene which fails to perform its normal function of initiating the synthesis of a particular enzyme or enzyme subunit. **Phenylpyruvic oligophrenia**, a disorder characterized by severe mental deficiency and the accumulation in the blood and tissues of large amounts of phenylalanine and its keto acid derivatives, is due to congenital absence of phenylalanine hydroxylase (Fig 13–3). This does not lead to a catecholamine deficiency because catecholamines are synthesized from ingested tyrosine. The mental deficiency must be secondary to the accumulation of phenylalanine derivatives; if the condition is diagnosed at birth and a phenylalanine-free diet is instituted immediately, the mental retardation is often at least partially prevented. There is evidence that high phenylalanine levels in the blood inhibit protein synthesis in the brain. There is an unexplained deficiency of serotonin (see Chapter 15) in this disease, and some investigators believe that the serotonin deficiency is a major factor in the production of the mental abnormality.

Catabolism of Catecholamines

Epinephrine and norepinephrine are metabolized to biologically inactive products by oxidation and methylation. The former reaction is catalyzed by **monoamine oxidase (MAO)** and the latter by **catechol-O-methyltransferase (COMT)** (Figs 13–4, 13–5). MAO is found in the mitochondria. It is widely distributed, being particularly plentiful in the brain, liver, and kidneys, and large amounts are found in the mitochondria of the adrenergic nerve endings. COMT is also widely distributed, with high concentrations in the liver and kidneys, but it is not found in adrenergic nerve endings. Consequently, there are 2 different patterns of catecholamine metabolism.

Circulating epinephrine and norepinephrine are for the most part O-methylated, and measurement of the O-methylated derivatives normetanephrine and metanephrine in the urine is a good index of the rate of secretion of norepinephrine and epinephrine. The O-methylated derivatives that are not excreted are largely oxidized, and, in man, VMA (Fig 13–5) is the most plentiful catecholamine metabolite in the urine.

In the adrenergic nerve endings, on the other hand, some of the norepinephrine is being constantly converted by MAO to the physiologically inactive deaminated derivatives 3,4-dihydroxymandelic acid and its corresponding glycol (Fig 13–4). These compounds enter the circulation and may subsequently be converted to their corresponding O-methyl derivatives.

The reuptake of released norepinephrine mentioned above is a major mechanism by which norepinephrine is removed from the vicinity of autonomic endings. The hypersensitivity of the sympathetically denervated structures (see Chapter 4) is probably explained in part on this basis. After the adrenergic neurons are cut, their endings degenerate; consequently, there is no reuptake, and more of a given dose of norepinephrine is available to stimulate the receptors of the autonomic effectors.

Chemical Divisions of the Autonomic Nervous System

On the basis of the chemical mediator released, the autonomic nervous system can be divided into cholinergic and adrenergic divisions. The neurons which are cholinergic are (1) all preganglionic neurons; (2) the anatomically parasympathetic postganglionic neurons; (3) the anatomically sympathetic postganglionic neurons which innervate sweat glands; and (4) the anatomically sympathetic neurons which end on blood vessels in skeletal muscles and produce vasodilatation when stimulated (sympathetic vasodilator nerves; see Chapter 31). The remaining postganglionic sympathetic neurons are adrenergic. The adrenal medulla is essentially a sympathetic ganglion in which the postganglionic cells have lost their axons and become specialized for secretion directly into the blood stream. The cholinergic preganglionic neurons to these cells have consequently become the secretomotor nerve supply of this gland.

RESPONSES OF EFFECTOR ORGANS TO AUTONOMIC NERVE IMPULSES

General Principles

The effects of stimulation of the adrenergic and cholinergic postganglionic nerve fibers to the viscera are listed in Table 13–1. The smooth muscle in the walls of the hollow viscera is generally innervated by both adrenergic and cholinergic fibers, and activity in one of these systems increases the intrinsic activity of the smooth muscle whereas activity in the other decreases it. However, there is no uniform rule about which system stimulates and which inhibits. In the case of sphincter muscles, both adrenergic and cholinergic innervations are excitatory, but one supplies the constrictor component of the sphincter and the other the dilator.

There is usually no acetylcholine in the circulating blood, and the effects of localized cholinergic discharge are generally discrete and of short duration because of the high concentration of acetylcholinesterase at cholinergic nerve endings. Norepinephrine spreads farther and has a more prolonged action than acetylcholine. Normal plasma contains about 0.2 ng of norepinephrine and 0.05 ng of epinephrine per ml. Some of this catecholamine titer is due to adrenal medullary secretion, but much of the norepinephrine is apparently liberated into the blood stream from adrenergic nerve endings.

Cholinergic Discharge

In a general way, the functions promoted by activity in the cholinergic division of the autonomic nervous system are those concerned with the vegetative aspects of day-to-day living. For example, cholinergic action favors digestion and absorption of food by increasing the activity of the intestinal musculature, increasing gastric secretion, and relaxing the pyloric

TABLE 13–1. Responses of effector organs to autonomic nerve impulses and circulating catecholamines.*

Effector Organs	Cholinergic Impulses Response	Adrenergic Impulses Receptor Type†	Adrenergic Impulses Response
Eye			
Radial muscle of iris	. . .	a	Contraction (mydriasis)
Sphincter muscle of iris	Contraction (miosis)		. . .
Ciliary muscle	Contraction for near vision	β	Relaxation for far vision
Heart			
S-A node	Decrease in heart rate; vagal arrest	β	Increase in heart rate
Atria	Decrease in contractility, and (usually) increase in conduction velocity	β	Increase in contractility and conduction velocity
A-V node and conduction system	Decrease in conduction velocity; A-V block		Increase in conduction velocity
Ventricles	. . .	β	Increase in contractility, conduction velocity, automaticity, and rate of idiopathic pacemakers
Blood vessels			
Coronary	Dilatation	a β	Constriction Dilatation
Skin and mucosa	. . .	a	Constriction
Skeletal muscle	Dilatation	a β	Constriction Dilatation
Cerebral	. . .	a	Constriction (slight)
Pulmonary	. . .	a	Constriction
Abdominal viscera	. . .	a β	Constriction Dilatation
Renal	. . .	a	Constriction
Salivary glands	Dilatation	a	Constriction
Lung			
Bronchial muscle	Contraction	β	Relaxation
Bronchial glands	Stimulation		Inhibition (?)
Stomach			
Motility and tone	Increase	β	Decrease (usually)
Sphincters	Relaxation (usually)	a	Contraction (usually)
Secretion	Stimulation		Inhibition (?)
Intestine			
Motility and tone	Increase	a, β	Decrease
Sphincters	Relaxation (usually)	a	Contraction (usually)
Secretion	Stimulation		Inhibition (?)
Gallbladder and ducts	Contraction		Relaxation
Urinary bladder			
Detrusor	Contraction	β	Relaxation (usually)
Trigone and sphincter	Relaxation	a	Contraction
Ureter			
Motility and tone	Increase (?)		Increase (usually)
Uterus	Variable‡	a, β	Variable‡
Male sex organs	Erection		Ejaculation
Skin			
Pilomotor muscles	. . .	a	Contraction
Sweat glands	Generalized secretion	a	Slight, localized secretion§
Spleen capsule	. . .	a	Contraction
Adrenal medulla	Secretion of epinephrine and norepinephrine		. . .
Liver	. . .	β	Glycogenolysis
Pancreas			
Acini	Secretion		. . .
Islets	Insulin secretion	a β	Inhibition of insulin secretion Insulin secretion
Salivary glands	Profuse, watery secretion	a	Thick, viscous secretion
Lacrimal glands	Secretion		. . .
Nasopharyngeal glands	Secretion		. . .
Adipose tissue	. . .	β	Lipolysis
Juxtaglomerular cells	. . .	β	Renin secretion

*Modified from Goodman & Gilman: *The Pharmacological Basis of Therapeutics,* 4th ed. Macmillan, 1970.

†Where adrenergic receptor type has been established.

‡Depends on stage of menstrual cycle, amount of circulating estrogen and progesterone, and other factors. Responses of pregnant uterus different from those of nonpregnant.

§On palms of hands and in some other locations ("adrenergic sweating").

sphincter. For this reason, and to contrast it with the "catabolic" adrenergic division, the cholinergic division is sometimes called the **anabolic nervous system**.

Adrenergic Discharge

The adrenergic division discharges as a unit in emergency situations. The effects of this discharge are of considerable value in preparing the individual to cope with the emergency, although it is important to avoid the teleologic fallacy involved in the statement that the system discharges in order to do this. For example, adrenergic discharge relaxes accommodation and dilates the pupil (letting more light into the eye), accelerates the heart beat and raises the blood pressure (providing better perfusion of the vital organs and muscles), and constricts the blood vessels of the skin (which limits bleeding if wounded). Adrenergic discharge also leads to lower thresholds in the reticular formation (reinforcing the alert, aroused state) and elevated blood glucose and free fatty acid levels (supplying more energy). On the basis of effects like these, Cannon called the emergency-induced discharge of the adrenergic nervous system the "preparation for flight or fight."

The emphasis on mass discharge in stressful situations should not obscure the fact that the adrenergic autonomic fibers also subserve other functions. Tonic adrenergic discharge to the arterioles maintains arterial pressure, and variations in this tonic discharge are the mechanism by which the carotid sinus feedback regulation of blood pressure is effected.

a & β Receptors

The effectors on which epinephrine and norepinephrine act can be separated into 2 categories on the basis of their different sensitivity to certain drugs. These differences are now accepted as being a reflection of the existence of 2 types of catecholamine receptors, the *a* and *β* receptors, in the effector organs. The *a* receptors mediate vasoconstriction, whereas the *β* receptors mediate such actions as increases in cardiac rate and strength of cardiac contraction (see Chapters 20 and 29). The effects of *β* receptor stimulation are brought about by activation of adenyl cyclase (see Chapter 17), and there is some evidence that *a* receptor activation inhibits adenyl cyclase.

Autonomic Pharmacology

The junctions in the peripheral autonomic motor pathways are a logical point of attack for pharmaco-

TABLE 13–2. Some drugs which affect sympathetic activity. Only the principal actions of the drugs are listed. Note that guanethidine is believed to have 2 principal actions.

Site of Action	Drugs Which Augment Sympathetic Activity	Drugs Which Depress Sympathetic Activity
Sympathetic ganglion	**Stimulate postganglionic neurons** Acetylcholine Nicotine Dimethphenylpiperazinium **Inhibit acetylcholinesterase** DFP (diisopropyl fluorophosphate) Physostigmine (eserine) Neostigmine (Prostigmin) Parathion	**Block conduction** Chlorisondamine (Ecolid) Hexamethonium (Bistrium, C-6) Mecamylamine (Inversine) Pentolinium (Ansolysen) Tetraethylammonium (Etamon, TEA) Trimethaphan (Arfonad) High concentrations of acetylcholine, anticholinesterase drugs
Endings of postganglionic neurons	**Release norepinephrine** Tyramine Ephedrine Amphetamine	**Block norepinephrine synthesis** a-Methyl-*p*-tyrosine **Interfere with norepinephrine storage** Reserpine Guanethidine (Ismelin) **Prevent norepinephrine release** Bretylium tosylate (Darenthin) Guanethidine (Ismelin) **Form false transmitters** a-Methyldopa (Aldomet)
a receptors	**Stimulate *a* receptors** Norepinephrine (levarterenol; Levophed) Epinephrine Metaraminol (Aramine) Methoxamine (Vasoxyl) Phenylephrine (Neo-Synephrine)	**Block *a* receptors** Phenoxybenzamine (Dibenzyline) Phentolamine (Regitine) Ergot alkaloids
β receptors	**Stimulate *β* receptors** Isoproterenol (Isuprel) Epinephrine Norepinephrine	**Block *β* receptors** Dichloroisoproterenol Pronethalol Propranolol (Inderal)

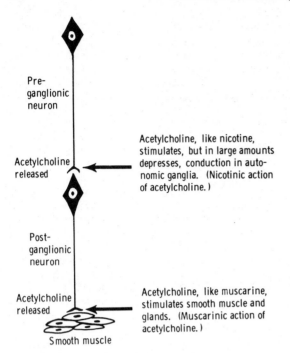

Pre-ganglionic neuron

Acetylcholine released

Acetylcholine, like nicotine, stimulates, but in large amounts depresses, conduction in autonomic ganglia. (Nicotinic action of acetylcholine.)

Post-ganglionic neuron

Acetylcholine released

Acetylcholine, like muscarine, stimulates smooth muscle and glands. (Muscarinic action of acetylcholine.)

Smooth muscle

FIG 13–6. Nicotinic and muscarinic actions of acetylcholine.

logic manipulation of visceral function because transmission across them is chemical. The transmitter agents are synthesized, stored in the nerve endings, and released near the neurons, muscle cells, or gland cells on which they act. They exert their action on these cells, and are then removed from the area by reuptake or metabolism. Each of these 5 steps can be stimulated or inhibited, with predictable consequences. In adrenergic endings, certain drugs also cause the formation of compounds which replace norepinephrine in the granules, and these weak or inactive "false transmitters" are released instead of norepinephrine by the action potentials reaching the endings.

Drugs that act on preganglionic neurons differ from those that act on postganglionic cholinergic neurons in spite of the similarities in transmitter chemistry at these 2 types of junctions. Muscarine, the alkaloid responsible for the toxicity of most toadstools, has little effect on autonomic ganglia but stimulates visceral effectors innervated by cholinergic postganglionic neurons. The actions of acetylcholine on these effec-

tors are therefore called **muscarinic actions** (Fig 13–6). Drugs with muscarinic actions include congeners of acetylcholine and drugs that inhibit acetylcholinesterase. Among the latter are diisopropyl fluorophosphate (DFP) and a number of other derivatives of the so-called nerve gases, chemical warfare agents which kill by producing massive inhibition of acetylcholinesterase. Atropine, scopolamine, and other natural and synthetic belladonna-like drugs block the muscarinic actions of acetylcholine by preventing the mediator from acting on visceral effector organs. Small doses of acetylcholine stimulate postganglionic cells, whereas large doses block the transmission of impulses from pre- to postganglionic neurons. These actions are unaffected by atropine. Nicotine has the same actions, and the actions of acetylcholine in the presence of atropine are called its **nicotinic actions.** Another category of drugs, the **curariform agents,** act by blocking transmission principally at the cholinergic endings of the motor neurons on skeletal muscle fibers.

A list of some of the commonly used drugs which affect sympathetic activity and the mechanisms by which they produce their effects are summarized in Table 13–2. The drugs which block the effects of norepinephrine on visceral effectors are referred to as adrenergic blocking agents, peripheral sympathetic blocking agents, adrenolytic agents, or sympatholytic agents. Monoamine oxidase inhibitors increase the catecholamine content of the brain but do not affect circulating levels of these amines. When COMT is inhibited, there is a slight prolongation of the physiologic effects of catecholamines; but even when both MAO and COMT are inhibited, the metabolism of epinephrine and norepinephrine is still rapid. Presumably the catecholamines are being inactivated via the other pathways (Fig 13–5) that normally account for only a small portion of their metabolism.

Nerve Growth Factor

The salivary glands of certain species of laboratory mammals contain **nerve growth factor,** a polypeptide factor or factors which is apparently necessary for the growth and development of the nervous system. This nerve growth factor exerts its greatest effect on the autonomic nervous system. Antiserum against it has been prepared, and injection of this antiserum in newborn animals leads to near total destruction of the sympathetic ganglia; it thus produces an **immunosympathectomy.**

14...

Neural Centers Regulating Visceral Function

The levels of autonomic integration within the CNS are arranged, like their somatic counterparts, in a hierarchy. Simple reflexes such as contraction of the full bladder are integrated in the spinal cord (see Chapter 12). The more complex reflexes that regulate respiration and blood pressure are integrated in the medulla oblongata. Those that control the pupillary responses to light and accommodation are integrated in the midbrain. The complex autonomic mechanisms that maintain the chemical constancy and temperature of the internal environment are integrated in the hypothalamus. The brain stem and diencephalic visceral regulatory centers are the subject of this chapter. The hypothalamus also functions with the limbic system as a unit that regulates emotional and instinctual behavior, and these aspects of hypothalamic function are discussed in the next chapter.

MEDULLA OBLONGATA

Control of Respiration, Heart Rate, & Blood Pressure

The medullary centers for the autonomic reflex control of the circulation, heart, and lungs are called the **vital centers** because damage to them is usually fatal. The afferent fibers to these centers originate in a number of instances in highly specialized visceral receptors. The specialized receptors include not only those of the carotid and aortic sinuses and bodies, but also receptor cells that are apparently located in the medulla itself. The motor responses are graded and delicately adjusted, and include somatic as well as visceral components. The details of the reflexes themselves are discussed in the chapters on the regulation of the circulation and respiration.

Other Medullary Autonomic Reflexes

Swallowing, coughing, sneezing, gagging, and vomiting are also reflex responses integrated in the medulla oblongata. The swallowing reflex is initiated by the voluntary act of propelling the oral contents toward the back of the pharynx (see Chapter 26). Coughing is initiated by irritation of the lining of the respiratory passages. The glottis closes and strong contraction of the respiratory muscles builds up intra-

pulmonary pressure, whereupon the glottis suddenly opens, causing an explosive discharge of air (see Chapter 36). Sneezing is a somewhat similar response to irritation of the nasal epithelium. It is initiated by stimulation of pain fibers in the trigeminal nerves.

Vomiting

Vomiting is another example of the way visceral reflexes integrated in the medulla include coordinated and carefully timed somatic as well as visceral components. Vomiting starts with salivation and the sensation of nausea. The glottis closes, preventing aspiration of vomitus into the trachea. The breath is held in mid-inspiration. The muscles of the abdominal wall contract, and because the chest is held in a fixed position the contraction increases intra-abdominal pressure. The esophagus and gastric cardiac sphincter relax, reverse peristalsis begins, and the gastric contents are ejected.

The "vomiting center" in the reticular formation of the medulla at the level of the olivary nuclei controls these activities (Fig 14—1).

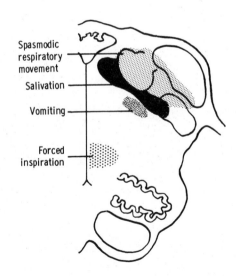

Spasmodic respiratory movement

Salivation

Vomiting

Forced inspiration

FIG 14—1. Cross-section of the medulla oblongata, showing approximate localization of areas concerned with components of the vomiting reflex. (Reproduced, with permission, from: *Research in the Service of Medicine*, Vol 44, Searle & Co, 1956.)

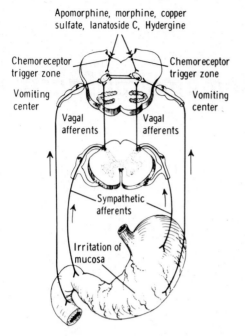

Apomorphine, morphine, copper
sulfate, lanatoside C, Hydergine

Chemoreceptor
trigger zone

Chemoreceptor
trigger zone

Vomiting
center

Vomiting
center

Vagal
afferents

Vagal
afferents

Sympathetic
afferents

Irritation of
mucosa

FIG 14—2. Afferent pathways for the vomiting reflex, showing the chemoreceptor trigger zone in the medulla. (Redrawn and reproduced, with permission, from: *Research in the Service of Medicine,* Vol 44, Searle & Co, 1956.)

Afferents

Irritation of the mucosa of the upper gastrointestinal tract causes vomiting. Impulses are relayed from the mucosa to the vomiting center over visceral afferent pathways in the sympathetic nerves and vagi. Other afferents presumably reach the vomiting center from the diencephalon and limbic system, because emetic responses also occur to emotionally charged stimuli. Thus, we speak of "nauseating smells" and "sickening sights."

It has been claimed that there are chemoreceptor cells in the medulla which initiate vomiting when they are stimulated by circulating chemical agents. The **chemoreceptor trigger zone** in which these cells are located is probably in or near the **area postrema**, a V-shaped band of tissue on the lateral walls of the fourth ventricle near the obex. This region is known to be more permeable to many substances than the underlying medulla (Fig 14—2). Lesions of the area postrema have little effect on the vomiting response to gastrointestinal irritation but abolish the vomiting that follows injection of apomorphine and a number of emetic drugs. Such lesions also decrease vomiting in uremia and radiation sickness, both of which may be associated with endogenous production of circulating emetic substances. A chemoreceptor mechanism stimulated by circulating toxins would explain vomiting in many clinical disorders.

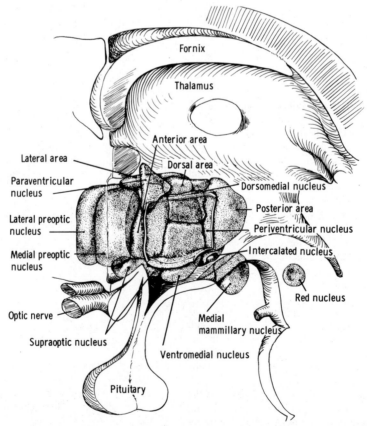

FIG 14—3. The human hypothalamus. (Redrawn from an original by Netter in Ciba Clinical Symposia. Copyright © 1956, Ciba Pharmaceutical Co. Reproduced with permission.)

Median eminence
Anterior lobe pars tuberalis
Anterior lobe pars distalis

Mammillary body
3rd ventricle
Pituitary stalk
Infundibulum
Posterior lobe
Intermediate lobe
Residual cleft

FIG 14—4. *Left:* Sagittal section of the ventral hypothalamus and pituitary of a dog (Gomori stain). *Right:* Diagram of same specimen to show anatomic landmarks. The small dark granules that are very abundant in the posterior pituitary and scattered along the hypothalamohypophysial nerve fibers in the median eminence are granules of "neurosecretory material."

HYPOTHALAMUS

ANATOMIC CONSIDERATIONS

The hypothalamus is that portion of the anterior end of the diencephalon that lies below the hypothalamic sulcus and in front of the interpeduncular nuclei. It is divided into the nuclei and nuclear areas shown in semidiagrammatic form in Fig 14—3. The supraoptic, the paraventricular, and, in some species, the ventromedial nuclei are clearly delineated, but most of the other nuclei and areas are rather ill-defined collections of small cells.

Relation to the Pituitary Gland

There are neural connections between the hypothalamus and the posterior lobe of the pituitary gland and vascular connections between the hypothalamus and the anterior lobe. The detailed anatomy of the pituitary and the adjacent ventral hypothalamus is shown in Fig 14—4. Embryologically, the posterior pituitary arises as an evagination of the floor of the third ventricle. In the adult it retains its essentially neural character. It receives an abundant supply of nerve fibers, the **hypothalamohypophysial tract,** from the supraoptic and paraventricular nuclei. Most of the supraoptic fibers end in the posterior lobe itself, whereas many of the paraventricular fibers end in the pituitary stalk. The anterior and intermediate lobes of the pituitary arise in the embryo from Rathke's pouch, an evagination from the roof of the pharynx (Fig 22—1). Sympathetic nerve fibers reach the anterior lobe from its capsule, and parasympathetic fibers reach it from the petrosal nerves, but very few nerve fibers pass to it from the hypothalamus. However, the portal hypophysial vessels form a direct vascular link between the hypothalamus and the anterior pituitary. Arterial twigs from the carotid arteries and circle of Willis end in a network of capillary loops in the ventral hypothalamus (Fig 14—5). The loops, which are called the primary plexus, drain into sinusoidal vessels which carry blood down the pituitary stalk to the capillaries of the anterior pituitary. This system begins and ends in capillaries without going through the heart, and is therefore a true portal system. In birds and some mammals, including man, there is no other anterior hypophysial arterial supply except capsular vessels and anastomotic connections from the capillaries of the

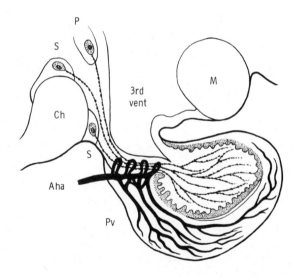

FIG 14—5. Diagram of the connections between the hypothalamus and pituitary in mammals. The capillary loops (primary plexus) in the median eminence of the hypothalamus drain into the portal hypophysial vessels. Ch, chiasm; S, supraoptic nucleus; Aha, anterior hypophysial artery; P, paraventricular nucleus; Pv, portal vessels; M, mammillary body; 3rd vent, third ventricle. (Based on a diagram by Ortman in: *Handbook of Physiology.* Field J, Magoun HW [editors]. Washington: The American Physiological Society, 1960. Section 1, pp 1039–1066.)

posterior pituitary. In other mammals, some blood reaches the anterior lobe through a separate set of anterior hypophysial arteries; but in all vertebrates a large fraction of the anterior lobe blood supply is carried by the portal vessels. The **median eminence** is generally defined as the portion of the ventral hypothalamus from which the portal vessels arise.

Afferent & Efferent Connections of the Hypothalamus

The principal afferent and efferent neural pathways to and from the hypothalamus are listed in Table 14–1. Most of the fibers are unmyelinated. Many connect the hypothalamus to the limbic system. There are also important connections between the hypothalamus and a group of nuclei in the midbrain tegmentum. The hypothalamus thus represents, to use Nauta's term, a "nodal point" on the circuits that connect the limbic system and the "limbic midbrain area."

Some of the nerve fibers ending in the hypothalamus are adrenergic (see Chapter 15). Norepinephrine-containing neurons with their cell bodies in the midbrain end in the supraoptic and paraventricular nuclei, the periventricular area, and the median eminence. There is also an intrahypothalamic system of dopamine-containing neurons which have their cell bodies in the arcuate nucleus and end on or near the capillaries that form the portal vessels in the median eminence (Fig 15–11).

HYPOTHALAMIC FUNCTION

The major functions of the hypothalamus are summarized in Table 14–2. Some are fairly clear-cut visceral reflexes, and others include complex behavioral and emotional reactions; but all involve a particular response to a particular stimulus. It is important to keep this pattern of stimulus-integration-response in mind in considering hypothalamic function.

RELATION OF HYPOTHALAMUS TO AUTONOMIC FUNCTION

Many years ago, Sherrington called the hypothalamus "the head ganglion of the autonomic system." Stimulation of the hypothalamus does produce autonomic responses, but there is little evidence that the hypothalamus is concerned with the regulation of visceral function per se. Rather, the autonomic responses triggered in the hypothalamus are part of more complex phenomena such as rage and other emotions.

"Parasympathetic Center"

Stimulation of the superior anterior hypothala-

TABLE 14–1. **Principal pathways to and from the hypothalamus.**

Tract		Description
Medial forebrain bundle	A, E	Connects limbic lobe and midbrain via lateral hypothalamus, where fibers enter and leave it; includes direct amygdalohypothalamic fibers, which are sometimes referred to as a separate pathway.
Fornix	A	Connects hippocampus to hypothalamus, mostly mammillary bodies; some efferent fibers (?)
Stria terminalis	A	Connects amygdala to hypothalamus, especially ventromedial region.
Mammillary penduncle	A	Diverges from sensory pathways in midbrain to enter hypothalamus; may be the pathway by which sensory stimuli enter.
Retinohypothalamic fibers	A	Optic nerve fibers entering hypothalamus from optic chiasm.
Thalamohypothalamic and pallidohypothalamic fibers	A	Connections from thalamus and lenticular nucleus.
Periventricular system (including dorsal longitudinal fasciculus of Schütz)	A, E	Interconnects hypothalamus and midbrain; efferent projections to spinal cord, afferent from sensory pathways.
Mammillothalamic tract of Vicq d'Azyr	E	Connects mammillary nuclei to anterior thalamic nuclei.
Mammillotegmental tract	E	Connects hypothalamus with reticular portions of midbrain.
Hypothalamohypophysial tract (supraopticohypophysial and paraventriculohypophysial tracts)	E	Connects supraoptic and paraventricular nuclei with pituitary stalk and posterior pituitary.

A = principally afferent; E = principally efferent.

mus occasionally causes contraction of the urinary bladder, a parasympathetic response. Largely on this basis, the statement is often made that there is a "parasympathetic center" in the anterior hypothalamus. However, bladder contraction can also be elicited by stimulation of other parts of the hypothalamus, and hypothalamic stimulation causes very few other parasympathetic responses. Thus, there is very little evidence that a localized "parasympathetic center" exists. Stimulation of the hypothalamus can cause cardiac arrhythmias, and there is reason to believe that these are due to simultaneous activation of vagal and sympathetic nerves to the heart (see Chapter 28).

Sympathetic Responses

Stimulation of various parts of the hypothalamus, especially the lateral areas, produces a rise in blood pressure, pupillary dilatation, piloerection, and other signs of diffuse adrenergic discharge. The stimuli which trigger this pattern of responses in the intact animal are not regulatory impulses from the viscera but emotional stimuli, especially rage and fear. Adrenergic responses are also triggered as part of the reactions which conserve heat (see below).

Low-voltage electrical stimulation of the mid-dorsal portion of the hypothalamus causes vasodilatation in muscle. Associated vasoconstriction in the skin and elsewhere maintains blood pressure at a fairly constant level. This observation and other evidence supports the conclusion that the hypothalamus is a way station on the so-called cholinergic sympathetic vasodilator system that originates in the cerebral cortex. It may be this system which is responsible for the dilatation of muscle blood vessels at the start of exercise (see Chapter 31).

Stimulation of the dorsomedial nuclei and posterior hypothalamic areas produces increased secretion of epinephrine and norepinephrine from the adrenal

TABLE 14–2. **Summary of hypothalamic regulatory mechanisms.**

Function	Afferents From	Integrating Areas
Temperature regulation	Cutaneous cold receptors; temperature-sensitive cells in hypothalamus	Anterior hypothalamus, response to heat; posterior hypothalamus, response to cold
Neuroendocrine control of: Catecholamines	Emotional stimuli, probably via limbic system	Dorsomedial and posterior hypothalamus
Vasopressin	Osmoreceptors, "volume receptors," others	Supraoptic nuclei
Oxytocin	Touch receptors in breast, uterus, genitalia	Paraventricular nuclei
Thyroid-stimulating hormone (TSH)	Temperature receptors, perhaps others (?)	Anterior median eminence and anterior hypothalamus
Adrenocorticotropic hormone (ACTH)	Limbic system (emotional stimuli); reticular formation ("systemic" stimuli); hypothalamic or anterior pituitary cells sensitive to circulating blood corticoid level; others (?)	Middle portion of median eminence
Follicle-stimulating hormone (FSH) and luteinizing hormone (LH)	Hypothalamic cells sensitive to estrogens; eyes, touch receptors in skin and genitalia of reflex ovulating species	Posterior median eminence, other areas
Prolactin	Touch receptors in breasts, other unknown receptors	Posterior median eminence (hypothalamus inhibits secretion)
Growth hormone	Unknown receptors	Anterior median eminence
"Appetitive" behavior Thirst	Osmoreceptors	Lateral superior hypothalamus
Hunger	"Glucostat" cells sensitive to rate of glucose utilization	Ventromedial satiety center, lateral hunger center, also limbic components
Sexual behavior	Cells sensitive to circulating estrogen and androgen, others	Anterior ventral hypothalamus, plus, in the male, pyriform cortex
Defensive reactions Fear, rage	Sense organs and neocortex, paths unknown	Diffuse, in limbic system and hypothalamus

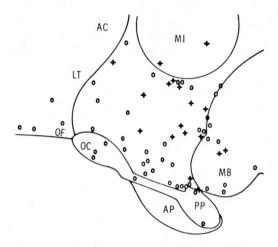

FIG 14–6. Points in the hypothalamus where low-intensity stimulation produces increased catecholamine secretion from the adrenal medulla of dogs. + = catecholamine output increased; 0 = catecholamine output unchanged. Points are projected on a midsagittal view of the hypothalamus. MI, massa intermedia; OC, optic chiasm; AP, anterior pituitary; PP, posterior pituitary; MB, mammillary body; OF, orbital surface of the frontal lobe; AC, anterior commissure; LT, lamina terminalis. (Reproduced, with permission, from Goldfien & Ganong: The adrenal medullary and adrenal cortical response to stimulation of the diencephalon. Am J Physiol 202:205, 1962.)

medulla (Fig 14–6). Increased adrenal medullary secretion is one of the physical changes associated with rage and fear, and may occur when the cholinergic sympathetic vasodilator system is activated. It has been claimed that there are separate hypothalamic centers for the control of epinephrine and norepinephrine secretion. Differential secretion of one or the other of these adrenal medullary catecholamines does occur in certain physiologic situations, but the evidence for separate hypothalamic control centers is scanty and unconfirmed.

RELATION TO SLEEP

Lesions of the posterior hypothalamus cause prolonged sleep, and stimulation of the dorsal hypothalamus in conscious animals causes them to go to sleep. These observations have led to considerable speculation about the existence of "sleep centers" and "wakefulness centers" in the hypothalamus, but study of the functions of the RAS and nonspecific projection nuclei of the thalamus (see Chapter 11) has provided alternative explanations.

The posterior hypothalamic lesions that cause coma involve fibers of the RAS as they pass to the thalamus and cortex. The sleep-producing effects of posterior hypothalamic lesions are therefore probably explicable on the basis of damage to the RAS rather than destruction of a hypothetical hypothalamic "wakefulness center."

The hypothalamic loci where stimulation produces sleep are close to the nonspecific projection nuclei of the thalamus. The stimulating frequency that produces sleep is approximately 8/sec. Stimulation at greater frequencies arouses rather than depresses the animal. As noted in Chapter 11, stimulation of the nonspecific projection nuclei of the thalamus, the orbital surface of the frontal lobe, and some parts of the brain stem at a frequency of 8/sec produces sleep. It therefore seems likely that the reported effects of hypothalamic stimulation are actually due to stimulation of a diffuse system, the slow frequency stimulation of which produces sleep. On the basis of these considerations, it seems unlikely that the hypothalamus plays any direct or unique role in the regulation of sleep.

HUNGER

Feeding & Satiety Centers

Hypothalamic regulation of the appetite for food depends primarily upon the interaction of 2 areas: a lateral **"feeding center"** in the bed nucleus of the medial forebrain bundle at its junction with the pallidohypothalamic fibers, and a medial **"satiety center"** in the ventromedial nucleus. Stimulation of the feeding center evokes eating behavior in conscious animals, and its destruction causes severe, fatal anorexia in otherwise healthy animals. Stimulation of the ventromedial nucleus causes cessation of eating, whereas lesions in this region cause hyperphagia and, if the food supply is abundant, the syndrome of **hypothalamic obesity** (Fig 14–7). Destruction of the feeding center in rats with lesions of the satiety center causes anorexia, which indicates that the satiety center functions by inhibiting the feeding center (Fig 14–8). Present evidence favors the view that the feeding center is chronically active and that its activity is transiently inhibited by activity in the satiety center after the ingestion of food.

Afferent Mechanisms

The activity of the satiety center is probably governed by the level of glucose utilization of cells within the center. These cells have therefore been called **glucostats**. It has been postulated that when their glucose utilization is low—and consequently when the arteriovenous blood glucose difference across them is low—their activity is decreased, the activity of the feeding center is unchecked, and the individual is hungry. When utilization is high, the activity of the glucostats is increased, the feeding center is inhibited, and the individual feels sated. This **glucostatic hypothesis** of appetite regulation is supported by an appre-

FIG 14—7. Hypothalamic obesity. The animal on the right, in which bilateral lesions had been placed in the ventromedial nuclei 4 months previously, weighs 1080 g. The control animal on the left weighs 520 g. (Reproduced, with permission, from Stevenson, in: *The Hypothalamus.* Haymaker W, Anderson E, Nauta WJH [editors]. Thomas, 1969.)

ciable body of experimental data. Other factors undoubtedly affect appetite, but it appears that the glucostatic mechanism is a major regulator. The glucostatic hypothesis has the merit of explaining the increased appetite in diabetes, in which the blood sugar is high but the glucose utilization of the cells is low because of the insulin deficiency. The objection has been raised that most neural tissue does not require

insulin to metabolize glucose. However, it now appears that the ventral hypothalamus is different from the rest of the brain in that its rate of glucose utilization does vary with the amount of insulin in the circulation.

Relatively large amounts of radioactive glucose are taken up by cells of the ventromedial nuclei. This affinity for glucose probably explains why injections of gold thioglucose produce obesity in mice. The ventromedial cells presumably take up the toxic gold-substituted glucose molecules, which destroy the cells and thus prevent inhibition of the lateral feeding center. Animals which have received gold thioglucose injections and have become obese have demonstrable lesions in the ventromedial nuclei.

The limbic system is also involved in the neural regulation of appetite. Lesions of the amygdaloid nuclei produce moderate hyperphagia. However, unlike animals with ventromedial hypothalamic lesions, animals with amygdaloid lesions will eat adulterated or tainted food. They are omniphagic and attempt to eat all sorts of objects (see Chapter 16). This suggests that fundamentally different mechanisms underlie the hyperphagia. Injection of norepinephrine into the hypothalamus and parts of the limbic system causes animals to eat, a finding which suggests that there are adrenergic components in the neural circuits regulating food intake.

Other Factors Regulating Food Intake

A cold environment stimulates and a hot environment depresses appetite. Distention of the gastrointestinal tract inhibits and contractions of the empty stomach (**hunger contractions**) stimulate appetite, but denervation of the stomach and intestines does not

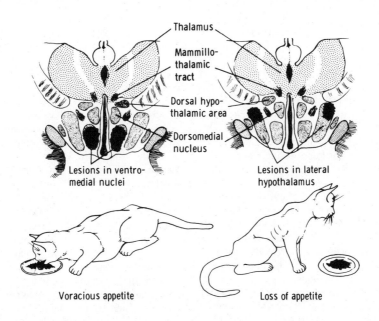

FIG 14—8. Diagrammatic summary of the effects of hypothalamic lesions on feeding. (Redrawn from an original by Netter in Ciba Clinical Symposia. Copyright 1956, Ciba Pharmaceutical Co. Reproduced with permission.)

affect the amount of food eaten. In animals with esophageal fistulas, chewing and swallowing food does cause some satiety even though the food never reaches the stomach. Especially in man, cultural factors, environment, and past experiences relative to the sight, smell, and taste of food also affect food intake.

The net effect of all the appetite-regulating mechanisms in normal adult animals and man is an adjustment of food intake to the point where caloric intake balances energy expenditures, with the result that body weight is maintained. In hyperthyroidism and diabetes mellitus, hunger increases as energy output increases. However, the link between energy needs and food intake is indirect, and in some situations intake is not correlated with immediate energy expenditure. For example, during growth, after exercise, and during recovery from debilitating illnesses, food intake is increased. How these long-term adjustments are brought about is not known.

THIRST

Another appetitive mechanism that is under hypothalamic control is thirst. Appropriately placed hypothalamic lesions diminish or abolish fluid intake, in some instances without any change in food intake, and electrical stimulation of the hypothalamus causes drinking. In the rat the area concerned with thirst is in the lateral hypothalamus posterior to the feeding center; in the dog and goat it is in the dorsal hypothalamus lateral and posterior to the paraventricular nuclei (Fig 14—9). Injection of hypertonic saline into these areas causes drinking in conscious animals. These observations suggest that in the hypothalamus there are **osmoreceptors**, cells that are stimulated by an increased osmotic pressure of the body fluids to initiate thirst and drinking. Decreases in ECF volume also stimulate thirst, and, in rats, hemorrhage causes increased drinking even though there is no change in the osmolality of the plasma. There is some evidence that angiotensin stimulates thirst, and circulating angiotensin levels are increased by hemorrhage. Injection of cholinergic agents into the hypothalamus and limbic system causes drinking in rats, and a cholinergic system regulating water intake has been postulated.

Whenever the sensation of thirst is obtunded, either by direct damage to the diencephalon or by depressed or altered states of consciousness, patients stop drinking adequate amounts of fluid. Dehydration results if appropriate measures are not instituted to maintain water balance. If the protein intake is high, the products of protein metabolism cause an osmotic diuresis (see Chapter 38), and the amounts of water required to maintain balance are large. Most cases of hypernatremia are actually due to simple dehydration in patients with psychoses or cerebral disease who do not or cannot increase their water intake when their thirst mechanism is stimulated.

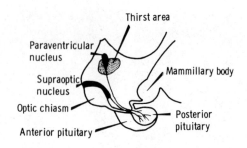

FIG 14—9. Hypothalamic areas concerned with water metabolism in the dog.

Other Factors Regulating Water Intake

A number of other well established factors contribute to the regulation of water intake. Dryness of the pharyngeal mucous membrane causes a sensation of thirst. Patients in whom fluid intake must be restricted sometimes get appreciable relief of thirst by sucking ice chips or a wet cloth. Rats with lesions in their thirst areas will drink small amounts of water when their throats become dry even though they do not respond to dehydration per se.

Dehydrated dogs, cats, camels, and some other animals rapidly drink just enough water to make up their water deficit. They stop drinking before the water is absorbed (while their plasma is still hypertonic), so some kind of pharyngeal or gastrointestinal "metering" must be involved. In man, this ability to drink just the right amount of water is not so well developed, and deficits are usually made up more slowly.

CONTROL OF POSTERIOR PITUITARY SECRETION

Posterior Pituitary Hormones

The 2 hormones in the posterior pituitary gland of all mammals studied except members of the pig family are **oxytocin** and **arginine vasopressin**. In the pig and the hippopotamus, arginine in the vasopressin molecule is replaced by lysine to form **lysine vasopressin**. The posterior pituitaries of some African warthogs and peccaries contain a mixture of arginine and lysine vasopressin. The posterior lobe hormones are nonapeptides (considering each half cystine as a single amino acid) with a disulfide ring at one end (Fig 14—10). Synthetic peptides more active than the naturally occurring substances have been produced by altering the amino acid residues.

In the posterior pituitary, oxytocin and vasopressin are stored bound to polypeptides called **neurophysins**. There is one neurophysin for oxytocin and another for vasopressin. The storage granules apparently contain oxytocin or vasopressin, ATP, and neurophysin, and when the posterior lobe is stimulated, all 3 are secreted. Neurophysins are present in the periph-

Cys-Tyr-Phe-Gln-Asn-Cys-Pro-Arg-Gly-NH$_2$
 1   2   3   4   5   6   7   8   9

Arginine vasopressin

┌S─────────S┐
Cys-Tyr-Ile-Gln-Asn-Cys-Pro-Leu-Gly-NH$_2$
 1   2   3   4   5   6   7   8   9

Oxytocin

FIG 14–10. Arginine vasopressin and oxytocin. In the pig and hippopotamus, lysine is substituted for arginine in position 8 of the vasopressin molecule.

TABLE 14–3. Summary of stimuli affecting vasopressin secretion.

Vasopressin Secretion Increased	Vasopressin Secretion Decreased
Increased effective osmotic pressure of plasma	Decreased effective osmotic pressure of plasma
Decreased extracellular fluid volume	Increased extracellular fluid volume
Morphine, nicotine, barbiturates	Alcohol
Pain, emotion, "stress," exercise	

eral blood, where they can be measured by immunoassay.

Effects of Vasopressin

Because its principal physiologic effect is the retention of water by the kidney, vasopressin is often called the antidiuretic hormone (ADH). It increases the permeability of the collecting ducts of the kidney, so that water enters the hypertonic interstitium of the renal pyramids (see Chapter 38). The urine becomes concentrated and its volume decreases. The overall effect is therefore retention of water in excess of solute; consequently, the effective osmotic pressure of the body fluids is decreased. In the absence of vasopressin, the urine is hypotonic to plasma, urine volume is increased, and there is a net water loss. Vasopressin also increases the permeability of the collecting ducts to urea and decreases blood flow in the renal medulla. In addition, it increases the permeability of the bladder of the toad and the skin of the frog to water.

In large doses, vasopressin elevates arterial blood pressure by an action on the smooth muscle of the arterioles. However, it is doubtful if enough endogenous vasopressin is ever secreted to exert any appreciable effect on blood pressure homeostasis. Hemorrhage is a potent stimulus to vasopressin secretion, but the blood pressure fall after hemorrhage is not significantly greater or more prolonged in the absence of the posterior pituitary than when it is present.

Circulating vasopressin is rapidly inactivated, principally in the liver and kidneys. It has a **biologic half-life** (time required for inactivation of half a given amount) of about 18 minutes in man. Its effects on the kidney develop rapidly but are of short duration.

Mechanism of Action

Vasopressin acts by increasing intracellular cyclic adenosine-3′,5′-monophosphate (cyclic AMP) in the cells of the collecting ducts. The cyclic AMP then acts in some undefined way to increase the permeability of

the renal epithelium. There is evidence that ACTH, TSH, LH, epinephrine, glucagon, and several other hormones also exert their effects by increasing cyclic AMP in their target organs (see Chapter 17).

Control of Vasopressin Secretion: Osmotic Stimuli

Vasopressin is stored in the posterior pituitary and released into the blood stream by impulses in the nerve fibers from the hypothalamus. Although there is some overlap, the fibers from the supraoptic nuclei are primarily concerned with vasopressin secretion, while those from the paraventricular nuclei control the release of oxytocin. When the effective osmotic pressure of the plasma is increased, the rate of discharge of the supraoptic neurons increases; when the effective osmotic pressure is decreased, supraoptic discharge is inhibited (Table 14–3, Fig 14–11). The changes are mediated via **osmoreceptor** cells sensitive to changes in the osmotic pressure of the plasma. These cells are located in the anterior hypothalamus. They may be the supraoptic neurons themselves, but they are more likely separate cells located in the perinuclear zone around the nucleus. It is not known if they are the same osmoreceptors that regulate water intake (see above).

Vasopressin secretion is thus controlled by a

FIG 14–11. Inhibition of water diuresis in a dog by injection of 10.5 ml of 1.5% NaCl (at A) and 11 ml of 1.5% NaCl (at B) into the carotid artery. (Redrawn and reproduced, with permission, from Verney: The antidiuretic hormone and the factors which determine its release. Proc Roy Soc London s.B 135:25, 1947.)

delicate feedback mechanism that operates continuously to defend the osmolality of the plasma. There is a steady, moderate level of vasopressin secretion when the plasma osmolality is normal, and the normal plasma vasopressin level is maintained at about 3 μU/ml. Whenever the effective osmotic pressure of plasma is increased, vasopressin secretion is increased; whenever plasma osmolality is decreased, vasopressin secretion is decreased. Significant changes in secretion occur when osmolality is changed as little as 2%. In this way, the osmolality of the plasma in normal individuals is maintained very close to 290 mOsm/liter.

Volume Effects

ECF volume also affects vasopressin secretion. Vasopressin secretion is increased when ECF volume is low and decreased when ECF volume is high (Table 14−3). There is an inverse relationship between the rate of vasopressin secretion and the rate of discharge in afferents from stretch receptors in the low and high pressure portions of the vascular system. The low pressure receptors are those in the great veins, right and left atria, and pulmonary vessels; the high pressure receptors are those in the carotid sinuses and aortic arch (see Chapter 31). The low pressure receptors monitor the fullness of the vascular system. Moderate decreases in ECF volume and, consequently, in blood volume increase vasopressin secretion without causing any change in arterial blood pressure; it therefore appears that the low pressure receptors are the primary mediators of volume effects on vasopressin secretion. However, when the volume changes are large enough to produce changes in blood pressure, the carotid and aortic receptors also play a role.

Hemorrhage causes the release of much greater amounts of vasopressin than plasma hyperosmolality, and hypovolemia causes vasopressin secretion even if the plasma is hypotonic.

Other Stimuli Affecting Vasopressin Secretion

A variety of stimuli in addition to osmotic pressure changes and ECF volume aberrations increase vasopressin secretion. These include pain, trauma, some emotions, and a number of drugs, including morphine, nicotine, and large doses of barbiturates. The pathways mediating the effects of noxious stimuli apparently include adrenergic neurons, since adrenergic blocking agents block the vasopressin stimulating effect of these stimuli.

Clinical Implications

In various clinical conditions, volume and other nonosmotic stimuli override the osmotic control of vasopressin secretion, producing water retention and a decrease in plasma osmolality. In patients with such hypersecretion, a high fluid intake can cause water intoxication. The water retention and hyponatremia seen after surgery are partly explained on this basis. Water retention occurs in addition to salt retention in patients with edema due to congestive heart failure, cirrhosis of the liver, and nephrosis. It has been argued

that the water retention is due to diminished removal of vasopressin from the plasma by the liver and kidney, prolonging the half-life of the hormone. This may be a factor, but water retention does not occur unless there is abnormal posterior pituitary secretion as well. If the osmoreceptor mechanism were normal, the decreased plasma osmolality would inhibit posterior pituitary secretion and the defect would correct itself. The cause of excess vasopressin secretion in diseases of the heart, liver, and kidneys is not known with certainty, but it is probably due to abnormal activity of the "volume-sensing" mechanism described above.

An "inappropriate" hypersecretion of vasopressin is believed to be responsible for the hyponatremia which occurs with high levels of salt excretion in some patients with cerebral or pulmonary disease. In these cases of "cerebral salt wasting" and "pulmonary salt wasting," water retention is sufficient to expand ECF volume. This inhibits the secretion of aldosterone by the adrenal cortex (see Chapter 20), and salt is lost in the urine. The syndrome is different from that seen in patients with edema because the latter retain salt and usually have a high level of aldosterone secretion. Hypersecretion of vasopressin in patients with pulmonary diseases such as lung cancer may be due in part to the interruption of inhibitory impulses in vagal afferents from the stretch receptors in the atria and great veins. However, it has been demonstrated that some lung tumors and other malignancies can secrete a substance with antidiuretic activity.

Diabetes insipidus is the syndrome that results when vasopressin deficiency develops due to disease processes in the supraoptic nuclei, the hypothalamo-hypophysial tract, or the posterior pituitary gland. It also develops after surgical removal of the posterior lobe of the pituitary, but in this situation it may be temporary because the remaining supraoptic fibers recover from the trauma and begin again to secrete vasopressin. The symptoms are passage of large amounts of dilute urine (**polyuria**) and the drinking of large amounts of fluid (**polydipsia**), provided the thirst mechanism is intact. It is the polydipsia that keeps these patients healthy. If their sense of thirst is depressed for any reason and their intake of dilute fluid decreases, they develop dehydration that can be fatal. The amelioration of diabetes insipidus produced by the development of concomitant anterior pituitary insufficiency is discussed in Chapter 22.

The well-known diuretic effect of alcoholic beverages has a 2-fold basis. The dilute liquids usually drunk with alcohol dilute the plasma, and the alcohol itself depresses vasopressin secretion.

Oxytocin

In mammals the principal physiologic effect of oxytocin is on the **myoepithelial cells**, smooth muscle-like cells that line the ducts of the breast. The hormone makes these cells contract, squeezing the milk out of the alveoli of the lactating breast into the large ducts (sinuses), and thence out the nipple (**milk ejection**). Many hormones acting in concert are responsible for breast growth and the secretion of milk into the ducts (see Chapter 23), but milk ejection in most species requires oxytocin.

The Milk Ejection Reflex

Milk ejection is normally initiated by a neuroendocrine reflex. The receptors involved are the touch receptors, which are plentiful in the breast—especially around the nipple. Impulses generated in these receptors are relayed from the somatic touch pathways via the bundle of Schütz and mammillary peduncle to the paraventricular nuclei. Discharge of the paraventricular neurons causes liberation of oxytocin from the posterior pituitary. The infant suckling at the breast stimulates the touch receptors, the paraventricular nuclei are stimulated, oxytocin is released, and the milk is expressed into the sinuses, ready to flow into the mouth of the waiting infant. In lactating women, genital stimulation and emotional stimuli also produce oxytocin secretion, sometimes causing milk to spurt from the breast.

Other Actions of Oxytocin

Oxytocin causes contraction of the smooth muscle of the uterus. The sensitivity of the uterine musculature to oxytocin varies. It is enhanced by estrogen and inhibited by progesterone. In late pregnancy, the uterus becomes very sensitive to oxytocin, and oxytocin secretion is increased during labor. After dilatation of the cervix, descent of the fetus down the birth canal probably initiates impulses in the afferent nerves which are relayed to the paraventricular nuclei, causing secretion of sufficient oxytocin to enhance labor. Oxytocin may also play some role in initiating labor. However, the mechanisms controlling the onset of labor are immensely complex, and neuroendocrine reflexes are certainly not the only mechanisms responsible for delivery.

Oxytocin may also act on the nonpregnant uterus to facilitate sperm transport. The passage of sperm up the female genital tract to the fallopian tubes where fertilization normally takes place depends not only on the motile powers of the sperm but, at least in some species, on uterine contractions as well. The genital stimulation involved in coitus releases oxytocin, but it has not been proved that it is oxytocin that initiates the rather specialized uterine contractions that transport the sperm. The secretion of oxytocin, like that of vasopressin, is inhibited by alcohol.

Site of Origin of Posterior Pituitary Hormones

When the hypothalamus and pituitary are treated with the Gomori stain or a number of other special stains, large granules thought to be aggregations of posterior lobe hormones bound to protein (Herring bodies) are seen in nerve endings in the posterior pituitary. There are similar granules along the axons of the supraoptic and paraventricular neurons, and in their cell bodies (Fig 14–4). The granules in both locations are depleted by stimuli known to increase the secretion of posterior pituitary hormones. After section of the

pituitary stalk, they disappear below the section and pile up above it. This and other evidence indicate that although vasopressin and oxytocin are stored in and released from the endings of the supraoptic and paraventricular neurons in the posterior lobe, the peptides are manufactured in the cell bodies of these neurons and transported down their axons.

Neurosecretion

Neurons which contain granules that stain with the Gomori stain are generally called neurosecretory neurons, and are believed to liberate chemical substances at their endings ("neurosecretion"). Although granule-containing neurons are found in the spinal cords of fish and in many parts of the nervous system of insects, the supraoptic and paraventricular neurons are the only neurons that normally contain abundant Herring bodies in mammals (Fig 14–4). However, it now appears that most if not all neurons liberate chemical agents. Most neurons secrete transmitter substances (see Chapter 4) that cross the synaptic clefts and act on the membrane of the postsynaptic cells. Others secrete substances that pass through the blood stream to affect distant organs. Some of these neurons contain Gomori-positive neurosecretory granules, but others do not. To avoid confusion, it seems wise to define the term **neurosecretion** as the secretion into the circulating body fluids by the endings of a neuron of chemical substances that act on other cells some distance away, whether or not the neuron contains Gomori-positive neurosecretory granules.

CONTROL OF ANTERIOR PITUITARY SECRETION

Anterior Pituitary Hormones

The anterior pituitary secretes 6 hormones: **adrenocorticotropic hormone** (corticotropin, ACTH), **thyroid-stimulating hormone** (thyrotropin, TSH), **growth hormone, follicle-stimulating hormone** (FSH), **luteinizing hormone** (LH), and **prolactin** (luteotropic hormone, LTH). The actions of these hormones are summarized in Fig 14–12, and other synonyms and abbreviations for them are listed in Table 22–1. They are discussed in detail in the chapters on the endocrine system. Other anterior pituitary hormones, including a lipid-mobilizing factor, may exist, but their existence has not been proved. Five of the hormones are **tropic hormones**, ie, they stimulate the secretion of substances from other glands. Prolactin promotes the formation of milk in the breast. The hypothalamus plays an important stimulatory role in regulating the secretion of ACTH, TSH, growth hormone, FSH, and LH. It also regulates prolactin secretion, but its effect is predominantly inhibitory rather than stimulatory.

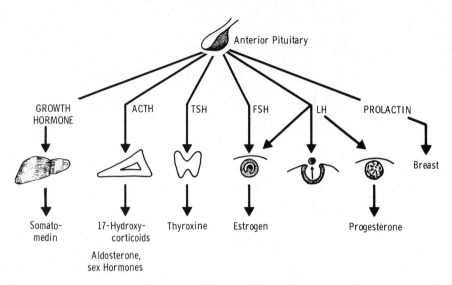

FIG 14–12. **Anterior pituitary hormones.** In women, FSH and LH act in sequence on the ovary to produce growth of the ovarian follicle, which secretes estrogen; ovulation; and formation and maintenance of the corpus luteum, which secretes estrogen and progesterone. In men, FSH and LH control the functions of the testes (see Chapter 23). Prolactin stimulates lactation.

Nature of Hypothalamic Control

There are probably a few nerve fibers that pass directly from the brain to the anterior pituitary, but they do not control anterior pituitary function. Instead, anterior pituitary secretion is controlled by chemical agents carried in the portal hypophysial vessels from the hypothalamus to the pituitary. These substances have generally been referred to as releasing and inhibiting factors, although there is an increasing tendency to refer to them as releasing and inhibiting hormones. The term factor is used in this book. **Corticotropin-releasing factor (CRF), thyrotropin-releasing factor (TRF), growth hormone-releasing factor (GHRF, SRF), follicle-stimulating hormone-releasing factor (FRF),** and **luteinizing hormone-releasing factor (LRF)** have been extracted from the hypothalamus. A factor which inhibits prolactin secretion (**prolactin inhibiting factor, PIF**) and a **growth hormone inhibiting factor (GIF)** have also been extracted, and there probably is a **prolactin-releasing factor (PRF)** as well.

TRF is a tripeptide (Fig 14–13). LRF is a decapeptide, and it has been reported that GIF is a tetradecapeptide (Fig 14–14). The other factors are probably also small polypeptides.

The area from which these releasing factors are secreted is the median eminence of the hypothalamus (Fig 14–4). This region contains few cells but many nerve endings in close proximity to the capillary loops from which the portal vessels originate. The releasing factors are probably secreted by these endings. Their release is therefore an example of neurosecretion as defined above. This type of neuroendocrine regulation is intermediate between that in the adrenal medulla, where nerve fibers stimulate gland cells, and that in the posterior pituitary, where substances secreted by neurons pass into the general circulation (Fig 14–15). The dopaminergic neurons in the median eminence (Fig 15–11) may end on the endings of the releasing factor-secreting neurons, and affect their secretion by a process akin to presynaptic inhibition (see Chapter 4).

There is considerable evidence in experimental animals that the various releasing factors are secreted from separate zones within the median eminence. In the dog, for example, TRF is secreted anteriorly, CRF

$$\text{(pyro)Glu-His-Trp-Ser-Tyr-Gly-Leu-Arg-Pro-Gly-NH}_2$$
$$12345678910$$

$$\text{Ala-Gly-Cys-Lys-Asn-Phe-Phe-Trp-Lys-Thr-Phe-Thr-Ser-Cys}$$
$$1234567891011121314$$

FIG 14–14. **Porcine LRF** (*top*) **and ovine GIF** (*bottom*).

(pyro)Glu-His-Pro-NH₂

FIG 14–13. **Structure of porcine and bovine TRF.** The structure of human TRF appears to be identical.

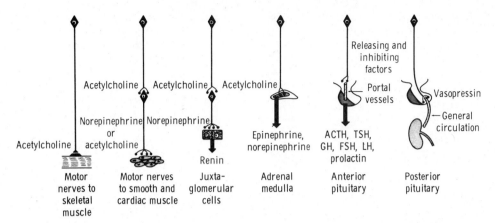

FIG 14–15. Diagrammatic representation of 6 situations in which humoral substances are released by neurons. The last 2 are examples of neurosecretion as this term is defined in the text. (Modified from Harris in: *Handbook of Physiology.* Field J, Magoun HW [editors]. Washington: The American Physiological Society, 1960. Section 1, pp 1007–1038.)

in the middle portion, and the gonadotropin-regulating factors posteriorly (Fig 14–16). A similar hypothalamic localization of releasing factor secretion in man has not been proved, but there is circumstantial evidence suggesting that the arrangement is similar to that in the dog.

The location of the cell bodies of the neurons that secrete releasing factors is an unresolved problem. The arcuate nucleus, a collection of cells along the bottom of the third ventricle near the infundibulum, is apparently involved in the secretion of the gonadotropin-stimulating factors. The CRF-secreting neurons appear to have their cell bodies throughout the hypothalamus. TRF-secreting neurons are probably located in the anterior hypothalamus and GRF-secreting neurons in or near the ventromedial nucleus. There is evidence that anterior pituitary hormones and, in the

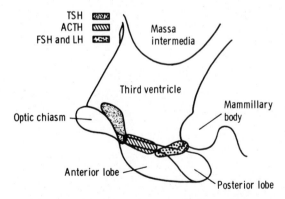

FIG 14–16. Hypothalamic localization. The areas involved in the control of anterior pituitary secretion in the dog are projected on a midsagittal section of the hypothalamus. (Redrawn and reproduced, with permission, from Ganong in: *Comparative Endocrinology.* Gorbman A [editor]. Wiley, 1959.)

case of the gonadotropins, gonadal steroids feed back on the hypothalamus to inhibit the secretion of the releasing factors.

Significance & Clinical Implications

The research delineating the multiple neuroendocrine regulatory functions of the hypothalamus is important because it explains how endocrine secretion is made appropriate to the demands of a changing environment. The nervous system receives information about changes in the internal and external environment from the sense organs. We now know that it brings about adjustments to these changes through effector mechanisms that include not only somatic movement but also changes in the rate at which hormones are secreted. There are many examples of the operation of the neuroendocrine effector pathways. In birds and many mammals, the increasing hours of daylight in the spring stimulate gonadotropin secretion, activating the quiescent gonads, and starting the breeding season. In some avian species, the sight of a member of the opposite sex in a mating dance apparently produces the gonadotropin secretion necessary to cause ovulation. It has been claimed that Eskimo women cease to ovulate during the long winter night and that regular menstrual cycles and sexual vigor return in the spring. In more temperate climates, menstruation in women is a year-round phenomenon, but its regularity can be markedly affected by somatic and emotional stimuli. The disappearance of regular periods when young girls move away from home (sometimes called "boarding school amenorrhea") and the inhibition of menstruation that can be produced by fear of pregnancy are examples of the many ways that psychic phenomena affect endocrine secretion.

Hypothalamic disease is not common, but it does occur. Its manifestations are neurologic defects, endocrine changes, and metabolic abnormalities such as hyperphagia and hyperthermia. The relative frequen-

TABLE 14–4. Symptoms and signs in 60 autopsied cases of hypothalamic disease.*

	Percentage of Cases
Endocrine and metabolic findings	
Precocious puberty	40
Hypogonadism	32
Diabetes insipidus	35
Obesity	25
Abnormalities of temperature regulation	22
Emaciation	18
Bulimia	8
Anorexia	7
Neurologic findings	
Eye signs	78
Pyramidal and sensory deficits	75
Headache	65
Extrapyramidal signs	62
Vomiting	40
Psychic disturbances, rage attacks, etc	35
Somnolence	30
Convulsions	15

*Data from Bauer: Endocrine and other manifestations of hypothalamic disease. J Clin Endocrinol 14:13, 1954. See also Kahana & others: Endocrine manifestations of intracranial extrasellar lesions. J Clin Endocrinol 22:304, 1962.

cies of the signs and symptoms of hypothalamic disease in one large series of cases are shown in Table 14–4. The possibility of hypothalamic pathology should be kept in mind in evaluating all patients with pituitary dysfunction, especially those with isolated deficiencies of single pituitary tropic hormones. Many of these deficiencies are proving to be due to hypothalamic rather than primary pituitary disease.

TEMPERATURE REGULATION

In the body, heat is produced by muscular exercise, assimilation of food, and all the vital processes that contribute to the basal metabolic rate (see Chapter 17). It is lost from the body by radiation, conduction, and vaporization of water in the respiratory passages and on the skin. Small amounts of heat are also removed in the urine and feces. The balance between heat production and heat loss determines the body temperature. Because the speed of chemical reactions varies with the temperature and because the enzyme systems of the body have narrow temperature ranges in which their function is optimal, normal body function depends upon a relatively constant body temperature.

Lower animals cannot adjust their body temperatures and so are at the mercy of the environment. In vertebrates, mechanisms for maintaining body temper-

ature by adjusting heat production and heat loss have evolved. In reptiles, amphibia, and fish, the adjusting mechanisms are rudimentary, and these species are called "cold-blooded" or **poikilothermic** because their body temperature fluctuates over a considerable range. In birds and mammals, the "warm-blooded" or **homeothermic** animals, a group of reflex responses integrated in the hypothalamus operate to maintain body temperature within a narrow range in spite of wide fluctuations in environmental temperature. The hibernating mammals are a partial exception. While awake, they are homeothermic, but during hibernation their body temperature falls.

Normal Body Temperature

In homeothermic animals the actual temperature at which the body is maintained varies from species to species and, to a lesser degree, from individual to individual. In man, the traditional normal value for the oral temperature is 37° C (98.6° F), but in one large series of normal young adults the morning oral temperature averaged 36.7° C, with a standard deviation of 0.2°. Therefore, 95% of all young adults would be expected to have a morning oral temperature of 36.3–37.1° C, or 97.3–98.8° F (mean ± 1.96 standard deviations; see Appendix). Various parts of the body are at different temperatures, and the magnitude of the temperature difference between the parts varies with the environmental temperature (Fig 14–17). The extremities are generally cooler than the rest of the body. The rectal temperature is representative of the temperature at the core of the body and varies least

FIG 14–17. Temperature of various parts of the body of a naked subject at various ambient temperatures in a calorimeter. (Redrawn and reproduced, with permission, from Hardy & Dubois: Basal metabolism, radiation, convection and vaporization at temperatures of 22–35° C. J Nutrition 15:477, 1938.)

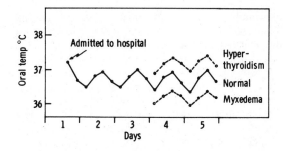

FIG 14—18. Typical temperature chart of a hospitalized patient who does not have a febrile disease. Note the slight rise in temperature, due to excitement and apprehension, at the time of admission to the hospital, and the regular diurnal temperature cycle.

FIG 14—19. Ranges in rectal and oral temperatures seen in normal humans. (Reproduced, with permission, from DuBois: *Fever and the Regulation of Body Temperature.* Thomas, 1948.)

with changes in environmental temperature. Oral temperature is normally 0.5° C lower than the rectal temperature, but it is affected by many factors, including ingestion of hot or cold fluids, gum-chewing, smoking, and mouth breathing.

The normal human core temperature undergoes a regular diurnal fluctuation of 0.5—0.7° C. In individuals who sleep at night and are awake during the day (even when hospitalized at bed rest), it is lowest at about 6:00 a.m. and highest in the evenings (Fig 14—18). It is lowest during sleep, slightly higher in the awake but relaxed state, and rises with activity. In women there is an additional monthly cycle of temperature variation characterized by a change in basal temperature at the time of ovulation (see Chapter 23, Fig 23—29). Temperature regulation is less precise in young children, and they may normally have a temperature that is 0.5° C or so above the established norm for adults.

During exercise the heat produced by muscular contraction accumulates in the body, and rectal temperature normally rises as high as 40° C (104° F). This rise is due in part to the inability of the heat-dissipating mechanisms to handle the greatly increased amount of heat that is produced, but there is evidence that in addition there is an elevation of the body temperature at which the heat-dissipating mechanisms are activated during exercise. Body temperature also rises slightly during emotional excitement, probably due to unconscious tensing of the muscles (Figs 14—18 and 14—19). It is chronically elevated by as much as 0.5° C when the metabolic rate is high, as in hyperthyroidism, and lowered when the metabolic rate is low, as in myxedema. Some apparently normal adults chronically have a temperature above the normal range (constitutional hyperthermia).

Heat Production

Heat production and energy balance are discussed in Chapter 17. A variety of basic chemical reactions contribute to body heat production at all times. Ingestion of food increases heat production because of the specific dynamic action of the food (see Chapter 17), but the major source of heat is the contraction of skeletal muscle (Table 14—5). Heat production can be varied in the absence of food intake or muscular exertion by endocrine mechanisms. Epinephrine and norepinephrine produce a rapid but short-lived increase in heat production; thyroxine causes a slowly developing but prolonged increase.

A source of considerable heat in human infants is a special type of fat, **brown fat**, which is located between and around the scapulas. This fat has a high rate of metabolism, and its function has been likened to that of an electric blanket. Brown fat is also found in a variety of animals, but, unlike ordinary white fat, it is not found in adult humans.

Heat Loss

The processes by which heat is lost from the body when the environmental temperature is below body temperature are listed in Table 14—5. **Radiation** is the transfer of heat from one object to another with which it is not in contact. **Conduction** is heat exchange between objects at different temperatures that are in contact with one another. The amount of heat transferred by conduction is proportionate to the temperature difference between the 2 objects (**thermal gradient**). **Convection**, the movement of the molecules of a

TABLE 14—5. Body heat production and heat loss.

Body heat is produced by:	
Basic metabolic processes	
Food intake (specific dynamic action)	
Muscular activity	

Body heat is lost by:	Percentage of Heat Lost at 21° C
Radiation and conduction	70
Vaporization of sweat	27
Respiration	2
Urination and defecation	1

gas or a liquid at one temperature to another location which is at a different temperature, aids conduction. When an individual is in a cold environment, he loses heat by conduction to the air around him and by radiation to cool objects in the vicinity. When he is in a hot environment, heat is transferred to him by these processes and adds to his heat load. Thus, in a sense, radiation and conduction work against the maintenance of body temperature. On a cold but sunny day, the heat of the sun reflected off bright objects exerts an appreciable warming effect. It is the heat reflected from the snow, for example, that makes it possible to ski in fairly light clothes even though the air temperature is below freezing.

Since conduction occurs from the surface of one object to the surface of another, the temperature of the skin determines to a large extent the degree to which body heat is lost or gained. The amount of heat reaching the skin from the deep tissues can be varied by changing the blood flow to the skin. When the cutaneous vessels are dilated, warm blood wells up into the skin, whereas in the maximally vasoconstricted state heat is held centrally in the body. The rate at which heat is transferred from the deep tissues to the skin is called the **tissue conductance**. Birds have a layer of feathers next to the skin, and most mammals have a significant layer of hair or fur. Heat is conducted from the skin to the air trapped in this layer, and from the trapped air to the exterior. When the thickness of the trapped layer is increased by fluffing the feathers or erection of the hairs **(horripilation)**, heat transfer across the layer is reduced and heat losses (or, in a hot environment, heat gains) are decreased. "Goose pimples" are the result of horripilation in man; they are the visible manifestation of cold-induced contraction of the piloerector muscles attached to the rather meager hair supply. Man usually supplements this layer of hair with a layer of clothes. Heat is conducted from the skin to the layer of air trapped by the clothes, from the inside of the clothes to the outside, and from the outside of the clothes to the exterior. The magnitude of the heat transfer across the clothing, a function of its texture and thickness, is the most important determinant of how warm or cool the clothes feel, but other factors, especially the size of the trapped layer of warm air, are important also. Dark clothes absorb radiated heat, and light-colored clothes reflect it back to the exterior.

The other major process transferring heat from the body in man and those animals that sweat is vaporization of water on the skin and mucous membranes of the mouth and respiratory passages. Vaporization of 1 g of water removes about 0.6 kcal of heat. A certain amount of water is vaporized at all times. This **insensible water loss** amounts to 50 ml/hour in man. When sweat secretion is increased, the degree to which the sweat vaporizes depends upon the humidity of the environment. It is common knowledge that one feels hotter on a humid day. This is due in part to the decreased vaporization of sweat, but even under conditions in which vaporization of sweat is complete an individual in a humid environment feels warmer than an individual in a dry environment. The reason for this difference is not known, but it seems related to the fact that in the humid environment sweat spreads over a greater area of skin before it evaporates. During muscular exertion in a hot environment, sweat secretion reaches values as high as 1600 ml/hour, and in a dry atmosphere most of this sweat is vaporized. Heat loss by vaporization of water therefore varies from 30 to over 900 kcal/hour.

Some mammals lose heat by **panting**. This rapid, shallow breathing greatly increases the amount of water vaporized in the mouth and respiratory passages, and therefore the amount of heat lost. Because the breathing is shallow, it produces relatively little change in the composition of alveolar air (Chapter 34).

The relative contribution of each of the processes that transfer heat away from the body (Table 14–5) varies with the environmental temperature. At 21° C, vaporization is a minor component in a man at rest. As the environmental temperature approaches body temperature, radiation losses decline and vaporization losses increase.

Temperature Regulating Mechanisms

The reflex and semireflex thermoregulatory responses are listed in Table 14–6. They include autonomic, somatic, endocrine, and behavioral changes. One group of responses increases heat loss and decreases heat production; the other decreases heat loss and increases heat production.

Curling up "in a ball" is a common reaction to cold in animals and has a counterpart in the position some people assume on climbing into a cold bed. Curling up decreases the body surface exposed to the environment. Shivering is an involuntary response of the skeletal muscles, but cold also causes a semiconscious

TABLE 14–6. Temperature regulating mechanisms.

Mechanisms activated by cold:	
Shivering	
Hunger	Increase
Increased voluntary activity	heat
Increased secretion of norepinephrine and epinephrine	production
Cutaneous vasoconstriction	Decrease
Curling up	heat
Horripilation	loss
Mechanisms activated by heat:	
Cutaneous vasodilatation	Increase
Sweating	heat
Increased respiration	loss
Anorexia	Decrease
Apathy and inertia	heat
Decreased secretion of TSH	production

general increase in motor activity. Examples include foot stamping and dancing up and down on a cold day. Increased catecholamine secretion is an important endocrine response to cold; adrenal medullectomized rats die faster than normal controls when exposed to cold. TSH secretion is increased by cold and decreased by heat in laboratory animals, but the change in TSH secretion produced by cold in adult humans is small and of questionable significance. It is common knowledge that activity is decreased in hot weather—the "it's too hot to move" reaction.

The reflex responses activated by cold are controlled from the posterior hypothalamus; those activated by warmth are controlled from the anterior hypothalamus. Stimulation of the anterior hypothalamus causes cutaneous vasodilatation and sweating, and lesions in this region cause hyperthermia, with rectal temperatures sometimes reaching 43° C (109° F). Posterior hypothalamic stimulation causes shivering, and the body temperature of animals with posterior hypothalamic lesions falls toward that of the environment. There is some evidence that serotonin is a synaptic mediator in the centers controlling the mechanisms activated by cold, and norepinephrine may play a similar role in those activated by heat.

Afferents

The signals which activate the hypothalamic temperature-regulating centers come from 2 sources: temperature-sensitive cells in the anterior hypothalamus, and cutaneous temperature receptors, especially cold receptors. Present evidence indicates that the stimuli which activate the defenses against high temperatures in man come mainly from the temperature-sensitive cells in the hypothalamus. This conclusion grew out of research in which the temperature of the back of the nasal cavity and the interior of the ear, near the hypothalamus, was correlated with thermoregulatory responses to changing environmental temperatures (Fig 14—20). This "head temperature" does not always correlate with rectal "body core" temperature, a fact which was often overlooked in previous research. The response of body heat production to cooling is modified by interactions between cutaneous and central stimuli. Heat production is increased when head temperature falls below a given threshold value, but the threshold for the response is lower and its magnitude decreased when the skin temperature is increased.

Fever

Fever is perhaps the oldest and most universally known hallmark of disease. When an individual develops a fever, his thermoregulatory mechanisms behave as if they were adjusted to maintain his body temperature at a higher than normal level, ie, "as if his thermostat had been reset" to a new set point above 37° C. His temperature receptors then signal that his actual temperature is below the new set point, and temperature-raising mechanisms are activated, producing chilly sensations due to cutaneous vasoconstric-

FIG 14—20. Quantitative relations in man between the temperature of the interior of the head (internal temperature) and cutaneous blood flow (squares, scale at the right), and sweating (circles and triangles, scale at the left). The arrow points to the sharp threshold at which these parameters start to rise. In this subject, the threshold was at 36.9° C. (Reproduced, with permission, from Benzinger: Receptor organs and quantitative mechanisms of human temperature control in a warm environment. Fed Proc 19:32, 1960.)

tion and occasionally enough shivering to produce a shaking chill. Salicylates such as aspirin appear to relieve fever by reducing the set point of the thermoregulatory mechanisms back toward normal.

Fever is produced in various ways. Many infections cause fever by causing the production of **endogenous pyrogen** from polymorphonuclear leukocytes in the blood (see Chapter 27). This fever-producing substance acts directly on the thermoregulatory centers in the hypothalamus to reset them. Other cells in the body can also release endogenous pyrogens, including monocytes, lymphocytes, and the Kupffer cells of the reticuloendothelial system. The endogenous pyrogens are proteins with molecular weights of 10,000–20,000. They are released from cells in response to viruses, antigens, antigen-antibody complexes, and even steroid hormones. They are also released in response to the endotoxin produced by some bacteria and as a result of phagocytosis of bacteria by endogenous pyrogen-producing cells.

The benefit of fever to the organism is unknown, although it is presumably beneficial in some way because it has evolved and persisted as a response to infections and other diseases in all homeothermic animals. Before the advent of antibiotics, fevers were artificially induced for the treatment of neurosyphilis. However, it is uncertain whether fever helps to kill the microorganisms that cause other infectious diseases. Very high temperatures are harmful. When the rectal temperature is over 41° C (106° F) for prolonged periods, some permanent brain damage results. When it is over 43° C, heat stroke develops and death is common.

Hypothermia

In hibernating mammals, body temperature drops to low levels without causing any ill effects which are demonstrable upon subsequent arousal. This observation led to experiments on induced hypothermia. When the skin or the blood is cooled enough to lower the body temperature in nonhibernating animals and in man, metabolic and physiologic processes slow down. Respiration and heart rate are very slow, blood pressure is low, and consciousness is lost. At rectal temperatures of about 28° C, ability to spontaneously return the temperature to normal is lost, but the individual continues to survive and, if rewarmed with external heat, returns to a normal state. If care is taken to prevent the formation of ice crystals in the tissues, the body temperature of experimental animals can be lowered to subfreezing levels without producing any damage that is detectable after subsequent rewarming.

Humans tolerate body temperatures of 21–24° C (70–75° F) without permanent ill effects, and induced hypothermia has been used extensively in surgery. In hypothermic patients the circulation can be stopped for relatively long periods because the O_2 needs of the tissues are greatly reduced. Blood pressure is low, and bleeding is minimal. It is possible under hypothermia to stop and open the heart and to perform other procedures, especially brain operations, that would have been impossible without cooling.

15...

Neurophysiologic Basis of Instinctual Behavior & Emotions

Emotions have both mental and physical components. They involve **cognition**, an awareness of the sensation and usually its cause; **affect**, the feeling itself; **conation**, the urge to take action; and **physical changes** such as hypertension, tachycardia, and sweating. Physiologists have been concerned for some time with the physical manifestations of emotional states, while psychologists have been concerned with emotions themselves. However, their interests merge in the hypothalamus and limbic systems since these parts of the brain are now known to be intimately concerned not only with emotional expression but with the genesis of emotions as well.

ANATOMIC CONSIDERATIONS

The term **limbic lobe** or **limbic system** is now generally applied to the part of the brain formerly called the rhinencephalon because it has become clear that only a small portion of this part of the brain is directly concerned with smell. Each limbic lobe consists of a rim of cortical tissue around the hilum of the cerebral hemisphere and a group of associated deep structures—the amygdala, the hippocampus, and the septal nuclei (Fig 15–1, 15–2).

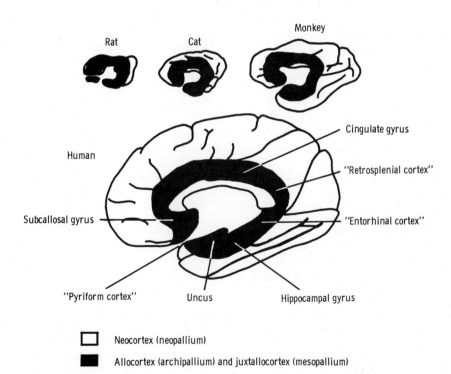

FIG 15–1. Relation of the limbic cortex to the rest of the cortex in the rat, the cat, the monkey, and the human. (Redrawn and reproduced, with permission, from MacLean: The limbic system and its hippocampal formation. J Neurosurg 11:29, 1954.)

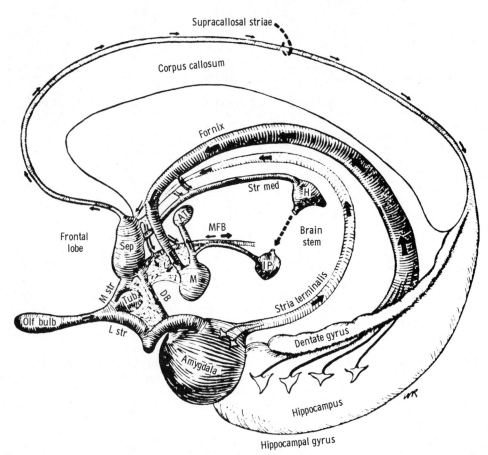

FIG 15—2. Diagram of the principal connections of the limbic system. M str, L str, medial and lateral olfactory striae; Str med, stria medullaris; Tub, olfactory tubercle; DB, diagonal band of Broca; Sep, septum; AT, anterior nucleus of the thalamus; M, mammillary body; H, habenula; IP, interpeduncular nucleus; MFB, medial forebrain bundle. (After Krieg. Reproduced, with permission, from MacLean: Psychosomatic disease and the visceral brain. Psychosom Med 11:338, 1949.)

Histology

The limbic cortex is phylogenetically the oldest part of the cerebral cortex. Histologically, it is made up of a primitive type of cortical tissue called **allocortex,** surrounding the hilum of the hemisphere, and a second ring of a transitional type of cortex called **juxtallocortex** between the allocortex and the rest of the cerebral hemisphere. The cortical tissue of the remaining nonlimbic portions of the hemisphere is called **neocortex.** The neocortex is the most highly developed type, and is characteristically 6-layered. The actual extent of the allocortical and juxtallocortical areas has changed little as mammals have evolved, but these regions have been overshadowed by the immense growth of the neocortex, which reaches its greatest development in man (Fig 15—1).

Afferent & Efferent Connections

The major connections of the limbic system are shown in Fig 15—2. The fornix connects the hippocampus to the mammillary bodies, which are in turn connected to the anterior nuclei of the thalamus by the mammillothalamic tract of Vicq d'Azyr. The anterior nuclei of the thalamus project to the cingulate cortex, and from the cingulate cortex there are connections to the hippocampus, completing a complex closed circuit. This circuit was originally described by Papez, and has been called the Papez circuit.

Correlations Between Structure & Function

One characteristic of the limbic system is the paucity of the connections between it and the neocortex. Nauta has aptly stated that, "The neocortex sits astride the limbic system like a rider on a horse without reins." Actually, there are a few reins; there are fibers from the frontal lobe to adjacent limbic structures, and probably some indirect connections via the thalamus. From a functional point of view, neocortical activity does modify emotional behavior and vice versa. However, one of the characteristics of emotion is that it cannot be turned on and off at will.

Another characteristic of limbic circuits is their prolonged afterdischarge following stimulation. This may explain in part the fact that emotional responses are generally prolonged rather than evanescent, and outlast the stimuli that initiate them.

LIMBIC FUNCTIONS

Stimulation and ablation experiments indicate that in addition to its role in olfaction (Chapter 10), the limbic system is concerned with feeding behavior. Along with the hypothalamus, it is also concerned with the control of biologic rhythms, sexual behavior, the emotions of rage and fear, and motivation.

Autonomic Responses & Feeding Behavior

Limbic stimulation produces autonomic effects, particularly changes in blood pressure and respiration. These responses are elicited from many limbic structures, and there is little evidence of localization of autonomic responses. This suggests that the autonomic effects are part of more complex phenomena, particularly emotional and behavioral responses. Stimulation of the amygdaloid nuclei causes movements such as chewing and licking and other activities related to feeding. Lesions in the amygdala cause moderate hyperphagia, with indiscriminate ingestion of all kinds of food. The relation of this type of omniphagia to the hypothalamic mechanisms regulating appetite is discussed in Chapter 14.

REGULATION OF BIOLOGIC RHYTHMS

Almost all plants and animals show cyclic variations in many of their functions. There are cycles of many different durations, but the most prominent are those about 24 hours long, the **circadian** or **diurnal rhythms**. In mammals and man, the diurnal fluctuations in body temperature, adrenocortical function, sodium and potassium excretion, and urine volume are among the best known, but there are many others. Although detailed discussion of these rhythms is outside the scope of this book, it is pertinent that the "biologic clocks" controlling some of them are apparently located in the limbic system. Lesions of the fornix seem to modify the adrenocortical rhythm. Abnormalities of sleep-wakefulness cycles and body temperature cycles without hypothermia or hyperthermia have also been reported after limbic lesions.

SEXUAL BEHAVIOR

Mating is a basic but complex phenomenon in which many parts of the nervous system are involved. Copulation itself is made up of a series of reflexes

integrated in spinal and lower brain stem centers, but the behavioral components that accompany it, the urge to copulate, and the coordinated sequence of events in the male and female that lead to pregnancy are regulated to a large degree in the limbic system and hypothalamus. Learning plays a part in the development of mating behavior, particularly in primates and man, but in lower animals courtship and successful mating can occur with no previous sexual experience. The basic responses are therefore innate and are undoubtedly present in all mammals. However, in humans the sexual functions have become extensively encephalized and conditioned by social and psychic factors. The basic physiologic mechanisms of sexual behavior in animals will therefore be considered first and then compared to the responses in humans.

Relation to Endocrine Function

In animals other than man, castration leads eventually to decreased or absent sexual activity in both the male and the female—although the loss is slow to develop in the males of some species. Injections of gonadal hormones in castrate animals revive sexual activity. Testosterone in the male and estrogen in the female have the most marked effect. Large doses of progesterone are also effective in the female, while in the presence of smaller doses of progesterone the dose of estrogen necessary to produce sexual activity is lowered. Large doses of testosterone and other androgens in castrate females initiate female behavior, and large doses of estrogens in castrate males trigger male mating responses. Why responses appropriate to the sex of the animal occur when the hormones of the opposite sex are injected is the subject of considerable debate. There is evidence that small doses of androgens produce male behavior in castrate females whereas large doses produce a female response, and the reverse relationship holds for the administration of estrogens to males.

Clinical Correlates

In adult women, ovariectomy does not necessarily reduce libido (defined in this context as sexual interest and drive) or sexual ability. Postmenopausal women continue to have sexual relations, often without much change in frequency from their premenopausal pattern. Some investigators claim that this persistence is due to continued secretion of estrogens and androgens from the adrenal cortex, but it is more likely due to the greater degree of encephalization of sexual functions in humans and their relative emancipation from instinctual and hormonal control. However, treatment with sex hormones increases sexual interest and drive in humans. Testosterone, for example, increases libido in males, and so does estrogen used to treat diseases such as carcinoma of the prostate. The behavioral pattern present before treatment is stimulated but not redirected. Thus, administration of testosterone to homosexuals intensifies their homosexual drive but does not convert it to a heterosexual drive.

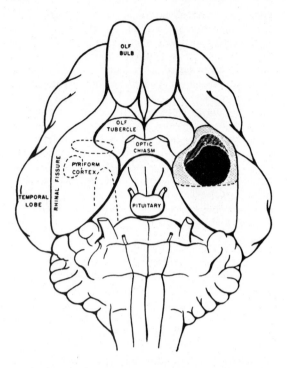

FIG 15—3. Site of lesions producing hypersexuality in male cats. When the black area was destroyed, hypersexuality was always present. The incidence of hypersexuality in animals with lesions in the surrounding lighter zones was not so high. Olf, olfactory. (Reproduced, with permission, from Green & others: Rhinencephalic lesions and behavior in cats. J Comp Neurol 108:505, 1957.)

Neural Control in the Male

In male animals, removal of the neocortex generally inhibits sexual behavior. Partial cortical ablations also produce some inhibition, the degree of the inhibition being independent of the coexisting motor deficit and most marked when the lesions are in the frontal lobes. On the other hand, cats and monkeys with bilateral limbic lesions localized to the pyriform cortex overlying the amygdala (Fig 15—3) develop a marked intensification of sexual activity. These animals not only mount adult females; they also mount immature females and other males, and attempt to copulate with animals of other species and with inanimate objects. Despite some claims to the contrary, such behavior is clearly outside the range of normal in the species studied. The behavior is dependent upon the presence of testosterone but is not due to any increase in its secretion.

The hypothalamus is also involved in the control of sexual activity in males. Stimulation along the medial forebrain bundle and in neighboring hypothalamic areas causes penile erection with considerable emotional display in monkeys. In castrated rats, intrahypothalamic implants of testosterone restore the complete pattern of sex behavior; and in intact rats, appropriately placed anterior hypothalamic lesions abolish interest in sex. It has been reported that lesions

in the mammillary region in male rats lead to increased sexual activity.

Sexual Behavior in the Female

In mammals the sexual activity of the male is more or less continuous, but in species other than man the sexual activity of the female is cyclic. Most of the time, the female avoids the male and repulses his sexual advances. Periodically, however, there is an abrupt change in behavior and the female seeks out the male, attempting to mate. These short episodes of **heat** or **estrus** are so characteristic that the sexual cycle in mammalian species that do not menstruate is named the **estrous cycle.**

This change in female sexual behavior is brought on by a rise in the circulating blood estrogen level. Some animals, notably the rabbit and the ferret, come into heat and remain estrous until pregnancy or pseudopregnancy results. In these species, ovulation is due to a neuroendocrine reflex. Stimulation of the genitalia and other sensory stimuli at the time of copulation provoke release from the pituitary of the gonadotropins that make the ovarian follicles rupture. In many other species, spontaneous ovulation occurs at regular intervals, and the periods of heat coincide with its occurrence. This is true even in monkeys and apes. In captivity, these species mate at any time; but in the wild state the females accept the male more frequently at the time of ovulation.

Neural Control in the Female

In female animals, removal of the neocortex and the limbic cortex abolishes active seeking out of the male ("enticement reactions") during estrus, but other aspects of heat are unaffected. Amygdaloid and periamygdaloid lesions do not produce hypersexuality as they do in the male. However, discrete anterior hypothalamic lesions abolish behavioral heat (Fig 15—4)

FIG 15—4. Sites of hypothalamic lesions which blocked behavioral heat without affecting ovarian cycles in ewes. MI, massa intermedia; MB, mammillary body; OC, optic chiasm; PIT, pituitary. (From data of Clegg & others: Endocrinology 62:790, 1958; and unpublished data of Clegg & Ganong.)

without affecting the regular pituitary-ovarian cycle (see Chapter 23).

Implantation of minute amounts of estrogen in the anterior hypothalamus causes heat in ovariectomized rats (Fig 23–29). Implantation into other parts of the brain and outside the brain does not have this effect. Apparently, therefore, some element in the hypothalamus is sensitive to the circulating estrogen titer and is stimulated by a high titer to initiate estrous behavior.

Effects of Sex Hormones in Infancy on Adult Behavior

In female experimental animals, exposure to sex steroids in utero or during early postnatal development causes marked abnormalities of sexual behavior when the animals reach adulthood. Female rats treated with a single relatively small dose of androgen before the fifth day of life do not have normal heat periods when they mature; they generally will not mate, even though they have cystic ovaries that secrete enough estrogen to cause the animals to have a persistently estrous type of vaginal smear (Chapter 23). These rats do not show the cyclic release of pituitary gonadotropins characteristic of the adult female, but rather the tonic, steady secretion characteristic of the adult male; their brains have been "masculinized" by the single brief exposure to androgens. Conversely, male rats castrated at birth develop the female pattern of cyclic gonadotropin secretion and show considerable female sexual behavior when given doses of ovarian hormones that do not have this effect in intact males. Thus, the development of a "female hypothalamus" depends simply on the absence of androgens in early life rather than on exposure to female hormones.

Rats are particularly immature at birth, and animals of other species in which the young are more fully developed at birth do not show these changes when exposed to androgens during the postnatal period. However, these animals develop genital abnormalities when exposed to androgens in utero (Chapter 23). Monkeys exposed to androgens in utero do not lose the female pattern of gonadotropin secretion but do develop abnormalities of sexual behavior in adulthood.

Clinical Correlates

The extent to which the findings in male animals with periamygdaloid lesions are applicable to man is, of course, difficult to determine, but there are reports of hypersexuality in men with bilateral lesions in the region of the amygdaloid nuclei.

In the human female, sexual activity is generally not confined to any period of heat, although some studies indicate an increase at about the time of ovulation. Others show some increase near the menses. There are reports of transient hypersexuality in women after surgical procedures involving manipulation of the anterior hypothalamus and neighboring structures. Because these reported effects were short-lived, they were probably due to inadvertent stimulation of diencephalic structures.

Early exposure to androgens in human females does not change the cyclic pattern of gonadotropin secretion in adulthood. However, there is evidence that masculinizing effects on behavior do occur.

Maternal Behavior

Maternal behavior is depressed by lesions of the cingulate and retrosplenial portions of the limbic cortex in animals. Hormones do not appear to be necessary for its occurrence, but certain hormones may facilitate its appearance. Prolactin from the anterior pituitary, which is secreted in large amounts during lactation, may exert a facilitatory effect by acting directly on the brain.

FEAR & RAGE

Fear and rage are in some ways closely related emotions. The external manifestations of the **fear, fleeing,** or **avoidance reaction** in animals are autonomic responses such as sweating and pupillary dilatation, cowering, and turning the head from side to side to seek escape. The **rage, fighting,** or **attack reaction** is associated in the cat with hissing, spitting, growling, piloerection, pupillary dilatation, and well-directed biting and clawing. Both reactions—and sometimes mixtures of the two—can be produced by hypothalamic stimulation. When an animal is threatened, it usually attempts to flee. If cornered, it fights. Thus, fear and rage reactions are probably related instinctual protective responses to threats in the environment.

Fear

The fear reaction can be produced in conscious animals by stimulation of the hypothalamus and the amygdaloid nuclei. Conversely, the fear reaction and its autonomic and endocrine manifestations are absent in situations in which they would normally be evoked when the amygdalae are destroyed. A dramatic example is the reaction of monkeys to snakes. Monkeys are normally terrified by snakes. After bilateral temporal lobectomy, monkeys approach snakes without fear, pick them up, and even eat them.

Rage & Placidity

Most animals and humans maintain a balance between rage and its opposite, the emotional state which for lack of a better name is called here placidity. Major irritations make the normal individual "lose his temper," but minor stimuli are ignored. In animals with certain brain lesions, this balance is altered. Some lesions produce a state in which the most minor stimuli evoke violent episodes of rage; others produce a state in which the most traumatic and anger-provoking stimuli fail to ruffle the animal's abnormal calm.

Rage responses to minor stimuli are observed after removal of the neocortex and after lesions of the ventromedial hypothalamic nuclei and septal nuclei in animals with intact cerebral cortices. On the other hand, bilateral destruction of the amygdaloid nuclei causes in monkeys a state of abnormal placidity. Similar responses are usually seen in cats and dogs. Wild rats which are vicious in captivity are transformed by this operation into animals that are as tractable and calm as ordinary laboratory white rats. Stimulation of some parts of the amygdala in cats produces rage. The placidity produced by amygdaloid lesions in animals is converted into rage by subsequent destruction of the ventromedial nuclei of the hypothalamus.

Rage can also be produced by stimulation of an area extending back through the lateral hypothalamus to the central gray area of the midbrain, and the rage response usually produced by amygdaloid stimulation is abolished by ipsilateral lesions in the lateral hypothalamus or rostral midbrain.

Gonadal hormones appear to affect aggressive behavior. In animals, aggression is decreased by castration and increased by androgens. It is also conditioned by social factors; it is more prominent in males that live with females, and increases when a stranger is introduced into an animal's territory.

"Sham Rage"

It was originally thought that rage attacks in animals with diencephalic and forebrain lesions represented only the physical, motor manifestations of anger, and the reaction was therefore called "sham rage." This now appears to be incorrect. Although rage attacks in animals with diencephalic lesions are induced by minor stimuli, they are usually directed with great accuracy at the source of the irritation. Furthermore, hypothalamic stimulation which produces the fear-rage reaction is apparently unpleasant to animals because they become conditioned against the place where the experiments are conducted and try to avoid the experimental sessions. They can easily be taught to press a lever or perform some other act to avoid a hypothalamic stimulus that produces the manifestations of fear or rage. It is difficult if not impossible to form conditioned reflex responses (see Chapter 16) by stimulation of purely motor systems, and it is also difficult if the unconditioned stimulus does not evoke either a pleasant or unpleasant feeling. The fact that hypothalamic stimulation is a potent unconditioned stimulus for the formation of conditioned avoidance responses and the fact that the avoidance responses are extremely persistent indicates that the stimulus is unpleasant. There is therefore little doubt that rage attacks include the mental as well as the physical manifestations of rage, and the term "sham rage" should be dropped.

Significance & Clinical Correlates

It is tempting on the basis of the evidence cited above to speculate that there are 2 intimately related mechanisms in the hypothalamus and limbic system, one promoting placidity and the other rage. If this is true, the emotional state is probably determined by afferent impulses which adjust the balance between them. An arrangement of this sort would be analogous to the systems controlling feeding and body temperature.

Although emotional responses are much more complex and subtle in humans than in animals, the neural substrates are probably the same. It is doubtful if placidity would be recognized as a clinical syndrome in our culture, but rage attacks in response to trivial stimuli have been observed many times in patients with brain damage. They are a complication of pituitary surgery when there is inadvertent damage to the base of the brain. They also follow a number of diseases of the nervous system, especially epidemic influenza and encephalitis, which destroy neurons in the limbic system and hypothalamus. Stimulation of the amygdaloid nuclei and parts of the hypothalamus in conscious humans produces sensations of anger and fear. In Japan, bilateral amygdaloid lesions have been produced in agitated, aggressive mental patients. The patients are said to have become placid and manageable, and it is of some interest that they were reported not to have developed hypersexuality or memory loss.

MOTIVATION

If an animal is placed in a box with a pedal or bar that can be pressed, the animal sooner or later accidentally presses it. Olds and his associates have shown that if the bar is connected in such a way that each press delivers a stimulus to an electrode implanted in certain parts of the brain (Fig 15–5), the animal returns to the bar and presses it again and again. Pressing the bar soon comes to occupy most of the animal's time. Some animals go without food and water to press the bar for brain stimulation, and some will continue until they fall over exhausted. Rats press the bar 5000–12,000 times per hour, and monkeys have been clocked at 17,000 bar presses per hour. On the other hand, when the electrode is in certain other areas the animals avoid pressing the bar, and stimulation of these areas is a potent unconditioned stimulus for the development of conditioned avoidance responses.

The points where stimulation leads to repeated bar pressing are located in a medial band of tissue passing from the amygdaloid nuclei through the hypothalamus to the midbrain tegmentum (Fig 15–6). The highest rates are generally obtained from points in the tegmentum, posterior hypothalamus, and septal nuclei. The points where stimulation is avoided are in the lateral portion of the posterior hypothalamus and dorsal midbrain and in the entorhinal cortex. The latter points are sometimes close to points where bar pressing is repeated, but they are part of a separate system. The areas where bar pressing is repeated are much more extensive than those where it is avoided. It has been calculated that in rats repeated pressing is obtained from 35% of the brain, avoidance from 5%,

FIG 15—5. Diagram of the apparatus in self-stimulation experiments. Each time the animal steps on the pedal, the electrical circuit is closed and a single current pulse is delivered to its brain through implanted electrodes. (Modified from Olds, in: *Electrical Stimulation of the Unanesthetized Brain.* Ramey E, O'Doherty J [editors]. Hoeber, 1960.)

FIG 15—6. Location of electrodes in self-stimulation studies, projected on parasagittal sections of the rat brain. The figures in the legend are percentages of time spent pressing the bar in a 6-hour test period. C, caudate; HPC, hippocampus; AM, amygdala; TH, thalamus; HTH, hypothalamus; MB, mammillary bodies; FX, fornix; TEG, tegmentum; S, septum; CB, cerebellum; EN, entorhinal cortex; CC, corpus callosum; C CORT, cerebral cortex; A, anterior commissure; MT, mammillothalamic tract; PREPYR, prepyriform cortex. (Reproduced, with permission, from Olds: A preliminary mapping of electrical reinforcing effects in the rat brain. J Comp Physiol Psychol 49:281, 1956.)

and indifferent responses (neither repetition nor avoidance) from 60%.

It is obvious that some effect of the stimulation causes the animals to stimulate themselves again and again, but what the animals feel is, of course, unknown. There are now a number of reports of bar-pressing experiments in humans with chronically implanted electrodes. Most of the subjects were schizophrenics or epileptics, but a few were patients with visceral malignancies and intractable pain. Like animals, humans press the bar repeatedly. They generally report that the sensations evoked are pleasurable, using phrases like "relief of tension" and "a quiet, relaxed feeling" to describe the experience. However, they rarely report "joy" or "ecstasy," and some persons with the highest self-stimulation rates cannot tell why they keep pushing the bar. When the electrodes are in the areas where stimulation is avoided, patients report sensations ranging from vague fear to terror. It is probably wise, therefore, to avoid vivid terms and call the brain systems involved the **reward** or **approach system** and the **punishment** or **avoidance system**.

Stimulation of the approach system provides a potent motivation for learning mazes or performing other tasks. Hungry rats will cross an electrified grid to obtain food only when the current in the grid is less than 70 microamperes, but when self-stimulation is the reward they will brave currents of 300 microamperes or more. A rat may even take a shock so strong that it will be stunned, but when it recovers consciousness will roll over and again struggle toward the bar.

To a certain extent, the reward system can be broken down into subsystems. In rats with certain lateral hypothalamic electrode placements, for example, self-stimulation rates are higher when the animals are hungry than when they are sated. In other hypothalamic locations, especially in the medial forebrain bundle, castration decreases and androgen treatment increases the self-stimulation rate. However, feeding and androgen treatment do not modify the responses in other locations.

Studies of the kind described above provide physiologic evidence that behavior is motivated not only by reduction or prevention of an unpleasant affect but also by primary rewards such as those produced by stimulation of the approach system of the brain. The implications of this fact are great in terms of the classical drive-reduction theory of motivation, in terms of the disruption and facilitation of ongoing behavior, and in terms of normal and abnormal emotional responses.

BRAIN CHEMISTRY, BEHAVIOR, & SYNAPTIC TRANSMISSION IN THE CNS

There is great current interest in drugs that modify human behavior. These drugs include **psychotomimetic agents,** drugs that produce hallucinations and other manifestations of the psychoses; **tranquilizers,** drugs that allay anxiety; and **psychic energizers,** antidepressant drugs that elevate mood and increase interest and drive. Many of these drugs appear to act by modifying transmission at synaptic junctions in the brain, and their discovery has stimulated great interest in the nature and properties of the transmitter agents involved.

Various agents have been suspected of being transmitters. Uneven distribution of a given substance in the various parts of the CNS and a parallel distribution of the enzymes responsible for the substance's synthesis and catabolism suggest that it may play a transmitter role. A change in behavior or some other CNS function coincident with a drug-induced change in the concentration of a substance is also indirect evidence that the substance is a transmitter. More direct evidence is provided by differential centrifugation of brain tissue, which has demonstrated the presence of a number of suspected mediators in fractions known to contain nerve endings. Agents found in nerve ending fractions in the CNS include acetylcholine, norepinephrine, dopamine, and serotonin. Additional evidence is provided by histochemical localization, which is now available for norepinephrine, serotonin, and dopamine. It has also been shown that certain of the suspected mediators are liberated from the brain in vitro, and that acetylcholine, glutamic acid, and some other suspected CNS mediators excite single neurons when applied to their membranes by means of a micropipet (**microelectrophoresis**). The substances currently known or suspected of being released from nerve endings are summarized in Table 15–1.

Serotonin

Serotonin (5-hydroxytryptamine, 5-HT) is present in highest concentration in blood platelets and in the gastrointestinal tract, where it is found in the enterochromaffin cells and the myenteric plexus (see Chapter 26). Lesser amounts are found in the brain, particularly in the hypothalamus (Table 15–2), and in the retina (see Chapter 8).

TABLE 15–1. Known and suspected synaptic transmitter agents and "neural hormones" in mammals.

Substance	Locations Where Substance Is Secreted	
	Known	Suspected
Acetylcholine	Myoneural junction Preganglionic autonomic endings Postganglionic parasympathetic endings Postganglionic sweat gland and muscle vasodilator endings Many parts of brain	Retina
Norepinephrine	Postganglionic sympathetic endings Brain stem, cerebellum	
Dopamine	Caudate nucleus, putamen, hypo- thalamus	Retina
Serotonin		Hypothalamus and environs, retina
Substance P		Hypothalamus, substantia nigra, retina, intestine
Histamine		Hypothalamus
Vasopressin	Posterior pituitary	
Oxytocin	Posterior pituitary	

Anterior pituitary hormone releasing
  and inhibiting factors (CRF,
  TRF, GRF, GIF, LRF, FRF,
  PRF, PIF; see Chapter 14)
	Median eminence of hypothalamus	

Glycine		Neurons mediating direct inhibi- tion in spinal cord

Gamma-aminobutyric acid (GABA)		Cerebral cortex; neurons mediat-
		  ing presynaptic inhibition in
		  spinal cord; retina

Glutamic acid (glutamate)		Excites many mammalian neurons

**TABLE 15–2. Brain content of GABA and a number of probable
transmitter agents at synapses in the CNS.**

	DOG					RAT
	Acetyl-choline µg/g*	Substance P units/g*	Sero-tonin µg/g*	Norepi-nephrine µg/g*	Hista-mine µg/g*	GABA µg/g†
Cerebral cortex—somesthetic	2.8	‡	‡	0	0	} 210
Cerebral cortex—motor	4.5	19	0.02	0.18	0	
Caudate nucleus	2.7	46	0.10	0.06	0	‡
Thalamus	3.0	13	0.02	0.16	0	‡
Hypothalamus	1.8	70	0.25	1.03	30	380
Hippocampus	‡	15	0.05	‡	‡	‡
Medulla	1.6	25	0.03	‡	‡	200
Cerebellum	0.2	2	0.01	0.07	0	160
Spinal cord	1.6	29	0	‡	0	‡
Sympathetic ganglia	30	7	0	6.00	5	‡
Area postrema	‡	460	0.24	1.04	‡	‡

*Data on dog from various authors, compiled by Paton: Ann Rev Physiol 20:431, 1958.
†Data on rat GABA (gamma-aminobutyric acid) from Berl & Waelsch: J Neurochem 3:161, 1958.
‡No data.

SEROTONIN

NOREPINEPHRINE

DOPAMINE

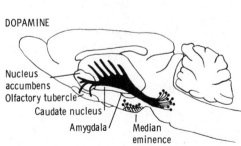

The monoamines in tissues can be demonstrated histochemically. The method makes serotonin, norepinephrine, epinephrine, and dopamine all fluoresce, but comparing the histologic pictures in animals treated with drugs that selectively deplete the various amines makes it possible to identify each amine. With this technic, it has been demonstrated that serotonin, norepinephrine, and dopamine are all localized in nerve endings. Serotonin is found in relatively high concentrations in the lateral gray horns of the spinal cord and in a number of areas in the brain. Histochemically, it can be shown that there is a system of serotonin-containing neurons that have their cell bodies in the raphe nuclei of the brain stem and project to portions of the hypothalamus, the limbic system, and the neocortex (Fig 15–7).

Serotonin is formed in the body by hydroxylation and decarboxylation of the essential amino acid tryptophan (Fig 15–8). It is inactivated principally by monoamine oxidase (Fig 15–9) to form 5-hydroxyindoleacetic acid (5-HIAA). This substance is the principal urinary metabolite of serotonin, and the urinary output of 5-HIAA is used as an index of the rate of serotonin metabolism in the body. In the pineal gland, serotonin is converted to melatonin (see Chapter 24).

◄——— FIG 15–7. Aminergic pathways in the brain of the rat. *Top:* Serotonin-secreting neurons. *Middle:* Norepinephrine-secreting neurons. *Bottom:* Dopamine-secreting neurons. (Modified and reproduced, with permission, from Ungerstedt: Stereotaxic mapping of the monoamine pathways in the rat brain. Acta physiologica scandinav Suppl 367:1, 1971.)

FIG 15–8. Biosynthesis of serotonin. PyPh = pyridoxal phosphate. Note that the same enzyme catalyzes the decarboxylation of 5-hydroxytryptophan and dopa (see Fig 13–3).

The psychotomimetic agent lysergic acid diethylamide (LSD) is a serotonin antagonist. The transient hallucinations and other mental aberrations produced by this drug were discovered when the chemist who synthesized it inhaled some by accident. Although the relation of LSD to brain serotonin remains unsettled, its discovery called attention to the correlation between behavior and variations in brain serotonin content. Several substances which, like serotonin, are derivatives of tryptamine have psychotomimetic actions; psilocybin, a hallucinogenic agent found in certain mushrooms, is the best known of these compounds. The tranquilizing drug reserpine causes a pronounced depletion of serotonin from body stores, including the brain; and if serotonin depletion is prevented the drug's tranquilizing action is blocked. However, reserpine also depletes brain norepinephrine and dopamine, and it is difficult to decide which of its effects are due to serotonin depletion and which to catecholamine depletion. Monoamine oxidase inhibitors, which are psychic energizers, increase brain serotonin, but they also increase brain norepinephrine and dopamine. Selective depletion of brain serotonin can be produced by administering p-chlorophenylalanine, a compound that blocks conversion of tryptophan to 5-hydroxytryptophan (Fig 15–8). This is the rate-limiting step in serotonin biosynthesis. In animals, p-chlorophenylalanine produces prolonged wakefulness, suggesting (along with other evidence) that serotonin plays a role in sleep. However, wakefulness is not produced in man, and no clear-cut psychic changes are produced even by large doses. Thus, the relation of serotonin to mental function remains uncertain. There is some evidence that serotonin is a mediator in descending fiber systems that inhibit the initiation of autonomic impulses in the lateral gray columns of the spinal cord.

Norepinephrine

The distribution of norepinephrine in the brain parallels that of serotonin (Tables 15–2 and 15–3). Large amounts are also found in the pineal gland. The cell bodies of most if not all of the norepinephrine-containing neurons are located in the locus ceruleus and other nuclei in the pons and medulla. Some of the axons descend in the spinal cord, and others enter the cerebellum. A large number ascend in 2 bundles to innervate the hypothalamus, limbic system, and neocortex (Fig 15–7).

Evidence has now accumulated that the norepinephrine in the brain is related to mental function. It has been known for some time that reserpine can produce depression and that monoamine oxidase inhibitors are psychic energizers. These drugs affect brain serotonin as well as brain catecholamines, but recent research with compounds that affect norepinephrine selectively indicates that mood is related to the amount of free norepinephrine available at synapses in the brain. When too little norepinephrine is available, depression results; and drugs such as monoamine oxidase inhibitors and amphetamine, which increase free norepinephrine, elevate mood. The tricyclic antidepressants such as desipramine appear to act in the same way; they decrease the reuptake of liberated norepinephrine (see Chapter 13), thus leaving more available to act on the postsynaptic structures.

In the cerebellum, adrenergic neurons inhibit Purkinje cells, and there is evidence that these inhibitory effects are mediated via β receptors and cyclic AMP.

The norepinephrine-containing neurons in the hypothalamus are involved in regulation of the secretion of anterior pituitary hormones (see Chapter 14), and they appear to inhibit the secretion of vasopressin and oxytocin. There is some evidence that norepinephrine is involved in the control of food intake and, along with serotonin, in the regulation of body temperature. An inhibitory effect on autonomic discharge from the spinal cord has also been suggested.

There are small amounts of epinephrine and appreciable quantities of tyramine in the CNS, but no

FIG 15–9. Catabolism of serotonin. In oxidative deaminations catalyzed by monoamine oxidase, an aldehyde is formed first and then oxidized to the corresponding acid. Some of the aldehyde is also reduced to the corresponding alcohol. The heavy arrow indicates the major metabolic pathway.

function has been assigned to these agents. The biosynthesis and metabolism of norepinephrine and epinephrine are discussed in Chapter 13.

Dopamine

Dopamine is the immediate precursor of norepinephrine (Fig 13–3). In certain parts of the brain, the concentration of norepinephrine is low and that of dopamine is very high (Table 15–3). These regions contain most of the enzymes found in parts of the brain that are rich in norepinephrine, but their dopamine β-hydroxylase activity is low. This is the enzyme that catalyzes the conversion of dopamine to norepinephrine; consequently, catecholamine synthesis stops at dopamine.

Dopamine is inactivated by monoamine oxidase and by catechol-O-methyltransferase (Fig 15–10) in a manner analogous to the inactivation of norepinephrine (Fig 13–5).

Dopaminergic neurons with their cell bodies in the midbrain project to the caudate, putamen, amygdala, and olfactory tubercle (Fig 15–7). A separate intrahypothalamic system of dopaminergic neurons projects from cell bodies in the arcuate nucleus to the external layer of the median eminence of the hypothalamus (Fig 15–11).

Evidence is accumulating that dopamine is related in some way to motor function. In Parkinson's disease (Chapter 12), the dopamine content of the caudate nucleus and putamen is about 50% of normal. Hypothalamic norepinephrine is also reduced, but not to so great a degree. Several drugs that produce parkin-

TABLE 15–3. Amine and substance P content of selected portions of the human brain.
Data compiled from various authors.

	Norepinephrine	Dopamine	Serotonin	Histamine	Substance P (U/g)
	(μg/g fresh tissue)				
Amygdala	0.21	0.6	0.26	*	*
Caudate nucleus	0.09	3.5	0.33	0.5	85
Putamen	0.12	3.7	0.32	0.7	*
Globus pallidus	0.15	0.5	0.23	0.6	*
Thalamus	0.13	0.3	0.26	0.4	12
Hypothalamus	1.25	0.8	0.29	2.5	102
Substantia nigra	0.21	0.9	0.55	*	699

*No data.

Dihydroxyphenylethylamine
(dopamine)

3,4-Dihydroxyphenylacetic acid
(DOPAC)

3-Methoxy-4-hydroxy-
phenylethylamine

Homovanillic acid
(HVA)

FIG 15–10. Catabolism of dopamine. MAO, mono-amine oxidase; COMT, catechol-O-methyltransfer-ase. See legend of Fig 15–9.

FIG 15–11. Dopaminergic neurons in the hypothalamus of the rat. *a*-Methylnorepinephrine injected before sacrifice to intensify fluorescence. Transverse section. Cell bodies can be seen above, in the arcuate nucleus on either side of the third ventricle, and the dense nerve terminals can be seen below in the external layer of the median eminence. (Reproduced, with permission, from Hökfelt & Fuxe: On the morphology and the neuroendocrine role of the hypothalamic cate-cholamine neurons. In: *Brain-Endocrine Interaction.* Knigge K, Scott D, Weindl A [editors]. Karger, 1972.)

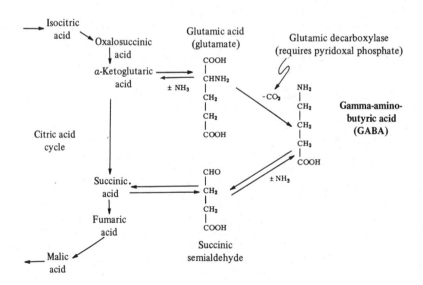

FIG 15–12. Formation and metabolism of gamma-aminobutyric acid.

sonism-like states as undesirable side-effects have been shown to alter the metabolism of dopamine in the brain. On the other hand, L-dopa (levodopa) has been found to be very effective in the treatment of Parkinson's disease when administered in large doses. This compound, unlike dopamine, crosses the blood-brain barrier (see Chapter 32) and produces a small but measurable increase in brain dopamine content.

There is some evidence that dopamine facilitates conditioned avoidance reflexes. The hallucinogen mescaline is a derivative of dopamine. The dopaminergic neurons in the hypothalamus seem to play a role in the control of the secretion of prolactin. L-Dopa inhibits prolactin secretion in humans, whereas reserpine and related drugs that deplete brain catecholamines have the opposite effect.

Acetylcholine

Acetylcholine is distributed throughout the CNS with the highest concentrations in the motor cortex and the thalamus (Tables 15–1 and 15–2). The distribution of choline acetylase and acetylcholinesterase parallels that of acetylcholine. Most of the acetylcholinesterase is in neurons, but some is found in glia. Pseudocholinesterase is also found in many parts of the CNS.

Acetylcholine has been linked directly or indirectly to a variety of brain functions. Many cholinergic neurons in the CNS form a large ascending system. The cell bodies of these neurons are in the reticular formation and their axons radiate to all parts of the forebrain, including the hypothalamus, thalamus, visual pathways, basal ganglia, hippocampus, and neocortex. This system appears to be the ascending reticular activating system, which produces EEG arousal and maintains consciousness (see Chapter 11).

A number of hallucinogenic agents are derivatives of atropine, a drug which blocks the effects of acetylcholine at postganglionic nerve endings. Injections of acetylcholine into the hypothalamus and parts of the limbic system cause drinking. Application of acetylcholine to the supraoptic nucleus in dogs causes increased secretion of vasopressin. In blinded rats, acetylcholinesterase activity is decreased in the superior colliculi and elevated in the occipital cortex. Cortical levels of acetylcholinesterase are greater in rats raised in a complex environment than in rats raised in isolation, but the significance of this type of correlation is uncertain. Acetylcholine appears to be an excitatory transmitter in the basal ganglia, whereas dopamine is an inhibitory transmitter in these structures. In parkinsonism, the loss of dopamine alters the cholinergic-dopaminergic balance, and anticholinergic drugs are of benefit along with L-dopa in the treatment of the disease.

Gamma-Aminobutyric Acid & Other Amino Acids

Gamma-aminobutyric acid (GABA) has been proved to be the synaptic transmitter at the inhibitory neuromuscular junctions in crustaceans. In mammals, it appears to be the mediator for presynaptic inhibition

in the spinal cord (see Chapter 4) and an inhibitory mediator in the brain and in the retina. Its action is antagonized by picrotoxin. There is an increase in the amount of GABA released from the brain when the EEG pattern is that of slow wave sleep.

GABA is formed by decarboxylation of glutamic acid, and it can reenter the citric acid cycle (see Chapter 17) by conversion to succinic acid (Fig 15–12). The citric acid cycle is the major pathway by which intermediates formed in the catabolism of carbohydrates, proteins, and fats are metabolized to CO_2 and H_2O. Pyridoxal phosphate, a derivative of the B complex vitamin pyridoxine, is a cofactor for the decarboxylase that catalyzes the formation of GABA from glutamic acid. The transaminases responsible for the formation of glutamic acid and for the formation of succinic semialdehyde are also pyridoxine-dependent. However, the decarboxylation, unlike the transaminations, is essentially irreversible. Consequently, the GABA content of the brain is reduced in pyridoxine deficiency. Pyridoxine deficiency is associated with signs of neural hyperexcitability and convulsions, although pyridoxine treatment is unfortunately of no value in most clinical cases of idiopathic epilepsy.

Glutamic acid (glutamate) has been shown to be the excitatory mediator at myoneural junctions in certain insects. It depolarizes mammalian neurons when placed directly on their membranes by microelectrophoresis, but it has not been proved to be a transmitter at any specific location in mammals.

Evidence is now accumulating that the ubiquitous amino acid **glycine** is the mediator responsible for direct inhibition in the spinal cord. When applied directly to the membranes of neurons, it produces hyperpolarization, and its action is antagonized by strychnine.

One conceptual objection to glycine and glutamate as transmitters is the fact that these amino acids probably occur not only in neurons but in most if not all living cells. However, the necessary specificity for chemical transmission is provided not by unique chemicals but by specialized neuronal mechanisms for the storage, release, and postsynaptic action of a particular substance. Thus, almost any small diffusible substance could be a transmitter.

Histamine

There are large amounts of histamine in the anterior and posterior lobes of the pituitary and in the adjacent median eminence of the hypothalamus. The heparin-containing tissue cells called **mast cells** have a high histamine content, and most of the histamine in the posterior pituitary is in mast cells although the histamine in the anterior pituitary and the hypothalamus is not. In other parts of the brain, the histamine content is very low. Histamine is formed by decarboxylation of the amino acid histidine (Fig 15–13). In the brain, it is converted to methylhistamine; outside the brain, to imidazoleacetic acid. The latter reaction requires the enzyme **diamine oxidase (histaminase)**

FIG 15–13. **Synthesis and catabolism of histamine.**

rather than monoamine oxidase, even though monoamine oxidase catalyzes the oxidation of methylhistamine to methylimidazoleacetic acid.

So far, there is relatively little evidence other than uneven distribution to suggest that histamine is a synaptic mediator in the brain. However, the histamine content of the brain is increased by the tremor-producing drug tremorine; by the psychotomimetic agent mescaline; and by the tranquilizer chlorpromazine. The content is decreased by reserpine.

Substance P

Substance P (Fig 15–14) is a polypeptide. It is found in appreciable quantities in the intestine, where it may be a chemical mediator in the myenteric reflex (Chapter 26). In the nervous system, high concentrations are found in the hypothalamus and the dorsal roots of the spinal nerves, and there are particularly large amounts in the substantia nigra (Tables 15–2 and 15–3). Little is known about the synthesis and catabolism of this polypeptide, although brain tissue apparently contains enzymes that are concerned with both processes. Injections of substance P alter potentials associated with transmission in the sensory pathways in the spinal cord.

$$\text{Arg-Pro-Lys-Pro-Gln-Gln-Phe-Phe-Gly-Leu-Met-NH}_2$$
$$\quad 1 \quad\ 2 \quad\ 3 \quad\ 4 \quad\ 5 \quad\ 6 \quad\ 7 \quad\ 8 \quad\ 9 \quad 10 \quad 11$$

FIG 15–14. **Bovine substance P**

Prostaglandins

Prostaglandins—fatty acid derivatives found in high concentration in semen (see Chapter 17)—are also found in the brain. They have been shown to be present in nerve ending fractions of brain homogenates and to be released from the cortex, the cerebellum, and the spinal cord. When administered by microelectrophoresis onto nerve cell membranes, they alter the firing rates of the neurons. This suggests that they may be synaptic mediators. However, they may also exert their effects by modulating reactions mediated by cyclic AMP. Their definitive role remains to be determined.

16...

"Higher Functions of the Nervous System": Conditioned Reflexes, Learning, & Related Phenomena

In previous chapters, somatic and visceral input to the brain and output from it have been discussed. The functions of the reticular core in maintaining an alert, awake state have been described, and the functions of the limbic-midbrain circuit in the maintenance of homeostatic equilibriums and the regulation of instinctual and emotional behavior have been catalogued (Fig 16–1). There remain the phenomena called, for lack of a better or more precise term, the "higher functions of the nervous system": learning, memory, judgment, language, and the other functions of the mind. As Penfield has said, those who study the neurophysiology of the mind are, ". . . like men at the foot of a mountain. They stand in the clearings they have made

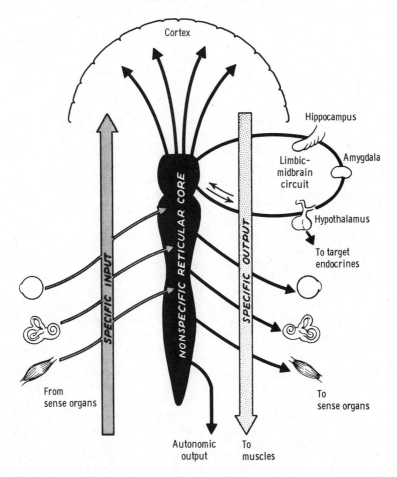

FIG 16–1. Organization of the nervous system. (Modified from Galambos & Morgan, in: *Handbook of Physiology*. Field J, Magoun HW [editors]. Washington: The American Physiological Society, 1960. Section 1, pp 1471–1500.)

on the foothills, looking up at the mountain they hope to scale. But the pinnacle is hidden in eternal clouds."* These "clearings on the foothills" are the subject of this chapter.

Methods

Some of the phenomena of the mind, such as learning and possibly memory, occur in many animal species, whereas others probably occur to a significant degree only in man. All are hard to study because it is difficult to communicate with animals and because moral and legal considerations rightly limit experimental studies in man. In general, the available data have been obtained by 4 methods. The oldest method consists of correlating clinical observations in humans with the site and extent of brain pathology discovered at autopsy. Information obtained in this way has been supplemented by studying the effects of stimulation of the exposed cerebral cortex during neurosurgical procedures under local anesthesia. More recently, the effects of stimulating subcortical structures with chronically implanted electrodes in patients with parkinsonism, schizophrenia, epilepsy, and incurable malignancies have been investigated. The fourth approach has been the study of conditioned reflexes in animals and man.

LEARNING

Learning is sometimes assumed to be a function of the cerebral hemispheres, but it also occurs in many animal species that have no cerebral cortex. It occurs readily in animals such as the octopus; it has been demonstrated in worms; and it may even occur in unicellular organisms. In addition, phenomena resembling learning occur at subcortical and spinal levels in mammals. Post-tetanic potentiation, the facilitation in a synaptic pathway that follows repeated stimulation (see Chapter 4), is such a phenomenon. Another is the long-term response to the injection of formalin into one paw in kittens. The inflammation and other visible effects of such an injection subside within a few weeks. However, it has been reported that if the kitten is decerebrated months or even years later, it develops flexor rather than extensor rigidity in the injected limb, even though the expected extensor response occurs in the other 3 extremities.

The rapidity with which persistent alterations in neural pathways can be produced in the spinal cord is illustrated by experiments on the effect of cord section in rats with unilateral cerebellar lesions. These lesions cause the rats to assume abnormal postures. The postural abnormalities in the limbs and trunk disappear if the spinal cord is transected in the cervical region up to

*From *Handbook of Physiology*. Field J, Magoun HW (editors). Washington: The American Physiological Society, 1960. Section 1, p 1441.

45 minutes after the production of the lesion. However, if the spinal cord is transected more than 45 minutes after the lesion has been produced, the abnormalities persist.

More advanced types of learning are largely cortical phenomena, but the brain stem is also involved in these processes. Some types of learning have been shown to produce structural changes in the cerebral cortex. For example, rats exposed to visually complex environments and trained to perform various tasks have thicker, heavier cerebral cortices than control rats exposed to monotonously uniform environments.

Conditioned Reflexes

Conditioned reflexes are an important type of learning. A conditioned reflex is a reflex response to a stimulus which did not previously elicit the response, acquired by repeatedly pairing the stimulus with another stimulus that normally does produce the response. In Pavlov's classical experiments, the salivation normally induced by placing meat in the mouth of a dog was studied. A bell was rung just before the meat was placed in the dog's mouth, and this was repeated a number of times until the animal would salivate when the bell was rung even though no meat was placed in its mouth. In this experiment the meat placed in the mouth was the **unconditioned stimulus** (US), the stimulus that normally produces a particular innate response. The **conditioned stimulus** (CS) was the bell-ringing. After the CS and US had been paired a sufficient number of times, the CS produced the response originally evoked only by the US. An immense number of somatic, visceral, and other neural phenomena can be made to occur as conditioned reflex responses.

If the CS is presented repeatedly without the US, the conditioned reflex eventually dies out. This process is called **extinction** or **internal inhibition**. If the animal is disturbed by an external stimulus immediately after the CS is applied, the conditioned response may not occur (**external inhibition**). However, if the conditioned reflex is **reinforced** from time to time by again pairing the CS and US, the conditioned reflex persists indefinitely.

When a conditioned reflex is first established, it can be evoked not only by the CS but also by similar stimuli. However, if only the CS is reinforced and the similar stimuli are not, the animal can be taught to discriminate between different signals with great accuracy. The elimination of the response to other stimuli is an example of internal inhibition. By means of such **discriminative conditioning** dogs can be taught, for example, to distinguish between a tone of 800 hz and one of 812 hz. Most of the data on pitch discrimination, color vision, and other sensory discriminations in animals have been obtained in this way.

For conditioning to occur, the CS must precede the US. If the CS follows the US, no conditioned response develops. The conditioned response follows the CS by the time interval that separated the CS and US during training. The delay between stimulus and response may be as long as 90 sec. When the time interval is appreciable, the response is called a **delayed conditioned reflex.**

As noted in Chapter 15, conditioned reflexes are difficult to form if the US provokes a purely motor response. They are relatively easily formed if the US is associated with a pleasant or unpleasant affect. Stimulation of the brain reward system is a powerful US (pleasant, or **positive reinforcement**), and so is stimulation of the avoidance system or a painful shock to the skin (unpleasant, or **negative reinforcement**).

Operant conditioning has been the subject of considerable research, especially in the United States. This is a form of conditioning in which the animal is taught to perform some task ("operate on the environment") in order to obtain a reward or avoid punishment. The US is the pleasant or unpleasant event, and the CS is a light or some other signal that alerts the animal to perform the task. Conditioned motor responses that permit an animal to avoid an unpleasant event are called **conditioned avoidance reflexes.** For example, an animal is taught that by pressing a bar it can prevent an electric shock to the feet. Reflexes of this type are extensively used in testing tranquilizers and other drugs that affect behavior.

Physiologic Basis of Conditioned Reflexes

The essential feature of the conditioned reflex is the formation of a new functional connection in the nervous system. In Pavlov's experiment, for example, salivation in response to bell-ringing indicates that a functional connection has developed between the auditory pathways and the autonomic centers controlling salivation. Because decortication depresses or interferes with the formation of many conditioned reflexes, it was originally thought that these new connections were intracortical. However, the effects of cortical ablation on conditioned reflexes are complex. When the CS is a complex sensory stimulus, the cortical sensory area for the sensory modality involved must be present. The rest of the cortex is not necessary, however, and nondiscriminative conditioned responses to simple sensory stimuli can be formed in the absence of the whole cortex. These and other experiments indicate that the new connections are formed in subcortical structures.

Electroencephalographic & Evoked Potential Changes During Conditioning

When a new sensory stimulus is first presented to an animal, it produces diffuse EEG arousal and prominent evoked secondary responses in many parts of the brain. Behaviorally, the human or animal becomes alert and attentive, a response that Pavlov called the **orienting reflex** (the "What is it?" response). If the stimulus is neither pleasurable nor noxious, it evokes less electrical response when repeated, and the EEG and other changes eventually cease to occur; the animal "becomes accustomed to" the stimulus and ignores it. These electrical and behavioral phenomena are thus examples of habituation. Changes in sensory stimuli also provoke arousal. For example, when an animal becomes habituated to a stimulus such as a regularly repeated tone, stopping the tone produces arousal.

If a signal to which an animal has become habituated is paired with another stimulus that evokes EEG arousal, conditioning occurs; after relatively few pairings, the previously neutral stimulus alone evokes desynchronization. This conditioned response to the neutral stimulus is an example of **electrocortical conditioning**, and is sometimes called the **alpha block conditioned reflex.** An example in the human of the alpha block conditioned reflex is shown in Fig 16–2. Electrocortical conditioning is unaffected by cutting the lateral connections of the cortical sensory areas but is prevented by lesions in the nonspecific projection nuclei of the thalamus, which indicates that the new connections involved are formed at or below the thalamic level. If an alpha block conditioned reflex is not reinforced, extinction occurs. Extinction is associated with the development of EEG hypersynchrony (extremely regular, large amplitude waves) in the cortical area concerned with the US that generated the reflex. This observation and various psychologic data suggest that extinction, or "unlearning," is not passive but,

FIG 16–2. Conditioned blocking of the alpha rhythm in the occipital region in a normal human. *A:* Lack of response to a tone to which the subject was habituated (thin black signal). *B:* Unconditioned alpha block (desynchronization) in response to a bright light (heavy black signal). *C:* Failure of the tone to produce desynchronization when first paired with the light. *D:* After ninth pairing of tone and light, the tone produces conditioned alpha block before the light is turned on. (Reproduced, with permission, from Morrell & Ross: Central inhibition in cortical reflexes. Arch Neurol Psychiat 70:611, 1953.)

like learning, involves an active process in the nervous system.

A stimulus produces EEG and behavioral arousal and widespread evoked potentials not only if it is new but also if it has been paired with a pleasant or unpleasant experience. For example, if a tone to which the animal has become habituated is paired a few times with an electric shock to the feet, the tone will produce large evoked responses in the brain stem reticular formation and throughout much of the cortex. A similar response is observed if the tone is positively reinforced. An example of these changes in a record of the electrical activity of the hippocampus is shown in Fig 16–3. The hippocampus is not in the direct sensory pathways, but evoked potentials are regularly produced in it by sensory stimuli, presumably via the RAS.

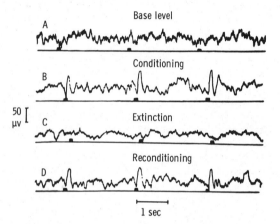

FIG 16–3. Records of the electrical activity of the hippocampus in a monkey exposed repeatedly to a tone stimulus (black signal marks). A: Control. B: After the tone was paired with a reward of food. C: After extinction of this response. D: After reconditioning by again pairing the tone with food. (Reproduced, with permission, from Hearst & others: Some electrophysiological correlates of conditioning in the monkey. Electroenceph Clin Neurophysiol 12:137, 1960.)

It is common knowledge that, at least at a behavioral level, similar conditioning of the arousal value of stimuli occurs in humans. The mother who sleeps through many kinds of noise but wakes promptly when her baby cries is one example. The intern who is unaware of the calls on the loudspeaker unless his own name is called is another example of a conditioned arousal response to a particular stimulus.

Attention

The generalized arousal response to a stimulus can progress to focused attention. When such focusing occurs, other sensory inputs are inhibited. This inhibition is common knowledge; we have all had the experi-

ence of having to say, "I'm sorry, but I didn't hear you. I was reading the newspaper." In animals this inhibition can occur at many levels, from the sense organs themselves to the cortex (see Chapter 11).

Intercortical Transfer of Learning

If a cat or monkey is conditioned to respond to a visual stimulus with one eye covered and then tested with the blindfold transferred to the other eye, it performs the conditioned response. This is true even if the optic chiasm has been cut, making the visual input from each eye go only to the ipsilateral cortex. If, in addition to the optic chiasm, the anterior and posterior commissures and the corpus callosum are sectioned ("split brain animal"), no transfer of learning occurs. This demonstrates that the neural coding necessary for "remembering with one eye what has been learned with the other" has been transferred somehow to the opposite cortex via the commissures. There is evidence for similar transfer of information acquired through other sensory pathways. "Split brain animals" can even be trained to respond to different and conflicting stimuli, one with one eye and another with the other—literally an example of not letting the right side know what the left side is doing. Attempts at such training in normal animals and humans lead to confusion, but they do not faze the animals with split brains. Similar results have been obtained in humans in whom the corpus callosum is congenitally absent or in whom it has been sectioned surgically in an effort to control epileptic seizures.

MEMORY

In discussions of the memory process, it is important to distinguish between remote and recent memories. It now appears that 3 mechanisms interact in the production of memories, one mediating immediate recall of the events of the moment, another mediating memories of events that occurred minutes to hours before, and a third mediating memories of the remote past. Memory for recent events is quite frequently impaired or lost in individuals with neurologic diseases, but remote memories are remarkably resistant and persist in the presence of severe brain damage.

Stimulation of portions of the temporal lobe in patients with temporal lobe epilepsy evokes detailed memories of events that occurred in the remote past, often beyond the power of voluntary recall. This response has not as yet been definitely proved to occur in individuals with normal temporal lobe function, but exposure of the temporal lobe has been carried out in relatively few individuals who were not suffering from temporal lobe disease. The memories produced by temporal lobe stimulation are "flashed back" complete, as if they were replays of a segment of experience. A particular memory is generally evoked by stimulation of a given point; it unfolds as long as the stimulus is applied, and stops when the stimulus is discontinued. For a number of reasons it seems unlikely that the memories themselves are localized in the temporal lobes. Instead, the temporal lobe points are probably "keys" that unlock memory traces stored elsewhere in the brain and the brain stem. Normally, a key is turned by some sort of comparing, associating circuit when there is a similarity between the memory and the current sensory input or stream of thought.

Stimulation of other parts of the temporal lobes sometimes causes a patient to change his interpretation of his surroundings. For example, when the stimulus is applied, he may feel strange in a familiar place or may feel that what is happening now has happened before. The occurrence of a sense of familiarity or a sense of strangeness in appropriate situations probably helps the normal individual adjust to the environment. In strange surroundings one is alert and on guard, whereas in familiar surroundings vigilance is relaxed. An inappropriate feeling of familiarity with new events or in new surroundings is known clinically as the *déjà vu phenomenon*, from the French words meaning "already seen." The phenomenon occurs from time to time in normal individuals, but it also may occur as an aura (a sensation immediately preceding a seizure) in patients with temporal lobe epilepsy.

Other data pertinent to the physiology of memory are the clinical and experimental observations showing that there is frequently a loss of memory for the events immediately preceding brain concussion or electroshock therapy (**retrograde amnesia**). In man this amnesia encompasses longer periods than it does in animals—sometimes days, weeks, and even years—but remote memory is not affected. In animals, acquisition of learned responses—or at least their retrieval—is prevented if, within 5 minutes after each training session, the animals are anesthetized, given electroshock treatment, or subjected to hypothermia. Such treatment 4 hours after the training sessions has no effect on acquisition. It thus appears that there is a period of "encoding" or "consolidation" of memory during which the memory trace is vulnerable, but following which a stable and remarkably resistant memory engram exists.

There is considerable evidence that the encoding process involves the hippocampus and its connections. Bilateral destruction of the ventral hippocampus in man and bilateral lesions of the same area in experimental animals cause striking defects in recent memory. Humans with such destruction have intact remote memory, and they perform adequately as long as they concentrate on what they are doing. However, if they are distracted for even a very short period, all memory of what they were doing and proposed to do is lost. They are thus capable of new learning and retain old memories, but they are deficient in forming new memories.

Additional evidence for the involvement of the hippocampus is the observation that in humans with chronically implanted electrodes, stimuli producing seizures in the hippocampus cause loss of recent memory. The hippocampal neurons are particularly prone to iterative discharge, and hippocampal seizures presumably disrupt the normal function of this structure. Several drugs which impair or alter recent memory produce abnormal electrical discharges in the hippocampus. Some alcoholics with brain damage develop considerable impairment of recent memory, and it has been claimed that the occurrence of this defect correlates well with the presence of pathologic changes in the mammillary bodies.

Ribonucleic Acid (RNA), Protein Synthesis, & Memory

The nature of the stable memory trace is largely unknown, but its resistance to electroshock and concussion suggests that memory might be stored as an actual biochemical change in the neurons. The ability of regenerated planarians to retain learned habits indicates that such changes occur in some animal species. Planarians are flatworms with rudimentary nervous systems and a remarkable ability to regenerate when cut in pieces. They can be taught to avoid certain visual stimuli. If a trained worm is divided in two, not only does the worm regenerated from the head piece retain the response but so does the worm regenerated from the tail.

One possible explanation of this phenomenon is the hypothesis that the acquisition of the learned response is associated with a change in the ribonucleic acid (RNA) of the cells. RNA provides a template for protein synthesis (see Chapters 1 and 17). If learning causes a stable alteration in the RNA, the learning response could conceivably be passed on to the new parts of the regenerated planarians. In support of this idea is the observation that treatment of the cut pieces of conditioned planarians with ribonuclease, the enzyme that destroys RNA, prevents the tail segments from regenerating into fully conditioned worms. Indeed, it has been claimed that if trained planarians are ground up and fed to untrained planarians, the untrained worms acquire with much greater facility than controls the responses the trained worms had learned. Several investigators have also reported that, in goldfish and rats, injection of brain extracts of trained animals improves learning in untrained animals.

There is additional evidence that protein synthesis is involved in some way in the processes responsible for memory. In rats, increased RNA turnover occurs in nerve cells subjected to intense stimulation. In cats, if an area in one cerebral hemisphere is frozen, a discharging epileptic focus forms around the area of damage and a similar focus ("mirror focus") appears at the homologous point on the opposite hemisphere. Forty-eight hours or more after the injury, the cells of the mirror focus have "learned" the pattern of epileptic discharge and continue it independently if isolated from all afferent connections. At this time, their RNA turnover appears to be increased. In goldfish the antibiotics puromycin and acetoxycycloheximide prevent the retention of conditioned avoidance responses when given up to 1 hour after the training session, although they have no effect on their acquisition. Puromycin also disrupts recent memory in mice. These antibiotics inhibit protein synthesis (see Chapter 17). However, it is a long way from these experiments to an understanding of the relationship of RNA and protein synthesis to the formation of the stable memory trace.

Drugs That Facilitate Learning

A variety of CNS stimulants have been shown to improve learning in animals when administered immediately before or after the learning sessions. These include caffeine, physostigmine, amphetamine, nicotine, and the convulsants picrotoxin, strychnine, and pentylenetetrazol (Metrazol). They seem to act by facilitating consolidation of the memory trace. In senile humans, small doses of pentylenetetrazol appear to improve memory and general awareness. The β-adrenergic blocking drug propranolol has been reported to improve learning in the elderly, and a theory has been advanced that decreased learning in these individuals is related to increased autonomic activity. Another drug that appears to facilitate learning in animals is pemoline (Cylert). This compound is a mild CNS stimulant, but it has attracted attention because it has also been shown to stimulate RNA synthesis.

FUNCTIONS OF THE NEOCORTEX

Memory and learning are functions of large parts of the brain, but the centers controlling some of the other "higher functions of the nervous system," particularly the mechanisms related to language, are more or less localized to the neocortex. It is interesting that speech and other intellectual functions are especially well developed in man—the animal species in which the neocortical mantle is most highly evolved.

Anatomic Considerations

There are 3 living species with brains larger than man's (the porpoise, the elephant, and the whale), but in man the ratio between brain weight and body weight far exceeds that of any of his animal relatives. From the comparative point of view, the most prominent gross feature of the human brain is the immense growth of the 3 major **association areas**: the **frontal**, in front of the motor cortex; the **temporal**, between the superior temporal gyrus and the limbic cortex; and the **parieto-occipital**, between the somesthetic and visual cortices.

The association areas are part of the 6-layered neocortical mantle of gray matter that spreads over the lateral surfaces of the cerebral hemispheres from the concentric allocortical and juxtallocortical rings around the hilum (see Chapter 15). The minor histologic differences in various portions of the cortex that are the basis for numbering cortical areas (Fig 16–4) are generally but not always correlated with differences in function.

FIG 16–4. Lateral view of the human cerebral cortex, showing various numbered areas of Brodmann. The shaded areas represent the primary sensory and motor areas. The remaining white areas are the association areas. (Reproduced, with permission, from Cobb: *Foundations of Neuropsychiatry,* 6th ed. Williams & Wilkins, 1958.)

The neuronal connections within the neocortex form a complicated network (Fig 11–2). The descending axons of the larger cells in the pyramidal cell layer give off collaterals that feed back via association neurons to the dendrites of the cells from which they originate, laying the foundation for complex reverberation. The recurrent collaterals also connect to neighboring cells and some end on inhibitory neurons which in turn end on the original cell, forming loops that mediate negative feedback inhibition (Chapter 4). The large, complex dendrites of the deep cells receive ascending fibers, nonspecific thalamic and reticular afferents and association fibers ending in all layers, and specific thalamic afferents ending in layer 4 of the cortex. The function of the intracortical association fibers is uncertain, but they can be cut with little evident effect. Thus, the term association areas is somewhat misleading; these areas must have a much more complex function than simple interconnection of cortical regions.

Aphasia & Allied Disorders

One group of functions which are more or less localized to the neocortex in man are those related to language, ie, to understanding the spoken and printed word and to expressing ideas in speech and writing. Abnormalities of these functions which are not due to defects of vision or hearing or to motor paralysis are called **aphasias**. Many different classifications of the aphasias have been published, and the nomenclature in this area is chaotic. In a general way, the aphasias can be divided into **sensory** (or **receptive**) aphasias and **motor** (or **expressive**) aphasias. They can be further subdivided into **word deafness**, inability to understand spoken words; **word blindness**, inability to understand written words; **agraphia**, inability to express ideas in writing; and the defect commonly signified by the term **motor aphasia**, inability to express ideas in speech. Motor aphasia is in turn divided into **nonfluent**

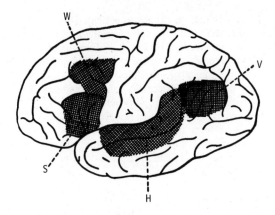

FIG 16—5. One theory of the localization of the language functions. In the hemisphere concerned with language functions, lesions at W are said to cause difficulty in expressing ideas in writing; at S, difficulty in oral expression; at H, difficulty in understanding spoken words; and at V, difficulty in understanding written words. (Reproduced, with permission, from *Physiology and Biophysics*, 19th ed. Ruch TC, Patton HD [editors]. Saunders, 1965.)

aphasia, in which speech is slow and words hard to come by; and **fluent aphasia**, in which speech is normal or even rapid but key words are missing. Patients with severe degrees of nonfluent aphasia are limited to 2 or 3 words with which they must attempt to express the whole range of meaning and emotion. Sometimes the words retained are those that were being spoken at the time of the injury or vascular accident that caused the aphasia. More commonly they are frequently used **automatic words** such as the days of the week, or, for some reason, "dirty" words and swear words.

Only one of the cerebral hemispheres is primarily concerned with the language function (see below). In this hemisphere, the locations said to be associated with the various forms of aphasia are shown in Fig 16—5. In clinical cases, however, more than one form of aphasia is usually present. Frequently, the aphasia is general, or **global**, involving both receptive and expressive functions. Lesions of area 44 in the inferior frontal gyrus (**Broca's area**, area S in Fig 16—5) cause nonfluent aphasia; in patients with fluent aphasia, Broca's area is intact and the lesions are generally in the temporal or parietal lobe.

Complementary Specialization of the Hemispheres vs "Cerebral Dominance"

It is a well-established fact that man's language functions depend more on one cerebral hemisphere than on the other. This hemisphere is concerned with categorization and symbolization and has often been called the **dominant hemisphere**. However, it is now clear that the other hemisphere is not simply less developed or "nondominant"; instead, it is specialized in the area of spatiotemporal relations. It is this hemisphere which is concerned, for example, with the recognition of faces, the identification of objects by their form, and the recognition of musical themes. Consequently, the concept of "cerebral dominance" and a dominant and nondominant hemisphere is being replaced by a concept of complementary specialization of the hemispheres, one for language functions (the categorical hemisphere) and one for spatiotemporal relations (the representational hemisphere).

Lesions in the categorical hemisphere produce aphasia, whereas extensive lesions of the representational hemisphere do not. Instead, lesions in the representational hemisphere produce **astereognosis**—inability to identify objects by feeling them—and other agnosias. **Agnosia** is the general term used for the inability to recognize objects by a particular sensory modality even though the sensory modality itself is intact. Lesions producing these defects are generally in the parietal lobe.

Hemispheric specialization is related to handedness. In right-handed individuals, it is the left hemisphere which is the dominant or categorical hemisphere; in approximately 30% of left-handed individuals, the right hemisphere is the categorical hemisphere. However, in the remaining 70% of left-handers, the left hemisphere is the categorical hemisphere. In adults, the characteristic defects produced by lesions in either the categorical or the representational hemisphere are long-lasting. However, in young children subjected to hemispherectomy for brain tumors or other diseases, the functions of the missing hemisphere may be largely taken over by the remaining hemisphere no matter which hemisphere is removed.

The Frontal Lobes

Some insight into the other functions of the various parts of the cerebral cortex is gained by ablation studies. Bilateral removal of the neocortical portions of the frontal lobes in primates produces, after a period of apathy, hyperactivity and constant pacing back and forth. General intelligence is little affected, and tests involving immediate responses to environmental stimuli are normal. However, responses requiring the use of previously acquired information are abnormal. In humans, frontal lobectomy leads to deficiencies in the temporal ordering of events. For example, humans who have been lobectomized have difficulty remembering how long ago they saw a particular stimulus card. Interestingly, left frontal lobectomy causes the biggest deficit in tests involving word stimuli, while right frontal lobectomy causes the biggest deficit in tests involving picture stimuli. Frontal lobectomy also abolishes the experimental neurosis.

Experimental Neurosis

As noted above, animals can be conditioned to respond to one stimulus and not to another even when the 2 stimuli are very much alike. However, when the stimuli are so nearly identical that they cannot be distinguished, the animal becomes upset, whines, fails to cooperate, and tries to escape. Pavlov called these symptoms the **experimental neurosis.** One may quarrel about whether this reaction is a true neurosis in the psychiatric sense, but the term is convenient. In some species the experimental neurosis affects not only behavior in conditioning tests but general behavior as well.

Frontal lobectomized animals are still capable of discriminating between like stimuli up to a point; but when they can no longer discriminate, their failure does not upset them. As a result of these experiments in animals, **prefrontal lobotomy** and various other procedures aimed at cutting the connections between the frontal lobes and the deeper portions of the brain were introduced for the treatment of various mental diseases in humans.

In some mental patients, tensions resulting from real or imagined failures of performance and the tensions caused by delusions, compulsions, and phobias are so great as to be incapacitating. Successful lobotomy blocks the tension. The delusions and other symptoms are still there, but they no longer bother the patient. A similar lack of concern over severe pain has led to the use of lobotomy in treating patients with intractable pain (see Chapter 7). Unfortunately, this lack of concern often extends to other aspects of the environment, including relations with associates, social amenities, and even toilet habits.

The effects which lobotomy can have on the personality were well described over 100 years ago by the physician who cared for a man named Phineas P. Gage. Gage was a construction foreman who was packing blasting powder into a hole with a tamping iron. The powder exploded, driving the tamping iron through his face and out the top of his skull, transecting his frontal lobes. After the accident, he became, in the words of his physician, ". . . fitful, irreverent, indulging at times in the grossest prcfanity (which was not previously his custom), manifesting but little deference to his fellows, impatient of restraint or advice when it conflicts with his desires, at times pertinaciously obstinate yet capricious and vacillating, devising many plans for future operation which are no sooner arranged than they are abandoned in turn for others appearing more feasible. . . .His mind was radically changed, so that his friends and acquaintances said he was no longer Gage."*

This description is classical, but it cannot be said to be typical. The effects of lobotomy in humans are highly variable from patient to patient. This variability has been attributed to variations in the milieu in which different patients are observed, and to differences in the extent and site of brain destruction. However, studies in which these variables were controlled make it clear that identical operations produce widely differing results that depend upon each patient's preoperative personality and past experiences. Because the desirable effects of lobotomy now can often be achieved with tranquilizers and other drugs, lobotomies are rarely, if ever, performed for the treatment of mental disease.

Temporal Lobes

The effects of bilateral temporal lobectomy were first described by Klüver and Bucy. Temporal lobectomized monkeys ("Klüver-Bucy animals") are docile and hyperphagic and the males are hypersexual, all of which effects are due to the removal of limbic structures. The animals also demonstrate visual agnosia, and a remarkable increase in oral activity. The monkeys repeatedly pick up all movable objects in their environment. They manipulate each object in a compulsive way, mouth, lick, and bite it, and then, unless it is edible, discard it. However, discarded objects are picked up again in a few minutes as if the animal had never seen them before and subjected to the same manipulation and oral exploration. It has been suggested that the cause of this pattern of behavior may be an inability to identify objects. It could well be a manifestation of a memory loss due to hippocampal ablation. In addition, the animals are easily distracted. They heed every stimulus, whether it is novel or not, and usually approach, explore, manipulate, and, if possible, bite its source. This failure to ignore peripheral stimuli is called **hypermetamorphosis.**

Clinical Implications & Significance

Various parts of the syndrome described by Klüver and Bucy in monkeys are seen in humans with temporal lobe disease. Impaired recent memory follows bilateral damage to the hippocampus. Hypersexuality may develop in some individuals with bilateral damage in the amygdaloid nuclei and pyriform cortex. It is obvious, however, that in the present state of our knowledge the abnormalities seen with temporal lobe lesions and, more generally, those produced by other neocortical lesions cannot be fitted into any general hypothesis of intellectual function. It is hoped that future research will provide such a synthesis and a better understanding of the neurophysiologic basis of mental phenomena.

---

*From. Harlow: Recovery from the passage of an iron bar through the head. Massachusetts Med Soc Publications 2:237, 1868.

•   •   •

References: Section III.
Functions of the Nervous System

Amols W, Merritt HJ: Vomiting. Neurology 5:645, 1955.

Atkins E, Bodel P: Fever. New England J Med 286:27, 1972.

Axelrod J: Noradrenaline: Fate and control of its biosynthesis. Science 173:598, 1971.

Axelrod J, Weinshilboum R: Catecholamines. New England J Med 287:237, 1972.

Basmajian JV: Electromyography comes of age. Science 176:603, 1972.

Beach FA: Cerebral and hormonal control of reflexive mechanisms involved in copulatory behavior. Physiol Rev 47:289, 1967.

Beets MGJ: The molecular parameters of olfactory response. Pharmacol Rev 22:1, 1970.

Benzinger TH: Heat regulation: Homeostasis of central temperature in man. Physiol Rev 49:671, 1969.

Bradshaw J, Geffen G, Nettleton N: Our two brains. New Scientist 54:62, 1972.

Brawley P, Duffield JC: The pharmacology of hallucinogens. Pharmacol Rev 24:31, 1972.

Bronisch FW: *The Clinically Important Reflexes.* Grune & Stratton, 1952.

Capps JA: *An Experimental and Clinical Study of Pain in the Pleura, Pericardium and Peritoneum.* Macmillan, 1932.

Catton WT: Mechanoreceptor function. Physiol Rev 50:297, 1970.

Chusid JG: *Correlative Neuroanatomy & Functional Neurology,* 15th ed. Lange, 1973.

Cotzias GC, Papavasiliou PS, Gellene R: Modification of parkinsonism: Chronic treatment with L-dopa. New England J Med 280:337, 1969.

De Reack AVS, Knight J (editors): *Hearing Mechanisms in Vertebrates.* Little, Brown, 1968.

Dollery CT, Patterson JW, Conolly ME: Clinical pharmacology of beta-receptor blocking drugs. Clin Pharmacol Therap 10:765, 1969.

Dow RS, Moruzzi G: *The Physiology and Pathology of the Cerebellum.* Univ of Minnesota Press, 1958.

Fitzsimons JT: Thirst. Physiol Rev 52:468, 1972.

Fjeringstad EJ (editor): *Chemical Transfer of Learned Information.* Elsevier, 1971.

Gaito J (editor): *Macromolecules and Behavior,* 2nd ed. Appleton-Century-Crofts, 1972.

Ganong WF, Martini L (editors): *Frontiers in Neuroendocrinology, 1973.* Oxford Univ Press, 1973.

Goldenberg M: Hyponatremia and the inappropriate secretion of antidiuretic hormone. Am J Med 35:293, 1963.

Granit R: *Mechanisms Regulating the Discharge of Motoneurons.* Thomas, 1972.

Hobson JA: Sleep. New England J Med 281:1343, 1468, 1969.

Hubel DH: Effects of distortion of sensory input on the visual system of kittens. The Physiologist 10:17, 1967.

Iverson LL: Neurotransmitters, neurohormones and other small molecules in neurons. *The Neurosciences Second Study Program.* Schmitt FO (editor). Rockefeller Univ Press, 1970.

Jacobson M, Hunt RK: The origins of nerve cell specificity. Scientific American 228:26, Feb 1973.

Knighton RS, Dumke PR (editors): *Pain.* Little, Brown, 1966.

Kornhuber HH: Motor functions of the cerebellum and basal ganglia: The cerebellocortical saccadic (ballistic) clock, the cerebellonuclear hold regulator, and the basal ganglia ramp (voluntary speed smooth movement) generator. Kybernetik 8:157, 1971.

Lasansky A: Nervous function at the cellular level: Glia. Ann Rev Physiol 33:84, 1971.

Levi-Montalcini R, Angeletti PU: Nerve growth factor. Physiol Rev 48:534, 1968.

Lowenstein OE (editor): *Mechanisms of Taste and Smell in Vertebrates.* Churchill, 1970.

Magoun HW: *The Waking Brain,* 2nd ed. Thomas, 1963.

Martini L, Ganong WF (editors): *Neuroendocrinology.* 2 vols. Academic Press, 1966, 1967.

Mayer J, Thomas DW: Regulation of food intake and obesity. Science 156:328, 1967.

Melzack R, Wall PD: Pain mechanism: A new theory. Science 150:971, 1965.

Money KE: Motion sickness. Physiol Rev 50:1, 1970.

Olds J: Hypothalamic substrates of reward. Physiol Rev 42:554, 1962.

Pavlov IP: *Conditioned Reflexes.* Oxford Univ Press, 1928.

Penfield W: Engrams in the human brain. Proc Roy Soc Med 61:831, 1968.

Rosenzweig MR, Bennett EL, Diamond MC: Brain changes in response to experience. Scientific American 226:22, Feb 1972.

Sawyer WH: Evolution of antidiuretic hormones and their functions. Am J Med 42:678, 1967.

Sherrington CS: *The Integrative Action of the Nervous System.* Cambridge Univ Press, 1947.

Straatsma BR & others (editors): *The Retina: Morphology, Function, and Clinical Characteristics.* Univ of California Press, 1969.

Ungerstedt U: Stereotaxic mapping of the monoamine pathways in the rat brain. Acta physiologica scandinav (Suppl) 367:1, 1971.

Van Harreveld A: *Brain Tissue Electrolytes.* Butterworth, 1965.

Wald G: Molecular basis of visual excitation. Science 162:230, 1968.

Symposium: Sensory receptors. Cold Spring Harbor Symposia on Quantitative Biology. Vol 30, 1965.

Symposium: Marijuana: Chemistry, pharmacology, and pattern social use. Ann New York Acad Sc 191:3, 1971.

Symposium: Central cholinergic transmission and its behavioral aspects. Fed Proc 28:89, 1969.

IV. Endocrinology & Metabolism

17...

Energy Balance, Metabolism, & Nutrition

The endocrine system, like the nervous system, adjusts and correlates the activities of the various body systems, making them appropriate to the changing demands of the external and internal environment. This integration is brought about by the secretion of **hormones**, chemical agents produced by ductless glands which pass into the circulation to regulate the metabolic processes of various cells. The term **metabolism**, meaning literally "change," is used to refer to all the chemical and energy transformations that occur in the body.

The animal organism oxidizes carbohydrates, proteins, and fats, producing principally CO_2, H_2O, and the energy necessary for life processes. CO_2, H_2O, and energy are also produced when food is burned outside the body. However, in the body, oxidation is not a one-step, semiexplosive reaction but a complex, slow, stepwise process called **catabolism**, which liberates energy in small, usable amounts. Energy can be stored in the body in the form of special energy-rich phosphate compounds and in the form of proteins, fats, and complex carbohydrates synthesized from simpler molecules. Formation of these substances by processes that take up rather than liberate energy is called **anabolism**.

ENERGY METABOLISM

METABOLIC RATE

An important advance in physiology was the demonstration that the amount of energy liberated by the catabolism of food in the body is the same as the amount liberated when food is burned outside the body. The energy liberated by catabolic processes in the body appears as external work, heat, and energy storage:

$$\frac{\text{Energy}}{\text{output}} = \frac{\text{External}}{\text{work}} + \frac{\text{Energy}}{\text{storage}} + \text{Heat}$$

The amount of energy liberated per unit of time is the **metabolic rate**. Isotonic muscle contractions perform work at a peak efficiency approximating 50%:

$$\text{Efficiency} = \frac{\text{Work done}}{\text{Total energy expended}}$$

Essentially all of the energy of isometric contractions appears as heat because little or no external work (the product of force times the distance the force moves a mass) is done (see Chapter 3). Energy is stored by forming energy-rich compounds. The amount of energy storage varies, but in fasting individuals it is zero or negative. Therefore, in an individual who is not moving and who has not eaten recently, essentially all of the energy output appears as heat. When food is burned outside the body, all of the energy liberated also appears as heat.

Calories

The standard unit of heat energy is the **calorie** (cal), defined as the amount of heat energy necessary to raise the temperature of 1 g of water 1 degree, from 15 to 16° C. This unit is also called the gram calorie, small calorie, or standard calorie. The unit commonly used in physiology and medicine is the **Calorie**, or **kilocalorie** (kcal), which equals 1000 cal.

Calorimetry

The energy released by combustion of foodstuffs outside the body can be measured directly (**direct calorimetry**) by oxidizing the compounds in an apparatus such as a **bomb calorimeter**, a metal vessel surrounded by water inside an insulated container. The food is ignited by an electric spark. The change in the temperature of the surrounding water is a measure of the calories produced. Similar measurements of the energy released by combustion of compounds in living animals and humans are much more complex, but large calorimeters have been constructed which can physically accommodate human beings. The heat produced

FIG 17–1. Diagram of Atwater-Benedict respiration calorimeter. Water flows from (1) to (4), and its temperature is measured at the inlet and the outlet. Air leaves at (8); water is removed from it by sulfuric acid, CO_2 is removed by soda lime, and O_2 is added at a measured rate; and the gas mixture reenters the chamber at (9). (2), inlet thermometer; (3), outlet thermometer; (6), porthole; (7), window; (9), air inlet; (10), air cushion. (Reproduced, with permission, from Bell, Davidson, & Scarborough: *Textbook of Physiology and Biochemistry*, 7th ed. Livingstone, 1969.)

by their bodies is measured by the change in temperature of the water circulating through the calorimeter (Fig 17–1).

The caloric values of the common foodstuffs, as measured in a bomb calorimeter, are found to be 4.1 kcal/g of carbohydrate, 9.3 kcal/g of fat, and 5.3 kcal/g of protein. In the body, similar values are obtained for carbohydrate and fat but the oxidation of protein is incomplete, the end products of protein catabolism being urea and related nitrogenous compounds in addition to CO_2 and H_2O (see below). Therefore, the caloric value of protein in the body is only 4.1 kcal/g.

Indirect Calorimetry

Energy production can also be calculated, at least in theory, by measuring the products of the energy-producing biologic oxidations—ie, the CO_2, H_2O, and the end products of protein catabolism produced—or by measuring the O_2 consumed. This is **indirect calorimetry**. It is difficult to measure all of the end products, but measurement of O_2 consumption is relatively easy. Since O_2 is not stored and since its consumption, except when an O_2 debt is being incurred or repaid, always keeps pace with immediate needs, the amount of O_2 consumed per unit of time is proportionate to the energy liberated.

One problem with using O_2 consumption as a measure of energy output is the fact that the amount of energy released per mol of O_2 consumed varies slightly with the type of compound being oxidized. The approximate energy liberation per liter of O_2 consumed is 4.82 kcal, and for many purposes this value is accurate enough. More accurate measurements require data on the foods being oxidized. Such data can be obtained from an analysis of the respiratory quotient and the nitrogen excretion.

Respiratory Quotient (RQ)

The respiratory quotient (RQ) is the ratio of the volume of CO_2 produced to the volume of O_2 consumed per unit of time. It can be calculated for reactions outside the body, for individual organs and tissues, and for the whole body. The RQ of carbohydrate is 1.00 and that of fat is about 0.70. This is because O_2 and hydrogen are present in carbohydrate in the same proportions as in water, whereas in the various fats extra O_2 is necessary for the formation of water.

Carbohydrate:

$$C_6H_{12}O_6 + 6O_2 \longrightarrow 6CO_2 + 6H_2O$$
(glucose)

$$RQ = 6/6 = 1.00$$

Fat:

$$2C_{51}H_{98}O_6 + 145O_2 \longrightarrow 102CO_2 + 98H_2O$$
(tripalmitin)

$$RQ = 102/145 = 0.703$$

Determining the RQ of protein in the body is a complex process, but an average value of 0.82 has been calculated.

RQs of some other important substances are:

Glycerol	0.86
β-Hydroxybutyric acid	0.89
Acetoacetic acid	1.00
Pyruvic acid	1.20
Ethyl alcohol	0.67

The approximate amounts of carbohydrate, protein, and fat being oxidized in the body at any given time can be calculated from the CO_2 expired, the O_2 inspired, and the urinary nitrogen excretion. However, the values calculated in this fashion are only approximations. Furthermore, the volume of CO_2 expired and the volume of O_2 inspired may vary with factors other than metabolism. For example, if the individual hyperventilates, the RQ rises because CO_2 is being blown off. During exercise, the RQ may reach 2.00 because of hyperventilation and blowing off of CO_2 while contracting an O_2 debt. After exercise, it falls for a while to 0.50 or less. In metabolic acidosis, the RQ rises because respiratory compensation for the acidosis causes the amount of CO_2 expired to rise (see Chapter 40). In severe acidosis, the RQ may be greater than 1.00. In metabolic alkalosis, the RQ falls. Because the RQ of the whole body is affected by respiratory factors as well as metabolism, many authors now refer to it as the **respiratory exchange ratio**, which they abbreviate R rather than RQ.

The O_2 consumption and CO_2 production of an organ can be calculated by multiplying its blood flow per unit of time by the arteriovenous differences for O_2 and CO_2 across the organ, and the RQ can then be calculated. Data on the RQ of individual organs are of considerable interest in drawing inferences about the metabolic processes occurring in them. For example, the RQ of the brain is regularly 0.97 to 0.99, indicating that its principal but not its only fuel is carbohydrate. During secretion of gastric juice, the stomach has a negative RQ because it takes up more CO_2 from the arterial blood than it puts into the venous blood (see Chapter 26).

Measuring the Metabolic Rate

In determining the metabolic rate, O_2 consumption is usually measured with some form of oxygen-filled spirometer and a CO_2 absorbing system. Such a device is illustrated in Fig 17–2. The spirometer bell is connected to a pen that writes on a rotating drum as the bell moves up and down. The slope of a line joining the ends of each of the spirometer excursions is proportionate to the O_2 consumption. The amount of O_2 (in ml) consumed per unit of time is corrected to standard temperature and pressure, and then converted to energy production by multiplying by 4.82 kcal/liter of O_2 consumed.

The metabolic rate is affected by many factors (Table 17–1). The most important is muscular exertion. O_2 consumption is elevated not only during exertion but for as long afterward as is necessary to repay the O_2 debt (see Chapter 3). Recently ingested foods also increase the metabolic rate because of their **specific dynamic action (SDA)**. The SDA of a food is the obligatory energy expenditure that occurs during its assimilation into the body. An amount of protein sufficient to provide 100 kcal increases the metabolic rate a total of 30 kcal; a similar amount of carbohydrate increases it 6 kcal; and a similar amount of fat,

FIG 17–2. Diagram of modified Benedict apparatus, a recording spirometer used for measuring human O_2 consumption, and record obtained with it. The slope of the line AB is proportionate to the O_2 consumption. V, V: one-way check valves.

TABLE 17–1. Factors affecting the metabolic rate. The first group of factors are eliminated by measuring the rate in the basal state or are accounted for in calculating the rate. The second group must be considered in interpreting the calculated value.

Muscular exertion during or just before measurement
Recent ingestion of food
High or low environmental temperature
Height, weight, and surface area

Sex
Age
Emotional state
Climate
Body temperature
Pregnancy or menstruation
Circulating level of thyroid hormones
Circulating epinephrine and norepinephrine level

TABLE 17–2. Effect of different environmental temperatures on O_2 consumption at rest. Subjects were clothed in "their usual attire."*

Room Temperature (°C)	Oxygen Consumption (ml/min)
0	330
10	290
20	240
30	250
40	255
45	260

*Data from Grollman: Physiologic variations of the cardiac output in man. Am J Physiol 95:263, 1930.

4 kcal. This means, of course, that the amount of calories available from the 3 foods is in effect reduced by this amount; the energy used in their assimilation must come from the food itself or the body energy stores. The cause of the SDA of proteins is probably related to the process of deamination of the constituent amino acids in the liver after their absorption. The SDA of fats may be due to a direct stimulation of metabolism by liberated fatty acids. That of carbohydrate may be a manifestation of the extra energy required to form glycogen. The stimulating effects of food on metabolism may last 6 hours or more.

Another factor which stimulates metabolism is the environmental temperature. When the environmental temperature is lower than body temperature, heat-conserving mechanisms such as shivering are activated and the metabolic rate rises. When the temperature is high enough to raise the body temperature, there is a general acceleration of metabolic processes and the metabolic rate also rises (Table 17–2).

Basal Metabolic Rate (BMR)

In order to make possible a comparison of the metabolic rates of different individuals and different species, metabolic rates are usually determined at as complete mental and physical rest as possible, in a room at a comfortable temperature, 12–14 hours after the last meal. The metabolic rate determined under these conditions is called the **basal metabolic rate (BMR)**. Actually, the rate is not truly "basal"; the metabolic rate during sleep is lower than the "basal" rate. What the term basal actually denotes is a set of widely known and accepted standard conditions.

The BMR of a man of average size is about 2000 kcal/day. This value is compared to that of other animal species in Table 17–3. Large animals have higher absolute BMRs, but the ratio of BMR to body weight in small animals is much greater. The one variable that correlates well with the BMR in different species is the body surface area. A constant ratio between the BMR and surface area might be expected in animals living in cool climates, since heat loss occurs at the body surface. However, this ratio is also rela-

TABLE 17–3. "Basal" metabolic rate in various animal species as a function of body weight and body surface area.*

Animal	Metabolic Rate (kcal/day)	Weight (kg)	Metabolic Rate (kcal/kg/day)	Metabolic Rate (kcal/sq m body surface/day)
Mouse	3.82	0.018	212	1185
Guinea pig		0.5		1246
Dog		3.19		1212
Dog	773	15	51.5	1039
Dog		31.2		1036
Man	2054	64	32.1	1042
Pig	2444	128	19.1	1074
Horse	4983	441	11.3	948

*Data largely from Rubner: *Ztschr f Biol* 19:535, 1883; 30:73, 1894.

tively constant in tropical animals. Consequently, the explanation of the correlation remains obscure.

The relationship in man between weight and height and body surface area can be expressed by the following formula:

$$S = 0.007184 \times W^{0.425} \times H^{0.725}$$

Where S = Surface area in sq meters
       W = Body weight in kg
       H = Height in cm

Nomograms constructed from this formula are often used for easy estimation of body surface area. For convenience, the BMR is usually expressed as a percentage of increase or decrease above or below a set of generally used standard normal values. Thus, a value of +65 means that the individual's BMR is 65% above the standard for his age and sex.

Factors Influencing the BMR

Factors affecting the BMR in man include age, sex, race, emotional state, climate, body temperature, and the circulating levels of the hormones epinephrine, norepinephrine, triiodothyronine, and thyroxine. In the female, the BMR at all ages is slightly lower than in the male. The rate is high in children and declines with age (Table 17–4). It is said that Chinese and Indians have lower BMRs than Caucasians. Anxiety and tension cause increased tensing of the muscles, even when the individual is quiet, and increased secretion of epinephrine. Both effects raise the BMR. On the other hand, apathetic, depressed patients may have low BMRs. In the tropics, BMRs are lower than in temperate climates and are more closely related to body weight than to surface area. An increase in body temperature speeds up chemical reactions, and the BMR rises approximately 14% for each degree C of fever (7% per degree F). The stimulatory effects of epinephrine and thyroid hormones on the BMR are discussed in the chapters on those hormones. It is said that during prolonged starvation the BMR falls. This is probably the explanation of the low BMR without

TABLE 17–4. Age and sex differences in BMR.*

Age in Years	BMR in kcal/sq m/hour	
	Male	Female
2	57.0	52.5
6	53.0	50.6
8	51.8	47.0
10	48.5	45.9
16	45.7	38.8
20	41.4	36.1
30	39.3	35.7
40	38.0	35.7
50	36.7	34.0
60	35.5	32.6

*Reproduced, with permission, from Keele & Neil: *Sampson Wright's Applied Physiology,* 12th ed. Oxford Univ Press, 1971.

depressed thyroid function that is occasionally seen in patients with chronic wasting disease. This also may be why, when an individual reduces, weight loss is initially rapid and then slows down.

ENERGY BALANCE

The first law of thermodynamics, the principle that states that energy is neither created nor destroyed when it is converted from one form to another, applies to living organisms as well as inanimate systems. One may therefore speak of an **energy balance** between caloric intake and energy output. If the caloric content of the food ingested is less than the energy output—ie, if the balance is negative—endogenous stores are utilized, glycogen, body protein, and fat are catabolized, and the individual loses weight. If the caloric value of the food intake exceeds energy loss due to heat and work and the food is properly digested and absorbed—ie, if the balance is positive—energy is stored and the individual gains weight. It is remarkable how often, in the wishful thinking of the obese, this law is forgotten. There are only 2 ways to lose weight: by increasing energy expenditure or by decreasing food intake.

Except in man and some hibernating and domesticated animals, the appetite mechanism regulates food intake with such precision that obesity is rare. Appetite is regulated as if it were determined by caloric needs. However, there is no evidence for a direct link between caloric consumption and appetite. As described in Chapter 14, food intake is regulated primarily by a mechanism that responds to changes in the level of glucose utilization in the cells of the hypothalamus.

To balance his basal output so that he can perform the energy-consuming tasks essential for life, the average adult must take in about 2000 kcal/day. Caloric requirements above the basal level depend upon the individual's activity. The average sedentary student (or professor) needs another 500 kcal, whereas a lumberjack needs up to 3000 additional kcal/day. Children require a lower absolute intake because of their smaller size, but a larger relative intake is essential to promote growth. Recommended dietary caloric allowances in various conditions are included in Table 17–12.

INTERMEDIARY METABOLISM

GENERAL CONSIDERATIONS

The end products of the digestive processes discussed in Chapters 25 and 26 are for the most part amino acids, fat derivatives, and hexoses such as fructose and glucose. These compounds are absorbed and metabolized in the body by various routes. The details of their metabolism are the concern of biochemistry and are not considered here. However, an outline of carbohydrate, protein, and fat metabolism is included for completeness and because some knowledge of the pathways involved is essential to an understanding of the action of thyroid, pancreatic, and adrenal hormones.

General Plan of Metabolism

The short-chain fragments produced by hexose, amino acid, and fat catabolism are very similar. From this **common metabolic pool** of intermediates, carbohydrates, proteins, and fats can be synthesized or the fragments can enter the citric acid cycle, a sort of final common pathway for catabolism, in which they are broken down to hydrogen atoms and CO_2. The hydrogen atoms are oxidized to form water by a chain of flavoprotein and cytochrome enzymes.

Energy Transfer

The energy liberated by catabolism is not used directly by cells but is applied instead to the formation of ester bonds between phosphoric acid residues and certain organic compounds. Because the energy of bond formation in these phosphates is particularly high, relatively large amounts of energy (10—12 kcal/mol) are released when the bond is hydrolyzed. Compounds containing such bonds are called **high-energy phosphate compounds**. Not all organic phosphates are of the high-energy type. Many, like glucose-6-phosphate, are low-energy phosphates which on hydrolysis liberate 2—3 kcal/mol. Some of the intermediates formed in carbohydrate metabolism are high-energy phosphates, but the most important high-energy phosphate compound is **adenosine triphosphate (ATP)**. This ubiquitous molecule (Fig 17—3) is the energy storehouse of the body. Upon hydrolysis to adenosine diphosphate (ADP), it liberates energy directly to such processes as muscle contraction, active transport, and the synthesis of many chemical compounds. Loss of another phosphate to form adenosine monophosphate (AMP) liberates more energy. Another energy-rich phosphate compound found in muscle is creatine phosphate (phosphocreatine, CrP; Fig 17—25). Other important phosphorylated compounds, at least some of which can serve as energy donors, include the triphosphate derivatives of pyrimidine or purine bases other than adenine (Fig 17—26). These include the guanine derivative, guanosine triphosphate (GTP); the cytosine derivative, cytidine triphosphate (CTP); the uracil derivative, uridine triphosphate (UTP); and the hypoxanthine derivative, inosine triphosphate (ITP). Many catabolic reactions are associated with the formation of energy-rich phosphates.

Another group of high-energy compounds are the thio esters, the acyl derivatives of mercaptans. **Coenzyme A (Co A)** is a widely distributed mercaptan containing adenine, ribose, pantothenic acid, and thioethanolamine (Fig 17—4). Reduced Co A (usually abbreviated HS-Co A) reacts with acyl groups (R—CO—) to form R—CO—S—Co A derivatives. A prime example is the reaction of HS-Co A with acetic acid to form acetylcoenzyme A (acetyl-Co A), a compound of pivotal importance in intermediary metabolism. Because acetyl-Co A has a much higher energy content than acetic acid, it combines readily with substances in reactions which would otherwise

Adenine   D-Ribose   Phosphoric acid residues

Adenosine triphosphate (ATP)

Adenosine diphosphate (ADP)

Adenosine-5-monophosphate (AMP)

Hydrolysis of energy-rich phosphate bonds

FIG 17—3. Energy-rich phosphate compounds.

Pantothenic acid   Thioethanolamine

$$CH_2-\underset{\underset{CH_3}{|}}{\overset{\overset{CH_3}{|}}{C}}-CHOH-\overset{O}{\overset{||}{C}}-NH-CH_2-CH_2-\overset{O}{\overset{||}{C}}-NH-CH_2-CH_2-SH$$

Diphosphate

Adenine

D-Ribose-3-phosphate

$$R-\overset{O}{\overset{||}{C}}-OH \;+\; HS-Co\,A \longrightarrow R-\overset{O}{\overset{||}{C}}-S-Co\,A \;+\; HOH$$

FIG 17–4. *Above:* Formula of reduced Co A (HS-Co A). *Below:* Type formula for reaction of Co A with biologically important compounds to form thio esters.

Biologic Oxidations

Oxidation is the combination of a substance with O_2, or loss of hydrogen, or loss of electrons. The corresponding reverse processes are called reduction. Biologic oxidations are catalyzed by enzymes, a particular protein enzyme being responsible in most cases for one particular reaction. Cofactors (simple ions) or coenzymes (organic, nonprotein substances) are accessory substances which usually act as carriers for products of the reaction. Unlike the enzymes, the coenzymes may catalyze a variety of reactions.

A number of coenzymes serve as hydrogen acceptors. One common form of biologic oxidation is removal of hydrogen from an R—OH group, forming R=O. In such dehydrogenation reactions, nicotinamide adenine dinucleotide (**NAD$^+$**) and nicotinamide adenine dinucleotide phosphate (**NADP$^+$**) pick up hydrogen, forming dihydronicotinamide adenine dinucleotide (**NADH**) and dihydronicotinamide adenine dinucleotide phosphate (**NADPH**) (Fig 17–5). The hydrogen is then transferred to the flavoprotein-cytochrome system, reoxidizing the NAD$^+$ and NADP$^+$. NAD$^+$ is also known as diphosphopyridine nucleotide (**DPN** or coenzyme I), NADH as reduced DPN or **DPNH**, NADP$^+$ as triphosphopyridine nucleotide (**TPN** or coenzyme II), and NADPH as reduced TPN or **TPNH**. The terms

require outside energy. Acetyl-Co A is therefore often called "active acetate." From the point of view of energetics, formation of 1 mol of any acyl-Co A compound is equivalent to the formation of 1 mol of ATP.

Adenine   Ribose   Diphosphate   Ribose   Nicotinamide

Oxidized coenzyme   Reduced coenzyme

$$NAD^+ \rightleftharpoons NADH$$
$$NADP^+ \rightleftharpoons NADPH$$

FIG 17–5. *Above:* Formula of oxidized form of nicotinamide adenine dinucleotide (NAD$^+$, DPN, coenzyme I). Nicotinamide adenine dinucleotide phosphate (NADP$^+$, TPN, coenzyme II) has an additional phosphate group at the location marked by the asterisk. *Below:* Reaction by which NAD$^+$ and NADP$^+$ become reduced to form NADH and NADPH. R, remainder of molecule; R′, hydrogen donor.

FIG 17−6. Outline of respiratory chain oxidation. Pi, inorganic phosphate; FAD, flavoprotein; Co Q, coenzyme Q; R, proton donor; Cyt, cytochrome.

DPN, DPNH, TPN, and TPNH are still widely used, but the newer terminology has gained such widespread acceptance that it seems appropriate to use NAD^+, NADH, $NADP^+$, and NADPH in this book.

The flavoprotein-cytochrome system is a chain of enzymes which transfer hydrogen to oxygen, forming water. Each enzyme in the chain is reduced, and then reoxidized as the hydrogen is passed down the line (Fig 17−6). Each of the enzymes is a protein with an attached nonprotein prosthetic group. The flavoprotein prosthetic group is a derivative of the B complex vitamin, riboflavin. The prosthetic groups of the cytochromes contain iron in a porphyrin configuration that resembles hemoglobin (see Chapter 27).

The transfer of hydrogen to flavoprotein is associated with the formation of ATP from ADP, and the further transfer along the flavoprotein-cytochrome system generates 2 more molecules of ATP per pair of protons transferred (Fig 17−6). Production of ATP coupled to oxidation in this situation is called **oxidative phosphorylation**. The process depends on an adequate supply of ADP, and consequently is under a form of feedback control; the more rapid the utilization of ATP in the tissues, the greater the accumulation of ADP and, consequently, the more rapid the rate of oxidative phosphorylation.

Cyclic AMP

In addition to its function in energy transfer, ATP

FIG 17−7. Cyclic adenosine-3′,5′-monophosphate. The numbers indicate the positions in the ribose molecule.

is the precursor of cyclic adenosine-3′,5′-monophosphate. This compound, the structure of which is shown in Fig 17−7, is also known as cyclic 3′,5′-AMP, cAMP, or, most commonly, **cyclic AMP**.

Cyclic AMP serves as a key intracellular mediator for the effects of many hormones and other substances that modify cellular function. It is formed from ATP by the action of the enzyme **adenyl cyclase**, which is more properly but less widely known as **adenylate cyclase**, or **adenylyl cyclase**. It is inactivated by con-

TABLE 17−5. Hormones and neurotransmitters that appear to exert their effects by increasing intracellular cyclic AMP. (For references, see Liddle & Hardman: Cyclic adenosine monophosphate as a mediator of hormone action. New England J Med 285:560, 1971.)

Substance	Effect
Catecholamines	Activation of phosphorylase in liver and heart Lipolysis Positive inotropic response in heart Increased renin secretion Inhibition of Purkinje cell discharge in cerebellum
Glucagon	Activation of phosphorylase in liver Lipolysis Positive inotropic effect Stimulation of insulin secretion
Vasopressin	Increased water permeability of renal collecting duct epithelium
ACTH	Steroidogenesis in adrenal cortex
LH	Steroidogenesis in ovary and testis
TSH	Increased secretion of thyroid hormones
TRF and some other releasing factors	Increased secretion of anterior pituitary hormones
Parathyroid hormone	Increased Ca^{++} mobilization from bone Increased renal tubular reabsorption of Ca^{++}; increased $PO_4^{\equiv}$ excretion Increased intestinal absorption of Ca^{++}
Gastrin	Increased gastric secretion of hydrochloric acid

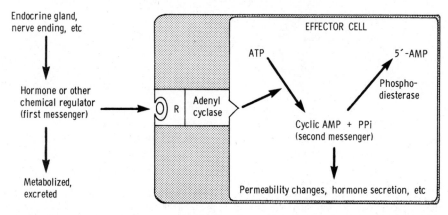

FIG 17–8. The role of cyclic AMP as a second messenger. R, receptor for the first messenger. (Based on Sutherland: Studies on the mechanism of hormone action. Science 177:401, 1972.)

version to 5'-AMP, a reaction catalyzed by the enzyme phosphodiesterase (Fig 17–8). Adenyl cyclase is located in cell membranes, and a specific receptor is associated with a part of the enzyme. Combination of the receptor with the hormone or other agent for which it is specific activates the adenyl cyclase, and cyclic AMP is released inside the cell. Thus, the hormone is a "first messenger" that remains outside the cell, and cyclic AMP is a "second messenger" that brings about the actual changes in permeability, secretion, and the like (Fig 17–8).

Originally, cyclic AMP was discovered as the mediator of the effects of epinephrine on liver glycogen (see below). However, it has now been demonstrated that cyclic AMP-mediated responses are exceedingly numerous and varied. Furthermore, cyclic AMP is found not only in mammals but throughout the animal kingdom, and it appears to have important functions in slime molds and bacteria. In mammals, it is responsible for the effects of many different hormones and appears to mediate responses to substances such as neurotransmitters. The effects of the principal hormones and neurotransmitters mediated by increases in cyclic AMP are summarized in Table 17–5. In addition, the effect of histamine on gastric acid is apparently mediated via cyclic AMP. The effects of catecholamines listed in Table 17–5 are mediated via β receptors (see Chapter 13). There is some evidence that the α receptor-mediated effects of catecholamines are

brought about by a decrease in intracellular cyclic AMP, and insulin decreases cyclic AMP in fat cells and the liver. Some prostaglandins (see below) antagonize the effects of agents that stimulate cyclic AMP.

It is worth noting that, although many different hormonal effects are mediated via cyclic AMP, the effects of hormones are specific. For example, ACTH stimulates adrenal corticoid secretion whereas TSH does not, and TSH stimulates thyroid hormone secretion whereas ACTH does not. The specificity of hormone responses apparently depends on the receptors associated with the adenyl cyclase; in each cell, the receptor is specific for the substance or substances that normally stimulate it. Some cyclic AMP does escape from cells upon stimulation by certain hormones, but the amounts are small compared to the intracellular concentration, and only small amounts of extracellular cyclic AMP enter cells.

In a number of tissues, the effects of cyclic AMP have been shown to be exerted by activation of **protein kinases**. Protein kinases catalyze the transfer of phosphate from ATP to various enzymes, thus activating– or in some cases inactivating–the enzymes. An example of such mediation, the stimulation of phosphorylase in the liver by epinephrine, is discussed below and illustrated in Fig 17–16. Observations on systems such as this have led to the general hypothesis that the effects of cyclic AMP are mediated via the protein kinases. Phosphorylation of certain proteins,

FIG 17–9. Interaction between protein kinase, cyclic AMP receptor protein, and cyclic AMP. Mg, magnesium ion. (Courtesy of J. Roth.)

for example, affects neurotransmitter activities, or the expression of genetic effects that would otherwise be repressed.

Current evidence indicates that, at least in some tissues, each protein kinase is associated with a cyclic AMP receptor protein, and when the receptor is unoccupied the protein kinase is inactive. Cyclic AMP (plus ATP and Mg^{++}) binds to this intracellular protein, and binding makes the kinase active (Fig 17–9). At the same time, intracellular binding protects the cyclic AMP from degradation. Thus, the intracellular concentration of active cyclic AMP depends on the equilibrium between the rate of its production by adenyl cyclase, the rate of its degradation by phosphodiesterase, and the amount of free receptor protein associated with protein kinase. Phosphodiesterase is inhibited by methyl xanthines such as caffeine and theophylline; consequently, these compounds augment hormonal effects mediated via cyclic AMP.

The clinical as well as the basic implications of cyclic AMP mediation of hormonal and other effects are obviously very great. At present, urinary cyclic AMP is being measured in various disease states, and the increase in this moiety normally produced by parathyroid hormone is being used in the evaluation of parathyroid disease. The urinary response to parathyroid hormone is deficient in pseudohypoparathyroidism and there is reason to believe that this disease is due to defective function of the adenyl cyclase system regulated by parathyroid hormone. Additional research will undoubtedly continue to define and elucidate the ubiquitous roles of cyclic AMP.

CARBOHYDRATE METABOLISM

Dietary carbohydrates are for the most part polymers of hexoses, of which the most important are galactose, fructose, and glucose (Fig 17–10). Most of the monosaccharides occurring in the body are the D-isomers. The principal product of carbohydrate digestion and the principal circulating sugar is glucose. The normal fasting level of glucose in peripheral venous blood, determined by the highly specific glucose oxidase method, is 60–80 mg/100 ml; substances other than glucose that cause similar reducing reactions are responsible for the higher values obtained with other methods. In arterial blood, the glucose level is 15–30 mg/100 ml higher than in venous blood.

Once it enters the cells, glucose is normally phosphorylated to form glucose-6-phosphate. The enzyme that catalyzes this reaction is **hexokinase**. In the liver, there is in addition an enzyme called **glucokinase**, which has greater specificity for glucose and which, unlike hexokinase, is increased by insulin and decreased in starvation and diabetes. The glucose-6-phosphate is either polymerized into glycogen or catabolized. The steps involved are outlined in Fig 17–11. The process of glycogen formation is called **glycogenesis**, and glycogen breakdown is called **glycogenolysis**. Glycogen, the storage form of glucose, is present in most body tissues, but the major supplies are in the liver and in skeletal muscle. The breakdown of glucose to CO_2 and water is called **glycolysis**. Glucose catabolism proceeds in 2 ways: via cleavage to trioses, or via oxidation and decarboxylation to pentoses. The pathway to pyruvic acid through the trioses is the **Embden-Meyerhof** pathway and the pathway through gluconic acid and the pentoses is the **direct oxidative pathway**, or **hexosemonophosphate shunt** (Fig 17–11). Pyruvic acid is converted to acetyl-Co A. Interconversions between carbohydrate, protein, and fat (see below) include the conversion of the glycerol from fats to dihydroxyacetone phosphate and the conversion of a number of amino acids with carbon skeletons resembling intermediates in the Embden-Meyerhof pathway and citric acid cycle to these intermediates by deamination. In this way, nonglucose molecules can be converted to glucose (**gluconeogenesis**). Glucose can be converted to fats through acetyl-Co A, but since the conversion of pyruvic acid to acetyl-Co A, unlike most of the reactions in glycolysis, is irreversible, fats are not converted to glucose via this pathway. There is therefore very little net conversion of fats to carbohydrate in the body because, except for the quantitatively unimportant production from glycerol, there is no pathway for conversion.

Citric Acid Cycle

The **citric acid cycle** (Krebs cycle, tricarboxylic acid cycle) is a sequence of reactions in which acetyl-Co A is metabolized to CO_2 and H atoms. Acetyl-Co A is first condensed with a 4-carbon acid, oxaloacetic acid, to form citric acid and HS-Co A. In a series of 7 subsequent reactions, 2 CO_2 molecules are split off, regenerating the oxaloacetic acid (Fig 17–12). Four pairs of H atoms are transferred to the flavoprotein-cytochrome chain, producing 12 ATP and 4 H_2O, of which 2 H_2O are used in the cycle. The citric acid cycle is the common pathway for oxidation to CO_2

```
H-C=O           H-C=O           CH₂OH
|               |               |
H-C-OH          H-C-OH          C=O
|               |               |
HO-C-H          HO-C-H          HO-C-H
|               |               |
H-C-OH          HO-C-H          H-C-OH
|               |               |
H-C-OH          H-C-OH          H-C-OH
|               |               |
CH₂OH           CH₂OH           CH₂OH

D-Glucose       D-Galactose     D-Fructose
```

FIG 17–10. Structure of principal dietary hexoses. The naturally occurring D isomers are shown.

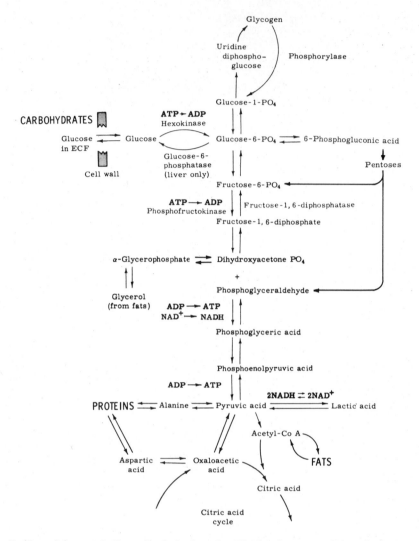

FIG 17–11. Outline of the metabolism of carbohydrate in cells showing some of the principal enzymes involved.

and H_2O of carbohydrate, fat, and some amino acids. The major entry into it is through acetyl-Co A, but pyruvic acid also enters by taking up CO_2 to form oxaloacetic acid, and a number of amino acids can be converted to citric acid cycle intermediates by de-amination (Figs 17–11, 17–24). The combination of pyruvic acid with CO_2 to form oxaloacetic acid is but one of a considerable number of metabolic reactions in which CO_2 is a building block rather than a waste substance. The citric acid cycle requires O_2, and does not function under anaerobic conditions.

Glycolysis to pyruvate occurs outside the mito-chondria. Pyruvic acid then enters the mitochondria and is metabolized. Oxidative phosphorylation occurs only in the mitochondria. Within the mitochondria, the enzymes involved in this process are arranged in orderly sequences along the shelves and inner walls.

Energy Production

The net production of energy-rich phosphate compounds during the metabolism of glucose and glycogen to pyruvic acid depends on whether metabo-lism occurs via the Embden-Meyerhof pathway or the hexosemonophosphate shunt. The conversion of 1 mol of phosphoglyceraldehyde to phosphoglyceric acid generates 1 mol of ATP, and the conversion of 1 mol of phosphoenolpyruvic acid to pyruvic acid another. Since each mol of glucose-6-phosphate produces, via the Embden-Meyerhof pathway, 2 mols of phospho-glyceraldehyde, 4 mols of ATP are generated per mol of glucose metabolized to pyruvate. All these reactions occur in the absence of O_2, and consequently rep-resent anaerobic production of energy or, more prop-erly, "anaerobic oxidation at the substrate level." However, 1 mol of ATP is used in forming fructose-1,6-diphosphate from fructose-6-phosphate, and 1 mol in phosphorylating glucose when it enters the cell. Consequently, when pyruvic acid is formed anaer-obically from glycogen, there is a **net** production of 3 mols of ATP per mol of glucose-6-phosphate; but when

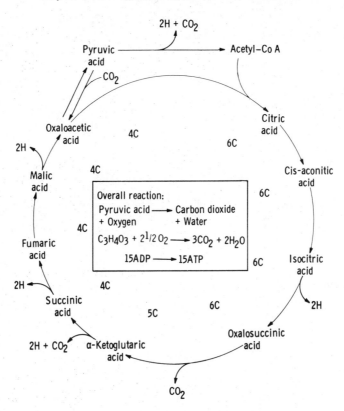

FIG 17–12. Citric acid cycle. The numbers in the circle (6C, 5C, 4C) indicate the number of carbon atoms in each of the acid intermediates. Note that 2 H atoms are transferred from the pyruvic acid → acetyl-Co A reaction and 8 H atoms are transferred for each turn of the cycle proper, generating by oxidative phosphorylation a total of 15 ATP.

pyruvic acid is formed from 1 mol of blood glucose, the net gain is only 2 mols of ATP. Another high-energy bond formed anaerobically is the thioester linkage of acetyl-Co A. Its energy is used in the further conversion of acetate in the citric acid cycle.

A supply of NAD$^+$ is necessary for the conversion of phosphoglyceraldehyde to phosphoglyceric acid. Under aerobic conditions, NADH is oxidized via the flavoprotein-cytochrome chain, regenerating NAD$^+$ and forming 6 additional mols of ATP per 2 mols of phosphoglyceric acid. Under anaerobic conditions (anaerobic glycolysis), a block of glycolysis at the phosphoglyceraldehyde conversion step might be expected to develop as soon as the available NAD$^+$ is converted to NADH. However, pyruvic acid can accept hydrogen from NADH, forming NAD$^+$ and lactic acid (Fig 17–13). In this way, glucose metabolism and energy production can continue for a while without O$_2$. The lactic acid that accumulates is converted back to pyruvic acid when the O$_2$ supply is restored, NADH transferring its hydrogen to the flavoprotein-cytochrome chain.

During aerobic glycolysis, the production of ATP is 19 times as great as it is under anaerobic conditions. Not only are 6 additional mols of ATP formed by NADH oxidation via the flavoprotein-cytochrome

chain, but similar oxidation of the 2 mols of NADH formed by the conversion of 2 mols of pyruvic acid to acetyl-Co A produces 6 mols of ATP, and each turn of the strictly aerobic citric acid cycle generates 12 mols of ATP. Therefore, the net production per mol of blood glucose metabolized aerobically via the Embden-Meyerhof pathway and citric acid cycle is 38 mols (2 + [2 × 3] + [2 × 3] + [2 × 12]) of ATP.

Glucose oxidation via the hexosemonophosphate shunt generates large amounts of NADPH. A supply of this reduced coenzyme is essential for many metabolic processes, especially steroid hormone synthesis. The pentoses formed in the process are building blocks for nucleotides (see below). The amount of ATP generated depends upon the amount of NADPH converted to NADH and then oxidized.

$$\underset{\text{Pyruvic acid}}{\overset{\displaystyle \mathrm{CH_3}}{\underset{\displaystyle \mathrm{COOH}}{\overset{|}{\underset{|}{\mathrm{C{=}O}}}}}} + 2\mathrm{NADH} \;\rightleftharpoons\; 2\mathrm{NAD^+} + \underset{\text{Lactic acid}}{\overset{\displaystyle \mathrm{CH_3}}{\underset{\displaystyle \mathrm{COOH}}{\overset{|}{\underset{|}{\mathrm{HCOH}}}}}}$$

FIG 17–13. Oxidation of NADH by reduction of pyruvic acid to lactic acid.

"Directional Flow Valves"

Metabolism is regulated by a variety of hormones and other factors. To bring about any net change in a particular metabolic process, regulatory factors obviously must drive a chemical reaction in one direction. Most of the reactions in intermediary metabolism are freely reversible, but there are a number of "directional flow valves," reactions which proceed in one direction under the influence of one enzyme or transport mechanism and in the opposite direction under the influence of another. Five examples in the intermediary metabolism of carbohydrate are shown in Fig 17–14. The different pathways for fatty acid synthesis and catabolism (see below) are another example. Regulatory factors exert their influence on metabolism by acting directly or indirectly at these "directional flow valves."

Phosphorylase

Glycogen breakdown is regulated by several hormones. Glycogen is synthesized from glucose-1-phosphate via uridine diphosphoglucose (UDPG; Fig 17–15), with the enzyme **glycogen synthetase** catalyzing the final step. Glycogen is a branched glucose polymer with 2 types of glucoside linkage. Cleavage of the 1:4a linkage in the polymer chain is catalyzed by

1. Glucose entry into cells and glucose exit from cells

2. Glucose ⇄ Glucose-6-phosphate
   (Hexokinase / Glucose-6-phosphatase)

3. Glucose-1-phosphate ⇄ Glycogen
   (Glycogen synthetase / Phosphorylase)

4. Fructose-6-phosphate ⇄ Fructose-1,6-diphosphate
   (Phosphofructokinase / Fructose-1,6-diphosphatase)

5. Phosphoenolpyruvic acid → Pyruvic acid
   (ADP → ATP, Pyruvate kinase)
   Phosphoenolpyruvate carboxykinase
   Oxaloacetic acid ← Malic acid (Malic enzyme)
   Malic acid dehydrogenase

FIG 17–14. Five examples of "directional flow valves" in carbohydrate metabolism: reactions which proceed in one direction by one mechanism and in the other direction by a different mechanism. Direct conversion of pyruvic acid to phosphoenolpyruvic acid is possible, but it is difficult because of the bioenergetics involved, and usually proceeds via malic acid.

phosphorylase, while cleavage of the 1:6a linkages at branching points is catalyzed by another enzyme.

Phorphorylase is activated by epinephrine in a sequence of reactions that provides a classic example of hormonal action via cyclic AMP. These reactions are summarized in Fig 17–16. Protein kinase is activated by cyclic AMP (Fig 17–9) and catalyzes the transfer of a phosphate group to phosphorylase kinase, converting it to its active form (Fig 17–16). The phosphorylase kinase in turn catalyzes the phosphorylation and consequent activation of phosphorylase. Inactive phosphorylase is known as phosphorylase b, or dephosphophosphorylase, and activated phosphorylase is known as phosphorylase a, or phosphophosphorylase.

Activation of protein kinase by cyclic AMP not only increases glycogen breakdown but also inhibits glycogen synthesis. Glycogen synthetase (Fig 17–15) is active in its dephosphorylated form and inactive when phosphorylated, and it is phosphorylated along with phosphorylase kinase when protein kinase is activated.

Because the liver contains the enzyme **glucose-6-phosphatase**, much of the glucose-6-phosphate which is formed in this organ can be converted to glucose and enter the blood stream, raising the blood glucose level. The kidneys can also contribute to the elevation. Other tissues do not contain this enzyme, so in them a large proportion of the glucose-6-phosphate is catabolized via the Embden-Meyerhof pathway and hexosemonophosphate shunt pathway. Increased glucose catabolism in skeletal muscle causes a rise in the blood lactic acid level (Chapter 3).

By stimulating adenyl cyclase, epinephrine causes activation of the phosphorylase in liver and skeletal muscle. The consequences of this activation are a rise in the blood glucose and lactic acid levels. Glucagon has a similar action, but it exerts its effect only on the phosphorylase in the liver. Consequently, glucagon causes a rise in blood glucose without any change in blood lactic acid.

McArdle's Syndrome

In the clinical condition known as **McArdle's syndrome**, or **myophosphorylase deficiency glycogenosis**, glycogen accumulates in skeletal muscles because of a deficiency of muscle phosphorylase. As would be predicted, patients with this disease have a greatly reduced exercise tolerance; they cannot break down their muscle glycogen to provide the energy for muscle contraction (Chapter 3), and the glucose reaching their muscles from the blood stream is sufficient only for the demands of very mild exercise. Patients with McArdle's syndrome respond with a normal rise in blood glucose when given glucagon or epinephrine, indicating that their hepatic phosphorylase is normal.

The "Hepatic Glucostat"

There is a net uptake of glucose by the liver when the blood glucose is high and a net discharge when it is low. The liver thus functions as a sort of "glucostat," maintaining a constant circulating glucose level. This

FIG 17-15. Glycogen formation and breakdown. The activation of phosphorylase a is summarized in Fig 17-16.

function is not automatic; glucose uptake and glucose discharge are affected by the actions of numerous hormones. Endocrine regulation of the blood glucose level and of carbohydrate metabolism in general are discussed in Chapter 19.

Effects of Glycogen on Hepatic Function

When the hepatic glycogen level is high, the rate of deamination of amino acids is depressed and the amino acids are thus preserved for other uses. Protein catabolism is decreased by the administration of glucose (**protein-sparing** effect of glucose; see below), and part of this sparing may be mediated via the effect of glycogen on deamination. Ketone body formation is also depressed when the liver glycogen content is high (see below). Acetylation and glucuronide conjugation of various substances in the liver progress at a faster rate when the glycogen content is high, and the glycogen-rich liver is more resistant to toxic agents and pathologic processes. This is why it is important in the treatment of infectious hepatitis to maintain a high carbohydrate intake.

Renal Handling of Glucose

In the kidney, glucose is freely filtered; but at normal blood glucose levels all but a very small amount is reabsorbed in the proximal tubules (see Chapter 38). When the amount filtered increases, reabsorption increases, but there is a limit to the amount of glucose

the proximal tubules can reabsorb. When the tubular maximum for glucose (Tm_G) is exceeded, appreciable amounts of glucose appear in the urine (**glycosuria**). The **renal threshold** for glucose, the arterial blood level at which glycosuria appears, is reached when the venous blood glucose concentration is normally about 180 mg/100 ml, but it may be higher if the glomerular filtration rate is low.

Glycosuria

Glycosuria occurs when the blood glucose is elevated because of relative insulin deficiency (diabetes mellitus) or because of excessive glycogenolysis after physical or emotional trauma. In some individuals, the glucose transport mechanism in the renal tubules is congenitally defective, so that glycosuria is present at normal blood glucose levels. This condition is called **renal glycosuria. Alimentary glycosuria,** glycosuria after ingestion of a high-carbohydrate meal, has been claimed to occur in normal individuals, but many of these people actually have mild diabetes mellitus. The maximal rate of glucose absorption from the intestine is about 120 g/hour.

Factors Determining the Blood Glucose Level

The blood glucose level at any given time is determined by the balance between the amount of glucose entering the blood stream and the amount leaving it. The principal determinants are therefore the dietary

FIG 17–16. Cascade sequence of reactions by which epinephrine activates phosphorylase. Glucagon has a similar action in liver but not in skeletal muscle. (Reproduced, with permission, from Peake: The role of cyclic nucleotides in the secretion of pituitary growth hormone. In: *Frontiers of Neuroendocrinology, 1973.* Ganong WF, Martini L (editors). Oxford Univ Press, 1973.)

intake, the rate of entry into the cells of muscle, adipose tissue, and other organs, and the glucostatic activity of the liver (Fig 17–17). Five percent of ingested glucose is promptly converted into glycogen in the liver and 30–40% is converted into fat. The remainder is metabolized in muscle and other tissues. If the blood glucose falls to low levels between meals, glycogenolysis occurs and the liver adds glucose to the

blood stream. When glycogen is depleted, gluconeogenesis from protein and glycerol occurs in the liver, and sufficient glucose is added to the blood stream to prevent hypoglycemia even during prolonged starvation.

Metabolism of Hexoses Other Than Glucose

Other hexoses which are absorbed from the intestine include galactose, which is liberated by the digestion of lactose; and fructose, part of which is ingested and part liberated by hydrolysis of sucrose. Galactose is converted to glucose in the liver. After phosphorylation, it reacts with uridine diphosphoglucose. The uridine diphosphogalactose formed is converted to uridine diphosphoglucose, which functions in glycogen synthesis. The latter reaction is reversible, and this is the way the galactose necessary for formation of glycolipids and mucoproteins is formed when dietary galactose intake is inadequate. The utilization of galactose, like that of glucose, is dependent upon insulin (see Chapter 19). In the inborn error of metabolism known as **galactosemia**, there is a congenital deficiency of phosphogalactose uridyl transferase, the enzyme responsible for the reaction between galactose-1-phosphate and uridine diphosphoglucose, so that ingested galactose accumulates in the circulation. Serious disturbances of growth and development result. Treatment with galactose-free diets improves this condition without leading to galactose deficiency because the enzymes necessary for the formation of uridine diphosphogalactose from uridine diphosphoglucose are present.

Fructose may be phosphorylated on the sixth carbon atom, competing with glucose for the hexokinase involved; or it may be phosphorylated on the first carbon atom, a reaction catalyzed by a specific fructokinase. Fructose-1-phosphate is then split into dihydroxyacetone phosphate and glyceraldehyde. The glyceraldehyde is phosphorylated, and it and the dihydroxyacetone phosphate enter the pathways for glucose metabolism. Fructose-1-phosphate may also be phosphorylated to form fructose-1,6-diphosphate (Fig 17–18). Since the reactions proceeding through phosphorylation of fructose in the one position can occur at a normal rate in the absence of insulin, it has been recommended that fructose be given to diabetics to replete their carbohydrate stores. However, because appreciable quantities of fructose are metabolized only in the intestines and the liver, fructose treatment is of limited value.

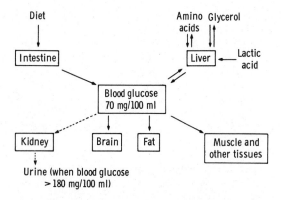

FIG 17–17. Blood glucose homeostasis, illustrating the glucostatic function of the liver.

PROTEIN METABOLISM

Proteins

Proteins are made up of amino acids (Fig 17–19) linked into chains by **peptide bonds** joining the amino group of one amino acid to the carboxyl group of the next. In addition, some proteins contain carbohydrates

FIG 17–18. **Metabolism of fructose, showing how fructose enters the Embden-Meyerhof pathway for glucose catabolism.**

(glycoproteins) and lipids (lipoproteins). The order of the amino acids in the chains is called the **primary structure** of a protein. The chains are twisted and folded in complex ways, and the term **secondary structure** of a protein refers to the spatial arrangement produced by the twisting and folding. The most common secondary structure is a regular coil with 3.7 amino acid residues per turn (α-helix). The **tertiary structure** of a protein is the arrangement of the twisted chains into layers, crystals, or fibers. Some protein molecules are made of subunits (eg, hemoglobin; see Chapter 27), and the term **quaternary structure** is used to refer to the arrangement of the subunits.

Amino Acids

The amino acids that are important in mammalian metabolism are shown in Table 17–6. In higher animals, the L-isomers are the only naturally occurring forms. The L-isomers of thyroxine and hormones such as epinephrine that are formed from amino acids are much more active than the D-isomers. Most of the amino acids are found in dietary proteins in large quantities, although a few with special functions, such as citrulline, ornithine, and 5-hydroxytryptophan, are not. They are acidic, neutral, or basic in reaction, depending upon the relative proportions of free acidic ($-COOH$) or basic ($-NH_2$) groups in the molecule.

The Amino Acid Pool

Proteins are absorbed from the gastrointestinal tract in infants, but only amino acids are absorbed in normal adults. The body's own proteins are being continuously hydrolyzed to amino acids and resynthesized. The turnover rate of endogenous proteins averages 80–100 g/day, being highest in the intestinal mucosa and practically nil in collagen. The amino acids formed by endogenous protein breakdown are in no way different from those derived from ingested protein. With the latter they form a common **amino acid pool** that supplies the needs of the body (Fig 17–20). In the kidney, most of the filtered amino acids are reabsorbed, but in diseases such as the Fanconi syndrome **aminoaciduria** is present, apparently as a result of congenital defects in the renal tubules. During growth, the equilibrium between amino acids and body proteins shifts toward the latter, so that synthesis exceeds breakdown. At all ages, a small amount of protein is lost as hair. There are small amounts of protein hormones in the urine, and unreabsorbed protein digestive secretions in the stools. These losses are made up by synthesis from the amino acid pool.

Specific Metabolic Functions of Amino Acids

Thyroxine, catecholamines, histamine, serotonin, melatonin, and intermediates in the urea cycle are formed from specific amino acids. Methionine, cystine, and cysteine provide the sulfur contained in proteins, coenzyme A, taurine, and other biologically important compounds. Methionine is converted into S-adenosylmethionine, which is the active methylating agent in

Amino acid   Polypeptide chain

FIG 17–19. **Amino acid structure and formation of peptide bonds.** The dotted lines show how the peptide bonds are formed, with the production of H_2O. R = remainder of amino acid. For example, in glycine, R = H; in glutamic acid, R = $-(CH_2)_2 -COOH$.

TABLE 17–6. Amino acids of biologic importance.
Those in bold type are essential amino acids.

Neutral Amino Acids.	Acidic Amino Acids. (Monoaminodicarboxylic acids)
Amino acids with unsubstituted chains.	Aspartic acid*
Glycine*	Asparagine*
Alanine*	Glutamic acid*
Valine*	Glutamine*
Leucine*	Basic Amino Acids. (Diaminomonocarboxylic acids)
Isoleucine*	Arginine*
Hydroxyl-substituted amino acids.	Citrulline†
Serine*	Ornithine†
Threonine*	Hydroxylysine
Sulfur-containing amino acids.	**Lysine***
Cysteine*	5-Hydroxylysine† (found in collagen in small amounts)
Cystine	Histidine*
Methionine*	Imino Acids. (Contain imino group but no amino group)
Homocysteine†	Proline*
Aromatic amino acids.	4-Hydroxyproline
Phenylalanine†	3-Hydroxyproline† (found in collagen in small amounts)
Tyrosine*	
Tryptophan*	
5-Hydroxytryptophan†	
Thyroxine and related compounds†	

*Has a specific tRNA.
†Not found in dietary proteins in appreciable amounts but has a role in metabolism.

the synthesis of compounds such as epinephrine, acetylcholine, and creatine. It is a major donor of biologically labile methyl groups, but methyl groups can also be synthesized from a derivative of formic acid bound to folic acid derivatives if the diet contains adequate amounts of folic acid and cyanocobalamin.

Urinary Sulfates

Sulfur-containing amino acids are the source of the sulfates in the urine. A few unoxidized sulfur-containing compounds are excreted (urinary **neutral sulfur**), but most of the urinary excretion is in the form of **sulfate** ($SO_4^=$) accompanied by corresponding amounts of cation (Na^+, K^+, NH_4^+, or H^+). The **ethereal sulfates** in the urine are organic sulfate esters ($R{-}O{-}SO_3H$) formed in the liver from endogenous and exogenous phenols, including estrogens and other steroids, indoles, and drugs.

Deamination, Amination, & Transamination

Interconversions between amino acids and the products of carbohydrate and fat catabolism at the level of the common metabolic pool and the citric acid cycle involve transfer, removal, or formation of amino groups. **Transamination** reactions, conversion of one amino acid to the corresponding keto acid with simultaneous conversion of another keto acid to an amino acid (Fig 17–21), occur in many tissues. The **transaminase** enzymes involved are also present in the circulation. When damage to many active cells occurs as a result of a pathologic process, serum transaminase levels rise. An example is the rise in **serum glutamic-oxaloacetic transaminase (SGOT)** following myocardial infarction.

Oxidative deamination of amino acids occurs in the liver. An imino acid is formed by dehydrogenation, and this compound is hydrolyzed to the corresponding

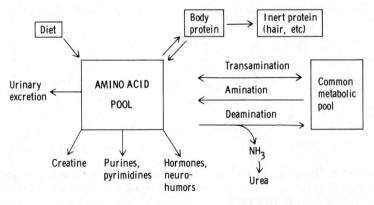

FIG 17–20. Amino acid metabolism. Sources and fates of amino acids.

$$CH_3 - CH - COOH \quad + \quad O=C - COOH \quad \rightleftharpoons \quad C=O \quad + \quad CH - COOH$$

Alanine   α-Ketoglutaric acid   Pyruvic acid   Glutamic acid

FIG 17–21. Transamination.

keto acid, with the liberation of ammonia (Fig 17–22). Amino acids can also take up NH_3, forming the corresponding amine (**amination**). An example is the binding of NH_3 in the brain by glutamic acid (Fig 17–23). The reverse reaction occurs in the kidney, with the liberation of NH_3 into the urine. The NH_3 reacts with H^+ to form NH_4^+, thus permitting more H^+ to be secreted into the urine (see Chapter 38).

Interconversions between the amino acid pool and the common metabolic pool are summarized in Fig 17–24. Leucine, isoleucine, phenylalanine, and tyrosine are said to be **ketogenic** because they are converted to the ketone body acetoacetic acid (see below). Threonine and valine (by an irreversible reaction) and many other amino acids (by reversible reactions) are **glucogenic** or **gluconeogenic**, ie, they give rise to compounds that can readily be converted to glucose.

Urea Formation

Most of the NH_3 formed by deamination of amino acids in the liver is converted to urea and the urea is excreted in the urine. Except for the brain, the liver is probably the only site of urea formation, and in severe hepatic disease the blood urea nitrogen level falls. The raw materials are 2 mols of NH_3 and 1 mol of CO_2 from the plasma HCO_3^-. The synthesis via the **urea cycle** (Krebs-Henseleit cycle) involves conversion of the amino acid ornithine to citrulline and then to arginine, following which urea is split off and ornithine is regenerated. CO_2 and NH_3 are introduced into the cycle by "carrier" molecules, the formation of which requires ATP.

Creatine & Creatinine

Creatine is synthesized in the liver from methionine, glycine, and arginine. In skeletal muscle it is phosphorylated to form phosphocreatine (Fig 17–25).

Phosphocreatine is the "back-up" energy store for ATP synthesis (see Chapter 3). The ATP formed by glycolysis and oxidative phosphorylation reacts with creatine to form ADP and large amounts of phosphocreatine. During exercise the reaction is reversed, maintaining the supply of ATP which is the immediate source of the energy for muscle contraction.

The creatinine in the urine is formed from phosphocreatine. Creatine is not converted directly to creatinine. The rate of creatinine excretion is relatively constant from day to day. Indeed, creatinine output is sometimes measured as a check on the accuracy of the urine collections in metabolic studies; an average daily creatinine output is calculated, and the values for the daily output of other substances are corrected to what they would have been at this creatinine output.

Creatinuria occurs normally in children, in women during and after pregnancy, and occasionally in nonpregnant women. There is very little if any creatine in the urine of normal men, but appreciable quantities are excreted in any condition associated with extensive muscle breakdown. Thus, creatinuria occurs in starvation, thyrotoxicosis, poorly controlled diabetes mellitus, and the various primary and secondary diseases of muscle (**myopathies**).

Purines & Pyrimidines

The physiologically important **purines** and **pyrimidines** are shown in Fig 17–26. **Nucleosides**—purines or pyrimidines combined with ribose—are components not only of a variety of coenzymes and related substances (NAD^+, $NADP^+$, ATP, UDPG, etc), but of ribonucleic acid (RNA) and deoxyribonucleic acid (DNA) as well (Table 17–7).

Nucleic acids in the diet are digested and their constituent purines and pyrimidines absorbed, but

$$CH_3 - CH - COOH \quad + \quad NAD^+ \longrightarrow CH_3 - C - COOH \quad + \quad NADH$$

Amino acid
(alanine)   Imino acid

$$CH_3 - C - COOH \quad + \quad H_2O \longrightarrow CH_3 - C - COOH \quad + \quad NH_3$$

Imino acid   Keto acid
(pyruvic acid)

FIG 17–22. Oxidative deamination.

$$NH_3 \quad + \quad \text{Glutamic acid} \quad \underset{\text{Glutaminase (kidney)}}{\overset{ATP \longrightarrow ADP \text{ (brain)}}{\rightleftharpoons}} \quad \text{Glutamine}$$

FIG 17–23. Uptake and release of NH_3 by interconversion of glutamic acid and glutamine. The reaction goes predominantly to the right in the brain, binding NH_3; and predominantly to the left in the kidney tubules, liberating NH_3 into the urine.

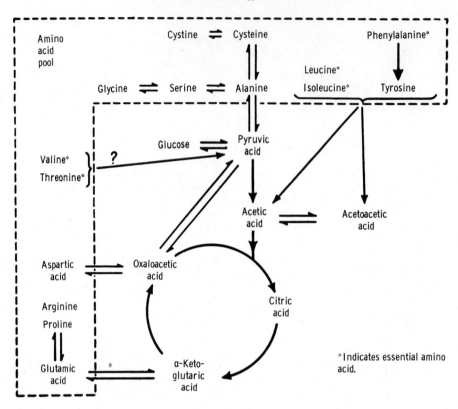

FIG 17—24. Interrelationships between the amino acid pool and the common metabolic pool (pyruvic acid and the citric acid cycle). (Reproduced, with permission, from Keele & Neil: *Sampson Wright's Applied Physiology,* 12th ed. Oxford Univ Press, 1971.)

most of the purines and pyrimidines are synthesized from amino acids, principally in the liver. The nucleotides and RNA and DNA are then synthesized. RNA is in dynamic equilibrium with the amino acid pool, but DNA, once formed, is metabolically stable throughout life.

The purines and pyrimidines liberated by the breakdown of nucleotides may be reused or catab-olized. Minor amounts are excreted unchanged in the urine. The pyrimidines are catabolized to CO_2 and NH_3, and the purines are converted to uric acid.

Adenine:	6-Aminopurine
Guanine:	2-Amino-6-oxypurine
Xanthine:	2,6-Dioxypurine
Uric acid:	2,6,8-Trioxypurine

Purine nucleus

Cytosine:	6-Amino-2-oxypyrimidine
Uracil:	2,6-Dioxypyrimidine
Thymine:	5-Methyl-2,6-dioxypyrimidine

Pyrimidine nucleus

FIG 17—26. Principal physiologically important purines and pyrimidines. Oxypurines and oxypyrimidines may form enol derivatives (hydroxypurines and hydroxypyrimidines) by migration of hydrogen to the oxygen substituents.

Creatine
(from arginine, glycine, and methionine)

Phosphocreatine

Creatinine

FIG 17—25. Creatine, phosphocreatine, and creatinine.

TABLE 17–7. Purine- and pyrimidine-containing compounds.

Purine or pyrimidine + Ribose = Nucleoside

Nucleoside + Phosphoric acid residue =
Nucleotide (mononucleotide)

Many nucleotides forming double helical structure of
2 polynucleotide chains = Nucleic acid

Nucleic acid + 1$^+$ Simple basic protein = Nucleoprotein

Ribonucleic acids (RNA) contain ribose

Deoxyribonucleic acids (DNA) contain 2-deoxyribose

Structure & Function of DNA & RNA

DNA is found in the nuclei of cells and in mitochondria. It is made up of 2 extremely long nucleotide chains containing adenine, guanine, thymine, and cytosine in various sequences (Fig 17–27). The chains are bound together by hydrogen bonding between the bases, adenine bonding to thymine and guanine to cytosine. The resultant double helical structure of the molecule is shown in Fig 17–28.

DNA is the component of the chromosomes that carries the "genetic message," the blueprint for all the heritable characteristics of the cell and its descendants. Each chromosome is in effect a segment of the DNA double helix. The genetic message is coded by the sequence of purine and pyrimidine bases in the nucleotide chains. The text of the message is the order in which the amino acids are lined up in the proteins manufactured by the cell. The message is transferred to the sites of protein synthesis in the cytoplasm by RNA. The proteins formed include all the enzymes,

FIG 17–27. Tetranucleotide portion of one strand of deoxyribonucleic acid. The strand is composed of adenine (A), thymine (T), cytosine (C), and guanine (G) deoxynucleotides.

and these in turn control the metabolism of the cell. It is generally believed that there is one gene for each enzyme or enzyme subunit in the body. Mutations occur when the base sequence in the DNA is altered by x-rays, cosmic rays, or other mutagenic agents.

At the time of each somatic cell division (**mitosis**), the 2 DNA chains separate and each serves as a template for the synthesis of a new complementary chain. **DNA polymerase** catalyzes this reaction. One of the double helices thus formed goes to one daughter cell and one to the other, so the amount of DNA in each daughter cell is the same as the amount in the parent cell. In the case of germ cells, reduction division (**meiosis**) takes place during maturation. The net result is that 1 DNA chain goes to each mature germ cell; consequently, each mature germ cell contains half the amount of chromosomal material found in somatic cells. Therefore, when a sperm unites with an ovum, the resulting zygote has the full complement of DNA, half of which came from the father and half from the mother. The chromosomal events that occur at the time of fertilization are discussed in more detail in Chapter 23.

The strands of the DNA double helix not only replicate themselves, but they serve as templates by lining up complementary bases for the formation in the nucleus of **messenger RNA (mRNA)** and **soluble** or **transfer RNA (tRNA)**. The formation of mRNA is catalyzed by the enzyme **RNA polymerase.** The mRNA molecules are smaller than the DNA molecules, and each represents a transcription of a small segment of the DNA chain. The molecules of tRNA are even smaller. They contain only 70–80 nitrogenous bases, compared to hundreds in mRNA and as many as 500,000,000 in DNA. tRNA and mRNA are single stranded, and they contain the base uracil in place of thymine. A third distinct type of RNA is the RNA in the ribosomes (**ribosomal RNA**).

Once mRNA is formed, it moves out of the nucleus and becomes associated with the ribosomes in the cytoplasm (Chapter 1). In the ribosomes, it serves as a template for the formation of a particular protein by the cell. tRNA attaches the amino acids to mRNA.

The functions of DNA and RNA in terms of formation of the individual and continuity of the species are summarized in Fig 17–29. DNA passes from one generation to the next in the germ cells, and in this sense it is immortal. RNA reads the information coded in the DNA and transcribes it so that a mortal individual is formed each generation, a process which has been called "budding off from the germ line."

Protein Synthesis

The process of protein synthesis is a complex but fascinating one. The first step is the reaction of an amino acid with ATP and an amino acid activating enzyme specific for that amino acid to form a complex made up of the amino acid, the enzyme, and adenosine monophosphate (adenylate). This **activated amino acid** then combines with a specific molecule of tRNA. There are 20 different kinds of tRNA molecules, one for each of the 20 amino acids found in large quantities in the body proteins of animals. The tRNA-amino acid-adenylate complex is next attached to the mRNA template, a process which occurs in the ribosomes. This process is shown diagrammatically in Fig 17–30. The tRNA "recognizes" the proper spot to attach on the mRNA template because it has on its active end a set of 3 bases which are complementary to a set of 3 in a particular spot on the mRNA chain. The genetic code

FIG 17–28. Diagram of the Watson and Crick model, slightly modified, of the double helical structure of DNA. On the left, the hydrogen bonding between the bases of the 2 nucleotide chains is shown. A, adenine; T, thymine; C, cytosine; G, guanine; S, deoxyribose; P, phosphate. (Reproduced, with permission, from Harper: *Review of Physiological Chemistry,* 14th ed. Lange, 1973.)

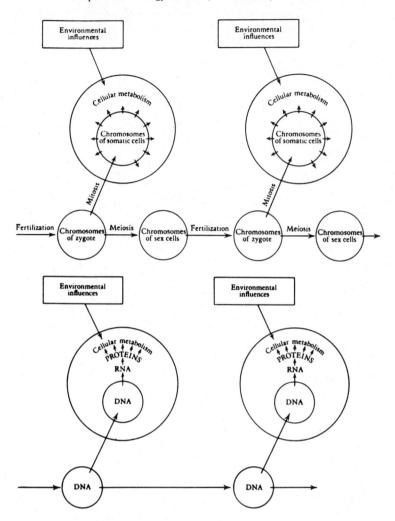

FIG 17−29. The functions of DNA and RNA in terms of the formation of the individual and the continuity of species. Germ plasm (DNA) passes from generation to generation via the germ cells. From this "germ line" the mortal soma, or body, buds off each generation. Formation of the individual depends upon transcription of the genetic message by RNA, thus determining the enzymes formed and consequently controlling the metabolism of the cell. (Reproduced, with permission, from Haggis & others: *Introduction to Molecular Biology.* Wiley, 1964.)

is made up of such **triplets,** sequences of 3 purine or pyrimidine bases each of which stands for a particular amino acid.

Proteins are formed in the ribosomes (see Chapter 1) beginning with the N-terminal amino acid, and the chain is lengthened one amino acid at a time. The messenger RNA attaches to the 30 S subunit of the ribosome during protein synthesis; the polypeptide chain being formed attaches to the 50 S subunit; and the tRNA attaches to both. As the amino acids are added in the order dictated by the triplet code, the ribosome moves along the mRNA molecule like a bead on a string. Typically, there is more than 1 ribosome on the mRNA chain at one time. The mRNA chain plus its collection of ribosomes is visible under the electron microscope as an aggregation of ribosomes

called a **polyribosome,** or **polysome.** When the ribosome reaches the end of the mRNA chain, it liberates the protein and the tRNA molecule is ready to be used again. The mRNA chains are also reused approximately 10 times before they are replaced by newly synthesized chains.

Effects of Antibiotics on Protein Synthesis

Many antibiotics inhibit protein synthesis. Some of them have this effect primarily in bacteria, but others inhibit protein synthesis in the cells of other animals, including mammals. This fact makes them of great value as research tools. Antibiotics have now been shown to disrupt a variety of different steps in the synthetic process (Table 17−8).

FIG 17−30. Diagrammatic outline of protein synthesis. The nucleic acids are represented as lines with multiple short projections representing the individual bases. (Reproduced, with permission, from Haggis & others: *Introduction to Molecular Biology.* Wiley, 1964.)

TABLE 17−8. Mechanisms by which antibiotics and related drugs inhibit protein synthesis.

Agent	Effect
Chloramphenicol (Chloromycetin)	Prevents normal association of mRNA with ribosomes
Streptomycin, neomycin, kanamycin	Cause misreading of genetic code
Tetracycline, cycloheximide	Inhibit transfer of tRNA-amino acid complex to polypeptide
Puromycin	Puromycin-amino acid complex substitutes for tRNA-amino acid complex and prevents addition of further amino acids to polypeptide
Actinomycin D (dactinomycin, Cosmegen)	Binds to DNA, preventing polymerization of RNA or DNA
Chloroquine, colchicine, novobiocin	Inhibit DNA polymerase
Nitrogen mustards, eg, mechlorethamine (Mustargen)	Binds to guanine in base pairs

Enzyme Induction

The velocity of enzyme-controlled reactions in the body can be increased by increasing the availability of substrate, by removing an inhibitor of the enzyme, by increasing the availability of a necessary coenzyme or energy source, by conversion of an inactive enzyme precursor into an active enzyme, or by the synthesis of more enzyme molecules. Increased enzyme activity can be induced by supplying cells with various organic substances (**inducers**). Addition of the substrate for the enzyme often brings on increased activity (**substrate induction**). This induction may be due in part to activation of preformed inactive enzyme molecules, but it may also be due to the formation of more enzyme molecules. Synthesis of more enzyme can be triggered by various substances, including some hormones. These substances bring out in the cell its latent ability to synthesize the particular enzyme by activating the appropriate gene to produce the appropriate mRNA.

Hormones That Act by Stimulating Enzyme Synthesis

The first concrete evidence that a hormone could act by stimulating the synthesis of certain enzymes came from studies of the insect hormone **ecdysone**, which controls moulting. This hormone was shown to induce increased mRNA synthesis in part of a chromosome. In some insect species, this area of increased synthetic activity on the chromosome is visible under the microscope as a local swelling called a **puff**. The demonstration that a hormone could stimulate the genetically controlled synthesis of enzymes in insects led to studies which demonstrated that many different hormones acted at the level of the genetic mechanism regulating protein synthesis. There is good evidence that at least some of the effects of the following hormones are due to an action at this level: all steroid hormones, ACTH, growth hormone, LH, thyroxine, insulin, and erythropoietin. The actions of the individual hormones are discussed in detail in succeeding chapters.

Relation to Cyclic AMP

It is interesting that the list of hormones thought to act by stimulation of enzyme synthesis includes some that appear to act via cyclic AMP. This other mechanism of hormone action, which is common to a variety of hormones, is discussed above. For any given hormone action, one might expect that one or the other of the mechanisms would be operative. However, in the adrenal cortex and the ovary, both appear to operate. In the adrenal, there is evidence that ACTH activates adenyl cyclase and that the resultant increase in intracellular cyclic AMP triggers the increased synthesis of a protein that increases the conversion of cholesterol to pregnenolone (see Chapter 20). There may be other situations in which hormones act on the cell membrane to cause release of an intracellular messenger which in turn activates the machinery controlling protein synthesis. However, most steroid hormones appear to enter the cell and act on the nucleus.

Uric Acid

Uric acid is formed by the breakdown of purines and by direct synthesis from 5-phosphoribosyl pyrophosphate (5-PRPP) and glutamic acid (Fig 17–31). In man, uric acid is excreted in the urine; but in other mammals—except, curiously, the Dalmatian coach dog—uric acid is further oxidized to allantoin before excretion. The normal blood uric acid level in man is approximately 4 mg/100 ml. In the kidney, uric acid is filtered, reabsorbed, and excreted. Normally, 98% of the filtered uric acid is reabsorbed and the remaining 2% makes up approximately 20% of the amount excreted. The remaining 80% comes from tubular secretion. The uric acid excretion in 24 hours on a purine-free diet is about 0.5 g and on a regular diet about 1 g.

"Primary" & "Secondary" Gout

Gout is a disease characterized by recurrent attacks of arthritis, urate deposits in the joints, kidneys, and other tissues, and elevated blood and urine uric acid levels. The joint most commonly affected initially is the metatarsophalangeal joint of the great toe. There are 2 forms of "primary" gout: one in which, for unknown reasons, uric acid production is increased; and another in which there is a selective

FIG 17–31. Uric acid metabolism.

deficit in renal tubular transport of uric acid. In "secondary" gout, the uric acid levels in the body fluids are elevated as a result of decreased excretion or increased production secondary to some other disease process. For example, excretion is decreased in renal disease and production is increased in leukemia and pneumonia due to increased breakdown of uric acid-rich white blood cells. Starvation also causes a rise in the blood uric acid level and may precipitate symptoms of gout, presumably because of increased nucleic acid breakdown. The treatment of gout is aimed at relieving the acute arthritis with drugs such as colchicine and decreasing the uric acid level in the blood. Colchicine does not affect uric acid metabolism, and it apparently relieves gouty attacks by inhibiting the phagocytosis of uric acid crystals by leukocytes, a process which in some way produces the joint symptoms. Adrenal glucocorticoid hormones and their synthetic derivatives increase uric acid excretion. So do salicylates and probenecid, which decrease tubular uric acid reabsorption. Allopurinol, which inhibits xanthine oxidase, is used to decrease uric acid production. Xanthine oxidase is the enzyme responsible for the conversion of xanthine to uric acid (Fig 17–31).

Nitrogen Balance

A moderate daily protein intake is necessary to replace protein and amino acid losses. This requirement is not for protein itself, but for the constituent amino acids, and the need can be met by feeding pure amino acids. Loss of protein and its derivatives in the stools is normally very small. Consequently, the amount of nitrogen in the urine is a reliable indicator of the amount of irreversible protein and amino acid breakdown. When the amount of nitrogen in the urine is equal to the nitrogen content of the protein in the diet, the individual is said to be in **nitrogen balance**. If protein intake is increased in a normal individual, the extra amino acids are deaminated and urea excretion increases, maintaining nitrogen balance. However, in conditions in which secretion of the catabolic hormones of the adrenal cortex is elevated or that of insulin is decreased, and during starvation and forced immobilization, nitrogen losses exceed intake and the nitrogen balance is **negative**. During growth or recovery from severe illnesses, or following administration of anabolic steroids such as testosterone, nitrogen intake exceeds excretion and nitrogen balance is **positive**.

Essential Amino Acids

Animals fed a protein-free but otherwise adequate diet become sick and eventually die. In humans, nitrogen balance is not maintained unless 8 amino acids—phenylalanine, valine, tryptophan, threonine, lysine, leucine, isoleucine, and methionine—are added to the diet. These amino acids are called the **essential amino acids** (Table 17–6). Histidine and arginine are not essential, but are required for normal growth. All other amino acids in the body can be synthesized in vivo at rates sufficient to meet needs by amination of carbohydrate and fat residues.

When any one of the amino acids necessary for synthesis of a particular protein is unavailable, the protein is not synthesized. The other amino acids that would have gone into the protein are deaminated, like other excess amino acids, and their nitrogen is excreted as urea. This is probably why nitrogen balance becomes negative whenever a single essential amino acid is omitted from the diet (Fig 17–32).

Response to Starvation

A syndrome called **kwashiorkor** is common in the tropics among those living on a diet adequate in

calories but grossly deficient in animal protein. It is characterized by anemia, a fatty, enlarged liver, edema, and many other disturbances, and is especially severe in children.

When an individual eats a diet that is low in protein but calorically adequate, excretion of urea and inorganic and ethereal sulfates declines. Uric acid excretion falls by 50%. Creatinine excretion is not affected (Table 17–9). The creatinine and about half of the uric acid in the urine must therefore be the result of "wear and tear" processes that are unaffected by the protein intake. Total nitrogen excretion fails to fall below 3.6 g/day during protein starvation when the diet is calorically adequate because of the negative nitrogen balance produced by essential amino acid deficiencies (Fig 17–32).

On a diet that is inadequate in calories as well, urea nitrogen excretion averages about 10 g/day as proteins are catabolized for energy. Small amounts of glucose counteract this catabolism to a marked degree (**protein-sparing** effect of glucose). This protein-sparing effect is probably due for the most part to the increased insulin secretion produced by the glucose. The insulin in turn inhibits the breakdown of protein in muscle.

Most of the protein burned during total starvation comes from the liver, spleen, and muscles, and relatively little from the heart and brain. The blood glucose falls somewhat after liver glycogen is depleted, but is maintained above levels that produce hypoglycemic symptoms by gluconeogenesis. Ketosis is present (see below), and the brain utilizes ketone bodies for energy. Neutral fat is rapidly catabolized. When fat stores are used up, protein catabolism increases even further and death soon follows. In hospitalized obese patients given nothing except water and vitamins, weight loss was observed to be about 1 kg/day for the first 10 days. It then declined and stabilized at about 0.3 kg/day. Some of these patients

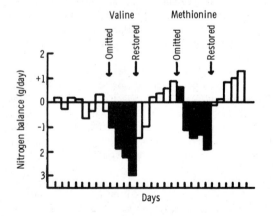

FIG 17–32. Effect on nitrogen balance of omitting single essential amino acids from the diet. (Redrawn and reproduced, with permission, from Rose & others: The amino acid requirements of man. J Biol Chem 182:541, 1950.)

TABLE 17–9. Effect of variations in protein intake on daily excretion of various protein and amino acid derivatives while consuming a calorically adequate diet.*

	Protein-Rich Diet	Protein-Poor Diet
Volume of urine (ml)	1170	385
Total nitrogen (g)	16.8	3.6
Urea nitrogen (g)	14.7	2.2
Uric acid nitrogen (g)	0.18	0.09
Ammonia nitrogen (g)	0.49	0.42
Creatinine nitrogen (g)	0.58	0.6
Inorganic SO_4 (g)	3.27	0.46
Ethereal SO_4 (g)	0.19	0.10
Neutral sulfur (g)	0.18	0.20

*Data from Folin: Laws governing the chemical composition of urine. Am J Physiol 13:66, 1905.

were starved for as long as 36 weeks. They did quite well on the whole, although postural hypotension and attacks of acute gouty arthritis were troublesome complications in some instances.

FAT METABOLISM

Lipids

The biologically important lipids are the neutral fats (triglycerides), the phospholipids and related compounds, and the sterols. The triglycerides are made up of 3 fatty acids bound to glycerol (Table 17–10). Naturally occurring fatty acids contain an even number of carbon atoms. They may be saturated (no double bonds) or unsaturated (dehydrogenated, with various numbers of double bonds). The phospholipids are constituents of cells, especially in the nervous system. The sterols include the various steroid hormones and cholesterol.

Plasma Lipids

The controversial subject of fat digestion and absorption is discussed in Chapter 25. Short-chain fatty acids liberated by hydrolysis of triglycerides in the intestine are absorbed into the portal blood. Long-chain fatty acids (more than 10 carbon atoms in length) are reesterified to form triglycerides in the intestinal mucosa. They are then complexed with lipoprotein, cholesterol ester, and phospholipid to form **chylomicrons**, which enter the lymphatic ducts. The chylomicrons are small fat globules about 1 μm in

TABLE 17–10. Lipids.

Typical fatty acids:

Palmitic acid:

$$CH_3(CH_2)_{14}-\overset{\overset{\text{O}}{\|}}{C}-OH$$

Stearic acid:

$$CH_3(CH_2)_{16}-\overset{\overset{\text{O}}{\|}}{C}-OH$$

Oleic acid:

$$CH_3(CH_2)_7CH = CH(CH_2)_7-\overset{\overset{\text{O}}{\|}}{C}-OH$$

(Unsaturated)

Triglycerides: Esters of glycerol and 3 fatty acids.

$$
\begin{array}{l}
CH_2-O-\overset{\overset{\text{O}}{\|}}{C}-R \\[4pt]
CH-O-\overset{\overset{\text{O}}{\|}}{C}-R \; + \; 3H_2O \;\rightleftharpoons\; CHOH \; + \; 3H\overset{\overset{\text{O}}{\|}}{O}-C-R \\[4pt]
CH_2-O-\overset{\overset{\text{O}}{\|}}{C}-R
\end{array}
\qquad
\begin{array}{l}
CH_2OH \\[4pt]
CHOH \\[4pt]
CH_2OH
\end{array}
$$

Triglyceride   Glycerol

R = Aliphatic chain of various lengths and degrees of saturation.

Phospholipids: Esters of glycerol, 2 fatty acids, and:
1. Phosphate = phosphatidic acid
2. Phosphate plus inositol = phosphatidyl inositol
3. Phosphate plus choline = lecithin
4. Phosphate plus ethanolamine = cephalin
5. Phosphate plus serine = phosphatidyl serine

Sphingomyelins: Esters of fatty acid, phosphate, choline, and the amino alcohol, sphingosine.

Cerebrosides: Compounds containing galactose, fatty acid, and sphingosine.

Sterols: Cholesterol and its derivatives, including steroid hormones, bile acids, and various vitamins.

TABLE 17–11. Plasma lipids and lipid-protein complexes. Of the total fatty acids, 20% are esterified to cholesterol, 50% are in phospholipids, 25% are in triglycerides, and 5% are free.

Plasma Lipid	Average Normal Value (mg/100 ml)	Proteins to Which Lipids Are Complexed	S_f Value	Density of Complexes
Triglycerides	140	β-Lipoproteins	40,000 ↑	Low
Cholesterol	200*		0	
Phospholipids	215†	α-Lipoproteins		↓
Free fatty acids	12	Albumin		High
Total lipids	570‡			

*Nonesterified cholesterol   55 mg/100 ml
†Lecithins   110 mg/100 ml
  Cephalins   80 mg/100 ml
  Sphingomyelins   25 mg/100 ml
‡Excluding fatty acids esterified to cholesterol

diameter which are visible under the microscope. After meals there are so many chylomicrons in the blood that the plasma has a milky appearance **(lipemia).** The chylomicrons are cleared from the plasma into the fat depots by the action of the enzyme **lipoprotein lipase,** which is also known as **clearing factor.** Heparin is a cofactor for this enzyme, which is believed to be located in the endothelium of the capillaries in adipose tissue and some other tissues. From the fat depots, unesterified **free fatty acids** (variously called **FFA, UFA,** or **NEFA**) are discharged into the blood stream.

In addition to triglycerides and free fatty acids, there are phospholipids and sterols in the circulation. All are bound to the albumin, α-globulin, and β-globulin fractions of the plasma proteins. The lipid-protein complexes containing the most lipid and the least protein are the least dense, and those containing the least lipid and the most protein are the most dense. On the basis of their density, the complexes are divided into **very low-density, low-density,** and **high-density lipoproteins.** In the ultracentrifuge the speed with which the various β-lipoprotein fractions rise to the top of the plasma can be measured. This speed is expressed in Svedberg units of flotation (S_f units). Triglycerides are bound to very low-density β-lipoproteins, cholesterol to low-density β-lipoproteins, phospholipids to α-lipoproteins, and free fatty acids to albumin (Table 17–11).

Cellular Lipids

The lipids in cells are of 2 main types: **structural lipids,** which are an inherent part of the membranes and other parts of cells; and **neutral fat,** stored in the adipose cells of the fat depots. A third special type of

Fatty acid   "Active" fatty acid

R = Rest of fatty acid chain.

FIG 17–33. Fatty acid oxidation. This process, splitting off 2 carbon fragments at a time, is repeated to the end of the chain.

fat is **brown fat,** which is found in infants but not in adult humans. It has a high metabolic rate and produces heat that aids in thermoregulation (see Chapter 14). Depot fat is mobilized during starvation, but structural lipid is preserved. The size of the fat depots obviously varies, but in nonobese individuals they make up about 10% of the body weight. They are not the inert lumps they were once thought to be but active, dynamic tissues undergoing continuous breakdown and resynthesis. In the depots, glucose is metabolized to fatty acids and neutral fats are synthesized. Neutral fat is also broken down, and free fatty acids are liberated into the circulation.

Fat Oxidation

The glycerol liberated when triglycerides are hydrolyzed can be converted to phosphoglyceraldehyde and thence to glucose or to CO_2 and H_2O. The fatty acids are broken down to acetyl-Co A, which enters the citric acid cycle. Fatty acid oxidation apparently occurs only in the mitochondria. The steps involved are shown in Fig 17–33. The energy yield of this process is large. For example, catabolism of 1 mol of a 6-carbon fatty acid through the citric acid cycle to CO_2 and H_2O generates 44 mols of ATP, compared to the 38 mols generated by catabolism of 1 mol of the 6-carbon carbohydrate, glucose.

Fat Synthesis

Many tissues can synthesize fatty acids from acetyl-Co A. Some synthesis of long-chain fatty acids

from short-chain fatty acids occurs in the mitochondria by simple reversal of the reactions shown in Fig 17–33. However, most of the synthesis of fatty acids occurs via a different pathway located principally outside the mitochondria, in the microsomes. The steps in this pathway are summarized in Fig 17–34.

For unknown reasons, fatty acid synthesis stops in practically all cells when the chain is 16 carbon atoms long. Only small amounts of 12- and 14-carbon fatty acids are formed, and none with more than 16 carbons. Particularly in fat depots, the fatty acids are combined with glycerol to form neutral fats. This combination takes place in the mitochondria.

Ketone Bodies

In many tissues, acetyl-Co A units condense to form acetoacetyl-Co A (Fig 17–35). In the liver, which (unlike other tissues) contains a deacylase, free acetoacetic acid is liberated. This β-keto acid is converted to β-hydroxybutyric acid and acetone, and because these compounds are metabolized with difficulty in the liver they diffuse into the circulation. Acetoacetic acid, β-hydroxybutyric acid, and acetone are called **ketone bodies.** Tissues other than liver transfer Co A from succinyl-Co A to acetoacetic acid, and metabolize the "active" acetoacetic acid to CO_2 and H_2O via the citric acid cycle. There are also other pathways via which ketone bodies are metabolized. The ketones are an important source of energy in some conditions. Acetone is discharged in the urine and expired air.

The normal blood ketone level in man is low

FIG 17–34. Fatty acid synthesis via pathway found in microsomes. ACP = acyl carrier protein, a protein to which the acyl residues are attached as fatty acid synthesis proceeds. The process shown here repeats itself, adding 1 acetyl-ACP unit to the butyryl-ACP to form a 6-carbon fatty acid-ACP derivative, then another acetyl-ACP to form an 8-carbon unit, etc.

$$CH_3-\overset{\overset{O}{\|}}{C}-S-Co\,A \;+\; CH_3-\overset{\overset{O}{\|}}{C}-S-Co\,A \;\underset{}{\overset{\beta\text{-Ketothiolase}}{\rightleftharpoons}}\; CH_3-\overset{\overset{O}{\|}}{C}-CH_2-\overset{\overset{O}{\|}}{C}-S-Co\,A \;+\; HS\text{-}Co\,A$$

2 Acetyl-Co A   Acetoacetyl-Co A + Reduced Co A

$$CH_3-\overset{\overset{O}{\|}}{C}-CH_2-\overset{\overset{O}{\|}}{C}-S-Co\,A \;\underset{\text{(liver only)}}{\overset{\text{Deacylase}}{\longrightarrow}}\; CH_3-\overset{\overset{O}{\|}}{C}-CH_2-\overset{\overset{O}{\|}}{C}-OH \;+\; HS\text{-}Co\,A$$

Acetoacetyl-Co A   Acetoacetic acid   Reduced Co A

Acetoacetic acid

$$CH_3-\overset{\overset{O}{\|}}{C}-CH_2-\overset{\overset{O}{\|}}{C}-OH \;\xrightarrow{\text{Tissues except liver}}\; CO_2 \;+\; ATP$$

$+2H \;\big\updownarrow\; -2H$ $-CO_2$

$$CH_3-CHOH-CH_2-\overset{\overset{O}{\|}}{C}-OH \qquad\qquad CH_3-\overset{\overset{O}{\|}}{C}-CH_3$$

β-Hydroxybutyric acid   Acetone

FIG 17–35. Formation and metabolism of ketone bodies.

(about 1 mg/100 ml), and less than 1 mg is excreted per 24 hours because the ketones are normally metabolized as rapidly as they are formed. However, if the entry of acetyl-Co A into the citric acid cycle is depressed, or if the entry does not increase when the supply of acetyl-Co A increases, acetyl-Co A accumulates, the rate of condensation to acetoacetyl-Co A increases, and more acetoacetic acid is formed in the liver. The ability of the tissues to oxidize the ketones is soon exceeded, and they accumulate in the blood stream **(ketosis)**. Buffering greatly reduces the decline in pH which would otherwise occur due to the increased amounts of acetoacetic acid and β-hydroxybutyric acid in the body fluids. However, the metabolic acidosis that develops in conditions such as diabetic ketosis can be severe and even fatal.

The main cause of relative or absolute impairment of the entrance of acetyl-Co A into the citric acid cycle is "intracellular carbohydrate starvation." When insufficient glucose is metabolized to pyruvic acid, the supply of oxaloacetic acid to condense with acetyl-Co A is inadequate relative to the supply of acetyl-Co A and the citric acid cycle cannot metabolize all of it. Furthermore, when glucose catabolism is deficient, less fat is synthesized from acetyl-Co A, adding to the accumulation of acetyl-Co A. In addition, the rate of fat oxidation is increased. Consequently, more acetoacetyl-Co A and more ketone bodies are formed.

There are 3 conditions which lead to deficient intracellular glucose supplies: starvation, diabetes mellitus, and a high-fat, low-carbohydrate diet. In diabetes, glucose entry into cells is impaired. When most of the caloric intake is supplied by fat, carbohydrate deficiency develops because there is no major pathway for converting fat to carbohydrate. The liver cells also become filled with fat, which damages them and displaces any glycogen that is formed. In all of these conditions ketosis develops primarily because the supply of ketones is overabundant.

The acetone odor on the breath of children who have been vomiting is due to the ketosis of starvation. Parenteral administration of relatively small amounts of glucose abolishes the ketosis, and it is for this reason that carbohydrate is said to be **antiketogenic**.

Conversion of Glucose to Fat

It used to be thought that fatty acids were synthesized from glucose in the liver, stored in fat depots, and returned to the liver where they were metabolized to ketone bodies for utilization by the tissues. It is now clear that glucose is also converted to fat by adipose tissue, that circulating free fatty acids are metabolized by many organs, and that fat formation is quantitatively a major pathway for carbohydrate utilization.

Free Fatty Acid Metabolism

The free fatty acids are an extremely labile circulating fat component, with a half-life of only a few minutes. They are a major source of energy for many organs, particularly the heart. Probably all tissues, including the brain, can oxidize free fatty acids to CO_2 and H_2O. The triglycerides stored in the fat droplet of fat cells are hydrolyzed and the free fatty acids liberated into the circulation. In the blood stream, they circulate bound to albumin. Norepinephrine and epinephrine promote the hydrolysis of triglycerides in adipose tissue, with a resultant increase in circulating free fatty acid levels. They exert this action by stimulating adenyl cyclase, which in turn stimulates the activity of the intracellular lipase in adipose tissue (Fig 17–36). This lipase is also called the hormone-sensitive lipase, and is different from lipoprotein lipase, which is apparently localized in the endothelium of the capillaries.

Catecholamines reach adipose tissue in the blood stream, but norepinephrine liberated at the endings of the postganglionic sympathetic nerves supplying the

FIG 17–36. Effect of various hormones on the lipase in adipose tissue. $\oplus$, stimulation; $\ominus$, inhibition; FFA, free fatty acids. (Courtesy of J Kane.)

FIG 17–37. The prostaglandin found in highest concentration (25 µg/ml) in human semen. This is 11a,15-dihydroxy-9-keto-prost-13-enoic acid, known as PGE$_1$. Other prostaglandins have very similar structures.

fat depots can also cause increased triglyceride hydrolysis. Thus there is a direct neural control of fat metabolism via the autonomic nervous system. The hydrolysis-promoting action of the norepinephrine and epinephrine is facilitated by ACTH, prolactin, growth hormone, adrenal glucocorticoids, and thyroid hormones. However, the physiologic significance of the FFA-mobilizing action of ACTH and prolactin is unsettled. Growth hormone and glucocorticoids apparently act by stimulating the synthesis of more lipase (Fig 17–36). The activity of the hormone-sensitive lipase is increased by fasting and stress and decreased by feeding and insulin. Conversely, feeding increases and fasting and stress decrease the activity of lipoprotein lipase. Glucagon initially increases circulating free fatty acid levels, but this is followed by a decline, presumably as a result of the increase in insulin secretion provoked by the hyperglycemia (Chapter 19). It has been claimed that another hormone which mobilizes triglycerides and free fatty acids is secreted by the pituitary, but the data supporting this claim are controversial.

There are 3 tissues that can liberate fats into the circulation: adipose tissue, the intestinal mucosa, and the liver. The function of the intestinal mucosa in fat absorption is discussed in Chapter 26. The liver takes up free fatty acids and forms triglycerides or ketone bodies. Normally, the triglycerides leave the liver and circulate bound to lipoproteins in the low-density lipoprotein fraction. Lipoprotein lipase in fat cells and other tissues breaks down these triglycerides to glycerol and fatty acids and the fatty acids are catabolized or used in the synthesis of new triglycerides.

Prostaglandins

A series of closely related fatty acids (Fig 17–37) are found in high concentration in semen. These **prostaglandins** are also found in the lungs, the brain, and a variety of other tissues. Fourteen naturally

occurring prostaglandins have been isolated, 8 of which are metabolites of the remaining 6. Thirteen of the 14 are found in man. They are divided into 3 main groups—PGA, PGE, and PGF—on the basis of the configuration of the ring. The number of double bonds in the side chains is indicated by a subscript number. For example, the prostaglandin illustrated in Fig 17–37 is PGE$_1$. Circulating prostaglandins are rapidly metabolized in the liver, lungs, and kidneys.

The prostaglandins have a bewildering array of actions. In general, members of the A and E groups lower blood pressure, whereas members of the F group raise it. They also inhibit gastric secretion, dilate bronchi, inhibit lipolysis, antagonize vasopressin-induced antidiuresis, constrict the pupil, increase intraocular pressure, and produce contraction of the uterus. Their use as abortifacients and agents to initiate labor is being explored. In the CNS, they may modify responses to synaptic transmitters. They mimic the actions of certain hormones and inhibit the actions of others, probably by an inhibitory effect on the cyclic AMP-generating mechanism. However, their exact physiologic role is uncertain.

Cholesterol Metabolism

Cholesterol is the precursor of the steroid hormones and bile acids. It is found only in animals. Related sterols occur in plants, but plant sterols are not absorbed from the gastrointestinal tract. Most of the dietary cholesterol is contained in egg yolks and animal fat.

Ingested cholesterol is rapidly absorbed. Most of it is esterified in the intestine, principally with fatty acids, and absorbed in this form into the lymph (see Chapter 25). Cholesterol is also synthesized in the liver from acetate in most animal species, including man. Most other tissues, except the adult brain, can also synthesize cholesterol, but the main site is the liver. There is an inverse relationship between the rate of synthesis and the dietary intake, presumably because a high circulating cholesterol level feeds back to inhibit cholesterol synthesis.

Cholesterol biosynthesis is outlined in Fig 17–38. Acetate is converted to mevalonic acid, and it is this reaction that is said to be inhibited by a high circulating cholesterol level. Isoprenoid units derived from

Acetyl-Co A + Acetoacetyl-Co A $\rightleftharpoons$ β-Hydroxy-β-methylglutaryl-Co A $\longrightarrow$ Mevalonic acid

Lanosterol $(C_{30}H_{50}O)$

Squalene $(C_{30}H_{50}O)$

14-Desmethyl lanosterol

Zymosterol

Δ-7,24-Cholestadienol

Desmosterol
(24-dehydrocholesterol)

Cholesterol $(C_{27}H_{46}O)$

FIG 17–38. Biosynthesis of cholesterol. The positions in the squalene molecule are numbered according to the conventional numbering of the steroid nucleus (see Chapter 20). The solid and open dots identify the various carbon atoms of the original isoprenoid units. (Slightly modified from Harper: *Review of Physiological Chemistry*, 14th ed. Lange, 1973.)

mevalonic acid combine to form 2 farnesyl pyrophosphate units of equal size, and these condense "tail to tail" (one end of one to the corresponding end of the other) to form squalene. Ring closure then produces the characteristic 4-membered steroid ring, and further alterations convert it to cholesterol.

Cholesterol is removed from the body by conversion to cholic acid in the liver. The cholic acid is combined with taurine or glycine and excreted in the bile (see Chapter 25).

Factors Influencing Plasma Cholesterol Levels

The plasma cholesterol level is decreased by thyroid hormones and estrogens. It is elevated when biliary flow is obstructed, and also in hereditary hypercholesterolemia and untreated diabetes mellitus. The elevation in diabetes occurs in spite of a decrease in cholesterol synthesis, apparently because hepatic destruction of cholesterol is depressed to a greater extent.

Restricting cholesterol in the diet has little effect on the plasma cholesterol in man because there is a compensating increase in cholesterol synthesis. However, a high neutral fat diet elevates plasma cholesterol levels and also reduces clotting time and fibrinolytic activity. If the saturated fats in the diet are replaced with polyunsaturated fats, the plasma cholesterol level falls and the effects on the clotting mechanism are reversed.

A subject of great current interest is the role of cholesterol in the etiology and course of **arteriosclerosis**. This extremely widespread disease of aging, which predisposes to myocardial infarction, cerebral thrombosis, and other serious illnesses, is characterized by infiltration of cholesterol into certain lesions of the arterial walls, distorting the vessels and making them rigid. There is considerable epidemiologic and clinical evidence suggesting that a low plasma cholesterol level slows down or prevents arteriosclerotic changes. On this basis, chronic administration of thyroxine or some of its less calorigenic derivatives (see Chapter 18) and replacement of saturated fats in the diet with polyunsaturated compounds have been recommended for the prevention of arteriosclerosis. Abnormalities of the plasma lipoproteins are associated with elevated plasma cholesterol and triglyceride levels, and 5 different, distinct abnormalities, 3 associated with a high incidence of coronary heart disease, have been described. The treatment that is most effective in lowering lipids varies with the abnormality. It is not yet proved that lowering blood lipid levels slows the progress of arteriosclerosis, but long-term studies designed for the purpose of determining whether this is so are under way.

Essential Fatty Acids

Animals fed a fat-free diet fail to grow, develop skin and kidney lesions, and become infertile. Adding linolenic acid to the diet restores growth to normal, and linoleic and arachidonic acids cure all the deficiency symptoms. These 3 acids are polyunsaturated fatty acids, and because of their action are called **essential fatty acids**. Similar deficiency symptoms have not been unequivocally demonstrated in man, but there is reason to believe that some unsaturated fats are essential dietary constituents, especially in children. Dehydrogenation of fats is known to occur in the body, but it is apparently impossible to synthesize carbon chains with the arrangement of double bonds found in the essential fatty acids.

NUTRITION

The aim of the science of nutrition is the determination of the kinds and amounts of foods that promote health and well-being. This includes not only the problems of undernutrition but those of overnutrition, taste, and availability. However, certain substances are essential constituents of any human diet. Many of these compounds have been mentioned in previous sections of this chapter, and a brief summary of the essential and desirable dietary components is presented below.

ESSENTIAL DIETARY COMPONENTS

An optimal diet includes, in addition to sufficient water (see Chapter 38), adequate calories, protein, fat, minerals, and vitamins.

Caloric Intake & Distribution

As noted above, the caloric value of the dietary intake must equal the energy expended as heat and work if body weight is to be maintained. When the caloric intake is insufficient, body stores of protein and fat are catabolized, and when the intake is excessive, obesity results. In addition to the 2000 kcal/day necessary to meet basal needs, 500–2500 or more kcal/day are required to meet the energy demands of daily activities.

The distribution of the calories among carbohydrate, protein, and fat foodstuffs is determined partly by physiologic factors and partly by taste and economic considerations. A daily protein intake of at least 1 g/kg body weight to supply the 8 essential amino acids and other amino acids is now regarded as desirable. The source of the protein is also important. **Grade I proteins**, the animal proteins of meat, fish, and eggs, are those which contain amino acids in approximately the proportions required for protein synthesis and other uses in the body. Some of the plant proteins are also grade I, but most are **grade II** because they supply different proportions of amino acids, and some lack one or more of the essential amino acids. Protein

TABLE 17–12. Recommended daily dietary allowances, revised 1968.*[1]

	Age[2] Years	Weight (kg)	(lb)	Height (cm)	(in)	Kcal	Protein (g)	Fat-Soluble Vitamins			Water-Soluble Vitamins								Minerals				
								Vitamin A Activity (IU)	Vitamin D Activity (IU)	Vitamin E Activity (IU)	Ascorbic Acid (mg)	Folates[3] (mg)	Niacin (mg eq[4])	Riboflavin (mg)	Thiamine (mg)	Vitamin B$_6$ (mg)	Vitamin B$_{12}$ (µg)	Calcium (g)	Phosphorus (g)	Iodine (µg)	Iron (mg)	Magnesium (mg)
Infants	0–1/6	4	9	55	22	kg × 120	kg × 2.2[5]	1500	400	5	35	0.05	5	0.4	0.2	0.2	1.0	0.4	0.2	25	6	40
	1/6–1/2	7	15	63	25	kg × 110	kg × 2.0[5]	1500	400	5	35	0.05	7	0.5	0.4	0.3	1.5	0.5	0.4	40	10	60
	1/2–1	9	20	72	28	kg × 100	kg × 1.8[5]	1500	400	5	35	0.1	8	0.6	0.5	0.4	2.0	0.6	0.5	45	15	70
Children	1–2	12	26	81	32	1100	25	2000	400	10	40	0.1	8	0.6	0.6	0.5	2.0	0.7	0.7	55	15	100
	2–3	14	31	91	36	1250	25	2000	400	10	40	0.2	8	0.7	0.6	0.6	2.5	0.8	0.8	60	15	150
	3–4	16	35	100	39	1400	30	2500	400	10	40	0.2	9	0.8	0.7	0.7	3	0.8	0.8	70	10	200
	4–6	19	42	110	43	1600	30	2500	400	10	40	0.2	11	0.9	0.8	0.9	4	0.8	0.8	80	10	200
	6–8	23	51	121	48	2000	35	3500	400	15	40	0.2	13	1.1	1.0	1.0	4	0.9	0.9	100	10	250
	8–10	28	62	131	52	2200	40	3500	400	15	40	0.3	15	1.2	1.1	1.2	5	1.0	1.0	110	10	250
Males	10–12	35	77	140	55	2500	45	4500	400	20	40	0.4	17	1.3	1.3	1.4	5	1.2	1.2	125	10	300
	12–14	43	95	151	59	2700	50	5000	400	20	45	0.4	18	1.4	1.4	1.6	5	1.4	1.4	135	18	350
	14–18	59	130	170	67	3000	60	5000	400	25	55	0.4	20	1.5	1.5	1.8	5	1.4	1.4	150	18	400
	18–22	67	147	175	69	2800	60	5000	400	30	60	0.4	18	1.6	1.4	2.0	5	0.8	0.8	140	10	400
	22–35	70	154	175	69	2800	65	5000	…	30	60	0.4	18	1.7	1.4	2.0	5	0.8	0.8	140	10	350
	35–55	70	154	173	68	2600	65	5000	…	30	60	0.4	17	1.7	1.3	2.0	5	0.8	0.8	125	10	350
	55–75+	70	154	171	67	2400	65	5000	…	30	60	0.4	14	1.7	1.2	2.0	6	0.8	0.8	110	10	350
Females	10–12	35	77	142	56	2250	50	4500	400	20	40	0.4	15	1.3	1.1	1.4	5	1.2	1.2	110	18	300
	12–14	44	97	154	61	2300	50	5000	400	20	45	0.4	15	1.4	1.2	1.6	5	1.3	1.3	115	18	350
	14–16	52	114	157	62	2400	55	5000	400	25	50	0.4	16	1.4	1.2	1.8	5	1.3	1.3	120	18	350
	16–18	54	119	160	63	2300	55	5000	400	25	50	0.4	15	1.5	1.2	2.0	5	1.3	1.3	115	18	350
	18–22	58	128	163	64	2000	55	5000	400	25	55	0.4	13	1.5	1.0	2.0	5	0.8	0.8	100	18	350
	22–35	58	128	163	64	2000	55	5000	…	25	55	0.4	13	1.5	1.0	2.0	5	0.8	0.8	100	18	300
	35–55	58	128	160	63	1850	55	5000	…	25	55	0.4	13	1.5	1.0	2.0	5	0.8	0.8	90	18	300
	55–75+	58	128	157	62	1700	55	5000	…	25	55	0.4	13	1.5	1.0	2.0	6	0.8	0.8	80	10	300
Pregnancy						+200	65	6000	400	30	60	0.8	15	1.8	+0.1	2.5	8	+0.4	+0.4	125	18	450
Lactation						+1000	75	8000	400	30	60	0.5	20	2.0	+0.5	2.5	6	+0.5	+0.5	150	18	450

*Reproduced from Publication 1694, Food and Nutrition Board, National Academy of Sciences, National Research Council, 1968.

[1]The allowance levels are intended to cover individual variations among most normal persons as they live in the USA under usual environmental stresses. The recommended allowances can be attained with a variety of common foods, providing other nutrients for which human requirements have been less well defined.

[2]Entries on lines for age range 22–35 years represent the reference man and woman at age 22. All other entries represent allowances for the midpoint of the specified age range.

[3]The folate allowances refer to dietary sources as determined by Lactobacillus casei assay. Pure forms of folic acid may be effective in doses less than ¼ of the recommended daily allowance.

[4]Niacin equivalents include dietary sources of the vitamin itself plus 1 mg equivalent for each 60 mg of dietary tryptophan.

[5]Assumes protein equivalent to human milk. For proteins not 100% utilized, factors should be increased proportionately.

needs can be met with a mixture of grade II proteins, but the intake must be large because of the amino acid wastage.

Fat is the most compact form of food since it supplies 9.3 kcal/g. However, it is also the most expensive. Indeed, there is a reasonably good positive correlation between fat intake and standard of living, and in the past western diets have contained moderately large amounts (100 g/day or more). The evidence suggesting that a high unsaturated/saturated fat ratio in the diet is of value in the prevention of arteriosclerosis and the current interest in preventing obesity may change this. In Central and South American Indian communities where corn (carbohydrate) is the dietary staple, adults live without ill effects for years on a very small fat intake. Therefore, provided the needs for essential fatty acids are met, a low fat intake does not seem to be harmful and a diet low in saturated fats may be desirable.

Carbohydrate is the cheapest source of calories, and makes up 50% or more of most diets. In practice, when calculating dietary needs, it is usual to meet the protein requirement first and then split the remaining calories between fat and carbohydrate depending upon taste, income, and other factors. For example, a 70 kg man who is moderately active needs about 2800 kcal/day. He should eat 70 g of protein/day, supplying 287 (70 × 4.1) kcal. Some of this should be grade I protein. Fat intake depends upon taste, but a reasonable figure is 60 g, supplying the essential fatty acids and 558 (60 × 9.3) kcal. The rest of the caloric requirement, 2800 − (287 + 558), or 1955 kcal, can be met by supplying 477 g (1955/4.1 kcal/g) of carbohydrate.

Mineral Requirements

A number of minerals must be ingested daily for the maintenance of health (Table 17−12). Copper deficiency causes neutropenia; iron deficiency causes anemia; iodine deficiency causes goiter (see Chapter 18); and calcium deficiency causes bone abnormalities (see Chapter 21). A variety of other minerals, including magnesium, manganese, cobalt, bromine, and zinc, are required in trace amounts; but any diet that is adequate in other respects easily supplies these traces. Sodium and potassium are also essential minerals, but listing them is academic because it is very difficult to prepare a sodium-free or a potassium-free diet. A low-salt diet is well tolerated for prolonged periods because of the compensatory mechanisms which conserve sodium, and salt depletion is a problem only when sodium is lost in excessive amounts in the stools, sweat, or urine.

Vitamins

Vitamins were discovered when it was observed that diets adequate in calories, essential amino acids, fats, and minerals failed to maintain health. The term **vitamin** has now come to refer to any organic dietary constituent necessary for life, health, and growth, which does not function by supplying energy.

Because there are minor differences in metabolism between mammalian species, some substances are vitamins in one species and not in another. The sources and functions of the major vitamins in man are listed in Table 17−13. Most of them have important functions in intermediary metabolism or the special metabolism of the various organ systems. Those that are water-soluble (vitamin B complex, vitamin C) are easily absorbed, but the fat-soluble vitamins (vitamins A, D, E, and K) are poorly absorbed in the absence of bile or pancreatic lipase. Some dietary fat intake is necessary for their absorption, and, in obstructive jaundice or in pancreatic disease, deficiencies of the fat-soluble vitamins can develop even if their intake is adequate (see Chapter 26).

The minimum daily requirements listed in Table 17−13 are for normal, healthy adults. In children, in pregnant and lactating women, and in various illnesses, the needs for vitamins and other dietary components are greater, and intake must be adjusted accordingly (Table 17−12).

The diseases caused by deficiency of each of these vitamins are listed in Table 17−13. It is worth remembering, however, particularly now that the well-advertised bottle of vitamin pills is frequently a fixture on the dinner table in the United States, that very large doses of vitamins A, D, and K are definitely toxic. **Hypervitaminosis A** is characterized by gastrointestinal disturbances, scaly dermatitis, patchy loss of hair, and bone pain. Acute vitamin A intoxication was first described by Arctic explorers, who found that men developed headache, diarrhea, and dizziness after eating polar bear liver. The liver of this animal is particularly rich in vitamin A. **Hypervitaminosis D** is associated with weight loss and calcification of many soft tissues, and excessive vitamin D intake eventually causes renal failure. **Hypervitaminosis K** is characterized by gastrointestinal disturbances and anemia.

TABLE 17–13. Vitamins essential or probably essential to human nutrition. Choline is not listed because it is synthesized in the body in adequate amounts except in special circumstances. MDR: minimum daily requirements, where such have been established.

Vitamin	Action	Deficiency Symptoms	Sources	MDR	Chemistry
A (A_1, A_2)	Constituents of visual pigments (Chapter 8); maintain epithelia.	Night blindness, dry skin	Yellow vegetables and fruit	5000 IU	Vitamin A_1 (alcohol)
B complex Thiamine (vitamin B_1)	Cofactor in pyruvic acid and α-ketoglutaric acid decarboxylation.	Beriberi, neuritis	Liver, unrefined cereal grains	0.5 mg/ 1000 kcal	
Riboflavin (vitamin B_2)	Constituent of flavoproteins.	Glossitis, cheilosis	Liver, milk	1.8 mg	
Niacin	Constituent of NAD^+, $NADP^+$.	Pellagra	Yeast, lean meat, liver	20 mg (or 1200 mg tryptophan)	Can be synthesized in body from tryptophan.
Pyridoxine (vitamin B_6)	Forms prosthetic group of certain decarboxylases and transaminases. Converted in body into pyridoxal phosphate and pyridoxamine phosphate.	Convulsions, hyperirritability	Yeast, wheat, corn, liver	2 mg	
Pantothenic acid	Constituent of Co A.	Dermatitis, enteritis, alopecia, adrenal insufficiency	Eggs, liver, yeast		
Biotin	Catalyzes CO_2 "fixation" (in fatty acid synthesis, etc).	Dermatitis, enteritis	Egg yolk, liver, tomatoes		
Folates (folic acid) and related compounds	Coenzymes for "one-carbon" transfer.	Sprue, anemia	Leafy green vegetables	500 μg	Folic acid

TABLE 17–13 (cont'd). Vitamins essential or probably essential to human nutrition.

Vitamin	Action	Deficiency Symptoms	Sources	MDR	Chemistry
Cyanoco-balamin (vitamin B_{12})	Coenzyme in amino acid metabolism? Stimulates erythropoiesis.	Pernicious anemia (Chapter 26)	Liver, meat, eggs, milk	2.8 μg	Complex of 4 substituted pyrrole rings around a cobalt atom (Chapter 26).
C	Necessary for hydroxylation of lysine in collagen synthesis.	Scurvy	Citrus fruits, leafy green vegetables	75 mg	Ascorbic acid (synthesized in all mammals except guinea pig and man).
D group	Increase intestinal absorption of calcium and phosphate (Chapter 21).	Rickets	Fish liver	400 IU	Family of sterols (see Chapter 21).
E group	? Cofactors in electron transport in cytochrome chain.	Muscular dystrophy and fetal death in animals; ? in man	Milk, eggs, meat, leafy vegetables		α-Tocopherol; β- and γ-tocopherol also active.
K group	Catalyze synthesis of prothrombin and several other clotting factors in the liver.	Hemorrhagic phenomena	Leafy green vegetables		Vitamin K_3; a large number of similar compounds have biologic activity.

18...

The Thyroid Gland

The thyroid gland maintains the level of metabolism in the tissues that is optimal for their normal function. Thyroid hormone stimulates the O_2 consumption of most of the cells in the body, helps regulate lipid and carbohydrate metabolism, and is necessary for normal growth and maturation. The thyroid gland is not essential for life, but in its absence there is poor resistance to cold, mental and physical slowing, and, in children, mental retardation and dwarfism. Conversely, excess thyroid secretion leads to body wasting, nervousness, tachycardia, tremor, and excess heat production. Thyroid function is controlled by the thyroid-stimulating hormone (TSH) of the anterior pituitary, and the secretion of this tropic hormone is in turn regulated in part by a direct inhibitory feedback of high circulating thyroid hormone levels on the pituitary and in part via neural mechanisms operating through the hypothalamus. In this way, changes in the internal and external environment bring about appropriate adjustments in the rate of thyroid secretion.

The thyroid gland also secretes calcitonin, a calcium-lowering hormone. This hormone is discussed in Chapter 21.

ANATOMIC CONSIDERATIONS

Thyroid tissue is present in all vertebrates. In mammals the thyroid originates from an evagination of the floor of the pharynx, and a **thyroglossal duct** marking the path of the thyroid from the tongue to the neck sometimes persists in the adult. The 2 lobes of the thyroid are connected in man by a bridge of tissue, the **thyroid isthmus,** and there is sometimes a **pyramidal lobe** arising from the isthmus in front of the larynx (Fig 18–1). The gland is well vascularized, and the thyroid has one of the highest rates of blood flow per gram of tissue of any organ in the body.

The thyroid is made up of multiple **acini,** or **follicles.** Each spherical follicle is surrounded by a single layer of cells and filled with pink-staining proteinaceous material called **colloid.** When the gland is inactive, the colloid is abundant, the follicles are large, and the cells lining them are flat. When the gland is active, the follicles are small, the cells are cuboidal or columnar, and the edge of the colloid is scalloped, forming many small "reabsorption lacunae" (Fig 18–2).

FIG 18–1. The human thyroid.

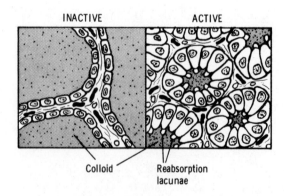

FIG 18–2. **Thyroid histology.** Notice the small, punched-out "reabsorption lacunae" in the colloid next to the cells in the active gland.

Microvilli project into the colloid from the apices of the thyroid cells, and canaliculi extend into them. There is a prominent endoplasmic reticulum, a feature common to most glandular cells, and secretory droplets of thyroglobulin are seen (Fig 18–3). The individual thyroid cells rest on a basement membrane which separates them from the adjacent capillaries. The endothelial cells are attenuated at places, forming gaps or fenestrations in the walls of the capillaries (Fig 18–3). This fenestration of the capillary walls also occurs in most other endocrine organs.

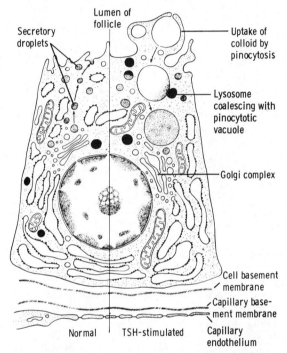

FIG 18–3. Thyroid cell. *Left:* Normal pattern. *Right:* After marked TSH stimulation. The arrows on the left show the secretion of thyroglobulin into colloid. On the right, pinocytosis of the colloid and merging of a pinocytotic vacuole with a lysosome are shown. The cell rests on a capillary with gaps (fenestrations) in the endothelial wall. (Modified and reproduced, with permission, from Fawcett, Long, & Jones: The ultrastructure of endocrine glands. Recent Progr Hormone Res 25:315, 1969.)

FORMATION & SECRETION OF THYROID HORMONES

Chemistry

The principal hormones secreted by the thyroid are **thyroxine** and **triiodothyronine**. Both are iodine-containing amino acids (Fig 18–4). Trace amounts of reverse triiodothyronine, monoiodotyrosine, and other compounds are also found in thyroid venous blood.

3,5,3',5'-Tetraiodothyronine (thyroxine, T_4)

3,5,3'-Triiodothyronine (T_3)

FIG 18–4. **Thyroid hormones.** The numbers in the rings in the thyroxine formula indicate the numbering of positions in the molecule.

The naturally occurring forms of thyroxine and its congeners with an asymmetric carbon atom are the L-isomers. D-Thyroxine has only a fraction of the activity of the L-form (see below).

Thyroglobulin

Current evidence indicates that thyroxine and triiodothyronine are synthesized in the colloid by iodination and condensation of tyrosine molecules that are bound in peptide linkage to **thyroglobulin**. This glycoprotein has 4 peptide chains and a molecular weight of approximately 650,000. The hormones remain in this bound form until secreted. When they are secreted, the peptide bonds are hydrolyzed and free thyroxine and triiodothyronine enter the thyroid cells, cross them, and are discharged into the capillaries. The thyroid cells thus have a dual function. They collect and transport the iodine and synthesize the thyroglobulin, then secrete it into the colloid; and they remove the thyroid hormones from thyroglobulin and secrete them into the circulation. Other iodinated proteins of uncertain function are also found in the thyroid.

Iodine Metabolism

Iodine is a raw material essential for thyroid hormone synthesis. Ingested iodine is converted to iodide and absorbed. Small amounts of iodide are excreted in the bile and appear in the feces, but 98% of the absorbed iodide is taken up by the thyroid or excreted in the urine. The thyroid iodide uptake is about 75 μg/day at normal rates of hormone synthesis and secretion in man. The normal plasma iodide level is about 0.3 μg/100 ml, and iodide is distributed in a "space" of approximately 25 liters (35% of body weight). Part of the circulating pool is iodide liberated from thyroid hormone broken down in the tissues and, to a minor extent, in the thyroid itself. In the kidneys, approximately 70% of the filtered iodide is reabsorbed, so that the loss from the body by this route at normal plasma iodide levels is small. To replace this and the other small losses from the body, a minimum daily intake of approximately 100–150 μg is required (Table 17–12).

Iodide Trapping

The thyroid concentrates iodide by actively transporting it from the circulation to the colloid. The transport mechanism is frequently called the "iodide trapping mechanism" or "iodide pump." The thyroid cell is about 50 mv negative to the interstitial area and the colloid; it has a resting membrane potential of −50 mv. Iodide is presumably pumped into the cell at its base against this electrical gradient, then diffuses down the electrical gradient into the colloid. Iodine uptake can be studied by administering radioactive iodine in **tracer doses,** amounts that are so small they do not significantly increase the amount of iodide in the body. The iodine isotope usually used is ^{131}I, which has a half-life of 8 days, although ^{132}I and ^{125}I are also available. The ratio of thyroid to plasma or serum free iodide (**T/S ratio**) ranges from 10 to over 100. In the gland, iodide is rapidly oxidized and bound to tyrosine. If binding is blocked by antithyroid drugs such as thiouracil (see below), the T/S ratio may rise to 250. Perchlorate and a number of other anions decrease iodide transport by competitive inhibition. The active transport mechanism is stimulated by TSH and inhibited by ouabain.

The salivary glands, the gastric mucosa, the placenta, the ciliary body of the eye, the choroid plexus, and the mammary glands also transport iodide against a concentration gradient, but their uptake is not affected by TSH. In addition, the mammary gland is the only one of these tissues which binds the iodine; diiodotyrosine is formed in the mammary gland, but thyroxine and triiodothyronine are not. There is a minor uptake of iodide by the posterior pituitary and adrenal cortex. The physiologic significance of all these extrathyroidal iodide-concentrating mechanisms is obscure. It has been claimed that traces of thyroxine may be formed by nonthyroidal tissues, but if such formation does occur the amount is insufficient to prevent the development of the full picture of hypothyroidism after surgical thyroidectomy.

Thyroid Hormone Synthesis

In the thyroid gland, iodide is oxidized to iodine and bound in a matter of seconds to the 3- position of tyrosine molecules attached to thyroglobulin (Fig 18–5). The enzyme responsible for the oxidation of iodide is a peroxidase, with hydrogen peroxide accepting the electrons. Monoiodotyrosine is next iodinated in the 5- position to form diiodotyrosine. Two diiodotyrosine molecules then undergo an oxidative condensation, with the liberation of an alanine residue and the formation of thyroxine, still in peptide linkage to thyroglobulin. Proof that the reactions occur in this sequence is the demonstration that injected radioactive iodine first appears in monoiodotyrosine, then in diiodotyrosine, and lastly in thyroxine. Triiodothyronine is probably formed by condensation of

monoiodotyrosine with diiodotyrosine. Some "reverse triiodothyronine" (3,3',5'-triiodothyronine) is formed, probably by condensation of diiodotyrosine and monoiodotyrosine. The condensation reaction is an aerobic, energy-requiring reaction. In the normal human thyroid, the average distribution of iodinated compounds is 23% monoiodotyrosine, 33% diiodotyrosine, 35% thyroxine, and 7% triiodothyronine. Only traces of reverse triiodothyronine and other components are present.

Secretion

About 80 μg/day of free thyroxine and up to 50 μg/day of triiodothyronine are secreted into the capillaries by the thyroid cells in man. The thyroid cells ingest colloid by pinocytosis (see Chapter 1). This chewing away at the edge of the colloid produces the reabsorption lacunae seen in active glands (Fig 18–2). In the cells, the globules of colloid merge with lysosomes (Fig 18–3). The peptide bonds between the iodinated residues and the thyroglobulin are broken by the proteases in the lysosomes, and thyroxine, triiodothyronine, diiodotyrosine, and monoiodotyrosine are liberated into the cytoplasm. The iodinated tyrosines are deiodinated by a microsomal **iodotyrosine dehalogenase,** but this enzyme does not attack iodinated thyronines, and thyroxine and triiodothyronine pass on into the circulation. The iodide liberated by deiodination of the tyrosines is reutilized.

Effects of TSH on the Thyroid

When the pituitary is removed, thyroid function is depressed (Table 18–1); when TSH is administered, thyroid function is stimulated. Within a few hours after the injection of TSH, iodide uptake is increased; monoiodotyrosine, diiodotyrosine, and thyroxine synthesis are enhanced; pinocytosis of colloid is increased; and more thyroxine and triiodothyronine are secreted. Later on, blood flow increases, and with chronic TSH treatment the cells hypertrophy and the weight of the gland rises. The primary action of TSH is now known to be activation of adenyl cyclase in thyroid cell membranes. The resultant increase in intracellular cyclic AMP (see Chapter 17) produces a rapid increase in the pinocytosis of colloid and a rapid increase in glucose oxidation in the gland, primarily via the hexosemonophosphate shunt. The other changes

TABLE 18–1. Effect of hypophysectomy on thyroid weight and radioactive iodine uptake in the dog.*

	Normal	Hypophysectomized
Thyroid weight (mg/kg)	84.4 ± 22.8	70.0 ± 31.4
Uptake of ^{131}I (%†)	31.5 ± 13.4	3.4 ± 2.4

*Values are means ± one standard deviation.
†Percentage of dose in thyroid 72 hours after injection.

FIG 18–5. Outline of thyroxine biosynthesis. Iodination of tyrosine and condensation reaction take place while molecules are bound in peptide linkage to thyroglobulin.

produced by TSH follow these. The increase in glucose oxidation presumably increases the formation of NADPH and other coenzymes necessary for a variety of reactions in hormone synthesis and secretion. TSH also increases thyroglobulin synthesis, and this action is blocked by actinomycin D (see Chapter 17). However, there is little evidence that the other effects of TSH on thyroid function are due to stimulation of protein synthesis per se.

Whenever TSH stimulation is prolonged, the thyroid becomes detectably enlarged. Enlargement of the thyroid is called **goiter**.

TRANSPORT & METABOLISM OF THYROID HORMONES

Protein-Bound Iodine (PBI)

The free thyroid hormones secreted by the thyroid are bound in the blood stream to plasma protein. The amount of **protein-bound iodine (PBI)** in the plasma normally ranges from 3.5–8.0 μg/100 ml and averages about 6.0 μg/100 ml (Table 18–2). Most of this is thyroxine, but some is triiodothyronine. The

TABLE 18–2. PBI and BEI levels in humans.*

	Protein-bound Iodine (PBI) (μg/100 ml)	Butanol-extractable Iodine (BEI) (μg/100 ml)
Normal humans	3.5–8.0 (mean, 5.8)	2.2–5.6 (mean, 4.0)
Ten hyperthyroid patients	9.4–18.9	8.6–13.7
Six hypothyroid patients	2.0–3.6	0–0.6

Iodine-containing nonthyroidal substances which elevate the PBI for 1 month or more after administration:

Potassium iodide (Lugol's solution)
Dyes used to outline the gallbladder
Dyes used for myelograms
Dyes used for angiograms
Iodopyracet (Diodrast) and other dyes used for intravenous urography

*Values in patients with thyroid disease courtesy of PH Forsham.

normal plasma total thyroxine is approximately 8 $\mu g/100$ ml, and the normal plasma total triiodothyronine is approximately 0.3 $\mu g/100$ ml. The iodine in thyroxine and triiodothyronine, but not that in monoiodotyrosine, diiodotyrosine, and thyroglobulin, is measured when the plasma is extracted with butanol, and for evaluating thyroid function the **butanol-extractable iodine (BEI)** level is preferred to the PBI in some clinics (Table 18–2). Unfortunately, both the PBI and BEI are elevated for months after the use of various radiopaque dyes and contrast media because of protein binding of the iodine they contain (Table 18–2). In patients receiving mercurial diuretics, the PBI and BEI levels may be falsely low.

Capacity & Affinity of Plasma Proteins for Thyroid Hormones

The plasma proteins which bind thyroid hormones are **albumin,** a prealbumin called **thyroxine-binding prealbumin (TBPA),** and a globulin with an electrophoretic mobility between a_1- and a_2-globulin, **thyroxine-binding globulin (TBG).** The **capacities** of these 3 proteins to bind thyroxine–the amounts of thyroxine they bind when saturated–are shown in Table 18–3. Albumin has by far the greatest capacity, and TBG the least. However, the **affinities** of the proteins for thyroxine–ie, the avidity with which they bind thyroxine under physiologic conditions–are such that most of the circulating thyroxine is bound to TBG, with over a third of the binding sites on the protein occupied. Only small amounts of thyroxine are bound to TBPA, and practically none to albumin.

Normally, 99.8% of the thyroxine in plasma is bound; the free thyroxine level is only about 2 ng/100 ml. There is very little thyroxine in the urine. Its biologic half-life is long (about 6–7 days), and its volume of distribution is less than that of ECF (10 liters, or about 15% of body weight). All of these properties are characteristic of a substance that is strongly bound to protein.

Triiodothyronine is not bound to as great an extent; of the 0.3 $\mu g/100$ ml normally found in plasma, 0.5% or 1.5 ng/100 ml is free. The rest is protein-bound, 75% to TBG and the remainder to albu-

min. Triiodothyronine does not bind to TBPA. The lesser binding to TBG and albumin correlates with the fact that triiodothyronine has a much shorter half-life than thyroxine and that its action on the tissues is much more rapid.

The free thyroid hormones in plasma are in equilibrium with the protein-bound thyroid hormones in the plasma and protein-bound thyroid hormones in the tissues. Free thyroid hormones are added to the circulating pool by the thyroid. It is the free thyroid hormones in plasma which are physiologically active, and in all probability it is this fraction which inhibits the pituitary secretion of TSH (see below). These relationships are summarized in Fig 18–6.

Because of the equilibriums shown in Fig 18–6, addition of free thyroid hormones to plasma increases the entry of thyroid hormones into cells. Conversely, addition of TBG decreases tissue uptake and, therefore, the rate of hormone metabolism (Table 18–4). Red blood cells bind thyroid hormones, and these effects can easily be demonstrated in vitro in suspensions of red cells in plasma. For example, red blood cell uptake of thyroxine can be used in the diagnosis of

FIG 18–6. Distribution of thyroxine in the body. The distribution of triiodothyronine is similar. The dashed arrow indicates inhibition of TSH secretion by increases in the free thyroxine level of ECF. Approximate concentrations in human blood are shown in parentheses.

TABLE 18–3. Thyroxine-binding capacity and affinity of plasma protein constituents.* (The values for plasma levels of the proteins and the amount of thyroxine bound on each in normal plasma are approximations.)

Protein	Plasma Level ($\mu g/ml$)	Thyroxine-binding Capacity ($\mu g/100$ ml)	Affinity for Thyroxine	Approximate Amount of Thyroxine Bound in Normal Plasma ($\mu g/100$ ml)
Thyroxine-binding globulin (TBG)	0.20	22	High	7
Thyroxine-binding prealbumin (TBPA)	1.20	120	Moderate	1
Albumin	. . .	1000	Low	None
Total protein-bound thyroxine in plasma	. . .	. . .	. . .	8

*Data partly from Deiss: Transport of thyroid hormones. Fed Proc 21:630, 1962.

various thyroid disorders. The plasma of hyperthyroid patients contains excess free thyroxine, and if this plasma is added to normal red blood cells, thyroxine uptake is greater than normal. Conversely, when the plasma of patients with elevated TBG levels is added to red cells, uptake is decreased. Similar results are obtained using a resin to take up triiodothyronine.

Fluctuations in Binding

TBG levels are elevated in estrogen-treated patients and during pregnancy (Table 18–4). They are depressed by methyltestosterone administration and are low in nephrosis. A few cases of congenital elevation or depression of TBG levels have been reported. When the TBG level is elevated, there is a transient drop in free thyroid hormone levels, TSH secretion is stimulated, and more thyroid hormones are secreted until a normal level is restored. Conversely, a drop in TBG levels transiently inhibits TSH secretion. Patients with abnormal TBG levels therefore do not usually show signs of hyper- or hypothyroidism, ie, they are **euthyroid**. Diphenylhydantoin (Dilantin) competes with thyroid hormones for binding sites on TBG, and in patients receiving this drug the PBI is low and TSH secretion is depressed without symptoms of hypothyroidism.

TBPA levels are nonspecifically depressed in severely ill patients, but rarely if ever to the point where measurable PBI changes are observed. However, depressed PBI values in patients treated with salicylates and dinitrophenol are apparently due to a decrease in thyroid hormone binding to TBPA.

Metabolism of Thyroid Hormones

Thyroxine and triiodothyronine are deiodinated and deaminated in many tissues. Deiodination of thyroxine to triiodothyronine has been demonstrated in man. Because triiodothyronine acts more rapidly and is more potent than thyroxine, it has been suggested that thyroxine is metabolically inert until it is deiodinated to triiodothyronine, ie, that it is a prohormone. The finding that the thyroxine-deiodinating activity of skeletal muscles parallels the metabolic rate supports this hypothesis. However, the more rapid action of triiodothyronine could be due simply to the

fact that it is less avidly bound in the circulation and consequently is more available.

Deamination in the tissues produces pyruvic acid analogues of thyroxine and triiodothyronine, and subsequent decarboxylation produces the acetic acid analogues, TETRAC and TRIAC (Table 18–5). TETRAC lowers the plasma cholesterol level in doses that do not affect the BMR, and a dose of this compound which stimulates cardiac O_2 consumption to the same degree as a given dose of thyroxine has a far less stimulating effect on kidney metabolism than the thyroxine. It is tempting to speculate that various tissues produce degradation products tailored to their special metabolic needs. However, there is no direct evidence for this hypothesis.

In the liver, thyroxine and triiodothyronine are conjugated to form sulfates and glucuronides. These conjugates enter the bile and pass into the intestine. The thyroid conjugates are hydrolyzed and some are reabsorbed (enterohepatic circulation), but some are excreted in the stool. The iodide lost in this way amounts to about 15% of the daily iodide loss.

EFFECTS OF THYROID HORMONES

Most of the widespread effects of thyroid hormones in the body are secondary to stimulation of O_2 consumption (**calorigenic action**), although they also affect growth and maturation in mammals, help regulate lipid metabolism, and increase the absorption of carbohydrates from the intestine. They also increase the dissociation of oxygen from hemoglobin by increasing red cell 2,3-DPG (see Chapter 35). In these actions, triiodothyronine is more potent than thyroxine (Fig 18–7), while the fatty acid analogues have selective effects (Table 18–5). Except for a cholesterol-lowering action and a slight inhibitory effect on radioactive iodine uptake, reverse triiodothyronine is metabolically inert.

Calorigenic Action

Thyroxine and triiodothyronine increase the O_2

TABLE 18–4. Effect of variations in the concentrations of thyroid hormone-binding proteins in the plasma on various parameters of thyroid function.

	Concentrations of Binding Proteins	PBI	Rate of Thyroid Hormone Metabolism	Clinical State
Hyperthyroidism	Normal	High	Increased	Hyperthyroid
Hypothyroidism	Normal	Low	Decreased	Hypothyroid
Pregnancy, estrogen treatment, congenital elevation of TBG	High	High	Decreased	Euthyroid
Nephrosis, methyltestosterone treatment, congenital depression of TBG	Low	Low	Increased	Euthyroid

TABLE 18–5. Relative potencies of thyroxine derivatives.* Note that in each column the potency of the derivatives is stated relative to an arbitrary value of 100 for thyroxine.

Chemical Structure	Name	Synonyms	[131]I†	Goiter Prev ‡	BMR §	Cholesterol Lowering
HO⟨ ⟩–O–⟨ ⟩–$CH_2CHCOOH$ (NH_2) (tetraiodo)	L-3,5,3',5'-Tetra-iodothyronine	L-Thyroxine; T_4	100	100	100	100
HO⟨ ⟩–O–⟨ ⟩–$CH_2CHCOOH$ (NH_2) (tetraiodo)	D-3,5,3',5'-Tetra-iodothyronine	D-Thyroxine; D-T_4	30	...	...	500
HO⟨ ⟩–O–⟨ ⟩–$CH_2CHCOOH$ (NH_2) (triiodo)	L-3,5,3'-Triiodo-thyronine	Triiodothyronine; TIT; T_3	300	800	800	...
HO⟨ ⟩–O–⟨ ⟩–$CH_2CHCOOH$ (NH_2) (triiodo)	3,3',5'-Triiodo-thyronine (D, L tested)	Reverse T_3	75	< 1	< 1	...
HO⟨ ⟩–O–⟨ ⟩–CH_2CH_2COOH (tetraiodo)	3,5,3',5'-Tetra-iodothyroprop-ionic acid	T_4 PROP	60	14	6	...
HO⟨ ⟩–O–⟨ ⟩–CH_2CH_2COOH (triiodo)	3,5,3'-Triiodo-thyropropionic acid	T_3 PROP	60	28	10	...
HO⟨ ⟩–O–⟨ ⟩–CH_2COOH (tetraiodo)	3,5,3',5'-Tetra-iodothyroacetic acid	TETRAC	75	63	9	250
HO⟨ ⟩–O–⟨ ⟩–CH_2COOH (triiodo)	3,5,3'-Triiodo-thyroacetic acid	TRIAC	75	51	21	...

*Data mostly from Money & others: Comparative effects of thyroxine analogues in experimental animals. Ann New York Acad Sci 86:512, 1960.
†Inhibition of radioactive iodine uptake.
‡Prevention of goiter in propylthiouracil treated animals (pituitary-inhibiting effect).
§Calorigenic effect.

consumption of almost all metabolically active tissues (Fig 18–8). The exceptions are the adult brain, testes, uterus, lymph nodes, spleen, and anterior pituitary. Thyroxine actually depresses the O_2 consumption of the anterior pituitary, presumably because it inhibits TSH secretion. The increase in metabolic rate produced by a single dose of thyroxine begins after a latent period of several hours and lasts 6 or more days (Fig 18–8). The magnitude of the calorigenic effect depends upon the level of catecholamine secretion and on the metabolic rate before injection. If the initial rate is low, the rise is great; but if it is high, the rise is small. This is true not only in euthyroid subjects but in athyreotic thyroxine-treated patients as well. The cause of the decreased effect at higher metabolic rates is obscure. The amounts of various thyroid preparations required to maintain a normal BMR in thyroid-ectomized humans are shown in Table 18–6.

Effects Secondary to Calorigenesis

When the metabolic rate is increased by thyroxine or triiodothyronine in adults, nitrogen excretion is

FIG 18—7. Calorigenic responses of thyroidectomized rats to subcutaneous injections of thyroxine and 3,5,3′-triiodothyronine. (Redrawn and reproduced, with permission, from Barker: Peripheral actions of thyroid hormones. Fed Proc 21:635, 1962.)

TABLE 18—6. Maintenance and suppressive doses of various thyroid preparations.* Sixty mg thyroid, USP, are approximately equal to 100 μg levothyroxine, but a rigid conversion cannot be made.

| | Dose (mg/day) Required To: | |
	Maintain Normal BMR in Athyreotic Humans	Suppress Thyroid [131]I Uptake in Euthyroid Humans
L-Triiodo-thyronine	0.05—0.1	0.07—0.1
Sodium levo-thyroxine	0.1—0.4	0.2—0.5
Desiccated thyroid	60—240	60—240

*Modified from Van Middlesworth in: Clinical Endocrinology I. Astwood EB (editor). Grune & Stratton, 1960.

increased; if food intake is not increased, endogenous protein and fat stores are catabolized and weight is lost. In hypothyroid children, small doses of thyroid hormones cause a positive nitrogen balance because they stimulate growth but large doses cause protein catabolism similar to that produced in the adult. The catabolic response in skeletal muscle is sometimes so severe that muscle weakness is a prominent symptom and creatinuria is marked (thyrotoxic myopathy). The potassium liberated during protein catabolism appears in the urine, and there is an increase in urinary hexosamine and uric acid excretion. The mobilization of bone protein leads to hypercalcemia and hypercalciuria with some degree of osteoporosis (see Chapter 21).

The skin normally contains a variety of proteins combined with polysaccharides, hyaluronic acid, and chondroitin sulfuric acid. In hypothyroidism these complexes accumulate, promoting water retention and the characteristic puffiness of the skin (myxedema). When thyroid hormones are administered, the proteins are mobilized and diuresis continues until the myxedema is cleared.

Large doses of thyroid hormones cause enough extra heat production to cause a slight rise in body temperature (see Chapter 14), which in turn activates heat-dissipating mechanisms. Peripheral resistance decreases because of cutaneous vasodilatation, but cardiac output is increased by the combined action of thyroid hormones and catecholamines on the heart, so that pulse pressure and cardiac rate are increased and circulation time is shortened.

In the absence of thyroid hormones, a moderate anemia occurs as a result of decreased bone marrow

FIG 18—8. Change in metabolism of various tissues of thyroidectomized rats after the injection of a single dose of thyroxine. (Redrawn and reproduced, with permission, from Barker & Klitgaard: Metabolism of tissues excised from thyroxine-injected rats. Am J Physiol 170:81, 1952.)

metabolism and poor absorption of cyanocobalamin (vitamin B_{12}) from the intestine. Thyroxine and triiodothyronine correct these defects.

When the metabolic rate is increased, the need for all vitamins is increased and vitamin deficiency syndromes may be precipitated. Thyroid hormones are necessary for hepatic conversion of carotene to vitamin A, and the accumulation of carotene in the blood stream (**carotenemia**) in hypothyroidism is responsible for the yellowish tint of the skin. Carotenemia can be distinguished from jaundice because in the former condition the scleras are not yellow.

Milk secretion is decreased in hypothyroidism and stimulated by thyroid hormones, a fact that is sometimes put to practical use in the dairy industry. Thyroid hormones do not stimulate the metabolism of the uterus but are essential for normal menstrual cycles and fertility.

Effects on the Nervous System

In adult hypothyroidism, mentation is slow and the CSF protein level elevated. Thyroid hormones reverse these changes, and large doses cause rapid mentation, irritability, and restlessness. This is somewhat surprising because it is generally agreed that cerebral blood flow and the glucose and O_2 consumption of the brain are normal in hypo- and hyperthyroidism, and only traces of thyroid hormones pass the blood-brain barrier (see Chapter 32). Some of the effects of thyroid hormones on the brain are probably secondary to increased sensitivity to circulating catecholamines, with consequent increased activation of the reticular activating system (see Chapter 11). In infants, thyroid hormones may stimulate the O_2 consumption of the brain and they appear to exert other actions on the nervous system, possibly because the blood-brain barrier is not developed. In hypothyroid infants, myelination is defective and mental development is seriously retarded. The mental changes are irreversible if replacement therapy is not instituted soon after birth.

Thyroid hormones also exert effects on the peripheral nervous system. The reaction time of stretch reflexes (see Chapter 6) is shortened in hyperthyroidism and prolonged in hypothyroidism. Measurement of the reaction time of the ankle jerk (Achilles reflex) has attracted considerable attention as a clinical test for evaluating thyroid function, but the reaction time is also affected by certain other diseases.

Effects on Carbohydrate Metabolism

Thyroid hormones increase the rate of absorption of carbohydrate from the gastrointestinal tract, an action that is probably independent of their calorigenic action. In hyperthyroidism, therefore, the blood glucose rises rapidly after a carbohydrate meal, sometimes exceeding the renal threshold. However, the increased catabolism and the elevated level of epinephrine secretion keep liver glycogen depleted. Therefore, the blood glucose falls again at a rapid rate as glucose is catabolized.

Effects on Cholesterol Metabolism

Thyroid hormones stimulate cholesterol synthesis and the hepatic mechanisms that remove cholesterol from the circulation. The decline in plasma cholesterol levels may occur because the rate of the latter process exceeds that of the former, or it may be secondary to changes in the plasma lipoprotein levels. The plasma cholesterol level drops before the metabolic rate rises, which indicates that this action is independent of the stimulation of O_2 consumption. Certain analogues of thyroxine have a clear-cut cholesterol-lowering effect with only slight calorigenic activity (Table 18–5).

Relation to Catecholamines

The actions of thyroid hormones and the catecholamines, norepinephrine and epinephrine, are intimately interrelated. Epinephrine increases the metabolic rate, stimulates the nervous system, and produces cardiovascular effects similar to those produced by thyroid hormones, although the duration of these actions is brief. Norepinephrine has generally similar actions. Catecholamines have no calorigenic effect in the absence of the thyroid, and the toxicity of the catecholamines is markedly increased in rats treated with thyroxine. Although catecholamine secretion is usually normal in hyperthyroidism, the cardiovascular effects, tremulousness, and sweating produced by thyroid hormones can be blocked by sympathectomy, drugs such as reserpine and guanethidine that deplete tissue stores of catecholamines, and drugs such as propranolol that block β-adrenergic receptors. Indeed, these drugs are used in the treatment of the severe exacerbations of hyperthyroidism called **thyroid storms**. There is also some inhibition of the calorigenic effect of thyroxine when sympathetic outflow is blocked. However, the plasma PBI does not change. Obviously, many of the effects of thyroid hormones, especially those on the nervous and cardiovascular systems, are due in large part to adrenergic nervous activity. It is also clear that thyroxine and triiodothyronine potentiate the effects of catecholamines, and vice versa, but the basis of this interaction is not known.

Effects on Growth & Development

Thyroid hormones are essential for normal growth and skeletal maturation (see Chapter 22). In hypothyroid children, bone growth is slowed and epiphysial closure delayed. In the absence of thyroid hormones, pituitary growth hormone content and secretion are depressed. Thyroid hormones also potentiate the effect of growth hormone on the tissues.

Another example of the role of thyroid hormones in growth and maturation is their effect on amphibian metamorphosis. Tadpoles treated with thyroxine or triiodothyronine metamorphose early into dwarf frogs, whereas hypothyroid tadpoles never become frogs. The effects of thyroxine on metamorphosis are probably independent of its effects on O_2 consumption, even though it raises the O_2 consumption of metamorphosing tadpole skin in vitro. The hormone also exerts a calorigenic effect on tadpoles in vivo.

MECHANISM OF ACTION OF THYROID HORMONES

Thyroxine and its analogues decrease the efficiency of energy transduction by uncoupling phosphorylation from oxidation in the mitochondria (see Chapter 17); therefore, less of the energy produced by catabolism is stored in energy-rich phosphate compounds and more appears as heat. Dinitrophenol, epinephrine, and some other compounds also uncouple oxidative phosphorylation, but they apparently do so by different mechanisms. Thyroxine causes swelling of the mitochondria, but it now appears that this effect is a toxic one produced only by large doses. Thyroxine also stimulates mitochondrial respiration and phosphorylation and the activity of the respiratory and other enzymes. The calorigenic effect of the hormone is blocked by puromycin and actinomycin D (dactinomycin, Cosmegen) (see Chapter 17). It seems possible, therefore, that the effect on the metabolic rate is secondary to an effect on RNA synthesis.

The situation is similar as far as the growth-promoting actions of thyroid hormones are concerned. The actions of the hormones on growth and development involve various actions on a number of different types of cells. There is good evidence that at least some of these effects are due to activation of genetic mechanisms. For example, the thyroid hormones are known to increase albumin synthesis, and this effect on protein synthesis appears to be brought about by increased production of ribosomal RNA and increased binding of this rRNA to the endoplasmic reticulum. Studies on isolated tadpole tails provide another example of an effect on protein synthesis. The tail of a tadpole will live as an isolated organ for some time if it is placed in a suitable medium as soon as it is cut off. If the tail is treated with thryoxine, it regresses in the same way that it does when attached to a thyroxine-treated tadpole. This regression-producing effect of thyroxine on the isolated tail is blocked by actinomycin D, and other studies indicate that thyroxine brings about regression of the tail by inducing the formation of tissue-destroying enzymes in the cells.

REGULATION OF THYROID SECRETION

Stimuli Which Alter Thyroid Secretion

Although a number of vasoactive hormones such as vasopressin and epinephrine can affect thyroid secretion by a direct action on the gland, the primary control is effected by variations in the circulating level

FIG 18–9. Relation between serum TSH (h-TSH) and serum free thyroxine (FT$_4$) in patients with myxedema given various doses of L-thyroxine. The horizontal dashed line indicates the normal upper range for TSH and the vertical dashed lines enclose the normal range for free thyroxine. The solid curved line is the regression line based on the mean values at each dose of L-thyroxine. (Reproduced, with permission, from Colton, Gorman, & Mayberry: Suppression of thyrotropin (h-TSH) in serums of patients with myxedema of varying etiology treated with thyroid hormones. New England J Med 285:529, 1971.)

of pituitary TSH. TSH secretion is inhibited by a rise in the circulating free thyroxine and triiodothyronine levels and stimulated when the free thyroid hormone levels drop (Fig 18–9.) TSH secretion is also increased by exposure to cold, at least in animals, and depressed by heat and stressful stimuli.

Chemistry & Metabolism of TSH

Human TSH, a glycoprotein with a molecular weight of about 28,000, contains hexoses, hexosamines, and sialic acid. It is made up of 2 subunits, designated a and β. TSH-a is very similar (possibly identical) in structure to the a subunit of LH and the a subunit of HCG (see Chapters 22 and 23); functional specificity is apparently conferred by the β unit. The structure of the subunits varies from species to species, but other mammalian TSHs are biologically active in man. The biologic half-life of human TSH is about 60 minutes. TSH is degraded for the most part in the kidney, and to a lesser extent in the liver.

One substance (and possibly 2) with TSH activity is secreted by the placenta. However, it apparently has little effect on maternal thyroid function since secretion of pituitary TSH appears to remain normal during pregnancy.

Control Mechanisms

Hypothalamic lesions prevent the increased TSH secretion usually provoked by exposure to cold in rats. Electrical stimulation of the hypothalamus causes increased TSH secretion. A tripeptide that stimulates TSH secretion has been isolated from hypothalamic tissue (thyrotropin-releasing factor, TRF; see Fig 14–13), and this releasing factor is normally secreted into the portal vessels in the median eminence (see Chapter 14). The part of the hypothalamus concerned with the regulation of TSH secretion is the region in and above the rostral end of the median eminence.

The negative feedback effect of thyroid hormones on TSH secretion may be exerted in part at the hypothalamic level, but it must be mainly on the pituitary, since thyroxine and triiodothyronine block the increase in TSH secretion produced by TRF. It seems likely that the day-to-day maintenance of thyroid secretion depends on the feedback interplay between thyroid hormones and TSH (Fig 18–10), while the hypothalamus adjusts TSH secretion in certain special situations. The principal adjustments that appear to be neurally mediated are the increased secretion produced by cold and, presumably, the decrease produced by heat. It is worth noting that although cold produces clear-cut increases in circulating TSH in experimental animals and human infants, the rise produced by cold

in adult humans is small. Consequently, in adults, increased heat production due to increased thyroid hormone secretion (**thyroid hormone thermogenesis**) plays little if any role in the response to cold. The inhibiting effect of stress on TSH secretion is probably due to an inhibiting effect of glucocorticoids on TRF secretion, but the effect of stress is a minor one.

CLINICAL CORRELATES

Hypothyroidism & Hyperthyroidism in Man

The signs, symptoms, and complications of hypothyroidism and hyperthyroidism in man are predictable consequences of the physiologic effects of thyroid hormones discussed above. The syndrome of adult hypothyroidism is generally called **myxedema**, although the term myxedema is also used to refer specifically to the skin changes in this syndrome. Hypothyroidism may be the end result of a number of diseases of the thyroid gland, or it may be secondary to pituitary failure ("pituitary hypothyroidism") or hypothalamic failure ("hypothalamic hypothyroidism"). In the latter 2 conditions, unlike the first, the thyroid responds to a test dose of TSH, and hypothalamic hypothyroidism can be distinguished from pituitary hypothyroidism by the presence in the former of a rise in plasma TSH following a test dose of TRF. In completely athyreotic humans, the BMR falls to about −40. The hair is coarse and sparse, the skin dry and yellowish (carotenemia), and cold is poorly tolerated. The voice is husky and slow, the basis of the aphorism that, "Myxedema is the one disease that can be diagnosed over the telephone." Mentation is slow and memory is poor, and in some patients severe mental symptoms develop ("myxedema madness").

Cretinism

Children who are hypothyroid from birth are called cretins. They are dwarfed, mentally retarded, and have enlarged, protruding tongues and pot bellies (Fig 18–11). Before the use of iodized salt became widespread, the most common cause of cretinism was maternal iodine deficiency. Increasing attention is now being paid to various congenital abnormalities of thyroid function which cause goiter and, in some instances, congenital hypothyroidism with cretinism. Unless the mother was severely hypothyroid, the stigmas of cretinism are preventable if treatment is started soon after birth; however, once the typical clinical picture has developed, it is usually too late to prevent permanent mental retardation.

Hyperthyroidism

Hyperthyroidism, or **thyrotoxicosis**, is characterized by nervousness, weight loss, hyperphagia, heat intolerance, increased pulse pressure, a fine tremor of the outstretched fingers, a warm, soft skin, and a metabolic rate from +10 to as high as +100. It may be

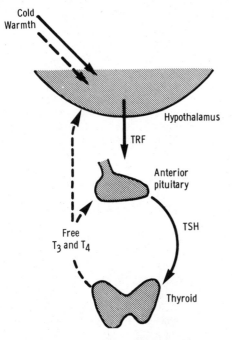

FIG 18–10. Diagram of the paths through which various physiologic stimuli presumably alter thyroid secretion. Solid arrows signify stimulation; dashed arrows, inhibition. T_3, triiodothyronine; T_4, thyroxine.

FIG 18–11. Fraternal twins, age 8 years. The boy has congenital hypothyroidism. (Reproduced, with permission, from Wilkins, in: *Clinical Endocrinology I.* Astwood EB [editor]. Grune & Stratton, 1960.)

FIG 18–12. Graves' disease. Note the goiter and the exophthalmos. (Courtesy of PH Forsham.)

caused by a variety of thyroid disorders, including, in rare instances, benign and malignant tumors, and cases due to TSH-secreting pituitary tumors have been reported. However, the most common form is **Graves' disease**, or **exophthalmic goiter**. In Graves' disease the thyroid is diffusely enlarged and hyperplastic, and there is a protrusion of the eyeballs called **exophthalmos** (Fig 18–12). Plasma TSH levels are actually subnormal in this disease. The thyroid hyperfunction is due to a circulating gamma globulin which has the unique property of stimulating the thyroid. Its effects resemble those of TSH, and it acts via cyclic AMP; however, its effects on the thyroid are of much longer duration (Fig 18–13). This substance, called **LATS** (long-acting thyroid stimulator), is an antibody that is formed against a component of thyroid tissue. The cause of its formation is an unsettled question. Neither this factor nor thyroid hormones are responsible for the exophthalmos. In fact, the exophthalmos not infrequently becomes worse if the thyroid is removed. A factor that produces exophthalmos in experimental animals (**exophthalmos-producing factor**) has been extracted from the plasma of patients with the disease. The factor is not TSH, but it may be of pituitary origin

FIG 18–13. Response of thyroxine-treated immature mice previously injected with tracer doses of radioactive iodine to TSH and to LATS in the serum of a patient with Graves' disease (thyrotoxic patient). The values are counts per minute in the serum of the mice at the stated intervals after injection of TSH or serum. (Data courtesy of F Greenspan.)

and is possibly a TSH derivative.

Thyrotoxicosis places a considerable load on the cardiovascular system, and in some patients with hyperthyroidism most or even all of the symptoms are cardiovascular. Thyrotoxic heart disease is a curable form of heart disease, but the diagnosis is often missed. It is important to remember that heart failure develops whenever the cardiac output, even though it is elevated, is inadequate to maintain tissue perfusion. The drop in peripheral resistance due to cutaneous vasodilatation in thyrotoxicosis is equivalent to opening a large arteriovenous fistula; if the compensatory increase in cardiac output is not great enough, "high-output failure" results.

Another complication of severe, long-term thyrotoxicosis is liver failure. The chronic liver glycogen depletion in hyperthyroid patients makes the liver abnormally susceptible to injury. If the increased demands for calories and vitamins are not met, malnutrition adds to the hepatic damage. Hepatic failure makes the thyrotoxicosis worse because the thyroid hormones are less rapidly removed from the circulation.

It has recently been demonstrated that, in some instances, Graves' disease is due to increased secretion of triiodothyronine with normal levels of plasma thyroxine. This syndrome has been called **T₃ thyrotoxicosis**.

Iodine Deficiency

When the dietary iodine intake falls below 10 μg/day, thyroid hormone synthesis is inadequate and secretion declines. As a result of increased TSH secretion, the thyroid hypertrophies, producing an **iodine deficiency goiter** which may become very large. Such "endemic goiters" have been known since ancient times. Before the practice of adding iodide to table salt became widespread, they were very common in Central Europe and the area around the Great Lakes in the United States, the inland "goiter belts" where iodine has been leached out of the soil by rain water so that food grown in the soil is iodine deficient.

Radioactive Iodine Uptake

Iodine uptake is a parameter of thyroid function that can be easily measured, using tracer doses of ^{131}I that have no known deleterious effect on the thyroid. For routine clinical tests, the tracer is administered orally and the thyroid uptake determined by placing a gamma ray counter over the neck. An area such as the thigh is also counted, and counts in this region are subtracted from the neck counts to correct for nonthyroidal radioactivity in the neck. The uptake in a normal subject is plotted in Fig 18–14. In hyperthyroidism, iodide is rapidly incorporated into thyroxine and triiodothyronine, and these hormones are released at an accelerated rate. Therefore, the amount of radioactivity in the thyroid rises sharply, but it then levels off and may start to decline within 24 hours, at a time when the uptake in normal subjects is still rising. The uptake at 3 hours is consequently more likely to

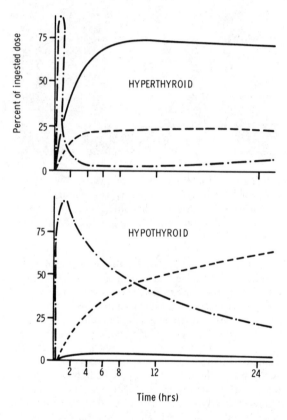

FIG 18–14. Radioactive iodine uptake in normal euthyroid, hyperthyroid, and hypothyroid subjects. Percentage of administered ^{131}I in thyroid, plasma, and urine are plotted against time after an oral dose of [131]I. In the hyperthyroid subject, plasma ^{131}I falls rapidly, then rises again as a result of release of ^{131}I-labeled thyroxine and triiodothyronine from the thyroid. (Reproduced, with permission, from Ingbar & Wooeber, in: *Textbook of Endocrinology*, 4th ed. Williams RH [editor]. Saunders, 1968.)

be abnormal than the 24-hour uptake in patients with hyperthyroidism. In hypothyroidism the uptake is low, and the rise to peak values is slower than normal. Uptake values must, of course, be interpreted with the physiology of iodine metabolism in mind. For example, on a diet high in iodine content, the ^{131}I uptake is low even though thyroid function may be normal because the iodide pool is so large that the tracer is excessively diluted. Conversely, ^{131}I uptake is high without hyperthyroidism in individuals whose daily iodine intake is adequate to prevent iodine deficiency goiter but chronically lower than the average intake. Variations in renal function also affect uptake because of differences in the amount of tracer excreted in the urine.

Large amounts of radioactive iodine destroy thyroid tissue because the radiation kills the cells. Radioiodine therapy is useful in some cases of thyroid cancer and can be used to treat benign thyroid diseases, although, especially in young patients, the dangers of possible radiation carcinogenesis and germ cell mutations must be kept in mind.

Antithyroid Drugs

Most of the drugs which inhibit thyroid function act either by interfering with the iodide trapping mechanism or by blocking the organic binding of iodine. In either case, TSH secretion is stimulated by the decline in circulating thyroid hormones, and goiter is produced. A number of monovalent anions compete with iodide for active transport into the thyroid, and therefore inhibit uptake to the point where the T/S ratio approaches unity; this inhibition of iodide transport can be overcome by administration of extra iodide. The anions include chlorate, pertechnetate, periodate, biiodate, nitrate, and perchlorate. Thiocyanate, another monovalent anion, inhibits iodide transport but is not itself concentrated within the gland. Thiocyanate and perchlorate are sometimes used clinically in the treatment of thyrotoxicosis. The activity of perchlorate is about 10 times that of thiocyanate.

The **thiocarbamides**, a group of compounds related to thiourea, were initially thought to block the oxidation of iodide to iodine. However, they are now known to inhibit the iodination of monoiodotyrosine and block the coupling reaction. They do not block iodide trapping. Because of the increase in TSH secretion, the initial ^{131}I uptake is actually increased during thiocarbamide therapy, and the T/S ratio may reach 250. However, since binding is inhibited, the ^{131}I is not retained, and 24 hours after administration of the isotope, uptake is subnormal.

Most of the thiocarbamides used in clinical practice are derivatives of thiouracil (Fig 18–15). Those in most common use are propylthiouracil and methimazole. Barbiturates and phentolamine are weak goitrogens because of their thiourea-like structure, but their antithyroid action is clinically of little importance.

Aminobenzenes inhibit the conversion of iodide

Thiouracil   Propylthiouracil   1-Methyl-2-mercapto-imidazole (methimazole, Tapazole)

FIG 18–15. Antithyroid thiocarbamides.

to iodine. Para-aminobenzoic acid (PABA) and the sulfonamide antibiotics have this action, but the doses used in the treatment of infections in humans have little goitrogenic effect.

Another substance which inhibits thyroid function under certain conditions is iodide itself. In hyperthyroidism, large doses of iodides regularly inhibit thyroid hormone secretion. The position of iodide in thyroid physiology is thus unique in that a minimal amount is necessary for normal thyroid function, whereas a large amount is inhibitory when the gland is hyperplastic. The inhibitory effect lasts for 1–4 weeks and then wears off in spite of continuing therapy. Colloid accumulates and the vascularity of the hyperplastic gland is decreased, making iodide treatment of considerable value in preparing thyrotoxic patients for surgery. By contrast, iodide has little, if any, effect on thyroid function in normal individuals. This is why, in doubtful cases of thyrotoxicosis, the clinical response to iodide therapy can be used as a diagnostic test. However, goiters sometimes develop in euthyroid patients taking large amounts of iodine in cough medicines. There are apparently several different mechanisms by which excess I^- inhibits thyroid function. It decreases the organic binding of iodine; it reduces the effect of TSH on the gland; and it inhibits proteolysis of thyroglobulin. There is no direct effect on the I^- trapping mechanism, but the total I^- uptake is low because of the inhibition of organic binding and, to a lesser extent, because the amount of circulating iodide is so great that added tracer is immensely diluted.

Naturally Occurring Goitrogens

Thiocyanates are sometimes ingested with food, and there are relatively large amounts of naturally occurring goitrogens in some foods. Vegetables of the Brassicaceae family, particularly rutabagas, cabbage, and turnips, contain **progoitrin** and a substance which converts this compound into **goitrin**, an active antithyroid agent (Fig 18–16). The progoitrin activator in vegetables is heat-labile; but because there are activators in the intestine (presumably of bacterial origin) goitrin is formed even if the vegetables are cooked. The goitrin intake on a normal mixed diet is usually not great enough to be harmful, but in vegetarians and food faddists "cabbage goiters" do occur. Other as yet unidentified plant goitrogens probably exist and may be responsible for the occasional small "goiter epidemics" reported from various parts of the world.

Progoitrin

$$H-N----CH_2.$$

$$S=C$$

$$O----C-C=CH_2$$
$$\quad\quad H \quad H$$

Goitrin
(L-5-vinyl-2-thiooxazolidone)

FIG 18—16. The naturally occurring goitrogen in vegetables of the family Brassicaceae.

Use of Thyroid Hormones in Nonthyroidal Diseases

When the pituitary-thyroid axis is normal, doses of exogenous thyroid hormone that provide less than the amount secreted endogenously have no significant effect on metabolism because there is a compensatory decline in endogenous secretion due to inhibition of TSH secretion. In euthyroid humans, the dose of desiccated thyroid that merely suppresses thyroid function (Table 18—6) is usually 60—180 mg/day, but in an occasional individual no metabolic stimulation will occur on 600 mg/day. Suppression of TSH secretion due to thyroxine treatment or pituitary disease leads eventually to thyroid atrophy. An atrophic gland initially responds sluggishly to TSH, and if the TSH suppression has been prolonged it may take some time for normal thyroid responsiveness to return. The adrenal cortex and other endocrine glands respond in an analogous fashion; when they are deprived of the support of their tropic hormones for some time, they become atrophic and only sluggishly responsive to their tropic hormone until the hormone has had some time to act on the gland.

In patients with so-called metabolic insufficiency—fatigued individuals who feel weak and have a slightly low BMR with a normal PBI and ^{131}I uptake—thyroid therapy has been proved to be of no more value than placebo medication. Use of thyroid to promote weight loss can be of value only if the patient pays the price of some nervousness and heat intolerance and curbs his appetite so that there is no compensatory increase in caloric intake.

Thyroxine and, more recently, its less calorigenic analogues such as TETRAC and D-thyroxine have been used to lower plasma cholesterol levels in an attempt to slow down or prevent arteriosclerotic vascular disease. Such treatment may be of some benefit, particularly in patients with hypercholesterolemia, but a definitive assessment of the value of the treatment must await the results of detailed, long-term studies.

19...

Endocrine Functions of the Pancreas & the Regulation of Carbohydrate Metabolism

The islets of Langerhans in the pancreas secrete the polypeptide hormones, **glucagon** and **insulin**, both of which have important functions in the regulation of the intermediary metabolism of carbohydrates, proteins, and fats. The 2 hormones have opposite effects. Glucagon elevates the blood glucose by stimulating hepatic glycogenolysis. Glucagon deficiency can cause hypoglycemia, but a clinical syndrome due to its excess has not been described. Insulin lowers the blood glucose and facilitates the entry of glucose into muscle and many other tissues. Insulin excess causes hypoglycemia, which leads to convulsions and coma. Insulin deficiency, either absolute or relative, is the cause of diabetes mellitus, a complex and debilitating disease which if untreated is eventually fatal.

The secretion of insulin is increased and that of glucagon decreased by an elevated blood glucose level, whereas hypoglycemia depresses insulin secretion and stimulates glucagon secretion. In this way, the endocrine portion of the pancreas functions to defend the constancy of the blood glucose level and maintain the flow of glucose into the cells. A variety of other hormones also have important roles in the regulation of carbohydrate metabolism.

ISLET CELL STRUCTURE

The islets of Langerhans (Fig 19–1) are ovoid, 75 × 175 μm collections of cells scattered throughout the pancreas, although they are more plentiful in the tail than in the body and head. They make up 1–2% of the weight of the pancreas. In man, there are 1–2 million islets. Each has a copious blood supply; and blood from the islets, like that from the gastrointestinal tract but unlike that from any other endocrine organs, drains into the portal vein.

The cells in the islets can be divided into types on the basis of their granulation and staining properties. In man and all mammals studied except the guinea pig, there are 3 types of cells: α, β, and δ. In man, 1–8% of the cells are δ cells, which have recently been reported to contain gastrin (see Chapter 26). Approximately 75% are the insulin-secreting β cells, which contain granules that stain bluish-purple with the modified Mallory aniline blue stain; and approximately 20% are the glucagon-secreting α cells, which contain granules that stain red with the Mallory stain.

FIG 19–1. **Islet of Langerhans, rat pancreas.** Darkly stained cells are β cells. Surrounding pancreatic acinar tissue is light colored. (× 400; courtesy of LL Bennett.)

FIG 19–2. **Electron micrograph of 2 adjoining β cells in human pancreas.** The β granules are the membrane-lined vesicles containing crystals that range from rhombic to round in shape. (× 26,000; courtesy of A Like. Reproduced, with permission, from Bloom & Fawcett: *A Textbook of Histology,* 9th ed. Saunders, 1968.)

Anti-insulin antibodies localize in the β cell granules, and on the basis of this and other evidence it seems clear that the granules are packets of insulin in the cell cytoplasm. Each packet is contained in a membrane-lined vesicle (Fig 19–2). The shape of the packets varies from species to species; in humans, some are round while others are rectangular. In the β cells the insulin molecule forms polymers and also complexes with zinc. The differences in shape of the packets are probably due to differences in the size of polymers or zinc aggregates of insulin. The α granules, presumably the storage form of glucagon, are relatively uniform from species to species (Fig 19–3).

The number of granules in the β cells parallels the insulin content of the pancreas. Stimuli which increase insulin secretion cause β cell degranulation. The regulation of insulin secretion is discussed below.

FIG 19–3. Electron micrograph of α cell in human pancreas. The granules are the dense round structures surrounded by membranes. (✕ 24,000; courtesy of A Like. Reproduced, with permission, from Bloom & Fawcett: *A Textbook of Histology,* 9th ed. Saunders, 1968.)

STRUCTURE, BIOSYNTHESIS, & SECRETION OF INSULIN

Structure & Species Specificity

Insulin is a polypeptide containing 2 chains of amino acids linked by disulfide bridges (Table 19–1). There are minor differences in the amino acid composition of the molecule from species to species. The differences are generally not sufficient to affect the biologic activity of a particular insulin in heterologous species but are sufficient to make the insulin antigenic.

TABLE 19–1. Structure of human insulin (molecular weight 5734) and (below) variations in this structure in other mammalian species. In the rat, the islet cells secrete 2 slightly different insulins, and in certain fish 4 different chains are found.*

	Variations From Human Amino Acid Sequence	
	A Chain Position	B Chain Position
Species	8 9 10	30
Pig, dog, sperm whale	Thr-Ser-Ile	Ala
Rabbit	Thr-Ser-Ile	Ser
Cattle, goat	Ala-Ser-Val	Ala
Sheep	Ala-Gly-Val	Ala
Horse	Thr-Gly-Ile	Ala
Sei whale	Ala-Ser-Thr	Ala

*Data mainly from Prout TE: The chemical structure of insulin in relation to biological activity and antigenicity. Metabolism 12:673, 1963; and Grodsky GM, Forsham PH: Insulin and the pancreas. Ann Rev Physiol 28:347, 1966.

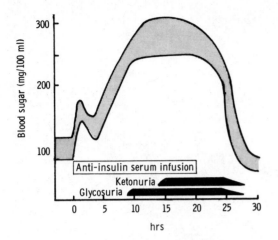

FIG 19–4. Hyperglycemia, glycosuria, and ketosis produced in rats by the injection of serum containing anti-insulin antibodies. The striped area includes all blood glucose values found in 3 rats. In this case, the rats were injected with sera of guinea pigs that had been injected with crystalline bovine insulin. (Redrawn and reproduced, with permission, from Armin & others: Experimental diabetes in rats produced by parenteral administration of anti-insulin serum. J Physiol 153:146, 1960.)

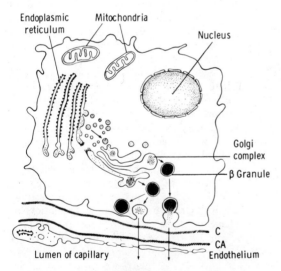

FIG 19–5. Schematic representation of insulin biosynthesis and secretion. Insulin is synthesized in the rough endoplasmic reticulum and translocated to the Golgi apparatus where the β granules are formed. The granules fuse to the cell membranes, and their contents pass through the basement membrane of the β cell (C), the basement membrane of the capillaries (CA), and the fenestrated capillary endothelium to enter the blood stream. (Modified from Orci & others: The ultrastructural events associated with the action of tolbutamide and glybenclamide on pancreatic β cells. Acta diab lat 6 [Suppl 1]:271, 1969.)

If the insulin of one species is injected for a prolonged period into another species, the anti-insulin antibodies formed inhibit endogenously secreted insulin when injected into an animal of the species from which the injected insulin was prepared (Fig 19–4). Almost all humans who have received commercial beef insulin for more than 2 months have antibodies against beef insulin, but the titer is usually low and presents no clinical problem. However, some patients develop high titers and become resistant to beef insulin on this basis. Such patients are usually responsive to insulins from other species.

Biosynthesis & Secretion

Insulin is synthesized in the endoplasmic reticulum of the β cells (Fig 19–5). It is then transported to the Golgi complex, where it is packaged in the membrane-bound β granules. These granules move to the cell wall, and their membranes fuse with the membrane of the cell, expelling the insulin to the exterior by exocytosis (see Chapter 1). The insulin must then cross the basement membranes of the β cell and a neighboring capillary and the fenestrated endothelium of the capillary (Fig 19–5) to reach the blood stream.

The insulin molecule is synthesized as a single chain. It is folded in the β cell, and the disulfide links are formed (Fig 19–6). The resultant large molecule, which has been named **proinsulin**, is secreted after prolonged stimulation and by some β cell tumors, but the peptide connecting the A and B chains (C peptide) is normally removed by hydrolysis before secretion. Without the connection, the proper folding of the molecule for the formation of the disulfide bridges would be difficult. The C peptide, which has little if any insulin-like activity, is then secreted along with the insulin in the β granule. The biologic activity of proinsulin is also slight, but it cross-reacts with insulin in the insulin immunoassay (see below). The process by which insulin is secreted normally requires glucose metabolism, possibly for the formation of ATP. It also depends on cyclic AMP, as do many other secretory processes in the endocrine system (see Chapter 17). Normal secretion also requires the presence of calcium and potassium ions.

FATE OF SECRETED INSULIN

Transportation & Distribution

From time to time, there have been claims that insulin is bound to plasma proteins, but recent research casts considerable doubt on this possibility. A circulating protein with anti-insulin activity called **synalbumin** has received considerable attention, but the significance and even the existence of this factor have also been questioned.

The half-life of insulin in the circulation in man is 10–25 minutes. Insulin is fixed to many tissues, but red blood cells and brain do not bind it. Large amounts are bound in the liver and kidneys.

FIG 19–6. **Porcine proinsulin.** The amino acid composition of the portion of the molecule connecting the A and B chains is considerably different in bovine and human proinsulin. (Reproduced, with permission, from Chance: Discussion of Steiner & others: Proinsulin and the biosynthesis of insulin. Recent Progr Hormone Res 25:207, 1969.)

Metabolism

Three insulin-inactivating systems have been described. Two break the disulfide linkages in the molecule—one enzymatically and one nonenzymatically—and one cleaves the peptide chains. The enzyme involved in the enzymatic disruption of the disulfide linkages is **hepatic glutathione insulin transhydrogenase**, which breaks the insulin molecule into A and B chains. Glutathione is a sulfur-containing tripeptide which in this case is acting as a coenzyme for the transhydrogenase. The enzymes responsible for the inactivation of insulin used to be grouped together under the term "insulinase." Variations in the rate of insulin inactivation in various tissues have been reported, but their significance is uncertain.

CONSEQUENCES OF INSULIN DEFICIENCY & ACTIONS OF INSULIN

Diabetes Mellitus

Insulin deficiency is a common and serious pathologic condition in man. In animals it can be produced by pancreatectomy or by the administration of alloxan (Fig 19–7), a compound which is relatively toxic to the liver and kidney but which in appropriate doses causes a selective destruction of the β cells of the

pancreatic islets. It can also be produced by drugs that inhibit insulin secretion or by administration of anti-insulin antibodies.

The constellation of abnormalities caused by insulin deficiency is called **diabetes mellitus.** Greek and Roman physicians used the term "diabetes" to refer to conditions in which the cardinal finding was a large urine volume, and 2 types were distinguished: "diabetes mellitus," in which the urine tasted sweet; and "diabetes insipidus," in which the urine was tasteless. Today the term diabetes insipidus is reserved for the condition produced by lesions of the supraoptic-posterior pituitary system (see Chapter 14), and the unmodified word diabetes is generally used as a synonym for diabetes mellitus.

Diabetes is characterized by polyuria, polydipsia, weight loss in spite of polyphagia (increased appetite), hyperglycemia, glycosuria, ketosis, acidosis, and coma. There are widespread biochemical abnormalities, but the fundamental defects to which most of the abnormalities can be traced are (1) a reduced entry of glucose into various "peripheral" tissues and (2) an increased liberation of glucose into the circulation from the liver (increased **hepatic glucogenesis**). There is therefore an extracellular glucose excess and an intracellular glucose deficiency, a situation which has been called "starvation in the midst of plenty."

Glucose Tolerance

In diabetes, glucose piles up in the blood stream, especially after meals. If a glucose load is given to a diabetic, the blood glucose rises higher and returns to the baseline more slowly than it normally does. The response to a standard oral test dose of glucose, the **oral glucose tolerance test,** is used in the clinical diagnosis of diabetes (Fig 19–8).

FIG 19–7. Alloxan.

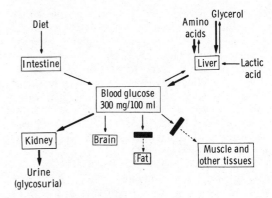

FIG 19—8. Glucose tolerance curves following oral administration of 1.75 g/kg of glucose after at least 3 days on a 300 g carbohydrate diet. Values falling below the shaded area are normal; those falling in it are "probable diabetes"; and those above it, diabetes. (Redrawn and reproduced, with permission, from Fajans & Conn: The early recognition of diabetes mellitus. Ann New York Acad Sci 82:208, 1959.)

The impaired glucose tolerance is due in part to reduced entry of glucose into cells (**decreased peripheral utilization**). In the absence of insulin, the entry of glucose into skeletal and cardiac muscle and other tissues is decreased (Table 19—2). However, intestinal absorption of glucose is unaffected, as is its reabsorption from the urine by the cells of the proximal tubules of the kidney. Glucose uptake by most of the brain and the red blood cells is also normal.

The second (and probably the major) cause of hyperglycemia in diabetes is derangement of the glucostatic function of the liver (see Chapter 17). The

TABLE 19—2. Effect of insulin on glucose uptake in tissues in which it has been investigated.

Tissues in which insulin increases glucose uptake
    Skeletal muscle
    Cardiac muscle
    Smooth muscle
    Adipose tissue
    Leukocytes
    Crystalline lens of the eye
    Pituitary
    Fibroblasts
    Mammary gland
    Aorta
    Liver
Tissues in which insulin does not affect glucose uptake
    Brain (except probably part of hypothalamus)
    Kidney tubules
    Intestinal mucosa
    Red blood cells

FIG 19—9. **Disordered blood glucose homeostasis in insulin deficiency.** Compare with Fig 17—17. The heavy arrows indicate reactions that are accentuated. The rectangles across arrows indicate reactions that are blocked.

liver takes up glucose from the blood stream and stores it as glycogen, but because the liver contains glucose-6-phosphatase it also discharges glucose into the blood stream. Indeed, Claude Bernard spoke of the liver as an endocrine gland that secreted glucose. Insulin facilitates glycogen synthesis and inhibits hepatic glucose output. When the blood glucose is high, insulin secretion is normally increased and hepatic glucogenesis is decreased. In diabetes, the glucose output remains elevated (Fig 19—9). The degree to which this contributes to the abnormal glucose tolerance is shown by experiments on hepatectomized animals. In fasted hepatectomized dogs, the blood glucose falls steadily, but if hepatectomized dogs are given glucose the glucose tolerance curves are of the diabetic type. This is true even if the pancreas is intact. However, pancreatectomized animals with intact livers given a constant infusion of insulin have essentially normal glucose tolerances.

Distribution of Endogenous & Exogenous Insulin

The action of insulin on the liver assumes added significance in view of the fact that endogenously secreted insulin enters the portal vein, so that the liver is normally exposed to higher concentrations of insulin than the peripheral tissues. The liver binds about half of a dose of insulin injected into the portal vein but only 25% of a peripherally injected dose. It is worth noting that the exogenous insulin injected in the treatment of diabetes enters the peripheral rather than the portal circulation, although it has not been determined whether the resultant unphysiologic distribution of insulin has any serious consequences in the control of the disease or its complications.

Effects of Hyperglycemia

Hyperglycemia by itself is relatively harmless unless it is so marked that there are symptoms due to the hyperosmolality of the blood. Even with relatively mild hyperglycemia, however, the glycosuria that occurs when the renal capacity for glucose reabsorption is exceeded causes polyuria and polydipsia. Excretion of the osmotically active glucose molecules entails the loss of large amounts of water (osmotic diuresis; see Chapter 38). This resultant dehydration activates the mechanisms regulating water intake, leading to polydipsia. There is an appreciable urinary loss of Na^+ and K^+ as well. For every gram of glucose excreted, 4.1 kcal are lost from the body. Increasing oral caloric intake to cover this loss raises the blood glucose further and increases the glycosuria, so mobilization of endogenous protein and fat stores and weight loss are for practical purposes unavoidable.

Hypoglycemic Action of Insulin

When insulin is injected into normal or diabetic persons, the blood glucose falls. With many commercial preparations there is an initial blood glucose rise because of contamination of the insulin with glucagon, but when specially prepared glucagon-free insulin is used the decline starts within minutes. Following intravenous administration, the decline is maximal in about 30 minutes; following subcutaneous administration, it is maximal in 2–4 hours. Insulin forms complexes with protamine and with zinc which delay its absorption, and a number of long-acting zinc and protamine complexes are commercially available (Table 19–3).

Relation to Potassium

Insulin causes K^+ to enter cells, with a resultant lowering of the ECF K^+ concentration. Infusions of insulin and glucose significantly lower the plasma K^+ level in normal individuals and are very effective for the temporary relief of hyperkalemia in patients with renal failure. Hypokalemia may develop when patients

TABLE 19–3. Characteristics of the blood glucose lowering effects of crystalline zinc insulin and several modified insulins.

Type of Insulin	Hours After Subcutaneous Administration	
	Peak Action	Duration of Action
Crystalline zinc insulin (CZI)	2–4	5–8
Globin zinc insulin	6–10	18–24
NPH insulin (neutral protamine-Hagedorn insulin)	8–12	28–30
Lente insulin	10–16	24–28
Protamine zinc insulin (PZI)	16–24	24–36+

with diabetic acidosis are treated with insulin. The reason for the intracellular migration of K^+ is still obscure. However, insulin has been shown to increase the resting membrane potential (see Chapter 1) of skeletal muscle and fat cells, and it has been argued that this increased electrical gradient into the cells is the cause of the increase in intracellular K^+. It is possible under certain experimental conditions to dissociate the movement of K^+ from the movement of glucose into cells. K^+ depletion decreases insulin secretion, and K^+-depleted patients such as those with primary hyperaldosteronism (see Chapter 20) develop diabetic glucose tolerance curves. These curves are restored to

FIG 19–10. Effect of insulin on the cells of muscle and other "peripheral" tissues. The cell is represented as a mill which obtains fuel (glucose) from a reservoir (blood glucose). Normally, as shown on the left, insulin is present and fuel enters through the pipeline in sufficient amounts to operate the turbine (citric acid cycle) and maintain a reserve supply in the storage tanks. When insulin is absent, the opening of the pipe is narrowed (figure on the right) and very little fuel gets into the cell. The turbine can now turn at a nearly normal rate only by depleting the reserves, the major source of energy being fats and proteins. (Modified, redrawn, and reproduced, with permission, from MacLeod: *Diabetes.* Upjohn Co., 1969.)

normal by K^+ repletion. The thiazide diuretics, which cause loss of K^+ as well as Na^+ in the urine (Table 38−9), decrease glucose tolerance and make diabetes worse. They apparently exert this effect principally because of their K^+-depleting effects, although some of them also cause pancreatic islet cell damage.

Exercise

The entry of glucose into skeletal muscle is increased during exercise in the absence of insulin. The cause of the increased muscle uptake is not definitely known. Relative O_2 deficiency may be a factor because glucose entry into cells is increased under anaerobic conditions. Exercise can precipitate hypoglycemia in diabetics taking insulin, and patients with this disease should take in extra calories or reduce their insulin dosage when they exercise.

Effects of Intracellular Glucose Deficiency

The plethora of glucose outside the cells in diabetes contrasts with the intracellular deficit. Glucose catabolism is normally a major source of energy for cellular processes (Fig 19−10), and in diabetes energy requirements can be met only by drawing on protein and fat reserves. Mechanisms are activated which greatly increase the catabolism of protein and fat, and one of the consequences of increased fat catabolism is ketosis.

Deficient glucose utilization in the cells of the hypothalamic ventromedial nuclei is probably the cause of the hyperphagia in diabetes. When the activity of the satiety center is decreased in response to decreased glucose utilization in its cells, the lateral appetite center operates unopposed and food intake is increased (see Chapter 14).

Glycogen depletion is a common consequence of intracellular glucose deficit, and the glycogen content of liver and skeletal muscle in diabetic animals is usually reduced. Insulin regularly increases the glycogen content of skeletal muscle, and it increases liver glycogen unless it produces sufficient hypoglycemia to also activate glycogenolytic mechanisms.

Changes in Protein Metabolism

In diabetes, the rate at which amino acids are catabolized to CO_2 and H_2O and the rate at which they are converted to glucose in the liver are both accelerated. These shifts are indicated in Fig 19−11, which also shows the other principal abnormalities of intermediary metabolism.

Some idea of the rate of gluconeogenesis in fasting diabetic animals is obtained by measuring the ratio of glucose (dextrose) to nitrogen in the urine (**D/N ratio**). In fasting animals, liver glycogen is depleted and glycerol is converted to glucose at a very limited rate, so that the only important source of plasma glucose is protein (see Chapter 17). It can be calculated that the amount of carbon in the protein represented by 1 g of urinary nitrogen is sufficient to form 8.3 g of glucose. Consequently, the D/N ratio of approximately 3 seen in diabetes indicates the conversion to glucose of about

33% of the carbon of the protein metabolized.

The causes of the increased gluconeogenesis are multiple. There is an increased supply of amino acids for gluconeogenesis because, in the absence of insulin, less protein synthesis occurs in muscle and blood amino acid levels rise. Alanine is particularly easily converted to glucose. In addition, the activity of the enzymes that catalyze the conversion of pyruvic acid and other 2-carbon metabolic fragments to glucose is increased. These include phosphoenolpyruvate carboxykinase, which facilitates conversion of oxaloacetic acid to phosphoenolpyruvic acid (see Chapter 17). They also include fructose-1,6-diphosphatase, which catalyzes the conversion of fructose diphosphate to fructose-6-phosphate, and glucose-6-phosphatase, which controls the entry of glucose into the circulation from the liver. Increased acetyl-Co A increases pyruvate carboxypeptidase activity, and insulin deficiency increases the supply of acetyl-Co A because lipogenesis is decreased.

Hormones contribute to the increased gluconeogenesis, but their role appears to be secondary. Adrenal glucocorticoids accelerate gluconeogenesis, but the level of adrenal cortical secretion is not elevated except in severely ill diabetics or in acidosis. Glucagon also stimulates gluconeogenesis, and there is a relative hyperglucagonemia in many diabetics. However, gluconeogenesis is also markedly increased in the diabetes produced by pancreatectomy.

Insulin & Growth

Not only is protein catabolism accelerated in the absence of insulin, but protein synthesis is depressed and insulin stimulates protein formation. This anabolic effect of insulin is explained in part by the protein-sparing action of adequate intracellular glucose supplies. Insulin also increases the incorporation of amino acids into proteins by an action that is independent of its effect on glucose metabolism. This action may be due to an activation of the ribosomes (see Chapter 17) by insulin, but insulin also increases the transport of amino acids into cells in which protein synthesis has been blocked by puromycin. Failure to grow is a symptom of diabetes in children, and insulin stimulates the growth of immature hypophysectomized rats to almost the same degree as growth hormone. Maximum insulin-induced growth is present, however, only when the protein-sparing action of glucose is fostered by feeding a high-carbohydrate diet.

Negative Nitrogen Balance

In diabetes, the net effect of accelerated protein catabolism to CO_2 and H_2O and to glucose, plus diminished protein synthesis, is a markedly negative nitrogen balance, protein depletion, and wasting. Protein depletion from any cause is associated with poor "resistance" to infections, and the sugar-rich body fluids are undoubtedly good culture media for microorganisms. This is probably why diabetics are particularly prone to bacterial infections.

FIG 19–11. Abnormalities of intermediary metabolism in diabetes mellitus. Reactions that are accentuated are indicated by heavy arrows; reactions that are blocked are indicated by rectangles across the small arrows. (Modified and reproduced, with permission, from Renold & others, in: *Principles of Internal Medicine,* 4th ed. Harrison TR & others [editors]. McGraw-Hill, 1962.)

Fat Metabolism in Diabetes

The principal abnormalities of fat metabolism in diabetes are acceleration of lipid catabolism, with increased formation of ketone bodies, and decreased synthesis of fatty acids and triglycerides. The manifestations of the disordered lipid metabolism are so prominent that diabetes has been called "more a disease of lipid than of carbohydrate metabolism."

Fifty percent of an ingested glucose load is normally burned to CO_2 and H_2O; 5% is converted to glycogen; and 30–40% is converted to fat in the fat depots. In diabetes, less than 5% is converted to fat even though the amount burned to CO_2 and H_2O is also decreased and the amount converted to glycogen is not increased. Therefore, glucose accumulates in the blood stream and spills over into the urine. Manifestations of the increased fat catabolism include an increase in circulating triglycerides. There is an increase in circulating chylomicrons, which may cause visible lipemia. It used to be thought that the diminished lipogenesis in diabetics was due to deficient oxidation of glucose-6-phosphate via the hexosemonophosphate shunt, which in turn led to a decrease in the formation of the NADPH required for fatty acid synthesis (see Chapter 17). However, it now seems clear that NADPH deficiency is not the cause of the defect in lipogenesis, and it is probably due instead to an enzyme deficiency that hinders the conversion of acetyl-Co A to malonyl-Co A.

Insulin inhibits the hormone-sensitive lipase in adipose tissue, and, in the absence of this hormone, the plasma level of **free fatty acids** (NEFA, UFA, FFA) is more than doubled (Fig 19–12). Thus, the FFA level parallels the blood glucose level in diabetes, and in some ways is a better indicator of the severity of the diabetic state. In the liver and other tissues, the fatty acids are catabolized to acetyl-Co A. Some of the acetyl-Co A is burned, along with amino acid residues, to yield CO_2 and H_2O in the citric acid cycle. However, the supply exceeds the capacity of the tissues to catabolize the acetyl-Co A.

FFAs diminish tissue oxidation of glucose and decrease the sensitivity of the tissues to insulin. In diabetes, there is a reduction in the suppressing action of insulin on FFA release as well as antagonism to the hypoglycemic action of the hormone. It has therefore been suggested that an abnormality in fat metabolism leading to an increase in FFA release might be the initial event which precipitates clinical diabetes.

Ketosis

When there is excess acetyl-Co A in the body, some of it is converted to acetoacetyl-Co A and then, in the liver, to acetoacetic acid. Acetoacetic acid and its derivatives, acetone and β-hydroxybutyric acid, enter the circulation in large quantities (see Chapter 17).

These circulating ketone bodies are an important source of energy in fasting. Half of the metabolic rate in fasted normal dogs is said to be due to metabolism of ketones. The rate of ketone utilization in diabetics

CONTROL

DIABETES

INSULIN

FIG 19–12. Effects of hormones on metabolic reactions in adipose tissue. The reactions in the absence of hormone excess or deficiency (control) are summarized in the top diagram. Glucose is phosphorylated to form glucose-6-phosphate (G-6-P), and some of the G-6-P is then catabolized via the Embden-Meyerhof pathway (path to left below G-6-P) or hexosemonophosphate shunt (path to right) to trioses. Some of the trioses are converted to a-glycerophosphate (a-GP). In each diagram, the width of the arrows is proportionate to the magnitude of a given reaction, and reactions proceeding at a very slow rate are indicated by dashed arrows. (Reproduced, with permission, from Cahill: Adipose tissue metabolism. In: *Fat as a Tissue.* Rodahl & Issekutz [editors]. McGraw-Hill, 1964.)

is also appreciable. It has been calculated that the maximal rate at which fat can be catabolized without significant ketosis is 2.5 g/kg body weight/day in diabetic humans. In untreated diabetes, production is much greater than this, and ketone bodies pile up in the blood stream. There is some evidence that in severe diabetes the rate of ketone utilization may also decline, making the ketosis worse.

Acidosis

Most of the hydrogen ions liberated from acetoacetic acid and β-hydroxybutyric acid are buffered, but severe metabolic acidosis still develops. The low plasma pH stimulates the respiratory center, producing the rapid, deep respirations described by Kussmaul as "air hunger" and named, for him, **Kussmaul breathing**. The urine becomes acid; but when the ability of the kidney to replace the plasma cations accompanying the organic anions with H^+ and NH_4^+ is exceeded, Na^+ and K^+ are lost in the urine. The electrolyte and water losses lead to dehydration, hypovolemia, and hypotension. Finally, the acidosis and dehydration depress consciousness to the point of coma. Diabetic acidosis is a medical emergency. Now that the infections which used to complicate the disease can be controlled with antibiotics, acidosis is the commonest cause of early death in clinical diabetes.

In severe acidosis, total body sodium is markedly depleted and plasma Na^+ is not infrequently low. Total body potassium is also low, but the plasma K^+ is usually normal, partly because the acidosis decreases K^+ excretion. Another factor tending to maintain the plasma K^+ is the lack of insulin-induced entry of K^+ into cells. This must be kept in mind in treating acidosis; when insulin is given, the K^+ in the ECF moves into cells in large quantities. Because total body stores of this ion are low, severe and even fatal hypokalemia may develop.

The degree to which ketoacidosis complicates experimental diabetes varies in different species. The size of the body fat stores is also a factor conditioning the response to diabetes. Thin, wasted pancreatectomized dogs rarely develop ketoacidosis, whereas well-fed, plump animals do so readily. It is pertinent that before the isolation of insulin by Banting and Best in 1921 the principal treatment of diabetes in man was a starvation diet **(Allen regimen)**. This not only lowered the blood glucose level but also reduced depot fat stores to the point where there was little fat to mobilize.

In **lipoatrophic diabetes**, a rare form of diabetes, subcutaneous fat depots are deficient. Patients with this disease become diabetic because, in all probability, the 30–40% of ingested glucose normally taken up by adipose tissue remains in the blood stream, and the resultant postprandial hyperglycemia eventually exhausts the β cells (see below). On the other hand, they rarely develop severe ketoacidosis, presumably because there is no large store of fats which can flood the liver with ketogenic lipids.

Coma in diabetes is not always due to ketoacido-sis. In some instances, the blood glucose is elevated to such a degree that the hyperosmolality of the plasma causes unconsciousness **(hyperosmolal coma)**. Accumulation of lactic acid in the blood **(lactic acidosis)** may also complicate diabetic ketoacidosis if the tissues become hypoxic (see Chapter 33), and lactic acidosis may itself cause coma.

Cholesterol Metabolism

In diabetes the plasma cholesterol level is usually elevated, and this may play a role in the accelerated development of the arteriosclerotic vascular disease which is a major long-term complication of diabetes in man. Although there has been some controversy on the point, it seems clear that, at least in severe diabetes, cholesterol synthesis is decreased. Part of the rise in plasma cholesterol level is due to an increase in the cholesterol containing very low-density and low-density β-lipoproteins secondary to the great increase in circulating triglycerides. Another factor may be a decline in hepatic degradation of cholesterol which, when it exceeds the decline in cholesterol synthesis, contributes to the rise.

Effect of Insulin on Adipose Tissue

Insulin reverses all the abnormalities of lipid metabolism, primarily by making glucose available intracellularly. The action of insulin on adipose tissue in vitro is especially striking (Fig 19–12). Glucose uptake is facilitated and its catabolism by the hexose-monophosphate shunt and the Embden-Meyerhof pathway is consequently stimulated to an equal degree. Fatty acids are synthesized from the acetyl-Co A and, because abundant glycerol phosphate is also formed by glycolysis, the fatty acids are esterified with glycerol rather than released. Insulin also has a lipolysis-inhibiting effect because it inhibits the hormone-sensitive lipase in adipose tissue. The liver is no longer flooded with the excess fats that it converts to ketones, acetyl-Co A no longer piles up, and the rate of ketone body formation falls to normal.

Insulin also activates lipoprotein lipase, aiding the removal of triglycerides from the circulation. Thus insulin promotes fat storage in 3 ways: by activating lipoprotein lipase, by inhibiting the hormone-sensitive lipase in adipose tissue, and by making glycerol phosphate abundantly available for triglyceride synthesis in the fat cells. Because insulin promotes the storage of carbohydrate, protein, and fat and is secreted after meals (see below), it has been called the "hormone of abundance."

Summary

Because of the complexities of the metabolic abnormalities in diabetes, a summary is in order. The key features of insulin deficiency are decreased entry of glucose into many tissues (decreased peripheral utilization) and increased net release of glucose from the liver (increased production). The resultant hyperglycemia leads to glycosuria and a dehydrating osmotic diuresis. Dehydration leads to polydipsia. In the face of intracellular glucose deficiency, appetite is stimulated, glucose is formed from protein (gluconeogenesis), and energy supplies are maintained by the metabolism of proteins and fats (Fig 19–10). Weight loss, debilitating protein deficiency, and inanition are the result.

Fat catabolism is increased, and the system is flooded with triglycerides and free fatty acids. Fat synthesis is inhibited, and the overloaded catabolic pathways cannot handle the excess acetyl-Co A formed. In the liver, the acetyl-Co A is converted to ketone bodies. The ketones are for the most part organic acids, which accumulate in the circulation (ketosis) because their production rate exceeds the ability of the body to utilize them. Therefore, metabolic acidosis develops as the ketones accumulate. Na^+ and K^+ depletion are added to the dehydration because these plasma cations are excreted with the organic anions not covered by the H^+ and NH_4^+ secreted by the kidney. Finally, the acidotic, hypovolemic, hypotensive, depleted animal or patient becomes comatose because of the toxic effects of acidosis and dehydration on the nervous system, and dies if treatment is not instituted.

All these abnormalities are due to insulin deficiency. Although emergency treatment of acidosis also includes administration of alkali to combat the acidosis and parenteral water, Na^+, and K^+ to replenish body stores, only insulin repairs the fundamental defects in a way that permits a return to normal.

INSULIN EXCESS

Symptoms

All the known consequences of insulin excess are manifestations, directly or indirectly, of the effects of hypoglycemia on the nervous system. Glucose is the only fuel normally used in appreciable quantities by the brain. The carbohydrate reserves in neural tissue are very limited, and normal function depends upon a continuous glucose supply. As the blood glucose level falls, the cortex and the other brain areas with high metabolic rates are affected first, followed by the more slowly respiring vegetative centers in the diencephalon and hindbrain (see Chapter 32). Thus, early cortical symptoms of confusion, weakness, dizziness, and hunger are followed by convulsions and coma. If the hypoglycemia is prolonged, irreversible changes develop in the same cortical-diencephalic-medullary sequence, and death results from depression of the respiratory center. Therefore, prompt treatment with glucose is in order. Although a dramatic disappearance of symptoms is the usual response, abnormalities ranging from some intellectual dulling to permanent coma may persist if hypoglycemia was severe or prolonged. Hypoglycemia is a potent stimulus to sympathetic discharge and increased catecholamine secretion (Fig 19–13). The tremors, palpitations, and nervousness in hypoglycemia are probably due to sympathetic overactivity. The blood glucose level at which symptoms appear is variable. A rapid decline to 20–30 mg/100 ml in humans does not cause symptoms until the cerebral carbohydrate reserves are depleted, but a slow or sustained decline usually causes symptoms at blood glucose levels of approximately 50 mg/100 ml.

FIG 19–13. Effect of insulin and subsequent glucose administration on the adrenal medullary secretion of epinephrine and norepinephrine in the dog. Catecholamine output from one adrenal was measured by cannulating the adrenal vein. (Reproduced, with permission, from Goldfien & others: The effect of hypoglycemia on the adrenal secretion of epinephrine and norepinephrine in the dog. Endocrinology 62:749, 1958.)

Compensatory Mechanisms

The increase in adrenal medullary secretion is accompanied by increased adrenocortical secretion, and both tend to compensate for the hypoglycemia: the epinephrine by causing glycogenolysis with consequent liberation of glucose from the liver, and the glucocorticoids by increasing gluconeogenesis and by their anti-insulin action. Insulin tolerance is significantly reduced in animals depleted of catecholamines by drug treatment. A decline in blood glucose also stimulates glucagon secretion, increasing gluconeogenesis and glycogenolysis. The blood glucose fall produced by insulin is more pronounced in fasting animals than in fed animals with abundant liver glycogen reserves. Finally, growth hormone secretion is also increased, and, by decreasing glucose utilization in peripheral tissues, the growth hormone helps to make more glucose available to the brain.

MECHANISM OF ACTION OF INSULIN

There is an appealing parsimony to the concept that insulin has a single action that underlies all its diverse effects on metabolism. However, at least 5 of the different actions mentioned above cannot be causally related to one another at this time: (1) The increase in the entry of glucose into muscle and certain other tissues (Table 19–2). (2) The inhibition of the hormone-sensitive lipase in adipose tissue. (3) The stimulation of protein synthesis, an effect that can occur in the absence of extracellular glucose. (4) The increase in the transport of amino acids into cells.

(5) The increase in the membrane potential of the cells in skeletal muscle and adipose tissue. Insulin may also have additional effects on the liver. However, much of what happens in diabetes can be explained by decreased entry of glucose into muscle.

An effect of insulin on the entry of sugars into cells is indicated by the observation that in hepatectomized nephrectomized animals the volume of distribution of galactose and several other sugars with similar structure is increased by insulin (Fig 19–14). In the absence of the liver and the kidneys, these sugars are not metabolized or excreted. Since their volume of distribution after insulin is greater than the ECF space, the sugars must have entered cells. Similar effects on the distribution of glucose can be demonstrated (Fig 19–15).

In the tissues in which insulin increases glucose uptake, it facilitates the entry of glucose into the cells by an action on the cell membranes. The rate of phosphorylation of the glucose, once it has entered the cells, is apparently controlled by other hormones. Growth hormone and cortisol both have been reported to inhibit phosphorylation in certain tissues. However, the process is normally so rapid that it is a rate-limiting step in glucose metabolism only when the rate of glucose entry is high.

Because of the rapid phosphorylation, the intracellular free glucose concentration is normally low and the concentration gradient for glucose is directed inward. Some glucose moves down this gradient into cells in the absence of insulin, but insulin greatly increases the rate of movement in a selective fashion. A carrier of some sort is probably involved because the process shows the saturation kinetics characteristic of a system in which there is limited availability of a specific carrier. It is thus an example of **facilitated diffusion**. The process is highly specific, being limited

FIG 19–14. The capacity of insulin to increase the volume of distribution of galactose. The sugar was infused in hepatectomized nephrectomized dogs, and the changes in its blood level followed. (Redrawn and reproduced, with permission, from Goldstein & others: Action of insulin on transfer of sugars across cell barriers. Am J Physiol 173:207, 1953.)

FIG 19–15. Volume of distribution of glucose in the perfused normal rat heart as a function of the glucose concentration in the perfusing medium. The horizontal bar indicates the size of the extracellular space. SEM = standard error of the mean. (Redrawn and reproduced, with permission, from Morgan & others: Regulation of glucose uptake in heart muscle from normal and alloxan-diabetic rats. Ann New York Acad Sci 82:387, 1959.)

for the most part to glucose and a few other sugars with the same configuration in the first 3 carbon atoms; furthermore, these sugars compete with one another for transport. Even though glucose transport does not involve movement against a concentration gradient, it is more sensitive to temperature changes than passive diffusion.

The effect of insulin on the liver is a facilitation of glycogen synthesis and a decrease in glucose output. Glycogen synthetase activity and glucokinase activity are increased, although it has not been proved that these increases are directly due to insulin.

REGULATION OF INSULIN SECRETION

Insulin secretion is now known to be influenced by a variety of stimulatory and inhibitory factors (Table 19–4). However, many of these factors are either substances related to glucose metabolism or agents that affect cyclic AMP. Normal secretion requires the presence of adequate quantities of calcium and potassium ions.

Effect of the Blood Glucose Level

The major control of insulin secretion is exerted by a feedback effect of the blood glucose level directly on the pancreas. Glucose penetrates the islets readily, and its rate of entrance is unaffected by insulin. When the level of glucose in the blood perfusing the pancreas is elevated (above 110 mg/100 ml in the rat), insulin secretion in the pancreatic venous blood is increased; when the level is normal or low, the rate of insulin secretion is low. Mannose also stimulates insulin secretion. Fructose has a moderate stimulatory effect, but it

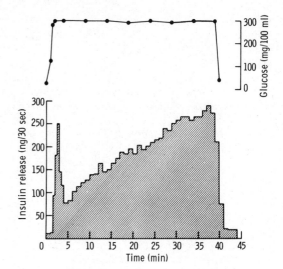

FIG 19–16. Insulin secretion from perfused rat pancreas in response to sustained glucose infusion. Values are means of 3 preparations. The top record shows the glucose concentration in the effluent perfusion mixture. (Reproduced, with permission, from Curry & others: Dynamics of insulin secretion by the perfused rat pancreas. Endocrinology 83:572, 1968.)

is converted intracellularly into glucose. Although the entry of galactose, D-xylose, and L-arabinose into cells is facilitated by insulin, these sugars do not stimulate insulin secretion. Neither do a variety of citric acid cycle intermediates and nonmetabolizable sugars. However, the stimulatory effect of glucose depends on its metabolism, since 2-deoxyglucose and mannoheptulose, agents that prevent glucose from being metabolized, also inhibit insulin secretion.

The action of glucose on insulin secretion in animals is biphasic (Fig 19–16); there is a rapid increase in secretion followed by a more slowly developing prolonged response. The former is inhibited by agents such as propranolol, which blocks β receptor-mediated increases in cyclic AMP formation. The latter is inhibited by inhibitors of protein synthesis. There is a similar biphasic response to glucose in humans.

The feedback control of blood glucose on insulin secretion normally operates with great precision, so that blood glucose and blood insulin levels parallel each other with remarkable consistency.

Protein & Fat Derivatives

Arginine, leucine, and certain other amino acids stimulate insulin secretion, and so do β-keto acids such as acetoacetic acid. The mechanisms by which the stimulation is produced are unknown. However, it is worth noting that insulin stimulates the incorporation of amino acids into proteins and combats the fat catabolism that produces the β-keto acids.

TABLE 19–4. Factors affecting insulin secretion.*

Stimulators	Inhibitors
Glucose	2-Deoxyglucose
Mannose	Mannoheptulose
Amino acids (leucine, arginine, others)	a-Adrenergic stimulating agents (norepinephrine, epinephrine)
β-Keto acids	
β-Adrenergic stimulating agents	β-Adrenergic blocking agents (propranolol)
Glucagon	Diazoxide
Cyclic AMP	Thiazide diuretics
Theophylline	Diphenylhydantoin
Sulfonylureas	
Stimulation of the right vagus	
Intestinal hormones (gastrin, secretin, CCK, GLI, others?)	

*Modified from Levine: Mechanism of insulin secretion. New England J Med 283:522, 1970.

Insulin Secretion & Cyclic AMP

Epinephrine and norepinephrine inhibit insulin secretion by a direct action on the pancreas. The inhibitory effect of epinephrine is blocked by drugs that block *a*-adrenergic receptors but not by drugs that block *β*-adrenergic receptors. Evidence is accumulating that *a*-adrenergic stimulating agents such as epinephrine and norepinephrine inhibit cyclic AMP. On the other hand, *β*-stimulating drugs stimulate insulin secretion. So does theophylline, which inhibits the phosphodiesterase that catalyzes the breakdown of cyclic AMP (see Chapter 17).

Oral Hypoglycemic Agents

Tolbutamide and other sulfonylurea derivatives (Fig 19–17) lower the blood glucose level, but only when a functioning pancreas is present. They act by stimulating the secretion of insulin, and there is some evidence that they do this by inhibiting phosphodiesterase, thus increasing the amount of cyclic AMP in *β* cells. It has also been claimed that they reduce glucagon secretion. Phenformin and the other biguanide oral hypoglycemic agents do not affect insulin secretion but increase glucose utilization, apparently because they inhibit oxidative reactions in the mitochondria.

Effect of the Vagus

Branches of the right vagus nerve innervate the pancreatic islets, and stimulation of the right vagus causes increased insulin secretion. However, the physiologic role, if any, of this neural pathway is uncertain.

CH_3—⬡—SO_2—NH—CO—NH—$(CH_2)_3$—CH_3

Tolbutamide

Cl—⬡—SO_2—NH—CO—NH—$(CH_2)_2$—CH_3

Chlorpropamide

⬡—$(CH_2)_2$—NH—$\overset{\overset{NH}{\|}}{C}$—NH—$\overset{\overset{NH}{\|}}{C}$—$NH_2$

Phenformin (phenethylbiguanide, DBI)

FIG 19–17. Commonly used oral hypoglycemic agents. Tolbutamide and chlorpropamide are sulfonylureas which stimulate endogenous insulin secretion. Phenformin and other biguanides act on the tissues to increase glucose utilization.

Intestinal Hormones

It has been clearly demonstrated that orally administered glucose exerts a greater insulin stimulating effect than intravenously administered glucose. This observation led to investigation of the possibility that a substance secreted by the gastrointestinal mucosa stimulated insulin secretion, and it has been claimed that secretin, CCK, gastrin, and glucagon all have such an action. The release of a substance that resembles glucagon (GLI) from the intestinal mucosa is discussed below. There is also evidence that other as yet unidentified "gut factors" stimulate insulin secretion. There is uncertainty about which factor is involved under physiologic conditions, but it does seem clear that insulin secretion is stimulated by an endocrine factor or factors released from the mucosa of the gastrointestinal tract by food reaching the stomach and small intestine.

Inhibitory Effect of Other Drugs

The drug diazoxide, which was originally developed for the treatment of hypertension, has been found to be diabetogenic, and it appears to exert this effect by inhibiting insulin secretion. A number of other drugs that inhibit insulin secretion have been reported, and in some individuals the commonly used thiazide diuretics may exert an inhibitory effect.

Long-Term Changes in *β* Cell Responses

The magnitude of the insulin response to a given stimulus is determined in part by the past secretory history of the *β* cells. Individuals fed a high-carbohydrate diet for several weeks not only have higher fasting plasma insulin levels but also show a greater secretory response to a glucose load than individuals fed an isocaloric low-carbohydrate diet.

Although the *β* cells respond to stimulation with hypertrophy like other endocrine cells, they become exhausted and stop secreting (*β* cell exhaustion) when the stimulation is marked or prolonged. With such stimulation, they become vacuolated and hyalinized (hydropic and hyaline degeneration). If the stimulation stops soon after the cells stop secreting, they can recover; but if it is continued the cells eventually die and disappear. In spite of some claims to the contrary, there is no convincing evidence that such "exhaustion atrophy" occurs in any other endocrine gland.

The pancreatic reserve is large, and it is difficult to produce *β* cell exhaustion in normal animals; but if the pancreatic reserve is reduced by partial pancreatectomy or small doses of alloxan, exhaustion of the remaining *β* cells can be produced by any procedure that chronically raises the blood glucose level. This is the cause of the diabetes produced in animals with limited pancreatic reserves by anterior pituitary extracts, growth hormone, thyroxine, or the prolonged continuous infusion of glucose alone. In rare instances, prolonged ingestion of a high-carbohydrate diet has been reported to cause hyperglycemia with glycosuria, dehydration, and coma in humans. The diabetes precipitated by hormones in animals is at first reversible, but with prolonged treatment it becomes permanent. The diabetes is usually named for the agent producing it, eg, "hypophysial diabetes," "thyroid diabetes." Permanent diabetes persisting after treatment has been discontinued is indicated by the prefix meta-, eg, "metahypophysial diabetes" or "metathyroid diabetes." When insulin is administered along with the diabetogenic hormones, the β cells are protected, probably because the blood glucose is lowered, and diabetes does not develop. Adrenal glucocorticoids raise the blood glucose level, but it has proved difficult to produce permanent diabetes in animals with adrenal steroid treatment alone. Exhaustion atrophy of the remaining β cells in diabetes treated with sulfonylureas has not been a problem; indeed, it has been claimed that these drugs induce islet cell hypergranulation and hypertrophy when administered for prolonged periods.

Effect of Exogenous Insulin

When insulin alone is administered to normal animals, the insulin content of the pancreas drops; but when treatment is stopped, the β cells are hyperresponsive, as if they had been "rested." This is probably the explanation of why, when many juvenile diabetics are first treated with insulin, their insulin requirement decreases as their condition improves. Sometimes it falls to zero and the diabetes "disappears" for some time, although it always reappears later on.

Measurement of Insulin in Body Fluids

There is hope that chemical methods may soon be developed for measuring protein hormones in body fluids, but none are available as yet for insulin. Insulin-like activity (ILA) in plasma has been bioassayed by comparing the effects of plasma samples with those of known amounts of insulin on a variety of physiologic parameters. These bioassays have now been replaced by insulin immunoassay. **Immunoassays** have come into extremely widespread use in the measurement of protein and polypeptide hormones. They depend on interference by unlabeled hormones with the binding of radioactivity-labeled hormones to antibodies. Immunoassays of nonprotein substances such as steroids have also been developed, using antibodies produced by injecting the substances bound to proteins.

The ILA values in plasma are generally higher than the values determined by immunoassay, and a significant ILA titer persists after pancreatectomy, so that factors other than insulin definitely contribute to the observed values. The more specific immunoassay gives values in the peripheral venous plasma of fasting normal humans of $0-70 \mu U/ml$. The amount of insulin secreted per day in a normal human has been calculated to be about 40 units.

GLUCAGON

Chemistry & Action

Human glucagon is a linear polypeptide with a molecular weight of 3485. It contains 29 amino acids (Fig 19–18) and has the same structure as porcine glucagon. However, bovine and porcine glucagon provoke the formation of antiglucagon antibodies in rabbits. These antibodies have been used to measure glucagon in dogs and humans.

A substance that cross-reacts with antiglucagon antibodies but is probably not identical with pancreatic glucagon is found in the walls of the duodenum and stomach. This material is secreted from the gastrointestinal tract into the circulation when glucose is placed in the intestinal lumen. It has been called glucagon-like immunoreactive factor (GLI). Both GLI and glucagon stimulate insulin secretion, so release of GLI into the circulation from the intestine may play a role in the increased insulin secretion produced by ingested glucose.

Glucagon raises the blood glucose level because it stimulates adenyl cyclase in the liver, leading to the activation of phosphorylase, and therefore to increased hepatic glycogenolysis. Glucagon also increases gluconeogenesis from available amino acids in the liver and elevates the metabolic rate. Its lipolytic activity is discussed in Chapter 17. The calorigenic action of glucagon is not due to the hyperglycemia per se but is probably due to the increased hepatic deamination of amino acids, with thyroid hormones stimulating the utilization of the deaminated residues. The calorigenic action requires the presence of thyroid and adrenocortical hormones, and fails to occur in their absence.

Glucagon exerts a positively inotropic effect on the heart (see Chapter 29) without producing increased myocardial irritability, and its use in the treatment of heart disease has been advocated.

Metabolism

Exogenous glucagon has a shorter half-life than insulin, disappearing from the circulation in a matter of minutes. It competes with insulin for degradation in vitro. A large proportion of the endogenously secreted glucagon is bound in the liver. Beef liver contains an enzyme which degrades glucagon by splitting off histidyl-serine from the N-terminal end of the glucagon molecule.

Secretion

Secretion of pancreatic glucagon is decreased by a rise in plasma glucose. In this respect it differs from GLI, the secretion of which is stimulated by glucose in the intestine. Glucagon secretion is increased during

His-Ser-Gln-Gly-Thr-Phe-Thr-Ser-Asp-Tyr-Ser-Lys-Tyr-Leu-Asp-Ser-Arg-Arg-Ala-Gln-Asp-Phe-Val-Gln-Trp-Leu-Met-Asn-Thr
 1   2   3   4   5   6   7   8   9 10 11 12 13 14 15 16 17 18 19 20 21 22 23 24 25 26 27 28 29

FIG 19–18. Human glucagon.

fasting, and it appears to mediate, at least in part, the increase in gluconeogenesis during fasting. Adrenocortical hormones play a permissive role in this response. Ingested protein and infusions of amino acids such as arginine also increase the secretion of glucagon. It has been suggested that the increase is appropriate since amino acids also increase insulin secretion, and a concomitant rise in glucagon secretion following a protein meal must help prevent the hypoglycemia that the insulin would otherwise produce. Glucagon secretion is also increased during exercise and may be decreased by sulfonylureas.

Insulin-Glucagon Molar Ratios

As noted above, insulin is glycogenic, antigluconeogenetic, and antilipolytic in its actions. It thus favors storage of absorbed nutrients and is a "hormone of energy storage." Glucagon, on the other hand, is glycogenolytic, gluconeogenetic, and lipolytic. It mobilizes energy stores and is a "hormone of energy release." Because of their opposite effects, the blood levels of both hormones must be considered in any given situation. It is convenient to think in terms of their molar ratios. The insulin-glucagon molar ratio in any given blood specimen can readily be calculated from the blood levels of the hormones, as determined by immunoassays, and their molecular weights.

It has been shown that the insulin-glucagon molar ratios fluctuate markedly because the secretion of glucagon and insulin are both modified by the conditions that preceded the application of any given stimulus. Thus, for example, the insulin-glucagon molar ratio on a balanced diet is approximately 2.3. An infusion of arginine increases the secretion of both hormones and raises the ratio to 3.0. After 3 days of starvation, the ratio falls to 0.4, and an infusion of arginine in this state lowers the ratio to 0.3. Conversely, the ratio is 25 in individuals receiving a constant infusion of glucose, and ingestion of a protein meal during the infusion causes the ratio to rise to 170. The rise is due to the fact that insulin secretion rises sharply, while the usual glucagon response to a protein meal is abolished. Thus, when energy is needed during starvation, the insulin-glucagon molar ratio is low, favoring glycogen breakdown and gluconeogenesis; conversely, when the need for energy mobilization is low, the ratio is high, favoring the deposition of glycogen, protein, and fat. However, the mechanisms that bring about these teleologically advantageous shifts in insulin and glucagon secretion are only partially understood and await further research.

Relation to Diabetes

Prolonged treatment with glucagon can produce β cell exhaustion in animals with diminished pancreatic reserves. The amount of insulin necessary to control hyperglycemia in an alloxan-diabetic animal is decreased if the pancreas is removed surgically. Alloxan kills the β cells but leaves the a cells unharmed. A partially pancreatectomized animal in which the hyperglycemia has caused β cell exhaustion

also requires more insulin than a totally pancreatectomized animal. The diabetes in patients who have had total pancreatectomies for carcinoma of the bile duct or pancreas is usually relatively mild. Fasting glucagon levels are normal in diabetes, but diabetics have higher blood sugars. At any given blood sugar level, glucagon levels in diabetics are higher than they are in nondiabetics. Furthermore, glucose fails to suppress glucagon secretion in diabetics while protein has its normal stimulating effect. Thus, there is a relative hyperglucagonemia in diabetes that contributes to the hyperglycemia. However, the question of whether glucagon has a more fundamental role in the pathogenesis of the disease is unanswered.

ENDOCRINE REGULATION OF CARBOHYDRATE METABOLISM

Many hormones other than insulin and glucagon have important roles in the regulation of carbohydrate metabolism. The other functions of these hormones are considered elsewhere, but it seems wise to summarize their effects on carbohydrate metabolism in the context of the present chapter.

Estrogens have a slight antidiabetogenic action in some species, but the major hormones, in addition to insulin and glucagon, that exert regulatory effects on carbohydrate metabolism are epinephrine, thyroid hormones, glucocorticoids, and growth hormone. The "directional flow valves" in metabolism at which these hormones act are discussed in Chapter 17.

Epinephrine

The activation of phosphorylase in liver and muscle by epinephrine is discussed in Chapter 17. Norepinephrine has much less effect. Hepatic glucose output is increased, producing hyperglycemia. In muscle, the glucose-6-phosphate formed can only be catabolized to pyruvate because of the absence of glucose-6-phosphatase. For reasons that are not entirely clear, large amounts of pyruvate are converted to lactic acid, which diffuses from the muscle into the circulation (Fig 19–19). The lactic acid is oxidized in the liver to pyruvic acid and converted to glycogen, so the response to epinephrine is an initial glycogenolysis followed by a rise in hepatic glycogen content. Lactic acid oxidation may be responsible for the calorigenic effect of epinephrine (see Chapter 20). Epinephrine also liberates fatty acids into the circulation.

Adrenal medullary tumors (pheochromocytomas) which secrete epinephrine cause hyperglycemia, glycosuria, and an elevated metabolic rate. However, the hyperglycemic effect of epinephrine is generally too transient to produce permanent diabetes, and the metabolic abnormalities disappear as soon as the tumors are removed.

FIG 19–19. Effect of epinephrine on tissue glycogen, blood glucose, and blood lactate levels in fed rats. (After Cori & Russell, in: *Physiology and Biophysics*, 19th ed. Ruch TC, Patton HD [editors]. Saunders, 1965.)

Thyroid Hormones

Thyroxine and triiodothyronine make experimental diabetes worse; thyrotoxicosis aggravates clinical diabetes; and metathyroid diabetes can be produced in animals with decreased pancreatic reserve. The principal diabetogenic effect of thyroid hormones is to increase absorption of glucose from the intestine, but the hormones also cause (probably through liberation of epinephrine) some degree of hepatic glycogen depletion. Glycogen-depleted liver cells are easily damaged. When the liver is damaged, the glucose tolerance curve is diabetic because the liver takes up less of the absorbed glucose. Thyroid hormones may also accelerate the degradation of insulin. All these actions have a hyperglycemic effect and, if the pancreatic reserve is low, may lead to β cell exhaustion.

Adrenal Glucocorticoids

The 17-hydroxycorticoids secreted by the adrenal cortex (see Chapter 20) elevate the blood glucose and produce a diabetic type of glucose tolerance curve. In humans this effect may occur only in individuals with a genetic predisposition to diabetes. Glucose tolerance is reduced in 80% of patients with Cushing's syndrome (see Chapter 20), and 20% of these patients have frank diabetes. The permissive action of the glucocorticoids in the maintenance of the blood glucose during fasting has been mentioned in the section on glucagon. In adrenal insufficiency the blood glucose is normal as long as food intake is maintained, but fasting precipitates hypoglycemia and collapse (Table 19–5). The blood glucose-lowering effect of insulin is greatly enhanced in patients with adrenal insufficiency. In animals with experimental diabetes, adrenalectomy markedly ameliorates the diabetes.

The complex actions of the glucocorticoids on intermediary metabolism are incompletely understood. Known or suspected actions which affect carbohydrate metabolism are summarized in Table 19–6. The major diabetogenic effects are an increase in protein catab-olism with increased gluconeogenesis in the liver; increased hepatic glycogenesis and ketogenesis; and a decrease in peripheral glucose utilization that may be due to inhibition of glucose phosphorylation (see below).

Growth Hormone

The diabetogenic effect of anterior pituitary extracts is due in part to the ACTH and TSH they contain, but it is also due to growth hormone. There is some species variation in the diabetogenicity of growth

TABLE 19–5. Effect of fasting on blood glucose levels in a patient with Addison's disease. When untreated, the patient developed symptoms of hypoglycemia at the time the 20-hour blood was drawn.*

	Blood Glucose (mg/100 ml) at Various Times After Start of Fast		
	15 hours	20 hours	24 hours
Untreated	60	43	. . .
During glucocorticoid treatment	70	69	66

*Data from Forsham & others: Am J Med 1:105, 1946.

TABLE 19–6. Actions of glucocorticoids which have a diabetogenic effect. Items 1–6 represent a possible sequence of reactions leading to an elevated blood glucose due to increased gluconeogenesis.*

1. Increased protein catabolism in liver and periphery
2. Increased hepatic uptake ("trapping") of amino acids
3. Increased deamination and transamination of amino acids in the liver
4. Increased hepatic CO_2 fixation, converting oxaloacetic acid to phosphopyruvic acid
5. Increased hepatic fructose diphosphatase activity, facilitating dephosphorylation of fructose-1,6-diphosphate
6. Increased hepatic glucose-6-phosphatase activity, releasing more glucose into the circulation
7. Decrease in glucose utilization peripherally and in the liver, possibly due to inhibition of phosphorylation
8. Increased blood lactate and pyruvate
9. Decreased hepatic lipogenesis
10. Increased plasma free fatty acid levels and increased ketone formation (when pancreatic reserve is low)
11. Presence necessary (permissive action) for growth hormone stimulation of plasma level of anti-insulin proteins

*Modified from Thorn & others: Diabetes 8:337, 1959.

hormone; but human growth hormone makes clinical diabetes worse, and 25% of patients with growth hormone-secreting tumors of the anterior pituitary have diabetes. In experimental animals and in man, hypophysectomy ameliorates diabetes and increases sensitivity to insulin even more than adrenalectomy; in man, growth hormone treatment has been shown to decrease sensitivity to insulin.

Growth hormone mobilizes free fatty acids from adipose tissue, thus favoring ketogenesis. It decreases glucose uptake into some tissues ("anti-insulin action"), increases hepatic glucose output, and may decrease tissue binding of insulin. Indeed, it has been suggested that the ketosis and decreased glucose tolerance produced by starvation are due to hypersecretion of growth hormone. Growth hormone does not stimulate insulin secretion directly, but the hyperglycemia it produces secondarily stimulates the pancreas and may eventually exhaust the β cells.

There is evidence that growth hormone and glucocorticoids affect the phosphorylation of glucose rather than its entry into cells. Glucocorticoids and growth hormone inhibit phosphorylation, whereas adrenalectomy and hypophysectomy accelerate it.

FIG 19–20. Typical glucose tolerance curves after an oral glucose load in liver disease and in conditions causing excessively rapid absorption of glucose from the intestine. Horizontal line is approximate blood glucose level at which hypoglycemic symptoms appear.

HYPOGLYCEMIA & DIABETES MELLITUS IN MAN

Hypoglycemia

"Insulin reactions" are common in juvenile diabetics, and in many diabetics occasional hypoglycemic episodes are the price of good diabetic control. The increase in the glucose uptake of skeletal muscle independently of insulin during exercise has been mentioned above. Diabetics taking insulin should be taught to anticipate this effect by adjusting their diet or insulin dose when they exercise.

Symptomatic hypoglycemia also occurs in nondiabetics, and a review of some of the more important causes serves to emphasize the variables affecting blood glucose homeostasis. Chronic mild hypoglycemia can cause incoordination and slurred speech, and the condition can be mistaken for drunkenness. Mental aberrations and convulsions in the absence of frank coma also occur. When the level of insulin secretion is chronically elevated due to an insulin-secreting tumor (**insulinoma**) or hyperplasia of the β cells, symptoms are most common in the morning, ie, after a night of fasting has depleted hepatic glycogen reserves. However, symptoms can develop at any time, and in such patients the diagnosis is often missed. Some cases of insulinoma have been erroneously diagnosed as epilepsy or psychosis. Hypoglycemia also occurs in some patients with large malignant tumors, and some of these tumors apparently secrete an insulin-like substance. In liver disease, the glucose tolerance curve is diabetic but the fasting blood glucose level is low (Fig 19–20). In **functional hypoglycemia**, the blood

glucose rise is normal after a test dose of glucose but the subsequent fall overshoots to hypoglycemic levels, producing symptoms 3–4 hours after meals. This pattern is sometimes seen in individuals who later develop diabetes. Most patients with this syndrome are tense, conscientious people with symptoms of autonomic overactivity. It has been postulated that the overshoot of the blood glucose is due to insulin secretion stimulated by impulses in the right vagus, but cholinergic blocking agents do not routinely correct the abnormality. In some thyrotoxic patients, and in patients who have had gastrectomies or other operations that speed the passage of food into the intestine, glucose absorption is abnormally rapid. The blood glucose rises to a high, early peak, but it then falls rapidly to hypoglycemic levels because the wave of hyperglycemia evokes a greater than normal rise in insulin secretion. Symptoms characteristically occur about 2 hours after meals.

Diabetes Mellitus

Spontaneously occurring diabetes is much more common in man than in other species. The evidence is clear that a predisposition to diabetes is inherited, and, although the genetic factors involved are complex, the inheritance resembles that of an autosomal recessive trait. Over 20% of the relatives of diabetic patients have abnormal glucose tolerance curves, compared to less than 1% of those without a family history of the disease. For unknown reasons, women who have the genetic predisposition to diabetes but no clinical evidence of the disease often have large babies. Many of these women subsequently develop overt diabetes.

It is generally stated that there are 2 types of diabetes in man. The type that has its onset in childhood or adolescence (**juvenile diabetes**) is often severe and is frequently complicated by ketoacidosis. The diabetes that develops late in life (**maturity onset diabetes**) is mild, and ketoacidosis is rare. Maturity onset diabetes occurs much more frequently in obese people, and weight reduction improves glucose tolerance. In juvenile diabetes, β cell pathology is common and the pancreatic insulin content is low, whereas in maturity onset diabetes the insulin content and β cell morphology are usually normal. However, these differences may be more apparent than real, because juvenile diabetics who die soon after the onset of their disease have a normal pancreatic insulin content and little evidence of β cell exhaustion. Since the sulfonylurea derivative oral hypoglycemic drugs apparently act by discharging endogenous insulin (see above), they would be expected to be clinically efficacious only in maturity onset diabetes and early juvenile diabetes, while there is still some insulin in the pancreas. This expectation has been borne out in clinical experience.

Diabetes used to be regarded as a disease of carbohydrate and fat metabolism which was complicated by accelerated arteriosclerosis and other blood vessel abnormalities, and it was argued that meticulous control of the disease with insulin and diet delayed or even prevented these vascular complications. This concept is no longer tenable; the onset and progression of the vascular disease is largely independent of the degree of diabetic control, although uncontrolled diabetes may intensify the vascular disease and good control is desirable to prevent the other complications of the disease. Indeed, diabetes is now viewed as a congenital disease in which disordered carbohydrate metabolism is a relatively late development. According to this view, diabetes can be divided into 4 stages: (1) **prediabetes**, the condition present from birth—or, actually, from conception—in which there are no readily detectable chemical abnormalities but in which changes in the basement membranes in some tissues can be detected; (2) **chemical diabetes**, in which symptoms are absent but the glucose tolerance test is diabetic in type; (3) **overt diabetes**, in which the classical, full-fledged syndrome of clinical diabetes is present; and (4) **chronic diabetes**, in which the effects of the vascular lesions as well as the diabetes are clinically manifest.

The cause of clinical diabetes is always insulin deficiency, but this deficiency may be relative rather than absolute. Insulin levels are elevated in patients with diabetes and acromegaly due to hypersecretion of growth hormone, and in Cushing's syndrome due to hypersecretion of adrenal glucocorticoids. However, the circulating growth hormone and glucocorticoid levels are generally normal in diabetes. In many patients with early maturity onset diabetes, fasting insulin levels are elevated and there is an exaggerated, prolonged increase in insulin levels following the administration of glucose. However, most patients with maturity onset diabetes are obese, and obese nondiabetic individuals also have elevated insulin levels and an exaggerated response to glucose. Obese subjects are resistant to the action of insulin, and have elevated plasma amino acid levels that may contribute to the hyperinsulinemia. Although there continues to be debate on the point, it now appears that, when obese diabetics are compared to obese subjects without diabetes and nonobese diabetics to nonobese normal subjects, the insulin levels in the diabetics are subnormal. Therefore, the presence of a circulating insulin antagonist seems unlikely, at least as a primary pathogenetic abnormality. The insulin levels in juvenile diabetes are usually low. Among the other possible causes of diabetes are abnormal storage or release of insulin, secretion of an abnormal insulin of some sort, or abnormal polymerization or binding of the insulin in the circulation. In prediabetes the initial phase of the biphasic increase in insulin secretion produced by glucose (see above) is deficient. This may be the defect that is inherited and later leads to overt diabetes.

The dose of insulin required to control the diabetes varies from patient to patient and from time to time in the same patient. The factors affecting insulin requirements are those which, as discussed in previous sections of this chapter, influence glucose tolerance. Thus, insulin requirements rise when patients gain weight; when they secrete or receive increased amounts of glucocorticoids and other hormones that are diabetogenic; during pregnancy; and in the presence of infection and fever. They fall when patients lose weight and during exercise.

20...

The Adrenal Medulla & Adrenal Cortex

There are 2 endocrine organs in the adrenal gland, one surrounding the other. The inner **adrenal medulla** (Fig 20–1) secretes the catecholamines, **epinephrine** and **norepinephrine**; the outer **adrenal cortex** secretes steroid hormones.

The adrenal medulla is in effect a sympathetic ganglion in which the postganglionic neurons have lost their axons and become secretory cells. The cells secrete when stimulated by the preganglionic nerve fibers that reach the gland via the splanchnic nerves. Adrenal medullary hormones are not essential for life, but they help to prepare the individual to deal with emergencies.

The adrenal cortex secretes **glucocorticoids,** steroids with widespread effects on the metabolism of carbohydrate and protein; a **mineralocorticoid** which is essential to the maintenance of sodium balance and ECF volume; and **sex hormones** which exert minor effects on reproductive function. Unless mineralocorticoid and glucocorticoid replacement therapy is administered postoperatively, adrenalectomy is followed by collapse and death. Adrenocortical secretion is controlled primarily by ACTH from the anterior pituitary, but mineralocorticoid secretion is also subject to independent control by circulating factors of which the most important is angiotensin II, a polypeptide formed in the blood stream. The formation of angiotensin is in turn dependent on renin, which is secreted by the kidney.

ADRENAL MORPHOLOGY

The adrenal medulla is made up of interlacing cords of densely innervated granule-containing cells which abut on venous sinuses. Two cell types can be distinguished morphologically, one of which secretes epinephrine and the other norepinephrine. **Paraganglia,** small groups of cells resembling those in the adrenal medulla, are found near the thoracic and abdominal sympathetic ganglia (Fig 20–1).

In adult mammals, the adrenal cortex is divided into 3 zones of variable distinctness. The outer **zona glomerulosa** is made up of whorls of large cells which rest on the columns of cells that form the **zona**

fasciculata. The columns are separated by venous sinuses. The inner portion of the zona fasciculata merges into the **zona reticularis,** where the cell columns become interlaced in a network. The cells contain abundant lipid, especially in the outer portion of the zona fasciculata. All 3 cortical zones secrete corticosterone (see below), but the enzymatic mechanism for aldosterone biosynthesis is limited to the zona glomerulosa, while the enzymatic mechanism for forming cortisol and sex hormones is found in the inner 2 zones.

Arterial blood reaches the adrenal from many small branches of the phrenic and renal arteries and the aorta. From a plexus in the capsule, blood flows to the

FIG 20–1. Human adrenal glands. Adrenocortical tissue is stippled; adrenal medullary tissue is black. Note location of adrenals at superior pole of each kidney. Also shown are extra-adrenal sites at which cortical and medullary tissue is sometimes found. (Reproduced, with permission, from Forsham, in: *Textbook of Endocrinology*, 4th ed. Williams RH [editor]. Saunders, 1968.)

sinusoids of the medulla. The medulla is also supplied by a few arterioles that pass directly to it from the capsule. In most species, including man, there is a single large adrenal vein. The blood flow through the adrenal is large, as it is in most endocrine glands.

During fetal life in the human, the adrenal is large and under pituitary control, but the 3 zones of the permanent cortex represent only 20% of the gland. The remaining 80% is the large **fetal adrenal cortex,** which undergoes rapid degeneration at the time of birth. A major function of this fetal adrenal is secretion of sulfate conjugates of androgens which are converted in the placenta to active androgens and estrogens that enter the maternal circulation. There is no structure comparable to the fetal adrenal in laboratory animals. In the mouse, cat, rabbit, and female hamster, there is a layer of cortical cells called the **X zone** between the zona reticularis and the medulla. This zone is maintained by pituitary gonadotropins, and it degenerates when androgen secretion increases during puberty in the male and during the first pregnancy in the female.

An important function of the zona glomerulosa, in addition to aldosterone biosynthesis, is the formation of new cortical cells. Like other tissues of neural origin, the adrenal medulla does not regenerate; but when the inner 2 zones of the cortex are removed a new zona fasciculata and zona reticularis regenerate from glomerular cells attached to the capsule. Small capsular remnants will regrow large pieces of adrenocortical tissue. After hypophysectomy, the zona fasciculata and zona reticularis atrophy, while the zona glomerulosa is unchanged (Fig 20–2), probably as a result of the action of nonpituitary factors on aldosterone biosynthesis. However, in long-standing hypo-

FIG 20–3. Diagrammatic representation of the cytologic features of steroid-secreting cells. Note the abundant agranular endoplasmic reticulum, the pleomorphic mitochondria, and the lipid droplets. (Reproduced, with permission, from Fawcett, Long, & Jones: The ultrastructure of endocrine glands. Recent Progr Hormone Res 25:315, 1969.)

pituitarism, degenerative changes also appear in the zona glomerulosa. In hypopituitarism the ability to conserve Na^+ is usually normal, but in patients who have had the disease for a long time aldosterone deficiency may develop. Injections of ACTH and stimuli which cause endogenous ACTH secretion produce hypertrophy of the zona fasciculata and zona reticularis but do not increase the size of the zona glomerulosa.

The cells of the adrenal cortex contain large amounts of smooth endoplasmic reticulum, which seems to be involved in the steroid-forming process. Other steps in steroid biosynthesis occur in the mitochondria. The structure of steroid-secreting cells is very similar throughout the body. The typical features of such cells are shown in Fig 20–3.

FIG 20–2. Effect of hypophysectomy on the morphology of the adrenal cortex of the dog. Note that the atrophy does not involve the zona glomerulosa. The morphology of the human adrenal is similar.

ADRENAL MEDULLA

STRUCTURE & FUNCTION OF MEDULLARY HORMONES

Biosynthesis, Metabolism, & Excretion

Norepinephrine and epinephrine are both secreted by the adrenal medulla. Cats and some other species secrete mainly norepinephrine, but in the dog and man 80% of the catecholamine output in the adrenal vein is epinephrine. Norepinephrine also enters the circulation from adrenergic nerve endings.

The details of the biosynthesis and catabolism of norepinephrine and epinephrine are described in Chapter 13 and summarized in Figs 13–3 and 13–5. Norepinephrine is formed by hydroxylation and decarboxylation of tyrosine, and epinephrine by the methylation of norepinephrine. Phenylethanolamine-N-methyltransferase (PNMT), the enzyme that catalyzes the formation of epinephrine from norepinephrine, is found in appreciable quantities only in the adrenal medulla. The normal human plasma norepinephrine level of 0.2 ng/ml is generally unchanged after adrenalectomy, but the epinephrine level, which is normally about 0.05 ng/ml, falls to essentially zero. The epinephrine found in tissues other than the adrenal medulla and the brain is for the most part absorbed from the blood stream rather than synthesized in situ.

In the medulla, the amines are stored in granules bound to ATP and protein. Their secretion is initiated by acetylcholine released from the preganglionic neurons that innervate the secretory cells. The acetylcholine increases the permeability of the cells, and the Ca^{++} which enters the cells from the ECF triggers exocytosis (reverse pinocytosis; see Chapter 1). In this fashion, the catecholamines, ATP, and proteins in the granules are all extruded from the cell.

The catecholamines have a very short half-life in the circulation. For the most part, they are methoxylated, then oxidized to 3-methoxy-4-hydroxymandelic acid (vanilmandelic acid, VMA). About 50% of the secreted catecholamines appear in the urine as free or conjugated metanephrine and normetanephrine, and 35% as VMA. Only small amounts of free norepinephrine and epinephrine are excreted. In normal humans, about 30 μg of norepinephrine, 6 μg of epinephrine, and 700 μg of VMA are excreted per day.

Effects of Epinephrine & Norepinephrine

In addition to mimicking the effects of adrenergic nervous discharge (Table 13–1), norepinephrine and epinephrine stimulate the nervous system and exert metabolic effects that include glycogenolysis in liver and skeletal muscle, mobilization of free fatty acids, and stimulation of the metabolic rate (Table 20–1).

Norepinephrine and epinephrine both increase the force and rate of contraction of the isolated heart. They also increase myocardial excitability, causing extrasystoles and, occasionally, more serious cardiac arrhythmias. Both amines dilate the coronary blood vessels. Norepinephrine produces vasoconstriction in most other organs, but epinephrine dilates the blood vessels in skeletal muscle. This overbalances the vasoconstriction it produces elsewhere, and the total peripheral resistance drops. When norepinephrine is infused slowly in normal animals or humans, the systolic and diastolic blood pressures rise. The hypertension stimulates the carotid and aortic pressorecep-

TABLE 20–1. Comparison of the effects of epinephrine and norepinephrine on some physiologic parameters. Where pertinent, the activity of the more active compound has been indicated as ++++ and the activity of the other is compared to it on a scale of + to ++++.

Norepinephrine	Parameter	Epinephrine
Decreased (due to reflex bradycardia)	Cardiac output	Increased
Increased	Peripheral resistance	Decreased
++++	Blood pressure elevation	++
++++	Free fatty acid release	+++
++++	Stimulation of CNS	++++
+++	Increased heat production	++++
+	Hyperglycemia	++++

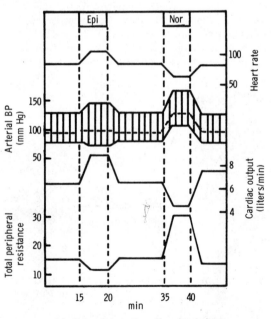

Epi = Epinephrine   Nor = Norepinephrine

FIG 20–4. Circulatory changes produced in man by the slow intravenous infusion of epinephrine and norepinephrine. (Slightly modified, redrawn, and reproduced, with permission, from Barcroft & Swan: *Sympathetic Control of Human Blood Vessels.* Arnold, 1953.)

tors, producing reflex bradycardia which overrides the direct cardio-acceleratory effect of norepinephrine. Consequently, cardiac output per minute falls. Epinephrine causes a widening of the pulse pressure; but because pressoreceptor stimulation is insufficient to obscure the direct effect of the hormone on the heart, cardiac rate and output increase. These changes are summarized in Fig 20–4.

The increased alertness that is produced by catecholamines is described in Chapter 11. Epinephrine and norepinephrine are equally potent in this regard, although in humans epinephrine usually evokes more anxiety and fear.

The one effect of epinephrine that is shared to only a small extent by norepinephrine is its glycogenolytic action. Epinephrine activates phosphorylase in liver and skeletal muscle (see Chapter 17), and the blood glucose rises. The blood lactic acid also rises. The liver glycogen first falls and then rises as the lactic acid is oxidized (Fig 19–19). The plasma potassium rises coincident with the glycogenolysis.

Norepinephrine and epinephrine are almost equally potent in their free fatty acid mobilizing activity (see Chapter 17) and their calorigenic action. They produce a prompt rise in the metabolic rate which is independent of the liver and a smaller, delayed rise which is abolished by hepatectomy and coincides with the rise in blood lactic acid. The calorigenic action does not occur in the absence of the thyroid and the adrenal cortex. The cause of the initial rise in metabolic rate is not clearly understood. It may be due to cutaneous vasoconstriction, which decreases heat loss and leads to a rise in body temperature, or to increased muscular activity, or to both. The second rise is probably due to oxidation of lactic acid in the liver.

On the basis of their differential sensitivity to drugs, the effects of epinephrine and norepinephrine have been divided into 2 groups. Those in one group are brought about by catecholamines interacting with "α receptors" in the effector organs, whereas those in the other group are brought about by catecholamines interacting with "β receptors" (see Table 13–1). This concept is probably an oversimplification, but drugs have been developed which inhibit with considerable selectivity one or the other group of responses. Drugs which are α blockers inhibit actions such as the pressor effects of the catecholamines. Drugs which are β blockers inhibit actions such as the chronotropic and inotropic effects of catecholamines on the heart and their glycogenolytic and free fatty acid mobilizing effects. β-Mediated effects are due to stimulation of adenyl cyclase, with resultant increased formation of cyclic AMP (see Chapter 17). Conversely, some α effects are apparently due to inhibition of cyclic AMP formation.

REGULATION OF ADRENAL MEDULLARY SECRETION

Neural Control

Certain drugs act directly on the adrenal medulla, but physiologic stimuli affect medullary secretion through the nervous system. Catecholamine secretion is low in basal states, but the secretion of epinephrine and, to a lesser extent, that of norepinephrine is reduced even further during sleep.

There is evidence that adrenal medullary secretion is increased when the "cholinergic sympathetic vasodilator" system discharges at the start of exercise, the increased epinephrine secretion reinforcing the vasodilatation produced by sympathetic vasodilator fibers to skeletal muscle (see Chapters 14 and 31).

Increased adrenal medullary secretion is part of the diffuse adrenergic discharge provoked in emergency situations, which Cannon called the "emergency function of the sympatho-adrenal system." The ways in which this discharge prepares the individual for flight or fight are described in Chapter 13. It is worth mentioning, however, that when adrenal medullary hormones are injected into control animals in the amounts secreted in response to splanchnic nerve stimulation, they exert effects on the musculature of the skin, kidneys, and spleen that are only 10–20% as great as the effects produced by comparable stimulation of the sympathetic innervation of these structures. Thus, the action of secreted catecholamines in augmenting the effects of adrenergic nerve discharges on the vascular system is relatively slight.

The metabolic effects of circulating catecholamines are probably more important, especially in certain situations. The calorigenic action of catecholamines in animals exposed to cold is an example. Animals with denervated adrenal glands shiver sooner and more vigorously than normal controls when exposed to cold. The glycogenolysis produced by epinephrine in hypoglycemic animals is another example. Hypoglycemia is a potent stimulus to catecholamine secretion (Fig 19–13), and insulin tolerance appears to be reduced when adrenal medullary secretion is blocked.

Selective Secretion

When adrenal medullary secretion is increased, the ratio of epinephrine to norepinephrine in the adrenal effluent is generally unchanged or elevated. However, asphyxia and hypoxia increase the ratio of norepinephrine to epinephrine (Fig 20–5). The fact that the output of norepinephrine can be increased selectively has unfortunately led to the teleologic speculation that the adrenal medulla secretes epinephrine or norepinephrine depending upon which hormone best equips the animal to meet the emergency it faces. The fallacy of such speculation is illustrated by the response to hemorrhage (Fig 20–6), in which the predominant catecholamine secreted is not norepinephrine but epinephrine, which lowers the peripheral

FIG 20–5. Effect of asphyxia and hypoxia on catecholamine secretion in the dog. The values shown are outputs from the right adrenal gland. (From Goldfien & Ganong: Unpublished data.)

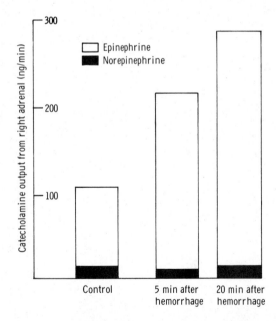

FIG 20–6. Mean epinephrine and norepinephrine output from the right adrenal gland in 8 pentobarbital-anesthetized normal dogs subjected to hemorrhage. (Data from Wise, Goldfien, & Ganong: Endocrine function in dogs after ablation of the area postrema. Acta neuroveg 22:1, 1960.)

resistance. Norepinephrine secretion is increased by emotional stresses with which the individual is familiar, whereas epinephrine secretion rises when the individual faces situations in which he does not know what to expect.

ADRENAL CORTEX

STRUCTURE & BIOSYNTHESIS OF ADRENOCORTICAL HORMONES

Classification & Structure

The hormones of the adrenal cortex are derivatives of cholesterol. Like cholesterol, bile acids, vitamin D, and ovarian and testicular steroids, they contain the **cyclopentenoperhydrophenanthrene nucleus** (Fig 20–7). The adrenocortical steroids are of 2 structural types (Fig 20–8): those which have a 2-carbon side chain attached at position 17 of the D ring and contain 21 carbon atoms ("C 21 steroids"), and those which have a keto or hydroxyl group at position 17 and contain 19 carbon atoms ("C 19 steroids"). Most of the C 19 steroids have a keto group at position 17 and are therefore called **17-ketosteroids**. The C 21 steroids which have a hydroxyl group at the 17 position in addition to the side chain are often called 17-hydroxycorticoids or 17-hydroxycorticosteroids.

FIG 20–7. The cyclopentenoperhydrophenanthrene nucleus.

The C 19 steroids have androgenic activity. The C 21 steroids are classified, using Selye's terminology, as mineralocorticoids or glucocorticoids. All secreted C 21 steroids have both mineralocorticoid and glucocorticoid activity; **mineralocorticoids** are those in which effects on Na$^+$ and K$^+$ excretion predominate, and **glucocorticoids** those in which effects on glucose and protein metabolism predominate.

Steroid Nomenclature & Isomerism

For the sake of simplicity, the steroid names used here and in Chapter 23 are the most commonly used trivial names. A few common synonyms are shown in Table 20–2. The details of steroid nomenclature and isomerism can be found in the texts listed in the refer-

"C 21" steroid (progesterone)   "C 19" steroid (dehydroepiandrosterone)

FIG 20–8. Structure of adrenocortical steroids. The letters in the formula for progesterone identify the A, B, C, and D rings; the numbers show the positions in the basic C 21 steroid structure. The angular methyl groups (positions 18 and 19) are usually indicated simply by straight lines, as in the formula on the right. Dehydroepiandrosterone is a "17-ketosteroid" formed by cleavage of the side chain of the C 21 steroid 17-hydroxypregnenolone and its replacement by an O atom. Similar conversion of other C 21 steroids to 17-ketosteroids occurs in the body.

ences, but it is pertinent to mention that the Greek letter Δ indicates a double bond and that the groups which lie above the plane of each of the steroid rings are indicated by the Greek letter β and a solid line (–OH), while those that lie below are indicated by a and a dotted line (⋯OH). Thus, the C 21 steroids secreted by the adrenal have a $\Delta4$,3-keto configuration in the A ring. In most naturally occurring adrenal steroids, 17-hydroxy groups are in the a configuration, while 3-, 11-, and 21-hydroxy groups are in the β configuration. The 18-aldehyde configuration on naturally occurring aldosterone is the D-form. L-Aldosterone is physiologically inactive.

Secreted Steroids

Innumerable steroids have been isolated from adrenal tissue, but the only steroids normally secreted in physiologically significant amounts are the mineralocorticoid **aldosterone**, the glucocorticoids **cortisol** and **corticosterone**, and the androgen **dehydroepiandros-**

TABLE 20–2. Steroids secreted in physiologically significant amounts from the adrenal cortex.

Name	Synonyms	Average Amount Secreted/Day in Adult Human (mg)
C 21 steroids		
Cortisol	Compound F, hydrocortisone	20
Corticosterone	Compound B	3
Aldosterone		0.15
C 19 steroids		
Dehydroepiandrosterone	DEA, DHEA	Males 21 Females 16

*Values for output of C 21 steroids are from secretion rate studies of EG Biglieri, PH Forsham, and associates.

terone. **Deoxycorticosterone** and **11-deoxycortisol** (the precursors of corticosterone and cortisol), 18-hydroxycorticosterone, estrogens such as **estradiol**, and some of the derivatives of dehydroepiandrosterone are secreted in small quantities, but they exert demonstrable effects only in pathologic situations. There is evidence that small amounts of progesterone and testosterone are also secreted. Dehydroepiandrosterone is secreted conjugated with sulfate, although most if not all the other steroids are secreted in the free, unconjugated form.

The rates at which the principal adrenocortical hormones are secreted in man are shown in Table 20–2. The secretion rate for each steroid in this table was determined by injecting a very small dose of isotopically labeled steroid and determining the degree to which the radioactive steroid excreted in the urine was diluted by unlabeled secreted hormone. This technic is used to measure the output of many different hormones.

Species Differences

In all species from fish to humans, the major C 21 steroid hormones secreted by adrenocortical tissue appear to be aldosterone, cortisol, and corticosterone, although the ratio of cortisol to corticosterone varies. Birds, mice, and rats secrete corticosterone almost exclusively; dogs secrete approximately equal amounts of the 2 glucocorticoids; and cats, cows, sheep, monkeys, and humans secrete predominantly cortisol. In man, the cortisol/corticosterone ratio is approximately 7.

Synthetic Steroids

The glucocorticoids are among the increasing number of naturally occurring substances that man has been able to improve upon. A number of synthetic steroids are now available that have many times the activity of cortisol. The relative glucocorticoid and mineralocorticoid potencies of the natural steroids are compared to those of the synthetic steroids 9a-fluoro-

TABLE 20–3. **Relative potencies of some natural and synthetic adrenocortical steroids.** Mineralocorticoid activities are compared to deoxycorticosterone, glucocorticoid to cortisol.*

9a-Fluorocortisol

Prednisolone

	Compared to Deoxycorticosterone = 100		Compared to Cortisol = 100	
	Maintenance of Adrenalectomized Dogs	Change in Urinary Na$^+$/K$^+$	Liver Glycogen Deposition	Thymus Involution
Cortisol	4	7	100	100
Cortisone	4	6	65	65
Corticosterone	15	14	35	28
Deoxycorticosterone	100	100	1	0
Aldosterone	3000	12000	25	slight
9a-Fluorocortisol	900	. . .	1200	900
Prednisolone	1	. . .	350	400

*Modified from Russell, in: *Physiology and Biophysics,* 19th ed. Ruch TC, Patton HD (editors). Saunders, 1965. Data from various authors.

cortisol and prednisolone in Table 20–3. Some of the synthetic steroids are slowly metabolized, but the reason for their increased potency is in most cases unknown.

Steroid Biosynthesis

The major paths by which the naturally occurring adrenocortical hormones are synthesized in the body are summarized in Fig 20–9. The major precursor of cortisol is 17a-hydroxypregnenolone and the major precursor of corticosterone and aldosterone is pregnenolone. The secreted steroids are synthesized by formation of the Δ4,3-keto configuration in the A ring and then hydroxylation in the 21 and, finally, the 11 position. Aldosterone is formed by replacement of the angular methyl group in position 18 of corticosterone with an aldehyde group. In the body fluids, most of the aldosterone is believed to be in the 11-hemiacetal form (Fig 20–10). Androgens are formed by side chain cleavage to form dehydroepiandrosterone and its derivatives, and estrogens are formed from androgens.

Action of ACTH

ACTH catalyzes a step in the conversion of cholesterol to pregnenolone. It acts on adenyl cyclase to increase the formation of cyclic AMP in the adrenal cortex, and cyclic AMP increases steroid secretion. Also, steroid secretion in response to ACTH is blocked by puromycin. It is postulated that the increase in intracellular cyclic AMP triggers the increased synthesis of a protein which in some way increases the conversion of cholesterol to pregnenolone.

The mechanism by which angiotensin II stimulates aldosterone biosynthesis is not known.

Enzyme Deficiencies

The consequences of inhibiting any of the enzyme systems involved in steroid biosynthesis can be predicted from Fig 20–9. Single enzyme defects can occur as congenital "inborn errors of metabolism" or can be produced by drugs. Congenital blockade of the formation of pregnenolone causes the syndrome of **lipoid adrenal hyperplasia,** with diffuse adrenal insufficiency and death soon after birth. Androgen formation is blocked, and female genitalia develop regardless of genetic sex (see Chapter 23). Congenital 3β-dehydrogenase, 21β-hydroxylase, and 11β-hydroxylase deficiency all cause various forms of the **adrenogenital syndrome.** In this syndrome, glucocorticoid secretion is deficient, and ACTH secretion is consequently stimulated. The steroid intermediates that pile up behind the block are converted via the remaining unblocked pathways to androgens. In 3β-dehydrogenase deficiency the glucocorticoid and mineralocorticoid deficiency is usually fatal. 21β-Hydroxylase deficiency is usually incomplete, so that enough glucocorticoids and mineralocorticoids are formed to sustain life; but 30% of the patients with this syndrome show abnormal sodium loss (**salt-losing form** of the adrenogenital syndrome). In 11β-hydroxylase deficiency there is excess secretion of 11-deoxycortisol and deoxycorticosterone; since the latter is an active mineralocorticoid, salt and water retention and hypertension result (**hypertensive form** of the adrenogenital syndrome). Glucocorticoid treatment is indicated in all of these forms of the syndrome because it repairs the glucocorticoid deficit and inhibits ACTH secretion (see below), thus preventing the abnormal secretion of androgens and other steroids.

FIG 20—9. Composite outline of major pathways in adrenocortical hormone biosynthesis. The major secretory products are underlined. In the zona fasciculata and zona reticularis, no aldosterone is formed. In the zona glomerulosa, aldosterone is produced but no 17-hydroxylated compounds or sex hormones are formed. The enzymes and cofactors for the reactions progressing down each column are shown on the left and from the first to the second column at the top of the chart. When a particular enzyme is deficient, hormone production is blocked at the points indicated by the shaded bars. (After Welikey, Mulrow, & others.)

17*a*-Hydroxylase deficiency is a rare condition which is apparently congenital in origin. Patients with this disorder secrete large amounts of corticosterone but no cortisol and no androgens or estrogens, since 17*a*-hydroxylation is a necessary step in the biosynthesis of these sex hormones (see Chapter 23).

FIG 20—10. 11-Hemiacetal form of aldosterone.

Enzyme Inhibition With Drugs

Metyrapone (methopyrapone, SU-4885, Metopirone) inhibits adrenal 11β-hydroxylase when administered in proper doses. It is used clinically to test pituitary reserve by producing a transient cortisol deficiency. The deficiency stimulates ACTH secretion, and the resultant increase in 11-deoxycortisol secretion is proportionate to the ability of the pituitary to respond. **Amphenone** and **DDD**, a derivative of DDT (Fig 20—11), block the secretion of all steroids. Amphenone causes adrenocortical hypertrophy, but DDD produces necrosis of cortical cells. Various other drugs which inhibit 17*a*-hydroxylase and other specific adrenocortical enzyme systems have been developed.

Adrenal Cholesterol & Ascorbic Acid

The adrenal cortex contains large amounts of cholesterol and ascorbic acid, and the content of both substances falls transiently when ACTH is injected. Adrenal ascorbic acid and cholesterol depletion have

Amphenone B (hydrochloride)

Metyrapone (SU-4885)

DDD (dichlorodiphenyldichloroethane)

FIG 20–11. Drugs which inhibit adrenocortical secretion. The active form of DDD is the ortho-para-prime isomer (o,p′DDD; mitotane; Lysodren).

both been used as indicators of increased ACTH secretion in animals. The cholesterol in the adrenal is presumably the store from which steroids are synthesized, but the function of the ascorbic acid in the adrenal is not known.

TRANSPORT, METABOLISM, & EXCRETION OF ADRENOCORTICAL HORMONES

Glucocorticoid Binding

Cortisol is bound in the circulation to an a globulin called **transcortin** or **corticosteroid-binding globulin (CBG)**. There is also a minor degree of binding to albumin. Corticosterone is similarly bound, but probably to a lesser degree. The half-life of cortisol in the circulation is therefore slightly longer (about 60–90 minutes) than that of corticosterone (50 minutes). Bound steroids appear to be physiologically inactive. Because of protein binding there is relatively little free cortisol and corticosterone in the urine.

The equilibrium between cortisol and its binding protein and the implications of binding in terms of tissue supplies and ACTH secretion are summarized in Fig 20–12. The bound cortisol probably functions as a circulating reservoir of hormone which keeps a supply of free cortisol available to the tissues. The relationship is similar to that of thyroxine and its binding protein (Fig 18–6). The usual methods for determining unconjugated "free 17-hydroxycorticoids" in the plasma measure both unbound and bound cortisol. At normal levels of cortisol secretion there is very little free

FIG 20–12. The interrelationships of free and bound cortisol. The dashed arrow indicates that cortisol inhibits ACTH secretion. The value for free cortisol is an approximation; in most studies it is calculated by subtracting the protein-bound cortisol from the total plasma cortisol. Some authors report lower or higher free cortisol values.

cortisol in the plasma, but the binding sites on CBG become saturated when the total plasma cortisol exceeds 20 $\mu g/100$ ml. At higher plasma levels, there is some increased binding to albumin, but the main increase is in the unbound fraction.

CBG is synthesized in the liver, and its production is increased by estrogen. CBG levels are elevated during pregnancy and depressed in cirrhosis, nephrosis, and multiple myeloma. When the CBG level rises, more cortisol is bound and the free cortisol level drops. This stimulates ACTH secretion, and a new equilibrium is reached at which the free cortisol level is normal but the bound cortisol level and the rate of adrenocortical secretion are elevated. Changes in the opposite direction occur when the CBG level falls. This explains why pregnant women have high rates of glucocorticoid secretion and high total plasma 17-hydroxycorticoid levels without symptoms of glucocorticoid excess; conversely, it also explains why some patients with nephrosis have low levels of glucocorticoid secretion and low plasma 17-hydroxycorticoids without adrenal insufficiency.

Metabolism & Excretion of Glucocorticoids

Cortisol is metabolized in the liver, which is the principal site of glucocorticoid catabolism. Most of the cortisol is reduced to dihydrocortisol and then to tetrahydrocortisol, which is conjugated to glucuronic acid (Fig 20–13). The glucuronyl transferase system responsible for this conversion also catalyzes the formation of the glucuronides of bilirubin (see Chapter 26) and a number of hormones and drugs. There is competitive inhibition between these substrates for the enzyme system.

Some of the cortisol in the liver is converted to cortisone. It should be emphasized that cortisone and other steroids with an 11-keto group are metabolites of

FIG 20−13. Outline of hepatic metabolism of cortisol.

the secreted glucocorticoids. Cortisone is an active glucocorticoid and is well known because of its extensive use in medicine, but it is not secreted by the adrenal gland. Little if any of the cortisone formed in the liver enters the circulation because it is promptly reduced and conjugated to form tetrahydrocortisone glucuronide. The tetrahydroglucuronide derivatives ("conjugates") of cortisol and corticosterone are freely soluble. They enter the circulation, where they do not become bound to protein. They are rapidly excreted in the urine, in part by tubular secretion.

About 10% of the secreted cortisol is converted in the liver to the 17-ketosteroid derivatives of cortisol and cortisone. The ketosteroids are conjugated for the most part to sulfate and then excreted in the urine. Other metabolites, including 20-hydroxy derivatives, are formed. About 15% of the secreted cortisol is excreted in the stool. The distribution of cortisol and its derivatives in the plasma and urine is summarized in Table 20−4.

The metabolism of corticosterone is similar to that of cortisol except that it does not form a 17-ketosteroid derivative. Other metabolites of the glucocorticoids are formed in small amounts. There is an enterohepatic circulation of glucocorticoids, but only minor amounts appear in the stools.

Variations in the Rate of Hepatic Metabolism

In some species, but not in man, the adrenals are larger in the female than in the male and the hepatic Δ4-hydrogenase level is higher in the female. Presumably, therefore, more rapid glucocorticoid metabolism in the female leads to a compensatory rise in ACTH secretion. The rate of hepatic inactivation of glucocorticoids is depressed in liver disease, and, interestingly, during surgery and other stresses. Thus, in the stressed animal, the plasma free cortisol level rises higher than it does with maximal ACTH stimulation in the absence of stress. Glucocorticoids apparently are not degraded in the process of exerting their physiologic effects.

Aldosterone

Aldosterone is bound to protein to only a slight extent, and its half-life is short (about 20 minutes). The amount secreted is small (Table 20−2), and the normal plasma aldosterone level is man is about 0.006 μg/100 ml, compared to a cortisol level (bound and free) of about 12 μg/100 ml. Much of the aldosterone is converted in the liver to the tetrahydro glucuronide derivative, but some is changed in the liver and in the kidney to an 18-glucuronide. This glucuronide, which is unlike the breakdown products of other steroids, is converted to free aldosterone by hydrolysis at pH 1.0, and it is therefore often referred to as the "acid-labile

TABLE 20–4. Distribution of cortisol and its principal derivatives in the plasma and urine. Note that the derivatives of corticosterone and the 17-ketosteroids from other sources are not included. The "plasma 17-hydroxycorticoids" include, in addition to cortisol and its derivatives, small amounts of other 17a-hydroxylated steroids.

Plasma: Average concentration in man at 8:00 a.m.

	µg/100 ml	
Free cortisol	0.5	
Protein-bound cortisol	12	90% of "plasma 17-hydroxy-corticoids"
Unconjugated dihydro- and tetrahydro-cortisol and -cortisone	Traces	
Tetrahydrocortisol glucuronide	10	"Conjugates"
Tetrahydrocortisone glucuronide	6	
17-Ketosteroids derived from cortisol and cortisone (mostly sulfate conjugates)		Actual plasma concentrations have not been measured

Urine: Average amount excreted per 24 hours

	(mg)
Free cortisol	0.03
Tetrahydrocortisol glucuronide	5
Tetrahydrocortisone glucuronide	3
20-Hydroxy derivatives of tetrahydro glucuronides	6
17-Ketosteroids derived from cortisol and cortisone (mostly sulfate conjugates)	1
Unidentified metabolites	7

conjugate." Less than 1% of the secreted aldosterone appears in the urine in the free form. Another 5% is in the form of the acid-labile conjugate, and up to 40% is conjugated to glucuronic acid.

17-Ketosteroids

The major adrenal androgen is the 17-ketosteroid, dehydroepiandrosterone, although its Δ4,3-keto and 11-hydroxy-Δ4,3-keto derivatives are also secreted. This last compound and the 17-ketosteroids formed from cortisol and cortisone by side chain cleavage in the liver are the only 17-ketosteroids which have an =O or an –OH group in the 11 position ("11-oxy-17-ketosteroids"). Testosterone is also converted to a 17-ketosteroid. Since the daily 17-ketosteroid excretion in normal adults is 15 mg in males and 10 mg in females, about two-thirds of the ketosteroids in the urine of males are secreted by the adrenal or formed from cortisol in the liver, and about one-third are of testicular origin.

Etiocholanolone, one of the metabolites of the adrenal androgens and testosterone (Fig 23–17), is capable of causing fever when it is unconjugated. This may be due to release of endogenous pyrogen (see Chapter 14). Certain individuals have episodic bouts of fever due to periodic accumulation in the blood of unconjugated etiocholanolone ("etiocholanolone fever").

EFFECTS OF ADRENAL ANDROGENS & ESTROGENS

Estrogens

It seems clear that estradiol is formed in the adrenals and secreted, although estrogens have not been isolated from adrenal venous blood. In ovariectomized women, urinary estrogen levels rise when ACTH is injected and fall when the adrenals are removed. The amount of estrogen secreted is normally too small to have any apparent physiologic effect. However, feminizing, estrogen-secreting tumors of the adrenal cortex have been described, and ovariectomized patients with estrogen-dependent breast cancers improve when their adrenals are removed or when they are treated with glucocorticoids in sufficient doses to inhibit ACTH secretion.

Androgens

Androgens are the hormones that exert masculinizing effects, and they promote protein anabolism

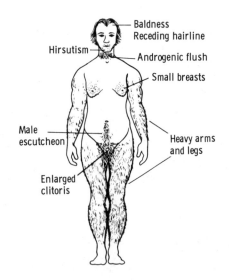

ADRENOGENITAL SYNDROME

FIG 20–14. Typical findings in the adrenogenital syndrome in an adult female. (Reproduced, with permission, from Forsham & Di Raimondo in: *Traumatic Medicine and Surgery for the Attorney.* Butterworth, 1960.)

and growth (see Chapter 23). Testosterone from the testes is the most active androgen, and the adrenal androgens have less than 20% of its activity. Secretion of the adrenal androgens is controlled by ACTH, not by gonadotropins. The amount of adrenal androgens secreted is almost as great in castrated males and females as in normal males, so it is clear that they exert no significant masculinizing effect when secreted in normal amounts. When secreted in abnormal amounts, as they are in patients with congenital enzyme deficiencies in the adrenal (see above) or adrenal tumors, they cause the stigmas of the adrenogenital syndrome.

In adult males, excess adrenal androgen secretion merely accentuates existing characteristics; but in prepuberal boys it causes precocious development of the secondary sex characteristics without testicular growth (**precocious pseudopuberty**). In prepuberal and adult females it causes masculinization which, when marked, produces the striking clinical picture of the **adrenogenital syndrome** (Fig 20–14). When excess androgen secretion occurs in genetically female fetuses before the 12th week of gestation, the development of male type external genitalia is stimulated and various degrees of female **pseudohermaphroditism** result. The role of hormones in the in utero development of the genitalia is discussed in Chapter 23.

PHYSIOLOGIC EFFECTS OF GLUCOCORTICOIDS

Adrenal Insufficiency

In untreated adrenalectomized animals and humans, there is Na$^+$ loss with circulatory insufficiency, hypotension, and, eventually, fatal shock due to the mineralocorticoid deficiency. Because glucocorticoids are absent, water, carbohydrate, protein, and fat metabolism are abnormal, and collapse and death follow exposure to even minor noxious stimuli. Small amounts of glucocorticoids correct the metabolic abnormalities, in part directly and in part by permitting other reactions to occur. It is important to separate these physiologic actions of glucocorticoids from the quite different effects produced by large amounts of the hormones.

Mechanism of Action

Evidence is accumulating that the multiple effects of glucocorticoids are due to an action on the genetic mechanism controlling protein synthesis. In most instances, the hormones appear to act by stimulating DNA-dependent mRNA synthesis (see Chapter 17) in the nucleus of their target cells. This in turn leads to the formation of enzymes that alter cell function. Aldosterone acts similarly (see below), and androgens, estrogens, and progesterone—indeed, all steroid hormones—appear to exert their effects in a similar way.

Effects on Intermediary Metabolism

The actions of glucocorticoids on the intermediary metabolism of carbohydrate, protein, and fat are discussed in Chapter 19. They include increased protein catabolism and increased hepatic glycogenesis and gluconeogenesis. Glucose-6-phosphatase activity is increased, and the blood glucose rises.

Glucocorticoids exert an anti-insulin action in peripheral tissues and make diabetes worse. In the diabetic, they raise plasma lipid levels and increase ketone body formation, but in normal individuals the increase in insulin secretion provoked by the rise in blood glucose obscures these actions. In adrenal insufficiency, the blood glucose is normal as long as an adequate caloric intake is maintained, but fasting causes hypoglycemia that can be fatal (Table 19–5). The adrenal cortex is not essential for the ketogenic response to fasting.

Permissive Action

Small amounts of glucocorticoids must be present for a number of metabolic reactions to occur, although the glucocorticoids do not produce the reactions by themselves. This effect is called their **permissive action**. For example, glucocorticoids must be present for glucagon and catecholamines to exert their calorigenic action (see above and Chapter 19).

Effects on ACTH Secretion

Glucocorticoids inhibit ACTH secretion, and ACTH secretion is increased in adrenalectomized animals. The consequences of the feedback action of cortisol on ACTH secretion are discussed below in the section on regulation of glucocorticoid secretion.

Vascular Reactivity

In adrenally insufficient animals, vascular smooth muscle becomes unresponsive to norepinephrine and epinephrine. The capillaries dilate and, terminally, become permeable to colloidal dyes. Failure to respond to the norepinephrine liberated at adrenergic nerve endings probably impairs vascular compensation for the hypovolemia of adrenal insufficiency and promotes vascular collapse. Glucocorticoids restore vascular reactivity.

Effects on Cardiac & Skeletal Muscle

In adrenalectomized animals, skeletal muscle becomes fatigued more rapidly than in normal animals, and glucocorticoid treatment is necessary to restore the muscles to normal. Glucocorticoids and mineralocorticoids have a positively inotropic effect on cardiac muscle in vitro, but there is no evidence that this digitalis-like action is of any significance in vivo. Heart failure is certainly not part of the clinical picture of adrenal insufficiency. The PR interval of the ECG is prolonged in adrenal insufficiency and shortened in patients who have excess circulating glucocorticoids.

Effects on the Nervous System

There are changes in the nervous system in

TABLE 20–5. Taste thresholds in adrenal insufficiency.*

| Substance | Lowest Concentration Detected (mM), Median Value | |
	Normal Subjects	Patients With Adrenal Insufficiency
Urea	90	0.8
HCl	0.3	0.006
Sucrose	12	0.1
KCl	12	0.1
NaHCO$_3$	12	0.1
NaCl	12	0.3

*Data from Henkin & others: Studies on taste thresholds in normal man and in patients with adrenal insufficiency: The role of adrenal cortical steroids and serum sodium concentration. J Clin Invest 42:727, 1963.

adrenal insufficiency that are reversed only by glucocorticoids. These include the appearance of EEG waves slower than the normal alpha rhythm, personality changes, and increased sensitivity to olfactory and gustatory stimuli. The mild but definite personality changes include irritability, apprehension, and inability to concentrate. The greater sensitivity of the taste mechanism, which includes all 4 taste modalities (Table 20–5), and of the olfactory apparatus is unexplained.

Glucocorticoids decrease the amount of current necessary to produce convulsions in rats (lower the **convulsive threshold**), whereas mineralocorticoids have the opposite effect. Indeed, mineralocorticoids have been used in the treatment of epilepsy. However, it is difficult to say what the convulsive threshold means in terms of normal brain function.

Effects on the Gastrointestinal System

Glucocorticoids and ACTH increase gastric acid and pepsin secretion in some species (see Chapter 26). In man, there is evidence that they alter the resistance of the mucosa to the irritant actions of the gastric secretions. Glucocorticoid treatment is contraindicated in patients with peptic ulcer. Absorption of water-insoluble fats from the intestine into the lymph is decreased in adrenal insufficiency and facilitated by glucocorticoids (see Chapter 25).

Effects on Water Metabolism

Adrenal insufficiency is characterized by inability to excrete a water load (Fig 20–15), and only glucocorticoids repair this deficit. The load is eventually excreted, but the excretion is so slow that there is danger of water intoxication. In patients with adrenal insufficiency who have not received glucocorticoids, glucose infusions may cause high fever ("glucose fever") followed by collapse and death. What presumably happens is that the glucose is metabolized, the water dilutes the plasma, and the resultant osmotic gradient between the plasma and the cells causes the cells of the thermoregulatory centers in the hypothalamus to swell to such an extent that their function is disrupted. It should be noted that water intoxication can occur in adrenal insufficiency even without an absolute excess of water in the body; the important factor is retention of water in excess of sodium.

The cause of defective water excretion in adrenal insufficiency is still the subject of much debate. There may be decreased hepatic inactivation of vasopressin, but this would only promote hemodilution which would in turn inhibit vasopressin secretion unless there were a coexisting defect in the osmoreceptor mechanism (see Chapter 14). Some investigators claim that in the absence of glucocorticoids there is an abnormally high rate of vasopressin secretion, but it has been reported that the plasma vasopressin level is lower in water-loaded adrenalectomized animals than in water-loaded controls. The glomerular filtration rate is low, and this probably contributes to the deficiency in water excretion. The selective effect of glucocorticoids

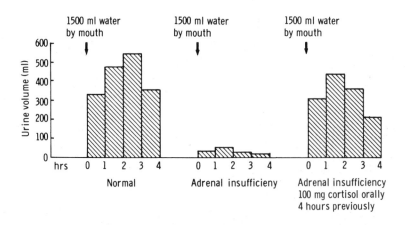

FIG 20–15. Response to a 1500 ml water load in a normal subject and a patient with adrenal insufficiency before and after cortisol treatment.

TABLE 20−6. Typical effects of cortisol on the white and red blood cell counts in man (values/µl).

	Normal	Cortisol-Treated
White blood cells		
Total	9000	10000
PMNs	5760	8330
Lymphocytes	2370	1080
Eosinophils	270	20
Basophils	60	30
Monocytes	450	540
Red blood cells	5 million	5.2 million

on the abnormal water excretion is consistent with this possibility because even though the mineralocorticoids improve filtration by restoring plasma volume, the glucocorticoids raise the glomerular filtration rate to a much greater degree. Another factor may be a direct effect of glucocorticoid deficiency on the distal tubules and collecting ducts, making them permeable to water in the absence of vasopressin (see Chapter 38).

Effects on the Blood Cells & Lymphatic Organs

Glucocorticoids decrease the number of circulating eosinophils by increasing their sequestration in the spleen and lungs. Changes in the eosinophil level have been used as an index of changes in ACTH secretion, but they are an unreliable indicator because some stresses cause eosinopenia in the absence of the adrenals. Glucocorticoids also lower the number of basophils in the circulation and increase the number of neutrophils, platelets, and red blood cells (Table 20−6). Moderate anemia is one of the findings in chronic adrenal insufficiency, but there is a brisk erythropoietic response to hypoxia (see Chapter 24) in the absence of the adrenals.

Glucocorticoids decrease the circulating lymphocyte count and the size of the lymph nodes and thymus, due both to an inhibition of lymphocyte mitotic activity and increased destruction of lymphocytes.

Resistance to "Stress"

When an animal or human is exposed to any of an immense variety of noxious or potentially noxious stimuli, there is an increased secretion of ACTH and, consequently, a rise in the circulating glucocorticoid level. This rise is essential for survival. Hypophysectomized animals, or adrenalectomized animals treated with maintenance doses of glucocorticoids, die when exposed to the same noxious stimuli.

Selye defined noxious stimuli which increase ACTH secretion as "stressors," and it is fashionable today to lump these stimuli together under the term "stress." This word is a short, emotionally charged word for something that otherwise takes many words to say, and it is a convenient term to use as long as it is

understood that, in the context of this book, it denotes only those stimuli which have been proved to increase ACTH secretion in normal animals and man.

Most of the stressful stimuli that increase ACTH secretion also activate the sympatho-adrenal medullary system, and part of the function of the circulating glucocorticoids may be the maintenance of vascular reactivity to catecholamines. In addition, glucocorticoids are necessary for the catecholamines to exert their full FFA-mobilizing action, and the FFAs are an important emergency energy supply. However, sympathectomized animals tolerate a variety of stresses with impunity. The reason why an elevated circulating glucocorticoid level is essential for resisting stress therefore remains for the most part unknown.

PHARMACOLOGIC & PATHOLOGIC EFFECTS OF GLUCOCORTICOIDS

Cushing's Syndrome

The clinical picture produced in man by glucocorticoid excess is called **Cushing's syndrome** (Fig 20−16). It may be caused not only by the administration of large amounts of exogenous hormones but also by glucocorticoid-producing adrenocortical tumors and by hypersecretion of ACTH. The most common cause of hypersecretion of ACTH is a poorly understood defect in the regulation of ACTH secretion. Cushing's syndrome also may be due to ACTH-secreting tumors of the pituitary or to tumors of nonendocrine tissues

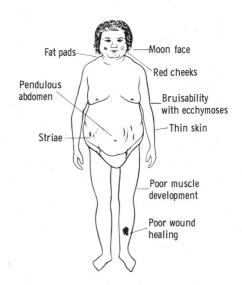

Fat pads

Pendulous abdomen

Striae

Moon face

Red cheeks

Bruisability with ecchymoses

Thin skin

Poor muscle development

Poor wound healing

CUSHING'S SYNDROME

FIG 20−16. Typical findings in Cushing's syndrome. (Reproduced, with permission, from Forsham & Di Raimondo in: *Traumatic Medicine and Surgery for the Attorney.* Butterworth, 1960.)

that secrete substances with CRF activity or substances very similar to and possibly identical with pituitary ACTH. Tumors of nonendocrine tissues have also been reported to secrete substances with actions like those of almost every known hormone.

Patients with Cushing's syndrome are protein depleted as a result of excess protein catabolism. The skin and subcutaneous tissues are therefore thin, and the muscles are poorly developed. Wounds heal poorly, and minor injuries cause bruises and ecchymoses. Hair growth is inhibited, and the hair is thin and scraggly.

Body fat is redistributed in a characteristic way. The extremities are thin, but fat collects in the abdominal wall, face, and upper back, where it produces a "buffalo hump." As the thin skin of the abdomen is stretched by the increased subcutaneous fat depots, the subdermal tissues rupture to form prominent reddish-purple **striae**. These scars are seen normally whenever there is rapid stretching of the skin (eg, around the breasts of girls at puberty or in the abdominal skin during pregnancy), but in normal individuals the striae are usually inconspicuous and lack the intense purplish color.

Many of the amino acids liberated from catabolized proteins are converted into glucose in the liver, and the resultant hyperglycemia and decreased peripheral utilization of glucose may be sufficient to precipitate insulin-resistant diabetes mellitus, especially in patients genetically predisposed to diabetes. Hyperlipemia and ketosis are associated with the diabetes, but acidosis is usually not severe.

The glucocorticoids are present in such large amounts in Cushing's syndrome that they exert a significant mineralocorticoid action. Deoxycorticosterone secretion is also elevated in those cases which are due to ACTH hypersecretion. The salt and water retention plus the facial obesity cause the characteristic plethoric, rounded "moon-faced" appearance, and there may be significant K^+ depletion and weakness. About 85% of patients with Cushing's syndrome are hypertensive. The hypertension may be due to increased deoxycorticosterone secretion or to a direct glucocorticoid effect on blood vessels.

Excess glucocorticoids lead to bone dissolution for 3 reasons: excess protein catabolism inhibits new bone formation and breaks down existing bone matrix; glucocorticoids exert an anti-vitamin D action; and glucocorticoids elevate the glomerular filtration rate, increasing calcium excretion. The result is **osteoporosis** (see Chapter 21), a softening and demineralization of bone that leads eventually to collapse of vertebral bodies and skeletal deformity.

Glucocorticoids in excess accelerate the basic EEG rhythms and produce mental aberrations ranging from increased appetite, insomnia, and euphoria to frank toxic psychoses. As noted above, glucocorticoid deficiency is also associated with mental symptoms, but the symptoms produced by glucocorticoid excess are more severe.

Anti-inflammatory & Antiallergic Effects of Glucocorticoids

In large doses, glucocorticoids inhibit the inflammatory response to tissue injury. This reaction is discussed in detail in Chapter 33. The glucocorticoids also suppress manifestations of allergic disease that are due to the release of histamine from tissues. Neither of these pharmacologic effects is produced by glucocorticoids in physiologic doses, and the effects cannot be produced without producing the other manifestations of glucocorticoid excess. Furthermore, large doses of exogenous glucocorticoids inhibit ACTH secretion to the point that severe adrenal insufficiency can be a dangerous problem when therapy is stopped.

Glucocorticoids inhibit fibroblastic activity, decrease local swelling, and block the systemic effects of bacterial toxins. The decreased local reaction may be due to inhibition of kinin release by the steroids (see Chapters 31, 33). There is evidence that by stabilizing the lysosomal membranes glucocorticoids inhibit the breakdown of lysosomes that takes place in inflamed tissue. They also appear to inhibit the release of endogenous pyrogen from granulocytes (see Chapter 14). Large doses of glucocorticoids in man initially elevate and later depress antibody levels. The effects on inflammation can be demonstrated in experimental animals with granulomas produced by the subcutaneous injection of turpentine or croton oil, or implantation of cotton pledgets. The inhibition of fibroblastic activity prevents the walling off of infections and also prevents such phenomena as keloid formation and the development of adhesions after abdominal surgery.

The actions of glucocorticoids in patients with bacterial infections are dramatic but dangerous. For example, in pneumococcal pneumonia or active tuberculosis, the febrile reaction, the toxicity, and the lung symptoms disappear, but unless antibiotics are given at the same time the bacteria spread throughout the body. It is important to remember that the symptoms are the warning that disease is present; when these symptoms are masked by glucocorticoid treatment, there may be serious and even fatal delays in diagnosis and the institution of antibiotic treatment.

When certain types of antibodies combine with their antigens they provoke the release of histamine from various tissues, and this in turn causes many of the symptoms of allergy. Glucocorticoids do not affect the combination of antigen with antibody and have no influence on the effects of histamine once it is released, but they prevent histamine release. Glucocorticoids therefore relieve the symptoms of asthma and delayed hypersensitivity reactions such as hives and serum sickness. They are also of symptomatic benefit in rheumatoid arthritis, disseminated lupus erythematosus, dermatomyositis, Guillain-Barré syndrome, and related diseases in which allergic and autoimmune reactions probably play a role.

REGULATION OF GLUCOCORTICOID SECRETION

Role of ACTH

Both basal secretion of glucocorticoids and the increased secretion provoked by stress are dependent upon ACTH from the anterior pituitary. Angiotensin II also stimulates the adrenal cortex, but its effect is mainly on aldosterone secretion. Large doses of a number of other naturally occurring substances, including vasopressin and serotonin, are capable of stimulating the adrenal directly, but there is no evidence that these agents play any role in the physiologic regulation of glucocorticoid secretion.

Chemistry & Metabolism of ACTH

ACTH is a single-chain polypeptide containing 39 amino acids. The first 23 amino acids in the chain, which are the same in all the species that have been examined, constitute the active "core" of the molecule, and a synthetic peptide containing these 23 amino acids has been shown to have the full activity of the 39 amino acid peptide. Amino acids 24—39 are therefore a "tail" which apparently stabilizes the molecule and which varies slightly in amino acid composition from species to species (Table 20—7). Each of the ACTHs that has been isolated is active in all species, but probably antigenic in heterologous species.

ACTH is inactivated in blood in vitro, but at a much slower rate than it is in vivo; its half-life in the circulation in man is about 10 minutes. A large part of an injected dose of ACTH is found in the kidneys, but neither nephrectomy nor evisceration appreciably enhances its in vivo activity, and the site of its inactivation is not known. ACTH is apparently not altered in the process of exerting its effect on adrenal tissue.

Effect of ACTH on the Adrenal

After hypophysectomy in animals and man, glucocorticoid synthesis and output decline within 1 hour to very low levels, although some hormone is still secreted. Within a short time after an injection of ACTH (in the dog, less than 2 minutes), glucocorticoid output rises (Fig 20—17). With low doses of ACTH there is a linear relationship between the log of the dose and the increase in glucocorticoid secretion. However, the maximal rate at which glucocorticoids can be secreted is rapidly reached, and in the dog doses larger than 10 milliunits (mU) only prolong the period of maximal secretion. A similar "ceiling on output" exists in the rat and man. The effects of ACTH on adrenal morphology and the mechanism by which it increases steroid secretion are discussed above.

Adrenal Responsiveness

In chronically hypophysectomized animals and patients with hypopituitarism, single doses of ACTH do not increase glucocorticoid secretion and repeated

FIG 20—17. Changes in cortisol output in the hypophysectomized dog following the administration of various doses of ACTH. (Reproduced, with permission, from Ganong: The central nervous system and the synthesis and release of ACTH. In: *Advances in Neuroendocrinology.* Nalbandov A [editor]. Univ of Illinois Press, 1963.)

TABLE 20—7. Structural differences among ACTHs isolated from the pituitaries of various species.*

Structure of human ACTH: (Straight chain containing 39 amino acids.)

Ser-Tyr-Ser-Met-Glu-His-Phe-Arg-Trp-Gly-Lys-Pro-Val-Gly-Lys-Lys-Arg-Arg-Pro-Val-Lys-Val-Tyr-
 1   2   3   4   5   6   7   8   9   10 11 12 13 14 15 16 17 18 19 20 21 22 23

Pro-Asp-Ala-Gly-Glu-Asp-Gln-Ser-Ala-Glu-Ala-Phe-Pro-Leu-Glu-Phe
24 25 26 27 28 29 30 31 32 33 34 35 36 37 38 39

Species	Amino Acid Residue in Position:								
	25	26	27	28	29	30	31	32	33
Pig	-Asp-	Gly-	Ala-	Glu-	Asp-	Gln-	Leu-	Ala-	Glu-
Sheep	-Ala-	Gly-	Glu-	Asp-	Asp-	Glu-	Ala-	Ser-	Gln-
Beef	-Asp-	Gly-	Glu-	Ala-	Glu-	Asp-	Ser-	Ala-	Gln-

*Data from Evans & others: The physiology and chemistry of adrenocorticotrophin. In: *The Pituitary Gland.* Harris GW, Donovan BT (editors). Univ of California Press, 1966.

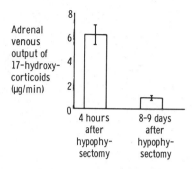

FIG 20–18. Loss of ACTH responsiveness in the dog after hypophysectomy. Values are mean outputs in the adrenal vein after injection of 1 IU of ACTH in 8 dogs. Vertical bars represent standard errors.

FIG 20–19. Fluctuations in plasma ACTH and glucocorticoids throughout the day in a normal girl (age 16). The ACTH was measured by immunoassay and the glucocorticoids as 11-oxy-steroids (11-OHCS). Note the greater ACTH and glucocorticoid rise in the morning, before awakening from sleep. (Reproduced, with permission, from Krieger & others: Characterization of the normal temporal pattern of plasma corticosteroid levels. J Clin Endocrinol 32:266, 1971.)

injections or prolonged infusions of ACTH are necessary to restore normal adrenal responses to ACTH. This decreased adrenal responsiveness to ACTH is detectable within 24 hours after hypophysectomy and increases progressively with time (Fig 20–18). It is marked when the adrenal is atrophic, but develops before there are visible changes in adrenal size or morphology.

Diurnal Rhythm

ACTH is secreted in irregular bursts throughout the day, and plasma cortisol tends to rise and fall in response to these bursts (Fig 20–19). However, in all mammalian species studied, most of the ACTH secretion occurs during one part of the day. In man, the bursts are most frequent in the early morning and least frequent in the evening. This diurnal rhythm in ACTH secretion is present in patients with adrenal insufficiency receiving constant doses of glucocorticoids. It is not due to the stress of getting up in the morning, traumatic as that may be, because the increased ACTH secretion occurs before waking up. If the "day" is lengthened experimentally to more than 24 hours—ie, if the individual is isolated and his day's activities are spread over more than 24 hours—the adrenal cycle also lengthens, but the increase in ACTH secretion still occurs during the period of sleep. The biologic clock responsible for diurnal ACTH rhythm is apparently located in the limbic lobes of the cerebral cortex (see Chapter 15). The diurnal rhythm is absent in patients with hypothalamic and temporal lobe disease.

The Response to Stress

Plasma ACTH levels in various conditions in man are shown in Fig 20–20. The values labeled "stress" in this illustration are those observed following stimuli of moderate strength. During severe stress the amount of ACTH secreted exceeds the amount necessary to produce maximal glucocorticoid output.

Increases in ACTH secretion to meet emergency situations are mediated almost exclusively through the hypothalamus. The median eminence-portal vessel system is the final common pathway to the pituitary; the release of CRF from the median eminence of the hypothalamus and its transport via the portal-hypophysial vessels to the anterior pituitary to stimulate ACTH secretion are discussed in Chapter 14. If the median eminence is destroyed, some basal glucocorticoid secretion continues and the adrenals do not atrophy, but increased secretion in response to many different stresses is blocked. Afferent nerve pathways from many parts of the brain converge on the median eminence. Fibers from the amygdaloid nuclei mediate responses to emotional stresses, and fear, anxiety, and apprehension cause marked increases in ACTH secretion. Input from the limbic system also provides the drive for the diurnal rhythm. Impulses ascending to the hypothalamus in the reticular formation trigger ACTH secretion in response to injury (Fig 20–21). There is also some evidence that the median eminence-anterior pituitary unit can be stimulated by humoral agents reaching it via the blood stream. Contrary to previously proposed theories, epinephrine and norepinephrine do not increase ACTH secretion (at least in the dog and man) and adrenocortical and adrenal medullary secretion are independently regulated from the hypothalamus.

Glucocorticoid Feedback

High circulating levels of free glucocorticoids inhibit ACTH secretion, and the degree of pituitary inhibition is apparently a linear function of the circulating glucocorticoid level. The inhibition appears to be rapid in onset but relatively prolonged. When a single dose of glucocorticoid is injected, peak inhibition

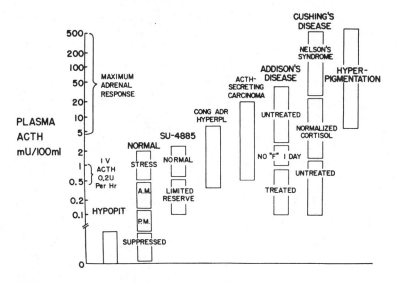

FIG 20–20. Estimates of the average ranges of plasma ACTH values one might expect to encounter in normal subjects and in various clinical conditions. (Reproduced, with permission, from Liddle & others: Normal and abnormal regulation of corticotropin secretion in man. Recent Progr Hormone Res 18:125, 1962.)

occurs after the circulating steroid level has fallen to its preinjection level. The explanation of the delay is not known, but it probably represents persistent hormone action on the tissues. There is a delay of similar magnitude in the peak eosinopenic and other actions of glucocorticoids.

The pituitary-inhibiting activity of the various steroids parallels their glucocorticoid potency. The site at which glucocorticoids act to inhibit ACTH secretion is still a matter of debate. It seems possible that they act on both the hypothalamus and the pituitary.

The dangers involved when prolonged treatment with therapeutic doses of glucocorticoids is stopped deserve emphasis. Not only is the adrenal atrophic and unresponsive after such treatment; even if its responsiveness is restored by injecting ACTH, the pituitary may be unable to secrete normal amounts of ACTH for as long as a month. The cause of the deficiency is presumably diminished ACTH synthesis.

It should be noted that the level of unbound glucocorticoids in the plasma is normally very low, so that there is little pituitary inhibition in the absence of stress. A drop from this level does stimulate increased ACTH secretion, and in chronic adrenal insufficiency there is a marked increase in the rate of ACTH synthesis and secretion. However, an acute drop in circulating glucocorticoid levels is not a potent stimulus to ACTH secretion.

It was once thought that stress stimulated ACTH secretion by initially lowering the plasma corticoid level, but this has been shown to be incorrect. In fact, an untreated adrenalectomized animal whose circulating corticoid level is zero responds to stress with a much greater than normal rise in plasma ACTH. Thus it seems clear that the rate of ACTH secretion is determined by 2 opposing forces: the sum of the neural and possibly other stimuli converging through the median

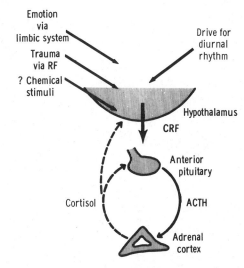

FIG 20–21. Diagram of current concepts of the control of ACTH secretion. The dashed arrows indicate inhibitory effects and the solid arrows stimulating effects. RF = reticular formation.

eminence to increase ACTH secretion, and the magnitude of the braking action of glucocorticoids on ACTH secretion, which is proportionate to their level in the circulating blood (Fig 20–21).

EFFECTS OF MINERALOCORTICOIDS

Actions

Aldosterone and other steroids with mineralocorticoid activity increase the reabsorption of Na^+ from

FIG 20–22. Effect of aldosterone (5 μg as a single dose injected into the aorta) on electrolyte excretion in an adrenalectomized dog. (Data from Ganong & Mulrow: Rate of change in sodium and potassium excretion after injection of aldosterone into the aorta and renal artery of the dog. Am J Physiol 195:337, 1958.)

FIG 20–23. Proposed mechanism of action of aldosterone. The theory is based on the results of experiments with the toad bladder, but it seems likely that it applies to mammalian cells as well. UTP, ATP, CTP, and GTP, purine and pyrimidine triphosphate derivatives; AA-tRNA, amino acid-tRNA complex; E, enzyme; E*, newly synthesized enzyme; Pi, phosphate. The Na^+ pumping mechanism is indicated by the small circle on the cell wall. (Reproduced, with permission, from Edelman & others: Specific action of aldosterone on RNA synthesis. Tr A Am Physicians 77:307, 1964.)

the urine, sweat, saliva, and gastric juice. They may also increase the K^+ and decrease the Na^+ in muscle and brain cells. An action on the distal renal tubule has been demonstrated, but there may be some proximal tubular effect as well. Under the influence of aldosterone, increased numbers of sodium ions are exchanged for K^+ and H^+ in the renal tubules, producing a moderate K^+ diuresis (Fig 20–22) and an increase in urine acidity.

Mechanism of Action

Aldosterone, like other steroids, acts by stimulating DNA-dependent mRNA synthesis (see Chapter 17). Sodium ions diffuse out of the urine (or saliva, sweat, or gastric juice) into the surrounding epithelial cells and are actively transported from these cells into the interstitial fluid. The amount of Na^+ removed from these fluids is proportionate to the rate of active transport of Na^+. The energy for the active transport is believed to be supplied by ATP, and ATP synthesis depends for the most part on the oxidation of substrate to CO_2 and H_2O via the citric acid cycle. Aldosterone apparently initiates an increase in mRNA synthesis at the level of transcription of DNA (Fig 20–23). The induced RNA stimulates protein synthesis at the ribosomal level. Aldosterone-induced proteins may then enhance substrate oxidation and

coupled ATP synthesis. Aldosterone fails to exert any effect on Na^+ excretion for 10–30 minutes or more even when injected directly into the renal artery. This latent period represents the time needed to increase enzyme synthesis.

Aldosterone is the principal mineralocorticoid secreted by the adrenal, although corticosterone is secreted in sufficient amounts to exert a minor mineralocorticoid effect (Tables 20–2 and 20–3). Deoxycorticosterone, which is secreted in appreciable amounts only in abnormal situations, has less than 3% of the activity of aldosterone. It is used clinically as a mineralocorticoid because its synthetic acetate (**deoxycorticosterone acetate, DOCA**) is cheaper and more readily available than aldosterone. It has been claimed that the adrenal secretes salt-losing steroids, but the existence of these substances has never been proved.

Effect of Adrenalectomy

In adrenal insufficiency, Na^+ is lost in the urine, K^+ is retained, and the plasma K^+ rises. When adrenal insufficiency develops rapidly, the decline in ECF Na^+ exceeds the amount excreted in the urine, indicating that Na^+ also must be entering the cells. When the posterior pituitary is intact, salt loss exceeds water loss, and the plasma Na^+ falls (Table 20–8). However, plasma volume also is reduced, resulting in hypo-

TABLE 20–8. Typical plasma electrolyte levels in normal humans and patients with adrenocortical diseases.

	Plasma Electrolytes (mEq/liter)			
	Na^+	K^+	Cl^-	HCO_3^-
Normal	142	4.5	105	25
Adrenal insufficiency	120	6.7	85	25
Primary hyper-aldosteronism	148	2.4	96	41

tension, circulatory insufficiency, and, eventually, fatal shock. These changes can be prevented to a degree by increasing the dietary salt intake. Rats survive indefinitely on extra salt alone, but in dogs and most humans the amount of supplementary salt needed is so large that it is almost impossible to prevent eventual collapse and death unless mineralocorticoid treatment is also instituted.

Secondary Effects of Excess Mineralocorticoids

K^+ depletion due to prolonged K^+ diuresis is a prominent feature of prolonged mineralocorticoid treatment (Table 20–8). When the K^+ loss is marked, intracellular K^+ is replaced by Na^+. This shift can be prevented by the administration of supplemental K^+ along with the mineralocorticoid. There is no net increase in body sodium if salt intake is restricted to the level of output, but on a normal diet total body sodium rises. However, the plasma Na^+ is elevated only slightly, if at all, because water is retained with the osmotically active sodium ions. Consequently, ECF volume is expanded and the blood pressure rises. It has also been claimed that aldosterone and deoxycorticosterone have a direct effect on blood vessels which contributes to the rise in blood pressure. Sometimes, ECF expansion is sufficient to cause heart failure and edema. However, when the expansion passes a certain point, Na^+ excretion is usually increased in spite of the continued action of mineralocorticoids on the renal tubules. This "escape phenomenon" (Fig 20–24) is mostly due to decreased reabsorption of Na^+ in the proximal tubule, but how this decrease is brought about is not known. It is because of this increased excretion of Na^+ when the ECF volume is expanded that mineralocorticoids do not produce edema in normal individuals and patients with hyperaldosteronism.

FIG 20–24. "Escape" from the sodium-retaining effect of deoxycorticosterone acetate (DCA) in an adrenalectomized patient. ECF, extracellular fluid volume; TBV, total blood volume; RCV, red cell volume; PV, plasma volume. (Courtesy of EG Biglieri.)

Primary Hyperaldosteronism

The effects of chronic mineralocorticoid excess are seen in patients with aldosterone-secreting tumors of the adrenal cortex that produce the syndrome of **primary hyperaldosteronism** (Conn's syndrome). These patients are severely K^+-depleted. They are hypertensive and their ECF volume is expanded, but they are not edematous or markedly hypernatremic because the escape phenomenon discussed in the preceding paragraph causes the excretion of any extra salt that is ingested.

Prolonged K^+ depletion damages the kidney, resulting in a loss of concentrating ability and polyuria **(hypokalemic nephropathy)**. The K^+ depletion also causes muscle weakness and metabolic alkalosis (see Chapter 38), and the alkalosis lowers the plasma Ca^{++} level to the point where latent or even frank tetany is present (see Chapter 21). For unknown reasons, the muscle weakness and tetany are much more common in females. The K^+ depletion causes a minor but detectable decrease in glucose tolerance that is corrected by K^+ repletion (see Chapter 19).

REGULATION OF ALDOSTERONE SECRETION

Stimuli

The stimuli which increase aldosterone secretion are summarized in Table 20–9. Some of them also increase glucocorticoid secretion; others selectively affect the output of aldosterone. The regulatory factors involved appear to be ACTH from the pituitary, renin from the kidney, and a direct stimulatory effect of a rise in plasma K^+, or a drop in plasma Na^+, on the adrenal cortex. Except in a few unusual situations such as a high-potassium diet, it seems unlikely that changes in plasma electrolyte levels are a major regulatory mechanism because it appears that the changes must be relatively large before any stimulating effect is seen. In the dog, the plasma K^+ concentration

TABLE 20–9. Stimuli which increase aldosterone secretion.

Glucocorticoid secretion also increased
    Surgery
    Anxiety
    Physical trauma
    Hemorrhage
Glucocorticoid secretion unaffected
    High potassium intake
    Low sodium intake
    Constriction of inferior vena cava in thorax
    Standing
    Secondary hyperaldosteronism (in some cases of congestive heart failure, cirrhosis, and nephrosis)

must rise by at least 1 mEq/liter or the plasma Na^+ fall by about 20 mEq/liter, and few of the stimuli which increase aldosterone secretion produce electrolyte changes of this magnitude.

Effect of ACTH on Aldosterone Secretion

It is now agreed that ACTH stimulates the output of aldosterone as well as that of glucocorticoids and sex hormones. Although the amount of ACTH required to increase aldosterone output is somewhat greater than the amount which stimulates maximal glucocorticoid secretion (Fig 20–25), it is well within the range of endogenous ACTH secretion. The effect is transient, and even if ACTH secretion stays elevated, aldosterone output begins to decline in 1 or 2 days. On the other hand, the output of the mineralocorticoid deoxycorticosterone remains elevated. After hypophysectomy, the basal rate of aldosterone secretion is normal and the rise produced by dietary salt restriction is unaffected for some time, but the increases normally produced by surgical trauma and other stresses are absent. The atrophy of the zona glomerulosa which complicates the picture in long-standing hypopituitarism has been discussed above.

FIG 20–25. Changes in adrenal venous output of steroids produced by ACTH in nephrectomized hypophysectomized dogs. (Data from Mulrow & Ganong, in Ganong: The central nervous system and the synthesis and release of ACTH. In: *Advances in Neuroendocrinology.* Nalbandov A [editor]. Univ of Illinois Press, 1963.)

Effects of Angiotensin II & Renin

The octapeptide, angiotensin II, is formed in the body from angiotensin I, which is liberated by the action of renin on a circulating a_2-globulin (see Chapter 24). Injections of renin or angiotensin II stimulate adrenocortical secretion and, in small doses, affect primarily the secretion of aldosterone (Fig 20–26). In humans, angiotensin II does not increase the secretion of deoxycorticosterone.

Renin is secreted from the juxtaglomerular cells that surround the renal afferent arterioles as they enter

No. of dogs   (5)*   (2)   (8)   (7)   (7)   *Aldosterone values on 3 dogs

FIG 20–26. Changes in adrenal venous output of steroids produced by angiotensin II in nephrectomized hypophysectomized dogs. (Data from Mulrow & others: The nature of the aldosterone-stimulating factor in dog kidneys. J Clin Invest 41:505, 1962.)

the glomeruli. The mechanism which regulates renin secretion is currently the subject of considerable debate (see Chapter 24), but it is clear that decreases in mean renal arterial pressure increase renin secretion. Thus, aldosterone secretion is regulated via the renin-angiotensin system in a feedback fashion (Fig 20–27). A drop in ECF volume or intra-arterial vascular volume decreases renal arterial pressure, increasing renin secretion, and the angiotensin II formed by the action of the renin increases the rate of secretion of aldosterone. The secreted aldosterone causes Na$^+$ and water retention, expanding ECF volume and shutting off the stimulus that initiated increased renin secretion.

Hemorrhage stimulates ACTH secretion, but it also increases aldosterone secretion in the absence of the pituitary. Like hemorrhage, standing and constriction of the thoracic inferior vena cava decrease intra-arterial vascular volume. Dietary sodium restriction also increases aldosterone secretion via the renin-angiotensin system (Fig 20–28). Such restriction reduces ECF volume, but aldosterone and renin secretion are increased before there is any measurable change in blood pressure. Consequently, dietary sodium restriction may increase renin secretion by some as yet unknown mechanism.

The Diencephalon & Aldosterone Secretion

The hypothalamus plays a role in the control of aldosterone secretion through its control of ACTH secretion. Lesions of the hypothalamus which affect ACTH secretion block stress-induced increases in aldosterone secretion. It has been claimed that the pineal gland plays a role in the regulatory process, but it now seems unlikely that any physiologically important aldosterone-regulating mechanism other than that controlling ACTH secretion operates through the diencephalon or pineal gland.

Clinical Correlates

It has been established that circulating renin and angiotensin II levels are elevated in many patients with congestive heart failure, nephrosis, or cirrhosis of the liver. It therefore seems likely that when elevated aldosterone secretion **(secondary hyperaldosteronism)** is seen in these diseases, it is mediated via the renin-angiotensin system. Changes in plasma electrolyte levels in patients are rarely great enough to act directly on the adrenal. Increased renin secretion is also found in individuals with the salt-losing form of the adrenogenital syndrome (see above), presumably because their ECF volume is low. In patients with elevated renin secretion due to renal artery constriction, aldosterone secretion is increased; in those in whom it is not elevated, aldosterone secretion is normal. The relationship of aldosterone to hypertension is discussed in Chapter 24.

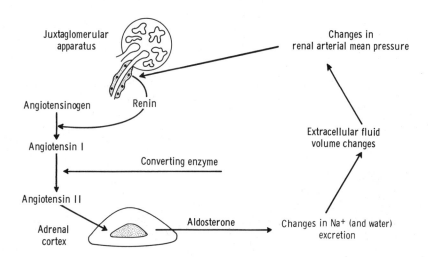

FIG 20–27. A postulated feedback mechanism regulating aldosterone secretion.

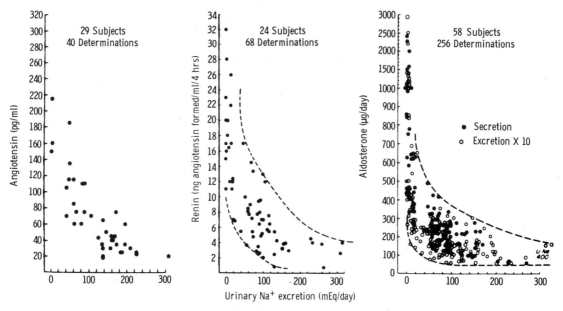

FIG 20–28. Correlation between urinary Na⁺ excretion and plasma angiotensin, plasma renin, and aldosterone secretion. In these normal subjects, the urinary Na⁺ excretion is in turn a reflection of dietary intake. (Courtesy of JA Laragh.)

ROLE OF MINERALOCORTICOIDS IN THE REGULATION OF SALT BALANCE

Variation in aldosterone secretion is only one of many factors affecting Na⁺ excretion. Other major factors include the glomerular filtration rate, the presence or absence of osmotic diuresis, and changes in tubular reabsorption of Na⁺ independent of aldosterone. It should also be remembered that it takes some time for aldosterone to act. Thus, for example, when one rises from the supine to the standing position, aldosterone secretion is increased and there is Na⁺ retention; but the decrease in Na⁺ excretion develops too rapidly to be explained solely by increased aldosterone secretion. The primary function of the aldosterone-secreting mechanism is probably the defense of intravascular volume, but it is only one of the homeostatic mechanisms involved.

SUMMARY OF THE EFFECTS OF ADRENOCORTICAL HYPER- & HYPO-FUNCTION IN MAN

Recapitulating the manifestations of excess and deficiency of the adrenocortical hormones in man is a convenient way to summarize the multiple and complex actions of these steroids. There is a characteristic clinical syndrome associated with excess secretion of each of the types of hormones. Excess androgen secre-

FIG 20–29. Pigmentation in Addison's disease. A, tan and vitiligo; B, pigmentation of scars; C, pigmentation of skin creases; D, darkening of areolas; E, pigmentation of pressure points; F, pigmentation of the gums. (Reproduced, with permission, from Forsham & Di Raimondo in: Traumatic Medicine and Surgery for the Attorney. Butterworth, 1960.)

tion causes masculinization, precocious pseudo-puberty, or female pseudohermaphroditism, depending upon the age at which androgen hypersecretion develops **(adrenogenital syndrome)**. Feminizing estrogen-secreting adrenal tumors are sometimes seen. Excess glucocorticoid secretion produces a moon-faced, plethoric appearance, with trunk obesity, purple abdominal striae, hypertension, osteoporosis, protein depletion, mental abnormalities, and, frequently, diabetes mellitus **(Cushing's syndrome)**.

Excess mineralocorticoid secretion leads to K^+ depletion and Na^+ retention, generally without edema but with weakness, hypertension, tetany, polyuria, and hypokalemic alkalosis **(Conn's syndrome)**.

If hormone treatment is stopped in a surgically adrenalectomized patient, the plasma K^+ rises and the plasma Na^+ falls as Na^+ excretion is increased and Na^+ enters the cells. The plasma volume declines, the blood pressure falls, and fatal shock develops in a few days if treatment is not reinstituted.

These changes can be prevented by mineralo-corticoids. Many adrenalectomized patients, provided they eat regularly, can be maintained for prolonged periods on mineralocorticoid replacement alone, but their existence is a precarious one. Fasting causes fatal hypoglycemia, and any stress causes collapse. Water is poorly excreted, and there is always the danger of water intoxication. Circulating ACTH levels are elevated. The diffuse tanning of the skin and the spotty pigmentation characteristic of chronic glucocorticoid deficiency (Fig 20–29) may be due in part to the MSH activity of the ACTH in the blood (see Chapter 22), but there is evidence that MSH secretion is also increased. Minor menstrual abnormalities occur in women, but the deficiency of adrenal sex hormones usually has little effect in the presence of normal testes or ovaries.

Adrenocortical insufficiency in cases of idiopathic adrenocortical atrophy or destruction of the adrenal glands by diseases such as tuberculosis and cancer is called **Addison's disease**. Total adrenal insufficiency is rapidly fatal, but the loss of adrenocortical function in these patients develops slowly. Because their adrenal insufficiency is relative rather than absolute, they have time to develop marked pigmentation and a decrease in cardiac size which is apparently secondary to chronic hypotension and a decrease in cardiac work. They often get along fairly well until some minor stress precipitates a collapse **(addisonian crisis)** which requires emergency medical treatment.

21...

The Parathyroid Glands, Calcium Metabolism, & the Physiology of Bone

The hormone secreted by the parathyroid glands raises the plasma calcium level, mobilizes calcium from bone, and increases urinary phosphate excretion. Its rate of secretion varies inversely with the plasma ionized calcium level, and the main function of the parathyroid glands is the maintenance of a constant Ca^{++} level in the ECF. Calcitonin, a calcium-lowering hormone which in mammals is secreted primarily by the thyroid gland, may also play a minor role in maintaining the Ca^{++} level.

CALCIUM METABOLISM

Parathyroid hormone is one of the most important factors affecting calcium metabolism. The adult human body contains about 1100 g of calcium (1.5% of body weight). Most of the calcium is in the skeleton. The plasma calcium, normally about 5 mEq/liter (10 mg/100 ml, 2.5 mM/liter), is partly bound to protein and partly diffusible (Fig 21–1).

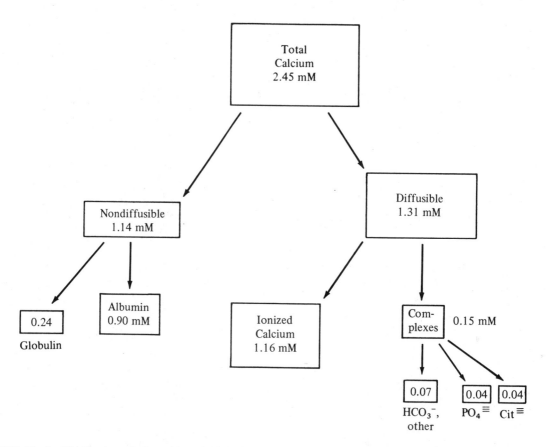

FIG 21–1. Distribution of the calcium in 1 liter of plasma. (Modified and reproduced, with permission, from Neuman & Neuman: *The Chemical Dynamics of Bone Mineral.* Univ of Chicago Press, 1958.)

It is the free, ionized calcium in the body fluids that is necessary for blood coagulation, normal cardiac and skeletal muscle contraction, and nerve function. A decrease in extracellular Ca^{++} at the myoneural junction inhibits transmission (see Chapter 4), but this effect is overbalanced by the excitatory effect of a low Ca^{++} level on nerve and muscle cells. The result is **hypocalcemic tetany**, which is due to increased activity of the motor nerve fibers. This condition is characterized by extensive spasms of skeletal muscle, involving especially the muscles of the extremities and the larynx. Laryngospasm becomes so severe that the airway is obstructed, and fatal asphyxia is produced. Calcium deficiency also has effects on clotting (see Chapter 27) and other systems; in vivo, however, the level of plasma calcium at which fatal tetany occurs is still above the level at which clotting defects would occur. In addition, calcium is an important constituent of the intercellular cement substance.

Since the extent of Ca^{++} binding by plasma proteins is proportionate to the plasma protein level, it is important to determine the plasma protein level at the same time total plasma calcium is measured. Reliable methods for measuring plasma ionized calcium are not available for routine use. Other electrolytes and pH affect the Ca^{++} level. The actions of the electrolytes in plasma are conveniently summarized in the following expression:

$$\text{Tendency to tetany} \cong \frac{[HCO_3^-][HPO_4^=]}{[Ca^{++}][Mg^{++}][H^+]}$$

Thus, for example, the symptoms of tetany appear at much higher Ca^{++} levels if the patient hyperventilates (decreased plasma H^+). Plasma proteins are more ionized when the pH is high, providing more protein anion to bind with Ca^{++}.

The calcium in bone is of 2 types: a readily exchangeable reservoir, and a larger pool of stable calcium that is only slowly exchangeable. The plasma calcium is in equilibrium with the readily exchangeable bone calcium.

The mechanisms regulating calcium absorption from the gastrointestinal tract are not completely understood. Absorption is decreased by substances which form insoluble salts with Ca^{++} (eg, phosphates and oxalates), or by alkalies, which favor formation of insoluble calcium soaps. A high-protein diet increases absorption in adults. Excess dietary calcium is excreted in the stools, but most of the calcium liberated during bone resorption is excreted in the urine. Calcium is actively transported out of the intestine by a system in the brush border of the epithelial cells that involves a calcium-dependent ATPase. Phosphate is transported secondary to the transport of calcium.

The active transport of calcium from the intestine is increased by vitamin D. The term vitamin D is used to refer to a group of closely related sterols produced by the action of ultraviolet light on certain provitamins (Fig 21−2). Vitamin D_3 is produced in the skin of

FIG 21−2. Vitamin D. Vitamin D_3 is formed from the provitamin 7-dehydrocholesterol in the skin of mammals and converted to the active metabolite, 1,25-dihydroxycholecalciferol.

mammals from 7-dehydrocholesterol by the action of sunlight. The vitamin D_3 is carried to the liver, where it is converted to a metabolite of the vitamin, 25-hydroxycholecalciferol. The 25-hydroxycholecalciferol is converted in turn in the kidney into the physiologically active metabolite, 1,25-dihydroxycholecalciferol. This metabolite acts on the nuclei of the epithelial cells to iniate the formation of mRNA. The mRNA dictates the formation of a protein which increases the activity of the calcium transport mechanism. Vitamin D has a similar action on bone, mobilizing calcium from old bone. However, the poor absorption of calcium in vitamin D deficiency often leads to hypocalcemia, and, because of the calcium deficiency, the protein of new bone fails to mineralize. The result in children and young animals is the disease called **rickets**. It is worth noting that rickets can be due to inadequate intake of the provitamins that are converted to vitamin D_3 by sunlight or to inadequate exposure to the sun. Rickets is also seen as a complication of renal disease, possibly because the kidney fails to produce normal amounts of 1,25-dihydroxycholecalciferol. Administration of large doses of vitamin D or the related compound **dihydrotachysterol** raises the plasma Ca^{++} level sufficiently to be of benefit in the treatment of hypoparathyroidism.

It has now been demonstrated that formation of 1,25-dihydroxycholecalciferol is regulated by plasma Ca^{++}, being increased when plasma Ca^{++} is decreased and decreased when plasma Ca^{++} is increased. There is evidence that the effect of decreased Ca^{++} is mediated by way of parathyroid hormone, which thus acts as a tropic hormone to the 1,25-dihydroxycholecalciferol-forming mechanism in the kidney. This is not the only action of parathyroid hormone on Ca^{++} metabolism, but it does make parathyroid hormone part of a feedback loop regulating Ca^{++} absorption.

In addition to parathyroid hormone and calcitonin, the hormones affecting calcium metabolism include adrenal glucocorticoids and growth hormone. The glucocorticoids lower plasma calcium levels, possibly by stabilizing lysosomal membranes in bone and thus decreasing bone resorption. They also tear down the protein matrix of bone, leading to osteoporosis (see below). They inhibit the action of vitamin D on the intestine and depress the hypercalcemia of vitamin D intoxication. Growth hormone increases calcium excretion in the urine, but it also increases intestinal absorption of calcium, and this effect may be greater than the effect on excretion with a resultant positive calcium balance.

BONE PHYSIOLOGY

Structure of Bone

Bone is a living tissue with a collagenous protein matrix that has been impregnated with mineral salts, especially phosphates of calcium. The protein in the collagen fibers that form bone matrix is complex. Adequate amounts of both protein and minerals must be available for the maintenance of normal bone structure. Mineral in bone is mostly in the form of a complex salt that resembles and may be identical with **hydroxyapatite**, $Ca_{10}(PO_4)_6(OH)_2$. This salt forms crystals that measure 20 by 3–7 nm. Sodium and small amounts of magnesium and carbonate are also present in bone.

Bone is cellular and well vascularized; the total bone blood flow in man has been estimated to be 200–400 ml/min. Throughout life, the mineral in the skeleton is being actively turned over, and bone is constantly being resorbed and reformed.

It is generally stated that the cells in bone that are primarily concerned with bone formation and resorption are the osteoblasts, the osteocytes, and the osteoclasts. However, these 3 cell types are apparently interconvertible, and it is probably appropriate to regard them as phases of a single cell type. **Osteoblasts** are the bone-forming cells that secrete collagen, forming a matrix around themselves that then calcifies. **Osteocytes** are bone cells surrounded by calcified matrix. They send processes into the canaliculi that ramify throughout the bone and are capable of considerable bone resorption. **Osteoclasts** are multinuclear cells that erode and resorb previously formed bone.

Bone Formation

The bones of the skull are formed by ossification of membranes (**intramembranous** bone formation). The long bones are first modeled in cartilage and then transformed into bone by ossification that begins in the shaft and in the ends of the bone (**enchondral** bone formation). Osteoblasts form a network of collagen fibers. This matrix then calcifies. In the meantime, the cartilage in the center of the shaft is invaded by osteoclasts which erode it away.

During growth, specialized areas at the ends of each long bone (**epiphyses**) are separated from the shaft of the bone by a plate of actively proliferating cartilage, the **epiphyseal plate**. Growth in bone length occurs as this plate lays down new bone on the end of the shaft. The width of the epiphyseal plate is proportionate to the rate of growth. Its width is affected by a number of hormones, but most markedly by the pituitary growth hormone. Changes in the width of the tibial epiphyseal plate are used as the endpoint in the "tibia test," a bioassay that has been used to measure growth hormone (see Chapter 22).

Linear bone growth can occur as long as the epiphyses are separated from the shaft of the bone, but such growth ceases after the epiphyses unite with the shaft (**epiphyseal closure**). The epiphyses of the various bones close in an orderly temporal sequence, the last epiphyses closing after puberty. In man, the normal age at which each of the epiphyses closes is known, and by x-raying the skeleton and noting which epiphyses are open and which are closed the "bone age" of an individual can be determined.

Calcification

The details of the process responsible for the calcification of newly formed bone matrix are uncertain despite intensive investigation. Whether or not calcium phosphate precipitates out of a solution depends upon the product of the concentrations of Ca^{++} and $PO_4^{\equiv}$. At a certain value for this product (the **solubility product**), the solution is saturated. Whenever $[Ca^{++}] \times [PO_4^{\equiv}]$ exceeds the solubility product, calcium phosphate precipitates. Associated with the osteoblasts in new bone is an alkaline phosphatase that hydrolyzes phosphate esters. It has been postulated that phosphates liberated by such ester hydrolysis increase the concentration of phosphate in the vicinity of the osteoblasts to a point where the solubility product is exceeded and calcium phosphate precipitates. This mechanism may be involved in the calcification process, but it is almost certainly only part of the story. There is some evidence that mineralization is a consequence of the stereochemical configuration of the collagen molecule itself.

In the same way that alkaline phosphatase is associated with the osteoblasts, acid phosphatase is associated with the osteoclasts. The significance of this association is not known, and the mechanisms by which the osteoclasts cause bone resorption are incompletely understood. They may secrete an acid which demineralizes the bone in their vicinity, or a chelating agent which ties up calcium, causing more bone calcium to go into solution. Other investigations suggest that osteoclasts phagocytize bone, digesting it in their cytoplasm.

Uptake of Other Minerals

Lead and some other toxic elements are taken up and released by bone in a manner similar to that in which calcium is turned over. The rapid bone uptake of these elements is sometimes called a "detoxifying mechanism" because it serves to remove them from the body fluids, thus ameliorating the toxic manifestations. One way to treat lead poisoning is to encourage the deposition of lead in bone by the use of such procedures as a high-calcium, low-phosphate diet and large doses of vitamin D. However, the lead in the bones is then subject to mobilization under any of the conditions in which calcium is mobilized. For example, if an individual becomes acidotic for any reason, the symptoms of lead intoxication may recur without any additional lead intake. For this reason, some authorities recommend that once the lead is in the bones, acid salts should be administered to promote its slow, steady release into the plasma and excretion in the urine.

The radioactive elements radium and plutonium (and the radioactive isotope of strontium that is a by-product of atomic bomb explosions) are also taken up by bone. In this situation, the uptake is definitely harmful, because radiation from these elements may cause malignant degeneration of bone cells and the formation of osteogenic sarcomas.

Fluoride is taken up by bone and is incorporated into the enamel of the teeth. When the amount incorporated is large, a discoloration of the enamel (**mottled enamel**) results. However, small amounts endow the teeth with a significantly increased resistance to dental caries.

Metabolic Bone Disease

There are a variety of diseases in which bone changes are secondary to generalized disturbances in metabolism. Terminology in this field has been changing and unsettled, but a number of names are in general use. **Osteosclerosis**, the presence of increased amounts of calcified bone, occurs in patients with metastatic tumors, lead poisoning, and hypoparathyroidism. **Osteoporosis**, a decrease in the amount of bone per unit volume, is a common abnormality which can be due to increased bone resorption or decreased bone formation. Bone formation is decreased in patients who are immobilized for any reason and in patients with excess glucocorticoid secretion (Cushing's syndrome). The term **osteomalacia** is usually used to refer to disorders such as rickets in which mineral accretion in bone is deficient.

ANATOMY OF THE PARATHYROIDS

In humans there are usually 4 parathyroid glands: 2 embedded in the superior poles of the thyroid and 2 in its inferior poles (Fig 21–3). However, the location of the individual parathyroids and their number vary considerably. Parathyroid tissue is sometimes found in the mediastinum.

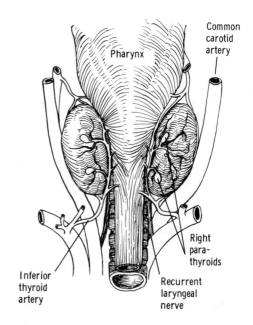

FIG 21–3. The human parathyroid glands, viewed from behind. (Redrawn and reproduced, with permission, from: *Gray's Anatomy of the Human Body,* 29th ed. Goss CM [editor]. Lea & Febiger, 1973.)

Each parathyroid gland is a richly vascularized disk, about 3 X 6 X 2 mm, containing 2 distinct types of cells. The abundant **chief cells**, which have a clear cytoplasm, secrete parathyroid hormone. The less frequent, larger **oxyphil cells**, which have oxyphil granules in their cytoplasm (Fig 21–4), contain large numbers of mitochondria. Their function is unknown.

FIG 21–4. Section of human parathyroid. (Reduced 50% from × 960.) Small cells are chief cells; large cells with granules in cytoplasm (especially prominent in lower left of picture) are oxyphil cells. (Reproduced, with permission, from Bloom & Fawcett: *A Textbook of Histology,* 9th ed. Saunders, 1968.)

In man, tetany is most often due to inadvertent parathyroidectomy during thyroid surgery. Symptoms usually develop 2–3 days postoperatively, but may not appear for several weeks or more. In rats on a low-calcium diet, tetany develops much more rapidly, and death occurs 6–10 hours after parathyroidectomy. Injections of parathyroid hormone correct the chemical abnormalities (Fig 21–5), and the symptoms disappear. Injections of calcium salts give temporary relief, and large doses of vitamin D or related sterols may maintain the plasma Ca^{++} at a level high enough to prevent symptoms.

The signs of tetany in man include **Chvostek's sign,** a quick contraction of the ipsilateral facial muscles elicited by tapping over the facial nerve at the angle of the jaw; and **Trousseau's sign,** a spasm of the muscles of the upper extremity that causes flexion of the wrist and thumb with extension of the fingers (Fig 21–6). In individuals with mild tetany in whom spasm is not evident, Trousseau's sign can sometimes be produced by occluding the circulation for a few minutes with a blood pressure cuff.

EFFECTS OF PARATHYROIDECTOMY & PARATHYROID EXTRACTS

Parathyroid hormone (parathormone, PTH) is essential for life. After parathyroidectomy, there is a steady decline in the plasma calcium level (Fig 21–5). Signs of neuromuscular hyperexcitability appear, followed by full-blown hypocalcemic tetany (see above). Plasma phosphate levels usually rise as the calcium falls after parathyroidectomy, but the rise does not always occur. In experimental animals, the rise is preceded by a fall.

FIG 21–6. Position of the hand in hypocalcemic tetany (Trousseau's sign). (After Aub. Drawn from a photograph in Adams: *Physical Diagnosis,* 14th ed. Williams & Wilkins, 1958.)

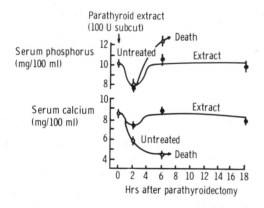

FIG 21–5. Effect of parathyroidectomy (open circles) and parathyroidectomy plus parathyroid extract (solid circles) in rats. Vertical bars are standard errors, each point being a mean of the values for 6 rats. (Redrawn and reproduced, with permission, from Munson: Recent advances in parathyroid hormone research. Fed Proc 19:593, 1960.)

Hyperparathyroidism due to injections of large doses of parathyroid extract in animals, or hypersecretion of a functioning parathyroid tumor in man, is characterized by hypercalcemia, hypophosphatemia, demineralization of the bones, hypercalciuria, and the formation of calcium-containing kidney stones. The bone disease caused by hyperparathyroidism is characterized by multiple bone cysts, and is known as **osteitis fibrosa cystica.** Bone resorption around the teeth with loss of the distinctness of the lamina dura in dental x-rays was once held to be an early and specific change in this disease, but it has now been shown that changes in the lamina dura do not occur regularly. Dental x-rays are therefore of questionable value in the diagnosis of hyperparathyroidism.

CHEMISTRY & METABOLISM OF PARATHYROID HORMONE

Bovine parathyroid hormone is a linear polypeptide with a molecular weight of 9500 that contains 84 amino acids (Fig 21–7). The biologic activity depends on the 34 amino acid residues nearest the N terminal. The half-life of parathyroid hormone in the circulation has been calculated to be 18 minutes in cows, and there is a significant decline in the plasma calcium level 1 hour after parathyroidectomy in calcium-depleted rats, indicating that it is metabolized rapidly. Some of the hormone is excreted in the urine.

FIG 21–7. Bovine parathyroid hormone.

In humans, parathyroid hormone is synthesized as part of a larger molecule (**pro-PTH**) in the parathyroid gland. Pro-PTH is cleaved in the gland, and a polypeptide with a molecular weight of 9500 is secreted into the blood. After secretion, there is a second rapid cleavage of the molecule to form a biologically inactive fragment with a molecular weight of 7500. This inactive molecule can also be detected in the circulation.

MECHANISM OF ACTION OF PARATHYROID HORMONE

In addition to increasing the plasma Ca^{++} and depressing the plasma phosphate, parathyroid hormone increases phosphate excretion in the urine. This **phosphaturic action** is due to a decrease in tubular reabsorption of phosphate. It was once believed that the increase in the plasma calcium level produced by parathyroid hormone was secondary to the decrease in plasma phosphate level, and, therefore, that the entire effect of the hormone could be explained by its phosphaturic action on the kidney. The rough reciprocal relationship between the plasma calcium and the plasma phosphate levels has been mentioned above. However, parathyroid hormone has a direct calcium-mobilizing action on bone in addition to its action on the kidney. It also increases renal reabsorption of calcium, although calcium excretion is usually increased in hyperparathyroidism because the increase in the amount filtered overwhelms the effect on reabsorption.

The actions of parathyroid hormone on the bones, the kidneys, and the intestine involve activation of adenyl cyclase, with consequent increased formation of cyclic AMP in the affected cells. How cyclic AMP affects calcium in bone is unsettled. The hormone promotes a rapid release of calcium and phosphorus from bone mineral into ECF, probably by stimulating bone resorption by the osteocytes. It also promotes on a more long-term basis increased osteoclastic activity, and may trigger the formation of more osteoclasts. There is some evidence that the cyclic AMP generated by parathyroid hormone increases the entry of calcium into the bone cells from bone matrix and that the calcium in turn activates—via the formation of mRNA—the synthesis of bone-resorbing enzymes. Vitamin D has an action on bone similar to parathyroid hormone and synergizes with it, but the vitamin does not affect cyclic AMP. Parathyroid hormone also increases the formation of 1,25-dihydroxy-cholecalciferol, the physiologically active metabolite of vitamin D (see above).

REGULATION OF PARATHYROID SECRETION

It has been proved by perfusion experiments that the circulating level of ionized calcium acts directly on the parathyroid glands in a feedback fashion to regulate the secretion of parathyroid hormone. When the plasma Ca^{++} level is high, secretion is inhibited, and the calcium is deposited in the bones. When it is low, secretion is increased, and calcium is mobilized from the bones. Magnesium appears to have a similar direct effect, with a decrease in plasma magnesium concentration stimulating parathyroid secretion. Another factor regulating the plasma Ca^{++} is the readily exchangeable bone calcium pool. However, this pool can only maintain the total plasma calcium at about 7 mg/100 ml in the absence of parathyroid hormone, and maintenance of the normal level of 10 mg/100 ml is due to the activity of the parathyroid. Elevated plasma phosphate levels stimulate parathyroid secretion, but only because they lower the plasma Ca⁺⁺ level; they do not act directly on the gland.

In conditions such as chronic renal disease and rickets, in which the plasma Ca⁺⁺ is chronically low, feedback stimulation of the parathyroid glands causes compensatory parathyroid hypertrophy and **secondary hyperparathyroidism.**

CALCITONIN

Origin

Perfusion of the thyroparathyroid region in the dog with solutions containing high concentrations of Ca^{++} leads to a fall in peripheral plasma Ca^{++}, after damage to this region, Ca^{++} infusions cause a greater increase in plasma Ca^{++} than they do in control animals. These and other observations led to the discovery that there is a calcium-lowering as well as a calcium-elevating hormone. The calcium-lowering hormone has been named **calcitonin.** In nonmammalian vertebrates, the source of calcitonin is the **ultimobranchial bodies,** a pair of glands which are derived embryologically from the fifth branchial arches. In mammals, these bodies have for the most part become incorporated into the thyroid gland, where the ultimobranchial tissue is distributed around the follicles as the **parafollicular cells.** Since these cells, which are also known as clear cells or C cells, secrete the hormone, it is often referred to as **thyrocalcitonin.** However, total thyroidectomy does not reduce the circulating level of the hormone to zero, and the hormone has been clearly demonstrated in the human thymus. Therefore, it seems more appropriate to refer to it by its original name, calcitonin.

Structure

The structure of human calcitonin (Fig 21–8) has been determined by analysis of extracts of medullary carcinomas of the thyroid. These are calcitonin-secreting tumors rich in parafollicular cells. The calcitonins of the other species that have been studied contain 32 amino acid residues, but the amino acid composition varies considerably. Salmon calcitonin is of some interest because it is 20 or more times as active in humans as human calcitonin.

Secretion

Secretion of calcitonin is increased when the thyroid gland is perfused with solutions containing a high Ca⁺⁺ concentration. Measurement of circulating calcitonin by immunoassay indicates that it is not secreted until the plasma calcium reaches approximately 9.5 mg/100 ml and that above this calcium level, plasma calcitonin is directly proportionate to plasma calcium (Fig 21–9). The normal rate of secretion appears to be about 0.5 mg/day. Cyclic AMP may be involved in the regulation of calcitonin secretion. There is some evidence that a "gut factor"—probably CCK (see Chapter 26)—stimulates calcitonin secretion, and it may be that calcium in the intestine initiates secretion of the calcium-lowering hormone before the calcium is absorbed.

FIG 21–9. Concentration of calcitonin (C) and parathyroid hormone (PTH) as a function of plasma calcium level. (Modified and reproduced, with permission, from Aurbach & others: Polypeptide hormones and calcium metabolism. Ann Int Med 70:1243, 1969).

Actions

Calcitonin lowers the circulating calcium and phosphate level. An example of its action is shown in Fig 21–10, which also shows that porcine calcitonin fails to affect the plasma magnesium level in man. It exerts its calcium-lowering effect by inhibiting bone resorption. This effect occurs in the absence of the parathyroid glands, gastrointestinal tract, and kidneys

Cys-Gly-Asn-Leu-Ser-Thr-Cys-Met-Leu-Gly-Thr-Tyr-Thr-Gln-Asp-Phe-Asn-
 1   2   3   4   5   6   7   8   9 10 11 12 13 14 15 16 17

Lys-Phe-His-Thr-Phe-Pro-Gln-Thr-Ala-Ile-Gly-Val-Gly-Ala-Pro-NH_2
 18 19 20 21 22 23 24 25 26 27 28 29 30 31 32

FIG 21–8. Human calcitonin.

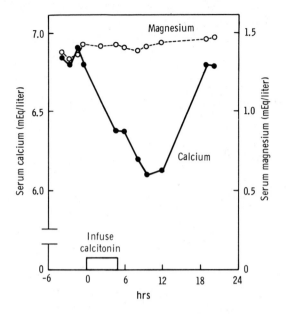

FIG 21–10. Effect of porcine calcitonin on serum calcium and magnesium in a patient with hypercalcemia. (Reproduced, with permission, from Foster & others: Effect of thyrocalcitonin in man. Lancet 1:107, 1966.)

and is due to a direct action of the hormone on bone. There is evidence that it acts by inhibiting the active transport of calcium from bone cells into the ECF. It does not appear to affect cyclic AMP or the genetic mechanism regulating protein synthesis.

The exact physiologic role of calcitonin is uncertain. The calcitonin content of the human thyroid is very low, and in thyroidectomized animals it is only after injecting calcium or parathyroid extract that any definite abnormality of calcium metabolism can be demonstrated. This may be explained in part by calcitonin from tissues other than the thyroid. However, there is general agreement that the hormone is relatively inactive in adult animals and humans. In addition, patients with medullary carcinoma of the thyroid and high circulating calcitonin levels have no symptoms directly attributable to the hormone. Similarly, a syndrome due to calcitonin deficiency has not been described. The hormone is more active in young individuals and may play a role in skeletal development.

22...

The Pituitary Gland

The anterior, intermediate and posterior lobes of the pituitary gland are actually 3 more or less separate endocrine organs that secrete in all at least 10 hormones. The 6 established hormones of the anterior pituitary are **TSH, ACTH, FSH, LH, prolactin**, and **growth hormone** (Table 22–1). All of these except growth hormone and prolactin regulate the function of other endocrine organs, and growth hormone causes the secretion of a peptide from the liver (see below). The hormones that are tropic to a particular endocrine gland are discussed in the chapter on that gland: TSH in Chapter 18; ACTH in Chapter 20; and the gonadotropins FSH and LH in Chapter 23, along with prolactin. The hormones secreted by the posterior pituitary in mammals (**oxytocin** and **vasopressin**) and the neural regulation of anterior and posterior pituitary secretion are discussed in Chapter 14. Growth hormone and the melanocyte-stimulating hormones of the intermediate lobe of the pituitary, a **MSH** and β **MSH**, are the subject of this chapter, along with a number of general considerations about the pituitary.

From time to time it has been claimed that other hormones are secreted by the anterior pituitary. There is some evidence that the pituitary produces a hormone concerned with the mobilization of fat, but—at least in man, the dog, and the rat—growth hormone is the only anterior pituitary hormone that has been proved to function as a fat-mobilizing hormone under physiologic conditions.

MORPHOLOGY

Gross Anatomy

The anatomy of the pituitary gland is summarized in Fig 22–1 and discussed in detail in Chapter 14. The posterior pituitary is innervated by fibers from the supraoptic and paraventricular nuclei of the hypothalamus, whereas the anterior pituitary has a special vascular connection with the brain, the portal hypophyseal vessels. The intermediate lobe is formed from the dorsal half of **Rathke's pouch** in the embryo, but is closely adherent to the posterior lobe in the adult. It is separated from the anterior lobe by the remains of Rathke's pouch, the **residual cleft**.

Histology

In the posterior lobe, the endings of the supra-

TABLE 22–1. Pituitary hormones.

Name and Source	Principal Actions
Anterior lobe	
Thyroid-stimulating hormone (TSH, thyrotropin)	Stimulates thyroid secretion and growth
Adrenocorticotropic hormone (ACTH, corticotropin)	Stimulates adrenocortical secretion and growth
Growth hormone (GH, somatotropin, STH)	Accelerates body growth
Follicle-stimulating hormone (FSH)	Stimulates ovarian follicle growth in female and spermatogenesis in male
Luteinizing hormone (LH, interstitial cell-stimulating hormone, ICSH)	Stimulates ovulation and luteinization of ovarian follicles in female and testosterone secretion in male
Prolactin (luteotropic hormone, LTH, luteotropin, lactogenic hormone, mammotropin)	Stimulates secretion of milk and maternal behavior. Maintains corpus luteum in female rodents but apparently not in other species
Intermediate lobe	
a- and β- Melanocyte-stimulating hormones (a- and β-MSH; referred to collectively as melanotropin or intermedin)	Expand melanophores
Posterior lobe	
Vasopressin (antidiuretic hormone, ADH)	Promotes water retention
Oxytocin	Causes milk ejection

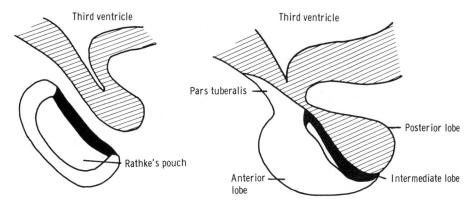

FIG 22–1. Diagrammatic outline of the formation of the pituitary and the various parts of the organ in the adult.

optic and paraventricular axons can be observed in close relation to blood vessels. In some species the endings are rod-like, palisaded structures. There are also neuroglial cells and **pituicytes**, stellate cells containing fat globules, which were once thought to secrete posterior lobe hormones but which are now believed to be modified astroglia.

The intermediate lobe is rudimentary in man. Most of its cells are agranular, although there are often a few basophilic elements that resemble anterior lobe cells. Along the residual cleft there are small thyroid-like follicles, some containing a little colloid.

The anterior pituitary is made up of interlacing cell cords and an extensive network of sinusoids. The endothelium of the sinusoids is fenestrated, like that in other endocrine organs. The cells contain granules of stored hormone which are extruded from the cells by exocytosis (Fig 22–2). The granules have not been seen entering the capillaries and they presumably dissolve in the perisinusoidal space. They contain an alkaline protease which might help them penetrate the basement membranes.

Cell Types in the Anterior Pituitary

In the rat, the cells that secrete each of the 6 anterior pituitary hormones can be identified histologically. In man, anterior pituitary cells have traditionally been divided on the basis of their staining reactions into agranular chromophobes and granular chromophils. The chromophobes are probably secretory cells that are quiescent and not forming secretory granules, or are secreting so rapidly that their stores of granules are exhausted. The chromophilic cells are subdivided into acidophils, which contain large granules that stain readily with acidic dyes, and basophils, which contain small glycoprotein granules with an affinity for basic dyes. Three of the hormones secreted by the basophils are glycoproteins. There has been debate about the ACTH-secreting cells. Tumors made up of what appear to be chromophobes secrete ACTH, but there is considerable evidence that the ACTH-secreting cells in normal humans are basophils (Table 22–2). It has now been established that there

FIG 22–2. Sinusoid in anterior pituitary of rat, surrounded by granule-containing anterior pituitary cells. *RC,* red cell in lumen of sinusoid; *E,* endothelial cell; *M,* macrophage in perisinusoidal space. *Inset:* Higher magnification of area such as that enclosed in the small rectangle showing release of granule by exocytosis. Structures are, from the left, pituitary cell containing granules, basement membrane of pituitary cell, perisinusoidal space, basement membrane of endothelial cell, endothelial cell, lumen of sinusoid. Note that at 2 locations in the inset the endothelial cell cytoplasm is attenuated (fenestrated) to form membrane-closed pores. (Redrawn and reproduced, with permission, from Farquhar: Fine structure and function in capillaries of the anterior pituitary gland. Angiology 12:270, 1961.)

TABLE 22–2. Hormone-secreting cells in the human anterior pituitary. PAS, periodic acid-Schiff reaction. (Courtesy of C Ezrin.)

Cell Type	Hormone Secreted	Staining Reactions		
		General	Orange G	PAS
Somatotrop	Growth hormone	Acidophil	+	–
Mammotrop	Prolactin	Acidophil	+	–
Corticotrop	ACTH	Basophil	–	+
FSH gonadotrop	FSH	Basophil	–	+
LH gonadotrop	LH	Basophil	–	+
Thyrotrop	TSH	Basophil	–	+

are 2 types of acidophils in humans, one secreting growth hormone and the other prolactin.

Two-Unit Structure of FSH, LH, & TSH

A recent discovery that bears on the question of the cells of origin of pituitary hormones is the demonstration that the 3 pituitary glycoprotein hormones are each made up of 2 subunits. The subunits, which have been designated a and β, have some activity, but must be combined for maximal physiologic activity. In addition, the placental glycoprotein gonadotropin HCG (see Chapter 23) has an a and a β subunit. All the a subunits of these hormones are similar to one another, even though they are produced in different cells. The β subunits, which differ in structure, confer hormonal specificity. The a units are remarkably interchangeable, and the hybrid molecule made up of TSH-a and LH-β, for example, has much more gonadotropic activity than LH-β alone. The physiologic and evolutionary significance of the unique 2-unit structure of these glycoprotein hormones remains to be determined.

INTERMEDIATE LOBE HORMONES

In the skins of fish, reptiles, and amphibians there are cells called melanophores which contain melanin granules. Others called iridophores contain reflecting platelets. When the granules aggregate around the nuclei of melanophores and the reflecting platelets disperse to the periphery of the iridophores, the color of the skin lightens; when the melanin granules disperse and the reflecting platelets aggregate, the skin darkens. Birds and mammals do not have pigment cells of this type, but their pituitaries contain 2 polypeptides called **melanotropins** or **melanocyte-stimulating hormones (MSHs)** which upon injection in lower vertebrates disperse melanophore granules and aggregate iridophore platelets. The structure of one of these polypeptides (a MSH) is the same in all mammalian species studied; the structure of the other (β MSH) varies from species to species (Table 22–3). The MSHs have amino acid sequences in common with ACTH, and pure ACTH has an MSH activity that is about 1/100 that of β MSH and 1/200 that of a MSH. On the other hand, the MSHs have no physiologically significant ACTH activity. In species which have melanophores, MSH activity is found in the intermediate lobe, but in mammals the MSHs are also found in anterior and posterior lobe tissue.

Changes in skin coloration in fish, reptiles, and amphibians are probably mediated in part via neuroendocrine reflex mechanisms. The receptor for these reflexes is the retina. The hypothalamus has been reported to contain an MSH-stimulating factor and an MSH-inhibiting factor, but the intermediate lobe is also believed to be innervated by fibers from the hypothalamus that inhibit MSH secretion. On a dark background, MSH secretion is not inhibited and the animal is dark. On a white background, release of MSH is inhibited and the animal's color lightens.

Melatonin, an indole derivative found in the pineal glands of mammals and other vertebrates (see Chapter 24), lightens the skin of embryonic fish and larval amphibians by causing aggregation of melanophore granules without any change in the iridophores. However, it does not exert a lightening effect in adult

TABLE 22–3. The relationship between the structure of the MSHs and amino acids 1–19 of the 39 amino acids in ACTH.*

		Ser-	Tyr-	Ser-	Met-Glu-His-Phe-Arg-Trp-Gly-	Lys-	Pro-	Val-	Gly-Lys-Lys-Arg-Arg-Pro
ACTH (pig, sheep, beef)		Ser-1	Tyr-2	Ser-3	Met-Glu-His-Phe-Arg-Trp-Gly- 4 5 6 7 8 9 10	Lys-11	Pro-12	Val-13	Gly-Lys-Lys-Arg-Arg-Pro 14 15 16 17 18 19
a MSH (pig, beef, horse)	CH₃CO-	Ser-1	Tyr-2	Ser-3	Met-Glu-His-Phe-Arg-Trp-Gly- 4 5 6 7 8 9 10	Lys-11	Pro-12	Val-13	NH₂
β MSH (pig)	Asp-Glu-Gly-Pro- 1 2 3 4	Tyr-5	Lys-6		Met-Glu-His-Phe-Arg-Trp-Gly- 7 8' 9 10 11 12 13	Ser-14	Pro-15	Pro-16	Lys-Asp 17 18
β MSH (beef)	Asp-Ser-Gly-Pro- 1 2 3 4	Tyr-5	Lys-6		Met-Glu-His-Phe-Arg-Trp-Gly- 7 8 9 10 11 12 13	Ser-14	Pro-15	Pro-16	Lys-Asp 17 18
β MSH (horse)	Asp-Glu-Gly-Pro- 1 2 3 4	Tyr-5	Lys-6		Met-Glu-His-Phe-Arg-Trp-Gly- 7 8 9 10 11 12 13	Ser-14	Pro-15	Arg-16	Lys-Asp 17 18
β MSH (human)	Ala-Glu-Lys-Lys-Asp-Glu-Gly-Pro- 1 2 3 4 5 6 7 8	Tyr-9	Arg-10		Met-Glu-His-Phe-Arg-Trp-Gly- 11 12 13 14 15 16 17	Ser-18	Pro-19	Pro-20	Lys-Asp 21 22

*Reproduced, with permission, from Li: Some aspects of the relation of peptide structure to activity in pituitary hormones. Vitamins & Hormones 19:313, 1961.

animals and apparently does not play any role in regulating their skin color.

In man and other mammals there are melanin-containing cells called **melanocytes**, but no melanophores containing pigment granules which move, and the functions of the MSHs and melatonin, if any, are uncertain. It has been claimed that the MSHs exert effects on the nervous system, but the physiologic significance of these effects is not known. All the hormones found in animals of a particular species or sex do not necessarily have a function. For example, there are no known functions for oxytocin and prolactin in the male. In addition, there is no reason that hormones as well as organs cannot become vestigial. This may be the case as far as the MSHs are concerned in mammals. On the other hand, there is evidence that MSH plays a role in disease states in humans. Prolonged treatment with natural and synthetic MSH preparations darkens the skin of Negroes, and such preparations have been reported to accelerate melanin synthesis. α MSH has not been detected in human plasma, but β MSH is normally present at a level of 0.02–0.1 ng/ml. It has been argued that the pigmentary changes in several endocrine diseases are due to changes in circulating ACTH, since ACTH has MSH activity. For example, abnormal pallor is a hallmark of hypopituitarism. Hyperpigmentation occurs in patients with ACTH-secreting tumors and in patients with adrenal insufficiency due to primary adrenal disease. Indeed, the presence of hyperpigmentation in association with adrenal insufficiency rules out the possibility that the insufficiency is secondary to pituitary disease because the pituitary must be intact for pigmentation to occur. However, a large amount of ACTH is required to produce pigmentation, and ACTH levels in the circulation are not high enough to account for the pigmentation seen in many cases. Furthermore, β MSH secretion appears to parallel ACTH secretion, and the ACTH-secreting nonendocrine tumors which have been tested (see Chapter 20) have been found to secrete an MSH-like compound in addition to ACTH. Therefore, the pigment changes appear to be due principally to β MSH rather than ACTH.

GROWTH HORMONE

Chemistry & Species Specificity

Growth hormone, like other protein hormones, varies considerably in structure from species to species. For example, the growth hormone of the rhesus monkey has a molecular weight of 25,400 and 4 disulfide bridges, while human growth hormone has a molecular weight of 21,500 and 2 disulfide bridges (Fig 22–3). Human growth hormone (HGH) has now been synthesized. Porcine and simian growth hormones have only a transient effect in the guinea pig, probably because they stimulate the rapid formation of anti-growth hormone antibodies. In man and monkeys, bovine and porcine growth hormones do not even have

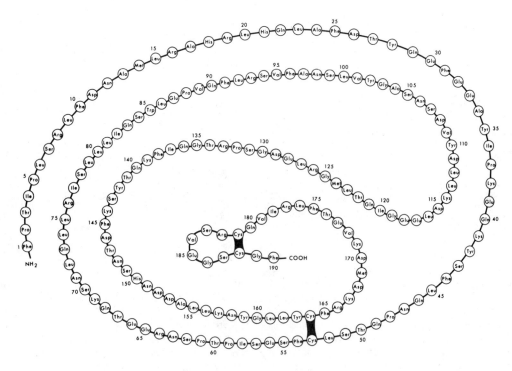

FIG 22–3. Structure of human growth hormone. The black bars indicate the disulfide bridges. (Courtesy of CH Li.)

TABLE 22–4. Activities of growth hormones in other species. (+), active; (−), inactive.

Growth Hormone From	Stimulates Growth In				
	Fish	Birds	Rats	Monkeys	Humans
Fish			−		
Reptiles			+		
Amphibia			+		
Birds			+		
Cows	+	−*	+	−	−†
Sheep	+		+		−
Pigs	+	−*	+	−	−†
Whales			+		−
Monkeys	+		+		+
Humans	+		+	+	

*Probable diabetogenic effect.
†Slight diabetogenic effect.

a significant transient effect on growth, although human and monkey growth hormones are fully active (Table 22–4). Human growth hormone has lactogenic activity, but it now seems clear that there is a separate human prolactin (see Chapter 23).

Plasma Levels & Metabolism

Plasma growth hormone levels are routinely measured by immunoassay. The basal growth hormone level in adult humans is normally less than 3 ng/ml, but it rises in response to a variety of stimuli (see below). Growth hormone is metabolized rapidly, probably at least in part in the liver. The half-life of circulating growth hormone in man is 20–30 minutes, and the daily growth hormone output has been calculated to be about 4 mg/day in adults.

Effects on Growth

The place of growth hormone in the complex of factors that promote growth is discussed below. In young animals in which the epiphyses have not as yet fused to the long bones (see Chapter 21), growth is inhibited by hypophysectomy (Fig 22–4) and stimulated by growth hormone. Chondrogenesis is accelerated, and as the cartilaginous epiphyseal plates widen they lay down more matrix at the ends of long bones (Fig 22–5). In this way, stature is increased, and prolonged treatment leads to gigantism. The possibility that the effects of growth hormone on cartilage are indirect is discussed below. Nevertheless, the increase in width of the tibial epiphyseal plate in hypophysectomized rats has been used as a bioassay for growth hormone ("tibia test"). When the epiphyses are closed, linear growth is no longer possible, and growth hormone produces the pattern of bone and soft tissue deformities (Fig 22–6) known in man as **acromegaly**. The size of most of the viscera is increased. Endocrine organs are not affected directly by growth hormone, but the hormone is said to synergize with ACTH in increasing adrenal size and

with androgens in increasing the size of accessory reproductive organs. The protein content of the body is increased and the fat content decreased.

Somatomedin

Evidence is accumulating that the effects of growth hormone on cartilage are indirect and are mediated, at

FIG 22–4. Effect of hypophysectomy on growth of the immature rhesus monkey. Both monkeys were the same size and weight 2 years previously when the one on the left was hypophysectomized. (Reproduced, with permission, from Knobil, in: *Growth in Living Systems.* Zarrow MX [editor]. Basic Books, 1961.)

FIG 22–5. Effect of growth hormone treatment for 4 days on the proximal tibial epiphysis of the hypophysectomized rat. Note the increased width of the unstained cartilage plate in the tibia of the treated animal on the right, compared with the control on the left. (Reproduced, with permission, from Evans & others: Bioassay of the pituitary growth hormone. Endocrinology 32:14, 1943.)

FIG 22–6. Effect of chronic treatment with anterior pituitary extract. The animal in the lower picture was treated from the sixth to the 32nd week of life. The animal in the upper picture is a littermate control. (Reproduced, with permission, from Evans & others: *Growth and Gonad-stimulating Hormones of the Anterior Hypophysis.* Univ of California Press, 1933.)

least in part, by a peptide secreted by the liver. Growth hormone stimulates the secretion of this peptide, which has a molecular weight of about 8000 and used to be called **sulfation factor** because it stimulates the incorporation of sulfate into cartilage. More recently, the factor has been renamed **somatomedin**, because it has been shown to have more widespread effects on the growth of cartilage. It may also be the mediator of some or even all of the other effects of growth hormone. However, its exact role in physiology remains to be determined.

Effects on Protein & Electrolyte Metabolism

Among the consequences of the increase in protein anabolism produced by growth hormone are a positive nitrogen and phosphorus balance (Fig 22–7), a rise in plasma phosphorus, and a fall in the blood urea nitrogen and amino acid levels. Gastrointestinal absorption of calcium is increased. Sodium and potassium excretion are reduced by an action independent of the adrenal glands, probably because these electrolytes are diverted from the kidney to the growing tissues. Excretion of the amino acid hydroxyproline is increased during growth and in acromegaly, but it is also increased in a number of other diseases. It is believed to come from collagen.

Mechanism of Anabolic Action

The effect of growth hormone on protein synthesis appears to be exerted at the ribosomal level, where it has been postulated to affect either ribosomal attachment or translation. It also increases the transport of neutral and basic amino acids into cells, and this action is said to occur even when protein synthesis is blocked by puromycin. Insulin stimulates the transport of amino acids into cells by a mechanism that is separate from that which is stimulated by growth hormone, and this action of insulin is also unaffected by puromycin.

Effects on Carbohydrate & Fat Metabolism

The actions of growth hormone on carbohydrate metabolism are discussed in Chapter 19. Growth hormone is diabetogenic because it increases hepatic glucose output and exerts an anti-insulin effect in muscle. It is ketogenic because it increases circulating free fatty acid levels (Fig 22–8). The increase in plasma free fatty acids, which takes several hours to develop, provides a ready source of energy for the tissues during hypoglycemia, fasting, and stressful stimuli. Growth hormone does not stimulate the β cells

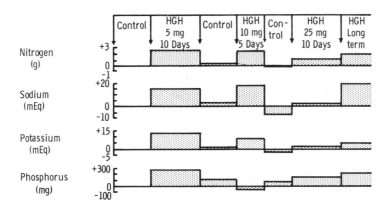

FIG 22–7. Effects of human growth hormone (HGH) on the daily balance (intake minus output) of nitrogen, sodium, potassium, and phosphorus in a female pituitary dwarf. A positive balance is plotted upward from the zero line and a negative balance is plotted downward. (Redrawn and reproduced, with permission, from Hutchings & others: Metabolic growth changes produced by human growth hormone [Li] in pituitary dwarf. J Clin Endocrinol 19:759, 1959.)

FIG 22-8. Effect of various hormones on plasma free fatty acid levels in fasting hypophysectomized rhesus monkeys. Pituitrin is an extract of posterior pituitary tissue. (Redrawn and reproduced, with permission, from Goodman & Knobil: The effects of fasting and of growth hormone administration on plasma fatty acid concentration in normal and hypophysectomized rhesus monkeys. Endocrinology 65:451, 1959.)

of the pancreas directly, but in animals with adequate pancreatic reserves the rise in blood glucose it provokes stimulates insulin secretion. This is one way growth hormone promotes growth, since insulin has a protein anabolic effect (see Chapter 19). Quantitatively, however, the direct effect of growth hormone on protein formation is much more important.

Another function of growth hormone may be the maintenance of cardiac muscle glycogen content. Unlike that of liver and skeletal muscle, the glycogen content of cardiac muscle rises during fasting, and this rise is prevented by hypophysectomy and restored by the administration of growth hormone in the presence of permissive doses of glucocorticoids.

Hypothalamic Control of Growth Hormone Secretion

The secretion of growth hormone is controlled, at least in part, via the hypothalamus. A growth hormone-releasing factor (GRF) and a growth hormone-inhibiting factor (GIF) have been extracted from hypothalamic tissue (see Chapter 14), and hypothalamic lesions or section of the pituitary stalk have been shown to inhibit growth hormone secretion. Anterior median eminence lesions not only inhibit growth; they also block the increase in growth hormone levels normally produced by hypoglycemia (see below). If growth hormone were secreted in a constant and continuous fashion and only in children, the hypothalamic control of its secretion might be surprising; however, it is now clear that, both in children and in adults, the rate of growth hormone secretion undergoes marked and rapid fluctuations in response to a variety of stimuli.

Stimuli Affecting Growth Hormone Secretion

As noted above, the basal plasma growth hormone concentration ranges from 0-3 ng/ml in normal adults. The values in newborn infants are higher, but plasma growth hormone levels throughout the rest of childhood have not been proved to be significantly greater than they are in adults. Furthermore, there are large quantities of growth hormone in the pituitaries of adults. It is not clear what these observations mean in terms of the physiology of growth, but they have focused attention on the possible functions of growth hormone in adults.

The stimuli which increase growth hormone secretion are summarized in Table 22-5. Most of them fall into 3 general categories: (1) conditions such as hypoglycemia and fasting, in which there is an actual or threatened decrease in the substrate for energy production in the cells; (2) conditions in which there are increased amounts of certain amino acids in the plasma; and (3) stressful stimuli. It has been claimed that the response to glucagon is useful as a test of the growth hormone secreting mechanism in patients with endocrine diseases. Although the growth hormone responses to the other stimuli are relatively reproducible (Fig 22-9), they may vary from individual to individual and are generally smaller in children than in adults. There are also irregular "spikes" in the plasma growth hormone level during the day in the absence of any identifiable stimulus to growth hormone secretion. Such a spike occurs with considerable regularity upon going to sleep, but the significance of the association between growth hormone and sleep is an enigma. Growth hormone secretion is increased in subjects deprived of REM sleep (see Chapter 11) and inhibited during normal REM sleep.

Glucose infusions lower plasma growth hormone levels and inhibit the response to exercise. The increase produced by 2-deoxyglucose is presumably due to intracellular glucose deficiency, since this compound blocks the catabolism of glucose-6-phosphate. Although the basal growth hormone levels and the

TABLE 22-5. Stimuli that have been reported to increase growth hormone secretion.

Deficiency of energy substrate
Hypoglycemia
2-Deoxyglucose
Exercise
Fasting
Increase in circulating levels of certain amino acids
Protein meal
Infusion of arginine and some other amino acids
Glucagon
Stressful stimuli
Pyrogen
Lysine vasopressin
Various psychologic stresses
Going to sleep
L-Dopa

FIG 22–9. **Changes in plasma human growth hormone (HGH) and blood glucose levels in 6 normal subjects and one hypophysectomized patient (PAR) following the administration of insulin, 0.1 U/kg body weight.** (Reproduced, with permission, from Roth & others: Hypoglycemia: A potent stimulus to secretion of growth hormone. Science 140[No. 3570]:987–988, 1963. Copyright 1963 by The American Association for the Advancement of Science.)

response to hypoglycemia are comparable in males and females, the responses to exercise and arginine are generally greater in women than in men, and the response to arginine in men is increased by estrogen treatment. Growth hormone feeds back to inhibit its own secretion; high plasma growth hormone levels reduce pituitary secretion of the hormone. Growth hormone secretion is also inhibited by cortisol, free fatty acids, and medroxyprogesterone.

The growth hormone responses to hypoglycemia, fasting, and exercise are reduced in obese subjects. The explanation of this reduction and its possible relationship to the pathogenesis of the obesity is currently unsettled.

PHYSIOLOGY OF GROWTH

Growth is a complex phenomenon that is affected not only by growth hormone but also by thyroid hormones, androgens, and insulin. It is also affected by extrinsic and genetic factors. It is normally accompa-

nied by an orderly sequence of maturational changes, and it involves accretion of protein and increase in length and size, not just an increase in weight, which may be due to the formation of fat or retention of salt and water.

Genetic & Extrinsic Factors

The food supply is the most important extrinsic factor affecting growth. The diet must be adequate not only in protein content but also in essential vitamins and minerals (see Chapter 17) and in calories, so that ingested protein is not burned for energy. Injury and disease stunt growth because they increase protein catabolism.

Following illnesses in children there is a period of "catch-up growth" during which the growth rate may be as much as 400% above normal. The acceleration continues until the previous growth curve is reached, at which point growth slows to normal. The mechanisms that bring about and control "catch-up growth" are not known.

Growth Periods

Patterns of growth vary somewhat from species to species. Rats continue to grow, although at a declining rate, throughout life. In humans there are 2 periods of rapid growth (Fig 22–10): the first is in infancy and the second is at the time of puberty just before growth stops. The first period of accelerated growth is partly a continuation of the fetal growth period. The second growth spurt and the subsequent cessation of growth are mainly due to the action of sex hormones.

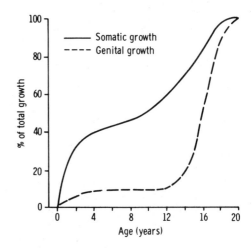

FIG 22–10. **Normal somatic and genital growth in male humans.** Growth of the whole body and of the testes is plotted as a percentage of total growth at ages up to 20 years. (Data from Harris & others: *The Measurement of Man.* Univ of Minnesota Press, 1930.)

Hormonal Effects

The contributions of hormones to growth after birth are shown diagrammatically in Fig 22–11. In

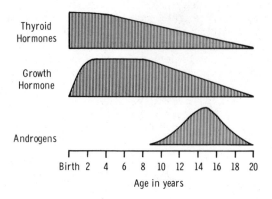

FIG 22–11. Relative importance of hormones in human growth at various ages. (Courtesy of DA Fisher.)

laboratory animals and in man, growth in utero is independent of fetal growth hormone. Rats hypophysectomized at birth continue to grow for about 30 days before they stop. Interestingly, the brain continues to grow in these rats after growth of

the skull stops, and the resulting compression of the brain may lead to death.

When growth hormone is administered to hypophysectomized animals, the animals do not grow as rapidly as they do when treated with growth hormone plus thyroid hormones. Thyroid hormones alone have no effect on growth in this situation. Their action is therefore permissive to that of growth hormone. Thyroid hormones also appear to be necessary for a normal rate of growth hormone secretion; the amount of growth hormone in the pituitary is decreased in thyroidectomized animals, and the growth hormone-secreting acidophils show regressive changes. Thyroid hormones have widespread effects on the ossification of cartilage, the growth of teeth, the contours of the face, and the proportions of the body. Cretins are therefore dwarfed and have infantile features (Fig 22–12). Patients who are dwarfed because of panhypopituitarism have features consistent with their chronologic age until puberty, but since they do not mature sexually they have juvenile features in adulthood.

The growth spurt at the time of puberty is due largely to the protein anabolic effect of androgens (see Chapter 23). The ovaries secrete small amounts of

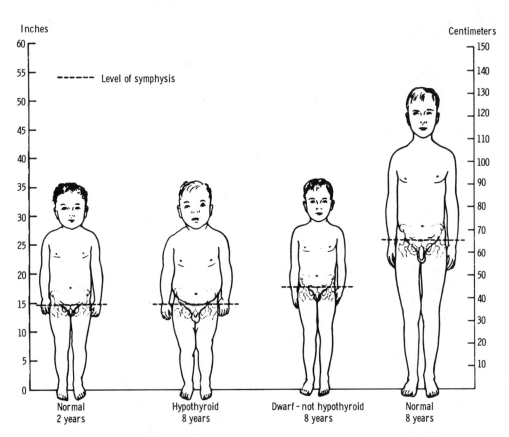

FIG 22–12. Normal and abnormal growth. Hypothyroid dwarfs retain their infantile proportions, whereas dwarfs of the constitutional type and, to a lesser extent, of the hypopituitary type have proportions characteristic of their chronologic age. (Reproduced, with permission, from Wilkins: *The Diagnosis and Treatment of Endocrine Disorders in Childhood and Adolescence,* 3rd ed. Thomas, 1966.)

androgens, but adolescent growth in females must be due primarily to androgens secreted from the adrenal cortex. At the time of puberty 17-ketosteroid excretion rises in females as well as males, although the rise in males is greater because testosterone begins to be secreted from the testes. The mechanism responsible for the increase in adrenal androgen secretion has not been identified with certainty. Other adrenocortical hormones exert a permissive action on growth in the sense that adrenalectomized animals fail to grow unless their blood pressure and circulation are maintained by replacement therapy.

Although androgens initially stimulate growth, they ultimately terminate growth by causing the epiphyses to fuse to the long bones (epiphyseal closure). Once the epiphyses have closed, linear growth ceases (see Chapter 21). This is why pituitary dwarfs treated with testosterone first grow a few inches and then stop. It is also why patients with sexual precocity are apt to be dwarfed. Estrogens have similar effects, but some investigators argue that the effects of estrogens are due to stimulation of androgen secretion by the adrenals.

African pygmies have been shown to have normal plasma growth hormone levels, but their tissues appear to be subnormally responsive to growth hormone. Other causes of short stature in man include, in addition to hypothyroidism, panhypopituitarism, and sexual precocity, the syndrome of congenital isolated growth hormone deficiency. These individuals, who are called **sexual ateliotic dwarfs**, remain short; however, they mature sexually, and women with the disease can become pregnant, deliver, and lactate normally. The disease appears to be inherited as an autosomal recessive. Dwarfism is part of the syndrome of **gonadal dysgenesis** seen in patients who have an XO chromosomal pattern instead of an XX or XY pattern (see Chapter 23). Various bone and metabolic diseases also cause stunted growth, and in many cases there is no known cause ("constitutional delayed growth").

The effect of insulin on growth is discussed in Chapter 19. Diabetic animals fail to grow; and insulin causes growth in hypophysectomized animals. However, the growth is appreciable only when large amounts of carbohydrate and protein are supplied with the insulin.

PITUITARY INSUFFICIENCY

Changes in Other Endocrines

The widespread changes that develop when the pituitary is removed surgically or destroyed by disease in humans or animals are predictable in terms of the known hormonal functions of the gland. The adrenal cortex atrophies, and the secretion of adrenal glucocorticoids and sex hormones falls to low levels although some secretion persists. Stress-induced rises in aldosterone secretion are absent, but basal aldosterone secretion and increases induced by salt depletion are normal, at least for some time. Since there is no mineralocorticoid deficiency, salt loss and hypovolemic shock do not develop, but the inability to increase glucocorticoid secretion makes patients with pituitary insufficiency sensitive to stress. Thyroid function is depressed to low levels, and cold is tolerated poorly. The gonads atrophy, sexual cycles stop, and secondary sexual characteristics disappear.

Insulin Sensitivity

Hypophysectomized animals have a tendency to become hypoglycemic, especially when fasted. In some species, but not in man, fatal hypoglycemic reactions are fairly common. Hypophysectomy ameliorates diabetes mellitus (see Chapter 19) and markedly increases the hypoglycemic effect of insulin. This is due in part to the deficiency of adrenocortical hormones, but hypophysectomized animals are more sensitive to insulin than adrenalectomized animals because they also lack the anti-insulin effect of growth hormone.

Water Metabolism

Although selective destruction of the supraopticposterior pituitary mechanism causes diabetes insipidus (see Chapter 14), removal of both the anterior and posterior pituitary usually causes no more than a transient polyuria. In the past, there was speculation that the anterior pituitary secreted a "diuretic hormone," but the amelioration of the diabetes insipidus is probably explained on the basis of a decrease in the osmotic load presented for excretion. Osmotically active particles hold water in the renal tubules (see Chapter 38). Because of the ACTH deficiency, the rate of protein catabolism is decreased in hypophysectomized animals. Because of the TSH deficiency, the metabolic rate is low. Consequently, fewer osmotically active products of catabolism are filtered and urine volume declines, even in the absence of vasopressin. Growth hormone deficiency contributes to the depression of the glomerular filtration rate in hypophysectomized animals, and human growth hormone increases the glomerular filtration rate and renal plasma flow in man. Finally, because of the glucocorticoid deficiency there is the same defective excretion of a water load that is seen in adrenalectomized animals. The "diuretic" activity of the anterior pituitary can thus be explained in terms of the actions of ACTH, TSH, and growth hormone.

Other Defects

The deficiency of β MSH secretion may be responsible for the pallor of the skin in patients with hypopituitarism. Growth hormone deficiency causes dwarfism in young individuals and may be responsible for some loss of protein in adults. However, it should be emphasized that wasting is not a feature of hypopituitarism in man, and most patients with pituitary insufficiency are well nourished (Fig 22–13). It used to be thought that cachexia was part of the clinical

FIG 22–13. Typical picture of hypopituitarism in adults. Note well-nourished appearance and pallor. (From Daughaday, in: *Textbook of Endocrinology*, 4th ed. Williams RH [editor]. Saunders, 1968.)

picture, but it is now generally accepted that emaciated patients described in the older literature had anorexia nervosa rather than hypopituitarism.

Causes of Pituitary Insufficiency in Man

Tumors of the anterior pituitary are generally classified on the basis of staining characteristics as chromophobe, acidophil, or basophil tumors. Most of the chromophobe tumors are nonsecreting, and produce hypopituitarism by destroying normal pituitary tissue. Suprasellar cysts, remnants of Rathke's pouch that enlarge and compress the pituitary, are another cause of hypopituitarism. In women who have an episode of shock in the course of pregnancy, the pituitary may become infarcted with the subsequent development of postpartum necrosis. The blood supply to the anterior lobe is vulnerable because it descends on the pituitary stalk through the rigid diaphragma sellae, and, during pregnancy, the pituitary is enlarged. Pituitary infarction is extremely rare in men, but it was fairly common in soldiers who contracted hemorrhagic fever in Korea. In hemorrhagic fever, there was a diffuse vasculitis which probably caused pituitary enlargement due to edema, and the patients who developed pituitary infarction were those who went into shock in the course of their disease.

TABLE 22–6. Effects of removing various amounts of pituitary tissue on endocrine function in male dogs.* (+) indicates that the finding was present and (0) that it was absent.

Number of Dogs	Gonadal Atrophy	Thyroid Atrophy	Adrenal Atrophy	Mean % Anterior Pituitary Remaining
6	0	0	0	27
3	+	0	0	11
2	+	+	0	5
19	+	+	+	2

*Data from Ganong & Hume: The effect of graded hypophysectomy on thyroid, gonadal, and adrenocortical function in the dog. Endocrinology 59:293, 1956.

Partial Pituitary Insufficiency

The anterior pituitary has a large reserve, and much of it can be destroyed without producing detectable endocrine abnormalities. It now appears that, with progressive loss of pituitary tissue, growth hormone secretion is the first function to be impaired. In the dog and the rat there is a depression of gonadotropin secretion when 70–90% of the anterior pituitary is removed or destroyed. When 90–95% is destroyed, thyroid function is also impaired, but almost 100% of the anterior pituitary must be destroyed before a marked degree of adrenal insufficiency is seen (Table 22–6). The same relationships hold in man. Isolated growth hormone deficiency occurs as a congenital abnormality (see above). Isolated corticotropin deficiency has also been described. However, in isolated pituitary tropin deficiencies such as these, the possibility of hypothalamic disease must be considered. For example, it has recently been shown that an appreciable number of patients with isolated TSH deficiency show an increase in TSH secretion when TRF is injected.

In the rat and in some other species, there appears to be some localization within the pituitary of the cells secreting the various hormones. It is not known if similar localization occurs in man.

PITUITARY HYPERFUNCTION IN MAN

Acromegaly

Acidophil cell tumors of the anterior pituitary secrete large amounts of growth hormone, leading in children to **gigantism** and in adults to **acromegaly**. The principal findings are those related to the local effects of the tumor (enlargement of the sella turcica, headache, visual disturbances) and those due to growth hormone secretion. In adults, there is enlargement of

Osteoarthritic vertebral changes

Visual field changes (bitemporal hemianopsia)

Prognathism and acromegalic facies

Hirsutism

Gynecomastia and lactation

Enlarged hands and feet

FIG 22−14. Typical findings in acromegaly.

the hands and feet (**acral** parts; hence the term acromegaly) and a protrusion of the lower jaw called **prognathism** (Fig 22−14). Overgrowth of the malar, frontal, and basal bones combines with prognathism to produce the coarse facial features called **acromegalic**

facies. Body hair is increased in amount. The skeletal changes predispose to osteoarthritis. About 25% of the patients have abnormal glucose tolerance tests, and 4% develop lactation in the absence of pregnancy.

Cushing's Syndrome

The clinical picture of Cushing's syndrome is described in Chapter 20. ACTH-secreting tumors of the pituitary can cause this syndrome, but such cases are rare. Most patients with bilaterally hyperplastic adrenals do not have detectable tumors as long as they have symptoms of glucocorticoid excess. However, a significant percentage of the patients who have bilaterally hyperplastic adrenals removed develop rapidly growing ACTH-secreting pituitary tumors (**Nelson's syndrome**). The tumors cause hyperpigmentation of the skin and neurologic signs due to pressure on structures in the sellar region. Most of them are made up of chromophobic cells rather than basophils, and some are malignant. Blood ACTH levels are extremely high, and the intrinsic MSH activity of the ACTH undoubtedly contributes to the cutaneous pigmentation, but the tumors also secrete MSHs. It is difficult to say whether these patients had undetected tumors to start with or developed neoplastic changes in the pituitary when the feedback check on ACTH secretion was removed. Animals sometimes develop TSH-secreting tumors after thyroidectomy and gonadotropin-secreting tumors after gonadectomy, but such tumors are rare in man.

23...

The Gonads: Development & Function of the Reproductive System

Modern genetics and experimental embryology make it clear that in higher animals the multiple differences between the male and the female depend ultimately upon a single chromosome (the Y chromosome) and a single pair of endocrine structures, the testes in the male and the ovaries in the female. The differentiation of the primitive gonads into testes or ovaries in utero is genetically determined in man, but the formation of male genitalia depends upon the presence of a functional testis. There is evidence that male sexual behavior and the male pattern of gonadotropin secretion are also due to the action of male hormones on the brain in early development. After birth, the gonads remain quiescent until adolescence, when they are activated by gonadotropins from the anterior pituitary. Hormones secreted by the gonads at this time cause the appearance of features typical of the adult male or female, and the onset of the sexual cycle in the female. In males the gonads remain more or less active from puberty onward. In the human female, ovarian function regresses after a period of time and sexual cycles cease (the menopause).

In both sexes, the gonads have a dual function: the production of germ cells (**gametogenesis**) and the secretion of **sex hormones**. The **androgens** are the steroid sex hormones which are masculinizing in their action; the **estrogens** are those which are feminizing. Both types of hormones are normally secreted in both sexes. The testes secrete large amounts of androgens, principally **testosterone**, but they also secrete small amounts of estrogens. The ovaries secrete large amounts of estrogens and small amounts of androgens. Androgens and, probably, small amounts of estrogens are secreted from the adrenal cortex in both sexes. The ovary also secretes **progesterone**, a steroid which has special functions in preparing the uterus for pregnancy. During pregnancy the ovary secretes a group of polypeptides, called collectively **relaxin**, which loosen the ligaments of the pubic symphysis and soften the cervix, facilitating delivery of the fetus.

The secretory and gametogenic functions of the gonads are both dependent upon the secretion of the anterior pituitary gonadotropins, FSH and LH. The sex hormones feed back through the hypothalamus to inhibit gonadotropin secretion. In the male, gonadotropin secretion is noncyclic; but in the postpuberal female an orderly, sequential secretion of gonadotropins is necessary for the occurrence of menstruation, pregnancy, and lactation.

SEX DIFFERENTIATION & DEVELOPMENT

CHROMOSOMAL SEX

The Sex Chromosomes

Sex is determined genetically by 2 chromosomes called the **sex chromosomes** to distinguish them from the other **somatic chromosomes (autosomes).** In many animals, the sex chromosomes are called the X and Y chromosomes. The Y chromosome has potent male determiners. Male cells with the diploid number of chromosomes contain an X and Y chromosome (XY pattern), whereas female cells contain 2 X chromosomes (XX pattern). As a consequence of meiosis during gametogenesis, each normal ovum contains a single X chromosome but half the normal sperms contain an X chromosome and half contain a Y chromosome (Fig 23–1). When a sperm containing a Y chromosome fertilizes an ovum, an XY pattern results and the zygote develops into a **genetic male.** When fertilization occurs with an X-containing sperm, an XX pattern and a **genetic female** result. Cell division and the chemical nature of chromosomes are discussed in Chapters 1 and 17.

Human Chromosomes

It is now possible to study human chromosomes in detail. Human cells are grown in tissue culture; treated with the drug colchicine, which arrests mitosis at the metaphase; exposed to a hypotonic solution which makes the chromosomes swell and disperse; and then "squashed" onto slides. New fluorescent and other staining technics make it possible to identify the individual chromosomes and study them in detail (Fig 23–2). There are 46 chromosomes: in males, 22 pairs of autosomes plus a large X chromosome and a small Y chromosome; in females, 22 pairs of autosomes plus 2 X chromosomes. The individual chromosomes are usually arranged in an arbitrary pattern or **karyotype.** The individual autosome pairs are identified by the numbers 1–22 on the basis of their morphology. Because the human Y chromosome is smaller than the X chromosome, it has been hypothesized that the sperms containing the Y chromosome are lighter and able to "swim" faster up the female genital tract, thus reach-

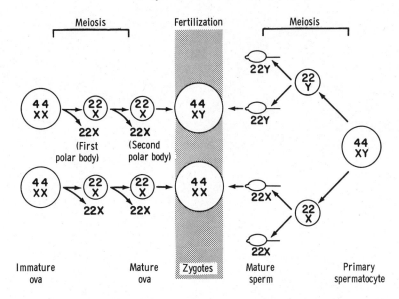

FIG 23-1. Basis of genetic sex determination. In the case of the 2-stage meiotic division in the female, 4 bodies form but only one survives as the mature ovum. In the case of the male, the meiotic division results in the formation of 4 sperms, 2 containing the X and 2 the Y chromosome. Fertilization thus produces a 44 XY (male) zygote or a 44 XX (female) zygote.

FIG 23-2. *Left:* Karyotype of chromosomes from normal male arranged in conventional groups (A–G). (Reproduced, with permission, from Barr: Some properties of the sex chromosomes and their bearing on normal and abnormal development. In: *Congenital Malformations.* International Medical Congress, 1964.) *Right:* Diagram of human chromosomes, idealized, showing one of each pair. Characteristic banding is produced by the new Giemsa method of staining. This banding, and the patterns produced by other technics, make it possible to identify individual chromosomes with great accuracy. (Reproduced, with permission, from Drets & Shaw: Specific banding patterns of human chromosomes. Proc Nat Acad Sci USA 68:2073, 1971.)

FIG 23–3. Sex chromatin (arrows) in epidermal spinous cell layer *(left)* and nuclear appendage ("drumstick") in white blood cells *(right)*. (Reproduced, with permission, from Grumbach & Barr: Cytologic tests of chromosomal sex in relation to sex anomalies in man. Recent Progr Hormone Res 14:255, 1958.)

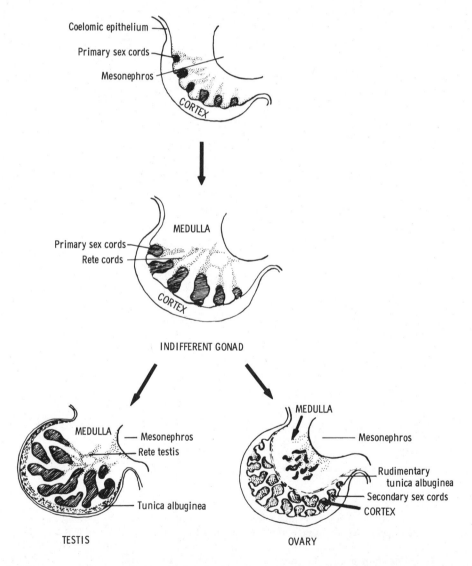

FIG 23–4. Diagrammatic representation of the development of an ovary from the cortex or a testis from the medulla of a bipotential primordial gonad in man. (After Burns. Reproduced, with permission, from Grumbach, in: *Clinical Endocrinology I.* Astwood EB [editor]. Grune & Stratton, 1960.)

ing the ovum more rapidly. This supposedly accounts for the fact that the number of males born is slightly greater than the number of females.

"Sex Chromatin"

The cells of individuals who have 2 X chromosomes contain an extra bit of chromatin, the "sex chromatin" or "Barr body." It can be seen in the nuclei, usually attached to the nuclear membrane (Fig 23–3). In almost all cells of females except ova, an X chromosome is partially inactive and condensed, and it is this chromosome which is visible as the sex chromatin. It is easily visible in over 25% of the cells in smears of the buccal mucosa and skin biopsies, although it is well developed in many other cells as well. Very few cells in preparations from individuals with only one X chromosome have nuclear material that resembles the sex chromatin. There is also a small "drumstick" of chromatin projecting from the nuclei of 1–15% of the polymorphonuclear leukocytes in females but not in males (Fig 23–3). Normal females thus have sex chromatin and are said to be **chromatin-positive.** Normal males are **chromatin-negative,** but so are individuals who have an abnormal XO chromosome pattern. Abnormal individuals who have extra X chromosomes have extra pieces of sex chromatin; there is one Barr body for each X chromosome in excess of one.

EMBRYOLOGY OF THE HUMAN REPRODUCTIVE SYSTEM

Development of the Gonads

On each side of the embryo, a primitive gonad arises from the genital ridge, a condensation of tissue near the adrenal gland. The gonad develops a **cortex** and a **medulla** (Figs 23–4 and 23–5). Until the sixth week of development these structures are identical in both sexes. In genetic males, the medulla develops during the seventh and eighth weeks into a testis and the cortex regresses. Leydig cells appear, and androgen is secreted. In genetic females, the cortex develops into an ovary and the medulla regresses. The embryonic ovary does not secrete hormones. Hormonal treatment of the mother has no effect on gonadal differentiation in man, although it does in some experimental animals.

Embryology of the Genitalia

In the seventh week of gestation the embryo has both male and female primordial genital ducts (Fig 23–6). One or the other of these duct systems develops, forming male or female internal genitalia, and the other regresses. The external genitalia are similarly bipotential until the eighth week (Fig 23–7). Thereafter, the urogenital slit disappears and male genitalia form, or, alternatively, it remains open and female genitalia form.

When there are functional testes in the embryo, male internal and external genitalia develop. The

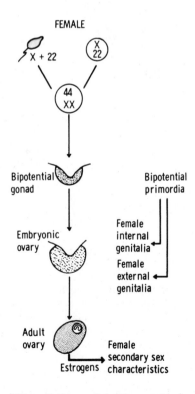

FIG 23–5. Diagrammatic summary of normal sex determination, differentiation, and development in humans.

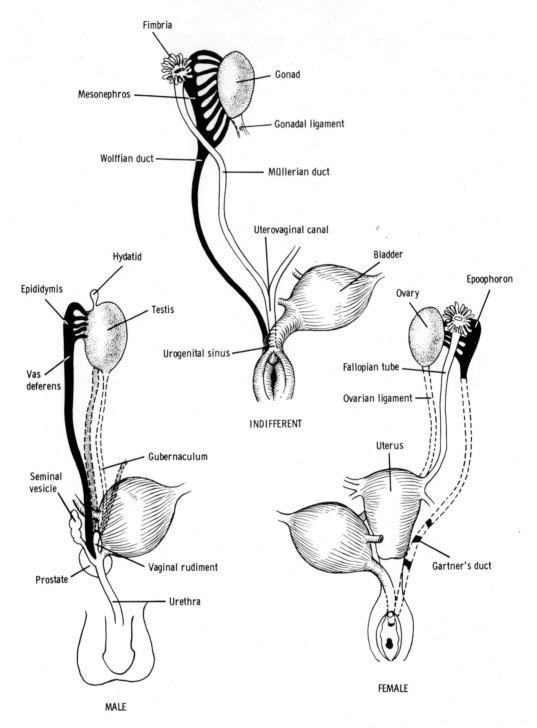

FIG 23-6. Embryonic differentiation of male and female internal genitalia (genital ducts) from wolffian (male) and müllerian (female) primordia. (After Corning & Wilkins. Redrawn and reproduced, with permission, from Van Wyk & Grumbach, in: *Textbook of Endocrinology,* 4th ed. Williams RH [editor]. Saunders, 1968.)

INDIFFERENT STAGE

SEVENTH TO EIGHTH WEEK

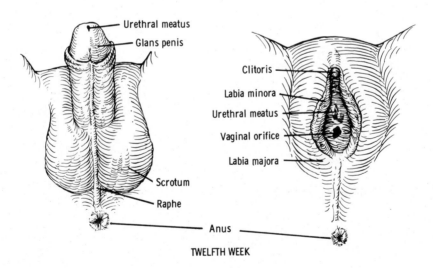

TWELFTH WEEK

FIG 23–7. Differentiation of male and female external genitalia from indifferent primordial structures in the embryo. (Redrawn from Spaulding: The development of the external genitalia in the human embryo. Contributions to Embryology 13:69, 1921.)

action of the testes is 2-fold. Male differentiation of the **internal** genitalia depends upon the action of an inductor substance elaborated by the embryonic testes. This substance, which may be a polypeptide, exerts its effect unilaterally; if there is a testis on one side only, male internal genitalia develop on that side and female on the other. Male differentiation of the **external** genitalia occurs in response to androgen secreted by the Leydig cells in the embryonic testes; this effect, unlike that of the inducers, is bilateral.

Development of the Brain

At least in some species, the development of the brain as well as the external genitalia is affected by androgens early in life. In rats, a brief exposure to androgens during the first few days of life causes the male pattern of sexual behavior and the male pattern of hypothalamic control of gonadotropin secretion to develop after puberty. In the absence of androgens, female patterns develop (see Chapter 15). In guinea pigs and monkeys, similar effects on sexual behavior are produced by exposure to androgens in utero. It has been argued that androgens exert masculinizing effects on behavior in humans, but human development is extremely complex and additional research is necessary before firm conclusions can be drawn.

ABERRANT SEXUAL DIFFERENTIATION

Chromosomal Abnormalities

From the preceding discussion, it might be expected that abnormalities of sexual development could be caused by genetic or hormonal abnormalities as well as by other nonspecific teratogenic influences, and this is indeed the case. The major classes of abnormalities are listed in Table 23–1.

An established defect in gametogenesis is **nondisjunction**, a phenomenon in which a pair of chromosomes fail to separate and both go to one of the daughter cells during meiosis. Four of the abnormal zygotes that can form as a result of nondisjunction of one of the X chromosomes during oogenesis are shown in Fig 23–8. In individuals with the XO chromosomal pattern, the gonads are rudimentary or absent, so that female external and internal genitalia develop. Stature is short, other congenital abnormalities are often present, and no maturation occurs at puberty. This syndrome is now called **gonadal dysgenesis** or, alternatively, **ovarian agenesis** or **Turner's syndrome**. Individuals with the XXY pattern, the most common sex chromosome disorder, have the genitalia of a normal male. Testosterone secretion at puberty is often great enough for the development of male characteristics. However, the seminiferous tubules are abnormal, and there is a higher than normal incidence of mental retardation. This syndrome is known as **seminiferous tubule dysgenesis**, or **Klinefelter's syndrome**. The XXX ("superfemale") pattern is second in frequency only to

TABLE 23–1. Classification of the major disorders of sex differentiation in man. Many of these syndromes can have great variation in degree, and consequently in manifestations.

Chromosomal disorders
  Gonadal dysgenesis (XO and variants)
  "Superfemales" (XXX)
  Seminiferous tubule dysgenesis (XXY and variants)
  True hermaphroditism
Developmental disorders
  Female pseudohermaphroditism
    Congenital virilizing adrenal hyperplasia of fetus
    Maternal androgen excess
      Virilizing ovarian tumor
      Iatrogenic: Treatment with androgens or certain synthetic progestational drugs
  Male pseudohermaphroditism
    Defective testicular development ("syndrome of the feminizing testis")
    Various nonhormonal anomalies

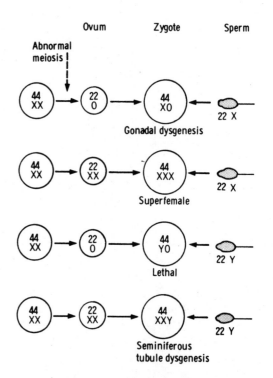

FIG 23–8. Summary of 4 possible defects produced by maternal nondisjunction of the sex chromosomes at the time of meiosis. The YO combination is believed to be lethal, and the fetus dies in utero.

the XXY pattern and may be even more common in the general population, since it does not seem to be associated with any characteristic abnormalities. The YO combination is probably lethal.

Meiosis is a 2-stage process, and nondisjunction can occur in both meiotic divisions, with the production of more complex chromosomal abnormalities. In addition, nondisjunction or simple loss of a sex chromosome can occur during the early mitotic divisions after fertilization. Chromosome loss occurs when a chromosome fails to line up properly during mitosis and is extruded from the cell rather than moving to one daughter cell **(anaphase lag).** The result of faulty mitoses in the early zygote is the production of a mosaic, an individual with 2 or more populations of cells with different chromosome complements. Some of the karyotypes that have been reported in patients with Klinefelter's syndrome, in addition to XXY, are XXYY, XXXY, XXXYY, XXXXY, and XY/XXY mosaicism. The cause of the condition in the vast majority of cases is at least one extra X chromosome in testicular tissue, but there are cases in which an extra X chromosome cannot be found. Gonadal dysgenesis has been reported in patients with XO/XX and XO/XX/XXX mosaicism. It also can occur in individuals who have the XX pattern, but in whom one of the X chromosomes is abnormal. **True hermaphroditism,** the condition in which the individual has both ovaries and testes, is probably due to XX/XY mosaicism and related mosaic patterns, although other genetic aberrations are possible.

A number of sex chromosome abnormalities are not associated with gonadal defects. The XXX pattern has been mentioned above. XXXX and XXXXX have also been reported in patients with mental retardation. There is currently a great deal of interest in the XYY pattern. The gonads of these males are usually normal, but they seem to have in common tall stature, mild mental deficiency, and a tendency to aggressive, antisocial behavior. Chromosome analyses are now being performed on criminals with increasing frequency, and the degree of responsibility of XYY individuals for violent crimes they have committed is currently being argued in the courts of a number of countries throughout the world.

Sex chromosome abnormalities are of course not the only abnormalities associated with disease states; nondisjunction of several different autosomal chromosomes is known to occur. For example, Down's syndrome (mongolism) is due to the presence of 3 chromosome 21s **(trisomy 21)** as a result of nondisjunction of this chromosome during meiosis.

Hormonal Abnormalities

Development of male external genitalia occurs normally in genetic males in response to androgen secreted by the embryonic testes, but male genital development may also occur in genetic females exposed to androgens from some other source during the eighth to the 13th weeks of gestation. The syndrome that results is **female pseudohermaphro-** **ditism.** A pseudohermaphrodite is an individual with the genetic constitution and gonads of one sex and the genitalia of the other. After the 13th week the genitalia are fully formed, but exposure to androgens can cause hypertrophy of the clitoris. Female pseudohermaphroditism may be due to congenital virilizing adrenal hyperplasia (see Chapter 20) or it may be caused by androgens administered to the mother. Conversely, female external genital development in genetic males **(male pseudohermaphroditism)** occurs when the embryonic testes are defective. Because the testes are also the source of the inductor substance governing development of the male internal genitalia, genetic males with defective testes have female internal genitalia. Genetic males with **lipoid adrenal hyperplasia** are pseudohermaphrodites because testicular as well as adrenal androgens are normally formed from pregnenolone, and pregnenolone formation is blocked in this syndrome (see Chapter 20).

PUBERTY

After birth, the androgen-secreting Leydig cells in the fetal testes disappear. There follows in all mammals a period in which the gonads of both sexes are quiescent until they are activated by gonadotropins from the pituitary to bring about the final maturation of the reproductive system. This period of growth and maturation is known as **adolescence.** It is often also called **puberty,** although puberty, strictly defined, is the period when the endocrine and gametogenic functions of the gonads have first developed to the point where reproduction is possible. **Menarche** is the first menstrual period at puberty. In humans as well as animals, castration increases gonadotropin secretion before there is any evident stimulation of the gonads, but the nature of the pituitary-inhibiting gonadal secretion is uncertain. In children between the ages of 7 and 10, a slow increase in estrogen and androgen secretion precedes the more rapid rise in the early teens (Fig 23–9). The age at the time of puberty is variable, but it averages 14 years in boys and 12 years in girls.

Control of the Onset of Puberty

The mechanism responsible for the onset of puberty is neural. The gonads of immature animals can be stimulated by gonadotropins, their pituitaries contain gonadotropins, and there is LH-releasing factor and FSH-releasing factor (see Chapter 14) in their hypothalami. The gonadotropins, however, are not secreted. When the pituitary of an immature animal is transplanted into an adult animal, it secretes gonadotropins like an adult pituitary. In experimental animals and in humans, lesions in the ventral hypothalamus near the infundibulum cause precocious puberty (Fig 23–10). This suggests that there is a hypothalamic mechanism which normally holds gonadotropin secretion in check until puberty. However, no substance

FIG 23–10. **Effect of brain lesions on the onset of puberty in female rats.** In rats the vagina stays closed until just before the onset of the first estrus. (Data of Gellert, from Ganong, in: *Control of Ovulation.* Villee C [editor]. Pergamon Press, 1961.)

FIG 23–9. **Estrogen (solid line) and 17-ketosteroid (dotted line) excretion as a function of age in humans.** 17-Ketosteroid excretion measures adrenal as well as testicular function, and not all 17-ketosteroids are androgens. (Data from various authors.)

that inhibits FSH and LH secretion has been extracted from the brain, and it is possible that the effect of lesions is due instead to chronic stimulation originating in irritative foci in tissue around the lesion. Another theory of the control of the onset of puberty is based on the observation that before puberty the brain is very sensitive to the inhibiting effects of gonadal steroids on gonadotropin secretion. According to this view, small amounts of steroids secreted by the gonads hold gonadotropin secretion in check, and puberty is due to a decrease in the sensitivity of the brain to this inhibition.

PRECOCIOUS & DELAYED PUBERTY

Sexual Precocity

The common causes of precocious sexual development in humans are listed in Table 23–2. Early development of secondary sexual characteristics without gametogenesis is caused by abnormal exposure of immature males to androgen or females to estrogen. This syndrome should be called **precocious pseudopuberty** to distinguish it from **true precocious puberty** due to an early but otherwise normal puberal pattern of gonadotropin secretion from the pituitary (Fig 23–11). In one large series of cases, precocious puberty was the commonest endocrine symptom of hypothalamic disease (see Chapter 14). Pineal tumors are sometimes associated with precocious puberty, and it was once thought that the pineal secreted a substance which inhibited the onset of puberty. There are still a few proponents of this view, but the bulk of the evidence indicates that pineal tumors are associated with precocious puberty only when there is secondary damage to the hypothalamus. Precocity due to this and other forms of hypothalamic damage probably occurs

TABLE 23–2. Classification of the causes of precocious sexual development in man.*

True precocious puberty
    Constitutional
    Cerebral: Disorders involving posterior hypothalamus
        Tumors
        Infections
        Developmental abnormalities

Precocious pseudopuberty (no spermatogenesis or ovarian development)
    Adrenal
        Congenital virilizing adrenal hyperplasia (in males)
        Androgen-secreting tumors (in males)
        Estrogen-secreting tumors (in females)
    Gonadal
        Interstitial cell tumors of testis
        Granulosa cell tumors of ovary
    Miscellaneous

*Modified from Jolly: *Sexual Precocity*. Thomas, 1955.

FIG 23–11. Constitutional precocious puberty in a 3½-year-old girl. The patient developed pubic hair and started to menstruate at the age of 17 months. (Reproduced, with permission, from Jolly: *Sexual Precocity*. Thomas, 1955.)

with equal frequency in both sexes, although the constitutional form of precocious puberty is more common in girls.

Delayed or Absent Puberty

The normal variation in the age at which adolescent changes occur is so wide that puberty cannot be considered to be pathologically delayed until the menarche has failed to occur by the age of 17 or testicular development by the age of 20. Failure of maturation due to panhypopituitarism or hypothyroidism is associated with dwarfing and evidence of other endocrine abnormalities. Patients with the XO chromosomal pattern and gonadal dysgenesis are also dwarfed. In some individuals, puberty is delayed even though the gonads are present and other endocrine functions are normal. In males, this clinical picture is called **eunuchoidism.** In females, it is called **primary amenorrhea** (see below).

MENOPAUSE

In humans, the ovary gradually becomes unresponsive to gonadotropins with advancing age, and its function declines, so that sexual cycles disappear **(menopause).** Old female mice and rats have long periods of diestrus and increased levels of gonadotropin secretion, but a clear-cut "menopause" has apparently not been described in animals.

In women, the menses usually become irregular and cease between the ages of 45 and 55. Sensations of warmth spreading from the trunk to the face ("hot flashes") and various psychic symptoms are common at this time. The hot flashes are prevented by estrogen treatment. They are not peculiar to females, and sometimes occur in males castrated in adulthood.

Although the function of the testes does tend to decline slowly with advancing age, the evidence is clear that there is no "male menopause" or **climacteric** similar to that occurring in women.

PITUITARY GONADOTROPINS & PROLACTIN

Actions

The testes and ovaries become atrophic when the pituitary is removed or destroyed. The actions of prolactin and the gonadotropins, FSH and LH, as well as those of the gonadotropin secreted by the placenta, are described in detail in succeeding sections of this chapter. In brief, FSH maintains the spermatogenic epithelium in the male and is responsible for the early growth of ovarian follicles in the female. LH is tropic

TABLE 23–3. Characteristics of pituitary gonadotropins.*

Hormone	Species	Molecular Weight	Hexose (%)	Hexosamine (%)	Fucose (%)	Sialic Acid (%)
FSH	Ovine	25–30,000	5.7	4.5	1.0	2.8
	Human	25–30,000	3.9	2.4	1.0	1.4
LH	Ovine	30,000	6.5	7.8	1.0	0?
	Human	26,000	5.9	5.1	1.0	0.7

*Data courtesy of H Papkoff.

to the Leydig cells, and testosterone output in the spermatic vein is increased within minutes after its injection in dogs. In females, LH is responsible for the final maturation of the ovarian follicles and estrogen secretion from them. It is also responsible for ovulation and the initial formation of the corpus luteum and secretion of progesterone. Prolactin causes milk secretion from the breast after estrogen and progesterone priming. Its stimulatory effect on maternal behavior is discussed in Chapter 15. The function, if any, of prolactin in males is unknown. In rodents, prolactin maintains the corpus luteum, but it is not luteotropic in man, and the corpus luteum appears to be maintained by LH.

Assay

Various methods have been used to bioassay FSH and LH. FSH has frequently been measured by its action in increasing ovarian weight in immature rats treated with a placental gonadotropin, the so-called **augmentation assay**. LH has been assayed by the increase it produces in the weight of the ventral prostate of hypophysectomized male rats or by the decrease it causes in the ascorbic acid content of the ovaries of suitably prepared female rats. However, FSH and LH are now generally being measured by radioimmunoassay.

An action of prolactin that has been used as the basis for bioassay of this hormone is stimulation of the growth and "secretion" of the crop sacs in pigeons and other birds. The paired crop sacs are outpouchings of the esophagus which form, by desquamation of their inner cell layers, a nutritious material ("milk") that the birds feed to their young. However, radioimmunoassays have now been developed for the measurement of prolactin.

Chemistry

FSH and LH are glycoproteins that contain the hexoses mannose and a galactose; the hexosamines N-acetylgalactosamine and N-acetylglycosamine; and the methyl pentose fucose (Table 23–3). Both hor-

FIG 23–12. Ovine prolactin. The black bars indicate disulfide bridges. (Courtesy of CH li.)

mones are made up of an *a* and a *β* subunit. The LH-*a* subunit appears to be very similar to and possibly identical with TSH-*a* and HCG-*a* (see Chapter 22). Very little is known about the metabolism of the pituitary gonadotropins. The half-life of human FSH is about 170 min; the half-life of LH is about 60 min.

Ovine prolactin is a simple protein with a ring containing cystine at one end (Fig 23—12). Bovine prolactin is slightly larger, with a molecular weight of 26,000.

Human Prolactin

It is difficult to separate human prolactin from growth hormone because human growth hormone has lactogenic activity and, except during pregnancy and lactation, there is very little prolactin in the human pituitary. Indeed, it was argued at one time that the 2 hormones were identical. However, experiments employing bioassays and immunoassays based on cross-reaction with ovine prolactin have demonstrated that there is a separate prolactin. Its chemical structure is not yet known, but its secretion is clearly independent of growth hormone. Prolactin secretion is increased during lactation, whereas growth hormone secretion is normal. It is also increased by stressful stimuli and after section of the pituitary stalk. A rise occurs during lactation in sexual ateliotic dwarfs who have congenital growth hormone deficiency (see Chapter 22). L-Dopa decreases the secretion of human prolactin while it increases the secretion of growth hormone, and, conversely, chlorpromazine and other phenothiazine tranquilizers increase prolactin secretion while they decrease growth hormone secretion.

THE MALE REPRODUCTIVE SYSTEM

STRUCTURE

The testes are made up of a series of convoluted **seminiferous tubules** along the walls of which the spermatozoa are formed from the primitive germ cells (**spermatogenesis**). The tubules drain into a network of ducts in the **epididymis**. From there, spermatozoa pass into the **vas deferens**. They enter through the **ejaculatory ducts** into the urethra in the body of the **prostate** at the time of ejaculation (Fig 23—13). Between the tubules in the testes are nests of cells containing lipid granules, the **interstitial cells of Leydig**, which secrete testosterone into the blood stream (Fig 23—14). The capillaries of the testes are unusual in that, unlike those in most other endocrine organs, they are not fenestrated.

GAMETOGENESIS & EJACULATION

Spermatogenesis

The **spermatogonia**, the primitive germ cells next to the basement membrane of the seminiferous tubules, mature into **primary spermatocytes**. This process begins during adolescence. The primary spermatocytes undergo meiotic division, reducing the number of chromosomes to the haploid number of 23. In the process, they divide into **secondary spermatocytes** and then into **spermatids**, which mature into **spermatozoa (sperms)**. In man, it takes an average of 74 days to form a mature sperm from a primitive germ cell by this orderly process of spermatogenesis. Each

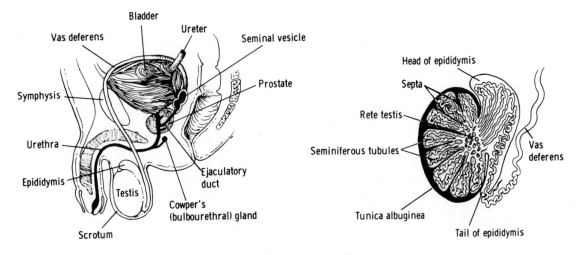

FIG 23—13. Male reproductive organs.

Primary spermatocyte

Spermato-gonium

Interstitial cell

Spermatid

Secondary spermatocyte

Sertoli cell

Sperm

FIG 23–14. Section of human testis, illustrating spermatogenesis in seminiferous tubule.

sperm is an intricate motile cell, rich in DNA, with a head that is made up mostly of chromosomal material (Fig 23–15). The sperms bury their heads in the **Sertoli cells,** glycogen-containing cells in the tubules from which the sperms apparently obtain nourishment. The Sertoli cells may also secrete estrogens.

Effect of Temperature

Spermatogenesis requires a temperature considerably lower than that of the interior of the body. When the testes are in the scrotum, they are kept cool enough for spermatogenesis to proceed normally. When they are retained in the abdomen or when, in experimental animals, they are held close to the body by tight cloth binders, degeneration of the tubular walls and sterility result.

Semen

The fluid that is ejaculated at the time of orgasm, the **semen,** contains sperms and the secretions of the seminal vesicles, prostate, Cowper's glands, and, probably, the urethral glands (Table 23–4). An average volume per ejaculate is 2.5–3.5 ml after several days of continence. Volume of semen and sperm count decrease rapidly with repeated ejaculation. Even though it takes only one sperm to fertilize the ovum, there are normally about 100 million sperms per ml of semen. Fifty percent of men with counts of 20–40 million/ml and essentially all of those with counts under 20 million/ml are sterile. The **prostaglandins** in semen, which actually come from the seminal vesicles, are in high concentration, but the function of these

TABLE 23–4. Composition of human semen.

Color: White, opalescent
Specific gravity: 1.028
pH: 7.35–7.50
Sperm count: Average about 100 million/ml, with
           fewer than 20% abnormal forms
Other components:

Fructose (1.5–6.5 mg/ml)	From seminal
Phosphorylcholine	vesicles (con-
Ergothioneine	tribute 60% of
Ascorbic acid	total volume)
Spermine	From prostate
Citric acid	(contributes
Cholesterol, phospholipids	20% of total
Fibrinolysin, fibrinogenase	volume)
Phosphate	Buffers
Bicarbonate	
Prostaglandins	
Hyaluronidase	

fatty acid derivatives in semen is not known. Their structure and actions are discussed in Chapter 17.

Human sperms move at a speed of about 3 mm/min through the female genital tract. In some species, contractions of the female organs facilitate the transport of the sperms to the fallopian tubes, but it is not known if such contractions occur in humans.

PROFILE

- Galea capitis (acrosome)
- Nucleus
- Cell membrane
- Centriole
- Mitochondrial sheath
- Axial fiber
- Fibrils in tail sheath
- Tail sheath

FRONTAL VIEW

- Head
- Middle piece
- Main piece of tail
- End piece of tail

CROSS-SECTION OF TAIL

FIG 23–15. Human spermatozoon. (Redrawn and reproduced, with permission, from Shultz-Larsen: The morphology of the human sperm. Acta path microbiol scandinav, Suppl 128, 1958.)

Ejaculation

Ejaculation is a 2-part spinal reflex that involves **emission,** the movement of the semen into the urethra; and **ejaculation** proper, the propulsion of the semen out of the urethra at the time of orgasm. The afferent pathways are mostly fibers from touch receptors in the glans penis that reach the spinal cord through the internal pudendal nerves. Emission is a sympathetic response, integrated in the upper lumbar segments of the spinal cord and effected by contraction of the smooth muscle of the vasa deferentia and seminal vesicles in response to stimuli in the hypogastric nerves. The semen is propelled out of the urethra by contraction of the bulbocavernosus muscle, a skeletal muscle. The spinal reflex centers for this part of the reflex are in the upper sacral and lowest lumbar segments of the spinal cord, and the motor pathways traverse the first to third sacral roots and the internal pudendal nerves.

Erection

Erection is initiated by dilatation of the arterioles of the penis. As the erectile tissue of the penis fills with blood, the veins are compressed, blocking outflow and adding to the turgor of the organ. The integrating centers in the lumbar segments of the spinal cord are activated by impulses in afferents from the genitalia and, in man, descending tracts that mediate erection in response to erotic psychic stimuli. The efferent fibers are in the pelvic splanchnic nerves (**nervi erigentes**). Sympathetic vasoconstrictor impulses to the arterioles terminate the erection.

ENDOCRINE FUNCTION OF THE TESTES

Chemistry & Biosynthesis of Testosterone

Testosterone, the principal hormone of the testes, is a C 19 steroid (see Chapter 20) with an –OH group in the 17 position (Fig 23–16). It is synthesized from cholesterol in the Leydig cells. According to current concepts, the biosynthetic pathways in all endocrine organs which form steroid hormones are similar, the organs differing from one another only in the enzyme systems they contain. In the Leydig cells, the 11- and 21-hydroxylases found in the adrenal cortex (Fig 20–9) are absent, but 17α-hydroxylase is present. Pregnenolone is therefore hydroxylated in the 17 position, then subjected to side chain cleavage to form 17-ketosteroids. These in turn are converted to testosterone. Testosterone secretion is under the control of LH, and the mechanism by which LH stimulates the Leydig cells appears to involve increased formation of cyclic AMP and increased protein synthesis (see Chapter 17). Testosterone is also formed in the adrenal cortex. Small amounts of estrogens are formed in the testes, although it is not certain whether they are products of the Leydig cells or the Sertoli cells.

Secretion

The testosterone secretion rate is 4–9 mg/day in the normal male. Small amounts of testosterone are also secreted in the female, probably from the ovary but possibly from the adrenal as well.

Transport & Metabolism

About two-thirds of the testosterone in plasma are bound to protein. Some is bound to albumin, and some to a β globulin that also binds estradiol. The latter protein is therefore known as gonadal steroid-binding globulin (GBG). The plasma testosterone level (free and bound) is approximately 0.65 μg/100 ml in normal men and 0.03 μg/100 ml in normal women. It declines somewhat with age in males.

A small amount of secreted testosterone is converted to estrogen somewhere in the body, but most of the testosterone is converted in the liver into 17-ketosteroids and excreted in the urine (Fig 23–17 and Table 23–5). About two-thirds of the urinary 17-ketosteroids are of adrenal origin, and one-third is of testicular origin. Although most of the 17-ketosteroids are weak androgens (they have 20% or less the potency of testosterone), it is worth emphasizing that not all

FIG 23–16. Biosynthesis of testosterone. Although testosterone is the main secretory product of the Leydig cells, some of the intermediates probably leak into the circulation. Compare with Fig 20–9.

FIG 23–17. Metabolism of testosterone. At least in some target tissues, it is dihydrotestosterone rather than testosterone that is physiologically active. Note that androsterone and the other 17-ketosteroids produced in the liver are isomers of one another.

TABLE 23–5. Origin of principal plasma and urinary 17-ketosteroids. The boldface compounds and their derivatives are 17-ketosteroids with an O or OH group in position 11 ("11-oxy-17-ketosteroids").

	Adrenal Androgens and Their Metabolites	Hepatic Metabolite of Cortisol	Hepatic Metabolite of Cortisone	Metabolite of Testosterone
Dehydroepiandrosterone	X			
△4-Androstene-3,17-dione	X			
11β-Hydroxy-△4-androstene-3,17-dione	X	X		X
Androsterone	X			X
Epiandrosterone	X			X
Etiocholanolone	X			X
Adrenosterone			X	

17-ketosteroids are androgens and not all androgens are 17-ketosteroids. Etiocholanolone, for example, has no androgenic activity, and testosterone itself is not a 17-ketosteroid.

Actions

• Testosterone and other androgens exert a feedback inhibitory effect on pituitary LH secretion; develop and maintain the male secondary sex characteristics; and exert an important protein anabolic, growth-promoting effect. Although FSH is normally responsible for the maintenance of gametogenesis, androgens are also capable of maintaining, at least to a degree, the integrity of the spermatogenic epithelium in hypophysectomized animals.

Secondary Sexual Characteristics

The widespread changes in hair distribution, body configuration, and genital size that develop in boys at puberty—the male **secondary sex characteristics**—are summarized in Table 23–6. Not only do the prostate and seminal vesicles enlarge, but fructose begins to be secreted from the seminal vesicles. This sugar appears to function as the main nutritional supply for the spermatozoa. The psychic effects of testosterone are difficult to define in man, but in experimental animals androgens provoke boisterous and aggressive play. The effects of androgens and estrogens on sex behavior are considered in detail in Chapter 15. Although body hair is increased by androgens, scalp hair is decreased. Hereditary baldness often fails to develop unless androgens are present (Fig 23–18).

TABLE 23–6. Body changes at puberty in boys (male secondary sex characteristics).

External genitalia: Penis increases in length and width. Scrotum becomes pigmented and rugose.

Internal genitalia: Seminal vesicles enlarge and secrete, and begin to form fructose. Prostate and bulbo-urethral glands enlarge and secrete.

Voice: Larynx enlarges, vocal cords increase in length and thickness, and voice becomes deeper.

Hair growth: Beard appears. Hair line on scalp recedes anterolaterally. Pubic hair grows with male (triangle with apex up) pattern. Hair appears in axillas, on chest, and around anus; general body hair increases.

Mental: More aggressive, active attitude. Interest in opposite sex develops.

Body conformation: Shoulders broaden, muscles enlarge.

Skin: Sebaceous gland secretion thickens and increases (predisposing to acne).

Anabolic Effects

Androgens increase the synthesis and decrease the breakdown of protein, leading to an increase in the rate of growth. They also cause the epiphyses to fuse to the long bones, thus eventually stopping growth. Their role in the adolescent growth spurt is discussed in Chapter 22. Secondary to their anabolic effect, they cause moderate sodium, potassium, water, calcium,

FIG 23–18. Hair line in children and adults. The hair line of the woman is like that of the child, whereas that of the man is indented in the lateral frontal region. (Reproduced, with permission, from Greulich & others: Somatic and endocrine studies of pubertal and adolescent boys. Monogr Soc Res Child Dev 7:1, 1942.)

sulfate, and phosphate retention, and they also increase the size of the kidneys. Doses of exogenous testosterone which exert significant anabolic effects are also masculinizing and increase libido, which limits the usefulness of the hormone as an anabolic agent in patients with wasting diseases. Attempts to develop synthetic steroids in which the anabolic action is divorced from the androgenic action have not been particularly successful.

In the prostate and presumably in other tissues, testosterone is converted (Fig 23–17) to dihydrotestosterone (DHT), and it is the DHT rather than the testosterone that is physiologically active. The DHT interacts with a protein in the cell. This triggers derepression of part of the genetic message, with resultant formation of new mRNA and stimulation of protein synthesis.

CONTROL OF
TESTICULAR FUNCTION

FSH maintains the gametogenic function of the testes, although androgens also contribute. LH is tropic to the Leydig cells. Testosterone inhibits LH secretion. Hypothalamic lesions in animals and hypothalamic disease in humans lead to atrophy of the testes and loss of their function.

A current "working hypothesis" of the way the functions of the testes are regulated is shown in Fig 23–19. Castration is followed by a rise in the pituitary content and secretion of FSH and LH, and hypothalamic lesions prevent this rise. Implantation of

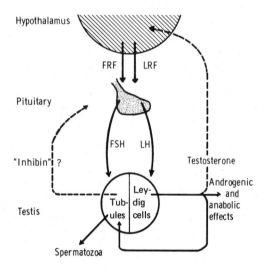

FIG 23–19. Postulated interrelationships between the hypothalamus, anterior pituitary, and testes. Solid arrows indicate excitatory effects; dashed arrows indicate inhibitory effects. Compare with Figs 18–10, 20–21, and 23–33.

minute amounts of testosterone in the hypothalamus but not in the pituitary causes testicular atrophy, indicating that the feedback effect of testosterone on gonadotropin secretion is at the level of the hypothalamus. Testosterone reduces plasma LH, but except in large doses it has no effect on plasma FSH. Castration in childhood leads to an increase in the excretion of gonadotropins, and gonadotropin excretion has been found to be elevated in patients who have atrophy of the seminiferous tubules but presumably normal levels of testosterone secretion. These studies suggest that, while testosterone feeds back to inhibit LH secretion (Fig 23–19), FSH secretion is independently controlled by the feedback of a hypothetical substance called "inhibin" which is secreted by some element in the seminiferous tubules. An alternative hypothesis is that the seminiferous tubules remove FSH from the circulation in the process of being stimulated by it. Estrogens lower plasma testosterone levels, presumably because they inhibit LH secretion. The estrogens from the testes might also play a role in the regulation of FSH secretion.

ABNORMALITIES OF
TESTICULAR FUNCTION

Cryptorchism
The testes develop in the abdominal cavity and normally migrate to the scrotum during fetal development. Testicular descent is incomplete on one or, less commonly, both sides in 10% of newborn males, the testes remaining in the abdominal cavity or inguinal canal. Spontaneous descent of these testes is the rule, however, and the proportion of boys with undescended testes **(cryptorchism)** falls to 2% at 1 year of age and 0.3% after puberty. Gonadotropic hormone treatment speeds descent in some cases, or the defect may be corrected surgically. Treatment should be instituted, probably before puberty, because there is a higher incidence of malignant tumors in undescended than in scrotal testes and because after puberty the higher temperature in the abdomen causes irreversible damage to the spermatogenic epithelium.

Effect of Spinal Cord Transection on the Testes
Over 50% of patients with paraplegia or quadriplegia due to spinal cord transection have degenerative changes of the seminiferous tubules. In most cases the Leydig cells are normal and androgen secretion is not decreased, although there have been reports of depressed gonadotropin excretion. Data on the effects of spinal cord transection on testicular function in experimental animals are contradictory. It has been claimed by some investigators that the changes in humans are due to the interruption of thermoregulatory pathways by cord transection, with resultant defective temperature regulation in the scrotum and increased testicular temperature.

Male Hypogonadism

The clinical picture of male hypogonadism depends upon whether testicular deficiency develops before or after puberty and whether the gametogenic or the endocrine function is compromised. The causes of testicular deficiency include hypothalamic and pituitary disease as well as a variety of primary testicular and chromosomal disorders. Loss or failure of maturation of the gametogenic function causes sterility. If the endocrine function is lost in adulthood, the secondary sex characteristics regress slowly because it takes very little androgen to maintain them once they are established. The growth of the larynx during adolescence is permanent, and the voice remains deep. Men castrated in adulthood suffer some loss of libido, although the ability to copulate persists for some time. They occasionally have hot flashes and are generally more irritable, passive, and depressed than men with intact testes. When the Leydig cell deficiency dates from childhood, the clinical picture is that of **eunuchoidism.** Eunuchoid individuals over the age of 20 are characteristically tall, although not so tall as hyperpituitary giants, because their epiphyses remain open and some growth continues past the normal age of puberty. They have narrow shoulders and small muscles, a body configuration resembling that of the adult female. The genitalia are small and the voice high-pitched. Pubic and axillary hair do appear, because of adrenocortical androgen secretion; but the hair is sparse and the pubic hair has the female "triangle with the base up" distribution rather than the "triangle with the base down" pattern seen in normal males.

Androgen-Secreting Tumors

"Hyperfunction" of the testes in the absence of tumor formation is not a recognized entity. Androgen-secreting testicular tumors are rare and cause detectable endocrine symptoms only in prepuberal boys, who develop precocious pseudopuberty (Table 23–2).

THE FEMALE REPRODUCTIVE SYSTEM

THE MENSTRUAL CYCLE

The reproductive system of the female (Fig 23–20), unlike that of the male, shows regular cyclic changes that teleologically may be regarded as periodic preparations for fertilization and pregnancy. In primates, the cycle is a **menstrual** cycle, and its most conspicuous feature is the periodic vaginal bleeding that occurs with the shedding of the uterine mucosa **(menstruation).** The length of the cycle is notoriously variable in women, but an average figure is 28 days from the start of one menstrual period to the start of the next. By common usage, the days of the cycle are identified by number, starting with the first day of menstruation.

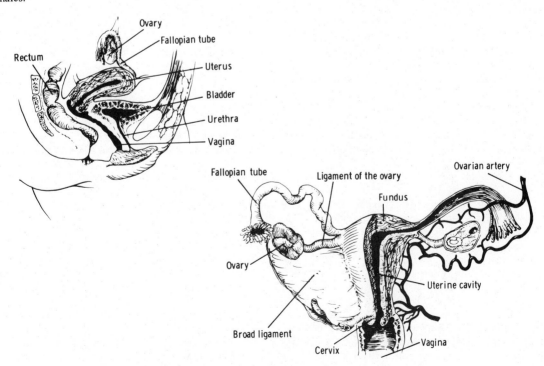

FIG 23–20. The female reproductive system.

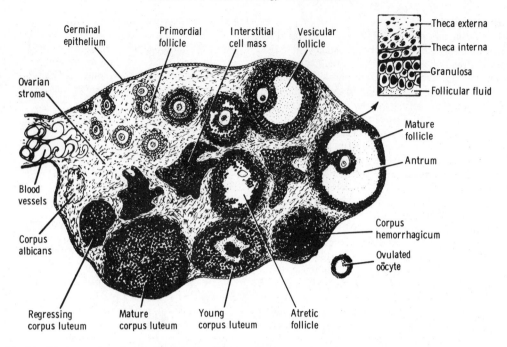

FIG 23—21. Diagram of a mammalian ovary, showing the sequential development of a follicle, formation of a corpus luteum, and, in the center, follicular atresia. A section of the wall of a mature follicle is enlarged at the upper right. The interstitial cell mass is not prominent in primates. (After Patten & Eakin. Reproduced, with permission, from Gorbman & Bern: *Textbook of Comparative Endocrinology.* Wiley, 1962.)

Ovarian Cycle

Under the ovarian capsule there are from the time of birth many **primordial follicles**, each containing an immature ovum (Fig 23—21). At the start of each cycle, several of these follicles enlarge and a cavity forms around the ovum (**antrum formation**). In humans, one of the follicles in one ovary starts to grow rapidly on about the sixth day, while the others regress. It is not known how one follicle is singled out for development. When women are given highly purified human pituitary gonadotropin preparations by injection, many follicles develop simultaneously. The structure of a maturing ovarian (**graafian**) follicle is shown in Fig 23—21. The cells of the **theca interna** of the follicle secrete estrogens. During follicular development, the ovum undergoes its meiotic reduction division.

At about the 14th day of the cycle, the distended follicle ruptures and the ovum is extruded into the abdominal cavity. This is the process of **ovulation.** The ovum is picked up by the fimbriated ends of the fallopian tubes and transported to the uterus, and, unless fertilization occurs, on out through the vagina. Follicles which enlarge but fail to ovulate degenerate, forming **atretic follicles** (Fig 23—21).

The follicle which ruptures at the time of ovulation promptly fills with blood, forming what is sometimes called a **corpus hemorrhagicum.** Minor bleeding from the follicle into the abdominal cavity may cause peritoneal irritation and fleeting lower abdominal pain ("mittelschmerz"). The granulosa and theca cells of the follicle lining promptly begin to proliferate, and the clotted blood is rapidly replaced with yellowish, lipid-rich **luteal** cells, forming the **corpus luteum.** The luteal cells secrete estrogens and progesterone. If pregnancy occurs, the corpus luteum persists and there are usually no more periods until after delivery. If there is no pregnancy, the corpus luteum begins to degenerate about 4 days before the next menses (24th day of the cycle) and is eventually replaced by scar tissue to form a **corpus albicans.**

The ovarian cycle in other mammals is similar, except that in many species more than one follicle ovulates and multiple births are the rule. Corpora lutea form in some submammalian species but not in others.

In humans, no new ova are formed after birth. At about the time of birth, the approximately 5 million that are present undergo the first part of the first meiotic division and then enter a stage of arrest in which approximately 500,000 of them persist until adulthood. Only one of these ova per cycle (or about 500 in the course of a normal reproductive life) is stimulated to mature; the remainder degenerate. Just before ovulation, the first meiotic division is completed and the second begins, but the second is completed only after a sperm penetrates the ovum.

Uterine Cycle

At the end of menstruation, all but the deep layers of the endometrium have sloughed. Under the influence of estrogens from the developing follicle, the endometrium increases rapidly in width during the

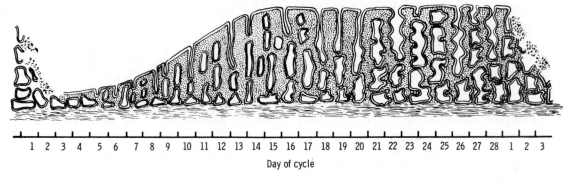

Day of cycle

FIG 23—22. Changes in the endometrium during the menstrual cycle.

period from the fifth to the 14th day of the menstrual cycle. The uterine glands increase in length but do not secrete to any degree (Fig 23—22). These endometrial changes are called **proliferative,** and this part of the menstrual cycle is sometimes called the **proliferative phase.** After ovulation, the endometrium becomes slightly edematous and the actively secreting glands become tightly coiled and folded under the influence of estrogen and progesterone from the corpus luteum. These are **secretory** or **progestational** changes, and this period is sometimes called the **secretory phase** of the menstrual cycle. When the corpus luteum regresses, hormonal support of the endometrium is withdrawn. The **spiral arteries** (Fig 23—23) constrict, and the part of the endometrium they supply becomes ischemic. This part is sometimes called the **stratum functionale** of the endometrium to distinguish it from the deeper **stratum basale,** supplied by straight **basal arteries.** The damaged tissue probably liberates an anticoagulant.

The spiral arteries then dilate one at a time and their necrotic walls rupture, producing hemorrhage, sloughing, and menstrual flow. Menstrual bleeding is predominantly arterial, only 25% of the blood in the flow being venous in origin. Unless the flow is excessive, it normally does not contain clots. The bleeding ends when the spiral arteries again constrict, and a new endometrium regenerates from the basal layers. The average duration of menstrual flow is 5 days. The average total blood loss is about 30 ml, although it varies considerably from woman to woman.

From the point of view of endometrial function, the proliferative phase represents the restoration of the epithelium from the preceding menstruation and the secretory phase the preparation of the uterus for the implantation of the fertilized ovum. When fertilization fails to occur, the endometrium is shed and a new cycle starts. Thus, to quote an old saying, "Menstruation is the uterus crying for lack of a baby."

The mucosa of the uterine cervix does not undergo cyclic desquamation, but there are regular changes in the cervical mucus. Estrogen makes the mucus thinner and more alkaline, changes which promote the survival and transport of sperms. Progesterone makes it thick, tenacious, and cellular. The mucus is thinnest at the time of ovulation, and dries in an arborizing, fernlike pattern (Fig 23—24) when a thin layer is spread on a slide. After ovulation and during pregnancy, it becomes thick and fails to form the fern pattern.

Vaginal Cycle

Under the influence of estrogens the vaginal epithelium becomes cornified, and cornified epithelial cells can be identified in the vaginal smear. Under the influence of progesterone, a thick mucus is secreted and the epithelium proliferates and becomes infiltrated with leukocytes. The cyclic changes in the vaginal smear in rats are particularly well known (Fig 23—25). The changes in humans and other species are similar, but unfortunately are not so clear-cut.

Clinical Applications

It is often important in clinical practice to know that ovulation has occurred and to know when during

Gland

Spiral arteries   Basal arteries

FIG 23—23. **Diagram of the vascular supply to the endometrium.**

Normal cycle, 14th day

Midluteal phase, normal cycle

Anovulatory cycle with
estrogen present

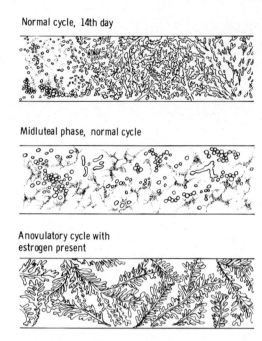

Vaginal   Cells in
epithelium   vaginal lumen

Diestrus

Proestrus

Estrus

Metestrus

FIG 23–24. Patterns formed when cervical mucus is smeared on a slide, permitted to dry, and examined under the microscope. Progesterone makes the mucus thick and cellular. In the smear from a patient who failed to ovulate *(bottom),* there is no progesterone to inhibit the estrogen-induced fern pattern.

the cycle it occurred. The finding of a secretory pattern in a biopsy of the endometrium (Fig 23–22) indicates that a functioning corpus luteum is present. Less reliably, finding thick, cellular cervical mucus that does not form a fern pattern in a woman who has regular menses is evidence of the same thing. A convenient and reasonably reliable indicator of the time of ovulation is a change—usually a rise—in the basal body temperature (Fig 23–28). Women interested in obtaining an accurate temperature chart should use a thermometer with wide gradations and take their temperatures (oral or rectal) in the morning before getting out of bed. The cause of the temperature change at the time of ovulation is not known.

The ovum lives for approximately 72 hours after it is extruded from the follicle, and sperms apparently survive in the female genital tract for no more than 48 hours. Consequently, the "fertile period" during a 28-day cycle is actually only 120 hours in length. Unfortunately for those interested in the "rhythm method" of contraception, the time of ovulation is rather variable even from one menstrual cycle to another in the same woman. Before the ninth and after the 20th day, there is relatively little chance of conception; but there are documented cases of pregnancy resulting from isolated coitus on every day of the cycle.

The Estrous Cycle

Mammals other than primates do not menstruate,

FIG 23–25. Changes in the vaginal wall (*left*) and type of cells found in the vaginal smear (*right*) during the estrous cycle in the rat. The vaginal smear pattern in man is similar, but not so clear-cut. (Redrawn and reproduced, with permission, from Turner & Bagnara: *General Endocrinology,* 5th ed. Saunders, 1971.)

and their sexual cycle is called an **estrous cycle.** It is named for the conspicuous period of "heat" or **estrus** at the time of ovulation, normally the only time during which the sexual interest of the female is aroused (see Chapter 15). The underlying endocrine events are essentially the same as those in the menstrual cycle, although the days of the cycle are numbered from the day of estrus (Fig 23–26).

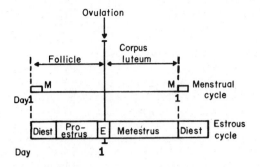

FIG 23–26. Timing of estrous cycle and menstrual cycle. M, menstruation; E, estrus, or "heat." Note that day 1 of a menstrual cycle is the first day of bleeding, while day 1 of an estrous cycle is the first day of heat.

OVARIAN HORMONES

Chemistry, Biosynthesis, & Metabolism of Estrogens

The naturally occurring estrogens are steroids which do not have an angular methyl group attached to the 10 position nor a Δ4,3-keto configuration in the A ring. They are secreted by the theca interna cells of the ovarian follicles, by the corpus luteum, by the

placenta, and, in small amounts, by the adrenal cortex and the testis. The biosynthetic pathway (Fig 23–27) involves their formation from androgens. The stromal tissues of the ovary also have the potential to make androgens and estrogens, but they probably do so in insignificant amounts in normal premenopausal women. **17β-Estradiol**, the major secreted estrogen, is in equilibrium in the circulation with **estrone**. Estrone is further metabolized to **estriol**, probably for the most part in the liver. Estradiol is the most potent estrogen of the three, and estriol the least. About 70% of the circulating estrogens are protein-bound. In the liver, the estrogens are oxidized or converted to glucuronide and sulfate conjugates. Appreciable amounts are secreted in the bile and reabsorbed into the blood stream (enterohepatic circulation). There are at least 10 different metabolites of estradiol in human urine.

Secretion

Estrogen secretion rates, estimated by isotope dilution, range from 200–500 µg/day in women at the time of ovulation. In men, the rate of secretion is approximately 50 µg/day. The urinary excretion of estradiol, estrone, and estriol is summarized in Table 23–7. Plasma levels, measured by radioimmunoassay, are shown in Fig 23–28. Estrogens are secreted throughout the menstrual cycle, but there are 2 peak

Pregnenolone ⟶ 17α-Hydroxypregnenolone ⟶ Dehydroepiandrosterone

Progesterone ⟶ 17α-Hydroxyprogesterone ⟶ Δ4-Androstene-3,17-dione

Testosterone

19-Hydroxytestosterone

Other metabolites

Estrone

16-Ketoestrone

16α-Hydroxyestrone

17β-Estradiol

Other metabolites

Estriol

FIG 23–27. Biosynthesis and metabolism of estrogens.

	Women, Age 18–41		Post- meno- pausal Women	Men	
	Prolif- erative Phase	Secre- tory Phase		Age 20– 48	Age 45– 65
Estriol	7	16	3	3	6
Estrone	5	7	2	4	6
Estradiol	2	4	1	1	2

*Data from Brown in: *Clinical Endocrinology I*. Astwood EB (editor). Grune & Stratton, 1960.

times of secretion: one at the time of ovulation and the other during the midluteal phase.

Effects on the Female Genitalia

The estrogens are said to facilitate the growth of the ovarian follicles and increase the motility of the fallopian tubes. Their role in the cyclic changes in the endometrium, cervix, and vagina are discussed above. They increase uterine blood flow and have important effects on the smooth muscle of the uterus. In immature and castrate females, the uterus is small and the myometrium atrophic and inactive. Estrogens increase the amount of muscle and its actomyosin content. Under the influence of estrogens, the uterine muscle becomes more active and excitable and action potentials in the individual fibers become more frequent (see Chapter 3). The "estrogen-dominated" uterus is also more sensitive to oxytocin. There is evidence that estrogen influences the excitability of uterine muscle

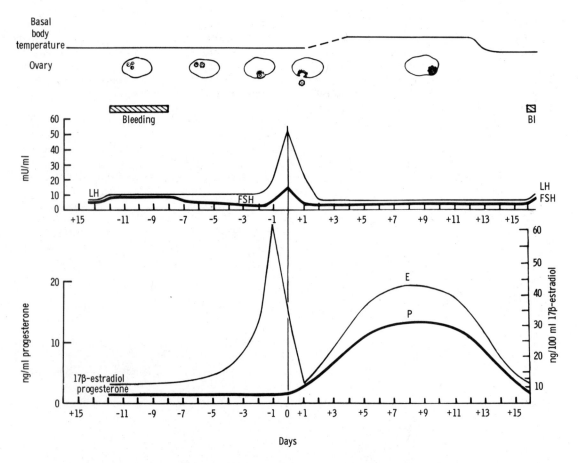

FIG 23–28. Changes in plasma hormone levels during the normal menstrual cycle. Horizontal axis, days before and after the peak LH concentration in plasma. Ovary: diagrammatic representation of ovarian changes. Note that ovulation occurs just after the LH peak. FSH and LH expressed in terms of the international reference standard used for measurement. (Courtesy of GW Harris and F Naftolin. Modified from Brit Med Bull 26:6, 1970.)

by changing the binding of Ca^{++} in the muscle.

Chronic treatment with estrogens causes the endometrium to hypertrophy. When estrogen therapy is discontinued, there is sloughing with **withdrawal bleeding**. Some "breakthrough" bleeding may occur during treatment when estrogens are given for long periods of time.

Effects on Endocrine Organs

Estrogens decrease FSH secretion. Under some circumstances, they inhibit LH secretion (negative feedback); under other circumstances, they may increase LH secretion (positive feedback; see below). Estrogens also increase the size of the pituitary. Female rats have a much greater diurnal variation in adrenocortical secretion than males, a difference that is abolished by castration and restored by estrogen treatment. They also secrete more ACTH in response to stress than males. There are other complex and as yet poorly understood effects of estrogens on thyroid and adrenocortical function. Estrogens exert an important protein anabolic effect in chickens and cattle, possibly by stimulating the secretion of androgens from the adrenal, and estrogen treatment has been used commercially to increase the weight of domestic animals. Estrogens have been reported to exert anabolic effects and to cause epiphyseal closure in humans, but these effects may also have been due to an increase in adrenal androgen secretion.

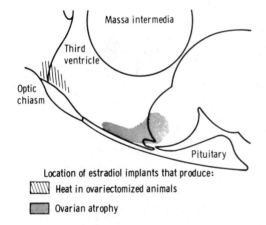

Location of estradiol implants that produce:

▨ Heat in ovariectomized animals

▨ Ovarian atrophy

FIG 23–29. **Loci where implantations of estrogen in the hypothalamus affect ovarian weight and sexual behavior, projected on a sagittal section of the hypothalamus of the rat.** Note that the implants which stimulate sex behavior are located in the suprachiasmatic area, whereas ovarian atrophy is produced by implants in the arcuate nucleus and surrounding ventral hypothalamus. (Drawn from data of Lisk: Estrogen-sensitive centers in the hypothalamus of the rat. J Exper Zool 145:197, 1960; and Diencephalic placement of estradiol and sexual receptivity in the female rat. Am J Physiol 203:493, 1962.)

Behavioral Effects

The estrogens are responsible for estrous behavior in animals, and they increase libido in humans. They apparently exert this action by a direct effect on certain neurons in the hypothalamus (Fig 23–29). The relation of estrogens, progesterone, and androgens to sexual behavior is discussed in detail in Chapter 15.

Effects on the Breast

Estrogens produce duct growth in the breasts and are largely responsible for breast enlargement at puberty in girls. Breast enlargement which occurs when estrogen-containing skin creams are applied locally is due primarily to systemic absorption of the estrogen, although a slight local effect is also produced. Estrogens are responsible for the pigmentation of the areolas, although pigmentation usually becomes more intense during the first pregnancy than it does at puberty. The role of the estrogens in the overall control of breast growth and lactation is discussed below.

Female Secondary Sex Characteristics

The body changes that develop in girls at puberty—in addition to enlargement of the breasts, uterus, and vagina—are in part due to estrogens, which are the "feminizing hormones," and in part due simply to the absence of testicular androgens. Women have narrow shoulders and broad hips, thighs that converge, and arms that diverge (wide **carrying angle**). This body configuration, plus the female distribution of fat in the breasts and buttocks, is seen also in castrate males. In women, the larynx retains its prepuberal proportions and the voice stays high-pitched. There is less body hair and more scalp hair, and the pubic hair has a characteristic flat-topped pattern. The growth of pubic and axillary hair in the female is due primarily to androgens rather than estrogens, although estrogen treatment may cause some hair growth. The androgens come from the adrenal cortex and, to a lesser extent, from the ovaries; the circulating level of dehydroepiandrosterone is about 0.17 μg/100 ml in adult women and about 0.12 μg in adult men.

Other Actions

Estrogens cause some degree of salt and water retention. Normal women retain salt and water and gain weight just before menstruation. They are somewhat irritable, tense, and uncomfortable at this time (**premenstrual tension**), and the symptoms are prevented if the weight gain is prevented. However, the role of estrogens in premenstrual tension is uncertain because the tension develops late in the cycle, not at the time of ovulation, when estrogen secretion is at its peak. It is possible that increased vasopressin secretion contributes to the premenstrual fluid retention.

Estrogens are said to make sebaceous gland secretions more fluid and thus to counter the effect of testosterone and inhibit formation of **comedones** ("blackheads") and acne. The liver palms, spider angiomas, and slight breast enlargement seen in advanced liver disease are generally said to be due to decreased hepatic metabolism of estrogens with a consequent rise in their circulating level. However, estrogen excretion is often normal in liver disease, and when it is elevated the elevation is usually due to a rise in the estriol fraction.

Estrogens have a significant plasma cholesterol lowering action, and they inhibit atherogenesis in chicks. The effect on cholesterol is probably due to an action of the hormone on the lipoproteins associated with cholesterol in the circulation. The higher estrogen level may be the reason for the lower incidence of myocardial infarction and other complications of arteriosclerotic vascular disease in women.

Mechanism of Action

The actions of estrogens on the uterus, vagina, and several other target tissues involve interaction with a protein which induces derepression of part of the genetic information coded in the nuclear DNA. New mRNA is formed, and protein synthesis is increased. It seems probable that all estrogen actions are produced in this fashion.

Synthetic Estrogens

The ethinyl derivative of estradiol (Fig 23–30) is a potent estrogen and, unlike the naturally occurring estrogens, it is relatively active when given by mouth. The activity of the naturally occurring hormones is low when they are administered by mouth because the portal venous drainage of the intestine carries them to the liver, where they are inactivated before they can reach the general circulation. Many other nonsteroidal substances and compounds found in plants have estrogenic activity. The plant estrogens are rarely a problem in human nutrition, but they may cause undesirable effects in farm animals. Diethylstilbestrol (Fig 23–30) and a number of related compounds are estrogenic, possibly because they are converted to a steroid-like ring structure in the body.

Ethinyl estradiol

Diethylstilbestrol

FIG 23–30. Synthetic estrogens.

Chemistry, Biosynthesis, & Metabolism of Progesterone

Progesterone is a C 21 steroid (Fig 23–31) secreted by the corpus luteum and the placenta. It is an important intermediate in steroid biosynthesis in all tissues that secrete steroid hormones, and small amounts apparently leak into the circulation from the testes and adrenal cortex. 17a-Hydroxyprogesterone is apparently secreted along with estrogens from the ovarian follicle, and its secretion parallels that of 17β-estradiol. The 20a- and 20β-hydroxy derivatives of progesterone are formed in the corpus luteum. Secreted progesterone is probably bound to protein, although little is known about the details of the binding. It is converted in the liver to pregnanediol, which is conjugated to glucuronic acid and excreted in the urine (Fig 23–31).

FIG 23–31. Biosynthesis of progesterone and major pathway for its metabolism. Other metabolites are also formed.

TABLE 23–8. Progesterone secretion rates.
Values are means of several determinations.*

	mg/day
Males	5
Females	
Follicular phase	4.7
Midluteal phase	31.8
Third trimester of pregnancy	335

*Data from Dominguez & others: *Progesterone Secretion in Man.* Abstracts, 44th Meeting of the Endocrine Society, 1962.

Secretion

The corpus luteum is apparently the only ovarian source of progesterone, because progesterone secretion is elevated during the luteal phase of the menstrual cycle whereas the progesterone secretion rate during the follicular phase is at the same low level as the secretion rate in men (Table 23–8). Measurements of plasma progesterone confirm this.

The stimulating effect of LH on progesterone secretion by the corpus luteum has been shown to be accompanied by an increased formation of cyclic AMP. The increase in progesterone secretion produced by LH or exogenous cyclic AMP is blocked by puromycin, which indicates that it depends upon the synthesis of new protein (see Chapter 17). However, the increase in the cyclic AMP content of the corpus luteum produced by LH is not blocked. The data suggest that LH activates adenyl cyclase in the corpus luteum and that, in a series of events analogous to that triggered by ACTH in the adrenal, the increased cyclic AMP initiates a reaction that involves protein synthesis and leads to steroid secretion.

Actions

Progesterone is responsible for the progestational changes in the endometrium and the cyclic changes in the cervix and vagina described above. It has an antiestrogenic effect on the myometrial cells, decreasing their excitability, their sensitivity to oxytocin, and their spontaneous electrical activity while increasing their membrane potential. In the breast it stimulates the development of lobules and alveoli.

Large doses of progesterone inhibit LH secretion, and progesterone injections can prevent ovulation in man; but smaller doses actually cause ovulation in the hen, rat, cow, and monkey. Progesterone does not induce heat in castrate animals, except possibly in huge doses, but in some species it lowers the dose of estrogen necessary to produce estrous behavior.

Progesterone stimulates respiration, and the fact that the alveolar P_{CO_2} ($P_{A_{CO_2}}$; see Chapter 34) in women during the luteal phase of the menstrual cycle is lower than in men is attributed to the action of secreted progesterone. In pregnancy, the $P_{A_{CO_2}}$ falls as progesterone secretion rises. Large doses of progesterone produce a natriuresis, probably by blocking the action of aldosterone on the kidney. The hormone does not have a significant anabolic effect. Most, and probably all of its effects, like those of other steroids, are brought about by an action on DNA to bring about synthesis of new mRNA.

Synthetic Progesterone Derivatives

Substances which mimic the action of progesterone are sometimes called **progestational agents**, **gestagens**, or **progestins**. Synthetic progestational agents (Fig 23–32) administered by mouth in suitable doses block the midcycle burst of LH secretion that causes ovulation (see below), thus acting as contraceptive agents. The blockade of LH release is apparently due to an inhibition of the neural events that normally trigger LRF secretion. This action is potentiated if the drugs are administered with small amounts of estrogens, and estrogens alone are contraceptive when given on a regular basis. The contraceptive regimens currently employed utilize either a combination of an estrogen and a progestational agent or sequential therapy with daily doses of an estrogen combined for the last 5–6 days of each treatment cycle with a progesterone derivative.

Δ4(5)-17a-Ethynyl-17-hydroxyestren-3-one
(norethindrone, Norlutin)

Δ5(10)-17a-Ethynyl-17-hydroxyestren-3-one

6a-Methyl-17a-acetoxyprogesterone
(medroxyprogesterone, Provera)

FIG 23–32. Some orally active synthetic progestational agents. Enovid is a mixture of 98.5% Δ5(10)-17a-ethynyl-17-hydroxyestren-3-one plus 1.5% estrogen (mestranol).

"Relaxin"

Aqueous extracts of the ovaries of sows and other animals relax the symphysis pubis and uterus and soften the cervix of estrogen-primed animals. These effects were originally thought to be due to a single factor which was called **relaxin** or **uterine relaxing factor (URF)**, but there are at least 3 closely related polypeptides with molecular weights of about 9000 which have relaxin activity. Relaxin also potentiates the stimulation of the endometrium produced by mixtures of estrogens and progesterone. The structure in the ovary that forms these peptides appears to be the corpus luteum. Relaxin activity has been demonstrated in the blood of pregnant women.

CONTROL OF OVARIAN FUNCTION

It is clear that FSH from the pituitary is responsible for the early maturation of the ovarian follicles; that FSH and LH together are responsible for their final maturation; and that a burst of LH secretion ("ovulating hormone" release) is responsible for ovulation and the initial formation of the corpus luteum (Fig 23–29). There is also a smaller midcycle burst of FSH secretion the significance of which is uncertain. In rats and mice, the function of the corpus luteum is then maintained by prolactin. However, prolactin does not have a luteotropic effect in rabbits, cattle, monkeys, and humans. In hypophysectomized rats, highly purified FSH preparations do not cause estrogen secretion unless a small amount of LH is also injected. LH and, presumably, prolactin stimulate progesterone secretion. Purified human FSH preparations have been reported to increase estrogen excretion in women, but the studies were carried out in women with intact pituitaries.

Neural Components

Observations on experimental animals and women with brain disorders show that the hypothalamus and probably also the limbic system are involved in the control of gonadotropin secretion in the female. Lesions of the arcuate nucleus in the ventral hypothalamus cause ovarian atrophy in experimental animals. An LH-releasing factor (LRF) has been isolated and synthesized and there is probably an FSH-releasing factor in the hypothalamus as well. These releasing factors are secreted into the portal-hypophysial vessels, passing directly to the pituitary to regulate its secretion.

The presence of another hypothalamic center affecting gonadotropin secretion in rats is indicated by the observation that lesions below the paraventricular nuclei are associated with the development of multiple follicular ovarian cysts and constant vaginal cornification. Injections of exogenous LH cause the cystic follicles to ovulate and luteinize. There must be a considerable chronic secretion of FSH and LH in these rats to produce the follicles and the estrogen secretion

responsible for the vaginal cornification, but the bursts of LH necessary to produce ovulation are apparently lacking. Stimulation of the amygdaloid nuclei causes ovulation in a number of species.

Reflex Ovulation

Female cats, rabbits, mink, and some other animals have long periods of estrus during which they ovulate only after copulation. Such **reflex ovulation** is brought about by afferent impulses from the genitalia and the eyes, ears, and nose which converge on the ventral hypothalamus and provoke an ovulation-inducing release of LH from the pituitary. In species such as the rat, monkey, and human, ovulation is a spontaneous periodic phenomenon, but neural mechanisms are also involved. Ovulation can be prevented in the rat by administering pentobarbital or various other neurally active drugs 12 hours before the expected time of ovulation. In women, menstrual cycles may be markedly influenced by emotional stimuli.

Feedback Effects

The site at which estrogens act to inhibit FSH secretion is apparently the hypothalamus. Small amounts of estrogen implanted in the hypothalamus cause ovarian atrophy (Fig 23–29). On the other hand, the rise in circulating estrogens just before ovulation is believed to initiate the burst of LH secretion that produces ovulation. It seems probable that the secretion of FSH and LH is inhibited by the high circulating estrogen and progesterone levels during the luteal phase of the menstrual cycle.

Control of Prolactin Secretion

Prolactin secretion is inhibited by the hypothalamus, and the secretion of this hormone is increased when the connections between the hypothalamus and the pituitary are severed. This increase is the probable explanation of the lactation seen after pituitary stalk section in nonpregnant women with breast cancer. The hypothalamus contains a hormonal factor (prolactin-inhibiting factor, PIF) which inhibits prolactin secretion (see Chapter 14). In general, there is a reciprocal relation between the secretion of LH and the secretion of prolactin.

Effects of Intrauterine Foreign Bodies

Implantation of foreign bodies in the uterus causes changes in the duration of the sexual cycle in a number of mammalian species. In humans, such foreign bodies do not alter the menstrual cycle, but they act as effective contraceptive devices. Intrauterine implantation of plastic spirals is currently seeing increasing use in programs aimed at controlling population growth. The mechanism by which these devices exert their contraceptive effect is unsettled, but there is some evidence that they speed the passage of the fertilized ovum through the uterus, preventing its implantation in the endometrium. They also disturb the orderly sequential changes in the endometrium during the menstrual cycle, and this may be a factor.

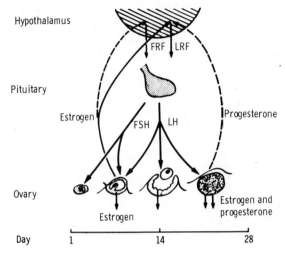

FIG 23–33. Summary of known and suspected endocrine changes during the menstrual cycle. The dashed arrows indicate inhibitory effects.

Summary

It is not possible at present to arrange the known hormonal events of the menstrual cycle summarized in Fig 23–33 into an automatically cycling mechanism. One of the key problems is what causes regression of the corpus luteum (**luteolysis**). Once luteolysis begins, the estrogen and progesterone levels fall and the secretion of FSH and LH increases. A new follicle develops, and estrogen secretion from it increases rapidly. This rise appears to trigger a burst of LH secretion via a positive feedback action on the nervous system. The resulting ovulation is followed by formation of a corpus luteum, and progesterone and estrogen levels rise. The high estrogen and progesterone levels inhibit FSH and LH secretion for a while, but luteolysis again occurs and a new cycle starts.

ABNORMALITIES OF OVARIAN FUNCTION

Menstrual Abnormalities

Some women who are infertile have **anovulatory cycles**; they fail to ovulate but have menstrual periods at fairly regular intervals. Such anovulatory cycles are the rule for the first 1–2 years after menarche, and again before the menopause. **Amenorrhea** is the absence of menstrual periods. If menstrual bleeding has never occurred, the condition is called **primary amenorrhea**. Women with primary amenorrhea usually have small breasts and other signs of failure to mature sexually. Cessation of cycles in a woman with previously normal periods is called **secondary amenorrhea**. The commonest cause of secondary amenorrhea is pregnancy, and the old clinical maxim that, "Secondary amenorrhea should be considered to be due to pregnancy until proved otherwise" has considerable merit. Other causes of amenorrhea include emotional stimuli and changes in the environment, hypothalamic diseases, pituitary disorders, primary ovarian disorders, and various systemic diseases. Women whose ovaries are removed surgically or destroyed by disease in adulthood usually have uncomfortable hot flashes, but there is little change in body conformation or libido. The terms **oligomenorrhea** and **menorrhagia** refer to scanty and abnormally profuse flow, respectively, during regular periods. **Metrorrhagia** is bleeding from the uterus between periods. **Dysmenorrhea** is painful menstruation. The severe menstrual cramps that are common in young women quite often disappear after the first pregnancy.

The Polycystic Ovary Syndrome

An interesting cause of infertility and amenorrhea is the **polycystic ovary syndrome** (Stein-Leventhal syndrome), a condition characterized by thickening of the ovarian capsule with the formation of multiple follicular cysts, usually in both ovaries. Stripping off the ovarian capsule usually brings at least transient relief, but the thick capsule is not the cause of the failure to ovulate because resection of a wedge of ovarian tissue provides equally effective relief. Many patients with polycystic ovaries also have moderate degrees of hirsutism and masculinization and excrete increased amounts of 17-ketosteroids. In some patients, the excretion of 17-ketosteroids is normal but plasma testosterone levels are elevated. The similarity between the cystic ovaries in this syndrome and the ovarian changes in rats exposed to androgen in early postnatal life (see Chapter 15) is obvious, but there is as yet no evidence that a similar exposure causes cystic ovaries in humans.

Ovarian Tumors

Androgen-secreting ovarian tumors can cause masculinization, and estrogen-secreting ovarian tumors in childhood can cause precocious sexual development (Table 23–2). Hormone-secreting ovarian tumors are rare, and there is no other syndrome related to "hyperfunction of the ovary."

PREGNANCY

Fertilization & Implantation

In humans, **fertilization** of the ovum by the sperm usually occurs in the midportion of the fallopian tube. The penetration of the ovum by the sperm and the initiation of cell division, which begins at once, may be brought about by lysosomal enzymes in the acrosome of the sperm. Only one sperm penetrates the ovum, because once the ovum has been fertilized a barrier forms around it that normally prevents other sperms from entering. The developing embryo, now called a

blastocyst, moves down the tube into the uterus. Once in contact with the endometrium, the blastocyst becomes surrounded by an outer layer of **syncytio-trophoblast**, a multinucleate mass with no discernible cell boundaries, and an inner layer of **cytotrophoblast** made up of individual cells. The syncytiotrophoblast erodes the endometrium, and the blastocyst burrows into it **(implantation)**. The implantation site is usually on the dorsal wall of the uterus. A placenta then develops and the trophoblast remains associated with it.

Endocrine Changes

In all mammals, the corpus luteum in the ovary at the time of fertilization fails to regress, and instead enlarges in response to stimulation by gonadotropic hormones secreted by the placenta. The placental gonadotropin in humans is called **human chorionic gonadotropin (HCG)**. The enlarged **corpus luteum of pregnancy** secretes estrogens and progesterone. In most species, removal of the ovaries at any time during pregnancy precipitates abortion. In humans, however, the placenta secretes sufficient estrogen and progesterone to take over the function of the corpus luteum after the third month of pregnancy. Ovariectomy before the third month leads to abortion, but after the third month has no effect on the pregnancy. There are degenerative changes in the corpus after the fifth month, but it persists throughout pregnancy. HCG secretion decreases after an initial marked rise, but estrogen and progesterone secretion increases until just before parturition (Fig 23–34).

FIG 23–34. Hormone levels during normal pregnancy. (Data from various authors.)

TABLE 23–9. Pregnancy tests. Note that all are based on detection of HCG in the urine in the early weeks of pregnancy.

Test	End Point
Aschheim-Zondek (A-Z)	Ovulation in immature mice
Hogben and related tests	Release of sperms or ova in various species of frogs and toads.
Immunoassay (agglutination inhibition)	
Latex particles (Gravindex)	Inhibition of agglutination of sheep red cells
Sheep red cells (Pregnosticon)	or latex particles coated with HCG.

HCG

HCG is a glycoprotein which contains galactose and hexosamine. Like the pituitary glycoprotein hormones, it is made up of a and β subunits. HCG-a is very similar to if not identical with LH-a and TSH-a. HCG has a molecular weight of about 100,000 and is antigenic in other animal species. Its actions are primarily luteinizing and luteotropic, but it has a little FSH activity. Its presence in the urine in early pregnancy is the basis for the various laboratory tests for pregnancy, and it can sometimes be detected as early as 14 days after conception (Table 23–9).

Pregnant Mare's Serum (PMS)

Another commercially available placental gonadotropin is that isolated from pregnant mare's serum (PMS). Unlike HCG, this substance has primarily follicle-stimulating activity and is a relatively weak luteinizing agent.

Other Placental Hormones

In addition to HCG, progesterone, and estrogens, the human placenta apparently secretes one or possibly 2 substances with TSH activity, renin and relaxin. It also secretes a protein hormone which is lactogenic and has a small amount of growth-stimulating activity. This hormone has been called **chorionic growth hormone-prolactin (CGP)**, **human placental lactogen (HPL)**, and **human chorionic somatomammotropin (HCS)**. All the placental hormones appear to be secreted by syncytiotrophoblast.

Like growth hormone, HCS contains 190 amino acid residues, and it has other structural similarities to growth hormone. Large quantities are found in maternal blood, but very little reaches the fetus. Secretion of growth hormone from the maternal pituitary is not increased during pregnancy. Indeed, there is some evidence that HCS inhibits growth hormone secretion. However, HCS has most of the actions of growth hormone and apparently functions as a "maternal growth hormone of pregnancy" to bring about the nitrogen, potassium, and calcium retention and decreased glucose utilization seen in this state. The amount of HCS secreted is proportionate to the size of the placenta, and low levels are a sign of placental insufficiency.

The interchange between maternal and fetal hormones is relatively slight. The nonprotein hormones cross the placenta to a slight degree, but as a general rule the movement of protein hormones in either direction is nil. However, the fetal adrenal gland secretes dehydroepiandrosterone sulfate (see Chapter 20), and the placenta converts this compound to androgens and estrogens which enter the maternal circulation.

Parturition

The duration of pregnancy in man averages 270 days from fertilization, or 284 days from the first day of the menstrual period preceding conception. In spite of intensive research, the mechanisms that initiate labor remain obscure. Irregular uterine contractions increase in frequency in the last month of pregnancy. The myometrium becomes increasingly sensitive to oxytocin late in pregnancy, and it seems clear that once labor is initiated, stimuli from the genital tract cause reflex secretion of the hormone (see Chapter 14). This in turn augments uterine contractions (Fig 23–35). Women with diabetes insipidus have given birth without incident, and experimental animals whose posterior pituitary glands have been removed do not have abnormal deliveries. However, removal of the

Onset of Labor

During Labor

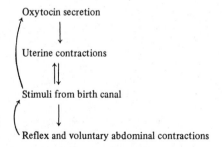

FIG 23–35. **Hypothetical scheme of factors involved in human parturition.** (Based in part on scheme of factors in rabbit, as outlined by Cross, in: *Recent Progress in the Endocrinology of Reproduction.* Lloyd CW [editor]. Academic Press, 1959.)

posterior pituitary alone leaves some oxytocin-secreting nerve endings in the pituitary stalk untouched; and hypothalamic lesions, which probably produce a more effective blockade of oxytocin secretion than posterior lobectomy, cause prolonged, desultory labor. Spinal reflexes and voluntary contractions of the abdominal muscles ("bearing down") also aid in expelling the uterine contents.

Pseudopregnancy

In rats, mice, and various other species, sterile coitus, stimulation of the cervix with a glass rod, or suckling a foster litter initiates a prolonged secretion of prolactin and retention of the corpus luteum with a consequent delay in the return of normal cycles for some time. This state is called **pseudopregnancy**. The release of prolactin that maintains pseudopregnancy is clearly a neuroendocrine reflex response.

During pseudopregnancy in rodents and during the luteal phase of the menstrual cycle in monkeys, implantation of a glass bead, a piece of thread, or other foreign body in the uterus evokes a local endometrial response called a **deciduoma**. The maternal portion of the placenta forms as a result of a similar endometrial response when the implanted object is a developing embryo.

The type of pseudopregnancy seen in rodents does not occur in women, but women do sometimes imagine themselves pregnant. In false pregnancy or **pseudocyesis**, there may be amenorrhea, abdominal enlargement, breast changes, and morning sickness. The fact that these changes can occur in the absence of pregnancy emphasizes the degree to which endocrine secretion can be affected by emotional states.

LACTATION

Development of the Breasts

Many hormones are necessary for full mammary development. In all species, estrogens are primarily responsible for proliferation of the mammary ducts and progesterone for the development of the lobules and alveoli. In hypophysectomized rats, adrenal glucocorticoids and growth hormone must be present before other hormones will act on the breast.

Secretion & Ejection of Milk

In estrogen and progesterone-primed rodents, injections of prolactin cause the formation of milk droplets and their secretion into the ducts. Oxytocin causes contraction of the myoepithelial cells lining the duct walls, with consequent ejection of the milk through the nipple (Fig 23–36). The reflex release of oxytocin initiated by touching the nipples and areolas (milk ejection reflex) is discussed in Chapter 14. Oxytocin is not essential for milk ejection in some

Anterior pituitary

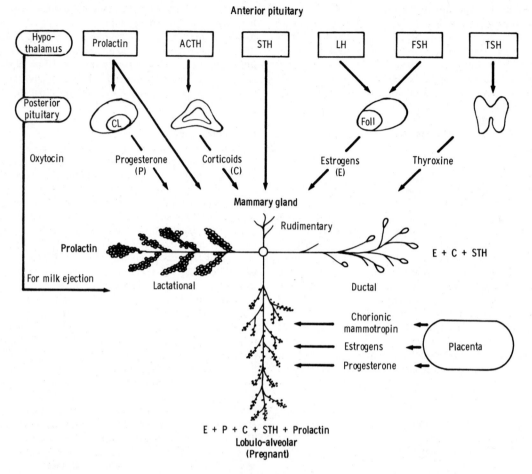

FIG 23–36. Hormonal control of breast development and lactation in the Long-Evans rat. Estrogens (plus some progesterone) in the presence of corticoids and growth hormone cause duct proliferation and growth at puberty (*right*). During pregnancy, all of these hormones plus some prolactin bring about full alveolar development and some milk secretion (*below*). After delivery, increased secretion of prolactin plus a decline in estrogen and progesterone levels bring about copious secretion and, in the presence of oxytocin, ejection of milk (*left*). Chorionic mammotropin is the lactogenic hormone presumably secreted by the placenta in rats and is analogous to human chorionic somatomammotropin. STH, growth hormone; CL, corpus luteum; Foll, follicle. (Modified and redrawn, with permission, from Lyons & others: Hormonal control of mammary growth and lactation. Recent Progr Hormone Res 14:219, 1958.)

species, but it is in humans. The other hormonal relations in humans are generally similar to those in rats, although normal lactation can occur in dwarfs with congenital growth hormone deficiency.

Initiation of Lactation After Delivery

The breasts enlarge during pregnancy in response to the high circulating level of estrogens and progesterone. Some milk is secreted into the ducts as early as the fifth month, but the amounts are small compared to the surge of milk secretion that follows delivery. A similar increase in milk secretion follows abortions after the fourth month, so expulsion of the uterine contents in some way stimulates milk secretion. In animals, milk is secreted within an hour after delivery, but in man it takes 1–3 days for the milk to "come in."

There still is considerable speculation and controversy about the mechanism that initiates lactation. Prolactin secretion rises after delivery. There is evidence that the levels of progesterone are high enough when estrogen is also present during pregnancy to inhibit prolactin secretion, and it has been claimed that progesterone inhibits the effect of prolactin on the breast. One theory of the initiation of lactation holds that, after the levels of progesterone drop, the small amounts of estrogen remaining stimulate prolactin secretion. The increase in circulating glucocorticoids associated with the stress of parturition is also said to contribute to the onset of lactation.

Maintenance of Lactation

Suckling not only evokes reflex oxytocin release and milk ejection; it also maintains and augments the secretion of milk, probably in response to prolactin secretion provoked by afferent neural stimuli from the breast. It was thought at one time that oxytocin acted on the pituitary as a neurohumor to stimulate prolactin secretion, but this hypothesis has been disproved.

Return of Menstrual Cycle After Delivery

Women who do not nurse their infants usually have their first menstrual period 6 weeks after delivery. Nursing stimulates prolactin secretion and apparently inhibits the secretion of FSH and LH, so that ovulation is delayed. The ovaries are inactive, and estrogen and progesterone output fall to low levels. Fifty percent of nursing mothers do not ovulate until the child is weaned. The mechanism responsible for the inhibition of FSH and LH secretion is unknown.

Chiari-Frommel Syndrome

An interesting although rare condition is persistence of lactation (**galactorrhea**) and amenorrhea in women who do not nurse after delivery. This condition, called the **Chiari-Frommel syndrome**, may be associated with some genital atrophy and is presumably due to persistent prolactin secretion without the secretion of the FSH and LH necessary to produce maturation of new follicles and ovulation. A similar pattern of galactorrhea and amenorrhea with high circulating prolactin levels is sometimes seen in nonpregnant women with chromophobe tumors of the pituitary and in women in whom the pituitary stalk has been sectioned in treatment of cancer.

Gynecomastia

Breast development in the male is called **gynecomastia**. It may be unilateral but is more commonly bilateral. It is seen in mild, transient form in 70% of normal boys at the time of puberty. It is a complication of estrogen therapy, and occurs in patients with estrogen-secreting tumors. It also occurs in a wide variety of seemingly unrelated conditions, including eunuchoidism due to primary testicular disease, hypothyroidism, hyperthyroidism, and cirrhosis of the liver. It occurs during initial digitalization in some patients with congestive heart failure and was seen in malnourished prisoners of war, but only after they were liberated and eating an adequate diet. There are many theories about the causes of gynecomastia, and probably many different etiologies.

Hormones & Cancer

About 35% of carcinomas of the breast in women of childbearing age are **estrogen-dependent**; their continued growth depends upon the presence of estrogens in the circulation, and they are made worse by pregnancy and inhibited by castration. The tumors are not destroyed by decreasing estrogen secretion, but symptoms are dramatically relieved and the tumor regresses for months or years before recurring. Women with estrogen-dependent tumors often have a remission when their ovaries are removed. When the disease recurs, another remission follows bilateral adrenalectomy or the administration of glucocorticoids in doses sufficient to inhibit ACTH secretion and thus reduce the secretion of estrogens from the adrenals. Since ovarian and adrenal estrogen secretion are both inhibited by hypophysectomy, this operation has been performed in many cancer patients. The number of remissions produced by hypophysectomy is at least as great as the number produced by castration. There also is some evidence that growth hormone stimulates the growth of breast carcinomas, and hypophysectomy removes this stimulus. Hypophysectomy induces a significant incidence of remissions in carcinoma of the male breast, an uncommon but serious disease. Some carcinomas of the prostate are **androgen-dependent** and regress temporarily after removal of the testes or hypophysectomy. The formation of pituitary tumors after removal of the target endocrine glands controlled by pituitary tropic hormones is discussed in Chapter 22.

24...

Other Organs With Established or Suggested Endocrine Functions

The organs with endocrine functions include a number of structures in addition to the posterior, intermediate, and anterior lobes of the pituitary, the thyroid, the parathyroids, the pancreas, the adrenal cortex, the adrenal medulla, and the gonads. "Releasing factors" which stimulate the secretion of anterior pituitary hormones are liberated from cells in the hypothalamus (see Chapter 14), and a number of hormones are secreted by the mucosa of the gastrointestinal tract (see Chapter 26). Two hormones are produced by the kidney, and there have been claims that the pineal, thymus, and spleen have endocrine functions.

THE ENDOCRINE FUNCTIONS OF THE KIDNEYS: RENIN & ERYTHROPOIETIN

Renin & Angiotensin

The rise in blood pressure produced by injection of kidney extracts is due to **renin**, a proteolytic enzyme which is secreted by the kidney. This enzyme is also found in the pregnant uterus. Only impure preparations of renin are presently available. Renin has a molecular weight of about 50,000, but very little is known about its structure. In the dog, it has a half-life in the circulation of about 80 minutes. In the blood stream, renin acts on a protein in the a_2 globulin fraction of the plasma proteins, releasing a decapeptide, **angiotensin I** (Fig 24–1). The a_2 globulin is synthesized in the liver and is called **angiotensinogen**, or **renin substrate**. Its circulating level is increased by glucocorticoid hormones and estrogens. **Converting enzyme** splits off histidyl-leucine from the physiologically inactive angiotensin I, forming the octapeptide **angiotensin II**. Most of this conversion occurs during the passage of the blood through the lungs.

Angiotensin II is destroyed rapidly, its half-life in man being 1–2 minutes. The enzymes that destroy angiotensin II are lumped together under the term **angiotensinase**. They are found in many tissues. They include aminopeptidases, and metabolism appears to proceed primarily via removal of amino acids from the N-terminal end of the peptide. There is a great deal of angiotensinase activity in red blood cells. In addition, angiotensin II appears to be removed from the circulation by some sort of trapping mechanism in the vascular beds of tissues other than the lungs.

Angiotensin II, which was previously called

```
┌──────────────────────────────┐   Renin     ┌───────────────┐  Converting   ┌────────────────┐ Peptidases,  ┌───────────────────┐
│Angiotensinogen (a₂-globulin) │ ─────────→ │ Angiotensin I │ ─── enzyme ──→ │ Angiotensin II │ ─── etc ───→ │ Inactive peptides │
└──────────────────────────────┘   Blood     └───────────────┘   Lungs       └────────────────┘  Vascular    └───────────────────┘
                                                                                                    beds
```

Converting enzyme splits this bond   Renin splits this bond
↓   ↓

Asp-Arg-Val-Tyr-Ile-His-Pro-Phe-His-Leu-Leu-Val-Tyr-Ser-R

Angiotensinogen

Asp-Arg-Val-Tyr-Ile-His-Pro-Phe
1   2   3   4   5   6   7   8

Angiotensin II

FIG 24–1. Formation of angiotensin II from angiotensinogen by renin and converting enzyme. R = remainder of protein. The structure shown is that of human, procine, and equine angiotensin II. Bovine angiotensin II has valine in position 5. The structure of angiotensin II in other species is not known. (Data largely from Skeggs & others: The preparation, purification and amino acid sequence of a polypeptide renin substrate. J Exper Med 106:439, 1957.)

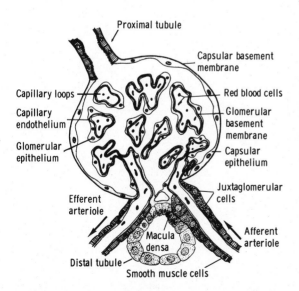

FIG 24—2. Pressor responses to intravenous injections of renin and angiotensin II in anesthetized dogs. Figures are drawings of records obtained with Grass polygraph.

hypertensin or **angiotonin**, produces arteriolar constriction and a rise in systolic and diastolic blood pressure (Fig 24—2). It is the most potent vasoconstrictor known, being on a weight basis 4—8 times as active as norepinephrine in normal individuals. However, its pressor activity is decreased in sodium-depleted individuals and in patients with cirrhosis and some other diseases. It also increases the secretion of glucocorticoids and aldosterone by a direct action on the adrenal cortex, and in small doses its predominant effect is on aldosterone secretion (see Chapter 20).

Renin is usually measured by incubating the sample to be assayed with substrate and measuring by immunoassay the amount of angiotensin I generated.

The Juxtaglomerular Apparatus

The source of the renin in kidney extracts is the **juxtaglomerular cells (JG cells)**. These granular epithelioid cells are located in the media of the afferent arterioles as they enter the glomeruli. A few granular cells are also found in the adjacent connective tissue. Evidence that the juxtaglomerular cells are the source of renin includes the observation that the number of granules in the cells correlates well with the renin content of the kidney and that fluorescent antirenin antibodies localize in the juxtaglomerular cells.

At the point where the afferent arteriole enters the glomerulus and the efferent arteriole leaves it, the tubule of the nephron touches the arteriole and the glomerulus from which it arose. At this point, which marks the start of the distal convolution, there is a modified region of tubular epithelium called the macula densa (Fig 24—3). The macula densa is in close proximity to the juxtaglomerular cells and, along with the adjacent glomerular cells, constitutes the juxtaglomerular apparatus.

FIG 24—3. *Left:* Diagram of glomerulus, showing the juxtaglomerular apparatus. (Reproduced, with permission, from Ham: *Histology,* 6th ed. Lippincott, 1969.) ***Right:*** Phase contrast photomicrograph of afferent arteriole in unstained, freeze-dried preparation of the kidney of a mouse. Note the red blood cell in the lumen of the arteriole, and the granulated juxtaglomerular cells in the wall. (Courtesy of C Peil.)

Regulation of Renin Secretion

The control of renin secretion is currently the subject of much research and debate. It appears that at least 3 separate mechanisms are involved. One is an intrarenal arteriolar baroreceptor mechanism which causes increased renin secretion when the intra-arteriolar pressure at the level of the juxtaglomerular cells is decreased and decreased renin secretion when this pressure is increased. It has been suggested that the juxtaglomerular cells themselves are the receptors and that their rate of secretion is inversely proportionate to the degree to which they are stretched. Another sensor involved in the regulatory process is the macula densa, with renin secretion being inversely proportionate to the rate of Na^+ transport across this portion of the distal tubule. The rate of transport is dependent not only on the Na^+ transport mechanisms in the macula densa cells but also on the amount of Na^+ reaching the macula densa. Therefore, decreased delivery of Na^+ to the distal tubules is associated with increased renin secretion. A third regulator is the sympathetic nervous system. Sympathetic stimulation increases renin secretion, and the increase is mediated both by way of increased circulating catecholamines and by way of the renal sympathetic nerves. The sympathetic effects on renin secretion are mediated via β-adrenergic receptors. Evidence is beginning to accumulate that the effects are direct and are exerted via adenyl cyclase and cyclic AMP in the juxtaglomerular cells. Renin secretion at any given time is apparently due to the combined activity of the arteriolar baroreceptor, macula densa, and sympathetic nervous mechanisms. Renin secretion also varies inversely with the plasma K^+ level, but the effect of K^+ may be mediated by the changes it produces in Na^+ transport at the macula densa.

Role of Renin in Hypertension

Constriction of one renal artery in the rat and man causes the development of sustained hypertension (**renal hypertension**). Since Goldblatt first demonstrated this effect of renal artery constriction, it has often been assumed that the hypertension is due to increased renin secretion. Removal of the ischemic kidney cures the hypertension if it has not persisted for too long. A similar hypertension can be produced in the dog, but it is sustained only if both renal arteries are constricted. Some patients with unilateral renal arterial stenosis have high circulating renin and angiotensin levels, hypokalemia, and high aldosterone secretion rates (see Chapter 20). However, most animals and humans with renal hypertension do not have high levels of aldosterone secretion. Furthermore, the circulating levels of renin and angiotensin are not elevated in chronic renal hypertension. These and other data indicate that after renal artery constriction the increase in renin secretion is transient and that, one day to several weeks later, renin secretion returns to normal while some other renal mechanism maintains the hypertension. The kidney contains a number of substances with vasodepressor activity (see Chapter 33), and decreased secretion of these might conceivably play a role.

An interesting syndrome occurs in patients with idiopathic hypertrophy and hyperplasia of their juxtaglomerular apparatuses. The findings associated with this abnormality are persistent hypokalemia, high levels of aldosterone secretion, and high circulating blood angiotensin II levels. However, the blood pressure is normal. The role of renin in a feedback mechanism that helps maintain the constancy of ECF volume through regulation of aldosterone secretion has been described in Chapter 20. A high level of renin secretion is apparently responsible for the elevated aldosterone secretion (**secondary hyperaldosteronism**) seen in some normotensive patients with cirrhosis and nephrosis. Indeed, it seems likely that the pressor effect produced by renin is a side issue and that its main physiologic function is the part it plays in the regulation of aldosterone secretion.

Erythropoietin

When an animal is bled or made hypoxic, hemoglobin synthesis is enhanced and production and release of red blood cells from the bone marrow (**erythropoiesis**) is increased (see Chapter 27). Conversely, when the red cell volume is increased above normal by transfusion, the erythropoietic activity of the bone marrow decreases. These adjustments are brought about by changes in the circulating level of **erythropoietin**, a circulating glycoprotein with a molecular weight of about 35,000. The hormone causes certain stem cells in the bone marrow to be converted to proerythroblasts (Fig 27–1). Although they resemble other stem cells, they are somewhat more differentiated, and are referred to as **erythropoietin-sensitive stem cells**. The action of erythropoietin is apparently mediated by stimulation of

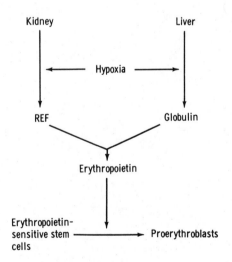

FIG 24–4. Proposed scheme for formation of erythropoietin. (Modified and reproduced, with permission, from Gordon & others: The kidney and erythropoiesis. Seminars in Hematology 4:337–358, 1967.)

mRNA synthesis. The fact that antierythropoietin antibodies cause anemia indicates that the hormone is essential for the maintenance of normal erythropoiesis.

Current evidence indicates that erythropoietin is formed by the action of a substance secreted by the kidneys on a globulin in the plasma (Fig 24–4). This renal factor has been called **renal erythropoietic factor (REF)**, or **erythrogenin**. Its production is increased by hypoxia of the kidneys, cobalt salts, and androgens. In dogs, REF appears to be formed only in the kidneys, but in rats, rabbits, and humans some erythropoietin can be formed in the absence of the kidneys. The globulin on which REF acts is apparently formed in the liver, and there is some evidence that its production is also increased by hypoxia. The action of REF on the plasma globulin appears to be enzymic, like that of renin on angiotensinogen. The principal site of inactivation of erythropoietin is the liver, and it has a half-life in the circulation of about 5 hours. However, the increase in circulating red cells that it triggers takes 2–3 days to appear, since red cell maturation is a relatively slow process.

The receptor in the kidney which responds to changes in oxygen tension is unknown. It has been claimed that REF is secreted by the juxtaglomerular cells, but some evidence suggests it is secreted by cells in the glomeruli. At any rate, it is clear that the REF-erythropoietin system and the renin-angiotensin system are separate; angiotensin II has no erythropoietic effect, and erythropoietin has no effect on blood pressure or aldosterone secretion.

Hypophysectomized animals become anemic, and pituitary extracts stimulate red blood cell production. However, hypophysectomy does not block the erythropoietic response to hemorrhage or hypoxia.

Glucocorticoids and thyroxine stimulate erythropoiesis, and the erythropoietic activity of pituitary extracts has been shown to be due in part to their ACTH and TSH content. It is also due in males to the LH in the pituitary extracts, since LH stimulates testosterone secretion and androgens increase REF secretion. On the other hand, estrogens inhibit erythropoiesis. This effect is not inhibited by nephrectomy, but it may be due in part to inhibition by estrogen of hepatic formation of the globulin substrate on which REF acts.

PINEAL

Anatomy

The **pineal**, or **epiphysis**, arises from the roof of the third ventricle under the posterior end of the corpus callosum and is connected by a stalk to the posterior commissure and habenular commissure. There are nerve fibers in the stalk, but few nerve cells are present in the pineal itself. The pineal stroma contains neuroglia and cells which have some features that suggest that they have a secretory function (Fig 24–5). In young animals and infants, the pineal is large and there is some tendency for the cells to be arranged in alveoli. The pineal begins to involute before puberty, and in man small concretions of calcium and magnesium phosphate and carbonate (**pineal sand**) appear in the tissue. Because the concretions are radiopaque, the normal pineal is often visible on x-ray films of the skull in adults. Displacement of a calcified pineal from its normal position indicates the presence of a space-

FIG 24–5. *Left:* Sagittal section of human brain stem, showing relations of pineal. *Right:* Histology of pineal. Drawing of hematoxylin and eosin-stained section. (Reproduced, with permission, from Bloom & Fawcett: *A Textbook of Histology,* 9th ed. Saunders, 1968.)

occupying lesion such as a tumor in the brain.

The pineal, like the area postrema and the posterior pituitary, takes up dyes and other substances more rapidly than the brain and is therefore "outside the blood-brain barrier" (see Chapter 32). Like the area postrema, it has a high norepinephrine and serotonin content. It also has a high rate of phosphorus turnover.

Pineal Function

The pineal, believed by Descartes to be the seat of the soul, has at one time or another been regarded as (1) a vestigial organ, probably homologous to the third eye found in reptiles; (2) the source of a growth-inhibiting factor; (3) the source of a compound that "cures" schizophrenia; (4) the source of a hormone that antagonizes the secretion or effects of ACTH; (5) the source of a substance that inhibits the onset of puberty; (6) the source of factors which regulate the adrenal secretion of aldosterone; and (7) the source of melatonin, a substance that causes lightening of the skin and may inhibit gonadotropin secretion. The phylogenetic evidence that the pineal is a vestigial organ in mammals is suggestive but not wholly convincing, and the evidence for functions (2) to (4) is too speculative and uncertain to merit further consideration. Item (5) has been discussed in Chapter 23 and item (6) in Chapter 20.

Melatonin

The pineal contains an indole, N-acetyl-5-methoxytryptamine, which has been named **melatonin** because it lightens the skin of tadpoles by an action on melanophores (see Chapter 22). Melatonin and the enzymes responsible for its synthesis from serotonin by N-acetylation and 5-methylation have been identified in mammalian pineal tissue (Fig 24–6). Small amounts of melatonin are found in peripheral nerves, and, since the nerves do not contain the enzymes required for melatonin synthesis, the presumption is that melatonin reaches them via the blood stream from the pineal. Hydroxyindole-O-methyltransferase (HIOMT), the enzyme catalyzing the final step in the synthesis of melatonin (Fig 24–6), is found mainly in the pineal. In rats, HIOMT activity is decreased by light, and this effect is prevented by sympathectomy. The sympathetic nerves to the pineal (nervi conarii) are prominent structures. It has been demonstrated that the N-acetyltransferase that catalyzes the formation of N-acetyl-5-hydroxytryptamine in the pineal is under excitatory control by these sympathetic nerves via a β-adrenergic mechanism. However, except for a slight inhibitory effect on the ovary, melatonin has no known effect in mammals.

THYMUS

The thymus is a bilobed structure in the anterior mediastinum which is large in infancy but undergoes

FIG 24–6. Formation and metabolism of melatonin. HIOMT, hydroxyindole-O-methyltransferase; MAO, monoamine oxidase.

progressive atrophy after puberty. Its outer layer, or **cortex,** is made up of lymphoid tissue; its inner portion, or **medulla,** contains lymphocytes and, within a coarse reticulum, cell clusters called **Hassall's corpuscles.** These corpuscles consist of granular cells surrounded by epithelioid cells, and are the remains of the tubes from the third branchial pouches which formed the thymus.

There is general agreement that the thymus is primarily a lymphoid organ. The general lysis of lymphoid tissue produced by adrenal glucocorticoids includes the thymus, and the degree of thymic atrophy in experimental animals has been used as an indicator of the level of adrenocortical secretion.

The lymphoid cells responsible for the production of antibodies that cause delayed hypersensitivity reactions and the rejection of homologous tissue transplants are formed under the influence of the thymus during infancy. In mice thymectomized in infancy and humans with congenital aplasia of the thymus (DiGeorge's syndrome), humoral immunity is normal but cellular immunity is deficient; tissue transplants from other individuals are not rejected, and delayed hypersensitivity reactions do not occur. Thymectomy later in life does not have these effects. If a thymus is transplanted into a thymectomized infant mouse, the recipient develops normally; and if the thymus is from another strain of mice, the recipient will later fail to reject tissue transplanted from the donor strain of animal. However, the "normalizing" effect of the thymus transplant occurs even if it is sealed within a chamber which has pores in its walls large enough to permit chemical agents to leave the chamber but too small to permit cells to escape. Thus, the effect appears to be humoral, and it is now believed that a thymus hormone of some sort circulates from this organ to stem cells in the lymphoid organs, inducing them to become immunologically competent lymphocytes capable of forming antibodies against foreign protein. A polypeptide extracted from the thymus has been shown to increase the number of lymphocytes in the circulation and accelerate rejection of skin grafts from other animals. This material has been given the name **thymosin.**

Some abnormality of the thymic mechanism is apparently involved in the "autoimmune diseases," in which there appear to be rejection-like reactions against some of the body's own tissues. At any rate, myasthenia gravis, hemolytic anemia, disseminated lupus erythematosus, rheumatoid arthritis, and thyroiditis (see Chapter 18) are all characterized by hyperplasia of the thymus with the formation within its substance of germinal centers like those normally found in lymph nodes.

SPLEEN

The spleen is one of the lymphoid organs in which lymphocytes and monocytes are formed. It is also part of the reticuloendothelial system, which removes old red blood cells from the circulation and contains the plasma cells that manufacture many of the antibodies. In dogs and other carnivores, but not to any extent in humans, the spleen serves as a blood reservoir, contracting in response to adrenergic stimulation and pumping extra blood into the circulation. In normal infants and in adults with fibrosis of the bone marrow, red blood cells are produced in the spleen and in the liver (**extramedullary hematopoiesis**). In pathologic states, the spleen may remove platelets from the circulation in excessive numbers, causing **thrombocytopenia** and extensive hemorrhages **(purpura)**. In some patients it also destroys excessive numbers of red and white blood cells.

The spleen also has poorly understood effects on the life of red blood cells and on the toxicity of certain drugs, and it has been suggested that these effects may be humoral. Other functions related to the control of adrenal secretion have been claimed. However, splenectomized animals and humans generally get along very well, and at present it cannot be said that the spleen has any established endocrine function.

•　　•　　•

References: Section IV.
Endocrinology & Metabolism

Berson SA, Yalow RS: Principles of immunoassay of peptide hormones in plasma. In: *Clinical Endocrinology*. Vol 2. Astwood EB, Cassidy CD (editors). Grune & Stratton, 1968.

Clermont Y: Kinetics of spermatogenesis in mammals: Seminiferous epithelium cycle and spermatogonial renewal. Physiol Rev 52:198, 1972.

Cohen H: Relaxin: Studies dealing with the isolation, purification, and characterization. Tr New York Acad Sci II 25:313, 1963.

Copp DH: Endocrine regulation of calcium metabolism and bone. Ann Rev Physiol 32:61, 1970.

Davis JO: The regulation of aldosterone secretion. In: *The Adrenal Cortex*. Eisenstein A (editor). Little, Brown, 1967.

Davson H: *The Physiology of the Eye*, 3rd ed. Academic Press, 1972.

Dietschy JM, Wilson JD: Regulation of cholesterol metabolism. New England J Med 282:1128, 1190, 1241, 1970.

Donovan BT, Van der Werff ten Bosch JJ: *Physiology of Puberty*. Williams & Wilkins, 1965.

Felig P: Glucagon: Physiologic and diabetogenic role. New England J Med 283:149, 1970.

Fieser LF, Fieser M: *Steroids*. Reinhold, 1959.

Fredrickson DS: A physician's guide to hyperlipidemia. Mod Concepts Cardiovas Dis 41:31, 1972.

Fuchs F, Klopper AI (editors): *Endocrinology of Pregnancy*. Harper, 1970.

Ganong WF, Martini L: *Frontiers in Neuroendocrinology, 1973*. Oxford Univ Press, 1973.

German J: Studying human chromosomes today. Am Scientist 58:182, 1970.

Greer MA: The natural occurrence of goitrogenic agents. Recent Progr Hormone Res 18:187, 1962.

Grodsky GM: Insulin and the pancreas. Vitamins Hormones 28:37, 1970.

Harper HA: *Review of Physiological Chemistry*, 14th ed. Lange, 1973.

Harris GW, Donovan BT (editors): *The Pituitary Gland*. 3 vols. Univ of California Press, 1966.

Havel RJ: Caloric homeostasis in health and disease. New England J Med 287:1186, 1972.

Hook EB: Behavioral implications of the human XYY genotype. Science 179:139, 1973.

Hershman JM, Pittman JA Jr: Control of thyrotropin secretion in man. New England J Med 285:997, 1971.

Kahana L & others: Endocrine manifestations of intracranial extrasellar lesions. J Clin Endocrinol 22:304, 1962.

Kleeman CR, Massoy SG, Coburn JW: The clinical physiology of calcium homeostasis, parathyroid hormone, and calcitonin. California Med 114:16, March 1971.

Liddle GW, Hardman JG: Cyclic adenosine monophosphate as a mediator of hormone action. New England J Med 285:560, 1971.

Lipman F: Polypeptide chain elongation in protein biosynthesis. Science 164:1024, 1969.

Macleod AG: *Diabetes*. Upjohn, 1969.

Martini L, Ganong WF (editors): *Neuroendocrinology*. Vols 1 & 2. Academic Press, 1966. 1967.

McKenzie JM: Humoral factors in the pathogenesis of Graves' disease. Physiol Rev 48:252, 1968.

Melby JC: Assessment of adrenocortical function. New England J Med 285:735, 1971.

Miller JFAP, Osaba D: Current concepts of the immunological function of the thymus. Physiol Rev 37:327, 1967.

Odell WD, Moyer DL: *Physiology of Reproduction*. Mosby, 1971.

O'Malley BW: Mechanisms of action of steroid hormones. New England J Med 284:370, 1971.

Page IH, McCubbin JW (editors): *Renal Hypertension*. Year Book, 1968.

Pierce JG: The subunits of pituitary thyrotropin: Their relationship to other glycoprotein hormones. Endocrinology 89:1331, 1971.

Rodahl K, Issekutz B Jr (editors): *Fats as Tissue*. McGraw-Hill, 1964.

Sawin CT: *The Hormones; Endocrine Physiology*. Little, Brown, 1969.

Sherwood LM: Human prolactin. New England J Med 284:774, 1971.

Stent G: *Molecular Genetics*. Freeman, 1971.

Sutherland EW: Studies on the mechanism of hormone action. Science 177:401, 1972.

Unger RH: Glucagon: Physiology and pathophysiology. New England J Med 285:443, 1971.

Villee DB: Development of endocrine function in the human placenta and fetus. New England J Med 281:473, 533, 1969.

Waldstein SS: Thyroid-catecholamine interrelations. Ann Rev Med 17:123, 1966.

Watson JD: *Molecular Biology of the Gene*, 2nd ed. Benjamin, 1970.

Werner SC, Ingbar SH (editors): *The Thyroid: A Fundamental and Clinical Text*, 3rd ed. Harper & Row, 1971.

Westphal U: *Steroid-Protein Interactions: Monographs in Endocrinology*. Vol 4. Springer-Verlag, 1971.

Williams RH (editor): *Textbook of Endocrinology*, 4th ed. Saunders, 1968.

Wolstenholme GEW, Knight J (editors): *Ciba Foundation Symposium on Lactogenic Hormones*. Churchill, 1972.

Wurtman RJ, Axelrod J, Kelly DE: *The Pineal*. Academic Press, 1968.

Young VC, Scrimshaw NS: The physiology of starvation. Scientific American 225:14, Oct 1971.

Symposium: Mechanism of Protein Synthesis. Cold Spring Harbor Symposium on Quantitative Biology, Vol 34, 1970.

Symposium: Transcription of Genetic Material. Cold Spring Harbor Symposium on Quantitative Biology, Vol 35, 1971.

Symposium: Growth hormone. Ann New York Acad Sci 148:289, 1968.

Symposium: Control of human fertility. Brit Med Bull 26:1, 1970.

Symposium: The pharmacology of bone. Fed Proc 29:1176, 1970.

Symposium: Cyclic AMP and cell function. Ann New York Acad Sci 185:5, 1971.

Symposium: Erythropoietin: Pharmacology, biogenesis and control of production. Pharmacol Rev 24:459, 1972.

V. Gastrointestinal Function

25...

Digestion & Absorption

The gastrointestinal system is the portal through which nutritive substances, vitamins, minerals, and fluids enter the body. Proteins, fats, and complex carbohydrates are broken down into absorbable units (**digested**), principally in the small intestine. The products of digestion and the vitamins, minerals, and fluids cross the mucosa of the stomach and intestines and enter the lymph or the blood (**absorption**). The digestive and absorptive processes are the subject of this chapter. The details of the function of the various

parts of the gastrointestinal system are considered in Chapter 26.

Digestion of the major foodstuffs is an orderly process involving the action of a large number of **digestive enzymes** (Table 25–1). Some of these enzymes are found in the secretions of the salivary glands, the stomach, and the exocrine portion of the pancreas. Other enzymes are found in the luminal membranes of the cells of the small intestine. The action of the enzymes is aided by the hydrochloric acid secreted by

TABLE 25–1. Principal digestive enzymes.
The corresponding proenzymes are shown in parentheses.

Source	Enzyme	Activator	Substrate	Catalytic Function or Products
Salivary glands	Salivary a-amylase	...	Starch	Hydrolyzes 1,4a linkages, producing a-limit dextrins, maltotriose, and maltose
Stomach	Pepsins (pepsinogens)	HCl	Proteins and polypeptides	Cleave peptide bonds adjacent to aromatic amino acids
Exocrine pancreas	Trypsin (trypsinogen)	Enterokinase	Proteins and polypeptides	Cleaves peptide bonds adjacent to basic amino acids
	Chymotrypsins (chymotrypsinogens)	Trypsin	Proteins and polypeptides	Cleave peptide bonds adjacent to aromatic amino acids
	Carboxypeptidase A (procarboxypeptidase A)	Trypsin	Proteins and polypeptides	Cleaves carboxy terminal amino acids with aromatic or branched aliphatic side chains
	Carboxypeptidase B (procarboxypeptidase B)	Trypsin	Proteins and polypeptides	Cleaves carboxy terminal amino acids with basic side chains
	Pancreatic lipase	Emulsifying agents	Triglycerides	Di- and monoglycerides and fatty acids
	Pancreatic a-amylase	Cl^-	Starch	Same as salivary a-amylase
	Elastase (proelastase)	Trypsin	Elastin, some other proteins	Cleaves bonds adjacent to neutral amino acids
	Ribonuclease	...	RNA	Nucleotides
	Deoxyribonuclease	...	DNA	Nucleotides
	Phospholipase A (prophospholipase A)	Trypsin	Lecithin	Lysolecithin
Intestinal mucosa	Enterokinase	...	Trypsinogen	Trypsin
	Aminopeptidases	...	Polypeptides	Cleave N-terminal amino acid from peptide
	Dipeptidases	...	Dipeptides	Two amino acids
	Maltase	...	Maltose, maltotriose	Glucose
	Lactase	...	Lactose	Galactose and glucose
	Sucrase	...	Sucrose	Fructose and glucose
	Isomaltase	...	a-Limit dextrins	Glucose
	Nuclease and related enzymes	...	Nucleic acids	Pentoses and purine and pyrimidine bases
	Intestinal lipase	...	Monoglycerides	Glycerol, fatty acids

the stomach and the bile secreted by the liver.

Substances pass from the lumen of the gastrointestinal tract to the circulation by diffusion, nonionic diffusion, facilitated diffusion, active transport, solvent drag, and pinocytosis. The dynamics of transport in all parts of the body are considered in Chapter 1. The cells of the jejunum in man act as if they contained pores about 0.75 nm in diameter, whereas those of the ileum act as if they contained pores 0.35 nm in diameter.

CARBOHYDRATES

Digestion

The principal dietary carbohydrates are polysaccharides, disaccharides, and monosaccharides. Starches (glucose polymers) and their derivatives are the only polysaccharides that are digested to any degree in man. In amylopectin, which comprises 80–90% of dietary starch, the glucose molecules are mostly in long chains (glucose molecules in 1,4 a linkage), but there is some chain branching (produced by 1,6 a linkages). Glycogen (see Chapter 17) is similar but more branched, whereas amylose is a straight chain with only 1,4 a linkages. The disaccharides **lactose** (milk sugar) and **sucrose** (table sugar) are also ingested, along with the monosaccharides fructose and glucose.

Starch is attacked by ptyalin, the a-amylase in the saliva. However, the optimal pH for this enzyme is 6.7 and its action is inhibited by the acid gastric juice

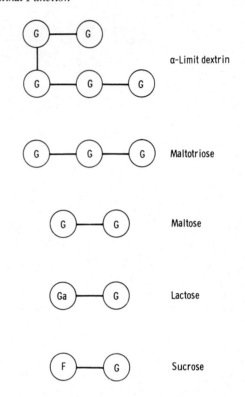

FIG 25–1. Principal end products of carbohydrate digestion in the intestinal lumen. Each circle represents a hexose molecule. G, glucose; F, fructose; Ga, galactose.

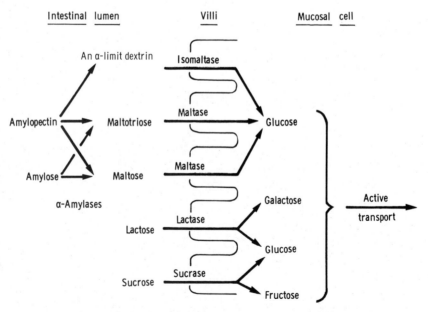

FIG 25–2. Outline of carbohydrate digestion and absorption. Some of the monosaccharides are also released into the intestinal lumen. (Redrawn and reproduced, with permission, from Gray: Malabsorption of carbohydrates. Fed Proc 26:1415, 1967.)

when food enters the stomach. In the small intestine, the potent pancreatic *a*-amylase also acts on the ingested polysaccharides. Both the salivary and the pancreatic *a*-amylases hydrolyze 1,4 *a* linkages but spare 1,6 *a* linkages, terminal 1,4 *a* linkages, and the 1,4 *a* linkages next to branching points. Consequently, the end products of *a*-amylase digestion are the disaccharide **maltose**, the trisaccharide **maltotriose**, and *a*-**limit dextrins**, branched polymers containing an average of about 8 glucose molecules (Fig 25–1).

The enzymes responsible for the further digestion of the starch derivatives are located on the surface of the mucosal cells, principally in the ileum. Isomaltase hydrolyzes the *a*-limit dextrins, and maltases hydrolyze maltotriose and maltose. Most of the glucose molecules that are formed enter the mucosal cells, although some reenter the intestinal lumen and are absorbed further along. Ingested disaccharides are hydrolyzed by lactase or sucrase on the luminal surface of mucosal cells (Fig 25–2). Deficiency of one or more of these disaccharidases leads to diarrhea, bloating, and flatulence after ingestion of sugar.

Lactase is of interest because, in most mammals and in many races of humans, intestinal lactase activity is high at birth, declines to low levels during childhood, and remains low in adulthood. The low lactase levels are associated with intolerance to milk (lactose intolerance). However, most Western Europeans and their American descendants retain their intestinal lactase activity in adulthood. Lactose tolerance is also found in a few African tribes, but most blacks are intolerant. In the USA, 70% of the black population and only 20% of the white population is intolerant to lactose.

Absorption

Hexoses and pentoses are rapidly absorbed across the wall of the duodenum and ileum. Essentially all of the hexoses are removed before the remains of a meal reach the terminal part of the ileum. The sugar molecules pass from the mucosal cells to the blood in the capillaries draining into the portal vein. Some hexoses and the pentoses are absorbed by diffusion, but glucose and galactose are absorbed by active transport (Table 25–2). Fructose is absorbed more slowly, but it may utilize the same carrier as glucose and simply have less affinity for the carrier.

The transport of sugars is uniquely affected by the amount of Na^+ in the intestinal lumen; a high concentration of Na^+ on the mucosal surface of the cells facilitates and a low concentration inhibits sugar influx

**TABLE 25–2. Active transport of substance by the intestine
and location of maximum absorption or secretion.***

	Location of Absorptive Capacity			
	Small Intestine			Colon
	Upper†	Mid	Lower	
Absorption				
Sugars (glucose, galactose, etc)	++	+++	++	0
Neutral amino acids	++	+++	++	0
Basic amino acids	++	++	++	?
Betaine, dimethylglycine, sarcosine	+	++ .	++	?
Gamma globulin (newborn animals)	+	++	+++	?
Pyrimidines (thymine and uracil)	+	+	?	?
Triglycerides	++	++	+	?
Fatty acid absorption and conversion to triglyceride	+++	++	+	0
Bile salts	0	+	+++	
Vitamin B_{12}	0	+	+++	0
Na^+	+++	++	+++	+++
H^+ (and/or HCO_3^- secretion)	0	+	++	++
Ca^{++}	+++	++	+	?
Fe^{++}	+++	++	+	?
Cl^-	+++	++	+	0
$SO_4^=$	++	+	0	?
Secretion				
K^+	0	0	+	++
H^+ (and/or HCO_3^- absorption)	++	+	0	0
Sr^{++}	0	0	+	?
Cl^- (under special conditions)	+	?	?	?
I^-	0	+	0	0

*Reproduced, with permission, from Wilson: *Intestinal Absorption.* Saunders, 1962. Amount of absorption or secretion is graded + to +++.
†Upper small intestine refers primarily to jejunum, although the duodenum is similar in most cases studied (with the notable exception that the duodenum secretes HCO_3^- and shows little net absorption or secretion of NaCl).

into the epithelial cells. This effect is apparently not due to a change in the affinity of the carrier for sugar, and it has been postulated that the carrier must bind both Na⁺ and sugar for transport to occur at the maximum rate. Hypoxia, metabolic inhibitors, and ouabain inhibit sugar transport, but it has been suggested that sugar transport is indirectly rather than directly dependent on metabolic energy. According to this hypothesis, the energy is required not for sugar transport per se but for the active transport of Na⁺ out of the mucosal cell. By keeping the intracellular Na⁺ low, this maintains the large Na⁺ concentration gradient across the mucosal cell membrane that is necessary for optimal sugar transport.

Insulin has little effect on intestinal transport of sugars. In this respect, intestinal absorption resembles glucose reabsorption in the proximal convoluted tubules of the kidneys (see Chapter 38); neither process requires phosphorylation, and both are essentially normal in diabetes but depressed by the drug phlorhizin. The maximal rate of glucose absorption from the intestine is about 120 g/hour.

PROTEINS & NUCLEIC ACIDS

Protein Digestion

Protein digestion begins in the stomach, where pepsins cleave some of the peptide linkages. Like many of the other enzymes concerned with protein digestion, pepsins are secreted in inactive precursor or **proenzyme** form and activated in the intestinal tract. The pepsin precursors are called pepsinogens and are activated by gastric hydrochloric acid. Human gastric mucosa contains 3 chromatographically distinct pepsinogens which produce 3 pepsins with slightly different properties (pepsins I, II, and III). Pepsins hydrolyze the bonds between aromatic amino acids such as phenylalanine or tyrosine and a second amino acid, so the products of peptic digestion are polypeptides of very diverse sizes. A **gelatinase** that liquefies gelatin is also found in the stomach. **Rennin,** a gastric enzyme that clots milk, is also found in the stomachs of young animals, but it is probably absent in man.

Because pepsins have a pH optimum of 1.6–3.2, their action is terminated when the gastric contents are mixed with the alkaline pancreatic juice in the duodenum. The pH of the duodenal contents is about 6.5. In the small intestine, small polypeptides and dipeptides are formed by the action of the powerful protein-splitting enzymes, trypsin and the chymotrypsins. The formation of trypsin and chymotrypsins from their precursors is discussed in Chapter 26. An elastase that hydrolyzes the fibrous proteins in structures such as ligaments is also present in pancreatic juice. The pancreatic carboxypeptidases and the intestinal aminopeptidases and dipeptidases split these fragments into their constituent free amino acids. Some free amino

acids are liberated in the intestinal lumen, but others are liberated at the cell surface by the aminopeptidases and dipeptidases that line the luminal border of the mucosal cells.

Protein Absorption

After ingestion of a protein meal there is a sharp transient rise in the amino nitrogen content of the portal blood. L-Amino acids are absorbed more rapidly than the corresponding isomers. The D-amino acids are apparently absorbed solely by passive diffusion, whereas most L-amino acids are actively transported out of the intestinal lumen. There are 3 separate transport systems: one that transports neutral amino acids, one that transports basic amino acids, and one that transports proline, hydroxyproline, and a few other compounds. Absorption of amino acids is coupled to Na⁺ transport in some as yet poorly understood fashion. Amino acid transport, like sugar transport, is facilitated by a high Na⁺ concentration on the mucosal side of the intestinal epithelial cells. However, the action of Na⁺ is different; Na⁺ increases the maximum velocity of sugar influx without affecting the apparent affinity of its carrier, whereas Na⁺ does not affect the maximum velocity of amino acid influx and does seem to increase carrier affinity. The transported amino acids accumulate in the mucosal cells, and from these cells they apparently diffuse passively into the blood.

Absorption of amino acids is rapid in the duodenum and jejunum but slow in the ileum. Approximately 50% of the digested protein comes from ingested food, 25% from proteins in digestive juices, and 25% from desquamated mucosal cells. Some of the ingested protein enters the colon and is eventually digested by bacterial action. The protein in the stools is not of dietary origin but comes from bacteria and cellular debris.

In infants, some undigested proteins are also absorbed. The protein antibodies in maternal colostrum which contribute to the passive immunity of infants against infections enter the circulation from the intestine. Foreign proteins that enter the circulation provoke the formation of antibodies (see Chapter 27), and the antigen-antibody reaction occurring upon subsequent entry of more of the same protein may cause allergic symptoms. There is evidence that the mucosal cells of young animals absorb whole proteins by pinocytosis and that as the cells mature they normally lose the ability to take in protein by this process. The situation is probably similar in humans. Infants are often allergic to protein foods such as eggs but lose this allergy as they grow older. However, some adults develop allergic symptoms after eating certain foods, and in these individuals the absorption of whole proteins presumably persists.

Nucleic Acids

Nucleic acids are split into nucleotides in the intestine by the pancreatic nucleases, and the nucleotides are split into the nucleosides and phosphoric acid by enzymes that appear to be located on the luminal surfaces of the mucosal cells. The nucleosides are then split into their constituent sugars and purine and pyrimidine bases. The bases are absorbed by active transport.

LIPIDS

Fat Digestion

Fat digestion begins in the duodenum, pancreatic lipase being the most important enzyme involved. The products of triglyceride digestion by this enzyme are monoglycerides, and it acts on fats that have been emulsified. There is a lipase in the gastric juice, but its action is physiologically of little importance. It is also claimed that there is a lipase secreted by the intestinal mucosa, but this may be the lipase present in desquamated epithelial cells.

Fats are finely emulsified in the small intestine by the detergent action of bile salts, fatty acids, and glycerides. Bile salts by themselves do not produce the fine emulsions seen in the upper small intestine. However, bile salts combine with monoglycerides and fatty acids to form micelles. These polymolecular aggregates are 3–10 nm in diameter (Fig 25–3). They effectively solubilize the monoglycerides and free fatty acids so that a clear aqueous solution rather than an emulsion is formed. The lipids are thus brought into close contact with the mucosal cells, permitting the monoglycerides and fatty acids to enter the cells and leaving the bile salts to pass on to the ileum, where they are reabsorbed.

Pancreatectomized animals and patients with diseases that destroy the exocrine portion of the pancreas have fatty, bulky, clay-colored stools (steatorrhea) because of the impaired digestion and absorption of fat. The steatorrhea is due in part to the lipase deficiency, but micelle formation is also depressed in pancreatic insufficiency because, in the absence of the bicarbonate that is secreted from the pancreas, the relatively acid milieu in the duodenum inhibits the incorporation of fatty acids in the micelles.

Fat Absorption

Forty to 50% of the triglycerides in the diet are hydrolyzed only to the monoglyceride and absorbed into the intestinal mucosal cells as such. Transport into the cells does not appear to require energy. The subsequent fate of the fatty acids depends on their size. Fatty acids containing less than 10–12 carbon atoms pass from the mucosal cells directly into the portal blood, where they are transported as free (unesterified) fatty acids. The fatty acids containing more than 10–12 carbon atoms are reesterified to triglycerides in the mucosal cells. They are then coated with a layer of lipoprotein, cholesterol, and phospholipid to form chylomicrons, which leave the cell and enter the lymphatics (Fig 25–4).

The biochemical reactions involved in esterification are summarized in Fig 25–5. Some of the absorbed monoglycerides are converted directly to diglycerides, while others are hydrolyzed by the intracellular lipase to fatty acids and glycerol. Most of the glycerol involved in the esterification of the free fatty acids is a-glycerophosphate produced from glucose via dihydroxyacetone phosphate (Fig 17–11), and rela-

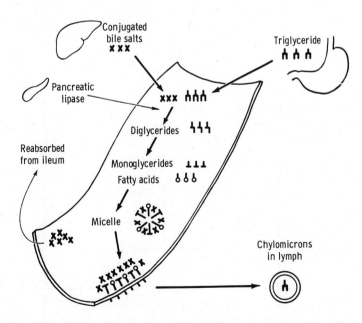

FIG 25–3. Intraluminal events during fat digestion and absorption. The micelles contain bile salts, fatty acids, and monoglycerides. (Reproduced, with permission, from Isselbacher: Biochemical aspects of lipid malabsorption. Fed Proc 26:1420, 1967.)

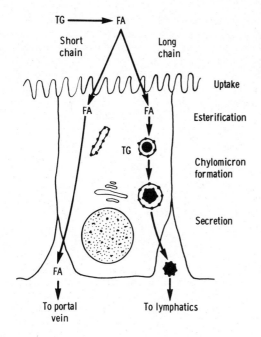

FIG 25—4. Absorption of fat by intestinal mucosal cells. Short chain fatty acids (FA) cross the cell and enter the portal vein. Long chain fatty acids become surrounded by smooth endoplasmic reticulum and are esterified to triglycerides (TG). The triglycerides in turn are surrounded by rough endoplasmic reticulum, which probably forms the lipoprotein that goes into the formation of the chylomicrons. The chylomicrons leave the cell and enter the lymphatics.

tively little is glycerol liberated in the intestinal lumen or mucosal cells by hydrolysis of triglycerides. Glycerol must be phosphorylated before it can combine with fatty acids. This reaction is catalyzed by the enzyme glycerokinase, and the intestinal mucosa has only weak glycerokinase activity. Adipose tissue also has little or no glycerokinase activity, but there are appreciable amounts in liver, kidney, and heart.

Current evidence indicates that esterification takes place within the smooth endoplasmic reticulum. The triglyceride droplets then become surrounded by rough endoplasmic reticulum, within which they become coated to form chylomicrons. The rough endoplasmic reticulum may synthesize the β-lipoprotein component of the coating. The chylomicrons are extruded from the lateral and basal aspects of the mucosal cells, cross the basement membrane underlying them, and enter the lymphatics.

Fat absorption is greatest in the upper parts of the small intestine, but appreciable amounts are also absorbed in the ileum. On a moderate fat intake, 95% or more of the ingested fat is absorbed (Fig 25—6). The stools contain 5% fat, but much of the fecal fat is probably derived from cellular debris and microorganisms rather than from the diet.

There is evidence that the hormones of the adrenal cortex affect the absorption of the fats that appear in the lymph but not the absorption of those appearing in portal blood. Absorption of the former is depressed in adrenalectomized animals and is increased by the administration of glucocorticoid hormones.

Absorption of Cholesterol & Other Sterols

Cholesterol is readily absorbed from the intestine if bile, fatty acids, and pancreatic juice are present. Closely related sterols of plant origin are poorly absorbed. The fatty acids and bile are probably neces-

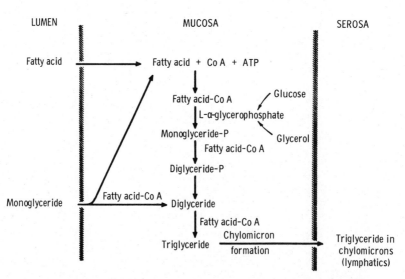

FIG 25—5. Major reactions in mucosal cells during fat absorption. P = phosphate. (Reproduced, with permission, from Isselbacher: Biochemical aspects of lipid malabsorption. Fed Proc 26:1420, 1967.)

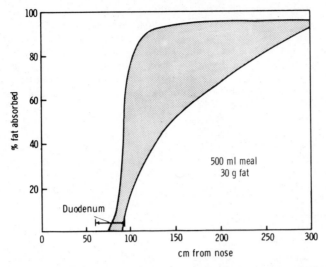

FIG 25–6. Fat absorption, based on measurement after a fat meal in humans. (Redrawn and reproduced, with permission, from Borgstrom & others: J Clin Invest 36:1521, 1957, and Gut 3:315, 1962; redrawn from diagram in Davenport: *Physiology of the Digestive Tract,* 2nd ed. Year Book, 1966.)

sary for emulsification and solubilization of the cholesterol, and they also facilitate esterification of cholesterol with fatty acids. Esterification facilitates absorption and is catalyzed by an enzyme in pancreatic juice. This is why cholesterol absorption is diminished in the absence of pancreatic juice. Absorption of cholesterol is said to be limited to the distal portions of the small intestine. Almost all the absorbed cholesterol is incorporated into chylomicrons which enter the circulation via the lymphatics, as noted above. Nonabsorbable plant sterols such as those found in soybeans reduce the absorption of cholesterol, probably by competing with cholesterol for esterification with fatty acids.

ABSORPTION OF VITAMINS, WATER, & MINERALS

Vitamins

Absorption of the water-soluble vitamins is rapid, but absorption of the fat-soluble vitamins, A, D, E, and K, is deficient if fat absorption is depressed due to lack of pancreatic enzymes or if bile is excluded from the intestine by obstruction of the bile duct. Most vitamins are absorbed in the upper small intestine. However, vitamin B_{12} is absorbed in the ileum. The absorptive process, which apparently involves pinocytosis, is discussed in Chapter 26.

Water & Sodium

Water moves freely in both directions across the mucosa of the small and large intestines and, to a lesser degree, across the gastric mucosa. Na^+ diffuses into or out of the small intestine depending upon the salinity of the intestinal contents; it is also actively transported out of the lumen in the small intestine and the colon. In the small intestine, its active transport appears to be important in bringing about the absorption of other substances. Appreciable quantities of the Na^+-K^+ ATPase associated with Na^+ pumping (see Chapter 1) are found in the brush border of the mucosal cells.

Water moves into or out of the stomach until the osmotic pressure of the intestinal contents equals that of the plasma. The osmolality of the duodenal contents may be hypertonic or hypotonic, depending on the meal ingested, but by the time the meal enters the jejunum its osmolality is close to that of plasma. This osmolality is maintained throughout the rest of the small intestine; the osmotically active particles produced by digestion are removed by absorption, and water moves passively out of the gut along the osmotic gradient thus generated. In the colon, Na^+ is pumped out and water moves passively with it, again along the osmotic gradient.

Calcium

Thirty to 80% of ingested calcium is absorbed. Active transport out of the intestinal lumen occurs primarily in the upper small intestine. The amount absorbed appears to depend in some way upon body needs rather than intake. Calcium absorption is facilitated by vitamin D, lactose, and protein. It is inhibited by phosphates and oxalates because these anions form insoluble salts with calcium. Magnesium absorption is facilitated by protein.

Iron

In normal adults, very little iron is lost from the body. Men lose about 0.6 mg/day, whereas women have an average loss of about twice this value because of the additional iron lost in the blood shed during menstruation. The average daily iron intake in America and Europe is about 20 mg, but the amount absorbed is equal only to the losses; if it were any greater, iron overload would develop. Thus, the amount of iron absorbed ranges normally from about 3–6% of the amount ingested.

Iron must apparently be in the ferrous state (Fe^{++}) to be absorbed, but most of the dietary iron is in the ferric form (Fe^{+++}). No more than a trace of iron is absorbed in the stomach, but the gastric secretions dissolve the iron and provide a milieu favorable to its reduction to the ferrous form. The importance of this function in humans is indicated by the fact that iron deficiency anemia is a troublesome and relatively frequent complication of partial gastrectomy. Ascorbic acid and other reducing substances in the diet facilitate conversion of ferric to ferrous iron. Other dietary factors affect the availability of iron for absorption; for example, the phytic acid found in cereals reacts with iron to form insoluble compounds in the intestine. So do phosphates and oxalates. Pancreatic juice inhibits iron absorption.

Iron absorption is an active process (Table 25–2). Most of the absorption occurs in the upper part of the small intestine. Other mucosal cells can transport iron, but the duodenum and adjacent jejunum contain most of the iron suitable for absorption. The mucosal cells pass part of the iron directly into the blood stream, but most of it is bound to **apoferritin**. This protein, which is found in many tissues, combines with iron to form **ferritin**. Apoferritin is a globular protein which appears to be made up of 24 subunits. Iron forms a micelle of ferric hydroxyphosphate, and in ferritin the subunits surround this micelle. Ferritin is readily visible under the electron microscope and has been used as a tracer in studies of phagocytosis and related phenomena. Ferritin is the principal storage form of iron in tissues, although hemosiderin, a granular protein-iron complex, also stores iron. Seventy percent of the iron in the body is in hemoglobin, 3% in myo-

globin, and the remainder in ferritin. Ferritin iron is in equilibrium with plasma iron. Ferritin is not normally found in plasma, where iron is transported bound for the most part to a β_1 globulin called **transferrin** or **siderophilin**. Normally, this protein is about 35% saturated with iron, and the normal plasma iron level is about 130 μg/100 ml in men and 110 μg/100 ml in women.

Iron absorption into the blood stream is increased when body iron stores are depleted or when erythropoiesis is increased, and decreased in the opposite conditions. When large quantities of iron are ingested, more iron is bound in the mucosal cells but absorption is increased very little. The iron in the mucosal cells stays bound in ferritin and is lost with the cells when they are shed into the intestinal lumen and passed in the stool. The mucosal cells also become loaded after parenteral administration of iron and reduce their uptake of dietary iron. Thus, one factor regulating iron uptake is the amount of iron in the mucosal cells, and the term "mucosal block" has been used to refer to the ability of the mucosa to prevent excess ingested iron from being absorbed.

The normal operation of the factors that maintain iron balance is essential for health. If more iron is absorbed than is excreted, iron overload results. Ferritin and hemosiderin accumulate in the tissues when the overload is prolonged. Large ferritin and hemosiderin deposits are associated with **hemochromatosis**, a syndrome characterized by pigmentation of the skin, pancreatic damage with diabetes ("bronze diabetes"), cirrhosis of the liver, a high incidence of hepatic carcinoma, and gonadal atrophy. Hemochromatosis can be produced by prolonged excessive iron intake and by a number of other conditions. Idiopathic hemochromatosis is a congenital disorder in which the mucosal regulatory mechanism behaves as if iron deficiency were present and absorbs iron at a high rate in the face of elevated rather than depleted body iron stores.

26...

Gastrointestinal Motility & Secretion

The digestive and absorptive functions of the gastrointestinal system outlined in the previous chapter depend upon a variety of mechanisms which propel the food through the gastrointestinal tract, soften it, and mix it with bile from the gallbladder and digestive enzymes secreted by the mucosal cells, salivary glands, and pancreas. Some of these mechanisms depend upon intrinsic properties of the intestinal smooth muscle. Others involve the operation of visceral reflexes or the actions of **gastrointestinal hormones**. The hormones are humoral agents secreted by parts of the mucosa and transported in the circulation to influence the functions of the stomach, the intestines, the pancreas, and the gallbladder.

The organization of the structures that make up the wall of the gastrointestinal tract from the posterior pharynx to the anus is shown in Fig 26–1. There is some local variation, but in general there are 3 layers of smooth muscle. The **myenteric nerve plexus**

(Auerbach's plexus) lies between the outer longitudinal and middle circular muscle layers; the **submucous plexus** (Meissner's plexus) lies between the middle layer and the longitudinal muscular fibers in the submucosa. The wall is lined by mucosa and, except in the case of the esophagus, is covered by serosa. The serosa continues onto the mesentery, which contains the nerves, lymphatics, and blood vessels supplying the tract.

MOUTH & ESOPHAGUS

In the mouth, food is mixed with saliva and propelled into the esophagus. Peristaltic waves in the esophagus move the food into the stomach.

Mastication

Chewing **(mastication)** breaks up large food particles and mixes the food with the secretions of the salivary glands. This wetting and homogenizing action aids subsequent digestion. Large food particles can be digested, but they cause strong and often painful contractions of the esophageal musculature. Edentulous patients are generally restricted to a soft diet and have considerable difficulty eating dry food.

Saliva

Saliva contains the digestive enzyme **ptyalin** or **salivary α-amylase** (see Chapter 25), which has a minor role in starch digestion; and **mucin**, a glycoprotein that lubricates the food. About 1500 ml of saliva are secreted per day. The pH of saliva is about 7.0. It performs a number of important functions. It facilitates swallowing, keeps the mouth moist, serves as a solvent for the molecules that stimulate the taste buds, aids speech by facilitating movements of the lips and tongue, and keeps the mouth and teeth clean. The saliva may also have some antibacterial action, and patients with deficient salivation **(xerostomia)** have a higher than normal incidence of dental caries. The buffers in saliva help maintain the oral pH at about 7.0. At this pH the saliva is saturated with calcium, and so the teeth do not lose calcium to the oral fluids. At more acid pHs, calcium loss is appreciable.

Serosa
Longitudinal muscle
Myenteric
Auerbach's } plexus
Circular muscle
Submucous
Meissner's } plexus
Submucosal muscle
(usually longitudinal)
Gut epithelium
Mucosa { with subepithelial
connective tissue
Submucosa

Mesentery
(arteries, veins,
nerves, lymphatics)

FIG 26–1. Diagrammatic representation of the layers of the wall of the stomach, small intestine, and colon. The structure of the esophagus is similar except that it has no mesentery. (Reproduced, with permission, from Bell, Davidson, & Scarborough: *Textbook of Physiology and Biochemistry,* 7th ed. Livingstone, 1969.)

TABLE 26–1. Nerve supply, histologic type, and relative contribution to total salivary output of each of the pairs of salivary glands in man. Serous cells secrete ptyalin, mucous cells secrete mucin.

Gland	Parasympathetic Nerve Supply Via	Histologic Type	Percentage of Total Salivary Secretion in Man (1.5 liters/day)
Parotid	Glossopharyngeal	Serous	25
Submaxillary	Facial	Mixed	70
Sublingual	Facial	Mucous	5

Control of Salivary Secretion

The characteristics of each of the 3 pairs of salivary glands in man are summarized in Table 26–1. In these alveolar glands, the secretory (zymogen) granules containing the salivary enzymes are discharged from the acinar cells into the ducts (Fig 26–2). The secretory process is under neural control. Stimulation of the parasympathetic nerve supply causes profuse secretion of watery saliva with a relatively low content of organic material. Associated with this secretion is a pronounced vasodilatation in the gland, which appears to be due to the local release of the vasodilator polypeptide **bradykinin**. This nonapeptide is formed from a_2 globulins in the plasma by the action of the enzyme kallikrein (see Chapter 31), and kallikrein is released in the salivary glands by stimulation of the parasympathetic nerves. Bradykinin is also released in sweat glands and the exocrine portion of the pancreas when they are active. Atropine and other cholinergic blocking agents reduce salivary secretion. The effect of stimulation of the sympathetic nerve supply varies from species to species. In man, it causes release of small amounts of saliva, rich in organic constituents, from the submaxillary glands; but it has no effect on parotid secretion.

Food in the mouth causes reflex secretion of saliva, and so does stimulation of vagal afferent fibers at the gastric end of the esophagus. Salivary secretion is easily conditioned, as shown in Pavlov's original experiments (see Chapter 16). In man, the sight, smell, and even thought of food causes salivary secretion ("makes the mouth water").

Like the thyroid gland, the salivary glands and the gastric mucosa concentrate iodide from the plasma, the salivary/plasma iodide ratio sometimes reaching 60. The physiologic significance of this iodide-trapping phenomenon is uncertain.

Deglutition

Swallowing (deglutition) is a reflex initiated by the voluntary action of collecting the oral contents on the tongue and propelling them backward into the pharynx. This initiates a wave of involuntary contraction in the pharyngeal muscles which pushes the material into the esophagus. Inhibition of respiration and glottic closure are part of the reflex response. Swallowing is difficult if not impossible when the mouth is open, as anyone who has spent time in the dentist's chair feeling saliva collect in his throat is well aware.

At the pharyngoesophageal junction, there is a 3 cm segment of esophagus in which the resting wall tension is high. This segment relaxes reflexly upon swallowing, permitting the swallowed material to enter the body of the esophagus. A ring contraction of the esophageal muscle forms behind the material, which is then swept down the esophagus by a peristaltic wave at a speed of approximately 4 cm/sec. The musculature of the gastroesophageal junction, like that of the pharyngoesophageal junction, is tonically active but relaxes upon swallowing. In the disease called **achalasia**, in which food accumulates in the esophagus, there is a failure of the gastroesophageal junction to relax. The normal coordinated peristalsis in the body of the esophagus also fails to occur, and the esophagus becomes massively dilated. Microscopic examination of the wall of the dilated portion of the esophagus reveals a deficient myenteric plexus.

FIG 26–2. Portion of a serous salivary gland, showing relation of ducts, lymphatics, and blood vessels. (Slightly modified and reproduced, with permission, from Bell, Davidson, & Scarborough: *Textbook of Physiology and Biochemistry*, 7th ed. Livingstone, 1969.)

Nervous persons who hyperventilate sometimes swallow large amounts of air, and some air is unavoidably swallowed in the process of eating and drinking (**aerophagia**). Some of the swallowed air is regurgitated (belching), and some of the gases it contains are absorbed, but much of it passes on to the colon. Here, some of the oxygen is absorbed, and hydrogen, hydrogen sulfide, carbon dioxide, and methane formed by the colonic bacteria are added to it. It is then expelled as **flatus**. Large amounts of gas in the intestines cause cramps, **borborygmi** (rumbling noises), and abdominal discomfort.

STOMACH

Food is stored in the stomach, mixed with acid, mucus, and pepsin, and released at a controlled, steady rate into the duodenum, where it is digested further and partially absorbed.

Anatomic Considerations

The gross anatomy of the stomach is shown in Fig 26–3. The gastric mucosa contains many deep glands. In the pyloric and cardiac regions, the glands secrete mucus. In the fundus and body of the stomach, the glands contain **parietal** or **oxyntic cells**, which secrete hydrochloric acid, and **chief** or **peptic cells**, which secrete pepsinogen (Fig 26–4). These secretions mix with mucus secreted by the cells in the necks of the glands. Several of the glands open on a common chamber that opens in turn on the surface of the mucosa (**gastric pits**).

The stomach has a very rich blood and lymphatic supply. Its parasympathetic nerve supply comes from the vagi, and its sympathetic supply from the celiac plexus.

Gastric Motility & Emptying

When food enters the stomach, the organ relaxes by the reflex process of **receptive relaxation**. This relaxation of the gastric musculature is triggered by

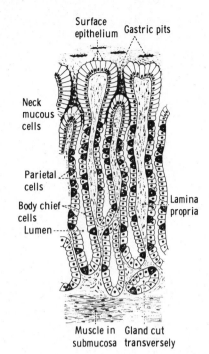

FIG 26–4. Diagram of glands in the mucosa of the body of the human stomach. (Reproduced, with permission, from Bell, Davidson, & Scarborough: *Textbook of Physiology and Biochemistry,* 6th ed. Livingstone, 1965.)

movement of the pharynx and esophagus. It is followed by **antral peristalsis**, which squirts food into the duodenum at a controlled rate. The peristaltic waves are most marked in the distal half of the stomach. When well developed, they occur at a rate of 3/min.

Despite its anatomic prominence, the pyloric sphincter has a remarkably limited function. Gastric emptying is normal if the pylorus is held open or even if it is surgically resected. The antrum, pylorus, and upper duodenum apparently function as a unit. Contraction of the antrum is followed by sequential contraction of the pyloric region and the duodenum. In the antrum, contraction ahead of the advancing gastric contents prevents solid masses from entering the duodenum. Regurgitation from the duodenum does not occur because the contraction of the pyloric segment tends to persist slightly longer than that of the duodenum. The gastric contents are thus squirted a bit at a time into the small intestine.

Gastric Slow Wave

Peristaltic contractions in the antrum are coordinated by the **gastric slow wave**, a wave of depolarization of smooth muscle cells proceeding from the middle of the stomach to the pylorus approximately every 20 seconds. This wave is the pacemaker for antral peristalsis; the wave and, consequently, peristalsis become chaotic and irregular after vagotomy or transection of the stomach wall. Thus, the slow wave

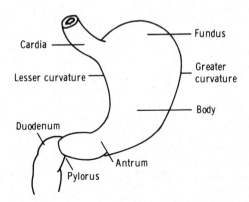

FIG 26–3. Gross anatomy of the stomach.

plays a major role in the control of gastric emptying. A similar aborally directed slow wave coordinates smooth muscle contractions in the small intestine and the colon (see below).

Hunger Contractions

The musculature of the stomach is rarely inactive. Soon after the stomach is emptied, mild peristaltic contractions begin. They gradually increase in intensity over a period of hours. The more intense contractions can be felt, and may even be mildly painful. These **hunger contractions** are associated with the sensation of hunger, and were once thought to be an important regulator of appetite. However, it has now been demonstrated that food intake is normal in animals after denervation of the stomach and intestines (see Chapter 14).

Gastric Secretion

The cells of the gastric glands secrete about 3000 ml/day of **gastric juice**. This juice contains a variety of substances (Table 26–2). The gastric enzymes are discussed in Chapter 25. **Mucus** is secreted by the glands in the pyloric region and the neck cells of the glands in the rest of the stomach. It appears to play an important protective function. The **hydrochloric acid** is secreted by the glands in the fundus of the stomach. This secretion is concentrated enough to cause tissue damage, and it is presumably the mucus coating the cells which in normal individuals prevents the gastric mucosa from being irritated or digested.

TABLE 26–2. Contents of normal gastric juice (fasting state).

Cations: Na^+, K^+, Mg^{++}, H^+ (pH approximately 1.0)
Anions: Cl^-, $HPO_4^{=}$, $SO_4^{=}$
Pepsins I–III
Mucus
Gastric lipase
Intrinsic factor
Rennin (in calves and many other young animals; probably not present in man)
Water

Pepsinogen Secretion

Pepsinogen, the precursor of the 3 pepsins in gastric juice (see Chapter 25), is secreted by the zymogen granule-containing **chief** or **peptic** cells of the stomach. The secretory process is apparently similar to that involved in the secretion of ptyalin by the salivary glands, and trypsinogen and the other pancreatic enzymes by the pancreas. Pepsinogen can be detected in the plasma and in the urine, where it is called **uropepsinogen**. The circulating and urinary levels of this enzyme generally parallel its secretion rate, although they are also influenced by other factors. They are often elevated in patients with peptic ulcer.

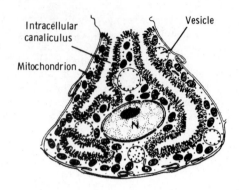

FIG 26–5. Parietal cell. Drawing of electron micrograph from mucosa of mouse after stimulation of acid secretion. In inactive parietal cells, the canaliculi are much narrower. N = nucleus. (Reproduced, with permission, from Hally in: *Physiology of the Digestive Tract,* 3rd ed. Davenport HW. Year Book, 1971.)

Hydrochloric Acid Secretion

Hydrochloric acid is secreted by the parietal cells of the gastric glands. The parietal cells contain small channels, or **canaliculi**, which communicate with the lumens of the gastric glands (Fig 26–5). When these cells are stained with appropriate indicator dyes, the canaliculi have an intensely acid reaction, while the pH of the interior of the cells, like that of other body cells, is 7.0–7.2. It therefore seems likely that H^+ is secreted into the canaliculi.

The amount of acid secreted under conditions of maximal stimulation varies with the number of parietal cells in the stomach. The rate has been calculated to be 20 mEq/hour/10^9 cells. It is difficult to obtain the products of parietal cell secretion free of contamination by other gastric secretions, but the purest specimens that have been analyzed are essentially isotonic. Their H^+ concentration is equivalent to approximately 0.17 N HCl with pHs as low as 0.87. Therefore, parietal cell secretion may well be an isotonic solution of essentially pure HCl containing 150 mEq of Cl^- and 150 mEq of H^+ per liter. The comparable concentrations per liter of plasma are about 100 mEq of Cl^- and 0.00004 mEq of H^+.

The mechanism in the cells that can actively transport H^+ against a concentration gradient of this magnitude is still incompletely understood. The primary source of the secreted H^+ is unsettled. It appears to be produced by the ionization of H_2O, although some H^+ may also come from substrates such as glucose via the flavoprotein-cytochrome respiratory enzyme chain (see Chapter 17). For each H^+ secreted, an OH^- remains in the cell (Fig 26–6). The OH^- is neutralized by an H^+ formed by the dissociation of carbonic acid (carbonic acid buffer system; see Chapters 35 and 40). The HCO_3^- formed by this dissociation enters the blood stream. The H_2CO_3 supply is replenished by the hydration of CO_2. The gastric mucosa contains an abundance of carbonic anhydrase,

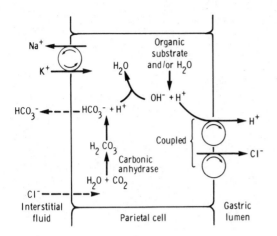

FIG 26—6. Principal chemical reactions believed to underlie HCl secretion by parietal cells in the stomach. H^+ and Cl^- are actively transported into the gastric lumen by pumps that are generally coupled in their operation. The solid arrows crossing cell membranes indicate active transport. The dashed arrows indicate diffusion. Compare to Fig 38—15.

the enzyme that catalyzes the hydration of CO_2, and the stomach has a negative RQ—ie, the amount of CO_2 in arterial blood is greater than the amount in gastric venous blood. Blood coming from the stomach is alkaline and has a high HCO_3^- content. When gastric acid secretion is elevated after a meal, sufficient H^+ may be secreted to raise the pH of systemic blood and make the urine alkaline. This is the probable explanation of the high pH of the urine excreted after a meal, the so-called **postprandial alkaline tide.**

The energy for the active transport of H^+ across the membrane of the parietal cell comes from aerobic glycolysis, since acid secretion ceases under anaerobic conditions. It is also inhibited by dinitrophenol, which indicates that oxidative phosphorylation is necessary for it to continue. Two mols of H^+ are secreted for each mol of O_2 consumed.

Cl^- is secreted by the parietal cells against an electrical gradient as well as a chemical gradient, since the luminal side of the gastric mucosa is about 60 mv negative to the serosal side. H^+ and Cl^- secretion are generally coupled, so that equivalent amounts are secreted, but there is also a basal Cl^- secretion in the absence of H^+ secretion.

Histamine has a potent stimulating effect on acid secretion. The effect of histamine is probably mediated via cyclic AMP. The gastric mucosa has a high histamine content, and it has been repeatedly suggested that stimuli that increase acid secretion act by liberating this amine in the mucosa. However, there are some data that do not completely fit this hypothesis, and other factors appear to play a role.

GASTROINTESTINAL HORMONES

Three of the variety of different gastrointestinal hormones that have been postulated to exist have now been obtained in pure form and have been synthesized. Experiments with these pure hormones have led to considerable revision of previous ideas about the regulation of gastrointestinal secretion and motility.

Gastrin

Gastrin is a hormone produced by cells in the lateral walls of the glands in the antral portion of the gastric mucosa. It is secreted in response to antral distention, protein and polypeptides in the stomach, vagal stimulation, and alcohol. Its secretion is inhibited by overdistention of the antrum and by acid. It stimulates gastric acid and pepsin secretion and motility, but it has other actions as well (see below). A significant amount of gastrin is also secreted by the human duodenal mucosa. In addition, the hormone appears to be present in the δ cells of the pancreatic islets (see Chapter 19). The structure of gastrin is shown in Fig 26—7.

In all species examined, approximately equal amounts of 2 gastrins are secreted; the structures of the 2 are identical except that one, gastrin II, contains a $-SO_3H$ group on the tyrosine residue in the 12 position, and the other, gastrin I, lacks the $-SO_3H$ group. Both forms are equally active. A biologically active "big gastrin," which consists of gastrin bound to an a_2 globulin, has also been found in the blood. A tetrapeptide made up of amino acid residues 14—17 of gastrin has all the activities of gastrin, although it has only about 10% of the potency of the whole molecule. Circulating gastrin can be measured by immunoassay.

Cholecystokinin-Pancreozymin

It was formerly thought that a hormone called cholecystokinin produced contraction of the gallbladder, while a separate hormone called pancreozymin increased the secretion of pancreatic juice rich in enzymes. It is now clear that a single hormone secreted by cells in the mucosa of the upper small intestine has both activities, and the hormone has therefore been named **cholecystokinin-pancreozymin.** It is also called **CCK-PZ, or CCK.** It is secreted when the products of fat and protein digestion are in the duodenal lumen. Porcine CCK contains 33 amino acid residues. The last 5 residues are identical with the last 5 in gastrin (Fig 26—7). There is also a sulfated tyrosine residue near the C-terminal in CCK, as there is in gastrin II. Removal of this $-SO_3H$ group changes the activity patterns of CCK into those of gastrin.

Secretin

Secretin occupies a unique position in the history of physiology. In 1902, Bayliss and Starling first demonstrated that the excitatory effect of duodenal stimulation on pancreatic secretion was due to a blood-borne factor. Their research led to the identification of

$$SO_3H$$
$$|$$
(pyro)Glu-Gly-Pro-Trp-Met-Glu-Glu-Glu-Glu-Glu-Ala-Tyr-Gly-Trp-Met-Asp-Phe-NH$_2$
  1   2   3   4   5   6   7   8   9   10   11   12   13   14   15   16   17

Gastrin II

Lys-Ala-Pro-Ser-Gly-Arg-Val-Ser-Met-Ile-Lys-Asn-
  1   2   3   4   5   6   7   8   9   10   11   12

$$SO_3H$$
$$|$$
Leu-Gln-Ser-Leu-Asp-Pro-Ser-His-Arg-Ile-Ser-Asp-Arg-Asp-Tyr-Met-Gly-Trp-Met-Asp-Phe-NH$_2$
  13   14   15   16   17   18   19   20   21   22 23   24   25   26   27   28   29   30   31   32   33

Cholecystokinin-pancreozymin (CCK)

His-Ser-Asp-Gly-Thr-Phe-Thr-Ser-Glu-Leu-Ser-Arg-Leu-Arg-Asp-Ser-Ala-Arg-Leu-Gln-Arg-Leu-Leu-Gln-Gly-Leu-Val-NH$_2$
  1   2   3   4   5   6   7   8   9   10   11   12   13   14   15   16   17   18   19   20   21   22   23   24   25   26   27

Secretin

FIG 26−7. Structure of porcine gastrointestinal hormones. Gastrin I is identical with gastrin II except that it lacks the −SO$_3$H group on the tyrosine in position 12. Human gastrin I and II are identical with porcine gastrin I and II except that they have leucine in place of methionine in position 5.

secretin. They also suggested that there might be many other chemical agents secreted by cells in the body which passed in the circulation to affect organs some distance away, and coined the term **hormone** to categorize such "chemical messengers." Modern endocrinology is the proof of the correctness of this hypothesis.

Secretin is secreted by cells that are located deep in the glands of the mucosa of the upper portion of the small intestine. It is secreted in response to free fatty acids in the duodenum, and causes the secretion of a dilute pancreatic juice rich in bicarbonate. The structure of porcine secretin (Fig 26−7) does not resemble that of gastrin or CCK, but it does bear a marked resemblance to porcine and human glucagon (Fig 19−18); indeed, although secretin contains 27 amino acid residues and glucagon 29, a total of 14 amino acid residues occupy the same positions in the 2 hormones.

Glucagon-Like Immunoreactive Factor

The presence of glucagon-like immunoreactive factor (intestinal glucagon, enteroglucagon, GLI) in the walls of the stomach and small intestine and its secretion in response to ingested glucose are described in Chapter 19. This material is probably not identical with pancreatic glucagon but appears to have very similar properties, including the ability to stimulate insulin secretion from the β cells of the pancreas.

Actions & Interactions

Although gastrin has a strong effect on gastric secretion and motility, CCK a strong effect on the gallbladder and pancreatic enzyme secretion, and secretin a strong effect on pancreatic bicarbonate secretion, it is now clear that, especially when large doses are given, the actions of these hormones overlap to a marked degree. Gastrin and CCK both stimulate gastric acid and pepsin secretion and gastric motility, pancreatic secretion of bicarbonate, hepatic secretion of bicarbonate in the bile, secretion by Brunner's glands in the duodenum, intestinal motility, and the secretion of insulin. Secretin is a weak inhibitor of gastric acid secretion and gastric and intestinal motility in man, but it stimulates all the other targets stimulated by gastrin and CCK. Pancreatic glucagon has been demonstrated to have almost all of the actions of secretin except stimulation of pepsin secretion. The stimulatory effects of the gastrointestinal hormones on insulin secretion are discussed in Chapter 19.

Not only do the gastrointestinal hormones have multiple actions, but they interact in complex ways. For example, as shown in Table 26−3, gastrin stimulates gastric acid secretion strongly and CCK stimulates it weakly; however, CCK actually inhibits acid secretion in gastrin-stimulated stomachs. Some of the inhibitory effects have the characteristics of competitive inhibition, while others have the characteristics of noncompetitive inhibition. In addition, 2 types of augmentation are observed: competitive augmentation, in which the maximal response to 2 hormones is no greater than the maximal response to either alone; and noncompetitive augmentation, in which the maximal response to 2 hormones may be greater than the response to either alone. To explain these interactions, it has been postulated that gastrin and CCK act on the same receptor, while gastrin and secretin act on different receptors. GLI resembles secretin and may act on the secretin receptor.

**TABLE 26–3. Effects of gastrointestinal
hormones alone and in combination.***

	Gastric Secretion of H^+	Pancreatic Secretion of	
		HCO_3^-	Enzymes
Gastrin	S	s	S
CCK	s	s	S
Secretin	I	S	s
Gastrin + CCK	CI	A	A
Gastrin + secretin	NI	P	P
CCK + secretin	NI	P	P

Legend: s = weak stimulation; S = strong stimulation; I = inhibition; CI = competitive inhibition; NI = non-competitive inhibition; A = stimulatory effects additive up to maximum produced by either alone; P = potentiation, with stimulatory effects of maximum doses of both greater than maximum stimulatory effect of either alone.
*Based primarily on experiments in the dog. In humans, gastrin-stimulated secretion of pancreatic enzymes has not been demonstrated, and secretin is only a weak inhibitor of gastrin-stimulated acid secretion. (Reproduced, with permission, from Grossman: Gastrointestinal hormones. Viewpoints on Digestive Diseases. Vol 2, No. 3, May 1970.)

Other Gastrointestinal Hormones

Acid in the duodenum has been claimed to release a hormone called **enterogastrone**, which inhibits gastric acid secretion and motility. Some of the inhibition attributed to this substance is probably due to secretin or, in the case of gastrin-stimulated acid secretion, to CCK. However, evidence is now accumulating that at least one acid-inhibiting peptide is also secreted by the intestinal mucosa.

Two other postulated hormones, villikinin and enterocrinin, have actions different from those mentioned above. They are believed to be liberated from the mucosa of the upper small intestine by chyme in the intestinal lumen. **Villikinin** is said to increase the contractions of the villi, while **enterocrinin** increases the secretion of intestinal juice. Proof of the existence of these hormones awaits their isolation and chemical characterization. Other gastrointestinal hormones have been proposed to exist, but their existence has not yet been proved.

Caerulein

An interesting decapeptide isolated from the skin of the Australian frog, *Hyla caerulea,* has the same 5 C-terminal and 2 N-terminal amino acid residues as gastrin and also has a sulfated tyrosyl residue. This material, which has been named **caerulein,** has all the properties of gastrin and CCK in mammals and is being used in humans to contract the gallbladder during cholecystography (see below).

Gastric motility and secretion are regulated by neural and humoral mechanisms. The neural components are local autonomic reflexes, involving cholinergic neurons, and impulses from the CNS by way of the vagus nerves. The humoral components are the hormones discussed above. Cholinergic stimulation increases gastrin secretion. Thus, the acetylcholine liberated at the endings of the postganglionic cholinergic neurons in the stomach increases gastric secretion in 2 ways: it acts directly on the cells in the fundus to increase acid and pepsin secretion; and it increases the secretion of gastrin. In their action on acid secretion, gastrin and acetylcholine potentiate each other. Stimulation of the vagus nerve in the chest or neck increases acid and pepsin secretion, but vagotomy does not abolish the secretory response to local stimuli.

Regulation of Gastric Motility & Emptying

The rate at which the stomach empties into the duodenum depends on the type of food ingested. Food rich in carbohydrate leaves the stomach in a few hours. Protein-rich food leaves more slowly, and emptying is slowest after a meal containing a large amount of fat. Products of protein digestion and hydrogen ions bathing the duodenal mucosa initiate a neurally mediated decrease in gastric motility, the **enterogastric reflex**. Distention of the duodenum also initiates this reflex. Fats, protein, and acid cause liberation from the duodenal mucosa of secretin and CCK, which pass in the circulation to the stomach where they inhibit gastric motility and secretion. Cutting the vagus nerves slows gastric emptying. In humans, vagotomy may cause relatively severe gastric atony and distention. Excitement is said to hasten gastric emptying, and fear to slow it.

Since fats are particularly effective in inhibiting gastric emptying, some people drink milk, cream, or even olive oil before a cocktail party. The fat keeps the alcohol in the stomach for a long time, where its absorption is relatively slow, and the intoxicant enters the small intestine in a slow, steady stream so that—theoretically, at least—a sudden rise of the blood alcohol to a high level and consequent embarrassing intoxication are avoided.

Regulation of Acid & Pepsin Secretion

The effects of acetylcholine and gastrointestinal hormones on gastric acid and pepsin secretion have been discussed above. The secretions of the adrenal cortex and adrenal medulla may also play a role in the control of gastric secretion. The increase in circulating adrenal glucocorticoids produced by ACTH stimulates increased gastric acid and pepsin secretion in the dog (Fig 26–8). However, stressful stimuli exert variable effects on gastric secretion. This variability may be due in part to release of catecholamines from the adrenal medulla. Epinephrine and norepinephrine inhibit

FIG 26–8. Stimulation of acid and pepsin secretion by ACTH in intact and vagally denervated dogs. Adrenalectomy blocks this gastric response to ACTH. (Reproduced, with permission, from Villareal & others: Effect of adrenocorticotropic hormone on gastric secretion. Am J Physiol 183:485, 1955.)

gastric secretion, and they are secreted in large amounts during stresses such as hypoglycemia.

Glucocorticoids also decrease the amount and alter the composition of the mucus secreted in the stomach. This mucus is an important barrier to the tissue-damaging effects of acid and pepsin, and glucocorticoids predispose to ulcer formation by decreasing this barrier. Peptic ulceration is thus a potentially dangerous side-effect of prolonged glucocorticoid therapy.

For convenience, the physiologic regulation of gastric secretion is usually discussed in terms of cephalic, gastric, and intestinal influences, although these overlap. The **cephalic** influences are vagally (and possibly pituitary-adrenally) mediated responses induced by activity in the CNS. The **gastric** influences are primarily local reflex responses and responses to gastrin. The **intestinal** influences are the reflex and hormonal feedback effects on gastric secretion initiated from the mucosa of the small intestine.

Cephalic Influences

The presence of food in the mouth reflexly stimulates gastric secretion. The efferent fibers for this reflex are in the vagus nerves. Vagally mediated increases in gastric secretion are easily conditioned. In humans, the sight, smell, and thought of food increase gastric secretion. These increases are due to alimentary conditioned reflexes which become established early in life.

The neural mechanisms involved in the formation of conditioned reflexes are discussed in Chapter 15. The impulses descending in the vagi originate in part in the diencephalon and limbic system. Stimulation of the anterior hypothalamus and parts of the adjacent orbital frontal cortex increases vagal efferent activity and gastric secretion. Hypoglycemia has a similar effect, presumably mediated via an action of hypoglycemia on the hypothalamus. The brain may also influence gastric secretion by way of ACTH secretion.

Emotional Responses

Psychic states have marked effects on gastric secretion and motility. These effects are principally mediated via the vagi. Among his famous observations on Alexis St. Martin, the Canadian with a permanent gastric fistula resulting from a gunshot wound, William Beaumont noted that anger and hostility were associated with turgor, hyperemia, and hypersecretion of the gastric mucosa. Similar observations have been made on other patients with gastric fistulas. Fear and depression decrease gastric secretion and blood flow and inhibit gastric motility.

Gastric Influences

Food in the stomach maintains the high level of gastric secretion produced by the sight and smell of food and the presence of food in the mouth. Much of this secretion is due to the continued release of gastrin, although local stimuli can still produce increased acid secretion over cholinergic reflex pathways after removal of the antrum.

It is worth noting that gastrin secretion is under a form of negative feedback control. Gastrin stimulates gastric hydrochloric acid secretion, but acid in the stomach inhibits gastrin secretion. In patients with pernicious anemia (see below), there is a marked atrophy of the acid-secreting cells in the stomach, and circulating gastrin levels are markedly elevated.

Intestinal Influences

There is some evidence that when the products of gastric protein digestion enter the duodenum they stimulate secretion from the duodenal mucosa of additional gastrin ("intestinal gastrin"). However, fats, carbohydrates, and acid in the duodenum inhibit gastric acid and pepsin secretion and gastric motility. These effects are probably due to secretin and CCK. Gastric acid secretion is increased following removal of large parts of the small intestine. The hypersecretion, which is roughly proportionate in degree to the amount of intestine removed, may be due in part to removal of secretin and CCK-secreting tissue. A substance called **urogastrone** with inhibitory effects on the stomach has been found in urine. Its origin is unknown.

Other Influences

The inhibiting effect of catecholamines on gastric secretion has been discussed above. Hypoglycemia stimulates acid and pepsin secretion and the stimulation produced by insulin is a result of hypoglycemia. Other stimulants include **alcohol** and **caffeine,** both of which act directly on the mucosa. The beneficial effects of moderate amounts of alcohol on appetite and digestion, due to this stimulatory effect on gastric secretion, have been known since ancient times.

Other Functions of the Stomach

The stomach has a number of functions in addition to the storage of food and the control of its release into the duodenum. The hydrochloric acid kills many of the ingested bacteria. The parietal cells in the gastric mucosa also secrete **intrinsic factor,** a substance necessary for the absorption of **cyanocobalamin** (vitamin B_{12}) from the small intestine.

Cyanocobalamin (Fig 26–9) is a complex cobalt-containing vitamin that is necessary for normal erythropoiesis. Inadequate absorption of this vitamin causes an anemia which is characterized by the appearance in the blood stream of large primitive red cell precursors called **megaloblasts.** A complete remission of the deficiency syndrome occurs when cyanocobalamin is injected parenterally but not when it is administered by mouth unless the intrinsic factor secreted by the gastric mucosa is also present. Anemia due to an inadequate dietary intake of cyanocobalamin is very rare, apparently because the minimal daily requirements are quite low and the vitamin is found in most foods of animal origin. The deficiency states seen clinically are therefore due primarily to defective cyanocobalamin absorption. Inadequate absorption may be due to primary intestinal diseases such as sprue, or it may be caused by intrinsic factor deficiency following gastrectomy. In patients with the specific megaloblastic anemia called **pernicious anemia,** there is intrinsic factor deficiency due to an idiopathic atrophy of the gastric mucosa.

Intrinsic factor is a glycoprotein with a molecular weight of 60,000. Cyanocobalamin becomes firmly bound to it in the intestine. The intrinsic factor-cyanocobalamin complex then becomes bound to specific receptors in the ileum, and the cyanocobalamin is transferred across the intestinal epithelium. The details of the absorptive process are uncertain, but it has been suggested that the role of intrinsic factor in the process is to stimulate pinocytosis. This would explain how such a large molecule can be absorbed. A syndrome has been described in which there is congenital absence of the ileal receptors for the cyanocobalamin-intrinsic factor complex.

In totally gastrectomized patients, the intrinsic factor deficiency must be circumvented by parenteral injection of cyanocobalamin. Protein digestion is normal in the absence of pepsin, and nutrition can be maintained. However, these patients are prone to develop iron deficiency anemia (see Chapter 25) and other abnormalities, and they must eat frequent small meals. Because of rapid absorption of glucose from the intestine and the resultant hyperglycemia and abrupt rise in insulin secretion, gastrectomized patients sometimes develop hypoglycemic symptoms about 2 hours after meals (see Fig 19–20). Weakness, dizziness, and sweating after meals due in part to hypoglycemia are part of the picture of the "dumping syndrome," a distressing syndrome which develops in patients in whom portions of the stomach have been removed or the jejunum anastomosed to the stomach. Another cause of the symptoms is rapid entry of hypertonic meals into the intestine; this provokes the movement of so much water into the gut that the resultant reduction of plasma volume is great enough to lead to a decrease in cardiac output.

Peptic Ulcer

Gastric and duodenal ulceration in humans is apparently related in some poorly understood way to a breakdown of the mucous barrier which presumably prevents irritation and autodigestion of the mucosa by the gastric secretions. Aspirin, which is known to be a gastric irritant, diminishes the barrier effect of the mucus in the stomachs of dogs. In patients with ulcers of the duodenum and prepyloric portion of the stomach—but not in those with ulcers of other portions of the stomach—prolonged, excessive acid secretion also plays a role (Fig 26–10). Another illustration of the importance of acid hypersecretion in the genesis of duodenal and prepyloric ulcers is provided by the **Zollinger-Ellison syndrome.** This syndrome is seen in patients with pancreatic adenomas that secrete gastrin. The gastrin causes prolonged hypersecretion of acid, and severe ulcers are produced. In the Zollinger-Ellison syndrome and in pernicious anemia, circulating gastrin levels are high. They do not seem to be elevated in most patients with gastric and duodenal ulcers; however, in the presence of excess acid secretion, they

FIG 26–9. Cyanocobalamin (vitamin B_{12}). Empiric formula: $C_{63}H_{88}O_{14}N_{14}PCo$.

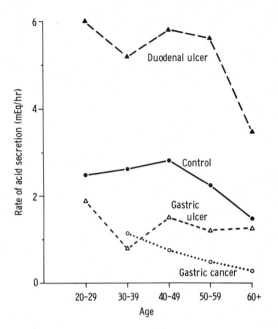

FIG 26—10. **Mean values for basal gastric acid secretion in men of various ages.** (Reproduced, with permission, from Grossman: Gastric secretion. Physiology for Physicians 1, No. 7, July 1963.)

should be depressed via the feedback control, and there is thus a relative if not an absolute hypergastrinemia.

More extensive discussions of the problem of peptic ulceration can be found in textbooks of pathophysiology. However, it is pertinent to note that most of the time-honored procedures used in the treatment of ulcers are aimed at decreasing gastric secretion or neutralizing secreted acid. Thus, atropine and other anticholinergic drugs are given to inhibit vagal effects on gastric glands and gastrin secretion. Antacids such as aluminum hydroxide gels are given to neutralize secreted hydrochloric acid. Frequent feedings of cream provide fat, which inhibits gastric secretion and motility via the duodenal feedback mechanism. A surgical procedure which is extensively used for the treatment of severe duodenal or prepyloric ulcer is vagotomy combined with removal of the gastrin-secreting antral mucosa. Vagotomy combined with a procedure such as pyloroplasty to prevent gastric stasis is popular, but the vagotomies are incomplete in about 20% of patients and recurrent ulcers are therefore a problem. Removal of the antral mucosa circumvents this difficulty because, in the absence of the potentiating action of gastrin, the effects of a few remaining vagal fibers on acid secretion are too small to be a problem.

SMALL INTESTINE

In the small intestine, the intestinal contents are mixed with the secretions of the mucosal cells and with pancreatic juice and bile. Digestion, which begins in the mouth and stomach, is completed in the lumen and mucosal cells of the small intestine, and the products of digestion are absorbed, along with most of the vitamins.

Anatomic Considerations

The general arrangement of the muscular layers, nerve plexuses, and mucosa in the small intestine is shown in Fig 26—1. The first portion of the duodenum is sometimes called the duodenal cap or bulb. It is the region struck by the acid gastric contents squirted through the pylorus, and is a common site of peptic ulceration. At the ligament of Treitz, the duodenum becomes the jejunum. Arbitrarily, the upper 40% of the small intestine below the duodenum is called the jejunum and the lower 60% is called the ileum, although there is no sharp anatomic boundary between the two. The ileocecal valve marks the point where the ileum ends in the colon.

The small intestine is shorter during life than it is in cadavers because it relaxes and elongates after death. In the living human, the distance from the pylorus to the ileocecal valve is about 280 cm (Table 26—4).

The mucosa of the small intestine contains **solitary lymph nodules** and, especially in the ileum, **aggregated lymphatic nodules** (Peyer's patches) along the antimesenteric border. Throughout the small intestine there are simple tubular **intestinal glands** (crypts of Lieberkühn). In the duodenum there are, in addition, the small, coiled acinotubular **duodenal glands** (Brunner's glands). The **enterochromaffin cells** in the mucosa of the intestine secrete serotonin (see Chapter 15). These cells are often located deep in the intestinal glands. There are many valve-like folds (**valvulae conniventes**) in the mucous membrane.

Throughout the length of the small intestine, the mucous membrane is covered by **villi**. There are 20—40 villi per sq mm of mucosa. Each intestinal villus is a finger-like projection, 0.5—1 mm in length, covered by a single layer of columnar epithelium and containing a network of capillaries and a lymphatic vessel (**lacteal**). Fine extensions of the smooth muscle of the sub-

TABLE 26—4. **Lengths of various segments of the gastrointestinal tract as measured by intubation in living humans.** *

Segment	Mean Length (cm)
Duodenum	22
Jejunum and ileum	258
Colon	110

*Data from Blankenhorn & others: Transintestinal intubation. Proc Soc Exper Biol Med 88:356, 1955.

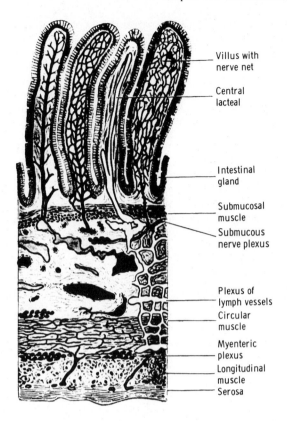

FIG 26—11. **Diagrammatic section of the wall of the human small intestine.** The villi show, from left to right, venous drainage, arterial supply, lymphatic drainage, and nerve supply only. (Reproduced, with permission, from Bell, Davidson, & Scarborough: *Textbook of Physiology and Biochemistry,* 7th ed. Livingstone, 1969.)

mucosa run longitudinally up each villus to its tip (Fig 26—11). The free edges of the cells of the epithelium of the villi are divided into minute **microvilli** (Fig 26—12). The valvulae conniventes, the villi, and the microvilli greatly increase the absorptive surface exposed to the contents of the small intestine. The total absorptive surface in the small intestine is about 300 sq m. The cells are connected to each other by tight junctions. The outer layer of the cell membrane of the mucosal cells contains many of the enzymes involved in the digestive processes initiated by salivary, gastric, and pancreatic enzymes. Enzymes found in this membrane include various disaccharidases, peptidases, and enzymes involved in the breakdown of nucleic acids (see Chapter 25).

The mucosal cells are sloughed into the intestinal lumen in large numbers and are rapidly replaced. The turnover rate of mucosal cells is 1—3 days, and the "secretion" of protein into the lumen due to cell sloughing has been calculated to be as great as 30 g/day. Mucosal cells are also rapidly sloughed and replaced in the stomach.

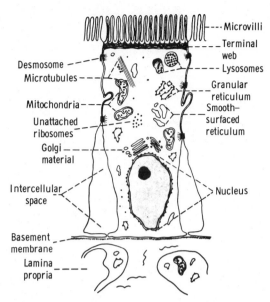

FIG 26—12. **Diagram of mucosal cells from human small intestine.** Note microvilli, tight connections of cells at mucosal edge (desmosomes), and space between cells at base (intercellular space). (Reproduced, with permission, from Trier: Structure of the mucosa of the small intestine as it relates to intestinal function. Fed Proc 26:1391, 1967.)

Intestinal Motility

The movements of the small intestine can be divided into peristaltic contractions, tonus changes, pendular movements, segmentation contractions, and movements of the villi. They mix and churn the intestinal contents, or **chyme,** and propel it toward the large intestine.

Tonus changes are local changes in the rate or degree of smooth muscle contraction occurring slowly in all parts of the digestive tract independently of the volume or nature of the contents. **Pendular movements** are 10—12/min lengthening and shortening motions of gut segments which fail to advance the intestinal contents. **Segmentation contractions** are ring-like contractions which appear at fairly regular intervals along the gut, then disappear and are replaced by another set of ring contractions in the segments between the previous contractions (Fig 26—13). These 3 types of movements occur after essentially complete denervation of the intestine. The first 2 are apparently manifestations of the intrinsic contractile activity of smooth muscle (see Chapter 3), but segmentation contractions and peristaltic contractions require an intact myenteric nerve plexus. Movements of the villi are believed to be under control of the gastrointestinal hormone villikinin.

The contractions of the small intestine are coordinated by the **small bowel slow wave,** a wave of smooth muscle depolarization that moves caudally in the longitudinal smooth muscle. The frequency of the

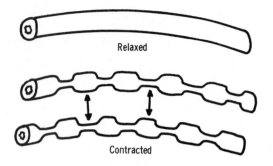

FIG 26—13. Diagram of segmentation contractions of the intestine. Arrows indicate how areas of relaxation become areas of constriction, and vice versa.

slow waves decreases from about 12/min in the jejunum to about 9/min in the ileum.

Peristalsis

Peristaltic contractions occur not only in the small intestine but also in the esophagus, stomach, colon, and ureters. They are easy to demonstrate in experimental animals, but there has been some debate about how big a role they play in the small intestine and colon of intact humans.

When the intestinal wall is stretched, a deep circular contraction (peristaltic wave) forms behind the point of stimulation and passes along the intestine toward the rectum at rates varying from 2—25 cm/sec. This response to stretch is called the **myenteric reflex**. It was originally believed that each peristaltic wave was preceded by a wave of smooth muscle relaxation, but such relaxation is often absent. Peristaltic waves differ in intensity and in the distance they travel. Very intense peristaltic waves are called **peristaltic rushes**. Weak antiperistalsis is sometimes seen in the colon, but most waves pass regularly in an oral-caudal direction. Removal and resuture of a segment of intestine in its original position does not block progression, and waves will even cross a small gap where the intestine has been replaced by a plastic tube. However, if an intestinal segment is reversed and sewed back into place, peristalsis stops at the reversed segment.

Peristaltic waves occur in the absence of extrinsic innervation but not in the absence of the myenteric (Auerbach's) plexus. The receptors for the myenteric reflex are apparently in the mucosa since removing the mucosa or painting it with a local anesthetic blocks peristalsis. One process of each bipolar ganglion cell in the submucous (Meissner's) plexus enters the mucosa and the other goes to the myenteric plexus. Therefore, the sequence of events in the myenteric reflex which initiates peristaltic contractions is probably mucosal stretch, transmission of impulses in the bipolar cells, activation of the neurons of the myenteric plexus, and contraction of the smooth muscle they innervate. Serotonin has been shown to be synthesized and bound in the myenteric plexus, and it has been suggested that it is the mediator at the junctions between

the bipolar cells and the neurons of the myenteric plexus. Substance P is also found in high concentrations in the intestine, and may play a role as a synaptic mediator in the myenteric reflex arc. The amount of this polypeptide in the different segments of the intestine parallels the number of ganglion cells in the myenteric submucous plexuses, and in disease states in which the number of ganglion cells is low in a particular region there is a parallel local decline in substance P content. Substance P and serotonin are discussed in more detail and their function in the brain is considered in Chapter 15.

Movements of the Villi

During digestion, the villi are apparently stimulated by villikinin and are in constant motion. Each villus shortens and lengthens in response to rhythmic contractions of the submucosal muscle fibers that extend into it.

Role of Autonomic Innervation

From the foregoing discussion it is apparent that the motility of the small intestine is relatively independent of extrinsic innervation. Vagal stimulation or local application of acetylcholine transiently increases movement of the villi. Sympathetic stimulation makes the villi blanch and remain motionless. Sympathectomy has no effect on intestinal motility; and although vagotomy may cause transient intestinal hypomotility, normal intestinal activity soon returns. However, the vagal connections may play a role in integrating the actions of the various parts of the intestine. If intestinal overdistention occurs or if the peritoneum is irritated, reflexes mediated via sympathetic pathways inhibit peristaltic activity.

Regulation of Intestinal Secretion

Brunner's glands in the duodenum secrete a thick alkaline mucus which probably protects the duodenal mucosa from the gastric acid. Their secretion is increased by gastrin, CCK, and secretin (see above). The intestinal glands secrete an isotonic fluid. Most of the enzymes usually found in this secretion are in desquamated mucosal cells; cell-free intestinal juice probably contains few if any enzymes. The chyme is believed to stimulate the secretion of a hormone, enterocrinin, from the intestinal mucosa. This hormone is believed to stimulate the secretion of intestinal juice without affecting intestinal motility or pancreatic secretion. Vagal stimulation increases the secretion of Brunner's glands but probably has no effect on that of the intestinal glands.

The Malabsorption Syndrome

The digestive and absorptive functions of the small intestine are essential for life. Removal of short segments of the jejunum or ileum generally does not cause severe symptoms, and there is compensatory hypertrophy and hyperplasia of the remaining mucosa with gradual return of the absorptive function toward normal. However, when more than 50% of the small intestine is resected or bypassed, the absorption of nutrients and vitamins is so compromised that it is very difficult to prevent malnutrition and wasting. Various disease processes also impair absorption (Table 26–5). The pattern of deficiencies that results is sometimes called the **malabsorption syndrome**. This pattern varies somewhat with the cause, but it can include deficient absorption of amino acids, with marked body wasting and, eventually, hypoproteinemia and edema. Carbohydrate and fat absorption are also depressed. Because of the defective fat absorption, the fat-soluble vitamins (vitamins A, D, E, and K) are not absorbed in adequate amounts. The amount of fat and protein in the stools is increased, and the stools become bulky, pale, foul-smelling, and greasy (**steatorrhea**).

The increased gastric acid secretion produced by intestinal resection has been mentioned above. Resection of the ileum also prevents the absorption of bile acids, and this leads in turn to deficient fat absorption and diarrhea. Other complications of intestinal resection or bypass include hypocalcemia and fatty infiltration of the liver, followed by cirrhosis. Operations in which large segments of the small intestine are bypassed have been recommended for the treatment of obesity, but in view of their complications and dangers they should not be undertaken lightly.

The defective intestinal function in tropical sprue is apparently due in part to folic acid deficiency. However, the intestinal changes in experimentally produced folic acid deficiency are less intense than those in tropical sprue, and patients with tropical sprue respond characteristically to treatment with antibiotics such as tetracycline. In celiac disease, the absorption defect is apparently caused by a congenital abnormality in the cells of the intestinal mucosa, which are harmed by the polypeptides formed by hydrolysis of gluten, the principal protein in wheat. When gluten is omitted from the diet, bowel function is generally restored to normal.

Adynamic Ileus

When the intestines are traumatized, there is a decrease in intestinal motility due to direct inhibition of smooth muscle. When the peritoneum is irritated, there is reflex inhibition due to increased discharge of adrenergic fibers in the splanchnic nerves. Both types of inhibition operate to cause **paralytic** or **adynamic ileus** after abdominal operations. Because of the diffuse decrease in peristaltic activity in the small intestine, its contents are not propelled into the colon and it becomes irregularly distended by pockets of gas and fluid. Adynamic ileus can be relieved by passing a tube through the nose down to the small intestine and aspirating the fluid and gas for a few days until the viscera heal and peristalsis returns.

Mechanical Obstruction of the Small Intestine

Localized mechanical obstruction of the small intestine causes severe cramping pain (**intestinal colic**), whereas adynamic ileus is often painless. The segment of intestine above the point of mechanical obstruction dilates and becomes filled with fluid and gas. The pressure in the segment rises and the blood vessels in its wall are compressed, causing local ischemia. Activity in visceral afferent nerve fibers from the distended segment causes sweating, a drop in blood pressure, and severe vomiting, with resultant metabolic alkalosis and dehydration. If the obstruction is not relieved, the condition can be fatal.

EXOCRINE PORTION OF
THE PANCREAS

The pancreatic juice contains enzymes which are of major importance in digestion (Table 25–1). Its secretion is controlled in part by a reflex mechanism and in part by secretin and CCK, 2 hormones secreted by the intestinal mucosa.

Anatomic Considerations

The portion of the pancreas that secretes pancreatic juice is a compound alveolar gland that resembles the salivary glands. Granules containing the digestive enzymes (**zymogen granules**) are formed in the cell and discharged by exocytosis (see Chapter 1) from the apexes of the cells into the lumens of the pancreatic ducts. The small duct radicles coalesce into a single duct (duct of Wirsung) which usually joins the common bile duct to form the ampulla of Vater (Fig 26–14). The ampulla opens through the duodenal papilla, and its orifice is encircled by the sphincter of Oddi. In some individuals there is an accessory pancreatic duct (duct of Santorini) which enters the duodenum more proximally. There is said to be a high incidence of nonpatency of the accessory pancreatic duct in patients with gastric acid hypersecretion and duodenal ulcer. It is possible that failure of the alkaline pancreatic secretion to enter the upper part of the duodenum via this duct contributes to the development of the ulcer.

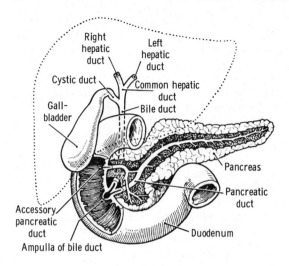

FIG 26−14. Connections of the ducts of the gallbladder, liver, and pancreas. (Reproduced, with permission, from Bell, Davidson, & Scarborough: *Textbook of Physiology and Biochemistry*, 7th ed. Livingstone, 1969.)

Composition of Pancreatic Juice

The pancreatic juice is alkaline and has a high bicarbonate content (Table 26−6 and Fig 26−15). About 2000 ml of pancreatic juice are secreted per day. The bile and intestinal juice are also neutral or alkaline, and these 3 secretions neutralize the gastric acid, raising the pH of the duodenal contents to 6.0−7.0. By the time the chyme reaches the jejunum, its reaction is nearly neutral, but the intestinal contents are rarely alkaline.

The powerful protein-splitting enzymes of the pancreatic juice are secreted as the inactive proenzymes, trypsinogen and several related chymotrypsinogens. Trypsinogen is converted to the active enzyme trypsin by **enterokinase**, an enzyme secreted by the duodenal mucosa. This enzyme also appears to convert procarboxypeptidase to active carboxypeptidase. Enterokinase contains 41% polysaccharide, and it

TABLE 26−6. Composition of normal human pancreatic juice.

Cations: Na^+, K^+, Ca^{++}, Mg^{++}; pH approximately 8.0
Anions: HCO_3^-, Cl^-, $SO_4^=$, $HPO_4^=$
Trypsinogen
Chymotrypsinogens
Procarboxypeptidase A and B
Elastase
Ribonuclease
Deoxyribonuclease
Prophospholipase A
Pancreatic lipase
Pancreatic a-amylase
Albumin and globulin

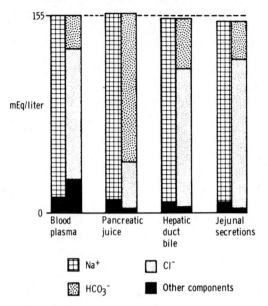

FIG 26−15. Electrolyte composition of pancreatic juice, bile, and intestinal juice. (Redrawn and reproduced, with permission, from Gamble: *Chemical Anatomy, Physiology and Pathology of the Extracellular Fluid,* 6th ed. Harvard Univ Press, 1954.)

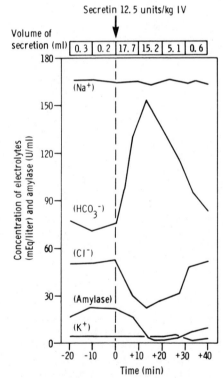

FIG 26−16. Effect of a single dose of secretin on the composition and volume of the pancreatic juice in man. (Redrawn and reproduced, with permission, from Janowitz: Pancreatic secretion. Physiology for Physicians 2, No. 11, Nov 1964.)

is this high polysaccharide content that apparently prevents it from being digested itself before it can exert its effect. Trypsin converts chymotrypsinogens into chymotrypsins.

Trypsin also converts prophospholipase A into the active enzyme, phospholipase A. This enzyme splits a fatty acid off lecithin, forming lysolecithin. Lysolecithin damages cell membranes. The cause of **acute pancreatitis**, a severe and sometimes fatal disease, may be activation of phospholipase in the pancreatic ducts, with the formation of lysolecithin from the lecithin which is a normal constituent of bile. This causes disruption of pancreatic tissue and necrosis of surrounding fat. A small amount of the pancreatic α-amylase normally leaks into the circulation, but in acute pancreatitis the circulating level of this enzyme rises markedly.

Regulation of the Secretion of Pancreatic Juice

Secretion of pancreatic juice is primarily under hormonal control. Secretin causes copious secretion of a very alkaline pancreatic juice poor in enzymes (Fig 26–16), and it is believed to act on epithelial cells of the small duct radicles rather than on the acinar cells. The duct cells probably secrete water and bicarbonate. Secretin also stimulates bile secretion. CCK causes secretion of pancreatic juice rich in enzymes by causing discharge of zymogen granules from the pancreatic acinar cells.

Stimulation of the vagi causes secretion of a small amount of pancreatic juice rich in enzymes, an effect that is blocked by atropine and denervation of the pancreas. The effects of secretin and CCK are not. There is some evidence for vagally mediated conditioned reflex secretion of pancreatic juice in response to the sight or smell of food.

Bradykinin (see Chapter 31) is liberated during active secretion in the exocrine portion of the pancreas and may be responsible for the increased blood flow that occurs at this time.

LIVER & BILIARY SYSTEM

Functions of the Liver

The liver, the largest gland in the body, has many complex functions. These include the formation of bile; carbohydrate storage, ketone body formation, and other functions in the control of carbohydrate metabolism; reduction and conjugation of adrenal and gonadal steroid hormones; detoxification of many drugs and toxins; manufacture of plasma proteins; inactivation of polypeptide hormones; urea formation; and many important functions in the metabolism of fat. Discussion of these functions in one place requires that they be taken out of their proper context at considerable cost in terms of clarity and integration of function. Therefore, in this book they are discussed individually in the chapters on the systems of which

each is a part. However, for the convenience of the reader, all hepatic functions are also listed in the index under the heading "liver functions."

Bile Secretion

Bile is secreted by the cells of the liver into the bile duct, which drains into the duodenum. Between meals, the duodenal orifice of this duct is closed and bile flows into the gallbladder, where it is stored. When food enters the mouth, the sphincter around the orifice relaxes; and when the gastric contents enter the duodenum, the hormone CCK from the intestinal mucosa causes the gallbladder to contract.

Anatomic Considerations

The intrahepatic portions of the biliary system are shown in Figs 26–17 and 26–18. The intrahepatic bile duct radicles coalesce to form the right and left hepatic ducts, which join outside the liver to form the common hepatic duct. The cystic duct drains the gallbladder. The hepatic duct unites with the cystic duct to form the common bile duct. The common bile duct enters the duodenum at the duodenal papilla. Its orifice is surrounded by the sphincter of Oddi, and it usually unites with the main pancreatic duct just before entering the duodenum (Fig 26–14).

The walls of the extrahepatic biliary ducts and the gallbladder contain fibrous tissue and smooth muscle. The mucous membrane contains mucous glands and is lined by a layer of columnar cells. In the gallbladder the mucous membrane is extensively folded; this increases its surface area and gives the interior of the gallbladder a honeycombed appearance. In primates, the mucous membranes of the cystic duct are also folded to form the so-called spiral valves.

Composition of Bile

Bile is a complex solution containing the substances listed in Table 26–7. It also contains electrolytes (Fig 26–15) and is generally somewhat alkaline. About 500 ml are secreted per day. Some of the components of the bile are reabsorbed in the intestine and then excreted again by the liver (**enterohepatic circulation**).

The glucuronides of the **bile pigments**, biliverdin and bilirubin, are responsible for the golden yellow color of bile. The formation of these breakdown

TABLE 26–7. Composition of human
hepatic duct bile.

Water	97.0%
Bile salts	0.7%
Bile pigments	0.2%
Cholesterol	0.06%
Inorganic salts	0.7%
Fatty acids	0.15%
Lecithin	0.1%
Fat	0.1%
Alkaline phosphatase	. . .

1 Lacuna	9 Periportal connective tissue	16 Bile canaliculi on the surface of
2 Central veins	10 Inlet venules	liver plates (not frequent)
3 Portal canal	11 Sinusoids	17 Intralobular cholangiole
4 Limiting plate	12 Sublobular vein	18 Cholangioles in portal canals
5 Portal vein	13 Perisinusoidal space of Disse	19 Arterial capillary emptying into
6 Hepatic artery	14 Periportal space of Mall	paraportal sinusoid
7 Bile ducts	15 Bile canaliculi within liver	20 Arterial capillary emptying into
8 Lymph vessel	plates	intralobular sinusoid

FIG 26–17. Synopsis of the structure of the normal human liver. (Reproduced, with permission, from Elias in: *Research in the Service of Medicine,* vol 37, 1953. Copyright © GD Searle & Co.)

products of hemoglobin is discussed in detail in Chapter 27, and their excretion is discussed below.

The **bile salts** are sodium and potassium salts of **bile acids** conjugated to glycine or taurine, a derivative of cystine. Four bile acids isolated from human bile are listed in Fig 26–19. Deoxycholic acid is now believed to be formed solely by the action of bacteria on cholic acid in the intestine. In common with vitamin D, cholesterol, a variety of steroid hormones, and the digitalis glycosides, the bile acids contain the cyclopentanoperhydrophenanthrene nucleus (see Chapter 20). Conjugation of the acids occurs in the liver, and the conjugates—eg, **glycocholic acid** and **taurocholic acid**—form sodium and potassium salts in the alkaline hepatic bile. The bile salts have a number of important actions. They combine with lipids to form micelles, water-soluble complexes from which the lipids can be more easily absorbed. This action is called their **hydrotropic** effect. They reduce surface tension and, in conjunction with fatty acids and glycerides, are

responsible for the emulsification of fat preparatory to its digestion and absorption in the small intestine (see Chapter 25). They also play a role in activating lipases in the intestines, and stimulate re-esterification of fatty acids and glycerol synthesis from glucose in the mucosal cells. When bile is excluded from the intestine as much as 25% of ingested fat appears in the feces. Agents that stimulate bile secretion by the liver are called **choleretic** agents. Bile salts themselves have this action when given by mouth.

Bilirubin Metabolism & Excretion

Most of the bilirubin formed in the tissues by the breakdown of hemoglobin (see Chapter 27) is bound to albumin in the circulation. Free bilirubin enters liver cells, where it is bound to cytoplasmic proteins (Fig 26–20). It is next conjugated to glucuronic acid in a reaction catalyzed by the enzyme **glucuronyl transferase.** This enzyme is located primarily in the smooth endoplasmic reticulum. Each bilirubin binds 2 glucu-

FIG 26–18. **Liver cell of rat, showing relation to blood vessels and bile canaliculi.** The desmosomes are areas of membrane thickening and increased density on either side of the bile canaliculi. Notice wide openings in the endothelium of the sinusoids next to the cell. (Redrawn and reproduced, with permission, from Porter & Bonneville: *Fine Structure of Cells and Tissues,* 3rd ed. Lea & Febiger, 1968.)

ronic acids. The source of the glucuronic acid is uridine diphosphoglucuronic acid (UDPGA). The bilirubin glucuronide, which is more water-soluble than the free bilirubin, is then transported against a concentration gradient by a presumably active process into the bile canaliculi. Some of the bilirubin glucuronide escapes into the blood, where it is bound less tightly to albumin than free bilirubin and is excreted in the urine. Most of the bilirubin glucuronide passes via the bile ducts to the intestine.

The intestinal mucosa is relatively impermeable to conjugated bilirubin but is permeable to unconjugated bilirubin and to urobilinogens, a series of colorless derivatives of bilirubin formed by the action of bacteria in the intestine. Consequently, some of the bile pigments are reabsorbed in the portal circulation. Some of the reabsorbed pigments are again excreted by the liver (**enterohepatic circulation**), whereas urobilinogens appear in the urine.

The total plasma bilirubin normally includes free bilirubin plus a small amount of conjugated bilirubin (Table 26–8). The free bilirubin is measured as the indirect-reacting bilirubin; the conjugated bilirubin is measured as the direct-reacting bilirubin.

Jaundice

When free or conjugated bilirubin accumulates in

the blood, the skin, scleras, and mucous membranes turn yellow. This yellowness is known as **jaundice** (icterus), and is usually detectable when the total plasma bilirubin is greater than 2 mg/100 ml. Hyperbilirubinemia may be due to (1) excess production (hemolytic anemia, etc); (2) decreased uptake of bilirubin into hepatic cells; (3) disturbed intracellular protein binding or conjugation; (4) disturbed secretion of bilirubin into the bile canaliculi; or (5) intrahepatic or extrahepatic bile duct obstruction. When it is due to processes (1)–(4), the free bilirubin rises, and it is primarily the indirect-reacting bilirubin that is elevated. When it is due to bile duct obstruction, bilirubin glucuronide regurgitates into the blood, and it is pre-

Cholic acid

Group at Position

	3	7	12
Cholic acid	OH	OH	OH
Deoxycholic acid	OH	H	OH
Chenodeoxycholic acid	OH	OH	H
Lithocholic acid	OH	H	H

FIG 26–19. **Bile acids isolated from human bile.** The numbers in the formula for cholic acid refer to the positions in the steroid ring.

FIG 26–20. **Metabolism of bilirubin in the liver.** P, intracellular binding proteins; UDPGA, uridine diphosphoglucuronic acid; UDP, uridine diphosphate.

TABLE 26–8. Normal plasma bilirubin levels (mg/100 ml).

	Free (Indirect-Reacting)	Conjugated (Direct-Reacting)	Total
Mean	0.51	0.11	0.62
Upper limit	1.2	0.3	1.2

TABLE 26–9. Comparison of human hepatic duct bile and gallbladder bile.

	Hepatic Duct Bile	Gallbladder Bile
Percent of solids	2–4	10–12
pH	7.8–8.6	7.0–7.4

dominantly the direct-reacting component of the plasma bilirubin that is elevated.

Other Substances Conjugated by Glucuronyl Transferase

The glucuronyl transferase system in the smooth endoplasmic reticulum catalyzes the formation of the glucuronides of a variety of substances in addition to bilirubin. The list includes steroids (see Chapters 20 and 23) and various drugs. These other compounds can compete with bilirubin for the enzyme system when they are present in appreciable amounts. In addition, several barbiturates, antihistamines, anticonvulsants, and other compounds have been found to cause marked proliferation of the smooth endoplasmic reticulum in the hepatic cells with a concurrent increase in hepatic glucuronyl transferase activity. Phenobarbital has been used successfully for the treatment of a congenital disease in which there is a relative deficiency of glucuronyl transferase (type 2 UDP glucuronyl transferase deficiency).

Other Substances Excreted in the Bile

Cholesterol and alkaline phosphatase are excreted in the bile. In patients with jaundice due to intra- or extrahepatic obstruction of the bile duct, the blood levels of these 2 substances usually rise; a much smaller rise is generally seen when the jaundice is due to non-obstructive hepatocellular disease. Adrenocortical and other steroid hormones and a number of drugs are excreted in the bile and subsequently reabsorbed (enterohepatic circulation). The dye sulfobromophthalein (Bromsulphalein, BSP) is removed from the blood stream by the liver cells and is excreted in the bile. Its rate of removal from the circulation is used as a test of hepatic function. This rate depends not only on the functional capacity of the liver cells but also on the hepatic blood flow.

Functions of the Gallbladder

In normal individuals bile flows into the gallbladder when the sphincter of Oddi is closed. In the gallbladder, the bile is concentrated by absorption of water. The degree of this concentration is shown by the fact that liver bile is 97% water, whereas the average water content of gallbladder bile is 89%. When the bile duct and cystic duct are clamped, the intrabiliary pressure rises to about 320 mm of bile in 30 minutes and bile secretion stops. However, when the bile duct is clamped and the cystic duct is left open, water is reabsorbed in the gallbladder and the intra-

biliary pressure rises only to about 100 mm of bile in several hours. Acidification of the bile appears to be another function of the gallbladder (Table 26–9).

Regulation of Biliary Secretion

When food enters the mouth, the resistance of the sphincter of Oddi decreases. Food in the stomach and duodenum releases CCK and other gastrointestinal hormones, which cause gallbladder contraction. Acid, the products of protein digestion, and magnesium sulfate also stimulate the secretion of CCK. Substances which cause contraction of the gallbladder are called **cholagogues**. Because painting the duodenal mucosa with procaine prevents release of CCK, it is probable that its secretion, like that of gastrin, depends upon a local reflex mechanism in the mucosa.

Effects of Cholecystectomy

The periodic discharge of bile from the gallbladder aids digestion but is not essential for it. Cholecystectomized patients maintain good health and nutrition with a constant slow discharge of bile into the duodenum, although eventually the bile duct becomes somewhat dilated and more bile tends to enter the duodenum after eating than at other times. Cholecystectomized patients can even tolerate fried foods quite well, although they generally have to avoid foods that are particularly high in fat content.

Cholecystography

Certain radiopaque iodine-containing dyes such as tetraiodophenolphthalein are excreted in the bile and concentrated with the bile in the gallbladder. When the gallbladder contains an adequate concentration of such dye, it can be visualized by x-ray (**cholecystography**). To determine if the gallbladder is capable of normal contraction, a fatty meal is fed. CCK is released and the gallbladder contracts, the size of its x-ray shadow normally decreasing to less than one-third of its original size within 30 minutes. When administered intravenously, certain other radiopaque dyes are excreted in the bile in sufficient quantities to permit x-ray visualization of the bile ducts (**intravenous cholangiography**).

Gallstones

Stones form in the gallbladder or bile ducts when foreign substances appear in the bile or when the relative composition of the bile changes so that a normal constituent precipitates. For example, calcium bilirubinate stones form if the conjugated bilirubin in

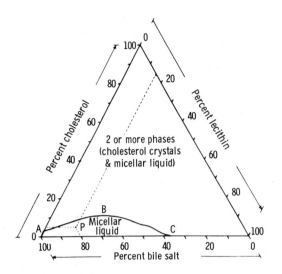

FIG 26—21. Cholesterol solubility in bile as a function of the proportions of lecithin, bile salts, and cholesterol. In bile which has a composition described by any point below line ABC (eg, point P), cholesterol is solely in micellar solution; points above line ABC describe bile in which there are cholesterol crystals as well. (Reproduced, with permission, from Small: Gallstones. New England J Med 279:588, 1968.)

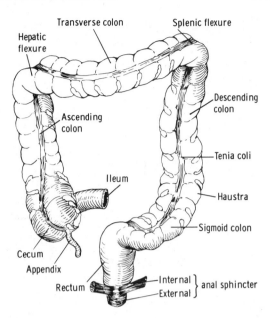

FIG 26—22. The human colon.

There are no villi on the mucosa. The colonic glands are short, inward projections of the mucosa that secrete mucus. Solitary lymph follicles are present, especially in the cecum and appendix.

Motility & Secretion of the Colon

The ileocecal valve is normally closed. Each time a peristaltic wave reaches it, it opens briefly, permitting some of the ileal chyme to squirt into the cecum. If the valve is resected in experimental animals, the chyme enters the colon so rapidly that absorption in the small intestine is reduced; however, a significant reduction does not occur in humans. When food leaves the stomach, the cecum relaxes and the passage of chyme through the ileocecal valve increases (**gastroileal reflex**). This is presumably a vagal reflex, although there is some argument about whether vagal stimulation affects the ileocecal valve. Sympathetic stimulation increases the tonic contraction of the valve.

The movements of the colon include intrinsic tonus changes and segmentation contractions like those occurring in the small intestine. These movements mix the contents of the colon and, by exposing more of the contents to the mucosa, facilitate absorption. Peristaltic waves propel the contents toward the rectum, although weak antiperistalsis is sometimes seen. **Mass movements**, very strong peristaltic rushes, occur 2—3 times a day. Like other peristaltic waves, the mass movements are initiated by local distention of the colon, are independent of extrinsic innervation, and do not occur if Auerbach's myenteric plexus is damaged. They effectively propel large amounts of the colonic contents for considerable distances. It normally takes 3—4 mass movements to propel colonic contents from ileum to rectum. However, they are not normally felt and are not directly related to defecation.

the bile is deconjugated by the action of the β-glucuronidase found in certain bacteria. The free bilirubin combines with calcium, and calcium bilirubinate is highly insoluble in bile. Cholesterol stones form when the proportions of cholesterol, lecithin, and bile salts in bile are altered. Cholesterol is normally present in bile in micelles made up of lecithin and bile salts, and relatively slight changes in bile composition lead to crystal formation (Fig 26—21). The crystals then gradually coalesce to form stones.

COLON

The main function of the colon is absorption of water, sodium, and other minerals, converting the 400—1500 ml of isotonic chyme entering it each day from the ileum to about 150 g of semisolid feces. Certain vitamins are also absorbed and some of them are synthesized by the large numbers of bacteria that grow in the colon.

Anatomic Considerations

The diameter of the colon is greater than that of the small intestine. The fibers of the external muscular layer are collected into 3 longitudinal bands, the **teniae coli**. Because these bands are shorter than the rest of the colon, the wall of the colon forms outpouchings (**haustra**) between the teniae (Fig 26—22).

The movements of the colon appear to be coordinated by a slow wave of the colon. The frequency of this wave, unlike the small intestine, increases from about 2/min at the ileocecal valve to 6/min at the sigmoid.

Mucus secretion by the colonic glands is stimulated by contact between the gland cells and the colonic contents. No hormonal or neural link is involved in the basic secretory response, although some additional secretion may be produced by local reflex responses via the pelvic and splanchnic nerves. No digestive enzymes are secreted in the colon.

Transit Time in the Small Intestine & Colon

The first part of a test meal reaches the cecum in about 4 hours, and all of the undigested portions have entered the colon in 8 or 9 hours. On the average, the first remnants of the meal reach the hepatic flexure in 6 hours, the splenic flexure in 9 hours, and the pelvic colon in 12 hours. From the pelvic colon to the anus, transport is much slower. As much as 25% of the residue of a test meal may still be in the rectum in 72 hours. When small colored beads are fed with a meal, an average of 70% of them are recovered in the stool in 72 hours; but total recovery requires more than a week.

Absorption in the Colon

The absorptive capacity of the mucosa of the large intestine is great. Na^+ is actively transported out of the colon, and water follows along the osmotic gradient thus generated. There is some net secretion of K^+ and HCO_3^- into the colon. The absorptive capacity of the colon makes rectal instillation a practical route for drug administration, especially in children. Many compounds, including anesthetics, sedatives, tranquilizers, and steroids, are absorbed rapidly by this route. Some of the water in an enema is absorbed, and if the volume of an enema is large, absorption may be rapid enough to cause water intoxication. Coma and death due to water intoxication have been reported following tap water enemas in children with megacolon.

Intestinal Bacteria

The chyme in the jejunum normally contains few if any bacteria. There are more organisms in the ileum, but it is only the colon that regularly contains large numbers of bacteria. The reason for the relative sterility of the jejunal contents is unsettled, although gastric acid and the comparatively rapid transit of the chyme through this region may inhibit bacterial growth.

The organisms present in the colon include not only bacilli such as *Escherichia coli* and *Enterobacter aerogenes* but also cocci of various types and organisms such as gas gangrene bacilli, which can cause serious disease in tissues outside the colon. Great masses of bacteria are passed in the stool. At birth the colon is sterile, but the intestinal bacterial flora becomes established early in life.

The effects of the intestinal bacteria on their host are complex, some being definitely beneficial and others possibly harmful.

Antibiotics improve growth rates in a variety of species, including man; and the addition of small amounts of antibiotics to the diets of domestic animals has become almost routine. Animals raised under sanitary but not germ-free conditions grow faster than controls. They assimilate food better, and do not require certain amino acids which are essential dietary constituents in other animals. They also have larger litters and a lower incidence of neonatal mortality.

The reason for the improved growth is unsettled. Nutritionally important substances such as ascorbic acid, cyanocobalamin, and choline are utilized by some intestinal bacteria. On the other hand, some enteric organisms synthesize vitamin K and a number of B complex vitamins. Appreciable quantities of the folic acid, biotin, vitamin K, and thiamine produced in the intestine were once thought to be absorbed. However, the experiments that led to this conclusion were largely performed on rats, and rats normally eat their own feces. When such coprophagy is prevented, only the folic acid produced by the bacteria can be shown to be absorbed in significant amounts.

The brown color of the stools is due to pigments formed from the bile pigments by the intestinal bacteria. When bile fails to enter the intestine, the stools become white (**acholic stools**). Bacteria produce some of the gases in the flatus (see above). Organic acids formed from carbohydrates by the bacteria are responsible for the slightly acid reaction of the stools (pH 5.0–7.0).

A number of amines, including such potentially toxic substances as histamine and tyramine, are formed in the colon by bacterial enzymes which decarboxylate amino acids. At one time, the symptoms seen in constipated patients were blamed on absorption of these amines, but this theory of "autointoxication" has now been thoroughly discredited. Other amines formed by the intestinal bacteria, especially indole and skatole, are responsible in large part for the odor of the feces.

Ammonia is also produced in the colon and absorbed. When the liver is diseased, the ammonia is not removed from the blood and severe neurologic symptoms result. In such individuals, removal of the colon or its isolation by anastomosing the ileum to the sigmoid has been reported to bring about remarkable improvement.

Adequate nutrition in herbivorous animals depends upon the action of gastrointestinal microorganisms that break down cellulose and related plant carbohydrates. In man, there is no appreciable digestion of these vegetable products. Cellulose, hemicellulose, and lignin in the diet are important components of the dietary **residue**, the material remaining after digestion and absorption. If the amount of residue is small, the diet is said to lack **bulk**. Since the amount of material in the colon is small, the colon is inactive and bowel movements are infrequent. So-called bulk laxatives work by providing a larger volume of indigestible material to the colon. It has been claimed that some individuals with chronic constipation have a greater than normal capacity to break down cellulose and related products, thus reducing the residue in their colons.

Work with animals raised from birth in a germ-free environment has uncovered further interesting data on the interaction between intestinal bacteria and their hosts. In germ-free guinea pigs, rats, and mice, the cecum becomes greatly enlarged, to the point where it may account for as much as 50% of the animal's weight. The cause of this cecal enlargement is not known.

When normal animals with the usual intestinal bacterial flora are exposed to ionizing radiation, the body defenses that prevent intestinal bacteria from invading the rest of the body break down, and a major cause of death in radiation poisoning is overwhelming sepsis. Germ-free animals have extremely hypoplastic lymphoid tissue and poorly developed immune mechanisms, probably because these mechanisms have never been challenged. However, they are much more resistant to radiation than animals with the usual intestinal flora because they have no intestinal bacteria to cause sepsis.

Blind Loop Syndrome

Overgrowth of bacteria within the intestinal lumen can cause definite harmful effects. Such overgrowth occurs when there is stasis of the contents of the small intestine, and it causes macrocytic anemia, malabsorption of cyanocobalamin (vitamin B_{12}), and steatorrhea. Because the condition is prominent in patients with surgically created blind intestinal loops, it has acquired the name **blind loop syndrome**; however, it can occur in any condition which promotes massive bacterial contamination of the small intestine. The cause of the anemia appears to be the cyanocobalamin deficiency, and the deficiency in cyanocobalamin absorption is probably due to uptake of ingested cyanocobalamin by the bacteria. The steatorrhea is probably due to excessive hydrolysis by the bacteria of conjugated bile salts. The important role of bile salts in fat digestion is discussed in Chapter 25.

Feces

The stools contain inorganic material, undigested plant fibers, bacteria, and water. Their composition (Table 26–10) is relatively unaffected by variations in diet because a large fraction of the fecal mass is of nondietary origin. This is also why appreciable amounts of feces continue to be passed during prolonged starvation.

Defecation

Distention of the rectum with feces initiates reflex contractions of its musculature and the desire to defecate. In man, the sympathetic nerve supply to the internal (involuntary) anal sphincter is excitatory, whereas the parasympathetic supply is inhibitory. This sphincter relaxes when the rectum is distended. The nerve supply to the striate muscle of the external anal sphincter comes from the pudendal nerve. The sphincter is maintained in a state of tonic contraction. It is

TABLE 26–10. Approximate composition of feces on an average diet.

	Percentage of Total Weight
Water	75
Solids	25

	Percentage of Total Solids
Cellulose and other indigestible fiber	Variable
Bacteria	30
Inorganic material (mostly calcium and phosphates)	15
Fat and fat derivatives	5

Also desquamated mucosal cells, mucus, and small amounts of digestive enzymes

relaxed by voluntary action, permitting the reflex contraction of the distended colon to expel the feces. Defecation is therefore a spinal reflex which can be voluntarily inhibited by keeping the external sphincter contracted, or facilitated by relaxing the sphincter and contracting the abdominal muscles (straining). Reflex evacuation of the distended rectum occurs in chronic spinal animals and humans if the sacral segments of the spinal cord are intact.

Distention of the stomach by food initiates contractions of the rectum and, frequently, a desire to defecate. This response is called the **gastrocolic reflex**, although there is some evidence that it is due to an action of gastrin on the colon and is not neurally mediated. Because of the response, defecation after meals is the rule in children. In adults, habit and cultural factors play a large role in determining when defecation occurs.

Effects of Colectomy

Humans can survive after total removal of the colon if fluid and electrolyte balance is maintained. When total colectomy is performed, the ileum is brought out through the abdominal wall (**ileostomy**) and the chyme expelled from the ileum is collected in a plastic bag fastened around the opening. If the diet is carefully regulated, the volume of ileal discharge decreases and its consistency increases over a period of time, but care of an ileostomy is at best a time-consuming, difficult job.

Constipation

In bowel-conscious America, the amount of misinformation and undue apprehension about constipation probably exceeds that about any other health topic. Patients with persistent constipation, and particularly those with a recent change in bowel habits, should of course be examined carefully to rule out underlying organic disease. However, many normal humans defecate only once every 2–3 days, even though others defecate once a day and some as often as 3 times a day. Furthermore, the only symptoms caused by constipation are slight anorexia and mild abdominal discomfort and distention. These symptoms are not due to absorption of "toxic substances" because they are promptly relieved by evacuating the rectum and can be reproduced experimentally by distending the rectum with inert material. Other symptoms attributed by laymen to constipation are due to anxiety or other causes.

Megacolon

The lack of harmful effects of infrequent bowel movements per se is emphasized by the relative absence for months and even years of symptoms other than abdominal distention, anorexia, and lassitude in children with **aganglionic megacolon** (Hirschsprung's disease). This disease is due to congenital absence of the ganglion cells in both the myenteric and submucous plexuses of a segment of the distal colon. The substance P content of the segment is low. Feces pass the aganglionic region with difficulty, and children with the disease may defecate as infrequently as once every 3 weeks. The condition can be cured if the agan-

glionic region is resected and the portion of the colon above it is anastomosed to the rectum.

About 40% of patients with megacolon have dilated bladders, and 4% have dilated ureters (**megalo-ureters**), which suggests that some deficiency of the parasympathetic nerve supply to the urinary tract is associated with the intestinal abnormality. A few cases of aganglionic megacolon in which symptoms first developed in adulthood have been reported. In these cases, the loss of ganglion cells was presumably not a congenital defect but an acquired abnormality of unknown cause.

Diarrhea

Severe diarrhea is debilitating and can be fatal, especially in infants. Large amounts of sodium, potassium, and water are washed out of the colon and the small intestine in the diarrheal stools, causing dehydration, hypovolemia, and, eventually, shock and cardiovascular collapse. A more insidious complication of chronic diarrhea, if fluid balance is maintained, is severe hypokalemia.

● ● ●

References: Section V.
Gastrointestinal Function

Botelho SY, Brooks FP, Shelley WB: *The Exocrine Glands.* Univ of Pennsylvania Press, 1970.

Brady JV: Behavior and physiological change: A comparative approach to the experimental analysis of some psychosomatic problems. Tr New York Acad Sc III 26:483, 1964.

Christensen RR: The controls of gastrointestinal movements: Some old and new views. New England J Med 285:85, 1971.

Crichton RR: Ferritin: Structure, synthesis and function. New England J Med 284:1413, 1971.

Davenport HW: *Physiology of the Digestive Tract,* 3rd ed. Year Book, 1971.

Dubos R, Schaedler RW: The digestive tract as an ecosystem. Tr A Am Physicians 77:110, 1964.

Gardner JD, Brown MS, Laster L: The columnar epithelial cell of the small intestine: Digestion and transport. New England J Med 283:1196, 1970.

Grossman MI: Gastrointestinal hormones. Viewpoints on Digestive Diseases. Vol 2, No. 3, May 1970.

Grossman MI: Integration of neural and hormonal control of gastric secretion. The Physiologist 6:349, 1963.

Kretchmer N: Lactose and lactase. Scientific American 227:70, October 1972.

Sachs G, Heinz E, Ullrich KJ (editors). *Gastric Secretion.* Academic Press, 1972.

Schmid R: Bilirubin metabolism in man. New England J Med 287:703, 1972.

Schultz SG, Curran PF: Coupled transport of sodium and organic solutes. Physiol Rev 50:637, 1970.

Smyth DH (editor): Intestinal absorption. Brit Med Bull 23:3, 1967.

Truelove SC: Movements of the large intestine. Physiol Rev 46:457, 1966.

Symposium: Structure and function of a digestive absorptive surface. Fed Proc 28:5, 1969.

Symposium: Nutritional and biochemical aspects of host-microflora interaction. Fed Proc 30:1772, 1971.

VI. Circulation

27...

Circulating Body Fluids

THE CIRCULATORY SYSTEM

The circulatory system is the transport system that supplies substances absorbed from the gastrointestinal tract and O_2 to the tissues, returns CO_2 to the lungs and other products of metabolism to the kidneys, functions in the regulation of body temperature, and distributes hormones and other agents that regulate cell function. The blood, the carrier of these substances, is pumped through a closed system of blood vessels by the heart, which in mammals is really 2 pumps in series with each other. From the left ventricle, blood is pumped through the arteries and arterioles to the capillaries, where the blood equilibrates with the interstitial fluid. The capillaries drain through venules into the veins and back to the right atrium. This is the **major** (or **systemic**) circulation. From the right atrium, blood flows to the right ventricle, which pumps it through the vessels of the lungs—the **lesser** (or **pulmonary**) **circulation**—and the left atrium to the left ventricle. In the pulmonary capillaries, the blood equilibrates with the O_2 and CO_2 in the alveolar air. Some tissue fluids enter another system of closed vessels, the lymphatics, which drain lymph via the thoracic duct and the right lymphatic duct into the venous system (the **lymphatic circulation**). The circulation is controlled by multiple regulatory systems which function in general to maintain adequate capillary blood flow—when possible, in all organs, but particularly in the heart and brain.

BLOOD

The cellular elements of the blood—white blood cells, red blood cells, and platelets—are suspended in the plasma. The normal total circulating blood volume is about 8% of the body weight, or 5600 ml in a 70 kg man. About 55% of this volume is plasma.

BONE MARROW

In the adult, red blood cells, many white blood cells, and platelets are formed in the bone marrow (Fig 27–1). In the fetus, blood cells are also formed in the liver and spleen, and in adults such **extramedullary hematopoiesis** may occur in diseases in which the bone marrow becomes destroyed or fibrosed. In children, blood cells are actively produced in the marrow cavities of all the bones. By age 20, the marrow in the cavities of the long bones, except for the upper humerus and femur, has become inactive (Fig 27–2). Active cellular marrow is called **red marrow**; inactive marrow that is infiltrated with fat is called **yellow marrow.**

The bone marrow is actually one of the largest organs in the body, approaching the size and weight of the liver. It is also one of the most active. Normally, 75% of the cells in the marrow belong to the white blood cell-producing myeloid series and only 25% are maturing red cells, even though there are over 500 times as many red cells in the circulation as there are white cells. This difference in the marrow probably reflects the fact that the average life span of white cells is short, whereas that of red cells is long.

WHITE BLOOD CELLS

In man there are normally 4000–11,000 white blood cells per μl of blood (Table 27–1). Of these, the **granulocytes**, or **polymorphonuclear leukocytes (PMNs)**, are the most numerous. Young granulocytes have horseshoe-shaped nuclei that become multilobed as the cells grow older. Most of them contain neutrophilic granules (**neutrophils**), but a few contain granules that stain with acid dyes (**eosinophils**) and some have basophilic granules (**basophils**). The other 2 cell types found normally in peripheral blood are **lymphocytes,** cells with large, round nuclei and scanty cytoplasm; and **monocytes,** cells with abundant agranular cytoplasm and kidney-shaped nuclei (Fig 27–1).

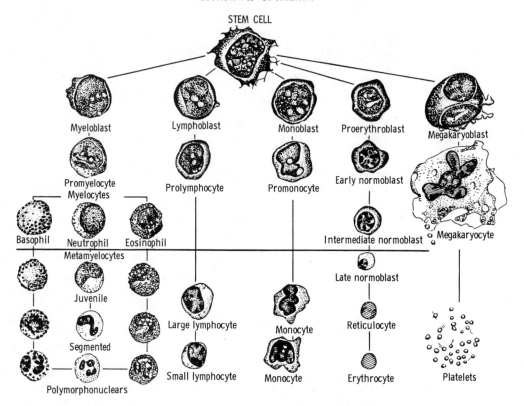

STEM CELL

FIG 27–1. The development of the various formed elements of the blood from bone marrow cells. Cells below the horizontal line, except for the late normoblast, may be found in normal peripheral blood. (Reproduced, with permission, from Whitby & Britton: *Disorders of the Blood,* 10th ed. Churchill, 1969.)

Functions & Life Cycle of Granulocytes

Neutrophils, eosinophils, and basophils are formed from stem cells in the bone marrow. All granulocytes contain histamine and the enzyme **peroxidase.** In the neutrophils, some of the granules are lysosomes that function in the digestion of material taken into the cells by phagocytosis. Phagocytosis and disposal of the ingested material in neutrophils has been shown to be an energy-requiring process that is associated with a marked stimulation of leukocyte respiration and glucose metabolism via the hexosemonophosphate shunt. The basophils contain heparin, but their role in

the maintenance of normal balance between the clotting and anticlotting systems (see below) is uncertain. The eosinophils apparently phagocytize antigen-antibody complexes, and the circulating eosinophil level is often elevated in patients with allergic diseases.

The number of neutrophils in the bone marrow is large relative to the number in the circulation. Those that enter the circulation and remain there throughout their life span survive about 30 hours. Senescent cells

FIG 27–2. Changes in red bone marrow cellularity with age. 100% equals degree of cellularity at birth. (Reproduced, with permission, from Whitby & Britton: *Disorders of the Blood,* 10th ed. Churchill, 1969.)

TABLE 27–1. Normal values for the cellular elements in human blood.

	Cells/μl (average)	Approximate Normal Range	Percentage of Total White Cells
Total WBC	9000	4000–11,000	. . .
Granulocytes			
Neutrophils	5400	3000–6000	50–70
Eosinophils	275	150–300	1–4
Basophils	35	0–100	0.4
Lymphocytes	2750	1500–4000	20–40
Monocytes	540	300–600	2–8
Erythrocytes			
Females	4.8×10^6	. . .	. . .
Males	5.4×10^6	. . .	. . .
Platelets	300,000	200,000–500,000	. . .

are presumably phagocytized by the cells of the reticuloendothelial system. However, many leave the circulation, and those that leave do not return; consequently, the average stay of a neutrophil in the circulation is about 7 hours. Many of those that leave the circulation enter the gastrointestinal tract and are lost from the body.

When bacteria invade the body, the bone marrow is stimulated to produce and to release large numbers of neutrophils. Bacterial products interact with plasma factors to attract these phagocytic cells to the infected area (**chemotaxis**), and the cells insinuate themselves through the walls of the capillaries to reach the infected tissues (**diapedesis**). Other plasma factors act on the bacteria to make them "tasty" to the phagocytes (**opsonization**). The neutrophils then ingest the bacteria (**phagocytosis**), and the phagocytic vesicles thus formed fuse with lysosomes (**degranulation**). Hydrogen peroxide is generated in the phagocytic vesicles, and the bacteria are killed. Phagocytosis by the neutrophils is the first line of defense against invading bacteria. Monocytes also invade areas of infection and are phagocytic, but they follow the neutrophils into the area and constitute a second line of defense.

It is worth noting that the number of circulating granulocytes is regulated with precision. In health, the number is held at a constant level; and when infection occurs, the number in the blood rises dramatically and rapidly. Granulocyte release from the bone marrow appears to be increased by a circulating factor in the blood, and another factor appears to regulate the multiplication of granulocyte precursors in the bone marrow. However, there is much that is still unknown about the regulation of granulocytopoiesis.

Lymphocytes

Some lymphocytes are formed in the bone marrow, but most are formed in the lymph nodes, thymus, and spleen from stem cells that originally come from the bone marrow. Lymphocytes enter the blood stream for the most part via the lymphatics. It has been calculated that, in man, 3.5×10^{10} lymphocytes per day enter the circulation via the thoracic duct alone; however, this count includes cells which reenter the lymphatics and thus traverse the thoracic duct more than once. There are large and small lymphocytes in the lymph nodes and blood. The large lymphocytes are probably simply the precursors of the small lymphocytes. The small lymphocytes contain the antibodies responsible for delayed hypersensitivity reactions. Their role in immune reactions is discussed below and in Chapter 24. The effects of adrenocortical hormones on the lymphoid organs, the circulating lymphocytes, and the granulocytes are discussed in Chapter 20.

Monocytes

The monocytes, like neutrophilic leukocytes, are actively phagocytic, but like lymphocytes they do not contain peroxidase. They invade areas of inflammation soon after the neutrophils and, by active phagocytosis, help remove bacteria and debris.

The Reticuloendothelial System

The phagocytes in the bone marrow and lymph nodes, together with those lining the sinusoids of the liver and spleen and the macrophages in the other tissues, are called collectively the **reticuloendothelial system**. The phagocytes in the liver sinusoids are called **Kupffer cells**. Reticuloendothelial cells ingest colloidal foreign particles and destroy old white and red blood cells.

PLATELETS

The platelets are small, granulated bodies $2-4$ μm in diameter (Fig 27–1). There are about $300,000/\mu$l of circulating blood. The **megakaryocytes,** giant cells in the bone marrow, form platelets by pinching off bits of cytoplasm and extruding them into the circulation. Platelet granules contain large amounts of serotonin, epinephrine, ADP, calcium, potassium, several clotting factors, various enzymes, and other less well characterized biologically active substances. When blood vessel walls are injured, platelets adhere to the site of injury. Adhesion is followed by the release, or more accurately, the secretion of the materials contained in the granules of the platelets. The serotonin and epinephrine probably assist in the vasoconstriction produced at the site of injury, and these amines plus ADP promote release of granule contents from other platelets. The ADP makes the platelets sticky and causes more platelets to aggregate, forming the hemostatic plug (see below). Platelet aggregation is an a-adrenergic reaction in that it is blocked by a-adrenergic blocking drugs and inhibited by cyclic AMP (see Chapter 17).

Platelet production is regulated by a circulating substance called **thrombopoietin** which increases the formation of megakaryocytes and their development. However, the origin and nature of the thrombopoietin are unknown.

RED BLOOD CELLS

The red blood cells, or **erythrocytes,** carry hemogloblin in the circulation. They are biconcave disks (Fig 27–3) that are manufactured in the bone marrow. In mammals they lose their nuclei before entering the circulation. In man, they survive in the circulation for an average of 120 days. The average normal red blood cell count is 5.4 million cells/μl in men and 4.8 million/μl in women. Each human red blood cell is about 7.5 μm in diameter and 2 μm thick, and each contains approximately 29 pg of hemoglobin (Table 27–2). There are thus about 3×10^{13} red blood cells and about 900 g of hemoglobin in the circulating blood of an adult man (Fig 27–4).

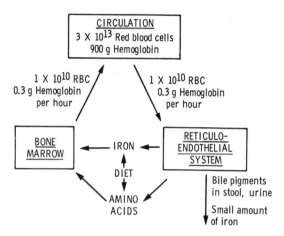

FIG 27–4. Red cell formation and destruction.

Fig 27–3. Human red blood cells and fibrin fibrils. Blood was placed on a polyvinyl chloride surface, then fixed and photographed, using a scanning electron microscope. Reduced from ×2590. (Courtesy of NF Rodman.)

Erythropoiesis

The formation of red blood cells (**erythropoiesis**), is subject to a feedback control. It is inhibited by a rise in the circulating red cell level to supernormal values and stimulated by anemia. It is also stimulated by hypoxia, and an increase in the number of circulating red cells is a prominent feature of acclimatization to altitude (see Chapter 37). Erythropoiesis is controlled by a circulating glycoprotein hormone called **erythropoietin**, which is probably formed by the action of a renal factor on a globulin in plasma (see Chapter 24). This hormone promotes the differentiation of certain stem cells into proerythroblasts.

Osmotic Fragility

Red blood cells, like other cells, shrink in solutions with an osmotic pressure greater than that of normal plasma. In solutions with a lower osmotic pressure they swell, becoming spherical rather than disk-shaped, and eventually lose their hemoglobin (**hemolysis**). The hemoglobin of hemolyzed red cells dissolves in the plasma, coloring it red. A 0.9% sodium chloride solution is isotonic with plasma. Normal red cells begin to hemolyze when suspended in 0.48% saline, and in 0.33% saline hemolysis is complete. In **hereditary spherocytosis** (congenital hemolytic icterus), the cells are spherocytic in normal plasma and hemolyze more readily than normal cells in hypotonic sodium chloride solutions (**abnormal red cell fragility**).

Hemoglobin

The red, oxygen-carrying pigment in the red blood cells of vertebrates is **hemoglobin**, a protein with a molecular weight of 64,450. Hemoglobin is a globular molecule made up of 4 subunits (Fig 27–5). Each subunit contains a **heme** moiety conjugated to a polypeptide. Heme is an iron-containing porphyrin derivative (Fig 27–6). The polypeptides are referred to collectively as the **globin** portion of the hemoglobin

TABLE 27–2. Characteristics of human red cells.* Cells with MCVs > 95 are called macrocytes; cells with MCVs < 80 are called microcytes; cells with MCHs < 25 are called hypochromic.

		Male	Female
Hematocrit (Hct) (%)		47	42
Red blood cells (RBC) (millions/μl)		5.4	4.8
Hemoglobin (Hb) (g/100 ml)		16	14
Mean corpuscular volume (MCV) (fl)	$= \dfrac{\text{Hct} \times 10}{\text{RBC } (10^6/\mu l)}$	87	87
Mean corpuscular hemoglobin (MCH) (pg)	$= \dfrac{\text{Hb} \times 10}{\text{RBC } (10^6/\mu l)}$	29	29
Mean corpuscular hemoglobin concentration (MCHC) (g/100 ml)	$= \dfrac{\text{Hb} \times 10}{\text{Hct}}$	34	34
Mean cell diameter (MCD) (μm)	$= \begin{array}{l}\text{Mean diameter of}\\ \text{500 cells in smear}\end{array}$	7.5	7.5

*Values are from Wintrobe: *Clinical Hematology*, 6th ed. Lea & Febiger, 1967.

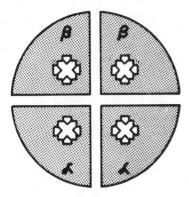

FIG 27–5. Diagrammatic representation of a molecule of hemoglobin A, showing the 4 subunits. There are 2 α and 2 β polypeptide chains, each containing a heme moiety.

molecule. There are 2 pairs of polypeptides in each hemoglobin molecule, 2 of the subunits containing one type of polypeptide and 2 containing another. In normal adult human hemoglobin (**hemoglobin A**), the 2 types of polypeptide are called the α chains, each of which contains 141 amino acid residues, and the β chains, each of which contains 146 amino acid residues. Not all the hemoglobin in the blood of normal adults is hemoglobin A. About 2.5% of the hemoglobin is hemoglobin A_2 in which β chains are replaced by δ chains. The δ chains also contain 146 amino acid residues, but 10 individual residues differ from those in the β chain.

Reactions of Hemoglobin

Hemoglobin binds O_2 to form **oxyhemoglobin**, O_2 attaching to the Fe^{++} in the heme. The affinity of hemoglobin for O_2 is affected by pH, temperature, and the concentration in the red cells of 2,3-diphospho-glycerate (2,3-DPG). 2,3-DPG and H^+ compete with O_2 for binding to deoxygenated hemoglobin, decreasing the affinity of hemoglobin for O_2. The details of the oxygenation and deoxygenation of hemoglobin and the physiologic role of these reactions in O_2 transport are discussed in Chapter 35. When blood is exposed to various drugs and other oxidizing agents in vitro or in vivo, the ferrous iron (Fe^{++}) in the molecule is converted to ferric iron (Fe^{+++}), forming **methemoglobin.** Methemoglobin is dark-colored, and when it is present in large quantities in the circulation it causes a dusky discoloration of the skin resembling cyanosis (see Chapter 37). Some oxidation of hemoglobin to methemoglobin occurs normally, but an enzyme system in the red cells, the NADH-methemoglobin reductase system, converts methemoglobin back to hemoglobin. Congenital absence of this system is one cause of hereditary methemoglobinemia.

Carbon monoxide reacts with hemoglobin to form **carbonmonoxyhemoglobin (carboxyhemoglobin).** The affinity of hemoglobin for O_2 is much less than its affinity for carbon monoxide, and carbon monoxide consequently displaces O_2 on hemoglobin, reducing the oxygen-carrying capacity of blood (see Chapter 37).

Heme is also part of the structure of **myoglobin,** an oxygen-binding pigment found in red, or slow, muscles (see Chapter 3) and in the respiratory enzyme, **cytochrome c** (see Chapter 17). Porphyrins other than that found in heme play a role in the pathogenesis of a number of metabolic diseases (congenital and acquired porphyria, etc).

Hemoglobin in the Fetus

The blood of the human fetus normally contains **fetal hemoglobin (hemoglobin F).** Its structure is similar to that of hemoglobin A except that the β chains are replaced by γ chains. The γ chains also contain 146 amino acid residues but have 37 that differ from those

FIG 27–6. Chemistry of hemoglobin. The hemoglobin molecule is made up of 4 of the units shown on the left. The abbreviations M, V, and P stand for the groups shown on the molecule on the left.

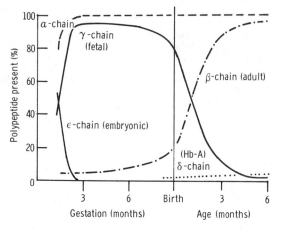

FIG 27—7. Development of human hemoglobin chains. (Reproduced, with permission, from Huehns ER & others: Human embryonic hemoglobin. Cold Spring Harbor Symp Quant Biol 29:327, 1964.)

in the β chain. Fetal hemoglobin is normally replaced by adult hemoglobin soon after birth (Fig 27—7). In certain individuals, it fails to disappear and persists throughout life. In the body, its O_2 content at a given P_{O_2} is greater than that of adult hemoglobin because it binds 2,3-DPG less avidly. This facilitates movement of O_2 from the maternal to the fetal circulation (see Chapter 32). In young embryos there is, in addition, Gower 2 or embryonic hemoglobin, in which the β chains are replaced by ϵ chains.

Abnormal Hemoglobins

The amino acid sequences in the polypeptide chains of hemoglobin are genetically determined. Mutant genes which cause the production of abnormal hemoglobins are widespread, and many abnormal hemoglobins have been described in humans. They are usually identified by letter—hemoglobin C, E, I, J, S,

etc. In most instances, the abnormal hemoglobins differ from normal hemoglobin A in the structure of the polypeptide chains. For example, in hemoglobin S, the a chains are normal but the β chains are abnormal because among the 146 amino acid residues in each β polypeptide chain one glutamic acid residue has been replaced by a valine residue (Table 27—3).

When an abnormal gene inherited from one parent dictates formation of an abnormal hemoglobin—ie, when the individual is heterozygous—half of his circulating hemoglobin is abnormal and half is normal. When identical abnormal genes are inherited from both parents, the individual is homozygous and all of his hemoglobin is abnormal. It is theoretically possible to inherit 2 different abnormal hemoglobins, one from the father and one from the mother. Studies of the inheritance and geographic distribution of abnormal hemoglobins have made it possible in some cases to decide where the mutant gene originated and approximately how long ago the mutation occurred. In general, mutations which are harmful tend to die out, but mutant genes which endow individuals with traits that have survival value persist and spread in the population.

Clinical Implications

Many of the abnormal hemoglobins are harmless. However, some cause anemia. For example, hemoglobin S is very insoluble at low O_2 tensions, and this causes the red cells to become sickle-shaped. These abnormal sickle cells hemolyze, producing the severe anemia known as **sickle cell anemia**. Those who are heterozygous have the **sickle cell trait** and rarely have severe symptoms, but those who are homozygous develop the full-blown disease. The sickle cell gene is an example of a gene that has persisted and spread in the population. It originated in the Negro population in Africa, and it confers resistance to one type of malaria. This is an important benefit in Africa, and in some parts of Africa 40% of the population have the sickle cell trait. In the American black population, its incidence is about 10%.

TABLE 27—3. Partial amino acid composition of normal human β chain, and some hemoglobins with abnormal β chains. Other hemoglobins have abnormal a chains. Hemoglobins which are very similar electrophoretically but still differ slightly in composition are indicated by the same letter with a subscript indicating the geographic location where they were first discovered; hence, $M_{Saskatoon}$ and $M_{Milwaukee}$.

Hemoglobin	Positions on β Polypeptide Chain of Hemoglobin							
	1 2 3	6	7	26	63	67	121	146
A (normal)	Val-His-Leu	Glu	Glu	Glu	His	Val	Glu	His
S (sickle cell)		Val						
C		Lys						
G$_{San Jose}$			Gly					
E				Lys				
M$_{Saskatoon}$					Tyr			
M$_{Milwaukee}$						Glu		
O$_{Arabia}$							Lys	

Heme

Opening of porphyrin ring between I and II
and elimination of a methylene carbon and iron.

$-Fe^{++}$

Biliverdin $(C_{33}H_{34}O_6N_4)$

$+ Fe$

Bilirubin $(C_{33}H_{36}O_6N_4)$

FIG 27—8. Catabolism of heme. The abbreviations M, V, and P stand for the groups shown on the molecule on the left in Fig 27—6.

Other hemoglobins have abnormal O_2 equilibriums. In the various forms of M hemoglobin, for example, the structural abnormality causes the heme iron in 25% or less of the hemoglobin to be oxidized, with the production of congenital methemoglobinemia. In other abnormal hemoglobins, the affinity for O_2 is increased, in some instances possibly because the structural change prevents the binding of 2,3-DPG (see Chapter 35). The resultant mild hypoxia leads to a chronic elevation in the red cell count (**erythrocytosis**).

Synthesis of Hemoglobin

The average normal hemoglobin content of blood is 16 g/100 ml in men and 14 g/100 ml in women, all of it in red cells. In the body of a 70 kg man there are about 900 g of hemoglobin, and 0.3 g of hemoglobin are destroyed and 0.3 g synthesized every hour (Fig 27—4). The heme portion of the hemoglobin molecule is synthesized from glycine and succinyl-Co A.

Catabolism of Hemoglobin

When old red blood cells are destroyed in the reticuloendothelial system, the globin portion of the hemoglobin molecule is split off and the heme is converted to **biliverdin** (Fig 27—8). In man, most of the biliverdin formed from heme is converted to **bilirubin**. The bilirubin is excreted in the bile (see Chapter 26). The iron from the heme is reused for hemoglobin synthesis. Iron is essential for hemoglobin synthesis; if blood is lost from the body and the iron deficiency is not corrected, **iron deficiency anemia** results. The metabolism of iron is discussed in Chapter 25.

BLOOD TYPES

The membranes of human red cells contain a variety of polysaccharide antigens called **agglutinogens**. The most important and best known of these are the A, B, and O agglutinogens, and individuals are divided into 4 major **blood types**, types A, B, AB, and O, on the basis of the agglutinogens present in their red cells. There are A, B, and O antigens in many tissues other than blood. They have been found in salivary glands, saliva, pancreas, kidney, liver, lungs, testes, semen, and amniotic fluid. Individuals with type A blood (ie, those who have agglutinogen A in their red cells) always have an appreciable titer in their plasma of an antibody against agglutinogen B called the β or anti-B **agglutinin**. When their plasma is mixed with type B cells, the agglutinins and the B cell agglutinogens react, causing the type B cells to become clumped (**agglutinated**) and subsequently hemolyzed (Fig 27—9). Similarly, individuals with type B blood have a circulating titer of an a or anti-A agglutinin. Individuals with type O blood have circulating anti-A and anti-B agglutinins, and those with type AB blood have no circulating agglutinins. The O agglutinogen is a very weak antigen and there is usually no circulating anti-O agglutinin, although in rare cases it may appear after repeated trans-

"A" cells in
"A" plasma

"B" cells in
"A" plasma

FIG 27—9. Red cell agglutination in incompatible plasma.

fusions of O cells. Some individuals have a variant of the A agglutinogen called A_2, and so A "proper" is often called A_1. Therefore, there are actually 6 ABO groups instead of 4: B, O, A_1, A_2, A_1B, and A_2B.

Transfusion Reactions

Dangerous **hemolytic transfusion reactions** occur when blood is transfused into an individual with an incompatible blood type, ie, an individual who has agglutinins against the red cells in the transfusion (Fig 27—9). The plasma in the transfusion is usually so diluted in the recipient that it rarely causes agglutination even when the titer of agglutinins against the recipient's cells is high. However, when the recipient's plasma has agglutinins against the donor's red cells, the cells agglutinate and hemolyze. Free hemoglobin is liberated into the plasma. The severity of the resulting transfusion reaction may vary from an asymptomatic minor rise in the plasma bilirubin level to severe jaundice and renal tubular damage (caused in some way by the products liberated from hemolyzed cells), with anuria and death.

Incompatibilities in the ABO blood group system are summarized in Table 27—4. Persons with type AB blood are sometimes called "universal recipients" because they have no circulating agglutinins and can be given blood of any type without developing a transfusion reaction due to ABO incompatibility. Con-

versely, type O individuals are sometimes called "universal donors" because there are no regular anti-O agglutinins and type O blood can therefore usually be given to anyone without producing a transfusion reaction due to ABO incompatibility. This does not mean, however, that blood should ever be transfused without being cross-matched except in the most extreme emergencies; the possibility of reactions or sensitization due to incompatibilities other than those due to ABO must be constantly kept in mind.

Inheritance of A, B, & O Antigens

The A_1, A_2, B, and O antigens are inherited as mendelian allelomorphs, A_1, A_2, and B being dominants. For example, an individual with type B blood may have inherited 2 B antigens or a B antigen from one parent and an O from the other; thus, an individual whose **phenotype** is B may have the **genotype** BB and be **homozygous** or the **genotype** BO and be **heterozygous.**

When the blood types of the parents are known, the possible genotypes of their children can be stated. For example, when both parents are type B, they could have children with genotype BB (B antigen from both parents), BO (B antigen from one parent, O from the other heterozygous parent), or OO (O antigen from both parents, both being heterozygous). When the blood types of a mother and her child are known, it is possible to state whether a man of a given blood type could or could not have been the father. This fact has obvious medicolegal importance in paternity cases. It should probably be emphasized that typing can only prove that a man is not the father, not that he is the father. The predictive value of such determinations is increased if the blood typing of the parties concerned includes identification of antigens other than the ABO agglutinogens.

Other Agglutinogens

In addition to the 6 antigens of the ABO system in human red cells, there are numerous other agglutinogen systems containing many individual antigens in red cells. Those which were known in 1959 are listed in

TABLE 27—4. Summary of ABO blood system.* Type O and type B individuals uniformly have antibodies that are active against the A_1 antigen in their plasma, but their anti-A_2 titer is variable and often low. Therefore, A_2 cells have been left out of the last column, even though they might be agglutinated in some instances.

Blood Type	Agglutinins in Plasma	Frequency in USA (%)	Plasma Agglutinates Red Cells of Type
O	Anti-A_1, anti-B	45	A_1, A_1B, B, A_2B
A_1	Anti-B	41	B, A_1B, A_2B
A_2			B, A_1B, A_2B
B	Anti-A_1	10	A_1, A_1B
A_1B	None	4	None
A_2B			

*Modified from Ham: *A Syllabus of Laboratory Examinations in Clinical Diagnosis.* Harvard Univ Press, 1953.

TABLE 27–5. Blood group factors (November, 1959).*

Blood Group Antigens	Numbers of Pheno-types in Each System	Theoretically Possible Number of Phenotype Combinations (Cumulative)
A_1, A_2, B, O	6	6(A_1, A_2, B, O, A_1B, A_2B)
M, N, S, s, Hu, He, Mi^a, Vw, U, Mg, Vr	98	588
P, Tj^a, Pk	4	2352
C, c, C^w, C^x, D, E, e, E^w, f, G, rh_i, Hr_o, V (The Rh system)	110	258,720
Lu^a, Lu^b (Lutheran)	3	776,160
K, k, Kp^a, Kp^b, Ku (Kell)	7	5,433,120
Le^a, Le^b (Lewis)	3	16,299,360
Fy^a, Fy^b (Duffy)	4	65,197,440
Jk^a, Jk^b (Kidd)	4	260,789,760
Unclassified Group (Levay, Vel, Ven, Wr^a, Be^a, Rm, By, Yt^a, Js, Di^a, I)	2048	> 500 billion

*Modified and reproduced, with permission, from Page & Culver: *A Syllabus of Laboratory Examinations in Clinical Diagnosis.* Harvard Univ Press, 1960.

Table 27–5. The list has now grown to 9 major and 24 minor antigen systems. Thus, there are well over 500 billion possible known blood group phenotypes, and other undiscovered antigens undoubtedly exist. This suggests that in the future it may be possible to identify people by their blood types in the way they now are identified by their fingerprints.

Agglutinins against the Rh antigens occur only in individuals who lack a particular antigen and develop the antibodies as an immune response when they are exposed to red cells containing the antigen.

Agglutinins against the other antigens are sometimes found without a history of sensitization by previous transfusions, but in general anti-A and anti-B are the only agglutinins that occur in high titer without sensitization. Transfusion reactions due to incompatibility in other systems can be avoided by routinely cross-matching blood before transfusion (see below).

The Rh Group

Aside from the antigens of the ABO system, those of the Rh system are of the greatest clinical importance. The "Rh factor," named for the rhesus monkey because it was first studied in the blood of this animal, is actually a system made up of 13 antigens (Table 27–5). Of these, D is by far the most antigenic, and the term "Rh positive" as it is generally used means that the individual has agglutinogen D. The "Rh-negative" individual has no D antigen and forms the anti-D agglutinin when injected with D-positive cells. The Rh typing serum used in routine blood typing is anti-D serum. Eighty-five percent of Caucasians are D-positive and 15% are D-negative, although over 99% of Orientals are D-positive. D-negative individuals who have received a transfusion of D-positive blood (even years previously) can have appreciable anti-D titers and thus may develop transfusion reactions when transfused again with D-positive blood.

Hemolytic Disease of the Newborn

Another complication due to "Rh incompatibility" arises when a D-negative mother carries a D-positive fetus. Small amounts of fetal blood regularly leak into the maternal circulation, and some mothers develop a titer of anti-D agglutinins. The mother's agglutinins then cross the placenta to the fetus, where they cause hemolysis and various forms of **hemolytic disease of the newborn (erythroblastosis fetalis).** If the hemolysis in the fetus is severe, the infant may die in utero or may develop anemia, severe jaundice, and edema **(hydrops fetalis). Kernicterus,** a neurologic syndrome in which bile pigments are deposited in the basal ganglia, may also develop, especially if birth is complicated by a period of hypoxia. Bile pigments do not enter the brain in the adult, but in the fetus and newborn infant the blood-brain barrier is not developed (see Chapter 32).

About 50% of D-negative individuals are sensitized (develop an anti-D titer) by a transfusion of D-positive blood. Only 5% of D-negative mothers are sensitized by carrying a D-positive fetus. Even in women who are sensitized during pregnancy, the first child is often normal. However, relatively large amounts of fetal blood enter the maternal circulation during delivery, and in subsequent pregnancies, hemolytic anemia is more likely to occur. Thus, the anti-D titer of a D-negative pregnant woman who has a D-positive husband should be checked frequently, but the overall chances of having an erythroblastotic child are low.

Erythroblastosis can also be due to incompatibility of C, E, Kell, Duffy, Lutheran, and Kidd factors, but such cases are rare. There are cases in which ABO incompatibility between the mother and the fetus (eg, a B fetus in an A mother) has caused hemolytic disease, but such transplacental sensitization is rarely a serious problem.

Blood Typing & Cross-Matching

In routine blood typing, tests are made only for the A, B, O, and D antigens by mixing the individual's cells with appropriate high titer anti-A, anti-B, and anti-D testing sera. When transfusions are to be given it is absolutely essential, except in the direst emergency, to also **cross-match** the blood of the donor and the recipient by mixing donor cells with recipient plasma or serum on a slide and observing for agglutination (Fig 27—9). It is probably advisable also to check the action of the donor's plasma on the recipient's cells even though, as noted above, this is rarely a source of trouble. Cross-matching is an important check on errors in typing and detects incompatibilities in other systems than the ABO and Rh systems. These incompatibilities can cause fatal transfusion reactions.

PLASMA

The fluid portion of the blood, the **plasma,** is a remarkable solution containing an immense number of ions, inorganic molecules, and organic molecules which are in transit to various parts of the body or which aid in the transport of other substances. The normal plasma volume is about 5% of body weight, or roughly 3500 ml in a 70 kg man. Plasma clots on standing, remaining fluid only if an anticoagulant is added. If whole blood is allowed to clot and the clot is removed, the remaining fluid is called **serum.** Serum has essentially the same composition as plasma, except that its fibrinogen and clotting factors II, V, and VIII (Table 27—7) have been removed, and it has a higher serotonin content because of the breakdown of platelets during clotting. The normal plasma levels of various substances are discussed in the chapters on the systems with which the substances are concerned, and summarized for convenience on the inside back cover.

Plasma Proteins

The plasma proteins are usually divided into **albumin, globulin,** and **fibrinogen** fractions. The globulin fraction is subdivided into numerous components. One classification divides it into a_1, a_2, β_1, β_2, and γ globulins and fibrinogen. Protein fractions can be separated and characterized by their relative speed of sedimentation in the ultracentrifuge. Electrophoresis is another technic for separating protein fractions. In this process, protein solutions in appropriate buffered solvents are placed on a medium such as paper or starch blocks and exposed to an electric current. Because of differences in electrical charge, the protein components migrate toward the anode or cathode at different rates. The molecular weights and configurations of several of the plasma proteins are shown in Fig 27—10.

The capillary walls are for the most part impermeable to the proteins in plasma, and the proteins therefore exert an osmotic force of about 25 mm Hg across the capillary wall (**oncotic pressure;** see Chapter 1) that tends to pull water into the blood. The plasma proteins are also responsible for 15% of the buffering capacity of the blood (see Chapter 35) because of the weak ionization of their substituent —COOH and —NH₂ groups. At the normal plasma pH of 7.40, the proteins are mostly in the anionic form (see Chapter 1) and constitute a significant part of the anionic complement of plasma. Plasma proteins such as

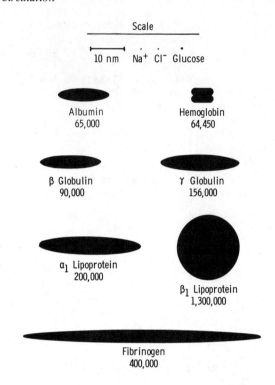

Scale

10 nm   Na⁺ Cl⁻ Glucose

Albumin
65,000

Hemoglobin
64,450

β Globulin
90,000

γ Globulin
156,000

a_1 Lipoprotein
200,000

β_1 Lipoprotein
1,300,000

Fibrinogen
400,000

FIG 27—10. Relative dimensions and molecular weights of some of the protein molecules in the blood. (After Oncley. Reproduced, with permission, from Harper: *Review of Physiological Chemistry,* 14th ed. Lange, 1973.)

the antibodies and the proteins concerned with blood clotting have specific functions. Some of the proteins function in the transport of thyroid, adrenocortical, and gonadal hormones. Binding keeps these hormones from being rapidly filtered through the glomeruli and provides a stable reservoir of hormones on which the tissues can draw. In addition, albumin serves as a carrier for metals, ions, fatty acids, amino acids, bilirubin, enzymes, and drugs.

Origin of Plasma Proteins

The circulating antibodies which are found in the γ globulin fraction of the plasma proteins are manufactured principally in the plasma cells of the reticuloendothelial system. The albumin fraction and the proteins concerned with blood clotting (fibrinogen, prothrombin) are manufactured in the liver. Data on the turnover of albumin provide an indication of the role played by synthesis in the maintenance of normal albumin levels. In a normal adult man, the plasma albumin level is 3.5—4.5 g/100 ml, and the total exchangeable albumin pool is 4.0—5.0 g/kg body weight; 38—45% of this albumin is intravascular, and much of the rest of it is in the skin. Six to 10% of the exchangeable pool is degraded per day, and the degraded albumin is replaced by hepatic synthesis of 120—200 mg/kg/day.

Hypoproteinemia

Plasma protein levels are maintained during starvation until body protein stores are markedly depleted; but in prolonged starvation and in the malabsorption syndrome due to intestinal diseases such as sprue, plasma protein levels are low (**hypoproteinemia**). They are also low in liver disease, because hepatic protein synthesis is depressed, and in nephrosis, because large amounts of albumin are lost in the urine. Because of the decrease in the plasma oncotic pressure, edema tends to develop (see Chapter 30). Rarely, there may be congenital absence of one or another plasma protein fraction. Examples of congenital protein deficiencies are **agammaglobulinemia**, a condition in which there is markedly lowered resistance to infections due to the absence of circulating antibodies; and the congenital form of **afibrinogenemia**, which is characterized by defective blood clotting.

IMMUNE MECHANISMS

Types

The 2 major types of immune mechanisms that respond to such foreign protein antigens as bacteria and foreign tissue are classified as humoral and cellular. **Humoral immunity** is immunity due to circulating antibodies in the γ globulin fraction of the plasma proteins. Immunoglobulins (Ig) of the type found in the a globulin fraction are also found in the secretions of the gastrointestinal tract and other external secretions such as tears and nasal mucus. The immunoglobulins are divided into 5 categories (Table 27–6). The basic unit of Ig structure is made up of 4 polypeptide chains: 2 shorter light chains and 2 longer heavy chains. The molecular weight of each light chain is approximately 25,000, and the molecular weight of each heavy chain is approximately 50,000. The form of IgA found in external secretions is a dimer made up of 2 of the units plus a connecting piece. IgM contains 5 of the units plus an additional piece of protein. The circulating antibodies are manufactured in the **plasma cells** in the reticuloendothelial system.

Cellular immunity is mediated via the small lymphocytes and is responsible for delayed allergic reactions, rejection of transplants from other individuals (see below), and graft-versus-host reactions. This form of immunity is dependent on the presence of the thymus in early life, whereas humoral immunity is not (see Chapter 24). In chickens, humoral immunity is abolished by removal of a lymphoid organ called the **bursa of Fabricius.** There is no comparable organ in mammals, but it has been suggested that Peyer's patches and related collections of lymphoid tissue in the gastrointestinal tract subserve the same function as the bursa. It appears that stem cells in the bone marrow differentiate in early life to form 2 distinct lymphocyte populations, one dependent on the thymus (T-lymphocytes) and the other independent of

the thymus (B-lymphocytes). The B-lymphocytes differentiate and mature into plasma cells.

When development of T-cells is defective—eg, in congenital aplasia of the thymus (DiGeorge's syndrome)—cellular immunity is deficient while humoral immunity is intact. When development of the B-cells is defective—eg, in X-linked agammaglobulinemia—the reverse is true. In certain other immunodeficiency disorders, both types of immunity are abnormal, presumably because of a defect in the lymphoid stem cell precursor of both the T- and the B-lymphocytes.

Tissue Incompatibility

When tissues such as skin or kidneys are transplanted from a donor to a recipient of the same species, the transplants "take" and function for a while but then become necrotic and are "rejected" because the recipient develops an immune response to the transplanted tissue. This is true even if the donor and recipient are close relatives, and the only transplants that are not rejected are those from an identical twin. The blood group antigens are found in some tissues, but their role in the rejection reactions must be minor. Unlike transfusion reactions, tissue incompatibility reactions are delayed rather than immediate. Practical methods to overcome the rejection of transplanted organs in humans are currently being developed. The transplant can be preserved by suppressing all immune responses with radiation and drugs, but this is hazardous. An antilymphocyte globulin prepared by immunizing animals with human lymphocytes is also used. This substance inhibits the lymphocytes responsible for cellular immune reactions. Additional technics are being sought.

TABLE 27–6. Human immunoglobulins.*

Immuno-globulin	Molecular Weight	Biologic Activity	Serum Concentration (μg/ml)
IgG	160,000	Major antibacterial and antiviral activity	12100
IgA	170,000	Antidiphtheria, antithyroid, etc	2600
	385,000†	Major Ig of external secretions	
IgM	900,000	Antipolysaccharide and initial antiprotein antibodies	930
IgD	180,000	Unknown	23
IgE	200,000	Reaginic antibodies involved in allergic diseases	0.5

*Data from Waldmann TA: Disorders of immunoglobulin metabolism. New England J Med 281:1170, 1969.

†In external secretions (tears, colostrum, gastrointestinal secretions, etc), IgA molecules exist as a dimer plus an additional piece of protein.

HEMOSTASIS

When a small blood vessel is transected or damaged, the injury initiates a series of events that leads to the formation of a clot. The end result of this process of **hemostasis** is generally a sealing off of the blood vessel and prevention of further blood loss. The initial event is constriction of the vessel and formation of a temporary hemostatic plug of platelets. This is followed by conversion of the plug into the definitive clot. The in vivo action of the clotting mechanism responsible for this conversion is balanced by limiting reactions that normally prevent clots from developing in uninjured vessels and maintain the blood in a fluid state.

Local Vasoconstriction

The constriction of an injured arteriole or small artery may be so marked that its lumen is obliterated. The vasoconstriction is probably due to serotonin and other vasoconstrictors liberated from platelets which adhere to the walls of the damaged vessels. It is claimed that, at least for a time after being divided transversely, arteries as large as the radial artery constrict and stop bleeding; however, this is no excuse for delay in ligating the damaged vessel. Furthermore, arterial walls that are cut longitudinally or irregularly do not constrict in such a way that the lumen of the artery is occluded, and bleeding continues.

The Temporary Hemostatic Plug

When a blood vessel is damaged, the endothelium is disrupted and an underlying layer of collagen is exposed. Collagen attracts platelets, which adhere to it and liberate serotonin and adenosine diphosphate (ADP). The ADP in turn rapidly attracts other platelets, and a loose plug of aggregated platelets is formed. Formation of this temporary plug is unaffected by clinically used doses of the anticoagulants heparin and dicumarol (see below).

The Clotting Mechanism

The loose aggregation of platelets in the temporary plug is bound together and converted into the definitive clot by **fibrin**. The clotting mechanism responsible for the formation of fibrin involves a complex series or "cascade" of reactions. The complexity of the system has in the past been compounded by variations in nomenclature, but acceptance of a numbering system for the various clotting factors (Table 27–7) has simplified the situation.

The fundamental reaction in the clotting of blood is conversion of the soluble plasma protein fibrinogen to fibrin (Fig 27–11). The fibrin molecules polymerize to form a loose mesh of insoluble interlacing strands (Fig 27–3), and this polymer is converted by the formation of covalent cross-linkages to a dense, tight aggregate. This latter reaction is catalyzed by factor XIII, the fibrin-stabilizing factor.

The conversion of fibrinogen to fibrin is catalyzed

TABLE 27–7. Numerical system for naming blood clotting factors. It is no longer felt that factor VI is a separate entity, and it has been dropped from the list.

Factor	
I	Fibrinogen
II	Prothrombin
III	Thromboplastin
IV	Calcium
V	Proaccelerin, labile factor, accelerator globulin
VII	Proconvertin, SPCA, stable factor
VIII	Antihemophilic factor (AHF), antihemophilic factor A, antihemophilic globulin (AHG)
IX	Plasma thromboplastic component (PTC), Christmas factor, antihemophilic factor B
X	Stuart-Prower factor
XI	Plasma thromboplastin antecedent (PTA), antihemophilic factor C
XII	Hageman factor, glass factor
XIII	Fibrin-stabilizing factor, Laki-Lorand factor

by thrombin. Thrombin is formed in turn from its circulating precursor, prothrombin, by the action of activated factor X. Factor X can be activated by reactions that proceed along either of 2 pathways, an intrinsic and an extrinsic pathway.

The initial reaction in the **intrinsic pathway** is conversion of inactive factor XII to active factor XII. This activation can be brought about in vitro by exposing the blood to electronegatively charged wettable surfaces such as glass, micelles of long-chain saturated fatty acids, and collagen fibers. Activation in vivo presumably occurs when blood is exposed to the collagen fibers underlying the endothelium in the blood vessels. Active factor XII then activates factor XI, active factor

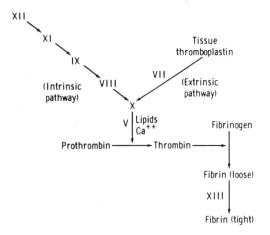

FIG 27–11. Diagrammatic summary of the clotting mechanism. (Modified and reproduced, with permission, from Deykin: Thrombogenesis. New England J Med 276:622, 1967.)

XI activates factor IX, active factor IX activates factor VIII, and active factor VIII activates factor X. In the presence of lipids from platelets, Ca^{++}, and factor V, activated factor X catalyzes the conversion of prothrombin to thrombin.

The **extrinsic pathway** involves the direct activation of factor X by tissue thromboplastin, a proteinlipid complex released from blood vessel walls and a variety of other tissues when they are damaged. The activation is catalyzed by factor VII. In the presence of Ca^{++} and factor V, the active factor X then catalyzes the conversion of prothrombin to thrombin. The tissue thromboplastin can meet the lipid requirements of this catalysis, and platelet lipids are not required, as they are in the case of the intrinsic system.

Anticlotting Mechanisms

The tendency of blood to clot is balanced in vivo by a number of limiting reactions which tend to prevent clotting inside the blood vessels and to break down any clots that do form. These reactions include the liberation from clotting blood of substances that inhibit further clotting, and removal of some activated clotting factors from the circulation by the liver. The supply of clotting factors is also reduced to the degree that they are used up during clotting. There is in addition a **fibrinolytic system** in the body that limits clotting.

The active component of the fibrinolytic system is **plasmin**, or **fibrinolysin** (Fig 27–12). This enzyme not only lyses fibrin; it also attacks factor V, factor VIII, and fibrinogen, with liberation from fibrinogen of substances that inhibit thrombin. Plasmin is formed from its inactive precursor, plasminogen, by activators that appear to include substances in tissues, activated factor XII, and thrombin.

The interaction of the various processes involved in hemostasis is summarized in Fig 27–13.

FIG 27–12. The fibrinolytic system. (Modified and reproduced, with permission, from Deykin: Thrombogenesis. New England J Med 276:622, 1967.)

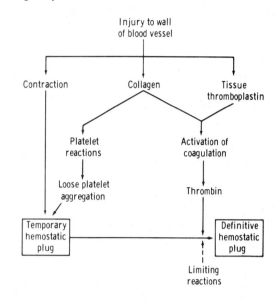

FIG 27–13. Summary of reaction involved in hemostasis. The dashed arrow indicates inhibition. (Modified and reproduced, with permission, from Deykin: Thrombogenesis. New England J Med 276:622, 1967.)

Anticoagulants

Heparin, a potent anticoagulant, is normally found in the body. This substance is a mixture of sulfate-containing mucopolysaccharides with a strongly acid reaction and a large electronegative charge. It acts as an anticoagulant by preventing the activation of factor IX, and, in conjunction with a plasma cofactor, inhibiting the action of thrombin. It is also a cofactor for lipoprotein lipase (clearing factor; see Chapter 17). Repeated large doses of heparin inhibit aldosterone secretion, apparently by a direct action on the adrenal cortex. When given for more than a year, they can also cause osteoporosis. The highly basic protein, protamine, forms an irreversible complex with heparin and is used clinically to neutralize heparin.

Heparin is found in the granules of the circulating basophils and in the granules of the **mast cells**, wandering cells that are found in most tissues but are most abundant in connective tissue. The mast cells also contain histamine, and may liberate this histamine in the tissues as part of the inflammatory reaction. The liver of the dog contains many mast cells which liberate their heparin into the blood stream when anaphylactic shock is induced; but the liver of other species contains little heparin, and it has not been proved that heparin has any physiologic role in maintaining blood in the fluid state.

Clotting can be prevented in vitro if Ca^{++} is removed from the blood by the addition of substances such as oxalates, which form insoluble salts with Ca^{++}, or substances such as citrate or other **chelating agents**, which bind Ca^{++}. Coumarin derivatives such as **dicumarol** competitively inhibit vitamin K. This

TABLE 27–8. Disease states due to deficiency of the various clotting factors.

Deficiency of Factor	Clinical Syndrome	Cause
I	Afibrinogenemia	Depletion during toxic pregnancy with premature separation of placenta; also congenital (rare)
II	Hypoprothrombinemia (hemorrhagic tendency in liver disease)	Decreased hepatic synthesis, usually secondary to vitamin K deficiency
V	Parahemophilia	Congenital
VII	Hypoconvertinemia	Congenital
VIII	Hemophilia A (classical hemophilia)	Congenital defect due to abnormal gene on X chromosome; disease is therefore inherited as sex-linked characteristic
IX	Hemophilia B (Christmas disease)	Congenital
X	Stuart-Prower factor deficiency	Congenital
XI	PTA deficiency	Congenital
XII	Hageman trait	Congenital

vitamin catalyzes the synthesis of prothrombin and factors VII, IX, and X in the liver. The coumarin derivatives are extensively used as anticoagulants.

Abnormalities of Hemostasis

In vivo, a plasma Ca^{++} level low enough to interfere with blood clotting is incompatible with life, but hemorrhagic diseases due to selective deficiencies of almost all the other clotting factors have been described (Table 27–8). The absorption of the K vitamins, along with that of the other fat-soluble vitamins, is depressed in obstructive jaundice because of the lack of bile in the intestine and consequent depression of fat absorption. The resultant depression of prothrombin synthesis may cause the development of a significant bleeding tendency.

When the platelet count is low, clot retraction is deficient and there is poor constriction of ruptured vessels. The resulting clinical syndrome (**thrombocytopenic purpura**) is characterized by easy bruisability and multiple subcutaneous hemorrhages. Purpura may also occur when the platelet count is normal, and in some of these cases the circulating platelets are in some way abnormal (**thrombasthenic purpura**).

Formation of clots inside the blood vessels is usually called **thrombosis** to distinguish it from the normal extravascular clotting of blood. The functions of the fibrinolytic system and the balance between it and the clotting mechanism are under intensive investi-gation in an effort to shed more light on the pathogenesis of intravascular clotting. Thromboses are a major medical problem. They are particularly prone to occur where blood flow is sluggish, eg, in the veins of the calves after operations and delivery, because the slow flow permits activated clotting factors to accumulate instead of being washed away. They also occur in vessels such as the coronary and cerebral arteries at sites where the intima is damaged by arteriosclerotic plaques, and over areas of damage to the endocardium. They frequently occlude the arterial supply to the organs in which they form, and bits of thrombus (**emboli**) sometimes break off and travel in the blood stream to distant sites, damaging other organs. Examples are obstruction of the pulmonary artery or its branches (**pulmonary embolism**) by thrombi from the leg veins, and embolism of cerebral or leg vessels by bits of clot breaking off from a thrombus in the left ventricle (**mural thrombus**) overlying a myocardial infarct.

LYMPH

Lymph is tissue fluid that enters the lymphatic vessels. It drains into the venous blood via the thoracic and right lymphatic ducts. It contains clotting factors and clots on standing. Its protein content is generally lower than that of plasma but varies with the region from which the lymph drains (Table 27–9). It should be noted that the interstitial fluid is not protein-free; it contains proteins which traverse the capillary walls and return to the blood via lymph. Water-insoluble fats are absorbed from the intestine into the lymphatics, and the lymph in the thoracic duct after a meal is milky because of its high fat content (see Chapter 25). Lymphocytes enter the circulation principally through the lymphatics, and there are appreciable numbers of lymphocytes in thoracic duct lymph.

TABLE 27–9. Probable approximate protein content of lymph in humans.*

Lymph From	Protein Content (g/100 ml)
Ankle	0.5
Limbs	2
Intestine	4
Liver	6
Thoracic duct	4

*Data based on studies of various authors in humans and animals.

28...

The Heart: Origin of the Heartbeat & the Electrical Activity of the Heart

ORIGIN & SPREAD OF CARDIAC EXCITATION

The parts of the heart normally beat in an orderly sequence: contraction of the atria **(atrial systole)** is followed by contraction of the ventricles **(ventricular systole)**, and during **diastole** all 4 chambers are relaxed. The **sino-atrial node** (SA node), the **atrioventricular node** (AV node), the **bundle of His** with its right and left branches, and the **Purkinje system**, the specialized structures that form the cardiac conduction system, discharge at a more rapid rate than the cardiac muscle. The SA node normally discharges most rapidly, depolarization spreading from it to the other regions before they discharge spontaneously. The SA node is therefore the normal **cardiac pacemaker**, its rate of discharge determining the rate at which the heart beats. Impulses generated in the SA node pass through the atrial muscle to the AV node; through this node to the bundle of His; and through the branches of the bundle of His via the Purkinje system to the ventricular muscle.

Anatomic Considerations

In 4-chambered mammalian hearts, the SA node is located at the junction of the superior vena cava with the right atrium. The AV node is located in the right posterior portion of the interatrial septum (Fig 28–1). There is no specialized conducting tissue connecting the 2 nodes, but the atrial muscle fibers converge on and interdigitate with the fibers in the AV node. The AV node is continuous with the bundle of His, which gives off a left bundle branch at the top of the interventricular septum and continues as the right bundle branch. The branches run subendocardially down either side of the septum and come into contact with the Purkinje system, the fibers of which spread to all parts of the ventricular myocardium.

The histology of cardiac muscle is described in Chapter 3. The SA and AV nodes and the bundle of His are composed of modified cardiac muscle which is striate but has indistinct boundaries. This tissue is richer in glycogen and has more sarcoplasm than the rest of the cardiac muscle fibers. The atrial muscle fibers are separated from those of the ventricles by a fibrous tissue ring, and normally the only conducting tissue between the atria and ventricles is the bundle of His.

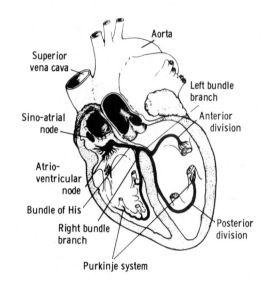

FIG 28–1. **Conducting system of the heart.** (Reproduced, with permission, from Goldman: *Principles of Clinical Electrocardiography,* 8th ed. Lange, 1973.)

The SA node develops from structures on the right side of the embryo, and the AV node from structures on the left. This is why in the adult the **right vagus** is distributed mainly to the SA node and the **left vagus** mainly to the AV node. Both areas receive adrenergic nerves from the cervical sympathetic ganglia via the cardiac nerves. Adrenergic fibers are distributed to the atrial and ventricular myocardium as well; the vagal fibers are probably distributed only to the nodal tissue and the atrial musculature.

Properties of Cardiac Muscle

The electrical responses of cardiac muscle and nodal tissue and the ionic fluxes which underlie them are discussed in Chapter 3. Myocardial fibers have a resting membrane potential of approximately −80 mv. The individual fibers are separated from one another by membranes, but depolarization spreads radially through them as if they were a syncytium. The transmembrane action potential of single cardiac muscle cells is characterized by rapid depolarization and a slow, triphasic repolarization process (Fig 28–2). Recorded extracellularly, the action potential resem-

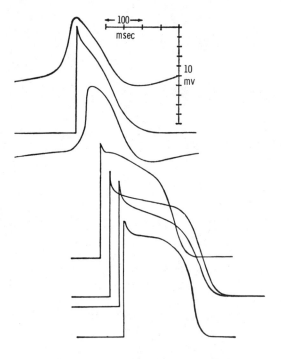

FIG 28–2. Typical transmembrane action potentials from (top to bottom) SA node, atrial muscle, AV node, bundle of His, Purkinje fiber of false tendon, terminal Purkinje fiber, and ventricular muscle fiber (all drawn on same time axis but with different zero points on the vertical scale). Note differences in configuration and sequence of activation. (Reproduced, with permission, from Hoffman & Cranefield: *Electrophysiology of the Heart*. McGraw-Hill, 1960.)

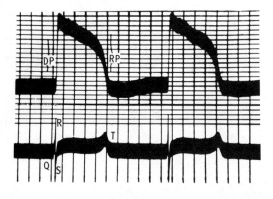

FIG 28–3. Action potential and surface electrocardiogram of cardiac muscle. Time lines, 0.1 sec; DP, depolarization; RP, repolarization. (Reproduced, with permission, from Hecht: Normal and abnormal transmembrane potentials of the spontaneously beating heart. Ann New York Acad Sci 65:700, 1957.)

bles the QRST pattern of the electrocardiogram (Fig 28–3). The ionic events responsible for the action potential are similar to those in skeletal muscle and nerve except that in cardiac muscle the slow repolarization is believed to be due to a prolonged increase in Na^+ permeability followed by a delayed increase in K^+ permeability.

Rhythmically discharging cells have an unstable membrane potential which after each impulse declines to the firing level (**prepotential** or **pacemaker potential**; see Chapter 3). This triggers the next impulse. The speed with which the membrane potential is reduced to the firing level determines the rate at which the tissue discharges. All parts of the myocardium are probably capable of spontaneous, rhythmic discharge and contraction, but prepotentials are prominent and the membrane potential declines rapidly only in nodal tissue (Fig 28–4).

When the cholinergic vagal fibers to nodal tissue are stimulated, the slope of the prepotentials is decreased, probably because the acetylcholine liberated at the nerve endings increases the permeability of nodal tissue to K^+. The rate of firing also decreases. Strong vagal stimulation may abolish spontaneous discharge for some time. Conversely, stimulation of the sympathetic cardiac nerves makes the membrane potential fall more rapidly and the rate of spontaneous discharge increases (Fig 28–4). This is apparently due to the adrenergic mediator, norepinephrine, which pro-

FIG 28–4. Effect of vagal stimulation *(A and B)* and sympathetic stimulation *(C)* on the pacemaker potentials of the sinus venosus of the frog heart. Stimulation periods are indicated by the breaks in the bottom trace in each case. Horizontal calibration marks, 1 sec. (Reproduced, with permission, from Hutter & Trautwein: Vagal and sympathetic effects on the pacemaker fibers in the sinus venosus of the heart. J Gen Physiol 39:715, 1956.)

duces an increase in the rate at which K$^+$ permeability declines between action potentials. It is this decline in K$^+$ permeability that produces the prepotentials (see Chapter 3).

The rate of discharge of the SA node and other nodal tissue is influenced by temperature and by drugs. The discharge frequency is increased when the temperature rises, and this may contribute to the tachycardia associated with fever. Digitalis depresses nodal tissue and exerts an effect like that of vagal stimulation, particularly on the AV node. The speeds of conduction in the various types of cardiac tissue are shown in Table 28–1.

TABLE 28–1. Conduction speeds in cardiac tissue.

Tissue	Conduction Rate (m/sec)
SA node	0.05
Atrial muscle	1
AV node	0.1
Right and left bundle branches	2
Purkinje system	1
Ventricular muscle	0.4

Spread of Cardiac Excitation

Depolarization initiated in the SA node spreads radially through the atria, converging on the AV node. Atrial depolarization is complete in about 0.1 sec. Because conduction in the AV node is slow, there is a delay of about 0.1 sec **(AV nodal delay)** before excitation spreads to the ventricles. This delay is shortened by stimulation of the sympathetic nerves to the heart and lengthened by stimulation of the vagi. From the top of the septum, the wave of depolarization spreads in the rapidly conducting Purkinje fibers to all parts of the ventricles in 0.08–0.1 sec. In man, depolarization of the ventricular muscle starts at the left side of the interventricular septum and moves first to the right across the midportion of the septum. The wave of depolarization then spreads down the septum to the apex of the heart. It returns along the ventricular walls to the AV groove, proceeding from the endocardial to the epicardial surface (Fig 28–5). The last parts of the heart to be depolarized are the posterobasal portion of the left ventricle, the pulmonary conus, and the uppermost portion of the septum.

THE ELECTROCARDIOGRAM

Because the body fluids are good conductors (ie, because the body is a **volume conductor**), fluctuations in potential that represent the algebraic sum of the action potentials of myocardial fibers can be recorded from the surface of the body. The record of these

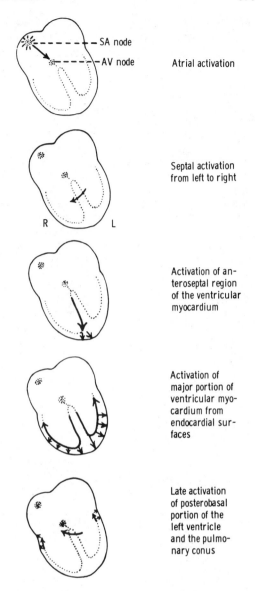

Atrial activation

Septal activation from left to right

Activation of anteroseptal region of the ventricular myocardium

Activation of major portion of ventricular myocardium from endocardial surfaces

Late activation of posterobasal portion of the left ventricle and the pulmonary conus

FIG 28–5. Normal spread of electrical activity in heart. (Reproduced, with permission, from Goldman: *Principles of Clinical Electrocardiography,* 8th ed. Lange, 1973.)

potential fluctuations during the cardiac cycle is the **electrocardiogram (ECG)**. Most electrocardiograph machines now in use record these fluctuations on a moving strip of paper.

The ECG may be recorded using an **active** or **exploring** electrode connected to an indifferent electrode at zero potential **(unipolar** recording), or between 2 active electrodes **(bipolar** recording). In a volume conductor, the sum of the potentials at the points of an equilateral triangle with a current source in the center is zero at all times. A triangle with the heart at its center **(Einthoven's triangle)** can be approximated by placing electrodes on both arms and on the left leg. If these electrodes are connected to a common terminal, an indifferent electrode that stays near zero potential is obtained. Depolarization moving toward an active electrode in a volume conductor produces a positive deflection, whereas depolarization moving in the opposite direction produces a negative deflection.

The names of the various waves of the ECG and their timing in man are shown in Fig 28–6. By convention, an upward deflection is written when the active electrode becomes positive relative to the indifferent; and when the active electrode becomes negative, a downward deflection is written. The P wave is produced by atrial depolarization, the QRS complex by ventricular depolarization, and the ST segment and T wave by ventricular repolarization. The manifestations of atrial repolarization are normally submerged in the QRS complex. The U wave is an inconstant finding, believed to be due to slow repolarization of the papillary muscles. The intervals between the various ECG waves and the events in the heart which occur during these intervals are shown in Table 28–2.

The magnitude and configuration of the individual ECG waves vary with the location of the electrodes. All the waves are small compared with the transmembrane potentials of single fibers because the ECG is being recorded at a considerable distance from the heart.

Unipolar (V) Leads

Nine standard locations for the exploring electrode (**leads**) are used for routine clinical electrocardiography. The 6 unipolar chest leads (precordial leads) are designated V_{1-6} (Fig 28–7). The 3 unipolar limb leads are VR (right arm), VL (left arm), and VF (left foot). Since current flows only in the body fluids, unipolar limb records are those which would be obtained if the electrodes were at the points of attachment of the limbs, no matter where on the limbs the electrodes are placed. **Augmented** limb leads, designated by the letter a (aVR, aVL, aVF), are generally used today. The augmented limb leads are recordings between one limb and the other 2 limbs. This increases the size of the potentials by 50% without any change in configuration from the nonaugmented record because each augmented limb lead equals 3/2 of the unaugmented lead:

$$aVR = VR - \frac{(VL + VF)}{2}$$

$$2aVR = 2VR - (VL + VF)$$

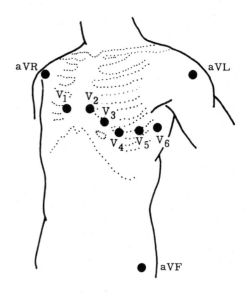

FIG 28–7. Unipolar ECG leads.

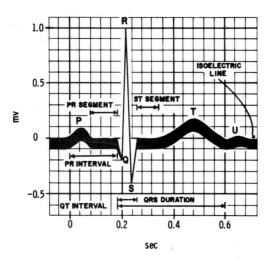

FIG 28–6. Waves of the ECG.

TABLE 28–2. ECG intervals.

| | Normal Duration (sec) | | Events in Heart During Interval |
	Average	Range	
PR interval*	0.18†	0.12–0.20	Atrial depolarization and conduction through AV node
QRS duration	0.08	to 0.10	Ventricular depolarization
QT interval	0.40	to 0.43	Ventricular depolarization plus ventricular repolarization
ST interval (QT minus QRS)	0.32	. . .	Ventricular repolarization

*Measured from the beginning of the P wave to the beginning of the QRS complex.
†Shortens as heart rate increases from average of 0.18 at rate of 70 to 0.14 at rate of 130.

Since VR + VL + VF = 0 (Einthoven's triangle),
$$VR = -(VL + VF)$$

Substituting for $-(VL + VF)$ in the second equation,
$$2aVR = 2VR + VR$$

Therefore, $aVR = 3/2 \, VR$

An esophageal electrode is sometimes used to study atrial activity. The electrode is inserted in a catheter and swallowed, and each esophageal lead is identified by the letter E followed by the number of centimeters from the teeth to the electrode tip. Thus, for example, lead E_{35} is a unipolar record in which the exploring electrode is 35 cm down the esophagus.

Bipolar Leads

Bipolar leads were used before unipolar leads were developed. The **standard limb leads**, leads I, II, and III, are records of the differences in potential

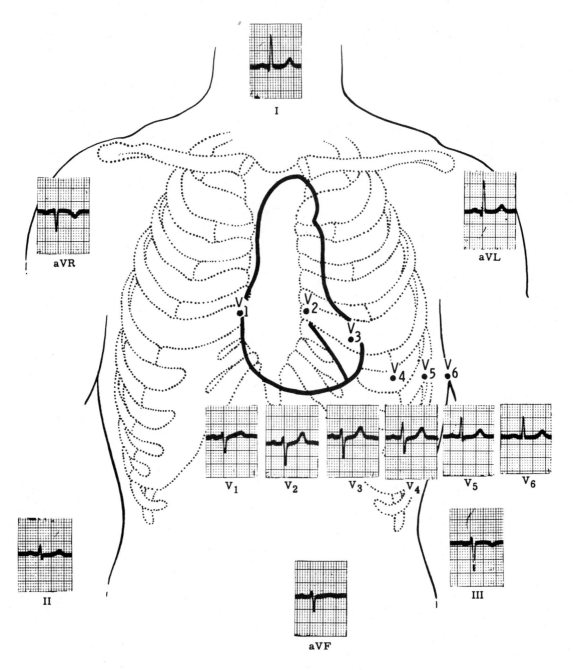

FIG 28–8. Normal ECG with heart in horizontal position. (Reproduced, with permission, from Goldman: *Principles of Clinical Electrocardiography,* 8th ed. Lange, 1973.)

between 2 limbs. In lead I, the electrodes are connected so that an upward deflection is inscribed when the left arm becomes positive to the right (left arm positive). In lead II, the electrodes are on the right arm and left leg with the leg positive; and in lead III, the electrodes are on the left arm and left leg with the leg positive.

Normal ECG

The ECG of a normal individual is shown in Fig 28–8. The sequence in which the parts of the heart are depolarized (Fig 28–5) and the position of the heart relative to the electrodes are the important considerations in interpreting the configurations of the waves in each lead. The atria are located posteriorly in the chest. The ventricles form the base and anterior surface of the heart, and the right ventricle is anterolateral to the left (Fig 28–9). Thus, aVR "looks at" the cavities of the ventricles. Atrial depolarization, ventricular depolarization, and ventricular repolarization move away from the exploring electrode, and the P wave, QRS complex, and T wave are therefore all negative

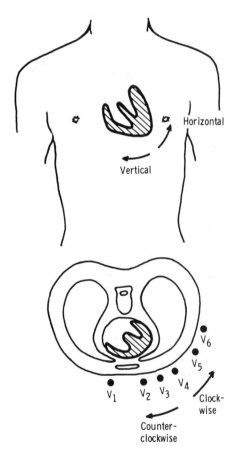

FIG 28–9. Diagram of position of heart in chest. Arrows indicate directions of cardiac rotation with normal variations in cardiac position. By convention, the direction of rotation in the horizontal plane is defined by its appearance as viewed from the inferior surface of the heart looking upward from the diaphragm.

(downward) deflections; aVL and aVF look at the ventricles, and the deflections are therefore predominantly positive or biphasic. There is no Q wave in V_1 and V_2, and the initial portion of the QRS complex is a small upward deflection because ventricular depolarization first moves across the midportion of the septum from left to right toward the exploring electrode. The wave of excitation then moves down the septum and into the left ventricle away from the electrode, producing a large S wave. Finally, it moves back along the ventricular wall toward the electrode, producing the return to the isoelectric line. Conversely, in the left ventricular leads (V_{4-6}), there may be an initial small Q wave (left to right septal depolarization), and there is a large R wave (septal and left ventricular depolarization) followed in V_4 and V_5 by a moderate S wave (late depolarization of the ventricular walls moving back toward the AV junction).

There is considerable variation in the position of the normal heart since the heart rotates on the 2 axes shown in Fig 28–9 plus the transverse axis (rotation forward and backward). These position changes affect the configuration of the ECG complexes in the various leads.

Bipolar Limb Leads & the Cardiac Vector

Because the standard limb leads are records of the potential differences between 2 points, the deflection in each lead at any instant indicates the magnitude and direction in the axis of the lead of the electromotive force generated in the heart (**cardiac vector** or **axis**). The vector at any given moment in the 2 dimensions of the frontal plane can be calculated from any 2 standard limb leads (Fig 28–10) if it is assumed that the 3 electrode locations form the points of an equilateral triangle (Einthoven's triangle) and that the heart lies in the center of the triangle. These assumptions are not completely warranted, but calculated vectors are useful approximations. An approximate **mean QRS vector** ("electrical axis of the heart") is often plotted using the average QRS deflection in each lead as shown in Fig 28–10. This is a **mean** vector as opposed to an **instantaneous** vector, and the average QRS deflections should be measured by integrating the QRS complexes. However, they can be approximated by measuring the net differences between the positive and negative peaks of the QRS. The normal direction of the mean QRS vector is generally said to be -30 to $+110°$ on the coordinate system shown in Fig 28–10. **Left** or **right axis deviation** is said to be present if the calculated axis falls to the left of $-30°$ to the right of $+110°$. Right axis deviation suggests right ventricular hypertrophy, and left axis deviation may be due to left ventricular hypertrophy. However, simple differences in heart position may produce axis values in the "abnormal" range, and there are better and more reliable ECG criteria for ventricular hypertrophy.

Vectorcardiography

If the tops of the arrows representing all of the **instantaneous** cardiac vectors in the frontal plane

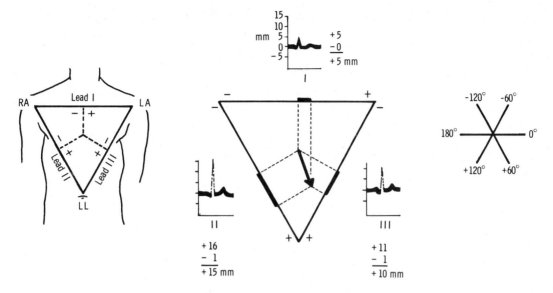

FIG 28–10. Cardiac vector. *Left:* Einthoven's triangle. Perpendiculars dropped from the midpoints of the sides of the equilateral triangle intersect at the center of electrical activity. RA, right arm; LA, left arm; LL, left leg. *Center:* Calculation of mean QRS vector. In each lead, distances equal to the height of the R wave minus the height of the largest negative deflection in the QRS complex are measured off from the midpoint of the side of the triangle representing that lead. An arrow drawn from the center of electrical activity to the point where perpendiculars extended from the distances measured off on the sides intersect represents the magnitude and direction of the mean QRS vector. *Right:* Reference axes for determining the direction of the vector.

during the cardiac cycle are connected, from first to last, the line connecting them forms a series of 3 loops: one for the P wave, one for the QRS complex, and one for the T wave. This can be done electronically, and the loops, called **vectorcardiograms**, projected on the face of a cathode ray oscilloscope. It is apparent that vectorcardiogram loops can be projected onto the horizontal and sagittal as well as the frontal planes (Fig 28–11).

CARDIAC ARRHYTHMIAS

Normal Cardiac Rate

In the normal human heart, each beat originates in the SA node (**normal sinus rhythm, NSR**). The heart beats about 70 times a minute at rest. The rate is slowed (**bradycardia**) during sleep and accelerated (**tachycardia**) by emotion, exercise, fever, and many other stimuli. The control of heart rate is discussed in Chapter 31. In healthy young individuals, the heart rate varies with the phases of respiration. The effect of respiration may be absent during quiet breathing but is readily seen when the depth of breathing is increased. During inspiration, impulses in the vagi from the stretch receptors in the lungs inhibit the cardioinhibitory center in the medulla oblongata (see Chapter 31). The tonic vagal discharge which keeps the

heart rate slow decreases, and the heart rate rises. An additional factor is irradiation of impulses from the inspiratory center to the cardioacceleratory center. During expiration, the rate decreases. This regular variation in rate is **sinus arrhythmia**, a normal phenomenon.

Abnormal Rhythms

Since all parts of the myocardium and conduction system have inherent rhythmicity, any part can in abnormal situations become the cardiac pacemaker. This happens when the SA node is depressed, when the bundle of His is interrupted, or when an abnormal (**ectopic**) focus in the atria or ventricles discharges faster than the SA node.

In experimental animals, stimulation of the hypothalamus can produce a variety of cardiac arrhythmias. There is evidence that their production is due to stimulation of sympathetic and parasympathetic pathways to the heart simultaneously. However, there is no evidence that hypothalamic discharge is an important cause of arrhythmias seen in patients.

Nodal & Idioventricular Rhythms

A simple but enlightening experiment that demonstrates the hierarchy of pacemakers in the heart can be performed in cold-blooded animals such as frogs and turtles. In these animals, the heartbeat originates in a separate cardiac chamber, the **sinus venosus**, instead of in an SA node. There is no coronary circula-

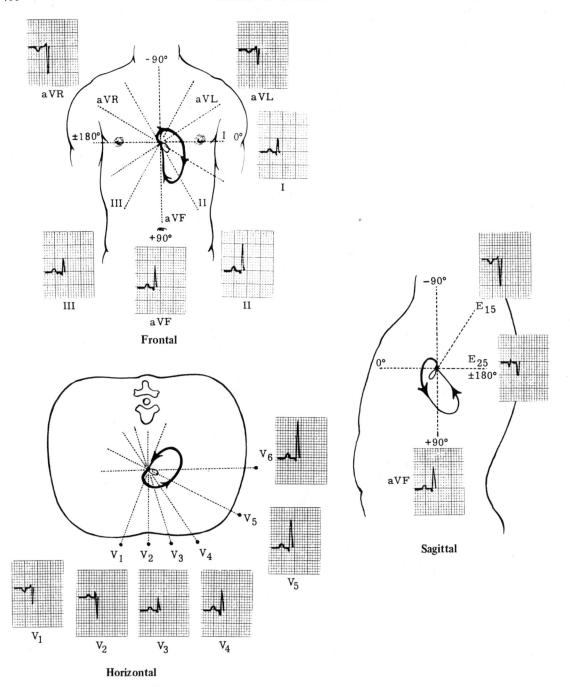

FIG 28–11. P (inner) and QRS (large outer) vectorcardiographic loops in a normal individual, with the corresponding standard and esophageal (E_{15} and E_{25}) leads of the ECG. (Reproduced, with permission, from Goldman: *Principles of Clinical Electrocardiography,* 8th ed. Lange, 1973.)

tion, the heart receiving O_2 by diffusion from the blood in the cardiac chambers. If a ligature (Stannius ligature I) is tied around the junction of the sinus venosus and right atrium, conduction from the sinus to the rest of the heart is prevented. The atria and ventricles stop for a moment, then resume beating at a slower rate as a focus in the atrium becomes the pacemaker for the portion of the heart below the ligature.

If a second ligature (Stannius ligature II) is tied between the atria and ventricles, the ventricles stop, then resume beating at an even slower rate than the atria. With both ligatures in place, there are 3 separate regions of the heart beating at 3 different rates.

It is not possible to perform the Stannius experiment in mammals because the SA node is embedded in the atrial wall, and tying a ligature between the atria

FIG 28–12. **High AV nodal extrasystole.** The first, second, and fourth complexes are normal; PR interval is 0.14 sec. The third complex originates in a high AV nodal focus and produces retrograde atrial stimulation. The P wave from this beat is upright in aVR and inverted in aVF; PR interval is 0.08 sec. (Reproduced, with permission, from Goldman: *Principles of Clinical Electrocardiography,* 8th ed. Lange, 1973.)

and the ventricles interrupts the coronary circulation, usually causing immediate ventricular fibrillation. However, experiments on laboratory mammals involving cooling or crushing of the SA and AV nodes and the "experiments of nature" in humans with diseased nodal tissue show that the same pacemaker hierarchy prevails.

When the function of the SA node is depressed, the more slowly discharging AV node takes over as pacemaker, producing a **nodal rhythm** (Fig 28–12). Depolarization spreads from the AV node into the atria and ventricles simultaneously, producing abnormal, inverted P waves and a short PR interval. Sometimes the P waves are buried in the QRS complexes and no ECG evidence of atrial depolarization is seen.

When the bundle of His is completely interrupted, the ventricles beat at their slow inherent rate (**idioventricular rhythm**). The atria continue to beat independently at the normal sinus rate (Fig 28–13), and **complete** or **third degree heart block** is said to be

PR = 0.16 sec

Normal complex

PR = 0.38 sec

First degree heart block

Second degree heart block
(2:1 heart block)

Second degree heart block
(Wenckebach phenomenon)

Complete heart block. Atrial rate, 107; ventricular rate, 43

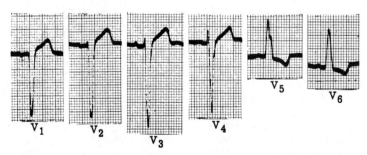

V leads in typical case of left bundle branch block

FIG 28–13. **Heart block.** (Tracings from Goldman: *Principles of Clinical Electrocardiography,* 8th ed. Lange, 1973.)

present. The idioventricular rate in man is usually regular at 30–45 beats/min, but there are sometimes periods of asystole lasting a minute or more. The resultant cerebral ischemia causes dizziness and fainting **(Stokes-Adams syndrome)**. Causes of third degree heart block include septal myocardial infarctions and damage to the bundle of His during surgical correction of congenital interventricular septal defects.

When the bundle of His is not completely interrupted, **incomplete heart block** is present. In the form called **first degree heart block**, all the atrial impulses reach the ventricles, but the PR interval is abnormally long. In the form called **second degree heart block**, not all atrial impulses are conducted to the ventricles. There may be, for example, a ventricular beat following every second or every third atrial beat (2:1 block, 3:1 block, etc). In another form of incomplete heart block there are repeated sequences of beats in which the PR interval lengthens progressively until a ventricular beat is dropped **(Wenckebach phenomenon)**. The PR interval of the cardiac cycle that follows each dropped beat is usually normal or only slightly prolonged (Fig 28–13).

Sometimes one branch of the bundle of His is interrupted, causing **right** or **left bundle branch block**. In bundle branch block, excitation passes normally down the bundle on the intact side and then sweeps back through the muscle to activate the ventricle on the blocked side. The ventricular rate is therefore normal, but the QRS complexes are prolonged and deformed (Fig 28–13).

Ectopic Foci of Excitation

A portion of the myocardium (or the AV node or bundle) sometimes becomes "irritable" and discharges independently **(ectopic focus)**. If it discharges once, the result is a beat which occurs before the expected next normal beat and transiently interrupts the cardiac rhythm (atrial, nodal, or ventricular **extrasystole** or **premature beat**). If the focus discharges repetitively at a rate more rapid than that of the SA node, it produces rapid, regular tachycardia (atrial, ventricular, or nodal **paroxysmal tachycardia** or **atrial flutter**). A very rapidly and irregularly discharging focus or, more likely, group of foci in the atria or ventricles are responsible for **atrial fibrillation** or **ventricular fibrillation**.

Atrial Arrhythmias

Excitation spreading from a focus in the atria stimulates the AV node and is conducted to the ventricles. The P waves of atrial extrasystoles are abnormal, but the QRST configurations are normal. The excitation depolarizes the SA node, which must repolarize and then depolarize to the firing level before it can initiate the next normal beat. Consequently, there is a pause between the extrasystole and the next normal beat which is usually equal in length to the interval between the normal beats preceding the extrasystole.

Atrial tachycardia occurs when an atrial focus discharges regularly at rates of 150–220/min (Table 28–3). Sometimes, especially in digitalized patients, some degree of atrioventricular block is associated with the tachycardia **(paroxysmal atrial tachycardia with block)**. When the atrial rate is 200–350/min, the condition is called atrial flutter. Atrial flutter is almost always associated with 2:1 or 3:1 AV block because the normal AV node has a long refractory period and, in adults, it cannot conduct more than about 230 impulses per minute.

In atrial fibrillation, the atria beat very rapidly (300–500/min) in a completely irregular and disorganized fashion. Because the AV node discharges at irregular intervals, the ventricles beat at a completely irregular rate, usually 80–160/min (Table 28–3). Atrial fibrillation has been attributed to a **circus movement**, a band of excitation that "chases its tail" in a continuous circular path through the atrial musculature. Data gathered using slow-motion movies of fibrillating atria appear to make this explanation unlikely, and suggest that fibrillation is due to very rapid, irregular discharges of multiple ectopic foci in the atria. However, the problem of the pathogenesis of atrial fibrillation remains unsettled.

Consequences of Atrial Arrhythmias

Occasional atrial extrasystoles occur from time to time in most normal humans and have no pathologic significance. In paroxysmal atrial tachycardia and flutter, the ventricular rate may be so high that diastole is too short for adequate filling of the ventricles with blood between contractions. Consequently, cardiac output is reduced and symptoms of heart failure appear. The relation between cardiac rate and cardiac output is discussed in detail in Chapter 29. Heart failure may also complicate atrial fibrillation when the ventricular rate is rapid. Acetylcholine liberated at vagal endings depresses conduction in the atrial musculature and AV node. This is why stimulating reflex vagal discharge by pressing on the eyeball **("oculocardiac reflex")** or massaging the carotid sinus often converts tachycardia and sometimes converts atrial flutter to normal sinus rhythm. Alternatively, vagal stimulation increases the degree of AV block, abruptly slowing the ventricular rate. Digitalis also depresses AV conduction, and is used to slow a rapid ventricular rate in atrial fibrillation.

Ventricular Arrhythmias

Extrasystoles that originate in an ectopic ventricular focus have bizarrely shaped prolonged QRS complexes (Fig 28–14) due to the slow spread of the impulse from the focus through the ventricular muscle to the rest of the ventricle. For unknown reasons, they are usually incapable of exciting the bundle of His, and so retrograde conduction to the atrium does not occur. In the meantime, the next succeeding normal SA nodal impulse depolarizes the atria. The P wave is usually buried in the QRS of the extrasystole. If the normal impulse reaches the ventricles, they are still in the refractory period following depolarization from the ectopic focus. However, the second succeeding impulse

TABLE 28–3. Atrial arrhythmias. The tracings are portions of the continuous esophageal (E_{35}) ECG of a patient who manifested all the rhythms illustrated within a single 5-minute period.*

Rate of Discharge of Atrial Ectopic Focus	Arrhythmia
Occasional discharge at a rate slower than the basic sinus rhythm Atrial premature contractions (at arrows)	E_{35}
About 160 to about 220 Atrial tachycardia (with 1:1 conduction)	E_{35}
About 220 to about 350 Atrial flutter (ie, atrial tachycardia with AV block)	E_{35}
Over 350 Atrial fibrillation	E_{35}

*Reproduced, with permission, from Goldman: *Principles of Clinical Electrocardiography*, 8th ed. Lange, 1973.

from the SA node produces a normal beat. Thus, ventricular extrasystoles are followed by a **compensatory pause** that is longer than the pause after an atrial extrasystole. Furthermore, ventricular extrasystoles do not interrupt the regular discharge of the SA node, whereas atrial extrasystoles interrupt and "reset" the normal rhythm. These differences make it possible to distinguish between atrial and ventricular premature beats by palpation of the pulse or auscultation of the heart at the bedside. If one taps his foot in time with the regular normal rhythm, the beats after an atrial premature beat occur early with respect to the previous regular beats. However, the first normal beat after a ventricular premature beat occurs on the second foot tap after the premature beat because the duration of a ventricular extrasystole plus the preceding normal beat is equal to the duration of 2 normal beats (Fig 28–14).

Atrial and ventricular extrasystoles are not strong enough to produce a pulse at the wrist if they occur

FIG 28–14. Ventricular premature beats (VPB). The lines under the tracing illustrate the compensatory pause and show that the duration of the premature beat plus the preceding normal beat is equal to the duration of 2 normal beats. (Tracing from Goldman: *Principles of Clinical Electrocardiography*, 8th ed. Lange, 1973.)

Ventricular tachycardia, rate 240. Lower record: After conversion to normal sinus rhythm, with one ventricular premature beat.

Ventricular fibrillation ending in asystole in a patient dying of a myocardial infarction.

FIG 28–15. Ventricular tachycardia and fibrillation. (Tracings from Goldman: *Principles of Clinical Electrocardiography*, 8th ed. Lange, 1973.)

FIG 28–16. Technic of external cardiac massage. The lines above are a diagrammatic representation of the cardiac output produced by slow massage (275 ml/stroke) and fast massage (125 ml/stroke). (After Gordon. Reproduced, with permission, from Whittenberger: *Artificial Respiration: Theory and Application.* Harper & Row, 1962.)

early in diastole, when the ventricles have not had time to fill with blood and the ventricular musculature is still in its relatively refractory period. They may not even open the aortic and pulmonary valves, in which case there is, in addition, no second heart sound (see Chapter 29).

Paroxysmal ventricular tachycardia is in effect a series of rapid, regular ventricular extrasystoles. In **ventricular fibrillation**, the ventricular muscle fibers contract in a totally irregular and ineffective way, probably because of the very rapid discharge of multiple ventricular ectopic foci (Fig 28–15). The fibrillating ventricles, like the fibrillating atria, are said to look like a quivering "bag of worms."

Ventricular extrasystoles are common and usually benign. Ventricular tachycardia is more serious because cardiac output is decreased, and ventricular fibrillation is an occasional complication of ventricular tachycardia. The fibrillating ventricles cannot pump blood effectively, and circulation of the blood stops. Therefore, in the absence of emergency treatment, ventricular fibrillation that lasts more than a few minutes is fatal. The most frequent cause of sudden death in patients with myocardial infarcts is ventricular fibrillation.

Ventricular fibrillation may be produced by electrocution, but, paradoxically, it can sometimes be stopped and converted to normal sinus rhythm by

Normal sinus beat

Usual accelerated conduction beat;
short PR interval, wide and
slurred QRS complex,
normal PJ interval.

FIG 28–17. Accelerated AV conduction. (Reproduced, with permission, from Goldman: *Principles of Clinical Electrocardiography*, 8th ed. Lange, 1973.)

means of electrical shocks. Electronic defibrillators are now kept in most hospital emergency rooms. Cardiac output can be maintained in a patient with fibrillating ventricles by **cardiac massage.** Effective massage can be carried out without opening the chest by pressing firmly upward and inward about 60 times per minute with the heel of the hand on the sternum, just above the xiphoid process (external cardiac massage; Fig 28–16). Manually squeezing the ventricles is also effective if the chest is already open, but emergency thoracotomies should not be performed.

Accelerated AV Conduction

An interesting condition seen in some otherwise normal individuals who are prone to attacks of paroxysmal atrial arrhythmias is **accelerated AV conduction (Wolff-Parkinson-White syndrome).** Normally, the only conducting pathway between the atria and the ventricles is the AV node. Individuals with the Wolff-Parkinson-White syndrome probably have an additional aberrant muscular or nodal tissue connection between the atria and ventricles. This conducts more rapidly than the slow-conducting AV node, and one ventricle is excited early. The manifestations of its activation merge with the normal QRS pattern, producing a short PR interval and a prolonged QRS deflection slurred on the upstroke (Fig 28–17), with a normal interval between the start of the P wave and the end of the QRS complex ("PJ interval").

ECG FINDINGS IN OTHER CARDIAC & SYSTEMIC DISEASES

Myocardial Ischemia

When the blood supply to a portion of myocardium is reduced and the cells are partially deprived of O_2, their repolarization becomes prolonged. The ECG manifestations of this change are negative or biphasic T waves over the ischemic area. T wave changes require careful interpretation. Many processes other than ischemia, some completely benign, cause T wave changes, and healthy patients have been made cardiac invalids by improper interpretation of minor changes.

Myocardial Infarction

When the blood supply to part of the myocardium is severely compromised, muscle cells die and the area becomes necrotic **(myocardial infarction).** The cause of myocardial infarction is usually occlusion of a coronary artery by a thrombus in a region narrowed by arteriosclerotic plaques (coronary thrombosis). The ECG is a very useful tool for diagnosing and localizing areas of infarction. The underlying electrical events and the resulting ECG changes are complex, and only a brief review can be presented here.

The 3 major abnormalities which cause ECG changes in acute myocardial infarction are summarized in Table 28–4. The first change, abnormally rapid repolarization of the infarcted muscle fibers, develops seconds after occlusion of a coronary artery in experimental animals. It lasts only a few minutes, but before it is over the resting membrane potential of the infarcted fibers declines. Starting about 30 minutes later, the infarcted fibers also begin to depolarize more slowly than the surrounding normal fibers.

All 3 of these changes cause current flow which produces elevation of the ST segment in ECG leads recorded with electrodes over the infarcted area. Because of the rapid repolarization in the infarct, the membrane potential of the infarcted area is greater than it is in the normal area during the latter part of repolarization, making the normal region negative to the infarct. Extracellularly, current therefore flows out of the infarct into the normal area (since, by convention, current flow is from positive to negative; see Chapters 2 and 3). This current flows toward electrodes over the injured area, causing increased positivity between the S and T waves of the ECG. Similarly, the delayed depolarization of the infarcted cells causes the infarcted area to be positive relative to the healthy tissue (Table 28–4) during the early part of repolarization, and the result is also ST segment elevation. The remaining change, the decline in resting membrane potential during diastole, causes a current flow into the infarct during ventricular diastole. The result of this current flow is a depression of the TQ segment of the ECG. However, the electronic arrangement in ECG recorders is such that a TQ segment depression is recorded as an ST segment elevation. Thus, the hallmark of acute myocardial infarction is elevation of the ST segments in the leads overlying the area of infarction (Fig 28–18). Leads on the opposite side of the heart show ST segment depression.

After some days or weeks, the ST segment abnormalities subside. The dead muscle and scar tissue become electrically silent. The infarcted area is there-

A. Normal tracing.

B. **Very Early Pattern (Hours After Infarction):** ST segment elevation in I, aVL, and V_{3-6}; reciprocal ST depression in II, III, and aVF.

C. **Later Pattern (Many Hours to a Few Days):** Q waves have appeared in I, aVL, and V_{5-6}. QS complexes are present in V_{3-4}. This indicates that the major transmural infarction is underlying the area recorded by V_{3-4}; ST segment changes persist, but are of lesser degree, and the T waves are beginning to invert in those leads in which the ST segments are elevated.

D. **Late Established Pattern (Many Days to Weeks):** The Q waves and QS complexes persist; the ST segments are isoelectric; the T waves are symmetrical, and deeply inverted in leads which had ST elevation and tall in leads which had ST depression. This pattern may persist for the remainder of the patient's life.

E. **Very Late Pattern:** This may occur many months to years after the infarct. The abnormal Q waves and QS complexes persist. The T waves have gradually returned to normal.

FIG 28–18. Diagram of the serial ECG changes following infarction of the anterior portion of the wall of the ventricles. (Reproduced, with permission, from Goldman: *Principles of Clinical Electrocardiography*, 8th ed. Lange, 1973.)

TABLE 28–4. Summary of the 3 major abnormalities of membrane polarization associated with acute myocardial infarction, and the ECG abnormalities they produce. Because of the characteristics of their input capacitors, ECG records show a TQ segment depression as an ST segment elevation.

Abnormality	Cause	Resultant Extracellular Current Flow (Positive to Negative)	Resultant ECG Change in Leads Over Infarct
During repolarization (late) – – + + – – + + ▦– –▦ + + + + ▦– –▦ + + – – + + – –	Rapid repolarization of infarcted cells	Out of infarct	ST segment elevation
At rest + + – – + + – – ▦+ +▦ – – – – ▦+ +▦ – – + + – – + +	Decreased resting membrane potential of infarcted cells	Into infarct	TQ segment depression (manifest as ST segment elevation)
During repolarization (early) – – + + – – + + ▦– –▦ + + + + ▦– –▦ + + – – + + – –	Delayed depolarization of infarcted cells	Out of infarct	ST segment elevation

Legend:
Extracellular fluid

Normal muscle	Infarcted muscle	Normal muscle

Extracellular fluid

fore negative relative to the normal myocardium during systole, and it fails to contribute its share of positivity to the ECG complexes. The manifestations of this negativity are multiple and subtle. Common changes include the appearance of a Q wave in some of the leads in which it was not previously present and an increase in the size of the normal Q wave in some of the other leads. Another finding in infarction of the anterior left ventricle is "failure of progression of the R wave"; the R wave fails to become successively larger in the precordial leads as the electrode is moved from right to left over the left ventricle. If the septum is infarcted, the conduction system may be damaged, causing bundle branch block or other forms of heart block.

Effects of Changes in the Ionic Composition of the Blood

Changes in ECF Na^+ and K^+ concentration would be expected to affect the potentials of the myocardial fibers because the electrical activity of the heart depends upon the distribution of these ions across the muscle cell membranes. Clinically, a fall in plasma Na^+ may be associated with low-voltage ECG complexes, but changes in the plasma K^+ level produce severe cardiac abnormalities. Hyperkalemia is a very dangerous and potentially lethal condition because of its effects on the heart. As the plasma K^+ level rises, the first change in the ECG is the appearance of tall peaked T waves, a manifestation of altered repolarization (Fig 28–19). At higher K^+ levels there is paralysis of the atria and prolongation of the QRS complexes. Ventricular arrhythmias may develop. The resting membrane potential of the muscle fibers decreases as the extracellular K^+ increases. The fibers eventually become unexcitable, and the heart stops in diastole. Conversely, a decrease in plasma K^+ causes prolongation of the PR interval, prominent U waves, and, occasionally, late T wave inversion in the precordial leads. If the T waves and U waves merge, the apparent QT interval is often prolonged; if the T and U waves are separated, the true QT interval is seen to be of normal duration. Hypokalemia is a serious condition, but it is not as rapidly fatal as hyperkalemia.

When large amounts of calcium are infused into experimental animals, the heart relaxes less during diastole and eventually stops in systole (**calcium rigor**). However, in clinical conditions associated with hypercalcemia, the plasma Ca^{++} level is rarely if ever high enough to affect the heart. Hypocalcemia causes prolongation of the ST segment and consequently of the QT interval, a nonspecific change also found in other clinical conditions.

Changes in plasma Ca^{++} and K^+ levels produce relatively marked changes in the sensitivity of the heart to digitalis. Hypercalcemia enhances digitalis toxicity,

Normal tracing (plasma K⁺ 4–5.5 mEq/liter). PR interval = 0.16 sec; QRS interval = 0.06 sec; QT interval = 0.4 sec (normal for an assumed heart rate of 60).

 Hypokalemia (plasma K⁺ ±3.5 mEq/liter). PR = 0.2 sec; QRS interval = 0.06 sec; ST segment depression. A prominent U wave is now present immediately following the T. The actual QT interval remains 0.4 sec. If the U wave is erroneously considered a part of the T, a falsely prolonged QT interval of 0.6 sec will be measured.

 Hypokalemia (plasma K⁺ ±2.5 mEq/liter). The PR is lengthened to 0.32 sec; the ST segment is depressed; the T wave is inverted; a prominent U wave is seen. The true QT interval remains normal.

 Hyperkalemia (plasma K⁺ ±7.0 mEq/liter). The PR and QRS intervals are within normal limits. Very tall, slender, peaked T waves are now present.

 Hyperkalemia (plasma K⁺ ±8.5 mEq/liter). There is no evidence of atrial activity; the QRS complex is broad and slurred and the QRS interval has widened to 0.2 sec. The T waves remain tall and slender. Further elevation of the plasma K⁺ may result in ventricular tachycardia and ventricular fibrillation.

FIG 28–19. Correlation of plasma K⁺ level and the ECG, assuming plasma Ca⁺⁺ is normal. The diagrammed complexes are left ventricular epicardial leads. (Reproduced, with permission, from Goldman: *Principles of Clinical Electrocardiography,* 8th ed. Lange, 1973.)

and hyperkalemia counteracts it. Mg⁺⁺, which depresses the myocardium, also counteracts digitalis toxicity.

In experimental animals, acidosis increases the duration of diastole and decreases the strength of the heartbeat, but no ECG abnormalities specifically due to the changes in H⁺ concentration of the body fluids in patients with acidosis or alkalosis have been demonstrated.

29...

The Heart as a Pump

MECHANICAL EVENTS OF THE CARDIAC CYCLE

The orderly depolarization process described in the previous chapter triggers a wave of contraction that spreads through the myocardium. In single muscle fibers, contraction starts just after depolarization and lasts until about 50 msec after repolarization is completed (Fig 3–13). Atrial systole starts after the P wave of the ECG; ventricular systole starts near the end of the R wave; and ventricular systole ends just after the T wave. The contraction produces sequential changes in pressures and flows in the heart chambers and blood vessels. It should be noted that the term **systolic pressure** in the vascular system refers to the peak pressure reached during systole, not the mean pressure; similarly, the **diastolic pressure** refers to the lowest pressure during diastole.

Events in Late Diastole

Late in diastole, the mitral and tricuspid valves between the atria and ventricles are open and the aortic and pulmonary valves are closed. Blood flows into the heart throughout diastole, filling the atria and ventricles. The rate of filling declines as the ventricles become distended, and—especially when the heart rate is slow—the cusps of the AV valves drift toward the closed position (Fig 29–1). The pressure in the ventricles remains low.

Atrial Systole

Contraction of the atria propels some additional blood into the ventricles, but about 70% of the ventricular filling occurs passively during diastole. Contraction of the atrial muscle that surrounds the orifices of the vena cavas and pulmonary veins narrows their orifices, and the inertia of the blood moving toward the heart tends to keep blood in it; however, there is some regurgitation of blood into the veins during atrial systole.

Ventricular Systole

The initial portion of ventricular systole, the period of **isometric** or **isovolumetric ventricular contraction**, lasts until the aortic and pulmonary valves open. The AV valves close at the start of isometric contraction, and the ventricles contract on their contained blood. There is little muscle shortening, but the intraventricular pressure rises rapidly. This period lasts about 0.05 sec. During isometric contraction, the mitral and tricuspid (AV) valves bulge into the atria, causing a small but sharp rise in atrial pressure (Fig 29–2).

When the rising pressure in the left ventricle exceeds the diastolic pressure in the aorta (80 mm Hg) and the right ventricular pressure exceeds the diastolic pressure in the pulmonary artery (10 mm Hg), the aortic and pulmonary valves open and the phase of **ventricular ejection** begins. Ejection is rapid at first, slowing down as systole progresses. The intraventricu-

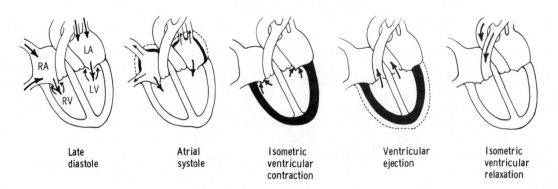

| Late diastole | Atrial systole | Isometric ventricular contraction | Ventricular ejection | Isometric ventricular relaxation |

FIG 29–1. Blood flow in the heart and great vessels during the cardiac cycle. The portions of the heart contracting in each phase are indicated in black. RA and LA, right and left atria; RV and LV, right and left ventricles.

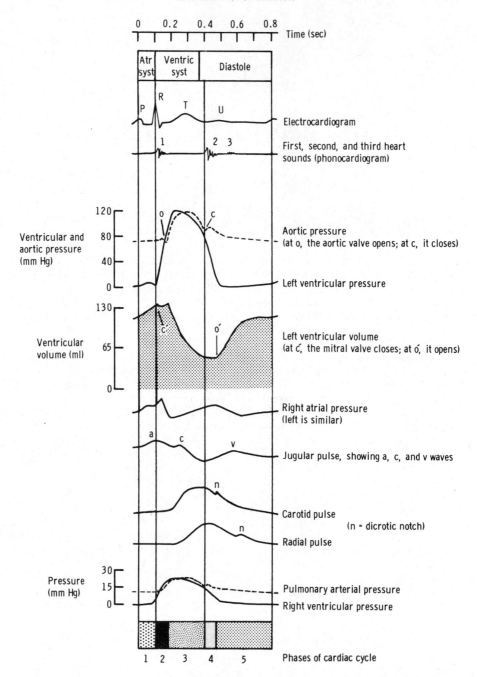

FIG 29–2. Events of the cardiac cycle at a heart rate of 75 beats/min. The phases of the cardiac cycle identified by the numbers at the bottom are: 1, atrial systole; 2, isometric ventricular contraction; 3, ventricular ejection; 4, isometric ventricular relaxation; 5, ventricular filling. Note that, late in systole, aortic pressure actually exceeds left ventricular pressure. However, the momentum of the blood keeps it flowing out of the ventricle for a short period of time. The pressure relationships in the right ventricle and pulmonary artery are similar. Atr syst, atrial systole. Ventric syst, ventricular systole.

lar pressure rises to a maximum and then declines somewhat before ventricular systole ends. Peak left ventricular pressure is about 120 mm Hg, and peak right ventricular pressure is 25 mm Hg or less. Late in systole, the aortic pressure actually exceeds the ventricular, but for a short period momentum keeps the blood moving forward. The AV valves are pulled down by the contractions of the ventricular muscle, and atrial pressure drops. The amount of blood ejected by each ventricle per stroke at rest is 70–90 ml. This leaves about 50 ml of blood in each ventricle at the end of systole (**end-systolic ventricular blood volume**).

Early Diastole

Once the ventricular muscle is fully contracted, the already falling ventricular pressures drop more rapidly. This is the period of **protodiastole**. It lasts about 0.04 sec. It ends when the momentum of the ejected blood is overcome and the aortic and pulmonary valves close, setting up transient vibrations in the blood and blood vessel walls. After the valves are closed, pressure continues to drop rapidly during the period of **isometric ventricular relaxation**. Isometric relaxation ends when the ventricular pressure falls below atrial pressure and the AV valves open, permitting the ventricles to fill. Filling is rapid at first, then slows down as the time of the next cardiac contraction approaches. Atrial pressure continues to rise after the end of ventricular systole until the AV valves open, then drops and slowly rises again until the next atrial systole.

Timing

Although events on the 2 sides of the heart are similar, they are somewhat asynchronous. Right atrial systole precedes left atrial systole, and contraction of the right ventricle starts after that of the left (see Chapter 28). However, since pulmonary arterial pressure is lower than aortic pressure, right ventricular ejection begins before left ventricular ejection. During expiration, the pulmonic and aortic valves close at the same time; but during inspiration the aortic valve closes slightly before the pulmonic. When measured over a period of minutes, the output of the 2 ventricles is, of course, equal, but there are transient differences in output during the respiratory cycle. These differences are believed to be responsible for the changes in the time of closure of the aortic and pulmonic valves.

Length of Systole & Diastole

Cardiac muscle has the unique property of contracting and repolarizing faster when the heart rate is rapid (see Chapter 3), and the duration of systole decreases from 0.3 sec at a heart rate of 65 to 0.16 sec at a rate of 200 (Table 29–1). The shortening is due mainly to a decrease in the duration of systolic ejection. However, the duration of systole is much more fixed than that of diastole, and when the heart rate is increased, diastole is shortened to a much greater degree. For example, at a heart rate of 65, the duration of diastole is 0.62 sec, whereas at a heart rate of 200 it

TABLE 29–1. Variation in length of action potential and associated phenomena with cardiac rate. All values are in seconds. (Courtesy of AC Barger and GS Richardson.)

	Heart Rate 75/min	Heart Rate 200/min	Skeletal Muscle
Duration, each cardiac cycle	0.80	0.30	. . .
Duration of systole	0.27	0.16	0.04
Duration of action potential	0.25	0.15	0.005
Duration of absolute refractory period	0.20	0.13	0.004
Duration of relative refractory period	0.05	0.02	0.003
Duration of diastole	0.53	0.14	. . .

is only 0.14 sec. This fact has important physiologic and clinical implications. It is during diastole that the heart muscle rests, and coronary blood flow to the subendocardial portions of the left ventricle occurs only during diastole (see Chapter 32). Furthermore, most of the ventricular filling occurs in diastole. At heart rates up to about 180 beats/min, filling is adequate as long as there is ample venous return, and cardiac output per minute is increased by an increase in rate. However, at very rapid heart rates, filling may be compromised to such a degree that cardiac output falls and symptoms of heart failure develop.

Because it has a prolonged action potential, cardiac muscle is refractory and will not contract in response to a second stimulus until near the end of the initial contraction. Therefore, cardiac muscle cannot be tetanized like skeletal muscle. The most rapid rate at which the ventricles can contract is theoretically about 400/min, but in adults the AV node will not conduct more than about 230 impulses/min because of its long refractory period. A ventricular rate of more than 230 is seen only in paroxysmal ventricular tachycardia (see Chapter 28).

Arterial Pulse

The blood forced into the aorta during systole not only moves the blood in the vessels forward but also sets up a pressure wave which travels down the arteries. The pressure wave expands the arterial walls as it travels, and the expansion is palpable as the **pulse**. The rate at which the wave travels, which is independent of and much faster than the velocity of blood flow, is 5–8 meters/sec depending upon the age of the individual (Table 29–2). In young adults, the pulse is felt in the radial artery at the wrist about 0.1 sec after the peak of systolic ejection into the aorta (Fig 29–2). With advancing age, the arteries become more rigid and the pulse wave moves faster.

The strength of the pulse is determined by the pulse pressure and bears little relation to the mean pressure. The pulse is weak ("thready") in shock. It is strong when stroke volume is large, eg, during exercise or after the administration of histamine. When the

TABLE 29–2. Relationship of pulse wave
velocity to aortic elasticity.*

Age (years)	Average Pulse Wave Velocity (meters/sec)	Aortic Elasticity (percentage increase in arterial volume per mm Hg rise in arterial pressure)
5	5.2	0.47
20	6.2	0.33
40	7.2	0.24
70	8.3	0.18

*Data from Keele & Neil, in *Samson Wright's Applied Physiology,* 11th ed. Oxford Univ Press, 1965.

pulse pressure is high, the pulse waves may be large enough to be felt or even heard by the individual (palpitation, "pounding heart"). When the aortic valve is incompetent (aortic insufficiency), the pulse is particularly strong and the force of systolic ejection may be sufficient to make the head nod with each heartbeat. The pulse in aortic insufficiency is called a **collapsing, Corrigan,** or **water-hammer pulse.** A water hammer is an evacuated glass tube half-filled with water that was a popular toy in the 19th century. When held in the hand and inverted, it delivers a short, hard knock.

The **dicrotic notch,** a small oscillation on the falling phase of the pulse wave due to vibrations set up when the aortic valve snaps shut (Fig 29–2), is visible if the pressure wave is recorded but is not palpable at the wrist.

Atrial Pressure Changes & the Jugular Pulse

Atrial pressure rises during atrial systole and continues to rise during isometric ventricular contraction when the AV valves bulge into the atria. When the AV valves are pulled down by the contracting ventricular muscle, pressure falls rapidly and then rises as blood flows into the atria until the AV valves open early in diastole. The return of the AV valves to their relaxed position also contributes to this pressure rise by reducing atrial capacity. The atrial pressure changes are transmitted to the great veins, producing 3 characteristic waves in the jugular pulse (Figs 29–2 and 29–3). The **a wave** is due to atrial systole. As noted above, some blood regurgitates into the great veins when the atria contract even though the orifices of the great veins are constricted. In addition, venous inflow stops, and the resultant rise in venous pressure contributes to the a wave. The **c wave** is the transmitted manifestation of the rise in atrial pressure produced by the bulging of the tricuspid valve into the atria during isometric ventricular contraction. The **v wave** mirrors the rise in atrial pressure before the tricuspid valve opens during diastole. The jugular pulse waves are superimposed on the respiratory fluctuations in venous pressure. Venous pressure falls during inspiration as a result of the increased negative intrathoracic pressure, and rises again during expiration.

FIG 29–3. Jugular venous pressure record (JVP), showing *a, c,* and *v* waves, compared with the simultaneously recorded ECG and carotid pressure record. (Redrawn and reproduced, with permission, from Wood: *Diseases of the Heart.* Lippincott, 1956.)

The jugular pulse can be recorded without catheterizing the vein by using a suitable tambour applied to the skin of the neck. Such recordings are rarely made today, but careful inspection at the bedside of the pulsations of the external jugular veins may give clinical information of some importance. For example, in tricuspid insufficiency there is a giant c wave with each ventricular systole. In complete heart block, when the atria and ventricles are beating at different rates, the a waves that are not synchronous with the radial pulse can be made out and there is a giant a wave ("cannon wave") whenever the atria contract while the tricuspid valve is closed. It may also be possible to distinguish atrial from ventricular extrasystoles by inspection of the jugular pulse because atrial premature beats produce an a wave, whereas ventricular premature beats do not.

Heart Sounds

Two sounds are normally heard through a stethoscope during each cardiac cycle: a low, slightly prolonged "lub" (**first sound**), caused by closure of the mitral and tricuspid valves at the start of ventricular systole; and a shorter, high-pitched "dup" (**second sound**), caused by closure of the aortic and pulmonic valves just after the end of ventricular systole. A soft, low-pitched **third sound** is heard about one-third of the way through diastole in many normal young individuals. It coincides with the period of rapid ventricular filling and is probably due to vibrations set up by the inrush of blood.

The first sound has a duration of about 0.15 sec and a frequency of 25–45 hz. It is soft when the heart rate is slow because the ventricles are well filled with blood and the leaflets of the AV valves float together before systole. The second sound lasts about 0.12 sec, with a frequency of 50 hz. It is loud and sharp when the diastolic pressure in the aorta or pulmonary artery is elevated, causing the respective valves to shut briskly at the end of systole. The interval between aortic and pulmonic valve closure during inspiration is frequently long enough for the second sound to be reduplicated, or "split." The third sound has a duration of 0.1 sec.

Murmurs

Murmurs and **bruits** are abnormal sounds heard in various parts of the vascular system. Blood flows silently as long as the flow is smooth. However, if blood strikes an obstruction or passes through a narrow orifice at high speed, swirling vortices are set up which generate **vortical sounds**. Turbulent flow may also generate sound. Examples of sounds outside the heart are the bruit heard over a large, highly vascular goiter and the murmurs heard over an aneurysmal dilatation of one of the large arteries, an A-V fistula, or a patent ductus arteriosus.

The major but certainly not the only cause of cardiac murmurs is disease of the heart valves. When a valve is narrowed (**stenosis**), blood flow through it in the normal direction is turbulent. When a valve is incompetent, blood leaks through it in the wrong direction (**regurgitation** or **insufficiency**). The timing (systolic or diastolic) of a murmur due to stenosis or insufficiency of any particular valve (Table 29–3) can

TABLE 29–3. Heart murmurs.

Valve	Abnormality	Timing of Murmur
Aortic or pulmonary	Stenosis	Systolic
	Insufficiency	Diastolic
Mitral or tricuspid	Stenosis	Diastolic
	Insufficiency	Systolic

be predicted from a knowledge of the mechanical events of the cardiac cycle. Murmurs due to disease of a particular valve can generally be heard best when the stethoscope is over that particular valve, and there are other aspects of the duration, character, accentuation, and transmission of the sound that help localize its origin in one valve or the other. One of the loudest murmurs is that produced when blood flows backward in diastole through a hole in a cusp of the aortic valve. Most murmurs can be heard only with the aid of the stethoscope, but this high-pitched musical diastolic murmur is sometimes audible to the unaided ear several feet from the patient.

In patients with congenital interventricular septal defects, flow from the left to the right ventricle causes a systolic murmur. Soft murmurs may also be heard in patients with interatrial septal defects, although they are not a constant finding.

It should be emphasized that soft systolic murmurs are common in individuals, especially children, who have no cardiac disease. Systolic murmurs are also common in anemic patients as a result of the low viscosity of the blood and the rapid flow (see Chapter 30).

CARDIAC OUTPUT

Methods of Measurement

Two methods of measuring the output of the heart that are applicable to humans are the **direct Fick method** and the **indicator dilution method**.

The **Fick principle** states that the amount of a substance taken up by an organ (or by the whole body) per unit of time is equal to the arterial level of the substance minus the venous level (**A-V difference**) times the blood flow. This principle can be applied, of course, only in situations in which the arterial blood is the sole source of the substance taken up. The principle can be used to determine cardiac output by measuring the amount of O_2 consumed by the body in a period of time and dividing this value by the A-V difference across the lungs. Because arterial blood has the same content in all parts of the body, the arterial O_2 content can be measured in a sample obtained from any convenient artery. A sample of venous blood in the pulmonary artery is obtained by means of a cardiac catheter. Right atrial blood has been used in the past, but mixing of this blood may be incomplete so that the sample is not representative of the whole body. An example of the calculation of cardiac output using a typical set of values is as follows:

$$\text{Output of left ventricle} = \frac{O_2 \text{ consumption (ml/min)}}{[AO_2] - [VO_2]}$$

$$= \frac{250 \text{ ml/min}}{\substack{190 \text{ ml/liter arterial blood} - \\ 140 \text{ ml/liter venous blood in} \\ \text{pulmonary artery}}}$$

$$= \frac{250 \text{ ml/min}}{50 \text{ ml/liter}}$$

$$= 5 \text{ liters/min}$$

It has now become commonplace to insert a long catheter through a forearm vein and to guide its tip into the heart with the aid of a fluoroscope. The idea of putting a catheter in the human heart so upset the superiors of the man who developed the technic of cardiac catheterization that he lost his job, but the procedure is now known to be essentially harmless. Catheters can be inserted not only into the right atrium but through the atrium down the inferior vena cava to the hepatic or renal vessels, and through the right ventricle into the small branches of the pulmonary artery.

In the indicator dilution technic, a known amount of dye or radioactive isotope is injected into an arm vein and the concentration of the indicator in serial samples of arterial blood is determined. The output of the heart is equal to the amount of indicator injected divided by its average concentration in arterial blood after a single circulation through the heart (Fig 29–4). The indicator must, of course, be a substance

$$F = \frac{E}{\int_0^\infty Cdt}$$

F = flow
E = amount of indicator injected
C = instantaneous concentration of indicator in
       arterial blood

In the **rest** example above,

$$\frac{\text{Flow in 39 sec}}{\text{(time of first passage)}} = \frac{5 \text{ mg injection}}{1.6 \text{ mg/liter}}$$
$$\text{(avg concentration)}$$

Flow = 3.1 liters in 39 sec

Flow (cardiac output)/min = $3.1 \times \dfrac{60}{39}$ = 4.7 liters

For the **exercise** example,

$$\text{Flow in 9 sec} = \frac{5 \text{ mg}}{1.51 \text{ mg/liter}} = 3.3 \text{ liters}$$

$$\text{Flow/min} = 3.3 \times \frac{60}{9} = 22.0 \text{ liters}$$

FIG 29–4. Determination of cardiac output by indicator (dye) dilution. (Data and graph from Asmussen & Nielsen: The cardiac output in rest and work determined by the acetylene and the dye injection methods. Acta physiologica scandinav 27:217, 1952.)

which stays in the blood stream during the test and which has no harmful or hemodynamic effects. In practice, the log of the indicator concentration in the serial arterial samples is plotted against time as the concentration rises, falls, and then rises again as the indicator recirculates. The initial decline in concentration, linear on a semilog plot, is extrapolated to the abscissa, giving the time for first passage of the indicator through the circulation. The cardiac output for that period of time is calculated (Fig 29–4), and then converted to output per minute.

Another method which has been used to measure cardiac output in humans is **ballistocardiography**. In accordance with Newton's third law of motion, the forces generated by the movements of the heart and the impact of the ejected blood on the aorta and pulmonary artery are opposed by "opposite and equal" recoil reactions. The operation of these forces has been observed by anyone who has stood on a scale and watched the pointer move with each heartbeat. The **ballistocardiogram** is a record of the to-and-fro movements of the body in the headward-footward direction when the subject lies on a suitably suspended table. However, values for stroke volume calculated from these records have proved to be unreliable.

Cardiac Output in Various Conditions

The amount of blood pumped out of each ventricle per beat, the **stroke volume**, is about 80 ml in a resting man of average size in the supine position (80 ml from the left ventricle and 80 ml from the right, with the 2 ventricular pumps in series). The output of the heart per unit time is the **cardiac output**. In a resting, supine male, it averages about 5.5 liters/min (80 ml × 69 beats/min). There is a correlation between resting cardiac output and body surface area. The output per minute per square meter of body surface (the **cardiac index**) averages 3.2 liters. The effects of various conditions on cardiac output are summarized in Table 29–4.

TABLE 29–4. Effect of various conditions on cardiac output. Approximate percentage changes are shown in parentheses.

	Condition or Factor
No change	Sleep
	Moderate changes in environmental temperature
Increase	Anxiety and excitement (50–100%)
	Eating (30%)
	Exercise (up to 700%)
	High environmental temperature
	Pregnancy (late)
	Epinephrine
	Histamine
Decrease	Sitting or standing from lying position (20–30%)
	Rapid arrhythmias
	Heart disease

Factors Controlling Cardiac Output

Variations in cardiac output can be produced by changes in cardiac rate or stroke volume. The cardiac rate is controlled primarily by the cardiac innervation, sympathetic stimulation increasing the rate and parasympathetic stimulation decreasing it (see Chapter 28). The stroke volume is determined in part by the length of the cardiac muscle fibers, but it is also influenced by the pressure in the aorta and by sympathetic stimuli which make the myocardial muscle fibers contract with greater strength at any given length. When the strength of contraction increases without an increase in fiber length, more of the blood that normally remains in the ventricles is expelled and the end-systolic ventricular blood volume falls. The cardiac accelerator action of the adrenergic mediator liberated by sympathetic stimulation is referred to as its chrono-tropic action, whereas its effect on the strength of cardiac contraction is called its **inotropic action**. Factors which increase the strength of cardiac contraction are said to be positively inotropic; those which decrease it are said to be negatively inotropic.

The force of contraction of cardiac muscle is dependent upon its preloading and its afterloading. These factors are illustrated in Fig 29–5, in which a muscle strip is stretched **(preloaded)** by a load that rests on a platform. The initial phase of the contraction is isometric; the elastic component in series with the contractile elements is stretched, and tension increases until it is just sufficient to lift the load **(afterload)**. The muscle then contracts isotonically without developing further tension.

Relation of Tension to Length in Cardiac Muscle

The length-tension relationship in cardiac muscle (Fig 3–14) is similar to that in skeletal muscle (Fig 3–9); as the muscle is stretched, the developed tension increases to a maximum and then declines as stretch becomes more extreme. Starling pointed this out when he stated that the "energy of contraction is proportional to the initial length of the cardiac muscle fiber." This pronouncement has come to be known as **Starling's law of the heart**, or the **Frank-Starling law**. For the heart, the length of the muscle fibers (ie, the extent of the preload) is proportionate to the end-diastolic volume. The relation between ventricular performance and end-diastolic volume that is brought about through the operation of the Frank-Starling mechanism is shown in Fig 29–6. This figure also lists

FIG 29–5. Model for isotonic contraction of afterloaded muscles. *A:* rest. *B:* partial contraction of the contractile element of the muscle (CE), with stretching of the series elastic element (SE) but no shortening. *C:* complete contraction, with shortening. (Reproduced, with permission, from Sonnenblick, in: *The Myocardial Cell; Structure, Function and Modifications.* Briller SA, Conn HL [editors]. Univ of Pennsylvania Press, 1966.)

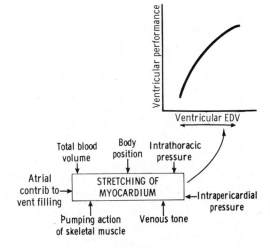

FIG 29–6. Relation between ventricular end-diastolic volume (EDV) and ventricular performance (Frank-Starling curve), with a summary of the major factors affecting EDV. (Reproduced, with permission, from Braunwald & others: Mechanisms of contraction of the normal and failing heart. New England J Med 277:794, 853, 910, 1012, 1967. Courtesy of Little, Brown, Inc.)

the principal factors that affect the end-diastolic volume. An increase in intrapericardial pressure limits the extent to which the ventricle can fill. Atrial contractions aid ventricular filling. The other factors affect the amount of blood returning to the heart and hence the degree of cardiac filling during diastole. A reduction in total blood volume reduces venous return. Constriction of the veins reduces the size of the venous reservoirs, decreasing venous pooling and thus increasing venous return. An increase in the normal negative intrathoracic pressure increases the pressure gradient along which blood flows to the heart, while a decrease impedes venous return.

Effect of Changes in Aortic Impedance

The strength of cardiac contractions is also determined by the resistance or impedance against which the ventricles pump blood. This impedance is low in the pulmonary artery, but the aortic impedance is high. It is proportionate to the resistance to flow through the aortic valve and the systemic blood pressure.

The effect of changes in aortic impedance can be demonstrated in the **heart-lung preparation.** In this preparation, the heart and lungs of an experimental animal, usually a dog, are cannulated in such a way that blood flows from the aorta through a system of tubing and reservoirs to the right atrium, and from there through the animal's heart and lungs back to the aorta. Deprived of its blood supply, the rest of the animal dies, so that the heart is functionally dener-

vated and the heart rate varies little if at all. By changing the caliber of the outflow tubing, the resistance against which the heart pumps (**"peripheral resistance"**) can be varied; and by raising or lowering the reservoir emptying into the right atrium, the amount of blood returning to the heart (**"venous return"**) can also be varied. One version of this preparation is shown in Fig 29–7. A **bell cardiometer** or, more recently, one of a variety of electronic devices is used to measure the volume of the heart. Cardiac volume varies with the amount of blood in the heart and is therefore a measure of the length to which the cardiac muscle fibers are stretched.

In the heart-lung preparation, when the pressure against which the heart is pumping is raised the heart puts out less blood than it receives for several beats. Blood accumulates in the ventricles, and the size of the heart increases. The distended heart beats more forcefully, and output returns to its previous level. Conversely, when the resistance is reduced, output rises transiently but the size of the heart decreases, and output falls to the previous constant level (Fig 29–8).

Myocardial Contractility

The third factor exerting a major influence on stroke volume is the contractility of the myocardium. When the sympathetic nerves to the heart are stimulated, the whole length-tension curve shifts upward and to the left (Fig 29–9). The positively inotropic effect of the norepinephrine liberated at the adrenergic endings is augmented by circulating norepinephrine, and epinephrine has a similar effect. A negatively

FIG 29–7. Heart-lung preparation.

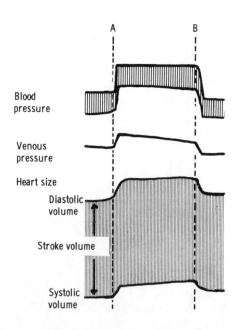

FIG 29–8. **Effect of increasing arterial resistance (at A) in heart-lung preparation.** At B, the resistance was reduced to its previous level. (Drawn from data of Patterson & others: The regulation of the heart beat. J Physiol 48:465, 1914.)

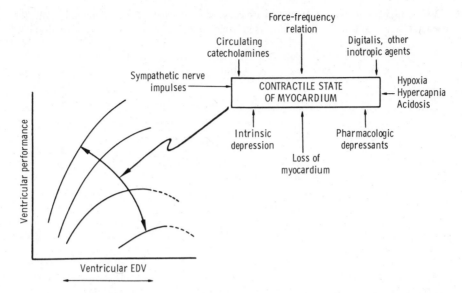

FIG 29–9. Effect of changes in myocardial contractility on the Frank-Starling curve. The major factors influencing contractility are summarized on the right. EDV = end-diastolic volume. (Reproduced, with permission, from Braunwald & others: Mechanisms of contraction of the normal and failing heart. New England J Med 277:794, 853, 910, 1012, 1967. Courtesy of Little, Brown, Inc.)

inotropic effect of vagal stimulation has been reported in dogs, but a role for the cholinergic innervation of the heart in the regulation of myocardial contractility has not been established.

Changes in cardiac rate and rhythm also affect myocardial contractility (force-frequency relation, Fig 29–9). Ventricular extrasystoles have a unique ability to condition the myocardium in such a way that the next succeeding contraction is stronger than the preceding normal contraction. This **postextrasystolic potentiation** is at least in part independent of ventricular filling since it occurs in isolated cardiac muscle. It has been postulated to be due to increased availability of intracellular Ca^{++}. A sustained increment in contractility can be produced by delivering paired electrical stimuli to the heart in such a way that the second stimulus is delivered shortly after the refractory period of the first. It has also been shown that myocardial contractility increases as the heart rate increases.

The catecholamines exert their inotropic effect via an action on cardiac β-adrenergic receptors, and β-receptor effects are probably mediated by cyclic AMP (see Chapter 17). Xanthines such as caffeine and theophylline which inhibit the breakdown of cyclic AMP are positively inotropic. Glucagon, which increases the formation of cyclic AMP, is positively inotropic, and it has been recommended for use in the treatment of some heart diseases. It acts via a different receptor than β-adrenergic agents and may be of benefit in treating patients with β-adrenergic blocking agent toxicity. It also accelerates AV conduction. The positively inotropic effect of digitalis and related drugs (Fig 29–9) is believed to be due to their inhibitory effect on the Na^+-K^+ ATPase in the myocardium. The

inhibition causes an increase in intracellular Na^+, which in turn increases the entry of Ca^{++} into the cell. The key role of Ca^{++} in the initiation of contraction in skeletal and cardiac muscle is discussed in Chapter 3. Hypercapnia, hypoxia, acidosis, and drugs such as quinidine, procainamide, and barbiturates depress myocardial contractility. The contractility of the myocardium is also reduced in heart failure (intrinsic depression). This depression is associated with a reduction in the catecholamine content of the myocardium, but its exact cause is not known. If part of the myocardium becomes fibrotic and nonfunctional as the result of a myocardial infarction, total ventricular performance is reduced.

Control of Cardiac Output in Vivo

In intact animals and humans, the mechanisms listed above operate in an integrated way to maintain cardiac output. During muscular exercise there is increased sympathetic discharge, so that myocardial contractility is increased and the heart rate rises. The increase in heart rate is particularly prominent in normal individuals, and there is little change in cardiac size (Table 29–5). However, patients with transplanted hearts are also able to increase their cardiac output during exercise in the absence of cardiac innervation through the operation of the Frank-Starling mechanism. The increase seen in these patients is not as rapid and their maximal increase is less than in normal individuals, but the increase is appreciable. It is important to note in this regard that the heart is the servant, rather than the master; it normally adjusts its function so that it expels all the blood that returns to the veins. If venous return increases and there is no change in

TABLE 29—5. Changes in cardiac function with exercise. Note that stroke volume levels off, then falls somewhat (as a result of the shortening of diastole) when the heart rate rises to high values.*

Work (kg m/min)	O_2 Usage (ml/min)	Pulse Rate (per min)	Cardiac Output (liters/min)	Stroke Volume (ml)	A-V O_2 Difference (ml/100 ml)
Rest	267	64	6.4	100	4.3
288	910	104	13.1	126	7.0
540	1430	122	15.2	125	9.4
900	2143	161	17.8	110	12.3
1260	3007	173	20.9	120	14.5

*Reproduced, with permission, from Asmussen & Nielsen: The cardiac output in rest and work determined by the acetylene and the dye injection methods. Acta physiologica scandinav 27:217, 1952.

sympathetic tone, venous pressure rises, diastolic inflow is greater, ventricular end-diastolic pressure increases, and the heart muscle contracts more forcefully. During muscular exercise, venous return is increased by the pumping action of the muscles and the increase in respiration (see Chapter 33). In addition, because of vasodilatation in the contracting muscles, peripheral resistance is decreased. The end result in both normal and transplanted hearts is thus a prompt and marked increase in cardiac output.

One of the differences between untrained individuals and trained athletes is that the athletes have lower heart rates, greater end-systolic ventricular volumes (Table 29—6), and greater stroke volumes at rest. Therefore, they can potentially achieve a given increase in cardiac output without increasing their heart rate to as great a degree as an untrained individual.

TABLE 29—6. Effect of training on some parameters of cardiac function.*

Subjects	Heart Volume (ml)	Estimated Heart Weight (g)	Left Ventricular End-systolic Blood Volume (ml)
1. Untrained	785	300	51
2. Trained for competition	1015	350	101
3. Professional cyclist	1437	500	177

*Modified from Reindell & others: *Schweiz Zeitschr f Sportmed* 1:97, 1953.

Oxygen Consumption of the Heart

The O_2 consumption of the heart is determined primarily by the intramyocardial tension, the contractile state of the myocardium, and the heart rate. Additional factors exerting minor effects are the external work performed by the heart, the activational energy involved in cardiac contraction, and the basal O_2 consumption of the myocardium. Intramyocardial tension is directly proportional to the intraventricular pressure, but it is also directly proportionate to the radius of the ventricle (law of Laplace; see Chapter 30) and inversely proportionate to the thickness of the ventricular wall. Thus, $T \cong Pr/h$, where T is the wall tension, P is the intraventricular pressure, r is the radius of the ventricle, and H is the thickness of the ventricular wall. Positively inotropic stimuli increase myocardial O_2 consumption both because they increase the tension the muscle can develop and because they increase the O_2 consumption for the same tension due to the energy cost of increasing contractility. The effects of heart rate on O_2 consumption depend primarily on the changes in tension development and contractile state. The increased number of beats causes more O_2 to be consumed per minute, but the stroke volume and end-diastolic volume decrease when the heart rate rises. This decreases the tension required to produce a given systolic pressure and tends to lower O_2 consumption. The work of the heart required to maintain the stroke volume against an increased aortic pressure utilizes considerably more O_2 than the work required to increase stroke volume against a constant aortic pressure. The former is "internal contractile element work," performed in stretching the series elastic elements in the myocardium; the latter is "external contractile element work," with the muscle expelling blood from the ventricle. The greater O_2 demand of expelling blood against an increased pressure explains the fact that angina pectoris, which is due to relative O_2 deficiency of the myocardium (see Chapter 7), is more common with aortic stenosis than it is with aortic regurgitation. The activation of myocardial contraction requires less than 1% of the myocardial O_2 consumption. The basal O_2 consumption of the heart is proportionate to the circulating level of thyroid hormones and normally accounts for 10–30% of the myocardial O_2 consumption.

30...

Dynamics of Blood & Lymph Flow

The blood vessels are a closed system of conduits which carry blood from the heart to the tissues and back to the heart. Some of the interstitial fluid enters the lymphatics and passes via these vessels to the vascular system. Blood flows through the vessels primarily because of the forward motion imparted to it by the pumping of the heart, although, in the case of the systemic circulation, diastolic recoil of the walls of the arteries, compression of the veins by skeletal muscles during exercise, and the negative pressure in the thorax during inspiration also move the blood forward. The resistance to flow depends to a minor degree upon the viscosity of the blood but mostly upon the diameter of the vessels, principally the arterioles. The blood flow to each tissue is regulated by local chemical and general neural mechanisms that dilate or constrict the vessels of the tissue. All of the blood flows through the lungs, but the systemic circulation is made up of numerous different circuits in parallel (Fig 30–1), an arrangement which permits wide variations in regional blood flow without changing total systemic flow.

This chapter is concerned with the general principles that apply to all parts of the circulation and with pressure and flow in the systemic circulation. The homeostatic mechanisms operating to adjust flow are the subject of Chapter 31. The special characteristics of pulmonary and renal circulation are discussed in Chapters 34 and 38, and the unique features of the circulation to other organs in Chapter 32.

ANATOMIC CONSIDERATIONS

Arteries & Arterioles

The characteristics of the various types of blood vessels are shown in Table 30–1. The walls of the aorta and other arteries of large diameter contain a relatively large amount of elastic tissue. They are stretched during systole, and recoil on the blood during diastole. The walls of the arterioles contain less elastic tissue but much more smooth muscle. The muscle is innervated by adrenergic nerve fibers, which are constrictor in function, and in some instances by cholinergic fibers, which dilate the vessels. The arterioles are the major site of the resistance to blood flow, and small changes in their caliber cause large changes in the total peripheral resistance.

Capillaries

The arterioles divide into smaller muscle-walled vessels, sometimes called **metarterioles**, and these in

FIG 30–1. Diagram of the circulation in the adult.

TABLE 30–1. Characteristics of various types of blood vessels in man.*

	Lumen Diameter	Wall Thickness	Approximate Total Cross-sectional Area (sq cm)	Percentage of Blood Volume Contained†
			All Vessels of Each Type	
Aorta	2.5 cm	2 mm	4.5	2
Artery	0.4 cm	1 mm	20	8
Arteriole	30 μm	20 μm	400	1
Capillary	6 μm	1 μm	4500	5
Venule	20 μm	2 μm	4000	
Vein	0.5 cm	0.5 mm	40	54
Vena cava	3 cm	1.5 mm	18	

*Data from Gregg, in: *The Physiological Basis of Medical Practice,* 8th ed. Best CH, Taylor NB (editors). Williams & Wilkins, 1966.

†In systemic vessels. There is an additional 12% in the heart and 18% in the pulmonary circulation.

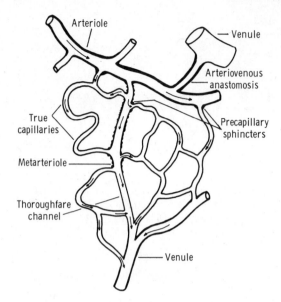

Arteriole

Venule

Arteriovenous anastomosis

True capillaries

Precapillary sphincters

Metarteriole

Thoroughfare channel

Venule

FIG 30–2. Portion of a capillary bed. The vessel walls are thickened in the areas where smooth muscle is found. (After Chambers & Zweifach: Capillary endothelial cement in relation to permeability. J Cell Comp Physiol 15:255, 1940.)

turn feed into capillaries. In some of the vascular beds that have been studied in detail, a metarteriole is connected directly with a venule by a capillary **thoroughfare vessel,** and the true capillaries are an anastomosing network of side branches of this thoroughfare vessel (Fig 30–2). The openings of the true capillaries are surrounded on the upstream side by minute smooth muscle **precapillary sphincters.** The vasoconstrictor fibers to the arterioles also innervate the metarterioles and precapillary sphincters. When the sphincters are dilated, the diameter of the capillaries is normally about 6 μm, just sufficient to permit red blood cells to squeeze through in "single file." As they pass through the capillaries, the red cells become thimble or parachute shaped with the concavity in the direction of flow. This configuration appears to be due simply to the pressure in the center of the vessel whether or not the edges of the red blood cell are in contact with the capillary walls.

The total area of all the capillary walls in the body exceeds 6300 sq m in the adult. The walls, which are about 1 μm thick, are made up of a single layer of endothelial cells joined by an **intercellular cement substance** which is probably a calcium proteinate and not, as was previously thought, hyaluronic acid. The connections between endothelial cells in the capillaries of some organs contain narrow areas where cells are tightly joined to each other, but these may be wide enough to permit passage of molecules 3 nm in diameter.

The anatomy of the capillaries varies considerably from organ to organ. In hepatic capillaries, "pores" are visible under the electron microscope, and the base-

ment membrane underlying the endothelial cells is interrupted as well; in other organs, the basement membrane is generally continuous. In most endocrine glands, the intestinal villi, and some portions of the kidney, there are definite gaps between the endothelial cells of the capillaries, but these gaps (fenestrations) are closed by a thin membrane (Fig 18–3).

Lymphatics

The lymphatics drain from the lungs and from the rest of the body tissues via a system of vessels that end in the venous system. The lymph vessels contain valves, and regularly traverse lymph nodes along their course. The ultrastructure of the small lymph vessels differs from that of the capillaries in several details: there are no visible fenestrations in the lymphatic endothelium; there is very little if any basement membrane under the endothelium; and the junctions between endothelial cells are open, with no tight intercellular connections.

A-V Anastomoses

In the fingers, palms, and ear lobes of humans and the paws and ears of animals there are short channels that connect arterioles to venules, bypassing the capillaries (Fig 30–2). These **A-V anastomoses** or **shunts** have thick, muscular walls and are abundantly innervated, presumably by vasoconstrictor nerve fibers. Similar shunts have been demonstrated in the kidneys and skeletal muscles of animals.

Venules & Veins

The walls of the venules are only slightly thicker than those of the capillaries. The walls of the veins are also thin and easily distended. They contain relatively little smooth muscle, but considerable venoconstriction is produced by activity in the adrenergic nerves to the veins and by chemical agents such as norepinephrine. Anyone who has had trouble making venipunctures has observed the marked local venospasm produced in superficial forearm veins by injury. Variations in venous tone are important in circulatory adjustments.

The intima of the limb veins is folded at intervals to form **venous valves** which prevent retrograde flow. The way these valves function in man was first demonstrated by William Harvey (Fig 30–3). There are no valves in the very small veins, the great veins, or the veins from the brain and viscera.

BIOPHYSICAL CONSIDERATIONS

Flow, Pressure, & Resistance

The relationship between mean flow, mean pressure, and resistance in the blood vessels is analogous in a general way to the relationship between the current, electromotive force, and resistance in an electrical circuit expressed in Ohm's law:

$$\text{Current (I)} = \frac{\text{Electromotive force (E)}}{\text{Resistance (R)}}$$

$$\text{Flow (F)} = \frac{\text{Pressure (P)}}{\text{Resistance (R)}}$$

Blood always flows, of course, from areas of high pressure to areas of low pressure, except in certain situations when momentum transiently sustains flow (Fig 29–2). Flow in any portion of the vascular system is equal to the **effective perfusion pressure** in that portion divided by the **resistance**. The effective perfusion pressure is the mean intraluminal pressure at the arterial end minus the mean pressure at the venous end. The units of resistance (pressure divided by flow) are dyne sec cm^{-5}. To avoid dealing with such complex units, resistance in the cardiovascular system is sometimes expressed in **R units** by dividing pressure in mm

FIG 30–3. Illustration showing the function of the venous valves in the human forearm, from William Harvey's book: *Exercitatio Anatomica de Motu Cordis et Sanguinis in Animalibus,* which was published in 1628. *A* is a tourniquet above the elbow, obstructing the venous return. If the vein (Fig 2) is milked from *G* to *H,* it fills from above only to the valve, *O.* If it is milked from *K* to *O* with another finger (Fig 3), it bulges above *O,* but *O* to *H* remains empty. If the vein is occluded at *L* (Fig 4) and milked with another finger *(M)* from *L* to the valve *N,* it remains empty from *L* to *N.* If the finger at *L* is removed, the vein fills from below.

Hg by flow in ml/sec (see also Table 32–1). Thus, for example, when the mean aortic pressure is 90 mm Hg and the left ventricular output is 90 ml/sec, the total peripheral resistance is:

$$\frac{90 \text{ mm Hg}}{90 \text{ ml/sec}} = 1 \text{ R unit}$$

Methods for Measuring Blood Flow

The blood flow of an organ can, of course, be measured directly by cannulating the vein draining the organ and collecting the effluent blood. The applicability of this technic is obviously limited, however, and numerous devices have been developed to measure the flow in arteries and veins without opening the vessels. All of them have limitations. **Electromagnetic flowmeters** are currently used in many experiments. The blood vessel is placed between the poles of an electromagnet and the flow is measured by an application of the principle that a voltage proportionate to the rate of flow is induced in a conductor (in this case, blood in a blood vessel) moving through a magnetic field at right angles to the magnetic lines of force. Sonar technics which measure the effect of velocity of flow on sound transmission through a blood vessel are also used.

The indirect methods used for measuring the blood flow of various organs in humans include adaptations of the Fick and indicator dilution technics described in Chapter 29. An ingenious example of the use of the Fick principle to measure flow in an organ is the Kety N_2O method for measuring cerebral blood flow (see Chapter 32). Another example is determination of the renal blood flow by measuring the clearance of para-aminohippuric acid (see Chapter 38). Considerable data on blood flow in the extremities have been obtained by **plethysmography** (Fig 30–4). The forearm, for example, is sealed in a watertight

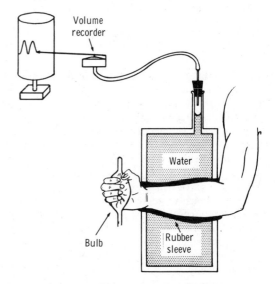

FIG 30–4. **Plethysmograph.** The hand is shown grasping the bulb of a dynamometer for measuring the strength and frequency of muscular contractions.

chamber (**plethysmograph**). Changes in the volume of the forearm, reflecting changes in the amount of blood and interstitial fluid it contains, displace the water, and this displacement is measured with a volume recorder. When the venous drainage of the forearm is occluded, the rate of increase in the volume of the forearm is a function of the arterial blood flow (**venous occlusion plethysmography**).

Applicability of Physical Principles to Flow in Blood Vessels

Physical principles and equations which are applicable to the description of the behavior of perfect fluids in rigid tubes have often been used indiscriminately to explain the behavior of blood in blood vessels. Blood vessels are not rigid tubes, and the blood is not a perfect fluid but a 2-phase system of liquid and cells. Therefore, the behavior of the circulation deviates, sometimes markedly, from that predicted by these principles. However, the physical principles are of value when used as an aid to understanding what goes on in the body rather than as an end in themselves or as a test of the memorizing ability of students.

Laminar Flow

The flow of blood in the blood vessels, like the flow of liquids in narrow, rigid tubes, is normally **laminar** or **streamline**. Within the blood vessels, an infinitely thin layer of blood in contact with the wall of the vessel does not move. The next layer within this layer has a small velocity, the next a higher velocity, and so forth, velocity being greatest in the center of the stream (Fig 30–5). Laminar flow occurs at velocities up to a certain **critical velocity**. At or above this velocity, flow is turbulent. Streamline flow is silent, but turbulent flow creates sounds.

The probability of turbulence is also related to the diameter of the vessel and the viscosity of the blood. This probability can be expressed as follows:

$$R = \frac{\rho DV}{\eta}$$

where R is the Reynolds number, named for the man who described the relationship; ρ is the density of the fluid; D is the diameter of the tube under consideration; V is the velocity of the flow; and η is the viscosity of the fluid. The higher the value of R, the greater the probability of turbulence.

In man, critical velocity is sometimes exceeded in the ascending aorta at the peak of systolic ejection, but it is usually exceeded only when an artery is constricted. Turbulence occurs more frequently in anemia because the viscosity of the blood is lower. This may be the explanation of the systolic murmurs that are common in anemia.

Average Velocity

The average velocity of fluid movement at any point in a system of tubes is inversely proportionate to the *total* cross-sectional area at that point. Therefore,

FIG 30–5. Diagram of the velocities of concentric laminas of a viscous fluid flowing in a tube, illustrating the parabolic distribution of velocities (streamline flow).

the average velocity of the blood is rapid in the aorta, declines steadily in the smaller vessels, and is slowest in the capillaries, which have 1000 times the *total* cross-sectional area of the aorta (Table 30–1). The average velocity of blood flow increases again as the blood enters the veins, and is relatively rapid in the vena cava, although not so rapid as in the aorta. Clinically, the velocity of the circulation is often measured by injecting a bile salt preparation into an arm vein and timing the first appearance of the bitter taste it produces (Fig 30–6). The average normal arm to tongue **circulation time** is 15 sec.

Poiseuille-Hagen Formula

The relation between the flow in a long, narrow tube, the viscosity of the fluid, and the radius of the

FIG 30–6. Arm to tongue circulation time.

tube is expressed mathematically in the **Poiseuille-Hagen formula:**

$$F = (P_A - P_B) \times (\frac{\pi}{8}) \times (\frac{1}{\eta}) \times (\frac{r^4}{L})$$

where F = flow
  $P_A - P_B$ = pressure difference between the 2 ends of the tube
  η = viscosity
  r = radius of tube
  L = length of tube

Since flow is equal to pressure difference divided by resistance (R),

$$R = \frac{8\eta L}{\pi r^4}$$

Since flow varies directly and resistance inversely with the 4th power of the radius, blood flow and resistance in vivo are markedly affected by small changes in the caliber of the vessels. Thus, for example, flow through a vessel is doubled by an increase of only 16% in its radius; and when the radius is doubled, resistance is reduced to 6% of its previous value. This is why organ blood flow is so effectively regulated by small changes in the caliber of the arterioles and why variations in arteriolar diameter have such a pronounced effect on systemic arterial pressure.

Viscosity & Resistance

Blood flow varies inversely and resistance directly with the viscosity of the blood in vivo, but the relationship deviates from that predicted by the Poiseuille-Hagen formula. Viscosity depends for the most part on the **hematocrit**, ie, the percentage of the volume of blood occupied by red blood cells. In large vessels, increases in hematocrit cause appreciable increases in viscosity. However, in vessels smaller than 100 μm in diameter, ie, in arterioles, capillaries, and venules, the viscosity change per unit change in hematocrit is much less than it is in large-bore vessels. This is due to a difference in the nature of flow through the small vessels. Therefore, the net change in viscosity per unit change in hematocrit is considerably less in the body than it is in vitro (Fig 30–7). This is why hematocrit changes have relatively little effect on the peripheral resistance except when the changes are large. In severe polycythemia, the increase in resistance does increase the work of the heart. Conversely, in severe anemia peripheral resistance is decreased, although the decreased resistance is only partly due to the decrease in viscosity. Cardiac output is increased, and as a result the work of the heart is also increased in anemia.

Viscosity is also affected by the composition of the plasma and the resistance of the cells to deformation. Clinically significant increases in viscosity are seen in diseases in which plasma proteins such as the immunoglobulins are markedly elevated and in diseases such as hereditary spherocytosis, in which the red blood cells are abnormally rigid.

In the vessels, red cells tend to accumulate in the center of the flowing stream. Consequently, the blood

FIG 30–7. Effect of changes in hematocrit on the relative viscosity of blood measured in a glass viscometer and in the hind leg of a dog. In each case, the middle line represents the mean and the upper and lower lines the standard deviation. (Reproduced, with permission, from Whittaker & Winton: The apparent viscosity of blood flowing in the isolated hind limb of the dog, and its variation with corpuscular concentration. J Physiol 78:338, 1933.)

along the side of the vessels has a low hematocrit, and branches leaving a large vessel at right angles may receive a disproportionate amount of this red cell-poor blood. This phenomenon, which has been called **plasma skimming,** may be the reason the hematocrit of capillary blood is regularly about 25% lower than the whole body hematocrit.

Critical Closing Pressure

In rigid tubes the relation between pressure and flow of homogeneous fluids is linear, but in blood vessels in vivo it is not. When the pressure in a small blood vessel is reduced, a point is reached at which there is no flow of blood even though the pressure is not zero (Fig 30–8). This is in part a manifestation of the fact that it takes some pressure to force red cells through capillaries which have diameters less than the red cells. Also, the vessels are surrounded by tissues which exert a small but definite pressure on the vessels, and when the intraluminal pressure falls below the tissue pressure the vessels collapse. In inactive tissues, for example, the pressure in many capillaries is low because the precapillary sphincters and metarterioles are constricted, and many of these capillaries are collapsed. The pressure at which flow ceases is called the **critical closing pressure.**

Law of Laplace

It is perhaps surprising that structures as thin-walled and delicate as the capillaries are not more prone to rupture. The principal reason for their relative

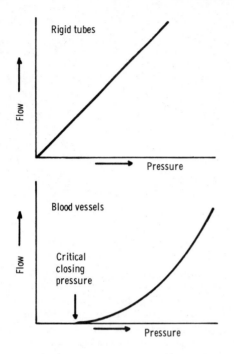

FIG 30–8. Relation of pressure to flow in a rigid-walled system *(above)* and the vascular system *(below)*.

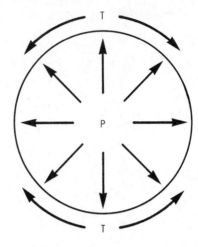

FIG 30–9. Relation between distending pressure *(P)* and wall tension *(T)* in a hollow viscus.

invulnerability is their small diameter. The protective effect of small size in this case is an example of the operation of the **law of Laplace,** an important physical principle with several other applications in physiology. This law states that the distending pressure (P) in a distensible hollow object is equal at equilibrium to the tension in the wall (T) divided by the 2 principal radii of curvature of the object (R_1 and R_2):

$$P = T(1/R_1 + 1/R_2)$$

The relation between distending pressure and tension is shown diagrammatically in Fig 30–9.

In the equation, P is actually the **transmural pressure,** the pressure on one side of the wall minus that on the other. T is expressed in dynes/cm and R_1 and R_2 in cm, so P is expressed in dynes/sq cm. In a sphere, $R_1 = R_2$, so

$$P = 2T/R$$

In a cylinder such as a blood vessel, one radius is infinite, so

$$P = T/R$$

Consequently, the less the radius of a blood vessel, the less the tension in the wall necessary to balance the distending pressure. In the human aorta, for example, the tension at normal pressures is about 170,000 dynes/cm, and in the vena cava it is about 21,000

dynes/cm; but in the capillaries, it is approximately 16 dynes/cm.

The law of Laplace also makes clear a disadvantage faced by dilated hearts. When the radius of a cardiac chamber is increased, a greater tension must be developed in the myocardium to produce any given pressure; consequently, a dilated heart must do more work than a nondilated heart. In the case of the lung, the radii of curvature of the alveoli become smaller during expiration, and these structures would tend to collapse due to the pull of surface tension if the tension were not reduced by the surface tension-lowering agent, surfactant (see Chapter 34). Another example of the operation of this law is seen in the urinary bladder (Chapter 39).

Pressure-Volume Relationships in Large Blood Vessels

When a segment of aorta is distended with increasing volumes of fluid, the pressure in the segment initially rises in a linear fashion (Fig 30–10). When the same experiment is carried out on a segment of the vena cava or another large distensible vein, the pressure does not rise rapidly until large volumes of fluid are injected. In vivo, the veins are an important blood reservoir. Normally they are partially collapsed, and oval in cross-section. A large amount of blood can be added to the venous system before the veins become distended to the point where further increments in volume produce a large rise in venous pressure. The veins are therefore called **capacitance vessels.** The arteries and arterioles are referred to as **resistance vessels.**

At rest, at least 50% of the circulating blood volume is in the systemic veins. Twelve percent is in the heart cavities and 18% is in the low-pressure pulmonary circulation. Only 2% is in the aorta, 8% in the arteries, 1% in the arterioles, and 5% in the capillaries (Table 30–1). When extra blood is administered by transfusion, less than 1% of it is distributed in the

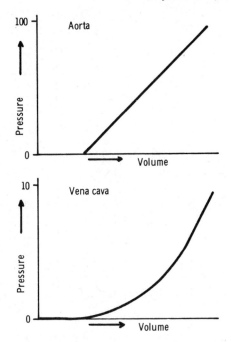

FIG 30–10. Shape of pressure-volume curves for human aorta and vena cava, based on measurements in cadavers. The curves are plotted on the same volume scale, but the pressure scale (indicated in arbitrary units) for the aorta is 10 times that for the vena cava. At pressures higher than those illustrated, the increments in volume per increment in pressure in the aorta also begin to decrease.

arterial system (the "high-pressure system"), and all the rest is found in the systemic veins, pulmonary circulation and heart chambers other than the left ventricle (the "low-pressure system").

ARTERIAL & ARTERIOLAR CIRCULATION

The pressure and velocities of the blood in the various parts of the systemic circulation are summarized in Fig 30–11. The general relationships in the pulmonary circulation are similar, but the pressure in the pulmonary artery is 25/10 mm Hg or less.

Velocity & Flow of Blood

Although the mean velocity of the blood in the aorta is 40 cm/sec, the flow is phasic, and velocity ranges from 120 cm/sec during systole to a negative value at the time of the transient backflow before the aortic valves close in diastole. In the distal portions of the aorta and in the arteries, velocity is also greater in systole than it is in diastole, but forward flow is continuous because of the recoil during diastole of the

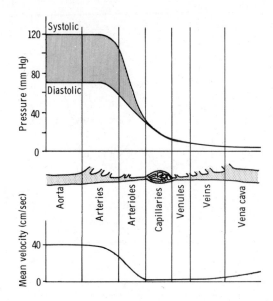

FIG 30–11. Diagram of the changes in pressure and velocity as blood flows through the systemic circulation.

vessel walls that have been stretched during systole (Fig 30–12). Pulsatile flow appears in some poorly understood way to maintain optimal function of the tissues. If an organ is perfused with a pump that delivers a nonpulsatile flow, there is a gradual rise in vascular resistance and tissue perfusion fails.

Arterial Pressure

The pressure in the aorta and in the brachial and other large arteries in a young adult human rises to a peak value (**systolic pressure**) of about 120 mm Hg during each heart cycle, and falls to a minimum value (**diastolic pressure**) of about 70 mm Hg. The arterial pressure is conventionally written as systolic pressure over diastolic pressure—eg, 120/70 mm Hg. The **pulse pressure**, the difference between the systolic and diastolic pressures, is normally about 50 mm Hg. The **mean pressure** is the average pressure throughout the cardiac cycle. Because systole is shorter than diastole, the mean pressure is slightly less than the value halfway between systolic and diastolic pressure. It can actually be determined only by integrating the area of the pressure curve (Fig 30–13); however, as an approximation, the diastolic pressure plus one-third of the pulse pressure is reasonably accurate.

The pressure falls very slightly in the large and medium sized arteries because their resistance to flow is small, but it falls rapidly in the small arteries and arterioles. The mean pressure at the end of the arterioles is 30–38 mm Hg. Pulse pressure also declines rapidly to about 5 mm Hg at the ends of the arterioles (Fig 30–11). The magnitude of the pressure drop along the arterioles varies considerably depending upon whether they are constricted or dilated.

FIG 30–12. Changes in blood flow during the cardiac
cycle in the dog. Systole at 0.2 and 0.6 sec. Flow
patterns in man are similar. Ao, aorta; PA, pulmonary artery; PV, pulmonary vein; IVC, inferior
vena cava; RA, renal artery. (Reproduced, with
permission, from Milnor, WR: Pulsatile blood
flow. New England J Med 287:27, 1972.)

Effect of Gravity

The pressures in Fig 30–11 are those in blood
vessels at heart level. The pressure in any vessel below
heart level is increased and that in any vessel above
heart level is decreased by the effect of gravity. The
magnitude of the gravitational effect—the product of
the density of the blood, the acceleration due to
gravity (980 cm/sec/sec), and the vertical distance
above or below the heart—is 0.77 mm Hg/cm at the
density of normal blood. Thus, in the upright position,
when the mean arterial pressure at heart level is 100

FIG 30–13. Brachial artery pressure curve of normal
young human, showing the relation of systolic
and diastolic pressure to mean pressure. The
shaded area above the mean pressure line is equal
to the shaded area below it.

FIG 30–14. Effects of gravity on arterial and venous
pressure. The scale on the right indicates the
increment (or decrement) in mean pressure in a
large artery at each level. The mean pressure in all
large arteries is approximately 100 mm Hg when
they are at the level of the left ventricle. The scale
on the left indicates the increment in venous pressure at each level due to gravity. The manometers
on the left of the figure indicate the height to
which a column of blood in a tube would rise if
connected to an ankle vein (A), the femoral vein
(B), or the right atrium (C), with the subject in
the standing position. The approximate pressures
in these locations in the recumbent position—ie,
when the ankle, groin, and right atrium are at the
same level—are (A), 10 mm Hg; (B), 7.5 mm Hg;
and (C), 5 mm Hg.

mm Hg, the mean pressure in a large artery in the head
(50 cm above the heart) is 62 mm Hg
(100 – [0.77 × 50]) and the pressure in a large artery
in the foot (105 cm below the heart) is 180 mm Hg
(100 + [0.77 × 105]) (Fig 30–14). The effect of
gravity on venous pressure is similar (see below).

Methods of Measuring Blood Pressure

If a cannula is inserted into an artery, the arterial
pressure can be measured directly with a mercury
manometer or a suitably calibrated strain gauge and an
oscillograph arranged to write directly on a moving
strip of paper. When an artery is tied off beyond the
point at which the cannula is inserted, an **end pressure**
is recorded. Flow in the artery is interrupted, and all
the kinetic energy of flow is converted into pressure
energy. If, alternatively, a T tube is inserted into a
vessel and the pressure is measured in the side arm of
the tube, under conditions where pressure drop due to

resistance is negligible, the recorded **side pressure** is less than the end pressure by the kinetic energy of flow. This is because in a tube or a blood vessel the total energy—the sum of the kinetic energy of flow and the pressure energy—is constant (**Bernoulli's principle**).

It is worth noting that the pressure drop in any segment of the arterial system is due both to resistance and to conversion of potential into kinetic energy. The pressure drop due to energy lost in overcoming resistance is irreversible, since the energy is dissipated as heat; but the pressure drop due to conversion of potential to kinetic energy as a vessel narrows is reversed when the vessel widens out again.

Bernoulli's principle also has a significant application in pathophysiology. According to the principle, the greater the velocity of flow in a vessel, the less the lateral pressure distending its walls. When a vessel is narrowed, the velocity of flow in the narrowed portion increases and the distending pressure decreases. Therefore, when a vessel is narrowed by a pathologic process such as an arteriosclerotic plaque, the lateral pressure at the constriction is decreased and the narrowing tends to maintain itself.

Auscultatory Method

The arterial blood pressure in humans is routinely measured by the **auscultatory method**. An inflatable cuff (**Riva-Rocci cuff**) attached to a mercury manometer (**sphygmomanometer**) is wrapped around the arm and a stethoscope is placed over the brachial artery at the elbow (Fig 30–15). The cuff is rapidly inflated until the pressure in it is well above the expected systolic pressure in the brachial artery. The artery is occluded by the cuff, and no sound is heard with the stethoscope. The pressure in the cuff is then lowered slowly. At the point at which systolic pressure in the artery just exceeds the cuff pressure, a spurt of blood

FIG 30–15. Determination of blood pressure by the auscultatory method. (Reproduced, with permission, from Tuttle & Schottelius: *Textbook of Physiology,* 16th ed. Mosby, 1969.)

passes through with each heartbeat and, synchronously with each beat, a tapping sound is heard below the cuff. The cuff pressure at which the sounds are first heard is the systolic pressure. As the cuff pressure is lowered further, the sounds become louder, then dull and muffled, and finally, in most individuals, they disappear. These are the **sounds of Korotkow**. When direct and indirect blood pressure measurements are made simultaneously, the diastolic pressure correlates better with the pressure at which the sounds become muffled than with the pressure at which they disappear.

The basis of the sounds of Korotkow is generally stated to be turbulent flow in the brachial artery. The streamline flow in the unconstricted artery is silent, but when the artery is narrowed the velocity of flow through the constriction exceeds the **critical velocity** (see above) and turbulent flow results. At cuff pressures just below the systolic pressure, flow through the artery occurs only at the peak of systole and the intermittent turbulence produces a tapping sound. As long as the pressure in the cuff is above the diastolic pressure in the artery, flow is interrupted at least during part of diastole and the intermittent sounds have a staccato quality. When the cuff pressure is just below the arterial diastolic pressure, the vessel is still constricted but the turbulent flow is continuous. Continuous sounds have a muffled rather than a staccato quality.

The auscultatory method is accurate when used properly, but a number of precautions must be observed. The cuff must be at heart level to obtain a pressure that is uninfluenced by gravity. The blood pressure in the thighs can be measured with the cuff around the thigh and the stethoscope over the popliteal artery, but there is more tissue between the cuff and the artery in the leg than there is in the arm, and some of the cuff pressure is dissipated. Therefore, pressures obtained using the standard arm cuff are falsely high. The same thing is true when brachial arterial pressures are measured in individuals with obese arms, the blanket of fat dissipating some of the cuff pressure. In both situations, accurate pressures can be obtained by using a cuff that is wider than the standard arm cuff. If the cuff is left inflated for some time, the discomfort may cause generalized reflex vasoconstriction, raising the blood pressure. It is always wise to compare the blood pressure in both arms when examining an individual for the first time. Persistent, major differences between the pressure on the 2 sides indicate the presence of vascular obstruction.

Palpation Method

The systolic pressure can be determined by inflating an arm cuff and then letting the pressure fall and determining the pressure at which the radial pulse first becomes palpable. Because of the difficulty in determining exactly when the first beat is felt, pressures obtained by this **palpation method** are usually 2–5 mm Hg lower than those measured by the auscultatory method.

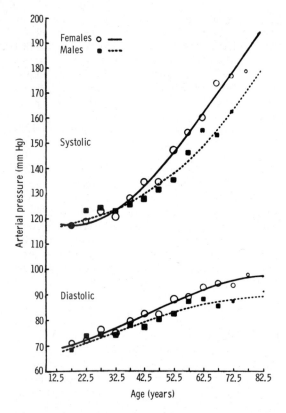

FIG 30–16. **Arterial pressure as a function of age in the general population.** The size of the squares and the circles is proportionate to the number of subjects studied in that age group. (Reproduced, with permission, from Hamilton & others: The aetiology of essential hypertension. I. The arterial pressure in the general population. Clin Sci 13:11, 1954.)

It is wise to form a habit of palpating the radial pulse while inflating the blood pressure cuff during measurement of the blood pressure by the auscultatory method. When the cuff pressure is lowered, the sounds of Korotkow sometimes disappear at pressures well above diastolic pressure, then reappear at lower pressures ("auscultatory gap"). If the cuff is initially inflated until the radial pulse disappears, the examiner can be sure that the cuff pressure is above systolic pressure, and falsely low pressure values will be avoided.

Normal Arterial Blood Pressure

The blood pressure in the brachial artery in young adults in the sitting or lying position at rest is approximately 120/70 mm Hg. Since the arterial pressure is the product of the cardiac output and the peripheral resistance, it is affected by conditions which affect either or both of these parameters. Emotion, for example, increases the cardiac output, and it may be difficult to obtain a truly resting blood pressure in an excited or tense individual. In general, increases in cardiac output increase the systolic pressure, whereas increases in peripheral resistance increase the diastolic pressure. There is a good deal of controversy about where to draw the line between normal and elevated blood pressure levels (**hypertension**), particularly in older patients. However the evidence seems incontrovertible that in apparently healthy humans both the systolic and the diastolic pressure rise with age (Fig 30–16). The systolic pressure increase is greater than the diastolic. An important cause of the rise in systolic pressure is decreased distensibility of the arteries as their walls become increasingly more rigid. At the same level of cardiac output, the systolic pressure is higher in old subjects than in young ones because there is less increase in the volume of the arterial system during systole to accommodate the same amount of blood.

CAPILLARY CIRCULATION

At any one time, only 5% of the circulating blood is in the capillaries, but this 5% is in a sense the most important part of the blood volume because it is across the systemic capillary walls that O_2 and nutrients enter the interstitial fluid and CO_2 and waste products enter the blood stream. The exchange across the capillary walls is essential to the survival of all the tissues in the body.

Methods of Study

It is difficult to obtain accurate measurements of capillary pressures and flows. The capillaries in the mesentery of experimental animals and the fingernail beds of humans are readily visible under the dissecting microscope, and observations on flow patterns under various conditions have been made in these and in some other tissues. Capillary pressure has been estimated by determining the amount of external pressure necessary to occlude the capillaries, or the amount of pressure necessary to make saline start to flow through a micropipet inserted so that its tip faces the arteriolar end of the capillary.

Capillary Pressure & Flow

Capillary pressures vary considerably, but typical values in human nail bed capillaries are 32 mm Hg at the arteriolar end and 15 mm Hg at the venous end. The pulse pressure is approximately 5 mm Hg at the arteriolar end and zero at the venous end. The capillaries are short, but blood moves slowly (about 0.07 cm/sec) because the total cross-sectional area of the capillary bed is large. Transit time from the arteriolar to the venous end of an average-sized capillary is 1–2 sec.

Equilibration With Interstitial Fluid

The capillary wall is a thin membrane that behaves as if it contained pores through which molecules smaller than proteins pass with ease. There is apparently no transfer of fluid and solutes across the walls of the rest of the vascular system, including the small arterioles and venules. The anatomy of the capillary wall has been described above. The cement substance-filled space between the endothelial cells is believed to be the site of transfer of fluids and small molecules. The postulated movement of proteins and other large molecules across the capillary walls in vesicles by a process resembling pinocytosis has been discussed in Chapter 1. On the basis of data on the movement of substances into skeletal muscle, it has been postulated that the walls of muscle capillaries contain "pores" about 3 nm in diameter. In the capillaries of the renal glomeruli the calculated average pore diameter is 10 nm. Hepatic capillaries have even larger pores which permit appreciable amounts of protein to leave and enter the circulation. The capillaries of the brain, on the other hand, are relatively impermeable to most substances in the blood (see Chapter 32).

The factors other than pinocytosis responsible for the movement of water and solutes across the capillary walls are diffusion and filtration (see Chapter 1). O_2 and glucose are in higher concentration in the blood stream than in the interstitial fluid, and diffuse into the interstitial fluid, whereas CO_2 diffuses in the opposite direction. Lipid soluble substances diffuse across the capillary walls with greater ease than lipid-insoluble substances, probably by passing directly through the endothelial cells. The rate of filtration at any point along a capillary depends upon the **filtration pressure** (the hydrostatic pressure in the capillary minus the hydrostatic pressure of the interstitial fluid) at that point. The filtration pressure is opposed by the inwardly directed osmotic gradient due to the presence of proteins in the plasma in the capillary (oncotic pressure). The interstitial tissue hydrostatic pressure normally averages about 1–2 mm Hg and the oncotic pressure 25 mm Hg, with some variation from tissue to tissue. Therefore, fluid moves into the interstitial space at the arteriolar end of the capillary, where the filtration pressure across its wall exceeds the oncotic pressure (Fig 30–17); and into the capillary at the venular end, where the oncotic pressure exceeds the filtration pressure. The amount of fluid that moves across the capillary walls is enormous. It is said that an amount equal to the entire plasma volume enters the tissues and an equal amount leaves them every minute.

Active & Inactive Capillaries

In resting tissues, most of the capillaries are collapsed and blood flows for the most part through the thoroughfare vessels from the arterioles to the venules. In active tissues, the metarterioles and the precapillary sphincters dilate. The intracapillary pressure rises, overcoming the critical closing pressure of the vessels, and blood flows through all the capillaries. Relaxation of the smooth muscle of the metarterioles and precapillary sphincters is due to the action of vasodilator metabolites formed in active tissue (see Chapter 31) and possibly also to a decrease in the activity of the sympathetic vasoconstrictor nerves that

FIG 30–17. Schematic representation of pressure gradients across the wall of a muscle capillary. The figures at the arteriolar and venular ends of the capillary are the hydrostatic pressures in mm Hg in these locations. The arrows indicate the approximate magnitude and direction of fluid movement. In this example, the pressure differential at the arteriolar end of the capillary is 11 mm Hg ([37−1] − 25) outward; at the opposite end, it is 9 mm Hg (25 − [17−1]) inward.

innervate the smooth muscle.

There is considerable debate about whether, in addition to passive dilatation of the capillaries secondary to dilatation of the arterioles, metarterioles, and sphincters, active capillary dilatation can occur. Certainly, in injured tissue, a substance is released which dilates the capillaries directly and increases their permeability ("H substance"; see Chapter 32). Bradykinin and histamine also increase capillary permeability. When capillaries are stimulated mechanically, they empty (white reaction; see Chapter 32), but this may well be due to contraction of the precapillary sphincters.

LYMPHATIC CIRCULATION & INTERSTITIAL FLUID VOLUME

Lymphatic Circulation

Fluid efflux normally exceeds influx across the capillary walls, but the extra fluid enters the lymphatics and drains through them back into the blood. This keeps the interstitial fluid pressure from rising and promotes the turnover of tissue fluid. The normal 24-hour lymph flow is 2–4 liters. The composition of lymph is discussed in Chapter 27.

Movements of skeletal muscles and pulsations transmitted from arteries undoubtedly compress lymphatics, and, since the valves in the lymph vessels prevent backflow, the compression propels the lymph toward the heart. The negative intrathoracic pressure during inspiration probably also aids lymphatic flow. However, it has now been demonstrated that the lymph vessels contract rhythmically. Furthermore, the rate of these contractions increases in direct proportion to the volume of lymph in the vessels. Evidence is now accumulating that the passive extralymphatic forces contribute relatively little to lymph flow and that the principal factor propelling the lymph is contraction of the vessels.

Agents which increase lymph flow are called **lymphagogues**. They include a variety of agents that increase capillary permeability. Agents that cause contraction of smooth muscle also increase lymph flow from the intestines.

Other Functions of the Lymphatic System

Appreciable quantities of protein enter the interstitial fluid in the liver and intestine, and smaller quantities enter from the blood in other tissues. These proteins are returned to the blood stream via the lymphatics. In the kidneys, formation of a maximally concentrated urine depends upon an intact lymphatic circulation; removal of reabsorbed water from the medullary pyramids is essential for the efficient operation of the countercurrent mechanism (see Chapter 38), and water enters the vasa recta only if an appreciable osmotic gradient is maintained between the medullary interstitium and the vasa recta blood by drainage of protein-containing interstitial fluid into the renal lymphatics. Some large enzymes—notably histaminase and lipase—may reach the circulation largely or even exclusively via the lymphatics after their secretion from cells into the interstitial fluid. The transport of absorbed long-chain fatty acids and cholesterol from the intestine via the lymphatics has been discussed in Chapter 25.

Interstitial Fluid Volume

The amount of fluid in the interstitial spaces depends upon the capillary pressure, the interstitial fluid pressure, the oncotic pressure, the permeability of the capillaries, the number of active capillaries, the lymph flow, and the total ECF volume. The ratio of precapillary to postcapillary venular resistance is also important. Precapillary constriction lowers filtration pressure, whereas postcapillary constriction raises it. Changes in any of these parameters lead to changes in the volume of interstitial fluid. Factors promoting an increase in this volume are summarized in Table 30–2. **Edema** is the accumulation of interstitial fluid in abnormally large amounts.

In active tissues, capillary pressure rises, often to the point where it exceeds the oncotic pressure throughout the length of the capillary. In addition, osmotically active metabolites may temporarily accumulate in the interstitial fluid because they cannot be washed away as rapidly as they are formed. To the extent that they accumulate, they exert an osmotic effect that decreases the magnitude of the osmotic gradient due to the oncotic pressure. The amount of fluid leaving the capillaries is therefore markedly increased, and the amount entering them reduced. Lymph flow is increased, decreasing the degree to which the fluid would otherwise accumulate, but exercising muscle, for example, still increases in volume by as much as 25%.

TABLE 30–2. Causes of increased interstitial fluid volume and edema.

Increased filtration pressure
    Arteriolar dilatation
    Venular constriction
    Increased venous pressure (heart failure, incompetent valves, venous obstruction, increased total ECF volume, effect of gravity, etc)

Decreased osmotic pressure gradient across capillary
    Decreased plasma protein level
    Accumulation of osmotically active substances in interstitial space

Increased capillary permeability
    Histamine and related substances
    Kinins, etc

Inadequate lymph flow

Interstitial fluid tends to accumulate in dependent parts due to the effect of gravity. In the upright position, the capillaries in the legs are protected from the high arterial pressure by the arterioles, but the high venous pressure is transmitted to them through the venules. Skeletal muscle contractions keep the venous pressure low by pumping blood toward the heart (see below) when the individual moves about; but if he stands still for long periods, fluid accumulates and edema eventually develops. The ankles also swell during long trips when travelers sit for prolonged periods with their feet in a dependent position. Venous obstruction may contribute to the edema in these situations.

Whenever there is abnormal retention of salt in the body, water is also retained. The salt and water are distributed throughout the ECF, and since the interstitial fluid volume is therefore increased there is a predisposition to edema. Salt and water retention is a factor in the edema seen in heart failure, nephrosis, and cirrhosis, but there are also variations in the mechanisms that govern fluid movement across the capillary walls in these diseases. In congestive heart failure, for example, there is usually an elevation in venous pressure, and capillary pressure is consequently elevated. In cirrhosis of the liver, oncotic pressure is low because hepatic synthesis of plasma proteins is depressed; and in nephrosis, oncotic pressure is low because large amounts of protein are lost in the urine.

Another cause of edema is inadequate lymphatic drainage. A not infrequent complication of **radical mastectomy**, an operation for cancer of the breast in which the axillary lymph nodes are also removed, is edema of the arm due to interruption of its lymph drainage. In filariasis, parasitic worms migrate into the lymphatics and obstruct them. Fluid accumulation plus tissue reaction lead in time to massive swelling, usually of the legs or scrotum (**elephantiasis**). The extent of the reaction is perhaps most graphically illustrated by the remarkable accounts of the man with elephantiasis whose scrotum was so edematous that he had to place it in a wheelbarrow and wheel it along with him when he walked.

VENOUS CIRCULATION

Blood flows through the blood vessels, including the veins, primarily because of the pumping action of the heart, although venous flow is aided by the heartbeat, the increase in the negative intrathoracic pressure during each inspiration, and contractions of skeletal muscles which compress the veins (**muscle pump**).

Venous Pressures & Flow

The pressure in the venules is 12–18 mm Hg. It falls steadily in the larger veins to about 5.5 mm Hg in the great veins outside the thorax. The pressure in the great veins at their entrance into the right atrium (**central venous pressure**) averages 4.6 mm Hg. but fluctuates with respiration and heart action.

The peripheral venous pressures, like the arterial, are affected by gravity. They are increased by 0.77 mm Hg for each cm below the right atrium and decreased a like amount for each cm above the right atrium the pressures are measured (Fig 30–13).

When blood flows from the venules to the large veins, its average velocity increases as the total cross-sectional area of the vessels decreases. In the great veins, the velocity of blood is about one-fourth as rapid as that in the aorta, averaging about 10 cm/sec.

Thoracic Pump

During inspiration, the intrapleural pressure falls from −2.5 mm Hg to −6 mm Hg. This negative pressure is transmitted to the great veins and, to a lesser extent, the atria, so that central venous pressure fluctuates from about 6 mm Hg during expiration to approximately 2 mm Hg during quiet inspiration. The drop in venous pressure during inspiration aids venous return. When the diaphragm descends during inspiration, intra-abdominal pressure rises, and this also squeezes blood toward the heart because backflow into the leg veins is prevented by the venous valves.

Effects of Heartbeat

The variations in atrial pressure are transmitted to the great veins to produce the a, c, and v waves of the venous pressure-pulse curve (see Chapter 29). Atrial pressure drops sharply during the ejection phase of ventricular systole because the AV valves are pulled downward, increasing the capacity of the atria. This action sucks blood into the atria from the great veins. The sucking of the blood into the atria during systole contributes appreciably to the venous return, especially at rapid heart rates.

Close to the heart, venous flow becomes pulsatile. When the heart rate is slow, 2 periods of peak flow are detectable: one during ventricular systole, due to pulling down of the AV valves; and one in early diastole, during the period of rapid ventricular filling (Fig 30–12).

Muscle Pump

In the limbs, the veins are surrounded by skeletal muscles, and contraction of these muscles during activity compresses the veins. Pulsations of nearby arteries may also compress veins. Since the venous valves prevent reverse flow, the blood moves toward the heart. During quiet standing, when the full effect of gravity is manifest, venous pressure at the ankle is 85–90 mm Hg (Fig 30–14). Pooling of blood in the leg veins reduces venous return, with the result that cardiac output is reduced, sometimes to the point where fainting occurs. Rhythmic contractions of the leg muscles while standing lower the venous pressure in the legs to less than 30 mm Hg by propelling blood toward the heart. This heartward movement of the blood is decreased in patients with **varicose veins**, whose valves are incompetent, and there may be venous stasis and ankle edema. However, even when the valves are incompetent, muscle contractions continue to produce heartward movement of the blood because the resistance of the larger veins in the direction of the heart is less than the resistance of the small vessels away from the heart.

Venous Pressure in the Head

In the upright position, the venous pressure in the parts of the body above the heart is decreased by the force of gravity. The neck veins collapse above the point where the venous pressure is zero, and the pressure all along the collapsed segments is zero rather than subatmospheric. However, the dural sinuses have rigid walls and cannot collapse. The pressure in them in the standing or sitting position is therefore subatmospheric. The magnitude of the negative pressure is proportionate to the vertical distance above the top of the collapsed neck veins, and in the superior sagittal sinus may be as much as −10 mm Hg. This fact must be kept in mind by neurosurgeons. Neurosurgical procedures are sometimes performed with the patient in the sitting position, and if one of the sinuses is opened during such a procedure it sucks air, causing **air embolism**.

Air Embolism

Because air, unlike fluid, is compressible, its presence in the circulation has serious consequences. The forward movement of the blood depends upon the fact that blood is incompressible. Large amounts of air fill the heart and effectively stop the circulation, causing sudden death, because most of the air is compressed by the contracting ventricles rather than propelled into the arteries. Small amounts of air are swept through the heart with the blood, but the bubbles lodge in the small blood vessels. The surface capillarity of the bubbles markedly increases the resistance to blood flow, and flow is reduced or abolished. Blockage of

Saline

Manometer

Level of right atrium

Alternate method using syringe, two-way stopcock, and spinal fluid manometer

FIG 30–18. Two technics of measuring peripheral venous pressure.

small vessels in the brain leads to serious and even fatal neurologic abnormalities. In experimental animals, the amount of air which produces fatal air embolism varies considerably, depending in part upon the rate at which it enters the veins. Sometimes as much as 100 ml can be injected without ill effects, whereas at other times as little as 5 ml are lethal.

Measuring Venous Pressure

Central venous pressure can be measured directly by inserting a catheter into the thoracic great veins. **Peripheral venous pressure** correlates well with central venous pressure in most conditions. To measure peripheral venous pressure, a needle attached to a manometer containing sterile saline is inserted into an arm vein (Fig 30–18). The peripheral vein should be at the level of the right atrium (a point 10 cm or half the chest diameter from the back). The values obtained in mm of saline can be converted into mm Hg by dividing by 13.6 (the density of mercury). The amount by which peripheral venous pressure exceeds central venous pressure increases with the distance from the heart along the veins. The mean pressure in the antecubital vein is normally 7.1 mm Hg, compared with a mean pressure of 4.6 mm Hg in the central veins.

A fairly accurate estimate of central venous pressure can be made without any equipment by simply noting the height to which the external jugular veins are distended when the subject lies with his head slightly above his heart. The vertical distance between the right atrium and the place the vein collapses (the place where the pressure in it is zero) is the venous pressure in mm of blood.

Central venous pressure is decreased during negative pressure breathing and shock. It is increased by positive pressure breathing, straining, expansion of the blood volume, and heart failure. In advanced congestive heart failure or obstruction of the superior vena cava, the pressure in the antecubital vein may reach values of 20 mm Hg or more.

31...

Cardiovascular Regulatory Mechanisms

In humans and other mammals, multiple cardiovascular regulatory mechanisms have evolved. These mechanisms increase the blood supply to active tissues and increase or decrease heat loss from the body by redistributing the blood. In the face of challenges such as hemorrhage, they maintain the blood flow to the heart and brain. When the challenge faced is severe, flow to these vital organs is maintained at the expense of the circulation to the rest of the body.

Circulatory adjustments are effected by local and systemic mechanisms that change the caliber of the arterioles and other resistance vessels and thus alter hydrostatic pressure in the capillaries. Systemic mechanisms also increase or decrease blood storage in venous reservoirs, and vary the rate and stroke output of the heart. In some situations, the capillaries may also be involved. The local autoregulatory mechanisms operate to maintain blood flow despite fluctuations in perfusion pressure and to dilate the arterioles and precapillary sphincters in active tissues. The systemic mechanisms synergize with the local mechanisms and adjust vascular responses throughout the body.

The terms vasoconstriction and vasodilatation are generally used to refer to constriction and dilatation of the resistance vessels. Changes in the caliber of the veins are referred to specifically as venoconstriction or venodilatation.

LOCAL REGULATORY MECHANISMS

Autoregulation

The capacity of tissues to regulate their own blood flow is referred to as **autoregulation**. Most vascular beds have an intrinsic capacity to compensate for moderate changes in perfusion pressure by changes in vascular resistance so that blood flow remains relatively constant. This capacity is well developed in the kidney (see Chapter 38), but it has also been observed in the mesentery, skeletal muscle, brain, liver, and myocardium. It is probably due in part to the intrinsic contractile response of smooth muscle to stretch: as the pressure rises, the blood vessels are distended, and the vascular smooth muscle fibers that surround the vessels contract (myogenic theory of autoregulation). If it is postulated that the muscle responds to the tension in the vessel wall, this theory could explain the greater degree of contraction at higher pressures; the wall tension is proportionate to the distending pressure times the radius of the vessel (law of Laplace; see Chapter 30), and the maintenance of a given wall tension as the pressure rises would require a decrease in radius. Vasodilator substances tend to accumulate in active tissues, and these "metabolites" also contribute to autoregulation (metabolic theory of autoregulation); when blood flow decreases, they accumulate and the vessels dilate, whereas when blood flow increases they tend to be washed away. It has also been argued that, as blood flow increases, the accumulation of interstitial fluid compresses the capillaries and venules; but the bulk of the available evidence is against this tissue pressure hypothesis of autoregulation.

"Vasodilator Metabolites"

The metabolic changes that produce vasodilatation include, in most tissues, decreases in O_2 tension and pH. These changes cause relaxation of the arterioles and precapillary sphincters. A rise in CO_2 tension also dilates the vessels. The direct dilator action of CO_2 is most pronounced in the skin and brain. The neurally mediated vasoconstrictor effects of systemic as opposed to local hypoxia and hypercapnia are discussed below. A rise in temperature exerts a direct vasodilator effect, and the temperature rise in active tissues (due to the heat of metabolism) may contribute to the vasodilatation. Other substances that accumulate locally, that have demonstrated dilator activity, and that may play a role in the dilatation include lactic acid, potassium ions, adenosine, and adenosine nucleotides. In injured tissues, histamine released from damaged cells dilates capillaries and increases their permeability.

Kinins

A vasodilator peptide called **bradykinin** (Fig 31–1) is formed during active secretion in sweat glands, salivary glands, and the exocrine portion of the pancreas (see Chapter 26). It may be responsible for the increase in blood flow in these secreting tissues. It is formed from a number of circulating a_2 globulins called **kininogens**, by the action of plasma **kallikrein**

Arg-Pro-Pro-Gly-Phe-Ser-Pro-Phe-Arg

FIG 31–1. Bradykinin.

FIG 31—2. Formation and breakdown of bradykinin. The dashed arrow indicates inhibition.

(Fig 31—2). A related kallikrein in the pancreas splits off lysyl bradykinin from kininogens, and plasma aminopeptidase converts this decapeptide to bradykinin. Lysyl bradykinin, which has some vasodilator activity, bradykinin, and related vasodilator peptides in blood and tissue are referred to collectively as **kinins**. The similarity between the action of the kallikreins and renin is apparent (see Chapter 24). Plasma kallikrein exists in the form of an inactive precursor, but when tissues are injured, various activators convert it to its active form. One of these activators is factor XII, the Hageman factor that plays a role in blood clotting (see Chapter 27). There are probably other kallikrein activators in the salivary glands and the pancreas. Bradykinin is metabolized by **kininases**, tissue enzymes which remove one or two amino acids from the C-terminal, converting the nonapeptide to an inactive octapeptide or septapeptide.

The actions of the kinins resemble those of histamine. They cause contraction of visceral smooth muscle, but they relax vascular smooth muscle and increase capillary permeability. They also attract leukocytes and cause pain upon injection under the skin.

The physiologic role of kinins is as yet speculative, but it seems likely that they are involved in the production of local vasodilation during activity in tissues other than glands. A role in thermoregulatory vascular adjustments is suggested by experiments on human volunteers in whom cutaneous vasodilatation was produced by warming the body while the subcutaneous tissue of the forearm was being perfused with saline. As the forearm vessels dilated, bradykinin appeared in the perfusate. The kinins may also participate, like histamine, in the normal inflammatory response (see Chapter 33) and in the genesis of allergic symptoms. In addition, there is some evidence that their release is responsible for the production of pain in injured tissues (see Chapter 7) and that they are responsible for the vasodilatation produced by the axon reflex (see Chapter 32).

Trypsin is capable of releasing bradykinin in plasma, and it has been suggested that the hypotension seen in acute pancreatitis may be due to liberation of bradykinin secondary to the elevation in the circulating trypsin level. Kinin release is inhibited by adrenal glucocorticoids. A kinin-like peptide has been implicated as a possible cause of migraine, and the kinins appear to be responsible for some episodes of vasodilatation in patients with carcinoid tumors.

Local Vasoconstrictors

Injured arteries and arterioles constrict strongly. The constriction appears to be due in part to the local liberation of serotonin from platelets which stick to the vessel wall in the injured area (see Chapter 27).

SYSTEMIC REGULATORY MECHANISMS

Circulating Vasoconstrictors

Norepinephrine, epinephrine, and angiotensin II are vasoconstrictor agents found in the circulation of normal individuals. Vasopressin is probably not secreted in amounts sufficient to produce appreciable vasoconstriction. Norepinephrine has a generalized vasoconstrictor action, whereas epinephrine dilates the vessels in skeletal muscle. The relative unimportance of circulating catecholamines in mediating cardiovascular (as opposed to metabolic) adjustments is pointed out in Chapter 20, in which their cardiovascular actions are discussed in detail.

The octapeptide angiotensin II has a generalized vasoconstrictor action. It is formed from the decapeptide angiotensin I liberated by the action of renin from the kidney on the circulating a_2 globulin, angiotensinogen (see Chapter 24). Angiotensin II is responsible for the initial rise in blood pressure produced by constriction of the renal artery, but it seems likely that other mechanisms take over to maintain the hypertension. Its formation is increased when the blood pressure falls, but its exact role in cardiovascular homeostasis is uncertain. Angiotensin II also stimulates aldosterone secretion, and increased formation of angiotensin II is part of a homeostatic mechanism that operates to maintain ECF volume (see Chapter 20).

Histamine, serotonin, and prostaglandins are also vasoactive and are found in the circulation. Histamine, serotonin, and catecholamines produce constriction of veins. Prostaglandins (see Chapter 17) have positively inotropic actions, and members of the PGE and PGA series lower blood pressure whereas members of the

PGF series raise it. However, the physiologic role of prostaglandins is unsettled.

Neural Regulatory Mechanisms

Although the arterioles and the other resistance vessels are most densely innervated, all blood vessels except capillaries contain smooth muscle and receive motor nerve fibers from the sympathetic division of the autonomic nervous system. The fibers to the resistance vessels regulate tissue blood flow and arterial pressure. The fibers to the venous capacitance vessels vary the volume of blood "stored" in the veins. Venoconstriction is produced by stimuli which also activate the vasoconstrictor nerves to the arterioles. The resultant decrease in venous capacity increases venous return, shifting blood to the arterial side of the circulation. In addition, increased vasoconstrictor discharge mobilizes blood from the splanchnic area because constriction of the arterioles of the gastrointestinal tract decreases inflow into the portal venous system, and changes that occur in the liver increase portal runoff (see Chapter 32).

Innervation of the Blood Vessels

Adrenergic fibers end on vessels in all parts of the body, although the innervation of the cerebral vessels is of little functional importance. The adrenergic fibers to the coronary vessels exert a vasodilator effect, but in other locations the adrenergic fibers are vasoconstrictor in function. In addition to their adrenergic vasoconstrictor innervation, the resistance vessels of the skeletal muscles are innervated by vasodilator fibers which, although they travel with the sympathetic nerves, are cholinergic (the **sympathetic vasodilator system**).

There is no tonic discharge in the vasodilator fibers, but the vasoconstrictor fibers to most vascular beds are tonically active. When the sympathetic nerves are cut (**sympathectomy**), the blood vessels dilate. In most tissues vasodilatation is therefore produced by decreasing the rate of tonic discharge in the vasoconstrictor nerves, although in skeletal muscles it can also be produced by activating the sympathetic vasodilator system (Table 31–1).

TABLE 31–1. Summary of factors affecting the caliber of the arterioles.

Constriction	Dilatation
Increased adrenergic discharge	Decreased adrenergic discharge
Circulating catecholamines (except epinephrine in skeletal muscle)	In muscle, activation of cholinergic dilators
Circulating angiotensin II	Histamine
Locally released serotonin	Kinins
Decreased local temperature	"Axon reflex"
	Decreased O_2 tension
	Increased CO_2 tension
	Decreased pH
	Lactic acid, etc
	Increased local temperature

There is evidence that afferent impulses in sensory nerves from the skin are relayed antidromically down branches of the sensory nerves that innervate blood vessels, and that these impulses produce vasodilatation. This local neural mechanism is called the **axon reflex** (Fig 32–10). Other cardiovascular reflexes are integrated in the CNS.

Cardiac Innervation

Impulses in the adrenergic sympathetic nerves to the heart increase the cardiac rate (chronotropic effect) and the force of cardiac contraction (inotropic effect). Impulses in the cholinergic vagal cardiac fibers decrease heart rate. Although there is some tonic discharge in the cardiac sympathetic nerves at rest, there is a good deal of tonic vagal discharge (**vagal tone**) in man and other large animals. When the vagi are cut in experimental animals, the heart rate rises, and after the administration of parasympatholytic drugs such as atropine the cardiac rate in humans increases from its normal resting value of 70 to 150–180 beats per minute. In humans in whom both adrenergic and cholinergic systems are blocked, the heart rate is approximately 100.

Cardioinhibitory Center

The dorsal motor nucleus of the vagus is the **cardioinhibitory center** that initiates the tonic vagal discharge at rest (Fig 31–3). It seems likely that there is no separate "cardioacceleratory center," and that

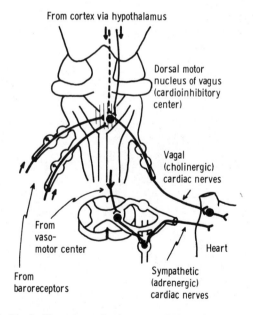

FIG 31–3. Neural mechanisms regulating the heart. The cholinergic fibers slow the heart, whereas the adrenergic fibers accelerate it and increase the force of contraction of cardiac muscle. Inhibitory pathways are indicated by the dashed neuron. The vasomotor center in the medulla is not shown.

the tachycardia produced by excitement, emotional states, and exercise is due to discharge in the sympathetic nerves to the heart. On the other hand, the afferents from the baroreceptors in the heart and great vessels (see below) pass directly to the cardioinhibitory center. The reflex bradycardia initiated by a rise in systemic arterial pressure is due to stimulation of the cardioinhibitory center, whereas the tachycardia produced by a fall in pressure is due for the most part to impulses in the sympathetic cardiac nerves. It is possible that other afferents converge on the cardioinhibitory center.

The Vasomotor Center

The discharge rate in the sympathetic vasoconstrictor nerves is influenced to a minor degree by spinal reflex activity but is controlled for the most part by the **vasomotor center** in the medulla oblongata. This center is a large, diffuse area in the reticular formation extending from just below the obex to the region of the vestibular nuclei, and from the floor of the fourth ventricle ventrally almost to the pyramids. Stimulation of the rostral and lateral portions of this center causes a rise in blood pressure and tachycardia, whereas stimulation of a smaller portion around the obex produces a fall in blood pressure and bradycardia (Fig 31–4). On the basis of these observations, it was originally postulated that there were separate vasoconstrictor and vasodilator centers with different efferent mechanisms, but it now seems clear that medullary influences are exerted solely through variations in the rate of tonic discharge in the vasoconstrictor nerves. The terms **pressor** and **depressor areas** within a single vasomotor center are therefore more

accurate. The details of the interaction between the 2 areas are unsettled, but it is known that excitatory fibers from the pressor area and inhibitory fibers from the depressor area descend in different portions of the spinal cord. These fibers presumably converge on and control the rate of discharge of the preganglionic vasoconstrictor neurons, the final common path to the blood vessels (Fig 31–5).

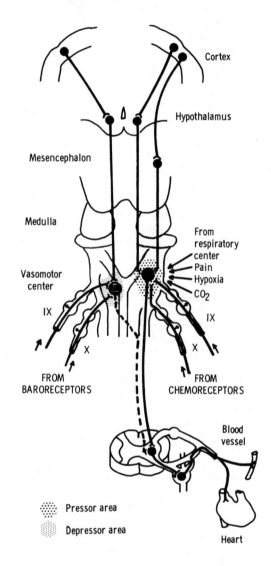

FIG 31–5. **Simplified diagram of the vasomotor center.** The principal factors affecting its activity are shown in capital letters. The inhibitory fibers are indicated by the neuron with the dashed axon. The excitatory fibers from the pressor area are mostly ipsilateral and travel in the ventrolateral portion of the cord. The inhibitory fibers from the depressor area cross extensively in the medulla. (Based in part on Uvnas, in: *Handbook of Physiology.* Field J, Magoun HW [editors]. Washington: The American Physiological Society, 1960. Section 1, pp 1131–1162.)

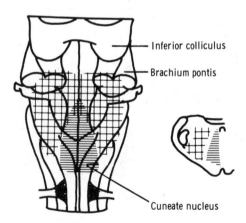

FIG 31–4. **The vasomotor center in the cat, showing the location of pressor (cross-hatched) and depressor (horizontal lined) areas.** *Left:* Dorsal view of brain stem with cerebellum removed. *Right:* Transverse section of medulla just above obex. (Modified, redrawn, and reproduced, with permission, from Alexander: Tonic and reflex functions of medullary sympathetic cardiovascular centers. J Neurophysiol 9:205, 1946.)

Summary of Effects of Variations in the Activity of the Vasomotor Center

When vasoconstrictor tone is increased by a decrease in the activity of the depressor area or an increase in the activity of the pressor area of the vasomotor center, there is increased arteriolar constriction and a rise in blood pressure. Venoconstriction and a decrease in the stores of blood in the venous reservoirs usually accompany these changes, although changes in the capacitance vessels do not always parallel changes in the resistance vessels. Heart rate and stroke volume are increased due to activity in the sympathetic nerves to the heart, and cardiac output is increased. There is usually an associated but separate decrease in the tonic activity of vagal fibers to the heart. Conversely, a decrease in the discharge rate of the vasoconstrictor fibers causes vasodilatation, a fall in blood pressure, and an increase in the storage of blood in the venous capacitance vessels. There is usually a concomitant decrease in heart rate, but this is mostly due to a separate direct stimulation of the cardioinhibitory center. There is relatively little tonic discharge in the cardiac sympathetic nerves at rest.

Afferents to the Vasomotor Center

The afferents that converge on the vasomotor center are summarized in Fig 31–5. They include not only the very important fibers from arterial baroreceptors, but fibers from other parts of the nervous system and from the carotid and aortic chemoreceptors as well. In addition, some stimuli act directly on the vasomotor center.

There are descending tracts to the vasomotor center from the cerebral cortex (particularly the limbic cortex) which relay in the hypothalamus and possibly also in the mesencephalon. These fibers are responsible for the blood pressure rise and tachycardia produced by emotions such as sexual excitement and anger. Pain usually causes a rise in blood pressure, presumably as a result of afferent impulses in the reticular formation converging on the vasomotor center. However, prolonged severe pain may cause vasodilatation and fainting.

Afferents from the chemoreceptors in the carotid and aortic bodies exert their main effect on respiration, and their function is discussed in Chapter 36. However, they also converge on the pressor area of the vasomotor center, and increased activity in them is responsible in part for the hypertension produced by hypoxia.

Cyclic activity in afferents from the chemoreceptors to the vasomotor center is responsible in part for the so-called **Mayer waves**. These are slow, regular oscillations in arterial pressure that occur at the rate of about one per 20–40 sec during hypotension. They are especially common after hemorrhage. Blood flow in the carotid and aortic bodies is poor when the blood pressure is low, and the resultant hypoxia stimulates the chemoreceptors. The stimulation raises the blood pressure, which improves the blood flow in the receptor organs and eliminates the stimulus to the chemoreceptors, so that the pressure falls and a new cycle is initiated. However, oscillation in the feedback control of blood pressure through the baroreceptors also plays a role in the genesis of these waves because they are reduced but not abolished by chemoreceptor denervation.

Hypoxia can also stimulate the vasomotor center directly. When the intracranial pressure is raised rapidly, the vessels supplying the medulla are compressed. The hypoxic cells in the vasomotor center increase their rate of discharge, and there is a rise in systemic arterial pressure which tends to restore the blood flow to the medulla. The local hypoxia also stimulates the cardioinhibitory center, and this is why bradycardia, rather than tachycardia, is characteristically seen in patients with increased intracranial pressure.

A rise in the CO_2 tension of the blood stimulates the vasomotor center, and a drop in P_{CO_2} inhibits it, partly by a direct effect on the center and partly via the carotid and aortic chemoreceptors. As noted above, the direct peripheral effect of hypercapnia is vasodilation, so the peripheral and central actions tend to cancel each other. Moderate hyperventilation, which significantly lowers the CO_2 tension of the blood, causes cutaneous and cerebral vasoconstriction in man, and there is often little change in blood pressure. Exposure to high concentrations of CO_2 is associated with marked cutaneous and cerebral vasodilatation, but there is vasoconstriction elsewhere and usually a slow rise in blood pressure.

Baroreceptors

The **baroreceptors** are stretch receptors in the walls of the heart and blood vessels. The **carotid sinus** and **aortic arch** receptors are the best known, but receptors are also located in the walls of the right and left atria at the entrance of the superior and inferior vena cava and the pulmonary veins, in the wall of the left ventricle, and in the pulmonary circulation. The receptors are stimulated by distention of the structures in which they are located, and so they discharge at an increased rate when the pressure in these structures rises. Their afferent fibers pass via the glossopharyngeal and vagus nerves to the depressor portion of the vasomotor center and the cardioinhibitory center. Impulses generated in the baroreceptors **inhibit** the tonic discharge of the vasoconstrictor nerves and **excite** the cardioinhibitory center, producing vasodilatation, a drop in blood pressure, bradycardia, and a decrease in cardiac output. The effects on cardiac rate are blocked by atropine. Some venodilatation also occurs, although it is still uncertain which receptors are responsible for reflex changes in venomotor tone.

Carotid Sinus & Aortic Arch

The carotid sinus is a small dilatation of the internal carotid artery just above the bifurcation of the common carotid into external and internal carotid branches (Fig 31–6). Baroreceptors are located in this dilatation, and are also found in the wall of the arch of the aorta. The receptors are located in the adventitia of the vessels. They are extensively branched, knobby, coiled and intertwined ends of myelinated nerve fibers that resemble Golgi tendon organs (Fig 6–5). Similar receptors have been found in various other parts of the large arteries of the thorax and neck in some species. The afferent nerve fibers from the carotid sinus and carotid body form a distinct branch of the glossopharyngeal nerve, the **carotid sinus nerve,** but the fibers from the aortic arch form a separate distinct branch of the vagus only in the rabbit. The carotid sinus nerves and vagal fibers from the aortic arch are commonly called the **buffer nerves.**

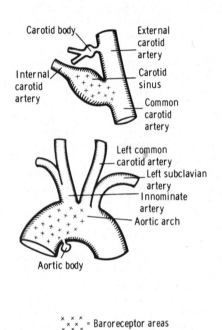

FIG 31–6. Baroreceptor areas in carotid sinus and aortic arch. (Courtesy of JH Comroe, Jr.)

Buffer Nerve Activity

At normal blood pressure levels, the fibers of the buffer nerves discharge at a slow rate. Sometimes they discharge only during systole (Fig 31–7). When the pressure in the sinus and aortic arch rises, the discharge rate increases, and when the pressure falls the rate declines. The compensatory response produced by increased discharge is a fall in blood pressure because activity in the baroreceptor afferents inhibits the tonic discharge in the vasoconstrictor nerves.

When one carotid sinus of a dog is isolated and perfused and the other baroreceptors are denervated, there is no discharge in the afferent fibers from the perfused sinus and no drop in the animal's arterial pressure or heart rate when the perfusion pressure is below 70 mm Hg. At perfusion pressures of 70–150 mm Hg there is an essentially linear relation between the perfusion pressure and the fall in blood pressure and heart

rate produced in the dog. At perfusion pressures above 150 mm Hg there is no further increase in response (Fig 31–8), presumably because the rate of baroreceptor discharge and the degree of inhibition of the vasomotor center are maximal.

The carotid receptors respond both to sustained pressure and to pulse pressure. A decline in carotid pulse pressure without any change in mean pressure

FIG 31–7. **Action potentials in a single fiber of the carotid sinus nerve of the rabbit.** When the mean arterial pressure was 40 mm Hg, the fiber fired 4 times with each systole. When the pressure was 135 mm Hg, the discharge was continuous and much more rapid. The baroreceptors of the rabbit respond at a lower pressure than those of the dog. (Drawn from oscillograph records of Bronk & Stella: Afferent impulses in carotid sinus nerve. J Cell Comp Physiol 1:113, 1932.)

FIG 31–8. **Relationships between pressure in the isolated carotid sinus and change in systemic blood pressure in the monkey (1), rabbit (2), dog (3), and cat (4).** The horizontal line on each curve represents the normal mean blood pressure for that species. Note that in each case the normal blood pressure is in the midportion of the curve, where variations in pressure produce the greatest reflex changes. (After Koch. Reproduced, with permission, from Keele & Neil: *Samson Wright's Applied Physiology,* 10th ed. Oxford Univ Press, 1961.)

decreases the rate of baroreceptor discharge and provokes a rise in blood pressure and tachycardia. The receptors also respond to change in the pressure; when the pressure is fluctuating, they sometimes discharge during the rises and are silent during the falls at mean pressures high enough so that, if there were no fluctuations, there would be a steady discharge.

The aortic receptors have not been studied in as great detail, but there is no reason to believe that their responses differ significantly from those of the receptors in the carotid sinus.

Function of the Arterial Baroreceptors

From the foregoing discussion, it is apparent that the baroreceptors on the arterial side of the circulation, their afferent fibers to the vasomotor and cardioinhibitory centers, and the efferent pathways from these centers constitute a reflex feedback mechanism that operates to stabilize the blood pressure and heart rate. Any drop in systemic arterial pressure decreases the inhibitory discharge in the buffer nerves, and there is a compensatory rise in blood pressure and cardiac output. Any rise in pressure produces dilatation of the arterioles and decreases cardiac output until the blood pressure returns to its previous normal level.

In chronic hypertension the baroreceptor reflex mechanism is "reset" to maintain an elevated rather than a normal blood pressure. In perfusion studies on hypertensive experimental animals, raising the pressure in the isolated carotid sinus lowers the systemic pressure and decreasing the perfusion pressure raises the systemic pressure. Little is known about how and why this resetting occurs. Since some forms of hypertension are curable, and since circulatory reflexes as well as blood pressure are apparently normal after treatment, it appears that the resetting is reversible.

If norepinephrine is painted on the carotid sinus, baroreceptor discharge increases and blood pressure falls. According to some investigators, stimulation of the sympathetic nerves to the sinus has a similar effect. The increased discharge is probably due to distortion of the receptors produced by contraction of the smooth muscle in the wall. However, there is considerable evidence that variations in the rate of sympathetic discharge and catecholamine secretion in intact animals have little if any effect on the sensitivity of the carotid sinus mechanism.

Effect of Carotid Clamping & Buffer Nerve Section

Bilateral clamping of the carotid arteries below the carotid sinuses elevates the blood pressure and heart rate because the procedure lowers the pressure in the sinuses. Cutting the carotid sinus nerves on each side has the same effect. The pressor response following these 2 procedures is moderate because the aortic baroreceptors are still functioning normally and they buffer the rise. If the vagi are also cut, blood pressure rises to 300/200 mm Hg or higher. Vagotomized animals develop fatal pulmonary edema, but if the carotid sinus nerves are cut and the aortic arch is carefully stripped, taking care not to damage other vagal

fibers, the animals survive and remain hypertensive indefinitely. This form of experimental hypertension is called "neurogenic hypertension."

Atrial Stretch Receptors

The stretch receptors in the atria are of 2 types: those that discharge primarily during atrial systole (type A), and those that discharge primarily late in diastole, at the time of peak atrial filling (type B). The discharge of type B baroreceptors is increased when venous return is increased, and decreased by positive pressure breathing, indicating that they respond primarily to distention of the atrial walls. The reflex circulatory adjustments initiated by increased discharge from these receptors are similar to those produced by carotid sinus stimulation. There is bradycardia, decreased cardiac output, and vasodilatation with a fall in blood pressure. The atrial baroreceptors are therefore probably part of a reflex mechanism which combats excessive rises in central venous pressure and venous return.

Bainbridge Effect

Rapid infusion of blood or saline in anesthetized animals sometimes produces a rise in heart rate if the initial heart rate is low. This effect was described by Bainbridge in 1915, and since then it has been known as the **Bainbridge reflex**. It should probably be called the Bainbridge effect, since there is some doubt that it is a reflex. It is blocked by atropine, but is diminished or absent whenever the initial heart rate is high. Indeed, an increase in heart rate can sometimes be produced in an isolated heart-lung preparation if the venous return is increased rapidly. Furthermore, the reflex response produced by stimulation of atrial stretch receptors and the baroreceptors in the pulmonary circulation is bradycardia, not tachycardia. Thus, the Bainbridge effect is an inconstant phenomenon of doubtful physiologic significance which may be due, when it occurs, to a direct effect of fluid injection on the cardiac muscle.

Left Ventricular Receptors

When the left ventricle is distended in experimental animals, there is a fall in systemic arterial pressure and heart rate. It takes considerable ventricular distention to produce this response, and its physiologic significance is uncertain. However, left ventricular stretch receptors may play a role in the maintenance of the vagal tone that keeps the heart rate slow at rest.

Coronary Chemoreflex

In experimental animals, injections of the drug **veratridine** into the branches of the coronary arteries that supply the left ventricle cause apnea, hypotension, and bradycardia (the **coronary chemoreflex**, or **Bezold-Jarisch reflex**). The response is prevented by vagotomy. Injections into the coronary arteries supplying the right ventricle and atria are ineffective. Nicotine produces a similar response when it is injected into the arterial supply of the left ventricle or applied to the surface of the left ventricle near the apex of the heart on pieces of filter paper. The response to nicotine by both routes is absent if procaine is first injected into the pericardial sac. The coronary chemoreflex might be triggered by chemical stimulation of the stretch receptors in the ventricular wall, or it might be due to stimulation of as yet unidentified chemoreceptors in the myocardium. There has been speculation that in patients with myocardial infarcts, substances released from the infarcted tissue stimulate ventricular receptors, contributing to the hypotension that is not infrequently a stubborn complication of this disease.

Pulmonary Stretch Receptors

Distention of the pulmonary vascular bed causes reflex bradycardia and systemic hypotension. The location of the receptors involved is not settled.

Pulmonary Chemoreflex

Injections of veratridine, phenyl biguanide, and serotonin into the pulmonary artery produce apnea, hypotension, and bradycardia. The response, which is blocked by vagotomy, is essentially the same as that produced by injection of veratridine into the arterial supply of the left ventricle, but it occurs too rapidly to be due to the drugs reaching the left ventricular receptors. The receptors are probably in the pulmonary veins, but their exact location has not been determined and it is not known whether they are different from the receptors for the response to distention of the pulmonary circulation.

Mesenteric Baroreceptors

There is some evidence that the pacinian corpuscles in the mesentery function as baroreceptors. They probably initiate reflexes that control the local blood flow in the viscera.

Effects of Baroreceptor Stimulation on Respiration

Increased activity in baroreceptor afferents inhibits respiration, but this effect is slight and of little physiologic importance.

Baroreceptor-Mediated Effects on Sodium & Water Metabolism

There is considerable evidence that impulses initiated in atrial stretch receptors are relayed to the hypothalamus, where they inhibit vasopressin secretion (see Chapter 14). The resultant diuresis helps reduce the venous distention which caused the stimulation. However, the decrease in intravascular and interstitial fluid volume is slight unless there is a concomitant increase in Na^+ excretion, and atrial distention does not appear to influence Na^+ excretion. A drop in systemic arterial pressure stimulates vasopressin secretion. The increase is inhibited if the carotid sinus nerves and the vagi are cut, but not by vagotomy alone. However, constriction of the carotid arteries does not regularly increase aldosterone secretion. Thus, the baroreceptors influence water metabolism, but have relatively little effect on Na^+ metabolism.

Clinical Testing & Stimulation

The changes in pulse rate and blood pressure that occur in humans on standing up or lying down (see Chapter 33) are due for the most part to baroreceptor reflexes. The function of the receptors can be tested by monitoring the changes in pulse and blood pressure that occur in response to brief periods of straining (forced expiration against a closed glottis: the **Valsalva maneuver**). The blood pressure rises at the onset of straining (Fig 31−9) because the increase in intrathoracic pressure is added to the pressure of the blood in the aorta. It then falls because the high intrathoracic pressure compresses the veins, decreasing venous return and cardiac output. The decrease in arterial pressure and pulse pressure inhibit the baroreceptors, causing tachycardia and a rise in peripheral resistance. When the glottis is opened and the intrathoracic pressure returns to normal, cardiac output is restored but the

FIG 31−9. Diagram of the response to straining (the Valsalva maneuver) in a normal man, recorded with a needle in the brachial artery. (Courtesy of M McIlroy.)

peripheral vessels are constricted. The blood pressure therefore rises above normal, and this stimulates the baroreceptors, causing bradycardia and a drop in pressure to normal levels.

In sympathectomized patients, the heart rate changes are present because the baroreceptors and the vagi are intact. However, in patients with autonomic insufficiency, a disease of unknown etiology in which there is widespread disruption of autonomic function, the heart rate changes are absent. For reasons that are still obscure, patients with primary hyperaldosteronism also fail to show the heart rate changes and the blood pressure rise when the intrathoracic pressure returns to normal. Their response to the Valsalva maneuver returns to normal after removal of the aldosterone-secreting tumor.

Stimulation of the carotid sinus nerves by means of a chronically implanted radiofrequency stimulator has recently been used with considerable success in the treatment of angina pectoris. The pain in this condition is due to the accumulation of a pain-producing substance in the myocardium when it is ischemic (see Chapter 7). When the patient feels pain coming on, he switches on his stimulator. The resulting decrease in cardiac rate and output reduces the load on the heart, relieving the attack.

Sympathetic Vasodilator System

The cholinergic sympathetic vasodilator fibers are part of a regulatory system that originates in the cerebral cortex, relays in the hypothalamus and mesencephalon, and passes through the medulla without interruption to the intermediate gray column of the spinal cord where the preganglionic sympathetic vasodilator fibers as well as the vasoconstrictor fibers originate (Fig 31–10). Stimulation of this system produces vasodilatation in skeletal muscle, but the resultant increase in blood flow is associated with a decrease rather than an increase in muscle O_2 consumption. This suggests that the blood is being diverted through thoroughfare channels rather than capillaries. Adrenal medullary secretion of norepinephrine and epinephrine is apparently increased when this system is stimulated, the epinephrine probably reinforcing the dilatation of muscle blood vessels. The system has been shown to discharge in response to emotional stimuli such as fear, apprehension, and rage, and the sudden drop in peripheral resistance that is produced may be responsible for fainting in emotional situations. It has also been argued that this system is responsible for the increase in muscle blood flow that occurs at or even before the start of muscular exercise (see Chapter 33). It is possible that the system increases muscle blood flow at the start of exercise and that the vasodilator metabolites that accumulate as exercise progresses then dilate precapillary sphincters, with a resultant increase in capillary blood flow.

Control of Heart Rate

Various conditions which affect the heart rate are listed in Table 31–2. The sympathetic and parasympa-

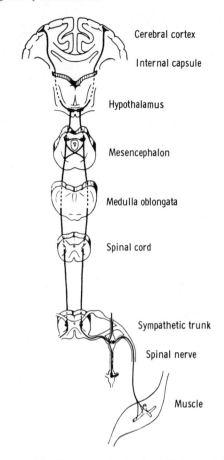

FIG 31–10. **The sympathetic vasodilator pathways.** (Reproduced, with permission, from Lindgren: The mesencephalic and vascular system. Acta physiol scandinav 35:Suppl 121, 1955.)

thetic nerves to the heart and the centers in the medulla which regulate the cardiac rate have been described above. Baroreceptor-mediated reflex changes in heart rate have also been considered in detail in preceding sections of this chapter. It is worth noting that, in general, stimuli which increase the heart rate also increase the blood pressure, whereas those which decrease the heart rate lower the blood pressure. Thus, for example, anger and excitement are associated with tachycardia and a rise in blood pressure, whereas fear and grief are usually associated with bradycardia and hypotension. The major exception to this generalization is the occurrence of hypertension and bradycardia when the intracranial pressure is increased. The 2 occur together in this condition because, as noted above, there is hypoxic stimulation of both the vasomotor center and the cardioinhibitory center. When the body temperature rises, the heart rate is increased, but the cutaneous vessels dilate and blood pressure is unchanged or lowered. When the SA node is warmed, its rate of discharge increases, and the effect of fever on the heart rate is probably due in part to the rise in cardiac temperature. Thyroid hormones increase the

TABLE 31–2. Factors affecting heart rate. Norepinephrine has a direct chronotropic effect on the heart, but in the intact animal its pressor action stimulates the baroreceptors, leading to enough reflex increase in vagal tone to overcome the direct effect and produce bradycardia.

Heart rate **accelerated** by:
Decreased activity of baroreceptors in the arteries, heart, and pulmonary circulation*
Inspiration*
Excitement*
Anger*
Most painful stimuli*
Hypoxia*
Exercise*
Norepinephrine*
Epinephrine
Thyroid hormones
Fever
Bainbridge effect
Heart rate **slowed** by:
Increased activity of baroreceptors†
Expiration†
Fear†
Grief†
Stimulation of pain fibers in trigeminal nerve
Increased intracranial pressure*

*Also produces a rise in blood pressure.
†Also produces a fall in blood pressure.

pulse pressure and accelerate the heart by potentiating the action of catecholamines. Epinephrine and norepinephrine both act directly on the heart to increase its rate, but the marked pressor response produced by norepinephrine stimulates the arterial baroreceptors, and the reflex bradycardia obscures the cardioacceleratory action.

The acceleration of the heart during inspiration (sinus arrhythmia; see Chapter 28) is partly due to impulses in afferents from vagal stretch receptors in the lung which inhibit the cardioinhibitory center, although increased sympathetic activity due to irradiation of impulses from the inspiratory center to the vasomotor center also contributes to the tachycardia.

Emotional stimuli converge through the hypothalamus on the cardioinhibitory center and probably exert their effects on heart rate by increasing or decreasing its rate of tonic discharge.

The rise in blood pressure produced by hypoxia is due to activity in chemoreceptor afferents that converge on the vasomotor center, but the explanation of the rise in heart rate is the subject of much debate. Stimulation of the carotid chemoreceptors in a dog on a respirator causes bradycardia; but chemoreceptor stimulation in a dog that can increase its breathing causes tachycardia, and mechanical production of increased breathing movements without chemoreceptor stimulation has a similar effect.

The heart rate increases promptly at the start of exercise and sometimes even in anticipation of it. The mechanisms responsible for the rapid onset of tachycardia are unsettled, although the increased heart rate is probably due to impulses from the cerebral cortex relayed via the hypothalamus to the cardioinhibitory and vasomotor centers. Increased activity in the cardiac sympathetic nerves as well as a decrease in vagal tone appear to be involved.

32...

Circulation Through Special Regions

The distribution of the cardiac output to various parts of the body at rest in a normal adult man is shown in Table 32–1. The general principles described in preceding chapters apply to the circulation of all these regions, but the vascular supplies of most organs have additional special features. The portal circulation of the anterior pituitary is discussed in Chapter 14, the renal circulation in Chapter 38, and the pulmonary circulation in Chapter 34. The circulation of skeletal muscle is discussed with the physiology of exercise in Chapter 33. This chapter is concerned with the circulation of the brain, the heart, the splanchnic area, the skin, the placenta, and the fetus.

CEREBRAL CIRCULATION

ANATOMIC CONSIDERATIONS

Vessels

Except for a small contribution from the anterior spinal artery to the medulla, the entire arterial inflow to the brain in man is via 4 arteries: 2 internal carotids and 2 vertebrals. The vertebral arteries unite to form the basilar artery; and the circle of Willis, formed by the carotids and the basilar artery, is the origin of the 6 large vessels supplying the cerebral cortex. In some animals the vertebrals are large and the internal carotids small, but in man a relatively small fraction of the total arterial flow is carried by the vertebral arteries. Substances injected into one carotid artery are distributed almost exclusively to the cerebral hemisphere on that side. There is normally no crossing over, probably because the pressure is equal on both sides. Even when it is not, the anastomotic channels in the circle do not permit a very large flow. Occlusion of one carotid artery, particularly in older patients, often causes serious symptoms of cerebral ischemia. There are precapillary anastomoses between the cerebral arterioles in man and some other species, but flow through these channels is generally insufficient to maintain the circulation and prevent infarction when a cerebral artery is occluded.

Venous drainage from the brain by way of the deep veins and dural sinuses empties principally into the internal jugular veins in man, although a small amount of venous blood drains through the ophthalmic and pterygoid venous plexuses, through emissary veins to the scalp, and down the system of paravertebral veins in the spinal canal. In other species, the internal jugular veins are small and the venous blood from the brain mixes with blood from other structures.

The cerebral vessels have a number of unique anatomic features. In the choroid plexuses there are gaps between the endothelial cells of the capillary wall, but the choroid epithelial cells are densely intermeshed and interlocked. The capillaries in the brain substance

TABLE 32–1. Blood flow and O_2 consumption of various organs in a 63 kg adult human with a mean arterial blood pressure of 90 mm Hg and an O_2 consumption of 250 ml/min. R units are pressure (mm Hg) divided by blood flow (ml/sec).*

Region	Mass (kg)	Blood Flow ml/min	Blood Flow ml/100 g/min	Arteriovenous Oxygen Difference (ml/liter)	Oxygen Consumption ml/min	Oxygen Consumption ml/100 g/min	Resistance in R units Absolute	Resistance in R units per kg	Percentage of Total Cardiac Output	Percentage of Total Oxygen Consumption
Liver	2.6	1500	57.7	34	51	2.0	3.6	9.4	27.8	20.4
Kidneys	0.3	1260	420.0	14	18	6.0	4.3	1.3	23.3	7.2
Brain	1.4	750	54.0	62	46	3.3	7.2	10.1	13.9	18.4
Skin	3.6	462	12.8	25	12	0.3	11.7	42.1	8.6	4.8
Skeletal muscle	31.0	840	2.7	60	50	0.2	6.4	198.4	15.6	20.0
Heart muscle	0.3	250	84.0	114	29	9.7	21.4	6.4	4.7	11.6
Rest of body	23.8	336	1.4	129	44	0.2	16.1	383.2	6.2	17.6
Whole body	63.0	5400	8.6	46	250	0.4	1.0	63.0	100.0	100.0

*Reproduced, with permission, from: *Medical Physiology*, 11th ed. Bard P (editor). Mosby, 1961.

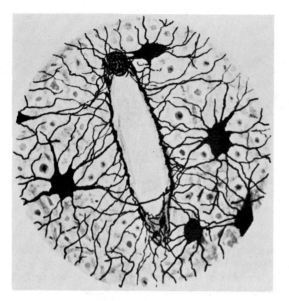

FIG 32–1. Membrane of end-feet of fibrous astrocytes (large dark cells) around a cerebral capillary. From occipital cortex of a monkey, silver carbonate stain. (Reproduced, with permission, from Glees: *Neuroglia, Morphology and Function.* Blackwell, 1955.)

resemble capillaries in other parts of the body, although there are no fenestrations in the endothelium as there are in some organs. The endothelial cells are tightly held together, and there is a thick basement membrane. In addition, the brain capillaries are surrounded by a membrane made up of the end-feet of astrocytes (Fig 32–1). These end-feet are closely applied to the basement membrane of the capillary (Fig 32–2) and cover almost all of the capillary wall. The protoplasm of astrocytes is also found around synapses, where it appears to be isolating the synapses in the brain from one another.

Innervation

There are numerous myelinated and unmyelinated nerve fibers on the cerebral vessels. The sympathetic fibers come from the cervical ganglia of the sympathetic ganglion chain. The parasympathetic fibers pass to the cerebral vessels from the facial nerve via the greater superficial petrosal nerve. The myelinated fibers are probably sensory in function, since touching or pulling on the cerebral vessels is known to cause pain.

FIG 32–2. Section of the brain and investing membranes. *Inset:* Detail of the barriers between blood in a capillary and cerebral tissue. (Reproduced, with permission, from Tschirgi in: *Handbook of Physiology.* Field J, Magoun HW [editors]. Washington: The American Physiological Society, 1960. Section 1, pp 1865–1890.)

THE BLOOD-BRAIN BARRIER

Over 50 years ago, it was first demonstrated that when acidic dyes such as trypan blue are injected into living animals all the tissues are stained except most of the brain and spinal cord. To explain the failure of the neural tissue to stain, the existence of a **blood-brain barrier** was postulated. The work with dyes has been criticized, but subsequent research has established the fact that only water, CO_2, and O_2 cross the cerebral capillaries with ease, and the exchange of other substances is slow.

The general features of exchange across capillary walls between the plasma and the interstitial fluid are described in Chapter 30. There is considerable variation in capillary permeability from organ to organ in the body. However, the exchange across the cerebral vessels is so different from that in other capillary beds—and the rate of exchange of many physiologically important substances is so slow—that it seems justifiable to speak specifically of a blood-brain barrier.

Penetration of Substances Into Brain

Water, CO_2, and O_2 cross the blood-brain barrier readily, while glucose crosses more slowly. Na^+, K^+, and Mg^{++}, Cl^-, HCO_3^-, and $HPO_4^=$ in plasma require 3–30 times as long to equilibrate with spinal fluid as they do with other portions of the interstitial fluid. The relatively slow penetration of urea into brain and the cerebrospinal fluid is illustrated in Fig 32–3. Bile salts and catecholamines do not enter the adult brain in more than minute amounts. Proteins cross the barrier to a very limited extent, and it is because they are bound to protein that acidic dyes fail to stain neural

FIG 32–3. Penetration of urea into muscle, brain, spinal cord, and cerebrospinal fluid. (Modified and reproduced, with permission, from Kleeman, Davson, & Levin: Urea transport in the central nervous system. Am J Physiol 203:739, 1962.)

tissue. It is worth noting that no substance is completely excluded from the brain, and the important consideration is the rate of transfer of the substance.

Substances move from the blood into the brain by diffusion, facilitated diffusion, and active transport. There is an H^+ gradient between brain ECF and blood; the pH of brain ECF is 7.32, whereas that of blood is 7.40. The rate of diffusion depends in part on molecular size, large or protein-bound molecules entering slowly. It also depends on lipid solubility, compounds with high lipid solubility entering more rapidly than substances with low lipid solubility. Glucose enters by facilitated diffusion and cations by active transport. Certain compounds cross the blood-brain barrier slowly, whereas closely related compounds enter rapidly. For example, the amines dopamine and serotonin penetrate to a very limited degree, but their corresponding acids, L-dopa and 5-hydroxytryptophan, enter with relative ease (see Chapter 15).

Development of the Blood-Brain Barrier

The cerebral capillaries are much more permeable at birth than in adulthood, and the blood-brain barrier develops during the early years of life. In severely jaundiced infants, bile pigments penetrate into the nervous system and, in the presence of asphyxia, damage the basal ganglia (kernicterus). However, in jaundiced adults, the nervous system is unstained and not directly affected.

Areas "Outside the Blood-Brain Barrier"

When an acidic dye is injected into an animal, 5 small areas in the brain stain like the tissues outside the brain. These areas are (1) the **pineal,** (2) the **posterior pituitary,** and the adjacent ventral part of the median eminence of the hypothalamus, (3) the **area postrema,** (4) the **supraoptic crest,** and (5) the **intercolumnar tubercle.** The physiologic significance of the fact that these areas have a much greater permeability than the rest of the brain is not known. There has been speculation that they may all be chemoreceptors of one sort or another. The area postrema is a chemoreceptor that initiates vomiting in response to chemical changes in the plasma. There is evidence that the osmoreceptor regulating vasopressin secretion is outside the blood-brain barrier, and circulating sex hormone and cortisol levels may act on the median eminence region to regulate anterior pituitary secretion of gonadotropins and ACTH. However, the function of the pineal is uncertain, and no function has as yet been assigned to the supraoptic crest and the intercolumnar tubercle.

Function of the Blood-Brain Barrier

The blood-brain barrier probably functions to maintain the constancy of the environment of the neurons in the CNS. These neurons are so dependent upon the ionic composition of the fluid bathing them that even minor variations have far-reaching consequences. The constancy of the composition of the ECF in all parts of the body is maintained by multiple homeostatic mechanisms (see Chapters 1 and 40), but because of the sensitivity of the cortical neurons to ionic change it is not surprising that an additional defense has evolved to protect them.

Clinical Implications

The physician must know the permeability of the blood-brain barrier to drugs in order to treat diseases of the nervous system intelligently. For example, among the antibiotics, penicillin and chlortetracycline enter the brain to a very limited degree. Sulfadiazine and erythromycin, on the other hand, enter quite readily.

Another important clinical consideration is the fact that the blood-brain barrier breaks down in areas of the brain that are irradiated, infected, or the site of tumors. The breakdown makes it possible to localize tumors with considerable accuracy. Substances such as radioactive iodine-labeled albumin penetrate normal brain tissue very slowly but they enter rapidly into tumor tissue, making the tumor stand out as an island of radioactivity in the surrounding normal brain.

CEREBROSPINAL FLUID

Formation & Absorption

About 50% of the cerebrospinal fluid (CSF) that fills the cerebral ventricles and subarachnoid space is formed in the choroid plexuses (Fig 32–2); the remaining 50% is formed around the cerebral vessels. Consequently, the composition of the CSF depends on filtration and diffusion from the blood, facilitated diffusion, and active transport. The composition (Table 32–2) is essentially the same as brain ECF, and there appears to be free communication between the brain extracellular space, the ventricles, and the sub-

FIG 32–4. CSF formation and absorption in humans at various CSF pressures. Note that at 112 mm CSF, formation and absorption are equal, and at 68 mm CSF, absorption is zero. (Modified and reproduced, with permission, from Cutler & others: Formation and absorption of cerebrospinal fluid in man. Brain 91:707, 1968.)

arachnoid space. The CSF flows out through the foramens of Magendie and Luschka and is absorbed through the arachnoid villi into the cerebral venus sinuses. Bulk flow via the villi is 500 ml/day in humans. Substances also leave the CSF by diffusion across adjacent membranes, and there is facilitated diffusion of glucose and active transport of cations and organic acids out of the CSF.

The rate of CSF formation is independent of intraventricular pressure, but the absorption, which takes place largely by bulk flow, is proportionate to the pressure (Fig 32–4). Below a pressure of approx-

TABLE 32–2. Concentration of various substances in human CSF and plasma.*

Substance		CSF	Plasma	Ratio CSF/Plasma
Na⁺	(mEq/kg H₂O)	147.0	150.0	0.98
K⁺	(mEq/kg H₂O)	2.9	4.6	0.62
Mg⁺⁺	(mEq/kg H₂O)	2.2	1.6	1.39
Ca⁺⁺	(mEq/kg H₂O)	2.3	4.7	0.49
Cl⁻	(mEq/kg H₂O)	113.0	99.0	1.14
HCO₃⁻	(mEq/liter)	25.1	24.8	1.01
PCO₂	(mm Hg)	50.2	39.5	1.28
pH		7.326	7.409	. . .
Osmolality	(mOsm/kg H₂O)	289.0	289.0	1.00
Protein	(mg/100 ml)	20.0	6000.0	0.003
Glucose	(mg/100 ml)	64.0	100.0	0.64
Inorganic P	(mg/100 ml)	3.4	4.7	0.73
Urea	(mg/100 ml)	12.0	15.0	0.80
Creatinine	(mg/100 ml)	1.5	1.2	1.25
Uric acid	(mg/100 ml)	1.5	5.0	0.30
Lactic acid	(mg/100 ml)	18.0	21.0	0.86
Cholesterol	(mg/100 ml)	0.2	175.0	0.001

*Data partly from Davson: *Physiology of the Cerebrospinal Fluid*, Churchill, 1967; and partly courtesy of R Mitchell & associates.

imately 68 mm CSF, absorption stops. Large amounts of fluid accumulate when the reabsorptive capacity of the arachnoid villi is decreased (**external, or communicating hydrocephalus**). Fluid also accumulates proximal to the block and distends the ventricles when the foramens of Luschka and Magendie are blocked or there is obstruction within the ventricular system (**internal hydrocephalus**).

Brain Extracellular Space

There has been considerable controversy about the size of the brain extracellular space. The sodium space in brain tissue is about 35% of brain volume and the chloride space is about 30%, but both ions are known to be present inside as well as outside of brain cells. Inulin and ferrocyanide, which do not enter cells, distribute in about 15% of brain volume. Under the electron microscope, brain cells appear very close together, and some electron microscopists have argued that the volume of the brain extracellular space could not be more than 4% of brain volume. However, asphyxia makes brain cells swell, and the brain extracellular space shrinks to 4% or less of brain volume when the brain is exposed to approximately the same amount of asphyxia as brain tissue prepared for electron photomicrography. These and other data indicate that there is an extracellular space in the living human which makes up about 15% of brain volume.

Protective Function

The meninges and the CSF protect the brain. The dura is attached firmly to bone. There is normally no "subdural space," the arachnoid being held to the dura by the surface tension of the thin layer of fluid between the 2 membranes. The brain itself is supported within the arachnoid by the blood vessels and nerve roots and by the multiple, fine fibrous **arachnoid trabeculae** (Fig 32–2). The brain weighs about 1400 g in air, but in its "water bath" of CSF it has a net weight of only 50 g. The buoyancy of the brain in the CSF permits its relatively flimsy attachments to suspend it very effectively. When the head receives a blow, the arachnoid slides on the dura and the brain moves, but its motion is gently checked by the CSF cushion and by the arachnoid trabeculae.

The pain produced by spinal fluid deficiency illustrates the importance of spinal fluid in supporting the brain. As a diagnostic procedure in patients suspected of having brain tumors, spinal fluid is removed and replaced by air to make the outline of the ventricles visible by x-ray (**pneumoencephalography**). This procedure causes a severe headache after the fluid is removed because the brain hangs on the vessels and nerve roots, and traction on them stimulates pain fibers. The pain can be relieved by intrathecal injection of sterile isotonic saline.

Head Injuries

Without the protection of the spinal fluid and the meninges, the brain would probably be unable to withstand even the minor traumas of everyday living, but with the protection afforded it takes a fairly severe blow to produce cerebral damage. The brain is damaged most commonly when the skull is fractured and bone is driven into neural tissue (depressed skull fracture); when the brain moves far enough to tear the delicate bridging veins from the cortex to the bone; or when the brain is accelerated by a blow on the head and is driven against the skull or the tentorium at a point opposite where the blow was struck (**contrecoup injury**).

CEREBRAL BLOOD FLOW

Kety Method

According to the **Fick principle** (see Chapter 29), the blood flow of any organ can be measured by determining the amount of a given substance (Q_X) removed from the blood stream by the organ per unit of time and dividing that value by the difference between the concentration of the substance in arterial blood and the concentration in the venous blood from the organ ($[A_X] - [V_X]$). Thus:

$$\text{Cerebral blood flow (CBF)} = \frac{Q_X}{[A_X] - [V_X]}$$

When an individual inhales small subanesthetic amounts of nitrous oxide (N_2O), this gas is taken up by the brain, and the brain N_2O equilibrates with the N_2O in blood in 9–11 minutes. After equilibration, the N_2O concentration in cerebral venous blood is equal to the concentration in the brain because the brain-blood partition coefficient for N_2O is 1. Therefore, the level in cerebral venous blood after equilibration divided by the mean A-V N_2O difference during equilibration equals the cerebral blood flow per unit of brain:

$$\text{CBF (ml/100 g brain/min)} = \frac{100 V_u S}{\int_0^u (A-V)dt}$$

where Q = Quantity taken up by brain
  u = Time of equilibrium (minutes)
  S = Partition coefficient of N_2O in blood and brain (= 1)
  A = Arterial N_2O concentration (vol/100 g)
  V = Cerebral venous N_2O concentration (vol/100 g)

The mean A-V difference can also be estimated from a plot of the differences at various times during equilibration (Fig 32–5). When blood N_2O concentrations are expressed in volumes/100 ml of blood or, more accurately, in volumes/100 g of blood, the cerebral blood flow values obtained are in ml/100 g of brain/min. The value per unit of brain tissue can be converted to an approximate value for total cerebral blood flow by multiplying by 1400 g, an average figure for brain weight in adult humans.

When the N_2O method (Kety method) is used to determine the cerebral blood flow in intact humans, arterial blood samples can be obtained from any convenient artery since the concentration of substances in systemic arterial blood is uniform throughout the body. To obtain cerebral venous blood, a needle is inserted into the jugular bulb. This expansion of the internal jugular vein at its point of exit from the skull is readily penetrated if the needle is inserted in a slightly headward direction half-way between the mastoid process and the angle of the mandible. The subject inhales N_2O for 10 minutes, and arterial and jugular venous blood samples are obtained repeatedly during this time. The N_2O content of the samples is determined, and the mean A-V N_2O difference is calculated.

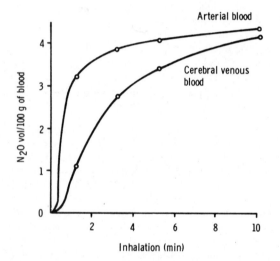

FIG 32–5. Arterial and cerebral venous blood N_2O levels while inhaling N_2O. (Redrawn and reproduced, with permission, from Kety, in: *Methods in Medical Research.* Vol I. Potter VR [editor]. Year Book, 1948.)

Normal Values

The average value for cerebral blood flow (CBF) in young adults is 54 ml/100 g/min (750 ml/min for the whole brain), with a range of approximately 40–67 ml/100 g/min. In children, the value averages about 105 ml/100 g/min. It falls to adult levels at the time of puberty in normal individuals but remains high in prepuberal castrates, suggesting that the sex hormones are responsible for the drop at puberty. However, castration in adulthood does not lead to a rise in CBF, and CBF is unaffected by the administration of sex and adrenal steroid hormones.

Limitations

The accuracy of the Kety method depends upon obtaining cerebral venous blood that is not significantly diluted with blood from other structures with different N_2O uptakes. In man, jugular venous blood is said to meet this requirement in over 95% of individuals, but it is not possible in most laboratory animals to obtain blood that comes only from the brain.

The value obtained with the Kety method is, of course, an average value for the flow during the 10 min equilibration period. Values for total CBF give no information about the relative blood flow in the various parts of the brain. Indeed, trying to draw conclusions about regional blood flow from total CBF measurements has been likened to trying to analyze the activity of individual tenants in a large apartment house by sampling the flow in the main water pipe and sewer pipe outside the apartment house. A reduction in flow to one part of the brain may be compensated by an increase in flow to another part, so that CBF remains unchanged (Fig 32–6). An uncompensated decrease in the blood flow to part of the brain results in decreased CBF, but the Kety method does not detect the decrease in total CBF produced by complete occlusion of the vessels supplying part of the brain.

FIG 32–6. Variations in intracerebral circulation.

This is true because the method measures only the flow per unit of brain, and the nonperfused area takes up no N_2O. The remaining normal brain extracts normal amounts, so that the CBF per unit of brain tissues is unaffected.

Blood Flow in Various Parts of the Brain

By determining the distribution of an inert radioactive gas in frozen sections of the brains of experimental animals and comparing these values with the level of the gas in the blood, it is possible to measure regional blood flow in the brain. The flow in the cerebral and cerebellar cortex is large, but the part of the brain with the highest blood flow is the inferior colliculus (Table 32–3). The blood flow in gray matter is about 6 times the flow in white matter.

TABLE 32–3. Blood flow of representative areas of the brain of unanesthetized cats.*

Area	Mean Blood Flow (ml/g/min)
Inferior colliculus	1.80
Sensorimotor cortex	1.38
Auditory cortex	1.30
Visual cortex	1.25
Medial geniculate body	1.22
Lateral geniculate body	1.21
Superior colliculus	1.15
Caudate nucleus	1.10
Thalamus	1.03
Association cortex	0.88
Cerebellar nuclei	0.87
Cerebellar white matter	0.24
Cerebral white matter	0.23
Spinal cord white matter	0.14

*Data from Landau & others: The local circulation of the living brain: Values in the unanesthetized cat. Tr Am Neurol A 80:125, 1955.

Cerebral Vascular Resistance

The cerebral vascular resistance (CVR) is equal to the cerebral perfusion pressure divided by the cerebral blood flow. The CVR in the supine position can be calculated on the basis of the mean brachial artery pressure (ignoring the relatively low cerebral venous pressure) without introducing a very large error. Calculated in this way, the normal CVR is approximately 100 "R units" (Table 32–1) per 100 g brain, or 7.2 R units for the whole brain.

REGULATION OF CEREBRAL CIRCULATION

Normal Flow

The cerebral circulation is regulated in such a way that a constant total CBF is generally maintained under varying conditions. For example, total cerebral blood flow is not increased by strenuous mental activity and is unchanged or even increased during sleep. However, when light is shone into the eyes of experimental animals, there is increased blood flow in the superior colliculi, lateral geniculate bodies, and occipital cortex, and there is evidence for increased regional blood flow in other parts of the brain when they become active.

The factors affecting the total CBF are the arterial pressure at brain level, the venous pressure at brain level, the intracranial pressure, the degree of active constriction or dilatation of the cerebral vessels, and the viscosity of the blood (Fig 32–7).

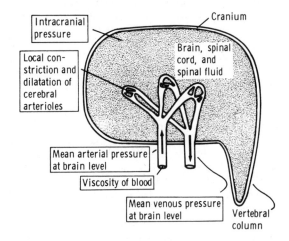

FIG 32–7. **Diagrammatic summary of the factors affecting cerebral blood flow.** (Modified from Patterson in: *Physiology and Biophysics*, 19th ed. Ruch TC, Patton HD [editors]. Saunders, 1965.)

Role of Intracranial Pressure

In adults, the brain, spinal cord, and spinal fluid are encased, along with the cerebral vessels, in a rigid bony enclosure. Because brain tissue and spinal fluid are essentially incompressible, the volume of blood, spinal fluid, and brain in the cranium at any time must be relatively constant (**Monro-Kellie doctrine**). More importantly, the cerebral vessels are compressed whenever the intracranial pressure rises. Any change in venous pressure promptly causes a similar change in intracranial pressure. Thus, a rise in venous pressure decreases cerebral blood flow both by decreasing the effective perfusion pressure and by compressing the cerebral vessels. This relationship helps to compensate for changes in arterial blood pressure at the level of the head. For example, if the body is accelerated upward ("positive *g*"), blood moves toward the feet and arterial pressure at the level of the head decreases. However, venous pressure also falls and intracranial pressure falls, so that the pressure on the vessels decreases and blood flow is much less severely compromised than it would otherwise be. Conversely, during acceleration downward, force acting toward the head ("negative *g*") increases arterial pressure at head level, but intracranial pressure also rises, so that the vessels are supported and do not rupture. The cerebral vessels are protected during the straining associated with defecation or delivery in the same way.

Effect of Intracranial Pressure Changes on Systemic Blood Pressure

When intracranial pressure is elevated to more than 450 mm of water (33 mm Hg) over a short period of time, cerebral blood flow is significantly reduced. The resultant ischemia stimulates the vasomotor center (see Chapter 31), and systemic blood pressure rises. Stimulation of the cardioinhibitory center produces bradycardia, and respiration is slowed. The blood pressure rise, which was described by Cushing and is sometimes called the **Cushing reflex**, helps to maintain the cerebral blood flow. Over a considerable range, the rise in systemic blood pressure is proportionate to the rise in intracranial pressure, although eventually a point is reached where the intracranial pressure exceeds the arterial pressure, and cerebral circulation ceases.

Chemical Effects on Cerebral Vessels

The arterioles in the brain, like those in other parts of the body, are directly affected by local changes in CO_2 and O_2 tension. A rise in P_{CO_2} exerts a particularly potent dilator effect on the cerebral vessels. A fall in P_{CO_2} has a constrictor effect, and cerebral vasoconstriction is an important factor in the production of the cerebral symptoms seen when the arterial P_{CO_2} falls during hyperventilation. A low P_{O_2} is associated with vasodilatation, and a high P_{O_2} with mild vasoconstriction. Hydrogen ions also exert a vasodilator effect, and a fall in pH is associated with increased flow whereas a rise in pH is associated with decreased flow.

These chemical effects on the cerebral vessels and the inherent response of their smooth muscle to stretch are the basis of considerable autoregulation of cerebral blood flow. The process of autoregulation is discussed in Chapter 31. When the blood flow decreases, the P_{CO_2} in the brain rises and the P_{O_2} and pH fall, dilating the vessels and helping to maintain tissue perfusion. Asphyxia is associated with a very great increase in cerebral blood flow because of the vasodilatation produced by the combination of hypoxia and hypercapnia.

Role of Vasomotor Nerves

The bulk of the evidence presently available indicates that even though cerebral vessels are innervated by adrenergic vasoconstrictor fibers and parasympathetic vasodilator fibers, vasomotor reflexes play little if any part in the regulation of cerebral blood flow in man. Stimulation of the cervical sympathetics does cause some constriction of pial vessels in animals, and injecting procaine into the stellate ganglion has had a considerable vogue in the treatment of cerebral thromboses in humans on the theory that the vasospasm associated with the thrombosis is mediated via vaso-

constrictor nerves. However, careful measurements clearly show that blocking the stellate ganglion has no effect on cerebral blood flow, and the therapeutic value of stellate ganglion block is questionable.

Integrated Operation of Regulatory Mechanisms

Several examples of the way the regulatory mechanisms discussed above maintain cerebral blood flow are discussed in Chapter 33. It is worth remembering that these mechanisms operate together to overcome such formidable challenges as the effect of gravity on the cerebral blood flow, not only in man but also in the giraffe when this animal stoops to drink water and when it raises its head to nibble leaves from the tops of trees.

BRAIN METABOLISM & OXYGEN REQUIREMENTS

Uptake & Release of Substances by the Brain

If the cerebral blood flow is known, it is possible to calculate the consumption or production by the brain of O_2, CO_2, glucose, or any other substance present in the blood stream by multiplying the cerebral blood flow by the difference between the concentration of the substance in arterial blood and its concentration in cerebral venous blood. When calculated in this fashion, a negative value indicates that the brain is producing the substance (Table 32–4).

TABLE 32–4. Utilization and production of substances by adult human brain in vivo.*

	Uptake (+) or output (−) per 100 g brain/min	Total/min
Substances utilized		
Oxygen	+3.5 ml	+49 ml
Glucose	+5.5 mg	+77 mg
Glutamic acid	+0.4 mg	+ 5.6 mg
Substances produced		
Carbon dioxide	−3.5 ml	−49 ml
Glutamine	−0.6 mg	− 8.4 mg

Substances not utilized or produced: lactic acid, pyruvic acid, total ketones, *a*-ketoglutarate.

*From data compiled by Sokoloff, in: *Handbook of Physiology.* Field J, Magoun HW (editors). Washington: The American Physiological Society, 1960. Section 1, pp 1843–1865.

Oxygen Consumption

The O_2 consumption of human brain, or **cerebral metabolic rate for O_2 ($CMRO_2$)**, averages about 3.5 ml/100 g brain/min, or 49 ml/min for the whole brain in an adult. This figure represents approximately 20%

of the total resting O_2 consumption (Table 32–1). The brain is extremely sensitive to hypoxia, and occlusion of its blood supply produces unconsciousness in as short a period as 10 sec. The vegetative structures in the brain stem are more resistant to hypoxia than the cerebral cortex, and patients may recover from accidents such as cardiac arrest and other conditions causing fairly prolonged hypoxia with normal vegetative functions but severe, permanent intellectual deficiencies. The basal ganglia also use O_2 at a very rapid rate. The values for in vitro O_2 consumption of various parts of the dog brain are shown in Table 32–5. The metabolic rate of the cerebral cortex relative to that of the basal ganglia may be higher in man than in the dog, but it is well to remember that the basal ganglia are sensitive to hypoxia in humans and that symptoms of Parkinson's disease as well as intellectual deficits can be produced by chronic hypoxia. The thalamus and the inferior colliculus are also very susceptible to hypoxic damage.

TABLE 32–5. Oxygen consumption of parts of adult dog brain in vitro.*

	Oxygen Consumption (μl/100 mg/hour)
Caudate nucleus	136
Cerebral cortex	116
Cerebellum	107
Thalamus	101
Midbrain	92
Medulla	69
Spinal cord	50

*Data from Himwich & Fazekas: Comparative studies of the metabolism of the brain. Am J Physiol 132:454, 1941.

Energy Sources

Glucose is the major ultimate source of energy for the brain under normal conditions. It is taken up from the blood in large amounts, and the RQ (respiratory quotient; see Chapter 17) of cerebral tissue is 0.95–0.99 in normal individuals. This does not mean that the immediate source of energy is always glucose. Indeed, there is evidence that as much as 30% of the glucose taken up under normal conditions is converted to amino acids, lipids, and proteins, and that substances other than glucose are metabolized for energy during convulsions. There may also be some utilization of amino acids from the circulation even though the amino acid A-V difference across the brain is normally minute. Insulin is not required for most cerebral cells to utilize glucose.

Hypoglycemia

The symptoms of hypoglycemia are mental changes, ataxia, confusion, sweating, coma, and convulsions (see Chapter 19). The total glycogen content of the brain is about 1.6 mg/g in fasted animals, and it

has been claimed that during hypoglycemia this amount is sufficient to sustain cerebral cells for 90 minutes. The figure is misleading because cortical symptoms appear in less than 90 minutes, but the brain can withstand hypoglycemia for longer periods than it can withstand hypoxia. The cortical regions are more sensitive to hypoglycemia than the vegetative centers in the brain stem, and sublethal exposures to hypoglycemia, like similar exposures to hypoxia, may cause irreversible cortical changes.

Glutamic Acid & Ammonia Removal

The brain uptake of glutamic acid is approximately balanced by its output of glutamine. It is probable that the glutamic acid entering the brain takes up ammonia and leaves as glutamine (see Chapter 17). The glutamic acid-glutamine conversion in the brain—the opposite of the reaction in the kidney which produces some of the ammonia that enters the tubules—probably serves as a detoxifying mechanism to keep the brain free of ammonia. Ammonia is very toxic to nerve cells, and ammonia intoxication is believed to be a major cause of the bizarre neurologic symptoms in hepatic coma.

CORONARY CIRCULATION

Anatomic Considerations

The 2 coronary arteries which supply the myocardium arise from the sinuses behind the cusps of the aortic valve at the root of the aorta. Eddy currents keep the valves away from the orifices of the arteries, and they are patent throughout the cardiac cycle. There are 2 venous drainage systems: a superficial system, ending in the coronary sinus and anterior cardiac veins, that drains the left ventricle; and a deep system draining the rest of the heart (Fig 32–8). The

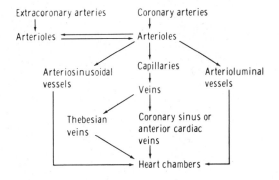

FIG 32–8. Diagram of the coronary circulation. (Based on Wearn & others: The nature of the vascular communications between the coronary arteries and the chambers of the heart. Am Heart J 9:143, 1933.)

deep system is made up in large part of the **arterio-sinusoidal vessels**, sinusoidal capillary-like vessels that empty directly into the heart chambers. There are also direct connections to the atria and ventricles from the coronary arterioles (**arterioluminal vessels**) and the veins (**thebesian veins**). There are a few anastomoses between the coronary arterioles and extracardiac arterioles, especially around the mouths of the great veins. Anastomoses between coronary arterioles in man only pass particles less than 40 μm in diameter, but there is evidence that these channels enlarge and increase in number in patients with coronary artery disease.

Pressure Gradients & Flow in the Coronary Vessels

The heart is a muscle which, like skeletal muscle, compresses its blood vessels when it contracts. The pressure inside the left ventricle is slightly greater than in the aorta during systole (Table 32–6). Conse-

TABLE 32–6. Pressures in aorta and left and right ventricles in systole and diastole.

	Pressure (mm Hg) in			Pressure Differential (mm Hg) Between Aorta and	
	Aorta	Left Vent	Right Vent	Left Vent	Right Vent
Systole	120	121	25	−1	95
Diastole	80	0	0	80	80

quently, flow occurs in the arteries supplying the subendocardial portion of the left ventricle only during diastole, although the force is sufficiently dissipated in the more superficial portions of the left ventricular myocardium to permit some flow in this region throughout the cardiac cycle. Since diastole is shorter when the heart rate is rapid, left ventricular coronary flow is reduced during tachycardia. On the other hand, the pressure differential between the aorta and the right ventricle, and the differential between the aorta and the atria, is somewhat greater during systole than during diastole. Consequently, coronary flow in those parts of the heart is not appreciably reduced during systole. Flow in the right and left coronary arteries of the dog is shown in Fig 32–9. Because there is no blood flow during systole in the subendocardial portion of the left ventricle, this region is prone to ischemic damage and is the most common site of myocardial infarction. Blood flow to the left ventricle is decreased in patients with stenotic aortic valves because in aortic stenosis the pressure in the left ventricle must be much greater than that in the aorta to eject the blood. Consequently, the coronary vessels are severely compressed during systole. Patients with this disease are particularly prone to develop symptoms of

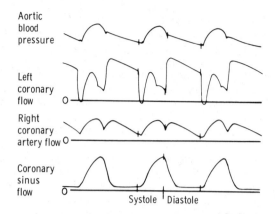

FIG 32–9. Schematic representation of blood flow in the left and right coronary arteries and the coronary sinus of the dog during phases of the cardiac cycle. (After Gregg. Reproduced, with permission, from: *Physiology and Biophysics,* 19th ed. Ruch TC, Patton HD [editors]. Saunders, 1965.)

myocardial ischemia, in part because of this compression and in part because more O_2 is required to expel blood through the stenotic aortic valve. Coronary flow is also decreased when the aortic diastolic pressure is low. The rise in venous pressure in conditions such as congestive heart failure reduces coronary flow because it decreases effective coronary perfusion pressure.

For technical reasons, accurate measurements of coronary flow are difficult to obtain. In humans, a venous catheter can be slipped into the coronary sinus without ill effects, and the Kety method applied to the heart, on the assumption that the N_2O content of coronary venous blood is typical of the entire myocardial effluent. The most reliable data indicate that coronary flow at rest in man is about 250 ml/min, or 5% of the cardiac output (Table 32–1).

Variations in Coronary Flow

The heart extracts large amounts of O_2 from each unit of blood at rest (Table 32–1). O_2 consumption can be increased significantly only by increasing blood flow. The caliber of the coronary vessels, and consequently the rate of coronary blood flow, is influenced not only by pressure changes in the aorta but also by chemical and neural factors. The coronary circulation shows considerable autoregulation.

Chemical Factors

Asphyxia, hypoxia, and intracoronary injections of cyanide all increase coronary blood flow 200–300% in denervated as well as intact hearts. The one feature common to these 3 stimuli is hypoxia of the myocardial fibers. Therefore, the increase is probably due to liberation of a vasodilator substance in the hypoxic tissue. It has been hypothesized that this vasodilator is adenosine. A similar increase in flow is produced in the area supplied by a coronary artery if the artery is occluded and then released. This **reactive hyperemia** is similar to that seen in the skin (see below). Hypercapnia alone does not affect coronary flow in the intact animal, and a fall in pH is associated with only a slight increase.

Neural Factors

The coronary arterioles contain α-adrenergic receptors, which mediate vasoconstriction; and β-adrenergic receptors, which mediate vasodilatation. Activity in the adrenergic nerves to the heart and injections of epinephrine cause coronary vasodilatation. However, it is difficult to prove that this is a direct effect of the adrenergic mediator on blood vessels. Adrenergic mediators increase the heart rate and the force of cardiac contraction, and the vasodilatation could be produced by chemical changes in the myocardium secondary to the increase in its activity. When the inotropic and chronotropic effects of adrenergic discharge are blocked by a β-adrenergic blocking drug, stimulation of the adrenergic nerves decreases coronary flow. Stimulation of vagal fibers to the heart dilates the coronaries.

When the systemic blood pressure falls, the reflex increase in adrenergic discharge causes coronary vasodilatation and increased coronary blood flow at a time when the cutaneous, renal, and splanchnic vessels are constricted. In this way the circulation of the heart, like that of the brain, is preserved when flow to other organs is compromised.

SPLANCHNIC CIRCULATION

The blood from the intestines, the pancreas, and the spleen drains via the portal vein and hepatic veins through the liver into the inferior vena cava. This large splanchnic vascular bed is a blood reservoir that plays an important role in homeostatic adjustments within the circulatory system.

Hepatic Circulation

The way the intrahepatic branches of the hepatic artery and portal vein converge on the sinusoids and drain into the central lobular veins of the liver is shown in Fig 26–17. The lobular veins drain via the hepatic veins to the inferior vena cava. Portal venous pressure is normally about 10 mm Hg in man, and hepatic venous pressure approximately 5 mm Hg. The mean pressure in the hepatic artery branches that converge on the sinusoids is about 90 mm Hg, but the pressure in the sinusoids is less than portal venous pressure, so there must be a marked pressure drop along the hepatic arterioles. The endothelium of the sinusoids is more permeable to protein than the capillary endothelium elsewhere in the body. The liver receives about one-fourth of the cardiac output in resting adults (1500 ml/min; Table 32–1). Eighty percent of its flow

reaches the liver via the portal vein and 20% via the hepatic artery.

The intrahepatic portal vein radicles have smooth muscle in their walls that is innervated by adrenergic vasoconstrictor nerve fibers reaching the liver via the third to 11th thoracic ventral roots and the splanchnic nerves. The vasoconstrictor innervation of the hepatic artery comes from the hepatic sympathetic plexus. There are no known vasodilator fibers reaching the liver. The hepatic veins are supplied with smooth muscle in the dog, but there is no good evidence for functioning "hepatic vein sphincters" in man. At rest, circulation in the peripheral portions of the liver is sluggish and only a portion of the organ is actively perfused. When systemic venous pressure rises, the portal vein radicles are dilated passively and the amount of blood in the liver increases. In congestive heart failure, this hepatic venous congestion may be extreme. Conversely, when there is diffuse adrenergic discharge in response to a drop in systemic blood pressure, the intrahepatic portal radicles constrict, portal pressure rises, and blood flow through the liver is brisk, bypassing most of the organ. Most of the blood in the liver enters the systemic circulation. Constriction of the hepatic arterioles diverts blood from the liver, and constriction of the mesenteric arterioles reduces portal inflow. In severe shock hepatic blood flow may be reduced to such a degree that there is patchy necrosis of the liver.

Reservoir Function of the Spleen

In dogs and other carnivores, there is a large amount of smooth muscle in the capsule of the spleen. The spleen traps blood, and rhythmic contractions of its capsule pump plasma into the lymphatics. The spleen therefore contains a reservoir of blood rich in cells. Adrenergic nerve discharge and epinephrine make the spleen contract strongly, discharging the blood into the circulation. However, this function of the spleen is quantitatively unimportant in man. Other functions of the spleen are discussed in Chapter 24.

Other important blood reservoirs which contain a large volume of blood at rest are the skin and lungs. During severe exercise, constriction of the vessels in these organs and decreased blood "storage" in the liver and other portions of the splanchnic bed, the skin, and the lungs may increase the volume of actively circulating blood perfusing the muscles by as much as 30%.

CIRCULATION OF THE SKIN

The amount of heat lost from the body is regulated to a large extent by varying the amount of blood flowing through the skin (see Chapter 14). The fingers, toes, palms, and ear lobes contain well innervated anastomotic connections between arterioles and venules (A-V anastomoses; Fig 30–2). Blood flow in response to thermoregulatory stimuli can vary from 1 to as much as 150 ml/100 g of skin/min, and it has been postulated that these variations are possible because blood can be shunted through the anastomoses. The subdermal capillary and venous plexus is a blood reservoir of some importance, and the skin is one of the few places where the reactions of blood vessels can be observed visually.

White Reaction

When a pointed object is drawn lightly over the skin, the stroke lines become pale **(white reaction)**. The mechanical stimulus apparently initiates contraction of the precapillary sphincters, and blood drains out of the capillaries. The response appears in about 15 seconds.

Triple Response

When the skin is stroked more firmly with a pointed instrument, instead of the white reaction there is reddening at the site that appears in about 10 seconds **(red reaction)**. This is followed in a few minutes by local swelling and diffuse, mottled reddening around the injury. The initial redness is due to capillary dilatation, a direct response of the capillaries to pressure. The swelling, or **wheal**, is local edema due to increased permeability of the capillaries and postcapillary venules. The redness spreading out from the injury **(flare)** is due to arteriolar dilatation. This three-part response, the red reaction, wheal, and flare, is called the **triple response**, and is part of the normal reaction to injury (see Chapter 20). It is present after total sympathectomy. The increase in vascular permeability **res**ponsible for wheal formation is produced by a substance ("H substance") or substances released locally. Histamine produces a wheal, and is probably one of the substances liberated. The flare is absent in locally anesthetized skin and in denervated skin after the nerves have degenerated, but it is present immediately after nerve block or section above the site of injury. Therefore, the flare is generally held to be due to an **axon reflex**, a response in which impulses initiated in sensory nerves by the injury are relayed antidromically down other branches of the sensory nerves (Fig 32–10). The antidromic impulses appear to release or activate proteolytic enzymes that cause the local formation of kinins, and these polypeptides in turn cause vasodilatation. This is the one situation in the body where there is substantial evidence for a physiologic effect due to antidromic conduction.

Reactive Hyperemia

A response of the blood vessels which occurs in many organs but is visible in the skin is **reactive hyperemia**, an increase in the amount of blood in a region when its circulation is reestablished after a period of occlusion. When the blood supply to a limb is occluded, the cutaneous arterioles below the occlusion dilate; and when the circulation is reestablished, blood flowing into the dilated vessels makes the skin become fiery red. O_2 diffuses a short distance through the skin, and reactive hyperemia is prevented if the circulation of the limb is occluded in an atmosphere of 100% O_2. Therefore, the arteriolar dilatation is apparently due to a local effect of hypoxia, and it is believed to be effected by the release of a chemical substance.

Generalized Responses

Adrenergic nerve stimulation and circulating epinephrine and norepinephrine constrict cutaneous blood vessels. There are no known vasodilator nerve fibers to the cutaneous vessels, and vasodilatation is brought about by decreasing constrictor tone. Skin color and temperature also depend on the state of the capillaries and venules. A cold blue or gray skin is one in which the arterioles are constricted and the capillaries dilated; a warm red skin is one in which both are dilated.

Because painful stimuli cause diffuse adrenergic discharge, a painful injury causes generalized cutaneous vasoconstriction in addition to the local triple response. When the body temperature rises during exercise, the cutaneous blood vessels dilate in spite of continuing adrenergic discharge in other parts of the body. Dilatation of cutaneous vessels in response to a rise in hypothalamic temperature (see Chapter 14) is a prepotent reflex response that overcomes other reflex activity. The vasodilatation may be due in part to the local liberation of the nonapeptide bradykinin (see Chapter 31). Cold causes cutaneous vasoconstriction; however, with severe cold, superficial vasodilatation may supervene. This vasodilatation is the cause of the ruddy complexions seen on a cold day.

Shock is more profound in patients with elevated temperatures because of the cutaneous vasodilatation, and patients in shock should not be warmed to the point that their body temperature rises. This is some-

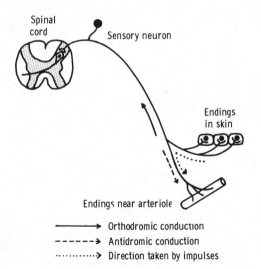

FIG 32–10. Axon reflex. Hypothetical pathway involved in the flare response.

times a problem because well-meaning laymen have read in first-aid books that "injured patients should be kept warm," and they pile blankets on accident victims who are in shock.

PLACENTAL & FETAL CIRCULATION

Uterine Circulation

The blood flow of the uterus parallels the metabolic activity of the myometrium and endometrium and undergoes cyclic fluctuations that correlate well with the menstrual cycle in the nonpregnant woman. The function of the spiral and basal arteries of the endometrium in menstruation is discussed in Chapter 23. During pregnancy, blood flow increases rapidly as the uterus increases in size (Fig 32–11). Metabolites with a vasodilator action are undoubtedly produced in the uterus, as they are in other active tissues; but in early pregnancy the A-V O_2 difference across the uterus is small, and it has been suggested that estrogens act on the blood vessels to increase uterine blood flow in excess of tissue O_2 needs. However, even though uterine blood flow increases 20-fold during pregnancy, the size of the conceptus increases much more, chang-

ing from a single cell to a fetus plus a placenta that weigh 4–5 kg at term in humans. Consequently, more O_2 is extracted from the uterine blood during the latter part of pregnancy and the O_2 saturation of uterine blood falls. Just before parturition there is a sharp decline in uterine blood flow, but the significance of this fact is not clear.

Placenta

The placenta is the "fetal lung." Its maternal portion is in effect a large blood sinus. Into this "lake" project the villi of the fetal portion containing the small branches of the fetal umbilical arteries and vein (Fig 32–12). O_2 is taken up by the fetal blood and CO_2 is discharged into the maternal circulation across the walls of the villi in a fashion analogous to O_2 and CO_2 exchange in the lungs (see Chapter 35), but the cellular layers covering the villi are thicker and less permeable than the alveolar membranes in the lung and exchange is much less efficient. The placenta is also the route by which all nutritive materials enter the fetus and by which fetal wastes are discharged to the maternal blood.

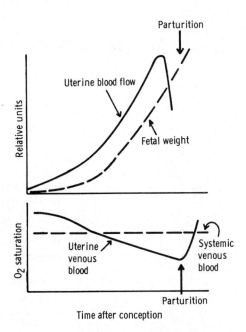

FIG 32–11. Changes in uterine blood flow and the amount of O_2 in uterine venous blood during pregnancy. (After Barcroft. Modified and redrawn, with permission, from Keele & Neil: *Samson Wright's Applied Physiology,* 12th ed. Oxford Univ Press, 1971.)

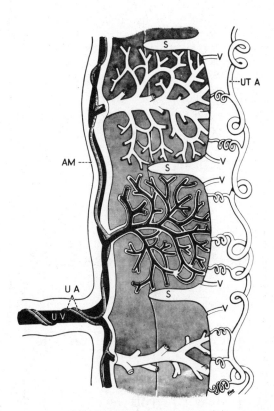

FIG 32–12. Diagram of a section through the human placenta. AM, amnion; S, septa; UA, umbilical arteries; UV, umbilical vein; UT A, uterine artery; V, veins. (Reproduced, with permission, from Harrison: *Textbook of Human Embryology,* 2nd ed. Blackwell, 1964.)

Section VI. Circulation

Fetal Circulation

The arrangement of the circulation in the fetus is shown diagrammatically in Fig 32–13. Fifty-five percent of the fetal cardiac output goes through the placenta. The blood in the umbilical vein in humans is believed to be about 80% saturated with O_2, compared with 98% saturation in the arterial circulation of the adult. The **ductus venosus** (Fig 32–14) diverts some of this blood directly to the inferior vena cava and the remainder mixes with the portal blood of the fetus. The portal and systemic venous blood of the fetus is only 26% saturated, and the saturation of the mixed blood in the inferior vena cava is approximately 67%. Most of the blood entering the heart through the inferior vena cava is diverted directly to the left atrium via the patent foramen ovale. Most of the blood from the superior vena cava enters the right ventricle and is expelled into the pulmonary artery. The resistance of the collapsed lungs is high, and the pressure in the pulmonary artery is several mm Hg higher than it is in the aorta, so that most of the blood in the pulmonary artery passes through the **ductus arteriosus** to the aorta. In this fashion, the relatively unsaturated blood from the right ventricle is diverted to the trunk and lower body of the fetus, while the head of the fetus receives the better oxygenated blood from the left ventricle. From the aorta, some of the blood is pumped into the umbilical arteries and back to the placenta. The O_2 saturation of the blood in the lower aorta and umbilical arteries of the fetus is approximately 60%.

Fetal Respiration

The tissues of fetal and newborn mammals have a remarkable but poorly understood resistance to hypoxia. However, the O_2 saturation of the maternal blood in the placenta is so low that the fetus might suffer hypoxic damage if fetal red cells did not have a greater O_2 affinity than adult red cells (Fig 32–15). The fetal red cells contain fetal hemoglobin (hemoglobin F), while the adult cells contain adult hemoglobin (hemoglobin A). The cause of the difference in O_2 affinity between the 2 is that hemoglobin F binds 2,3-DPG less effectively than hemoglobin A. The decrease in O_2 affinity due to the binding of 2,3-DPG is discussed in detail in Chapter 35. The quantitative aspects of gas exchange across the placenta, based on experiments on the cow, are shown in Table 32–7.

In humans, hemoglobin A first appears in the fetal circulation at about the 20th week, when the bone marrow first begins to function (Fig 27–7). At birth, only 20% of the circulating hemoglobin is of the adult type. However, no more hemoglobin F is normally formed after birth, and by the age of 4 months 90% of the circulating hemoglobin is hemoglobin A.

TABLE 32–7. Summary of gaseous interchange across the placenta in the cow.*

	Hemoglobin % Saturation	Partial Pressure (mm Hg)	
		O_2	CO_2
Maternal artery	90	70	41
Uterine vein	70	41.5	46.5
Umbilical vein		11.5	48
Umbilical artery		5.5	50

*Data of Roos & Romijn: J Physiol 92:261, 1938.

FIG 32–13. Diagram of the circulation in the fetus, the newborn infant, and the adult. DA, ductus arteriosus; FO, foramen ovale. (Redrawn and reproduced, with permission, from Born & others: Changes in the heart and lungs at birth. Cold Spring Harbor Symposia on Quantitative Biology 19:102, 1954.)

FETUS   NEWBORN   ADULT

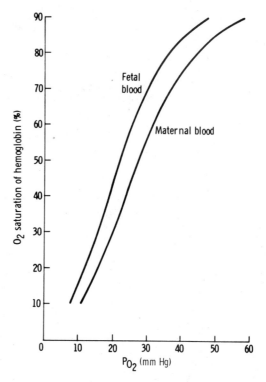

FIG 32–15. **Dissociation curves for hemoglobin in fetal and adult blood in the human.** (Reproduced, with permission, from Darling & others: Some properties of human fetal and maternal blood. J Clin Invest 20:739, 1941.)

FIG 32–14. **Circulation in the fetus.** Most of the oxygenated blood reaching the heart via the umbilical vein and inferior vena cava is diverted through the foramen ovale and pumped out the aorta to the head, while the deoxygenated blood returned via the superior vena cava is mostly pumped through the pulmonary artery and ductus arteriosus to the feet and the umbilical arteries.

Changes in Fetal Circulation & Respiration at Birth

Because of the patent ductus arteriosus and foramen ovale (Fig 32–14), the left and right heart pump in parallel in the fetus rather than in series as they do in the adult. At birth, the placental circulation is cut off and the peripheral resistance suddenly rises. The pressure in the aorta rises until it exceeds that in the pulmonary artery. Meanwhile, because the placental circulation has been cut off, the infant becomes increasingly asphyxic. Finally, he gasps several times, and the lungs expand. The markedly negative intrapleural pressure (−30 to −50 mm Hg) during the gasps

contributes to the expansion of the lungs, but other poorly understood factors are also involved. The sucking action of the first breath plus constriction of the umbilical veins squeezes as much as 100 ml of blood from the placenta (the "placental transfusion").

Once the lungs are expanded, the pulmonary vascular resistance falls to less than 20% of the in utero value and pulmonary blood flow increases markedly. Blood returning from the lungs raises the pressure in the left atrium, closing the foramen ovale by pushing the valve which guards it against the interatrial septum. The ductus arteriosus constricts within a few minutes after birth but, at least in sheep, does not close completely for 24–48 hours. The mechanism responsible for obliteration of the ductus arteriosus, like that responsible for expansion of the lungs, is incompletely understood, although there is evidence that a rise in arterial P_{O_2} and asphyxia are both capable of making the ductus constrict. There is also some evidence that kinins are involved. Eventually, the foramen ovale and the ductus arteriosus both fuse shut in normal infants, and by the end of the first few days of life the adult circulatory pattern is established.

33...

Cardiovascular Homeostasis in Health & Disease

The compensatory adjustments of the cardiovascular system to the challenges the circulation faces normally in everyday life and abnormally in disease illustrate the integrated operation of the cardiovascular regulatory mechanisms described in the preceding chapters.

COMPENSATIONS FOR GRAVITATIONAL EFFECTS

In the standing position, as a result of the effect of gravity on the blood (see Chapter 30), the mean arterial blood pressure in the feet of a normal adult is 180–200 mm Hg and venous pressure is 85–90 mm Hg. The arterial pressure at head level is 60–75 mm Hg and the venous pressure is zero. Blood pools in the venous capacitance vessels of the lower extremities, and stroke volume is decreased up to 40%. Symptoms of cerebral ischemia develop when the cerebral blood flow decreases to less than about 60% of the flow in the recumbent position. If there were no compensatory cardiovascular changes, the reduction in cardiac output due to pooling on standing would lead to a reduction of cerebral flow of this magnitude and consciousness would be lost.

The major compensations on assuming the upright position are triggered by the drop in blood pressure in the carotid sinus and aortic arch. The heart rate increases, helping to maintain cardiac output. There is little if any venoconstriction, but there is a prompt increase in the circulating levels of renin and aldosterone. The arterioles constrict helping to maintain blood pressure. The actual blood pressure change at heart level is variable, depending upon the balance between the degree of arteriolar constriction and the drop in cardiac output (Fig 33–1).

In the cerebral circulation there are additional compensatory changes. The arterial pressure at head level drops 20–30 mm Hg but jugular venous pressure falls 5–8 mm Hg, reducing the drop in perfusion pressure (arterial pressure minus venous pressure). Cerebral vascular resistance is reduced because intracranial pressure falls as venous pressure falls, decreasing the pressure on the cerebral vessels. The decline in cerebral blood flow increases the partial pressure of CO_2 (P_{CO_2}) and decreases the P_{O_2} and the pH in brain tissue, further actively dilating the cerebral vessels. Because of the operation of these autoregulatory mechanisms, cerebral blood flow declines only 20% on standing. In addition, the amount of O_2 extracted from each unit of blood increases, and the net effect is that cerebral O_2 consumption is about the same in the supine and the upright position.

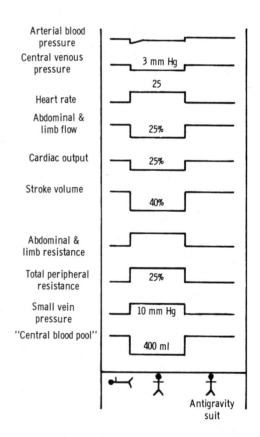

FIG 33–1. Effect on the cardiovascular system of rising from the supine to the upright position. Figures shown are average changes. Changes in abdominal and limb resistance and in blood pressure are variable from individual to individual. (Redrawn and reproduced, with permission, from Gregg, in: *The Physiological Basis of Medical Practice,* 8th ed. Best CH, Taylor NB [editors]. Williams & Wilkins, 1966.)

Prolonged standing presents an additional problem because of increasing interstitial fluid volume in the lower extremities. Plasma volume decreases about 15% in the standing position. As long as the individual moves about, the operation of the muscle pump (see Chapter 30) keeps the venous pressure below 30 mm Hg in the feet, and venous return is adequate. However, with prolonged quiet standing (eg, in military personnel standing at attention for long periods) fainting may result. In a sense, the fainting is a "homeostatic mechanism" because falling to the horizontal position promptly restores venous return, cardiac output, and cerebral blood flow to adequate levels.

The effects of gravity on the circulation in humans depend in part upon the blood volume. When the blood volume is low, these effects are marked; when it is high, they are minimal.

The compensatory mechanisms that operate on assumption of the erect posture are better developed in man than in quadrupeds even though these animals have sensitive carotid sinus mechanisms. Quadrupeds tolerate tilting to the upright position poorly.

Postural Hypotension

In some individuals, sudden standing causes a fall in blood pressure, dizziness, dimness of vision, and even fainting. Such **orthostatic** or **postural hypotension** is common after surgical sympathectomy and in patients receiving sympatholytic drugs. It also occurs in diseases such as diabetes and syphilis, in which there is damage to the sympathetic nervous system, underscoring the importance of the sympathetic vasoconstrictor fibers in compensating for the effects of gravity on the circulation. Another cause of postural hypotension is **primary autonomic insufficiency**, a disease of unknown etiology in which, in addition to other signs of deficient autonomic function, there are diminished responses to baroreceptor stimulation (see Chapter 31). Baroreceptor reflexes are also abnormal in patients with primary hyperaldosteronism. However, these patients generally do not have postural hypotension because their blood volumes are expanded sufficiently to maintain cardiac output in spite of changes in position. Indeed, mineralocorticoids are used to treat patients with postural hypotension.

Effects of Acceleration

The effects of gravity on the circulation are multiplied during acceleration or deceleration in vehicles which in modern civilization range from elevators to rockets. Force acting on the body due to acceleration is commonly expressed in *g* units, 1 *g* being the force of gravity on the earth's surface. "Positive *g*" is force due to acceleration acting in the long axis of the body from head to foot; "negative *g*" is force due to acceleration acting in the opposite direction. During exposure to positive *g*, blood is "thrown" into the lower part of the body. The cerebral circulation is protected by the fall in venous pressure and intracranial pressure. Cardiac output is maintained for a time because blood is drawn from the pulmonary venous reservoir and because the force of cardiac contraction is increased. At accelerations producing more than 5 *g*, however, vision fails ("blackout") in about 5 sec and unconsciousness follows almost immediately thereafter. The effects of positive *g* are effectively cushioned by the use of "*g* suits," double-walled pressure suits containing water or compressed air and regulated in such a way that they compress the abdomen and legs with a force proportionate to the positive *g*. This decreases venous pooling and helps maintain venous return (Fig 33–1).

Negative *g* causes increased cardiac output, a rise in cerebral arterial pressure, intense congestion of the head and neck vessels, ecchymoses around the eyes, severe throbbing head pain, and, eventually, mental confusion ("red-out"). In spite of the great rise in cerebral arterial pressure, the vessels in the brain do not rupture because there is a corresponding increase in intracranial pressure and their walls are supported in the same way as during straining (see Chapter 32). The tolerance for *g* forces exerted across the body is much greater than it is for axial *g*. Men tolerate 11 *g* acting in a back-to-chest direction for 3 minutes, and 17 *g* acting in a chest-to-back direction for 4 minutes. Astronauts are therefore positioned to take the *g* forces of rocket flight in the chest-to-back direction. The tolerances in this position are sufficiently large to permit acceleration to orbital or escape velocity and deceleration back into the earth's atmosphere without ill effects.

Effects of Zero Gravity

From the data available to date, weightlessness for up to 19 days appears to have only transient adverse effects on the circulation. One would expect that the circulation in zero gravity would be essentially similar to that in the recumbent position at sea level, with possible minor variations due to changes in the position of viscera. Transient postural hypotension has been present after return to earth from orbital flights. There has been speculation that prolonged weightlessness during future trips to the planets may lead to more severe "disuse atrophy" of the cardiovascular and somatic reflex mechanisms (see Chapter 12) responsible for postural adjustments. Muscular effort will, of course, be much reduced when the objects to be moved are weightless, and the decrease in the extensive normal proprioceptive input due to the action of gravity on the body may lead to flaccidity of skeletal muscles. In the absence of the increases in cardiac output normally occasioned by the efforts of everyday living, it is possible that there may even be some atrophy of the myocardium. A program of regular exercises against resistance, eg, pushing against a wall or stretching a heavy rubber band, might prevent this.

Other changes that have been observed during long space flights include extreme bradycardia, with heart rates as low as 35 beats/min during sleep; bone demineralization; diuresis; and a decrease in red blood cell volume.

EXERCISE

Muscle Blood Flow

When a muscle contracts, it compresses the vessels in it if it develops more than 10% of its maximal tension (Fig 33–2); when it develops more than 70% of its maximal tension, blood flow is completely stopped. Between contractions, however, flow is so greatly increased that blood flow per unit of time in a rhythmically contracting muscle is increased as much as 30-fold. Because the blood flow increase occurs at or even before the start of exercise, the initial rise must be a neurally mediated response. Impulses in the sympathetic vasodilator system (see Chapter 31) may be involved. The blood flow in resting muscle doubles after sympathectomy, and so some decrease in tonic vasoconstrictor discharge may also be involved. However, once exercise has started, local mechanisms maintain the high blood flow and there is no difference in flow in normal and sympathectomized animals.

Local mechanisms maintaining a high blood flow in exercising muscle include a fall in tissue P_{O_2}, a rise in tissue P_{CO_2}, and accumulation of "vasodilator metabolites" (see Chapter 31). The temperature rises in active muscle, and this further dilates the vessels. Dilatation of the arterioles, metarterioles, and precapillary sphincters causes a 10–100-fold increase in the number of open capillaries. The average distance between the blood and the active cells—and the distance O_2 and metabolic products must diffuse—is thus greatly decreased. The dilatation increases the cross-sectional area of the vascular bed, and the velocity of flow therefore decreases. The capillary pressure increases until it exceeds the oncotic pressure throughout the length of the capillaries. In addition, the accumulation of osmotically active metabolites at a more rapid rate than they can be carried away

decreases the osmotic gradient across the capillary walls. Therefore, fluid transudation into the interstitial spaces is tremendously increased. Lymph flow is also greatly increased, limiting the accumulation of interstitial fluid and in effect greatly increasing its turnover. The decreased pH and increased temperature shift the dissociation curve for hemoglobin to the right, so that more O_2 is given up by the blood. Increased concentration of 2,3-DPG in the red blood cells has been reported, and this would further decrease the O_2 affinity of hemoglobin (see Chapters 27 and 35). The net result is an up to 3-fold increase in the A-V O_2 difference, and the transport of CO_2 out of the tissue is also facilitated. All of these changes combine to make it possible for the O_2 consumption of skeletal muscle to increase 100-fold during exercise. An even greater increase in energy output is possible for short periods during which the energy stores are replenished by anaerobic metabolism of glucose and the muscle incurs an O_2 debt (see Chapter 3).

Systemic Circulatory Changes

The systemic cardiovascular response to exercise depends on whether the muscle contractions are primarily isometric or primarily isotonic with the performance of external work. With the start of an isometric muscle contraction, heart rate rises. This increase still occurs if the muscle contraction is prevented by local infusion of a neuromuscular blocking drug. It also occurs with just the thought of performing a muscle contraction, so it is probably the result of psychic stimuli acting on the medulla. The increase is largely due to decreased vagal tone, although increased discharge of the cardiac sympathetic nerves plays some role. Within a few seconds of the onset of an isometric muscle contraction, systolic and diastolic blood pressure rise sharply. Stroke volume changes relatively little, and blood flow to the steadily contracting muscles is reduced as a result of compression of their blood vessels.

The response to exercise involving isotonic muscle contraction is similar in that there is a prompt increase in heart rate but different in that there is a marked increase in stroke volume. However, there is a fall in total peripheral resistance (Fig 33–3) due to vasodilatation in exercising muscles (Table 33–1). Consequently, systolic blood pressure rises only moderately, whereas diastolic pressure may remain unchanged or even fall.

Cardiac output is increased during exercise to values that may exceed 35 liters/min, the amount being proportionate to the increase in O_2 consumption. The mechanisms responsible for this increase are discussed in Chapter 29. The increase is due to an increase in heart rate and stroke volume, the heart muscle contracting more forcibly and discharging more of the end-systolic volume of blood in the ventricles. These chronotropic and inotropic effects on the heart are both due to increased activity in the adrenergic sympathetic nerves to the heart. The activity is apparently initiated by psychic stimuli. The increase in heart

FIG 33–2. Blood flow through a portion of the calf muscles during rhythmic contraction. (Reproduced, with permission, from Barcroft & Swan: *Sympathetic Control of Human Blood Vessels.* Arnold, 1953.)

FIG 33–3. **Effects of different levels of exercise on cardiovascular function.** (Reproduced, with permission, from Berne & Levy: *Cardiovascular Physiology,* 2nd ed, Mosby, 1972; data from Carlsten & Grimby: *The Circulatory Response to Muscular Exercise in Man.* Thomas, 1966.)

TABLE 33–1. **Cardiac output and regional blood flow in a sedentary man.*** Values are at rest and during exercise at maximal oxygen uptake.

	ml/min	
	Quiet Standing	Exercise
Cardiac output	5900	24,000
Blood flow to:		
Heart	250	1000
Brain	750	750
Active skeletal muscle	650	20,850
Inactive skeletal muscle	650	300
Skin	500	500
Kidney, liver, gastrointestinal tract, etc	3100	600

*Data from Mitchell & Blomquist: Maximal oxygen uptake. New England J Med 284:1018, 1971.

After exercise, the blood pressure may transiently drop to subnormal levels, presumably because accumulated metabolites keep the muscle vessels dilated for a short period. However, it soon returns to the preexercise level. The heart rate returns to normal more slowly.

Temperature Regulation

The quantitative aspects of heat dissipation during exercise are summarized in Fig 33–4. In many locations, the skin is supplied by branches of muscle arteries, so that some of the blood warmed in the

rate is sustained by the autonomic changes plus the stimulatory effect of the increase in P_{CO_2} on the medulla. To the extent that it operates, the Bainbridge effect may also contribute to the increase in heart rate. The maximal heart rate achieved during exercise decreases with age. In children, it rises to 200 or more beats per minute; in adults it rarely exceeds 195 beats per minute, and in elderly individuals the rise is even less.

A great increase in venous return is necessary to supply the extra blood put out by the heart, although the increase in venous return is not, as was once thought, the cause of the increase in cardiac output (see Chapter 29). Venous return is increased by the great increase in the activity of the muscle and thoracic pumps; by mobilization of blood from the viscera; by increased pressure transmitted through the dilated arterioles to the veins; and by adrenergically mediated venoconstriction, which decreases the volume of blood in the veins. The amount of blood mobilized from the splanchnic area and other reservoirs may increase the amount of blood in the arterial portion of the circulation by as much as 30% during strenuous exercise.

FIG 33–4. **Energy exchange in muscular exercise.** The shaded area represents the excess of heat production over heat loss. The total energy output equals the heat production plus the work done. (Redrawn and reproduced, with permission, from Nielsen: *Die Regulation der Korpertemperatur bei Muskelarbeit.* Skand Arch Physiol 79:193, 1938.)

muscles is transported directly to the skin where some of the heat is radiated to the environment. There is a marked increase in ventilation (see Chapter 37), and some heat is lost in the expired air. The body temperature rises and the hypothalamic centers that control heat-dissipating mechanisms are activated. The increase is due in part to inability of the heat-dissipating mechanisms to handle the great increase in heat production, but there is evidence that during exercise there is in addition a "resetting of the thermostat"—ie, an increase in the body temperature at which the heat-dissipating mechanisms are activated. Sweat secretion is greatly increased, and vaporization of this sweat is the major path for heat loss. The cutaneous vessels also dilate. In some regions, this dilatation is due to inhibition of vasoconstrictor tone; but in the forearms and possibly elsewhere it appears to be due to local release of the vasodilator peptide bradykinin (see Chapter 31).

Training

Trained athletes have a larger stroke volume and slower heart rate at rest than untrained individuals, and they tend to have larger hearts (see Chapter 29). During exercise, their stroke volume and heart rate increase, but a given increase in cardiac output can be effected with a smaller increase in heart rate. The maximal possible increase in cardiac output is also greater in athletes, and there is evidence that the A-V O_2 difference in athletes during exertion is greater than the difference in untrained individuals.

In view of the current vogue for jogging and other forms of exercise, it is worth noting that one of the clear-cut benefits of exercise regimens is psychologic; patients who exercise regularly "feel better." Regular physical exertion also increases the probability that an individual can remain active past the standard age of retirement. In addition, there is evidence that exercise decreases the incidence and severity of myocardial infarction, but this beneficial effect cannot as yet be regarded as established.

INFLAMMATION

The Normal Inflammatory Response

When the tissues are invaded by bacteria, polypeptides are liberated locally which attract white blood cells, cause white cells to stick to the blood vessel walls in the area, produce local vasodilatation, and increase vascular permeability. The kinins are probably the principal factors involved, but histamine and other substances may also play a role. The increase in permeability is greatest in the venules, although the capillaries are also involved. The area becomes warm, red, and swollen. The gaps at the junctions between endothelial cells enlarge, and polymorphonuclear cells leave the blood stream by insinuating themselves through these gaps (diapedesis). They collect in the area and, along with other phagocytes and dead bacteria, form the

fluid known as pus. Fibroblasts in the area are stimulated to wall off the bacteria with connective tissue, and the antigenic foreign proteins of the bacteria stimulate the formation of antibodies. There is also an increase in the entry of white blood cells into the blood stream; and the number of circulating leukocytes, especially neutrophils, is increased (leukocytosis). Bacterial toxins that are absorbed into the circulation act on the hypothalamus to produce fever. In the case of viral infections, the infected cells liberate a protein called **interferon** which inhibits virus replication.

The polymorphonuclear leukocytes in a wound are joined in 12–24 hours by monocytes, which actively remove debris. Fibroblasts that enter the wound form strands made up of the protein **collagen,** and the collagen fibers become parallelly oriented to form a scar. New blood vessels form as buds from the walls of existing vessels, and the area becomes revascularized.

HEMORRHAGE & HEMORRHAGIC SHOCK

Effects of Hemorrhage

The decline in blood volume produced by bleeding decreases venous return, and cardiac output falls. Numerous compensatory mechanisms are activated (Table 33–2). The heart rate is increased and, with severe hemorrhage, there is always a fall in blood pressure. With moderate hemorrhage (5–15 ml/kg body weight), pulse pressure is reduced, but mean arterial pressure may be normal. The blood pressure changes vary from individual to individual, even when exactly the same amount of blood is lost. The skin is cool and pale, and may have a grayish tinge because of stasis in the capillaries and a small amount of cyanosis. Respiration is rapid, and intense thirst is a prominent symptom. This combination of findings constitutes the clinical syndrome known as **hypovolemic shock.** **Hemorrhagic shock** is the form of hypovolemic shock due to hemorrhage. Other causes of this type of shock are discussed below.

TABLE 33–2. Compensatory reactions activated by hemorrhage.

Vasoconstriction
Tachycardia
Venoconstriction
Increased thoracic pumping
Increased skeletal muscle pumping (in some cases)
Increased movement of interstitial fluid into capillaries
Increased secretion of norepinephrine and epinephrine
Increased secretion of vasopressin
Increased secretion of glucocorticoids
Increased secretion of renin and aldosterone
Increased plasma protein synthesis
Increased formation of erythropoietin

In hypovolemic and other forms of shock, the inadequate perfusion of the tissues leads to increased anaerobic glycolysis with the production of large amounts of lactic acid. In severe cases, the blood lactic acid level rises from the normal value of about 1 mM/liter to 9 mM/liter or more. The resulting **lactic acidosis** depresses the myocardium, decreases peripheral vascular responsiveness to catecholamines, and may be severe enough to cause coma.

Immediate Compensatory Reactions

When blood volume is reduced and venous return is decreased, the arterial baroreceptors are stretched to a lesser degree and their tonic inhibitory effect on the vasomotor center and cardiac rate decreases. Even if there is no drop in mean arterial pressure, the decrease in pulse pressure decreases the rate of discharge in the arterial baroreceptors and reflex tachycardia and vasoconstriction result.

The vasoconstriction is generalized, sparing only the vessels of the brain and heart. The cerebral arterioles are not constricted because their vasoconstrictor innervation is functionally insignificant, and the coronary vessels are dilated because impulses in the adrenergic nerves which innervate them generally cause dilatation rather than constriction (see Chapter 32). Vasoconstriction is most marked in the skin, where it accounts for the coolness and pallor, and in the kidneys and viscera.

Hemorrhage also evokes a widespread reflex venoconstriction that helps maintain the filling pressure of the heart, although the receptors that initiate the venoconstriction are unsettled. The intense vasoconstriction in the splanchnic area shifts blood from the visceral reservoir into the systemic circulation. Blood is also shifted out of the subcutaneous and pulmonary veins. Contraction of the spleen discharges more "stored" blood into the circulation, although the volume mobilized in man is small.

In the kidneys, both afferent and efferent arterioles are constricted, but the efferent vessels are constricted to a greater degree. Glomerular filtration rate is depressed but renal plasma flow is decreased to a greater extent, so that the filtration fraction (glomerular filtration rate/renal plasma flow) increases. There may be shunting of the blood through the medullary portions of the kidneys, bypassing the cortical glomeruli. Very little urine is formed. Sodium retention is marked, and there is retention of the nitrogenous products of metabolism in the blood (**azotemia** or **uremia**). Especially when the hypotension is prolonged, there may be severe renal tubular damage (**lower nephron nephrosis**).

Hemorrhage is a potent stimulus to adrenal medullary secretion (see Chapter 20). Circulating norepinephrine is also increased because of the increased discharge of sympathetic adrenergic neurons. The increase in circulating catecholamines probably contributes relatively little to the generalized vasoconstriction, but it may lead to stimulation of the reticular formation (see Chapter 11). Possibly because of such

reticular stimulation, some patients in hemorrhagic shock are restless and apprehensive. Others are quiet and apathetic, and their sensorium is dulled, probably because of cerebral ischemia and acidosis. When restlessness is present, increased motor activity and increased respiratory movements increase the muscular and thoracic pumping of venous blood.

The loss of red cells decreases the O_2-carrying power of the blood, and the blood flow in the carotid and aortic bodies is reduced. The resultant anemia and stagnant hypoxia (see Chapter 37) as well as the acidosis stimulate the chemoreceptors. Increased activity in chemoreceptor afferents is probably the main cause of respiratory stimulation in shock. Chemoreceptor activity also excites the vasomotor center, increasing vasoconstrictor discharge. In fact, in hemorrhaged dogs with arterial pressures of less than 70 mm Hg, cutting the nerves to the carotid baroreceptors and chemoreceptors may cause a further fall in blood pressure rather than a rise. This paradoxic result is due to the fact that there is no baroreceptor discharge at pressures below 70 mm Hg and activity in fibers from the carotid chemoreceptors is driving the vasomotor center beyond the maximal rate produced by release of baroreceptor inhibition.

Long-Term Compensatory Reactions

When the arterioles constrict and the venous pressure falls because of the decrease in blood volume, capillary pressure drops. Fluid moves into the capillaries along most of their course, helping to maintain the circulating blood volume. This dehydrates the interstitial tissues, and fluid moves out of the cells. Decreased ECF volume has been shown to cause thirst, and thirst is intense in patients in shock. Thirst can occur without any change in plasma osmolality after hemorrhage, but it may be the interstitial or intracellular dehydration that stimulates the thirst mechanism (see Chapter 14).

After a moderate hemorrhage in man, the circulating plasma volume is restored in 12–72 hours. There is also a rapid entry of preformed albumin from extravascular stores, but most of the tissue fluids that are mobilized are protein-free. They dilute the plasma proteins and cells, but when whole blood is lost the hematocrit may not fall for several hours after the onset of bleeding (Fig 33–5). After the initial influx of preformed albumin, the rest of the plasma protein losses are replaced, presumably by hepatic synthesis, over a period of 3–4 days. Erythropoietin appears in the circulation and the reticulocyte count increases, reaching a peak in 10 days. The red cell mass is restored to normal in 4–8 weeks. However, a low hematocrit is remarkably well tolerated because of various compensatory mechanisms. One of these is an increase in the concentration of 2,3-DPG in the red blood cells, which causes hemoglobin to give up more O_2 to the tissues (see Chapters 27 and 35). In long-standing anemia in otherwise healthy individuals, exertional dyspnea is not observed until the hemoglobin concentration is about 7.5 g/100 ml. Weakness

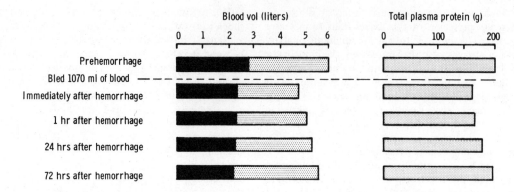

FIG 33–5. Changes in plasma volume (dotted bars), red cell volume (black bars), and total plasma protein following hemorrhage in a normal human subject. (From data in Keele & Neil: *Samson Wright's Applied Physiology,* 11th ed. Oxford Univ Press, 1965.)

becomes appreciable at a level of about 6 g/100 ml; dyspnea at rest appears at about 3 g/100 ml; and the heart finally fails when the hemoglobin level falls to 2 g/100 ml.

Hemorrhage causes an increase in aldosterone secretion, due in part to increased secretion of renin and in part to increased secretion of ACTH (see Chapter 20). It also produces a marked rise in vasopressin secretion which is triggered by the decrease in discharge from the arterial and atrial baroreceptors (see Chapters 14 and 31). The increased circulating levels of aldosterone and vasopressin cause retention of Na^+ and water, which helps reexpand the blood volume. However, the initial decline in urine volume and Na^+ excretion is certainly due for the most part to the hemodynamic alterations in the kidney.

The angiotensin II liberated during hemorrhage apparently plays a minor role in maintaining the blood pressure. Vasopressin is also a pressor agent when administered in large doses, but it is doubtful if increased vasopressin secretion contributes to the restoration of the blood pressure. In one series of experiments, the mean blood pressure fall after a standard hemorrhage was essentially the same in acutely hypophysectomized dogs as in normal animals. The fall in nephrectomized hypophysectomized dogs was greater than in normal animals, but the difference was not statistically significant (Table 33–3).

Irreversible Shock

Depending largely upon the amount of blood lost, some patients die soon after hemorrhage and others recover as the compensatory mechanisms, aided by appropriate treatment, gradually restore the circulation to normal. In an intermediate group of patients, shock persists for hours and gradually progresses to a state in which there is no longer any response to vasopressor drugs and in which, even if the blood volume is returned to normal, cardiac output remains depressed. This is known as **irreversible shock.** The peripheral resistance falls, the heart slows, and the patients eventually die.

There has been much discussion about what makes shock become irreversible. It seems clear that a number of deleterious positive feedback mechanisms become operative in this stage. For example, severe cerebral ischemia leads eventually to depression of the vasomotor and cardiac center, with slowing of the heart rate and vasodilatation. These both make the blood pressure drop further, with a further reduction in cerebral blood flow and further depression of the vasomotor and cardiac centers.

Another important example of positive feedback is myocardial depression. In severe shock, the coronary blood flow is reduced because of the hypotension and tachycardia (see Chapter 32), even though the coronary vessels are dilated. If the reduction is marked and

TABLE 33–3. Effects of hemorrhage (15 ml/kg body weight) in pentobarbital-anesthetized dogs.*

	Mean Arterial Pressure (mm Hg)		
	Normal	Hypophys-ectomized	Hypophysectomized and Nephrectomized
Control	136/81	133/87	123/65
10 minutes after hemorrhage	80/47	83/52	64/32
70 minutes after hemorrhage	115/70	111/68	96/54
10 minutes after reinfusion of shed blood	146/90	137/84	127/81
Number of dogs studied	6	10	10

*Data partly from Ganong & Mulrow: Role of the kidney in adrenocortical response to hemorrhage in hypophysectomized dogs. Endocrinology 70:182, 1962.

prolonged, the myocardium may be damaged to the point where cardiac output cannot be restored to normal in spite of reexpansion of the blood volume. The myocardial failure makes the shock and the acidosis worse, which in turn leads to further depression of myocardial function.

Spasm of the precapillary sphincters and venules, especially in the splanchnic region, is apparently a prominent feature of reversible shock. The reduced capillary perfusion due to the constriction of the precapillary sphincters leads to hypoxic tissue damage. Irreversible shock begins to develop when, after 3–5 hours, the precapillary sphincters dilate while the venules remain constricted. Blood now enters the capillaries but stagnates in these vessels, so that the tissue hypoxia continues. Capillary hydrostatic pressure rises and fluid leaves the vascular system in increasing amounts. The capillary walls eventually lose their integrity and slough, permitting whole blood to enter the tissues. At this stage, administered fluids leak out of the vascular system almost as fast as they can be given. Circulating bacterial toxins may contribute to the paralysis of the precapillary sphincters. There is evidence that, presumably as a result of stagnant hypoxia in the gastrointestinal tract, the barriers to the entry of bacteria into the circulation from the intestinal tract and liver break down.

On the theory that the imbalance between precapillary sphincter and venular tone is the key to the development of the irreversibility, treatment of shock with adrenergic blocking agents such as phenoxybenzamine to reduce the vascular spasm has been recommended. Results with such treatment are striking in the dog, but there is some uncertainty about the value of the blocking agents in the treatment of shock in humans. It is also claimed that glucocorticoids in large doses prevent the development of the abnormalities in the capillary bed.

OTHER FORMS OF SHOCK

General Considerations

Hemorrhage has been considered in detail as an example of a condition that produces the syndrome of shock. There has been a great deal of confusion and controversy about this syndrome. Part of the difficulty lies in the loose use of the term by physiologists and physicians as well as laymen. **Electric shock** and **spinal shock**, for example, bear no resemblance to the condition produced by hemorrhage. Shock, in the restricted sense of "circulatory shock," is still a collection of different entities which share certain common features. The feature that appears to be common to all cases is inadequate tissue perfusion. The cardiac output may be inadequate because the heart is damaged or the volume of circulating blood may be less than the capacity of the circulation, either because the blood volume is reduced or because the capacity is increased.

On this basis, 3 general types of shock are often delineated: (1) **hypovolemic shock**, in which blood or plasma has been lost from the circulation to the exterior or into the tissues; (2) **cardiogenic shock**, in which the pumping action of the heart is inadequate; and (3) **low-resistance shock**, in which there is vasodilatation in the face of a normal cardiac output and blood volume.

Hypovolemic Shock

Hypovolemic shock is also called "cold shock." It is characterized in the typical case by hypotension, a rapid thready pulse, a cold, pale, clammy skin, intense thirst, rapid respiration, and restlessness or, alternatively, torpor. None of these findings, however, are invariably present. The hypotension may be relative. A hypertensive patient whose blood pressure is regularly 240/140, for example, may be in severe shock when his blood pressure is 120/90.

Hypovolemic shock is commonly subdivided into categories on the basis of etiology. The use of terms such as hemorrhagic shock, wound shock, surgical shock, traumatic shock, and burn shock is of some benefit because although there are similarities between these various forms of shock, there are important features that are unique to each type. Hemorrhagic shock is discussed above.

Traumatic shock develops when there is severe damage to muscle and bone. This is the type of shock seen in battle casualties and automobile accident victims. Frank bleeding into the injured areas is the principal cause of the shock, although some plasma also enters the tissues. The amount of blood which can be lost into an injury that appears relatively minor is remarkable; the thigh muscles can accommodate 1 liter of extravasated blood, for example, with an increase in the diameter of the thigh of only 1 cm.

When there is extensive soft tissue and muscle crushing, myoglobin leaks into the circulation. It is said to precipitate in the renal tubules, causing renal damage, and the combination of traumatic shock and renal damage due to myoglobinuria has been called the **crush syndrome**. However, myoglobinuria is only one of the factors causing renal damage, and in all forms of shock renal insufficiency is a potential complication.

Surgical shock and **wound shock** are due to the combination in various proportions of external hemorrhage, bleeding into injured tissues, and dehydration.

In **burn shock** the most apparent abnormality is loss of plasma as exudate from the burned surfaces. Since the loss in this situation is plasma rather than whole blood, the hematocrit rises and **hemoconcentration** is a prominent finding. Burns also cause complex, poorly understood metabolic changes in addition to fluid loss. For example, there is a 50% rise in metabolic rate of nonthyroidal origin, and some burned patients develop hemolytic anemia. Because of these complications, plus the severity of the shock and the problems of sepsis and kidney damage, the mortality rate when third degree burns cover more than 75% of the body is still essentially 100%.

Cardiogenic Shock

When there is a gross decline in cardiac output due to disease of the heart rather than to inadequate blood volume, the condition that results is called cardiogenic shock. The symptoms are those of shock plus congestion of the lungs and viscera due to failure of the heart to put out all the venous blood returned to it. Consequently, the condition is sometimes called "congested shock." The incidence of this type of shock in patients with myocardial infarction is about 10%, and it usually occurs when there is extensive damage to the left ventricular myocardium. It has been suggested that release of chemical agents such as serotonin from the infarcted area activates ventricular receptors which trigger a reflex inhibition of the vasomotor center (Bezold-Jarisch reflex; see Chapter 31). This limits the compensatory vasoconstrictor responses and makes the shock worse.

Low-Resistance Shock

Low-resistance shock includes a number of entities in which the blood volume is normal while the capacity of the circulation is increased by massive vasodilatation. For this reason, it is also called "warm shock." Examples include fainting in response to strong emotion and the reaction produced by overwhelming fear and grief. Another form is the poorly understood, immediate, stunned reaction in injured individuals. The most common form, however, is that produced by endotoxin from gram-negative bacteria. This toxin may be liberated in the body in large amounts in certain infections.

Anaphylactic shock is a rapidly developing, severe allergic reaction that sometimes occurs when an individual is exposed to an antigen to which he has been sensitized. The resultant antigen-antibody reaction releases large quantities of histamine, causing increased capillary permeability and widespread dilatation of arterioles and capillaries. Various other circulatory abnormalities contribute to the shock in animals, but phenomena such as bronchospasm and changes in hepatic blood flow are usually not prominent in man.

Shock is a complication of various metabolic and infectious diseases. Low vascular resistance is a factor in these cases, but there is also an element of hypovolemia. For example, although the mechanism is different in each case, adrenal insufficiency, diabetic ketoacidosis, and severe diarrhea are all characterized by loss of Na^+ from the circulation. The resultant decline in plasma volume may be severe enough to precipitate cardiovascular collapse. In severe infections, shock may occur as a result of diffuse vasculitis with leakage of plasma into the tissues (Rocky Mountain spotted fever, Korean hemorrhagic fever), circulating "toxins" which paralyze vascular smooth muscle, dehydration, or, very rarely, bilateral hemorrhage into the adrenal glands and acute adrenal insufficiency. In febrile patients, shock is apt to be more severe because the cutaneous blood vessels are often dilated (see Chapter 32), increasing the disparity between the capacity of the vascular system and the available circulating blood volume.

Treatment of Shock

The treatment of shock should be aimed at correcting the cause and helping the physiologic compensatory mechanisms to restore an adequate level of tissue perfusion. In hemorrhagic, traumatic, wound, and surgical shock, for example, the cause of the shock is blood loss, and the treatment should include early and rapid transfusion of adequate amounts of compatible whole blood. Saline is of limited temporary value. The immediate goal is restoration of an adequate circulating blood volume, and since saline is distributed in ECF, only 25% of the amount administered stays in the vascular system. In burn shock and other conditions in which there is hemoconcentration, plasma is the treatment of choice to restore the fundamental defect, the loss of plasma. "Plasma expanders," solutions of sugars of high molecular weight and related substances which do not cross capillary walls, have some merit. Concentrated human serum albumin and other hypertonic solutions expand the blood volume by drawing fluid out of the interstitial spaces. They are valuable in emergency treatment but have the disadvantage of further dehydrating the tissues of an already dehydrated patient.

In anaphylactic shock, epinephrine has a highly beneficial and almost specific effect that must represent more than just constriction of the dilated vessels. In all types of shock, restoration of an adequate arterial pressure is important to maintain coronary blood flow. Vasopressor agents such as norepinephrine are of value for this purpose, but their use should be discontinued as soon as possible.

A number of measures sometimes used in the treatment of shock inhibit the operation of the physiologic compensatory mechanisms. Sedatives and other drugs that depress the CNS should be used as sparingly as possible because they depress the discharge of the vasomotor center. Alcohol is particularly unphysiologic because it depresses the CNS and, through a central action, dilates cutaneous vessels. Care should be taken to avoid overheating and resultant cutaneous vasodilatation. Further compromising the circulation by permitting the patient to sit or stand is, of course, detrimental, and gravity should be put to work to help rather than hinder the compensatory mechanisms. Raising the foot of the bed 6–12 inches with "shock blocks" is a simple but valuable therapeutic maneuver which aids venous return from the lower half of the body and improves cerebral blood flow. However, the head-down position also causes the abdominal viscera to press on the diaphragm, making adequate ventilation more difficult to maintain and favoring the development of pulmonary complications. Consequently, it should not be used for prolonged periods.

FAINTING

Sudden loss of consciousness due to cerebral ischemia has many causes. Probably the most common cause of fainting or **syncope** is hypotension due to sudden, diffuse vasodilatation and bradycardia, often in association with a strong emotion. The attacks are short-lived, and consciousness is restored in a few minutes. The term **vasovagal syncope** has been coined to denote this entity. The fall in blood pressure is due in part to the decreased cardiac output caused by the marked bradycardia. However, diffuse discharge of the sympathetic vasodilator system also occurs, decreasing the vascular resistance in skeletal muscle. Sudden loss of consciousness due to decreased cardiac output also occurs in patients who have short runs of ventricular fibrillation or episodes of cardiac asystole (Stokes-Adams syndrome; see Chapter 28). **Postural syncope** is fainting due to pooling of blood in the dependent parts of the body on standing. **Micturition syncope**, fainting during urination, occurs in patients with orthostatic hypotension. It is due to the combination of the ortho-stasis and reflex bradycardia induced by voiding in these patients. Pressure on the carotid sinus produced, for example, by a tight collar, can cause such marked bradycardia and vasodilatation that fainting results (**carotid sinus syncope**). **Cough syncope** occurs when the increase in intrathoracic pressure during straining or coughing is sufficient to block venous return. **Effort syncope** is fainting on exertion due to inability to increase the cardiac output to meet the increased demands of the tissues, and is particularly common in patients with aortic or pulmonary stenosis.

HEART FAILURE

Manifestations

The manifestations of heart failure range from sudden death (eg, in ventricular fibrillation or air embolism), through the shock-like state called cardio-genic shock, to chronic **congestive heart failure**, depending upon the degree of circulatory inadequacy and the rapidity with which it develops. The principal symptoms and signs of congestive failure are cardiac enlargement, weakness, edema (particularly of the dependent portions of the body), a prolonged circula-tion time, hepatic enlargement (**hepatomegaly**), a sensation of shortness of breath and suffocation (**dyspnea**), and distention of the neck veins. Dyspnea on exertion is a prominent symptom. In advanced cases, a common finding is dyspnea which is precipi-tated by lying flat and relieved by sitting up (**orthop-nea**). The dyspnea may be paroxysmal, and sometimes progresses to frank **pulmonary edema**. Some of these abnormalities are due to "backward failure"—failure of the left and right heart pumps to put out all the blood returned to them in the veins, with a resultant rise in venous pressure and congestion of the lungs and viscera. Others are due to "forward failure"—failure of the heart to maintain a cardiac output that is adequate for normal perfusion of all the tissues (Table 33–4). The decline in cardiac output may be relative rather

TABLE 33–4. Simplified summary of pathogenesis of major findings in congestive heart failure.

Abnormality	Cause
Ankle, sacral edema	"Backward failure" of right ventricle → increased venous pressure → fluid trans-udation.
Hepatomegaly	Increased venous pressure → increased resistance to portal flow.
Pulmonary congestion	"Backward failure" of left ventricle → increased pulmonary venous pressure → pulmonary venous distention and trans-udation of fluid into air spaces.
Dyspnea on exertion	Failure of left ventricular output to rise during exercise → increased pulmonary venous pressure.
Paroxysmal dyspnea, pulmonary edema	Probably sudden failure of left heart output to keep up with right heart out-put → acute rise in pulmonary venous and capillary pressure → transudation of fluid into air spaces.
Orthopnea	Normal pooling of blood in lungs in supine position added to already con-gested pulmonary vascular system; increased venous return not put out by left ventricle. (Relieved by sitting up, raising head of bed, lying on extra pil-lows.)
Weakness, exercise intolerance	"Forward failure"; cardiac output in-adequate to perfuse muscles; especially, failure of output to rise with exercise.
Cardiac dilatation	Greater ventricular end-diastolic volume.

than absolute. In thyrotoxicosis and thiamine defi-ciency, for example, output may be elevated in absolute terms, but when it is inadequate relative to the needs of the tissues, heart failure is present ("high-output failure").

Pathogenesis & Pathophysiology

The pathophysiology of heart failure is a complex and, in some areas, controversial subject. One of the earliest and most constant findings in chronic conges-tive failure is abnormal retention of Na^+ and water. This expands the ECF, predisposing to the formation of edema and increasing the load on the heart by in-creasing venous return.

The key to the abnormal Na^+ retention in early heart failure may be the circulatory abnormalities which occur during exercise. At this stage, cardiac out-put, venous pressure, glomerular filtration rate, and renal blood flow are normal at rest. However, when the patient exercises, the increase in cardiac output is subnormal. This initiates, probably via the barorecep-tors, reflex changes in the circulation that include constriction of the cutaneous, splanchnic, and renal vessels and a marked decline in renal blood flow.

Circulating renin levels are increased in congestive heart failure, and the aldosterone secretion rate is elevated in some patients. However, it now seems clear that in most cases of heart failure aldosterone secretion remains unchanged. Furthermore, salt retention occurs when the heart fails in bilaterally adrenalectomized animals maintained on constant doses of deoxycorticosterone. On the other hand, mineralocorticoids are metabolized at an abnormally slow rate in patients with heart failure, and the plasma aldosterone level is often high even when the secretion rate is normal. Other possible mechanisms for the Na^+ retention have been suggested, but the cause of the abnormal Na^+ retention in early congestive failure remains unsettled.

HYPERTENSION

Hypertension is a sustained elevation of the systemic arterial pressure. **Pulmonary hypertension** can also occur, but the pressure in the pulmonary artery (see Chapter 34) is relatively independent of that in the systemic arteries.

Experimental Hypertension

The arterial pressure is determined by the cardiac output and the peripheral resistance (pressure = flow × resistance; see Chapter 30). The peripheral resistance is determined by the viscosity of the blood and, more importantly, by the caliber of the resistance vessels. Hypertension can be produced by elevating the cardiac output, but sustained hypertension is usually due to increased peripheral resistance. Procedures that have been reported to produce sustained hypertension in experimental animals range from injection of kaolin into the cisterna magna to production of the experimental neurosis (Table 33–5). For the most part, the procedures involve manipulations of the kidneys, the

TABLE 33–5. **Some procedures that have been reported to produce sustained hypertension in experimental animals.**

1. Interference with renal blood flow (renal hypertension).
   a. Constriction of one or both renal arteries.
   b. Constriction of aorta just above origin of renal arteries.
   c. Compression of kidney by rubber capsules, etc.
2. Removal of both kidneys (renoprival hypertension).
3. Denervation of arterial baroreceptors (neurogenic hypertension).
4. Exposure to loud noises (rats).
5. Production of experimental neurosis by conditioned reflex technics.
6. Injection of inert substances (kaolin) into the cisterna magna.
7. Chronic injection of deoxycorticosterone (DOC) or aldosterone.
8. Partial adrenalectomy (adrenal regeneration hypertension; rats).
9. High salt intake (rats); high salt intake combined with unilateral nephrectomy.

nervous system, or the adrenals. Some forms of experimental hypertension have counterparts in clinical medicine, while others do not.

The hypertension that follows constriction of the renal arterial blood supply or compression of the kidney is called **renal hypertension**. The role of renin in its pathogenesis is discussed in Chapter 24. Interestingly, hypertension also develops in bilaterally nephrectomized animals maintained by technics such as peritoneal dialysis which remove accumulated waste products from the blood. This form of hypertension is called **renoprival hypertension**. When the ureters are implanted into the colon so that all the urine is reabsorbed into the circulation, a similar degree of uremia is produced but there is no hypertension. This suggests that the kidneys normally secrete a vasodepressor agent and that the hypertension produced by compromising the renal circulation is actually due to decreased secretion of the depressor substance. Extracts of the renal medulla have depressor activity, and medullary tissue has been shown to contain prostaglandins with vasodepressor activity. Other renal vasodepressor substances have been reported, but the function of all such agents remains obscure.

Neurogenic hypertension is discussed in Chapter 31. There is some evidence that renal factors as well as sustained vasoconstriction are responsible for the elevation in blood pressure produced by denervation of the arterial baroreceptors. The pressor response due to hypoxia of the vasomotor center when its blood supply is compressed by a rise in intracranial pressure is discussed in Chapter 32. The hypertension produced by injecting kaolin or other inert materials into the subarachnoid space around the medulla is probably due to sustained interference with the blood supply of the vasomotor center. Provided salt intake is normal or high, deoxycorticosterone generally causes hypertension in experimental animals which may persist after treatment is stopped. The hypertension is more severe in unilaterally nephrectomized animals.

Hypertension in Man

Hypertension is a common abnormality in humans. It can be produced by a variety of disease processes (Table 33–6). Hypertension is also a prominent symptom of **toxemia of pregnancy**, a condition which may be caused by a pressor polypeptide secreted by the placenta.

Hypertension causes a number of serious disorders. When the resistance against which the left ventricle must pump is elevated for a long period, the cardiac muscle hypertrophies. The total O_2 consumption of the heart, already increased by the work of expelling blood against a raised pressure (see Chapter 29), is increased further because there is more muscle. Therefore, any decrease in coronary blood flow has more serious consequences in hypertensive patients than it does in normal individuals, and degrees of coronary narrowing that do not produce symptoms when the size of the heart is normal may produce myocardial infarction when the heart is enlarged. Myocardial

TABLE 33–6. **Causes of sustained diastolic hypertension in man.** The diseases marked by the asterisk are quite often curable. In all of them except Cushing's syndrome, sustained hypertension may be the only physical finding.

1. Unknown (essential hypertension)
2. Adrenocortical diseases
   a. Aldosterone-secreting tumor (Conn's syndrome)*
   b. Excess secretion of other mineralocorticoids
   c. Glucocorticoid hypersecretion (Cushing's syndrome)*
3. Tumor of adrenal medullary or paraganglionic origin (pheochromocytoma)*
4. Narrowing of one or both renal arteries*
5. Narrowing (coarctation) of the aorta*
6. Severe polycythemia
7. Renal disease
   a. Glomerulonephritis
   b. Pyelonephritis
   c. Polycystic disease
8. Oral contraceptives

infarcts are especially common in patients with hypertension. The "Starling mechanism" (see Chapter 29) probably operates in hypertension, dilatation of the heart stretching the muscle fibers and increasing their strength of contraction. However, the ability to compensate for the high peripheral resistance is eventually exceeded, and the heart fails. Hypertensives are also predisposed to thromboses of cerebral vessels and cerebral hemorrhage.

Malignant Hypertension

Chronic hypertension can enter an accelerated phase in which necrotic arteriolar lesions develop and there is a rapid downhill course with papilledema, cerebral symptoms, and progressive renal failure. This syndrome is known as **malignant hypertension,** and without vigorous treatment it is fatal in less than 2 years. It appears to be due to a pathologic process which can be triggered by hypertension due to any cause, but the nature of this process and why it develops are not known.

Essential Hypertension

Essential hypertension is by far the commonest form of hypertensive disease. The elevation of the arterial pressure in essential hypertension is due to a diffuse constriction of the arterioles the cause of which is unknown. Early in the course of the disease, the hypertension is intermittent and there is an exaggerated pressor response to stimuli such as cold and excitement which produce only a moderate blood pressure elevation in normal individuals. This suggests that overactive autonomic reactions are responsible for the arteriolar spasm, and treatment with drugs that block sympathetic outflow markedly slows the progress of the disease. Later on, the blood pressure elevation becomes sustained. The baroreceptor mechanism

becomes "reset," so that the blood pressure is maintained at the elevated level (see Chapter 31). The spasm of the arterioles leads to hypertrophy of their musculature, and there is probably some degree of organic narrowing of the vessels. At this stage, even a normal rate of autonomic discharge is associated with an elevated pressure.

The progression of untreated essential hypertension is variable. Particularly in women, it is often benign, with elevated pressure being the only finding for many years. However, it may also progress rapidly into the malignant phase.

Essential hypertension is not at present a curable disease, although even after it has entered the malignant phase its progression can be stopped with modern drug treatment. On the other hand, several of the other disease processes that cause hypertension in man are curable. It is therefore of great importance to recognize these latter diseases and institute appropriate definitive treatment.

Other Causes of Hypertension

In humans, deoxycorticosterone and aldosterone both elevate the blood pressure, and hypertension is a prominent feature of primary hyperaldosteronism. It is also seen in patients who secrete excess deoxycorticosterone (see Chapter 20). The hypokalemia that these hormones produce damages the kidneys (**hypokalemic nephropathy**), and the hypertension may be partly renal in origin. Expansion of the blood volume due to Na^+ retention may also play a role.

Plasma renin activity is low in hypertension due to excess secretion of aldosterone and deoxycorticosterone. It has also been found to be low in the presence of normal or low aldosterone and deoxycorticosterone secretion rates in 25–30% of patients with what otherwise appears to be essential hypertension ("**low-renin hypertension**"). This raises the interesting possibility that an as yet unidentified mineralocorticoid is being secreted in excess in these patients.

Hypertension is also seen in Cushing's syndrome, in which aldosterone secretion is usually normal. The cause of the hypertension in this syndrome is uncertain; it may be due to the increased secretion of deoxycorticosterone produced by increased circulating ACTH, or it may be due to a direct action of glucocorticoids on the arterioles.

Pheochromocytomas–tumors of the adrenal medulla or of cathecholamine-secreting tissue elsewhere in the body–also produce hypertension. The hypertension is often episodic, and, particularly when the tumors secrete predominantly epinephrine, the blood glucose level and the metabolic rate are intermittently elevated. However, in some patients with pheochromocytomas, sustained hypertension is the only finding.

Renal hypertension due to narrowing of the renal arteries is discussed above and in Chapter 24. Various other types of renal disease are associated with hypertension, but it is not known whether the association is due to renin secretion, to secretion of other vasoactive substances of renal origin, or to nonhumoral mechanisms. **Coarctation of the aorta,** a congenital narrowing of a segment of the thoracic aorta, increases the resistance to flow, producing severe hypertension in the upper part of the body. The blood pressure in the lower part of the body is usually normal.

Increased cardiac output is sometimes a cause of diastolic as well as systolic hypertension. The elevated pressure seen in thyrotoxicosis and in anxious, tense patients is explained on this basis. In severe polycythemia, the increase in blood viscosity may raise the peripheral resistance enough to cause significant hypertension.

Chronic treatment with oral contraceptives containing progestins and estrogens produces significant hypertension in some women. The hypertension is probably due, at least in part, to an increase in circulating levels of angiotensinogen, the production of which is stimulated by estrogens (see Chapter 24). There is some evidence that women developing "pill hypertension" are those predisposed to hypertension in any case. Certainly, the occurrence of hypertension is not a reason for normotensive women to avoid oral contraceptives, but it would seem wise for them to have their blood pressures checked at 6-month intervals.

●　●　●

References: Section VI.
Circulation

Berne RM: Regulation of coronary blood flow. Physiol Rev 44:1, 1964.

Bock KD (editor): *Shock: Pathogenesis and Therapy.* Springer, 1962.

Dayhoff MO: *Atlas of Protein Sequence and Structure.* Vol 5. National Biomedical Research Foundation, 1972.

Dobbing J: The blood-brain barrier. Physiol Rev 41:130, 1961.

Ebert RV: Syncope. Circulation 27:1148, 1963.

Edelman GM: The structure and function of antibodies. Scientific American 223:34, Aug 1970.

Folkow B, Neil E: *Circulation.* Oxford Univ Press, 1971.

Goldman MJ: *Principles of Clinical Electrocardiography,* 8th ed. Lange, 1973.

Gordon AS (editor): *Regulation of Hematopoiesis.* 2 vols. Appleton-Century-Crofts, 1970.

Greenway CV, Stark RD: Hepatic vascular bed. Physiol Rev 51:23, 1971.

Haddy FJ, Scott JB: Metabolically linked vasoactive chemicals in local regulation of blood flow. Physiol Rev 48:688, 1968.

Hall JG: The flow of lymph. New England J Med 281:720, 1969.

Heymans C, Neil E: *Reflexogenic Areas of the Cardiovascular System.* Little, Brown, 1958.

Kety SS: Blood flow and metabolism of the human brain in health and disease. In: *Neurochemistry,* 2nd ed. Page & Quastel (editors). Thomas, 1962.

Lee KS, Kalus W: The subcellular basis for the mechanism of inotropic action of cardiac glycosides. Pharmacol 23:193, 1971.

Macleod AG: *Aspects of Acute Inflammation.* Upjohn, 1970.

McIlwain H: *Biochemistry and the Central Nervous System,* 3rd ed. Churchill, 1966.

Metcalf J & others: Gas exchange in the pregnant uterus. Physiol Rev 47:782, 1967.

Nakano J: Prostaglandins and the circulation. Mod Concepts Cardiovas Dis 40:49, 1971.

Nutter DO, Schlant RC, Hurst JW: Isometric exercise and the cardiovascular system. Mod Concepts Cardiovas Dis 41:11, 1972.

Perry S: Appraisal of myelopoiesis. New England J Med 285:214, 1971.

Ranney HM: Clinically important variants of human hemoglobin. New England J Med 282:144, 1970.

Rhodin JAG: Fine structure of capillaries. In: *Topics in the Study of Life.* Kramer A (editor). Harper, 1971.

Riley JF: The mast cells. Physiology for Physicians Vol 1, No. 4, April 1963.

Rothschild MA, Oratz M, Schreiber SS: Albumin synthesis. New England J Med 286:748, 1972.

Schachter M: Kallikreins and kinins. Physiol Rev 49:510, 1969.

Scheer AM: Excitation of the ventricles. The Physiologist 10:381, 1967.

Schilling J: Wound healing. Physiol Rev 48:374, 1968.

Smith HW: Salt and water volume receptors. Am J Med 23:623, 1957.

Sonnenblick EH, Skelton CC: Oxygen consumption of the heart: Physiological principles and clinical implications. Mod Concepts Cardiovas Dis 40:9, 1971.

Spann JF Jr, Mason DJ, Zelis RF: Recent advances in the understanding of congestive heart failure. Mod Concepts Cardiovas Dis 39:73, 79, 1970.

Webb-Peploe MM, Shepherd JT: Veins and their control. New England J Med 278:317, 1968.

Wilson DB: Lymphocytes and immunity. In: *Topics in the Study of Life.* Kramer A (editor). Harper, 1971.

Symposium: Immunoglobulins. Ann New York Acad Sci 190:5, 1971.

Symposium: Platelets and their role in hemostasis. Ann New York Acad Sci 201:1, 1972.

VII. Respiration

34...

Pulmonary Function

Respiration, as the term is generally used, includes 2 processes: **external respiration,** the absorption of O_2 and removal of CO_2 from the body as a whole; and **internal respiration,** the gaseous exchanges between the cells and their fluid medium. Details of the uptake of O_2 by cells and the formation and liberation of CO_2 by cells are considered in the section on intermediary metabolism (see Chapter 17). This chapter is concerned with the processes responsible for the uptake of O_2 and excretion of CO_2 in the lungs. Chapter 35 is concerned with the transport of O_2 and CO_2 to and from the tissues.

At rest, a normal human breathes 12–15 times a minute. Five hundred ml of air per breath, or 6–8 liters/min, are inspired and expired. This air mixes with the gas in the alveoli and, by simple diffusion, O_2 enters the blood in the pulmonary capillaries while CO_2 enters the alveoli. In this manner, 250 ml of O_2 enter the body per minute and 200 ml of CO_2 are excreted.

PROPERTIES OF GASES

Partial Pressures

Unlike liquids, gases expand to fill the volume available to them, and the volume occupied by a given number of gas molecules at a given temperature and pressure is (ideally) the same regardless of the composition of the gas.

$$P = \frac{nRT}{V} \quad \text{(from equation of state of ideal gas)}$$

P = Pressure
n = Number of mols
R = Gas constant
T = Absolute temperature
V = Volume

Therefore, the pressure exerted by any one gas in a mixture of gases (its **partial pressure**) is equal to the total pressure times the fraction of the total amount of gas it represents.

The composition of dry air is 20.98% O_2, 0.04% CO_2, 78.06% N_2, and 0.92% other inert constituents such as argon and helium. The barometric pressure

(P_B) at sea level is 760 mm Hg (one atmosphere). The partial pressure (indicated by the symbol P) of O_2 in dry air is therefore 0.21 × 760, or 160 mm Hg at sea level. The partial pressure of N_2 and the other inert gases is 0.79 × 760, or 600 mm Hg; and the P_{CO_2} is 0.0004 × 760, or 0.3 mm Hg. The water vapor in the air in most climates reduces these percentages, and therefore the partial pressures, to a slight degree. Air equilibrated with water is saturated with water vapor, and inspired air is saturated by the time it reaches the lungs. The P_{H_2O} at body temperature (37° C) is 47 mm Hg. Therefore, the partial pressures at sea level of the other gases in the air reaching the lungs are: P_{O_2}, 149 mm Hg; P_{CO_2}, 0.3 mm Hg; and P_{N_2} (including the other inert gases), 564 mm Hg.

Gas diffuses from areas of high pressure to areas of low pressure, the rate of diffusion depending upon the concentration gradient and the nature of the barrier between the 2 areas. When a mixture of gases is in contact with and permitted to equilibrate with a liquid, each gas in the mixture dissolves in the liquid to an extent determined by its partial pressure and its solubility in the fluid. The partial pressure of a gas in a liquid is that pressure at which it would produce the concentration of gas molecules found in the liquid if it were in the gaseous phase in equilibrium with the liquid.

Methods of Quantitating Respiratory Phenomena

Respiratory excursions can be recorded, using devices which measure chest expansion or recording spirometers (Fig 17–2), which also permit measurement of gas intake and output. Since gas volumes vary with temperature and pressure and since the amount of water vapor in them varies, it is important to correct respiratory measurements involving volume to a stated set of standard conditions. The 3 most commonly used standards and their abbreviations are shown in Table 34–1. Modern refinements of standard technics for gas analysis make possible rapid, reliable measurements of the composition of gas mixtures and the gas content of body fluids. N_2, for example, emits light in an electrical field in vacuo, and, by using a meter which continuously measures and records the light emitted, it is possible to obtain a graphic record of the fluctuations in P_{N_2} of the expired air while breathing various gas mixtures. O_2 and CO_2 electrodes, small probes sensitive to O_2 or CO_2, can be inserted into the airway or into blood vessels or tissues and the P_{O_2} and P_{CO_2}

recorded continuously. CO_2, carbon monoxide (CO), and many anesthetic gases can be measured rapidly by infrared absorption spectroscopy.

MECHANICS OF RESPIRATION

Inspiration & Expiration

The lungs and the chest wall are elastic structures. Normally, the space between the lungs and the chest wall contains no more than a thin layer of fluid. The pressure in this intrapleural space is subatmospheric (Fig 34–1), and the lungs are closely applied to the chest wall. The lungs are stretched when they are expanded at birth, and at the end of quiet expiration their tendency to recoil from the chest wall is just balanced by the tendency of the chest wall to recoil in the opposite direction. If the chest wall is opened, the lungs collapse; and if the lungs lose their elasticity, the chest expands and becomes barrel-shaped.

Inspiration is an active process. The contraction of the inspiratory muscles increases intrathoracic volume. During quiet breathing the intrapleural pressure, which is about −2.5 mm Hg (relative to atmospheric) at the start of inspiration, decreases to about −6 mm Hg, and the lungs are pulled into a more expanded position. The pressure in the airway becomes slightly negative, and air flows into the lungs (Fig 34–1). At the end of inspiration, the lung recoil pulls the chest back to the expiratory position where the recoil pressures of the lungs and chest wall balance. The pressure in the airway becomes slightly positive, and air flows out of the lungs. Expiration during quiet breathing is passive in the sense that no muscles which decrease intrathoracic volume contract. However, there is some contraction of the inspiratory muscles in the early part of expiration. This contraction exerts a braking action on the recoil forces and slows expiration.

Strong inspiratory efforts reduce intrapleural pressure to values as low as −30 mm Hg, producing correspondingly greater degrees of lung inflation. When ventilation is increased, the extent of lung deflation is also increased by active contraction of expiratory muscles which decrease intrathoracic volume.

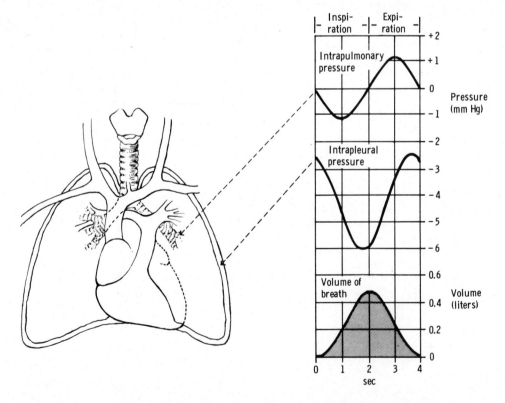

FIG 34–1. Changes in intrapleural (intrathoracic) and intrapulmonary pressure during inspiration and expiration. (Based in part on data in Perkins: Respiration. *Encyclopaedia Britannica,* 1961.)

Air Passages

After passing through the nasal passages and pharynx, where it is warmed and takes up water vapor, the inspired air passes down the trachea and through the bronchioles, respiratory bronchioles, and alveolar ducts to the alveoli (Fig 34–2). The alveoli are surrounded by pulmonary capillaries, and in most areas, the structures between the air and the capillary blood across which O_2 and CO_2 diffuse are exceedingly thin (Fig 34–3). There are 300 million alveoli in man, and the total area of the alveolar walls in contact with capillaries in both lungs is about 70 sq m.

Lung Volumes

The amount of air that moves into the lungs with each inspiration (or the amount that moves out with each expiration) is called the **tidal volume**. The air inspired with a maximal inspiratory effort in excess of the tidal volume is the **inspiratory reserve volume**. The volume expelled by an active expiratory effort after passive expiration is the **expiratory reserve volume**, and the air left in the lungs after a maximal expiratory effort is the **residual volume**. Normal values for these lung volumes, and names applied to combinations of them, are shown in Fig 34–4. The space occupied by gas that does not exchange with blood in the pulmonary vessels is the **respiratory dead space**. The **vital capacity**, the greatest amount of air that can be expired after a maximal inspiratory effort, is frequently measured clinically as an index of pulmonary function. The fraction of the vital capacity expired in 1 sec (**timed vital capacity**; also called forced expired volume in 1 sec, or FEV 1″) gives additional valuable information. The vital capacity may be normal but the timed vital capacity greatly reduced in diseases such as asthma, in which, due to bronchial constriction, the resistance of the airways is increased. The amount of air inspired per minute (**pulmonary ventilation**, or **respiratory minute volume**) is normally about 6 liters/min (500 ml/breath × 12 breaths/min). The **maximal voluntary ventilation (MVV)** or, as it was formerly called, the **maximal breathing capacity**, is the largest volume of gas that can be moved into and out of the lungs in one minute by voluntary effort. The normal MVV is 125–170 liters/min.

Respiratory Muscles

Movement of the **diaphragm** accounts for 75% of the change in intrathoracic volume during quiet inspiration. Attached around the bottom of the thoracic cage, this muscle arches over the liver and moves downward like a piston when it contracts. The distance it moves ranges from 1.5 cm to as much as 7 cm with deep inspiration. The other major **inspiratory muscles** are the **external intercostal muscles,** which run obliquely downward and forward from rib to rib. The ribs pivot as if hinged at the back, so that when the external intercostals contract they elevate the lower ribs. This pushes the sternum outward and increases the anteroposterior diameter of the chest (Fig 34–5). The transverse diameter is actually changed little if at

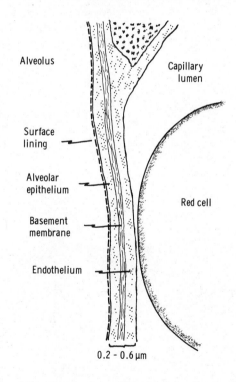

FIG 34–3. The alveolo-capillary membrane. To reach the red cell, O_2 traverses the surface lining, the alveolar epithelial cytoplasm, the basement membrane, the endothelial cell cytoplasm, and the plasma. In some locations, there is also loose interstitial tissue between the epithelium and the endothelium. (Approximate magnification × 20,000.)

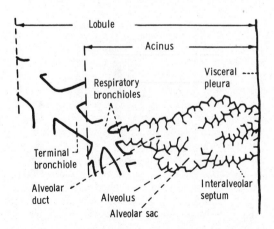

FIG 34–2. Air passages in the mammalian lung. The alveolar sacs are formed by major partitions projecting into the alveolar ducts, and the alveoli are formed by the interalveolar septa which project into the sacs. (Reproduced, with permission, from *Physiology and Biophysics,* 19th ed. Ruch TC, Patton HD [editors]. Saunders, 1965.)

IRV = Inspiratory reserve volume   TV = Tidal volume
ERV = Expiratory reserve volume   RV = Residual volume

		Volume (liters)		
		Men	Women	
Vital capacity	IRV	3.3	1.9	Inspiratory capacity
	TV	0.5	0.5	
	ERV	1.0	0.7	Functional residual capacity
	RV	1.2	1.1	
Total lung capacity		6.0	4.2	

Respiratory minute volume (rest): 6 liters/min
Alveolar ventilation (rest): 4.2 liters/min
Maximal voluntary ventilation (BTPS): 125–170 liters/min
Timed vital capacity: 83% of total in 1 sec; 97% in 3 sec
Work of quiet breathing: 0.5 kg-m/min
Maximal work of breathing: 10 kg-m/breath

FIG 34–4. Lung volumes and some measurements related to the mechanics of breathing. The diagram at the upper right represents the excursions of a spirometer plotted against time. (Data and graph, slightly modified, from Comroe & others: *The Lung, Clinical Physiology and Pulmonary Function Tests,* 2nd ed. Year Book, 1962.)

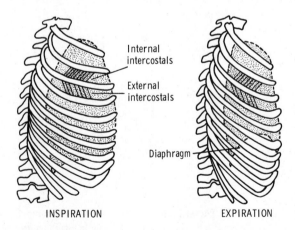

FIG 34–5. Action of the diaphragm and external intercostal muscles.

all. Either the diaphragm or the external intercostal muscles alone can maintain adequate ventilation at rest. Transection of the spinal cord above the third cervical segment is fatal without artificial respiration, but transection below the origin of the phrenic nerves that innervate the diaphragm (third to fifth cervical segments) is not; conversely, in patients with bilateral phrenic nerve palsy, respiration is adequate to maintain life. The scalene and sternocleidomastoid muscles in the neck are accessory inspiratory muscles which help to elevate the thoracic cage during deep labored respiration.

A decrease in intrathoracic volume and forced expiration result when the **expiratory muscles** contract. The internal intercostals have this action because they pass obliquely downward and posteriorly from rib to rib and therefore pull the rib cage downward when they contract. Contractions of the muscles of the anterior abdominal wall also aid expiration by pulling the rib cage downward and inward; and by increasing the intra-abdominal pressure, which pushes the diaphragm upward.

Glottis

The abductor muscles in the larynx contract early in inspiration, pulling the vocal cords apart and opening the glottis. During swallowing or gagging, there is reflex contraction of the adductor muscles which close the glottis and prevent aspiration of food, fluid, or vomitus into the lungs. In unconscious or anesthetized patients, glottic closure may be incomplete and vomitus may enter the trachea, causing an inflammatory reaction in the lung (**aspiration pneumonia**).

The laryngeal muscles are supplied by the vagi. When the abductors are paralyzed, there is inspiratory stridor. When the adductors are paralyzed, food and fluid enter the trachea, causing aspiration pneumonia and edema. Bilateral cervical vagotomy in animals causes the slow development of fatal pulmonary congestion and edema. The edema is due at least in part to aspiration, although some edema develops even if a tracheostomy is performed before the vagotomy.

Compliance of the Lungs & Chest Wall

The interaction between the recoil of the lungs and recoil of the chest can be demonstrated in living subjects. The nostrils are clipped shut and the subject breathes through an apparatus that contains a valve just beyond the mouthpiece. The mouthpiece contains a pressure measuring device. After the subject inhales a given amount, the valve is shut, closing off the airway. He then relaxes his respiratory muscles while the pressure in the airway is recorded. The procedure is repeated after inhaling or actively exhaling various volumes. The curve of airway pressure obtained in this way, plotted against volume, is the relaxation pressure curve of the total respiratory system (Fig 34–6). The pressure is zero at a lung volume that corresponds to the volume of gas in the lungs at the end of quiet expiration (functional residual capacity; see below), positive at greater volumes, and negative at smaller volumes. The change in lung volume per unit change in airway pressure ($\Delta V/\Delta P$) is the stretchability or **compliance** of the lungs and chest wall. It is normally measured in the pressure range where the relaxation pressure curve is steepest. The normal value is about 0.1 liter/cm of H_2O. When the rigidity of the lungs or the chest wall increases, the value drops; it is low in conditions in which the airways are obstructed, pulmonary fibrosis, and pulmonary congestion.

Alveolar Surface Tension

An important factor affecting the compliance of the lungs is the surface tension of the film of fluid that lines the alveoli. The magnitude of this component at various lung volumes can be measured by removing the lungs from the body and distending them alternately with saline and with air while measuring the intrapulmonary pressure. Because saline reduces the surface tension to nearly zero, the pressure volume curve obtained with saline measures the tissue elasticity (Fig

FIG 34–6. Relation between intrapulmonary pressure and volume. The middle curve is the static pressure curve of values obtained when the lungs are inflated or deflated by various amounts and the intrapulmonary pressure is measured with the airway closed. The relaxation volume is the point where the recoil of the chest and the recoil of the lungs balance. The slope of the curve is the compliance of the lungs and chest wall. The maximal inspiratory and expiratory curves are the airway pressures that can be developed during maximal inspiratory and expiratory efforts. The dashed lines, the horizontal distances between the inspiratory and expiratory curves and the relaxation pressure curve, represent the net pressure exerted by the inspiratory and expiratory muscles. (Modified from Lambertsen, in: *Medical Physiology,* 12th ed. Mountcastle VB [editor]. Mosby, 1968.)

FIG 34–7. **Pressure volume relations in the lungs of a cat after removal from the body.** *Air:* lungs inflated (Inf) and deflated (Def) with air. *Saline:* lungs inflated and deflated with saline. (Reproduced, with permission, from Morgan: Pulmonary surfactant. New England J Med 284:1158, 1971.)

34–7), while the curve obtained with air measures both components. The difference between the 2 curves, the elasticity due to surface tension, is much smaller at small than at large lung volumes. The surface tension is also much less than the expected surface tension at a water-air interface of the same dimensions.

The low surface tension when the alveoli are small is due to the presence in the fluid lining the alveoli of **surfactant**, a lipid surface tension-lowering agent. Surfactant is a complex mixture of protein and lipids, but the major component is dipalmitoyl lecithin (DPL). This phospholipid has a hydrophilic "head" and 2 parallel hydrophobic fatty acid "tails" like phospholipids in cell membranes (see Chapters 1 and 17). Presumably, the molecules are parallelly oriented at the air-fluid interface in the alveoli, and surface tension is inversely proportionate to their concentration. The molecules of surfactant are spread apart as alveolar size increases during inspiration but move together during expiration, thus adjusting surface tension during breathing. If the surface tension is not kept low when the alveoli become smaller during expiration, they collapse in accordance with the law of Laplace (see Chapter 30). In spherical structures like the alveoli, the distending pressure equals 2 times the tension divided by the radius ($P = 2T/R$); if T is not reduced as R is reduced, the tension overcomes the distending pressure. Surfactant also helps to prevent pulmonary edema. It has been calculated that if it were not present the unopposed surface tension in the alveoli would produce a 20 mm Hg force favoring transudation of fluid from the blood into the alveoli.

Surfactant appears to be produced by one of the 2 types of epithelial cells lining the alveoli. The type I cells are the thin cells which line much of the alveolar surface, whereas the type II cells, also called **granular**

pneumocytes, are round and contain large lamellar inclusions. These inclusions are believed to be surfactant which is secreted from the type II cells by exocytosis. The size and number of granules in the type II cells are increased by thyroxine.

There is a surfactant deficiency in **hyaline membrane disease**, a serious disease of newborn infants. Surface tension in the lungs of these infants is high, and there are many areas in which the alveoli are collapsed (atelectasis). Similar changes are associated with surfactant deficiency in patients who have undergone cardiac surgery during which a pump oxygenator was used and the pulmonary circulation was interrupted. In bilaterally vagotomized guinea pigs the amount of surfactant decreases, and it is possible that this contributes to the fatal pulmonary congestion and edema that develop in such animals. Surfactant deficiency may also play a causal role in some of the abnormalities that develop following occlusion of a main bronchus, occlusion of one pulmonary artery, and long-term inhalation of 100% O_2.

Work of Breathing

Work is performed by the respiratory muscles in stretching the elastic tissues of the chest wall and lungs, moving inelastic tissues, and moving air through the respiratory passages. Since pressure times volume (g/sq cm × cu cm = g × cm) has the same dimensions as work (force × distance), the work of breathing can be calculated from the relaxation pressure curve (Figs 34–6 and 34–8). In Fig 34–8, the total elastic work required for inspiration is area ABCA. It is worth noting that the relaxation pressure curve of the total

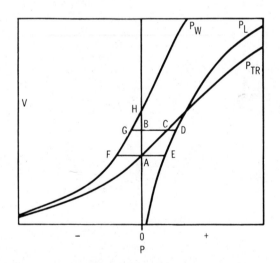

FIG 34–8. **Relaxation pressure curve of total respiratory system (P_{TR}) and its components, the relaxation pressure curve of the lungs (P_L) and the chest (P_W).** (Reproduced, with permission, from Otis: The work of breathing. In: *Handbook of Physiology.* Fenn WO, Rahn H [editors]. Washington: The American Physiological Society, 1964. Section 3, vol 1, pp 463–476.)

respiratory system differs from that of the lungs alone. The actual elastic work required to increase the volume of the lungs alone is area ABDEA. The amount of elastic work required to inflate the whole respiratory system is less than the amount required to inflate the lungs alone because part of the work comes from elastic energy stored in the thorax. The elastic energy lost from the thorax (area AFGBA) is equal to that gained by the lungs (area AEDCA).

The frictional resistance to air movement is relatively small during quiet breathing, but it does cause the intrapleural pressure changes to lead the lung volume changes during inspiration and expiration, producing a **hysteresis loop** rather than a straight line when pressure is plotted against volume (Fig 34–9). In this diagram, area AXBYA represents the work done to overcome airway resistance and lung viscosity.

Estimates of the total work of quiet breathing range from 0.3 up to 0.8 kg-m/min. The value rises markedly during exercise, but the energy cost of breathing in normal individuals represents less than 3% of the total energy expenditure during exercise. The work of breathing is greatly increased in diseases such as emphysema, asthma, and congestive heart failure with dyspnea and orthopnea.

Dead Space & Uneven Ventilation

Since gaseous exchange in the respiratory system occurs only in the alveoli, the gas that occupies the rest of the respiratory system is not available for gas exchange with pulmonary capillary blood. Normally, the volume of this dead space is approximately equal to the body weight in pounds. Thus, in a 150 lb man, only the first 350 ml of the 500 ml inspired with each breath at rest mixes with the air in the alveoli. Conversely, with each expiration, the first 150 ml expired is gas that occupied the dead space, and only the last 350 ml is gas from the alveoli.

It is wise to distinguish between the anatomic dead space (volume of the respiratory system exclusive

FIG 34–10. Method of measuring anatomic dead space. *Ordinate:* Percentage of N_2 in inspired and expired gas. *Abscissa:* Volume of gas inspired (to dotted line) and expired (beyond dotted line). The subject takes a deep breath of pure O_2 and then exhales steadily. The percentage of N_2 in the expired gas is initially zero because of the inhalation of O_2. It rises sharply to a plateau when alveolar air begins to be expired. A vertical line is drawn in such a way that A and B are equal. The distance along the abscissa between this line and the dotted line marking the start of expiration indicates the volume of gas which occupies the anatomic dead space. % Alv N_2 = % N_2 in alveolar gas. (Reproduced, with permission, from Comroe & others: *The Lung, Clinical Physiology and Pulmonary Function Tests,* 2nd ed. Year Book, 1962.)

of alveoli) and the **total,** or **physiologic dead space** (volume of gas not equilibrating with blood, ie, wasted ventilation). In health, the 2 dead spaces are identical; but in disease states there may be no exchange between the gas in some of the alveoli and the blood, and some of the alveoli may be overventilated. The volume of gas in nonperfused alveoli and any volume of air in the alveoli in excess of that necessary to arterialize the blood in the alveolar capillaries is part of the dead space (nonequilibrating) gas volume. The anatomic dead space can be measured by single breath analyses of nitrogen content as shown in Fig 34–10. The total dead space can be calculated from the P_{CO_2} of expired air, the P_{CO_2} of alveolar gas, and the tidal volume. The tidal volume (V_T) times the P_{CO_2} of the expired gas ($P_{E_{CO_2}}$) equals the alveolar P_{CO_2} ($P_{A_{CO_2}}$) times the difference between the tidal volume and the dead space (V_D) plus the P_{CO_2} of inspired air ($P_{I_{CO_2}}$) times V_D:

$$P_{E_{CO_2}} \times V_T = P_{A_{CO_2}} \times (V_T - V_D) +$$
$$P_{I_{CO_2}} \times V_D \text{ (Bohr's equation).}$$

However, the term $P_{I_{CO_2}} \times V_D$ is so small that it can be ignored and the equation solved for V_D. If, for example,

FIG 34–9. Diagrammatic representation of pressure and volume changes during quiet inspiration (line AXB) and expiration (line BZA). Line AYB is the compliance line.

$$P_{E_{CO_2}} = 28 \text{ mm Hg}$$
$$P_{A_{CO_2}} = 40 \text{ mm Hg}$$
$$V_T = 500 \text{ ml}$$
then, $\quad V_D = 150 \text{ ml}$

Although it is possible to stand underwater and breathe through a tube that projects above the surface, it may be worth noting that such a tube is in effect an extension of the respiratory dead space. For each ml of tube volume, the depth of inspiration would have to be increased 1 ml to supply the same volume of air to the alveoli. Thus, if the volume of the tube were at all large, breathing would become very laborious. Additional effort is also required to expand the chest against the pressure of the surrounding water.

Alveolar Ventilation

Because of the dead space, the amount of air reaching the alveoli (**alveolar ventilation**) at a respiratory minute volume of 6 liters/min is 500–150 ml times 12 breath/min, or 4.2 liters/min. Because of the dead space, rapid, shallow respiration produces much less alveolar ventilation than slow, deep respiration at the same respiratory minute volume (Table 34–2).

TABLE 34–2. Effect of variations in respiratory rate and depth on alveolar ventilation.

Respiratory rate	30/min	10/min
Tidal volume	200 ml	600 ml
Minute volume	6 liters	6 liters
Alveolar ventilation	(200–150) × 30 = 1500 ml	(600–150) × 10 = 4500 ml

Composition of Alveolar Air

Oxygen continuously diffuses out of the gas in the alveoli (**alveolar gas**) into the blood stream, and CO_2 continuously diffuses into the alveoli from the blood. In the steady state, inspired air mixes with the alveolar gas, replacing the O_2 that has entered the blood and diluting the CO_2 that has entered the alveoli. Part of this mixture is expired. The O_2 content of the alveolar gas then falls and its CO_2 content rises until the next inspiration. Since the volume of gas in the alveoli is about 2 liters at the end of expiration (functional residual capacity; Fig 34–4), each 350 ml increment of inspired and expired air changes the P_{O_2} and P_{CO_2} very little. Indeed, the composition of alveolar gas remains remarkably constant, not only at rest but in a variety of other conditions as well (see Chapter 36).

Sampling Alveolar Air

Theoretically, all but the first 150 ml expired with each expiration is alveolar air, but there is always some mixing at the interface between the dead space gas and the alveolar air. The last portion of expired air is therefore the portion taken for analysis. Using

FIG 34–11. Partial pressures of gases (mm Hg). (Values from Lambertsen, in: *Medical Physiology,* 12th ed. Mountcastle VB [editor]. Mosby, 1968.)

modern apparatus with a suitable automatic valve, it is possible to collect the last 10 ml expired during quiet breathing. Larger samples can be obtained by collecting the last portion of the expired gas when the subject expires maximally (Haldane-Priestley method), but this technic interrupts the breathing pattern and is not necessary with modern equipment. The composition of alveolar gas is compared with that of inspired and expired air in Fig 34–11.

Metabolic Functions of the Lung

In addition to their respiratory functions, the lungs are involved in a number of metabolic processes. They not only synthesize surfactant, but they appear to be the major site of conversion of angiotensin I to angiotensin II in vivo (see Chapter 24). They inactivate bradykinin, 5-hydroxytryptamine, and prostaglandins. They store megakaryocytes, and histamine is both taken up and discharged by the lungs, which are rich in mast cells.

The Upper Respiratory Tract

The respiratory passages that lead from the exterior to the alveoli do more than serve as gas conduits. They humidify and cool or warm the inspired air so that even very hot or very cold air is at or near body temperature by the time it reaches the alveoli. They also contain mechanisms that do much to prevent foreign matter from reaching the alveoli. The hairs in the nostrils strain out many particles larger than 10 μm in diameter, and most of the remaining particles of this size settle on mucous membranes in the nose and pharynx. Particles 2–10 μm in diameter generally fall on the walls of the trachea and bronchi, where they initiate reflex bronchial constriction and coughing (see Chapter 14). They are also moved away from the lungs by the "ciliary escalator." The epithelium of the respiratory passages from the anterior third of the nose to the beginning of the respiratory bronchioles is ciliated, and the cilia, which are covered with mucus, beat in a coordinated fashion. The ciliary mechanism is capable of moving particles at a rate of at least 16 mm/min. Particles less than 2 μm in diameter generally reach the alveoli, where they are ingested by the macrophages ("dust cells") and carried to the lymph nodes. The importance of these defense mechanisms is evident when one remembers that, in modern cities, each liter of air may contain several million particles of dust and irritants.

PULMONARY CIRCULATION

Anatomic Considerations

The pulmonary vascular bed resembles the systemic (see Chapter 30) except that the walls of the pulmonary artery and its large branches are about 30% as thick as the wall of the aorta, and the small arterial vessels, unlike the systemic arterioles, are endothelial tubes with very little muscle in their walls. The pulmonary capillaries are large and there are multiple anastomoses, so that each alveolus sits in a capillary basket. The pulmonary lymphatics normally drain some interstitial fluid from the lungs, but lymphatics extend only as far as the terminal bronchioles and are not found in the alveolar walls.

Pressure, Volume, & Flow

The output per minute of the right ventricle is, of course, equal to that of the left ventricle and, like that of the left ventricle, averages 5.5 liters/min at rest. The ratio of alveolar ventilation to pulmonary blood flow at rest is therefore about 0.8 (4.2/5.5). It should be noted that this ratio may be normal in patients with severe hypoxia because in disease states there may be nonuniform ventilation and nonuniform perfusion of alveoli. The extreme case of such nonuniformity would be that in which all the ventilation went to one lung and all the blood flow to the other, a state which would, of course, be rapidly fatal even though the ventilation/blood flow ratio would be normal.

The entire pulmonary vascular system is a distensible low-pressure system. The pulmonary arterial pressure is 25/10 mm Hg or less. The mean pressure is about 15 mm Hg. The pressure in the left atrium is about 7 mm Hg during diastole, so that the pressure gradient in the pulmonary system is about 8 mm Hg compared with a gradient of about 90 mm Hg in the systemic circulation (Fig 34–12).

The volume of blood in the pulmonary vessels at any one time is about 1 liter, of which less than 100 ml are in the capillaries. The mean velocity of the blood in the root of the pulmonary artery is the same as that in the aorta (about 40 cm/sec). It falls off rapidly, then rises slightly again in the larger pulmonary veins. It takes a red cell about 0.75 sec to traverse the pulmonary capillaries at rest, and 0.3 sec or less during exercise.

"Physiologic Shunt"

About 2% of the blood in the systemic arteries is blood that has bypassed the pulmonary capillaries. The

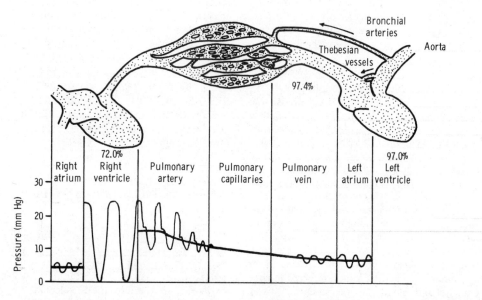

FIG 34–12. The pulmonary circulation. The percentage values are percentage saturation of hemoglobin in the various locations. The heavy line indicates the mean pressure in the various vessels. The light line indicates the superimposed pressure curves with each cardiac cycle. The arrows indicate the flow through the bronchial arteries and thebesian vessels which bypass the lung ("physiologic shunt").

bronchial arteries, branches of the thoracic aorta, provide blood that nourishes parts of the lung parenchyma, and some of this blood returns to the heart via the pulmonary veins. There is further dilution of the oxygenated blood in the heart by blood that flows from the coronary arteries directly into the chambers of the left side of the heart (see Chapter 32). It is because of this small "physiologic shunt" that the blood in the systemic arteries contains less O_2 per 100 ml than the blood that has equilibrated with the alveolar air.

Capillary Pressure

Pulmonary capillary pressure is about 10 mm Hg, whereas the oncotic pressure is 25 mm Hg, so that there is an inward-directed pressure gradient of about 15 mm Hg which keeps the alveoli free of fluid. When the pulmonary capillary pressure is more than 25 mm Hg—as it may be, for example, when there is "backward failure" of the left ventricle—pulmonary congestion and edema result. Patients with mitral stenosis also have a chronic, progressive rise in pulmonary capillary pressure and extensive fibrotic changes in the pulmonary vessels. Pulmonary edema is not as prominent a symptom in mitral stenosis as in frank congestive heart failure, probably because the fibrosis and constriction of the pulmonary arterial vessels "protect" the capillaries. It has been claimed that the increased arterial resistance is reflex in origin, but this has not been proved.

Pulmonary Reservoir

Because of their distensibility, the pulmonary veins are an important blood reservoir. Pulmonary blood volume increases by up to 400 ml in a normal individual when he lies down, and this blood is discharged into the general circulation when he stands up. This shift is the cause of the decrease in vital capacity in the supine position, and is responsible for the occurrence of orthopnea in heart failure (see Chapter 33).

Dilatation & Constriction of the Pulmonary Vessels

The pulmonary vessels are capable of considerable passive dilatation. When the blood supply to one normal lung is obstructed by inflating a balloon in a main branch of the pulmonary artery, the flow through the other lung is doubled, but there is only a small rise in pulmonary arterial pressure. The vessels are plentifully supplied with sympathetic vasoconstrictor nerve fibers, and stimulation of the cervical sympathetic ganglia decreases pulmonary blood flow by as much as 30%. The fibers serve in part to decrease the capacity of the pulmonary circulation, thus mobilizing blood from the pulmonary reservoir. Pressure in the pulmonary artery is increased by hypoxia. It is little affected by stimuli which alter the systemic pressure. In exercise, for example, pulmonary blood flow increases by the same amount as systemic blood flow (as much as 7-fold), but pulmonary arterial pressure changes very little. The pulmonary arterial pressure is usually normal in essential hypertension, and pressor drugs cause little change in pulmonary pressure.

When a bronchus is obstructed, the vessels supplying the poorly ventilated alveoli constrict, and blood is shunted to other areas. The constriction is due to a local effect of the low alveolar P_{O_2} on the vessels. Accumulation of CO_2 leads to a drop in pH in the area and a decline in pH also produces constriction. Conversely, obstruction of the blood flow to a portion of the lung lowers the alveolar P_{CO_2} in that area, and this leads to constriction of the bronchi supplying it.

Pulmonary Embolization

Emboli that block small branches of the pulmonary artery provoke a marked rise in pulmonary arterial pressure and cause rapid, shallow respiration (tachypnea). The rise in pulmonary arterial pressure is apparently due to reflex vasoconstriction via the sympathetic nerve fibers, although there is controversy on this point and reflex vasoconstriction appears to be absent when large branches of the pulmonary artery are blocked. The tachypnea is a reflex response to activation of vagally innervated pulmonary deflation receptors close to the vessel walls. There is some evidence that serotonin is released from platelets at the site of embolization, and that serotonin stimulates or "sensitizes" these receptors.

The pattern of ventilation in the lungs can be assessed by having the subject inhale a radioactive isotope of the inert gas, xenon (^{133}Xe), while monitoring his chest with a battery of radiation detectors. Areas that show little radioactivity are poorly ventilated. ^{133}Xe can also be used to survey pulmonary blood flow by injecting a saline solution of the gas intravenously while monitoring the chest. The gas rapidly enters the alveoli that are perfused normally but fails to enter those that are not perfused. Another technic for locating poorly perfused areas is injection of macroaggregates of albumin labeled with radioactive iodine. These aggregates are large enough to block capillaries and small arterioles, and they lodge only in vessels in which blood was flowing when they reached the lungs. Although it seems paradoxical to study patients with pulmonary vascular obstruction by producing additional obstruction, the technic is safe because relatively few particles are injected. The particles block only a small number of pulmonary vessels and are rapidly removed by the body.

DIFFUSION CAPACITY

The P_{O_2} of alveolar air is 100 mm Hg, whereas that in the venous blood in the pulmonary artery is 40 mm Hg (Fig 34–11). There is no evidence that any process other than passive diffusion is involved in the movement of O_2 into the blood along this pressure gradient. O_2 dissolves in the plasma and enters the red cells, where it combines with hemoglobin, a reaction considered in detail in the next chapter. Diffusion into the blood must be very rapid, since the time each ml of blood is in the capillaries is short. Nevertheless, O_2 diffusion is adequate in health to raise the P_{O_2} of the blood to 97 mm Hg, a value just under the alveolar P_{O_2}.

The **diffusion capacity** of the lungs for O_2 is the amount of O_2 which crosses the alveolar membrane per min per mm Hg difference in P_{O_2} between the alveolar gas and the blood in the pulmonary capillaries. Expressed in terms of STPD (see Table 34–1), it is normally about 20 ml/min/mm Hg at rest. As a result of capillary dilatation and an increase in the number of active capillaries, it rises to values of 65 or more during exercise. The diffusion capacity for O_2 is decreased in diseases such as sarcoidosis and beryllium poisoning (berylliosis) which cause fibrosis of the alveolar walls and produce **alveolar-capillary block**.

The P_{CO_2} of venous blood is 46 mm Hg, whereas that of alveolar air is 40 mm Hg, and CO_2 diffuses from the blood into the alveoli along this gradient. The P_{CO_2} of blood leaving the lungs is 40 mm Hg. CO_2 passes through all biologic membranes with ease, and the pulmonary diffusion capacity for CO_2 is much greater than the capacity for O_2. It is for this reason that CO_2 retention is rarely a problem in patients with alveolar-capillary block even when the reduction in diffusion capacity for O_2 is severe.

35...

Gas Transport Between the Lungs & the Tissues

The partial pressure gradients for O_2 and CO_2 have been plotted in graphic form in Fig 35–1 to emphasize that they are the key to gas movement, and that O_2 "flows downhill" from the air through the alveoli and blood into the tissues whereas CO_2 flows downhill from the tissues to the alveoli. However, the amount of both of these gases transported to and from the tissues would be grossly inadequate if it were not that the O_2 that dissolves in the blood combines with the O_2-carrying protein, hemoglobin, and that the CO_2 that dissolves enters into a series of reversible chemical reactions which convert it into other compounds. The presence of hemoglobin increases the O_2-carrying capacity of the blood 70-fold, and the reactions of CO_2 increase the blood CO_2 content 17-fold (Table 35–1).

TABLE 35–1. Gas content of blood.

| Gas | ml/100 ml of blood containing 15 g of hemoglobin | | | |
| | Arterial Blood (P_{O_2} 95 mm Hg; P_{CO_2} 40 mm Hg; Hb 97% saturated) | | Venous Blood (P_{O_2} 40 mm Hg; P_{CO_2} 46 mm Hg; Hb 75% saturated) | |
	Dissolved	Combined	Dissolved	Combined
O_2	0.29	19.5	0.12	15.1
CO_2	3.0	47.0	3.5	51.5
N_2	1.04	0	1.04	0

OXYGEN TRANSPORT

Oxygen Delivery to the Tissues

The O_2 delivery system in the body consists of the lungs and the cardiovascular system. O_2 delivery to a particular tissue depends on the amount of O_2

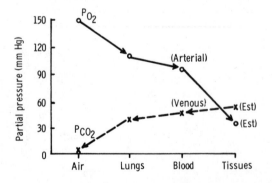

FIG 35–1. Summary of P_{O_2} and P_{CO_2} values in air, lungs, blood, and tissues, graphed to emphasize the fact that both O_2 and CO_2 diffuse "downhill" along gradients of decreasing partial pressure. (Redrawn and reproduced, with permission, from Kinney: Transport of carbon dioxide in blood. Anesthesiology 21:615, 1960.)

entering the lungs, the adequacy of pulmonary gas exchange, the blood flow to the tissue, and the capacity of the blood to carry O_2. The blood flow depends on the degree of constriction of the vascular bed in the tissue and the cardiac output. The amount of O_2 in the blood is determined by the amount of dissolved O_2, the amount of hemoglobin in the blood, and the affinity of the hemoglobin for O_2.

Reaction of Hemoglobin & Oxygen

The dynamics of the reaction of hemoglobin with O_2 make it a particularly suitable O_2 carrier. Hemoglobin (see Chapter 27) is a protein made up of 4 subunits, each of which contains a **heme** moiety attached to a polypeptide chain. Heme (Fig 27–6) is a complex made up of a porphyrin and one atom of ferrous iron. Each of the 4 iron atoms can bind reversibly one O_2 molecule. The iron stays in the ferrous state, so that the reaction is an **oxygenation**, not an oxidation. It has been customary to write the reaction of hemoglobin with O_2 as $Hb + O_2 \rightleftarrows HbO_2$. Since it contains 4 Hb units, the hemoglobin molecule actually reacts with 4 molecules of O_2 to form Hb_4O_8.

$$Hb_4 + O_2 \leftrightarrows Hb_4O_2$$
$$Hb_4O_2 + O_2 \leftrightarrows Hb_4O_4$$
$$Hb_4O_4 + O_2 \rightleftarrows Hb_4O_6$$
$$Hb_4O_6 + O_2 \rightleftarrows Hb_4O_8$$

The reaction is rapid, requiring less than 0.01 sec. The deoxygenation (reduction) of Hb_4O_8 is also very

PO₂ (mm Hg)	% Sat of Hb	Dissolved O₂ (ml/100 ml)
10	13.5	0.03
20	35	0.06
30	57	0.09
40	75	0.12
50	83.5	0.15
60	89	0.18
70	92.7	0.21
80	94.5	0.24
90	96.5	0.27
100	97.5	0.30

FIG 35−2. Oxygen hemoglobin dissociation curve. pH 7.40, temperature 38° C. (Redrawn and reproduced, with permission, from Comroe & others: *The Lung, Clinical Physiology and Pulmonary Function Tests,* 2nd ed. Year Book, 1962.)

in normal blood is about 15 g/100 ml (14 g/100 ml in women and 16 g/100 ml in men; see Chapter 27). Therefore, 100 ml of blood contains 20.1 ml (1.34 ml × 15) of O_2 bound to hemoglobin when the hemoglobin is 100% saturated. The amount of dissolved O_2 is a linear function of the P_{O_2} (0.003 ml/100 ml blood per mm Hg P_{O_2}).

In vivo the hemoglobin in the blood at the ends of the pulmonary capillaries is about 97.5% saturated with O_2 (P_{O_2} = 97 mm Hg). Because of a slight admixture with venous blood that bypasses the lungs ("physiologic shunt"), the hemoglobin in systemic arterial blood is only 97% saturated. The arterial blood therefore contains a total of about 19.8 ml of O_2 per 100 ml; 0.29 ml in solution and 19.5 ml bound to hemoglobin. In venous blood at rest, the hemoglobin is 75% saturated, and the total O_2 content is about 15.2 ml/100 ml. Thus, at rest the tissues remove about 4.6 ml of O_2 from each 100 ml of blood passing through them (Table 35−1); 0.17 ml of this total represents O_2 that was in solution in the blood, and the remainder represents O_2 that was liberated from hemoglobin. In this way, 250 ml of O_2 per minute are transported from the blood to the tissues at rest.

rapid. The **oxygen hemoglobin dissociation curve,** the curve relating percentage saturation of the O_2-carrying power of hemoglobin to the P_{O_2} (Fig 35−2), has a characteristic sigmoid shape. Combination of the first heme in the Hb molecule with O_2 increases the affinity of the second heme for O_2, and oxygenation of the second increases the affinity of the third, etc, so that the affinity of Hb for the fourth O_2 molecule is many times that for the first. This shifting affinity for O_2 is what makes the dissociation curve sigmoid in shape. When hemoglobin takes up O_2, the 2 β chains move closer together; when O_2 is given up, they move farther apart. This shift is apparently essential for the shift in affinity for O_2 to occur.

When blood is equilibrated with 100% O_2 (P_{O_2} = 760 mm Hg), the hemoglobin becomes 100% saturated. When fully saturated, each gram of hemoglobin contains 1.34 ml of O_2. The hemoglobin concentration

Factors Affecting the Affinity of Hemoglobin for Oxygen

Three important conditions affect the O_2-hemoglobin dissociation curve: the pH, the temperature, and the concentration of 2,3-diphosphoglycerate (**DPG, 2,3-DPG**). A rise in temperature or a fall in pH shifts the curve "to the right" (Fig 35−3). When the curve is shifted in this direction, a higher P_{O_2} is required for hemoglobin to bind a given amount of O_2. Conversely, a fall in temperature or a rise in pH shifts the curve to the left, and a lower P_{O_2} is required to bind a given amount of O_2. A convenient index of such shifts is the P_{50}, the P_{O_2} at which the hemoglobin is half-saturated with O_2; the higher the P_{50}, the lower the affinity of hemoglobin for O_2.

The decrease in O_2 affinity of hemoglobin when the pH of blood falls is called the **Bohr effect** and is closely related to the fact that deoxyhemoglobin binds

$$pH = 6.10 + \log \frac{[HCO_3^-]}{0.0301\, P_{CO_2}}$$

pH arterial blood $\cong$ 7.40
pH venous blood $\cong$ 7.36

FIG 35−3. Effect of temperature and pH on hemoglobin dissociation curve. Ordinates and abscissas as in Fig 35−2. (Redrawn and reproduced, with permission, from Comroe & others: *The Lung, Clinical Physiology and Pulmonary Function Tests,* 2nd ed. Year Book, 1962.)

FIG 35—4. Formation and catabolism of 2,3-DPG.

H^+ more actively than oxyhemoglobin. The pH of blood falls as its CO_2 content increases (see below), so that when the P_{CO_2} rises, the curve shifts to the right and the P_{50} rises. Most of the unsaturation of hemoglobin that occurs in the tissues is secondary to the decline in the P_{O_2}, but an extra 1—2% unsaturation is due to the rise in P_{CO_2} and consequent shift of the dissociation curve to the right.

2,3-DPG is very plentiful in red cells. It is formed (Fig 35—4) from 3-phosphoglyceraldehyde, which is a product of glycolysis via the Embden-Meyerhof pathway (see Chapter 17). It is a highly charged anion which binds to the β chains of deoxygenated hemoglobin but not to those of oxyhemoglobin. One mol of deoxygenated hemoglobin binds 1 mol of 2,3-DPG. In effect:

$$HbO_2 + 2,3\text{-}DPG \rightleftarrows Hb\text{-}2,3\text{-}DPG + O_2$$

In this equilibrium, an increase in the concentration of 2,3-DPG shifts the reaction to the right, causing more O_2 to be liberated. ATP binds to deoxygenated hemoglobin to a lesser extent, and some other organic phosphates bind to a minor degree.

Factors affecting the concentration of 2,3-DPG in the red cells include pH. Because acidosis inhibits red cell glycolysis, the 2,3-DPG concentration falls when the pH is low. Thyroid hormones, growth hormone, and androgens increase the concentration of 2,3-DPG and the P_{50}.

Exercise has been reported to produce an increase in 2,3-DPG within 60 minutes. The P_{50} is also increased during exercise because the temperature rises in active tissues and CO_2 and metabolites accumulate, lowering the pH. In addition, much more O_2 is removed from each unit of blood flowing through active tissues because the tissue P_{O_2} declines. Finally, at low P_{O_2} values, the O_2 hemoglobin dissociation

curve is steep, and large amounts of O_2 are liberated per unit drop in P_{O_2}.

Ascent to high altitude triggers a substantial rise in red cell 2,3-DPG concentration, with a consequent increase in P_{50} and increase in the availability of O_2 to tissues. The rise in 2,3-DPG, which has a half-life of 6 hours, is secondary to the rise in blood pH (see Chapter 37). 2,3-DPG levels drop to normal upon return to sea level.

The greater affinity of fetal hemoglobin (hemoglobin F) than adult hemoglobin (hemoglobin A) for O_2 facilitates the movement of O_2 from the mother to the fetus (see Chapters 27 and 32). The cause of this greater affinity is the poor binding of 2,3-DPG by the γ polypeptide chains that replace β chains in fetal hemoglobin. The changes in P_{50} produced by 2,3-DPG in hemoglobin F and hemoglobin A are shown in Fig 35—5. Some abnormal hemoglobins found in adults also have low P_{50} values, and the resulting high O_2 affinity of the hemoglobin causes enough tissue hypoxia to stimulate increased red cell formation with resulting polycythemia (see Chapter 24). It is interesting to speculate that these hemoglobins may not bind 2,3-DPG.

Red cell 2,3-DPG concentration is increased in anemia and in a variety of diseases in which there is chronic hypoxia. This facilitates the delivery of O_2 to the tissues by raising the P_{O_2} at which O_2 is released in peripheral capillaries. In bank blood that is stored, the 2,3-DPG level falls, and the ability of this blood to release O_2 to the tissues is consequently reduced. This decrease, which obviously limits the benefit of the blood if it is transfused into a hypoxic patient, is less if the blood is stored in citrate-phosphate-dextrose solution rather than the usual acid-citrate-dextrose solution.

FIG 35—5. Effect of 2,3-DPG on P_{50} values for human fetal (F) and adult (A) hemoglobin. (Reproduced, with permission, from Bunn & Jandl: Control of hemoglobin function within the red cell. New England J Med 282:1414, 1970.)

Other aspects of the chemistry of hemoglobin are discussed in Chapter 27. Fetal hemoglobin and transplacental O_2 exchange are discussed in Chapter 32.

Myoglobin

Myoglobin is an iron-containing pigment found in skeletal muscle. It resembles hemoglobin but binds one rather than 4 mols of O_2 per mol. Its dissociation curve is a rectangular hyperbola rather than a sigmoid curve. Because its curve is to the left of the hemoglobin curve (Fig 35–6), it takes up O_2 from hemoglobin in the blood. It releases O_2 only at low P_{O_2} values, but the P_{O_2} in exercising muscle is close to zero. The myoglobin content is greatest in muscles specialized for sustained contraction. The muscle blood supply is compressed during such contractions, and myoglobin may provide O_2 when blood flow is cut off. There is also evidence that myoglobin facilitates the diffusion of O_2 from the blood to the mitochondria, where the oxidative reactions occur.

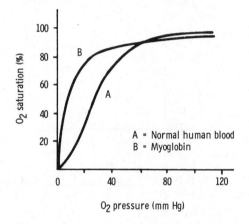

FIG 35–6. Dissociation curve of oxyhemoglobin and myoglobin at 38° C, pH 7.40. (Redrawn and reproduced, with permission, from Roughton: *Handbook of Respiratory Physiology.* USAF School of Aviation Medicine, 1954.)

BUFFERS IN BLOOD

Since CO_2 forms carbonic acid in the blood, a discussion of the buffer systems in the blood is a necessary preliminary to a consideration of CO_2 transport.

The Henderson-Hasselbalch Equation

The general equation for a buffer system is

$$HA \rightleftarrows H^+ + A^-$$

A^- represents any anion, and HA the undissociated acid. If an acid stronger than HA is added to a solution containing this system, the equilibrium is shifted to the left. Hydrogen ions are "tied up" in the formation of

more undissociated HA, so the increase in H^+ concentration is much less than it would otherwise be. Conversely, if a base is added to the solution, H^+ and OH^- react to form H_2O but more HA dissociates, limiting the decrease in H^+ concentration. By the law of mass action, the product of the concentrations of the products in a chemical reaction divided by the product of the concentration of the reactants at equilibrium is a constant.

$$\frac{[H^+] [A^-]}{[HA]} = K$$

If this equation is solved for H^+ and put in pH notation (pH is the negative log of $[H^+]$), the resulting equation is that originally derived by Henderson and Hasselbalch to describe the pH changes resulting from addition of H^+ or OH^- to any buffer system (**Henderson-Hasselbalch equation**):

$$pH = pK + \log \frac{[A^-]}{[HA]}$$

It is apparent from these equations that the buffering capacity of a system is greatest when the amount of free anion is equal to the amount of undissociated HA, ie, when $[A^-]/[HA] = 1$, so that $\log [A^-]/[HA] = 0$, and pH = pK. This is why the most effective buffers in the body would be expected to be those with pKs close to the pH in which they operate. The pH of the blood is normally 7.40; that of the cells is probably about 7.2; and that of the urine varies from 4.5–8.0.

Buffers in Blood

In the blood, proteins—particularly the **plasma proteins**—are effective buffers because both their free carboxyl and their free amino groups dissociate.

$$RCOOH \rightleftarrows RCOO^- + H^+$$

$$pH = pK_{RCOOH} + \log \frac{[RCOO^-]}{[RCOOH]}$$

$$RNH_3^+ \rightleftarrows RNH_2 + H^+$$

$$pH = pK_{RNH_3^+} + \log \frac{[RNH_2]}{[RNH_3^+]}$$

Another important buffer system is provided by the dissociation of the imidazole groups of the histidine residues in **hemoglobin**.

Indeed, in the pH 7.0–7.7 range, the free carboxyl and amino groups of hemoglobin contribute relatively little to its buffering capacity. However, the hemoglobin molecule contains 38 histidine residues, and on this basis—plus the fact that it is present in large amounts—the hemoglobin in blood has 6 times the buffering capacity of the plasma proteins. In addition, the action of hemoglobin is unique because the imidazole groups of deoxygenated hemoglobin dissociate less than those of oxyhemoglobin, making Hb a weaker acid and therefore a better buffer than HbO_2. Titration curves for Hb and HbO_2 are shown in Fig 35–7.

FIG 35–7. Titration curves of Hb and HbO_2. The arrow from *a* to *c* indicates the mM of H^+ which can be added without pH shift. The arrow from *a* to *b* indicates the pH shift on deoxygenation. (Curves drawn, from data of German & Wyman, by Davenport, in: *The ABC of Acid-Base Chemistry*, 4th ed. Univ of Chicago Press, 1958.)

The third major buffer system in blood is the **carbonic acid-bicarbonate** system:

$$H_2CO_3 \rightleftarrows H^+ + HCO_3^-$$

$$pH = pK_{H_2CO_3} + \log \frac{[HCO_3^-]}{[H_2CO_3]}$$

The pK of this system is low relative to blood pH, and yet it is one of the most effective systems because the H_2CO_3 level in plasma is in equilibrium with dissolved CO_2, and the amount of dissolved CO_2 is controlled by respiration:

$$H_2CO_3 \rightleftarrows CO_2 + H_2O$$

In addition, the plasma concentration of HCO_3^- is regulated by the kidneys. When H^+ is added to the blood, HCO_3^- declines as more H_2CO_3 is formed. If the extra H_2CO_3 were not converted to CO_2 and H_2O and the CO_2 excreted in the lungs, the H_2CO_3 concentration would rise. When enough H^+ had been added to halve the plasma HCO_3^-, the pH would have dropped from 7.4 to 6.0. However, not only is all the

extra H_2CO_3 that is formed removed, but the H^+ rise stimulates respiration and therefore produces a drop in P_{CO_2}, so that some additional H_2CO_3 is removed. The pH thus falls only to 7.2 or 7.3 (Fig 40–3).

The reaction $CO_2 + H_2O \rightleftarrows H_2CO_3$ proceeds slowly in either direction unless the enzyme **carbonic anhydrase** is present. There is no carbonic anhydrase in plasma, but there is an abundant supply in red blood cells. It is also found in high concentration in gastric acid-secreting cells (see Chapter 26) and in renal tubular cells (see Chapter 38). Carbonic anhydrase is a protein with a molecular weight of 30,000 that contains an atom of zinc in each molecule. It is inhibited by cyanide, azide, and sulfide. The sulfonamides also inhibit this enzyme, and sulfonamide derivatives have been used clinically as diuretics because of their inhibitory effects on carbonic anhydrase in the kidney (see Chapter 38).

The system $H_2PO_4^- \rightleftarrows H^+ + HPO_4^=$ has a pK of 6.80. In the plasma, the phosphate concentration is too low for this system to be a quantitatively important buffer, but in the urine it frequently plays a significant role (see Chapter 38).

Buffering in Vivo

Buffering in vivo is of course not limited to the blood. Indeed, in metabolic acidosis, only 15–20% of the acid load is buffered in the blood. Another 20–25% is buffered by the H_2CO_3-HCO_3^- system in the interstitial fluid, and the remainder is buffered in cells. The principal intracellular buffers are proteins and organic phosphates. They bind H^+ and liberate Na^+ and K^+; thus, in acidosis, the total extracellular Na^+ and K^+ rise. In metabolic alkalosis, about 30–35% of the OH^- load is buffered in cells, whereas in respiratory acidosis and alkalosis (see Chapter 40) almost all the buffering is intracellular.

Summary

When a strong acid is added to the blood, the 3 major buffer reactions are driven to the left.

$$HHb \rightleftarrows H^+ + Hb^-$$

$$HProt \rightleftarrows H^+ + Prot^-$$

$$H_2CO_3 \rightleftarrows H^+ + HCO_3^-$$

The blood levels of the 3 "buffer anions"—Hb^- (hemoglobin), $Prot^-$ (protein), and HCO_3^-—consequently drop (Fig 35–8). The anions of the added acid are filtered into the renal tubules. They are accompanied ("covered") by cations, particularly Na^+, because electrochemical neutrality is maintained. By processes which are discussed in Chapter 38, the tubules replace the Na^+ with H^+ and in so doing reabsorb equimolar amounts of Na^+ and HCO_3^-, thus conserving the cations, eliminating the acid, and restoring the supply of buffer anions to normal. When CO_2 is added to the blood, similar reactions occur except that since it is H_2CO_3 that is formed, the plasma HCO_3^- rises rather than falls.

FIG 35–8. Distribution of cations and anions in whole blood, pH 7.39, P_{CO_2} 41 mm Hg. Hb^-, hemoglobin; $Prot^-$, plasma protein; X^-, remaining anions. (Reproduced, with permission, from Singer, in Altman & others: *Handbook of Respiration.* Saunders, 1958.)

CARBON DIOXIDE TRANSPORT

Fate of Carbon Dioxide in Blood

The solubility of CO_2 in blood is about 20 times that of O_2, so that there is considerably more CO_2 than O_2 in simple solution. The CO_2 that diffuses into red blood cells is rapidly hydrated to H_2CO_3 because of the presence of carbonic anhydrase. The H_2CO_3 dissociates to H^+ and HCO_3^-, and the H^+ is buffered, primarily by hemoglobin, while the HCO_3^- diffuses into the plasma. The decline in the O_2 saturation of the hemoglobin as the blood passes through the tissue capillaries improves its buffering capacity because deoxygenated hemoglobin binds more H^+ than oxyhemoglobin (see above). Some of the CO_2 in the red cells reacts with the amino groups of proteins, principally hemoglobin, to form **carbamino compounds:**

$$CO_2 + R-N\overset{H}{\underset{H}{\diagdown}} \;\rightleftarrows\; R-N\overset{H}{\underset{COOH}{\diagdown}}$$

At P_{CO_2} values above 10 mm Hg, the amount of carbamino-Hb formed is relatively constant and independent of the P_{CO_2} because the tendency to form more as the amount of available CO_2 increases is offset by the formation of more H^+, which ties up RNH_2 groups by forming RNH_3^+. Since deoxygenated hemoglobin forms carbamino compounds much more readily than HbO_2, transport of CO_2 is facilitated in

venous blood. About 20% of the CO_2 added to the blood in the systemic capillaries is carried to the lungs as carbamino-CO_2.

In the plasma, CO_2 reacts with plasma proteins to form small amounts of carbamino compounds, and small amounts of CO_2 are hydrated; but the hydration reaction is slow in the absence of carbonic anhydrase.

Chloride Shift

Since the rise in the HCO_3^- content of red cells is much greater than that in plasma as the blood passes through the capillaries, HCO_3^- diffuses into the plasma. About 70% of the HCO_3^- formed in the red cells enters the plasma. Normally, the protein anions cannot cross the cell membrane, and owing to the operation of the sodium-potassium pump, Na^+ and K^+ do not diffuse freely. Electrochemical neutrality is maintained by diffusion of Cl^- into the red cells (the **chloride shift**). The Cl^- content of the red cells in venous blood is therefore significantly greater than in arterial blood. The chloride shift occurs rapidly, and is essentially complete in 1 sec.

Because there are many negative charges on each protein molecule but only one on each HCO_3^- and Cl^-, the number of osmotically active particles in the red cells increases as the hydrogen ions are buffered and the HCO_3^- accumulates (Fig 35–9). The red cells take up water, and the resultant increase in red cell size is the reason the hematocrit of venous blood is normally 3% greater than that of the arterial blood. In the lungs, the Cl^- moves out of the cells and they shrink.

Summary of Carbon Dioxide Transport

For convenience, the various fates of CO_2 in the plasma and red cells are summarized in Fig 35–10. The extent to which they increase the capacity of the

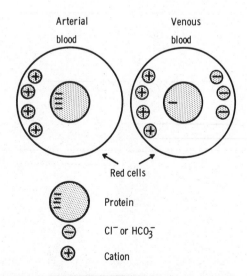

FIG 35–9. Simplified scheme showing why there are more osmotically active particles in the red cells in venous blood than in arterial blood. For explanation, see text.

FIG 35–10. Fate of CO$_2$ in the blood. (Modified and redrawn, with permission, from Kinney: Transport of carbon dioxide in blood. Anesthesiology 21:615, 1960.)

FIG 35–11. CO$_2$ dissociation curves. The arterial point (A) and the venous point (V) indicate the total CO$_2$ content found in arterial blood and venous blood of normal resting humans. (Modified and reproduced, with permission, from Kinney: Transport of carbon dioxide in blood. Anesthesiology 21:615, 1960.)

blood to carry CO_2 is indicated by the difference between the dissolved CO_2 line and the total CO_2 content lines in the "dissociation curves" for CO_2 shown in Fig 35−11.

Of the approximately 50 ml of CO_2 in each 100 ml of arterial blood (Table 35−1), 3 ml are dissolved, 3 ml are in carbamino compounds, and 44 ml are in HCO_3^-. In the tissues, 5 ml of CO_2 per 100 ml of blood are added; 0.5 ml stays in solution, 1 ml forms carbamino compounds, and 3.5 ml form HCO_3^-. The pH of the blood drops from 7.40 to 7.36. In the lungs, the processes are reversed and the 5 ml of CO_2 are discharged into the alveoli. In this fashion, 200 ml of CO_2 per minute at rest and much larger amounts during exercise are transported from the tissues to the lungs and excreted. It is worth noting that this amount of CO_2 is equivalent in 24 hours to over 12,500 mEq of H^+.

36 . . .

Regulation of Respiration

RESPIRATORY CENTER

Neural Control of Breathing

Spontaneous respiration is completely dependent, at least in adult mammals, upon the rhythmic discharge of the **respiratory center** in the medulla oblongata. If the efferent connections from the center to the respiratory muscles are interrupted, or if the center is destroyed, voluntary respiratory movements are still possible, but automatic breathing stops. Intermittent bursts of impulses in the nerves to the inspiratory muscles are responsible for the respiratory excursions at rest. Increases in ventilation are effected by increases in the rate and intensity of these discharges and by activation of the expiratory muscles after each inspiratory burst.

There is evidence that the motor neurons to the expiratory muscles are inhibited when those supplying the inspiratory muscles are active, and vice versa. The neural substrate for this **reciprocal innervation** is not known, but it might well be mediated, like the reciprocal innervation of the limb flexors and extensors (see Chapter 6), via collaterals from excitatory pathways that synapse on inhibitory interneurons, producing direct inhibition of the motor neurons supplying the antagonistic muscles when the motor neurons innervating the protagonists are excited.

Location of the Respiratory Center

The respiratory center is in the reticular formation of the caudal medulla. It is made up of an **inspiratory center**, containing neurons which when stimulated produce inspiration; and an overlapping **expiratory center**, containing neurons which when stimulated produce active expiration (Figs 36–1, 36–2).

Genesis of Rhythmicity

The mechanism that generates the rhythmic inspiratory discharges responsible for spontaneous respiration is still incompletely understood. In intact animals, the inspiratory neurons are characterized by bursts of activity interspersed with periods of quiescence 12–15 times/min. Unlike the inspiratory neurons, the expiratory neurons do not discharge spontaneously, but they can be excited via afferents which converge on them and the inspiratory neurons from many sources.

The discharge of the respiratory center is influenced by centers in the pons and by afferents in the vagus nerves from receptors in the lungs. The interactions of these components can be analyzed by evaluating the results of the experiments summarized diagramatically in Fig 36–3. Complete transection of the brain stem below the obex (section 4 in Fig 36–3) stops all respiration. When all the cranial nerves (including the vagi) are cut and the brain stem is transected above the pons (section 1 in Fig 36–3), regular breathing continues. However, when an additional transection is made in the inferior portion of the pons (section 2 in Fig 36–3), the inspiratory neurons discharge continuously and there is a sustained contraction of the inspiratory muscles. This arrest of respiration in inspiration is called **apneusis**. Its occurrence has led to the hypothesis that there is a feedback circuit which operates to make the discharge of the inspiratory neurons intermittent. According to this hypothesis, impulses in the efferent fibers from the inspiratory center to the spinal motor neurons relay via

FIG 36–1. **Respiratory center in the cat.** Cross-section of the medulla, showing overlapping and intermingling of points which on stimulation produce expiration with those which on stimulation produce inspiration. (Redrawn and reproduced, with permission, from Pitts: The differentiation of respiratory centers. Am J Physiol 134:192, 1941.)

490

FIG 36–2. Brain stem of the cat, showing areas concerned with respiration. *Left:* Dorsal view; *right,* ventral view. EC, expiratory center; IC, inspiratory center; CSA, chemosensitive areas. (Modified and reproduced, with permission, from Mitchell & Severinghaus: Cerebrospinal fluid and the regulation of respiration. Physiol Physicians 3, No. 3 [March], 1965.)

recurrent collaterals to cells in the rostral pons (the **pneumotaxic center**). Impulses in the cells of the pneumotaxic center in turn exert an inhibitory influence on the inspiratory center neurons.

When the brain stem is transected in the inferior portion of the pons and the vagus nerves are left intact, regular respiration continues. In an apneustic animal, stimulation of the proximal stump of one of the cut vagi produces, after a moderate latent period, a relatively prolonged inhibition of inspiratory neuron dis-

FIG 36–3. Changes in respiration produced by transecting the brain stem at various levels. The spirometer tracings on the right indicate the depth and rate of breathing. The numbers identify the level of transection (see text). SC, superior colliculus; IC, inferior colliculus; CP, cerebellar peduncle. (From Comroe: *The Physiology of Respiration,* 2nd ed. Copyright © by Year Book Medical Publications. In press, 1973. Used by permission.)

charge (Fig 36–4). There are stretch receptors in the lung parenchyma that relay to the medulla via afferents in the vagi, and rapid inflation of the lung inhibits inspiratory discharge (Hering-Breuer reflex; see below). Thus, stretching of the lungs during inspiration reflexly inhibits the inspiratory center, reinforcing the action of the pneumotaxic center in producing intermittency of inspiratory neuron discharge. This is why the depth of inspiration is increased after vagotomy in otherwise intact experimental animals, although breathing continues as long as the pneumotaxic center is intact.

More recently, it has been demonstrated that when all pontine tissue is separated from the medulla (section 3 in Fig 36–3) and respiration is observed for a sufficient length of time in vagotomized animals, apneusis is replaced by rhythmic gasping respirations. To explain this result, the hypothesis has been advanced that there is a group of tonically discharging neurons in the caudal portion of the pons (**apneustic center**) which drives the inspiratory neurons. According to this view, the periodic inhibition via vagal afferents and afferents from the pneumotaxic center is exerted on the apneustic center rather than directly on the inspiratory neurons.

The reappearance of rhythmic respiration when the pons is separated from the medulla in an apneustic animal suggests that the inspiratory neurons are capable of autonomous rhythmic discharge after all, and studies with microelectrodes also support this view. However, the physiologic significance of this discharge is uncertain.

When the activity of the inspiratory neurons is increased in intact animals, the rate and the depth of breathing are increased. The depth of respiration is increased because the lungs are stretched to a greater

Time 0.2 sec

FIG 36—4. Effect of vagal stimulation (between arrows) on discharge rate in phrenic nerve fibers in an "isolated inspiratory center preparation." The cat had been prepared by cutting both vagi and transecting the medulla at the caudal border of the pons, thus cutting off the pneumotaxic center. In *A*, the continuous discharge of the inspiratory neurons is shown. In *B* and *C*, stimulation of the proximal stump of one vagus produces, after a considerable latent period, inhibition of inspiratory discharge. The animal exhales when the inspiratory discharge stops, as is shown by the record of respiratory excursions (upper line in *B* and *C*; inspiration upward). (Reproduced, with permission, from Pitts: The function of components of the respiratory complex. J Neurophysiol 5:407, 1942.)

degree before the amount of vagal and pneumotaxic center inhibitory activity is sufficient to overcome the more intense inspiratory neuron discharge. The respiratory rate is increased because the after-discharge in the vagal and pneumotaxic afferents is rapidly overcome.

REGULATION OF RESPIRATORY CENTER ACTIVITY

A rise in the P_{CO_2} or H^+ concentration of arterial blood or a drop in its P_{O_2} increases the level of respiratory center activity, and changes in the opposite direction have a slight inhibitory effect. The effects of variations in blood chemistry on ventilation are mediated via respiratory **chemoreceptors**—receptor cells in the medulla and the carotid and aortic bodies sensitive to changes in the chemistry of the blood which initiate impulses that stimulate the respiratory center. Superimposed on this basic **chemical control of respiration,** other afferents provide the "fine adjustments" that affect breathing in particular situations (Fig 36—5).

CHEMICAL CONTROL OF BREATHING

The chemical regulatory mechanisms adjust ventilation in such a way that the alveolar P_{CO_2} is normally held constant, the effects of excess H^+ in the blood are combated, and the P_{O_2} is raised when it falls to a potentially dangerous level. The respiratory minute volume is proportionate to the metabolic rate, but the link between metabolism and ventilation is CO_2, not O_2. The receptors in the carotid and aortic bodies are stimulated by a rise in the P_{CO_2} or H^+ concentration of arterial blood or a decline in its P_{O_2}. After denervation of these chemoreceptors, the response to a drop in P_{O_2} is abolished; the predominant effect of hypoxia after denervation of the carotid and aortic bodies is a direct depression of the respiratory center. The response to changes in arterial blood H^+ concentration in the pH 7.3—7.5 range is also abolished, although larger changes do exert some effect. The response to changes in arterial P_{CO_2}, on

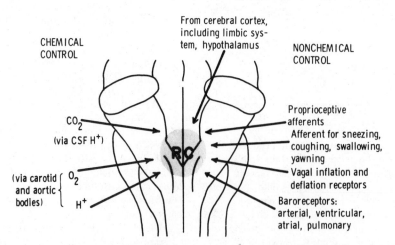

CHEMICAL CONTROL

From cerebral cortex, including limbic system, hypothalamus

NONCHEMICAL CONTROL

CO_2
(via CSF H^+)

(via carotid and aortic bodies) { O_2

H^+

RC

Proprioceptive afferents
Afferent for sneezing, coughing, swallowing, yawning
Vagal inflation and deflation receptors
Baroreceptors: arterial, ventricular, atrial, pulmonary

FIG 36—5. Diagram of chemical and nonchemical stimuli which converge on the respiratory center and regulate respiration.

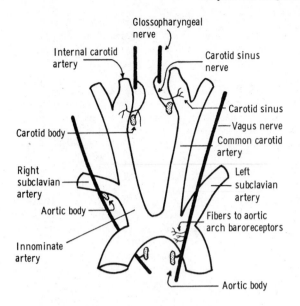

FIG 36–6. Diagram showing location and innervation of carotid and aortic bodies.

is reason to believe that the chemoreceptors that sense O_2 tension are these nerve endings. The staining reactions of glomus tissue suggest that both acetylcholine and catecholamines are present, but the functional role of these agents, if any, is unknown. Outside the capsule of each body, the nerve fibers acquire a myelin sheath; however, they are only 2–5 μm in diameter and conduct at the relatively slow rate of 7–12 m/sec. Afferents from the carotid bodies ascend to the medulla via the carotid sinus and glossopharyngeal nerves, and fibers from the aortic bodies ascend in the vagi. Studies in which one carotid body has been isolated and perfused while recordings are being taken from its afferent nerve fibers show that there is a graded increase in impulse traffic in these afferent fibers as the P_{O_2} of the perfusing blood is lowered or the P_{CO_2} raised (Fig 36–7). There is evidence for a sympathetic efferent nerve supply to the carotid body which increases its excitability, and an efferent component in the sinus nerve which seems to decrease its excitability.

The blood flow of each 2 mg carotid body is about 0.04 ml/min, or 2000 ml/100 g of tissue per minute, compared with a blood flow per 100 g/min of 54 ml in the brain and 420 ml in the kidney (Table 32–1). Because the blood flow per unit of tissue is so enormous, the O_2 needs of the cells can be met largely by dissolved O_2 alone. Therefore, the receptors are not stimulated in conditions such as anemia and carbon monoxide poisoning, in which the amount of dissolved O_2 in the blood reaching the receptors is generally normal even though the combined O_2 in the blood is markedly decreased. The receptors are stimulated when the arterial P_{O_2} is low or when, because of vascular stasis, the amount of O_2 delivered to the receptors per unit of time is decreased. Powerful stimulation is also produced by drugs such as cyanide, which prevent O_2 utilization at the tissue level. In sufficient doses nicotine and lobeline activate the chemo-

the other hand, is affected only slightly; it is reduced no more than 20%.

Carotid & Aortic Bodies

There is a carotid body near the carotid bifurcation on each side, and there are usually 2 or more aortic bodies near the arch of the aorta (Fig 36–6). Each carotid and aortic body, or **glomus**, contains islands of 2 types of cells, surrounded by sinusoidal vessels. The cell types have received various names, but since their function is uncertain it seems wise to simply refer to them as type I and type II cells. The type II cells surround the type I cells, and unmyelinated nerve endings are found at intervals between the two. There

FIG 36–7. Changes in "impulse traffic" in the carotid sinus nerve of the cat, produced by changes in arterial P_{CO_2} *(A)* and P_{O_2} *(B)*. (After Witzleb, Bartels, & associates. Reproduced, with permission, from Lambertsen, in: *Medical Physiology,* 11th ed. Bard P [editor]. Mosby, 1961.)

receptors.

Because of their anatomic location, the aortic bodies have not been studied in as great detail as the carotid bodies. Their responses are probably similar but of less magnitude. In humans in whom both carotid bodies have been removed but the aortic bodies have been left intact, the responses are essentially the same as those following denervation of both carotid and aortic bodies in animals; there is little change in ventilation at rest, but the ventilatory response to hypoxia is lost and there is a 30% reduction in the ventilatory response to CO_2. The humans who were studied had had their carotid bodies removed in an effort to relieve severe asthma, but it now appears that bilateral carotid body resection is of little benefit in this disease.

Chemoreceptors in the Brain Stem

The chemoreceptors that mediate the hyperventilation produced by increases in arterial P_{CO_2} after the carotid and aortic bodies are denervated are located near the respiratory center itself. It has been suggested that the chemical stimuli act directly on the inspiratory center neurons, but it now appears that there are separate receptor cells. The response to CO_2, for example, is depressed during anesthesia and natural sleep, but the response to hypoxia is unchanged. This experimental observation is difficult to explain if CO_2 acts directly on the inspiratory neurons.

The medullary chemoreceptors are now believed to be located on the ventral surface of the brain stem (Fig 36–2), and to monitor the H^+ concentration of the cerebrospinal fluid or, possibly, the brain interstitial fluid. CO_2 readily penetrates membranes, including the blood-brain and blood-CSF barriers, while H^+ and HCO_3^- penetrate slowly. The CO_2 that enters the brain and CSF is promptly hydrated. The H_2CO_3 dissociates, so that the local H^+ concentration rises. The spinal fluid H^+ concentration parallels the arterial P_{CO_2}. Experimentally produced changes in the P_{CO_2} of spinal fluid have minor, variable effects on respiration as long as the H^+ is held constant, but any increase in spinal fluid H^+ concentration stimulates respiration. The magnitude of the stimulation is proportionate to the rise in H^+. Thus, it seems likely that the effects of CO_2 on respiration are mainly due to its movement into the spinal fluid, where it increases the H^+ concentration and stimulates receptors sensitive to H^+.

The effects of CO_2 on ventilation cannot be explained solely on the basis of changes in arterial H^+ concentration produced by the CO_2 because, after denervation of the carotid and aortic bodies, pH changes in the 7.3–7.5 range have no effect on ventilation.

Pulmonary & Myocardial "Chemoreceptors"

Bradycardia and hypotension produced by injections of veratridine and nicotine into the coronary circulation (Bezold-Jarisch reflex) and the pulmonary circulation are due to stimulation of "chemoreceptors" of some type in the coronary and pulmonary vessels

(see Chapter 31). Such injections also produce brief periods of respiratory arrest (**apnea**), but the effects on respiration of stimuli from these receptors in physiologic situations are probably insignificant.

Ventilatory Responses to Changes in Acid-Base Balance

In metabolic acidosis due, for example, to the accumulation of the acid ketone bodies in the circulation in diabetes mellitus, there is pronounced respiratory stimulation (Kussmaul breathing; see Chapter 19). The hyperventilation decreases alveolar P_{CO_2} ("blows off CO_2") and thus produces a compensatory fall in blood H^+ concentration (see Chapter 40). Conversely, in metabolic alkalosis due, for example, to protracted vomiting with loss of HCl from the body, ventilation is depressed and the arterial P_{CO_2} rises, raising the H^+ concentration toward normal (see Chapter 40). If there is an increase in ventilation that is not secondary to a rise in arterial H^+ concentration, the drop in P_{CO_2} lowers the H^+ concentration below normal (**respiratory alkalosis**); conversely, hypoventilation that is not secondary to a fall in plasma H^+ concentration causes **respiratory acidosis**.

Ventilatory Responses to CO_2

When there is a rise in arterial P_{CO_2} due to increased tissue metabolism, ventilation is stimulated and the rate of pulmonary excretion of CO_2 is increased until the arterial P_{CO_2} falls to normal, shutting off the stimulus. The operation of this feedback mechanism keeps CO_2 excretion and production in balance.

When a gas mixture containing CO_2 is inhaled, the alveolar P_{CO_2} rises, elevating the arterial P_{CO_2} and stimulating ventilation as soon as the blood which contains more CO_2 reaches the medulla. CO_2 elimination is increased and the alveolar P_{CO_2} drops toward normal. This is why relatively large increments in the P_{CO_2} of inspired air (eg, 15 mm Hg) produce relatively slight increments in alveolar P_{CO_2} (eg, 3 mm Hg). However, the P_{CO_2} does not drop to normal, and a new equilibrium is reached at which the alveolar P_{CO_2} is slightly elevated and the hyperventilation persists as long as CO_2 is inhaled. The essentially linear relationship between respiratory minute volume and the alveolar P_{CO_2} is shown in Fig 36–8.

There is, of course, an upper limit to this linearity. When the P_{CO_2} of the inspired gas is close to the alveolar P_{CO_2}, elimination of CO_2 becomes difficult. When the CO_2 content of the inspired gas is more than 7%, the alveolar and arterial P_{CO_2} begin to rise abruptly in spite of hyperventilation. The resultant accumulation of CO_2 in the body (**hypercapnia**) depresses the CNS, including the respiratory center, and produces headache, confusion, and, eventually, coma (**CO_2 narcosis**).

Ventilatory Response to Oxygen Lack

When the O_2 content of the inspired air is decreased, there is an increase in respiratory minute vol-

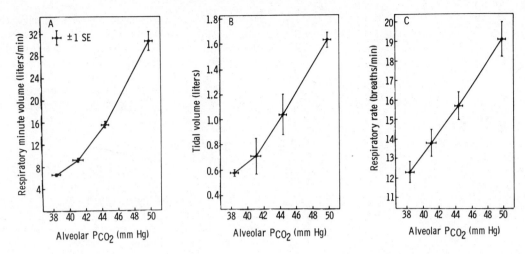

FIG 36–8. Responses of normal subjects to inhaling 0 and approximately 2, 4, and 6% CO$_2$. Note that the increase in respiratory minute volume *(A)* is due to an increase in both the depth *(B)* and rate *(C)* of respiration. (Reproduced, with permission, from Lambertsen, in: *Medical Physiology*, 12th ed. Mountcastle VB [editor]. Mosby, 1968.)

ume. The stimulation is slight when the P$_{O_2}$ of the inspired air is more than 60 mm Hg, and marked stimulation of respiration occurs only at lower P$_{O_2}$ values (Fig 36–9). However, any decline in arterial P$_{O_2}$ below 100 mm Hg produces increased discharge in the nerves from the carotid and aortic chemoreceptors. There are 2 reasons why in normal individuals this increase in impulse traffic does not increase ventilation to any extent until the P$_{O_2}$ is less than 60 mm Hg. Because Hb is a weaker acid than HbO$_2$ (see Chapter 35), there is a slight decrease in the H$^+$ concentration of arterial blood when the arterial P$_{O_2}$ falls and hemoglobin becomes less saturated with O$_2$. The fall in H$^+$ concentration tends to inhibit respiration. In addition, any increase in ventilation that does occur lowers the alveolar P$_{CO_2}$, and this also tends to inhibit respiration. Therefore, the stimulatory effects of hypoxia on ventilation are not clearly manifest until they become strong enough to override the counterbalancing inhibitory effects of a decline in arterial H$^+$ concentration and P$_{CO_2}$.

The effects on ventilation of decreasing the alveolar P$_{O_2}$ while holding the alveolar P$_{CO_2}$ constant are shown in Fig 36–10. When the alveolar P$_{CO_2}$ is stabilized at a level 2–3 mm Hg above normal, there is an inverse relationship between ventilation and the alveolar P$_{O_2}$ even in the 90–110 mm Hg range; but when the alveolar P$_{CO_2}$ is fixed at lower than normal values there is no stimulation of ventilation by hypoxia until the alveolar P$_{O_2}$ falls below 60 mm Hg.

Effects of Hypoxia on the CO$_2$ Response Curve

When the converse experiment is performed, ie, when the alveolar P$_{O_2}$ is held constant while the response to varying amounts of inspired CO$_2$ is tested, it is found that the slope of the CO$_2$ response curve increases when the alveolar P$_{O_2}$ is decreased (Fig

FIG 36–9. *Above:* Average respiratory minute volume during the first half hour of exposure to gases containing various amounts of O$_2$. The horizontal line in each case indicates the mean; the vertical bar indicates one standard deviation. *Below:* Alveolar P$_{O_2}$ and P$_{CO_2}$ values when breathing air at various barometric pressures. The 2 graphs are aligned so that the P$_{O_2}$s of the inspired gas mixtures in the upper graph correspond to the P$_{O_2}$s at the various barometric pressures in the lower graph. (Data from various authors, compiled by RH Kellogg.)

FIG 36–10. Ventilation at various alveolar P_{O_2} values in a subject in whom the alveolar P_{CO_2} was held constant at 48.7, 43.7, and 35.8 mm Hg and, in one experiment, varied as shown by the individual values along this curve *(R)*. (Slightly modified and reproduced, with permission, from Loeschke & Gertz: Einfluss des O_2-Druckes in der Einatmungsluft auf die Atemtätigkeit des Menschen, geprüft unter Konstanthaltung des alveolaren CO_2-Druckes. Arch Ges Physiol Pflügers 267:460, 1958.)

Alveolar P_{CO_2} (mm Hg)

FIG 36–11. Fan of lines representing linear segments of CO_2 response curves at the alveolar P_{O_2} values indicated by the small figures near each line. *Experiment 1:* Control. *Experiment 2:* Metabolic acidosis. (Redrawn and reproduced, with permission, from Cunningham & others: The effect of maintained ammonium chloride acidosis on the relation between pulmonary ventilation and alveolar oxygen and carbon dioxide in man. Quart J Exper Physiol 46:323, 1961.)

36–11). In other words, hypoxia makes the individual more sensitive to increases in arterial P_{CO_2}. However, the alveolar P_{CO_2} level at which the curves in Fig 36–11 intersect is unaffected. In the normal individual, this threshold value is just below the normal alveolar P_{CO_2}, indicating that normally there is a very slight but definite "CO_2 drive" of the respiratory center.

Effect of H^+ on the CO_2 Response

The stimulatory effects of H^+ and CO_2 on respiration appear to be additive and not, like those of CO_2 and O_2, complexly interrelated. Fig 36–11 shows this additive effect; when the subject became acidotic by ingesting $NH_4 Cl$, his CO_2 response curves "shifted to the left" without a change in slope. In other words, the same amount of respiratory stimulation was produced by lower arterial P_{CO_2} levels. It has been calculated that the CO_2 response curve shifts 0.8 mm Hg to the left for each millimicromol rise in arterial H^+. About 40% of the ventilatory response to CO_2 is removed if the increase in arterial H^+ produced by CO_2 is prevented. As noted above, the remaining 60% is probably due to the effect of CO_2 on spinal fluid or brain interstitial fluid H^+ concentration.

Breath Holding

Respiration can be voluntarily inhibited for some time, but eventually the voluntary control is overridden. The point at which breathing can no longer be voluntarily inhibited is called the **breaking point**. Breaking is due to the rise in arterial P_{CO_2} and the fall in P_{O_2}. If a subject breathes 100% O_2 before he holds his breath, his alveolar P_{O_2} is initially elevated, and he can hold his breath for a longer period. However, if he hyperventilates room air before holding his breath, he can also inhibit breathing for a longer period because he blows off CO_2 and his arterial P_{CO_2} is lower at the start. Reflex or mechanical factors appear to influence the breaking point, since subjects who hold their breaths as long as possible and then breathe a gas mixture low in O_2 and high in CO_2 can hold their breath for an additional 20 sec or more. Psychic factors also play a role, and subjects can hold their breath longer when they are told their performance is very good than when they are not.

NONCHEMICAL INFLUENCES ON RESPIRATION

Afferents From "Higher Centers"

There are undoubtedly excitatory and inhibitory afferents from the neocortex to the motor neurons innervating the respiratory muscles, since even though breathing is not usually a conscious event, both inspiration and expiration are under voluntary control. Pain and emotional stimuli affect respiration, so there must also be afferents from the limbic system and hypothalamus.

The voluntary and the automatic control of respiration are separate, and automatic control can be disrupted without loss of voluntary control. The clinical condition that results has been called **Ondine's curse.** In German legend, Ondine was a water nymph who punished an unfaithful lover by casting a curse upon him which took away all his automatic functions. In this state, he could stay alive only by staying awake and remembering to breathe. He eventually fell asleep from sheer exhaustion and his respiration stopped. Patients with this intriguing condition generally have disease processes which compress the medulla, or bulbar poliomyelitis. The condition has also been produced, however, in patients who have been subjected to bilateral ventrolateral cervical cordotomy for pain (see Chapter 7). The fact that automatic respiration ceases in such patients while voluntary respiration remains intact indicates that the pathways for the former descend in the ventral quadrant of the cord while the pathways for the latter descend more dorsally, presumably in the corticospinal tracts.

Afferents From Proprioceptors

Carefully controlled experiments have shown that active and passive movements of joints stimulate respiration, presumably because impulses in afferent pathways from proprioceptors in muscles, tendons, and joints stimulate the respiratory center. This effect probably helps increase ventilation during exercise.

Responses to Irritation of the Air Passages

Sneezing and coughing are reflex responses to irritation of receptors in the mucosa of the large respiratory passages (see Chapter 14). Irritation of the walls of the trachea or large bronchi produces coughing, which begins with a deep inspiration followed by forced expiration against a closed glottis. The glottis is then suddenly opened, producing an explosive outflow of air at velocities up to 600 miles per hour. Sneezing is a similar expiratory effort with a continuously open glottis. These reflexes help expel irritants and keep airway clear.

Other Pulmonary Receptors

The vagally mediated inhibition of inspiration produced by inflation of the lung has been mentioned above. The response is due to stimulation of stretch receptors located in the smooth muscle of the airways. Pulmonary deflation receptors which trigger inflation have also been described, and the expiratory and inspiratory reflex responses to pulmonary inflation and deflation, respectively, have been known as the **Hering-Breuer reflexes.** However, the deflation receptors respond better to pulmonary congestion and embolization, producing shallow, rapid breathing, and they have come to be called **type J receptors** instead, because of their juxtacapillary location. There are also **lung irritant receptors** located between the epithelial cells in the bronchi and bronchioles. When stimulated, they initiate hyperventilation and bronchoconstriction, but their function in normal breathing is not known.

Respiratory Components of Other Visceral Reflexes

The respiratory adjustments during vomiting, swallowing, and gagging are discussed in Chapters 14 and 26. Inhibition of respiration and closure of the glottis during these activities not only prevent the aspiration of food or vomitus into the trachea but, in the case of vomiting, fix the chest so that contraction of the abdominal muscles increases the intra-abdominal pressure. Similar glottic closure and inhibition of respiration occur during voluntary and involuntary straining.

Hiccup is a spasmodic contraction of the diaphragm which produces an inspiration during which the glottis suddenly closes. The glottic closure is responsible for the characteristic sensation and sound. Yawning is a peculiar "infectious" respiratory act the physiologic basis and significance of which are uncertain. However, underventilated alveoli have a tendency to collapse and it has been suggested that the deep inspiration and stretching open up alveoli and prevent the development of atelectasis.

Respiratory Effects of Baroreceptor Stimulation

Afferent fibers from the baroreceptors in the carotid sinuses, aortic arch, atria, and ventricles relay to the respiratory center as well as the vasomotor and cardioinhibitory centers. Impulses in them inhibit respiration, but the inhibitory effect is slight and of little physiologic importance. The hyperventilation in shock is due to chemoreceptor stimulation caused by acidosis and hypoxia secondary to local stagnation of blood flow, and is not baroreceptor mediated. The activity of the inspiratory neurons affects the blood pressure and heart rate (see Chapters 28 and 31), and activity in the vasomotor center and the cardiac centers in the medulla may have minor effects on respiration.

37...
Respiratory Adjustments in Health & Disease

EFFECTS OF EXERCISE

Many cardiovascular respiratory mechanisms must operate in an integrated fashion if the O_2 needs of the active tissues are to be met and the extra CO_2 and heat removed from the body during exercise. There is an increase in ventilation that provides extra O_2, eliminates some of the heat, and excretes extra CO_2; there are circulatory changes that increase tissue blood flow while maintaining an adequate circulation in the rest of the body (see Chapter 33); and there is an increase in the extraction of O_2 from the blood in the tissues.

Changes in Ventilation

During exercise, the amount of O_2 entering the blood in the lungs is increased because the amount of O_2 added to each unit of blood and the pulmonary blood flow per minute is increased. The P_{O_2} of blood flowing into the pulmonary capillaries falls from 40 mm Hg to 25 mm Hg or less, so that the alveolar-capillary P_{O_2} gradient is increased and more O_2 enters the blood. Blood flow per minute is increased from 5.5 liters/min to as much as 20–35 liters/min. The total amount of O_2 entering the blood therefore increases from 250 ml/min at rest to values as high as 4000 ml/min. The amount of CO_2 removed from each unit of blood is increased, and CO_2 excretion increases from 200 ml/min to as much as 8000 ml/min. The increase in O_2 uptake is proportionate to work load up to a maximum. Above this maximum, O_2 consumption levels off and blood lactic acid rises precipitously (Fig 37–1). The lactic acid comes from muscles in which aerobic resynthesis of energy stores cannot keep pace with their utilization and an **oxygen debt** is being incurred (see Chapter 3).

There is an abrupt increase in ventilation with the onset of exercise, followed by a further, more gradual increase (Fig 37–2). Similarly, there is an abrupt decrease when exercise ceases, followed by a more gradual decline to preexercise values. The abrupt increase is presumably due to psychic stimuli and afferent impulses from proprioceptors in muscles, tendons, and joints. The more gradual increase is presumably humoral. The increase in ventilation is proportionate to the increase in O_2 consumption (Fig 37–3), but the mechanisms responsible for the stimulation of respiration are still the subject of much debate. Arterial P_{CO_2} and P_{O_2} stay constant with moderate exercise, and the former actually falls while the latter rises with severe exercise as a result of the increase in ventilation. Arterial pH is constant with moderate exercise, and only falls when the exercise is severe. The increase in body temperature may play a role. In addition, it

FIG 37–1. Relation between work load, blood lactic acid, and O_2 uptake. I–VI, increasing work loads produced by increasing the speed and grade of a treadmill on which the subjects worked. (Reproduced, with permission, from Mitchell & Blomqvist: Maximal oxygen uptake. New England J Med 284:1018, 1971.)

FIG 37–2. Changes in ventilation during exercise. (Reproduced, with permission, from Dejours, in: *Regulation of Human Respiration.* Cunningham DJC, Lloyd BB [editors]. Blackwell, 1963.)

FIG 37–3. Relation of ventilation to O_2 consumption during exercise in man. The solid line is the mean and the dotted lines the range of many determinations from different investigators. STPD, BTPS: See Table 34–1. (Redrawn and reproduced from: *Handbook of Respiratory Data in Aviation.* Committee on Aviation Medicine, 1944.)

may be that the sensitivity of the respiratory center to CO_2 is increased or that the respiratory fluctuations in arterial P_{CO_2} increase so that, even though the mean arterial P_{CO_2} does not rise, it is CO_2 that is responsible for the increase in ventilation. O_2 also seems to play some role despite the lack of a decrease in arterial P_{O_2}, since during the performance of a given amount of work, the increase in ventilation while breathing 100% O_2 is 10–20% less than the increase while breathing air (Fig 37–4). It currently appears that a number of different factors combine to produce the increase in ventilation seen during exercise.

FIG 37–4. Effect of 100% O_2 on ventilation during work at various levels on the bicycle ergometer. (Reproduced, with permission, from Astrand: The respiratory activity in man exposed to prolonged hypoxia. Acta physiol scandinav 30:343, 1954.)

The respiratory rate after exercise does not reach basal levels until the O_2 debt is repaid. This may take as long as 90 minutes. The stimulus to ventilation is not the arterial P_{CO_2}, which is normal or low, or the arterial P_{O_2}, which is normal or high, but the elevated arterial H^+ concentration due to the lactic acidemia. The magnitude of the O_2 debt is the amount by which O_2 consumption exceeds basal consumption from the end of exertion until the O_2 consumption has returned to preexercise vasal levels. Buffering of the lactic acid by the carbonic acid-bicarbonate system during exercise results in the formation of extra CO_2, and the RQ rises, values reaching 1.5–2.0. After exertion, while the O_2 debt is being repaid, the RQ falls to 0.5 or less.

Changes in the Tissues

During exercise, the contracting muscles use more O_2 and the tissue P_{O_2} falls nearly to zero. More O_2 diffuses from the blood, the blood P_{O_2} drops, and more O_2 is removed from hemoglobin. Because the capillary bed is dilated and many previously closed capillaries are open, the mean distance from the blood to the tissue cells is greatly decreased; this facilitates the movement of O_2 from blood to cells. The O_2 hemoglobin dissociation curve is steep in the P_{O_2} range below 60 mm Hg, and a relatively large amount of O_2 is supplied for each mm Hg drop in P_{O_2} (Fig 35–2). Additional O_2 is supplied because, as a result of the accumulation of CO_2 and the rise in temperature in active tissues—and perhaps because of a rise in red blood cell 2,3-DPG—the dissociation curve shifts to the right (Fig 35–3). The net effect is a 3-fold increase in O_2 extraction from each unit of blood (Table 37–1). Since this increase is accompanied by a 30-fold or greater increase in blood flow, it permits the metabolic rate of muscle to rise as much as 100-fold during exercise (see Chapter 3).

Fatigue

Fatigue is a poorly understood phenomenon to which, undoubtedly, many factors contribute. The subjective hardness or "heaviness" of exercise correlates with the rate of O_2 consumption, not with the actual work performed in kg-m/min. Barrages of impulses in afferents from proprioceptors in muscles are said to make one feel "tired." The effects of the acidosis on the brain may contribute to the sensation of fatigue. Sustained muscle contractions are painful because the muscle becomes ischemic, and a substance

TABLE 37–1. Oxygen in venous blood from resting and exercising muscle.

	Rest	Strenuous Exercise
P_{O_2} (mm Hg)	40	15
Percentage saturation of Hb	70	16
O_2 content (ml/100 ml)	15	3
O_2 extracted (ml/100 ml blood)	5	17

which stimulates pain endings accumulates ("P substance"; see Chapter 7), but intermittent contractions are not painful because the P substance is washed away. Muscle stiffness may be due in part to the accumulation of interstitial fluid in the muscles during exertion.

Heat dissipation during exercise is discussed in Chapter 33 and summarized in Fig 33–4.

HYPOXIA

Hypoxia is O_2 deficiency at the tissue level. It is a more correct term than **anoxia**, there rarely being no O_2 at all left in the tissues, but the term anoxia is still widely used.

Traditionally, hypoxia has been divided into 4 types. Numerous other classifications are currently in use, but the 4-type system still has considerable utility if the definitions of the terms are kept clearly in mind. The 4 categories are as follows: (1) **hypoxic hypoxia (anoxic anoxia),** in which the P_{O_2} of the arterial blood is reduced; (2) **anemic hypoxia,** in which the arterial P_{O_2} is normal but the amount of hemoglobin available to carry O_2 is reduced; (3) **stagnant,** or **ischemic hypoxia,** in which the blood flow to a tissue is so low that adequate O_2 is not delivered to it despite a normal P_{O_2} and hemoglobin concentration; and (4) **histotoxic hypoxia,** in which the amount of O_2 delivered to a tissue is adequate but, due to the action of a toxic agent, the tissue cells cannot make use of the O_2 supplied to them.

Effects of Hypoxia

The effects of stagnant hypoxia depend upon the tissue affected. In hypoxic hypoxia and the other generalized forms of hypoxia, the brain is affected first. A sudden drop in the inspired P_{O_2} to less than 20 mm Hg, which occurs, for example, when cabin pressure is suddenly lost in a plane flying over 16,000 m, causes loss of consciousness in about 20 sec and death in 4–5 minutes. Less severe hypoxia causes a variety of mental aberrations not unlike those produced by alcohol: impaired judgment, drowsiness, dulled pain sensibility, excitement, disorientation, loss of time sense, and headache. Other symptoms include anorexia, nausea, vomiting, tachycardia, and, when the hypoxia is severe, hypertension. Ventilation is increased in proportion to the severity of the hypoxia of the aortic and carotid chemoreceptor cells.

Respiratory Stimulation

Dyspnea is by definition labored breathing in which the subject is conscious of shortness of breath; **hyperpnea** is the general term for an increase in the rate or depth of breathing regardless of the patient's subjective sensations. **Tachypnea** is rapid, shallow breathing. In general, a normal individual is not conscious of his respiration until ventilation is doubled,

and breathing is not uncomfortable (ie, the **dyspnea point** is not reached) until ventilation is tripled or quadrupled. Whether or not a given level of ventilation is uncomfortable also depends upon the respiratory reserve. This factor is taken into account in the **dyspneic index,** which measures the fraction of the respiratory capacity that is not being used at a given respiratory minute volume.

$$\text{Dyspneic Index} = \% \text{ Breathing Reserve} = \frac{\text{MVV} - \text{RMV}}{\text{MVV}} \times 100$$

MVV = Maximal voluntary ventilation, liters/min (see Chapter 34)
RMV = Respiratory minute volume, liters/min, in state under consideration

When the dyspneic index is less than about 0.7, dyspnea is usually present. A third factor is the effort involved in moving the air in and out of the lungs (the work of breathing). In asthma, for example, the bronchi are constricted, especially during expiration, and breathing against this increased airway resistance is uncomfortable work. Additional factors producing dyspnea may be increased discharge in vagal afferents from lung irritant receptors and increased discharge in the γ efferents to the respiratory muscles.

Cyanosis

Reduced hemoglobin has a dark color, and a dusky bluish discoloration of the tissues called **cyanosis** appears when the reduced hemoglobin concentration of the blood in the capillaries is more than 5 g/100 ml. Cyanosis is most easily seen in the nail beds and mucous membranes and in the ear lobes, lips, and fingers, where the skin is thin. Its occurrence depends upon the total amount of hemoglobin in the blood, the degree of hemoglobin unsaturation, and the state of the capillary circulation.

One might think that cyanosis would be more marked when the cutaneous vessels were dilated. However, when there is cutaneous arteriolar and venous constriction, blood flow through the capillaries is very slow and more O_2 is removed from the hemoglobin. This is why moderate cold causes cyanosis in exposed areas even in normal individuals. In very cold weather cyanosis does not develop because the drop in skin temperature inhibits the dissociation of oxyhemoglobin and the O_2 consumption of the cold tissues is decreased. Cyanosis does not occur in anemic hypoxia when the total hemoglobin content is low; in carbon monoxide poisoning, because the color of reduced hemoglobin is obscured by the cherry-red color of carbonmonoxyhemoglobin (see below); nor in histotoxic hypoxia, because the blood gas content is normal. A discoloration of the skin and mucous membranes similar to cyanosis is produced by high circulating levels of methemoglobin (see Chapter 27).

HYPOXIC HYPOXIA

Hypoxic hypoxia is a problem in normal individuals at high altitudes and is a complication of pneumonia and a number of other common diseases (Table 37–2).

Effects of Decreased Barometric Pressure

The composition of air stays the same, but the total barometric pressure falls with increasing altitude (Fig 37–5). Therefore, the P_{O_2} also falls. At 3000 m (approximately 10,000 feet) above sea level, the alveolar P_{O_2} is about 60 mm Hg and there is enough hypoxic stimulation of the chemoreceptors to definitely increase ventilation. As one ascends higher, the alveolar P_{O_2} falls less rapidly and the alveolar P_{CO_2} declines somewhat because of the hyperventilation. The resulting fall in arterial P_{CO_2} produces respiratory alkalosis.

Hypoxic Symptoms Breathing Air

There are a number of compensatory mechanisms that operate over a period of time to increase altitude tolerance (**acclimatization**), but in unacclimatized subjects mental symptoms such as irritability appear at about 3700 m. At 5500 m, the hypoxic symptoms are severe; and at altitudes above 6100 m (20,000 ft), consciousness is usually lost (Fig 37–6).

TABLE 37–2. Causes of hypoxic hypoxia.

1. Decreased P_{O_2} in inspired air (high altitude, breathing O_2-poor gas mixture)
2. Hypoventilation
   Airway obstruction (foreign body, etc)
   Paralysis of respiratory muscles (poliomyelitis)
   Skeletal deformities (kyphoscoliosis)
   Depression of respiratory center (morphine, etc)
   Shallow breathing (pain on inspiration due to pleurisy)
   Increased airway resistance (asthma, emphysema)
   Increased pulmonary tissue resistance (pulmonary sarcoidosis)
   Decreased elastic recoil (emphysema)
   Large pneumothorax
3. Alveolar-capillary diffusion block
   Decrease in total area of normal alveolar membrane (pneumonia, pulmonary congestion)
   Fibrosis of alveolar or pulmonary capillary walls (pulmonary fibrosis, berylliosis)
4. Abnormal ventilation-perfusion ratio or ventilation-perfusion imbalance
   Areas of underventilation and overperfusion of alveoli (emphysema)
   Perfusion of completely unventilated alveoli (emphysema, atelectasis)
   Shunting of venous blood into the arterial circulation, bypassing the lungs (cyanotic congenital heart disease)

FIG 37–5. Composition of alveolar air breathing air (0–6100 m) and 100% O_2 (6100–13,700 m). The minimal alveolar P_{O_2} that an unacclimatized subject can tolerate without loss of consciousness is about 35–40 mm Hg. Note that with increasing altitude, the alveolar P_{CO_2} drops because of the hyperventilation due to hypoxic stimulation of the carotid and aortic chemoreceptors. The fall in barometric pressure with increasing altitude is not linear because air is compressible.

FIG 37–6. Acute effects of hypoxia at various arterial O₂ saturation levels. (Modified and reproduced, with permission, from Pace, in: *The Air We Breathe: A Study of Man and His Environment.* Farber SM, Wilson RHL [editors]. Thomas, 1961.)

Hypoxic Symptoms Breathing Oxygen

The total atmospheric pressure becomes the limiting factor in altitude tolerance when breathing 100% O_2. The partial pressure of water vapor in the alveolar air is constant at 47 mm Hg, and that of CO_2 is normally 40 mm Hg, so that the lowest barometric pressure at which a normal alveolar P_{O_2} of 100 mm Hg is possible is 187 mm Hg, the pressure at about 10,400 m (34,000 ft). At greater altitudes, the increased ventilation due to the decline in alveolar P_{O_2} lowers the alveolar P_{CO_2} somewhat, but the maximal alveolar P_{O_2} that can be attained breathing 100% O_2 at the ambient barometric pressure of 100 mm Hg at 13,700 m is about 40 mm Hg. At about 14,000 m, consciousness is lost in spite of the administration of 100% O_2 (Fig 37–7). It is possible, however, to create an artificial atmosphere around an individual; in a pressurized suit or cabin supplied with O_2 and a system to remove CO_2, ascent to any altitude is possible.

At 19,200 m the barometric pressure is 47 mm Hg, and at or below this pressure the body fluids boil at body temperature. The point is largely academic, however, because any individual exposed to such a low pressure would be dead of hypoxia before the bubbles of steam could kill him.

Delayed Effects of High Altitude

Many individuals, when they first arrive at a high altitude, develop transient "mountain sickness." This syndrome develops 8–24 hours after arrival at altitude and lasts 4–8 days. It is characterized by headache, irritability, insomnia, breathlessness, and nausea and vomiting. Its cause is unknown, but the symptoms are reduced or prevented if alkalosis is reduced by proce-

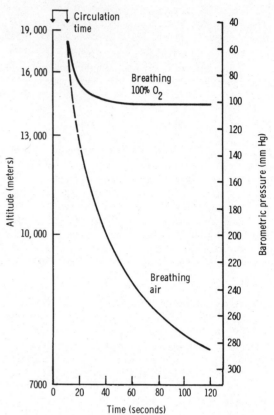

FIG 37–7. Duration of useful consciousness upon sudden exposure to the ambient pressure at various altitudes. Note that 10 sec is the approximate lung-to-brain circulation time. (After Benzinger & others, from: *Flight Surgeon's Manual,* USAF Manual No. 160–5, 1954.)

dures such as treatment with acetazolamide.

High altitude pulmonary edema is an interesting condition that is prone to occur in individuals who ascend quickly to altitudes above 2500 m and engage in heavy physical activity during the first 3 days after arrival. It is also seen in individuals acclimatized to high altitudes who spend 2 weeks or more at sea level and then reascend. It occurs in the absence of cardiovascular or pulmonary disease. It is associated with marked pulmonary hypertension, but left atrial pressures are normal. The mechanism responsible for its production is unknown. It responds to rest and O_2 treatment, and does not develop in individuals who ascend to high altitudes gradually and avoid physical exertion for the first few days of high-altitude exposure.

Acclimatization

Acclimatization to altitude is due to the operation of a variety of compensatory mechanisms. The respiratory alkalosis produced by the hyperventilation shifts the O_2-hemoglobin dissociation curve to the left, but there is a concomitant increase in red blood cell 2,3-DPG, which tends to decrease the O_2 affinity of hemoglobin. The net effect is an increase in P_{50} (see Chapter 35). The decrease in O_2 affinity makes more O_2 available to the tissues. However, it should be noted that the value of the increase in P_{50} is lost at very high altitudes because when the arterial P_{O_2} is markedly reduced the decreased O_2 affinity also interferes with O_2 uptake by hemoglobin in the lungs.

The initial ventilatory response to altitude is relatively small because the alkalosis tends to counteract the stimulating effect of hypoxia. However, there is a steady increase in ventilation over the next 4 days (Fig 37–8) because the active transport of H^+ into CSF and the resultant fall in CSF pH increase the response to hypoxia. After 4 days, the ventilatory response begins to decline slowly, but it takes years of residence at altitude for it to decline to the initial level. Associated with this decline is a gradual desensitization to the stimulatory effects of hypoxia.

Erythropoietin secretion increases promptly on ascent to altitude (see Chapter 24) and then falls somewhat over the following 4 days as the ventilatory response increases and the arterial P_{O_2} rises. The increase in circulating red blood cells triggered by the erythropoietin begins in 2–3 days and is sustained as long as the individual remains at high altitude.

There are also compensatory changes in the tissues. The mitochondria, which are the site of oxidative reactions, increase in number, and there is an increase in myoglobin (see Chapter 35) which facilitates the movement of O_2 in the tissues. There is also an increase in the tissue content of cytochrome oxidase.

The effectiveness of the acclimatization processes is indicated by the fact that in the Andes and Himalayas there are permanent human habitations at elevations above 5500 m (18,000 ft). The Indians who live in these villages are markedly polycythemic and have low alveolar P_{O_2} values, but in most other ways they are remarkably normal.

Diseases Causing Hypoxic Hypoxia

Hypoxic hypoxia is the most common form of hypoxia seen clinically. The diseases which cause it can be roughly divided into those in which inadequate amounts of O_2 reach the alveoli; those in which there is uneven ventilation in relation to blood flow; those in which diffusion from the alveoli to the capillaries is blocked; and those in which venous blood bypasses the lungs (see Table 37–2). However, there is a good deal of overlap.

Ventilation-Perfusion Imbalance

In disease processes which prevent ventilation of some of the alveoli, the ventilation/blood flow ratios in different parts of the lung determine the extent to which systemic arterial P_{O_2} declines. If nonventilated alveoli are perfused, the nonventilated but perfused portion of the lung is in effect a right-to-left shunt, dumping unoxygenated blood into the left side of the heart; but if blood is diverted from the diseased areas to better ventilated portions of the lung, the arterial P_{O_2} may remain essentially normal. Such shifts occur when a portion of the lung is collapsed. Lesser degrees of ventilation-perfusion imbalance are much more common. In the example illustrated in Fig 37–9, the underventilated alveoli (B) have a low alveolar P_{O_2} whereas the overventilated alveoli (A) have a high alveolar P_{O_2}. However, the unsaturation of the hemoglobin of the blood coming from B is not completely compensated by the greater saturation of the blood coming from A because hemoglobin is normally nearly saturated in the lungs, and the higher alveolar P_{O_2} adds only a little more O_2 to the hemoglobin than it normally carries. Consequently, the arterial blood is unsaturated. On the other hand, the CO_2 content of the arterial blood is generally normal in such situations since extra loss of CO_2 in overventilated regions can balance off diminished loss in underventilated areas.

Collapse of the Lung

When a bronchus or bronchiole is obstructed, the gas in the alveoli beyond the obstruction is absorbed and the lung segment collapses. Collapse of alveoli is called **atelectasis**. The atelectatic area may range in size from a small patch to a whole lung. When a large part of the lung is collapsed, there is an appreciable decrease in lung volume. The intrapleural pressure therefore becomes more negative and pulls the mediastinum, which in man is a fairly flexible structure, to the affected side.

Another cause of atelectasis is absence or inactivation of surfactant, the surface tension depressing agent normally found in the thin fluid film lining the alveoli (see Chapter 34). This abnormality may be a major cause of failure of the lungs to expand normally at birth.

Collapse of the lung may also be due to the pres-

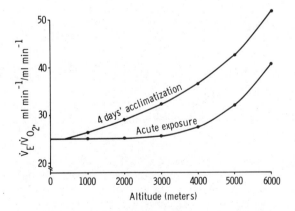

FIG 37–8. Effect of acclimatization on the ventilatory response at various altitudes. $\dot{V}_E/\dot{V}_{O_2}$ is the ventilatory equivalent, the ratio of expired minute volume ($\dot{V}_E$) to the O_2 consumption ($\dot{V}_{O_2}$). (Reproduced, with permission, from Lenfant & Sullivan: Adaptation to high altitude. New England J Med 284:1298, 1971.)

	A	B	A + B			A	B	A + B
Alveolar ventilation (liters/min)	2.0	2.0	4.0		Alveolar ventilation (liters/min)	3.2	0.8	4.0
Pulmonary blood flow (liters/min)	2.5	2.5	5.0		Pulmonary blood flow (liters/min)	2.5	2.5	5.0
Ventilation/blood flow ratio	0.8	0.8	0.8		Ventilation/blood flow ratio	1.3	0.3	0.8
Mixed venous O_2 saturation (%)	75.0	75.0	75.0		Mixed venous O_2 saturation (%)	75.0	75.0	75.0
Arterial O_2 saturation (%)	97.4	97.4	97.4		Arterial O_2 saturation (%)	98.2	91.7	95.0
Mixed venous O_2 tension (mm Hg)	40.0	40.0	40.0		Mixed venous O_2 tension (mm Hg)	40.0	40.0	40.0
Alveolar O_2 tension (mm Hg)	104.0	104.0	104.0		Alveolar O_2 tension (mm Hg)	116.0	66.0	106.0
Arterial O_2 tension (mm Hg)	104.0	104.0	104.0		Arterial O_2 tension (mm Hg)	116.0	66.0	84.0

FIG 37–9. *Left:* "Ideal" ventilation/blood flow relationship. *Right:* Nonuniform ventilation and uniform blood flow, uncompensated. V_A, alveolar ventilation; MV, respiratory minute volume. (Reproduced, with permission, from Comroe & others: *The Lung, Clinical Physiology and Pulmonary Function Tests,* 2nd ed. Year Book, 1962.)

ence in the pleural space of air **(pneumothorax)**, tissue fluids **(hydrothorax, chylothorax)**, or blood **(hemothorax)**.

Pneumothorax

When air is admitted to the pleural space, either through a rupture in the lung or a hole in the chest wall, the lung on the affected side collapses due to its elastic recoil. Since the intrapleural pressure on the affected side is atmospheric, the mediastinum shifts toward the normal side. If the communication between the pleural space and the exterior remains open **(open or sucking pneumothorax)**, more air moves in and out of the pleural space each time the patient breathes. If the hole is large, the resistance to air flow into the pleural cavity is less than the resistance to air flow into the intact lung, and little air enters the lung during inspiration. The mediastinum shifts farther to the intact side, kinking the great vessels until it flaps back during expiration. There is marked stimulation of respiration due to hypoxia, hypercapnia, and activation of pulmonary deflation receptors, and respiratory distress is severe.

If there is a flap of tissue over the hole in the lung

or chest wall that acts as a flutter valve, permitting air to enter during inspiration but preventing its exit during expiration, the pressure in the pleural space rises above atmospheric **(tension pneumothorax)**. The hypoxic stimulus to respiration causes deeper inspiratory efforts, which further increase the pressure in the pleural cavity, kinking the great veins and causing further hypoxia. Intrapleural pressure in such cases may rise to 20–30 mm Hg. The peripheral veins become distended, there is intense cyanosis, and the condition is potentially fatal if the pneumothorax is not decompressed by removing the air.

On the other hand, if the hole through which air enters the pleural space seals off **(closed pneumothorax)**, respiratory distress is not great because, with each inspiration, air flows into the lung on the unaffected side rather than into the pleural space. Because the vascular resistance is increased in the collapsed lung, blood is diverted to the other lung. Consequently, unless the pneumothorax is very large, it does not cause much hypoxia.

The air in a closed pneumothorax is absorbed. Since it is at atmospheric pressure, its total pressure, P_{O_2}, and P_{N_2} are greater than the corresponding values in venous blood (compare values for air and venous blood in Fig 34–11), and gas diffuses down these gradients into the blood. After 1–2 weeks, all of the gas disappears.

Spontaneous pneumothorax, the formation of a small closed pneumothorax due to rupture of congenital blebs on the surface of the visceral pleura, is a common benign condition. Indeed, production of an artificial pneumothorax by injecting air through the chest wall was at one time used extensively in the treatment of pulmonary tuberculosis, the aim being to collapse and thus "rest" the diseased lung.

Emphysema

In the degenerative pulmonary disease called **emphysema,** the lungs lose their elasticity and the walls between the alveoli break down so that the alveoli are replaced by large air sacs. The physiologic dead space is greatly increased, and, because of inadequate and uneven alveolar ventilation and perfusion of underventilated alveoli, severe hypoxia develops. Hypercapnia also develops. Inspiration and expiration are labored, and the work of breathing is greatly increased. The chest becomes enlarged and barrel-shaped because the chest wall expands as the opposing elastic recoil of the lungs declines (see Chapter 34). The hypoxia leads to polycythemia. Pulmonary hypertension develops, and the right side of the heart enlarges (**cor pulmonale**), then fails.

Venous to Arterial Shunts

When a cardiovascular abnormality such as an interatrial septal defect permits large amounts of unoxygenated venous blood to bypass the pulmonary capillaries and dilute the oxygenated blood in the systemic arteries ("right-to-left shunt"), chronic hypoxic hypoxia and cyanosis (**cyanotic congenital heart disease**) result. Administration of 100% O_2 raises the O_2 content of alveolar air and improves the hypoxia due to hypoventilation, impaired diffusion, or ventilation-perfusion imbalance (short of perfusion of totally unventilated segments) by increasing the amount of O_2 in the blood leaving the lungs. However, in patients with venous to arterial shunts and normal lungs, any beneficial effect of 100% O_2 is slight and due solely to an increase in the amount of dissolved O_2 in the blood.

OTHER FORMS OF HYPOXIA

Anemic Hypoxia

Hypoxia due to anemia is rarely severe at rest because red blood cell 2,3-DPG increases and the hemoglobin deficiency must be very marked before the tissue O_2 supplies at rest are compromised. However, anemic patients may have considerable difficulty during exercise because of limited ability to increase O_2 delivery to the active tissues.

Carbon Monoxide Poisoning

Carbon monoxide (CO), a gas formed by incomplete combustion of carbon, was used by the Greeks and Romans to execute criminals. Today it causes more deaths than any other gas. CO poisoning is less common in America since natural gas, which does not contain CO, replaced artificial gases such as coal gas, which contains large amounts. However, the exhaust of gasoline engines is 6% or more CO.

CO is toxic because it reacts with hemoglobin to form **carbonmonoxyhemoglobin (carboxyhemoglobin, COHb),** and COHb cannot take up O_2. Carbon monoxide poisoning is often listed as a form of anemic hypoxia because there is a deficiency of hemoglobin that can carry O_2, but the total hemoglobin content of the blood is unaffected by CO. The affinity of hemoglobin for CO is 210 times its affinity for O_2, but COHb liberates CO very slowly. An additional difficulty is that when COHb is present the dissociation curve of the remaining HbO_2 shifts to the left, decreasing the amount of O_2 released. This is why an anemic individual who has 50% of the normal amount of HbO_2 may be able to perform moderate work, whereas an individual whose HbO_2 is reduced to the same level because of the formation of COHb is seriously incapacitated.

Because of the affinity of CO for hemoglobin, there is progressive COHb formation when the alveolar P_{CO} is greater than 0.4 mm Hg. However, the amount of COHb formed depends upon the duration of exposure to CO as well as the concentration of CO in the inspired air and the alveolar ventilation.

CO is also toxic to the cytochromes in the tissues, but the amount of CO required to poison the cytochromes is 1000 times the lethal dose; tissue toxicity thus plays no role in clinical CO poisoning.

The symptoms of CO poisoning are those of any type of hypoxia, especially headache and nausea, but there is little stimulation of respiration since the arterial P_{O_2} remains normal and the carotid and aortic chemoreceptors are not stimulated (see Chapter 36). The cherry-red color of COHb is visible in the skin, nail beds, and mucous membranes. Death results when about 70–80% of the circulating hemoglobin is converted to COHb. The symptoms produced by chronic exposure to sublethal concentrations of CO are those of progressive brain damage, including mental changes and, sometimes, a parkinsonian-like state (see Chapter 32).

Treatment of CO poisoning consists of immediate termination of the exposure and adequate ventilation, by artificial respiration if necessary. Ventilation with O_2 is preferable to ventilation with fresh air, since O_2 hastens the dissociation of COHb, and hyperbaric oxygenation (see below) is useful.

Stagnant Hypoxia

Hypoxia due to slow circulation is a problem in organs such as the kidneys and heart during shock (see Chapter 33). The liver and possibly the brain are damaged by stagnant hypoxia in congestive heart failure.

Histotoxic Hypoxia

Hypoxia due to inhibition of tissue oxidative processes is most commonly the result of cyanide poisoning. Cyanide inhibits cytochrome oxidase and possibly other enzymes. Nitrites or methylene blue are used to treat cyanide poisoning. They act by forming **methemoglobin,** which then reacts with cyanide to form **cyanmethemoglobin,** a nontoxic compound. The extent of treatment with these compounds is, of course, limited by the amount of methemoglobin that can be safely formed. Hyperbaric oxygenation may also be useful.

OXYGEN TREATMENT

Administration of oxygen-rich gas mixtures is of very limited value in stagnant, anemic, and histotoxic hypoxia because all that can be accomplished in this way is an increase in the amount of dissolved O_2 in the arterial blood. This is also true in hypoxic hypoxia due to shunting of unoxygenated venous blood past the lungs. In other forms of hypoxic hypoxia, O_2 is of great benefit. However, it must be remembered that in hypercapnic patients in severe pulmonary failure the CO_2 level may be so high that it depresses rather than stimulates respiration. Some of these patients keep breathing only because the carotid and aortic chemoreceptors drive the respiratory center. If the hypoxic drive is withdrawn by administering O_2, breathing may stop. During the resultant apnea, the arterial P_{O_2} drops, but breathing may not start again because the increase in P_{CO_2} further depresses the respiratory center. Therefore, O_2 therapy in this situation may be fatal.

When 100% O_2 is first inhaled, there may be a slight decrease in respiration in normal individuals, suggesting that there is normally some hypoxic chemoreceptor drive. However, the effect is minor and can only be demonstrated by special technics. In addition, it is offset by a slight accumulation of H^+ ions, since the concentration of deoxygenated hemoglobin in the blood is reduced, and Hb is a better buffer than HbO_2 (see Chapter 35).

Oxygen Toxicity

When 80–100% O_2 is administered for periods of 8 hours or more the respiratory passages become irritated, causing substernal distress, nasal congestion, sore throat, and coughing. The reason O_2 produces the irritation is not completely understood, although O_2 treatment appears to inhibit the ability of lung macrophages to kill bacteria, and surfactant production is reduced. In animals, more prolonged administration without irritation is possible if treatment is briefly interrupted from time to time, but it is not certain that periodic interruptions are of benefit in man.

No other untoward symptoms have been reported from the administration of 100% O_2 to adult humans at atmospheric pressure; but 100% O_2 administered at pressures greater than atmospheric produces muscle twitching, ringing in the ears, dizziness, convulsions, and coma. The speed with which these symptoms develop is proportionate to the pressure at which the O_2 is administered; eg, at 4 atmospheres, symptoms develop in half the subjects in 30 minutes, whereas at 6 atmospheres convulsions develop in a few minutes. Administration of other gases at increased pressure also causes CNS symptoms (see below). Administration of O_2 to rats at elevated pressures decreases their brain γ-aminobutyric acid (GABA) content (see Chapter 15) and their brain, liver, and kidney ATP content. Succinate has been reported to protect animals from this type of oxygen toxicity.

Exposure to O_2 at increased pressures **(hyperbaric oxygenation)** can produce marked increases in the dissolved O_2 in blood. It has proved useful during surgery for certain forms of congenital heart disease. It is also of value in the treatment of gas gangrene, carbon monoxide poisoning, and probably cyanide poisoning. However, oxygen toxicity limits exposures to less than 5 hours and pressures to 3 atmospheres or less.

HYPERCAPNIA & HYPOCAPNIA

Hypercapnia

Retention of CO_2 in the body (hypercapnia) is characterized by symptoms due to depression of the CNS: confusion, diminished sensory acuity, and, eventually, coma with respiratory depression and death. In patients with these symptoms, the P_{CO_2} is markedly elevated, there is severe respiratory acidosis, and the plasma HCO_3^- may exceed 40 mEq/liter. Large amounts of HCO_3^- are excreted, partially compensating for the acidosis (see Chapter 40).

CO_2 is so much more soluble than O_2 that hypercapnia is rarely a problem in patients with hypoxia due to alveolar-capillary block, but it is a problem when for any reason alveolar ventilation is inadequate.

Asphyxia

In asphyxia produced by occlusion of the airway, acute hypercapnia and hypoxia develop together. There is pronounced stimulation of respiration, with violent respiratory efforts. Blood pressure and heart rate rise sharply, and blood pH drops. Catecholamine secretion is stimulated, the stimulation of norepinephrine secretion being proportionately greater than the stimulation of epinephrine secretion. Eventually the respiratory efforts cease, the blood pressure falls, and the heart slows. Asphyxiated animals can still be revived at this point by artificial respiration, although they are prone to ventricular fibrillation, probably owing to the combination of hypoxic myocardial damage and high circulating catecholamine levels. If artificial respiration is not started, cardiac arrest occurs in 4–5 minutes.

Drowning

In about 10% of drownings, the first gasp of water after the losing struggle not to breathe triggers laryngospasm, and death results from asphyxia without any water in the lungs. In the remaining cases, the glottic muscles eventually relax and the lungs are flooded. Fresh water is rapidly absorbed, diluting the plasma and causing intravascular hemolysis. Ocean water is markedly hypertonic, and draws fluid from the vascular system into the lungs, decreasing plasma volume. The immediate goal in the treatment of drowning is, of course, resuscitation, but long-term treatment must also take into account the circulatory effects of the water in the lungs.

Hypocapnia

Hypocapnia is the result of hyperventilation. During voluntary hyperventilation, the arterial P_{CO_2} falls from 40 to as low as 15 mm Hg while the alveolar P_{O_2} rises to 120–140 mm Hg.

The acute effects of voluntary hyperventilation demonstrate the interaction of the chemical respiratory regulating mechanisms. When an individual hyperventilates for 2–3 minutes, then stops and permits his respiration to continue without exerting any voluntary control over it, there is a period of apnea. This is followed by a few shallow breaths, and then by another period of apnea, followed again by a few breaths **(periodic breathing)**. The cycles may last for some time before normal breathing is resumed (Fig 37–10). The apnea apparently is due to CO_2 lack because it does not occur following hyperventilation with gas mixtures containing 5% CO_2. During the apnea, the alveolar P_{O_2} falls and the P_{CO_2} rises. Breathing resumes because of hypoxic stimulation of the carotid and aortic chemoreceptors before the CO_2 level has returned to normal. A few breaths eliminate the hypoxic stimulus, and breathing stops until the alveolar P_{O_2} falls again. Gradually, however, the P_{CO_2} returns to normal, and normal breathing resumes.

FIG 37–10. Changes in breathing and composition of alveolar air after forced hyperventilation for 2 minutes. (Redrawn and reproduced, with permission, from Douglas & Haldane: The causes of periodic or Cheyne-Stokes breathing. J Physiol 38:401, 1909.)

Cheyne-Stokes Respiration

Periodic breathing in disease states is called **Cheyne-Stokes respiration**. It is seen most commonly in congestive heart failure and uremia, but it occurs also in patients with brain injuries and during sleep in some normal individuals at high altitudes. Some of the patients with Cheyne-Stokes respiration have been shown to have increased sensitivity to CO_2, or at least an increased ventilatory response to CO_2. The increased response may be due to disruption of pathways or mechanisms that normally inhibit respiration. In these individuals, CO_2 causes relative hyperventilation, lowering the arterial P_{CO_2}. During the resultant apnea, the arterial P_{CO_2} again rises to normal, but the respiratory mechanism again overresponds to CO_2. Breathing ceases, and the cycle repeats.

Another cause of periodic breathing in patients with cardiac disease is prolongation of the lung-to-brain circulation time, so that the feedback from the lungs to the brain via the circulation is delayed. When such an individual hyperventilates, he lowers the P_{CO_2} of his blood in his lungs, but it takes a longer time than normal for the blood with a low P_{CO_2} to reach his brain. During this time, he continues to lower the P_{CO_2} in his pulmonary capillary blood, and when this blood reaches the brain the low P_{CO_2} inhibits the respiratory center, producing apnea. In other words, his respiratory control system oscillates because his negative feedback loop from lungs to brain is abnormally long.

Other Effects of Hypocapnia

The more chronic effects of hypocapnia are seen in neurotic patients who chronically hyperventilate. Cerebral blood flow may be reduced 30% or more because of the direct constrictor effect of hypocapnia on the cerebral vessels (see Chapter 32). The cerebral ischemia causes lightheadedness, dizziness, and paresthesias. Hypocapnia also increases cardiac output. It has a direct constrictor effect on many vessels, but it depresses the vasomotor center, so that the blood pressure is usually unchanged or only slightly elevated.

Other consequences of hypocapnia are due to the associated respiratory alkalosis, the blood pH being increased to 7.5 or 7.6. The plasma HCO_3^- is low, but bicarbonate reabsorption is decreased because of the inhibition of renal acid secretion by the low P_{CO_2}. The plasma total calcium level does not change, but, presumably, the plasma ionized calcium level falls. At any rate, carpopedal spasm, a positive Chvostek sign, and the other manifestations of frank tetany appear (see Chapter 21).

EFFECTS OF INCREASED BAROMETRIC PRESSURE

The ambient pressure increases by 1 atmosphere for every 10 m of depth in sea water and every 10.4 m of depth in fresh water. Therefore, at a depth of 31 m (100 ft) in the ocean, a diver is exposed to a pressure of 4 atmospheres. Men who dig underwater tunnels are also exposed to the same hazards because the pressure in the chambers (caissons) in which they work is increased to keep out the water.

The hazards of exposure to increased barometric pressure used to be the concern largely of the specialists who cared for deep sea divers and tunnel workers. However, the invention of SCUBA gear (self-contained underwater breathing apparatus, a tank and valve system carried by the diver) has transformed diving from a business into a sport. The popularity of skin diving is so great that all physicians should be aware of its potential dangers. The current interest in performing certain surgical procedures in high pressure tanks (see above) also focuses attention on the effects of increased barometric pressure.

When an individual is exposed to increased atmospheric pressure, the pressure of the gas he breathes must be as great as the pressure on his chest or he has difficulty breathing. CO_2 is routinely removed from the environment to prevent its accumulation. The P_{O_2} and P_{N_2} are increased in proportion to the rise in total pressure. The increased amount of dissolved O_2 is used by the tissues, while the increased amount of dissolved N_2 distributes mainly in fatty tissues because N_2 is 5 times more soluble in fat than it is in water.

Nitrogen Narcosis

The harmful effects of breathing 100% O_2 at increased pressure (see above) are proportionate to the P_{O_2}, and can therefore be obviated by decreasing the concentration of O_2 in the gas mixture to 20% or less. However, N_2 and the other gases which are physiologically nonreactive at atmospheric pressure depress the nervous system when administered at high pressures. Xenon has an anesthetic effect at atmospheric pressure. The basis of these effects is not known, although they appear to be correlated with the lipid solubility of the gases. The pressure of 80% N_2 required to produce anesthesia is about 38 atmospheres, but at pressures as low as 4–5 atmospheres (ie, at depths of 30–40 m in the ocean) N_2 produces definite euphoria. At greater depths, the symptoms resemble alcohol intoxication (**nitrogen narcosis,** or "rapture of the deep"). It has been claimed that this narcosis can be prevented by treatment with certain tranquilizers. Helium has less anesthetic effect than N_2, and deep dives are possible without narcotic effects if the diver breathes a helium-O_2 mixture.

Decompression Sickness

As a diver breathing 80% N_2 ascends from a dive, the elevated alveolar P_{N_2} falls. N_2 diffuses from the tissues into the blood stream and from the blood stream into the lungs along the partial pressure gradient. If the return to atmospheric pressure (decompression) is gradual, no harmful effects are observed; but if the ascent is rapid, N_2 escapes from solution.

Bubbles form in the tissues and blood, causing the symptoms of **decompression sickness (the bends, caisson disease).** Bubbles in the tissues cause severe pains, particularly around joints, and neurologic symptoms that include paresthesias and itching. Bubbles in the blood stream, which occur in more severe cases, obstruct the arteries to the brain, causing major paralyses and respiratory failure. Bubbles in the pulmonary capillaries are apparently responsible for the dyspnea that divers call the "chokes," and bubbles in the coronary arteries may cause myocardial damage.

Treatment of this disease is prompt recompression in a pressure chamber followed by slow decompression. Recompression is frequently lifesaving. Recovery is often complete, but there may be residual neurologic sequelae due to irreversible damage to the nervous system.

It should be noted that ascent in an airplane is equivalent to ascent from a dive. The decompression during a climb from sea level to 8550 m in the unpressurized cabin of an airplane (pressure drop from 1 down to one-third atmosphere) is the same as that during ascent to the surface after spending a period of time in 20 m of sea water (pressure drop from 3 down to 1 atmosphere). A rapid ascent in either situation can cause decompression sickness.

Air Embolism

If, during a dive, a diver breathing from a tank at increased pressure holds his breath and suddenly heads for the surface—as he may do if he gets into trouble and panics—the gas in his lungs may expand rapidly enough to rupture the pulmonary veins. This drives air into the vessels, causing air embolism. Fatal air embolism has occurred during rapid ascent from as shallow a depth as 5 m. The consequences of air in the circulatory system are discussed in Chapter 30. This cannot happen, of course, to an individual who takes a breath on the surface, dives, and returns to the surface still holding his breath, no matter how deep he dives.

Air embolism also occurs as a result of rapid expansion of the gas in the lungs when the external pressure is suddenly reduced from atmospheric to subatmospheric, as it is when the wall of the pressurized cabin of an airplane or rocket at high altitude is breached (**explosive decompression**).

ARTIFICIAL RESPIRATION

In acute asphyxia due to drowning, CO or other forms of gas poisoning, electrocution, anesthetic accidents, and other similar causes, artificial respiration after breathing has ceased may be lifesaving. It should always be attempted because the respiratory center fails before the vasomotor center and heart. There are numerous methods of emergency artificial respiration, but the method presently recommended to produce adequate ventilation in all cases is mouth-to-mouth breathing.

Mouth-to-Mouth Breathing

The operator in this form of resuscitation quickly wipes vomitus or water out of the airway, then covers the victim's mouth with his own, occludes the victim's nostrils, and exhales a volume about 2 times the tidal

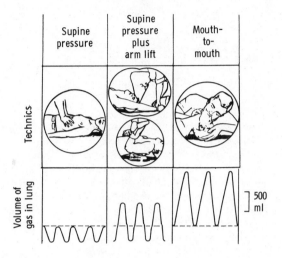

FIG 37–11. Technics of artificial respiration. The prone pressure plus arm lift method moves about the same amount of air as the supine pressure plus arm lift method. The dotted line indicates the volume of gas in the lung in the subject whose respiration has ceased. (Modified and reproduced, with permission, from Gordon, in Whittenberger: *Artificial Respiration: Theory and Applications.* Harper, 1962.)

volume 12–20 times a minute. The elastic recoil of the victim's lungs produces passive expiration. One thumb is put in the victim's mouth, his neck is extended, and his jaw is held forward and up to keep the airway open. The nostrils can be occluded by the operator's cheek as shown in Fig 37–11, or they can be held shut with the operator's other hand. Any gas blown into the stomach can be expelled by applying upward pressure on the abdomen from time to time. The advantages of mouth-to-mouth resuscitation lie not only in its simplicity but in the fact that it works by expanding the lungs. In the prone or supine pressure methods of artificial respiration, the lungs are compressed by pressure on the thorax and passive recoil of the chest wall pulls air into them (Fig 37–11). Some expansion of the lungs can be achieved by raising the arms, but even when arm raising and pressure are alternated the effective ventilation is not so great as that produced by the mouth-to-mouth method.

Mechanical Respirators

For treatment of chronic respiratory insufficiency due to inadequate ventilation in such conditions as bulbar poliomyelitis, mechanical respirators such as the Drinker tank respirator are available. These are airtight metal or plastic containers enclosing the body except for the head. By means of a motor, negative pressure is applied to the chest at regular intervals, moving the chest wall in a way that resembles normal breathing. Modern, portable models that cover only the chest are now in use. Intermittent positive pressure breathing machines are also used. These machines produce intermittent increases in intrapulmonary pressure by means of "pulses" of air delivered via a face mask.

● ● ●

References: Section VII.
Respiration

Biscoe TJ: Carotid body: Structure and function. Physiol Rev 51:427, 1971.

Clark JM, Lambertson CJ: Pulmonary oxygen toxicity: A review. Pharmacol Rev 23:37, 1971.

Comroe JH Jr, Nadel JA: Screening tests of pulmonary function. New England J Med 282:1249, 1970.

Cunningham DJC, Lloyd BB (editors): *Regulation of Human Respiration.* Blackwell, 1963.

Davenport HW: *The ABC of Acid-Base Chemistry,* 5th ed. Univ of Chicago Press, 1969.

Finch CA, Lenfant C: Oxygen transport in man. New England J Med 286:407, 1972.

Forster RE: Exchange of gases between alveolar air and pulmonary capillary blood. Pulmonary diffusing capacity. Physiol Rev 37:391, 1957.

Heinemann HO, Fishman AP: Nonrespiratory functions of mammalian lung. Physiol Rev 49:1, 1969.

Hultgren HN, Flamm MD: Pulmonary edema. Mod Concepts Cardiovas Dis 38:1, 1969.

Lambertsen CJ (editor): *Underwater Physiology.* Academic Press, 1971.

Lenfant C, Sullivan K: Adaptation to high altitude. New England J Med 284:1298, 1971.

Leusen I: Regulation of cerebrospinal fluid composition with reference to breathing. Physiol Rev 52:1, 1972.

Mitchell RA: Control of respiration. In: *Pathophysiology.* Frohlich ED (editor). Lippincott, 1972.

Porter R (editor): *Breathing: Hering-Breuer Centenary Symposium.* Churchill, 1970.

Respiration and circulation. Biological Handbook FASEB, 1971.

Robin ED, Cross CE, Zelis R: Pulmonary edema. New England J Med 288:239, 1973.

Staub NC: Respiration. Ann Rev Physiol 31:173, 1969.

Steen JB: *Comparative Physiology of Respiration Mechanisms.* Academic Press, 1971.

Whittenberger JL: Myoglobin-facilitated oxygen diffusion: Role of myoglobin in oxygen entry into muscle. Physiol Rev 50:559, 1970.

Winter PM, Lowenstein E: Acute respiratory failure. Scientific American 221:23, Nov 1969.

VIII. Formation & Excretion of Urine

38...

Renal Function

In the kidneys, a fluid that resembles plasma is filtered through the glomerular capillaries into the renal tubules **(glomerular filtration)**. As this glomerular filtrate passes down the tubules, its volume is reduced and its composition altered by the processes of **tubular reabsorption** (removal of water and solutes from the tubular fluid) and **tubular secretion** (secretion of solutes into the tubular fluid) to form urine. A comparison of the composition of the plasma and an average urine specimen illustrates the magnitude of some of these changes (Table 38–1) and emphasizes the manner in which wastes are eliminated while water and important electrolytes and metabolites are conserved. Furthermore, the composition of the urine can be varied, and many homeostatic regulatory mechanisms minimize or prevent changes in the composition of the ECF by changing the amount of water and various specific solutes in the urine. The kidneys are also endocrine organs, secreting renin (see Chapter 24) and the renal erythropoietic factor (see Chapters 24 and 27).

nephrons they contain. There are approximately 1 million nephrons in each human kidney. The parts of the nephron are illustrated in Fig 38–1.

The glomerulus, which is about 200 μm in diameter, is formed by the invagination of a tuft of capillaries into the dilated, blind end of the nephron **(Bowman's capsule)**. The capillaries are supplied by an **afferent arteriole** and drained by a slightly smaller **efferent arteriole** (Fig 38–1). There are 2 cell layers separating the blood from the glomerular filtrate in Bowman's capsule, the capillary endothelium and the epithelium of the tubule. Under the electron microscope, the endothelium is seen to be fenestrated and the pseudopodia of the epithelial cells are seen to form slits along the capillary wall (Fig 38–2). However, the basement membrane between the endothelial and epithelial cells does not contain visible pores. The total area of glomerular capillary endothelium across which filtration occurs in man is about 1.5 sq m.

The **proximal convoluted tubule** is about 15 mm long and 55 μm in diameter in man. Its wall is made up of a single layer of cells that interdigitate with one

FUNCTIONAL ANATOMY

The Nephron

Each individual renal tubule and its glomerulus is a unit, or **nephron**. The size of the kidneys in various species is largely determined by the number of

TABLE 38–1. Urinary and plasma concentrations of some physiologically important substances.

| Substance | Concentration in | | U/P Ratio |
	Urine (U)	Plasma (P)	
Glucose (mg/100 ml)	0	100	0
Na$^+$ (mEq/liter)	150	150	1
Urea (mg/100 ml)	900	15	60
Creatinine (mg/100 ml)	150	1	150

FIG 38–1. Diagram of a juxtamedullary nephron. (Details of the cells based on studies of Rhodin: Anatomy of kidney tubules. Internat Rev Cytol 7:485, 1958.)

FIG 38−2. Ultrastructure of the glomerulus. Ep, epithelial cell of tubule; end, endothelial cell of capillary; 1, processes of epithelial cells; 2, cement layer; 3, basement membrane; 4, inner cement layer; 5, endothelial cytoplasm, fenestrated, with thin areas about 10 nm in diameter. (Reproduced, with permission, from Pease: Fine structure of the kidney as seen by electron microscopy. J Histochem 3:295, 1955.)

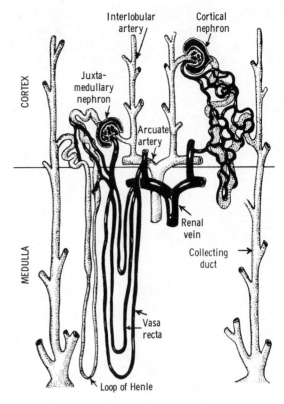

FIG 38−3. Cortical and juxtamedullary nephrons, showing renal circulation. (Reproduced, with permission, from Smith: *The Kidney.* Oxford Univ Press, 1951.)

another. The luminal edges of the cells have a striate **brush border** due to the presence of innumerable 1 × 0.7 μm microvilli.

The convoluted portion of the proximal tubule (pars convoluta) drains into the straight portion (pars recta), which forms the first part of the **loop of Henle** (Figs 38−1 and 38−3). The proximal tubule terminates in the thin segment of the descending limb of the loop of Henle, which has an epithelium made up of attenuated, flat cells. The nephrons with glomeruli in the outer portions of the renal cortex have short loops of Henle (Fig 38−3), whereas those with glomeruli in the juxtamedullary region of the cortex have long loops extending down into the medullary pyramids. In humans only 15% of the nephrons have long loops. The total length of the thin segment of the loop varies from 2−14 mm in length. It ends in the thick segment of the ascending limb, which is about 12 mm in length.

The ascending limb of the loop of Henle doubles back to the glomerulus of the nephron from which the tubule arose and passes close to its afferent arteriole. At this point, some of the cells of the juxtaglomerular apparatus are piled up around the tubule and the tubular epithelium is modified histologically to form the **macula densa** (see Chapter 24). The macula densa is arbitrarily designated as the point where the loop of Henle ends and the distal convoluted tubule begins.

The **distal convoluted tubule** is about 5 mm long. Its epithelium is lower than that of the proximal tubule, and although there are a few microvilli there is no distinct brush border. The distal tubules coalesce to

form **collecting ducts** which are about 20 mm long and pass through the renal cortex and medulla to empty into the pelvis of the kidney at the apices of the medullary pyramids. The total length of the nephrons, including the collecting ducts, ranges from 45−65 mm.

Blood Vessels

The renal circulation is diagrammed in Fig 38−3. The afferent arterioles are short, straight branches of the interlobular arteries. The efferent arterioles break up into capillaries which supply the tubules before draining into the renal vein. The arterial segments between glomeruli and tubules are thus technically a portal system and the glomerular capillaries are the only capillaries in the body that drain into arterioles.

The capillaries draining the tubules of the cortical nephrons form a peritubular network, but the efferent arterioles from the juxtamedullary glomeruli drain into a network of vessels that form hairpin loops (the **vasa recta**). These loops dip into the medullary pyramids alongside the loops of Henle (Fig 38−3). The efferent arteriole from each cortical glomerulus breaks up into capillaries that generally supply the same nephron, but in the case of juxtamedullary nephrons the capillaries may supply a number of different nephrons. This fact must be kept in mind when considering mechanisms responsible for glomerulotubular balance (see below).

In man, the total surface of the renal capillaries is approximately equal to the total surface area of the tubules, both being about 12 sq m. The volume of blood in the capillaries at any given time is 30–40 ml.

Lymphatics

The kidney has an abundant lymphatic supply which drains via the thoracic duct into the venous circulation in the thorax.

Capsule

The renal capsule is a thin but tough structure. If the kidney becomes edematous, the capsule limits the swelling and the tissue pressure (**renal interstitial pressure**) rises. This decreases the glomerular filtration rate and is claimed to be a factor in enhancing and prolonging the anuria in the lower nephron syndrome (see Chapter 33).

Innervation of the Renal Vessels

The renal nerves travel along the renal blood vessels as they enter the kidney. They contain many sympathetic efferent fibers and a few afferent fibers of unknown function. There also appears to be a cholinergic component, but its function is uncertain. In man, the sympathetic innervation comes primarily from the 12th thoracic to the second lumbar segments of the spinal cord. The sympathetic fibers are predominantly vasoconstrictor in function and are distributed particularly to the afferent and efferent arterioles. However, nerve fibers can also be demonstrated ending in close proximity to the renal tubular cells and the juxtaglomerular cells.

RENAL CIRCULATION

Blood Flow

In a resting adult the kidneys receive 1.2–1.3 liters of blood per minute, or just under 25% of the cardiac output (Table 32–1). Renal blood flow can be measured with electromagnetic or other types of flow meters, or it can be determined by applying the Fick principle (see Chapter 29) to the kidney—ie, by measuring the amount of a given substance taken up per unit of time and dividing this value by the A-V difference for the substance across the kidney. Since the kidney filters plasma, the **renal plasma flow** equals the amount of a substance excreted per unit of time divided by the renal A-V difference as long as the amount in the red cells is unaltered during passage through the kidney. Any excreted substance can be used if its concentration in arterial and renal venous plasma can be measured and if it is not metabolized, not stored nor produced by the kidney, and does not itself affect blood flow. From the renal plasma flow, the renal blood flow can be calculated by dividing by one minus the hematocrit.

Renal plasma flow is commonly measured by infusing para-aminohippuric acid (PAH) or iodopyracet (Diodrast) and determining their urine and plasma concentrations. These substances are filtered by the glomeruli and secreted by the tubular cells so that their **extraction ratio** (arterial concentration minus renal venous concentration/arterial concentration) is high. For example, when infused at low doses, 90% of the PAH in arterial blood is removed in a single circulation through the kidney. It has therefore become commonplace to calculate the "renal plasma flow" by dividing the amount of PAH in the urine by the plasma PAH level, ignoring the level in renal venous blood. Peripheral venous plasma can be used because its PAH concentration is essentially identical to that in the arterial plasma reaching the kidney. The value obtained should be called the **effective renal plasma flow (ERPF)** to indicate that the level in renal venous plasma was not measured. Average values are about 625 ml/min in man.

Effective renal plasma flow (ERPF) =

$$\frac{U_{PAH}V}{P_{PAH}} = \text{Clearance of PAH } (C_{PAH})$$

Example:

Concentration of PAH in urine (U_{PAH}): 14 mg/ml

Urine volume (V): 0.9 ml/min

Concentration of PAH in plasma (P_{PAH}): 0.02 mg/ml

$$\text{ERPF} = \frac{14 \times 0.9}{0.02} = 630 \text{ ml/min}$$

It should be noted that the ERPF determined in this way is the **clearance** of PAH. The concept of clearance is discussed in detail below.

ERPF can be converted to actual renal plasma flow (RPF):

Average PAH extraction ratio: 0.9

$$\frac{\text{ERPF}}{\text{Extraction ratio}} = \frac{630}{0.9} = \text{Actual RPF} = 700 \text{ ml/min}$$

Hematocrit (Hct): 45%

$$\text{Renal blood flow} = \text{RPF} \times \frac{1}{1-\text{Hct}} =$$
$$700 \times \frac{1}{0.55} = 1273 \text{ ml/min}$$

Regional Blood Flow

The blood flow in the renal cortex is much greater than in the medulla. Values obtained in dogs are 4–5 ml/g of kidney tissue per minute in the cortex, 1–2 ml/g/min in the outer medulla, and less than 0.3 ml/g/min in the inner medulla.

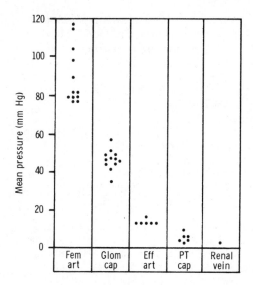

FIG 38−4. Mean pressures in the blood vessels of rats. Dots represent individual values in the femoral artery (Fem art), glomerular capillaries (Glom cap), efferent arterioles (Eff art), peritubular capillaries (PT cap), and renal vein. (Reproduced, with permission, from Brenner, Troy, & Daugharty: The dynamics of glomerular filtration in the rat. J Clin Invest 50:1176, 1971.)

Pressure in Renal Vessels

The pressure in the glomerular capillaries has now been measured directly in rats and has been found to be considerably lower than predicted on the basis of indirect measurements. Directly measured values in a systemic artery, glomerular capillaries, efferent arterioles, peritubular capillaries, and the renal vein are shown in Fig 38−4. Pressure gradients are presumably similar in man, with a glomerular capillary pressure that is about 50% of systemic arterial pressure and a peritubular capillary pressure of about 15 mm Hg.

Renal Vasoconstriction

Stimulation of the renal nerves causes a marked decrease in renal blood flow. Similar renal vasoconstriction can be produced by stimulating the vasomotor center in the medulla, parts of the brain stem, and the cerebral cortex, especially the anterior tip of the temporal lobe. There is debate about whether there is tonic discharge in the renal nerves at rest in animals and humans; however, when the systemic pressure falls, the vasoconstrictor response produced by decreased discharge in the baroreceptor nerves includes renal vasoconstriction.

Hypoxia is another stimulus to renal vasoconstriction, but only when the arterial O_2 content falls to less than 50% of normal. The response is mediated via the chemoreceptors, which stimulate the vasomotor center to produce renal vasoconstriction when the renal nerves are intact. Catecholamines constrict the renal vessels. Small doses of epinephrine and norepinephrine have a greater effect on the efferent than on the afferent arterioles, so that glomerular capillary pressure and, consequently, the glomerular filtration rate are maintained while renal blood flow is decreased; large doses depress the glomerular filtration rate. Epinephrine also constricts the renal veins, making the kidneys swell. Renal blood flow is decreased during exercise and, to a lesser extent, on rising from the supine to the standing position.

Renal Vasodilatation

Bacterial pyrogens cause renal vasodilatation. The response is not due to the fever they produce, because it occurs when the febrile response is blocked by the administration of antipyretic drugs. In fact, fever due to other causes is usually associated with moderate renal vasoconstriction. Hydralazine (Apresoline), a drug used to treat hypertension, has the unique property of lowering blood pressure and increasing renal blood flow. For unknown reasons, a high-protein diet increases renal blood flow.

Other Functions of the Renal Nerves

There are a number of observations in the literature that suggest that increased activity in the renal nerves decreases salt excretion by an action independent of its effect on the afferent arterioles and hence on glomerular filtration. This could be due to a direct effect on the tubular cells or could be secondary to changes in medullary blood flow. It could also be due to stimulation of the juxtaglomerular cells, with increased secretion of renin and consequently of aldosterone. However, most renal functions that have been tested appear to be normal after renal denervation in man.

Autoregulation of Renal Blood Flow

When the kidney is perfused at moderate pressures (90−220 mm Hg in the dog), the renal vascular resistance varies with the pressure so that renal blood flow is relatively constant (Fig 38−5). Autoregulation of this type occurs in other organs, and many theories have been advanced to explain it (see Chapter 31). Renal autoregulation is present in denervated and in isolated, perfused kidneys, but is prevented by the administration of drugs which paralyze vascular smooth muscle; it is therefore probably due to a direct response of the vascular smooth muscle, especially that of the afferent arterioles.

Cell Separation Theory

A theory has been offered as an explanation of renal autoregulation. This theory holds that, due to plasma skimming (see Chapter 30), the hematocrit—and, consequently, the viscosity of the blood in the afferent arterioles—varies with the perfusion pressure. Such changes in viscosity might explain autoregulation. However, autoregulation occurs in kidneys perfused with cell-free solutions of the plasma substitute dextran. Moreover, red cells pass through the kidney as

FIG 38—5. Autoregulation in the dog kidney. GFR, glomerular filtration rate; RPF, renal plasma flow. (Modified and reproduced, with permission, from Shipley & Study: Changes in renal blood flow . . . Am J Physiol 167:676, 1951.)

TABLE 38—2. Characteristics of a substance suitable for measuring the GFR by determining its clearance.

Freely filtered
Not reabsorbed or secreted by tubules
Not metabolized
Not stored in kidney
Not protein-bound (substances bound to albumin and globulin not filtered)
Not toxic
Has no effect on filtration rate
Preferably easy to measure in plasma and urine

rapidly as plasma; and the O_2 saturation of the blood in the peritubular capillaries is no lower than it is in renal venous blood. It therefore seems doubtful that cell separation occurs to any degree in the kidney.

Renal Oxygen Consumption

The O_2 consumption of the kidneys in man is about 18 ml/min. The renal blood flow per g of tissue is very large, and it is therefore not surprising that the A-V O_2 difference is only 14 ml/liter of blood, compared with 62 ml/liter for the brain and 114 ml/liter for the heart (Table 32—1). The renal function with which the O_2 consumption correlates best is the rate of active transport of sodium. The O_2 consumption of the cortex is about 9 ml/100 g/min, whereas that of the inner medulla is only 0.4 ml/100 g/min. The tubular fluid passes through the medulla on its way to the renal pelvis, and the P_{O_2} of the urine is also low.

GLOMERULAR FILTRATION

Measuring GFR

The **glomerular filtration rate (GFR)** can be measured in intact animals and humans by measuring the excretion and plasma level of a substance which is freely filtered through the glomeruli and neither secreted nor reabsorbed by the tubules. The amount of such a substance in the urine per unit of time must have been provided by filtering exactly the number of ml of plasma which contained this amount. Therefore, if the substance is designated by the letter x, the GFR is equal to the **concentration** of x in urine (U_X) times the **urine flow** per unit of time (V) divided by the **arterial plasma level** of x (P_X), or U_XV/P_X. This value is called the **clearance** of x (C_X). P_X is, of course, the

same in all parts of the arterial circulation, and if x is not metabolized to any extent in the tissues the level of x in peripheral venous plasma can be substituted for the arterial plasma level.

Substances Used to Measure GFR

In addition to the requirement that it be freely filtered and neither reabsorbed nor secreted in the tubules, a substance suitable for measuring the GFR should meet other criteria (Table 38—2). Inulin, a polymer of fructose with a molecular weight of 5200 that is found in dahlia tubers, meets these criteria in man and most animals and is extensively used to measure GFR. In practice, a loading dose of inulin is administered intravenously, followed by a sustaining infusion to keep the arterial plasma level constant. After the inulin has equilibrated with body fluids, an accurately timed urine specimen is collected and a plasma sample obtained half-way through the collection. Plasma and urinary inulin concentrations are determined and the clearance calculated.

Example:

$$U_{In} = 29 \text{ mg/ml}$$

$$V = 1.1 \text{ ml/min}$$

$$P_{In} = 0.25 \text{ mg/ml}$$

$$C_{In} = \frac{U_{In}V}{P_{In}} = \frac{29 \times 1.1}{0.25}$$

$$C_{In} = 128 \text{ ml/min}$$

In the dog, cat, rabbit, and a number of other mammals, clearance of creatinine (C_{Cr}) can also be used to determine the GFR, but in primates, including man, some creatinine is secreted by the tubules, and some may be reabsorbed. In addition, plasma creatinine determinations are inaccurate at low creatinine levels because the method for determining creatinine measures small amounts of other plasma constituents. In spite of this, the clearance of endogenous creatinine is frequently measured in patients. The values agree quite well with the GFR values measured with inulin because, although the value for $U_{Cr}V$ is high as a result of tubular secretion, the value for P_{Cr} is also high as a result of nonspecific chromogens and the errors thus tend to cancel. Endogenous creatinine clearance is easy to measure and is a worthwhile index of renal function, but when precise measurements of GFR are needed it seems unwise to rely on a method that owes what accuracy it has to compensating errors.

Normal GFR

The GFR in an average-sized normal man is approximately 125 ml/min. Its magnitude correlates fairly well with surface area, but values in women are 10% lower than those in men even after correction for surface area. It should be noted that 125 ml/min is 7.5 liters/hour, or 180 liters/day, whereas the normal urine volume is about 1 liter/day. Thus, 99% or more of the filtrate is normally reabsorbed. At the rate of 125 ml/min, the kidneys filter in 1 day an amount of fluid equal to 4 times the total body water, 15 times the ECF volume, and 60 times the plasma volume.

Control of GFR

The factors governing filtration across the glomerular capillaries are the same as those governing filtration across all other capillaries (see Chapter 30), ie, the size of the capillary bed, the permeability of the capillaries, and the hydrostatic and osmotic pressure gradients across the capillary wall.

Permeability

The glomerular filter behaves as if it had pores about 10 nm in diameter. It is more than 400 times more permeable than the capillaries in skeletal muscle. Depending upon the shape of the molecules, substances with molecular weights as great as 70,000 appear in the glomerular filtrate. The globulins in the plasma, which generally have molecular weights of 90,000+, are not filtered to any extent, but there is evidence that small amounts of plasma albumin (molecular weight 65,000) are filtered and reabsorbed in the proximal tubules. The reabsorption may be by the process of pinocytosis. When, as a result of hemolysis, hemoglobin (molecular weight 64,450) is present in the plasma, it appears in glomerular filtrate at about 5% of its plasma concentration. Smaller molecules, including small proteins and polypeptides, pass much more readily. However, their concentration in plasma is normally very low, and the glomerular filtrate normally contains only traces of protein. Because of the nondiffusibility of plasma proteins, there is a Donnan effect (see Chapter 1) on the monovalent diffusible ion distribution, the concentration of anions being about 5% greater in the glomerular filtrate than in plasma and the concentration of monovalent cations 5% less. However, for most purposes this effect can be ignored, and in all other respects the composition of the filtrate is similar to that of plasma.

Capillary permeability is increased in many renal diseases, permitting plasma proteins to pass into the urine. Albumin escapes in the largest quantities, and the term **albuminuria** is often used; however, since other proteins are often present also, the term **proteinuria** is more correct.

Hydrostatic & Osmotic Pressure

The pressure in the glomerular capillaries—presumably about 50 mm Hg in man—is higher than that in other capillary beds because the afferent arterioles are short, straight branches of the interlobular arteries. Furthermore, the vessels "downstream" from the glomeruli, the efferent arterioles, have a relatively high resistance. The capillary hydrostatic pressure is opposed by the hydrostatic pressure in Bowman's capsule. This is normally about 10 mm Hg. Filtration is also opposed by the 25 mm Hg osmotic pressure gradient across the capillaries due to the oncotic pressure of the plasma proteins. The net pressure producing filtration at the glomeruli when the systemic arterial pressure is normal is therefore about 15 mm Hg (50−10−25). The total GFR is also affected by variations in the total area of the glomerular capillary membrane in both kidneys. In frogs, some of the glomeruli are inactive at any given time; but in mammals, including man, the bulk of the evidence indicates that all of the nephrons are continuously active. In many kidney diseases, the total glomerular area is reduced because individual nephrons are destroyed.

Changes in GFR

Variations in the factors listed in the preceding paragraphs have predictable effects on the GFR (Table 38−3). Changes in renal vascular resistance due to autoregulation may tend to stabilize filtration pressure, but when the mean systemic arterial pressure drops below 90 mm Hg there is a sharp drop in GFR. This effect is magnified by baroreceptor-mediated reflex renal vasoconstriction. The GFR rises when efferent arteriolar constriction is greater than afferent constriction, and falls when the reverse is true, although either type of constriction decreases the tubular blood flow.

TABLE 38−3. Factors affecting the glomerular filtration rate.

1. Changes in glomerular capillary hydrostatic pressure
   a. Changes in systemic blood pressure
   b. Afferent or efferent arteriolar constriction
2. Changes in hydrostatic pressure in Bowman's capsule
   a. Ureteral obstruction
   b. Edema of kidney inside tight renal capsule
3. Changes in oncotic pressure of plasma proteins: Dehydration, hypoproteinemia, etc (minor factors)
4. Increased permeability of glomerular filter: Various diseases
5. Decrease in total area of glomerular capillary bed
   a. Diseases which destroy glomeruli with or without destruction of tubules
   b. Partial nephrectomy

Filtration Fraction

The ratio of the GFR to the renal plasma flow (RPF), the **filtration fraction,** is normally 0.16–0.20 in man. The GFR varies less than the RPF. When there is a fall in systemic blood pressure, GFR falls less than the RPF and the filtration fraction consequently rises. A rise in filtration fraction is also observed early in congestive heart failure, and this fact may have significance in the genesis of the salt and water retention in that disorder (see Chapter 33).

TUBULAR FUNCTION

General Considerations

The amount of any substance that is filtered is the product of the GFR and the plasma level of the substance ($C_{In}P_X$). The tubular cells may add more of the substance to the filtrate (tubular secretion), may remove some or all of the substance from the filtrate (tubular reabsorption), or may do both. The amount of the substance excreted (U_XV) equals the amount filtered plus the **net amount transferred** by the tubules. This latter quantity is conveniently indicated by the symbol T_X. When there is net tubular secretion, T_X is positive; when there is net tubular reabsorption, T_X is negative (Fig 38–6).

Since the clearance of any substance is UV/P, the clearance equals the GFR if there is no net tubular secretion or reabsorption; exceeds the GFR if there is net tubular secretion; and is less than the GFR if there is net tubular reabsorption. It should be noted that in the latter 2 cases the clearance is a "virtual volume," an index of renal function, rather than an actual volume.

Much of our knowledge about glomerular filtration and tubular function has been obtained by the use of micropuncture technics. It was first demonstrated some years ago that micropipets could be inserted into the tubules of the living kidney and the composition of aspirated tubular fluid determined by the use of microchemical technics. Recent technical advances have made it possible to study in this way the kidneys of a variety of mammals. In the rat, data are now available on samples from the first 70% of the proximal tubule, the tip of the loop of Henle, and all parts of the distal tubule and collecting ducts as well as all parts of the renal vasculature. Using microelectrodes, it has been possible to measure the membrane potentials of the tubular cells. The potential difference of −70 mv between the tubular lumen and the interior of proximal tubular cells is the same, or nearly the same, as that between the cells and the ECF. Consequently, the potential between the tubular lumen and the ECF in the proximal tubule is only about 2 mv (tubular lumen negative). However, the potential difference between the distal tubular lumen and the tubular cells has been claimed to be only −30 mv. Thus, there is a net potential difference between the distal tubular lumen and the ECF of about 40 mv (tubular lumen negative). A 20 mv potential difference has been reported in the collecting ducts.

Mechanisms of Tubular Reabsorption & Secretion

The possibility that proximal cells reabsorb protein by pinocytosis has been mentioned above. Other substances are secreted or reabsorbed by passive diffusion down chemical or electrical gradients or actively transported against such gradients (see Chapter 1). Like transport systems elsewhere, each renal active transport system has a maximal rate, or **transport maximum (Tm)** at which it can transport a particular

$$GFR \times P_X + T_X = U_XV$$

FIG 38–6. **Tubular function.** For explanation of symbols, see text.

solute. Thus, the amount of a particular solute transported is proportionate to the amount present up to the Tm for the solute, but at higher concentrations the transport mechanism is **saturated** and there is no appreciable increment in the amount transported. However, the Tm for some systems is so high that it is almost impossible to saturate them.

Glucose Reabsorption

Glucose is typical of substances removed from the urine by active transport. It is filtered at a rate of approximately 100 mg/min (80 mg/100 ml of plasma × 125 ml/min). Micropuncture studies demonstrate that reabsorption occurs in the first part of the proximal tubule. Essentially all of the glucose is reabsorbed, and no more than a few mg appear in the urine per 24 hours. The amount reabsorbed is proportionate to the amount filtered and hence to the plasma glucose level (P_G) up to the transfer maximum (Tm_G); but when the Tm_G is exceeded the amount of glucose in the urine rises (Fig 38–7). The Tm_G is about 375 mg/min in men and 300 mg/min in women.

The **renal threshold** for glucose is the plasma level at which the glucose first appears in the urine in more than the normal minute amounts. One would predict that the renal threshold would be about 300 mg/100 ml—ie, 375 mg/min (Tm_G) divided by 125 ml/min (GFR). However, the actual renal threshold is about 200 mg/100 ml of arterial plasma, which corresponds to a venous level of about 180 mg/100 ml.

Fig 38–7 shows why the actual renal threshold is less than the predicted threshold. The "ideal" curve shown in this diagram would be obtained if the Tm_Gs in all the tubules were identical and if all the glucose were removed from each tubule when the amount filtered was below the Tm_G. The curve of data actually obtained in man is not sharply angulated, and deviates considerably from the "ideal" curve. This deviation is called **splay**. It is present for 2 reasons. In the first place, not all of the 2 million nephrons in the kidneys have exactly the same Tm_G or filtration rate; in some, Tm_G is exceeded at low levels of P_G. In the second place, some glucose escapes reabsorption when the amount filtered is below the Tm_G because the reactions involved in glucose transport are not completely irreversible. Indeed, the dynamics of all the active transport systems that remove substances from the tubules are probably such that, for each, the curve relating amount transported to the plasma level of the substance is rounded rather than sharply angulated. The degree of rounding is inversely proportionate to the avidity with which the transport mechanism binds the substance it transports.

Glucose Transport Mechanism

The details of the operation of the renal glucose transport mechanism are still obscure. The same mechanism transports fructose, galactose, and xylose. It is unaffected by insulin, Tm_G being normal in diabetes; but it is inhibited, as is the transport of glucose across the intestinal mucosa, by the plant glycoside **phlorhizin**.

Other Substances Reabsorbed Actively

Other substances that are actively reabsorbed include Na^+, K^+, $PO_4^{\equiv}$, amino acids, creatine, sulfate, uric acid, ascorbic acid, and the ketone bodies acetoacetic acid and β-hydroxybutyric acid. The Tm's of these substances range from very low values to values so high that they have not yet been accurately measured. There are several different systems that transport amino acids. Some of the transport mechanisms appear to share a common step. Some transport in either direction, depending on circumstances, and some may exchange one substance for another.

Most of the active transport mechanisms responsible for reabsorbing particular solutes are located in the proximal tubules. The major exception is the transport mechanism responsible for the reabsorption of Na^+. Na^+ is actively transported out of the tubular fluid in the distal tubule and collecting ducts. It is probably actively transported in the thick ascending limb of Henle's loop as well, although recent evidence suggests that it may be Cl^- rather than Na^+ that is transported. There is also some uncertainty about whether Na^+ is actively transported out of the proximal tubule.

The renal active transport mechanisms, like active transport systems elsewhere, can be inhibited competitively or noncompetitively. For example, the mechanism responsible for the reabsorption of uric acid can be inhibited by probenecid (Benemid) and phenylbutazone (Butazolidin), a fact of practical importance in the treatment of gout (see Chapter 17).

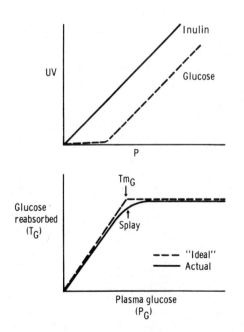

FIG 38–7. *Above:* Relation between plasma level (P) and excretion (UV) of glucose and inulin. *Below:* Relation between plasma glucose level (P_G) and amount of glucose reabsorbed (T_G).

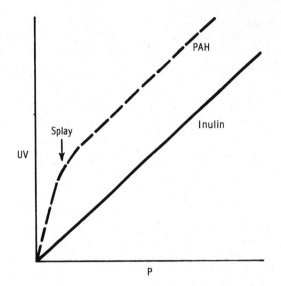

FIG 38–8. Relation between plasma levels (P) and excretion (UV) of PAH and inulin.

PAH Transport

The dynamics of PAH transport illustrate the operation of the active transport mechanisms that secrete substances into the tubular fluid. The filtered load of PAH is a linear function of the plasma level, but PAH secretion increases as P_{PAH} rises only until a maximal secretion rate (Tm_{PAH}) is reached (Fig 38–8). When P_{PAH} is low, C_{PAH} is high; but as P_{PAH} rises above Tm_{PAH}, C_{PAH} falls progressively. It eventually approaches the clearance of inulin (C_{In}) (Fig 38–9) because the amount of PAH secreted becomes a smaller and smaller fraction of the total amount excreted. Conversely, the clearance of glucose is essentially zero at P_G levels below the renal threshold; but above the threshold, C_G rises to approach C_{In} as P_G is raised.

The use of C_{PAH} to measure effective renal plasma flow (ERPF) is discussed above. It should again be emphasized that the excretion of any substance that is not stored or metabolized in the kidney can be used to measure renal plasma flow if the level in arterial and renal venous plasma can be measured, and the only advantage of PAH is that its extraction ratio is so high that renal plasma flow can be approximated without measuring the PAH concentration in renal venous blood.

Other Substances Secreted by the Tubules

Derivatives of hippuric acid in addition to PAH, phenol red and other sulfonphthalein dyes, penicillin, and a variety of iodinated dyes such as iodopyracet (Diodrast) are actively secreted into the tubular fluid. Substances that are normally produced in the body and secreted by the tubules include various ethereal sulfates, steroid and other glucuronides, and 5-hydroxyindoleacetic acid, the principal metabolite of serotonin (see Chapter 15). All of these secreted substances are weak anions and compete with each other for secretion; for example, PAH reduces the excretion of both the 18-glucuronide and the tetrahydroglucuronide derivatives of aldosterone (see Chapter 20). Thus, a single transport system appears to be involved. This transport system is limited to the proximal tubule. PAH transport and, presumably, the transport of the other weak anions are facilitated by acetate and lactate and inhibited by various Krebs cycle intermediates, probenecid, phenylbutazone, dinitrophenol, and, in man, by mercurial diuretics. Probenecid has been used clinically to inhibit penicillin excretion and thus to maintain the blood levels after a given dose for a longer period of time. A separate proximal tubular transport mechanism secretes certain drugs which are organic bases. A third, which secretes ethylenediaminetetraacetic acid (EDTA), has also been described.

WATER EXCRETION

Normally, 180 liters of fluid are filtered through the glomeruli each day, while the average daily urine volume is about 1 liter. The same load of solute can be excreted per 24 hours in a urine volume of 500 ml with a concentration of 1400 mOsm/liter; or in a volume of 23.3 liters, with a concentration of 30 mOsm/liter (Table 38–4). These figures demonstrate 2 important facts: first, that at least 88% of the filtered water is reabsorbed, even when the urine volume is 23 liters; and second, that the reabsorption of the remainder of the filtered water can be varied without affecting total solute excretion. Therefore, when the urine is concentrated, water is retained in excess of solute; and when it is dilute, water is lost from the body in excess of solute. Both facts have great importance in the body economy and the regulation of the osmolality of the body fluids.

FIG 38–9. Clearance of inulin, glucose, and PAH at various plasma levels of each substance in man.

TABLE 38–4. Alterations in water metabolism produced by vasopressin. In each case, the osmotic load excreted is 700 mOsm/day.

	GFR (ml/min)	Percentage of Filtered Water Reabsorbed	24-Hour Urine Volume	Urine Concentration (mOsm/liter)	Gain or Loss of Water in Excess of Solute (liters/day)
Urine isotonic to plasma	125	98.8	2.3	300	. . .
Vasopressin (maximal anti-diuresis)	125	99.7	0.5	1400	1.8 gain
No vasopressin ("complete" diabetes insipidus)	125	88	23.3	30	21.0 loss

Proximal Tubule

Many substances are actively transported out of the fluid in the proximal tubule, but fluid obtained from the first 70% of the proximal tubule by micropuncture is isosmotic with plasma, and it presumably remains isosmotic to the end of the proximal tubule (Fig 38–10). Therefore, in the proximal tubule water moves passively out of the tubule along the osmotic gradients set up by active transport of solutes, and isotonicity is maintained. Since the ratio of the con-

FIG 38–10. Osmolality of proximal tubular fluid (TF) obtained by micropuncture and osmolality of ureteral urine (U) compared with plasma osmolality (P) in rats. (From Gottschalk & Mylle: Study of mammalian urinary concentrating mechanism. Am J Physiol 196:927, 1959.)

centration in tubular fluid to the concentration in plasma (TF/P) of the nonreabsorbable substance inulin is approximately 4 at the end of the proximal tubule, it follows that approximately 75% of the filtered solute and 75% of the filtered water have been removed by the time the filtrate reaches this point (Table 38–5).

Loop of Henle

As noted above, the loops of Henle of the juxtamedullary nephrons dip deeply into the medullary pyramids before draining into the distal convoluted tubules in the cortex, and all of the collecting ducts descend back through the medullary pyramids to drain at the tips of the pyramids into the renal pelvis. It is now established that there is a graded increase in the osmolality of the interstitium of the pyramids, the osmolality at the tips of the papillae normally being many times that of plasma. It is also generally believed that the ascending limb of the loop of Henle is impermeable to water and that Na^+ is actively pumped out of the thick segment of the ascending limb. Therefore, the fluid in the descending limb of the loop of Henle becomes hypertonic as water moves into the hypertonic interstitium. In the ascending limb, it becomes more dilute, and when it reaches the top of the limb it is hypotonic to plasma because of the active transport of Na^+ out of the tubular lumen (Fig 38–11). In the process of passing through the loop of Henle, there is a net reduction of the volume of fluid of about 5%, so that by the time the fluid enters the distal tubule about 80% of the amount originally filtered has been reabsorbed (Table 38–5).

Distal Tubule & Collecting Duct

The changes in the osmolality and volume of the fluid in the distal tubule and collecting duct depend upon whether or not vasopressin, the antidiuretic hormone of the posterior pituitary (see Chapter 14), is present. This hormone increases the permeability of the epithelium of the collecting ducts to water. In the monkey and presumably in man, it acts only on the collecting ducts, but in other species it also increases the permeability of the distal tubule. When it is present, small volumes of concentrated urine are excreted; but when it is absent, large volumes of dilute urine are excreted.

TABLE 38–5. Water reabsorption in various portions of the nephron in hydropenic rats (maximal anti-diuresis), based on micropuncture studies in which the tubular fluid/plasma ratio of C^{14} inulin was determined. Because it is not as yet possible to puncture the distal third of the proximal tubule, the values for "end of proximal tubule" are calculated rather than observed.*

Location	Ratio of C^{14} Inulin, Tubular Fluid/Plasma	Percentage of Glomerular Filtrate Remaining	Percentage of Filtered Water Reabsorbed in Segment
Bowman's capsule	1	100	
Junction middle and distal third of proximal tubule	3	33	75 in proximal tubule
End proximal tubule (calculated)	4	25	
Start distal tubule	5	20	5 in loop
End distal tubule	20	5	15 in distal tubule
Ureter	690	0.14	4.86 in collecting ducts

*Based on data of Gottschalk: Micropuncture studies of tubular function in the mammalian kidney. The Physiologist 4:35, 1961.

In the presence of vasopressin in the rat, water leaves the distal tubule and the fluid in it is isosmotic from the midportion of the tubule on (Fig 38–11). Na^+ is pumped out and water moves with it, further reducing the volume of filtrate. The isotonic fluid then enters the collecting duct system and passes down

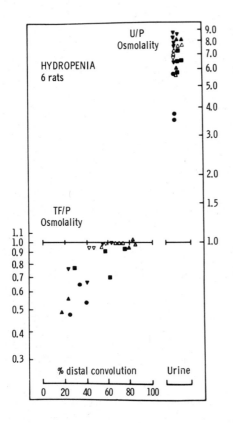

FIG 38–11. Osmolality ratios of fluid from distal convoluted tubules of rats during hydropenia. See legend for Fig 38–10. (From Gottschalk & Mylle: Study of mammalian urinary concentrating mechanism. Am J Physiol 196:927, 1959.)

through the hypertonic medullary pyramids, where water moves out of the lumen along the osmotic gradient, making the fluid concentrated. Fifteen percent of the filtrate is reabsorbed in the distal tubule by isosmotic reabsorption. A final 4+% is reabsorbed from the collecting ducts, forming a concentrated urine. The total amount of water reabsorbed during maximal antidiuresis is therefore 99.86% in the water-deprived rat (Table 38–5), and the urine is 6.4 times as concentrated as the plasma. In man, in whom the concentrating process presumably occurs only in the cortical and medullary portions of the collecting ducts, the concentrating power is not quite so great; however, 99.7% of the filtered water can be reabsorbed, and the final urine can contain 1400 mOsm/liter, a concentration that is almost 5 times that of plasma. Maximal urine osmolality in the dog is about 2500 mOsm/liter; in the laboratory rat, about 3200 mOsm/liter; and in certain desert rodents, as high as 5000 mOsm/liter.

When vasopressin is absent, the distal tubule and collecting duct epithelium is relatively impermeable to water. The fluid therefore remains hypotonic, and large amounts flow into the renal pelvis. In man, the urine osmolality may be as low as 30 mOsm/liter. The impermeability of the distal portions of the nephron is not absolute; along with the salt that is pumped out of the distal tubular and collecting duct fluid, about 8% of the filtered fluid is reabsorbed in the absence of vasopressin. However, as much as 12% of the filtered fluid may be excreted in man, and urine flow may reach 16 ml/min or more. The effects on daily water metabolism of the absence and the presence of vasopressin are summarized in Table 38–4.

Since it is much easier to drop a hydrometer into a urine specimen than to determine its osmolality, the **specific gravity** is the index of urine concentration that is generally used clinically. The specific gravity of an ultrafiltrate of plasma is 1.010, while that of a maximally concentrated urine specimen is about 1.035. However, it should be remembered that the specific gravity of a solution depends upon the nature as well as the number of solute particles in it. Thus, for example, a subject excreting radiographic contrast medium may have a specific gravity at 1.040–1.050, with relatively little increase in osmolality. Consequently, it is more accurate to measure osmolality.

The Countercurrent Mechanism

The concentrating mechanism depends upon the maintenance of a gradient of increasing osmolality along the medullary pyramids. This gradient exists because of the operation of the loops of Henle as **countercurrent multipliers** and the vasa recta as **countercurrent exchangers**. A countercurrent system is a system in which the inflow runs parallel to, counter to, and in close proximity to the outflow for some distance. The operation of such a system in increasing the heating at the apex of a loop of pipe is shown in Fig 38–12. The heat in the outgoing fluid heats the incoming fluid so that by the time it reaches the heater its temperature is 90° instead of 30°, and the heater therefore raises the fluid temperature from 90° to 100° rather than from 30° to 40°. The loop of Henle operates in an analogous fashion. The key to the maintenance of the osmotic gradients is the active transport of Na^+ out of the thick portion of the ascending limb of the loop of Henle. There is debate about the further details of the way the countercurrent mechanism operates. One current theory based on perfusion experiments in isolated tubules is illustrated in Fig 38–13. According to this view, the descending limb of the loop of Henle is relatively impermeable to solute but highly permeable to water. Consequently, water moves into the interstitium and the concentration of Na^+ in the tubular fluid rises markedly. The thin ascending limb of the loop is relatively impermeable to water and more permeable to Na^+ than to urea. Consequently, Na^+ moves passively into the interstitium along a concentration gradient. The thick ascending limb is relatively impermeable to both water and solute, but in this segment Na^+ is actively transported out of the tubular fluid. The distal tubule and outer portions of the collecting duct are relatively impermeable to urea but permeable to water in the presence of vasopressin. Consequently, water leaves the lumen and the urea concentration of the fluid increases markedly. Finally, the inner medullary portion of the collecting duct is permeable to urea and, in the presence of vasopressin, to water. Consequently, urea moves passively into the interstitium, maintaining the high osmolality of the medullary pyramid. Additional water is also removed, and the fluid in the tubule becomes highly concentrated.

Recent evidence indicates that the pump in the thick portion of the ascending limb of the loop of Henle is a Cl^- rather than Na^+ pump, with Na^+ passively following the Cl^- out of the tubular lumen.

The osmotic gradient in the medullary pyramids would not last long if the Na^+ and urea in the interstitial spaces were removed by the circulation. These solutes remain in the pyramids primarily because the vasa recta operate as countercurrent exchangers. The solutes diffuse out of the vessels conducting blood

FIG 38–12. Operation of a countercurrent system. On the left, a heater surrounds a pipe and raises the temperature of the water flowing in it 10°. On the right, the same heater is applied to a pipe bent to form a **U**, with the inflow close to the outflow. The heater still raises the temperature of the water 10°, but the heated water flowing away from the heater warms the inflow. A gradient of temperature is thus set up along the pipe, so that at the bend the temperature is raised not from 30° to 40° but from 90° to 100°. (Modified, redrawn, and reproduced, with permission, from Berliner: Dilution and concentration of the urine and the action of antidiuretic hormone. *Am J Med* 24:730, 1958.)

toward the cortex and into the vessels descending into the pyramid. Conversely, water diffuses out of the descending vessels and into the ascending vessels. Therefore, the solutes tend to recirculate in the medulla and water tends to bypass it, so that the hypertonicity is maintained. The meagerness and sluggishness of the blood flow of the medulla also contribute to the maintenance of the osmotic gradient. It should be noted that countercurrent exchange is a passive process; it depends upon diffusion of water and solutes in both directions across the permeable walls of the vasa recta, and could not maintain the osmotic gradient along the pyramids if the process of countercurrent multiplication in the loops of Henle were to cease.

FIG 38–13. Diagrammatic summary of one theory of the operation of the countercurrent mechanism in the renal medulla. All concentrations ([ ]) are in mOsm/liter. CD, collecting duct; X, nonreabsorbable solute. (Reproduced, with permission, from Kokko & Rector: Countercurrent multiplication system without active transport in inner medulla. Kidney Internat 2:214, 1972.)

It is also worth noting that there is a very large osmotic gradient in the renal tubules, and it is the countercurrent system that makes this gradient possible by spreading it along a system of tubules 1 cm or more in length rather than across a single layer of cells that is only a few μm thick. There are other examples of the operation of countercurrent systems in animals. One is the heat exchange between the arteries and venae comitantes of the limbs. To a minor degree in man, but to a major degree in mammals living in cold water, heat is transferred from the arterial blood flowing into the limbs to the adjacent veins draining blood back into the body, making the tips of the limbs cold while conserving body heat.

FACTORS AFFECTING URINE CONCENTRATION

Water Diuresis

The feedback mechanism controlling vasopressin secretion and the way vasopressin secretion is stimu-

lated by a rise and inhibited by a drop in the effective osmotic pressure of the plasma are discussed in Chapter 14. The **water diuresis** produced by drinking large amounts of hypotonic fluids begins about 15 minutes after ingestion of a water load and reaches its maximum in about 40 minutes. The delay represents the time required for the water to be absorbed, the vasopressin secretory mechanism inhibited, and the previously circulating vasopressin metabolized.

Water Intoxication

While excreting an average osmotic load, the maximal urine flow that can be produced during a water diuresis is about 16 ml/min. If water is ingested at a more rapid rate than this for any length of time, the swelling of the cells due to the uptake of water from the hypotonic ECF becomes severe, and the symptoms of **water intoxication** develop. Swelling of the cells in the brain causes convulsions and coma and leads eventually to death. Water intoxication can also occur when water intake is not reduced after administration of exogenous vasopressin or secretion of endogenous vasopressin in response to nonosmotic stimuli such as surgical trauma.

Urea Excretion

Although active transport of urea apparently occurs in some species, it has not been demonstrated in man. However, the urea in the glomerular filtrate diffuses out of the tubules as its concentration is increased by the progressive reduction of filtrate volume. This is hardly surprising, since urea diffuses rapidly through most membranes in the body except the blood-brain barrier. When urine flows are low, there is more opportunity for urea to leave the tubules, and only 10–20% of the filtered urea is excreted; at high urine flows, 50–70% is excreted.

Urea accumulates in the interstitium of the medullary pyramids, where it tends to remain trapped by the countercurrent exchange in the vasa recta. The urea concentration of the tubular fluid as it issues from the collecting ducts is still much higher than it would be if the fluid passed only through tissue with the low urea content of the rest of the kidney. Because the walls of the collecting ducts are very permeable to urea, relatively little difference in urea concentration develops across them and urea exerts only a slight inhibitory effect on the reabsorption of water from the collecting ducts. Therefore, the nonurea solutes can be concentrated almost as if urea were not present. The amount of urea in the medullary interstitium and, consequently, in the urine varies with the amount of urea filtered, and this in turn varies with the dietary intake of protein. A high-protein diet increases the ability of the kidney to concentrate the urine, and this increase is due, at least in part, to increased urea in the urine. However, urea has also been shown to increase the ability of the kidney to concentrate the nonurea solutes, so urea presumably has some additional unknown action on the concentrating mechanism.

The clearance of endogenous urea is sometimes measured as a clinical test of renal function. It has been demonstrated empirically that, when the urine flow is less than 2 ml/min, urea clearance is relatively independent of urine flow if $\sqrt{V}$ is used in the clearance formula instead of V.

Therefore, 2 arbitrary types of clearance, maximal and standard, are used:

Maximal urea clearance $= \dfrac{UV}{B}$ (Used when urine flow > 2 ml/min)

B = Whole blood urea level (approximately the same as the plasma level, but more frequently measured clinically)

Normal value: 75 ml/min

Standard urea clearance $= \dfrac{U\sqrt{V}}{B}$ (Used when urine flow < 2 ml/min)

Normal value: 54 ml/min

Osmotic Diuresis

Solutes that are not reabsorbed in the proximal tubules exert an appreciable osmotic effect as the volume of tubular fluid decreases and their concentration rises. They therefore "hold water in the tubules" and increase the volume of isotonic fluid presented to the countercurrent mechanism. There is a limit to the amount of Na^+ that can be actively transported out of the ascending limbs of the loops of Henle. When the loops are presented with greatly increased volumes of isotonic fluid from the proximal tubules, this amount of Na^+ becomes inadequate to prevent dilution by isotonic fluid of the hypertonic fluid in the medullary interstitium. More fluid passes through the loops, and because of the decrease in the osmotic gradient along the medullary pyramids, less water is reabsorbed in the collecting ducts. The resulting increase in urine volume is called **osmotic diuresis**. Osmotic diuresis is produced by the administration of compounds such as mannitol and related polysaccharides that are filtered but not reabsorbed. It is also produced by naturally occurring substances when they are present in amounts exceeding the capacity of the tubules to reabsorb them. In diabetes, for example, the glucose that remains in the tubules when the filtered load exceeds the Tm_G causes polyuria. Osmotic diuresis can also be produced by the infusion of large amounts of sodium chloride or urea.

It is important to recognize the difference between osmotic diuresis and water diuresis. In water diuresis, the amount of water reabsorbed in the proximal portions of the nephron is normal, and the maximal urine flow that can be produced is about 16 ml/min. In osmotic diuresis, increased urine flow is due to decreased water reabsorption in the proximal tubules, and very large urine flows can be produced. As the load of excreted solute is increased, the concentration of the urine approaches that of plasma (Fig 38–14) in spite of maximal vasopressin secretion because an increasingly large fraction of the excreted urine is isotonic proximal tubular fluid. If osmotic diuresis is produced in an animal with diabetes insipidus, the urine concentration rises for the same reason.

Appreciable amounts of water are lost during osmotic diuresis. Significant amounts of electrolytes, especially Na^+, are also lost in the urine. There is a limiting concentration gradient against which Na^+ can be actively transported out of the tubular fluid. Normally, the movement of water out of the proximal tubule prevents any appreciable gradient from developing; but Na^+ concentration in the fluid falls when water reabsorption is decreased because of the presence in the tubular fluid of increased amounts of unreabsorbable solutes. The limiting concentration gradient is reached, and further proximal Na^+ reabsorption is prevented; more Na^+ is therefore lost in the urine.

Relation of Urine Concentration to GFR

The magnitude of the osmotic gradient along the medullary pyramids is increased when the rate of flow

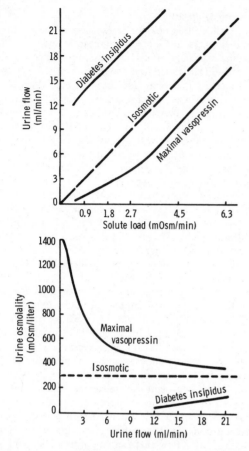

FIG 38–14. **Approximate relationship between urine concentration and urine flow in osmotic diuresis in man.** The dashed line in the lower diagram indicates the concentration at which the urine is isosmotic with plasma. (Slightly modified, redrawn, and reproduced, with permission, from Berliner, in: *The Physiological Basis of Medical Practice,* 8th ed. Best CH, Taylor NB [editors]. Williams & Wilkins, 1966.)

of fluid through the loops of Henle is decreased. A reduction in GFR such as that caused by dehydration produces a decrease in the volume of fluid presented to the countercurrent mechanism, so that the rate of flow in the loops declines and the urine becomes more concentrated. When the GFR is low, the urine can become quite concentrated in the absence of vasopressin; if one renal artery is constricted in an animal with diabetes insipidus, the urine excreted on the side of the constriction becomes hypertonic because of the reduction in GFR, whereas that excreted on the opposite side remains hypotonic.

Disruption of the renal lymphatics decreases renal concentrating ability, presumably because it permits protein to accumulate in the interstitium of the medullary pyramids, reducing the osmotic gradient along which reabsorbed water moves into the vasa recta for return to the general circulation (see Chapter 30).

"Free Water Clearance"

In order to quantitate the gain or loss of water by excretion of a concentrated or dilute urine, the "free water clearance" (C_{H_2O}) is sometimes calculated. This is the difference between the urine volume and the clearance of osmols (C_{Osm}):

$$CH_2O = V - \frac{U_{Osm}V}{P_{Osm}}$$

where V is the urine volume and U_{Osm} and P_{Osm} the urine and plasma osmolality. C_{Osm} is the amount of water necessary to excrete the osmotic load in a urine that is isotonic with plasma. Therefore, C_{H_2O} is negative when the urine is hypertonic and positive when the urine is hypotonic. In Table 38–4, for example, the values for C_{H_2O} are –1.3 ml/min (–1.8 liters/day) during maximal antidiuresis, and 14.6 ml/min (21.0 liters/day) in the absence of vasopressin.

ACIDIFICATION OF THE URINE & BICARBONATE EXCRETION

H⁺ Secretion

The cells of the proximal and distal tubules, like the cells of the gastric glands, secrete hydrogen ions (see Chapter 26). Acidification also occurs in the collecting ducts. The reactions believed to occur in the cells are shown in Fig 38–15. Like other cells, the renal tubular cells have a Na⁺-K⁺ exchange pump (see Chapter 1), but this pump is believed to be absent from the membrane that faces the tubular lumen. H⁺ is actively transported across this membrane, and for

FIG 38–15. **Probable chemical reactions involved in secretion of H⁺ by proximal and distal tubular cells in the kidney.** Solid arrows crossing cell membranes indicate active transport. Dashed arrows indicate diffusion. The circle containing arrows in the cell wall represents a coupled active transport mechanism. Compare with Fig 26–6.

each H^+ secreted an Na^+ enters the cell. In this case, Na^+ is moving down its electrical and its chemical gradients. There is no evidence that H^+ efflux and Na^+ influx are linked by utilization of a common carrier, and it appears that Na^+ simply diffuses into the cell to maintain electroneutrality. For each H^+ secreted, one HCO_3^- and one Na^+ enter the interstitial fluid and diffuse from there into the blood stream.

The source of the H^+ secreted by the tubular cells is uncertain. It may be produced simply by dissociation of H_2CO_3, as shown in Fig 38–15, or it may be produced by the ionization of H_2O or more complex reactions such as those postulated to occur in the stomach, with the H^+ from H_2CO_3 buffering the OH^- that is formed. The acid-secreting cells contain the enzyme **carbonic anhydrase**, which catalyzes the reaction $CO_2 + H_2O \rightleftarrows H_2CO_3$. This makes possible the rapid formation of H_2CO_3 (see Chapter 35). Drugs which inhibit carbonic anhydrase depress renal acid secretion and the reactions in the kidney that depend on it.

Fate of H^+ in the Urine

The amount of acid secreted depends upon the subsequent events in the tubular urine. The maximal H^+ gradient against which the transport mechanism can secrete in man corresponds to a urine pH of about 4.5, which is thus the **limiting pH**. If there were no buffers or other substances that "tied up" H^+ in the urine, this pH would be reached rapidly and H^+ secretion would stop. However, 3 important reactions in the tubular fluid remove free H^+, permitting more acid to be secreted (Fig 38–16). These are the reactions with

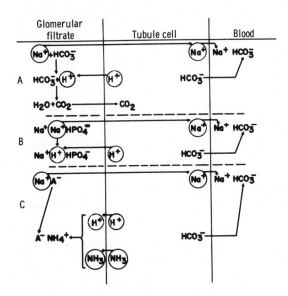

FIG 38–16. Fate of H^+ secreted into tubule in exchange for Na^+. *A:* Reabsorption of filtered bicarbonate. *B:* Formation of titratable acid. *C:* Ammonium formation. Note that in each instance one Na^+ and one HCO_3^- enter the blood stream for each H^+ secreted. A^-, anion.

HCO_3^- to form CO_2 and H_2O, with $HPO_4^=$ to form $H_2PO_4^-$, and with NH_3 to form NH_4^+.

Reaction With Buffers

The dynamics of buffering are discussed in Chapter 35. The major buffers in the glomerular filtrate are the bicarbonate (pK 6.1) and dibasic phosphate (pK 6.8) systems. The concentration of HCO_3^- in the plasma, and consequently in the glomerular filtrate, is normally about 24 mEq/liter, whereas that of phosphate is only 1.5 mEq/liter. Therefore, in the proximal tubule, most of the secreted H^+ reacts with HCO_3^- to form H_2CO_3 (Fig 38–16). The H_2CO_3 breaks down to form CO_2 and H_2O. In the proximal (but not in the distal) tubule, there is carbonic anhydrase in the brush border of the cells; this facilitates the formation of CO_2 and H_2O in the tubular fluid. The CO_2, which diffuses readily across all biologic membranes, enters the tubular cells, where it adds to the pool of CO_2 available to form H_2CO_3. Since the H^+ is removed from the tubule, the pH of the fluid is unchanged. This is the mechanism by which HCO_3^- is reabsorbed; for each mol of HCO_3^- removed from the tubular fluid, 1 mol of HCO_3^- diffuses from the tubular cells into the blood even though it is not the same mol that disappeared from the tubular fluid.

Secreted H^+ also reacts with dibasic phosphate ($HPO_4^=$) to form monobasic phosphate ($H_2PO_4^-$). This happens to the greatest extent in the distal tubules and collecting ducts because it is here that the phosphate which escapes proximal reabsorption is greatly concentrated by the reabsorption of water. H^+ also combines to a minor degree with other buffer anions.

Each H^+ that reacts with buffer anions other than HCO_3^- contributes to the urinary **titratable acidity**, which is measured by determining the amount of alkali that must be added to the urine to return its pH to 7.4, the pH of the glomerular filtrate. The titratable acidity obviously measures only a fraction of the acid secreted since it does not measure the H^+ that combines with HCO_3^- nor that which combines with NH_3.

Ammonia Secretion

NH_3 is secreted in the proximal and distal tubules and the collecting ducts. The reactions forming NH_3 in the cells are summarized in Fig 38–17. Glutamine is converted to glutamic acid and ammonia (Fig 17–23). This reaction is catalyzed by the enzyme **glutaminase**, which is abundant in tubular cells. More NH_3 is formed by the deamination of glutamic acid and small amounts by deamination of other amino acids. In addition, some comes directly from arterial blood. The NH_3 diffuses into the tubular fluid because it is lipid-soluble, and crosses the lipid-containing membranes of the cells with ease. In the fluid, it reacts with secreted H^+ to form ammonium ions (NH_4^+). Unlike NH_3, NH_4^+ is relatively lipid-insoluble and thus stays in the tubular fluid.

The amount of NH_4^+ formed depends upon the pH of the tubular fluid and the rate of NH_3 production. At any given rate of NH_3 production, the amount

$$\text{Glutamine} + \text{H}_2\text{O} \xrightarrow{\text{Glutaminase}} \text{Glutamic acid} + \text{NH}_3$$

$$\text{Glutamic acid} \xrightarrow[\text{dehydrogenase}]{\text{Glutamic}} \alpha\text{-Ketoglutaric acid} + \text{NH}_3$$

$$\text{Deamination of} \xrightarrow{} \alpha\text{-Keto acids} + \text{NH}_3$$
$$\text{other amino acids}$$

$$\text{NH}_3 + \text{H}^+ \rightleftharpoons \text{NH}_4^+$$

FIG 38–17. Major reactions involved in ammonia production in the kidney. See also Figs 17–22 and 17–23.

of NH_4^+ formed is proportionate to the amount of H^+ available and therefore to the rate of H^+ secretion. Thus, the NH_4^+ content of an alkaline urine is nil whereas that of a maximally acid urine is high.

The production of NH_3 is gradually increased over a period of 3–5 days in chronic acidosis. This **adaptation** of NH_3 production is brought about by an increase in tissue glutaminase activity, but the mechanism responsible for this increase is not known. The increase is independent of changes in urinary pH, and occurs even in compensated acidosis in which the pH of the plasma is nearly normal (see Chapter 40).

The process by which NH_3 is secreted is called **nonionic diffusion** (see Chapter 1). Salicylates and a number of other drugs that are weak bases or weak acids are also secreted by nonionic diffusion. They diffuse into the tubular fluid at a rate which is dependent upon the urine pH, and the amount of each drug excreted therefore varies with the pH of the urine.

pH Changes Along the Nephrons

Micropuncture studies indicate that an appreciable drop in pH occurs in the proximal tubule in mammalian kidneys, although there is further acidification in the distal tubule (Fig 38–18). Since most of the HCO_3^- is absorbed in the proximal tubule and the H^+ secretion responsible for its reabsorption does not change the pH of the fluid, it is apparent that there is considerably more acid secretion in the proximal than in the distal tubule. The acid-secreting mechanism in the distal tubules, and particularly in the collecting ducts, has a lower secretory capacity but is capable of generating a large pH difference between the tubular lumen and the cells. The pH of the tubular urine also depends upon the relation between the amount of HCO_3^- reabsorbed and the reduction in the volume of the filtrate. The urinary pH, like that of the blood, depends upon the ratio $[\text{HCO}_3^-]/[\text{H}_2\text{CO}_3]$, since

$$\text{pH} = \text{pK}_{\text{H}_2\text{CO}_3} + \log \frac{[\text{HCO}_3^-]}{[\text{H}_2\text{CO}_3]}$$

and $[\text{H}_2\text{CO}_3]$ is proportionate to P_{CO_2}. Therefore, if the amount of fluid in the tubule decreases less rapidly than the amount of HCO_3^- at any given P_{CO_2}, the

concentration of HCO_3^- falls and so does the pH. Conversely, when the HCO_3^- concentration rises, the pH rises.

Factors Affecting Acid Secretion

Renal acid secretion is altered by changes in the intracellular P_{CO_2}, K^+ concentration, carbonic anhydrase level, and adrenocortical hormone concentration. When the P_{CO_2} is high (respiratory acidosis), more intracellular H_2CO_3 is available to buffer the hydroxyl ions and acid secretion is enhanced, whereas the reverse is true when the P_{CO_2} falls. K^+ depletion enhances acid secretion, apparently because the loss of K^+ causes intracellular acidosis even though the plasma pH may be elevated. Conversely, K^+ excess in the cells inhibits acid secretion. When carbonic anhydrase is inhibited, acid secretion is inhibited because the formation of H_2CO_3 is decreased. Aldosterone and the other adrenocortical steroids that enhance tubular reabsorption of Na^+ also increase the secretion of H^+ and K^+.

FIG 38–18. Changes in pH in the renal tubules. The values are plotted as changes in pH relative to plasma pH. (Reproduced, with permission, from Gottschalk & others: Location of urine acidification in the mammalian kidney. Am J Physiol 198:581, 1960.)

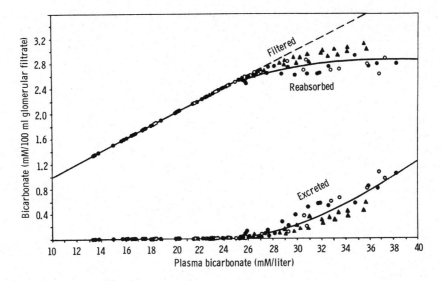

FIG 38–19. Reabsorption and excretion of bicarbonate at various plasma bicarbonate levels in man. The different symbols represent values from different subjects. (Reproduced, with permission, from Pitts & others: The renal regulation of acid-base balance in man. III. The reabsorption and excretion of bicarbonate. J Clin Invest 28:35, 1949.)

Bicarbonate Excretion

Although the process of HCO_3^- reabsorption does not actually involve transport of this ion into the tubular cells, HCO_3^- behaves as if it had a Tm that is exceeded when the plasma HCO_3^- concentration exceeds 28 mEq/liter (mM/liter). At lower HCO_3^- levels, all the HCO_3^- is reabsorbed; but at values above this threshold, HCO_3^- appears in the urine and urine becomes alkaline (Fig 38–19).

When the plasma HCO_3^- is 28 mEq/liter, H^+ is being secreted at its maximal rate and all of it is being used to reabsorb HCO_3^-; but as the plasma HCO_3^- drops, more H^+ becomes available to appear as titratable acidity and NH_4^+. Therefore, the further the plasma HCO_3^- drops, the more acid the urine becomes and the greater its NH_4^+ content. For unknown reasons, the capacity of the tubules to reabsorb HCO_3^- rises when the GFR rises.

Implications of Urinary pH Changes

Depending upon the rates of the interrelated processes of acid secretion, NH_4^+ production, and HCO_3^- excretion, the pH of the urine varies from an extreme of 4.5 to about 8.0 in man. Excretion of a urine that is at a pH different from that of the body fluids has important implications for the body's electrolyte and acid-base economy which are discussed in detail in Chapter 40. Acids are buffered in the plasma and cells, the overall reaction being $HA + NaHCO_3 \rightleftarrows$ NaA and H_2CO_3. The H_2CO_3 forms CO_2 and H_2O, and the CO_2 is expired, while the NaA appears in the glomerular filtrate. To the extent that the Na^+ is replaced by H^+ as titratable acidity or NH_4^+, Na^+ is conserved in the body. Furthermore, for each H^+ excreted as titratable acidity or NH_4^+, there is a net

gain of one HCO_3^- in the blood, replenishing the supply of this important buffer anion. Conversely, when base is added to the body fluids, the OH^- ions are buffered, raising the plasma HCO_3^-. When the plasma level exceeds 28 mEq/liter, the urine becomes alkaline and the extra HCO_3^- is excreted in the urine. Because the rate of maximum H^+ secretion by the tubules varies directly with the arterial P_{CO_2}, HCO_3^- reabsorption also is affected by the P_{CO_2}. This relationship is discussed in detail in Chapter 40.

SODIUM & CHLORIDE EXCRETION

Na^+ is filtered in large amounts, but it appears to be actively transported out of many portions of the tubules (see above). Normally, 96% to well over 99% of the filtered Na^+ is reabsorbed. Most of the Na^+ is reabsorbed with Cl^- (Table 38–6), but some is reabsorbed in the processes by which one Na^+ enters the blood stream for each H^+ secreted by the tubules, and a small amount is reabsorbed in association with the secretion of K^+.

Regulation of Na⁺ Excretion

Because Na^+ is the most abundant cation in ECF and because sodium salts account for over 90% of the osmotically active solute in the plasma and interstitial fluid, the amount of Na^+ in the body is a prime determinant of the ECF volume. Therefore, it is not surprising that multiple regulatory mechanisms have evolved in terrestrial animals to control the excretion of this ion. Through the operation of these regulatory

TABLE 38–6. Quantitative aspects of Na⁺ reabsorption in a normal man.

GFR = 125 ml/minute
Plasma HCO_3^- = 27 mEq/liter
Plasma Na⁺ = 145 mEq/liter

Na⁺ filtered per minute . . . . 18,125 μEq

Reabsorbed with Cl⁻ . . . . 14,585 μEq
Reabsorbed while
  reabsorbing 3375 } . . . . 3,375 μEq
  μEq HCO_3^-
Reabsorbed in asso-
  ciation with
  formation of } . . . . 50 μEq
  titratable acidity
  and ammonia
Reabsorbed in asso-
  ciation with . . . . 50 μEq
  secretion of K⁺

Total Na⁺ reabsorbed per minute . . . . 18,060 μEq

mechanisms, the amount of Na⁺ excreted is adjusted to equal the amount ingested over a wide range of dietary intakes, and the individual stays in Na⁺ balance. Thus, urinary Na⁺ output ranges from less than 1 mEq/day on a low-salt diet to 400 mEq/day or more when the dietary Na⁺ intake is high. In addition, there is a natriuresis when saline is infused intravenously and a decrease in Na⁺ excretion when ECF volume is reduced. Variations in Na⁺ excretion are effected by changes in the amount filtered and the amount reabsorbed in the tubules. The factors affecting the GFR are discussed above. The factors affecting Na⁺ reabsorption include the oncotic and hydrostatic pressures in the peritubular capillaries, the circulating level of aldosterone and other adrenocortical hormones, the rate of tubular secretion of H⁺ and K⁺, and possibly other factors which are as yet incompletely identified.

Importance of the Filtered Na⁺ Load

The amount of Na⁺ filtered is so large (over 26,000 mEq/day) that—if the total amount of Na⁺ reabsorbed stayed constant—a rise in GFR of only 2 ml/min would more than double the amount excreted (Table 38–7) and a small fall in GFR would reduce Na⁺ excretion to zero. These figures are theoretical rather than actual because the total amount reabsorbed rises when the GFR rises and falls when it falls. Most

of the change in reabsorption occurs in the proximal tubule. However, the compensation is rarely complete, and fluctuations in GFR play an important role in determining the amount of Na⁺ excreted.

The Reabsorptive Process

Na⁺ diffuses passively from the tubular lumen into tubular epithelial cells and is pumped actively from them into the interstitial space. The tubular cells are connected at their luminal surface by tight junctions, but there is space between the cells along the rest of their lateral borders. It now appears that much of the Na⁺ is actively transported into these extensions of the interstitial space, which are called the **lateral intercellular spaces** (Fig 38–20). This creates a hyperosmotic local environment in the spaces, and water moves passively into it from cells. From the lateral intercellular spaces and the rest of the interstitium, the rate at which solutes and water move into the capillaries is determined by the forces determining movement across the walls of all capillaries, ie, the hydrostatic and osmotic pressures in the interstitium and the capillaries (see Chapter 30). Thus, when renal capillary hydrostatic pressure is high and oncotic pressure in the capillary is low, movement of fluid out of the interstitial space is slowed and the space expands. Especially when it is expanded, there appears to be bulk flow of interstitial fluid and solute across the tight junctions from the lateral intercellular spaces to

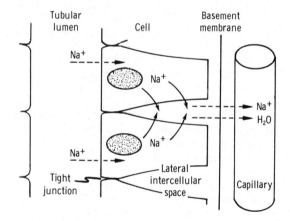

FIG 38–20. Diagrammatic summary of the movement of Na⁺ from the tubular lumen to the renal capillaries. Dashed arrows represent passive movement and solid arrows indicate active transport.

TABLE 38–7. Changes in Na⁺ excretion that would occur as a result of changes in GFR if there were no concomitant changes in Na⁺ reabsorption.

GFR (ml/min)	Plasma Na⁺ (μEq/ml)	Amount Filtered (μEq/min)	Amount Reabsorbed (μEq/min)	Amount Excreted (μEq/min)
125	145	18,125	18,000	125
127	145	18,415	18,000	415
124.1	145	18,000	18,000	0

FIG 38–21. **Two mechanisms that actively transport Na^+ from renal tubular cells into the lateral intercellular spaces and the other parts of the interstitium.** Solid arrows represent active transport; dashed arrows, passive movement. Pump A transports only Na^+, whereas pump B is a coupled Na^+-K^+ exchange pump. (Modified and reproduced, with permission, from Giebisch: Coupled ion and fluid transport in the kidney. New England J Med 287:913, 1972.)

the tubular lumen. Thus, there is an appreciable leakage of Na^+ back into the tubule and net Na^+ reabsorption is decreased.

There appear to be 2 separate Na^+ pumps in the renal tubules. One (pump A in Fig 38–21) extrudes Na^+ into the interstitium, and Cl^- moves passively with the Na^+. The Cl^- in the cells is replenished by diffusion from the tubular fluid. This pump is an **electrogenic Na^+ pump** in that it extrudes positively charged Na^+ ions and consequently contributes to the maintenance of the electronegativity of the cell interior. The other pump (pump B in Fig 38–21) is a coupled exchange pump which transports a K^+ into the cell for each Na^+ it transports into the interstitium. It therefore produces no net movement of charge and has no direct effect on the membrane potential of the renal tubular cells.

The electrogenic Na^+ pump is inhibited by ethacrynic acid or by the replacement of Cl^- in the tubular fluid with anions that penetrate tubular cells poorly. The Na^+-K^+ exchange pump is inhibited by ouabain and by a low extracellular K^+ concentration.

Glomerulotubular Balance

The proximal tubular reabsorption of a number of substances is proportionate to the load delivered to the tubule by filtration. This proportionality, which is especially apparent in the case of Na^+ and, consequently, of water reabsorption, has come to be referred to as **glomerulotubular balance**. The mechanism by which the change in proximal reabsorption is brought about is currently the subject of intensive research. The change in Na^+ reabsorption occurs within seconds after a change in filtration, so it seems unlikely that an extrarenal humoral factor is involved. However,

intrarenal mechanisms that bring about the change have not as yet been identified.

Hemodynamic Effects on Tubular Reabsorption

Changes in renal capillary hydrostatic and oncotic pressure appear to be important in the response to salt loading. Intravenous saline produces a natriuresis with decreased Na^+ reabsorption in the proximal tubule. Saline dilutes the blood, lowering the oncotic pressure, and volume expansion also appears to decrease renal vascular resistance, with a consequent increase in hydrostatic pressure. Conversely, conditions which reduce ECF volume cause renal vasoconstriction, with a consequent reduction in hydrostatic pressure in the capillaries, and proximal tubular Na^+ reabsorption is increased. Changes in hydrostatic and osmotic pressures may also play a role in glomerulotubular balance and in the "escape phenomenon" (see Chapter 20).

Effects of Adrenocortical Steroids

Adrenal mineralocorticoids such as aldosterone increase tubular reabsorption of Na^+ in association with secretion of K^+ and H^+, and also Na^+ reabsorption with Cl^- (see Chapter 20). When these hormones are injected into adrenalectomized animals, there is a latent period of 10–30 minutes before their effects on Na^+ reabsorption become manifest. There is evidence that they act on both the proximal and distal tubules, but their main action is unquestionably on the distal tubule. The glucocorticoids such as cortisol also increase Na^+ reabsorption; but, unlike the mineralocorticoids, they increase the GFR. They may therefore increase, rather than decrease, Na^+ excretion because the increase they produce in the filtered load of Na^+ may exceed the increase in reabsorption.

Reduction of the dietary intake of salt increases aldosterone secretion (Fig 20–28). Changes in aldosterone secretion can explain changes in Na^+ excretion that occur over days or even hours, but, because of the latent period before its effects are manifest, rapid changes in Na^+ excretion cannot be attributed to this hormone.

Relation to Acid & K^+ Secretion

Na^+ excretion is increased by drugs which decrease renal acid secretion by inhibiting carbonic anhydrase. After CO_2 or acid is buffered in the blood, Na^+ filtered with acid anions is lost in the urine if the amount in the filtrate exceeds the capacity of the tubules to exchange the Na^+ for H^+. Changes in Na^+ excretion due to changes in the rate of K^+ secretion are small (Table 38–6).

Other Factors

The factors affecting proximal Na^+ reabsorption are important because proximal reabsorption is increased when ECF volume is reduced, and decreased when it is expanded. The role of hydrostatic and oncotic pressures in mediating these changes is discussed above. Other investigators argue that an as yet unisolated hormone, an elusive **"third factor,"** acts along with the adrenocortical hormones and the GFR to regulate Na⁺ excretion. It has been suggested that such a hormone acts primarily on proximal Na⁺ reabsorption. There is some evidence that the renal nerves affect Na⁺ reabsorption (see above). However, the role of each of these factors, if any, must await further research.

Chloride Excretion

Chloride reabsorption is increased when HCO_3^- reabsorption is decreased, and vice versa, so that Cl^- concentration in plasma varies inversely with the HCO_3^- concentration, keeping the total anion concentration constant. Passive diffusion can explain the movements of Cl^- in most situations. However, in some micropuncture studies, Cl^- concentrations have been observed in tubular fluid which are difficult to explain except in terms of the active transport of Cl^-.

POTASSIUM EXCRETION

Much of the filtered K⁺ is removed from the tubular fluid by active reabsorption in the proximal tubules (Table 38–8), and K⁺ is then secreted into the fluid by the distal tubular cells. In the absence of complicating factors, the amount secreted is approximately equal to the K⁺ intake and K⁺ balance is maintained. The distal secretory mechanism involves an exchange process by which Na⁺ is reabsorbed as K⁺ is secreted. Current evidence indicates that the secretion of K⁺ is passive, not active, and that there is no carrier-coupled exchange of Na⁺ for K⁺. However, electrical coupling exists in the sense that intracellular migration of Na⁺ tends to lower the potential difference across the tubular cell, and this favors movement of K⁺ into the tubular lumen. Since Na⁺ is also reabsorbed in association with H⁺ secretion, there is competition for

the Na⁺ in the distal tubular fluid. K⁺ excretion is decreased when the amount of Na⁺ reaching the distal tubule is low, and K⁺ excretion is also decreased when H⁺ secretion is increased. When total body K⁺ is high, H⁺ secretion is inhibited, apparently because of intracellular alkalosis; and K⁺ secretion and excretion is therefore facilitated. Conversely, the cells are acid in K⁺ depletion, and K⁺ secretion declines. Apparently the K⁺ secretory mechanism is capable of "adaptation" because the amount of K⁺ excreted gradually increases when a constant large dose of a potassium salt is administered for a prolonged period of time.

DIURETICS

Although a detailed discussion of diuretic agents is outside the scope of this book, consideration of their mechanisms of action constitutes an informative review of the factors affecting urine volume and electrolyte excretion. These mechanisms are summarized in Table 38–9. Water, alcohol, osmotic diuretics, xanthines, and acidifying salts have limited clinical usefulness, but the other agents on the list are used extensively in medical practice.

Water diuresis and osmotic diuresis have been discussed above. Ethyl alcohol acts directly on the hypothalamus. The diuretic action of the xanthines is weak. When NH_4Cl is ingested, the NH_4^+ dissociates to H^+ and NH_3 and the NH_3 is converted to urea, so that ingesting NH_4Cl is equivalent to adding HCl to the body. The H⁺ is buffered and the Cl⁻ filtered along with Na⁺, thus maintaining electrical neutrality. To the extent that any of the Na⁺ is not replaced by H⁺ from the renal tubules, Na⁺ and water are lost in the urine. Other acidifying salts produce diuresis in a similar way.

The carbonic anhydrase inhibiting drugs are only

TABLE 38–8. Renal handling of various plasma constituents in a normal adult human on an average diet.
P, proximal tubules; L, loops of Henle; D, distal tubules; C, collecting ducts.

Substance	Per 24 Hours				Percentage Reabsorbed	Location
	Filtered	Reabsorbed	Secreted	Excreted		
Na⁺ (mEq)	26,000	25,850		150	99.4	P, L, D, C
K⁺ (mEq)	900	900*	100	100	100*	P, D*
Cl⁻ (mEq)	18,000	17,850		150	99.2	P, L, D, C
HCO₃⁻ (mEq)	4,900	4,900		0	100	P, D
Urea (mM)	870	460†		410	53	P, L, D, C
Creatinine (mM)	12	1‡	1‡	12	...	...
Uric acid (mM)	50	49	4	5	98	P
Glucose (mM)	800	800		0	100	P
Total solute (mOsm)	54,000	53,400	100	700	87	P, L, D, C
Water (ml)	180,000	179,000		1000	99.4	P, L, D, C

*K⁺ is reabsorbed proximally and secreted distally. It is not certain that all of the filtered K⁺ is reabsorbed proximally.

†Urea diffuses into as well as out of some portions of the nephron.

‡Variable secretion and probable reabsorption of creatinine in man.

TABLE 38–9. Mechanism of action of various diuretics.

Agent	Mechanism of Action
Water	Inhibits vasopressin secretion.
Ethyl alcohol	Inhibits vasopressin secretion.
Large quantities of osmotically active substances such as mannitol and glucose	Produce osmotic diuresis.
Xanthines such as caffeine and theophylline	Probably decrease tubular reabsorption of Na^+ and increase GFR.
Acidifying salts such as $CaCl_2$ and NH_4Cl	Supply acid load; H^+ is buffered, and anion is excreted with Na^+ when the ability of the kidney to replace Na^+ with H^+ is exceeded.
Organic salts of mercury such as mercaptomerin (Thiomerin) and meralluride (Mercuhydrin)	Inhibit Na^+ reabsorption "beyond the proximal tubule"; inhibit K^+ secretion.
Carbonic anhydrase inhibitors such as acetazolamide (Diamox)	Decrease H^+ secretion, with resultant increase in Na^+ and K^+ excretion.
Thiazides such as chlorothiazide (Diuril)	Inhibit Na^+ reabsorption in the distal portion of the loop of Henle and proximal portion of the distal tubule; large doses also inhibit carbonic anhydrase.
Furosemide (Lasix)	Inhibits Na^+ reabsorption in the loop of Henle.
Ethacrynic acid (Edecrin)	Inhibits Na^+ reabsorption in the loop of Henle.
K^+-retaining natriuretics such as spironolactone (Aldactone) and triamterene (Dyrenium)	Inhibit Na^+-K^+ "exchange" in the distal tubule by inhibiting the action of aldosterone (spironolactone) or directly (triamterene).

moderately effective as diuretic agents, but because they inhibit acid secretion by decreasing the supply of carbonic acid they have far-reaching effects. Not only is Na^+ excretion increased because H^+ secretion is decreased, but HCO_3^- reabsorption is also depressed; and because H^+ and K^+ compete with each other and with Na^+, the decrease in H^+ secretion facilitates the secretion and excretion of K^+.

Another determinant of the rate of K^+ secretion is the amount of Na^+ delivered to the Na^+-K^+ "exchange" site in the distal tubule. Thiazides, furosemide, and ethacrynic acid act proximal to this site, and the resultant increase in Na^+ delivery increases K^+ secretion. The K^+ loss is appreciable, and K^+ depletion is one of the common complications of treatment with these agents. The mercurial diuretics probably also act proximal to the exchange site, but they have the additional action of inhibiting K^+ secretion, so that K^+ depletion is not marked. Spironolactone and triamterene act on the exchange mechanism itself, causing K^+ retention and, in some cases, mild hyperkalemia.

Furosemide and ethacrynic acid both inhibit the Na^+-K^+ ATPase that is intimately related to Na^+ transport (see Chapter 1), but the relation of this inhibitory action to their diuretic effect is unsettled.

EFFECTS OF DISORDERED RENAL FUNCTION

A number of abnormalities are common to many different types of renal disease. The secretion of renin by the kidneys and the relation of the kidneys to hypertension are discussed in Chapters 24 and 33. A frequent finding in various forms of renal disease is the presence in the urine of protein, leukocytes, red cells, and **casts**, which are bits of proteinaceous material precipitated in the tubules and washed into the bladder. Other important consequences of renal disease are loss of the ability to concentrate or dilute the urine, uremia, acidosis, and abnormal retention of Na^+.

Proteinuria

In many renal diseases and in one benign condition, the permeability of the glomerular capillaries is increased and protein is found in the urine in more than the usual trace amounts (**proteinuria**). Most of this protein is albumin, and the defect is commonly called **albuminuria**, although other plasma proteins are also present. The amount of protein in the urine may be very large, and, especially in nephrosis, the urinary protein loss may exceed the rate at which the liver can synthesize plasma proteins. The resulting hypoproteinemia reduces the oncotic pressure and the plasma volume declines, sometimes to dangerously low levels, while edema fluid accumulates in the tissues.

The one benign condition that causes proteinuria is a poorly understood change in renal hemodynamics which in some otherwise normal individuals causes protein to appear in urine formed when they are in the standing position (**orthostatic albuminuria**). Urine formed when they are lying down is protein-free.

Loss of Concentrating & Diluting Ability

In renal disease, the urine becomes less concentrated and urine volume is often increased, producing the symptoms of **polyuria** and **nocturia** (waking up at night to void). The ability to form a dilute urine is often retained, but in advanced renal disease the osmolality of the urine becomes fixed at about that of plasma, indicating that the diluting and concentrating functions of the kidney have both been lost. The loss is due in part to disruption of the countercurrent mechanism, but a more important cause is a loss of functioning nephrons. When one kidney is removed surgically, the number of functioning nephrons is halved. The number of osmols excreted is not reduced to this extent, and so the remaining nephrons must each be filtering and excreting more osmotically active substances, producing what is in effect an osmotic diuresis. In osmotic diuresis, the osmolality of the urine approaches that of plasma (see above); the same thing happens when the number of functioning nephrons is reduced by disease. Of course, when most of the nephrons are destroyed, urine volume falls and **oliguria** or even **anuria** is present.

Uremia

When the breakdown products of protein metabolism accumulate in the blood, the syndrome known as **uremia** develops. The symptoms of uremia include lethargy, anorexia, nausea and vomiting, mental deterioration and confusion, muscle twitching, convulsions, and coma. Because erythropoiesis is depressed, anemia is a prominent feature of chronic uremia. The blood urea nitrogen (BUN), nonprotein nitrogen (NPN), and creatinine levels are high, and the blood levels of these substances are used as an index of the severity of the uremia. It is often stated that it is not the accumulation of urea and creatinine per se but rather the accumulation of other toxic substances—possibly organic acids or phenols—that produces the symptoms of uremia. Because urea crosses the blood-brain barrier slowly, it is administered intravenously to neurosurgical patients to make the ECF outside the brain hypertonic and shrink the brain during surgery. However, urea infusions cause changes in the electrical activity of the brain in experimental animals and may not be as innocuous as they appear to be. In dogs, prolonged infusions of urea cause anorexia, weakness, vomiting, and diarrhea.

The toxic substances which cause the symptoms of uremia can be removed by dialyzing the blood of uremic patients against a bath of suitable composition in an artificial kidney. By repeated dialysis patients can be kept alive and in reasonable health for many months, even when they are completely anuric or have had both kidneys removed.

Acidosis

Acidosis is common in chronic renal disease due to failure to excrete the acid products of digestion and metabolism (see Chapter 40). In the rare syndrome of **renal tubular acidosis**, there is specific impairment of the ability to make the urine acid, and other renal functions are usually normal. However, in most cases of chronic renal disease, the urine is maximally acidified, and acidosis develops because the total amount of H^+ that can be secreted is reduced because of impaired renal tubular production of NH_3.

Abnormal Na⁺ Metabolism

Many patients with renal disease retain excessive amounts of Na^+ and become edematous. There are at least 3 causes of Na^+ retention in renal disease. In acute glomerulonephritis, a disease which primarily affects the glomeruli, there is a marked decrease in the amount of Na^+ filtered without a corresponding decrease in Na^+ reabsorption. In nephrosis, an increase in aldosterone secretion contributes to the salt retention. The plasma protein is low in this condition, and so fluid moves from the plasma into the interstitial spaces and the plasma volume falls. The decline in plasma volume triggers the increase in aldosterone secretion, probably via the renin-angiotensin system.

A third cause of Na^+ retention and edema in renal disease is **heart failure**. The relationship between heart failure and abnormal salt retention is discussed in Chapter 33. Renal disease predisposes to heart failure, partly because of the hypertension it frequently produces.

A rare but interesting syndrome is **salt-losing nephritis**. In this condition there is marked loss of Na^+ in the urine, unresponsiveness to endogenous and exogenous mineralocorticoids, and symptoms and signs of hypovolemia that may lead to the mistaken diagnosis of adrenocortical insufficiency. The syndrome is apparently the result of relatively selective damage to the Na^+-reabsorbing mechanisms. In patients with this condition, a very high salt intake is necessary to prevent cardiovascular collapse.

Variations in the Response to Aldosterone

An interesting problem is why aldosterone-treated normal individuals and patients with primary hyperaldosteronism become severely K^+ depleted, while edematous patients with nephrosis, cirrhosis, or heart failure who have secondary hyperaldosteronism do not. One factor seems to be the amount of Na^+ reaching the distal tubule; Na^+ in the tubular fluid helps maintain the potential difference between the tubular lumen and the cells, and this favors K^+ secretion. In patients with primary hyperaldosteronism, "escape" has taken place and proximal tubular Na^+ reabsorption is decreased, so that large quantities of Na^+ reach the distal tubule. In patients with edema, the filtered Na^+ load may be small because the plasma Na^+ is low due to "dilutional hyponatremia," or the GFR is low, or both. However, the amount of Na^+ reaching the distal tubules may be low even when the plasma Na^+ and GFR are apparently normal because there is increased Na^+ reabsorption in the proximal tubule. Another factor in patients with edema is the flow of fluid in the distal tubule. K^+ excretion appears to be flow-limited, and in these patients the amount of fluid reaching the distal tubules is often reduced.

39...

Micturition

FILLING OF THE BLADDER

The walls of the ureters contain smooth muscle arranged in 3 distinct layers. Regular peristaltic contractions occurring 1–5 times per minute move the urine from the renal pelvis to the bladder, where it enters in spurts synchronous with each peristaltic wave. The ureters pass obliquely through the bladder wall and, although there are no ureteral sphincters as such, the oblique passage tends to keep the ureters closed except during peristaltic waves, preventing reflux of urine from the bladder.

EMPTYING OF THE BLADDER

Anatomic Considerations

The smooth muscle of the bladder, like that of the ureters, is arranged in 3 layers. Contraction of the outer layer, which is called the **detrusor muscle**, is mainly responsible for emptying the bladder during urination (micturition). Extensions of the middle layer pass on either side of the urethra. These fibers are sometimes called the **internal urethral sphincter**. Farther along the urethra is a sphincter of skeletal muscle, the sphincter of the membranous urethra, or **external urethral sphincter**. The bladder epithelium is made up of a superficial layer of flat cells and a deep layer of cuboidal cells. The innervation of the bladder is summarized in Table 39–1.

Micturition

The physiology of micturition and its disorders are subjects about which there is much confusion. Micturition is fundamentally a spinal reflex facilitated and inhibited by higher brain centers and, like defecation, subject to voluntary facilitation and inhibition. Urine enters the bladder without producing much increase in intravesical pressure until the viscus is well filled. In addition, like other types of smooth muscle, the bladder muscle has the property of plasticity; when it is stretched, the tension initially produced is not maintained. The relation between intravesical pressure and volume can be studied by inserting a catheter and emptying the bladder, then recording the pressure while the bladder is filled with 50 ml increments of water or air **(cystometry)**. A plot of intravesical pressure against the volume of fluid in the bladder is called a **cystometrogram** (Fig 39–1). The curve shows an initial slight rise in pressure when the first increments in volume are produced; a long, nearly flat segment as further increments are produced; and a sudden, sharp rise in pressure as the micturition reflex is triggered. These 3 components are sometimes called segments Ia, Ib, and II (Fig 39–1). The first urge to void is felt at a bladder volume of about 150 ml, and a marked sense of fullness at about 400 ml. The flatness of segment Ib is a manifestation of the law of Laplace (see Chapter 30). This law states that the pressure in a spherical viscus is equal to twice the wall tension divided by the radius. In the case of the bladder, the tension increases as the organ fills—but so does the radius, so that, until the organ is relatively full, the pressure increase is slight.

TABLE 39–1. Innervation of the bladder and urethra in man.

Efferent Fibers	Spinal Nerve Roots	Peripheral Nerves	Structures Innervated
Sympathetic	Upper lumbar, lower thoracic	Superior hypogastric plexus ("presacral nerve") and hypogastric nerves	Bladder generally; internal sphincter
Parasympathetic	S_2–S_4	Pelvic nerves	Detrusor, internal sphincter
Somatic	S_3–S_4	Pudendal nerves	External sphincter

Afferent Pain Fibers From	Peripheral Nerves
Dome of bladder	Hypogastric nerves
Detrusor	Pelvic nerves (also transmit afferent impulses that initiate micturition)
Urethra	Pudendal nerves

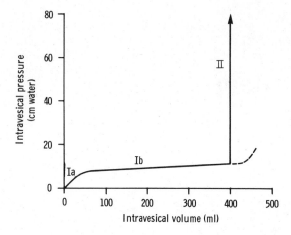

FIG 39–1. **Cystometrogram in normal human.** The numerals identify the 3 components of the curve described in the text. The dotted line indicates the pressure-volume relations that would have been found had micturition not occurred and produced component II. (Modified and reproduced, with permission, from Smith: *General Urology,* 7th ed. Lange, 1972.)

During micturition, the perineal muscles and external urethral sphincter are relaxed; the detrusor muscle contracts; and urine passes out through the urethra. The internal urethral sphincter apparently plays no role in micturition, and its main function is believed to be the prevention of reflux of semen into the bladder during ejaculation.

The mechanism by which voluntary urination is initiated remains unsettled. One of the initial events is relaxation of the muscles of the pelvic floor, and this may cause a sufficient downward tug on the detrusor muscle to initiate its contraction. The perineal muscles and external sphincter can be contracted voluntarily, preventing urine from passing down the urethra or interrupting the flow, once urination has begun. It is through the learned ability to maintain the external sphincter in a contracted state that adults are able to delay urination until the opportunity to void presents itself. After urination, the female urethra empties by gravity. Urine remaining in the urethra of the male is expelled by several contractions of the bulbocavernosus muscle.

Reflex Control

The bladder smooth muscle has some inherent contractile activity; however, when its nerve supply is intact, stretch receptors in the bladder wall initiate a reflex contraction which has a lower threshold than the inherent contractile response of the muscle. Fibers in the pelvic nerves are the afferent limb of the voiding reflex, and the efferent parasympathetic fibers to the bladder also travel in these nerves. The reflex is integrated in the sacral portion of the spinal cord. In the adult, the volume of urine in the bladder that normally initiates a reflex contraction is about 300–400 ml. There is no good evidence that the sympathetic nerves play any part in micturition.

There is no small motor nerve system to the stretch receptors in the bladder wall; but the threshold for the voiding reflex, like the stretch reflexes, is adjusted by the activity of facilitatory and inhibitory centers in the brain stem. There is a facilitatory area in the pontine region and an inhibitory area in the midbrain. After transection of the brain stem just above the pons, the threshold is lowered, and less bladder filling is required to trigger it; whereas after transection at the top of the midbrain the threshold for the reflex is essentially normal. There is another facilitatory area in the posterior hypothalamus. In humans with lesions in the superior frontal gyrus, the desire to urinate is reduced and there is also difficulty in stopping micturition once it has commenced. However, stimulation experiments in animals indicate that other cortical areas also affect the process. The bladder can be made to contract when it contains only a few ml of urine by voluntary facilitation of the spinal voiding reflex. Voluntary contraction of the abdominal muscles aids the expulsion of urine by increasing the intra-abdominal pressure, but voiding can be initiated without straining even when the bladder is nearly empty.

ABNORMALITIES OF MICTURITION

There are 3 major types of bladder dysfunction due to neural lesions: (1) the type due to interruption of the afferent nerves from the bladder; (2) the type due to interruption of both afferent and efferent nerves; and (3) the type due to interruption of facilitatory and inhibitory pathways descending from the brain. In all 3 types the bladder contracts, but the contractions are generally not sufficient to empty the viscus completely and residual urine is left in the bladder.

Effects of Deafferentation

When the sacral dorsal roots are cut in experimental animals or interrupted by diseases of the dorsal roots such as **tabes dorsalis** in humans, all reflex contractions of the bladder are abolished. The bladder becomes distended, thin-walled, and hypotonic, but there are some contractions because of the intrinsic response of the smooth muscle to stretch.

Effects of Denervation

When the afferent and efferent nerves are both destroyed, as they may be by tumors of the cauda equina or filum terminale, the bladder is flaccid and distended for a while. Gradually, however, the muscle of the "decentralized bladder" becomes active, with many contraction waves which expel dribbles of urine out of the urethra. The bladder becomes shrunken and the bladder wall hypertrophied. The reason for the difference between the small, hypertrophic bladder seen in this condition and the distended, hypotonic bladder seen when only the afferent nerves are interrupted is not known. The hyperactive state in the former condition suggests the development of denervation hypersensitization even though the neurons interrupted are preganglionic rather than postganglionic.

Effects of Spinal Cord Transection

During spinal shock, the bladder is flaccid and unresponsive. It becomes overfilled and urine dribbles through the sphincters **(overflow incontinence)**. After spinal shock has passed the voiding reflex returns, although there is, of course, no voluntary control and no inhibition or facilitation from higher centers when the spinal cord is transected. Some paraplegic patients train themselves to initiate voiding by pinching or stroking their thighs, provoking a mild mass reflex (see Chapter 12). In some instances, the voiding reflex becomes hyperactive. Bladder capacity is reduced, and the wall becomes hypertrophied. This type of bladder is sometimes called the **spastic neurogenic bladder**. The reflex hyperactivity is made worse by, and may possibly be caused by, infection in the bladder wall.

40...

Regulation of Extracellular Fluid Composition & Volume

This chapter is a review of the major homeostatic mechanisms that operate, primarily through the kidneys, to maintain the **tonicity,** the **volume,** and the **specific ionic composition,** particularly the **H⁺ concentration,** of the ECF. The interstitial portion of this fluid is the fluid environment of the cells, and life depends upon the constancy of this "internal sea" (see Chapter 1).

DEFENSE OF TONICITY

The defense of the tonicity of the ECF is primarily the function of the vasopressin-secreting and thirst mechanisms. The total body osmolality is directly proportionate to the total body sodium plus the total body potassium divided by the total body water, so that changes in the osmolality of the body fluids occur when there is a disproportion between the amount of these electrolytes and the amount of water ingested or lost from the body (see Chapter 1). When the effective osmotic pressure of the plasma rises, vasopressin secretion is increased and the thirst mechanism is stimulated. Water is retained in the body, diluting the hypertonic plasma, and water intake is increased (Fig 40–1). Conversely, when the plasma becomes hypotonic, vasopressin secretion is decreased and "solute-free water" (water in excess of solute) is excreted. In this way, the tonicity of the body fluids is maintained within a narrow normal range. The details of the way these mecha-

nisms operate and the disorders that result when their function is disrupted are considered in Chapters 14 and 38.

DEFENSE OF VOLUME

The volume of the ECF is determined primarily by the total amount of osmotically active solute in the ECF. The composition of the ECF is discussed in Chapter 1. Since Na⁺ and Cl⁻ are by far the most abundant osmotically active solutes in ECF, and since changes in Cl⁻ are to a great extent secondary to changes in Na⁺, the amount of Na⁺ in the ECF is the most important determinant of ECF volume, and the mechanisms that control Na⁺ balance are the major mechanisms defending ECF volume. There is, however, a volume control of water excretion as well; a rise in ECF volume inhibits vasopressin secretion, and a decline in ECF volume produces an increase in the secretion of this hormone. Volume stimuli override the osmotic regulation of vasopressin secretion.

In disease states, loss of water from the body **(dehydration)** causes a moderate decrease in ECF volume because water is lost from both the intracellular and extracellular fluid compartments; but loss of Na⁺ in the stools (diarrhea), urine (severe acidosis, adrenal insufficiency), or sweat (heat prostration) decreases ECF volume markedly and eventually leads to shock. The immediate compensations in shock operate principally to maintain intravascular volume (see Chapter 33), but the long-term mechanisms affect Na⁺ balance. In adrenal insufficiency, the decline in ECF volume is due not only to loss of Na⁺ in the urine but also to its movement into cells (see Chapter 20).

Because of the key position of Na⁺ in volume homeostasis, it is not surprising that more than one mechanism operates to control the excretion of this ion. The filtration and reabsorption of Na⁺ in the kidneys and the effects of these processes on Na⁺ excretion are discussed in Chapter 38. When ECF volume is decreased, blood pressure falls. Glomerular capillary pressure declines, and the GFR therefore falls, reducing the amount of Na⁺ filtered. Tubular reabsorption of Na⁺ is increased, in part because the secretion of

FIG 40–1. Mechanisms defending ECF tonicity. The dashed arrow indicates inhibition. (Courtesy of J Fitzsimons.)

aldosterone is increased but in part also because other poorly understood mechanisms increase its transport out of the tubular fluid. Aldosterone secretion is controlled in part by a feedback system in which the change which initiates increased secretion is a decline in mean intravascular pressure, probably in the renal artery (see Chapters 20 and 24). There are, however, changes in Na⁺ excretion which occur too rapidly to be due solely to changes in aldosterone secretion. For example, rising from the supine to the standing position increases aldosterone secretion. However, Na⁺ excretion is decreased within a few minutes, and this rapid change in Na⁺ excretion occurs in adrenalecto- mized subjects. Some investigators believe that the effect of standing is due to a slight decrease in GFR, but others have presented evidence that an increase in tubular reabsorption is also involved.

Elimination of excess Na⁺ also appears to operate through a volume-sensing mechanism of some sort that affects GFR but also decreases the reabsorption of Na⁺ in the proximal tubules. Natriuresis follows the infusion of hypo-, iso-, and hypertonic saline, so that the concentration of Na⁺ in the ECF does not appear to be the important factor. For reasons that remain obscure, a patient who has received a water load up to 24 hours before a salt load excretes the salt load more rapidly than a control who has not received a water load, even though the administered water has long since been excreted.

DEFENSE OF SPECIFIC IONIC COMPOSITION

Special regulatory mechanisms maintain the levels of certain specific ions in the ECF as well as the level of glucose and other nonionized substances important in metabolism (see Chapters 17 and 19). The feedback of Ca^{++} on the parathyroids and the calcitonin-secreting cells to adjust their secretion maintains the ionized calcium level of the ECF (see Chapter 21). Magnesium concentration is subject to close regulation, but the mechanisms controlling Mg^{++} metabolism are incom- pletely understood.

The mechanisms controlling Na⁺ and K⁺ content are part of those determining the volume and tonicity of ECF, and are discussed above. The level of these ions is also dependent upon the H⁺ concentration, and the pH is one of the major factors affecting the anion composition of ECF.

DEFENSE OF H⁺ CONCENTRATION

The mystique which has grown up around the subject of acid-base balance makes it necessary to point out that the core of the problem is not "buffer base" or "fixed cation" or the like but simply the maintenance of the H⁺ concentration of the ECF. The mechanisms regulating the composition of the ECF are particularly important as far as this specific ion is con- cerned because the machinery of the cells is very sensitive to changes in H⁺ concentration and because the intracellular H⁺ concentration, although not identi- cal with the ECF H⁺ concentration, is dependent upon it.

The pH notation is a useful means of expressing H⁺ concentrations in the body because the H⁺ concen- trations happen to be low relative to those of other cations. Thus, the normal Na⁺ concentration of arterial plasma that has been equilibrated with red blood cells is 145 mEq/liter, whereas the H⁺ concentration is 0.00004 mEq/liter (Table 40−1). The pH, the negative logarithm of 0.00004, is therefore 7.4. Of course, a **decrease** in pH of 1 unit, eg, from 7.0 to 6.0, repre- sents a **tenfold increase** in H⁺ concentration. It is also important to remember that the pH of blood is the pH of **true plasma**—plasma that has been in equilibrium with red cells—because the red cells contain hemoglo- bin, which is quantitatively one of the most important blood buffers (see Chapter 35).

TABLE 40−1. H⁺ concentration and pH of body fluids.

		H⁺ Concentration		pH
		mEq/liter	mol/liter	
Gastric HCl		150	0.15	0.8
Maximal urine acidity		0.03	3×10^{-5}	4.5
Plasma	Extreme acidosis	0.0001	1×10^{-7}	7.0
	Normal	0.00004	4×10^{-8}	7.4
	Extreme alkalosis	0.00002	2×10^{-8}	7.7
Pancreatic juice		0.00001	1×10^{-8}	8.0

H⁺ Balance

The pH of the arterial plasma is normally 7.40, and that of venous plasma slightly lower. Technically, **acidosis** is present whenever the arterial pH is below 7.40 and **alkalosis** is present whenever it is above 7.40, although variations of up to 0.05 pH units occur with- out untoward effects. The H⁺ concentrations in the ECF that are compatible with life cover an approxi- mately 5-fold range from 0.00002 mEq/liter (pH 7.70) to 0.0001 mEq/liter (pH 7.00).

Dietary proteins contain sulfate and phosphate groups which, when the protein is metabolized, remain as H_2SO_4 and H_3PO_4. The H⁺ load from this source is normally about 150 mEq/day. The CO_2 formed by metabolism in the tissues is in large part hydrated to H_2CO_3 (see Chapter 35), and the total H⁺ load from this source is over 12,500 mEq/day. Most of the CO_2 is excreted in the lungs, and only small quantities of the H⁺ from this source are excreted by the kidneys. Common sources of extra acid loads are strenuous exercise (lactic acid), diabetic ketosis (acetoacetic and β-hydroxybutyric acid), and ingestion of acidifying salts such as NH_4Cl and $CaCl_2$, which in effect add HCl to the body. Failure of diseased kidneys to excrete the normal acid load is also a cause of acidosis. Fruits are the main dietary source of alkali. They contain Na^+ and K^+ salts of weak organic acids, and the anions of these salts are metabolized to CO_2, leaving $NaHCO_3$ and $KHCO_3$ in the body. $NaHCO_3$ and other alkalinizing salts are sometimes ingested in large amounts, but a more common cause of alkalosis is loss of acid from the body due to vomiting of gastric juice rich in HCl. This is, of course, equivalent to adding alkali to the body.

Buffering

Buffering and the buffer systems in the body are discussed in Chapters 1 and 35. The principal buffers in the ECF are hemoglobin (Hb^-), protein ($Prot^-$), and H_2CO_3:

$$HHb \rightleftarrows H^+ + Hb^-$$

$$HProt \rightleftarrows H^+ + Prot^-$$

$$H_2CO_3 \rightleftarrows H^+ + HCO_3^-$$

The position of H_2CO_3 is unique because it is converted to H_2O and CO_2 and the CO_2 is then excreted in the lungs. The Henderson-Hasselbalch equation for the equilibrium in this system is:

$$pH = pK_{H_2CO_3} + \log \frac{[HCO_3^-]}{[H_2CO_3]}$$

When the symbol $[H_2CO_3]$ stands not for the concentration of carbonic acid alone but for the **concentration of carbonic acid plus dissolved CO_2**, the normal $[HCO_3^-]/[H_2CO_3]$ ratio is 20 and the pK is 6.1.

$$pH = 6.1 + \log \frac{[HCO_3^-]}{[H_2CO_3]}$$

The amount of carbonic acid and dissolved CO_2 is proportionate to the P_{CO_2}. The plasma HCO_3^- actually equals the total CO_2 of plasma minus the dissolved CO_2, the H_2CO_3, and the carbamino-CO_2, but constants have been derived experimentally to permit writing the Henderson-Hasselbalch equation for the bicarbonate system in plasma in the following special form:

$$pH = 6.10 + \log \frac{[Total\ CO_2] - aP_{CO_2}}{aP_{CO_2}}$$

When total CO_2 of true plasma ($[total\ CO_2]$) is in mM/liter, and P_{CO_2} is in mm Hg, a = 0.0314. This is the clinically applicable form of the equation because the HCO_3^- cannot be measured directly, but the total CO_2 and P_{CO_2} can be measured.

Respiratory Acidosis & Alkalosis

It is apparent from the Henderson-Hasselbalch equation for the bicarbonate system that the primary changes in arterial P_{CO_2} that occur with disorders of

FIG 40–2. **Changes in true plasma pH, HCO_3^-, and P_{CO_2} in respiratory acidosis and alkalosis.** Note that with this plot the addition of CO_2 moves the point up and to the left along the line indicated by the arrow, and removal of CO_2 moves it down and to the right. On the other hand, addition of stronger acid moves the point down the dashed "iso-CO_2" line to the left, whereas removal of stronger acid (or addition of alkali) moves the point up the iso-CO_2 line to the right. (Based on Davenport: *The ABC of Acid-Base Chemistry*, 5th ed. Univ of Chicago Press, 1969.)

respiration change the $[HCO_3^-]/[H_2CO_3]$ ratio and, therefore, the pH. A rise in arterial P_{CO_2} due to decreased ventilation causes **respiratory acidosis**. The CO_2 that is retained is in equilibrium with H_2CO_3, which in turn is in equilibrium with HCO_3^-, so that the plasma HCO_3^- rises and a new equilibrium is reached at a lower pH. This can be indicated graphically on a plot of plasma HCO_3^- concentration versus pH (Fig 40–2). Conversely, a decline in P_{CO_2} causes **respiratory alkalosis**.

The initial changes shown in Fig 40–2 are those which occur independently of any compensatory mechanism, ie, they are those of **uncompensated** respiratory acidosis or alkalosis. In either situation, changes are produced in the kidneys, which then tend to **compensate** for the acidosis or alkalosis, adjusting the pH toward normal.

Renal Compensation

HCO_3^- reabsorption in the renal tubules depends not only upon the plasma HCO_3^- level but also upon the rate of H^+ secretion by the renal tubular cells, since HCO_3^- is reabsorbed by exchange for H^+. The rate of H^+ secretion—and hence the rate of HCO_3^- reabsorption—is proportionate to the arterial P_{CO_2}, probably because the greater the amount of CO_2 that is available to form H_2CO_3 in the cells, the greater the amount of

H⁺ that can be secreted (see Chapter 38). Furthermore, when the P_{CO_2} is high, the interior of most cells becomes more acid (see Chapter 35). In respiratory acidosis, renal tubular H⁺ secretion is therefore increased, removing H⁺ from the body; and even though the plasma HCO_3^- is elevated, HCO_3^- reabsorption is increased, further raising the plasma HCO_3^-. This "renal compensation for respiratory acidosis" is shown graphically in Fig 40–2. Cl⁻ excretion is increased and plasma Cl⁻ falls as plasma HCO_3^- is increased. Conversely, in respiratory alkalosis, the low P_{CO_2} hinders renal H⁺ secretion, HCO_3^- reabsorption is depressed, and HCO_3^- is excreted, further reducing the already low plasma HCO_3^- and lowering the pH toward normal (Fig 40–2).

Metabolic Acidosis

When acids stronger than the buffer acids are added to blood, **metabolic acidosis** is produced; and when the free H⁺ level falls as a result of addition of alkali or removal of acid, **metabolic alkalosis** results. If, for example, HCl is added, the H⁺ is buffered and the Hb^-, $Prot^-$, and HCO_3^- levels in plasma drop. The H_2CO_3 formed is converted to H_2O and CO_2, and the CO_2 is rapidly excreted via the lungs. The importance of this fact is demonstrated in Fig 40–3. If enough acid were added to halve the HCO_3^- in plasma and CO_2 were not formed and excreted, the pH would fall to approximately 6.0 and death would result. If the H_2CO_3 level were so regulated that it remained **constant**, the pH would fall only to about 7.1. This is the

FIG 40–4. Changes in true plasma pH, HCO_3^-, and P_{CO_2} in metabolic acidosis and alkalosis. (Based on Davenport: *The ABC of Acid-Base Chemistry*, 5th ed. Univ of Chicago Press, 1969.)

situation in **uncompensated** metabolic acidosis (Fig 40–4). Actually, the rise in plasma H⁺ stimulates respiration, so that H_2CO_3 level, instead of rising or remaining constant, is reduced. This **respiratory compensation** raises the pH even further. The renal compensatory mechanisms then excrete the extra H⁺ and return the buffer anion supply to normal.

Renal Compensation

The acid anions that replace HCO_3^- in the plasma in metabolic acidosis are filtered, each with a cation (principally Na⁺), thus maintaining electrical neutrality. The renal tubular cells secrete H⁺ into the glomerular filtrate; and for each H⁺ secreted, 1 Na⁺ and 1 HCO_3^- are added to the blood (see Chapter 38). The limiting urinary pH of 4.5 would be reached rapidly and the total amount of H⁺ secreted would be small if there were no substances in the urine that "tied up" H⁺. However, secreted H⁺ reacts with HCO_3^- to form CO_2 and H_2O (bicarbonate reabsorption); with $HPO_4^=$ to form $H_2PO_4^-$ (titratable acidity); and with NH_3 to form NH_4^+. In this way large amounts of H⁺ can be secreted, permitting correspondingly large amounts of HCO_3^- to be returned to (in the case of bicarbonate reabsorption) or added to the depleted body stores and large numbers of the cations filtered with the acid anions to be reabsorbed. It is only when the acid load is very large that Na⁺ is lost with the anions, producing diuresis and depletion of body cation stores. In chronic acidosis, NH_3 secretion increases over a period of days (adaptation of NH_3 secretion; see Chapter 38), further improving the renal compensation for acidosis.

The overall reaction in blood when a strong acid such as HCl is added is as follows:

FIG 40–3. Buffering by the H_2CO_3-HCO_3^- system in blood. The bars are drawn as if buffering occurred in separate steps in order to show the effect of the initial reaction, the reduction of H_2CO_3 to its previous value, and its further reduction by the increase in ventilation. In this case, [H_2CO_3] is actually the concentration of H_2CO_3 plus dissolved CO_2 (see text), so that the mEq/liter values for it are arbitrary. (Based on Gamble: *Chemical Anatomy, Physiology and Pathology of Extracellular Fluid*, 6th ed. Harvard Univ Press, 1954.)

$$NaHCO_3 + HCl \rightarrow NaCl + H_2CO_3$$

For each mol of HCl added, 1 mol of $NaHCO_3$ is lost. The kidney in effect reverses the reaction:

$$NaCl + H_2CO_3 \rightarrow NaHCO_3 + H^+ + Cl^-$$

Of course; HCl is not excreted as such, the H^+ appearing in the urine as titratable acidity and NH_4^+.

In metabolic acidosis, the respiratory compensation tends to inhibit the renal response in the sense that the induced drop in P_{CO_2} hinders acid secretion, but it also decreases the filtered load of HCO_3^- and so its net inhibitory effect is not great.

Metabolic Alkalosis

In metabolic alkalosis, the plasma HCO_3^- and pH rise (Fig 40−4). The respiratory compensation is a decrease in ventilation due to decline in H^+ concentration, which elevates the P_{CO_2}. This brings the pH back toward normal, while elevating the plasma HCO_3^- still further. The magnitude of this compensation is limited by the carotid and aortic chemoreceptor mechanisms, which drive the respiratory center if there is any appreciable fall in the arterial P_{O_2}. In metabolic alkalosis, more renal H^+ secretion is expended in reabsorbing the increased filtered load of HCO_3^-; and if the HCO_3^- level in plasma exceeds 28 mEq/liter, HCO_3^- appears in the urine. The rise in P_{CO_2} inhibits the renal compensation by facilitating acid secretion, but its effect is relatively slight.

Clinical Evaluation of Acid-Base Status

In evaluating disturbances of acid-base balance, it is important to know the pH and HCO_3^- content of arterial plasma. The P_{CO_2} is higher and the pH lower in venous plasma because it contains the CO_2 being carried from the tissues to the lungs for excretion (see Chapter 35); but if this is kept in mind in evaluating the results, free-flowing venous blood can be substituted for arterial blood. Reliable pH determinations using a pH meter and a glass pH electrode are now available in most hospitals. The HCO_3^- content of plasma cannot be measured directly, but the total CO_2 content can; and if the pH is known, the P_{CO_2} can be calculated using the special form of the Henderson-Hasselbalch equation discussed above in the section on buffering.

Alternatively, the total CO_2 content and the arterial P_{CO_2} can be measured and the pH calculated. A second alternative is use of the Siggaard-Andersen curve nomogram (see below). In these ways, the precise form of acid-base disturbance and its magnitude can be determined and proper treatment instituted.

When neither the pH nor the arterial P_{CO_2} can be measured, the plasma total CO_2 alone is a valuable datum. If 1.2 mM/liter for dissolved CO_2 are subtracted from this figure, a value that is approximately equal to the plasma HCO_3^- concentration is obtained; and with this value, plus clinical observations, the acid-base problem and its magnitude can usually be evaluated with considerable reliability. However, treatment is more precise and mistakes are less frequent when the pH is also measured.

The Siggaard-Andersen Curve Nomogram

Use of the Siggaard-Andersen curve nomogram (Fig 40−5) to plot the acid-base characteristics of arterial blood is becoming increasingly widespread. This nomogram has log P_{CO_2} on the vertical scale and pH on the horizontal scale. Thus, any point to the left of a vertical line through pH 7.40 indicates acidosis and any point to the right indicates alkalosis. The position of the point above or below the horizontal line through a P_{CO_2} of 40 mm Hg defines the effective degree of hypoventilation or hyperventilation.

If a solution containing $NaHCO_3$ and no buffers were equilibrated with gas mixtures containing various amounts of CO_2, the pH and P_{CO_2} values at equilibrium would fall along the dashed line on the left in Fig 40−5 or a line parallel to it. If buffers were present, the slope of the line would be greater; and the greater the buffering capacity of the solution, the steeper the line. For normal blood containing 15 g of hemoglobin per 100 ml, the **CO_2 titration line** passes through the 15 g/100 ml mark on the hemoglobin scale (on the under side of the upper curved scale) and the point where the P_{CO_2} = 40 mm Hg and pH = 7.40 lines intersect, as shown in Fig 40−5. When the hemoglobin content of the blood is low, there is significant loss of buffering capacity and the slope of the CO_2 titration line diminishes. However, blood of course contains buffers in addition to hemoglobin, so that even the line drawn from the zero point on the hemoglobin scale through the normal P_{CO_2}-pH intercept is steeper than the curve for a solution containing no buffers.

The nomogram is very useful clinically. Arterial blood or arterialized capillary blood is drawn anaerobically and its pH measured. The pHs of the same blood after equilibration with each of 2 gas mixtures containing different known amounts of CO_2 are also determined. The pH values at the known P_{CO_2} levels are plotted and connected to provide the CO_2 titration line for the blood sample. The pH of the blood sample before equilibration is plotted on this line, and the P_{CO_2} of the sample is read off the vertical scale. The **standard bicarbonate** content of the sample is indicated by the point at which the CO_2 titration line intersects the bicarbonate scale on the P_{CO_2} = 40 mm Hg line. The standard bicarbonate is not the actual bicarbonate concentration of the sample but rather what the bicarbonate concentration would be after elimination of any respiratory component. It is a measure of the alkali reserve of the blood, except that it is measured by determining the pH rather than the total CO_2 content of the sample after equilibration. Like the alkali reserve, it is an index of the degree of metabolic acidosis or alkalosis present.

Additional graduations on the upper curved scale of the nomogram (Fig 40−5) are provided for measuring **buffer base** content; the point where the CO_2

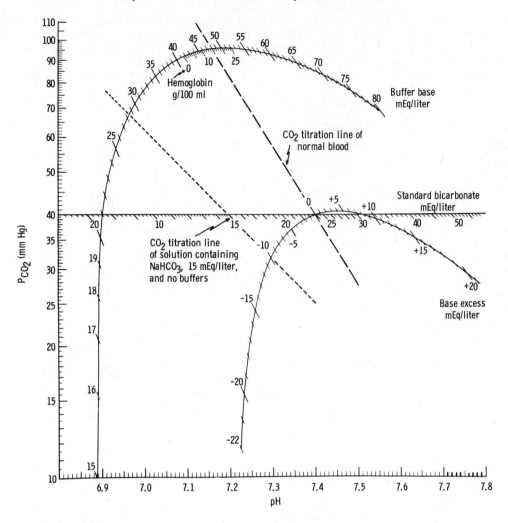

FIG 40−5. Siggaard-Andersen curve nomogram. (Reproduced with the permission of O Siggaard-Andersen and Radiometer, Copenhagen, Denmark.)

calibration line of the arterial blood sample intersects this scale shows the mEq/liter of buffer base in the sample. The buffer base is equal to the total amount of buffer anions (principally $Prot^-$, HCO_3^-, and Hb^-; see Chapter 35) which can accept hydrogen ions in the blood. The normal value in an individual with 15 g of hemoglobin/100 ml of blood is 48 mEq/liter.

The point at which the CO_2 calibration line intersects the lower curved scale on the nomogram indicates the **base excess**. This value, which is positive in alkalosis and negative in acidosis, is the amount of acid or base which would restore 1 liter of blood to normal acid-base composition at a P_{CO_2} of 40 mm Hg. It should be noted that a base deficiency cannot be completely corrected simply by calculating the difference between the normal standard bicarbonate (24 mEq/liter) and the actual standard bicarbonate and administering this amount of $NaHCO_3$ per liter of blood; some of the added HCO_3^- is converted to CO_2 and H_2O, and the CO_2 is lost in the lungs. The actual amount which must be added is roughly 1.2 times the standard bicarbonate deficit, but the lower curved scale on the nomogram, which has been developed empirically by analyzing many blood samples, is more accurate.

Some examples of clinical acid-base disturbances are shown in Table 40−2.

In treating acid-base disturbances, one must, of course, consider not only the blood but all the body fluid compartments. The other fluid compartments have markedly different concentrations of buffers. It has been determined empirically that administration of an amount of acid (in alkalosis) or base (in acidosis) equal to 50% of the body weight in kg times the blood base excess per liter will correct the acid-base disturbance in the whole body. At least when the abnormality is severe, however, it is unwise to attempt such a large correction in a single step; instead, about half the indicated amount should be given, and the arterial blood acid-base values determined again. The amount

TABLE 40–2. Plasma pH, HCO$_3^-$, and P$_{CO_2}$ values in various typical disturbances of acid-base balance. In the diabetic acidosis and prolonged vomiting examples, respiratory compensation for primary metabolic acidosis and alkalosis has occurred and the P$_{CO_2}$ has shifted from 40 mm Hg. In the emphysema and high altitude examples, renal compensation for primary respiratory acidosis and alkalosis has occurred and has made the deviations from normal of the plasma HCO$_3^-$ larger than they would otherwise be. Data from various authors.

| Condition | Arterial Plasma | | | Cause |
	pH	HCO$_3^-$ (mEq/liter)	P$_{CO_2}$ (mm Hg)	
NORMAL	7.40	24.1	40	
Metabolic	7.26	18.1	40	NH$_4$Cl ingestion
acidosis	6.94	5.0	23	Diabetic acidosis
Metabolic	7.48	30.1	40	NaHCO$_3$ ingestion
alkalosis	7.54	49.8	58	Prolonged vomiting
Respiratory	7.35	25.0	48	Breathing 7% CO$_2$
acidosis	7.32	33.5	64	Emphysema
Respiratory	7.50	22.0	27	Voluntary hyperventilation
alkalosis	7.46	18.7	26	Three-week residence at 14,000 ft altitude

required for final correction can then be calculated and administered.

Relation Between Potassium Metabolism & Acid-Base Balance

The K$^+$ and H$^+$ concentration of the ECF parallel each other, in part because of the effects of K$^+$ on renal H$^+$ secretion (see Chapter 38). K$^+$ depletion apparently produces an intracellular acidosis, promoting H$^+$ secretion into the urine. H$^+$ is thus removed from the body and HCO$_3^-$ reabsorption increased, producing an extracellular alkalosis. Conversely, K$^+$ excess increases K$^+$ secretion by the renal tubular cells. Since both H$^+$ and K$^+$ are secreted in exchange for Na$^+$ and compete for the available Na$^+$ in the tubular fluid, H$^+$ secretion is inhibited, promoting extracellular acidosis.

• • •

References: Section VIII.
Formation & Excretion of Urine

Barger AC, Herd JA: The renal circulation. New England J Med 284:482, 1971.

Davenport HW: *The ABC of Acid-Base Chemistry,* 5th ed. Univ of Chicago Press, 1969.

Fisher JW (editor): *Kidney Hormones.* Academic Press, 1971.

Frazier HS, Yager H: Drug therapy: The clinical use of diuretics. New England J Med 288:246, 1973.

Hutch JA: *Anatomy and Physiology of the Bladder, Trigone and Urethra.* Appleton-Century-Crofts, 1972.

Pitts RF: The role of ammonia production in regulation of acid-base balance. New England J Med 284:32, 1971.

Rouiller C, Muller AF (editors): *The Kidney.* 3 vols. Academic Press, 1969.

Scholander RF: The wonderful net. Scientific American 196:96, April 1957.

Siggaard-Andersen O: *The New Acid-Base Status of Blood.* Williams & Wilkins, 1965.

Waddell WJ, Bates RG: Intracellular pH. Physiol Rev 49:285, 1969.

Welt L: *Clinical Disorders of Hydration and Acid-Base Equilibrium,* 3rd ed. Little, Brown, 1971.

Wesson LG Jr: *Physiology of the Human Kidney.* Grune & Stratton, 1969.

Windhager EE: Kidney, water, and electrolytes. Ann Rev Physiol 31:198, 1969.

Appendix

GENERAL REFERENCES

Many large, comprehensive textbooks of physiology are available. The following are among the best of the recently revised volumes:

Guyton AC: *Textbook of Medical Physiology*, 4th ed. Saunders, 1971.

Keele CA, Neil E: *Samson Wright's Applied Physiology*, 12th ed. Oxford Univ Press, 1971.

Mountcastle VB (editor): *Medical Physiology*, 13th ed. 2 vols. Mosby, 1973.

Year Book Medical Publishers, Inc, has published a series of monographs on various aspects of physiology. The volumes, which are generally excellent, are collectively equivalent to a comprehensive text on physiology.

Excellent summaries of current research on selected aspects of physiology can be found in the symposia now being published with increasing frequency in Federation Proceedings and in the Annals of the New York Academy of Sciences. Various types of valuable reviews appear in the New England Journal of Medicine. These include the Physiology in Medicine Series, articles which review current topics in physiology with the aim of providing up-to-date information for practicing physicians. The most pertinent serial review publications are Physiological Reviews, Pharmacological Reviews, Recent Progress in Hormone Research (the proceedings of each annual Laurentian Hormone Conference), Annual Review of Physiology, and other volumes of the Annual Review series. The American Physiological Society is currently publishing a *Handbook of Physiology*, separate volumes of which will eventually cover all aspects of physiology. The volumes published to date cover Neurophysiology, Circulation, Respiration, Adaptation to the Environment, Adipose Tissue, the Alimentary Canal, and Endocrinology. A volume on renal and electrolyte physiology is being prepared. The articles in them are valuable but extremely detailed reviews.

• • •

NORMAL VALUES & THE STATISTICAL
EVALUATION OF DATA

The approximate ranges of values in normal humans for some commonly measured plasma constituents are summarized in the table on the inside back cover. The accuracy of the methods used for these and other measurements varies. It is important in evaluating any single measurement to know the possible errors in making the measurement. In the case of chemical determinations on body fluids, these include errors in obtaining the sample and the inherent error of the chemical method. However, the values obtained using even the most accurate methods vary from one normal individual to the next as a result of what is usually called **biologic variation**. This variation is due to the fact that in any system as complex as a living organism or tissue there are many variables that affect the particular measurement. Variables such as age, sex, time of day, time since last meal, etc can be controlled. Numerous other variables cannot, and for this reason the values obtained differ from individual to individual.

The magnitude of the normal range for any given physiologic or clinical measurement can be calculated by standard statistical technics if the measurement has been made on a suitable sample of the normal population (preferably more than 20 individuals). It is important to know not only the average value in this sample but also the extent of the deviation of the individual values from the average.

The average, or **arithmetic mean (M)**, of the series of values is readily calculated:

$$M = \frac{\Sigma X}{n}$$

Where Σ = Sum of
      X = The individual values
      n = Number of individual values in the series

The average deviation is the mean of the deviations of each of the values from the mean. From a mathematical point of view, a better measure of the deviation is the **geometric mean** of the deviations from the mean. This is called the **standard deviation** (σ):

$$\sigma = \sqrt{\frac{\Sigma (M - X)^2}{n-1}}$$

The term $n-1$ rather than n is used in the denominator of this equation because the σ of a sample of the population rather than the σ of the whole population is being calculated. The following form of the equation for σ can be derived algebraically, and is convenient for those using a calculator to compute σ:

$$\sigma = \sqrt{\frac{\Sigma X^2 - \frac{(\Sigma X)^2}{n}}{n-1}}$$

Here, ΣX^2 is the sum of the squares of the individual values, and $(\Sigma X)^2$ is the square of the sum of the items, ie, the items added together and then squared.

Another commonly used index of the variation is the **standard error of the mean** (SE, SEM):

$$SE = \frac{\sigma}{\sqrt{n}}$$

Strictly speaking, the SE indicates the reliability of the sample mean as representative of the true mean of the general population from which the sample was drawn.

A **frequency distribution** curve can be constructed from the individual values in the sample by plotting the frequency with which any particular value occurs in the series against the values. If the group of individuals tested was homogeneous, the frequency distribution curve is usually symmetric (Fig 1) with the

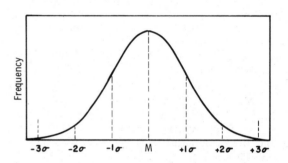

FIG 1. Curve of normal distribution (frequency distribution curve of values from a homogeneous sample of a population).

highest frequency corresponding to the mean and the width of the curve varying with σ (curve of **normal distribution**). Within an ideal curve of normal distribution, the percentage of observations which fall within various ranges are shown in Table 1. The mean and σ of a representative sample are approximately those of the whole population. It is therefore possible to predict from the mean and σ of the sample the probability that any particular value in the general population is normal. For example, if the difference between such a value and the mean is equal to 1.96 σ, the chances are

TABLE 1. Percentage of values in a population which will fall within various ranges within an ideal curve of normal distribution.

Mean ± 1 σ	68.27%
Mean ± 1.96 σ	95.00%
Mean ± 2 σ	95.45%
Mean ± 3 σ	99.73%

1 out of 20 (5 out of 100) that it is normal. Conversely, of course, the chances are 19 out of 20 that it is abnormal. It is unfortunate that data on normal means and σs are not more generally available for the important plasma and urinary constituents in man.

Statistical analysis is also useful in evaluating the significance of the difference between 2 means. In physiologic and clinical research, measurements are often made on a group of animals or patients given a particular treatment. These measurements are compared with similar measurements made on a control group which ideally has been exposed to exactly the same conditions except that the treatment has not been given. If a particular mean value in the treated group is different from the corresponding mean for the control group, the question arises whether the difference is due to the treatment or to chance variation. The probability that the difference represents chance variation can be estimated by using **"Student's"** *t* **test.** The value *t* is the ratio of the difference in the means of 2 series (M_a and M_b) to the uncertainty in these means. The formula used to calculate *t* is:

$$t = \frac{M_a - M_b}{\sqrt{\dfrac{(n_a + n_b)[(n_a - 1)\,\sigma_a{}^2 + (n_b - 1)\,\sigma_b{}^2]}{n_a n_b (n_a + n_b - 2)}}}$$

where n_a and n_b are the number of individual values in series a and b, respectively. When $n_a = n_b$, the equation for *t* becomes simplified to:

$$t = \frac{M_a - M_b}{\sqrt{(SE_a)^2 + (SE_b)^2}}$$

The higher the value of *t*, the less the probability that the difference represents chance variation. This probability also decreases as the number of individuals (n) in each group rises because the greater the number of measurements, the smaller the error in the measurements. A mathematical expression of the probability (*P*) for any value of *t* at different values of n can be found in tables in most texts on statistics. *P* is a fraction which expresses the probability that the difference between 2 means was due to chance variation. Thus, for example, if the *P* value is 0.10, the probability that the difference was due to chance is 10% (1 chance in 10). A *P* value of < 0.001 means that the chances that the difference was due to random variation are less than 1 in 1000. When the *P* value is < 0.05, most investigators call the difference "statistically significant," ie, it is concluded that the difference is due to the operation of some factor other than chance—presumably the treatment.

These elementary statistical methods and many others are available for analyzing data in the research laboratory and the clinic. They provide a valuable objective means of evaluation. Statistical significance does not arbitrarily mean physiologic significance, and the reverse may sometimes be true; but replacement of evaluation by subjective impression with analysis by statistical methods is certainly an important goal in the medical sciences.

● ● ●

References: Appendix

Hill AB: *Principles of Medical Statistics,* 9th ed. Oxford Univ Press, 1971.

Ipsen J, Feigl P: *Bancroft's Introduction to Biostatistics,* 2nd ed. Harper & Row, 1970.

ABBREVIATIONS & SYMBOLS
COMMONLY USED IN PHYSIOLOGY

[ ]	Concentration of
Δ	Change in. (*Example:* ΔV = change in volume.) In steroid nomenclature, Δ followed by a number (eg, Δ4-) indicates the position of a double bond
σ	Standard deviation
Ia, Ib, II, III, IV nerve fibers:	Types of fibers in sensory nerves (see Chapter 2)
μ	Micro, 10^{-6}; see units of measurement, below.
A (Å)	Angstrom unit(s) (10^{-10} m, 0.1 nm)
a	atto-, 10^{-18}; see units of measurement, below
A, B, and C nerve fibers:	Types of fibers in peripheral nerves (see Chapter 2)
A^-	General symbol for anion
A_1, A_2, A_1B, A_2B, B, O:	Major blood groups
Acetyl-Co A	Acetyl-coenzyme A
ACH, Ach	Acetylcholine
ACTH	Adrenocorticotropic hormone
Acyl-Co A	General symbol for an organic compound—coenzyme A ester
ADH	Antidiuretic hormone (vasopressin)
ADP	Adenosine diphosphate
AHG	Antihemophilic globulin
Ala	Alanine
AMP	Adenosine-5-monophosphate
Arg	Arginine
$\underset{\mid}{NH_2}$	
Asn, Asp	Asparagine
Asp	Aspartic acid
atm	Atmosphere: 1 atm = 760 torr = mean atmospheric pressure at sea level
ATP	Adenosine triphosphate
A-V difference	Arteriovenous concentration difference of any given substance
AV node	Atrioventricular node
aVR, aVF, aVL:	Augmented unipolar electrocardiographic leads
AV valves	Atrioventricular valves of heart
BEI	Butanol-extractable iodine
BMR	Basal metabolic rate
BSP	Sulfobromophthalein
c	Centi-, 10^{-2}; see units of measurement, below
C	Centigrade
C followed by subscript:	Clearance; eg, C_{In} = clearance of inulin
C 19 steroids	Steroids containing 19 carbon atoms
C 21 steroids	Steroids containing 21 carbon atoms
cal	The calorie (gram calorie)
Cal	1000 calories; kilocalorie
cAMP	Cyclic adenosine-3′,5′-monophosphate
CBF	Cerebral blood flow

CBG	Corticosteroid-binding globulin; transcortin
cc	Cubic centimeters
CCK, CCK-PZ	Cholecystokinin-pancreozymin
CGP	Chorionic growth hormone-prolactin (same as HCS)
C_{H_2O}	"Free water clearance"
Ci	Curie
$CMRO_2$	Cerebral metabolic rate for oxygen
CNS	Central nervous system
Co A	Coenzyme A
COHb	Carbonmonoxyhemoglobin
Compound A	11-Dehydrocorticosterone
Compound B	Corticosterone
Compound E	Cortisone
Compound F	Cortisol
Compound S	11-Deoxycortisol
COMT	Catechol-O-methyltransferase
cps	Cycles per second, hertz
CR	Conditioned reflex
Cr	Creatinine
CRF	Corticotropin-releasing factor
CRO	Cathode ray oscilloscope
CrP	Creatinine phosphate (phosphocreatine, PC)
CS	Conditioned stimulus
CSF	Cerebrospinal fluid
C terminal	End of peptide or protein having a free —COOH group
CTP	Cytidine triphosphate
CVR	Cerebral vascular resistance
cyclic AMP	Cyclic adenosine-3′,5′-monophosphate
Cys	Half-cystine
CZI	Crystalline zinc insulin
D	Geometric isomer of L form of chemical compound
dalton	Unit of mass, equal to one twelfth the mass of the carbon-12 atom, or approximately 1.65×10^{-24} g
dB	Decibel
DDD	Derivative of DDT that inhibits adrenocortical function
DEA, DHEA	Dehydroepiandrosterone
DHT	Dihydrotestosterone
DIT	Diiodotyrosine
DNA	Deoxyribonucleic acid
D/N ratio	Ratio of dextrose (glucose) to nitrogen in the urine
D_2O	Deuterium oxide (heavy water)
DOCA	Deoxycorticosterone acetate
DOPA	Dihydroxyphenylalanine, L-dopa
DPG, 2,3-DPG	2,3-Diphosphoglycerate
DPN	Diphosphopyridine nucleotide
DPNH	Reduced diphosphopyridine nucleotide
e	Base for natural logarithms = 2.7182818...
E followed by subscript number:	Esophageal electrocardiographic lead, followed by number of cm it is inserted in esophagus
EACA	Epsilon-aminocaproic acid
ECF	Extracellular fluid

ECG	Electrocardiogram	Ile, Ileu	Isoleucine
ECoG	Electrocorticogram	In	Inulin
EDTA	Ethylenediaminetetraacetic acid	IPSP	Inhibitory postsynaptic potential
EEG	Electroencephalogram	ITP	Inosine triphosphate
EJP	Excitatory junction potential	IU	International unit(s)
EKG	Electrocardiogram	k	Kilo-, 10^3; see units of measurement, below
EMG	Electromyogram		
EPSP	Excitatory postsynaptic potential	kcal (Cal)	Kilocalorie (1000 calories)
Eq	Equivalent(s)	K_E	Exchangeable body potassium
ERG	Electroretinogram	L	Geometric isomer of D form of chemical compound
ERPF	Effective renal plasma flow		
ETP	Electron transport particle	LATS	Long-acting thyroid stimulator
f	Femto-, 10^{-15}; see units of measurement, below	Leu	Leucine
		LH	Luteinizing hormone
F	Fahrenheit	ln	Natural logarithm
FEV 1″	Forced expiratory volume in 1 sec	log	Logarithm to base 10
FFA	Unesterified, free fatty acid (also called NEFA, UFA)	LRF	Luteinizing hormone-releasing factor
		LSD	Lysergic acid diethylamide
FRF, FSHRF	FSH-releasing factor	LTH	Luteotropic hormone (prolactin)
FSH	Follicle-stimulating hormone	Lys	Lysine
ft	Foot or feet	m	Meter(s); also milli-, 10^{-3}; see units of measurement, below
g, gm	Gram(s)		
g	Unit of force; 1 g equals the force of gravity on the earth's surface	M	Mol(s), molar; also mega-, 10^6; see units of measurement, below
G	Glucose; also giga-, 10^9; see units of measurement, below	MAO	Monoamine oxidase
		MBC	Maximal breathing capacity (same as MVV)
GABA	Gamma-aminobutyric acid		
GBG	Gonadal steroid-binding globulin	Met	Methionine
GFR	Glomerular filtration rate	mho	Unit of conductance; the reciprocal of the ohm
GH	Growth hormone		
GIF, GRIF	Growth hormone-inhibiting factor	min	Minute(s)
GLI	Glucagon-like immunoreactive factor from gastrointestinal mucosa	MIT	Monoiodotyrosine
		mRNA	Messenger RNA
		MSH	Melanocyte-stimulating hormone
	$\underset{|}{NH_2}$	MVV	Maximal voluntary ventilation
Gln, Glu	Glutamine	n	nano-, 10^{-9}; see units of measurement, below
Glu	Glutamic acid		
Gly	Glycine	N	Normality (of a solution)
GRF, GHRF	Growth hormone-releasing factor	NAD^+	Nicotinamide adenine dinucleotide; same as DPN
GTP	Guanosine triphosphate		
HA	General symbol for an acid	NADH	Dihydronicotinamide adenine dinucleotide; same as DPNH
Hb	Deoxygenated hemoglobin		
HbO_2	Oxyhemoglobin	$NADP^+$	Nicotinamide adenine dinucleotide phosphate; same as TPN
HCC, 25-HCC	25-Hydroxycholecalciferol, an active metabolite of vitamin D_3		
		NADPH	Dihydronicotinamide adenine dinucleotide phosphate; same as TPNH
HCG	Human chorionic gonadotropin		
HCS	Human chorionic somatomammotropin	Na_E	Exchangeable body sodium
Hct	Hematocrit	NEFA	Unesterified (nonesterified) free fatty acid (same as FFA)
HGH	Human growth hormone		
HIOMT	Hydroxyindole-O-methyltransferase	NPH insulin	Neutral protamine Hagedorn insulin
His	Histidine	NPN	Nonprotein nitrogen
HPL	Human placental lactogen (same as HCS)	NREM sleep	Nonrapid eye movement (spindle) sleep
		N terminal	End of peptide or protein having a free $-NH_2$ group
HS-Co A	Reduced coenzyme A		
H substance	Histamine-like capillary vasodilator	O	The symbol O indicates absence of a sex chromosome, eg, XO as opposed to XX or XY
5-HT	Serotonin		
Hyl	Hydroxylysine		
Hyp	4-Hydroxyproline	Osm	Osmol(s)
hz	hertz, unit of frequency. 1 cycle per second = 1 hertz	p	Pico-, 10^{-12}; see units of measurement, below
IJP	Inhibitory junction potential		

P followed by subscript: Plasma concentration, eg, P_{Cr} = plasma creatinine concentration; also permeability coefficient, eg, P_{Na^+} = permeability coefficient for Na^+; also pressure (see respiratory symbols, below)

P_{50} — Partial pressure of O_2 at which hemoglobin is half-saturated with O_2

PAH — Para-aminohippuric acid

PBI — Protein-bound iodine

P factor — Hypothetical pain-producing substance produced in ischemic muscle

pH — Negative logarithm of the hydrogen ion concentration of a solution

Phe — Phenylalanine

PIF — Prolactin inhibiting factor

pK — Negative logarithm of the equilibrium constant for a chemical reaction

PMN — Polymorphonuclear neutrophilic leukocyte

PMS — Pregnant mare's serum gonadotropin

PRF — Prolactin-releasing factor

Pro — Proline

$Prot^-$ — Protein anion

5-PRPP — 5-phosphoribosyl pyrophosphate

PTA — Plasma thromboplastin antecedent (clotting factor XI)

PTC — Plasma thromboplastin component (clotting factor IX); also phenylthiocarbamide

(pyro)Glu — pyroglutamic acid

PZI — Protamine zinc insulin

R — General symbol for remainder of a chemical formula, eg, an alcohol is $R-OH$; also gas constant; also respiratory exchange ratio; also Reynolds' number

RAS — Reticular activating system

rbc — Red blood cell(s)

REF — Renal erythropoietic factor

REM sleep — Rapid eye movement (paradoxical) sleep

Reverse T_3 — 3,3′,5′-Triiodothyronine; isomer of triiodothyronine

Rh factor — Rhesus group of red cell agglutinogens

RMV — Respiratory minute volume

RNA — Ribonucleic acid

RPF — Renal plasma flow

RQ — Respiratory quotient

R unit — Unit of resistance in cardiovascular system; mm Hg divided by ml/sec

SA — Specific activity

SA node — Sinoatrial node

SCUBA — Self-contained underwater breathing apparatus

SDA — Specific dynamic action

sec — Second(s)

Ser — Serine

SE (SEM) — Standard error of the mean

S_f units — Svedberg units of flotation

SGOT — Serum glutamic-oxaloacetic transaminase

SH — Sulfhydryl

SPCA — Proconvertin (clotting factor VII)

sq cm — Square centimeter(s)

SRIF — Somatotropin release-inhibiting factor; same as GIF

sRNA — Soluble or transfer RNA

STH — Somatotropin, growth hormone

Substance P — Polypeptide found in brain

T — Absolute temperature

T_3 — 3,5,3′-Triiodothyronine

T_4 — Thyroxine

TBG — Thyroxine-binding globulin

TBPA — Thyroxine-binding prealbumin

TBW — Total body water

TETRAC — Tetraiodothyroacetic acid

TF/P — Concentration of a substance in renal tubular fluid divided by its concentration in plasma

Thr — Threonine

Tm — Renal tubular maximum

torr — 1/760 atm = 1.00000014 mm Hg; unit for various pressures in the body

TPN — Triphosphopyridine nucleotide

TPNH — Reduced triphosphopyridine nucleotide

TRF — Thyrotropin-releasing factor

tRNA — Transfer RNA; same as sRNA

Trp, Try, Tryp — Tryptophan

TSH — Thyroid-stimulating hormone

T/S ratio — Thyroid/serum iodide ratio

Tyr — Tyrosine

U — Unit(s)

U followed by subscript: Urine concentration, eg, U_{Cr} = urine creatinine concentration

UDPG — Uridine diphosphoglucose

UFA — Unesterified free fatty acid (same as FFA)

URF — Uterine-relaxing factor; relaxin

US — Unconditioned stimulus

UTP — Uridine triphosphate

V — Urine volume/unit time

v — Volt

V_1, V_2, etc — Unipolar chest electrocardiographic leads

Val — Valine

VF — Unipolar left leg electrocardiographic lead

VL — Left arm unipolar electrocardiographic lead

VMA — Vanilmandelic acid (3-methoxy-4-hydroxymandelic acid)

VR — Unipolar right arm electrocardiographic lead

wbc — White blood cell(s)

X chromosome: One of the sex chromosomes in humans

X zone — Inner zone of adrenal cortex in some young mammals

Y chromosome: One of the sex chromosomes in humans

STANDARD RESPIRATORY SYMBOLS
(See Fed Proc 9:602, 1950)

General Variables

V	Gas volume
$\dot{V}$	Gas volume/unit of time. (Dot over a symbol indicates rate.)
P	Gas pressure
$\bar{P}$	Mean gas pressure
f	Respiratory frequency (breaths/unit of time)
D	Diffusing capacity
F	Fractional concentration in dry gas phase
C	Concentration in blood phase
R	Respiratory exchange ratio = $\dot{V}_{CO_2}/\dot{V}_{O_2}$
Q	Volume of blood
$\dot{Q}$	Volume flow of blood/unit of time

Localization (Subscript letters.)

I	Inspired gas
E	Expired gas
A	Alveolar gas
T	Tidal gas
D	Dead space gas
B	Barometric
a	Arterial blood
c	Capillary blood
v	Venous blood

Special Symbols

STPD	Standard temperature and pressure, dry (0° C, 760 mm Hg)
BTPS	Body temperature and pressure, saturated with water vapor
ATPD	Ambient temperature and pressure, dry
ATPS	Ambient temperature and pressure, saturated with water vapor

Molecular Species

Indicated by chemical formula printed as subscript.

Examples

$P_{I_{O_2}}$ = Pressure of oxygen in inspired air
V_D = Dead space gas volume

● ● ●

Units of Measurement

Prefix	Abbreviation	Magnitude
tera-	T	10^{12}
giga-	G	10^9
mega-	M	10^6
kilo-	k	10^3
deci-	–	10^{-1}
centi-	c	10^{-2}
milli-	m	10^{-3}
micro-	μ	10^{-6}
nano-	n, mμ	10^{-9}
pico-	p, $\mu\mu$	10^{-12}
femto-	f	10^{-15}
atto-	a	10^{-18}

These prefixes are applied to metric and other units. For example, a micrometer (μm) is 10^{-6} meter (also called a micron); a picoliter (pl) is 10^{-12} liter; and a kilogram (kg) is 10^3 grams. Also applied to seconds, units, mols, hertz, volts, farads, ohms, curies, equivalents, osmols, etc.

Index

*In general, phrases are indexed under the first word in the normal order of speech—eg, *Inborn errors of metabolism, Inhibitory mediator*, not *Metabolism, inborn errors of*, nor *Mediator, inhibitory*. Extensive cross-indexing has been done under major headings—eg, under *Insulin* are listed most of the subjects relating to insulin which are dealt with in the text, and the reader will be able to find specific references by scanning the column under the word.

Equivalents of Metric, United States, and English Measures
(Values rounded off to 2 decimal places.)

Length
    1 kilometer = 0.62 mile
    1 mile = 5280 feet = 1.61 kilometers
    1 meter = 39.37 inches
    1 inch = 1/12 foot = 2.54 centimeters

Volume
    1 liter = 1.06 US liquid quart
    1 US liquid quart = 32 fluid ounces = 1/4 US gallon = 0.95 liter
    1 milliliter = 0.03 fluid ounce
    1 fluid ounce = 29.57 milliliters
    1 US gallon = 0.83 English (Imperial) gallon

Weight
    1 kilogram = 2.20 pounds (avoirdupois) = 2.68 pounds (apothecaries')
    1 pound (avoirdupois) = 16 ounces = 453.60 grams
    1 grain = 65 milligrams

Energy
    1 kilogram-meter = 7.25 foot-pounds
    1 foot-pound = 0.14 kilogram-meters

Temperature
    To convert centigrade degrees into Fahrenheit, multiply by 9/5 and add 32
    To convert Fahrenheit degrees into centigrade, subtract 32 and multiply by 5/9

Greek Alphabet

Symbol		Name	Symbol		Name
A	α	alpha	N	ν	nu
B	β	beta	Ξ	ξ	xi
Γ	γ	gamma	O	o	omicron
Δ	δ	delta	Π	π	pi
E	ϵ	epsilon	P	ρ	rho
Z	ζ	zeta	Σ	σ, ς	sigma
H	η	eta	T	τ	tau
Θ	θ	theta	Υ	υ	upsilon
I	ι	iota	Φ	ϕ	phi
K	κ	kappa	X	χ	chi
Λ	λ	lambda	Ψ	ψ	psi
M	μ	mu	Ω	ω	omega